Quilters' Travel Companion

Published by:

Chalet PUBLISHING
32 Grand Avenue
Manitou Springs, CO 80829
(719) 685-5041

Edited by:
Audrey Swales Anderson
& Thomas Culp

Check out our website:
www.chalet-publishing.com
E-mail:
info@chalet-publishing.com
Fax: (719) 685-2347

Chalet Publishing is the Home of the *Quilters' Travel Companion* and the *Needlecrafters' Travel Companion*

With all our love,
this book is dedicated to
Audrey's husband, Marlow and
Tom's wife, Rona.
Thank you for your hours of
assistance and support.

Thanks for your help, Ruth O'Riley

Illustrations from Clip Art:
Winter Weather & Garden Party
by Rebecca Carter,
Countryside Collection & Four Seasons
by Kathy Distefano Griffiths
From My Hands to Warm Your Heart
by Lori Gardner
All Occasions & Everyday by Annette Ward
At The Cabin by Leeré Aldrich
and Whimsy for all Seasons by Jeff Goddsell
Distributed by Provo Crafts, Salt Lake City

How to Use this Guide

General Purpose: Whenever you're away from home be sure to take your *Quilters' Travel Companion* (QTC). You never know when you might have an opportunity to check out a shop. This guide includes featured listings for over 1750 quilt shops in the United States and Canada.
Lots of customers have told us that they have the shops sign their book along the way--great fun!

Layout of the Book: The shop listings are organized by state. We provide a state map which will enable you to tell at a glance where each of the featured shops is located. The number on the state map will also be found in the shop listing.
In addition, for each state we include a listing of other shops located in that state. A phone number is included for these shops, please call before venturing there as our information on these shops is not as good as for the featured shops. We have made every effort for the information in this book to be up-to-date and accurate. Unfortunately shops do move, change hours, or go out of business; so if you want to be sure before you go a phone call might be prudent. All the 'featured shops' information was correct when published. Also note that many new telephone area codes have been added across the country and many more new ones are planned.

Send us Info: We've tried hard to include every shop in the country, but we're sure that we've missed some. If you know of one we've missed drop us a note or call us at (719) 685-5041, Fax: (719) 685-2347 email--info@chalet-publishing.com or visit our website at: www.chalet-publishing.com

Plan your Trips: There are two basic ways we see you using our 'travel companion'
1) Whenever you're traveling on business or vacation check out your route and see what shops you may be close to. The state maps should give you an idea if you'll be in the vicinity of a store. Then if you have time or can make time give yourself a break and STOP !
Since beginning these guides in 1992, I have certainly realized that I used to drive right by shops on my travels, but not stop because I didn't realize they were close.
2) Or go WILD and take a few days with family or friends and plan a whole trip going from shop to shop. Many shops are in historic / tourist places so your trip just may lead you into an unexpected adventure. Either way, enjoy exploring all the great shops scattered across this country. We would be grateful if you'd tell them that QTC got you there.

New treatment of the Guilds: With this issue of the QTC we are no longer including the guilds. However, we are still collecting this information, and if you'd like the list of guilds it is a nominal $5 charge just to cover our costs. We weren't really sure if our travelers were using this information.

Chalet Publishing's mascot, Max.

Map Conventions used in the QTC:
a) Our state maps only include major roads; please use our maps in conjunction with commercial maps.
b) All maps are oriented with North at the top.
c) The shops are marked either by a square with the street address inside (i.e. 100) or by a star ☆

* = traffic light | ■ =Business or landmark
-┼┼┼┼┼┼┼- = Railroad | A Gray line or area = water
Dashed line = state border | ● = City

www.chalet-publishing.com

CONTENTS

U.S.A. Featured Shops

Canadian Featured Shops

Have a Great Trip

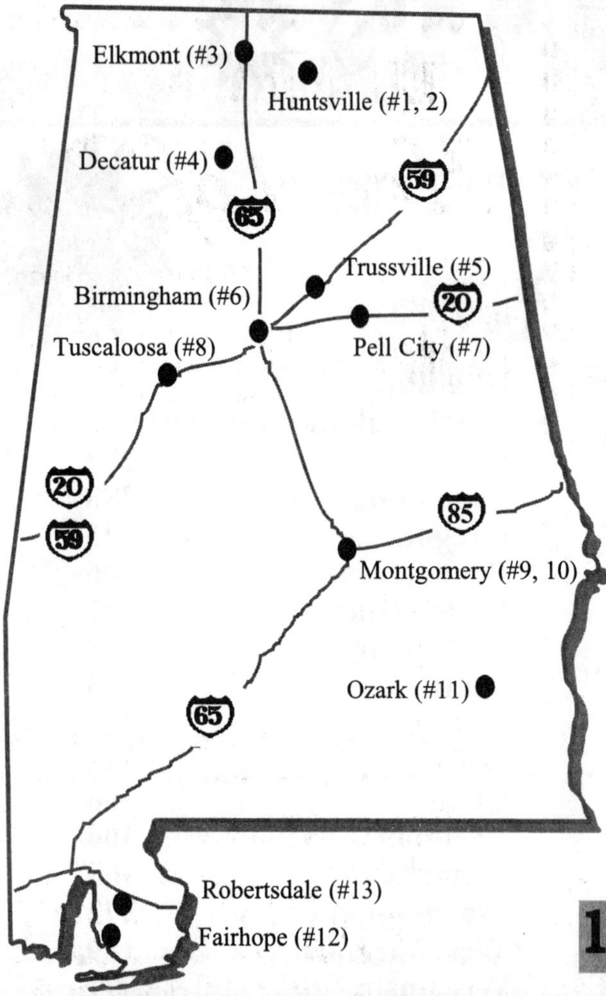

ALABAMA

13 Featured Shops

Huntsville, AL #1

Mon - Fri
9:30 - 5:30
Thur til 6
Sat 9:30-4:30

Patches & Stitches

603 Humes Avenue 35801 (256) 533-3886
e-mail: patchesand@knology.net
Visit our Web Site at: www.patches&stitches.com
Owner: Linda Worley Est: 1978 2500 sq.ft.

Toll Free # 1-877-SHE-SEWS
Complete line of quilt supplies;
Also cross-stitch and needlepoint.
Extensive Fibers. Mail order.

We are located in one of Huntsville's Historic Mill Villages. Call for directions if you can't find us. We are off of Andrew Jackson behind the CVS Pharmacy.

Huntsville, AL #2

Mon - Fri 10 - 5
Sat 10 - 4

Lydia's

518 Madison St. 35801
(256) 536-9700 Est: 1992
E-Mail: Lydiashsv@aol.com
Web Site: www.Lydias.com
Owners: Michael & Mary Penton 3000 sq.ft.

Quilting & Heirloom Sewing Classes & Supplies
Husqvarna Viking Sewing Machines
2 Blocks from Downtown Historic District.

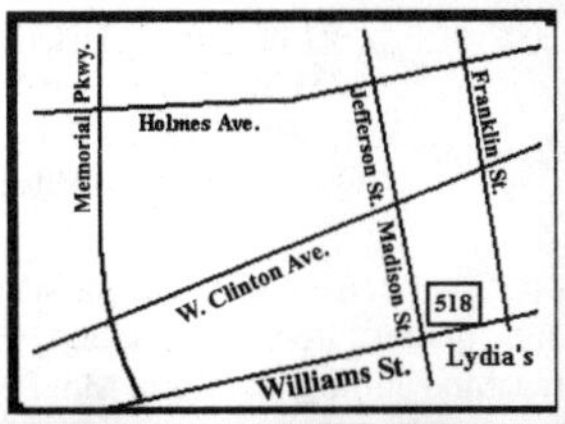

Elkmont, AL #3

Heart of Dixie

Mon - Sat 10 - 5

23640 Hwy. 99 35620
(888) 239-0941
E-Mail: maquilt@companet.net
Web Site: www.heartofdixiequiltshop.com
Owner: Brenda Armstrong
Est: 1998 6400 sq.ft. 5000+ bolts.

- RV parking
- Machine quilting service
- Quilt Kits
- Original patterns
- Reproduction ™ Signs

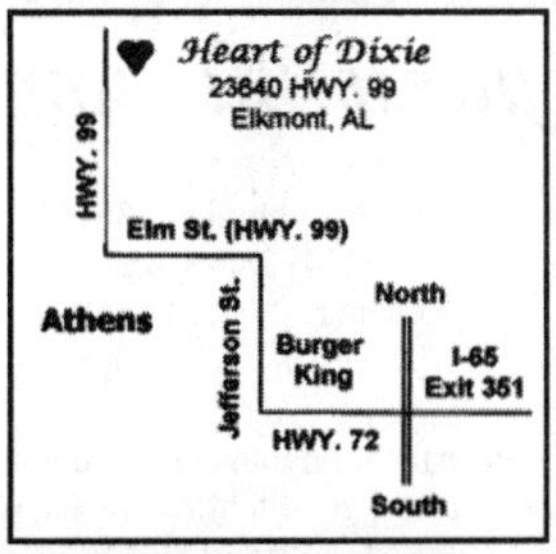

Decatur, AL #4

Mon - Fri 10 - 5
Sat 10 - 4

Crafty Bear Quilt Shop

2208 Danville Rd. S.W. 35601
(256) 351-0420 Est: 1988
E-Mail: cbearshop@mindspring.com
Owner: Helen DeButy 2500 sq.ft.

Cotton Fabrics, books, patterns, supplies, and lots of classes. The friendliest quilt shop for service, inspiration and sharing of ideas.

Trussville, AL #5

Heart to Heart Quilt Shop

1110 N. Chalkville Rd. 35173
(205) 661-0537 Fax: (205) 661-9497
E-Mail: h2hquilt@earthlink.net Est: 1998
Web Site: www.hearttoheartquiltshop.com
Owners: Terry Cates & Cindy Wilson 2500 sq.ft.

Mon- Sat 9 - 5 Tues 9 - 8

Located in Valley View Shopping Center.
Newest Designer 100% cotton Fabrics, Books, Notions, Patterns, Classes. Helpful, friendly staff.

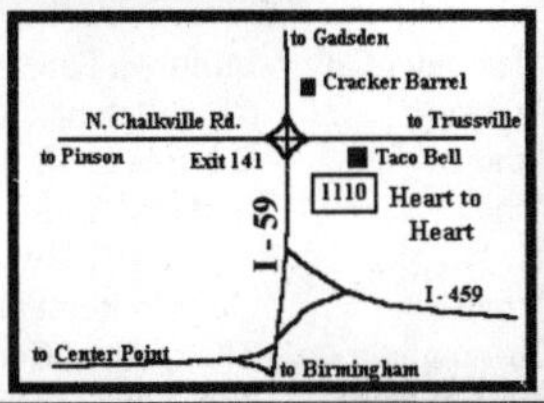

Birmingham, AL #6

Quiltmaker's Workshop

A Quilter's Quilt Shop

1930 Edwards Lake Rd. #132 35235
(205) 661-9780
Owner: Annie Woods

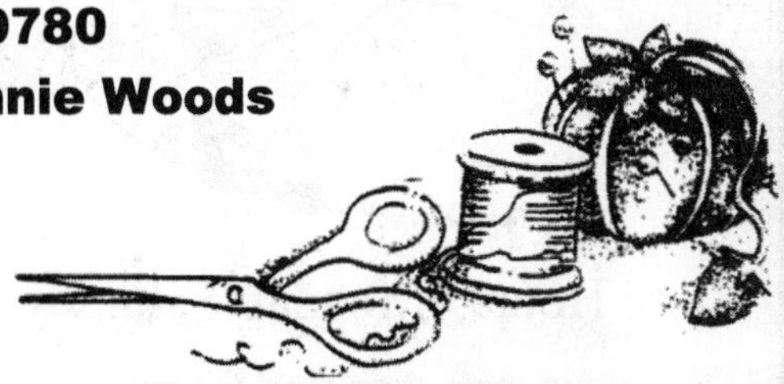

Serving the Greater Birmingham Area since 1994

Mon - Sat
10 - 5
Thur til 8

Over 3000 bolts of the latest cotton fabrics
Great Books
Patterns
Notions
Gadgets
Gifts

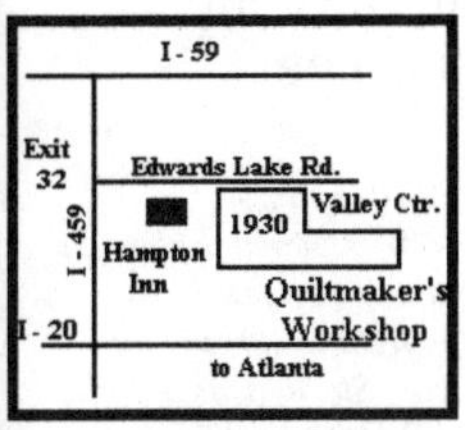

Friendly service and free advice
Classes for all levels.

Pell City, AL #7

Mon - Fri 10 - 6
Thur til 8
Sat 9 - 5

Heart N Home Quilts

1605 Martin St. S, Suite 1 35128
(205) 814-0063
E-Mail: heartnhome@pell.net
Web Site: heartnhomequilts.edenonline2.com
Owners: Kathy Kirby & Nan Ramsey

Quality 100% cotton fabrics, books, notions & quilting supplies. Classes for ages 10 & up. Friendly, personal service. Janome sales & service. Kathy is a certified *Quilt in a Day* Inst.

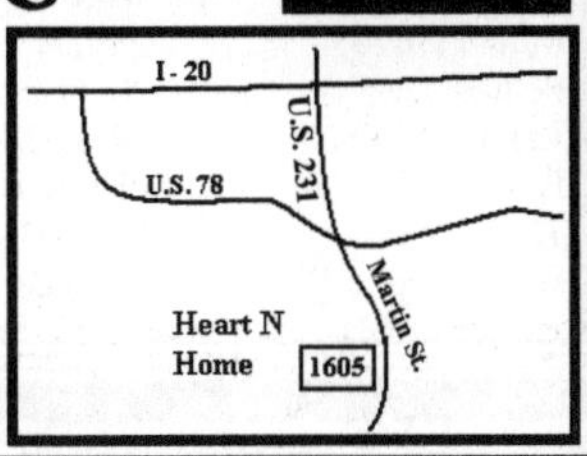

Tuscaloosa, AL #8

Mon - Fri 10 - 5 Sat 10 - 3

Carolina Lily Quilt Shop

2120 7th St. 35401
(205) 349-8899
Owner: Joy W. Robertson
Est: 1997
E-Mail: joyandleon@earthlink.net

100% cotton fabrics from all leading manufacturers, books, patterns, frames and quilting notions. Classes and machine quilting also available.

Montgomery, AL #9

Mon - Fri 9 - 4:30 Sat by Appt.

Rose of Sharon

Mulberry District
1721 W. 2nd St. 36106
(334) 281-9775 Est: 1994
Owner: Sharon Wilson

100% cotton fabrics, thread, stencils, notions and quilted items for sale. Hand guided machine quilting by Susan Moseley.

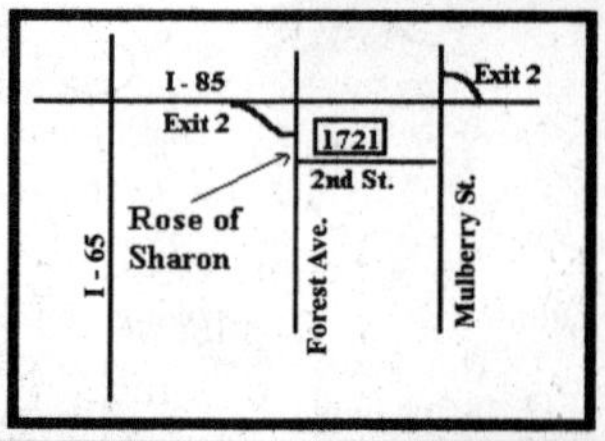

Montgomery, AL #10

Mon - Fri 9:30 - 5 Sat 9:30 - 3

Kudzu Blossom Quilt Shop

3666-E Debby Dr. 36111
(334) 288-8108
Owner: Janice Jarrett
Est: 1997 1500 sq.ft.

A wonderful shop to meet all your quilting needs. Lots of great fabrics, books, patterns, and quilting supplies.

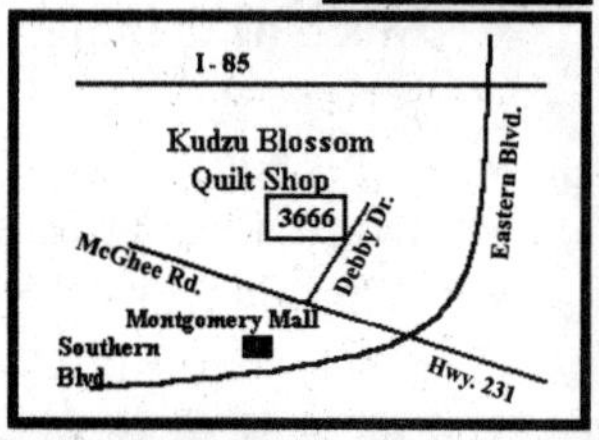

Ozark, AL #11

Mon - Sat 9:30 - 5

Front Porch Quilt Shoppe

227 D Hwy. 231 N 36360
(334) 445-3521
Owner: Melanie Simpson
Est: 1999

This charming shop is located in Deloney's Verandas. "Where quilters gather" for fabric - books - patterns - notions - classes and fun.

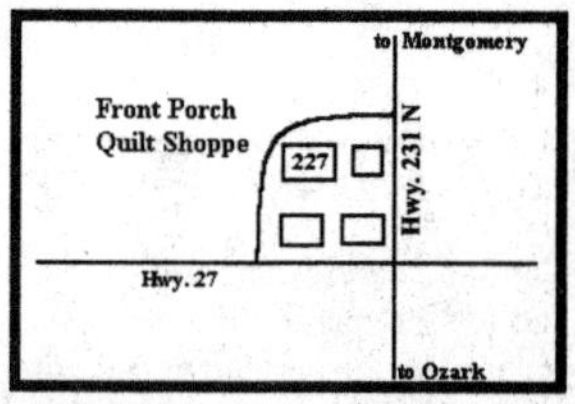

Bears & Quilting By The Bay

212 1/2
Fairhope Ave.
36532
(251) 928-8989
Fax: Same
Owner:
Nancy Scott
Est: 1994
2000 sq.ft.

Store Hours: Monday-Saturday 10:00 - 5:00

Your one stop shopping for bears, fabrics, quilting books, notions, kits, BOM's and quilting classes.

Over 2,500 bolts of fabrics and more arriving daily. Lots of new books and old time favorites and many different BOM's (block of the month) to choose from.

All bear lovers and fabricholics welcome !!
e-mail: nancy@bearsandquilting.com
http://www.bearsandquilting.com

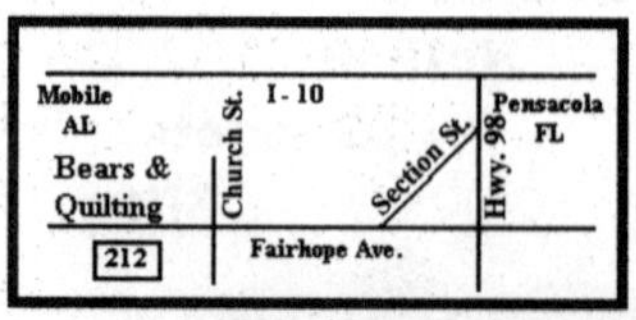

I - 10, Exit 35A
7.5 miles to "Welcome to Fairhope" veer to right will become Section St. 4th traffic light turn right onto Fairhope Ave. Store located on left hand side, 1/2 block past Church St.

Fairhope, AL #12

Robertsdale, AL #13

Mon - Sat 10 - 5

Build-A-Quilt

21783-C Hwy. 59 36567
(251) 947-6275 Fax: (251) 947-6277
E-Mail: BuildAQuilt@aol.com
Web Site: www.Build-A-Quilt.com
Owners: Bonnie & Gary Sides
Est: 2001 1200 sq.ft.

We stock Fabrics, Notions, & Books. We offer great Classes. Travelers Welcome. Located on Highway 59, Behind Express Lube across from the High School.

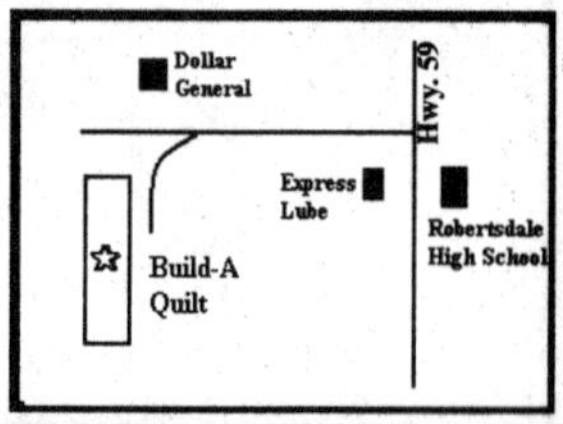

Other Shops in Alabama: We suggest calling first

Alexander City	Midtown Fabrics & Crafts, 26 Main St.	205-234-2394
Anniston	Cloth Patch, 2120 Noble St.	205-237-9972
Athens	Do' Bea Craft Shop, 15392 Elk River Mills Rd.	205-233-1915
Athens	Hickory House Gift Shoppe & Antique Mall 23101 Hwy. 72 E	205-232-9860
Athens	Quilt to Remember, 27344 Elkins Rd.	256-233-2585
Birmingham	The Quilted Cat, 63 Church	205-871-4741
Birmingham	The Attic Antiques, 5620 Cahaba Valley Rd.	205-991-6887
Birmingham	Glory Bee Designs, P.O. Box 26231	205-942-5145
Foley	Quilt Connection, 21188 Miflin Rd.	334-943-4641
Gadsden	Thornton Lake Cloth Barn, 576 Thornton Lake	205-492-2773
Homewood	Prime Time Treasures, 1755 Oxmoor Rd.	205-870-5555
Jasper	Grandma's Treasures & Fabrics Parkland Shopping Center	205-221-5263
Mobile	Fabric Works, 5441 Highway 90 W.	334-666-0285
Mount Olive	L & L Quilt & Gifts, 1325 McConnell Ln.	205-631-4910
Pelham	Harry's Southern Textiles, 2775 Hwy. 31 S	205-664-1811
Rainbow City	Stitchin Post, 3805 Rainbow Dr.	256-442-0933
Russellville	Parker's Discount Hwy., 24 E	205-332-4539
Tuscaloosa	Cloth Patch, 4331 University Blvd. E.	205-553-0705
Wetumpka	Creations Galore, Inc., 105 E. Main	334-567-6096

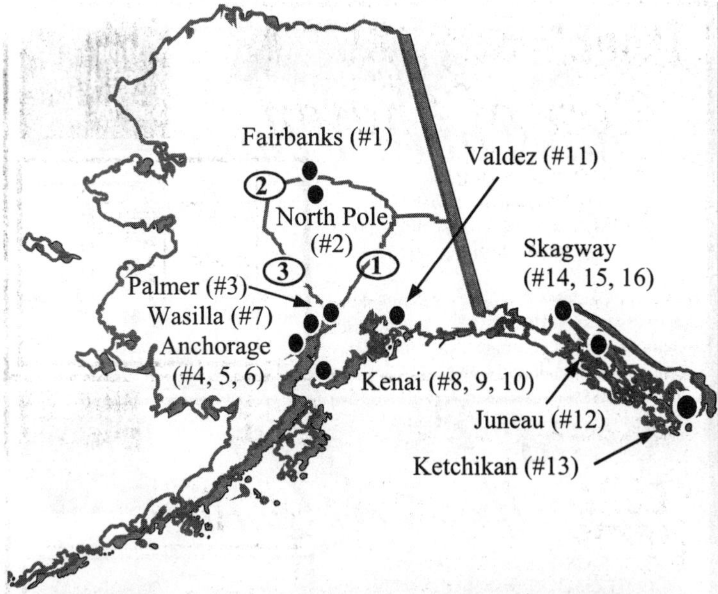

Alaska

16 Featured Shops

Fairbanks, AK #1

Mon - Sat 9:30 - 6
Sun 12 - 5

Snow Goose Fibers

1875 University Ave. 99709
(907) 474-8118
E-Mail: snogoose@eagle.ptialaska.net
Web Site: www.snogoose.com

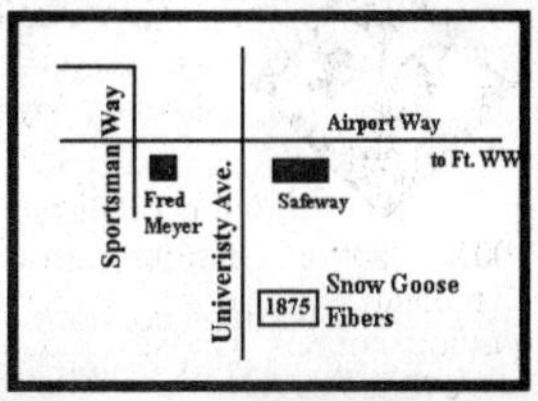

Wonderful Alaskan Kits, Patterns, Fabric featuring our wildlife. Beautiful New Store; 4000 bolts of 100% cottons. Call or email for summer hours! Don't miss this shop!

North Pole, AK #2

Mon - Fri 10:30 - 6
Sat 10:30 - 4

The Quilting Trail

3136 Dyke Rd. 99705
(907) 488-8091
E-Mail: qtrail@alaska.com
Web Site: www.quiltingtrail.com
Owner: Marie Noah

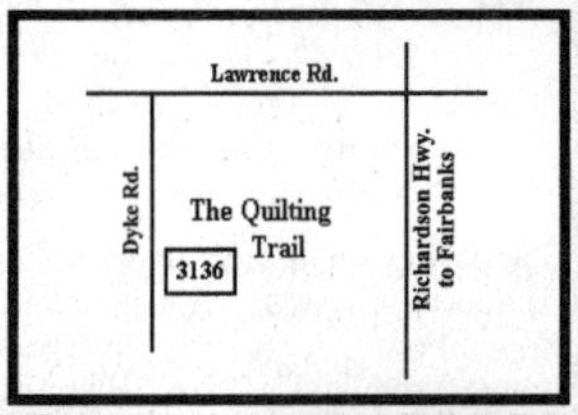

Over 1000 Bolts of 100% cottons & flannels, quilting supplies & Alaskan Gifts.

Palmer, AK #3

Mon - Fri 10 - 6
Sat 10 - 5
Sun 1 - 5

Just Sew

579 S. Alaska 99645
(907) 745-3649
Owners: Jim & Cheri Cooper
2400 sq.ft.

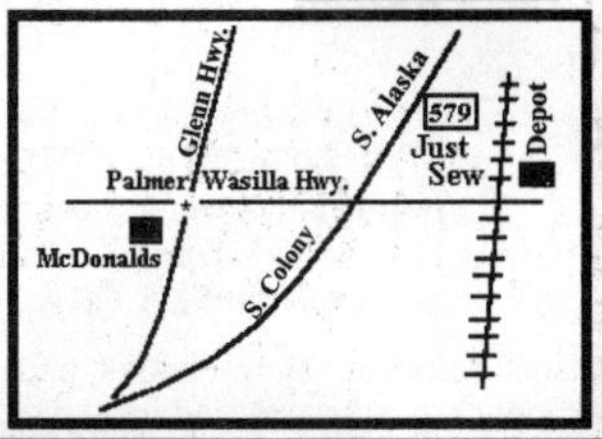

All your quilting and needlework supplies. 100% cottons, books, patterns, notions, cross-stitch supplies, yarn, and lots more!

Anchorage, AK #4

Mon - Fri 10 - 6:30
Sat 10 - 6
Sun 12 - 5

Quilt Works

3120 Denali St. #4 99503
(907) 563-9773 Fax: (907) 563-9772
E-Mail: vwquilt@alaska.net
Web Site: www.alaskaquiltworks.com
Owner: Sue Bergerson
Manager: Julie Dolan

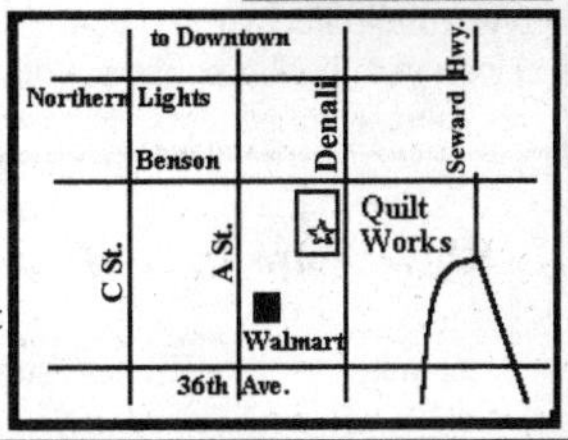

Over 6000 bolts of 100% cotton fabric. Excellent selection of books, patterns, & Alaskan patterns. 10% off on Thurs. Open late on class nights.

Anchorage, AK #5

The Quilt Tree

5520 Lake Otis Pkwy,
Suite 105 99507
(907) 561-4115
Fax: (907) 561-4406
3000 sq.ft. 4500 Bolts
E-Mail: quiltree@alaskalife.net

Mon- Fri 10 - 9 Sat 10 - 6 Sun 12 - 5

Large selection of quality 100% cotton fabric, unique Alaskan patterns, books, notions & supplies. Experienced, helpful staff.

Anchorage, AK #6

Mon - Sat 9 - 7
Sun 12 - 5

1041 E. 76th, Suite B 99516
(907) 677-8790
Fax: (907) 677-8791
E-Mail: akseams@yahoo.com
Web Site: www.seamslikehome.com
Owner: Maret Anderson

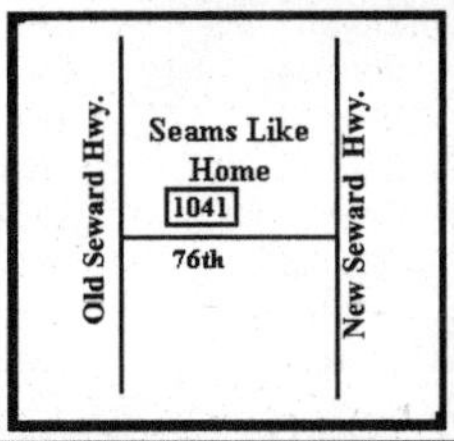

A quilt shop for fabric artists. Distinctive fabrics, Alaskan patterns, books, patterns, notions & supplies, classes for all abilities.

Wasilla, AK #7

Mon - Fri 10 - 6
Sat 10 - 5

Sylvia's Quilt Depot

490 Carpenter Circle 99654
(907) 376-6468 Fax: (907) 376-6403
E-Mail: sylviasquilt@gci.net
Web Site: www.sylviasquiltdepot.com
1000 Bolts

We offer a friendly, cozy atmosphere for all quilters, with quality cotton fabrics, notions, books and gifts including Alaskan designs.

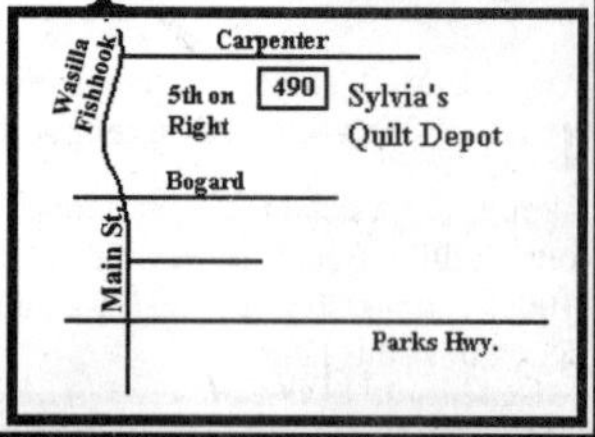

Kenai, AK #8

Mon - Sat 9 - 6
Sun 1 - 4

Kenai Fabric Center

115 N. Willow 99611
(907) 283-4595 Fax: (907) 283-5609
Est: 1970 4000+ Bolts

Quilting Fabrics & Classes, Fashion & Outerwear fabrics, Husqvarna/Viking & White Sewing Machines & Sergers, Notions, Yarns, Books, Family-owned.

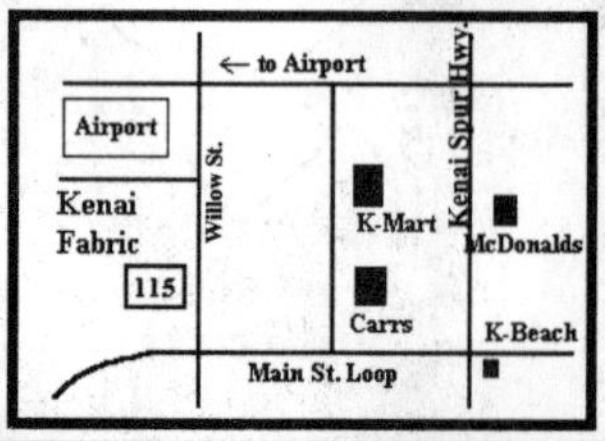

Kenai, AK #9

Mon - Fri 10 - 6
Sat 10 - 5

Quilt Kits Alaska

49926 Douglas Ln. 99611
(907) 776-8858
Web Site: www.quiltkitsalaska.com
Owner: Terry DiBetta

Quilt Kits - Quilting Fabrics (including 500+ Batiks) - Classes - Alaskan Patterns - Books Machines for Rent - Sewing Space Avail. Quilt Samples for Sale. Beautiful Lake Front Setting. Motorhome Turn Around Space.

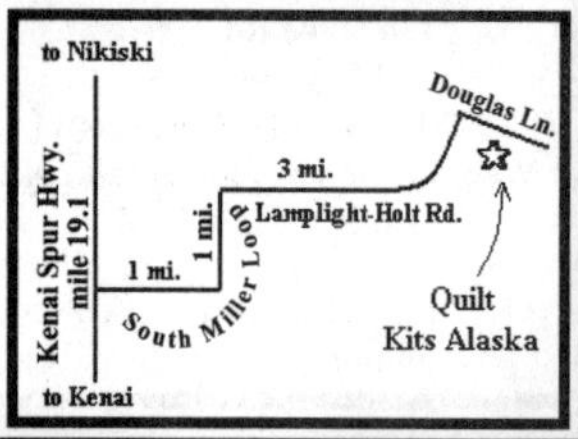

Kenai, AK #10

Tues - Sat 8 - 4:30

Forget-Me-Knot Quilting

12498 Spur Highway; Suite 2 99611
(907) 283-2687 or (866) 538-7739
Fax: (907) 283-3179
E-Mail: mcgrady2@alaska.net
Owners: Jenni and Kathy McGrady
Est: 1996 1600 sq.ft.

Two Gammill Longarm Quilting Machines. Quilt classes and Basic Sewing Instructions. Custom Quilting Designs. Memory Quilts our Specialty.

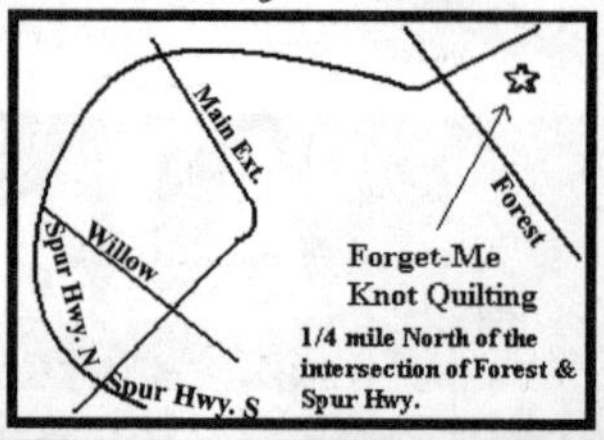

Valdez, AK #11

Mon - Sat 10 - 5

The Calico Whale

354 Fairbanks Dr. 99686
(907) 835-4263 Fax: (907) 835-5263
E-Mail: calicowhale@cvinternet.net
Owner: Trudy Koszarek
Est: 1995 1500 sq.ft.

Good selection fabrics, books, patterns, quilting supplies, needlework and local handmade gifts.

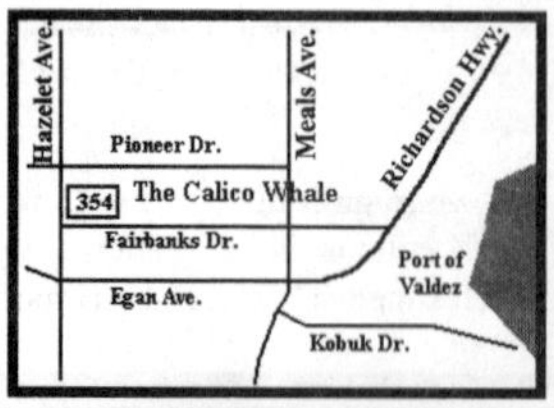

Juneau, AK #12

Mon - Sat 10 - 6
Sun 12 - 5
Closed Sun June, July, Aug

RainTree Quilting

9131 Glacier Hwy. #7 99801
9 miles from cruise ship dock
(907) 789-7900 Fax: (907) 789-1940
E-Mail: quilt@raintreequilting.com
Web Site: www.raintreequilting.com

Over 1500 bolts of 100% cotton fabrics. Large selection of books, patterns, notions. Alaskan fabrics and patterns. Bernina Dealer.

Ketchikan, AK #13

Winter
Mon - Sat 10 - 5:30
Summer
7 Days 9 - 6

Silver Thimble Fabric Shoppe

5 Salmon Landing #204 99901
(907) 225-5422
Owner: Betty T. Gale Est: 1984

Available: Quilting fabrics, supplies, Alaskan patterns and sewing machines.

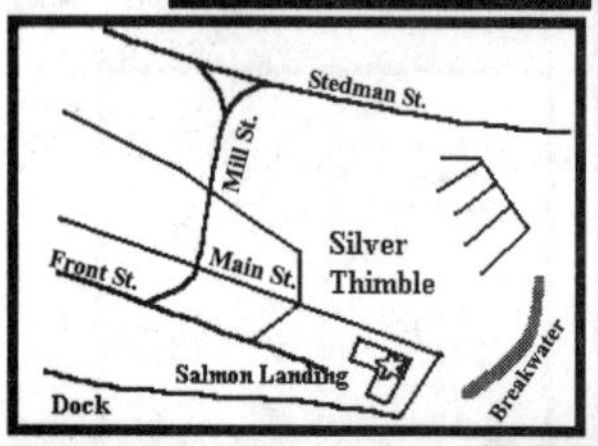

Skagway, AK #14

Mon - Sat 10 - 5

Dirce Ann's Fabrics

P.O. Box 284 412 8th Ave. 99840
(907) 983-2376 Fax: (907) 983-3114
E-Mail: dirceann@aptalaska.net
Owners: Dirce & Dennis Spurrier
Est: 1993

Alaskan Wildlife Fabrics, 100% Cotton Quilting Fabrics, Northern Patterns, Quilting Supplies, Yarns, Homemade Gifts & More.

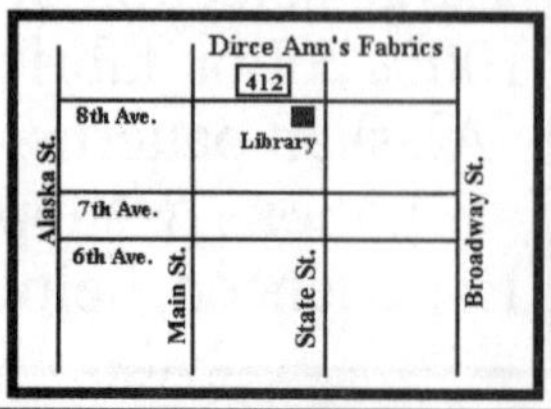

Other Shops in Alaska: We suggest calling first

Anchorage	Three Sisters Fabric Boutique, 1120 Huffman #10	907-345-8041
Anchorage	The Whiffletree, 9420 Old Seward Hwy.	907-344-5922
Anchorage	Debbie's Created Moments, 4801 Jumar Rd.	907-346-3779
Anchorage	Great Alaskan Quilt Co., 837 W. 56th Ave.	907-562-8183
Cordova	Forget-Me-Not Fabrics, P.O. Box 1109	907-424-3656
Cordova	Calico Corner, P.O. Box 320	907-424-3285
Craig	Attic Treasures Quilt Shop, 1 Easy St.	907-826-2535
Eagle River	Sleeping Lady Quilts, 10970 Corrie Way	907-694-4571
Fairbanks	Quilts Unlimited, 1918 Jack St.	907-452-1918
Fairbanks	Hands All Around, 731 Eton Blvd	907-452-2347
Haines	Seams Like Yesterday, P.O. Box 1167	907-766-2265
Kenai	Lasting Stitches, 11472 Kenai Spur Hwy. #3	907-283-9470
Kodiak	The Stitchery, P.O. Box 3809	907-486-5580
Petersburg	Island Bound Quilting, P.O. Box 358	907-772-3249
Petersburg	Fabric Basket, P.O. Box 1636	907-772-4576
Sitka	Calico Cross Stitch, 231 Lincoln St.	907-747-5122
Sitka	Abby's Reflection, 231 Lincoln St.	907-747-3510
Skagway	Crocus Creek Quilts, P.O. Box 37	867-668-7699
Skagway	The White House, 8 & Main St., P.O. Box 41	907-983-9000
Soldotna	Robin Place Fabrics, 105 Robin Pl.	907-262-5438
Tok	The Quails Nest, P.O. Box 480	907-883-4353
Wasilla	Alaska Dyeworks, 300 W. Swanson Ave. #106	907-373-6562
Wrangell	Angerman's Special-Tees, P.O. Box 849	907-874-3611

Changing Tides

Quilting and Needlework Emporium

3rd & Broadway
907 983-3349

Email: changingtides@iname.com
Web site: www.alaskastitching.com

est. 1994

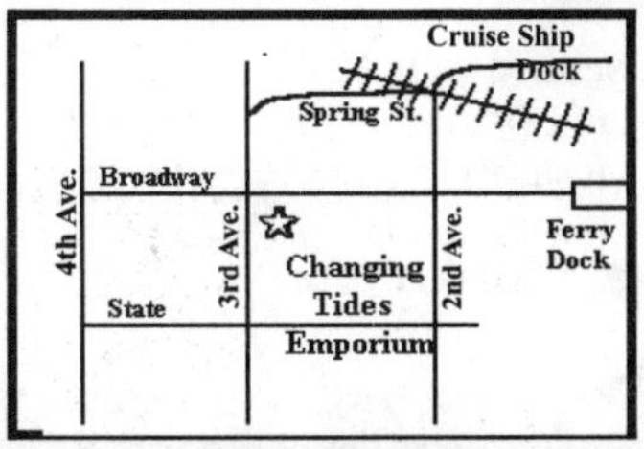

A unique needlework store located in the heart of historic downtown Skagway. Featuring Alaskan Motif Fabrics and the largest selection of patterns, needlework charts and kits by Alaskan Designer.
On staff quilters and designers to help you bring home a keepsake of your tip to "The Last Frontier."

Skagway, AK #15

Mon - Sat 8:30 - 7
Sun 9 - 5

The Rushin' Tailor

Quilting & Needlework

Downtown Skagway
Est: 1989

636 Broadway
P.O. Box 135 99840
(800) 981-5432 or (907) 983-2397
rtailor@aptalaska.net
www.rtailor.com
www.quiltalaska.com

Daily 8:30 - 5:30 May - Sept.
Thur, Fri, Sat 12 - 5 Oct. - April

Visit an "Alaskan themed" quilt Shop with quilt kits and patterns by Alaskan designers!
GREAT QUILTS ON DISPLAY worth seeing!
We offer loads of FQ's & bolts in Alaskan wildlife, floral & batik fabrics.
Bonus!! Cross Stitch by Alaskan Artists
New!! Needlepoint!

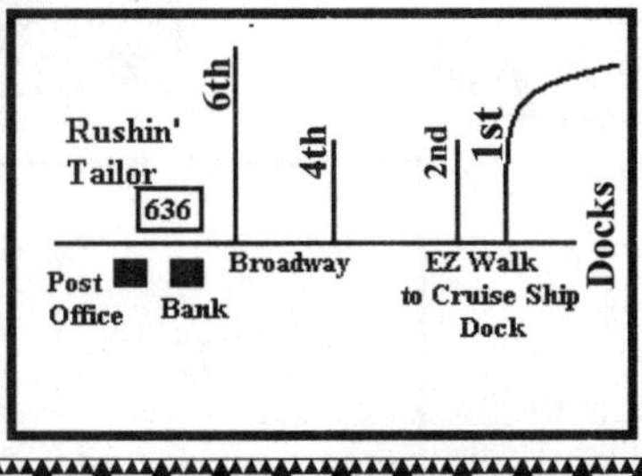

Skagway, AK #16

ARIZONA

25 Featured Shops

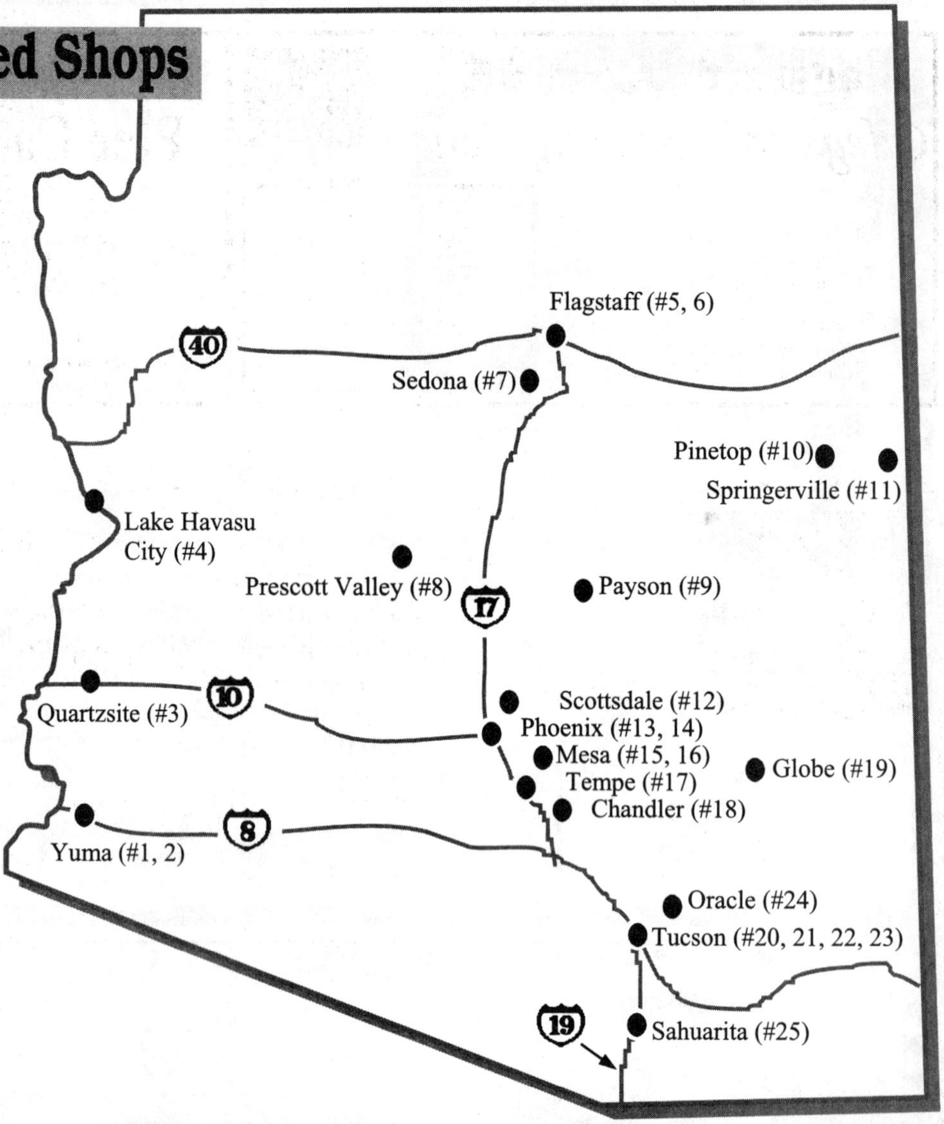

Yuma, AZ #1

Mon - Sat 9 - 5
Sun 11 - 4

Quilt & Sew House

102 E. 3rd St. 85364
(928) 376-0911
Fax: Same
Est: 1997
2500 sq.ft.
Owner:
Wanda Hinkhouse
E-Mail: quiltwand@prodigy.net
Web Site: www.quiltandsewhouse.com

We are Premier Husqvarna Viking Dealers. Large Class room for quilters. 10% Discount if you show Guild card before purchase.

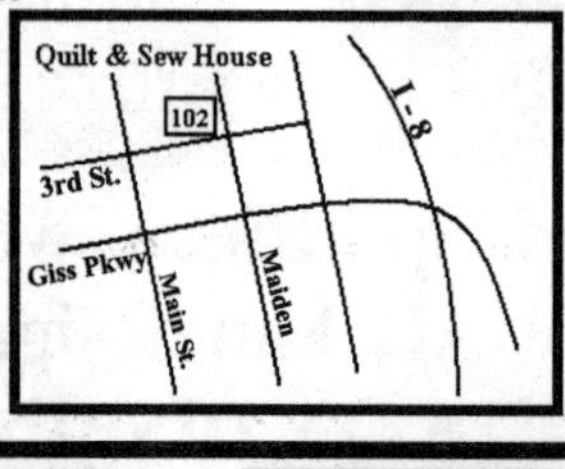

Yuma, AZ #2

Tues - Sat 9:30 - 4:30

Cactus Creek Quilting

11805 S. Fortuna Rd., Suite A-1 85367
(928) 345-9390 Fax: (928) 345-9392
E-Mail: ccquilting@c.s.com
Est: 2000 1500+ Bolts.

100% Cotton Fabrics. Quilting books and supplies. Long Arm Machine. Quilting Threads.

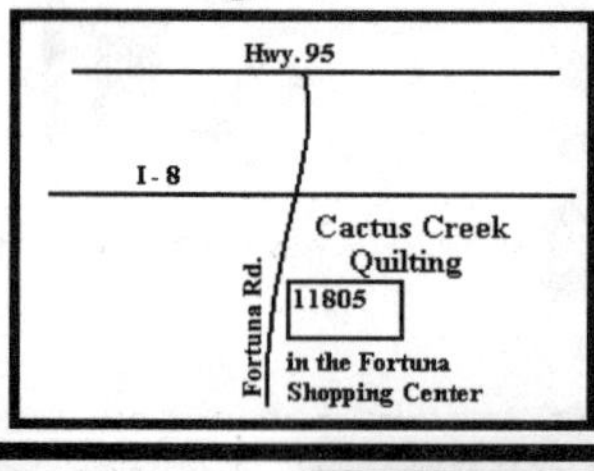

Quartzsite, AZ #3

Mon - Sat 9 - 5
Closed May thru Aug

Desert Fabric

185 Washington Ave 85346
(520) 927-7447 Fax: (928) 927-3416
E-Mail: jbarc@tds.net
1400 sq. ft. 1100+ Bolts

Quality fabric selection to satisfy any quilters taste. Excellent selection of southwest prints to remember your Arizona visit.

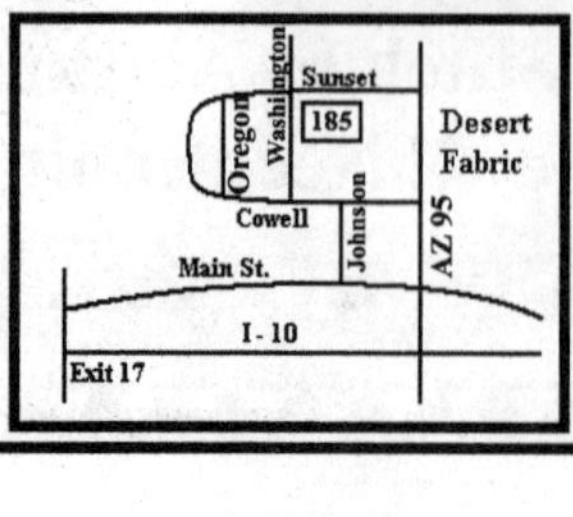

Lake Havasu City, AZ #4

Mon - Fri 9 - 5
Sat 9 - 4

Sew What?

1685 Mesquite Ave. #E 86403
(928) 453-4040 Fax: (928) 453-3023
E-Mail: SewWhatJK@aol.com
Owner: Jeanette Kennedy
Est: 1995 4000 Bolts

Largest selection of fabrics, books, patterns, & quilting supplies on the Colorado River and the American Home of the London Bridge.

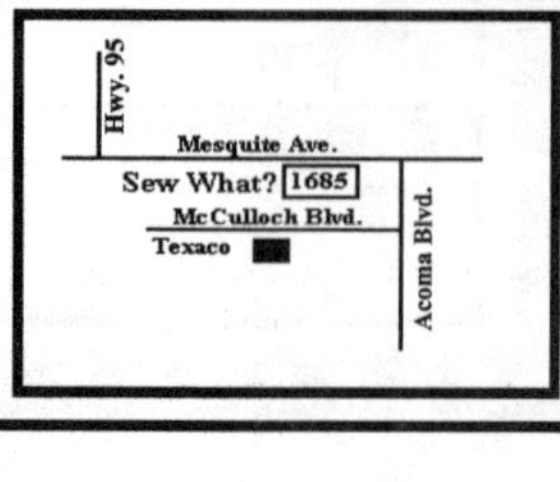

Flagstaff, AZ #5

Mon - Sat 9 - 5:30

Odegaard's Sewing Center

19 W. Aspen 86001
(520) 774-2331 In AZ (800) 360-2331
Fax: (520) 774-4668
Bernina, Pfaff, Viking, Singer

Large selection of 100% Cotton Fabrics,
Quilting Books & Patterns.
Southwest Fabrics and Notions.

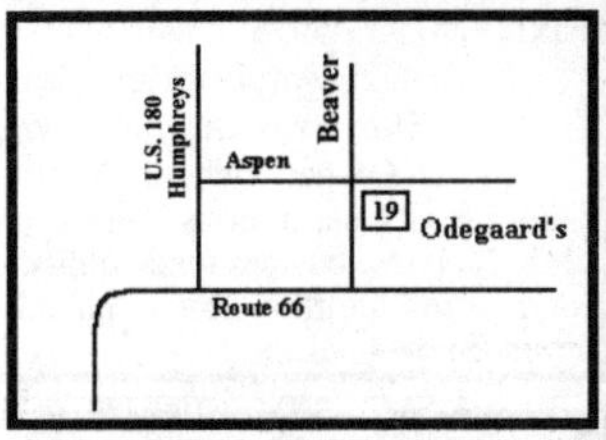

Flagstaff, AZ #6

Mon - Sat 10 - 5 Sun 1 - 4

Pine Country Quilts

1800 S. Milton Rd., #13 86001
(928) 779-2194 Green Tree Village
Owner: Shelly & Keith Breunig
Est: 1985 1300 sq.ft. 1000 Bolts

Fabrics, books, and notions for the traditional and contemporary quilter. Pure quilting fun on the way to the Grand Canyon!

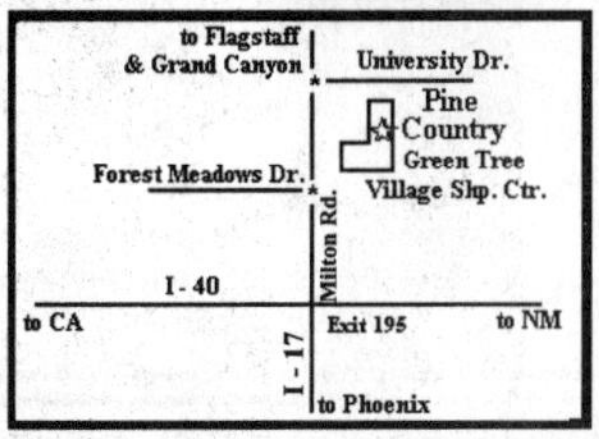

**Not only do we have beautiful fabrics,
we also have beautiful views!
We've added a Quilters' Gallery with artwork
and traditional & antique quilts.
Come Visit!**

The Quilter's Store & Gallery

Quilting Supplies — Classes — 100% Cotton Fabrics
Personalized Instruction Available

(928) 282-2057
Marge Elson, Proprietor
3075 West Highway 89A 86336

Sedona, AZ #7

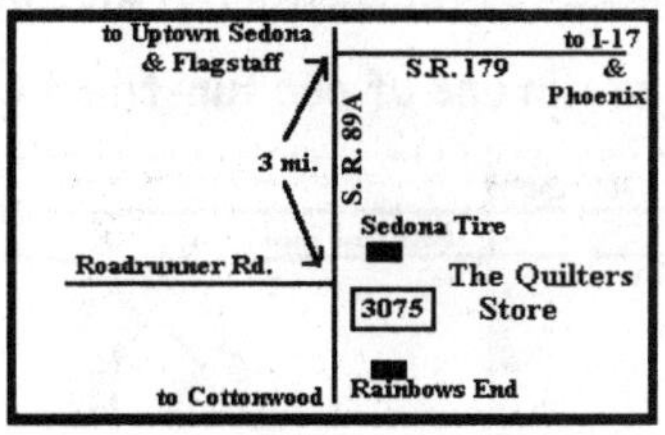

Monday - Friday: 9 a.m. - 5 p.m.
Saturday: 9 a.m. - 4 p.m. **Sunday**: 12 p.m. - 4 p.m.

Prescott Valley, AZ #8

Mon - Fri 9 - 5 Sat 9 - 4

A Quilter's Dream

8732 E. Hwy. 69 86314
(928) 772-0864
Owner: Muriel L. Gregg

Beautiful 100% Cotton Fabrics. Great Selections of Books, Patterns & Notions. Unique Gifts. Classes for all Levels of Quilting.

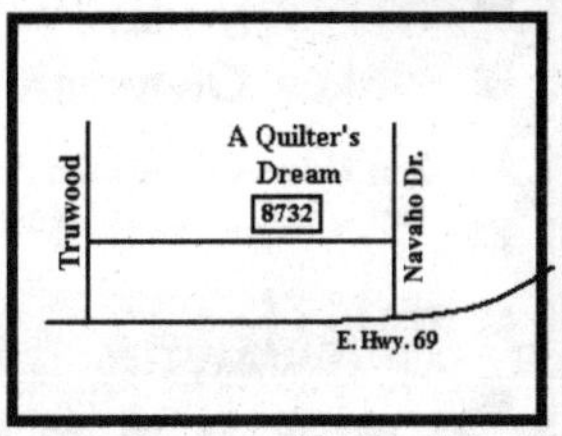

Payson, AZ #9

Mon - Fri 10 - 5 Sat 10 - 4

The Quilters Outpost

904 N. Beeline, Suite E 85541
(928) 468-6360 Fax: (928) 474-9550
Est: 2001 2000 sq.ft. 1600 Bolts

Fabrics, Books, Patterns, Notions, Silk Ribbon, Yarns and Specialty Threads.
Horn Furniture

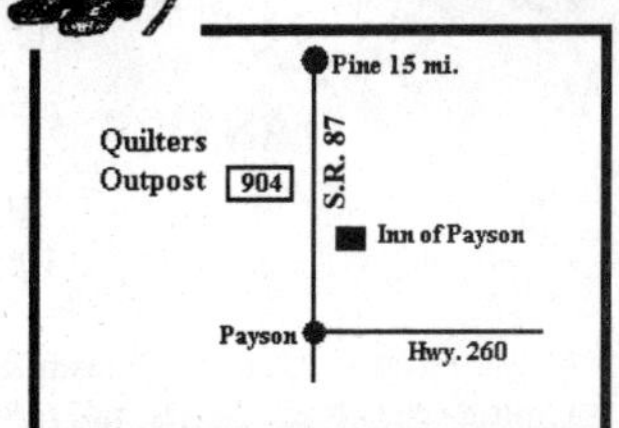

Pinetop, AZ #10

Mon - Sat 10 - 5

Bear Hollow Quilters Den

846 A E. White Mountain Blvd. 85935
(520) 367-2770
Fax: (520) 367-4346
Est: 1997 1800 sq.ft. 2000+ Bolts

Complete Quilt Store. Fabrics, Notions, Books & Patterns. In store long arm quilting. Fun and Friendly

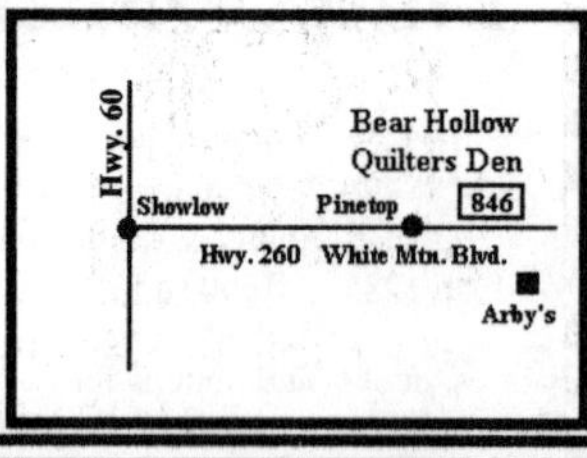

Springerville, AZ #11

Tues - Sat 10 - 5

Crazy Quilt Shoppe & Gifts

310 E Main St., P.O. Box 299 85938
(928) 333-2739 or (800) 707-2739 (2SEW)
Fax: (928) 333-5933 Est: 2002 2100 sq. ft.
E-Mail: crazyquiltshoppe@yahoo.com
Web Site: www.crazyquiltshoppe.com
Owner: Deborah Martin

Quilting fabrics, notions, books, patterns, kits, clubs, classes, custom made quilts, embroidery, long arm quilting, faux chenille blankets, Trunk Shows.

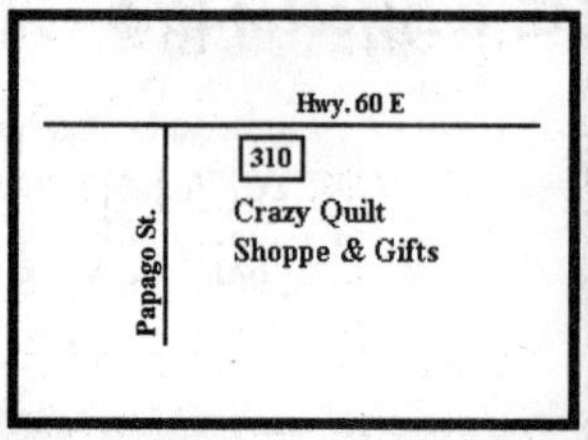

♥ *Quilting from the Heart* ♥

Quilters Delight

480 368-9598

Hours
Mon - Fri.
9:30am to 5:30pm
Saturdays
9:30am to 4:30pm
Sunday
11:00am to 4:00pm
Closed Sundays July and August

8230 E. Raintree Dr. #106
Scottsdale, AZ 85260

COME AND SHARE
ALL 100% COTTON FABRICS (approx 3000 BOLTS)
BOOKS-PATTERNS-NOTIONS-GIFTS
Participate in one of our fun-filled CLASSES

www.quiltersdelight.net

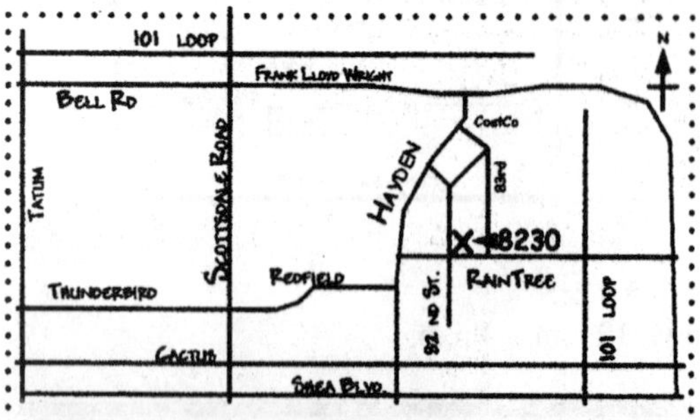

Scottsdale, AZ #12

The Quilted Apple

3043 North 24th St. 85016
(602) 956-0904
E-Mail: q-apple@swlink.net
Web Site: www.quiltedapple.com
Owner: Laurene Sinema
Est: 1978 4600 sq.ft. 2400 Bolts

100 % cotton fabrics, books, patterns, notions, classes.

Mon - Sat 9:30 - 5:30 Tues till 9

Specialize in fine hand quilting. Bernina Sewing Machines. Free Catalog

Phoenix, AZ #13

The Quilter's Koop

Fine Fabric
Classes
Notions
Patterns
Books & Gifts
Supplies

Shop Hours
Monday - Saturday 9:30 AM - 5:30 PM
Thurs. Evening until 9:00 PM
Sundays Closed
(480) 785-0710

EASY FREEWAY ACCESS
Elliot Road, 1 block West of I-10

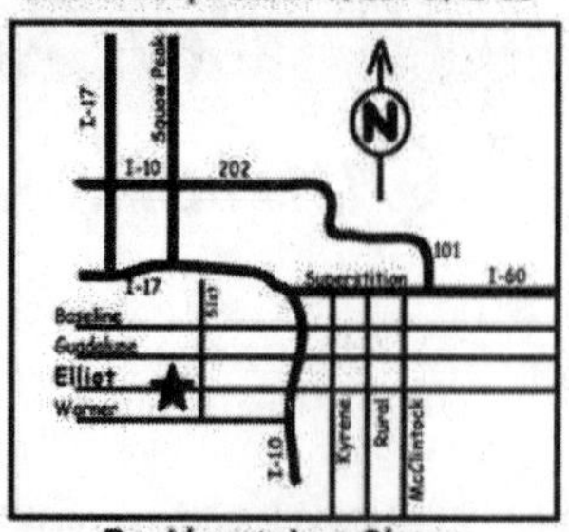

Under New Ownership!
Jan Morris & Sandra Turley
Darlene Johannis, Manager

In Ahwatukee Plaza,
5053 E. Elliot Rd., Phoenix, AZ 85044

Phoenix, AZ #14

Mesa, AZ #15

Mon - Fri 9 - 9 Sat 9 - 6

Sally's FABRICS

1235 E. Main 85203
(480) 833-7201
Fax:
(480) 833-4694
Est: 1952
20,000 sq.ft.
1000's of Bolts

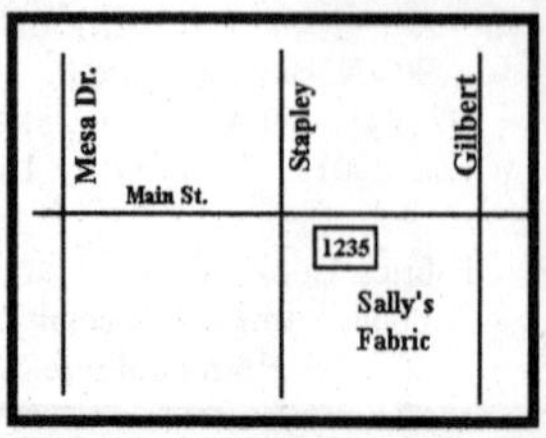

All your fabric needs and dreams in one location. Quilting & Bridal. Largest full service fabric shop in Arizona.

Mesa, AZ #16

Quilter's Emporium

7516 E. Main St. #3 85207
(480) 654-8143 Fax: (480) 654-8165
E-Mail: QuiltrsEmporium@juno.com
Owners: Rosie Lefkowitz & Lois Smith

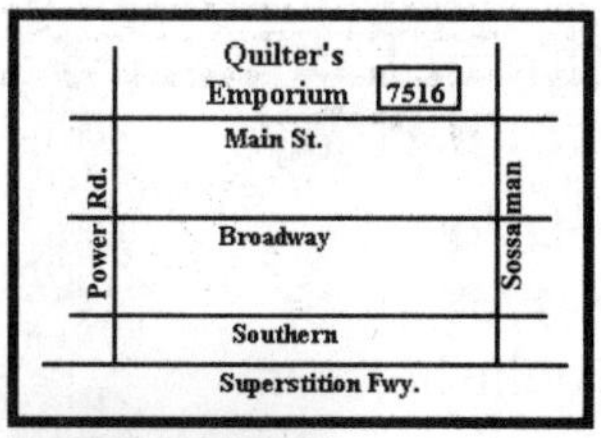

Large selection of fabric (2000+ bolts), books, patterns & quilting supplies. The friendliest quilt shop for service, inspiration and sharing of ideas.

Mon - Fri 9:30 - 5:30 Sat 9:30 - 4

Tempe, AZ #17

Est: 1982

the Quilter's Ranch

1030 E. Baseline Road $178 85283
(In Mill Towne Center)

Friendly, knowledgeable staff
Cozy and inviting environment
From batiks to southwest to homespuns;
something for everyone!

(480) 838-8350
E-Mail:
quiltersranch@juno.com

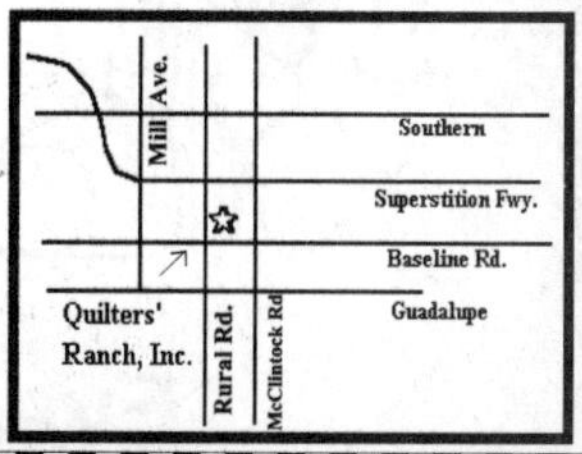

Mon - Sat 9:30 - 5:30 Thurs til 9 (Sept. - May) Sun 12 - 4

Owner: Susan Visotsky

Chandler, AZ #18

Mon - Fri 10 - 6 Thur til 8 Sat 10 - 5 Labor to Mem Sun 12 - 4

1949 W. Ray Rd. #38 85224
(480) 857-3443 Fax: (480) 857-6945
E-Mail: CuttingEdgeQ@aol.com
Est: 2001

Cutting Edge QUILTWORKS

Premium Quality Fabric for Quilters. Take Ray Rd. Exit from I - 10 or 101. East on Ray to Dobson (SE corner)

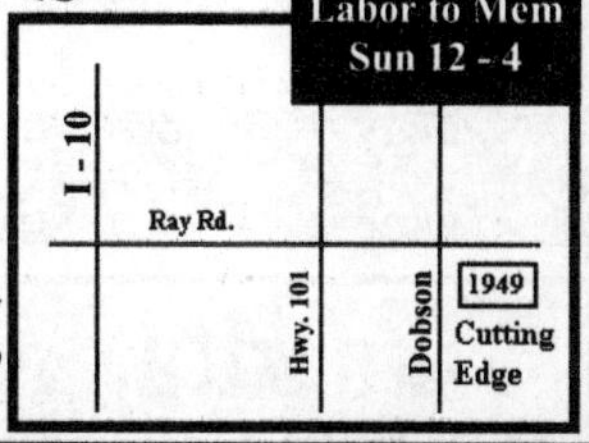

Globe, AZ #19

Tues- Sat 9 - 5:30

Country Corner

383 South Hill Street 85501
(928) 425-8208
Owners: Johnny & Janice McInturff
Est: 1986 6000 sq.ft.

Quilts, Fabric, Notions--Antiques Hardware, Tack, Boots, Vet Supplies, Chain saws--parts and service.

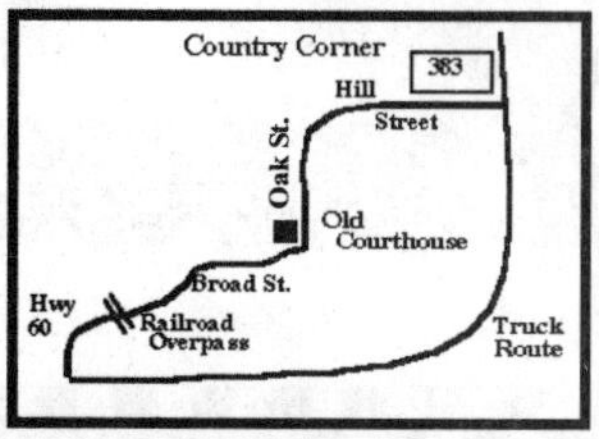

Tucson, AZ #20

Mon - Sat 9 - 5

Bernina Sewing Center

4500 E. Speedway #39 85712
(520) 795-7786 Est: 1976
E-Mail: bernina@mindspring.com
Web Site: www.mindspring.com/~bernina

quilting cottons * heirloom laces & embroideries
* books * threads * classes *
* Bernina Sales & Service *

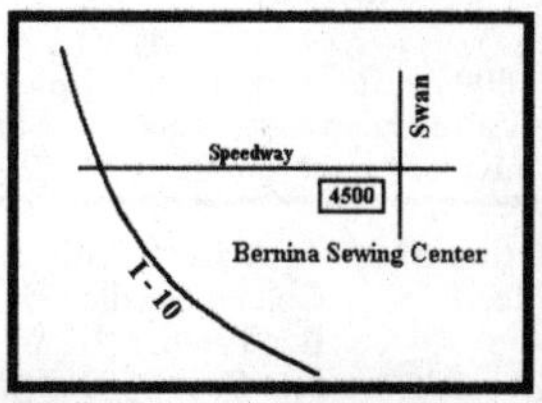

Tucson, AZ #22

Mon - Sat 9:30 - 5

Quilt Basket, Inc.

6538 C E. Tanque Verde Rd. 85715
(520) 722-8810 Fax: (520) 722-7720
Owner: Peggy Peck
Est: 1990 1500 sq.ft.

Lots & Lots of beautiful fabrics ....
Everything for today's busy quilter ....
Come see us !
"A friendly place for all your quilting needs"

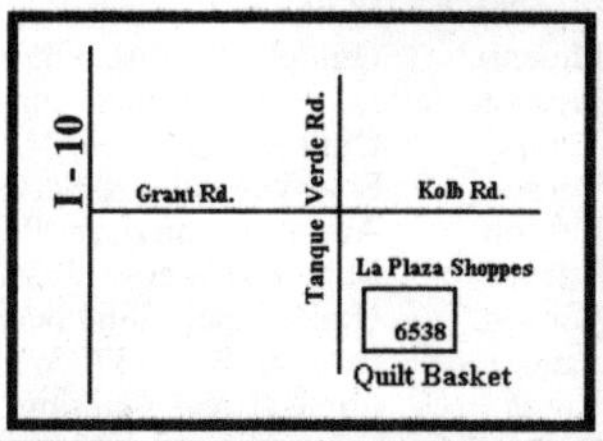

Tucson, AZ #21

Precious Hands Needleworks

2917 E. Grant Rd. 85716
(520) 325-8010
E-Mail: cdargel@theriver.com
Web Site: www.immaquilter.com
Owner: Cathy Dargel
Est: 1994 2000 sq.ft.

Mon - Sat 9 - 5 Thur til 8

Bountiful Cotton Fabrics, Quilting Supplies, Classes, & Notions. We specialize in Southwestern Fabrics & Patterns, Batiks, Flannels & Brights. We also offer machine quilting, come see a demonstration!

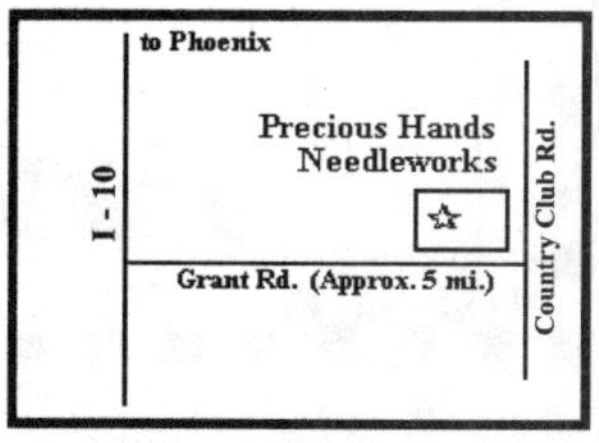

Tucson, AZ #23

Cactus Quilt Shop

Mon - Fri 9:30 - 5
Sat 9:30 - 4:30

6482 N. Oracle Rd.
Plaza Del Oro Shopping Center
In The NE Corner - Under the Clock
(520) 498-4698
Fax: (520) 498-4708
Web Site: www.cactusquiltshop.com
Owner: Nancy Landon
Est: 1997 1890 sq.ft. 3000 plus Bolts

Everything for the Quilter
Plus Treasures.
We specialize in reproduction fabrics--largest collection in the South West!
And don't miss our Kitty Corner.

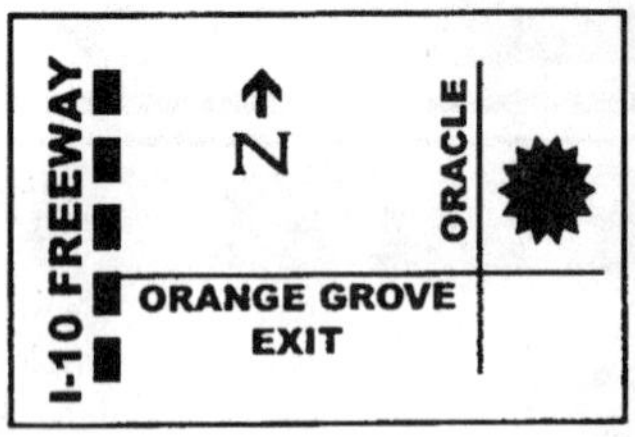

Purr-fect Quilters Cottage

Fabric Gifts
Notions Fudge

1575 W. American Ave. Oracle, AZ 85623
(520) 896-2414
E-Mail: quilters@theriver.com
Est: 2001 2100 sq.ft. 1300 Bolts

We are a friendly shop with great tasting fudge. We have a selection of gifts, books, notions, patterns and of course a wonderful selection of fabric! Come in and visit us.
We love show and tell

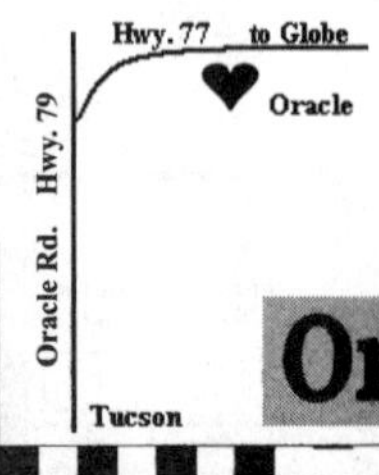

Mon - Sat 10 - 5
Thur til 7

Oracle, AZ #24

Sahuarita, AZ #25

Mon - Fri 9 - 5
Sat 9 - 12
Summer Hours
(June, July, August)
Fri & Mon 9 - 5
or by Appt.

QUILTERS DESERT PATCH

16121 S. Country Club Rd. 85629
(520) 648-1533
E-Mail: trvlnqltr@aol.com
Owner: Phyllis Sirrine Est: 1985

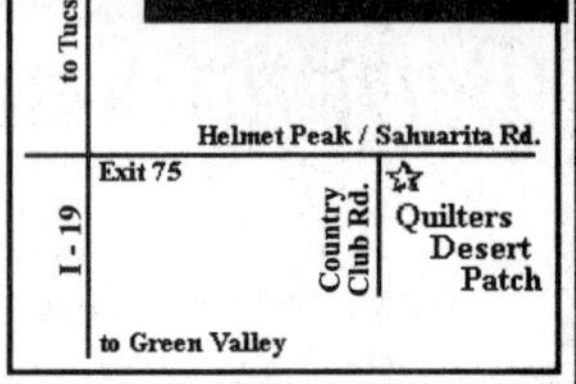

1800 sq.ft. stuffed with Bolts & Flat Folds. We're happy to open by appointment for travelers in the summer call (520) 393-1237

Other Shops in Arizona: We suggest calling first

Mesa	Golden Needle, 7516 E. Main St. #4	480-985-2534
Ajo	Bee Patch, 1161 W. Snyder Rd.	520-387-7765
Dewey	Sun Country Quilts, 12 Smoki Trail, HC 61, Box 446	520-632-7422
Flagstaff	Rosamond's, 6090 E. Robles Rd.	520-527-4658
Flagstaff	Suzie's Quilting Bee, 5850 Silver Saddle Rd.	928-526-8031
Gilbert	Patchwork Pieces Quilt Co., 1250 N. Sailors Way	480-545-7096
Glendale	Heart Strings, 7157 N. 58th Dr.	602-937-3713
Glendale	Craftmart, 5644 W. Soft Wind Dr.	623-581-8008
Mesa	Sally's Fabrics, 2647 W. Baseline Rd.	602-839-0154
Phoenix	Enriquez Materials & Quilting, 1423 N. 27th Ln.	602-484-9254
Phoenix	Mom's Quilting & Yarn Shop, 6842 N 14th St.	602-265-1953
Phoenix	Quilters Paradise, 3639 W. Juniper Ave	602-993-2590
Prescott Valley	Sew Much More, 2517 N. Great Western Dr.	928-772-3454
Tempe	Quilt Kits & More, 2436 E. Balboa Dr.	480-897-3430
Tucson	Sew-Vac Sales & Service, 5933 E. 22nd St.	
Tucson	Antiques American, P.O. Box 13709	520-745-5631
Tucson	Material Things, 1527 N. Wilmot Rd.	520-733-3718
Tucson	Quilters Bee, 3860 N. El Moraga Dr.	520-743-0391
Yuma	Quilting Bee, 2370 W. 32nd St.	520-726-3000
Yuma	Cactus Creek Quilting, 11411 S. Fortuna Rd. #205B	928-345-9390

16 Featured Shops

ARKANSAS

Spinning Star Fabrics

205 W. Rock
72701
(479) 443-2243
Fax:
(479) 443-2236

Fayetteville, AR #1

- 100% Cotton Prints for Quilting & Apparel
- Buttons, Lace & Trims
- Linens, Silks, Organically Grown Cotton & Heirloom Fabrics
- Notions, Tools & Patterns
- Classes for All Ages & Skill Levels

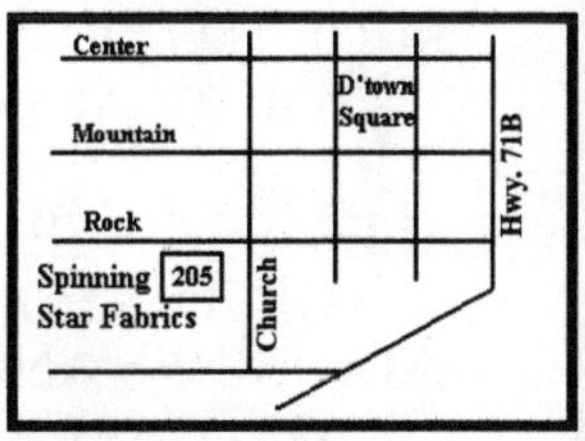

Mon - Sat 9 - 6
Thur til 9

www.spinning starfabrics.com
spinstarfab@aol.com

Fayetteville, AR #2

Quilt Your Heart Out

Mon - Sat 10 - 5

125 E. Township #11 72703
(501) 587-0307
Owner: Lila Rostenberg
Est: 1993 1000 sq.ft.

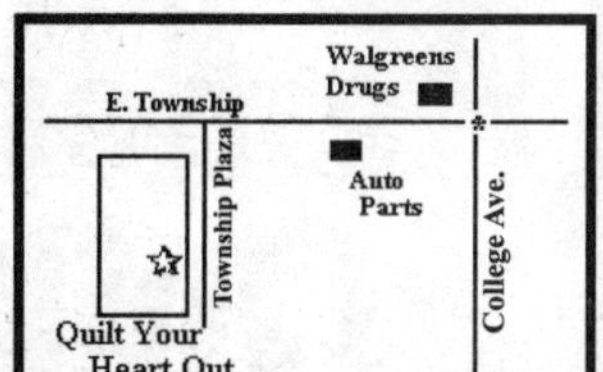

800 Bolts of 100% cotton fabric. Lots of patterns, books & notions. Homespuns, 1930's & 1800's reproduction pieces.

Gentry, AR #3

Tapestry Gardens

Mon - Fri 9 - 5
Sat 9-4

1021 S. Gentry Blvd. 72747
(479) 736-3100 or (800) 773-7953
Fax: (479) 736-3101
Owner: Marci Nichols
Est: 1996 5000 sq.ft.

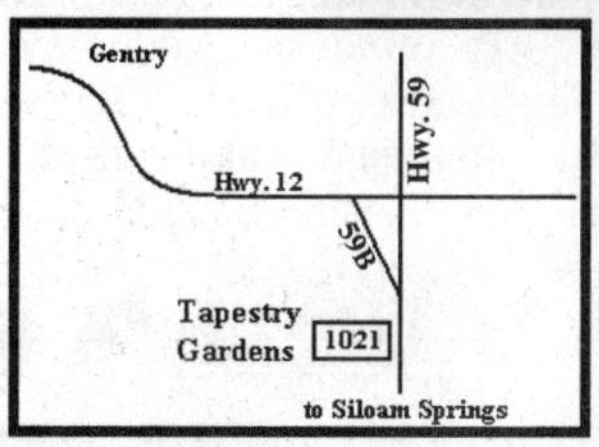

Quilt fabrics, Clothing fabrics, Gifts, Bakery/ tearoom. Amish furniture and stoves.

Rogers, AR #4

Mon - Sat 9 - 5

Patchwork Emporium

218 S. 1st St. 72756
(479) 636-3385 Est: 1981
Owner: Nancy Daniel
"A Complete Quilt Shop !"
4000 Bolts of Fabric—100% Cottons,
Notions. Felted Wool Kits. Handmade Gifts.
Lots of Quilts! Models! Ideas! Classes!

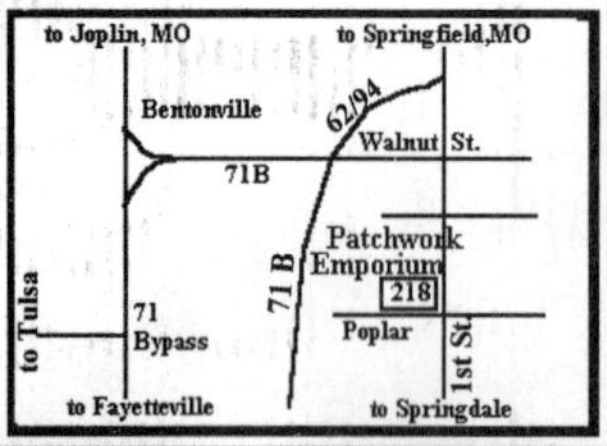

Eureka Springs, AR #5

Mon- Fri 9 - 5 Sat by Appt.

Warren Electronics & Digital Quiltz

36 Hwy. 23 S 72632
(479) 253-9049 Est: 1995
E-Mail: warren@ipa.net
Owners: John & Martha Ann Warren

Inspiration for Quilters through high quality cotton fabrics. We demonstrate computer design software in our shop. Tourists welcome & appreciated

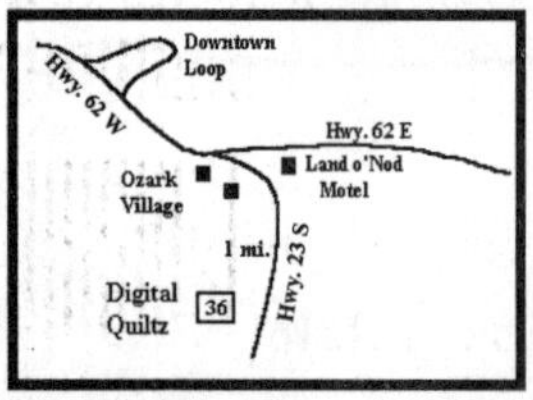

Wall to Wall Samples & Quilts for Sale

**Tues - Fri 9:30 - 5
Sat 9:30 - 3**

Full Service Quilting Shop!

Fabric, Books, Patterns, Notions, Class schedule available on the internet with free pattern at www.mtncom.com/quilts. Babylock, Bernina and Elna sewing machines sales & repairs. Classes. In an historic 2-story rock house built in 1908 with a new classroom.

Remember Me Quilt Shop

914 S. Main 72653 (870) 425-7670
rememberme@cox_internet.com

P&B, Hoffman, Monarch, Moda, RJR, South Seas, Kings Road. Embroidery headquarters, classes, software machines, thread & stabilizers etc.

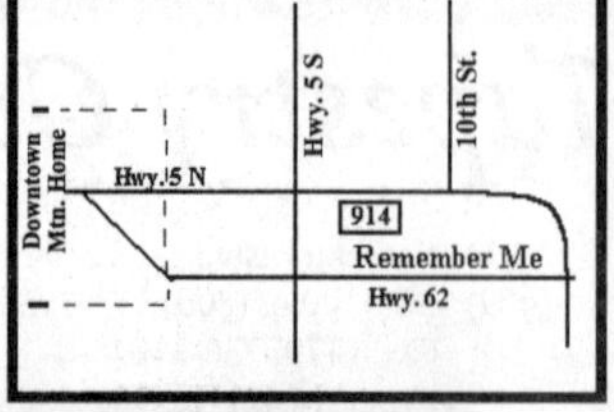

Mountain Home, AR #6

Harrison, AR #7

Country Corner Quilt Shop

We Meet All Your Quilting Needs!

10872 Hwy. 392
Harrison, AR 72601
870-437-2299
E-mail: QuiltShop@eritter.net
Est: 1986 4000+ Bolts

Mon - Sat 8 - 5

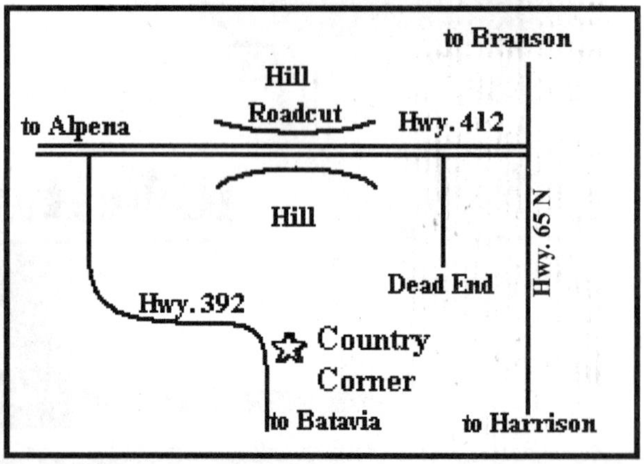

4000 BOLTS OF FABRIC * 100% COTTON
CHOSEN WITH THE QUILTER IN MIND

PATTERNS & BOOKS GALORE
STENCILS SULKY THREAD NOTIONS

CLASSES
BLOCK OF THE MONTH PATTERNS AND KITS

HAND GUIDED MACHINE QUILTING
WE DO QUALITY CUSTOM WORK IN OUR SHOP TO FIT YOUR SPECIFIC NEEDS.
STOP BY AND WATCH US WORK.

SALES, SERVICE AND INSTRUCTION ON NOLTING LONG ARM QUILTING MACHINES AND SIMPLICITY HOME SEWING MACHINES AND SERGERS.

Heart Quilt Shop

Harrison, AR #8

HOME OF THE HEART QUILT

We make all kinds of quilts: Moose, Deer, Eagles, Birds, Angels, Tractors, Horses, Fishing, Trains, Lighthouses and Reversable Ones.
We also have traditional Quilts: Lone Star, Double Wedding Ring, Log Cabin, Christmas Tree Skirts, Angels, Quilted Angels.
Stop by and get a Free Quilt Pattern

COME BY AND SEE US!

8874 Hwy. 62 West,
Harrison, AR 72601
870-437-5400
Brian & Trena Johnson

Daily 9 - 5 Closed Sundays in Jan & Feb

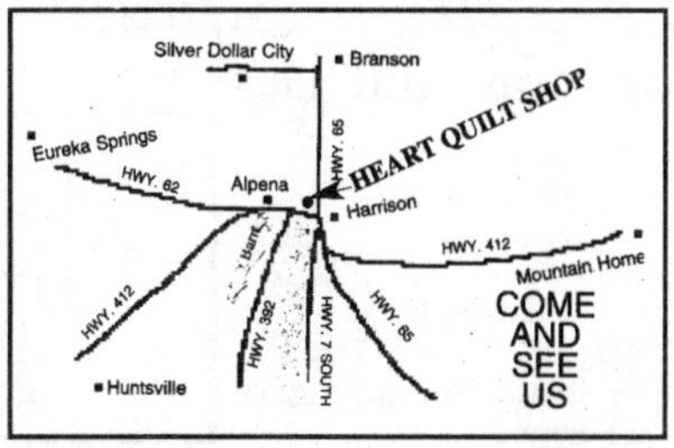

To reach us off Hwy. 65, turn West on Hwy. 62-412 from Bear Creek Springs, drive about 2 miles on the right.

Jonesboro, AR #9

Tues - Fri 10 - 5:30 Sat 10 - 4 Mon by Appt.

Quilters Corner

2010 Wilkins 72401
(870) 931-1138 Est: 1996
E-Mail: padavis@cox-internet.com
Owners: Leonard & Ann Davis

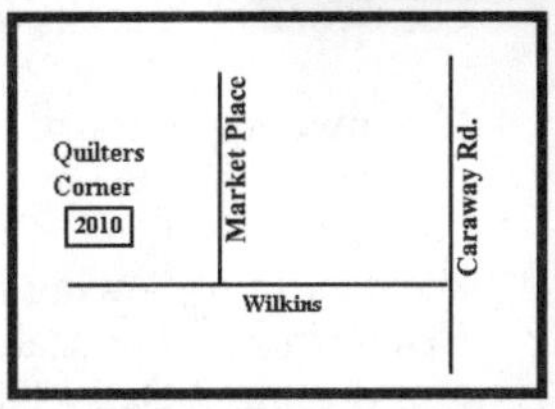

Fabrics, Notions, Books & Patterns. Machine Quilting. Classes for beginners and advanced. Friendly Service and a great place to visit.

Russellville, AR #10

Mon - Fri 10 - 5 Sat 9 - 4

Donna's Sew 'n Quilt

1610 S. Arkansas Ave. 72801
(479) 967-9591 Fax: Same
E-Mail: sewmuch@cswnet.com
Web Site: www.donnassewnquilt.com
Est: 1995 1000+ Bolts

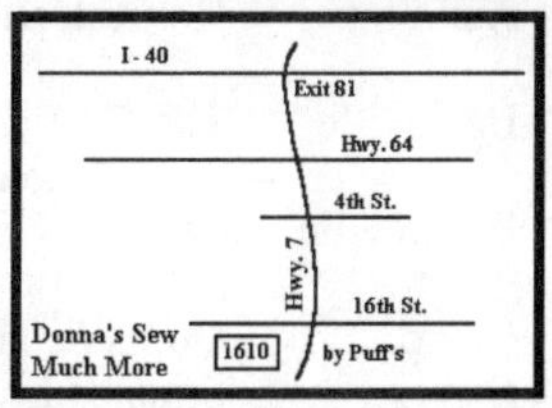

The River Valley's place for quilters to learn, quilt, and have fun and get the finest available for their quilting needs. Husqvarna Viking Dealer.

Historic Van Buren, AR #11

Mon - Sat 9:30 - 5:30 Winter 10 - 5

Olde Towne Quilt Shoppe

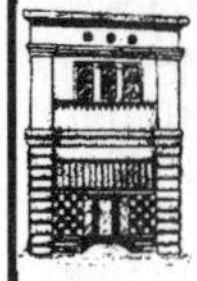

814 Main St. 72956
(479) 474-6378
Web Site: wwwthequiltshoppe.com
Est: 1997 1800 sq.ft.
Owner: Yolanda Mullins & Winona Bishop

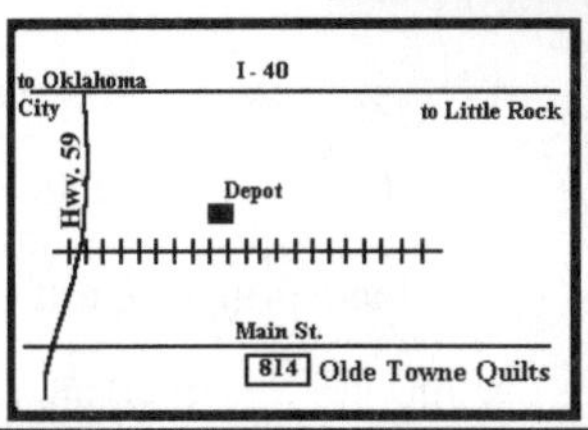

Where family heirlooms are created. Custom quilts & home décor. Located across from the depot in Historic Van Buren, AR

Greenwood, AR #12

Mon - Fri 9 - 5 Sat 10 - 3

Main Street Fabric

20 N. Main, P.O. Box 908 72936
(479) 996-7349
Owner: Oleta Kennedy
Est: 1990
1600 sq.ft. 1600 Bolts

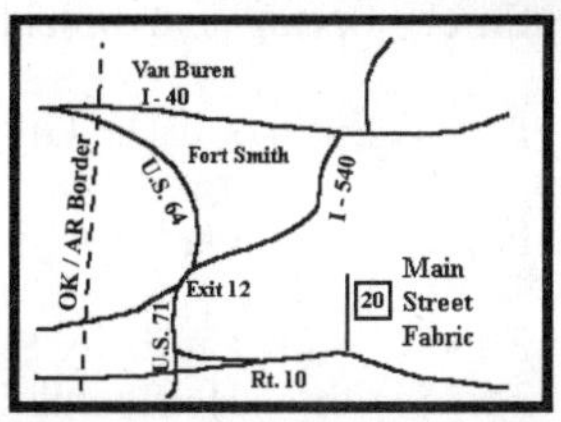

Great selection of 100% Cotton Fabric, Books, Patterns, Notions, Supplies. Classes Avail.
Approximately 10 miles south of Exit 12

Huntington, AR #13

Wed & Sat 9:30 - 5

MAMA'S LOG HOUSE

3715 E. Clarks Chapel Rd.
72940
(479) 928-5059 or
(479) 883-0254 Est: 1982
E-mail: mamaslog@valuelinx.net

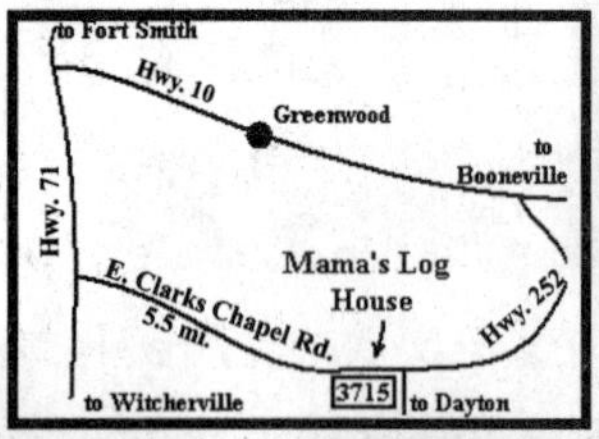

Quilting Supplies - Crafts - Split Oak Baskets 100% Cotton Fabric

Hot Springs, AR #15

Mon - Fri 9 - 5:30 Sat 9 - 3

Cathy's Quiltin' Square

& Monogrammin' Designs

3256 Albert Pike 71913
Est: 1999
(501) 760-6099
Owner: Cathy Anderson
3600 sq.ft. 1200 Bolts
Catalog $12.95

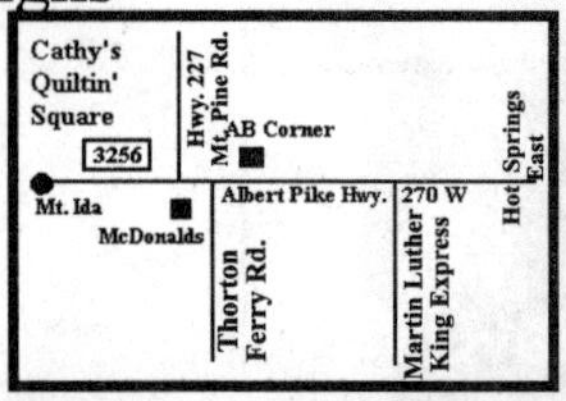

Quilt Fabric, Patterns, Books, Notions, Custom Machine Quilting, & Embroidery

Stuttgart, AR #16

Mon - Fri 9:30 - 5:30 Sat 10 - 2

The French Seam

2014 S. Main St. 72160
(870) 673-8156 Fax: (870) 673-6280
E-Mail: frenchseam@arkansascounty.com

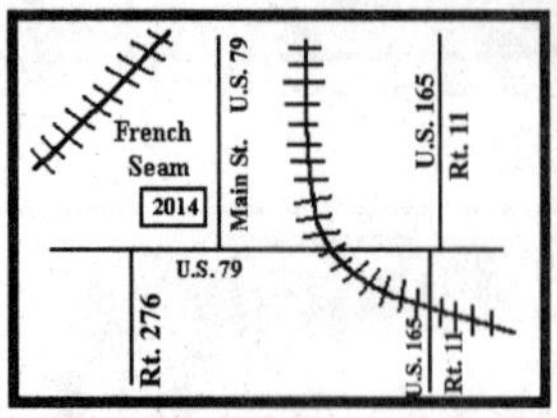

Authorized Bernina dealer. Quilting, heirloom, silk ribbon, fashion fabric and notions.
Machine embroidery supplies
Machine repair.

The Stitchin' Post

Little Rock, AR #14

10301 Rodney Parham Rd.
(In Breckenridge Village)
Little Rock, AR 72227
(501) 227-0288
Est: 1972 3600 sq.ft.

Mon - Fri 10 - 5:30 Sat 10 - 5

VIKING Husqvarna

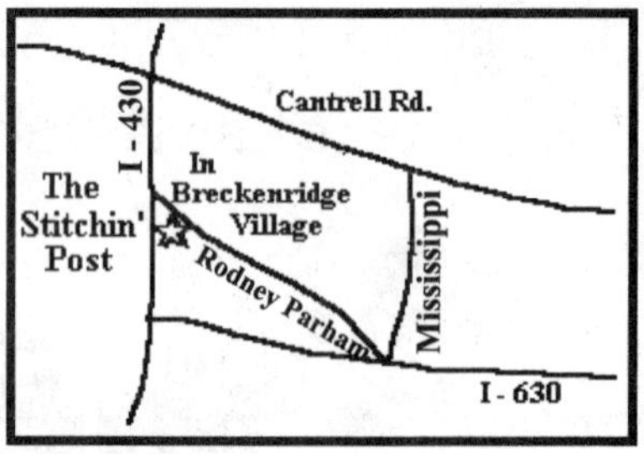

Serving quilters for over 30 years.
Domestic and imported cottons.
Quilting supplies and classes.

Other Shops in Arkansas: We suggest calling first

Ash Flat	Homestead Stitches, HC 67, Box 256	870-994-2033
Batesville	The Fabric Connection, 151 W. Main St. PO Box 2313	870-793-2405
Booneville	Cheryl's General Store, 200 W. Main St.	501-675-4017
Camp	Quilts & Things, R.R. #1, Box 573	870-895-2518
Dover	Stitches Etc., 331 Water St.	501-331-3656
Dover	Bear Bluff Quilts, 28958 SR 7 N	501-331-3511
Dover	Linda's, 253 Rentfro	501-331-4957
Eureka Springs	The Cotton Patch Quilts, 1 Center St.	501-253-9894
Eureka Springs	Vicky's Too, 2039B E. Van Buren	501-253-7889
Eureka Springs	The Quilt Shop, 2 Center St.	501-253-2093
Eureka Springs	Honeysuckle Rose Quilts & Gifts, 1 Spring St.	501-253-5148
Eureka Springs	Tropical Threads, 435 W. Van Buren	501-253-8681
Eureka Springs	The Gingham Goose, P.O. Box 2186	501-253-9141
Flippin	Ogden's Quilts & Collectibles, 204 Main St. #B	870-453-3783
Flippin	Curiosity Shop 9084 Hwy. 62 E	870-453-5300
Fort Smith	Heirlooms Quilt Shop II, 1415 N. 38th	501-782-6839
Glenwood	Creekside Farm Country Store, Hwy. 70 W	870-356-5123
Greenwood	Crooked Creek Quilts, 909 Fairview Ln.	501-996-5808
Gurdon	Linda Calley, Hwy. 67	870-353-2618
Harrison	Sewing Place, 1065 Zinc Rd.	870-743-6739
Hot Springs	Log Cabin Crafts, 450 S. Rogers	501-767-6624
Hot Springs	Daisy Patch, 111 Murray Hill Pl.	501-362-8988
Little Rock	Sew Smart, 9700 N. Rodney Parham Rd.	501-223-2317
Lowell	Makin Memories Fabric Shop, 5731 Primrose Rd.	501-756-9502
Omaha	Quilting Bee, 24790 U.S. Hwy. 65 N	501-426-5466
Paragould	Hillcrest Quilt Shop, 8802 Hwy 412 W	501-236-1988
Pea Ridge	Country House Quilting, 16324 N. Hwy 94	501-451-8978
Pelsor	Country Palace Ozark Crafts, HC 30 Box 108	870-294-5366
Pelsor	Nellie's Craft Shop, HC 30 Box 102	870-294-5317
Sulphur Springs	Quilt Corner, 128 N. Hibler Ave.	501-298-3006
Yellville	Sleeping Owl Crafts, Hwy. 14 S	870-449-5299

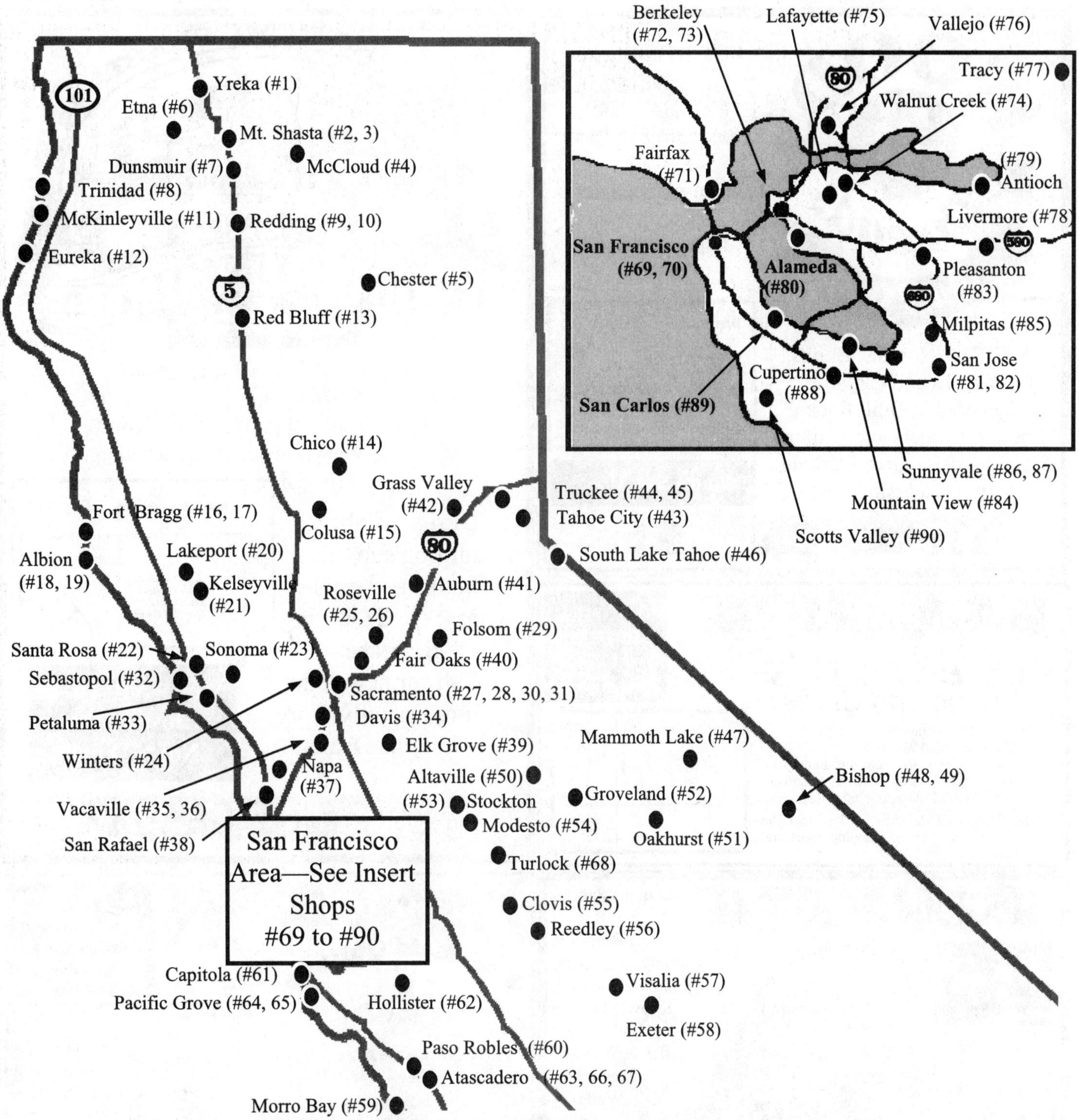

For Southern California See Page 37 Shops #91 thru #155

CALIFORNIA

155 Featured Shops

The Fabric Train

Dunsmuir, CA #7

5853 Sacramento Ave. 96025
(530) 235-4519
E-Mail: thefabrictra@earthlink.net
Web Site: www.thefabrictrain.com
Owners: Bill & Ann Sanford

Jan 1st thru March 1st
10 am to 4 pm
March thru December
10 am to 5 pm
Closed Sunday & Monday

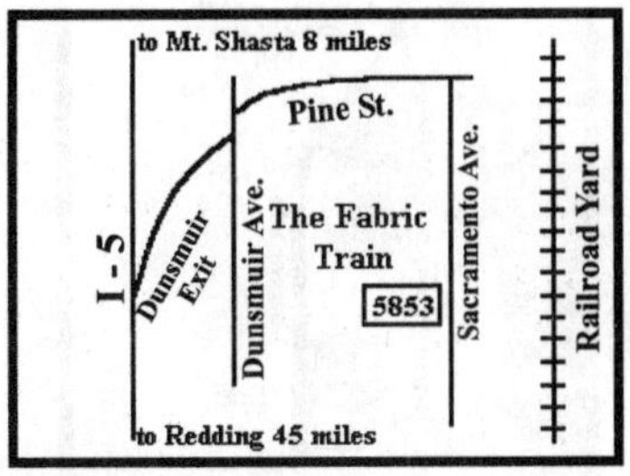

Full Service Fabric Store.
Large selection of Hoffman, Moda, Northcott, & Flannels, David Textiles & Fleece.

Located in historic Dunsmuir. "The Railroad Town"

Trinidad, CA #8

Ocean Wave Quilts

529 Trinity St. 95570
(707) 677-3770 Fax: (707) 677-3795
Owner: Sandi Globus
Est: 1994 800 sq.ft. 1000 Bolts

Open 6 days
9:30 - 5:30
Closed Tues

A unique shop containing fabulous fabrics, books and notions located in a historic fishing village nestled between redwoods and beaches.

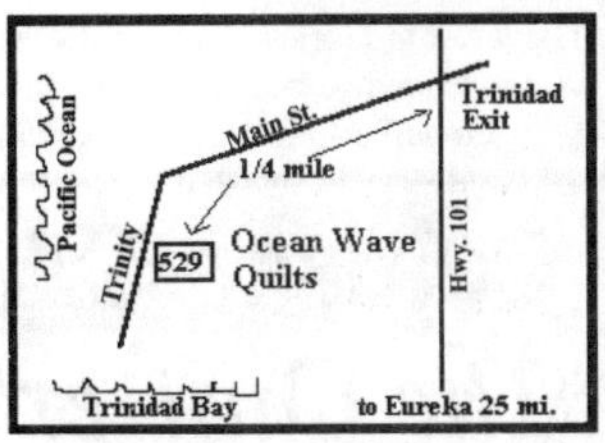

Redding, CA #9

Mon - Fri
9 - 6:30
Sat 9 - 6

The Fabric & Yarn CONNECTION

5200 Churn Creek Rd.
96002
(530) 221-0785

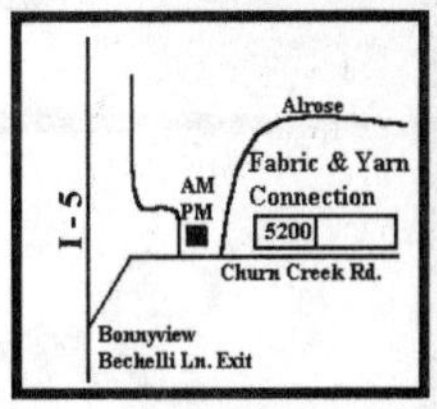

Owner: Jeri Webster Est: 1999 5400 sq.ft.

Full Service Fabric, Large Selection of Yarn, Quilting, Needlework, Friendly Service Just off I-5

Redding, CA #10

Mon - Sat
9 - 6
Sun 10 - 5

Ben Franklin Crafts

961 Dana Dr. 96003
(530) 221-8313 Fax: (530) 221-8387
Owners: Fred & Judy Zerull
Est: 1965 9000 sq.ft. 3500 Bolts

Visit our complete quilt department; stitchery, patterns, books, notions and fabrics: P&B, Benartex, Hoffman, Nancy Crow, Moda and many more.

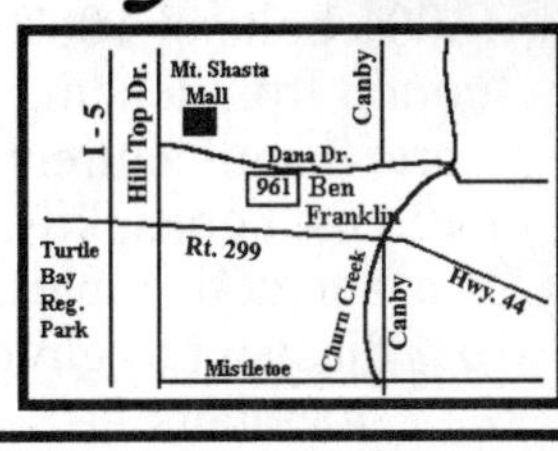

McKinleyville, CA #11

Serendipity
QUILTS & CRAFTS

1977 Central Avenue
McKinleyville, CA 95519
www.serendipityquilts.com
PH: (707) 839-9015 FAX: (707) 839-9016

HOURS:
Tues- Sat, 10 am-5:30 pm, Sunday, Noon-4 pm
2000+ Bolts 2200 sq. ft.

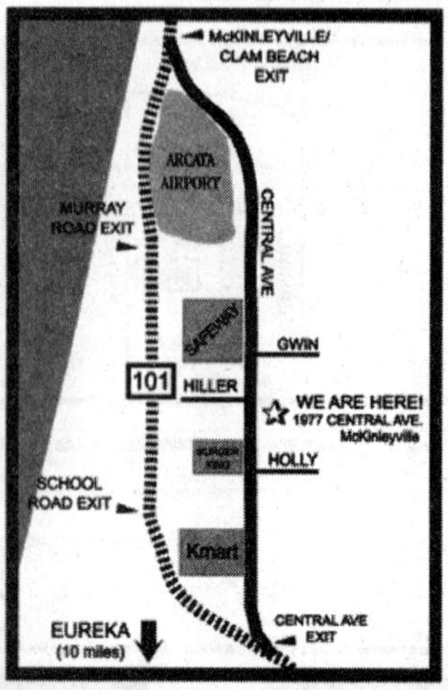

- SPECIALIZING IN FLANNELS!
- Kits Available
- Classes - All Levels
- Quilt Fabric & Supplies
- Books & Patterns
- Racks & Ladders

Monthly Fat Quarter Raffle and Color of the Week Sale!

Craft Supplies & Gifts Also Available!

We will sell your quilts on consignment!

Scottie Dog Quilts

301 W. Harris St. Eureka, CA 95503
(707) 444-9662 Fax: (707) 443-6649
E-Mail: ScottieDogQuilts@aol.com
Owner: BrendaLou Scott

Mon - Fri
10 - 5:30
Sat 10 - 4

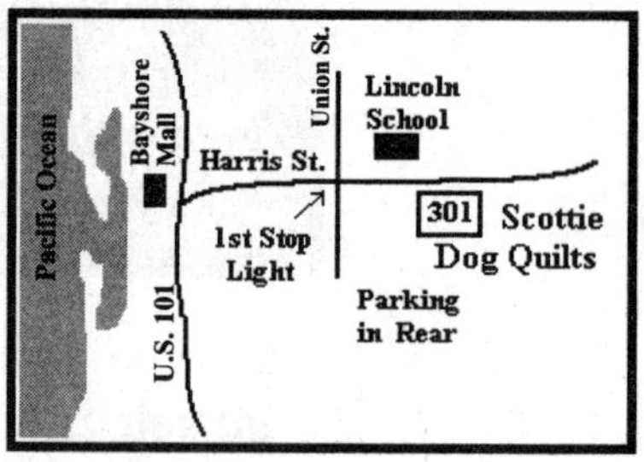

Wonderful selection of 100% Cotton Fabrics.
1200+ Bolts
Full line of Patterns, Books, Notions & Gifts.
Classes and Retreats for beginning through advanced quilters.
HandiQuilter Dealer.

Eureka, CA #12

Red Bluff, CA #13

In Stitches

208 Elm St. 96080
(530) 529-1436
instiches@snowcrest.net
Est: 2001 1400 sq.ft.

Tues - Sat
10 - 5

1300+ bolts of 100% cotton from leading fabric manufacturers. Patterns, books, kits, gifts and collectibles. 10% discount to guild members.

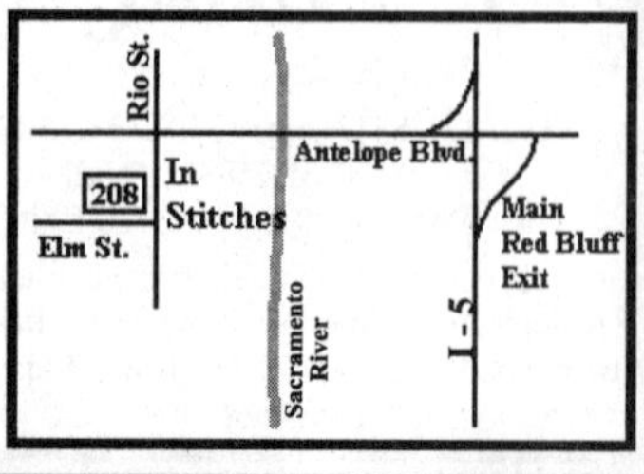

Chico, CA #14

Honey Run Quilters

Mon - Sat
10 - 5:30
Sun 11 - 4

1230 Esplanade 95926
(530) 342-5464
Web Site: www.honeyrunquilters.com
Owner: Sharon Berg

The latest in fabrics, books, patterns & notions.
Friendly, knowledgeable service.
Good Parking. Coffee's always on!

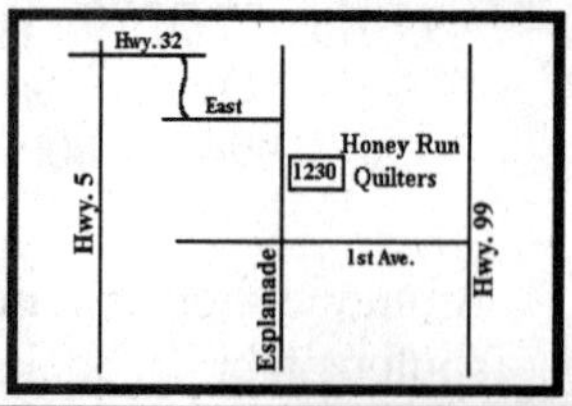

Colusa, CA #15

The Quilter's Garden

Mon - Fri
10 - 5:30
Sat 10 - 4

624 Fremont St 95932
(530) 458-4580
E-Mail: quiltersgarden@colusanet.com
Owner: Gail Ellersick
Est: 1999 2000 sq. ft. 1500 Bolts

We have quilt fabrics, notions, books, patterns, flannels and classes. We simply are the friendliest shop.

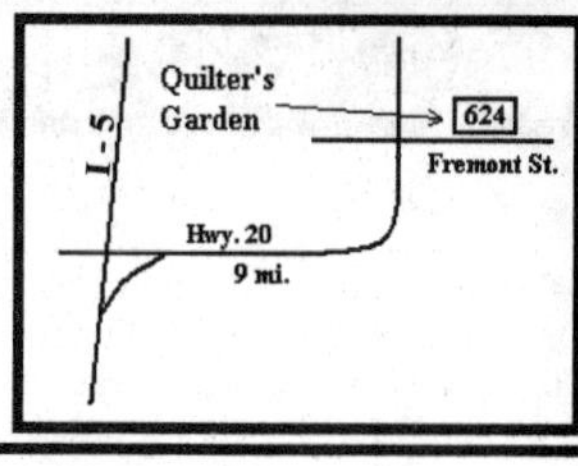

Fort Bragg, CA #16

Open Daily

FABRIC *Indulgence* & Art Supply

544 S. Main St. 95437
(707) 964-6365 Fax: (707) 964-6365
Est: 2000 3000 sq.ft. 3000 Bolts

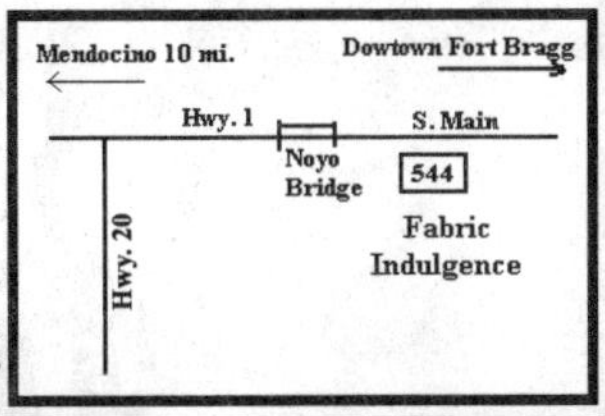

E-Mail: lunarain@mcn.org
Owners: Erin Severi & Tabitha Korhummel

Fine fabrics, notions, books, patterns, natural fibers, dyes, silk painting supplies & inspiration.

Fort Bragg, CA #17

Mon - Fri 9:30 - 5 Sat 10 - 4:30

Sew'n Sew Fabrics

115 E. Laurel St. 95437
(707) 964-4152
Fax: (707) 964-7046
Owner: Nancy Lamphear

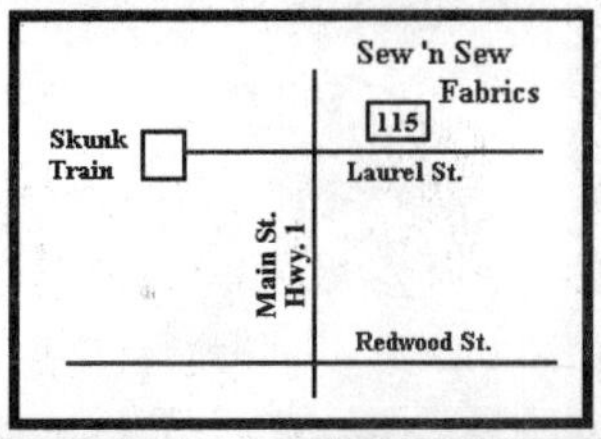

Quilting Fabrics including: Batiks, Japanese, Kids/Brights, Flannel & locally screened prints. Large selection of books & Patterns. Husband Friendly.

Albion, CA #18

Phone for Appointment

Rainbow Resource Co.

P.O. Box 222 95410
(707) 937-0431
E-Mail: rainbow@mcn.org
Owner: Charlene Younker
Est: 1969 Send LSASE for Catalog

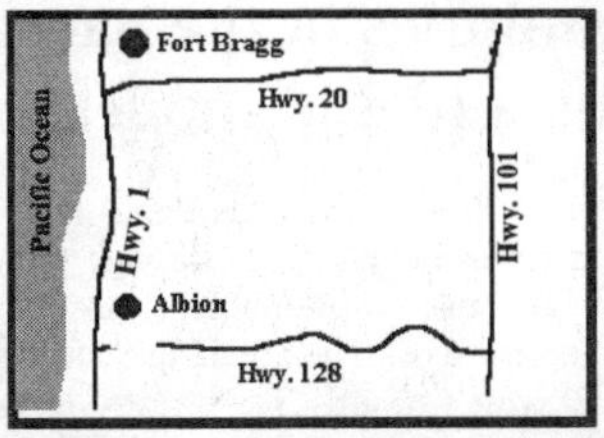

My own line of hand silk-screened fabric for quilters, along with related fabrics from various companies. Unusual Buttons, & Fun Stuff.

Albion, CA #19

By Appointment Only

The Quilt Complex

30701 Middle Ridge Rd. 95410
(707) 937-0739
E-mail: qultcomplex@starband.net
Web Site: www.thequiltcomplex.com
Owners: Julie Silber & Jean Demeter

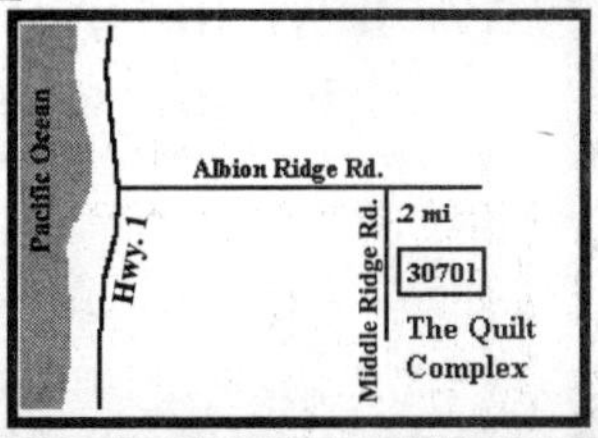

Antique and Vintage Quilts for Sale.
Exhibitions, Professional Appraisals.
Lectures and Workshops

Lakeport, CA #20

Tues - Sat 10 - 4

Kerrie's Quilting

1853 N. High St. 95453
(707) 263-8555
Owner: Harry & Kerrie Hershey

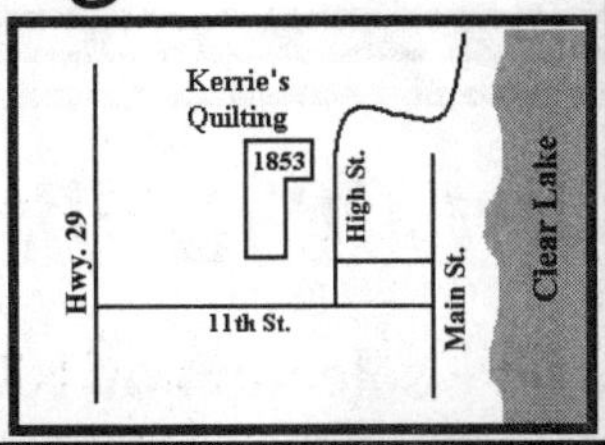

A friendly, small town shop at the lake. Cotton fabrics, books, notions, classes & retreats. Authorized Elna dealer.

Kelseyville, CA #21

Quilted Treasures

www.quilted-treasures.com

3925 Main St., P.O. Box 1189 95451
(707) 279-0324 Fax: (707) 279-4430
Pamela Francis, President
Anne Barquist, Vice President

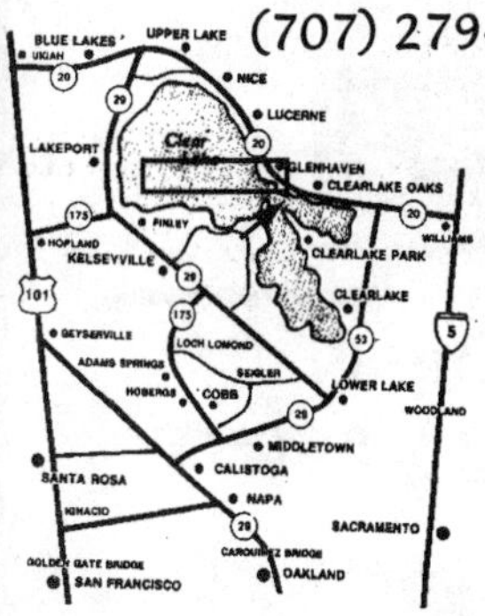

- Thousands of premium cotton fabrics
- Flannel is our specialty: 100's to choose from
- Batiks, ikats, silk, rayons, and fleece
- Quilts on display
- Knowledgeable, friendly staff

1 hour from Hwy. 5
45 min. from Hwy. 101

Mon - Fri 10 - 5:30 Sat 10 - 4

For all your Quilting needs!

Santa Rosa, CA #22

Mon - Fri 9:30 - 8 Sat 9:30 - 6 Sun 10 - 5

Ben Franklin Crafts

1793 Marlow Rd. 95401
(707) 539-5473 Fax: (707) 539-9346
Est: 1992 15,000 sq.ft.

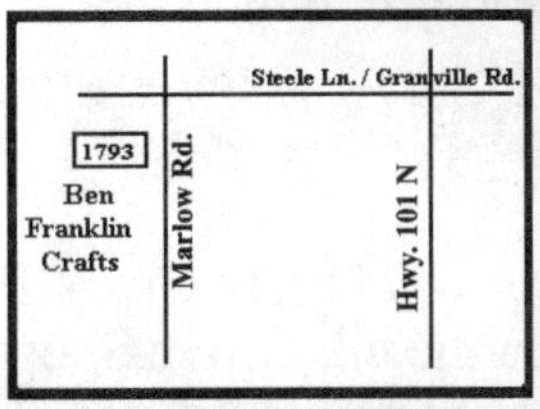

Quilt corner is located in full line craft store. Best quilt fabric from the best companies. Books, patterns, notions and lots of good ideas.

Sonoma, CA #23

Mon - Fri 9:30 - 6 Sat 10 - 5:30 Sun 11 - 4

Kay's Fabrics

201 W. Napa St. #14
Sonoma Mkt.Pl. 95476
(707) 996-3515
Est: 1963 2600 sq.ft.
4000 Bolts
We do Mail Orders & Invite Fabric Requests.

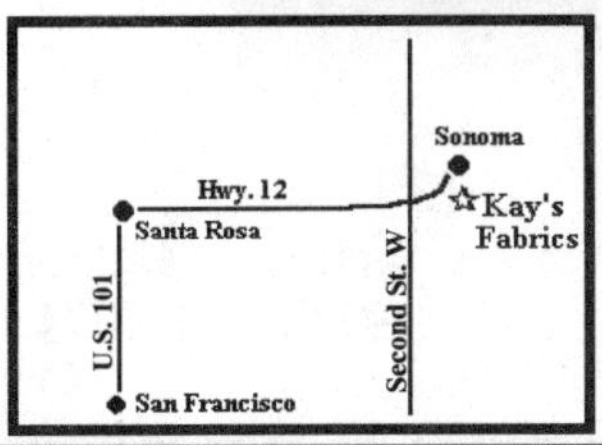

Complete line of quilting fabrics, books, patterns and notions. Hoffman, RJR, VIP, Kona & Many Unusual Fabrics.

Winters, CA #24

Tues - Sat 10 - 4:30 Fri til 9

Cloth Carousel & Quiltworks

9 Main St. 95694
(530) 795-2580
Owner: Laurie A. Sengo & Diane Falera
Est: 1995

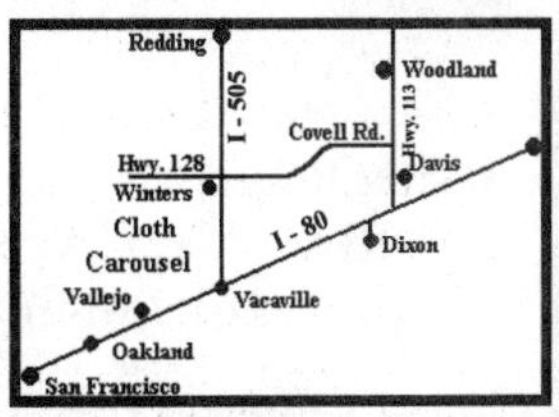

Specializing in service. 1200 bolts, notions, books, classes. We offer quality custom machine quilting. Eleven miles North of Vacaville off I - 505.

Largest Selection of Patterns in Northern California

Roseville, CA #25

The Stitching Station

1000 Sunrise Ave. 95661
(916) 773-0296
Fax: (916) 773-0294
Owner: Sandra Satnowski
Est: 1989 2400 sq.ft.

Mon - Fri 10 - 6
Sat 10 - 5:30
Sun 12 - 4

If you're a quilter, you've heard about The Stitching Station. We have the most unique array of Quilting supplies in the Sacramento area, with a large selection of show quality quilts and doll models on display.

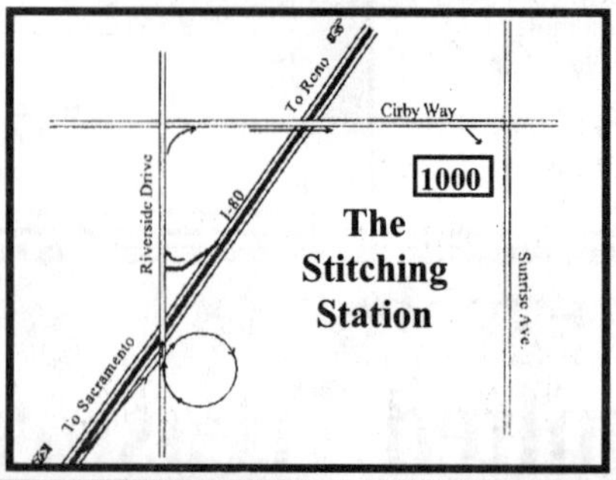

From Sacramento: Take I - 80 east (towards Reno) to the first Roseville exit, Riverside Dr./Auburn Blvd. Follow the signs to Riverside Dr. (pass through the underpass, circle around and cross over the freeway). Turn right again at the second stoplight, Cirby Way. Follow Cirby Way approximately 1 mile, and turn right just before Sunrise Ave. The Stitching Station is on the right.
From Reno: Take I - 80 west (towards Sacramento) to the Riverside Dr. off-ramp. Turn right onto Riverside. Turn right again at the first stoplight, Cirby Way. Follow Cirby Way approximately 1 mile, and turn right just before Sunrise Ave. The Stitching Station is on the right.

Fabric, Books, Supplies, Notions, Doll Patterns, Quilting Classes. Large selection of 30's reproduction fabrics and a great collection of Homespuns.

Meissner

Sewing & Learning Centers

4 Great Locations!

Mon - Fri 9 - 6
Sat 9 - 5 Sun 12 - 5

Extensive selection of 100% cotton designer fabrics, books, notions, accessories for quilters and classes for all levels of sewers.
Toll Free: 800-521-2332
www.meissnersewing.com
email: info@meissnersewing.com Fax: 916-920-9186

Sacramento, CA #27

2417 Cormorant Way
Sacramento, CA 95815
(916) 920-2121
Est: 1974
20,000 sq.ft. 3000 Bolts

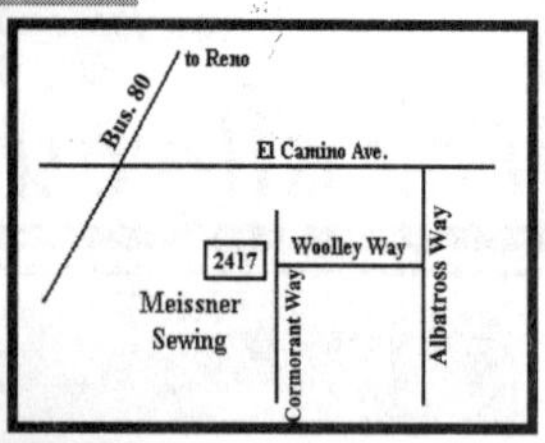

Sacramento, CA #28

8771 Elk Grove Blvd.
(In the elk Grove Shopping Ctr.)
Sacramento, CA 95624
(916) 686-1108

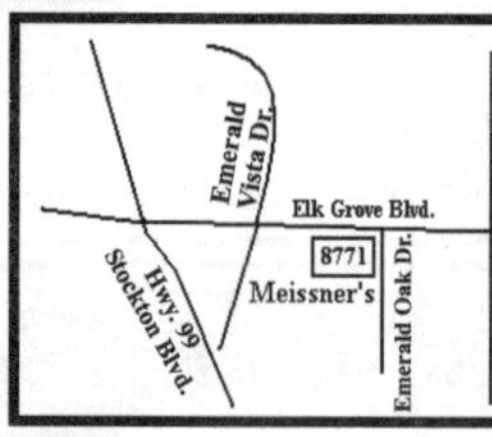

Roseville, CA #26

1850 Douglas Blvd., Suite 904
Roseville, CA 95661
(916) 786-3630

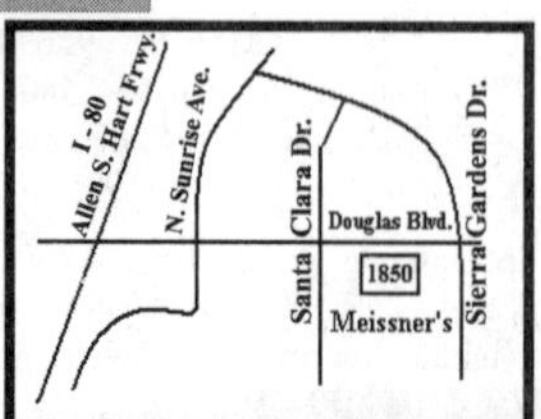

Folsom, CA #29

1013 Riley St., Suite 200
Folsom, CA 95630
(916) 984-7071

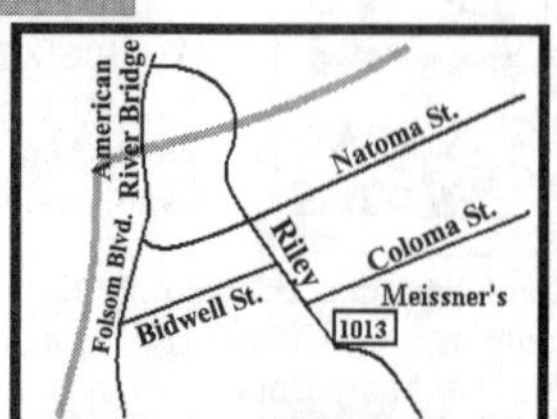

Material Girls

Sacramento, CA #30

2617 Alta Arden Expressway 95825
(916) 485-4252 Fax: (916) 485-4272
Owner: Terri Lanning
Est: 1997 3500 sq.ft.
4500 Bolts
www.matgirls.com

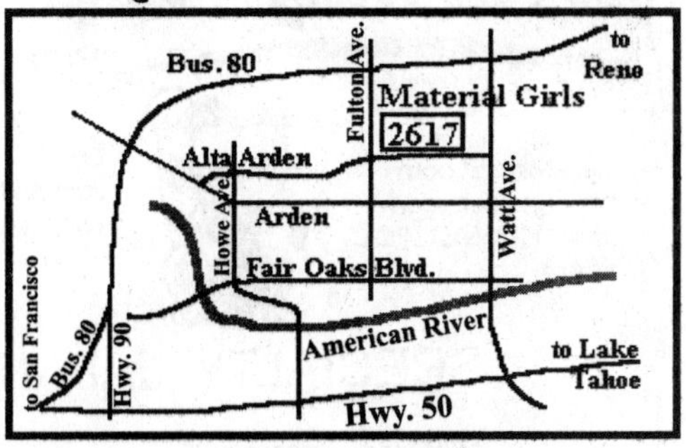

Mon - Sat 10 - 6
Sunday 12 - 4

A great selection of :

- Quality 100% cotton fabric
- Books & Patterns
- Notions
- Classes Offered
- Quilting Machine on Premises.

"Friendliest Shop in Town"

Quilters' Corner, Inc.

QC

Sacramento, CA #31

9792 B. Business Park Dr., Sacramento, CA 95827
(916) 366-6136 Fax: (916) 366-6105
E-Mail: quilterscorner@rcip.com

Sacramento's newest quilt shop.

Over 3,000 sq.ft. of fabrics, books, patterns, notions, and gifts. We have Thimbleberries Club, Quiltsitter Circle and Jan Patek Girl Gang.

Mon - Fri 10 - 6
Sat 10 - 4 Sun 12 - 4

www.quilterscornersac.com

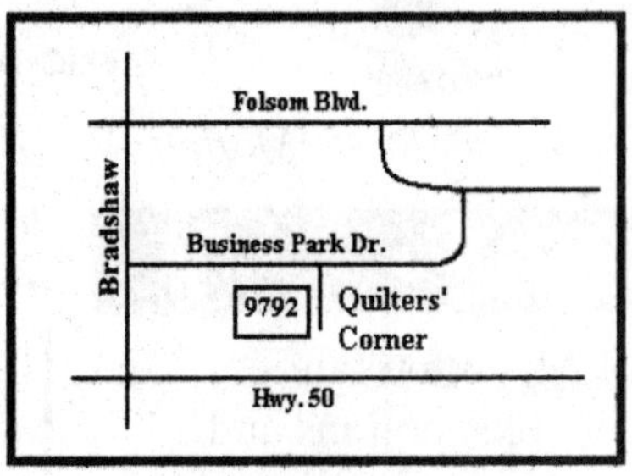

Take Hwy. 50 to Bradshaw Rd., We are north of the Freeway. Turn on Business Park Dr. About 1/2 mi. turn into Driveway 9792 (Across from Marsh's Carpets)

いろはにほへといろはにほへと

Sebastopol, CA #32

Phone for Appt.

Eastwind Art

(707) 829-3536

www.eastwindart.com
kitagami@telocity.com
P.O. Box 811 SEBASTOPOL, CA 95473

Owner: Joanne Newcomb
Established 1973

SPECIALTY: JAPAN

VISIT OUR JAPANESE GARDEN

Patterns: Japanese crafts, clothing, quilts.

Fabrics: Japanese cotton prints, kimono scraps.

Sashiko: Needles, thread, stencils, indigo fabric.

Books: Japanese designs, sashiko, reference.

Gifts: Note cards, charms, maneki neko, etc.

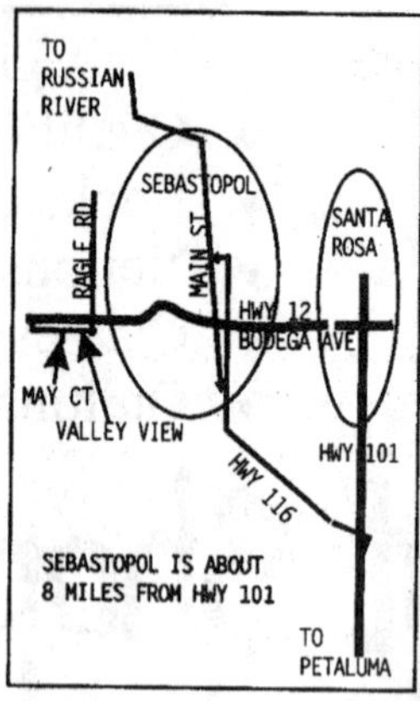

Petaluma, CA #33

Mon - Sat 10 - 5:30
Sun 12 - 4

Quilted Angel

200 G St. 94952
(707) 763-0945
E-Mail: angels@QuiltedAngel.com
Web Site: www.QuiltedAngel.com
Owner: Susie Ernst
Est: 1991 3600 sq.ft. 4000+ Bolts

A "destination" Quilt Store. Fabrics from all major suppliers, books (800 titles), notions, patterns & classes.

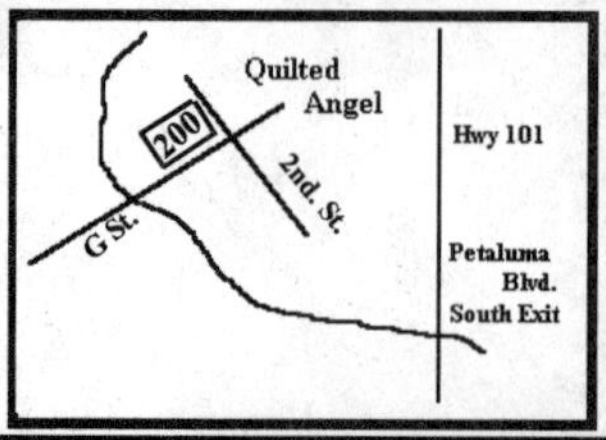

Davis, CA #34

Mon 10 - 8
Tues - Fri 10 - 5:30
Sat 10 - 5
Sun 11 - 5

Pincushion Boutique

2827 Spafford St. 95616
(530) 758-3488 or (800) 758-3488
E-Mail: sweettrt@pacbell.net
Web Site: www.sweettreat.com
Owner: Beth Murphy
Est: 1977 5000 sq.ft.
3000 Bolts + 10,000 fabrics in 1/2 yd. Cuts.
Home of Sweet Treat™.
Helpful quilters on staff.
Mail Order & Sweet Treat™ Subscription.

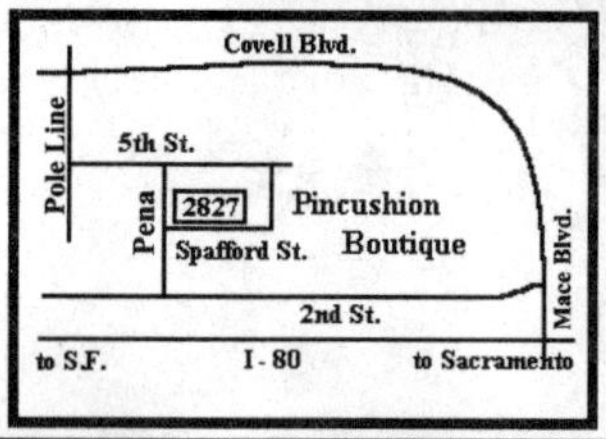

Vacaville, CA #35

Hours by Appt.

The Unique Spool

407 Corte Majorca 95688
(707) 448-1538
Web Site: www.uniquespool.com
Owner: Roberta Dent

African, animal, Australian fabrics plus domestic prints, ethnic quilt patterns, puppet patterns & more.

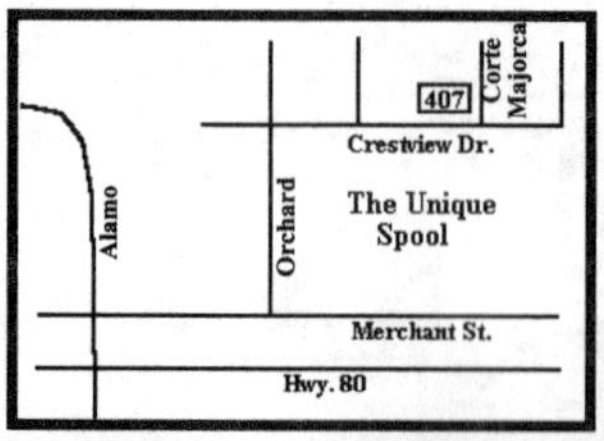

Vacaville, CA #36

Stacy's Quilt Shop

878 Alamo Dr. 95688
(707) 447-9000

FABRIC•NOTIONS•CLASSES

Owner: Stacy Moffett

Pfaff & Brother Sewing Machines
In-house service all makes.

Mon - Fri 10 - 6 Sat 10 - 5

All cotton fabrics, books, notions and classes. Full line of Kona Cotton solids. Original patterns from our home town teachers.

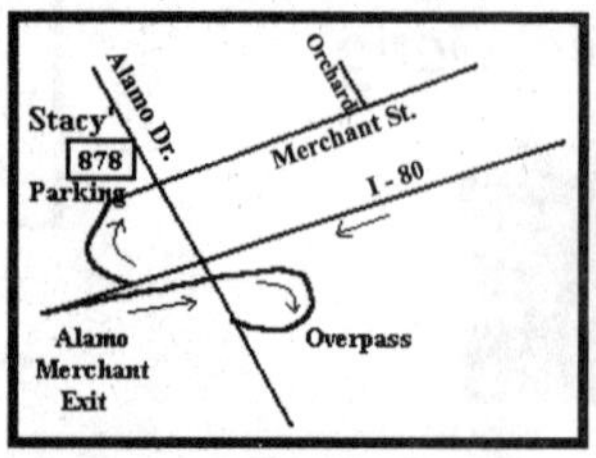

From Sacramento, exit Merchant St.
From San Francisco, exit Alamo Dr.

Napa, CA #37

Mon - Fri 10 - 5
Tues til 7
Sat 10 - 3

QUILTMAKER

1275 Napa Town Center 94559
(707) 252-6793 Fax: (707) 252-3552
Owners: Diane Massey-Todd & Nancy Eberlin
Est: 1996 1500 sq.ft. 3000+ bolts

Quiltmaker says it all! We are all things quilting! Fabulous fabrics, classes, assistance, tools and books.

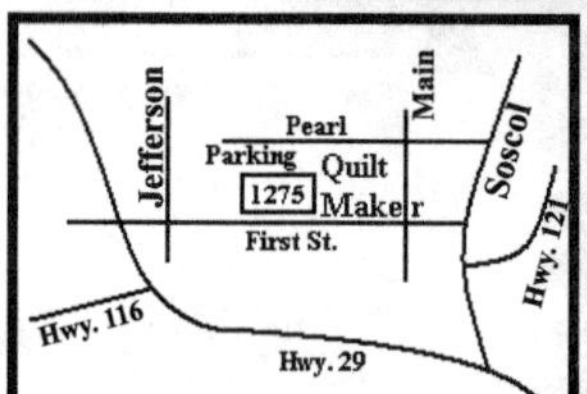

Pumpkin Seed
Quilts & Textiles

1414 - 4th St. San Rafael, CA 94901
(415) 453-4758 Fax: (415) 453-4768
Owner: Jennifer Una McCoy
Est: 2001 1800 sq.ft. 2500 Bolts
Newsletter 3x/yr with catalog of classes

T, W, F 10 - 6 Th 10 - 9 Sat 10 - 5 Sun 12 - 5

Full service quilt shop with classroom and gallery. Exciting "downtown" atmosphere with friendly and helpful staff. Fabric favorites include: batiks, asian, brights, K. Fassett, reproductions and over 200 solids.

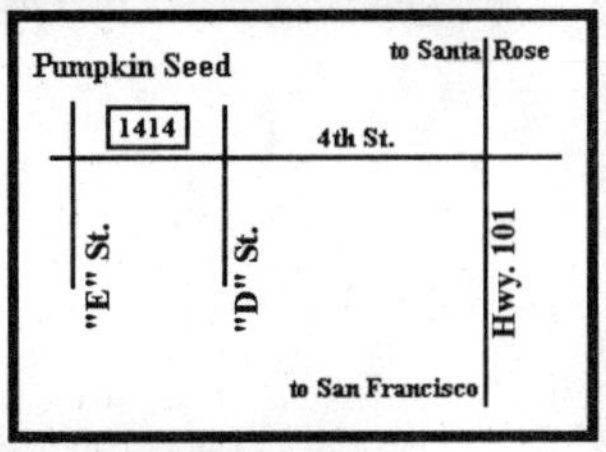

San Rafael, CA #38

Elk Grove, CA #39

Country Sewing Center

9639 E. Stockton Blvd. 95624
(916) 685-8500
E-Mail: cntrysew@elkgrove.net
Visit our Web-Site: www.elkgrove.net/csc
Owners: Susan & Bill Zimlich
Est: 1993 2400 sq.ft. 3000+ Bolts

Mon - Fri 10 - 6
Sat 10 - 5

Great selection of 100% cotton fabrics, books & notions. Friendly, small-town service. Elk Grove exit from 99 or I - 5 then East.

Fair Oaks, CA #40

Mon - Sat 9 - 5

Tayo's Fabrics & Quilts

10127 Fair Oaks Blvd. 95628
(916) 967-5479
E-Mail: info@tayosfabrics.com
Web Site: www.tayosfabrics.com
Owner: Shenna Mealey Est: 1983

Fabrics, books, patterns & notions for traditional & contemporary quilting, cloth dolls, wearable art & fashion sewing. Classes. Personal & friendly service.

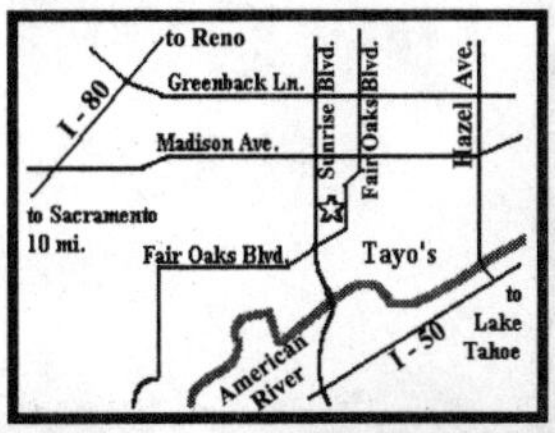

Auburn, CA #41

Mon - Fri 9:30 - 6
Sat 9:30 - 4
Sun 10 - 3

Cabin Fever Quilt Shoppe

826 Lincoln Way 95603
(530) 885-5500 Fax: (530) 878-8030
E-Mail: frostie111@msn.com
Est: 2002 3000 sq.ft.

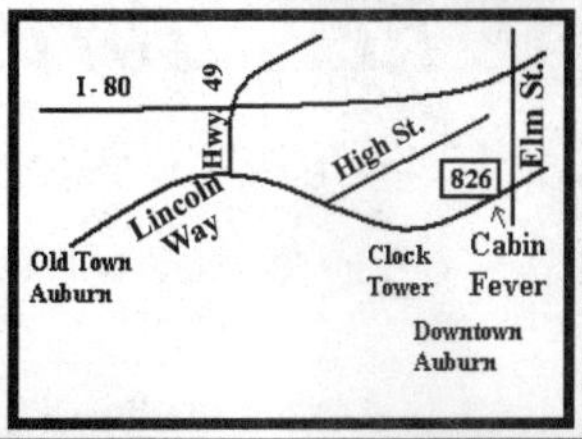

Cabin Fever Quilt Shoppe offers friendly, knowledgeable staff - a wide variety of fabrics, notions, books & classes to meet all you quilting needs.

Grass Valley, CA #42

Mon - Fri 10 - 5:30
Sat 10 - 5
Sun 11 - 3

The Quillted Feather

239 E. Main St. 95945
(530) 477-1497 Fax: (530) 477-1499
E-Mail: qfeather@jps.net
Est: 1998 1900 sq.ft. 2200+ Bolts

Classes, Books, Notions, Fabrics, Knowledgeable Staff.
Housed in a 100 year old Victorian.
Come Say "Hi" to Stitches, our cat.

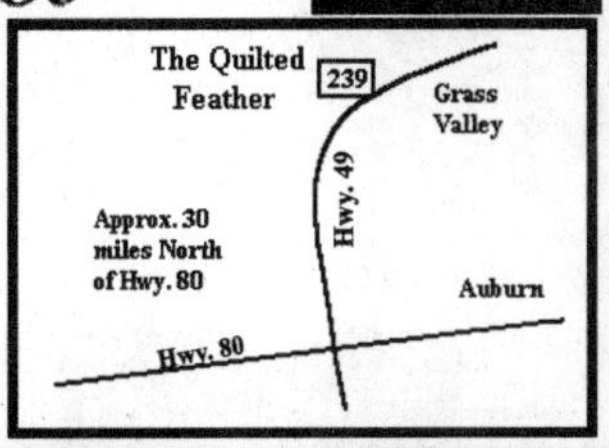

Tahoe City, CA #43

10 - 5
Closed Wed.

Mountain Stitchery

295 N. Lake Blvd., P.O. Box 1420 96145
(530) 583-9301
Est: 1978 700 sq.ft. 700 Bolts

Large variety of gorgeous quilts in stock or we'll make yours to order! Great selection of unique fabrics, wallhangings and dolls.

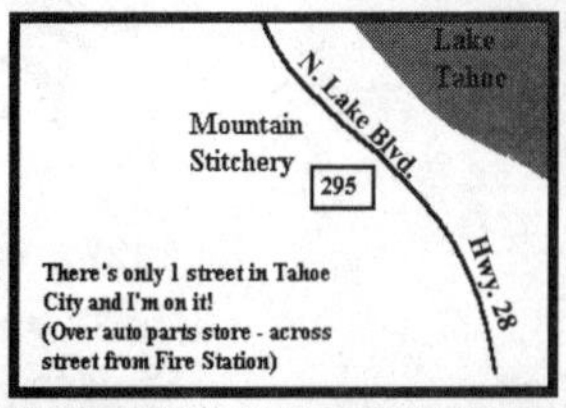

Truckee, CA #44

Mon - Sat 9:30 - 5:30
Sun 10 - 5

Donna's Stitchery

10075 Jibboom St.
96161
(530) 587-6708

Est: 1979

100% cotton fabrics including Jinny Beyer, Nancy Crow, Moda, Debbie Mumm, Hoffman & P&B. Books and Notions. The friendliest quilt shop for service, inspiration and sharing of ideas.

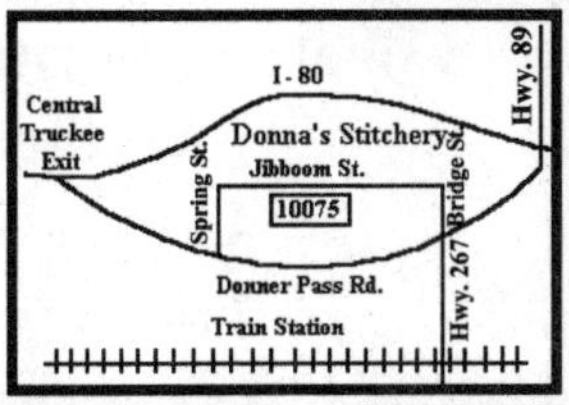

Truckee, CA #45

Mon - Sat 10 - 5:30
Sun 12 - 4

Truckee Fabrics

11429 Donner Pass Rd. 96161
(530) 582 - 8618
2000 + Bolts

Over 2000 Bolts of Cotton Fabrics including Flannels and Mountain Theme Prints. A large Selection of the Latest Books and Notions.

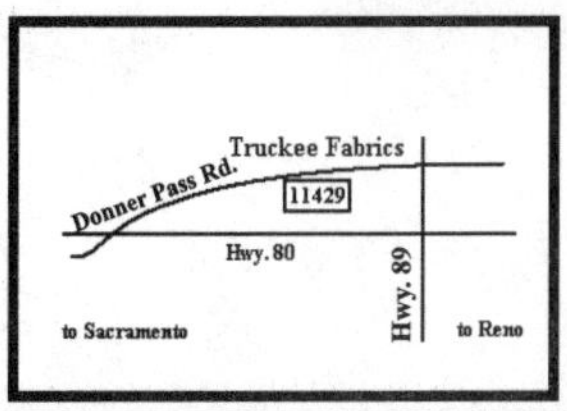

South Lake Tahoe, CA #46

Sierra Tahoe Fabrics

3097 Harrison Ave.
S. Lake Tahoe, CA 96150
530-542-0500
www.sierratahoefabrics.com
Est: 1999 1400 sq.ft. 1000 Bolts

High quality quilting fabrics, batiks, flannels, fleece and tapestries. Books, patterns, notions & classes. Terrific Lodge-Look fabrics.

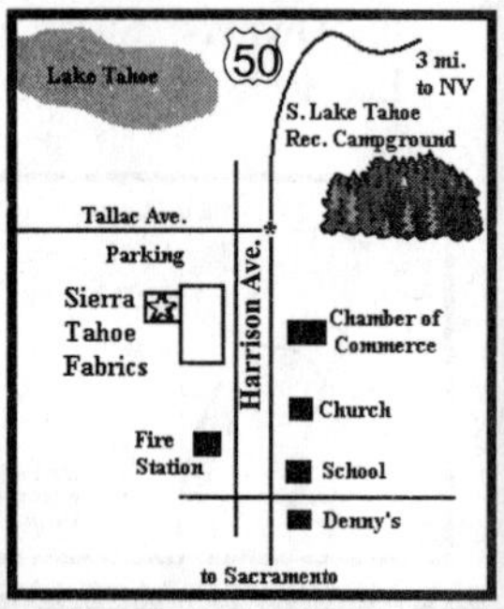

Mon - Sat 10 - 5 Sun 11 - 4

Mammoth Lakes, CA #47

Mon - Sat 11 - 5:30 Sun 11 - 4

FABRICATIONS

126 Old Mammoth Rd. 93546
(760) 934-5682
E-Mail: Fabric@qnet.com
Owner: Lesley Byberg
Est: 1988 900 sq.ft.

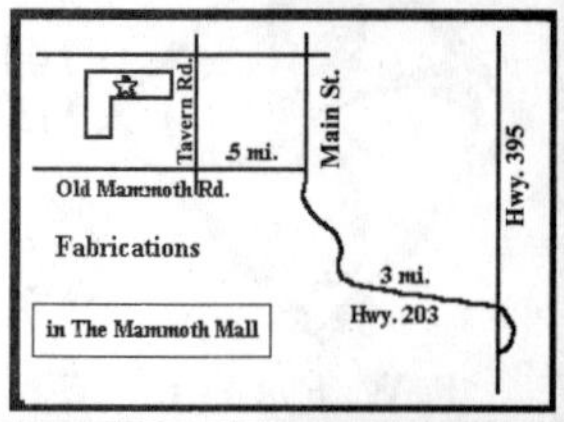

We're a small & friendly quilt shop in the most beautiful little mountain town!

Bishop, CA #48

Mon - Sat 10 - 5:30

Sew It Seams

124 N. Main St. 93514
(760) 873-5635
Owner: Nancy Wood
Est: 1995 2200 sq.ft. 1100 Bolts

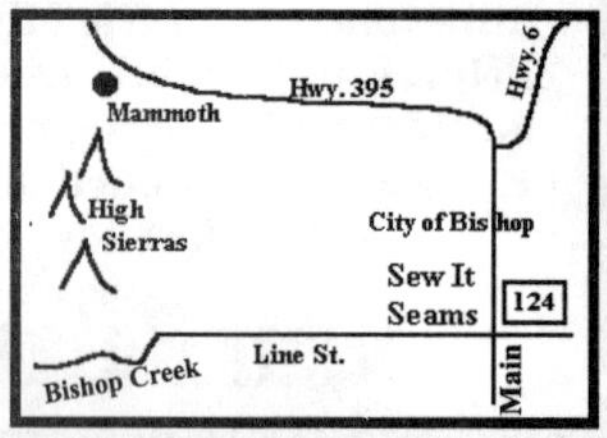

Large Selection of Quality Fabric. Books, Patterns and Quilting Supplies. Classes Available. Machine Sales & Service. Friendly & Personal Service.

Bishop, CA #49

Mon - Sat 10 - 5

The Fabric Store

1335 Rocking W. Dr. 93514
(760) 873-6808
Owners: Charlie & John Waldriff
Est: 1982 1280 sq.ft. 1000 Bolts

A Sewer's Haven
Classes in Quilting & Sewing

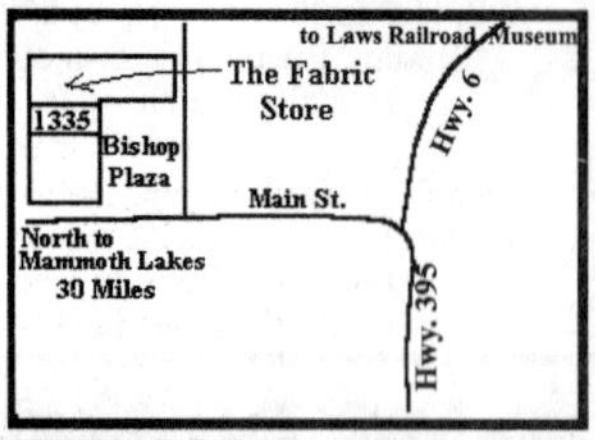

Altaville, CA #50

The Country Cloth Shop

457 S. Main St. P.O. Box 868
"Angels Camp" 95221
(209) 736-4998

Fax: (209) 736-9519
E-Mail: ccshop @goldrush.com
Owners:
Ginger & Chuck Duffy
Est: 1980 1600 sq.ft.

Mon - Sat 10 - 5

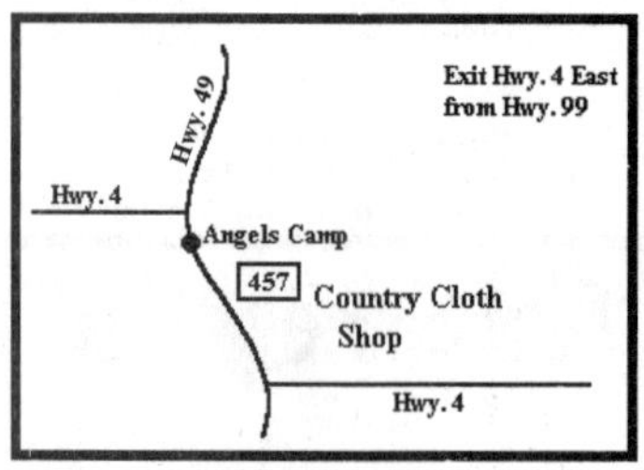

Authorized Bernina Dealer
Located in historic Angels Camp in the Mother Lode foothills.
Good selection of fabrics, books, patterns & threads.

Oakhurst, CA #51

Bear Paw Quilts & More

40282 Hwy. 41 #5
(559) 683-7397
Owners: Donna Henning
Bonnie McClintock

Special selection of nature fabrics, books, patterns, quilting supplies, general sewing notions, classes

2000 bolts of fabric

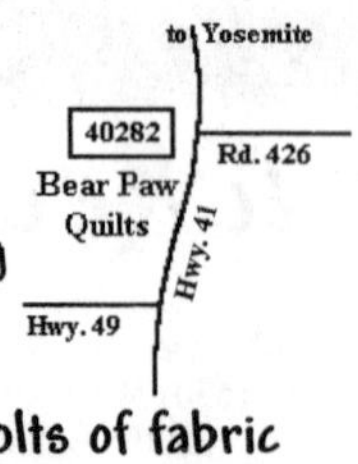

Mon - Sat 9:30 - 6 Tues til 8

Groveland, CA #52

Mon - Sat
9 - 4
Closed Wed.

Bunny Rose & Co.

18282 Hwy. 120, Suite D, P.O. Box 1063
(209) 962-5702 95321
Owner: Bunny Kite

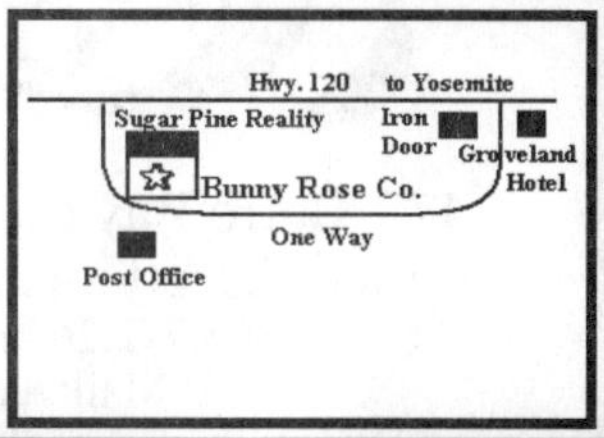

Specializing in quilting fabrics & notions
Long Arm Quilting & Classes also available.
Come visit on your way to Yosemite.

Modesto, CA #54

Mon - Fri
9:30 - 5:30
Sat 10 - 5
Sun 12 - 4

R. Lily Stem Quilts

909 W. Roseburg Ave. Suite B 95350
(209) 577-1919 Fax: (209) 577-1412
Owner: Marilyn Nelson
Est: 1986 3200 sq.ft.

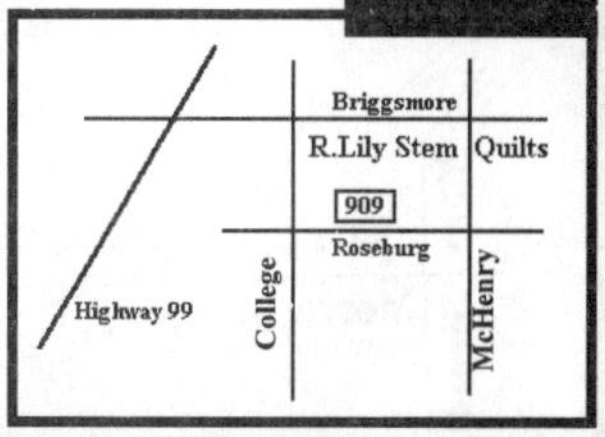

Fabulous fabrics, books, patterns, classes and great service ! Authorized Bernina Dealer.

Clovis, CA #55

QUILTERS' PARADISE

339 Pollasky
93612
(559) 297-7817
Fax: 297-0838
E-Mail:
qpshop@aol.com
Web Site:
www.quilters-paradise.com
Owner:
Jennifer Wheeler
Est: 1978
5000 sq.ft.

- helpful, friendly service
- great selection of newest fabrics, books, patterns and notions
- silk ribbon and doll making supplies
- block of the months
- new merchandise arriving daily
- mail orders & special orders welcome
- Visa, Mastercard, Discover & Am. Express

Just What the Shop Name Says!!

Mon - Fri
10 - 6
Sat 10 - 5
Sun 12 - 4

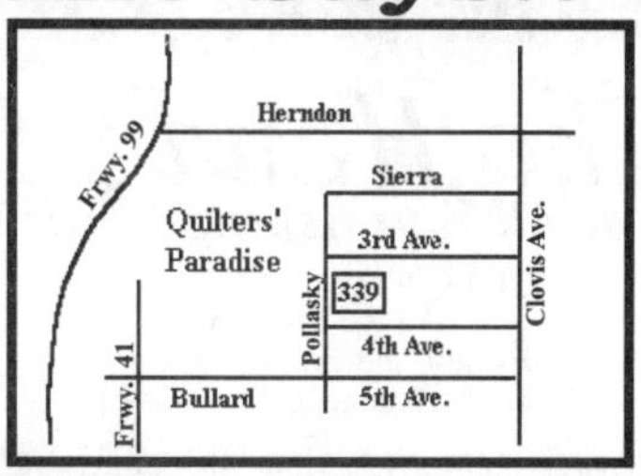

Stockton, CA #53

QUILTERS QUARTERS

1517 N. Lincoln St. 95204
(209) 462-0161
Stockton's <u>only</u> Quilt Shop

Fabric, Classes & Supplies for the Contemporary Quilter

Over 3,000 bolts in a small space
150 Kona Cotton solids always in stock,
Batiks, Brights, Kaffee Fasset Stripes & Homespun Plaids

E-Mail: quiltquarters@attbi.com
Owner: Debbie Chase

www.quiltersquarters-stkn.com

Reg Hours:
Mon, Tue, Thurs, Fri 10 - 6,
Wed 1 - 7,
Sat 10 - 4

Located at Harding Way & Lincoln St.

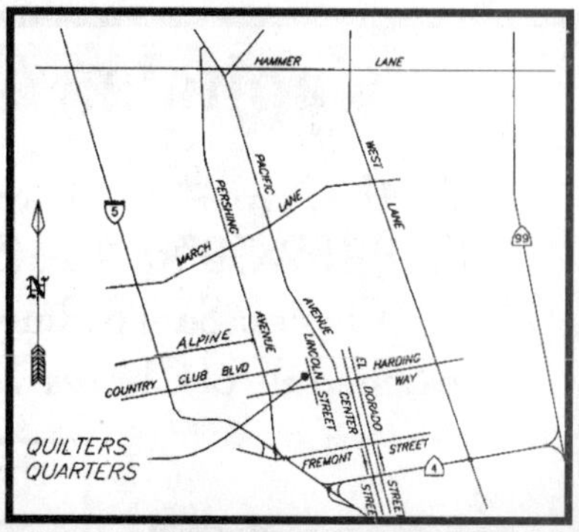

Reedley, CA #56

Mon - Fri
9:30 - 4:30
Sat 10 - 2

Mennonite Quilt Center

1012 "G" St. 93654
(209) 638-3560 2500 sq.ft.
Mgr: Mary Elizondo & Ruth Buxman
& Kathleen Heinrichs 450 Bolts

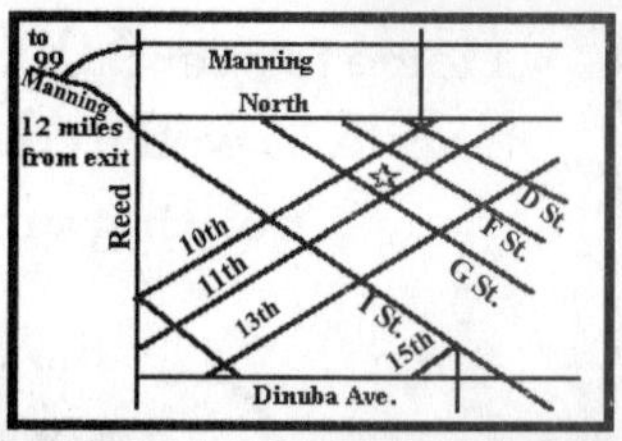

100% Cotton Fabrics, notions, Books, Patterns, & Battings. Quilters on site Monday mornings. Quilt show year around. Tours Avail.

Visalia, CA #57

Mon - Fri
9:30 - 5:30
Thur til 7
Sat 9:30 - 4:30

Thimble Towne

400 W. Caldwell Ave. #F 93277
(559) 627-5778
Est: 2000
E-Mail:
thimbletowne
@aol.com
Owner: Kathy &
Stu Veltkamp

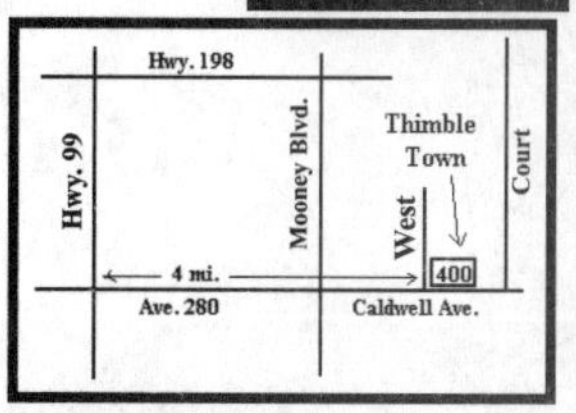

100% cotton fabrics; books and patterns galore;
mail order welcome; newsletter; classes
Bernina Sewing Machines

Exeter, CA #58

Tues - Sat 10 - 5

The Quilt Store

161 N. "E" St.
93221
(559) 594-4450
Owner: Pat Baker
2000 sq.ft.

Top quality 100% cotton fabrics (1400 bolts), books, notions. Elna Sewing Machines, buttons, doll kits, classes.

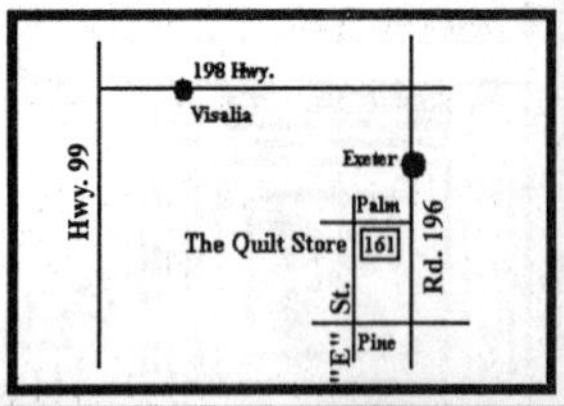

The Cotton Ball

Named one of the top 10 Quilt Shops In North America by Better Homes & Gardens Quilt Sampler Magazine

475 Morro Bay Blvd., Morro Bay, CA 93442
www.thecottonball.com 1.800.895.7402
805.772.2646 Fax: 805.772.6357
E-Mail: cottonball@thegrid.net
Owner: Judi Appell Est: 1969 7000 Sq.ft.

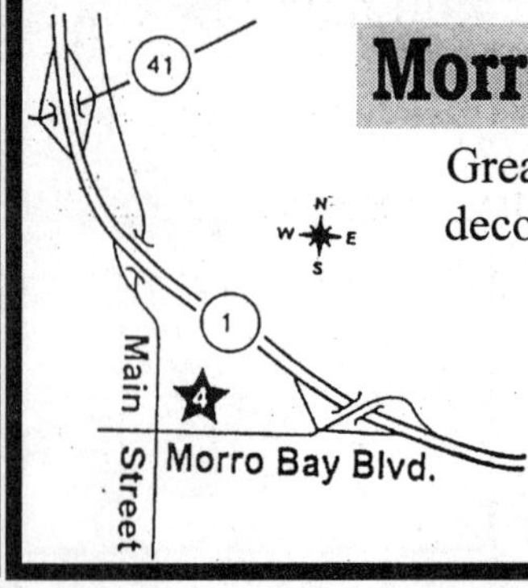

Morro Bay, CA #59

Great selection of quilting fabric, decorating fabric, books, patterns and notions.

Great, friendly service!

Pfaff Sewing Machine Dealer

Mon - Sat 10 - 5 Sun 12 - 4

Paso Robles, CA #60

Tues - Sat 10 - 5

The Quiltery

715 24th #V (Upper Level) 93446
(805) 227-4561
E-mail: machinequilter@thegrid.net
Owner: Sherline Lockhart
Est: 1999 600 sq.ft. 500 Bolts

500 Bolts of Maywoods, Timeless Treasures, etc. at $5 yd. Custom machine quilting. Quilters' Retreats. Always Friendly Service.

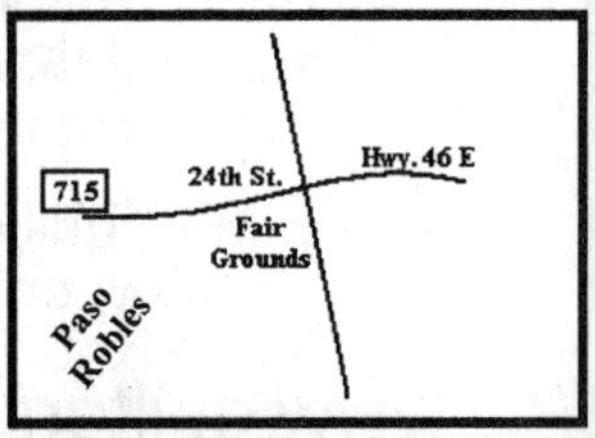

Capitola, CA #61

1475 41st Ave. #A1, Capitola, CA 95010
(831) 462-3930 Fax: (831) 462-9403
Owner: Sam Ridino Est: 1979
Free Schedule of Classes "Sewing by the Sea"

Mon - Fri 10 - 8
Saturday 10 - 6
Sunday 11 - 5

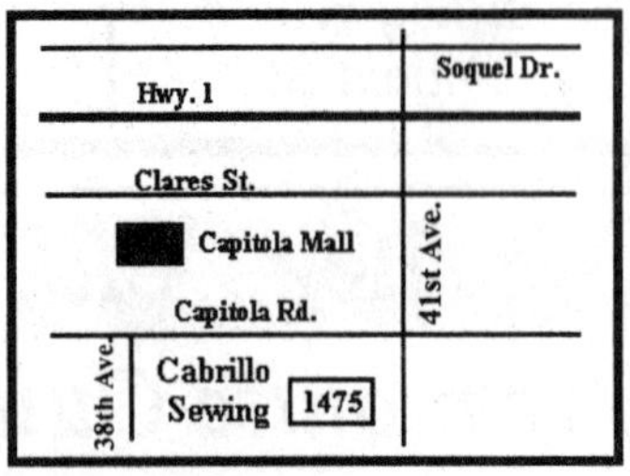

Home to over 3,000 bolts of quality quilting fabric, as well as the latest in books, notions, quilting supplies and classes.

Hollister, CA #62

Mon - Fri 9 - 6
Sat 10 - 4

Creative Friends Craft Supplies

191 San Felipe Rd. #M1 95023
(831) 636-7773 Fax: (831) 636-1965
Web Site: www.creativefriends.net
Owners: Karen Coatsworth & Mary Lundquist

We specialize in Quilting Supplies & 100% Cottons. We also have classes. And we carry Craft Supplies. Yarns and beads.

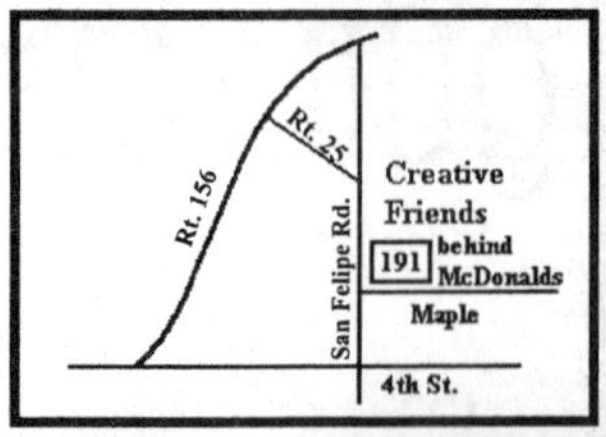

Atascadero, CA #63

Mon - Fri 10 - 6
Sat 10 - 5
Sun 12 - 5

Sew Fun

8775 El Camino Real 93422 (805) 462-9739
Owner: Marilyn (Lynn) J. Barksdale
Est: 1996 2400 sq.ft. 3500 Bolts

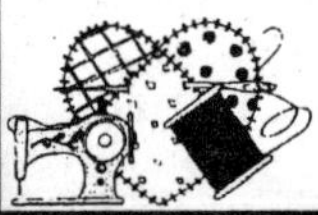

Great selection of fabrics, books, patterns. The latest in quilting supplies.
Friendly and helpful staff.
Janome sewing machine sales & service.

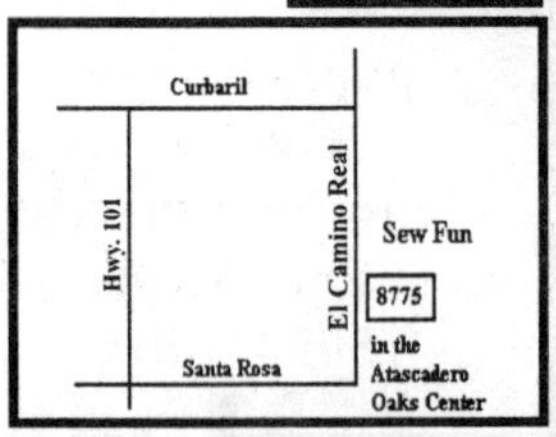

Pacific Grove, CA #64

Mon - Sat 10 - 5:30
Sun 10:30 - 4

The Hand Maden

"For All Your Sewing Needs"

620 Lighthouse Ave. at 17th
(831) 373-5353
E-Mail: thm@redshift.com
Owners: Jeanne & Jim Graham

Extensive fabric selection for quilters & wearable artists. Books, Patterns, Notions, Buttons and Sew Much More. Husqvarna Viking Machines.

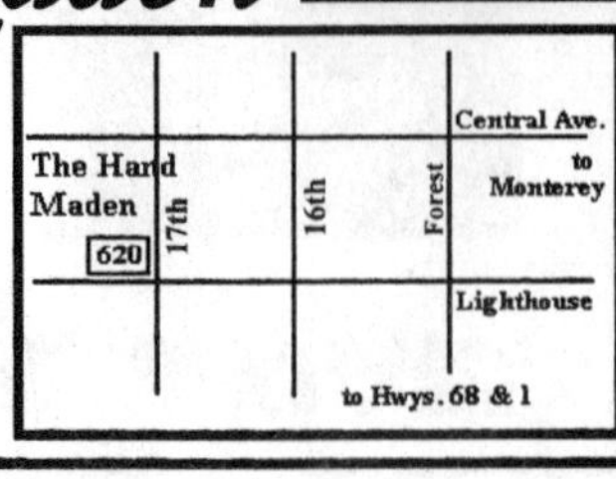

Back Porch Fabrics

157 Grand Ave. at Central 93950
(831) 375-4453 Fax: (831) 375-3755
E-Mail: info@backporchfabrics.com
Owner: Gail Abeloe Est: 1996

Mon - Sat
10 - 5
Sun 12 - 4

Pacific Grove, CA #65

- **Unique fabrics, books and patterns for quilting and wearable art.**
- **Home of the "Back Porch Press" pattern company.**
- **Try on model garments for sizing and inspiration.**
- **Continuous shows in our Quilt Gallery featuring prominent, local quilters.**

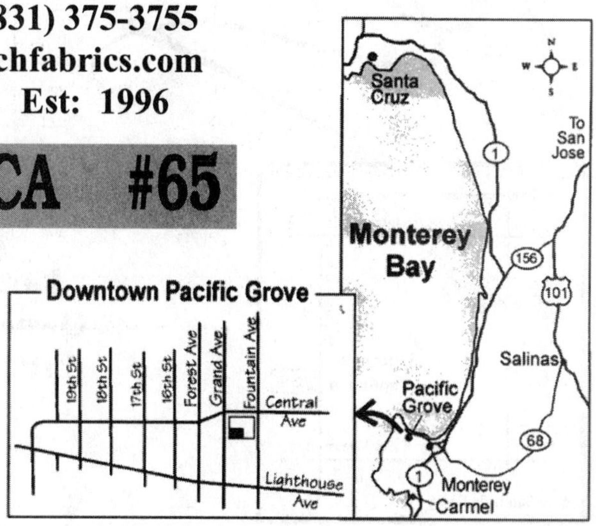

Located 90 miles south of San Francisco on the Monterey Peninsula.

Visit Us on the Web At: www.backporchfabrics.com

Atascadero, CA #66

The Country Sampler

New Address

5880 Traffic Way, Atascadero, California
805-466-7282

Web site: www.countrysampler.net E-mail: Contrysmpl@aol.com

Monday thru Saturday 10-5:30 PM

The Shop that feeds a Quilter's soul!

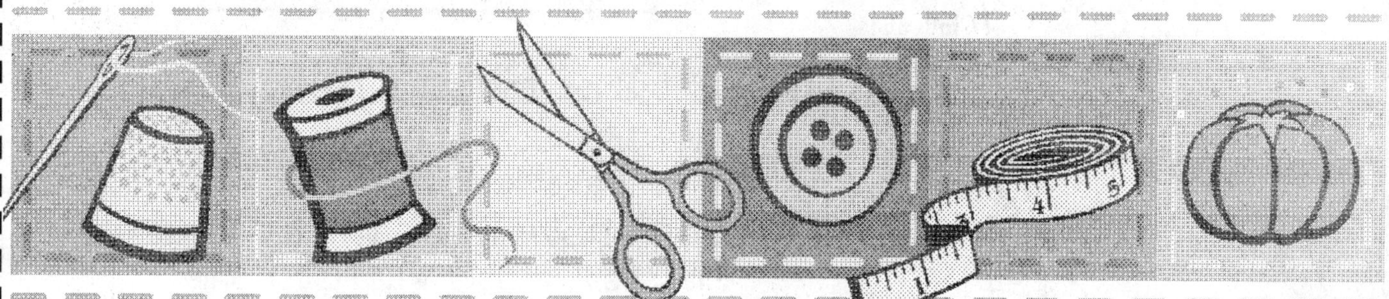

Quilter's Cupboard

Atascadero, CA #67

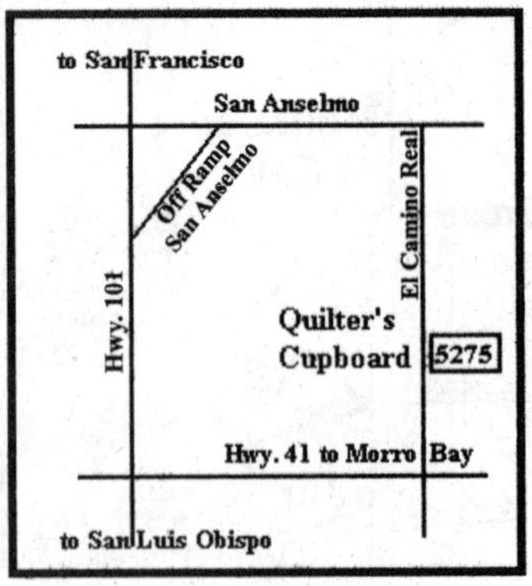

5275 El Camino Real 93422
(805) 466-6996
Fax: (805) 466-6555
Owner: Lorraine Lowe
Est: 1997 2000 sq.ft.

Monday - Saturday
10 - 5
Closed Sundays.

COMPLETE QUILT STORE
with over 2500 bolts of 100% cotton fabric, stencils, notions, books, patterns, classes & gifts.

Turlock, CA #68

Cloth and Quilts

625 E. Main St.
Turlock, CA 95380
(209) 632-3225

E-mail: clothandquilts@worldnet.att.net
Fax: (209) 632-3354
Est: 2001 3900 sq.ft.
Owners: Cindy Kooistra, Debbie Sanders, & Margaret Labno

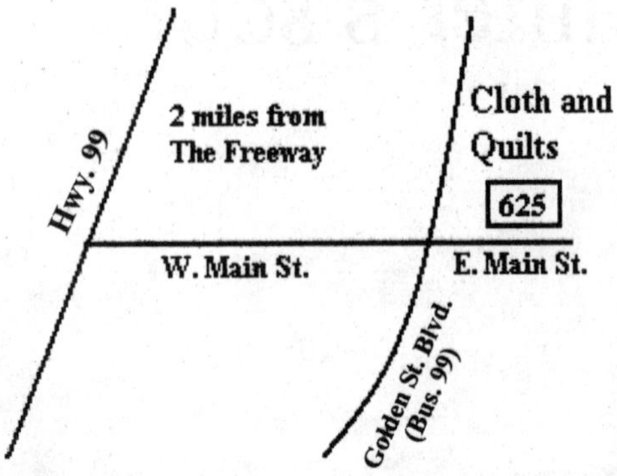

Mon - Sat 9:30 - 5:30

Your One Stop Quilt Shop!

Over 3500 Bolts of Fabrics, Books, Patterns and Notions.

If we don't have it, we will try to get it.

Classes Available -- Quilts for Sale

San Francisco, CA #69

Mon - Fri 10 - 6
Sat 10 - 5:30
Sun 12 - 5

Mendels Far~Out Fabrics

1556 Haight St. 94117
(415) 621-1287 E-Mail: sales@mendels.com
Web-Site: http://www.mendels.com
Owner: Bette Mosias 3900 sq.ft.

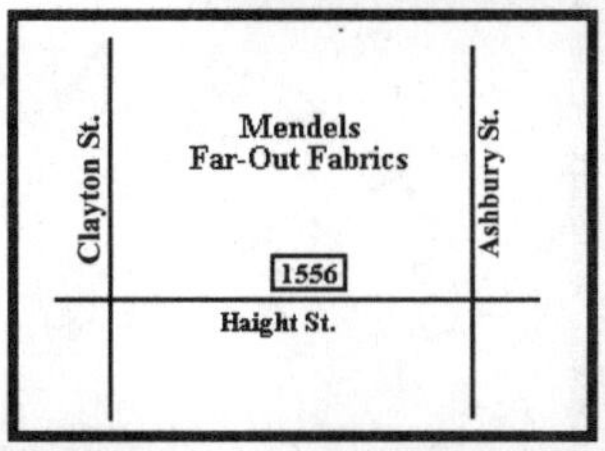

Lots of wonderful cotton fabrics, unusual ethnic - large selection textile dyes, paints, great buttons, trims and an art supply store.

San Francisco, CA #70

Mon, Wed, & Fri 10 - 6
Thur 11 - 7
Sat 10 - 5
Sun 12 - 4

Black Cat QUILTS

2608 Ocean Ave. 94132
(415) 337-1355 Fax: (415) 337-1383
Owner: Gretchen G. Nelson
Est: 1996 1500 sq.ft.

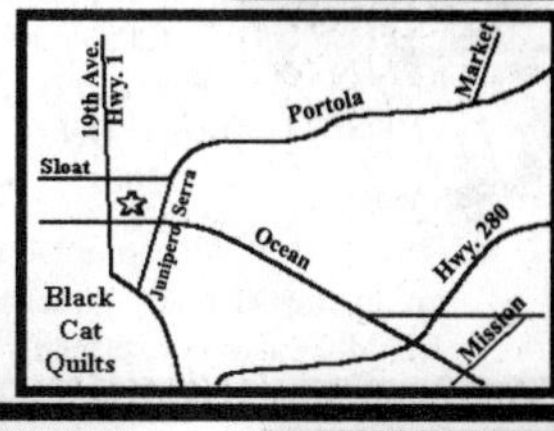

The only store in San Francisco devoted exclusively to meeting your quiltmaking needs. Featuring fabrics, books, patterns, notions & classes.

Fairfax, CA #71

Mon - Sat 10 - 6
Sun 12 - 4

Rainbow Fabrics

50 Bolinas Rd. 94930
(415) 459-5100
Owner: Rose Taber

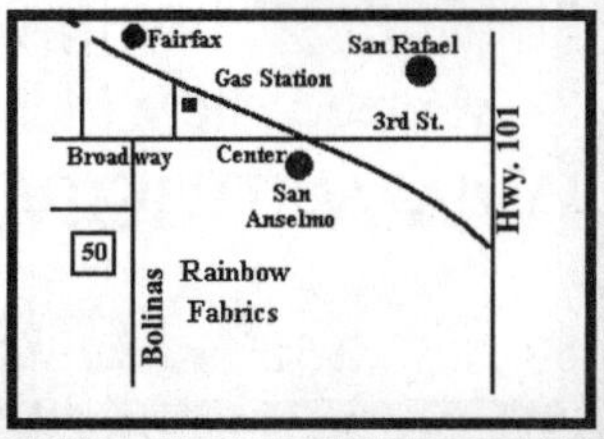

Unique country store. Cotton, Rayons, Books, Beads, Notions. Helpful staff. Classes for Adults and Children. Sewing Machine Service.

Berkeley, CA #72

Mon - Sat 10 - 6
Tues & Thur til 9
Sun 12 - 5

New Pieces

1597 & 1605 Solano Ave. 94707
(510) 527-6779 Fax: (925) 253-9000
E-Mail: sally@newpieces.com
Web Site: www.newpieces.com
Est: 1984 2800 sq.ft. 3000 Bolts

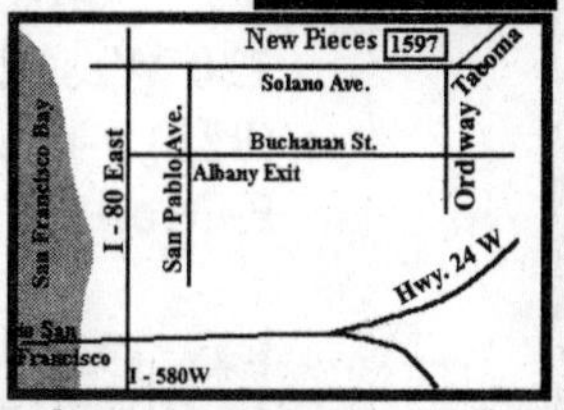

Contemporary Art Quilt & Doll Shop and Gallery. Commission quilts & quilt service & workshops.

Berkeley, CA #73

Mon - Fri 10 - 6:30
Sat 10 - 6
Sun 11 - 5:30

Stonemountain & Daughter Fabrics

2518 Shattuck Ave. 94704
(510) 845-6106 Est: 1981
Web Site: www.stonemountainfabric.com
Owners: Suzan & Bob Steinberg
6000 sq.ft. Thousands of Bolts

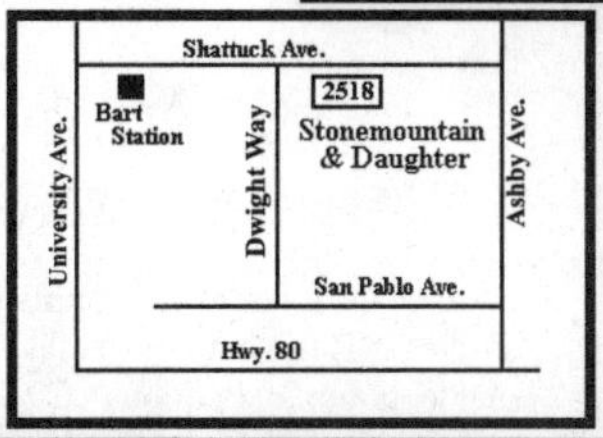

Huge Selection of Quality, Unique Cottons at affordable prices! Ethnic, Quilting & Basic Cottons. Wools, Silks, Rayons, & Linens also Available.

Walnut Creek, CA #74

Thimble Creek

1536 Newell Ave.
94596
(925) 946-9970
Owners:
Roxie & Joe Wood
Est: 1994 6000 sq.ft.
4000 Bolts

Wonderful quilts on display in a spacious, friendly, atmosphere. Great selection of books, patterns, notions, fabric & classes !

Mon - Fri 9:30 - 5:30
Tues & Thur til 8
Sat 9:30 - 5
Sun 12 - 4

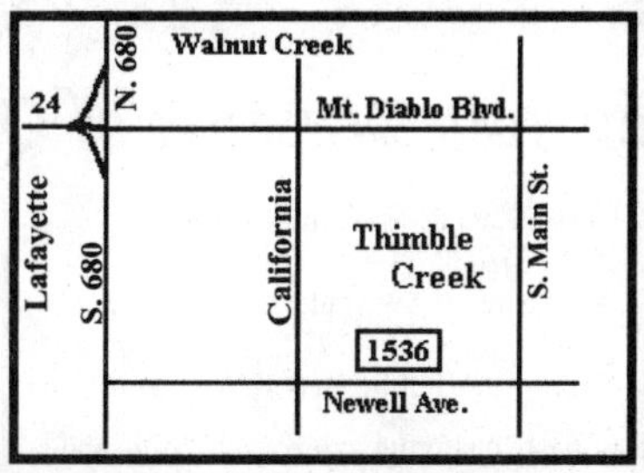

Lafayette, CA #75

Mon - Fri 9:30 - 5:30
Tues & Thur til 9
Sat 10 - 5
Sun 12 - 4

The Cotton Patch

1025 Brown Avenue 94549
(925) 284-1177 Est: 1978
Web Sites: www.quiltusa.com
and www.quiltusa.yahoo.com
Proprietor: Carolie Hensley

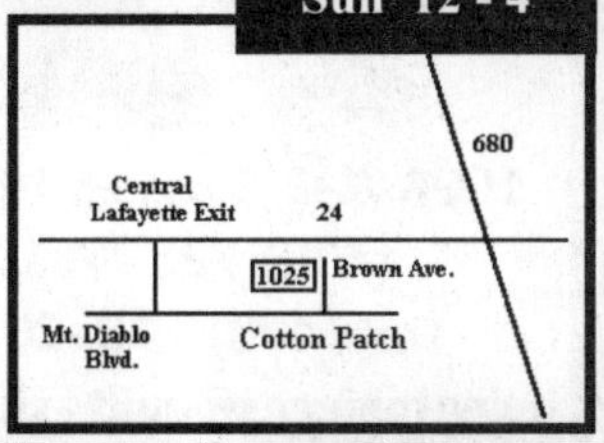

Cotton prints, solids, batiks, Japanese fabrics. 800 book titles, gifts, notions, etc.

Vallejo, CA #76

M, Wed - Fri 10 - 6
Sat - Sun 11 - 5

Seams Like Art

318 Georgia St. 94590
(707) 647-1222
Owner: Sandy Hager Est: 2002
3000 sq.ft. 700 Bolts & Growing!

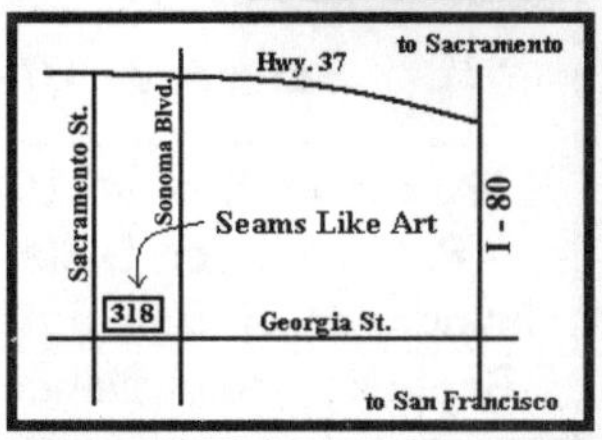

Two blocks from San Francisco/Vallejo Ferry in Oldtown Vallejo. 100% Cotton Fabrics, Notions, Books, Patterns, Classes, A Fun Shop!

Tracy, CA #77

Mon - Sat 10 - 5:30 Wed til 7

The Quilt Lady

71 E 10th Street 95376
(209) 836-5426
Fax: (209) 836-5584
Owner: Debra Middleton
Est: 2001 2000 sq. ft.

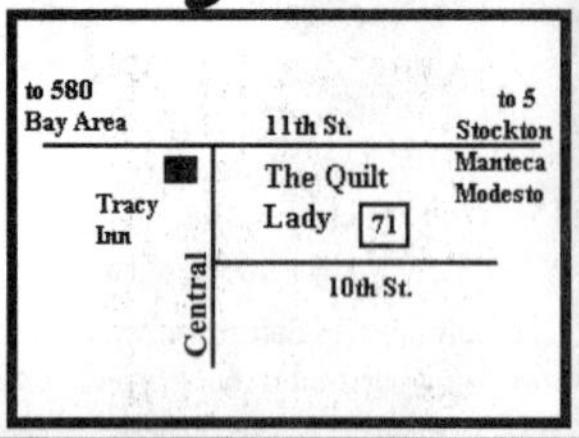

1,200 plus bolts from top companies. Books, patterns, notions and friendly customer service. Classes

The Quilting Queens

720 West 2nd Street 94509
(925) 9-QUILTS (978-4587)
E-Mail: TheQuilting Queens@prodigy.net
Fax: (925) 756-2445
Owners: Bernie & Alexandra
Est: 2001 1550 sq.ft. 3000 bolts

We Are A Full Service Quilting Store.

- Friendly, knowledgeable & helpful staff
- Fabric galore & more arriving daily
- Patterns, books, notions & supplies
- Classes for all levels
- Professional custom machine quilting
- Visa & Master Card welcome

Antioch, CA #79

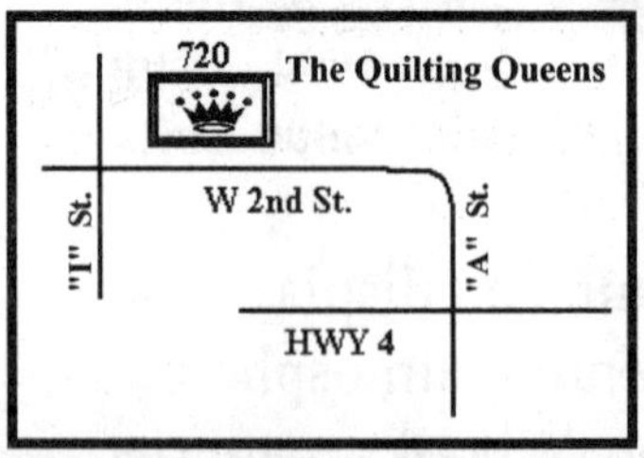

Mon - Sat 10 - 5:30

2033 Railroad Ave.
Livermore, CA 94550
(925) 371-7064

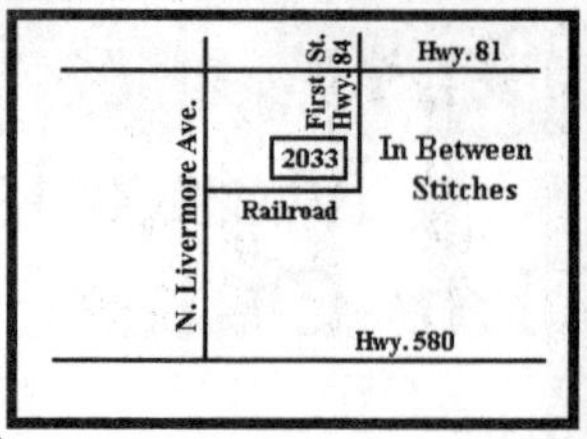

IN BETWEEN STITCHES
QUILT & GIFT STORE

Mon - Sat 9 - 6
Sun 11 - 3

Fax: (925) 371-7065
Est: 2002

A place where friendships grow

www.inbetweenstitches.com

Livermore, CA #78

Alameda, CA #80

Tues - Sat 10 - 6
Thur til 9
Sun 12 - 5

Quilt Fans

1716 Lincoln Ave. 94501
(510) 749-6717
Owner: Cathy Rodriguez

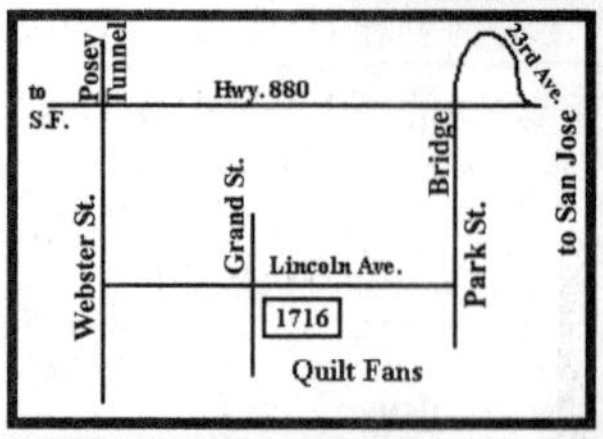

Fan-tastic quilt fabric and supplies for quilt fan-ciers. 100% cottons, batiks, flannels, plaids, books and notions. Classes too!

Going To Pieces

GREAT LOCATION

San Jose, CA #81

1008 G-2 Blossom Hill Rd.
(408) 723-4133
fax (408) 723-2025
goingtopieces@quilt-shop.com
www.quilt-shop.com
Owner: Judie Eichenbaum
Free Newsletter

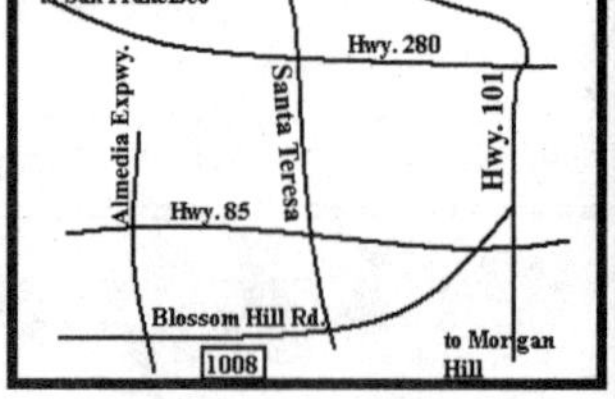

Store Hours: Monday - Friday 10-7pm
Saturday 10-6pm Sunday 11-5pm

Large selection of 100% Cotton Fabrics, Books and Patterns for Dolls, Quilts and Wearable Art. Hundreds of Bali Batiks. Surface Design Supplies. Beginning to Advanced Classes. Quarterly Sales.

San Jose, CA #82

Tues - Sun 10 - 5
Thur til 8

San Jose Museum of Quilts & Textiles

110 Paseo de San Antonio 95112
(408) 971-0323 Fax: (408) 971-7226
Web Site: www.sjquiltmuseum.org
Est: 1977
Non-profit Public Benefit Museum

Regularly changing exhibits of Quilts and Textiles. Museum Store has extensive assortment of books on quilting.

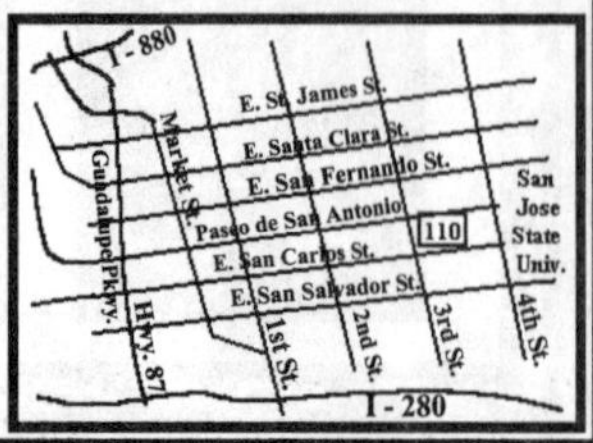

The Village Quilt Shop

Pleasanton, CA #83

Mon - Fri 10 - 6
Sat 10 - 5
Sun 12 - 4

1989 "F" Santa Rita Rd., Pleasanton, CA 94566
(925) 462-9340 Fax: (925) 462-4135
Owner: Tammy MacLean
Est: 1981 2400 sq.ft. 2000+ Bolts
E-mail: thevillagequiltshop@att.net
Web Site: www.TheVillageQuiltShop.net

Welcome to our Quilt Shop.

We offer a large selection of 100% cotton Fabrics, notions, books, patterns and classes, beginning to advanced.

Mountain View, CA #84

Check out our **bias**! We have enough **backing** and **stash** to make us arguably the **Best One-Stop Quilting Solutions Store**!

Eddie's Quilting Bee

FAMILY OWNED SINCE 1976; Eddie Leone

264 Castro St • Mountain View, CA 94041 • (650) 969-1714 • (888) 784-5837
web site: www.quiltingbee.com • e-mail: quiltbee@quiltingbee.com

We feature:

- ★ 4,000 bolts of cotton fabric
- ★ Books, patterns, notions, threads, ribbons, machine accessories, cabinets, irons, you name it... if we don't have it, we can get it
- ★ Three brands of sergers, embroidery, and sewing machines
- ★ Hours of operations
  Mon-Fri 9am-8:30pm
  Sat 9am-5:30pm
  Sun 11am-5:00pm

baby lock®

... and others.

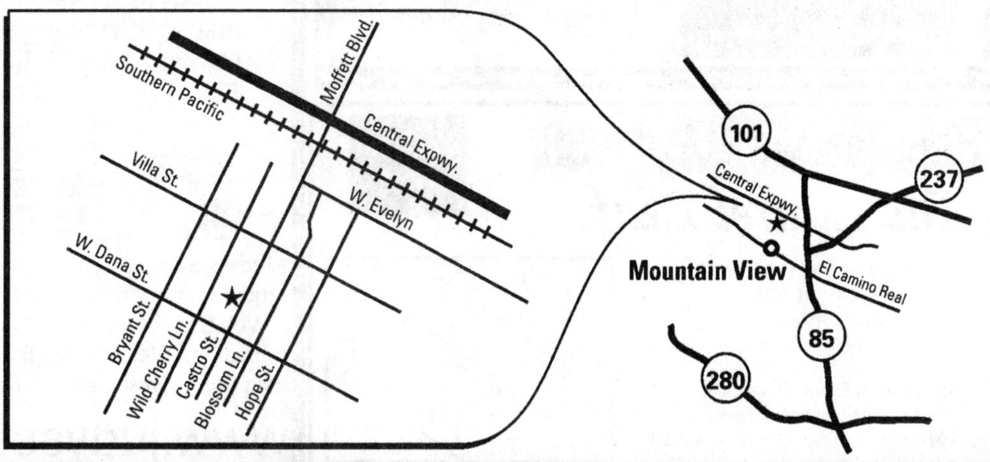

Milpitas, CA #85

Mon - Fri 10 - 7
Thur til 9
Sat 10 - 5
Sun 11 - 5

Fabrics 'n' Fun

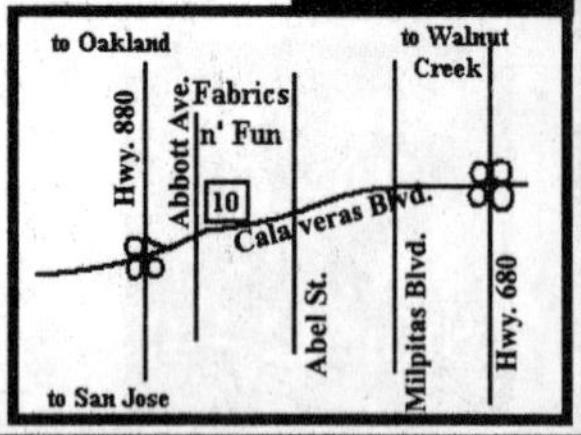

10 S. Abbott Ave., Suite A 95035
(408) 946-3860 Fax: (408) 946-3844
E-Mail: lillian@fabricnfun.com
Web site: www.fabricsnfun.com
Owner: Lillian Sienknecht 3300 sq.ft.
Colorful fabrics, wonderful books, patterns, notions, samples, great classes, knowledgeable helpful staff. A fun place to visit. Everything for the quilter's resources.

Sunnyvale, CA #86

Mon - Fri 10 - 6
Sat 10 - 5

Carolea's Knitche

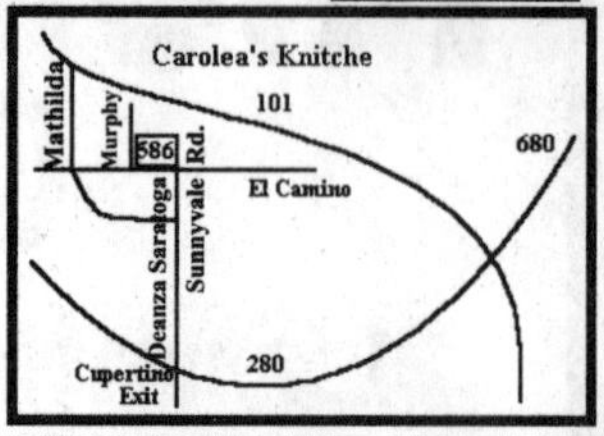

586 South Murphy Ave. 94086
(408) 736-2800
Owner: Carolea Peterson
Est: 1973 1400 sq.ft.

The very latest in Hoffman, Alex Henry, Jinny Beyer, Kaufman, Tony Wentzel, Gutcheon . . . Mail orders welcome.

1326 S. Mary Ave., Sunnyvale, CA 94087
♥(408) 735-9830♥www.thegranaryquilts.com

Sunnyvale, CA #87

Your Friendly Neighboryhood Quilt Shop!

- ♥ 100% Cotton Fabrics
- ♥ Quilting Supplies
- ♥ Books & Patterns
- ♥ Gifts for Quilters
- ♥ Notions
- ♥ Classes

Owner: Paula Ivers

Shop Hours:
Mon - Thur 10am - 6pm
Fri & Sat 10am - 5pm
Last Sunday of the Month 10am - 4pm

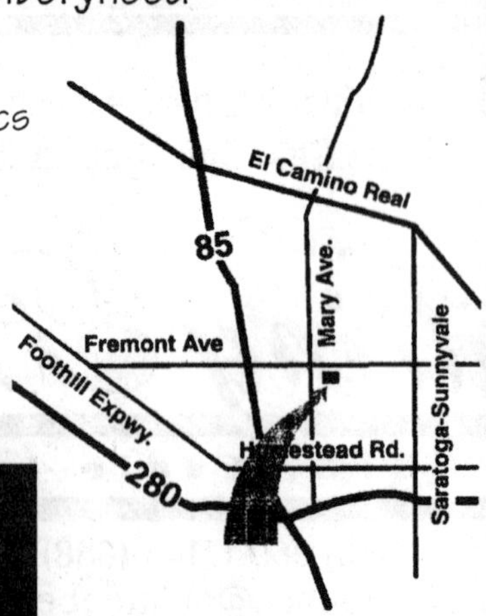

Easy Freeway Access!

Whiffle Tree Quilts

10261 S. DeAnza Blvd. 95014
(408) 255-5270
Web-Site: www.whiffletreequilts.com
Owner: Louise Horkey
Est: 1982 1280 sq.ft.

Mon - Fri 9:30 - 6
Thur til 8
Sat 9:30 - 5

Cupertino, CA #88

A terrific store full of fabric, patterns, & notions & books. The user-Friendly quilt shop in the heart of Silicon Valley!

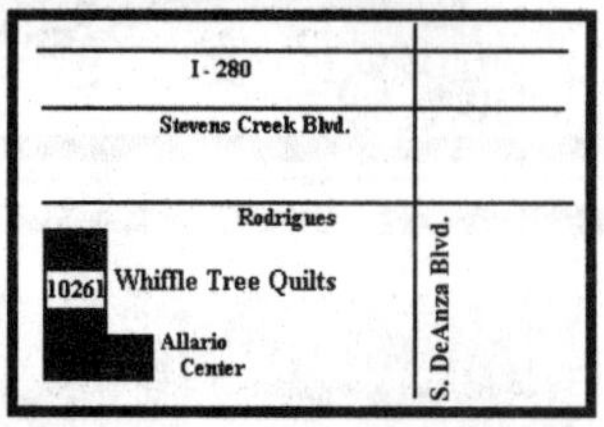

San Carlos, CA #89

Mon - Sat 10 - 5

The Laurel Leaf

648 Laurel Street 94070
(650) 591-6790
Owner: Julie Murphy
Est: 1983 2200 sq.ft.

100% Cotton Fabric, Books, Patterns, Quilting Supplies, Classes.
10 Min. South of San Francisco Airport

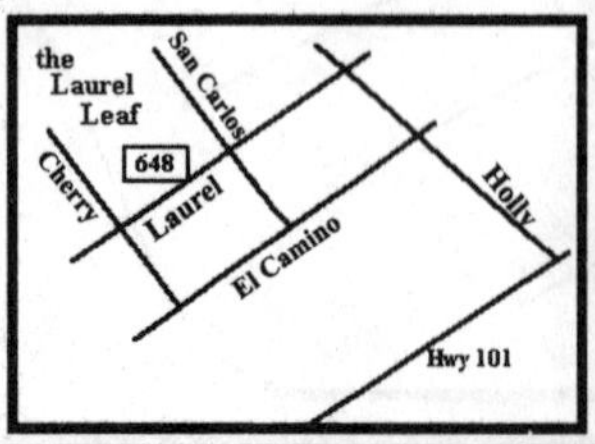

Scotts Valley, CA #90

Judy's Sewing Center

222 G Mt. Hermon Rd. 95066
(831) 440-1050
Fax: (831) 440-1709
E-mail: JHSewing@aol.com
Owner: Judy Hollaway
Est: 1997 2500 sq.ft.

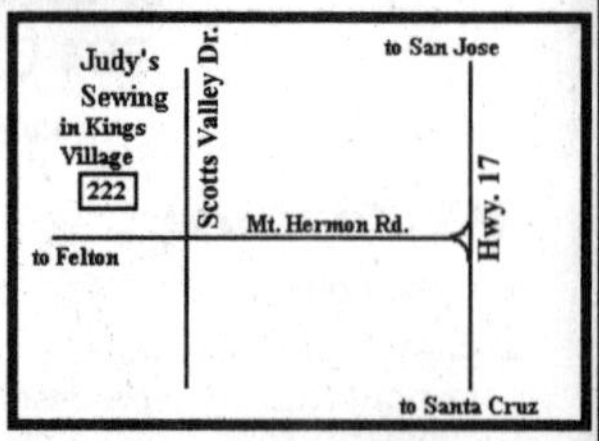

Judy's Sewing Center is a quilt shop just for you. Judy's offers friendly, helpful service. Check our Web Site for our annual quilt retreat & our class schedule. We carry the finest in quilting fabrics & supplies. Husqvarna / Viking Sewing Machines.

Mon - Sat 10 - 6
Sun 12 - 5

www.judyssewingcenter.com

SOUTHERN CALIFORNIA

23 Featured Shops #91 to #113

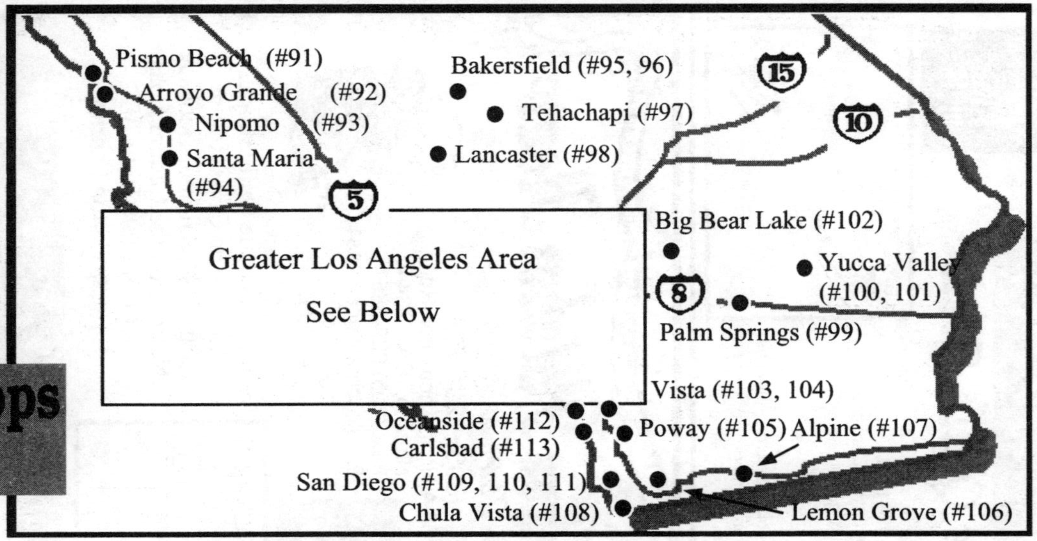

Greater Los Angeles Area

42 Featured Shops #114 to #155

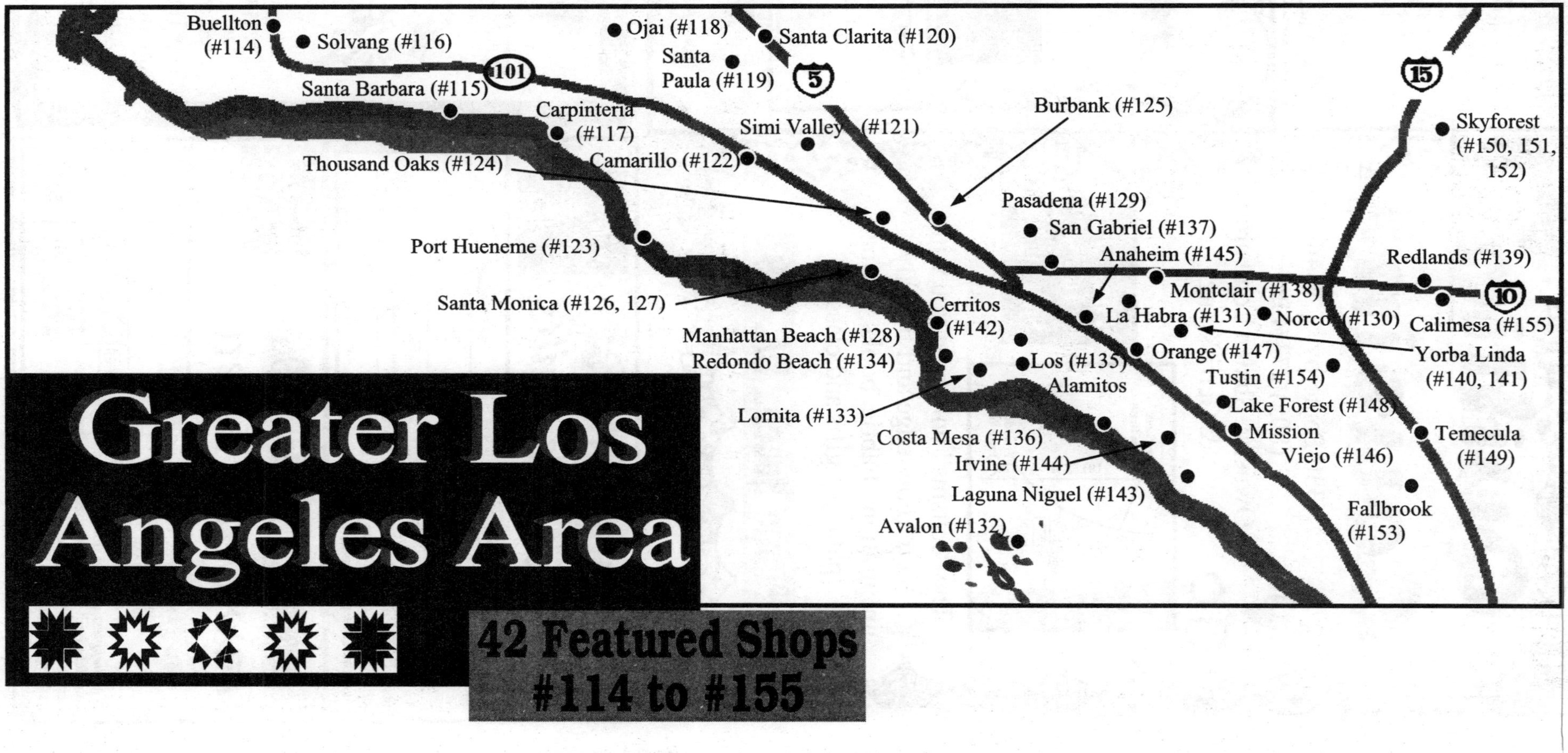

Quiltin' Cousins

330 Pomeroy 93449
(805) 773-4988
Owners: Shawn Lombardo & Gerri Kautz

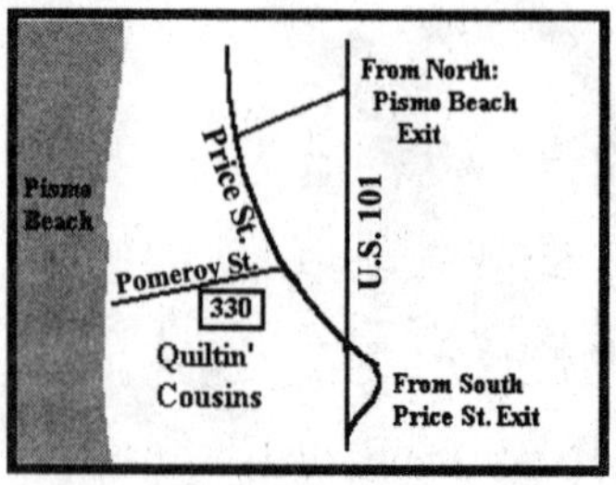

Tues - Fri 10 - 5
Sat 10 - 4

The "cousins" will greet you with their knowledge and friendly inspiration. Fabric, books, notions, patterns, gifts and classes.

Pismo Beach, CA #91

Arroyo Grande, CA #92

The Quilt Attic

Mon - Sat 10 - 5
Sun 12 - 4

106 Bridge St. 93420
(805) 474-0717
E-Mail: TheQuiltAttic@aol.com
Website: www.quiltspot.com
Est: 1998 2000 sq.ft.

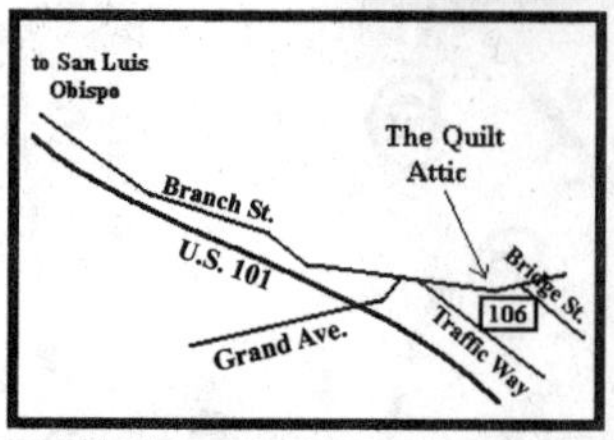

Cotton fabrics, books, patterns, notions, gifts and classes for quilters. We have Computer Software to design your quilts.

Creative Patches House

Patricia Hughes
(805) 929-3704
136 A North Thompson Rd.
Nipomo, CA 93444
Fax: (805) 929-3857
Email: creativepatches1@aol.com
Est: 1997

Mon - Sat 10 - 5
Wed til 8

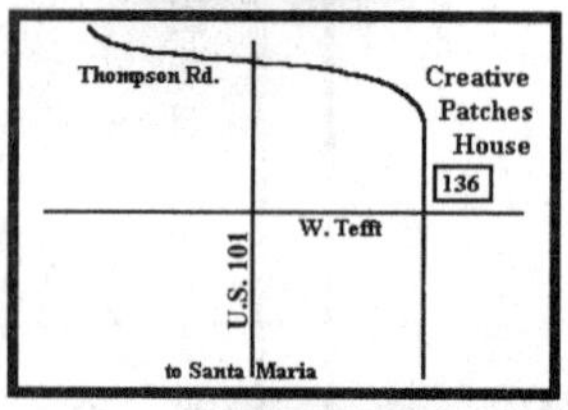

....A Unique Quilt Shop....
....Fantastic Class Room....
Largest Selection of Books & Notions on the Central Coast
Over 3000 Bolts of 100% Cotton Fabrics

Nipomo, CA #93

Also Visit "Janeels Ribbon Works" Jan Lee (Owner) featuring Brazilian & Silk Embroidery

Santa Maria, CA #94

Sophie Ann's Quilts

Mon - Fri 10 - 5
Sat 10 - 4

1765 - B South Broadway 93458
(805) 925-1888
Owner: Jaime Cummings & Helga Trampush
Est: 1986 950 sq.ft.

Finest in contemporary and traditional fabrics. Bolts of 100% Cotton Fabric, books, notions, classes and always friendly Service !

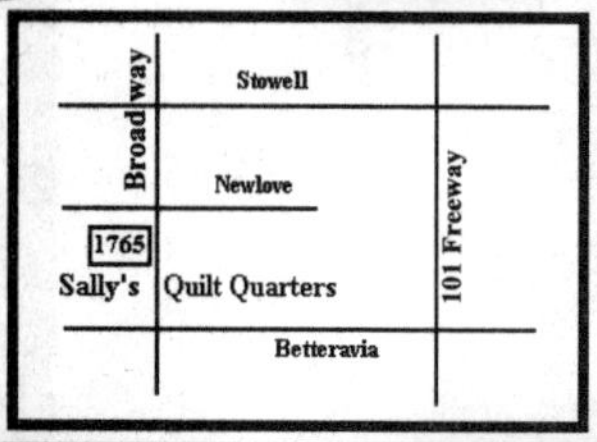

Bakersfield, CA #96

Two Quilt 'n Sew

Mon - Sat 9 - 6

2701 Calloway Dr., Suite 414 93312
(661) 589-8863 Fax: (661) 587-3974
E-Mail: 2quilt@etcrier.net
Owner: Robin Laiblin
Est: 2000 1900 sq.ft. 2000+ Bolts

"The happiest quilting store in Kern County"
Complete quilt store specializing in customer service. 200+ book titles and 200+ distinct Quilting stencils and patterns. Classes for beginners to advanced.

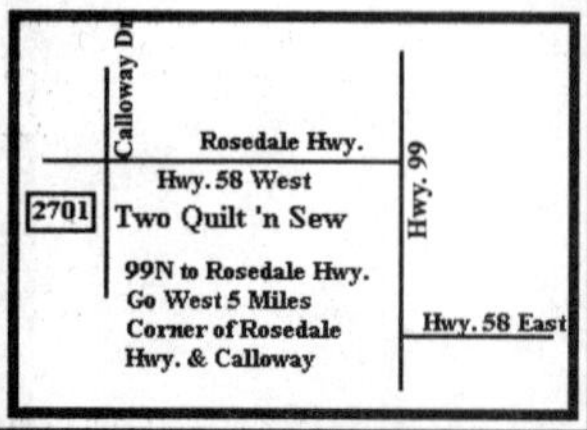

Bakersfield, CA #95

STRAWBERRY PATCHES

6439 Ming Ave. #C
Bakersfield, CA 93309
(661) 835-1738
Fax: (661) 835-0406
Owner: Suzanne Zingg
Est: 1985 2500 sq.ft.

Mon - Fri 10 - 5:30
Sat 10 - 5

www.strawberry-patches.com

Voted one of America's Top Ten quilt shops by American Patchwork & Quilting Magazine. Selection, Service, Smiles.

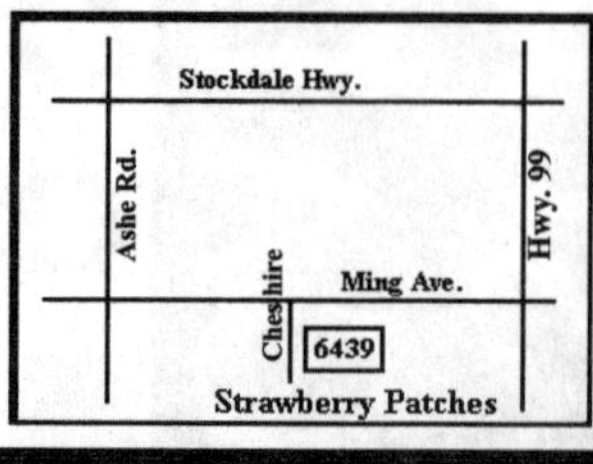

Tehachapi, CA #97

Tues - Fri 9:30 - 3:30
Sat 10 - 3

*** 5 Heart ***
Quilts & Fabric

Est: 1993
1900 sq.ft.
1600 Bolts

104 W. Tehachapi Blvd.
(661) 822-8709 93561
Owner: Claudia Blodget - Lye

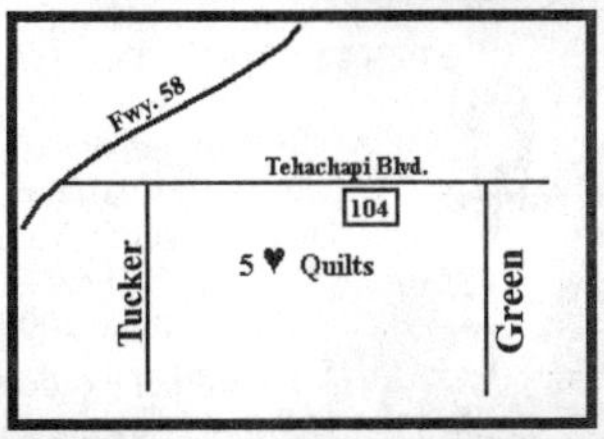

A Quilters Heaven with all of the Colors - 100% Cotton, Hoffman, Alex. Henry, Northcott, Benartex, Books, Notions and Classes - For Your Needs.

Lancaster, CA #98

Mon 12 - 5
Tues - Thur 9:30 - 6
Fri 9:30 - 5
Sat 9:30 - 4

Quilters' Cabin

QUILTERS CABIN

1832 W. Avenue K, Ste. 6
(frwy side of Arco) 93534
(661) 948-2118
Fax: (661) 948-0391
Est: 1988

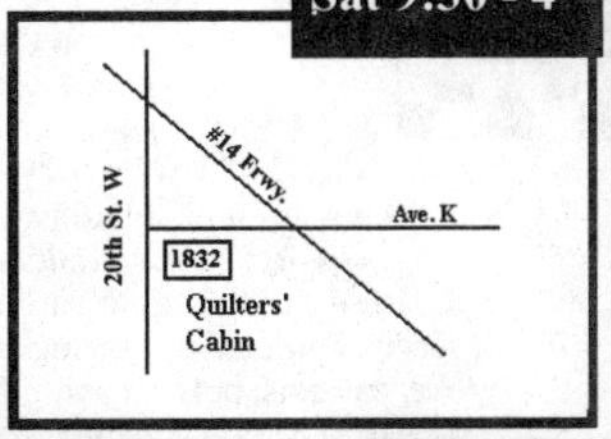

E-Mail: cabin@antelecom.net
Stop by for quilting supplies, 100% cottons, and Authorized dealer for *Unique Sewing Furniture.*

BERNINA

Yucca Valley, CA #100

Mon - Sat 9 - 4

Stitchin & Quiltin

57353-A 29 Palms Hwy. 92284
(760) 365-1744
Owner: Loreli Hagedorn

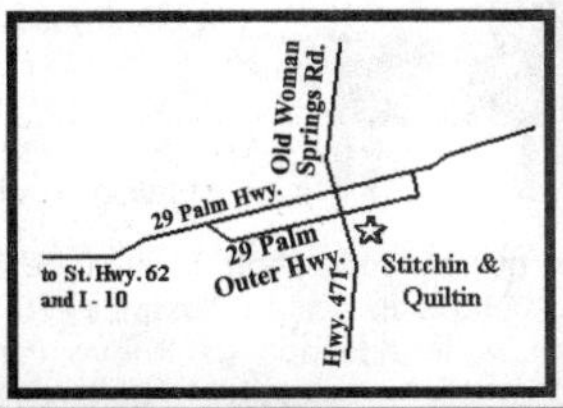

Quilting Supplies.
Free Classes with purchase of Materials.
Sewing Machine Repairs

Yucca Valley, CA #101

Donna's Country Store

55879 29 Palms Hwy. 92284
(760) 365-0577
Fax: (760) 369-2237
Owner: Donna Wightman
Est: 1992

Mon - Sat 10 - 5:30
Sun 10 - 4

2500 bolts of quilting Fabric, Books, Notions and classes. For your gift needs we carry Boyd Bears, Candles, Lotions, Jellys and Salsa's.

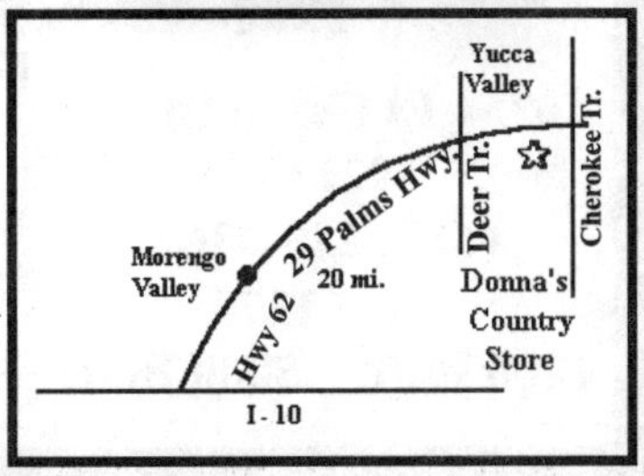

#99

Creative Expressions OF PALM SPRINGS

1111 South Palm Canyon Drive
Palm Springs, CA 92264
Tel: 760-327-2587
Fax: 760-322-2319
www.creativeexpressionsps.com
vmgonzales@AOL.com

All your Quilting needs:

Bali Batiks ▪ Novelties ▪ Solids ▪ Prints ▪ Reproductions

Notions — Patterns — Books — Threads — Embellishments

3,000+ bolts of high-quality, 100% cotton fabrics

All your Beading needs:

Exquisite ▪ Exotic ▪ Ethnic ▪ Contemporary

Beads from around the world — Seed Beads — Semi-Precious Stones — African Trade Beads — Crystals — Sterling Silver — Books — and much more

Fast, Friendly, Professional Service provided by our excellent staff.

Classes available in quiltmaking, beaded jewelry, wearable art, and more. Call for a free class schedule.

We are about 11.7 miles from I-10 when taking Palm Springs/ Hwy. 111 exit.

We are about 8.5 miles from I-10 when taking the Ramon exit.

Hwy. 111 becomes Palm Canyon Dr. after you enter the City of Palm Springs.

We share a building with Club Liquors. Parking is in the rear.

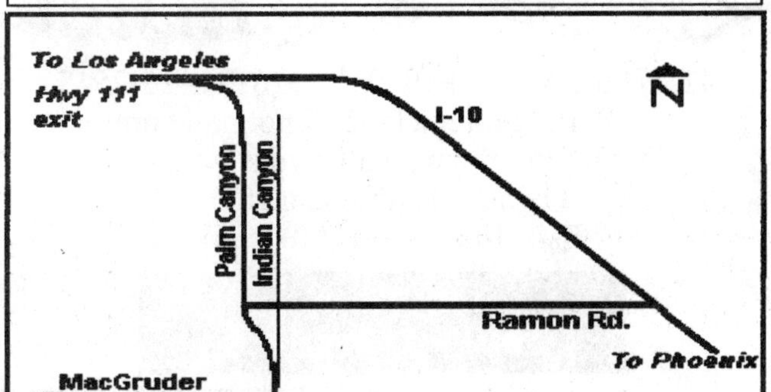

Map not to scale

Big Bear Lake, CA #102

Mon - Sat 10 - 5

The Patchwork Peddler

582 Paine Rd. 92315
(909) 878-4629
Fax: (909) 878-4729
E-Mail: candace@bbv.net
Owner: Candace Wright - Wilkerson

A Shop for Quilters
Fine Fabrics — Notions — Patterns
Classes — Specializing in Beginning Quilting

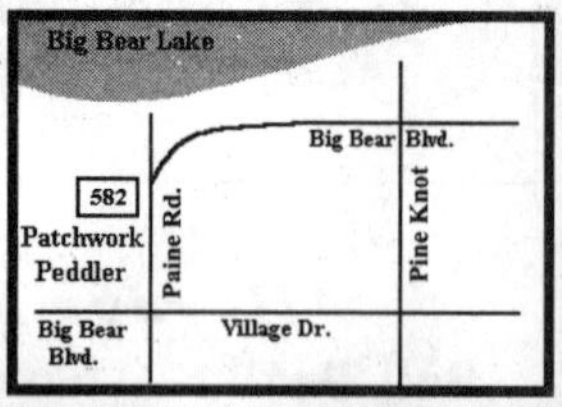

Vista, CA #103

Mon - Sat 10 - 5

Sew Special

777 E. Vista Way, Suite 205 92084
(760) 940-0363 Fax: (760) 431-6846
Orders: (888) 940-0663
E-Mail: sewspecial@adelphia.net
www.sewspecialfabrics.com
Owner: Wendy Mathews
Est: 1982
1500 sq.ft. 1000+ Bolts
Mail & Phone orders welcome
Heirloom Sewing and Quilting

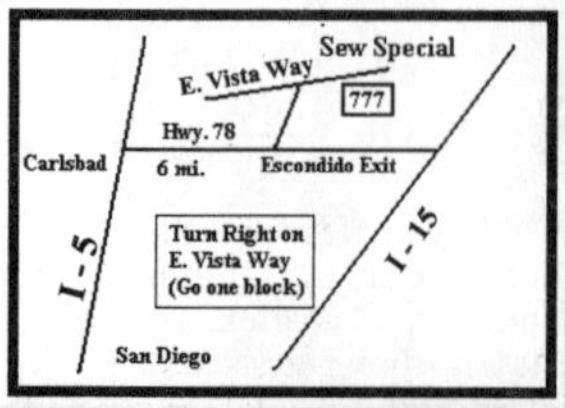

Vista, CA #104

Mon - Fri 10 - 5:30 Sat 10 - 4

Fat Quarters Quilt Shop

728 Escondido Ave. 92084
(760) 758-8308
Owners: Kelly & Mary Sullivan

Charming house filled with primitive country quilts. Lots of fabrics, quilting supplies, gifts, antiques & friendly people.

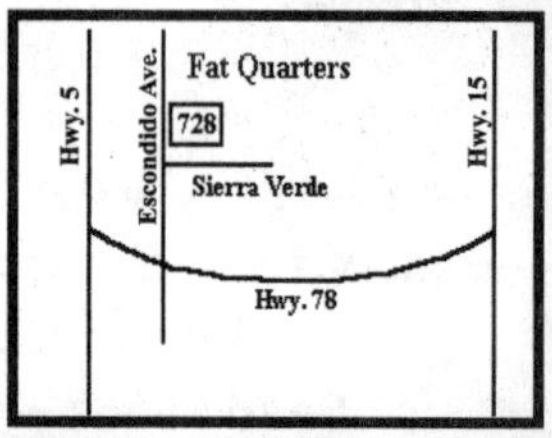

Poway, CA #105

Mon, Fri Sat 9 - 5 Tues, Wed Thur 9 - 8

Amidon Quiltworks

12625 Danielson Ct. #111
92064
(858) 486-0696
Fax: (858) 486-1618
Web Site: www.amidonquiltworks.com
Owner: Nancy Amidon
Est: 1994 3800 sq.ft. 1700 Bolts
A full service quilt shop carrying fabrics, books, patterns, notions and gifts.
Mail Order Available.

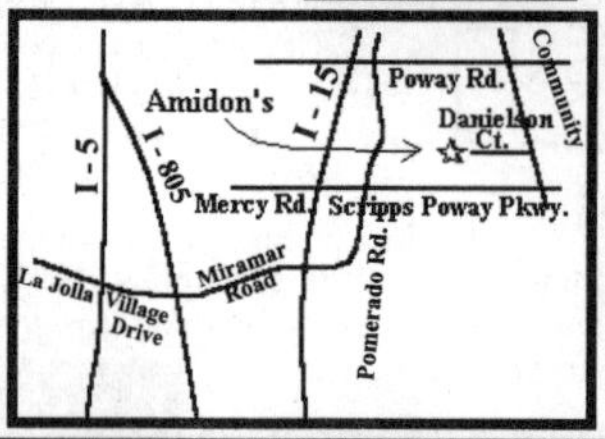

Lemon Grove, CA #106

Tues - Fri 9 - 4 Sat 10 - 6

Ethnic Quilts & Fabrics

2607-09 Lemon Grove Ave. 91977
(619) 461-0783
E-Mail: enbriggs@aol.com
Web Site: www.ethnicquilts-fabrics.com
Est: 1999 1400 sq.ft.

Beautiful African Fabric and Custom Machine Quilting Available.

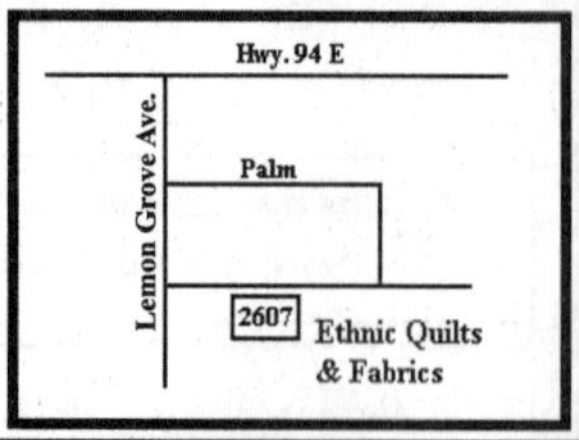

Alpine, CA #107

Wed - Sun 10 - 5

Kat's Cottage

2526 Alpine Blvd 91901
(619) 445-2877 2000+ Bolts
E-Mail: katsews@flash.net
Web Site: www.katscottage.com
Owner: Kathie Passarino

A quaint quilt shop located next to a B&B and restaurant in beautiful Alpine. 100% cotton fabrics. A wide selection of Robyn Pandolph, Batiks & Orientals. 50+ samples of quilts & clothes.

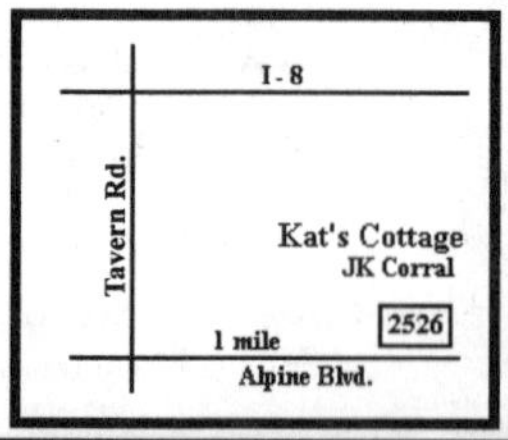

Chula Vista, CA #108

Quilters' Choice

423 Third Ave. 91910 (619) 425-2545
E-Mail: Quilterschoice@hotmail.com
Web Site: www.Quiltsbydesign.com
Owner: Kathy Schaeffer
Est: 1992 1500+ sq.ft.

Tues - Fri 10 - 7
Sat 10 - 5 Sun 12 - 4

Fabric, Books, Patterns, Notions, Classes, Kits, Mail Order, Special Orders.
Authorized Bernina Dealership.

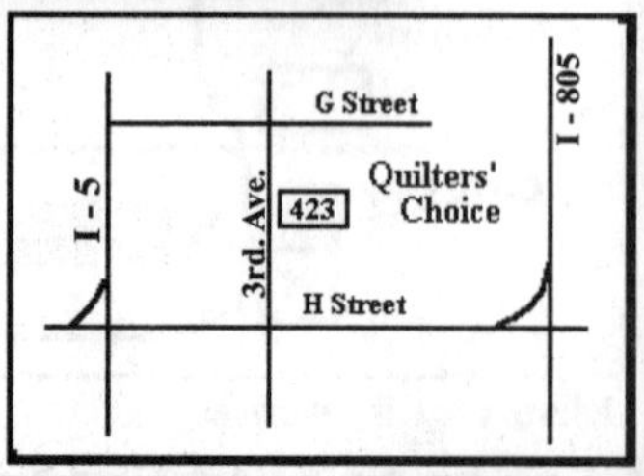

FABRIC VILLA - IMPORTS

San Diego, CA #109

Hand-loomed Cottons from Guatemala & India, African Prints, Batiks, Ethnic Braids, Cuna Indian Molas, Unique Assortment of Printed Cottons.

Mon - Fri 10 - 6
Closed Sat Sun 11 - 3

6364 El Cajon Blvd.
92115
(619) 286-4364
Est: 1974
1200 sq.ft. 5000 Bolts

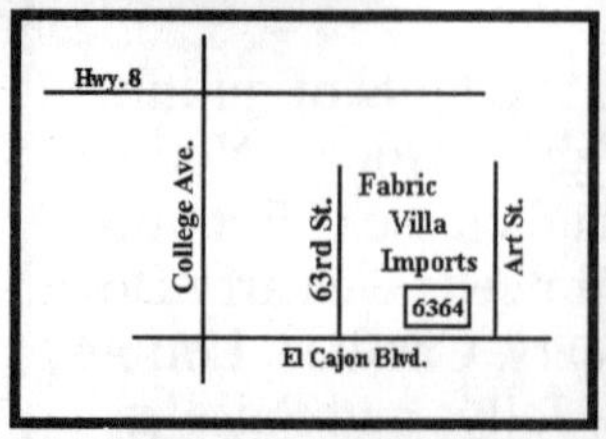

San Diego, CA #110

Rosie's Calico Cupboard

7151 El Cajon Blvd. Suite 'F' 92115 (619) 697-5758
Fax: (619) 465-8298 E-Mail: rozgonzalez@cox.net
Web Site: www.rosiescalicocupboard.com

Offering over 4900 sq.ft. (stocked to the brim) with over **10,000** bolts of **First Quality** 100% Cotton Prints, plus Books, Batting, Notions, Patterns, Thread, Silk Ribbon, Quilting & Crafting related gift items, New & Old Antique Quilts, a 'Trunk Full of over 500 lbs of Buttons', plus much, much more and all at Everyday **DISCOUNT** prices.

Monday - Friday 9 - 5 Wednesday til 8
Saturday 8 - 5 Sunday 11 - 5

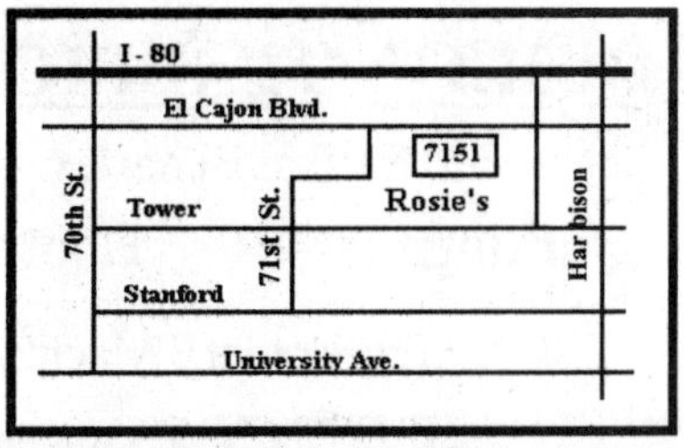

- Well stocked sale rack with values from 25 to 75% off suggested Retail Prices.
- New stock arriving daily.
- 1100 sq.ft. Classroom with a full calendar or Quilting & Crafting Classes year round.
- Mail Orders and Special Orders Welcome
- Visa, MC, Discover, American Express, ATM Cards Accepted

Hwy. 8 (East or West) — take 70th St. exit, travel south on 70th St. for 1/2 mile to El Cajon Blvd., turn left (east) onto El Cajon Blvd., travel for 1 1/2 blocks.
Hwy. 94 (East or West) — take the Mass. exit, travel north to University Ave., turn left, follow to 70th St., turn right, follow to El Cajon Blvd., turn right.

A Full Service Quilt Shop
Catering to Quilters and Crafters Since 1983

WEST COAST DEALER OF GAMMILL QUILTING MACHINES

WE TRAIN YOU! 13 YEARS EXPERIENCE WITH GAMMILL MACHINES

❖ Sales ❖ Service ❖ Training

Call today for a complimentary video or to set up an appointment for a free hands-on demonstration. Experience first hand how easy and smooth Gammill Quilting Machines are to operate. While visiting our shop, you will be able to try the *Premier, Classic or Optimum Quilting Machines* to determine which one best suits your needs. Our two day training class is included with purchase of your machine through The Quilted Rose.

We offer various workshops for those interested in purchasing a longarm quilting machine as well as workshops for new or experienced longarm quilters. We also carry a line of quilting supplies, including original continuous line quilting patterns. Check out our website for workshop, supply and pattern information.

Contact us regarding the free package of accessories that come with delivery of your machine only from our shop....

Mon - Sat
10am - 5pm

THE QUILTED ROSE

Web Site: www.thequiltedrose.com

7151 El Cajon Blvd. Suite H 92115
(619) 462-1848 or (800) 660-8282 Fax: (619) 462-1389
Owner: Barbara Vanice E-Mail: info@thequiltedrose.com

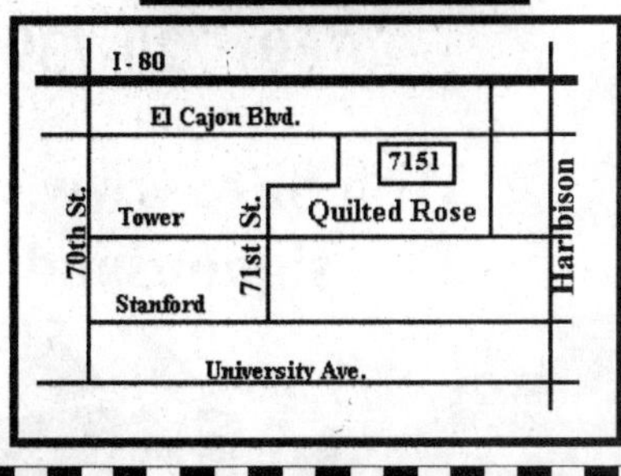

San Diego, CA #111

SEW MUCH BETTER

1824-A Oceanside Blvd. 92054
(Boney's Center — one block east of I - 5)
760-433-5151

Owners:
Larry & Mary Danielson

30 miles North of San Diego
5 miles North of Legoland
60 miles South of Disneyland

Oceanside, CA #112

Tues - Sat 9:30 - 5:00

QUILTING FABRIC 1000+ BOLTS @ DISCOUNT PRICES
Hoffman, Batiks, Benartex, Kona Bay, South Seas, RJR, P&B, others
Quilting classes Books, Patterns, Notions Antique Quilts
Embroidery Machine Supplies and Design Patterns
BERNINA Sales & Service **FEATHERWEIGHTS**

Web Site: www.sewmuchbetter.com

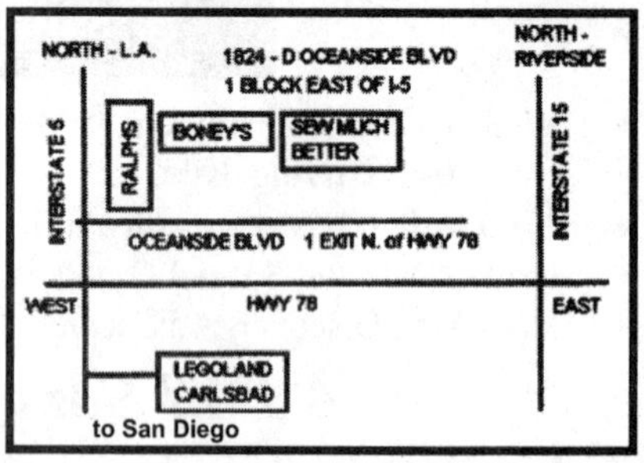

Sowing Sisters

QUILTING & ARTISAN CENTER

Carlsbad, CA #113

Sowing the Seeds of Creativity

2956 Roosevelt St., Suite 1 92008
(760) 720-7397 **Fax: (760) 720-7627**

Web Site: www.sowingsisters.signonsandiego.com

Mon - Sat 9 - 5

Friendly experienced staff make you feel at home! Cozy Cottage fully stocked with a large assortment of books, patterns, notions, tools, mats — everything a quilter needs. Great collection of 100% cottons and batiks. Classes offered every day.

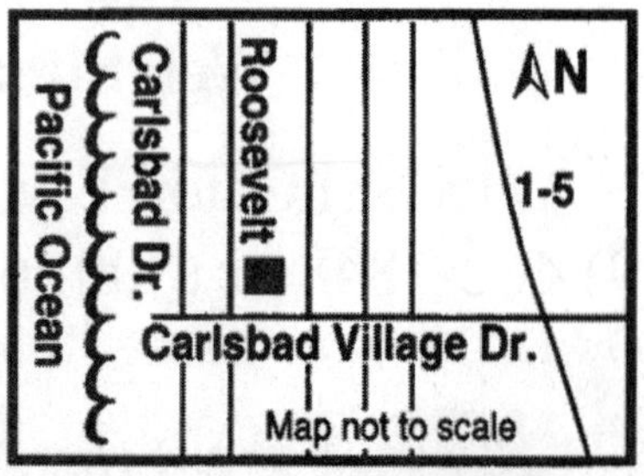

Buellton, CA #114

www.thecreationstation.com

252 E. Hwy. 246, Unit A
Buellton, CA 93427
(805) 693-0174

The Creation Station FABRIC & Quilt Shop

Wed - Sat 10 - 5
Sun 10 - 4

Fax: (805) 693-0164
Owner: Dawn Farrier
Est: 2002 2600 sq.ft.

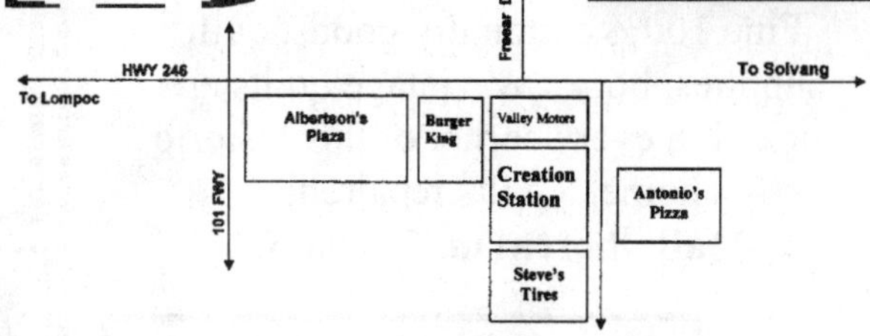

All fabric $5.00 per yard!

Unique selection of 100% cotton & flannel fabrics amidst our fun & funky nostalgic setting

Blue Island Quilts

Mon - Fri 10 - 6
Sat 10 - 5

"Looking for the Unusual?"

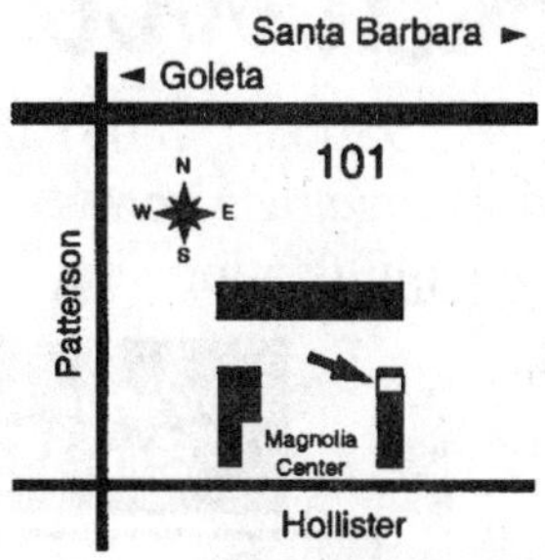

- Fabrics - carefully selected, top quality cottons including tropical, asian, australian, batik & one-of-a-kind
- Patterns - our own original designs as well as the mainland's best selection of Hawaiian Quilt patterns
- Books, notions, specialty items & gifts

Santa Barbara, CA #115

5140 Hollister Avenue, Santa Barbara, CA 93111
805 683-0112

Solvang, CA #116

Rasmussen's Solvang

Mon - Sat 9 - 5:30
Sun 9 - 5

1697 Copenhagen Dr. 93463
(805) 688-6636 Fax: (805) 688-2847
E-Mail: ras1sol@aol.com

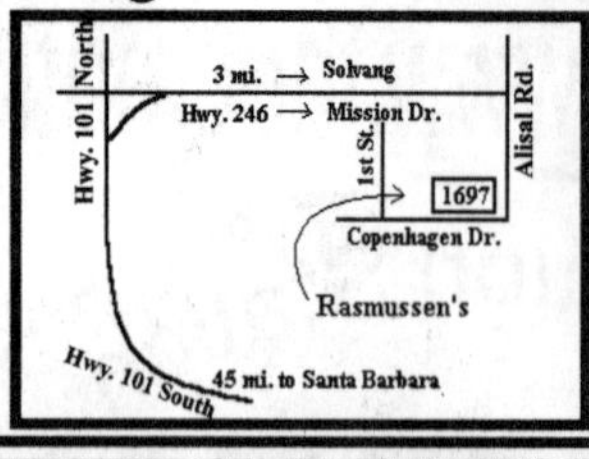

We offer a large selection of quilting fabric, patterns, and books; as well as needlework and knitting supplies. We welcome phone and mail orders.

The Treasure Hunt

Folk Art ❤ Gifts
Special Treasures
Greeting Cards
Collectibles
Good Times

Fabric ❤ Quilting
Stenciling ❤ Painting
Knitting ❤ Crochet
Country Crafts
Floral Designs
Needlework

Mon - Sat 10 - 5
Sun 11 - 4

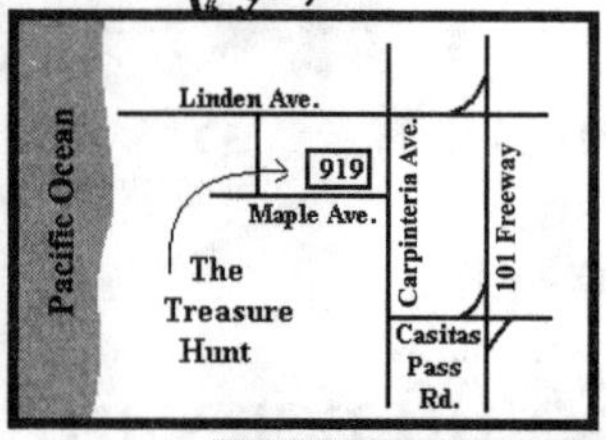

919 Maple Ave.
93013
(805) 684-3360
Owner: Roxanne Barbieri
Est: 1982

Carpinteria, CA #117

HEARTWARMERS Mercantile

"Where it feels good to shop"

Wed - Sat 10 - 5:30
Sun 11 - 4

Fine 100% cotton dry goods, quilt supplies, books, & vintage quilts are tucked in every corner of this historic home. Quilts repaired.

E-Mail: hartwrmr@west.net

310 E. Matilija St.
93023
(805) 640-1187
Proprietress:
Lou Ann Schlichter
Est: 1994

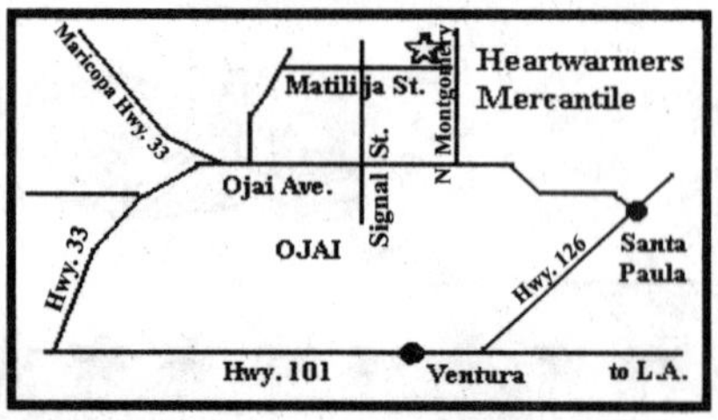

Ojai, CA #118

Santa Paula, CA #119

Brownie's Basement

Mon - Fri 10 - 6
Sat 10 - 5
Sun 12 - 4

866 E. Main St. 93060
(805) 525-4556 Fax: (805) 525-5113
E-mail: baudwink@aol.com
Owners: Allen and Cheryl Baudizzon
Est: 2001 2400 sq.ft. 3000 Bolts

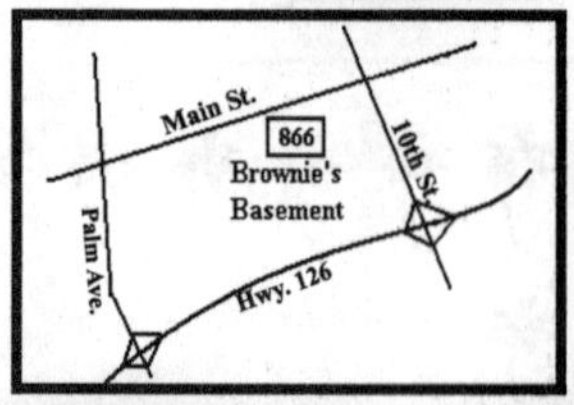

Visit the friendliest Quilt Shop around. We have over 3000 Bolts of Cotton with over 200 Bolts of Flannels.

Loving Stitches QUILT SHOPPE

Mon - Fri 10 - 5
Thur til 7:30
Sat 10 - 4

21515 Soledad Canyon Rd. #110
Santa Clarita, CA 91350
(661) 254-1296

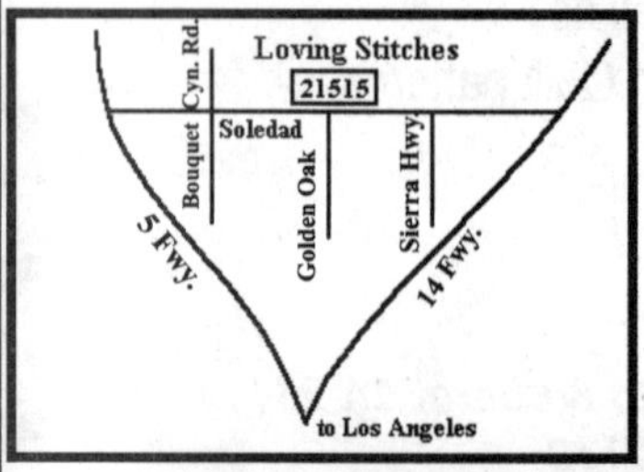

Over 1500 bolts of fabric - all in a charming country atmosphere. Large selection of plaids, 30's Reproductions, Flannels, and Batiks.

Santa Clarita, CA #120

Simi Valley, CA #121

Owner: Linda Patton

Quilt Station

4210 E. Los Angeles Ave. 93063 (805) 584-6915
E-Mail: 97diggem@msn.com
Web Site: www.quiltstation.com

A Complete quilt Store . . .
We carry the finest quality 100% Cotton Fabrics in prints and solids. A complete line of Books, Patterns and Notions to round out your quilting needs along with gift items for your Quilting Friends. We offer a wide variety of classes for all levels of quilters. Our friendly staff is here to help you.

Mon - Sat 10 - 5:30
Sun 12 - 4

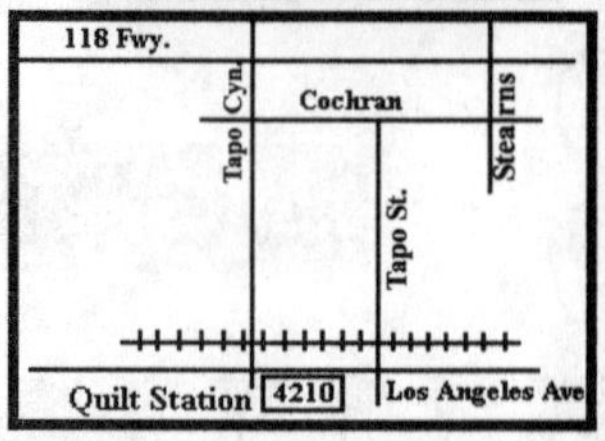

Camarillo, CA #122

Stitcherz

2117 Pickwick Drive
93010
(805) 445-8875
www.stitcherz.com
Janet & Jaye Killian, owners

Mon. - Sat. 10-5:30

Stitcherz has a friendly, knowledgeable staff; a large selection of quality 100% cotton fabrics; quilting books, supplies, & notions. Ventura County's largest selection of Thimbleberries products.

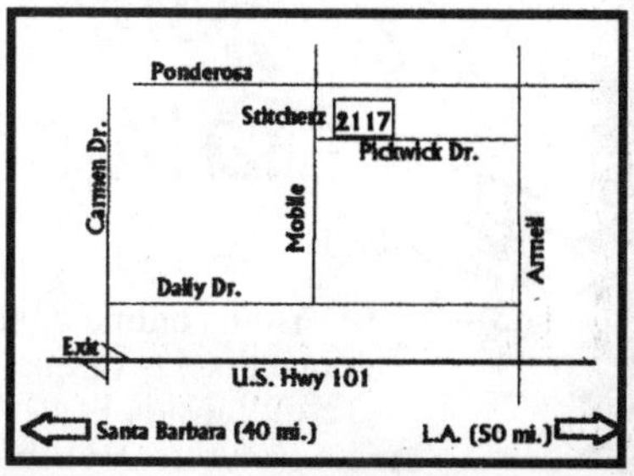

Port Hueneme, CA #123

All roads lead to...

The posie patch

475 Channel Islands Blvd.
Port Hueneme, CA 93041
(805) 984-8818
Tues. - Sat. 10-5

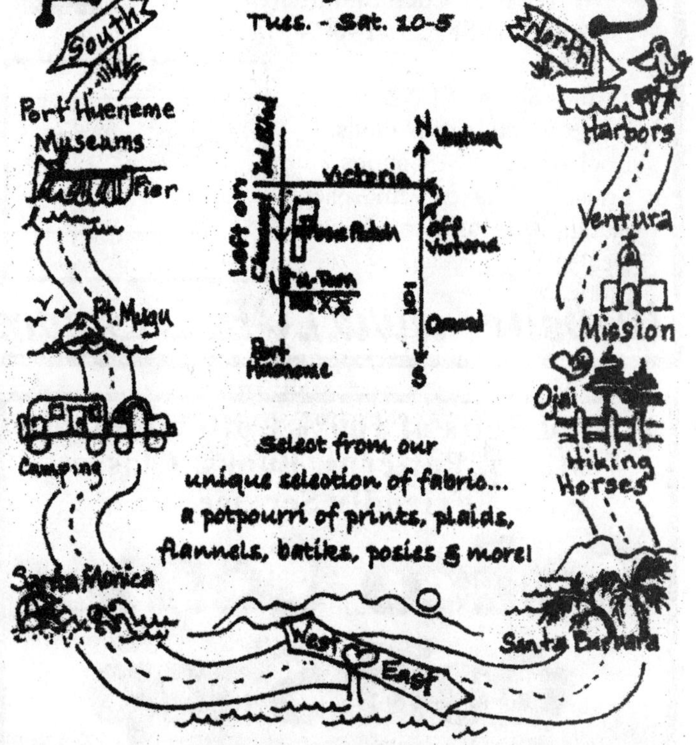

Select from our unique selection of fabric... a potpourri of prints, plaids, flannels, batiks, posies & more!

Thousand Oaks, CA #124

Mon - Thur 10 - 6
Fri & Sat 10 - 5
Sun 12 - 4

Mary's Quilt Inn

1772 Avenida de los Arboles #E 91362
(805) 241-0061 Owner: Mary Freeman
Est: 1978 1575 sq.ft. 1250+ Bolts

We offer a large variety of fabrics, classes, quilting supplies, books & patterns.

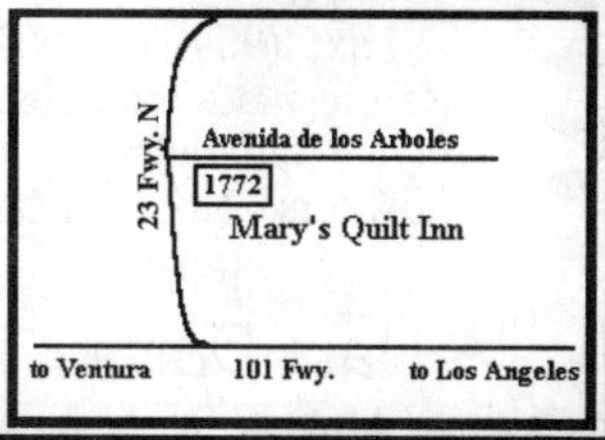

Burbank, CA #125

Mon - Fri 10 - 6
Sat 10 - 5
Sun 12 - 4

Q is For Quilts

620 S. Glenoaks Blvd. 91502
(818) 567-0267
Fax: (818) 567-1793

Come see our large variety of over 6,500 bolts of fabric. Our friendly staff is eager to help you find what you're looking for!

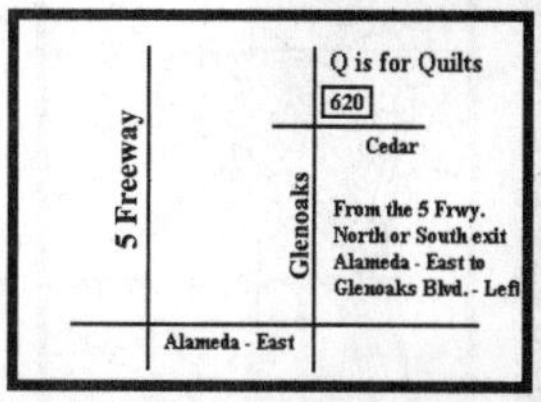

When you're ready for the best, we're ready for you!

Santa Monica, CA #126

Sewing Arts Center

Extraordinary Quilting Fabrics, including over 600 Batiks! Extensive Selection of Threads & Notions. Southern California's Husqvarna Viking Sewing Machine Specialist, Reliable Repairs, Cabinets & Over 100 Classes Per Quarter!

3306 Pico Blvd. 90405
310-450-4300 Est: 1955
Fax: 310-399-3406
info@sewingartscenter.com
www.sewingartscenter.com
2400 sq.ft. 2400 Bolts

Mon - Sat 10 - 6:30

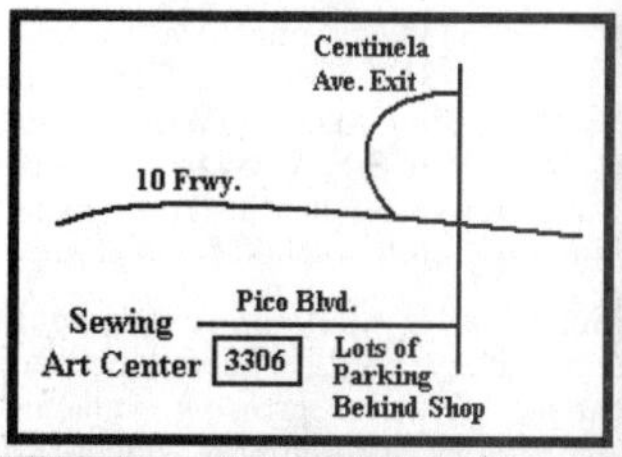

Santa Monica, CA #127

Mon - Sat 10:30 - 5:30

Crazy Ladies & Friends

2451 Santa Monica Blvd. 90404
(310) 828-3122
Owner: Karin Sheard
Est: 1977 1300 sq.ft. Classes

The Quilt Shop that offers words of encouragement. 3000 Bolts of Cotton Fabric chosen with the Quilter in mind.

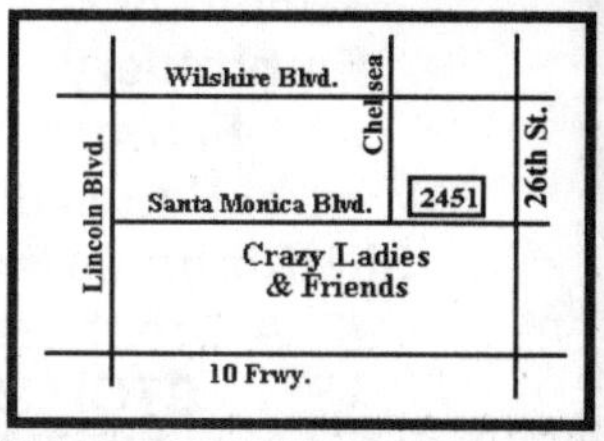

Manhattan Beach, CA #128

Luella's Quilt Basket

1840 N. Sepulveda Blvd. 90266
(310) 545-3436 Fax: (310) 545-8047
E-Mail: LUELLAS@gte.net
Owner: Luella Fournell
Est: 1988 1400 sq.ft.

Mon - Sat 10 - 6

- 3 Miles South of LAX
- Large selection of Notions, Books, and 100% Cottons
- Friendly, Relaxed Atmosphere
- Authorized Husqvarna Viking Dealer

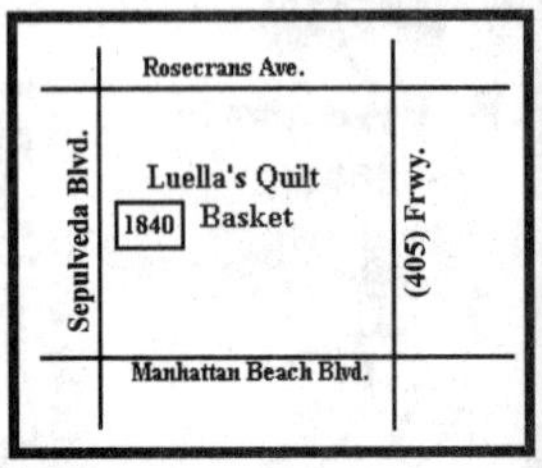

Website: www.LUELLAS.com

Pasadena, CA #129

Mon - Fri 9:30 - 7
Sat 9:30 - 6
Sun 12 - 5

Bearly Stitchin Sewing Center

2245 E. Colorado Blvd. A-106 91107
(626) 796-2118 Fax: (626) 796-3966
E-Mail: bstitchin@earthlink.net
Est: 1986 3100 sq.ft. 2000 Bolts

Complete selection of 100% cotton fabrics. Bernina and Husqvarna Viking sewing machines, books, notions, machine accessories and cabinets.

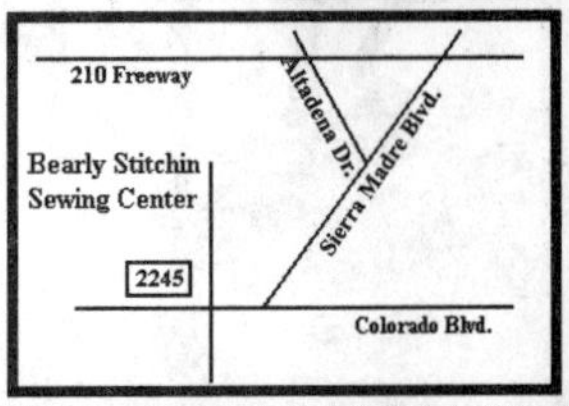

Norco, CA #130

The Tattered Rabbit Quilt Shop

Visit us online or stop by and see our completely unique display of quality 100% cotton fabrics and quilting supplies. We carry all your favorite manufacturers: Hoffman, Moda, Benartex, Michael Miller, Timeless Treasures, South Seas & many others.

Mon - Fri 11 - 6 Sat 10 - 4

1660 Hamner Ave., Suite 16
Norco, CA 92860
(909) 278-9108
Fax: (909) 278-9073
4fabric@tatteredrabbit.com
www.tatteredrabbit.com
Owners: Noel & Martha Hardcastle

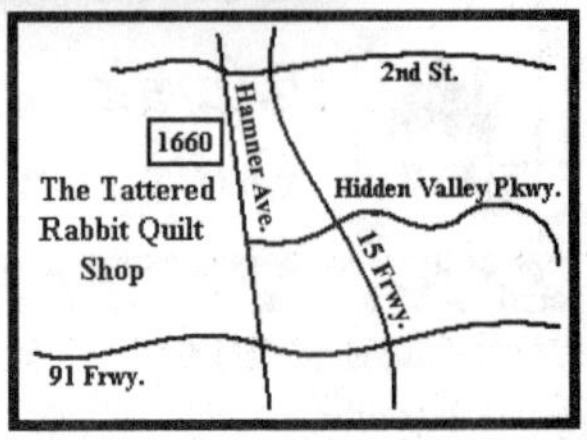

"A Hare Better Than Other Quilt shops"

3500 Bolts of 100% Cotton Fabric
Notions, Patterns, Books, Classes, Friendly Service.

Calico Corner Quilt Shop

2094 W. LaHabra Blvd.
90631 Est: 1984
(562) 694-3384
Owner: Sheila Ingersoll

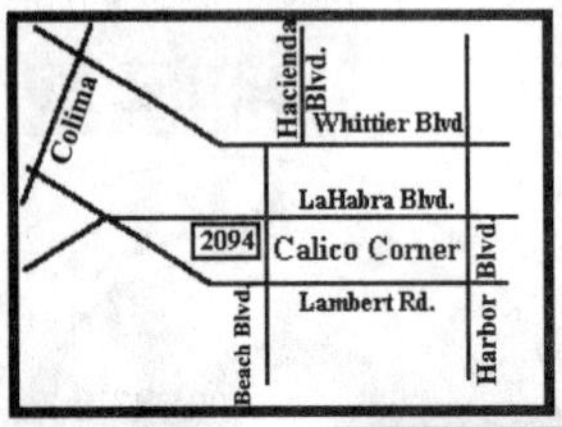

LaHabra, CA #131

Mon - Sat 10 - 5

Avalon, CA #132

CATALINA

CRAFTERS

115 Sumner Ave. 90704
(310) 510-3590
Est: 1995

Catalina Island's only complete Needlecraft store!

Open 7 Days 9:30 - 5:30

Everything for
Quilting - Crocheting - Cross Stitch
Embroidery - Needlepoint - Knitting
Fabrics, Yarns, DMC Floss
Patterns, Notions, Books
Silk Ribbon, Handcrafted Gifts, Classes
A Great Staff here to help You
STOP BY AND SEE US!

Lomita, CA #133

Tues - Thur 10 - 6
Fri & Sat 10 - 5
Sun 12 - 5

TREADLEART

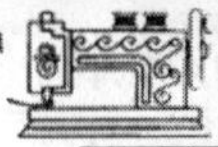

25834 Narbonne Ave. 90717
(310) 534-5122 Fax: Same
E-Mail: treadleart@treadleart.com
Web Site: www.treadleart.com
Owner: Janet Stocker Est: 1978
7000 sq.ft. 5000 Bolts Free Catalog

Supplies for all your sewing, quilting and embroidery needs. Fabric, books, patterns, rulers, cutters, sewing machines and accessories. Tour groups Welcome.

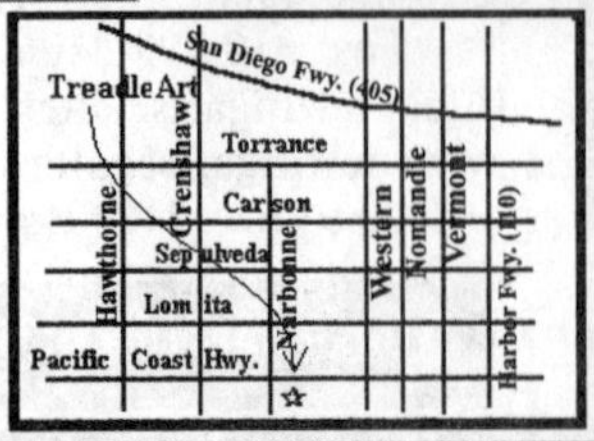

FRESH FABRIC ARRIVING DAILY

Redondo Beach, CA #134

- -Hoffman
- -Alexander Henry
- -P & B
- -Moda
- -Timeless Treasures

Hawaiian & Tropical Prints
Flannel Prints & Novelties
Exquisite Decorator Fabrics
Bridal & Special Occasion

~ Since 1959 ~

THE COTTON SHOP
FINE FABRICS

1922 Artesia Blvd Redondo Beach, CA 90278

Open Mon-Thurs 10-7 Fri-Sat 10-6 Sun 11-5 Visa Mastercard American Express Discover

(310) 376-3518 www.thecottonshop.com

Los Alamitos, CA #135

Cornerstone Quilt Shop

Everything for the Quilt Enthusiast !

4470 Cerritos Avenue 90720
(714) 226-9647 or (562) 630-0330
Come peek into our Cupboard on the web
www.thequiltcupboard.net
Owner: Sheri Siedentop

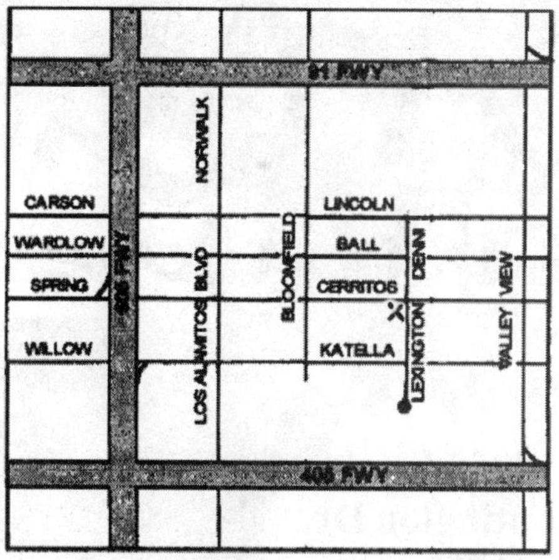

Mon - Fri 10 - 6
Sat 10 - 5
Sun 12 - 4
Evenings by appt.

Southern California's Newest Quilt Shop!

We offer the finest quality books, notions, and 100% cotton fabrics in a friendly, relaxed atmosphere with old-fashioned personal service. We have a wonderful teaching staff and offer a variety of classes for Beginning through advanced skill levels. Bernina sewing machine. Information about local guilds, shows and classes.
*Wheelchair accessible*Easy Parking*Children's play area*
10 minutes West of Disneyland! Excellent stop for field trips with restaurant and banquet facilities new door. Call for details.

Piecemakers — The Wonderful World of Sewing

Home is where your threads are!

Walk through Piecemakers door and be greeted with a cozy fireplace which sets the mood. Quilts and wallhangings, patterns and fabric all stir the creative juices. Knowledgeable "Santa's helpers" answer every need. And, oh yes, a tea room like back home, back in time. Piecemakers — an experience that harkens old memories, stirs up old creativity, refreshes the spirit.

Outside Piecemakers' front door, a yellow brick road leads to yet another experience — Piecemakers Village. Thirty-five artisans with special handcrafted collectibles you just cannot live without!

Costa Mesa, CA #136

- **Handmade Quilts**
- **Unique Country Gifts ❧ Fabrics**
- **Patterns, Books & Calendars**
- **Quilting Supplies ❧ Hair Salon**
- **Quilt, Doll, Needlework & Kids' Classes**
- **Four Handcrafts Fairs Yearly**

Store Hours

Weekdays	9:00 to 8:00
Weekends	10:00 to 5:30

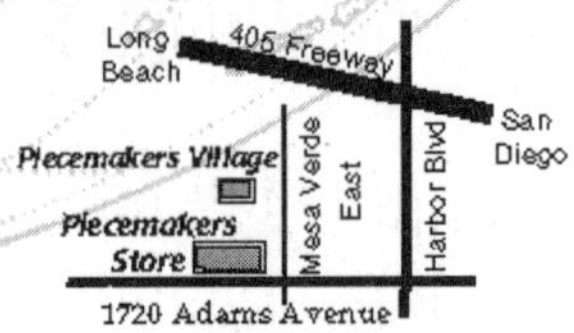

Piecemakers Country Store
1720 Adams Avenue, Costa Mesa, CA 92626

phone: (714) 641–3112 *fax:* (714) 641–2883 *email:* mail@piecemakers.com *website:* www.piecemakers.com

A Quilter's Dream

...if you love to quilt or love a quilter.

8958 E. Huntington Dr. 91775
Owner: Susan Prescott

Mon - Sat 10 - 5:30
Sun 12 - 4

(626) 286-2822

Quilt@aquiltersdream.com
www.aquiltersdream.com

Come visit our ever-growing 100% cotton fabric selection. We specialize in batiks, flannels, kits, quality notions and offer a full range of classes.

San Gabriel, CA #137

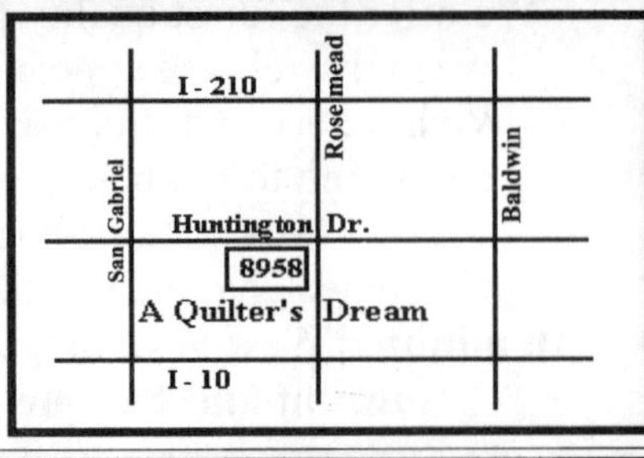

Montclair, CA #138

"Your Idea Place"

500 Books
Gifts for Quilters
Notions and Supplies
Classes for all Skill Levels
4,000 Bolts of Cotton Fabric
Over 1,000 Doll, Critter & Quilt Patterns
Featured in Quilt Sampler Magazine

(909) 985-9000
Mon - Sat 10 - 5
Sun 12 - 3

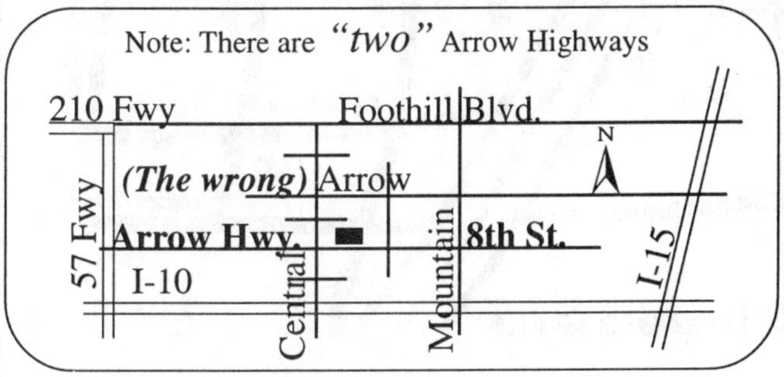

5436D Arrow Hwy., ✷ Montclair CA 91763
www.thefabricpatch.com

Redlands, CA #139

Est: 1986

The Calico Horse

461 Tennessee St. Suite J 92373
(909) 793-1868 or 824-6198
Fax: (909) 793-5868
E-Mail: calhrse@aol.com
Owners: Debra & Doug Grantz
Beverly & Bill Dean
1580 sq.ft.

Mon - Fri 10 - 6
Sat 10 - 5

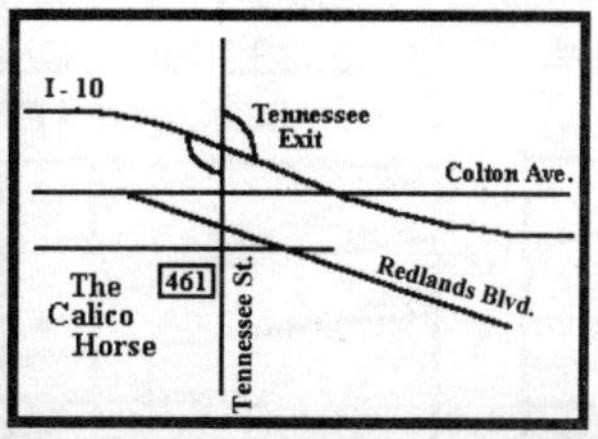

Large selection of 100% cotton fabrics and supplies including flannels & reproduction fabrics. Patterns & Books. Orange crate labels on muslin. Friendly, expert advice. Mail Order Available.

Yorba Linda, CA #140

The Calico House

Mon - Sat 9:30 - 5:00
Sun 11:30 - 3:30

4825-D Valley View Ave. 92886
(714) 993-3091 Fax: (714) 993-2316
E-mail: calicohus@aol.com
Owners: Jane, Janice, Cari
Est: 1981 1500+ Bolts

Complete Quilt Shop.
Books, Fabrics, Notions, Classes.
Helpful, Friendly Staff

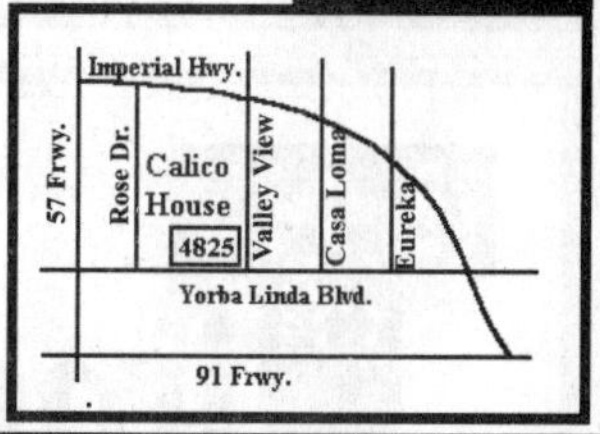

TALL MOUSE

Arts, Crafts & Custom Framing

Crafts. Discover life's little pleasures.

The **Tall Mouse Quilt Shoppe** has a large assortment of the finest 100% cotton fabrics, complete quilting supplies, notions, books and patterns. PLUS cross-stitch, ribbons, buttons, beads, stencils and a complete scrapbook department with die-cut machines are only just a few of the perks to the Tall Mouse shopping experience . Classes are also offered throughout the year.

Yorba Linda #141
17506 Yorba Linda Blvd.
714-996-0101

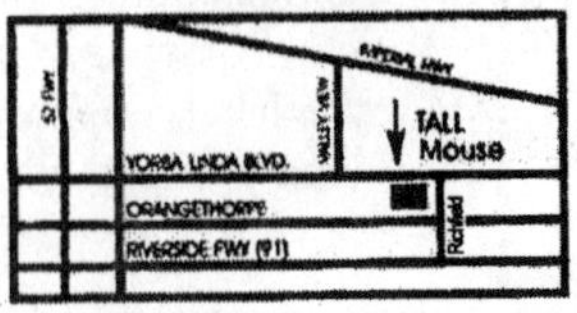

Laguna Niguel #143
23932 Aliso Creek
949-360-5777

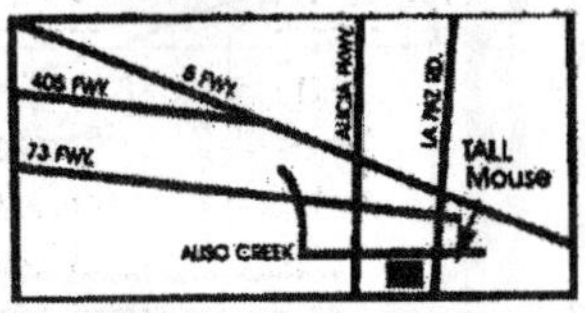

Cerritos #142
13233 South St.
562-865-0800

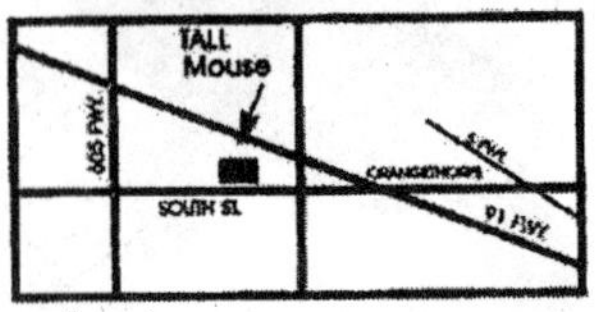

Irvine #144
5695 Alton Pkwy.
949-551-3300

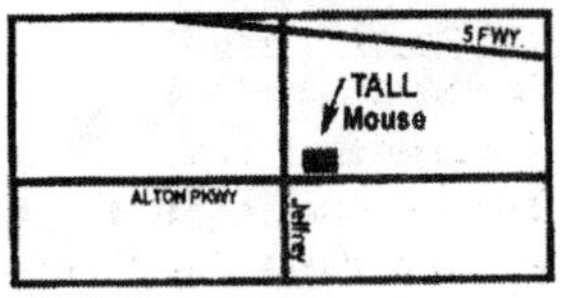

Family Owned & Operated for 35 YEARS!

Vistit us at www.tallmouse.com

Tall Mouse is Your Family Place for Creativity!

OPEN 7 DAYS
Mon. - Fri. 9:00am-9:00pm
Sat. 9:00am-6:00pm
Sun. 10:00am-6:00pm

Timeless Quilts™

Anaheim, CA #145

A unique quilt shop in a restored 1924 "craftsman" home with a large selection of quality fabric, quilt kits & quilting supplies. The shop has warmth and charm... a perfect setting for quilting!

128 W. Sycamore St. 92805

Tuesday - Saturday
10:00am - 5:00pm

Toll free: (877)997-8458
or local #: (714)520-5304
E-mail: arlene@timelessquilts.com
On the web: www.timelessquilts.com

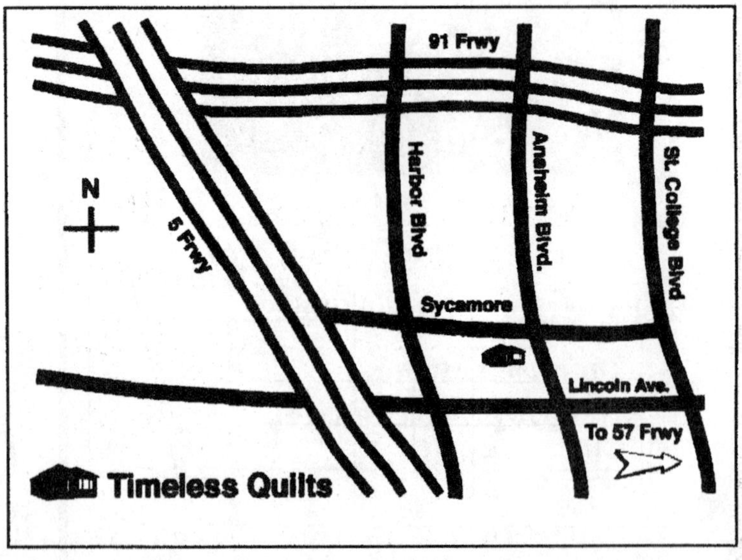

Timeless Quilts is located South of the 91 Freeway and East of I-5, between Harbor Blvd, and N. Anaheim Blvd on Sycamore St. The shop is just 5 minutes from the Disneyland Resort area.

Owner: Arlene Taormina Est:2001

Leah's fabric gallery

FOR QUALITY, SELECTION & SERVICE

since 1969

Open 7 days

Convenient Store Hours

Mon-Fri	10 AM – 8 PM
Sat	10 AM – 6 PM
Sun	Noon – 5 PM

e-mail: lfg4quilting@usa.net

Leah's for Quilting:

- **400+ Book titles & 250+ patterns**
- **4000+ bolts of quality cotton fabric**
- **Extensive selection of quilting accessories**
- **Inspiring quilt models**
- **Large class selection with outstanding teachers**
- **Unique gift items**
- **FRIENDLY & KNOWLEDGEABLE SALES STAFF**

2 Great Locations

Leah's in Mission Viejo
Corner of Avery &
Marguerite Pkwy
28641 Marguerite Pkwy
Mission Viejo, Ca. 92692
(949) 364-6372
4 miles N of Mission San Juan Capistrano

Mission Viejo, CA #146

Leah's in Orange
W of Tustin Ave on Katella
1321 E. Katella Ave.
Orange, Ca. 92867
(714) 639-3245
4.7 miles EAST of Disneyland

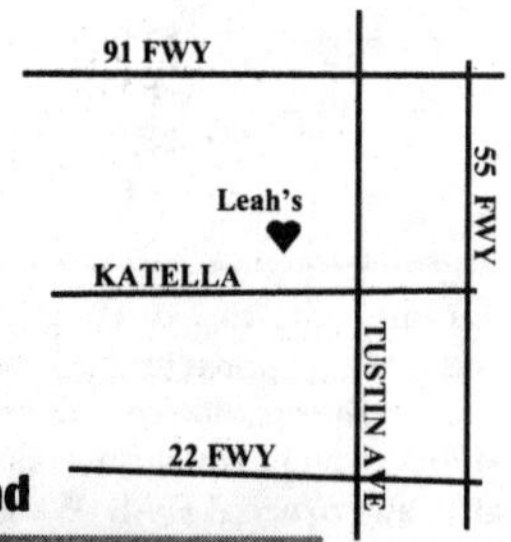

Orange, CA #147

REMEMBER: At Leah's, Guild Members always receive a 10% discount on all purchases. Excludes sale merchandise

Material Possessions Quilt Shop

22600-C Lambert St., Suite 905
Lake Forest, Calif. 92630
949.586.3418 fax 949.586.7125
www.quiltessentials.com e-mail quilt@quiltessentials.com

Lake Forest, CA #148

Visit the largest quilt shop in Southern California.
Featured in Better Homes and Gardens
Quilt Sampler 1999.

Monday through Saturday 10:00 AM to 5:30 PM
Wednesday 10:00 AM - 9:00 PM Closed Sunday

How to find us: From the Intertsate 405 or 5 freeway take Bake Parkway exit. Turn east on Bake Parkway. Turn right at Muirlands Blvd. Turn right on Aspan. We are located on the right side of the street in an industrial complex The building number is 22600-C.

Woerth Stitching

28780 Old Town Front St. #D2
(909) 693-3213 92590
Fax: (909) 693-3216
Website: www.woerthstitching.com
Owner: Aileen Woerth

Mon - Sat 9:30 - 5:30
Sun 12 - 4

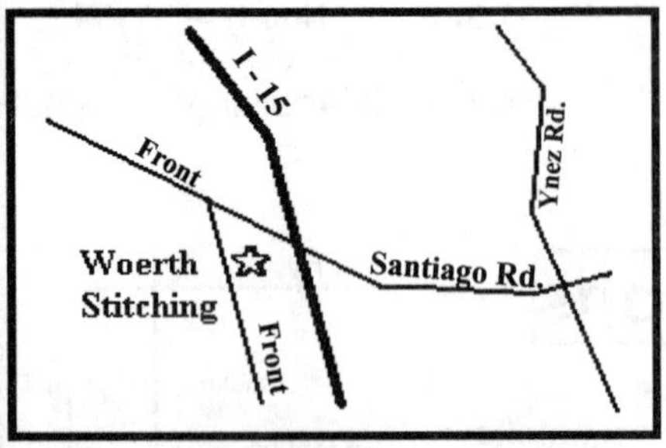

From Interstate 15, exit Hwy. 79 South and proceed West approximately 7/10 of a mile. Make a right turn into South Creek Mall, the first driveway north of the Harley Davidson dealer, and proceed East. We are in Suite D-2 and we face the freeway.

3500 Bolts of Fabric
Books & Patterns
Notions & Classes
Gifts & Quilts
Bernina Sewing Machines

Temecula, CA #149

Sky Forest, CA #150

Willow Woods
Quilters Cottage

28589 Hwy. 18 (Valley Side)
P.O. Box 192 Sky Forest, CA 92385
(909) 337-1521
E-Mail: kwiltin@earthlink.net
Owner: Cyndee Dvorak
Est: 1998 1100 sq.ft.
Annual Outdoor Quilt Show the Saturday of Labor Day Weekend

Everyday 10 - 5
Winter 10 - 4:30

Quality Fabrics. Quilting Supplies and Notions. Large selection of Books. Hand-Guided Custom Machine Quilting done on a Gammill Classic
Lots of Flannels

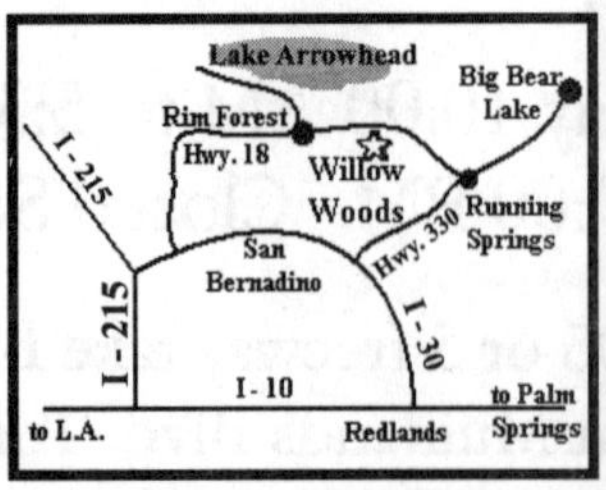

Sky Forest, CA #151

By Chance or Appointment

Laguna Mountain Needleworks

28589 Hwy. 18, P.O. Box 906 92385
(909) 337-7555
E-Mail: LagunaMountain@aol.com
Owner: Janet Chapman Est: 2002

Custom machine embroidery. Thousands of designs - perfect for baby gifts, weddings, sports teams. Motifs for quilt blocks and quilt labels.

In the Same House as Willow Woods Quilter's Cottage

Sky Forest, CA #152

Sat & Sun 10 - 4:30 or by Chance Or Appt.

Uniquely Janniece

28589 Hwy. 18, P.O. Box 908 92385
(909) 337-7555 Fax: (909) 336-2480
E-Mail: ujquilts@earthlink.net
Owner: Janniece Stanley-MacDonald Est: 2002

Vintage Quilts, tops & blocks. New American quilts & wall hangings. Gifts for the quilter; unique pincushions, silver chatelaines & tools, nice things made with lavender & goats milk.

Located Above Willow Woods Quilter's Cottage

We Cater to Quilters !

Sharon Walters — Owner

Mon - Sat 9:30 - 4:30

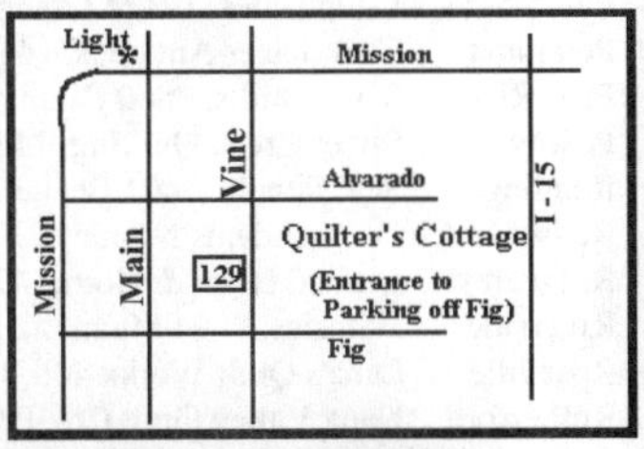

129 S. Vine St 92028
(760) 723-3060
Est: 1990 800 sq.ft.
1500 Bolts

Fallbrook, CA #153

- Quilting Supplies - Books Fabrics - Classes - Quilt Magazines - Woven Plaids - Patterns - Home Decor - Notions - Ribbons -

FLYING GEESE FABRICS

307 El Camino Real
Tustin, CA 92780
(714) 544-9349

...in the heart of Old Towne Tustin with tree lined streets, cozy tea houses and quaint antique shops...

GREAT CLASSES AVAILABLE

- Beginner and Intermediate Quilting
- Hand and Machine Quilting
- Hand and Machine Applique
- Beginner and Intermediate Sewing
- Clothing Classes
- Home Décor
- Children's Sewing (ages 7 - 17)

BETHANY SERVICE PROJECT
2nd and 4th Friday Mornings

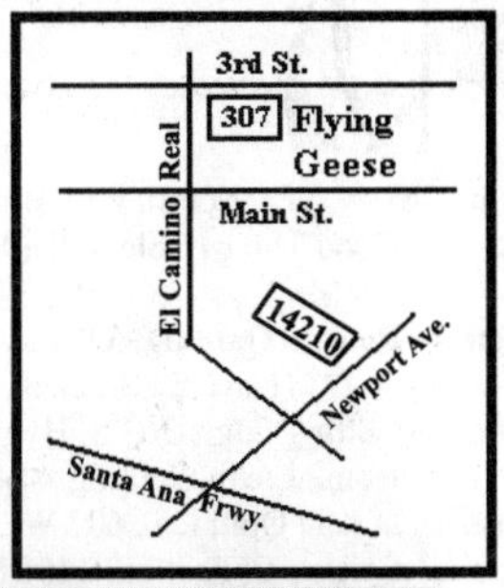

Tustin, CA #154

New Store Hours
Mon - Thurs 10 - 6 Fri & Sat 10 - 5
Closed Sundays and Holidays.

- Quilting Supplies - Books Fabrics - Classes - Quilt Magazines - Woven Plaids - Patterns - Home Decor - Notions - Ribbons -

Calimesa, CA #155

Everything Nice

1007 Calimesa Blvd., # J
Calimesa, CA 92320
909-795-2778
Owners: Judy DeBoer & Cathy Brown
Est: 1999 2000 sq.ft.

A really fun Quilt Shop featuring a unique selection of fun 100% cotton fabrics. Books, patterns, magazines and notions. Authorized Elna and Babylock dealers.

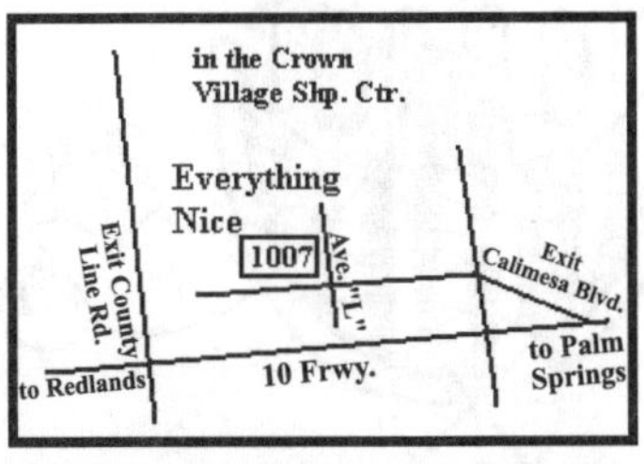

Mon 10 - 8
Tues - Fri 10 - 6
Sat 10 - 3
Closed Sun

Other Shops in California:
We suggest calling first

Alta Loma	Quilt Affair, 7219 Cosenza Pl.	909-989-4968
Anaheim	M & L Fabrics, 3430 W. Ball Rd.	714-995-3178
Anderson	Carol's Quilt Shop, 17456 Flowers Ln.	530-357-2575
Antioch	Cottontales, 601 W. 2nd St.	925-757-7787
Antioch	Ben Franklin Crafts, 2710 Delta Fair Blvd.	925-778-3850
Arcata	Fabric Temptations, 942 `G' St.	707-822-7782
Arroyo Grande	Chameleon Fabric & Gifts, 107 Nelson St.	805-481-4104
Auburn	Thyme to Sew, 884 Lincoln Way	530-888-6420
Bakersfield	Quilters Garden, 930 Olive Dr. #13	661-387-0628
Berkeley	Kasuri Dyeworks, 1959 Shattuck Ave.	510-841-4509
Berkeley	Ninepatch, 2001 Hopkins	510-527-1700
Blocksburg	In Stitches, P.O. Box 257	707-926-0306
Bridgeport	Hampton House, 261 Main St.	760-932-9138
Camarillo	Baron's Fabric, 379 Carmen Dr.	805-482-9848
Camarillo	David Sanders Co., 1221 Calle Suerte	805-389-4699
Campbell	Golden State Sewing Center 2435 S. Winchester	408-866-1181
Cardiff by Sea	Fabricraft, P.O. Box 962	619-436-1281
Chatsworth	Good Things Tole & Quilt Shoppe, 10218 Mason Ave.	818-407-1312
Compton	Becerra Quilting, 3221 N. Alameda St.	310-638-7141
Crescent City	Heavenly Stitches, 1981 Northcrest Dr.	707-465-3565
Crestline	Cutting Edge, 363 S. Hwy. 138, P.O. Box 4141	909-338-0357
Dublin	Home Lovin Quilting, 8544 Valencia St.	510-833-9640
El Centro	D & D Quilt Co., 607 W. Main St.	760-352-2712
Encinitas	Claire's Collection, 3461 Bumann Rd.	619-756-5718
Escondido	The Quilter's Cottage, 2253 E. Valley Pkwy.	
Escondido	Little Stitches, 1750 W. Citracado Pkwy.	760-480-0624
Eureka	Heart of Folk Art, 301 W. Harris St.	707-445-9412
Fair Oaks	Jeanette's Fabrics, 11045 Fair Oaks Blvd	916-482-1899
Fairfield	Let's Make Quilts, 2452 Sawgrass Ct.	707-426-6016
Fort Bragg	The Todd Farm House, 100 Highway 20	707-964-1742
Fort Bragg	Sharon's Sew N Vac, 338 N. Main St.	707-964-6226
Fremont	Quilting Bee Sewing Center, 39161 Farwell Dr.	510-494-9040
Gilroy	Nimble Thimble, 55 W. 6th St.	408-842-6501
Goleta	Finely Quilted, 150 Verona Ave.	805-967-5011
Granada Hills	Patchwork N' Things, 12355 Jolette Ave.	818-360-2828
Grass Valley	Ben Franklin Crafts, 11598 Sutton Way	530-273-1348
Healdsburg	Fabrications, 118 Matheson St.	707-433-6243
Julian	Julian Yarn Basket, 2122 Main St.	760-765-0849
Kernville	Sewing for You, 142 Tobias St., P.O. Box 821	760-376-3220
Kirk	Benay's Country Quiltin', 32131 Cty. Rd. HH	970-362-4650
La Mesa	The Country Loft, 4685 Date Ave.	619-466-5411
La Mesa	Save Nine Quilting, 4679 68th St.	619-644-1445
Laguna Beach	Klassic Creations, 157 Canyon Acres Dr.	949-494-7966
Laguna Hills	Brooks Woodworking, 23291 A-2 Peralta Dr.	714-770-2037
Lake Forest	Penache, 24611 Shadowfax Dr.	949-768-5979
Lancaster	Cozy Quilts, 42555 32nd St. W	805-945-1207
Los Angeles	Azabu-Ya, 1894 Westwood Blvd.	310-446-1831
Magalia	Seams To B, 14543 Grinnell Ct.	530-873-2670
Manhattan Beach	Once Upon a Quilt, 312 Manhattan Beach	310-379-1264
McCloud	Judy's Wedge, 233 Main St.	530-964-2801
McKinleyville	Redwood Quilting Studio, 1805 Central Ave.	707-839-5566
Mendocino	Ocean Quilts, 45156 Main St., P.O. Box 1692	707-937-4201
Modesto	Helens Yardage, 1331 Crows Landing Rd.	209-526-0903
Montebello	Robbin's Fabrics, Inc., 2524 W. Beverly Blvd.	213-724-6180
Montrose	Quilt 'n' Things, Inc., 2411 Honolulu Ave.	818-957-2287
Mountain View	Buttons & Bolts Factory Outlet, 264 Castro St.	650-965-9712
Napa	A Stitch in Time, 2101 Russell St.	707-252-6925
Needles	Quilters Therphy, 224 G St. #D	760-326-6966
Newark	No Thimbles Quilting, 8192 Idlewild Ct.	510-739-6931
Newbury Park	Quilters' Studio, 3327 Kimber Dr. #C	805-480-3550
Newhall	Blazing Star Quilt Com., 22940 1/2 Lyons Ave.	661-253-0399
North Highlands	Athena's Thimble, 6424 Larry Way	916-331-9295
North Hollywood	Tilt & Quilt, 12836 Waddell St.	818-508-6898
North San Juan	Small Patches, P.O. Box 329	530-292-1159
Oakland	Poppy Fabric, 5151 Broadway	510-655-5151
Oroville	Something to Crow About, 1637 Montgomery St.	530-533-7635
Oxnard	Fabric Well, 3075 Saviers Rd.	805-486-7826
Paradise	Fabric Friends Studio, 148 Pearson Rd.	916-877-3564
Paramont	Estephanies, 14124 Orange Ave.	562-531-0445
Petaluma	Chanticleer Antiques, 145 Petaluma Blvd. N	
Pico Rivera	S & J Quilts, 7860 Paramount Blvd.	310-942-7784
Poway	Silver Creek Quilting, 14655 Deerwood St.	858-679-6980
Redding	Sew Simple, 3001 Bechelli Ln.	916-246-9310
Redwood City	Adams Notion & Yardage, 2090 Broadway	415-366-1711
Ridgecrest	Quilted Heart & Home, 425 E. Ridgecrest Blvd.	760-371-1116
Riverside	Wimsies, 9892 Magnolia Ave.	909-687-2462
Roseville	Lana's Quilt Works 406 Yosemite St	209-745-9446
Rutherford	Napa Valley Quilt Co., P.O. Box 566	707-967-9677
Sacramento	Electric Texture, 972 Robertson Way	916-492-2111
San Andreas	Last Camp by the Creek, P.O. Box 991	209-754-0213
San Anselmo	San Anselmo Country Store, 312 Sir Francis Drake Blvd.	415-258-0922
San Anselmo	Dove Place Quilts & Antiques, 610 Sir Francis Drake Blvd.	415-459-2002
San Clemente	Nine Patch, 1501 Avenida Hacienda	949-361-9145
San Diego	Treasures of the Gypsy, 3435 Texas St.	619-294-2586
San Diego	Desert Quilts, 2820 Chatsworth Blvd.	619-523-5027
San Diego	The Shepherdess, 2802 Juan St.	619-297-4110
San Diego	Kojo, 9654 Siempre Viva Rd. #1	714-841-5656
San Luis Obispo	Betty's Fabrics, 1229 Carmel St.	805-543-1990
San Pedro	Quilt Sails, 1312 W. 37th	310-548-7094
San Rafael	Beverly Fabrics & Crafts, 836 4th Street	415-256-8121
Santa Ana	Quilting Possibilities, 2207 S. Grand Ave.	714-546-9949
Santa Cruz	Hart's Fabric Center, 1620 Seabright	408-423-5434
Santa Maria	Betty's Fabrics, 1627 S. Broadway, P.O. Box 5257	805-922-2181
Santa Marie	Santa Maria Sewing, 709 E. Main St. #D	805-922-1784
Solvang	Arbor Rose Quilts, 485 Alisal Rd. #F1	805-693-0124
Solvang	Quilts Galore & More, 1693 Mission Dr.	805-693-1028
Sonoma	Quilts of the Past, P.O. Box 2279	707-938-9535
Tracy	Quilts by Rita, 1741 Summertime Ct.	209-833-6240
Ukiah	Sharin Stitches & Strokes, 163 E. Gobbie St. #A	707-462-7397
Upper Lake	Gracious Ladies, 9479 Main St., P.O. Box 975	707-275-2307
Vacaville	Cowtown Quilters, 631 Harvard Ave.	707-448-8656
Valencia	Quilted Heart, 24201 Valencia Blvd. #1371	805-255-0771
Walnut Creek	Home Town Quilting, 230 Summit Rd.	925-939-8728
Weaverville	Stitch Witchery, 1310 Nugget Ln.	916-623-6891
Woodland Hills	Baron's Sewing Center, 22635 Ventura Blvd	818-348-7012
Woodland Hills	The Quilt Emporium, 4918 Topanga Canyon Blvd.	818-704-8238
Yorba Linda	Cranberry Quiltworks 3960 Prospect Ave. #M	714-223-1701
Yucaipa	Apple Tree Gifts and Country Things 38392 Oak Glen Rd.	909-797-3130
Yucca Valley	Quilting Between Friends 7379 Hopi Tr.	760-365-4519

COLORADO

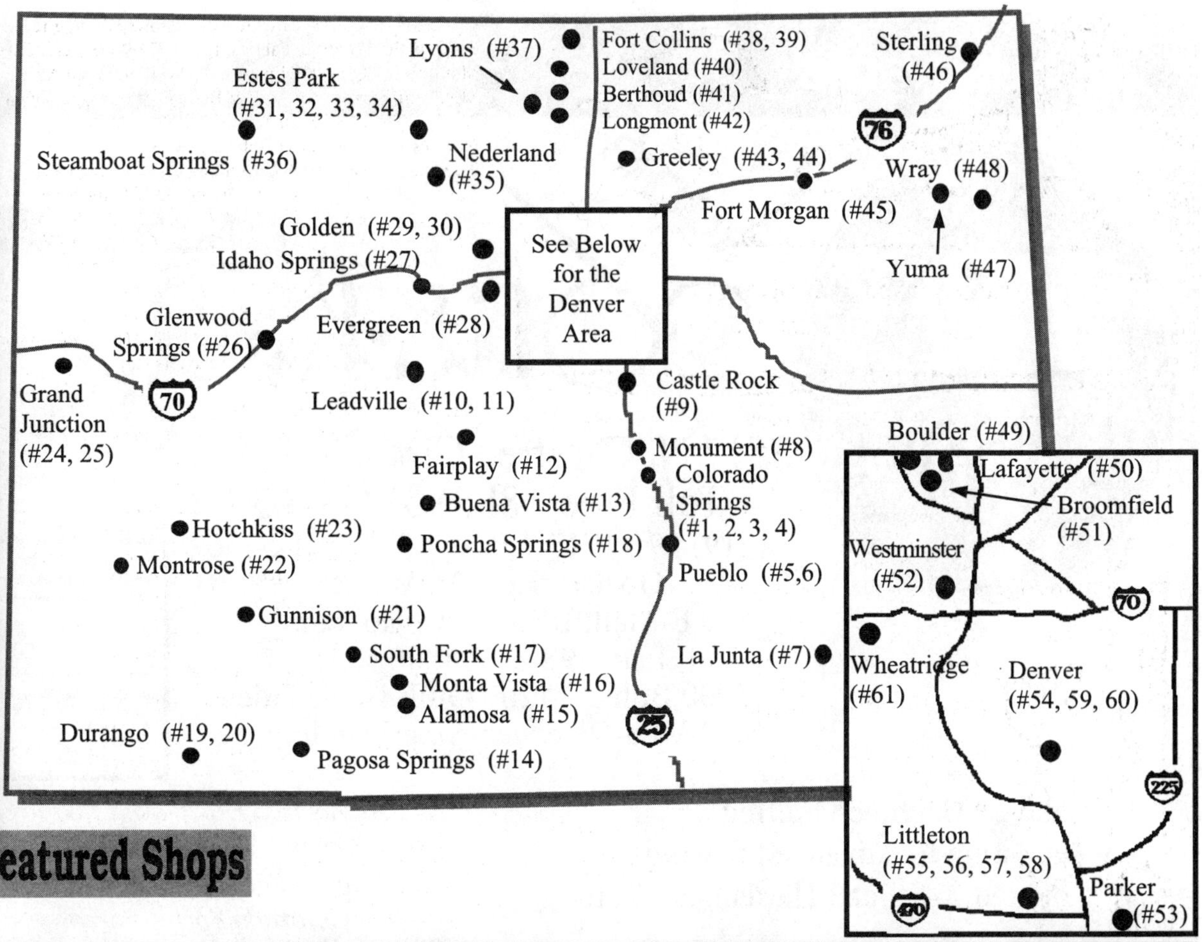

61 Featured Shops

High Country Quilts

Colorado Springs, CO #1

4771 N. Academy Blvd.
(719) 598-1312 80918
Owner: Barbara L. Blutt Est: 1983

Email: hcquilts@frii.com
Web: www.frii.com/~hcquilts

Monday-Saturday	9:30 a.m.-6:00 p.m.
Tuesday	9:30 a.m.-7:00 p.m.
Sunday	1:00 p.m.-5:00 p.m.

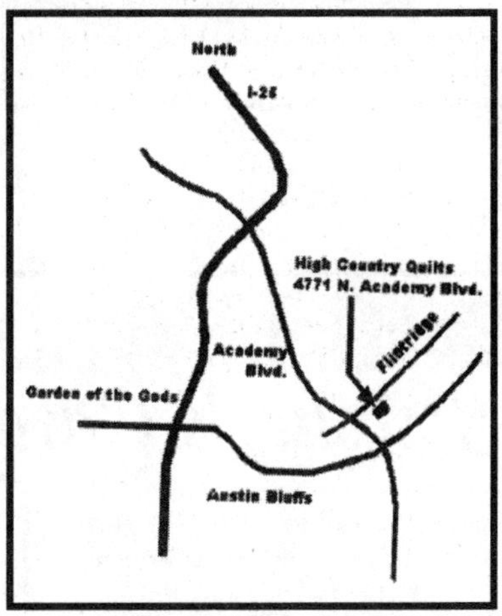

4 mi. from N. Academy Exit
8 mi. from S. Academy Exit
Enter off Flintridge

QUILTING SUPPLIES & INSTRUCTIONS
Large assortment of Cotton Fabrics, Books, Patterns, & Notions.

Husqvarna VIKING

Web Site: www.ruthonline.net

Colorado Springs, CO #2

KEEP AMERICA SEWING

Ruth's Stitchery

Mon - Sat 9 - 6
Thur til 9
Sun 12 - 5

3517 N. Carefree Circle 80917
Toll Free (888) 591-8803
(719) 591-1717 Fax: (719) 591-5356
Owner: Ruth V. Warren
E-Mail: RStichery@aol.com
Est: 1984 4800 sq.ft.
5000 Bolts 1200 Quilt Book Titles
M/C-Visa-Discover-American Express

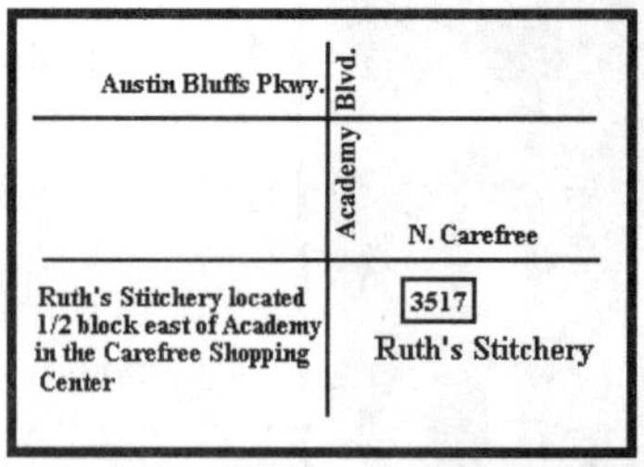

- Hand & Machine Quilting
- Beginning to Advanced Sewing
- Counted X-Stitch / Hardanger / Tatting

Authorized Husqvarna Viking Sewing Machine / Serger Dealer and Service center for Colorado Springs area.

Colorado Springs, CO #3

Mon - Fri 10 - 6
Sat 9:30 - 5
Sun 12 - 5

Lady Bug Hill Quilts.com

618 N. Tejon 80903
(719) 593-5949
website: www.ladybughillquilts.com

1000+ bolts of 100% cotton fabric, books, patterns, notions and fun classes.

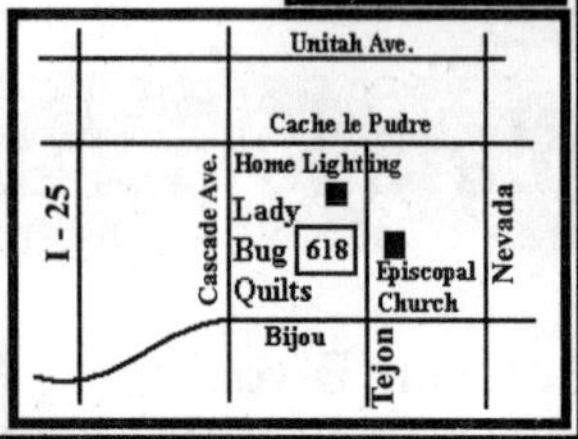

Colorado Springs, CO #4

Mon 8 - 8
Tue - Sat 8 - 6

Mill Outlet Fabric Shop

2906 N. Prospect Street 80907
(719) 632-6296
Web Site: www.MillOutletFabric.com
Est: 1965 11000 sq. ft.

Quilting, Dress, Bridal, Notions, Drape, Upholstery, Vinyl, Home Decorating, Buttons, Books & Batting! Colorado's Best Selection of Fabric & Supplies!

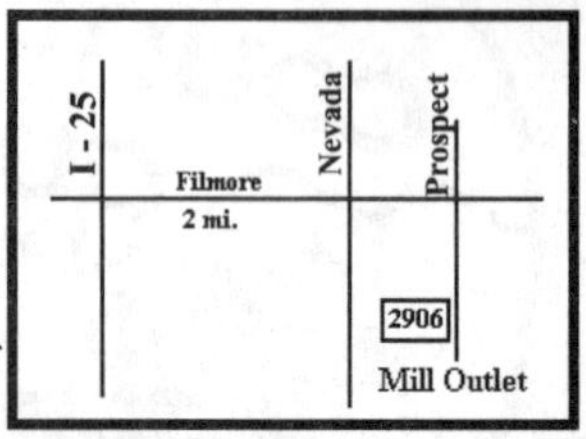

Pueblo, CO #5

Tues - Sat 10 - 5

Stitcher's Garden

319 S. Union Ave. 81003
(719) 545-3320 Fax: (719) 545-3307
Web Site: www.stitchers-garden.com
Owners: Susie Cunningham
& Nancy Piazza

Located in the historic district, we feature fine cotton fabrics, patterns, books, and supplies for quilting and cross stitch.

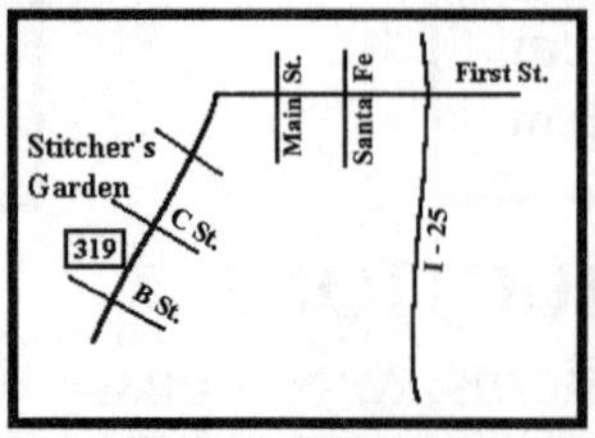

Pueblo, CO #6

Mon 12 - 6
Tues - Fri 10 - 6
Sat 10 - 5

Grandma's Quilting Threads

2648 Santa Fe Dr. #8 81006
(719) 544-8897
Owner: Kibbie Balsick
Est: 2000

Great variety of 100% cotton fabrics, books, notions, patterns and friendly service. Classes available.

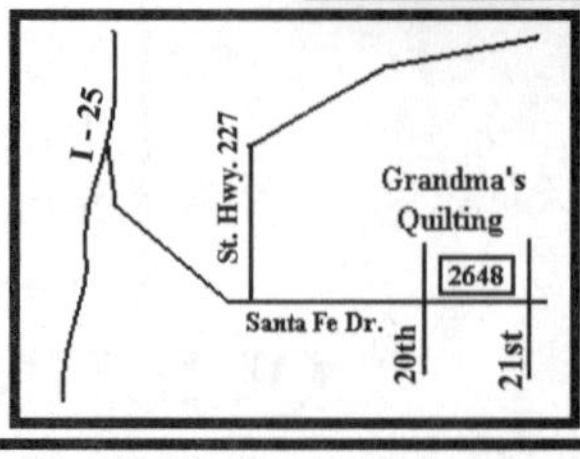

La Junta, CO #7

Itchin' to Stitch
Quilting Fabric & Supplies

**Mon - Fri 9 - 5:30
Mon til 9
Sat 9 - 5**

We specialize in quality quilting fabrics, notions & classes. Friendly service always available. Stop in anytime, we enjoy meeting new people and sharing ideas.

Est: 2000
1800 sq.ft.
750+ bolts

409 W. 3rd St. 81050
(719) 384-9050
or (888) 384-9050
Fax: (719) 384-9050
Owner: Debbie Autry
E-mail: Debbie_Autry@hotmail.com

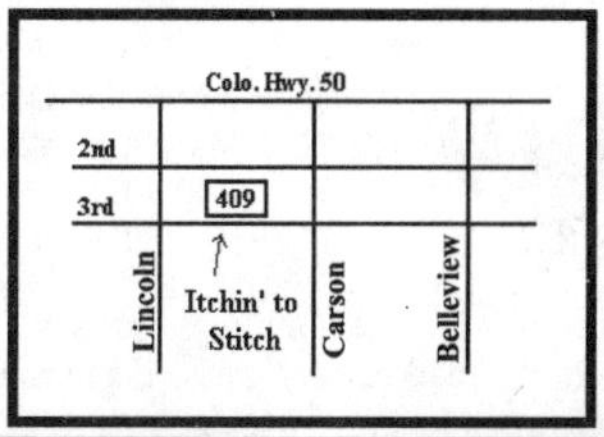

Monument, CO #8

Tues - Sat 10 - 5

The Quilted Cottage

341 Front St.
P.O. Box 237 80132
(719) 481-4887
Owner: Karen Hadfield
Est: 1997 1500 sq.ft.

Quality quilting fabrics & notions, quilt classes. Enjoy the old world charm of shopping in Historic Monument Village!

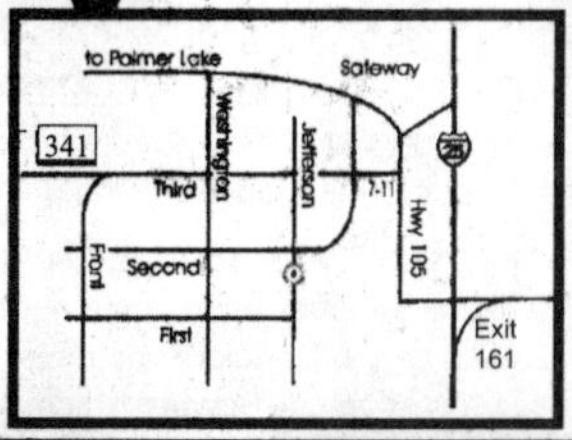

Castle Rock, CO #9

**Mon - Fri 10 - 6
Sat 10 - 4**

PLUM CREEK Quilts

981 N. Park St.
80104
(303) 663-9181
Est: 1998
Owner:
Mardean Haines
Web Site: www.plumcreekquilts.net

100% cotton Fabric, Books, Patterns, Notions, Classes.

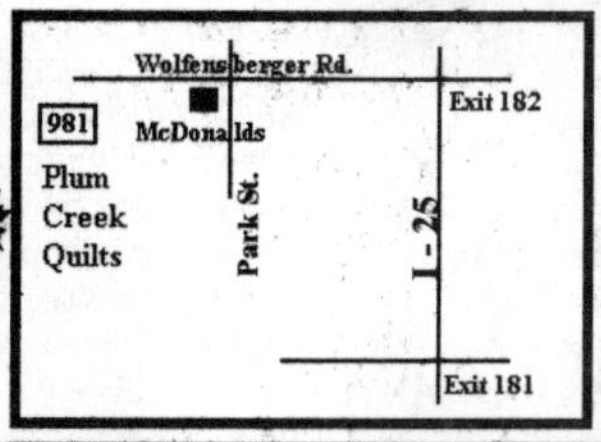

Leadville, CO #10

Mon - Sat 9 - 5

Mt. Elbert Patchwork

721 Harrison Ave. 80461
(719) 486-3243 Est: 1997
E-mail: ggg@Chaffee.net
Owner: Jane Crocker 2000 sq.ft. 2000+ Bolts

100% Cotton fabrics, notions, books, machine quilting.

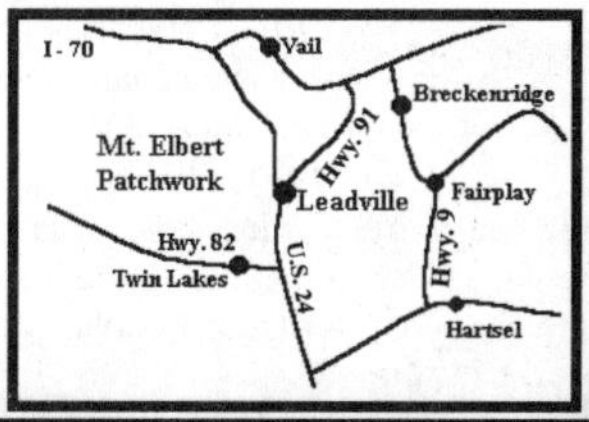

Leadville, CO #11

Hrs. Vary Please Call First

Mtn. Top Quilts

129 E. 7th St. 80461
(719) 486-3454
Owner: Gwendolyn Shepherd
Est: 1983 E-Mail: ccsmtq@sni.net

Quilts—old and new, vintage fabric, old quilt blocks and quilt tops. Hundreds of antique buttons. Vintage clothes & sewing collectables.

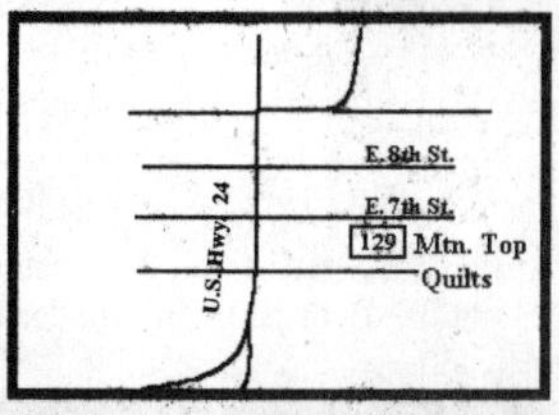

Fairplay, CO #12

**6 Days A Week
Tues - Sun
10 - 5
Closed Mon**

Treadle House

443 Front St., P.O. Box 557 80440
(719) 836-0985
E-Mail: treadle443@aol.com
Owner: Tricia Benes
Est: 1995 3000 sq.ft. 1000+ Bolts

Quality fabrics, notions, books for quilting but we also have cross stitch supplies and we're a gift shop too!

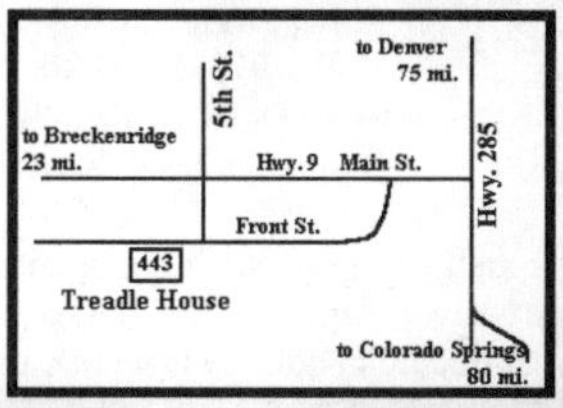

Buena Vista, CO #13

**Mon - Fri 9:30 - 5
Sat 9:30 - 3**

Bev's Stitchery

202 Tabor St. P.O. Box 1773 81211
(719) 395-8780
Owner: Bev Zabloudil Est: 1977

Quilting, Fabrics, Notions & Tools. Fine Needlework Supplies. Large Selection of Books. Quilting, Counted Cross-Stitch, Crochet & Knitting. Classes too!

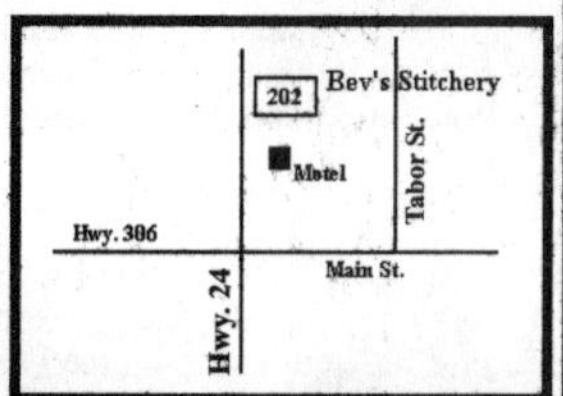

Pagosa Springs, CO #14

Mon - Sat 7 - 6

2435 W. Hwy. 160, P.O. Box 1800 81147
(970) 731-4111 Fax: (970) 731-4455
E-Mail: Ponderosa@pagosa.net

PONDEROSA
Do it Best
HomeCenter
Web Site: www.ponderosa.doitbest.com

You'll be pleasantly surprised at the wonderful quilt fabrics, patterns, etc., tucked away inside our Do It Best hardware store.

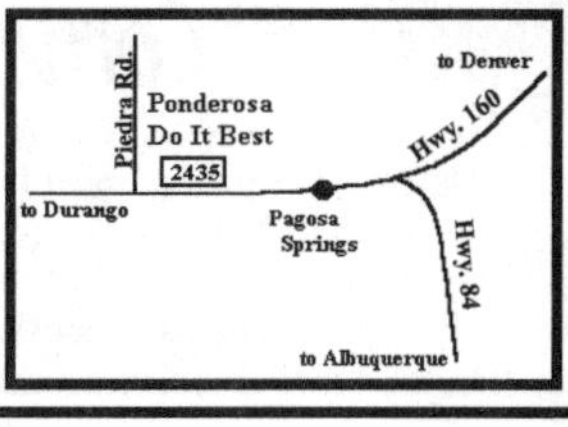

Alamosa, CO #15

**Mon - Fri 9:30 - 5:30
Sat 9:30 - 4**

Gray Goose Fashion Fabric

614 Main St. 81101
(719) 589-6982
Owner: Gail Mattive & Kerry Worley
2000+ Bolts 800 Books / Patterns

100% Cottons & Fashion Fabrics, notions, quilting supplies, books, and patterns.
Daytime, evening and Saturday Classes.

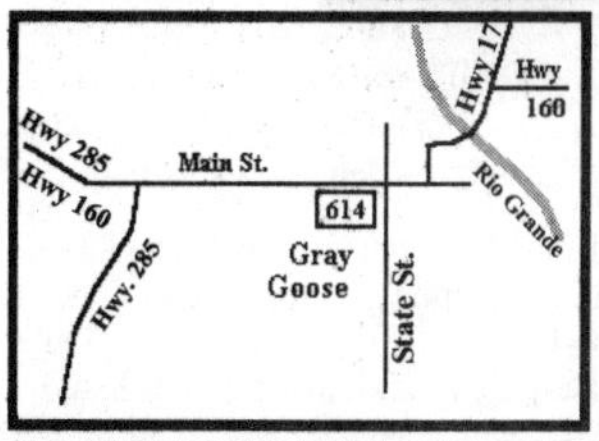

Monte Vista, CO #16

Mon - Fri 10 - 5
Sat 10 - 3

Shades, Quilts & Etc.

129 Adams St. 81144
(719) 852-2179 Fax: Same
E-Mail: jadavey@amigo.net

Window Covering & Quilt Shop. Quilting Supplies including a wide selection of fabrics, notions, books & patterns. DMC Floss, Janome Sewing Machines.

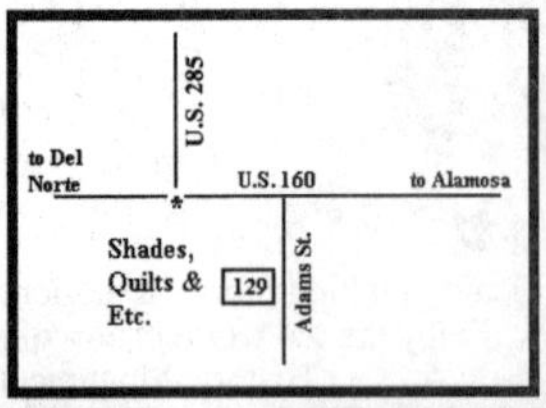

South Fork, CO #17

Mon - Sat 10 - 5
Winter 10 - 4

Kathy's Fabric Trunk

0203 W. Frontage Rd. 81154
(719) 873-0211 Fax: (719) 873-5539
Owner: Kathy Black
Est: 2001 1200 sq.ft.

Fabrics, Patterns, Notions, Classes, Books, Floss
One day classes for busy travelers.
Come see our selection!

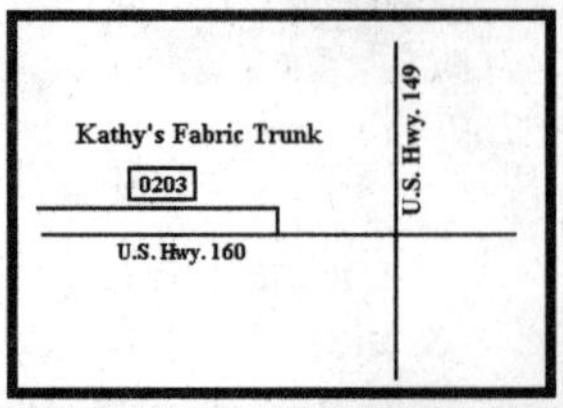

Poncha Springs, CO #18

Mon - Sat 9:30 - 5
Wed til 6

Quilt Studio

145 Sabeta Ave., P.O. Box 339 81242
(719) 530-9900 Fax: (719) 530-9901
E-Mail: mail@quilt-studio.com
Web Site: www.quilt-studio.com
Owners: Fran & Jack Switzer

Quilt Studio is a full service shop, offering an extensive collection of fabrics, and a wide variety of notions, books, classes and machine embroidery supplies. We also carry Janome and Singer sewing machines.

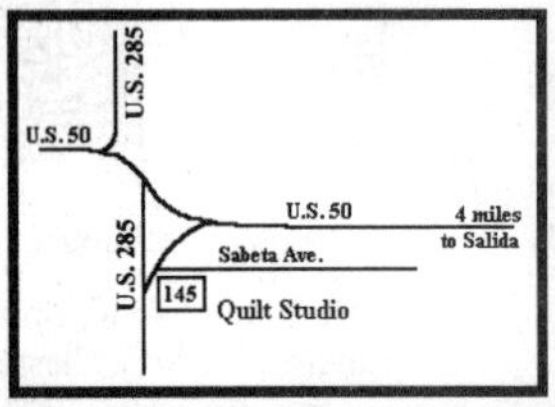

Durango, CO #19

Mon - Fri 10 - 6

All For The Love of Quilts

Long Arm Machine Quilting
1474 Main Ave. #205
81301
(970) 259-1454

Custom Machine Quilting Service (in the ditch or marked designs); Custom Quilts; Quilt Completion or Repair.

Durango, CO #20

Summer 9:30 - 6
Winter 10 - 5:30

Animas Quilts

600 Main Avenue 81301
(970) 247-2582
Web Site: www.animasquilts.com
Owner: Pat Nicholas
Est: 1988 2600 sq.ft.

"A quilter's paradise" on the western slope of Colorado. 3000 Bolts of wonderful cottons! Plus quilt kits and classes.

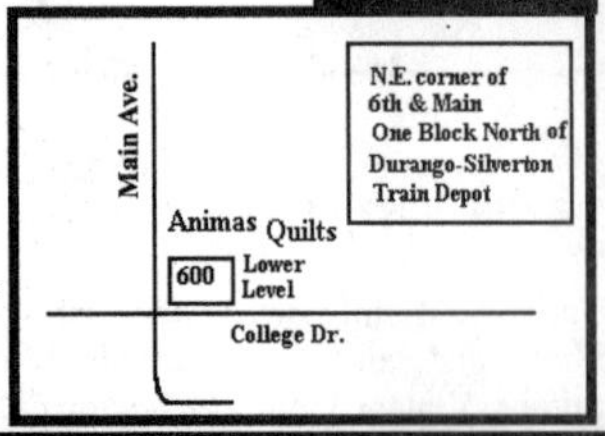

Gunnison, CO #21

Mon - Sat
Summer 9 - 6
Winter 10 - 5:30
Sun 12 - 4

E & P Sewing Emporium

135 N. Main St. 81230
(970) 641-0474
E-Mail: epsewing@gunnison.com
Owner: Mary Spann
Est: 1985 2000 sq.ft.

We are a full-service store offering Janome Sewing Machines, Quilting and Yarn Supplies and Classes. Our Quilt Festival is the 1st two weeks in August.

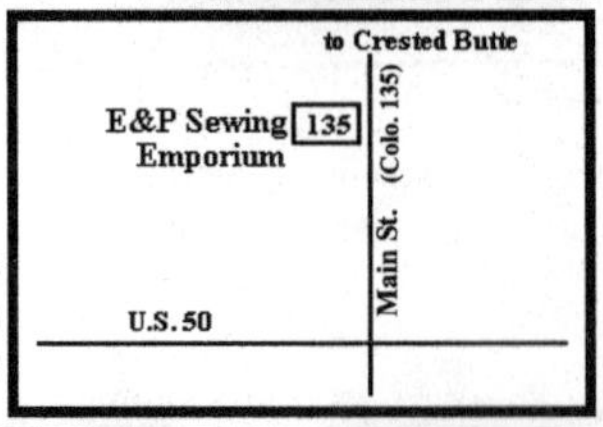

Montrose, CO #22

Mon - Sat 10 - 5:30

The Quilter's Cottage

1425 Hawk Parkway 81401
(970) 240-8132 Fax: (970) 240-9735
E-Mail: iquilt@thequilterscottage.com
Web Site: www.thequilterscottage.com
Owner: Jan Ogg
Est: 1999 1400 sq. ft. 1000 Bolts

High quality fabrics, books, and patterns. Machine quilting. Friendly, experienced staff. The best little quilt shop on the Western Slope.

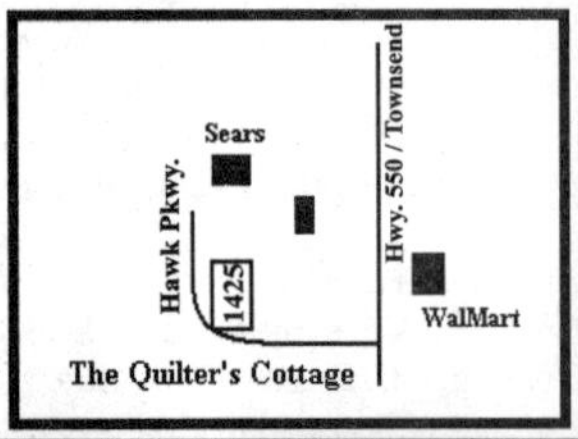

Hotchkiss, CO #23

Mon - Sat 9 - 5

D. C. Fabric

148 Bridge St. 81419
(970) 872-2688
Owner: Della Collins Est: 1990
Twenty miles west of Delta

Small town country store atmosphere. Pull up a chair and visit. Over 1100 bolts. Commercial quilting machine.

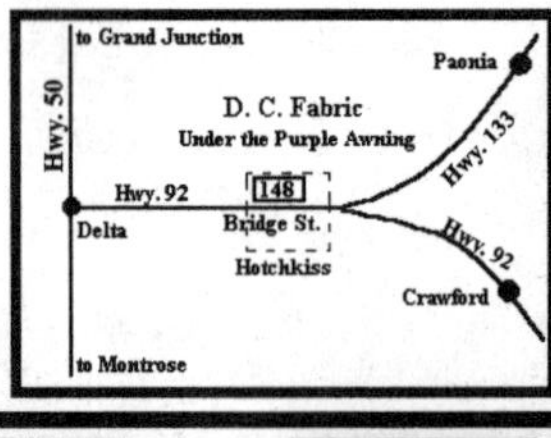

Grand Junction, CO #24

Mon - Sat 9:30 - 5:30

Hi Fashion **Fabrics, Inc.**

2586 Patterson Rd. 81505
(970) 242-1890 Fax: (970) 243-0360
E-Mail: jpvlefty@aol.com
Owners: Arlene & Jeff Vogel 18,000 sq.ft.

Huge Selection of Quilting Cottons, Books, and Supplies. Complete Line of Other Fabrics: Bridal, Fashion, Outer Wear, Drapery & Upholstery, Boat Vinyl.

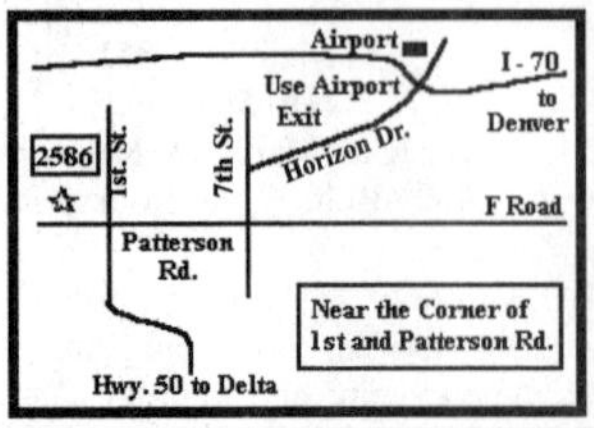

Grand Junction, CO #25

Open 7 Days a week.

Quilters' Corner, Inc.

443 Main St. 81501
Downtown Historic Grand Junction
(970) 255-8838 or (800) 255-4863

Over 3000 bolts, hundreds of books and patterns.

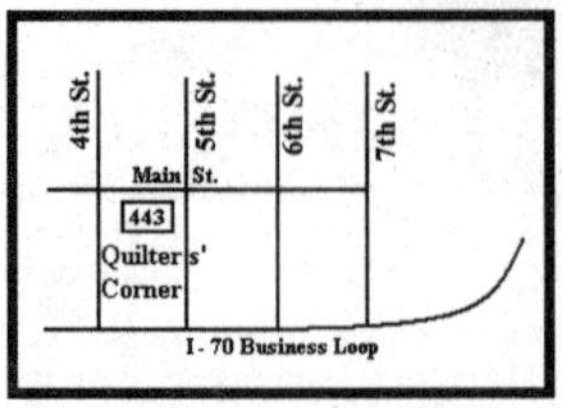

GLENWOOD SEWING CENTER

822 Grand Ave., Glenwood Springs, CO 81601
(970) 945-5900 or (800) 371-5967
E-Mail: glenwoodsew@compuserve.com
Owners: Bob & Sandy Boyd
Est: 1977 5000 sq.ft. 2500 Bolts

Mon - Sat 10 - 6 Sun 11 - 4

Glenwood Springs, CO #26

- Over 2,500 bolts
- Full line of books & notions
- Quilting classes & workshops

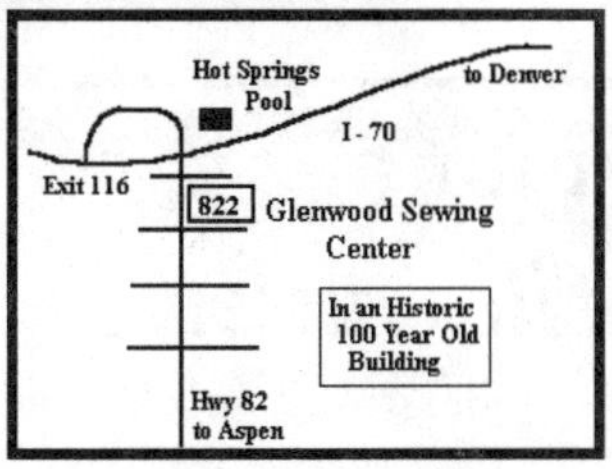

Take 1 - 70 to exit 116. First block after the bridge in downtown.

Idaho Springs, CO #27

Mon - Sat 11 - 5

Gold Nugget Fabrics and Quilts

1800 Colorado Blvd #8, P.O. Box 216 80452
(303) 567-9793
E-Mail: tom27454@hotmail.com
Owner: Mary A. Flowers
Est: 2000 800 sq. ft.

Stop and visit on your way through Colorado. Just 20 minutes west of Golden. Silk thread, appliqué patterns a favorite.

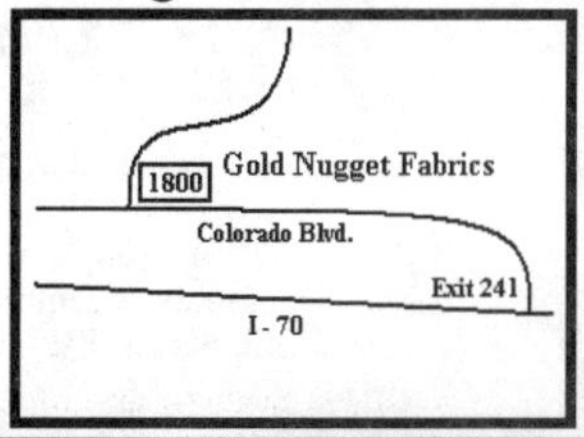

Evergreen, CO #28

Mon - Fri 9:30 - 5:30 Sat 9:30 - 4:30 Sun 12 - 4

The Quilt Cabin

6947 Hwy. 73 80439
(303) 670-4798
Owner: Holly Engelken
Est: 1996

Great Selection Quilting Fabrics and Supplies. Reproductions, Flannels and Plaids our speciality.

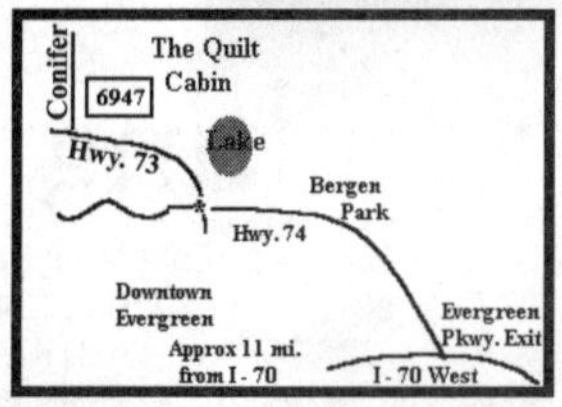

Golden, CO #29

Mon - Fri 10 - 5 Closed Weekends

Primedia Quilt Gallery

741 Corporate Circle, Suite A 80401
(303) 278-1010
Fax: (303) 277-0370

Enjoy the current quilt exhibit at the home offices of Quilter's Newsletter Magazine, Quiltmaker, and McCall's Quilting. Free Admission.

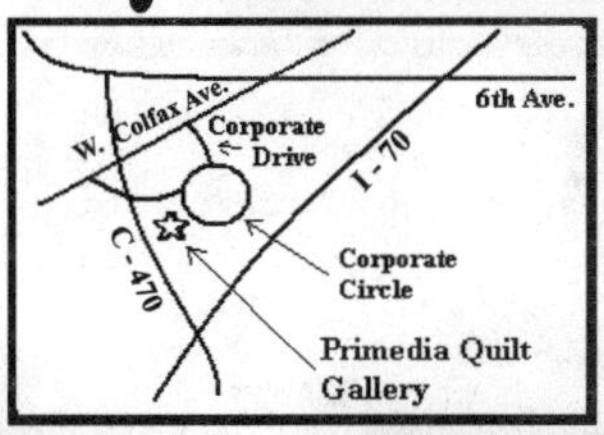

Golden, CO #30

Mon - Sat 10 - 4

Rocky Mountain Quilt Museum

1111 Washington Ave. 80401
(303) 277-0377
Non-Profit Self Supporting Museum
Web Site: www.RMQM.org
Adm: Janet E. Finley Est: 1990
Quilt Market - Gift Shop

The only Quilt Museum in the Rocky Mountains. Exhibits change 5 times a year. Send S.A.S.E. for schedule. Admission Charged

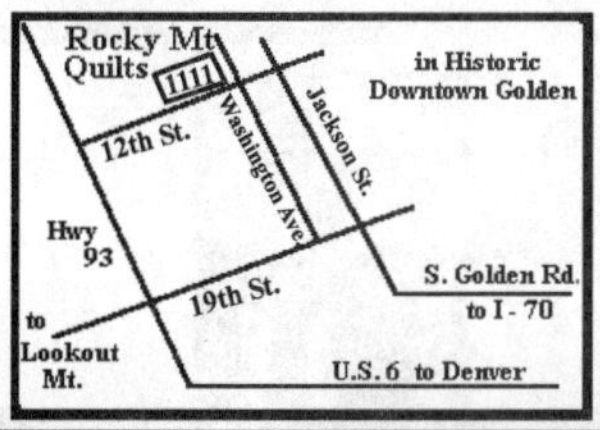

Estes Park, CO #31

Wed, Thur Fri 12 - 5 Sat & Sun 9 - 5

Around The Block Quilts

433 C. West Elkhorn 80517
(970) 577-7100
Owner: Judy Edwards Est: 2001
2500 sq.ft.
1000 Bolts

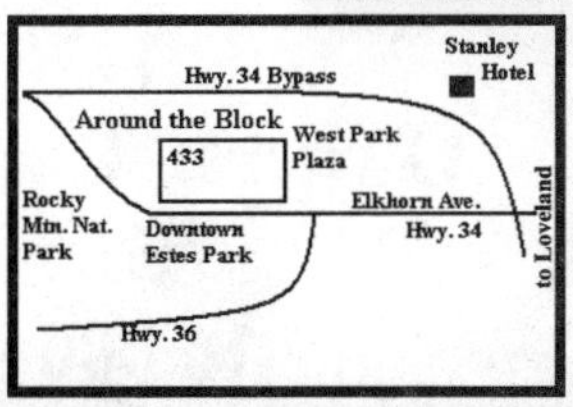

Lots of flannels and Lots of florals.
Large selection of gifts, candles and baskets.

Estes Park, CO #32

Summer Open Daily 10 - 5 Winter Open Mon - Sat 10 - 5

Mountain Lady Quilt Shop LLC

205 Park Ln., P.O. Box 436 80517
(970) 586-5330
Owner: Connie Westley
mtnladyqult@aol.com

Quality supplies for Quilters.
Custom machine and hand quilting.
Classes, mail order.

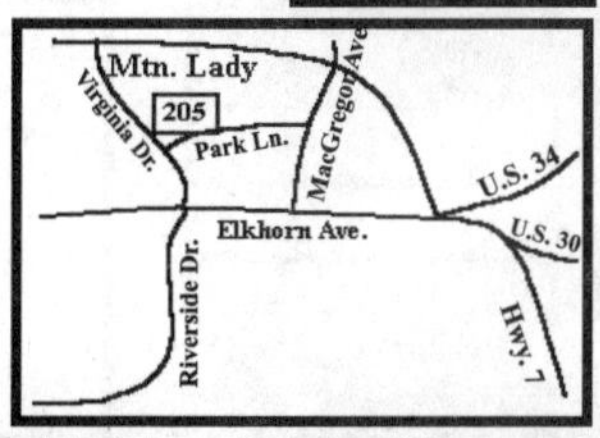

Estes Park, CO #33

Mon - Sat 10 - 5

High Country Amish Quilts

800-B Moraine Ave./ Hwy. 36
P.O. Box 3107 80517
(Near the South Entrance to Rocky Mtn. National Park)
(970) 577-1557 1.1 miles from downtown

Come and visit Colorado's largest selection of Amish quilts and wallhangings. Our Amish Country Store is filled with Amish art, dolls and handcrafts, candles, cookbooks, rugs, pottery, florals and other fine gifts.

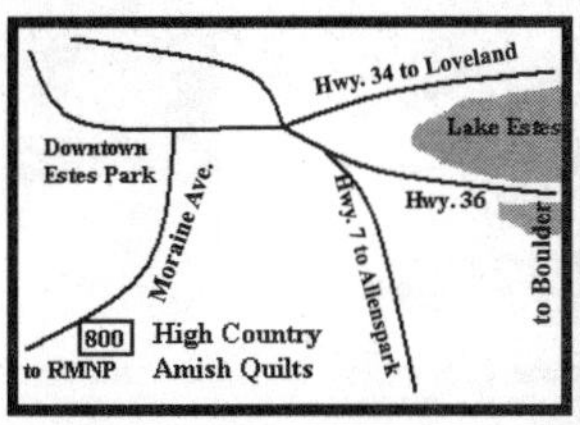

Estes Park, CO #34

Year 'round 10 - 5 Closed Wed.

Maggie Mae's Quilts 'N

242 Moraine Ave. P.O. Box 3580
(970) 586-4257 80517
Owner: Margaret McCormick
Est: 1990 1200 sq.ft.

Featuring Patterns by Colorado Designers, both quilting and cross stitch. Kits - Handmade Wooden Quilt Racks - Fabrics - Christmas Projects & Unique Wearables.

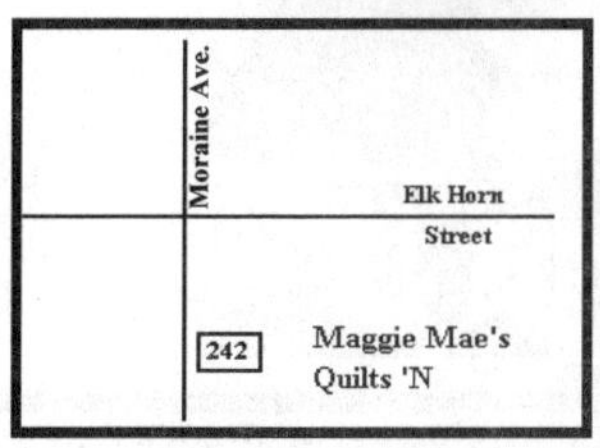

Nederland, CO #35

Flexible Please call ahead for hours

Fabric Peddlers

1 West First St. 80466-3061
(303) 258-0626
E-Mail: Fabped@peoplepc.com
Owner: Frances Smith
Mgr: Billie Bishop Est: 1996

Friendly Fabric store in the mountains above Boulder. Beautiful fabrics, batiks, batting, patterns, yarn & quilts. Come visit us.

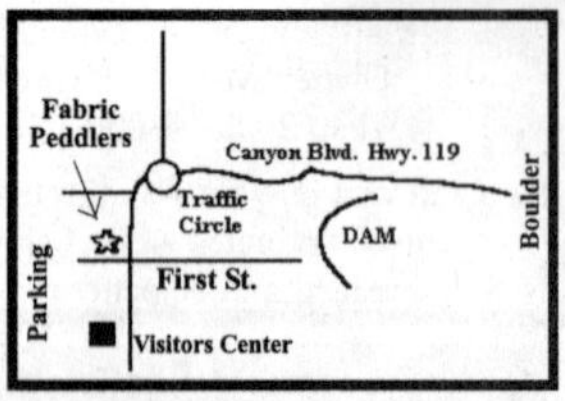

Steamboat Springs, CO #36

Mon - Sat 10 - 7

Pieces Of The Past

626 Lincoln Ave., P.O. Box 776209 80477
(970) 870-8684
E-Mail: quilts@quiltedlegends.com
Web Site: www.quiltedlegends.com
Owner: Kimberley L. Mosher

We are a full service quilt shop with terrific Fabric, Unique Gifts and One of a Kind Antiques. Self published line of patterns called "Legends of the West".

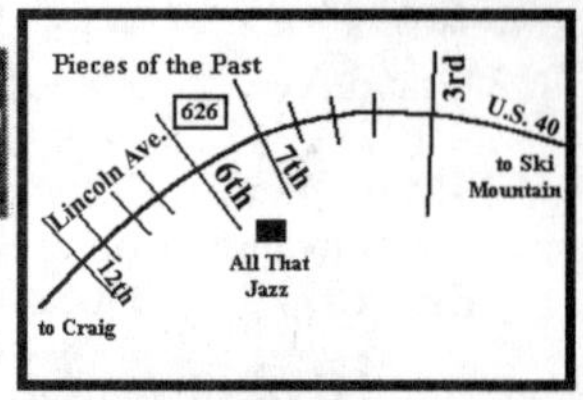

Lyons, CO #37

Mon - Sat 9:30 - 6:30 Sun 1 - 5

Quilting Hands

304 Main St., Suite C
P.O. Box 1342 80540
(303) 823-6067
Owner: Jan Rold
Est: 2000 1000 sq.ft.
1700 Bolts

Inspiration, Instruction, Fabrics, and Supplies for Quilters.

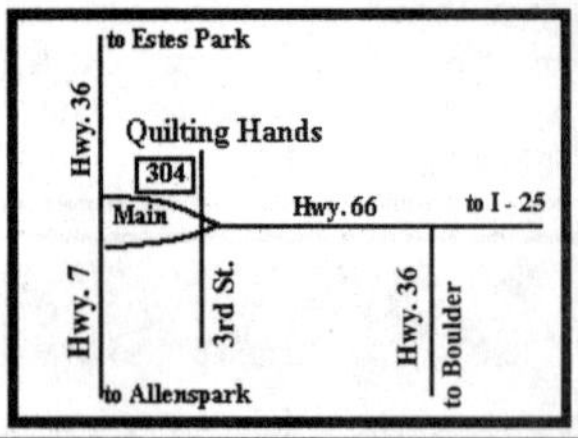

Fort Collins, CO #38

Mon - Thurs 9 - 6 Fri & Sat 9 - 5

Mill Outlet Fabric Shop

2317 E. Mulberry 80521
(970) 221-0998
Web Site: www.MillOutletFabric.com
Est: 1965 4000 sq. ft.

Quilting, Dress, Bridal, Notions, Drape, Upholstery, Vinyl, Home Decorating, Buttons, Books & Batting! Colorado's Best Selection of Fabric & Supplies!

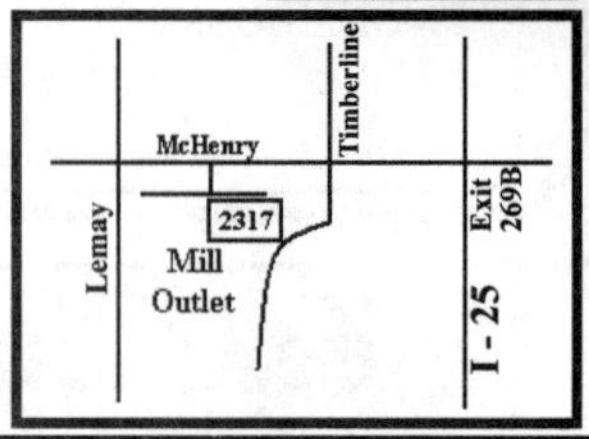

Ft. Collins, CO #39

The Fig Leaf

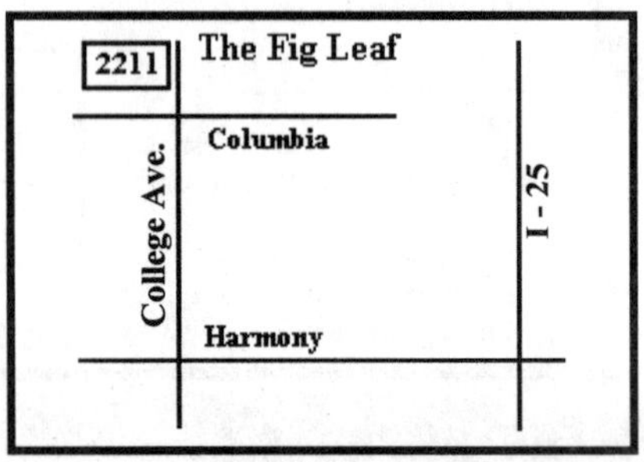

2211 S. College 80525
(970) 495-1766
Owners: Rob & Laura Shotwell
Est: 1982
16,000 sq.ft.

Over 3500 Bolts of Fabric
(includes 500 Bolts of Flannel)
Books, Patterns, Notions.
Full Line Furniture Store with Gifts and Accessories.

Mon - Sat 10 - 6 Sun 12 - 5

MJ's Quilt Shop

265 H E. 29th St. 80538 Orchards Shopping Center
Toll Free 877.657.8458 (1.877.mjquilt)
970.663.1300 Fax: 970.663.1300
E-Mail: mjsquiltshop@yahoo.com
Web Site: www.mjsquiltshop.com
Owner: M.J. Olinger 2500 sq.ft. Est: 1998

Loveland, CO #40

Loveland's full service quilt shop

- 2000+ bolts of fabric
- 100% Cotton Quality Fabric
- Books--all the latest
- Notions--everything you need
- Stencils--great selection
- Classes--all levels
- Machine Quilting by Juliana Olinger

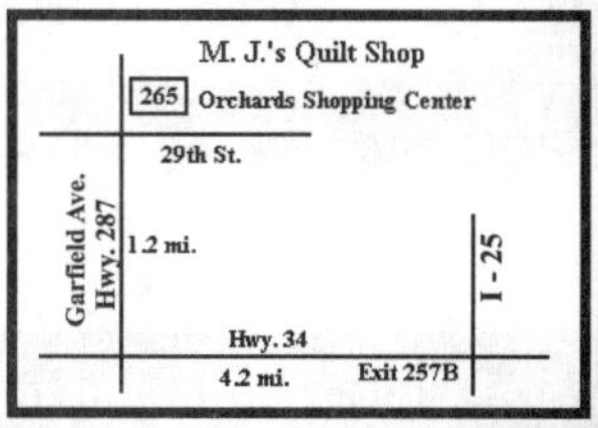

Mon - Fri 10 - 5:30
Sat 10 - 4:30

We wish you the best in your quilting adventure!

Berthoud, CO #41

Mountain Prairie Quilts

516 Mountain Ave., Berthoud CO 80513
(970) 532-3386 or (866) 532-3386
e-mail- mtprairie@frii.com
Owner: Dana Richardson
Est: 2000 2000 sq.ft.

Mon - Fri 10 - 6
Sat 9 - 5

Quilt supplies, classes, books, 100% cotton fabrics featuring brights, orientals, southwest, western, batiks, the entire line of Moda marbles and much more!

We are "the Quilter Friendly Store."

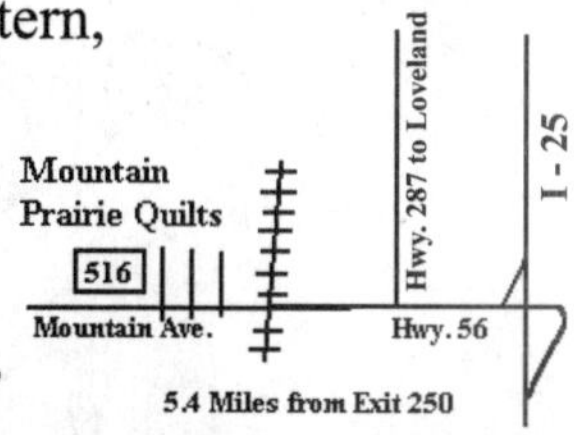

Longmont, CO #42

Mon- Sat 10 - 5:30
Mon & Thur til 7
Sun 12 - 4

The Patch Works

700 Ken Pratt Blvd. #101 80501
(303) 772-3002
Owner: Terri Miller Est: 1988
2000 sq.ft. 1600+ Bolts

Friendly atmosphere, clean bathroom, lots of fabric, books, patterns, notions.
Some one-day classes available.
Block of the Month Kits Available.

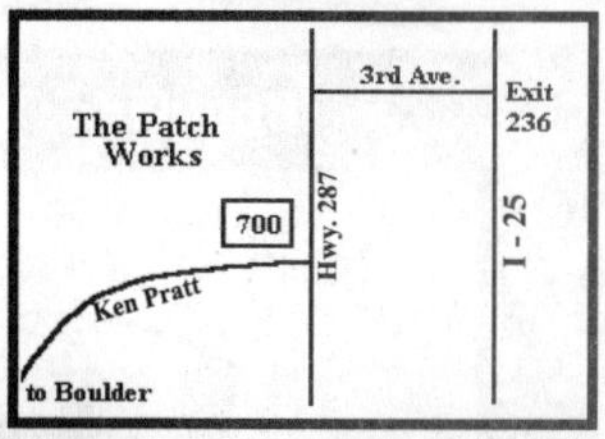

Greeley, CO #43

Mon - Fri 10 - 5:30
Sat 10 - 4

wild'n woolly

2308 W. 17th St. 80634
(970) 356-0335
Owner: Ruth Dixon
Est: 1978 1800 Bolts

Needlework Shop. Quilting Supplies, Hand Knitting Yarns. Needlepoint, Hardanger and Cross Stitch

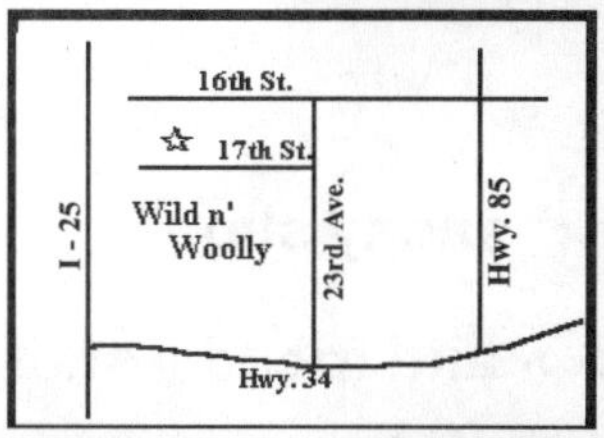

Greeley, CO #44

Mon - Fri 10 - 5:30
Sat 10 - 4

Quilter's Stash

3512 W. 10th St., #2 80634
(970) 353-6264
Fax: (970) 330-5762
Owner: Patty Winkelman
Est: 2002

Fabric, Notions, Quilt Kits, Books & Patterns, BOM

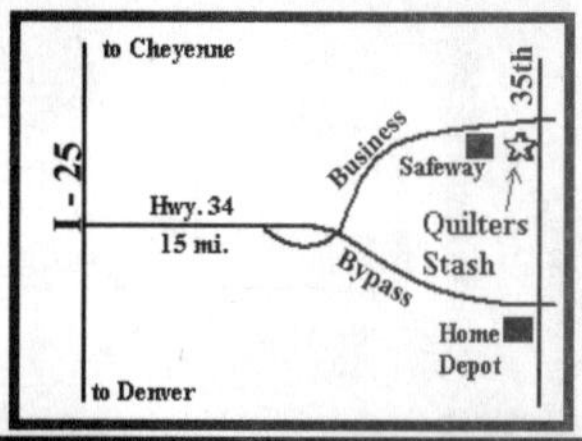

Ft. Morgan, CO #45

Mon - Sat 10 - 5

423 Main St. #300 80701
(970) 542-0810
Web Site: www.inspirations-quilts.com

inspirations

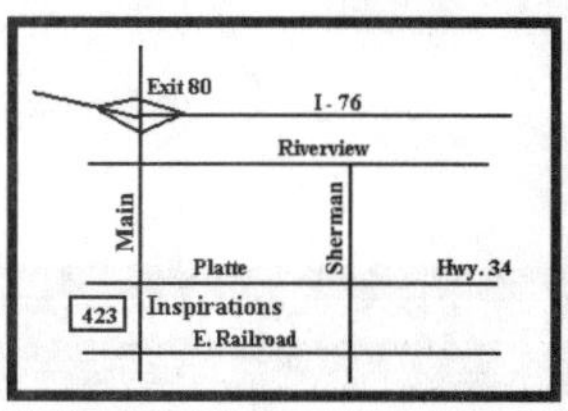

Owners: Ginger McCafferty & Nancy Hocheder
Top quality fabrics, quilt books & patterns; kits; doll & critter patterns & many quilting supplies. You'll enjoy seeing our large selection of models.

Sterling, CO #46

Mon - Sat 9 - 5:30

Quilts-N-Creations

201 Ash P.O. Box 991 80751
(970) 522-0146 Est: 1987

1000 Bolts of Printed & Solid Cottons
Bridal Headquarters for N.E. Colorado including Bridal Fabric & Trims. Tuxedo Rentals with over 70 varieties to choose from. Authorized Bernina Dealer. Custom sewing including crafts, quilts, garments or Bridal. Custom, Traditional & Heirloom Quilting.

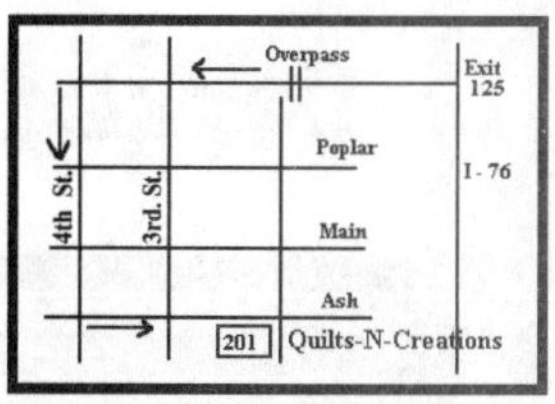

Yuma, CO #47

Tues - Fri
10 - 5:30
Sat 9:30 - 12:30

Stitches In Time

201 E. 8th Ave. 80759
(970) 848-0555 Fax: (970) 848-3230
E-mail: junger@plains.net
Owner: Carole J. Unger
Est: 1998 700+ Bolts

A cozy quilt shop carrying 100% cotton fabrics, quilt books, patterns and notions. Classes and Machine Quilting Available.

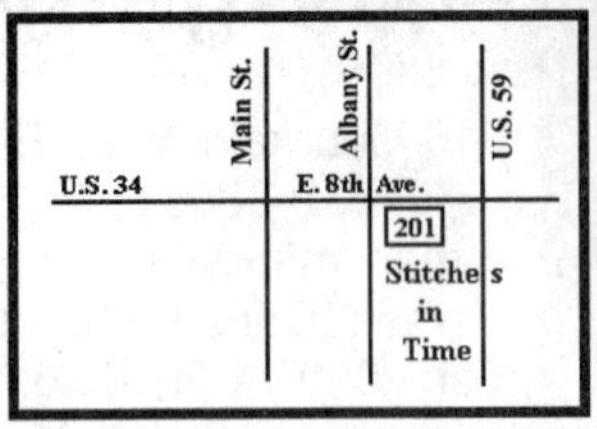

Wray, CO #48

Patchwork County

Mon - Fri
9:30 - 5
Sat 9:30 - 3

Located in charming renovated house built in 1902 one block east off Main.
Latest fabric, patterns, books, notions.
Patchwork County— "*Where The Inspiration Is Free!*"

Featured in Quilt Sampler 2001

140 E. 4th St. 80758
(970) 332-5676
Owners: Dana Barnett & Claudia Fix
E-mail: patchworkcounty@plains.net
Est: 1994

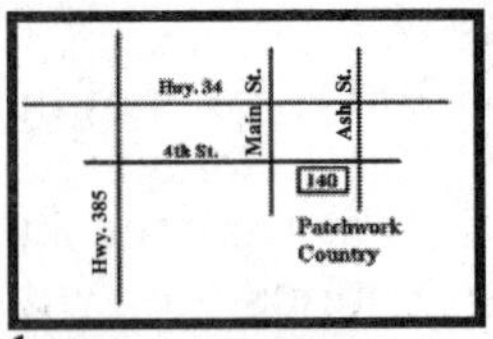

Web: www.patchworkcounty.com

Boulder's ONLY independent quilting supply store! Only 30 minutes from downtown Denver.

Prosperity Quilt Shoppe

Mon - Sat
10 - 6

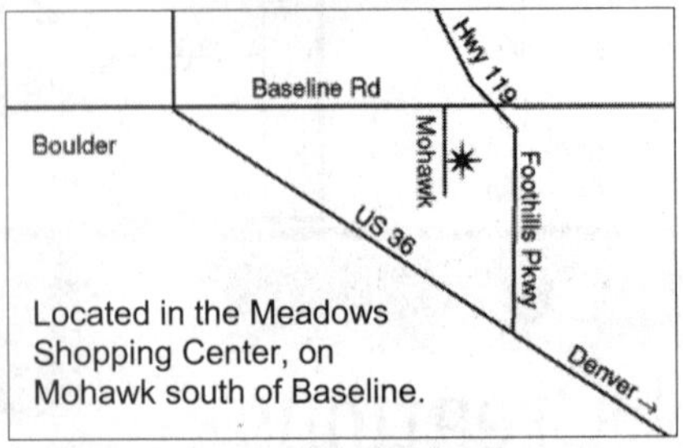

Inviting, sunny shop.
Fun and friendly staff.
Eclectic mix of fabrics.
Decorative embellishments.
Innovative classes for all levels.
Janome sewing machines.

Boulder, CO #49

4800 Baseline Rd. E-108 • Boulder, CO 80303 • 303-494-0541 • www.prosperityquiltshoppe.com

Cabin Fever Quilts & More

2695 N. Park Dr. #102 Lafayette, CO 80026
(303) 664-1877 Fax: (303) 664-1887
Owners: Kathy Lewis & Monika Koenig
Est: 1996 2500+ Bolts

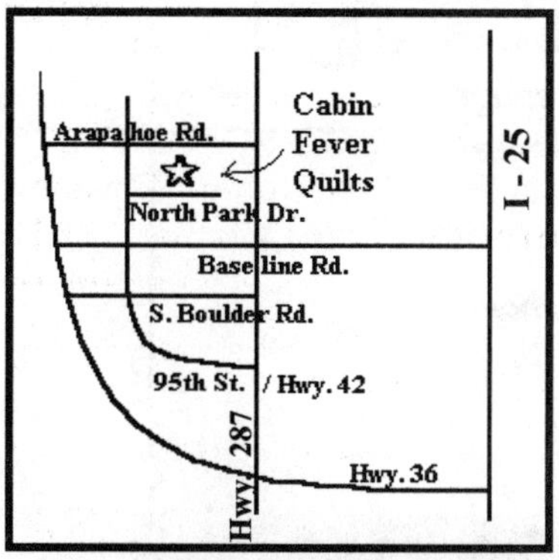

E-Mail:
cabinfever@mho.com
Web Site: www.
cabinfeverquilts.com

Over 2500 bolts of gorgeous fabrics. Classes Galore. Books, Patterns, & Notions, Pfaff Machines. Tons of Fat Quarters. Friendly, Expert Staff. 30 minutes from downtown Denver.

Mon - Fri 10 - 6
Sat 10 - 5 Sun 12 - 4

Great "homey" atmosphere. Sit by the fireplace and check out our newest books. Classes nearly every day.

Lafayette, CO #50

Broomfield, CO #51

DRY CREEK QUILTS

FABRICS · SUPPLIES · CLASSES

COME VISIT US!

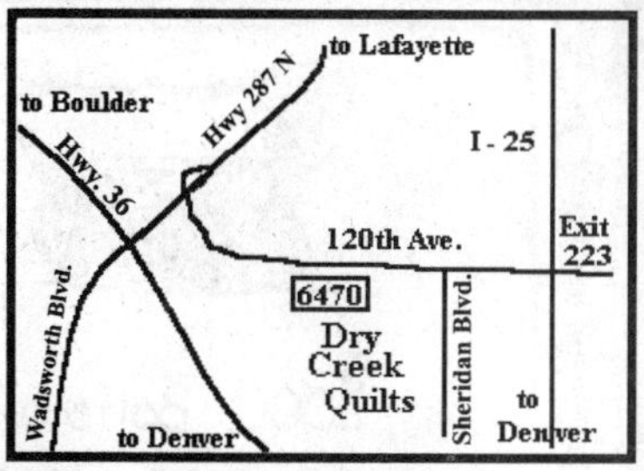

VILLAGER SQUARE SHOPPING CENTER
One mile West of Sheridan Blvd.
6470 W. 120th Ave., Unit D-3
Broomfield, CO 80020
(303) 465-2526
E-Mail: drycreekquilts@att.net
Owner: Jo-Anne Ginther

Over 3,000+ Bolts of Fabric

Everything for Quilters: Quilting Books, Patterns, Notions, Viking Sewing Machines & Classes. FREE Inspiration and Advice.

Tomorrow's Heirlooms

A Gourmet Quiltmaking Establishment

Located at 1005 W 120th, Suite 500
2 blocks west of I-25 at Huron St.
In the Village at Park Centre
Phone 303-457-3888
Fax 303-457-0964

Quilt Racks, Spool Cabinets, Quilt Hangers, and Sewing Cabinets

100% cotton and flannel fabrics

A large selection of Mettler, YLI, and Oliver Twist cotton, YLI silk, Superior and Isacord Polyester Threads

Premium Cotton and Wool Battings

Gift Certificates Available in any Denomination

Store Hours:
M-F 9:30 am—6:00 pm
Sat 9:30 am— 5:00 pm
Sun 12:00 pm—5:00 pm

Representing Bernina Sewing Machines and Accessories through authorized dealer, Studio Bernina of Boulder Colorado

Fully Equiped Bernina Classroom featuring the Virtuosa 153 Quilters Edition

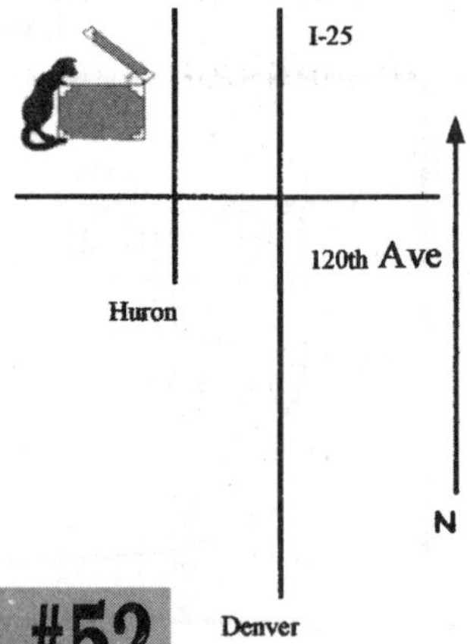

Westminster, CO #52

Rhonda Anderson, Owner

HIGH PRAIRIE QUILTS

2000+ Bolts of fabric, books, patterns, notions. Classes for everyone, from beginner to the most advanced quilter. A variety of Block of the Month quilt programs. Come visit our newly expanded, customer friendly shop. Now with over 3500 sq. ft. of quilting heaven.
Our Store Hours:
Mon - Sat 9:30 - 5:30.
Sun. 12- 4:30
Wed. evening now open till 8pm

Visit our website at
www.highprairiequilts.com

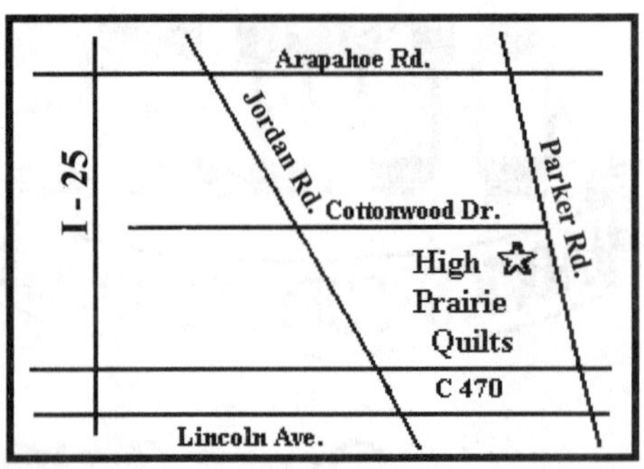

Parker, CO #53

17920 Cottonwood Dr., Parker, Colorado 80134
303- 627-0878

Denver, CO #54

8970 East Hampden Ave. 80231

(303) 740-6206 or (800) 474-2665 Fax: (303) 220-7424

Owners: Nancy Smith & Lynda Milligan Est: 1981 3000 sq.ft.

Great American Quilt Factory

Welcome !

4000+ Fabrics, Books, Notions, Patterns, Classes.
Photo transfer and machine quilting services.

Mon - Fri 9:30 - 6
Wed til 8:30
Sat 9:30 - 5
Sun 12 - 5

Home of: POSSIBILITIES®

Publishers of:
Dream Spinners, I'll Teach Myself, and Possibilities books.

Web Site: www.greatamericanquilt.com

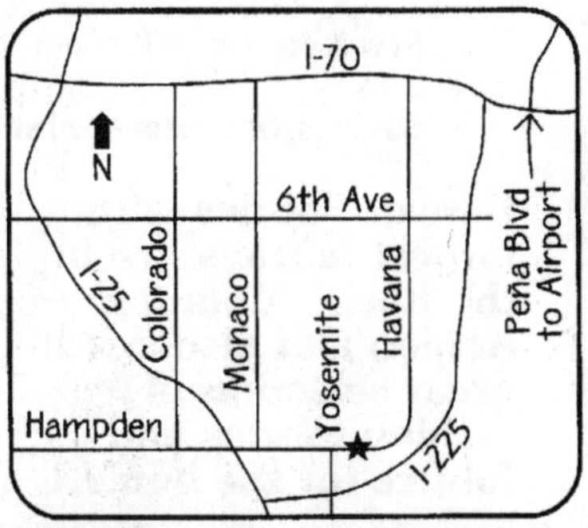

Littleton, CO #55

fabric EXPRESSIONS
A Unique Quilt Shop

5950 S. Platte Canyon Rd. #D12 80123
(303) 798-2556
E-Mail: fabexp@aol.com
Owners: Toni Phillips & Juanita Simonich
Est: 1994 4200 sq.ft.

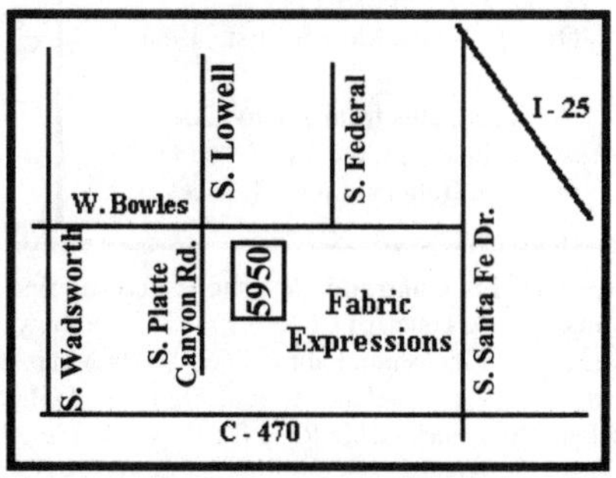

Mon - Fri 9:30 - 6
Tues til 8
Sat 10 - 5

100% Cottons! Homespuns, Flannels, Plaids, Prints, Solids.
Books, Notions, Classes.
www.fabricexpressions.com

Catalog of Our Patterns SASE
Monthly Block of the Month Club

Home of "Fabric Expressions" patterns & books.

Littleton, CO #56

Denver Fabrics Quilting Department

- The best prints from your favorite companies: Moda, Hoffman, South Seas, P&B, RJR, Marcus Brothers, Bali Fabrications, Timeless Treasures, & many more.
- Basics including Moda Marbles, Fossil Fern, Staples and white-on-white prints.
- Hand dyed & batik fabrics, homespun, flannels, floral prints & asian prints.
- Special section of great quality cotton prints at half price every day.
- New & classic quilt books, and notions.
- Battings, both packaged and by the yard.

Denver Fabrics is the largest fabric store in the Rocky Mountain Region and also has a great selection of fashion fabrics and fabrics for the home.

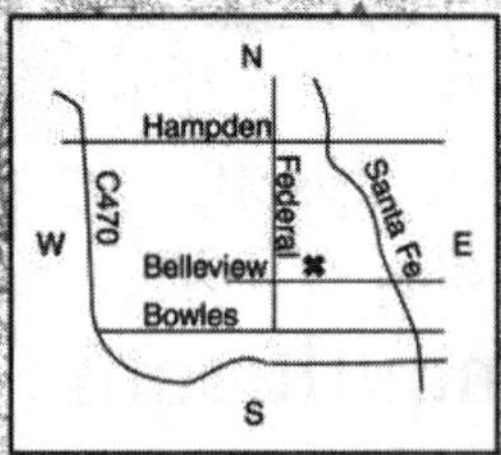

Denver Fabrics

2777 W. Belleview • 303-730-2777
(Between Santa Fe & Federal)
M-F 10-8 Sat 10-6 Sun 12-5

Littleton, CO #57

Mon - Wed 10 - 8
Thurs - Sat 10 - 5
Sun 12 - 4

The Creative Needle

6905 South Broadway #113 80122
(303) 794-7312
Web Site: www.thecreativeneedle.com
Owner: Marge Serck
Est: 1978 3500 sq.ft. 2000 Bolts

One stop for quilting, cross-stitch, heirloom and smocking. Elna machine sales and service.

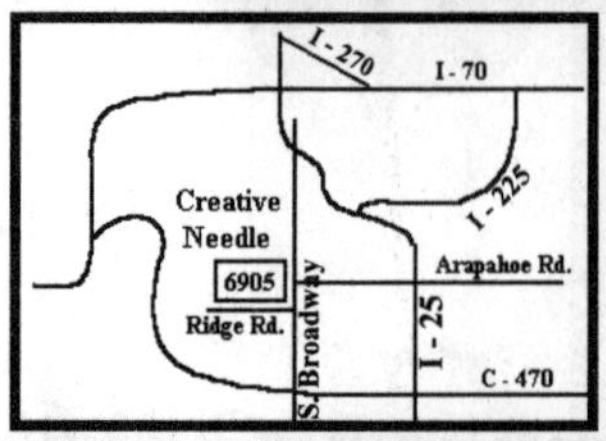

Littleton, CO #58

Mon - Sat
10 - 6
Tues til 7:30
Sun 12 - 4

Quilting up a Storm

7424 S. University, Suite D 80122
(720) 529-9659
Owner: Holly Engelken

Fabric - All 100% Cotton, Books, Patterns, Batting, Notions, Quilting Services, Classes. Ideas and Friendly Service.

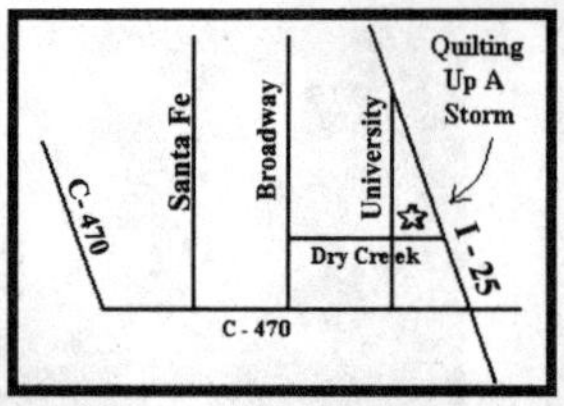

Denver, CO #59

Mon - Sat
9:30-5:30
Tues til 7:30
Sun 12 - 4

Quilts in the Attic

1025 South Gaylord St. 80209
(303) 744-8796
Est: 1972 1500 sq.ft.
Owner: Holly Engelken

Fabric - all 100% cotton - Books, Patterns, Batting, Notions, Quilting Services. Ideas and Friendly Service. Classes.

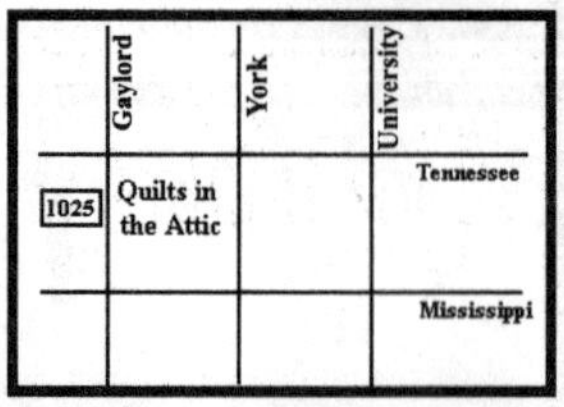

Denver, CO #60

Mon - Sat
11 - 5
Sun by Appt.

The Country Line Antiques & Quilts

1067 S. Gaylord St. 80209
(303) 733-1143
Owner: Genna Morrow Est: 1988

Antique Quilts from $20 to $2000
Also—quilt scraps, pieces, & "cutters".
Vintage Buttons, Linen & Laces.

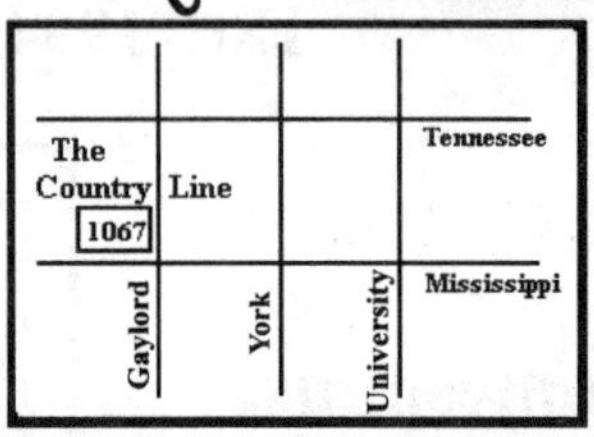

Wheatridge, CO #61

Mon - Fri
9:30 - 5
Sat 9:30 - 4

Harriet's Treadle Arts

6390 West 44th Ave. 80033
(303) 424-2742
Web Site: www.harriethargrave.com
Owner: Harriet Hargrave
3600 sq.ft. Est: 1981

Over 5000 bolts - largest selection of vintage reproduction fabrics in Colorado.
Come See Us ! !

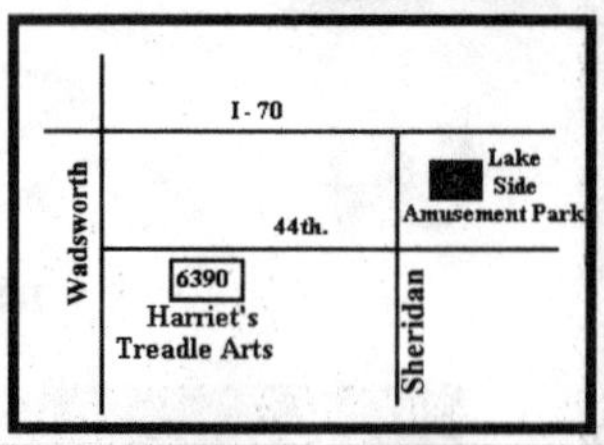

Other Shops in Colorado: We suggest calling first

Arvada	A Touch of Country, 7317 Grandview Ave.	303-422-2878
Arvada	Pincushion Fabric, 8662 W. 84th Circle	303-426-9967
Aspen	Katie Ingham Antique Quilts, 257 Glen Eagles Dr.	970-925-2595
Breckenridge	Honeysuckle Rose Quilts & Friends, 211 S. Main	970-547-9654
Cahone	Ann Neely's Quilting Shop, 14064 Hwy. 666	970-562-4655
Cedaredge	Katie's Kloth & Kreations, 2012 2375 Rd.	970-856-7878
Conifer	Old Glory Antiques, 11825 Hwy. 285	303-838-4600
Craig	Rose of Sharon Quilt Shop, 485 Yampa Ave.	970-824-7414
Denver	D'Leas Fabric Affair, 2719 E. 3rd. Ave.	303-388-5665
Denver	Exeter River Trader, 1212 S. Broadway	303-744-7049
Estes Park	The Sampler--Lakeview Plz., P.O. Box 1771	970-577-1750
Fort Collins	Calico Country, 4604 Terry Lake Rd.	970-493-2751
Fort Morgan	Quilting Corner, 328 Main St.	970-867-9066
Indian Hills	Log Cabin Patchworks, P.O. Box 186	303-838-7343
Lafayette	Artistic Creations, 825 Sparta Dr.	303-665-2388
Lakewood	Cabin Quilts & Creations, 6245 W. Harvard Dr.	303-646-1388
Lakewood	Sew Far Sew Good, 10555 W. Jewell Ave. Apt. #14-208	907-279-7656
Littleton	A Touch of Country Joy, 6878 S. University	303-741-3799
Littleton	Designer Fabrics, 8966 W. Bowles Ave .	303-978-9914
Longmont	Bernina Sewing Center, 1744 Collyer St	303-776-6704
Loveland	Country Wishes & Wants, 120 E. 4th St.	970-635-0132
Merino	D & J Country Antiques, P.O. Box 29	970-842-5813
Niwot	Berry Patch, 300 2nd Ave., P.O. Box 893	303-652-1500
Pueblo	Quilt Shop Antiques, 111 E. Abriendo Ave.	719-544-4906
Pueblo	Only Friends, 1418 Berkley Ave.	719-545-6160
Sterling	Sew Together, 320 N. 4th	970-521-0258
Walden	Never Summer Designs, 454 1/2 Main St., P.O. Box 626	970-723-4473
Westminster	Konfetti's, 9160 W. 96th Dr.	303-424-6488
Windsor	Blacksmith Carriage Shop, 128 Walnut St.	970-686-1191

CONNECTICUT

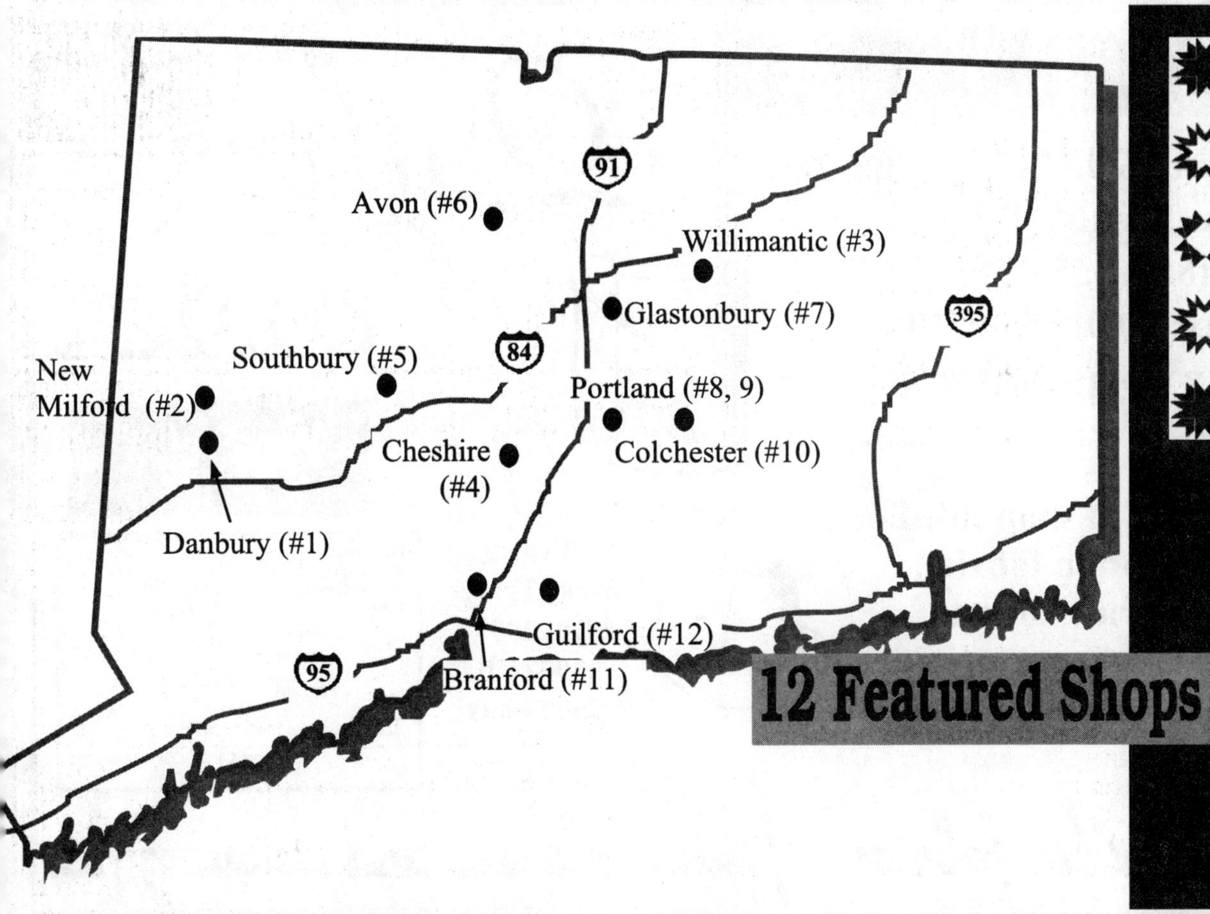

New Milford, CT #2

Quilter's Corner

312 Danbury Rd. (Rt. 7) 06776
In The Red Barn
(860) 355-4516
Fax: (860) 355-9510
Web Site: www.quilterscorner.com

Mon - Sat 10 - 5
Wed til 8

Spacious, well lit shop filled with 100% cotton fabrics, books, patterns, notions, gift items and a friendly, helpful staff.

Owner:
Becky Frazer
Est: 1999
2300 sq.ft.
2500 Bolts

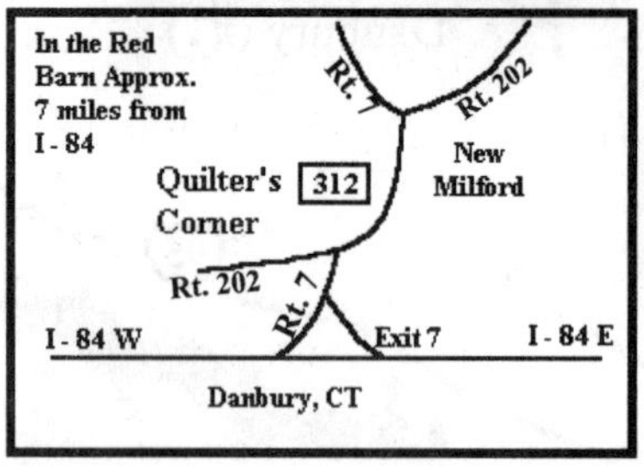

Your source for fabrics supplies, classes and unique gifts.

"Everything You Need To Make Your Quilting Experience A Dream"

Nearly 4000 Bolts of Fabric

Including Hoffman, Benartex, P & B, Moda, Maywood South Seas, Kona Bay and many more.

We Carry Tons of Books, Supplies, Patterns, Batiks, Gadgets and Quilters Tools. Sign up for our Quarterly Newsletter where you will learn more about ...

- Our Extensive Class Schedule (Over 35 - for all levels)
- Block of the Month Program (We ship anywhere!)
- Workshops and Lectures featuring nationally renowned speakers such as: Karen Stone, Becky Goldsmith John Flynn, Jackie Robinson

One of 10 featured Shops in Quilt Sampler 2000 Magazine!

Visit our Web Site at
www.quiltersdream.com
Monday - Saturday, 10 AM - 6 PM
Thursday, 10 AM - 8 PM,
Sunday, 12 Noon - 5 PM

Quilter's Dream

Located in a lovely Victorian building situated in the downtown of an historic mill town, blocks from the Windham Textile and History Museum

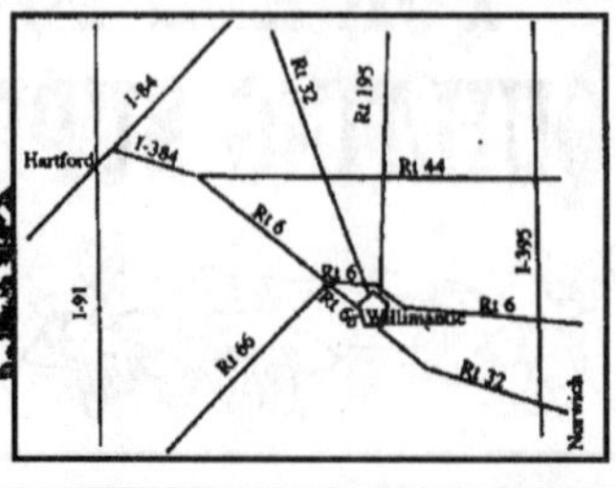

Bus Tours Welcome* • Free Gift to All
(*Please call ahead if you wish to plan a group visit.)

1158 Main Street
Willimantic, CT 06226
(860) 456-7629

#3

Larisa and James Key

calico, etc.

The Watch Factory Shoppes
116 Elm Street
Cheshire, CT 06410
203 272-2443
calicoetcquilt@aol.com
www.calicoetc.com

Fabrics & Quality Quilting Supplies

For all your Quilting needs.
Over 3,600 Bolts of Fabric,
Including our wall of Balis,
Japanese Fabrics, Brights and more.
Kits, Books, Patterns, Notions
Classes with a friendly and
Knowledgeable staff.
Call for Summer Hours
New Owner - Marty Child

Cheshire, CT #4

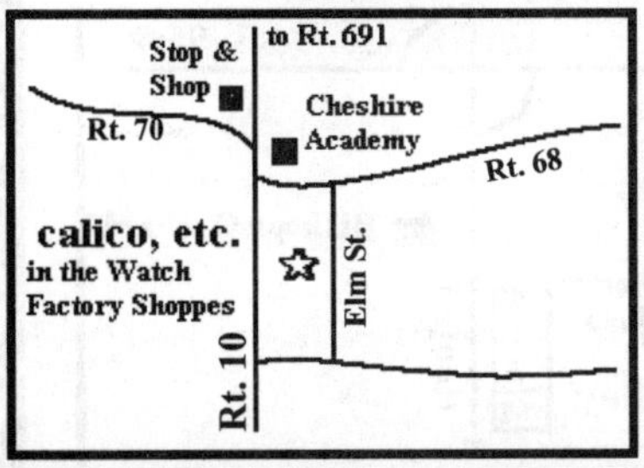

Mon & Tues 10 - 4
Wed, Fri & Sat 10 - 5
Thur 10 - 8
Sun 12 - 4

Southbury, CT #5

Dagmar's Fabrics

1481-6 Southford Rd. (Route 67) 06488
(203) 262-1206
Owner: Dagmar Ferguson
Est: 1989 2500+ sq.ft.

Mon - Fri 9:30 - 6 Sat 9 - 5

Area's largest selection of quilting books, patterns, & supplies. Knowledgeable, Friendly Staff, Quality Fabrics - over 3000 bolts. Classes. Gift Certificates Authorized Viking Dealer

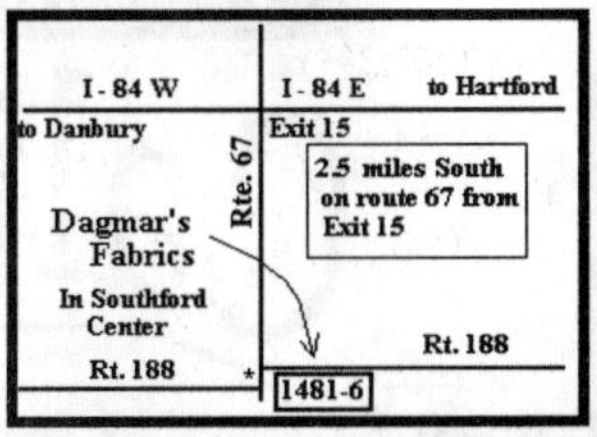

Avon, CT #6

Tues - Sat 10 - 5

Patchwork Cottage

17 E. Main St. (Rt. 44) 06001
(860) 678-0580
E-Mail: Patcottage@aol.com
Owner: Patricia-Anne Barker
Est: 1997

Beautiful 100% Cotton Fabrics
Books, Patterns, Notions, Classes.
Handmade Gifts.

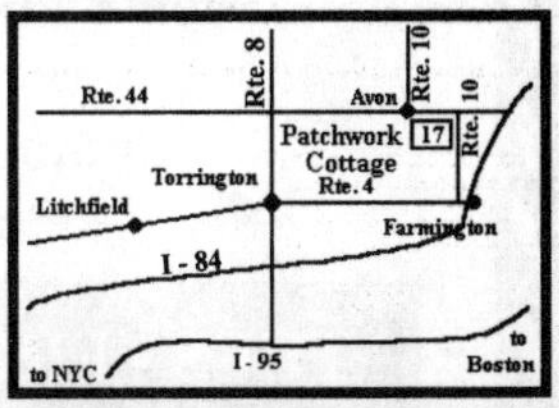

Glastonbury, CT #7

Mon - Sat 9:30 - 6
Thur til 8
Sun 12 - 4

Close To Home

2717 Main St. 06033
(860) 633-0721 Fax: (860) 657-0354
E-Mail: rgattinella@yahoo.com
Web Site: www.sewland-usa.com or www.northeastquiltfestival.com
Owner: Ron & Marilyn Gattinella
Est: 1982 6000 sq.ft. 4000+ Bolts
The most complete Quilt Shop Around. Tons of Books, Fabric, Notions, Sewing Accessories, Sewing Machines, Sergers and Cabinets.

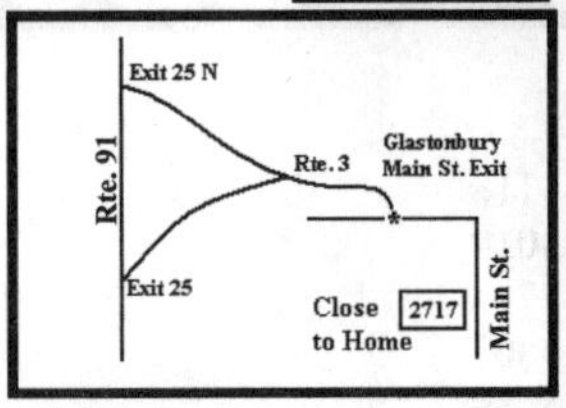

Portland, CT #8

By Appointment

Carolyn's Quilting Bee

73 Ames Hollow Rd. 06480
(860) 342-1949
Owner: Carolyn Johnson
Est: 1980

Located in the Blacksmith Shop of an 18th Century Farm.
Visitors are always welcome.

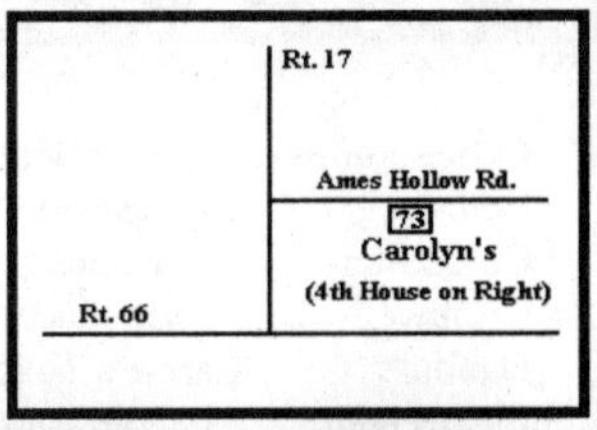

Portland, CT #9

Tues - Fri 10 - 5
Sat 10 - 3

Patches & Patchwork

216 Main St. 06480
(860) 342-4567 Fax: (860) 342-1615
E-Mail: pjsatpp@aol.com Est: 1980
Owner: Jane Wilk Sterry 1200 sq.ft.

We carry the unusual in fabrics. Latest books, patterns and notions. Classes. Antique quilt repair! Commission quilts. We are in our 22nd year!

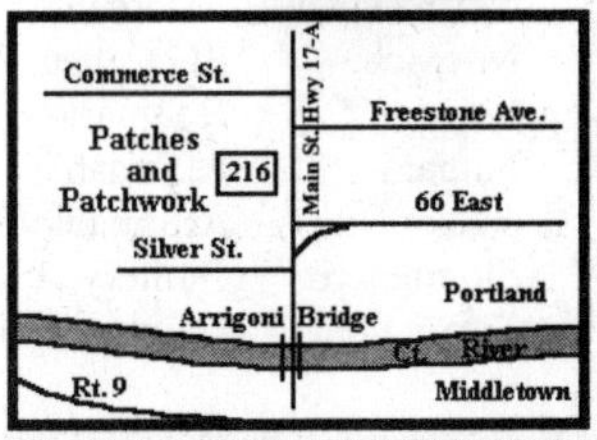

Colchester, CT #10

Mon - Fri 9 - 6
Thur til 8
Sat 9:30 - 5
Sun 10 - 5

Colchester Mill Fabrics

120 Lebanon Ave. 06415
(860) 537-2004 Fax: (860) 537-5239
E-Mail: cherylcmf@cs.com
Est: 1974 16,000 sq.ft.

Full Line Fabric Store specializing in Quilting Name brand fabrics, battings, books, gifts and quilting supplies.

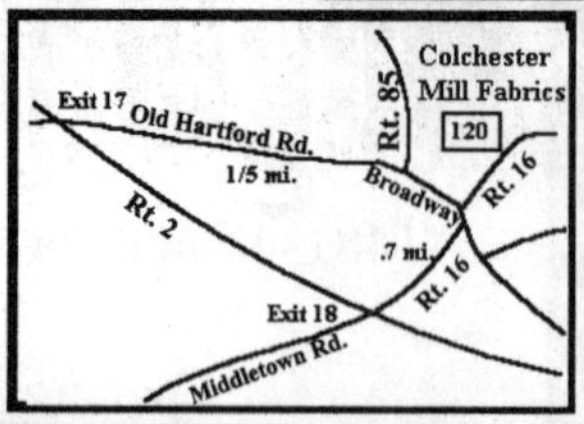

Branford, CT #11

Tues - Sat 10 - 5

Quilter's Habitat

131 Montowese St. 06405
(203) 488-2321
E-Mail: QHabitat@aol.com
Owner: Cher Hurney
Est: 1998 650 sq.ft.
1000 Bolts

Charming, friendly, Colorful store, Classes, Custom orders, Hard to find tools and fabrics (all 100% cotton), Patterns & Books.

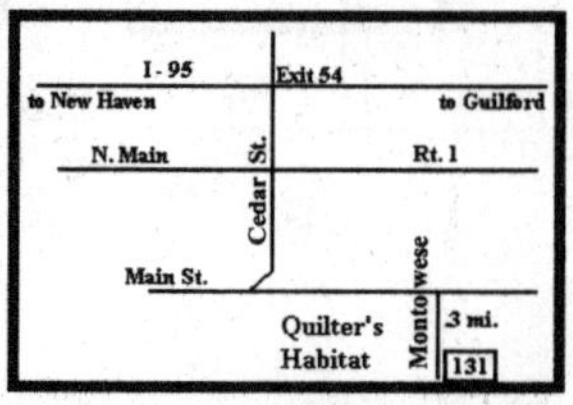

Guilford, CT #12

Calico Alley

1310 Boston Post Rd.
Guilford, CT 06437
Strawberry Hill Plaza
(203) 458-6122
Est: 1992

www.calicoalley.com

IT'S WORTH THE DRIVE

2500+ Bolts of Designer Fabric & 100% Cottons, Notions, & Supplies.
Unique Block of the Month Programs—Check them out on our Website

TUES - FRI 10 - 5 SAT 10 - 4 SUN 12 - 4

Your Fat Quarter Headquarters 8000+ Fat Quarters

COME SEE US SOON !

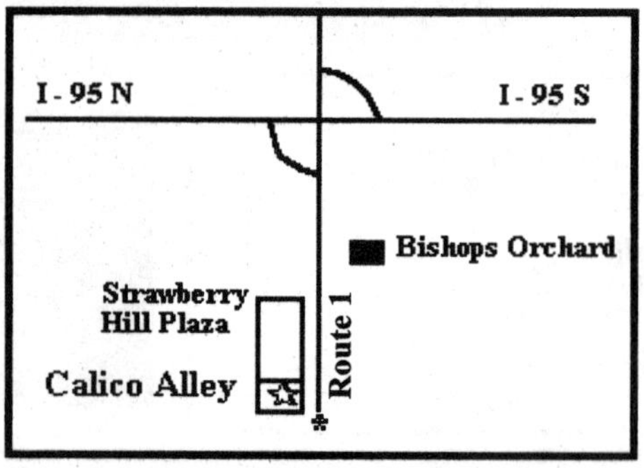

Within minutes of Shoreline Trolley Museum & Thimble Islands
45 minutes from Mystic Seaport
60 minutes from Foxwoods Casino.
From I - 95N take Exit 57. Take a Right.

Other Shops in Connecticut: We suggest calling first

Bethel	Homestead Quilts, 5 Front St.	203-744-3118
Colchester	Wild Geese, 119 Lebanon Ave.	860-537-4010
Cromwell	Fabric Place, 136 Berlin Rd.	203-632-5744
Danbury	Carole's Textiles Inc., 16 Chesokee Dr	203-775-4807
East Haven	The Tail End Workshop, 37 Martin Rd.	203-469-8489
Milford	Affordable Fabrics, 487 Bridgeport Ave.	203-877-0177
Monroe	The Quiltmaker, 24 Countryside Dr.	203-459-1122
New Britain	Ready or Knot Quilts, 311 Lewis Rd.	860-826-7681
New Canaan	Main Street Cellar Antiques, 120 Main	203-966-8348
New Milford	Wild Irish Rows, 135 Carmen Hill Rd. #2	860-355-7131
North Haven	Affordable Fabrics, 151 Washington Ave.	203-239-2301
Norwich	BG Calico, 294 Asylum St.	860-859-3417
Putnam	Jeanmarie's Country Calicos, 42 Chapman St.	860-928-9382
Putnam	Affordable Fabrics, 247 Kennedy Dr.	860-928-4317
Rocky Hill	Affordable Fabrics, 2119 Silar Deane Hwy.	860-563-7647
Stonington	Quiltery, 252 S. Broad St.	860-599-3553
Torrington	Gingham Rocker, 84 Main	860-482-9364

DELAWARE

6 Featured Shops

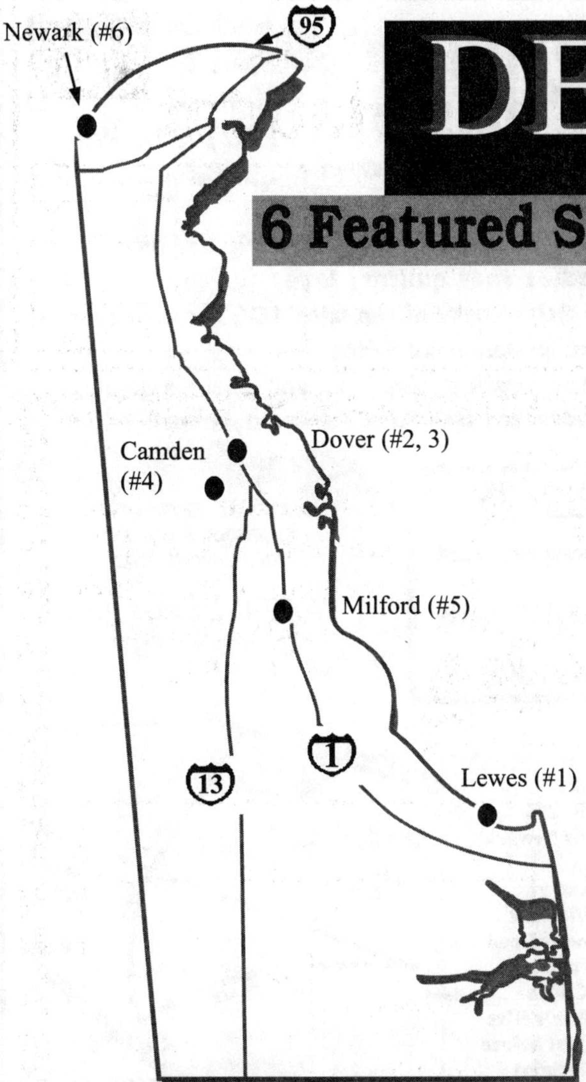

Mare's Bears

QUILT SHOP

Mon - Sat Open 10 am
Sun Open 12 noon

- Fabric
- Notions
- Books & Patterns
- Classes
- Bernina Dealer

At the "Beacon Motel"
528 E. Savannah Rd.
19958
(302) 644-0556
www.maresbearsquiltshop.com
Owner: Maryann McFee
Est: 1995 2000 sq.ft.

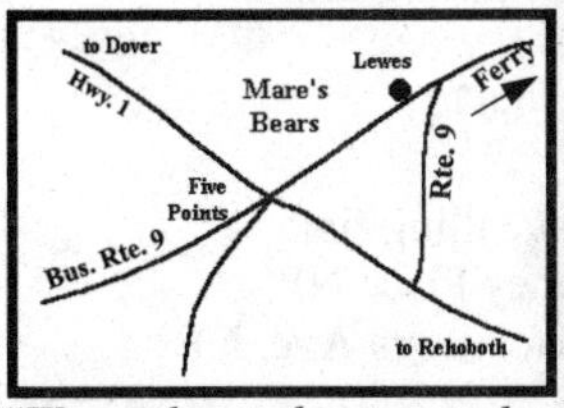

"We are located just over the drawbridge on Savannah Road @ The Beacon Motel"

Lewes, DE #1

Dover, DE #2

Shady Lane Selections

Mon, Tues, Wed 8 - 5
Fri 8 - 7
Sat 8 - 4

1121 Victory Chapel Rd. 19904
Owner: Salina Yoder
Est: 1982 moved to new location in Jan 2001
1500 sq.ft. 500+ Bolts

Quilts in all sizes — We do special orders. Custom Hand Quilting. Lots of small crafts, rag rugs, etc. Fabric from Hoffman, RJR, P&B, etc.

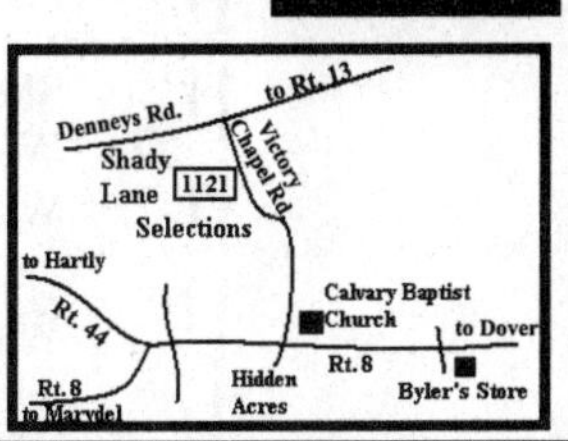

Delaware Sewing Centers, Inc.

Mon - Sat 10 - 5:30

3 Great Locations to Serve You

Owners: Wilson & Joan Reed
(800) 231-9030
E-Mail: crystaland company@hotmail.com
Web: www.delawaresewing.com

Dover, DE #3 (302) 674-9030
Rodney Village Shop. Ctr.

Camden, DE #4 (302) 697-2445
8 N. Main St.

Milford, DE #5 (302) 422-9009
235 Milford Shop. Ctr.

While visiting Delaware's beaches, take time to see each one of our shops. Authorized Singer and Janome dealers, computer software and a complete line of cabinets, sergers and accessories. Classes every day. Full line of quilting, bridal and children fabrics. Stop by to say Hi.

Quilter's Hive

fabric classes supplies

1800 Capitol Trail, Suite 2
Newark, DE 19711
(302) 737-5699
quilthive@aol.com

2800 sq. ft. of all the fabric, gadgets and goodies that quilters love
- over 2000 bolts of the latest 100% cotton fabrics
- books, patterns and notions
- classes frombeginning hand and machine quilting to advanced Baltimore Album- style applique

HOURS
10 - 5 Monday thru Saturday
Open til 8 PM Wednesday
1 - 5 Sunday

Newark, DE #6
LOCATED AT THE CORNER OF KIRKWOOD HIGHWAY AND HARMONY ROAD

TAX FREE SHOPPING CLOSE TO I-95

From I-95 take Exit 3 on to Rt 273 West (towards Newark) Turn right on Harmony Road at the first traffic light Follow Harmony Road for 2.1 miles and turn left into the Calico Corners/Quilter's Hive parking lot (just before the 5th traffic light)

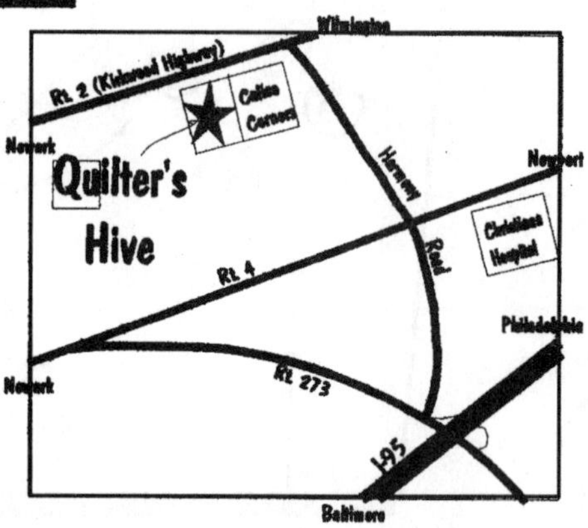

Other Shops in Delaware: We suggest calling first

Laurel Homestead Shoppe, Rt. 64, Box 179 302-875-2017
Newark Quilting Factory, 27 Albe Dr. 302-838-8677

Shops in the District of Columbia: We suggest calling first

Washington Daughter of Dorcas, 1109 Abbey Place NE
Washington Appalachian Spring, 50 Massachusetts Ave. NE 202-682-0505
Washington Applachian Spring, 1415 Wisconsin Ave. NW 202-337-5780
Washington Kathryn Berenson Quilts, 3453 Newark St. NW 301-718-0570

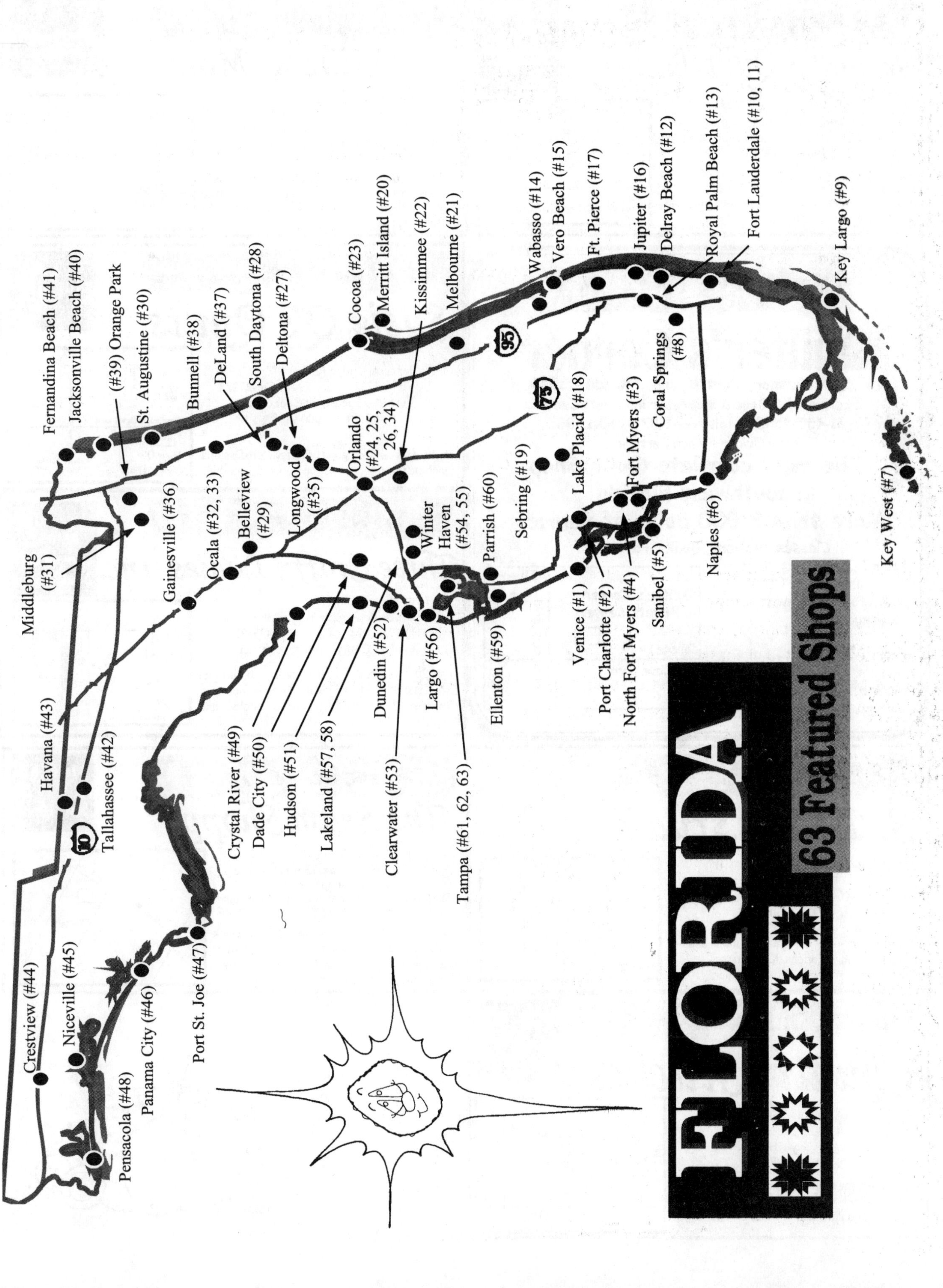
FLORIDA
63 Featured Shops
Fernandina Beach (#41)
Jacksonville Beach (#40)
(#39) Orange Park
St. Augustine (#30)
Bunnell (#38)
DeLand (#37)
South Daytona (#28)
Deltona (#27)
Cocoa (#23)
Merritt Island (#20)
Kissimmee (#22)
Melbourne (#21)
Wabasso (#14)
Vero Beach (#15)
Ft. Pierce (#17)
Jupiter (#16)
Delray Beach (#12)
Royal Palm Beach (#13)
Fort Lauderdale (#10, 11)
Key Largo (#9)
Key West (#7)
Coral Springs (#8)
Fort Myers (#3)
Lake Placid (#18)
Sebring (#19)
Parrish (#60)
Winter Haven (#54, 55)
Orlando (#24, 25, 26, 34)
Longwood (#35)
Belleview (#29)
Ocala (#32, 33)
Gainesville (#36)
Middleburg (#31)
Naples (#6)
Sanibel (#5)
North Fort Myers (#4)
Port Charlotte (#2)
Venice (#1)
Ellenton (#59)
Tampa (#61, 62, 63)
Largo (#56)
Clearwater (#53)
Dunedin (#52)
Lakeland (#57, 58)
Hudson (#51)
Dade City (#50)
Crystal River (#49)
Havana (#43)
Tallahassee (#42)
Port St. Joe (#47)
Panama City (#46)
Niceville (#45)
Crestview (#44)
Pensacola (#48)
10
75
95

Venice, FL #1

Mon - Fri 10 - 5
Sat 10 - 2
Closed Sat. May - Sept.

Deborah's Quilt Basket

337 W. Venice Ave. 34285
(941) 488-6866 Fax: Same
E-Mail: debsquiltbasket@aol.com
Est: 1984 2000 Bolts

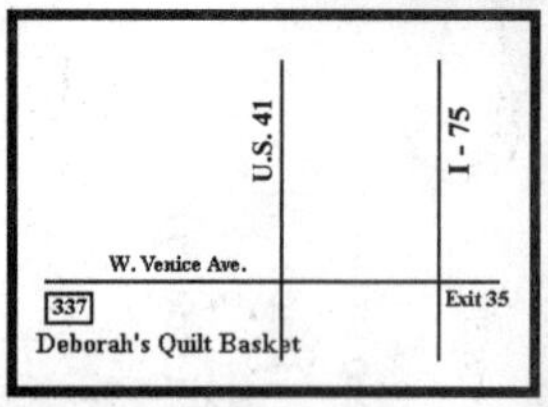

Visit historic downtown Venice. See a large variety of fabrics in addition to lots of books, patterns, notions and gifts.

Port Charlotte, FL #2

Mon - Fri 9:30 - 5
Sat 9:30 - 4

Quilts n' More

17753 Toledo Blade Blvd #4D 33948
(941) 255-9330
E-Mail: quiltsnmore@earthlink.net
Owner: Elaine L. Hamlin
Est: 2000 1800 sq. ft.

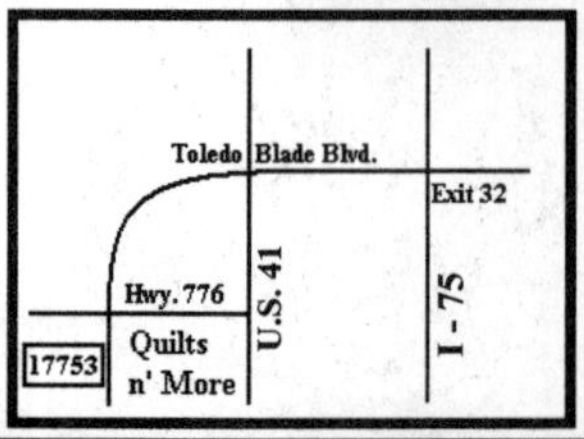

2000+ bolts of 100% cotton fabrics, books, notions, patterns, classes. Janome authorized dealer. Horn cabinets. Friendly, helpful customer service.

Ft. Myers, FL #3

Quilter's Corner

12729 McGregor, Fort Myers, Florida 33919
NE corner of College & McGregor in Pewett Center
941-437-4555 or toll-free 1-877-265-2996
New Owner - Alice Ferriola

The most complete Quilt Shop in southwest Florida

More than 3,000 bolts of fabric

Classes, Notions, Books, Patterns

From I-75 S - exit 22 at Colonial. West to US 41, south to College, west to McGregor.

From I-75 N, exit 21 at Daniels. West on Daniels to McGregor, then north to College.

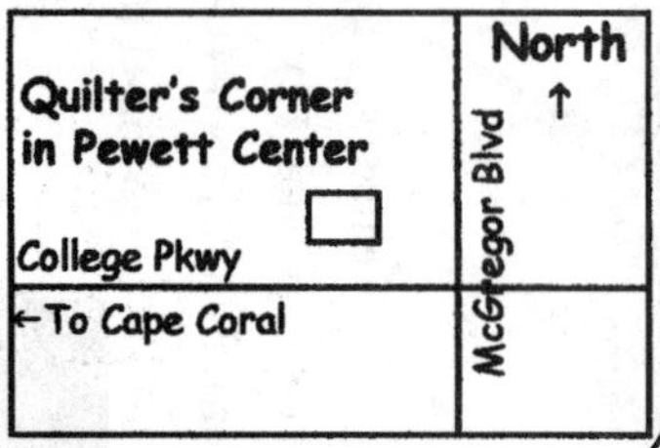

North Fort Myers, FL #4

Tues - Sat 10 - 4:30
Tues 7- 9

Susie Q's Quilts

4150 Hancock Bridge Pkwy. #17 33903
(941) 656-2722 Fax: (941) 656-2722
E-Mail: susieqsquilt@aol.com
Est: 2001 1000 sq. ft.

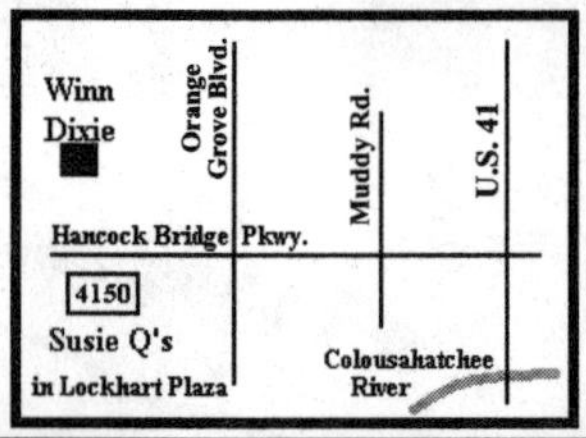

Susie Q's - for great fabrics, professional machine quilting, classes and good fellowship!

Sanibel, FL #5

Everyday 9:30 - 5
Closed Sun May - Sept

Three Crafty Ladies, Inc.

1620 Periwinkle Way 33957
(941) 472-2893 Fax: (941) 433-9316
E-Mail: Craftyladies@webtv.net

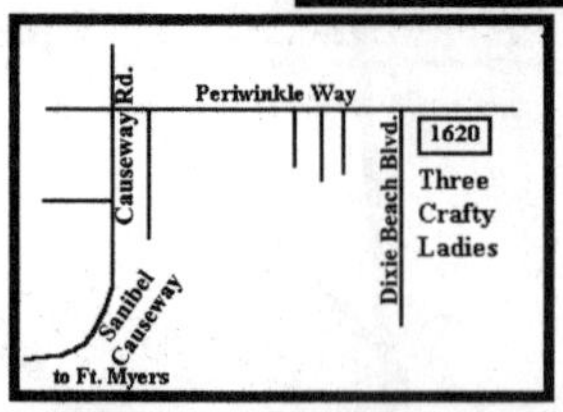

Over 2000 Quilting Fabrics featuring batiks and fish, shell, and tropical prints—including Hoffman. Quilting patterns, books and supplies.

Naples, FL #6

S. E. W. Studio

2360 Immokalee Rd. 34110
(941) 598-3752 Fax: Same
Owner: Rita Decker
Est: 1992 1600 sq.ft.

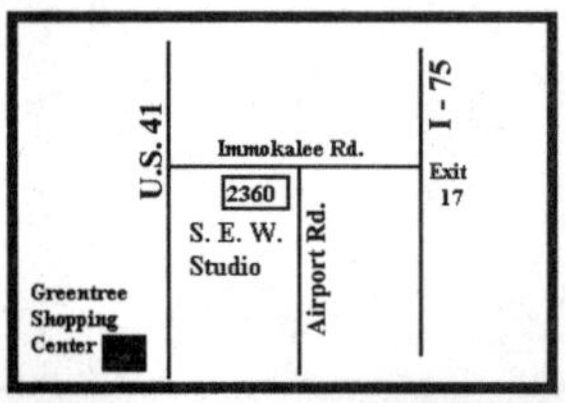

Unique collection of top quality cottons and silks for quilting, Notions, Kits, Classes. Authorized PFAFF and Brother Dealer.

Key West, FL #7

Mon - Fri 9 - 6
Sat 10 - 2

The Seam Shoppe

1114 Truman Ave. 33040
(305) 296-9830 Fax: (305) 296-9630
E-Mail: seamshoppe@aol.com
Web site: www.tropicalfabricsonline.com
Owners: Cindy & Doug Meyer Est: 1986

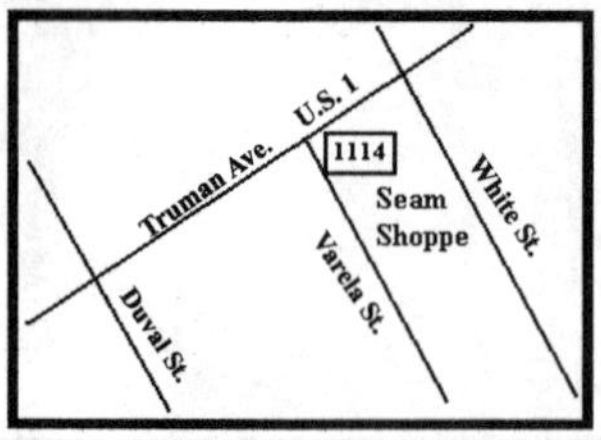

Quilters and Fabric Collectors ! We stock mostly tropical fabrics for fashion, quilting and upholstery including palms, batiks, florals and vintage look.

Coral Springs, FL #8

Mon - Sat 10 - 5
Sun 12 - 4

Country Stitches

11471 W. Sample Road 33065
(954) 755-2411
Owner: Gayle Boshek
Est: 1982 3200 sq.ft.

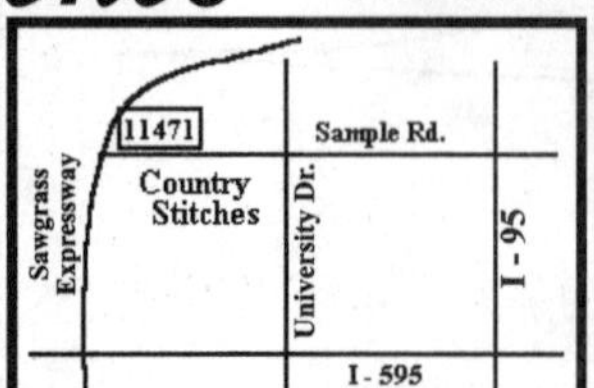

Your one stop Quilting Shoppe.
Over 3000 bolts of fabric and patterns !
You'll be glad you came !

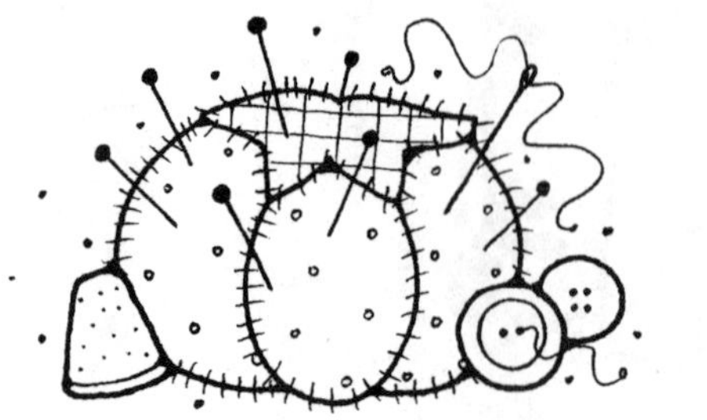

LARGEST QUILT SHOP IN SOUTH FLORIDA

EXOTIC TREASURES

Mile Marker 103 Bayside
103100 Overseas Hwy.,
Suite 53, Key Largo, FL
33037
(305) 451-0268
E-mail: adyjen@aol.com

Key Largo, FL #9

Mon - Sat 10:00 AM to 6:00 PM

Unique and Unusual Fabrics from Around the World specializing in Indonesian Batik and Czech Beads.

Also Hoffman, Kaufman,
Paula Nedlestern Fabrics and Many More.

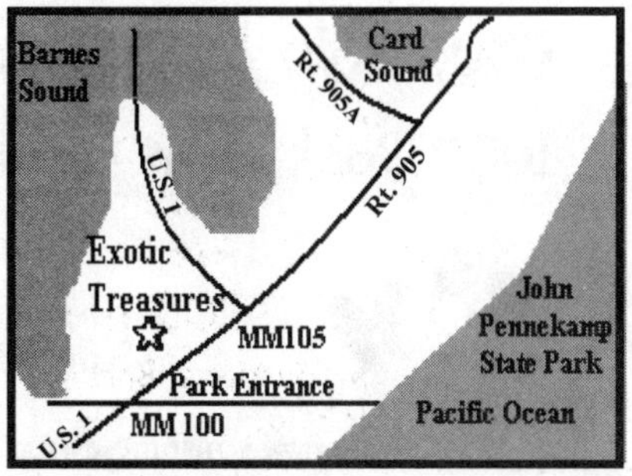

ONCE UPON A QUILT, CO.

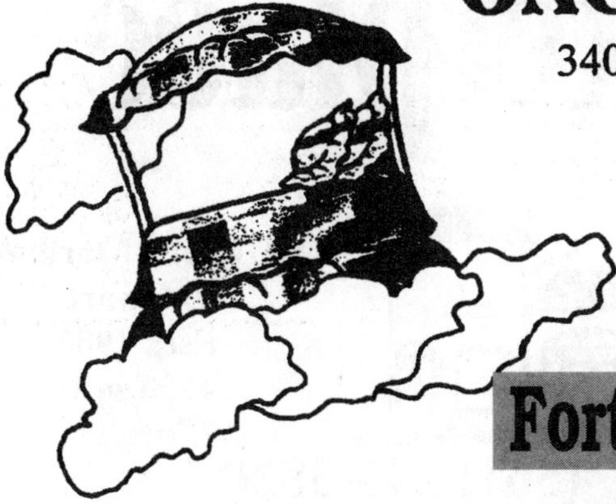

3404 Griffin Road * Ft. Lauderdale * Florida * 33312
954/987-8827 email: ouaq@aol.com

We invite you to visit us in person or
shop with us online 24/7 at...
www.onceuponaquilt.com

SHOP HOURS
9:30 – 4:30
Monday – Saturday

Fort Lauderdale, FL #10

2500 Bolts of 100 % Cotton Fabrics

Books * Videos * Software * Patterns
Notions * Silk & Wire Edged Ribbon
Embellishments* Unique Gift Items
Classes and much more...

A Friendly Staff and a
Warm & Welcome Atmosphere

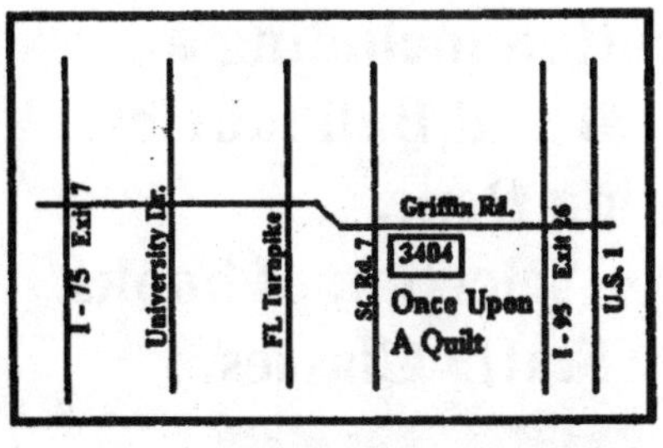

4 Miles From The Hlwd/Ft. Lauderdale Airport

PROUD SPONSORS OF QUILT SHOW BY THE SEA
Shows on the even # Years
Next show March 2004

Visit our website
www.onceuponaquilt.com

click the Lighthouse for up – to – date show information.

Fort Lauderdale, FL #11

SUNSHINE SEWING COMPANY

Authorized Janome Dealer

1312 N. State Rd. 7, Margate, FL 33063

* Fort Lauderdale Area *

Tel: (954) 971-4810 ~ Fax: (954) 972-0035

LARGEST QUILT SHOP IN SOUTH FLORIDA

6000 Bolts of 100% Cotton Fabric ~ 1000 Batiks

1000 Book Titles ~ Classes ~ Computer Programs

Notions ~ Patterns

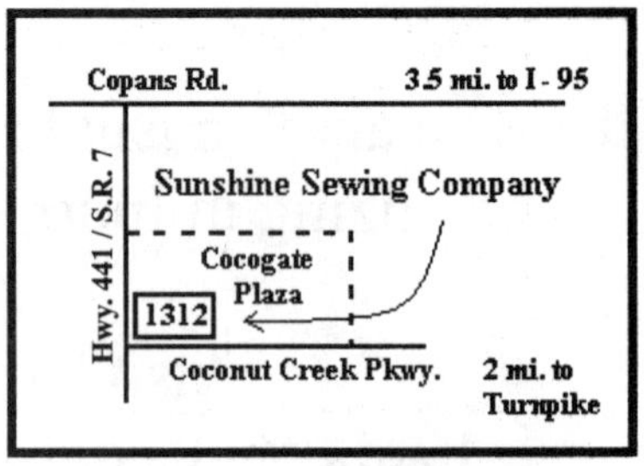

Store Hours: M,T,W,F 10-5; Th 10-9; Sat 10-4

Web Site: www.sunshinesewing.com

Email: sewwithfay@aol.com

Quilters Marketplace

Mon - Sat
10 - 5

Owner: Marilyn Dorwart
Est: 1987
4000 sq.ft

524 E. Atlantic Avenue 33483 (561) 243-3820

Web Site: www.quiltersmaketplace.net

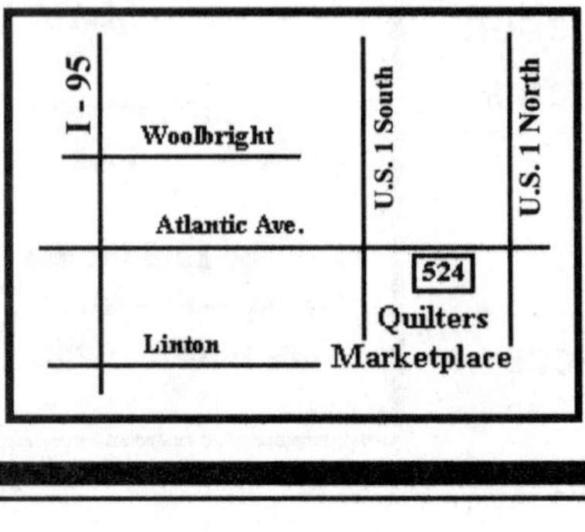

1200 bolts of 100% cotton including a beautiful array of tropical and Bali fabrics.
Complete Notion Dept.
Many patterns and a large selection of books.
Gifts and a Friendly Staff. Classes.

Delray Beach, FL #12

Est: 1988

follow me to ...

Suzanne's QUILT SHOP Inc

Shop our online catalog, secure transactions & worldwide shipping
www.suzannesquilts.com

Owner: Suzanne Leimer

1112 Royal Palm Beach Blvd. 33411
(561) 798-0934
Fax: (561) 798-3767

Monday - Saturday 10 - 5:30
Evenings During Classes

Royal Palm Beach, FL #13

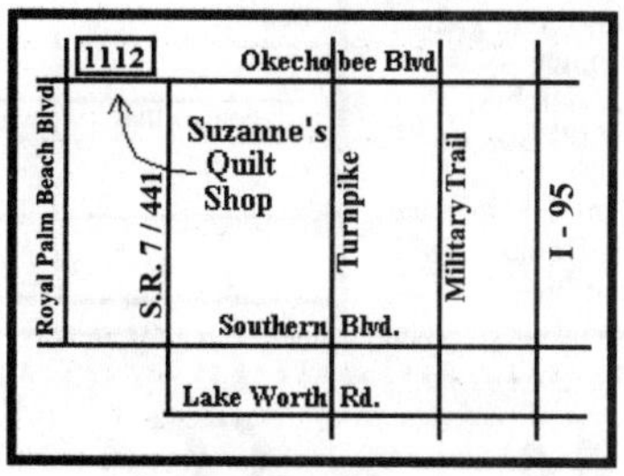

6 miles West of Florida Turnpike West Palm Beach exit

4000 Bolts of 100% Cotton Fabrics
Antique Reproductions, Aunt Grace's, Batiks, Orientals, Florals, Thimbleberries, Debbie Mumm, Flannels, Felt, Tropicals, Juvenile Prints, Plaids & Christmas.
Paper Foundations * Silk Ribbon Embroidery * Wire Edged Ribbon
Electric Quilt Software & Books
Books & Patterns for Quilts, Clothing, Dolls, Santas, Bears & Bunnies
Quilt Planning * Classes & Private Lessons

Marilou's Quilting & Sewing Centers

TWO GREAT SHOPS!

Custom Machine Quilting, Quilting Supplies, Fabric, Books, Classes, Husqvarna Viking Sewing Machines, Sales and Service. Quilts for sale.

Wabasso, FL #14

8802 N U.S. Hwy 1, P.O. Box 337
Wabasso, FL 32970
(772) 589-0011
Fax: (772) 388-5722
Est: 1996

Mon - Fri 10 - 6
Sat 10 - 5

Vero Beach, FL #15

2122 58th Avenue, Ryanwood Sq.
Vero Beach, FL 32966
(772) 770-5883
Fax: (772) 770-5773
Est: 2001

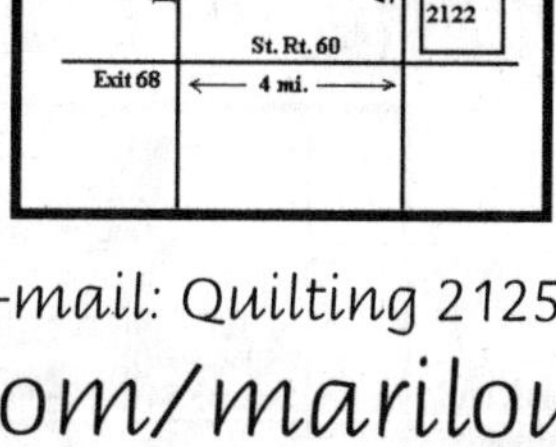

Owners: Stan Kahn & Marilou Keen e-mail: Quilting 2125@aol.com
www.vikingdealer.com/marilous

1500 bolts of 100% cotton. Complete selection of Notions, Books & Patterns. Authorized Bernina Dealer. Great classes and friendly service. Machine Quilting Service Provided on our Gammill Quilt Machine.

Quilters' Choice

661 Maplewood Dr. #14 33458
(561) 747-0525 Fax: (561) 747-0267
E-Mail: quilterschoicefl@aol.com Est: 1992
Owner: Vivian Irwin 3000 sq.ft.

Mon - Fri 10 - 5
Sat 10 - 4

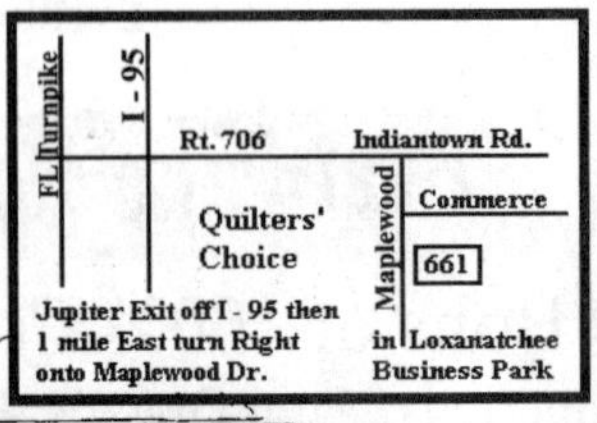

Jupiter, FL #16

Ft. Pierce, FL #17

Mon & Wed - Sat 9 - 5

Tomorrow's Heirlooms

1840 S. King's Hwy. 34945
(561) 461-9510
Owners: Theresa & Earle Field
800 Bolts

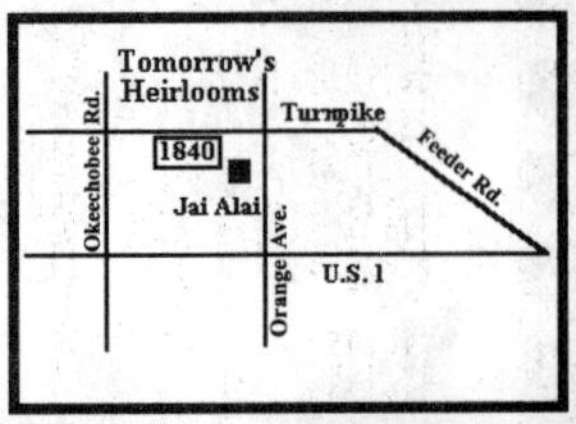

100% Cottons, Quilting Patterns, Quilting Supplies, Instruction Books.

Lake Placid, FL #18

Tues - Fri 10 - 5
Sat 9 - 1

Sew-Biz

299 Interlake Blvd. 33852
(863) 699-2228 Fax: (863) 699-2272
E-Mail: sewbiz@htn.net
Owner: Paul & Nancy Vasilchik
Est: 1992 2400 sq. ft. 1000 Bolts.

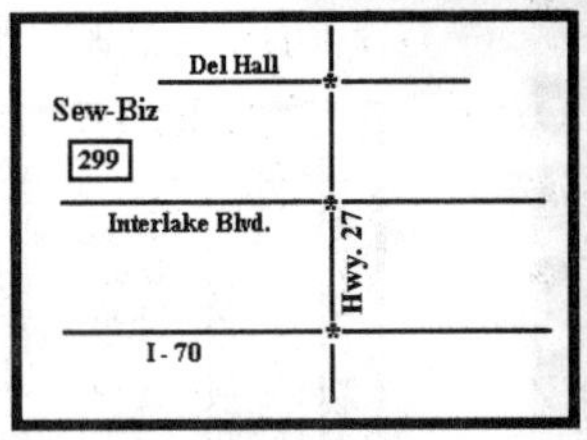

Home of Fish Bowl Fun, Little Fishie and many other Quilt Patterns & Books. Enjoy fellowship with fellow fabricholics.

Sebring, FL #19

Crafty Quilters

4920 U.S. 27 South 33870
(863) 382-4422 Est: 1990
E-Mail: shdee@strato.net
Owner: Dee Dee Bedard

Mon - Fri 9 - 5
Sat 9 - 3

For all your Quilting Needs.
Quilting Frames.
Classes Available.
Factory Authorized Dealer of New Home & Janome.
Repairs on all Machines.

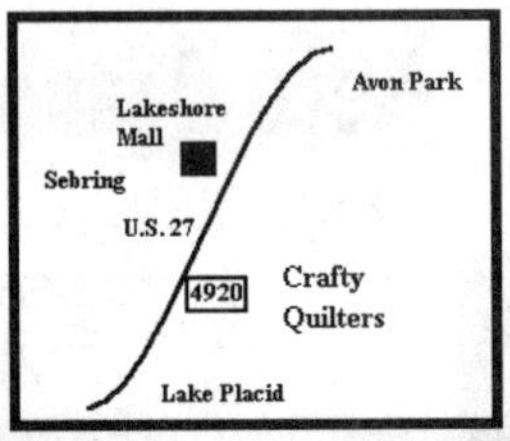

Thimbles & Thread

275 Magnolia Ave. #6 32952
(321) 456-5685
Fax: (321) 456-5774
E-Mail: Quilts1999@aol.com
Web: www.thimblesandthread.com
Est: 1996 2000 sq.ft.

Mon - Sat 10 - 5
Tues & Thur 10 til 7

Books - Patterns
Notions - Classes
Mail Order - Decorative Thread
100% Cotton thread in 1200 yards and 6000 yd. spools.

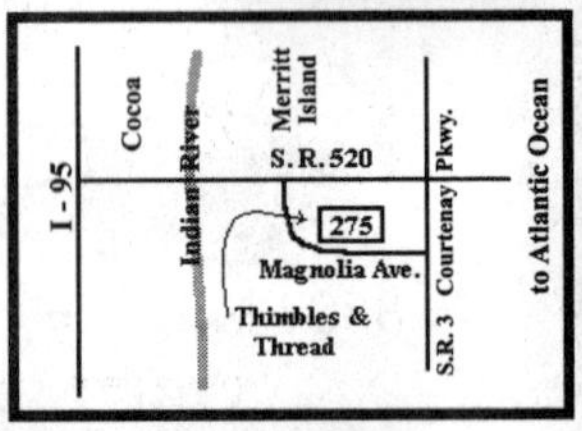

Merritt Island, FL #20

Melbourne, FL #21

Mon - Fri 9:30 - 6
Sat 9:30 - 4

Willow n Hare Quiltworks

1800 W Hibiscus Blvd #108 32901
(321) 951-7977
Owner: Susan A. Schering
Est: 2002 2000+ sq. ft.

Nestled in "The Oaks", we offer a wonderful selection of cotton fabrics, patterns, notions & classes with a friendly experienced staff.

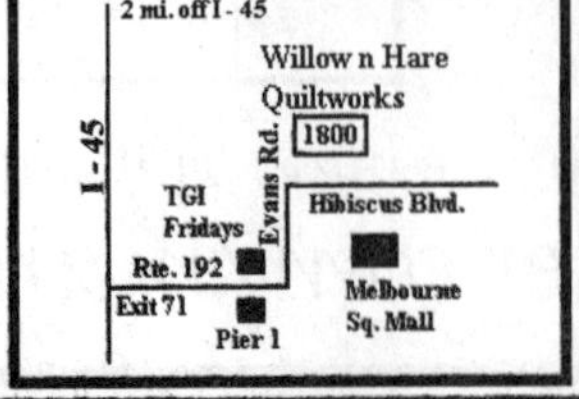

Kissimmee, FL #22

Mon - Sat 10 - 5
Tues til 9

Queen Ann's Lace

715 East Vine Street 34744
(407) 846-7998
Owners: Ginny & Tom King
Est: 1991 4500 sq.ft.

3500 Bolts of 100% Cotton
plus supplies, notions, & patterns
Everything you'll need.
Decorative Art Painting & Doll Supplies.

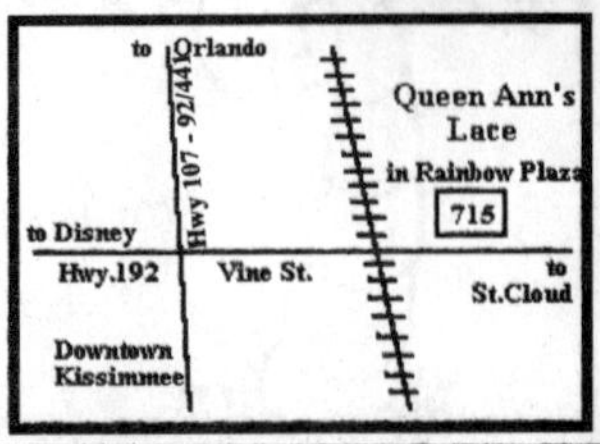

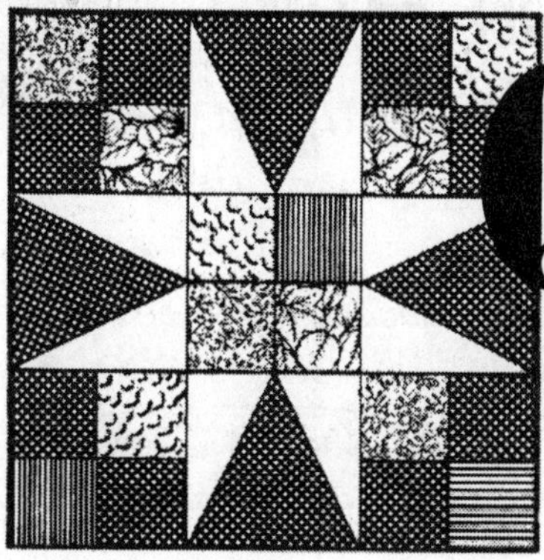

Cocoa, FL #23

Quilting Folks

(321) 631-8601

1300 N. Cocoa Blvd. Suite C

Owners: Linda Joseph & Bernadette Schecher

E-Mail: FLQuilts@aol.com

Authorized Dealer For Bernina, Janome, Elna

Full Line Quilt & Sew Shop

Over 2,000 Bolts of 100% Cotton Fabric

- Hoffman
- Batiks
- RJR & Thimbleberries
- Moda
- South Seas
- Large selection of Flannel & Homespuns
- Much, much more!

BERNINA

JANOME

elna

Mon - Fri 10 - 5
Sat 10 - 4

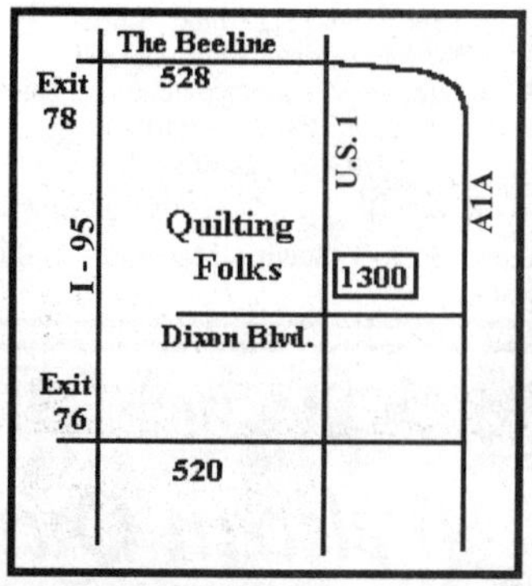

Orlando, FL #24

Sewing Gallery

407-281-0446

11913 E. Colonial Dr. (Alafaya Cummins)

E-Mail: FLQuilts@aol.com **2000 sq.ft. showroom**

Owners: Linda & Gabe Joseph

Mon - Fri
10 - 6
Sat 10 - 4

Fabric Companies:

- Hoffman
- RJR
- South Seas
- P & B
- Benartex
- Kona Bay

Fully Stocked With:

- Fabrics
- Patterns
- Books
- Notions
- Mats
- Everything A Quilter Needs.

Factory Authorized Dealer For:

♦ Janome ♦ New Home ♦ Singer

We also specialize in: Bernina, Viking, Elna, PFAFF, White, Babylock & Brother

"L☺☺k"

We also have our own 12 foot Long Arm Quilting Machine

We ship all over the World!

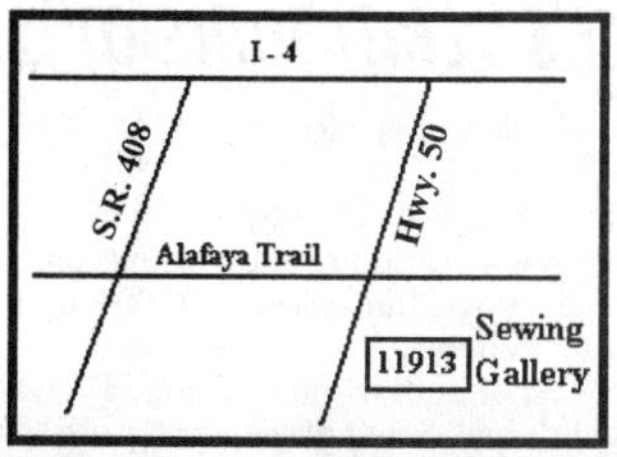

Orlando, FL #25

Please call first
We may be moving
Mon - Sat 11 - 5

Firefly Antiques

929 N. Mills Ave. 32803
(407) 898-7888 Est: 1985
Owners: John Roberts & Chris Lee

A Full-Line Antique Shop Generally with 15 - 20 Older Quilts The Most Eclectic Selection In The Mickey Mouse Region Collectibles, Vintage Clothing & Jewelry

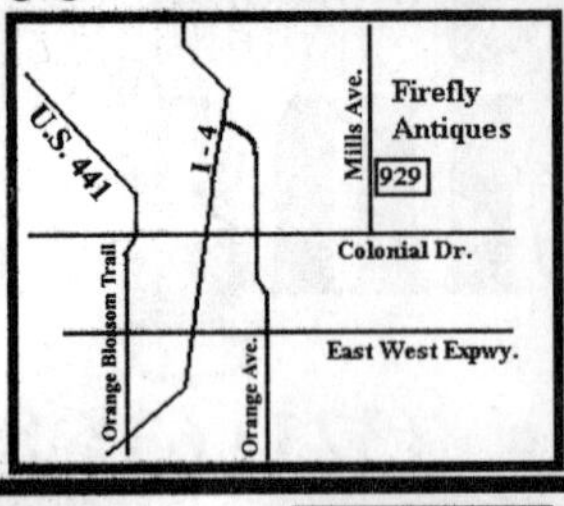

Deltona, FL #27

Mon - Sat
9:30 - 5

Country Patch Quilt Shop

777 Deltona Blvd., Suite 28 32725
(386) 860-7272 Fax: Same
E-Mail: eearthal@mpinet.net
Web Site: www.countrypatchquilts.com
Owner: Estaleen Earthal
Est: 1996 1800 sq.ft.

1200 Bolts of quality Fabric. Quilt/Sewing Classes. PFAFF Sewing Machines. Software Classes.

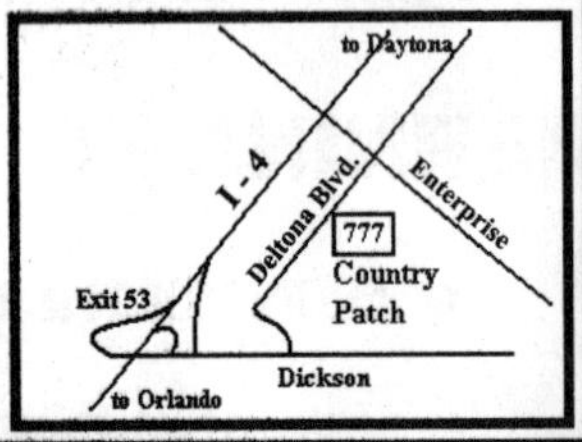

The Good Home Quilt Company

Mon - Sat
9:30 - 5:30
Thur til 7

5600 W. Colonial Dr. #309 32808
(407) 523-3612 Fax: (407) 523-3613
E-Mail: goodhomequiltco@aol.com
Owner: Carol Crago Est: 1999 1000+ Bolts

Primitive folkart look, traditional and reproduction fabrics, patterns, books, rughooking, hand-dyed wool, stitchery and much more.

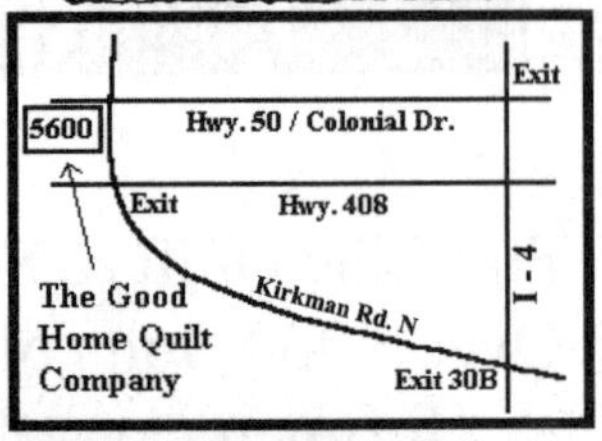

Orlando, FL #26

South Daytona, FL #28

Mon - Fri
9:30 - 4:30
Sat 9:30 - 3

Pelican Quiltworks

905 Big Tree Rd. 32119
(386) 761-8879 or (888) 566-8879
Web Site: www.pelicanquiltworks.com
Owner: Michelle Ross

Quilting, Cloth Dolls & Silk Ribbon. We stock 100% Premium Quality Cotton. Fabrics and Kits for small projects. A wide variety of Books, Patterns & Cloth Doll Supplies available. Classes & Workshop offered. Several B.O.M. Programs

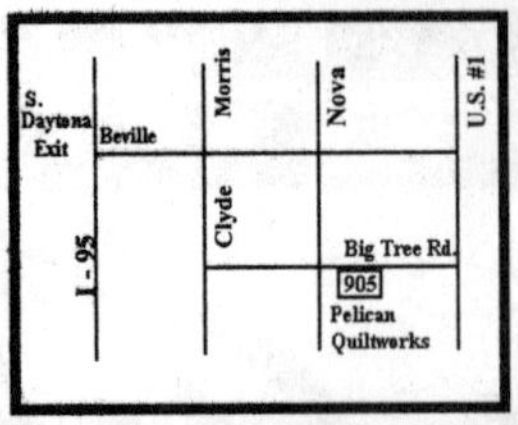

Belleview, FL #29

Mon - Fri
9 - 5
Sat 9 - 3

Fabric Stash
Quilting and Heirloom Shop

11781 SE U.S. Hwy. 441 34420
(352) 245-3989
E-Mail: fabricstash@bigfoot.com
Web Site: www.fabricstashusa.com
Owner: Janet Bunn
A Quilt Shop and More!
Quality notions, books, patterns & upscale 100% cotton fabrics, warm & personal assistance. Viking Dealer.

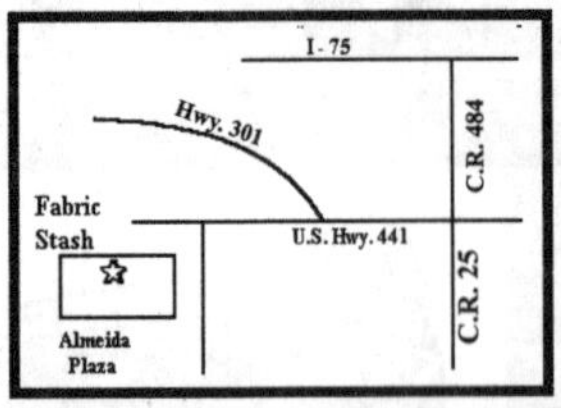

Saint Augustine, FL #30

Mon- Fri
10 - 5
Sat 10 - 4

Material Things

77 Saragossa St. 32084
(904) 829-3778
Owner: Joyce Snyder
E-mail: Materialthings quiltshop@yahoo.com
Est: 1991 1575 sq.ft. 1000+ Bolts

Most beautiful selection of 100% cottons in the area. Wide variety of books, patterns, notions and classes.

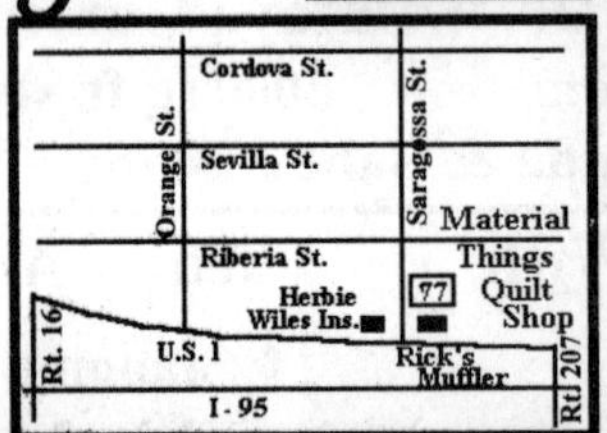

Ocala, FL #32

M, W, F
9:30 - 5
T, Th til 6
Sat 9:30 - 3

Peggy's Heirlooms of Tomorrow

2400 SW College Rd. 34474
(352) 351-8282 fax: (352) 351-3926
E-Mail: peggysheirlooms@aol.com
Web Site: www.heirloomsoftomorrow.com
Owner: Peggy Vogt, Licensed 3700+ sq.ft.
Martha Pullen Heirloom Instructor.
Enjoy the best of both worlds: "Quilting" and "Heirloom" Sewing! Featuring Thimbleberries, Northcott, Hoffman, RJR, Chanteclaire; Homespuns to Batiste!

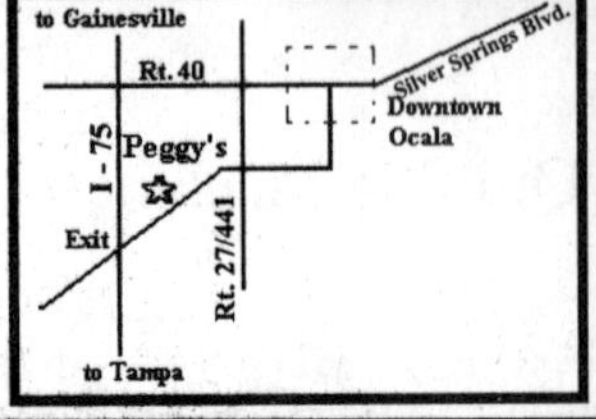

LADY BUG QUILT SHOP

Tues - Fri
11 - 6
Sat 10 - 4

We are located 13.5 miles south from 295 & Blanding Blvd. Left side of the road in the Watson Realty Shopping Center. We carry 100% cotton fabric and a unique line of animal prints. Northcott, Michael Miller, Moda, Hi Fashion, Benartex, South Seas and many other varieties. We have a great line of Batiks & Flannels. We carry books, patterns, notions, offer classes and completed quilts & wall hangings for sale. We have excellent customer service. Hope to see you soon and travel safe.

2751 Blanding Blvd., #106 32068
(904) 282-2120
E-Mail: Flyingx@bellsouth.net
www.ladybugquiltshop.com
Est: 2001 1500+ Bolts.

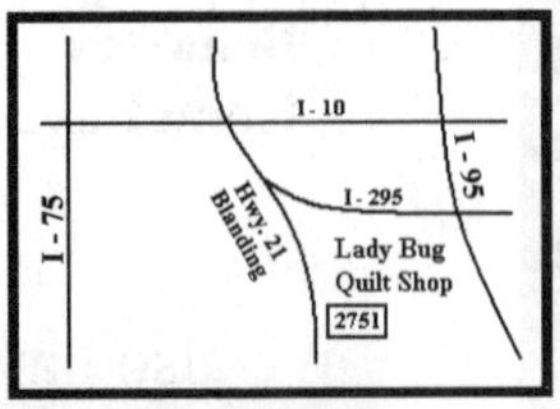

Middleburg, FL #31

Whippoorwill Station

Hours: Mon - Fri 9:30 - 5:30
Sat 9:30 - 3 PM

Ocala, FL #33

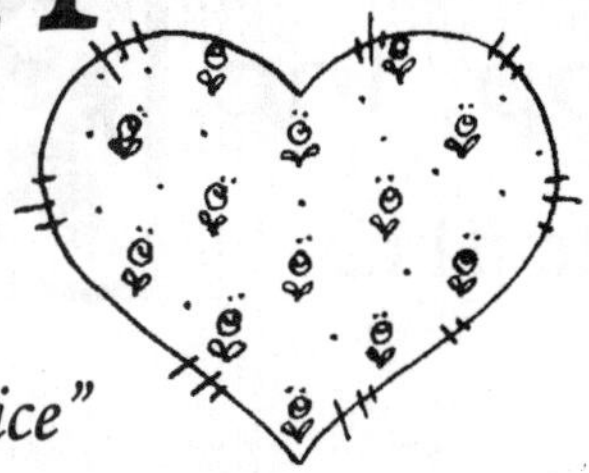

"Great, friendly service"

3115 E. Silver Springs Blvd. 34470
(352) 690-1914 E-Mail ~ Whip3437@aol.com
Owner: Billie J. Clark
Ocala's foremost Quilt shop

Distinctively different comes to mind when you explore our quilt and gift shop, you will find 100% cotton fabric for the Quilter's dream. We also have a wonderful selection of fabric for your next craft or sewing project. Over 3,500 bolts of fabric and growing.

Northcott.... Hoffman.... RJR.... P&B....
Moda.... Kings Road.... Thimbleberries...
In The Beginning.... Clothworks....
Vintage & Reproductions.... Much, Much More....

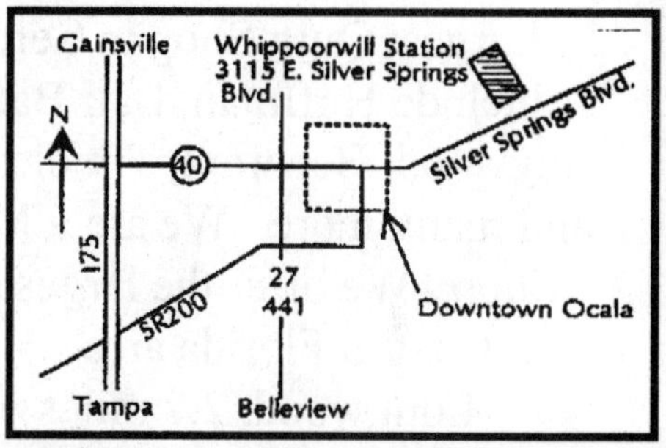

Classes forming.... Call for a schedule....

Visiting Orlando ? Don't miss - - -

The Sewing Studio

FABRIC SUPERSTORE

Central Florida's Largest Selection of Quilting Fabrics

Orlando, FL #34

9605 S. Hwy. 17-92 Maitland, FL 32751
800-831-1492 407-831-6488
www.sewing.net

Mon - Fri 9:00 - 8:30
Sat 9:00 - 5:30 Sun 12 - 5

- ★Full Quilting Dept.: Fabrics, Patterns, and Books
- ★Full Line of Quilting Notions
- ★Smocking & Heirloom: Fabrics, Patterns and Plates
- ★Huge Selection of Bridal & Evening Wear Fabrics
- ★Lycra, Spandex, Stretch Velvets, Crushed Velvets
- ★Silks, Linens, Trims, Notions
- ★Buttons, Buttons, Buttons
- ★Don't Forget to Visit our Bargain Annex—Next Door!
- ★We have many 'Hard to Find' Items!

1/4 miles N. of Maitland Overpass on Hwy. 17-92

Busy Fingers

Quilt Shop, Inc.

460 North C. R. 427, Suite #112
Longwood, FL 32750
(407) 767-5123
www.ourbusyfingers.com

Mon - Fri
10 - 5
Sat 9 - 3

Longwood, FL #35

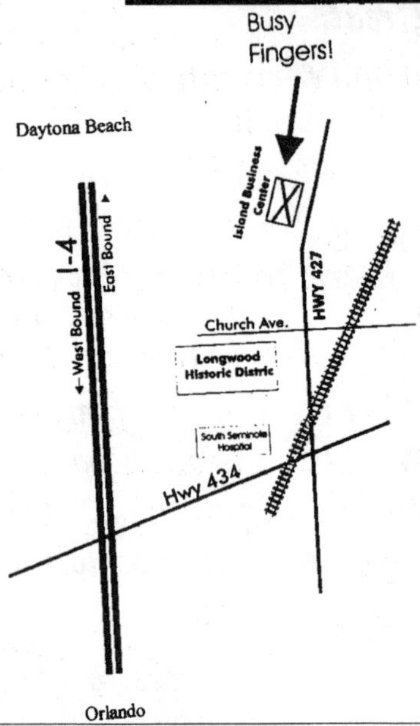

Largest Quilt Shop in Seminole County. Our fabrics include Hoffman, Bali Batiks, Moda, RJR, Orientals, Maywood, Benartex, Timeless Treasures, Marcus Brothers and many more. We are a Martingale Publishing Premier Shop. We offer the largest class selection in the entire Central Florida area. We are located in Historic Longwood, 2.7 miles east of I - 4 off S.R. 434.

My Favorite Quilt Shop

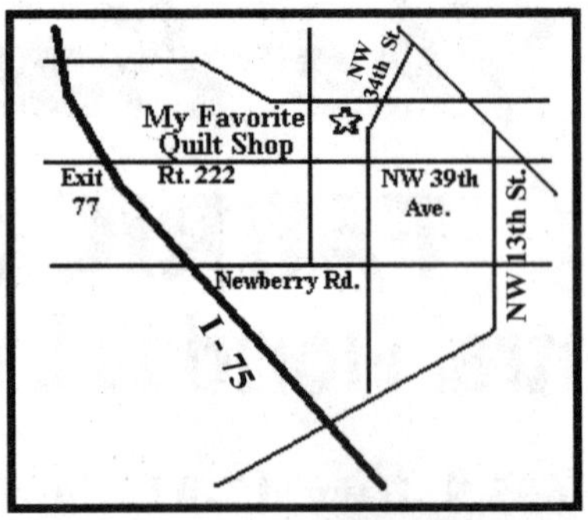

5110 NW 34th St. 32605
(352) 372-4720 Fax: (352) 372-1222
Owner: Mary E. Derry Est: 1995 4000 sq.ft.
E-Mail: MaryEDerry@msn.com

M, T, W, F
10 - 5:30
Th 12 - 8:30
Sat 10 - 4

North Central Florida's finest Quilt Shop.
4000 sq. ft. filled with the world's Best Quilting Fabrics, Notions, Books and Patterns.
Gold Standard Bernina Dealer
E-Z on-off I - 75 Take Exit #77 (New#390)
WE LOVE QUILTERS

Gainesville, FL #36

DeLand, FL #37

Quilt Shop of DeLand, Inc.

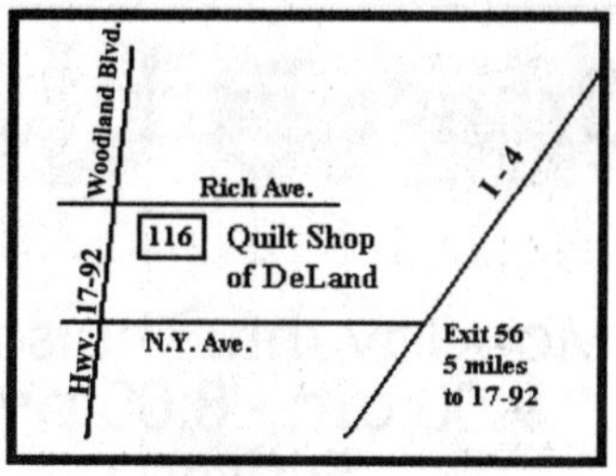

Featuring the Newest Fabrics, Patterns & Books on the Market
Located in the beautiful downtown Historic District.
And within walking distance of Stetson University

Come by for some refreshments and leisurely browse through our selection of 100% cotton fabrics.

Ask about our upcoming class schedules.

116 E. Rich Ave.
DeLand, FL 32724
386-734-8782
Owner: Judy Hansen
Est: 2001
quiltshopofdeland@hotmail.com
www.quiltshopofdeland.com

EXPERIENCE THE PERSONAL TOUCH

Mon - Sat 10 - 5

Bunnell, FL #38

The Sew & Quilt Shop

Authorized Bernina® Dealer

(386) 586-5409
4601 E. Hwy. 100 32110
Fax (386) 586-5291
Email: info@sewandquiltshop.com
Web site: www.sewandquiltshop.com
Est: 2001 3300 sq.ft.

Free Inspiration & Advice Always Available

- 2000 bolts and growing
- "Block of the Month"
- "Thimbleberries Club"
- Large selection of Quality 100% cotton fabrics, "Kits", gift items, books, patterns, and notions
- Knowledgeable and Friendly staff and welcoming and Fun atmosphere
- Quality classes and teachers
- Gift Certificates
- Bus Tours and Quilt Guilds welcome (please call ahead) so we can have the coffee on!
- Professional Machine Quilting

Make sure and visit us while in the area. We've been told that we're worth the trip!

Mon - Fri 10 - 5
Tues 10 - 8 Sat 10 - 3

BERNINA

Bernina Sewing & Embroidery Machines & Sergers & Horn of America Cabinets.

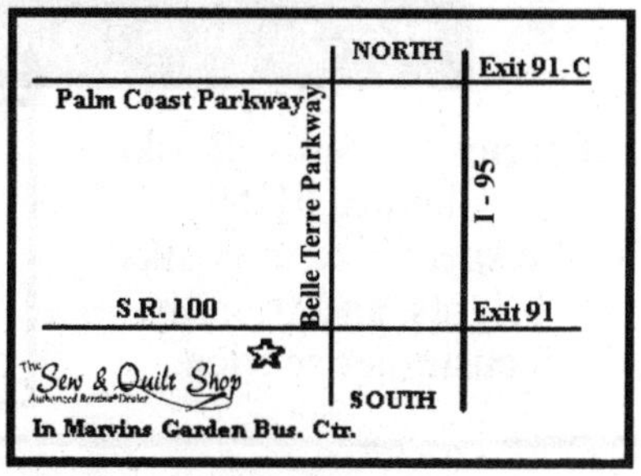

2 miles West of I - 95,
20 miles north of Daytona Beach
20 miles South of St. Augustine

Orange Park, FL #39

Monday thru Thursday
9:00 am - 8:00 pm
Friday
9:00 am - 5:00 pm
Saturday
10:00 am - 5:00 pm

Calico Station

1857 Wells Road
Orange Park, Florida
32073
1-904-269-6911

www.calicostation.com

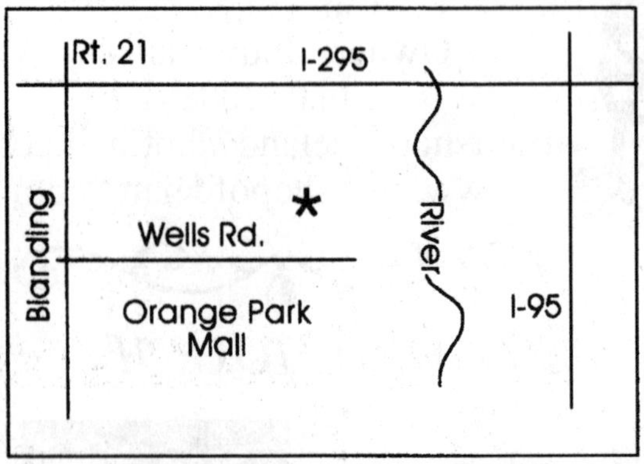

Exit Route 21 south off Interstate 295
turn left on Wells Road
turn left at the second light

North Florida's largest quilt shop.
In business for 22 years!

Over 2500 bolts of premium 100% cotton fabrics
Patterns, books, kits, threads
Long Arm quilting machine

Email: calstation1@aol.com
Website: www.calicostation.com

Jacksonville Beach, FL #40

BEACHES QUILT SHOP

1486 South 3rd St. 32250
(904) 246-6644
www.geocities.com/beachesquiltshop
Owners: Beth Nielsen-Gildea, Cheryl Wills & Nancy Trumbull
E-Mail: Beachesqlt@aol.com Est: 1998 1000 Bolts

Mon - Sat 10 - 5 Tues & Thur til 9

Fabrics, Patterns, Books, Classes, FUN!
We specialize in Batiks, brights, and friendly customer service.

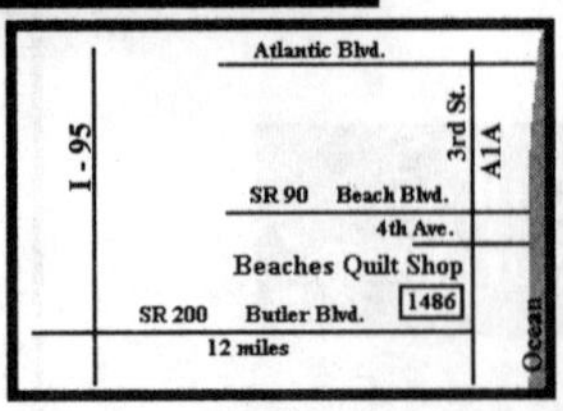

Fernandina Beach, FL #41

Jan's Quilt Shop

Wed, Fri, Sat 10 - 4 or by appt.

599 Nassauville Rd. (CR 107 S) 32034
(904) 261-9432 (800) 261-9698
E-Mail: jan@jansquiltshop.com
Web Site: www.jansquiltshop.com
Owner: Jan Stokes

Nestled in the pines, a warm welcome awaits you at Northeast Florida's newest quilt shop -- 1300+ bolts of 100% quality fabrics -- plus notions -- patterns -- books.

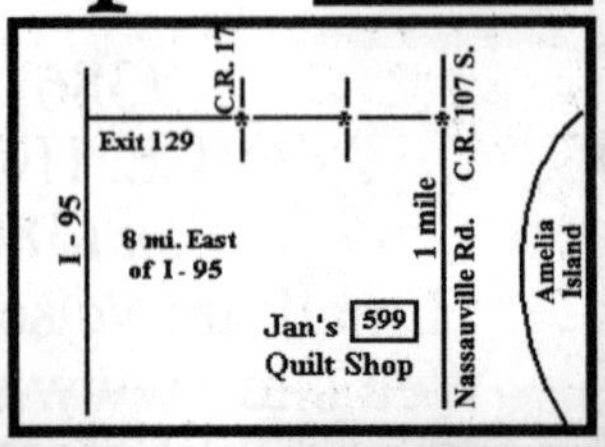

Tallahassee, FL #42

The Quilting Patch

Tues - Fri 9:30 - 5:30
Sat 9:30 - 4:30

1989 Capital Circle, NE #9 32308
(850) 553-4650 Fax: (850) 553-4672
E-Mail: quiltpatch@nettally.com
Owner: Kris Hebert
Est: 1999 2600 sq.ft. 1400 Bolts

100% cotton fabrics, notions, books, patterns, silk ribbon, threads. Husqvarna Viking Sewing Machines. Classes, Classes, Classes!

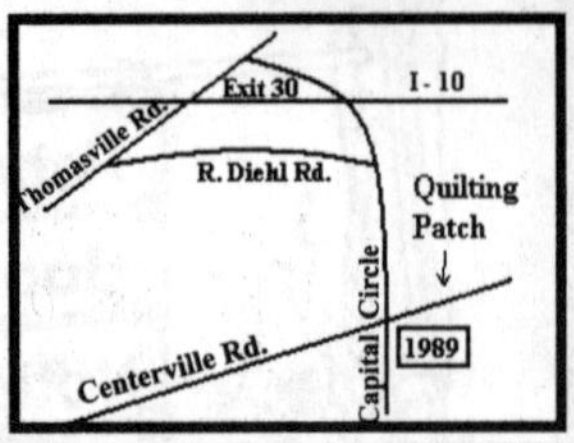

Pieceful Quilting

11350 Florida/Georgia Hwy.
(Route 27N) 32333
(850) 539-6522
Fax: (229) 872-3763
PiecefulQuilting@allteal.net
Est: 2001 1000 sq.ft.

Mon - Thurs 10 - 7
Fri 10 - 5 Sat 11 - 5

- 2000+ Bolts of 100% cotton at discount prices
- Books & Patterns
- Sewing Notions
- Classes
- Gifts for Quilters
- Friendly, helpful Customer Service.

Havana, FL #43

Constantly Growing
to be Your
Premier Quilt Shop

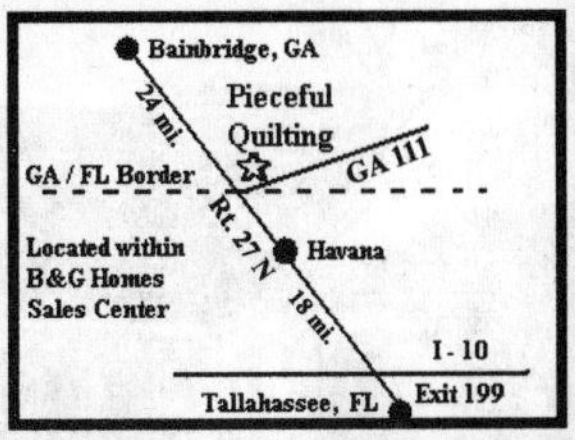

Margie's Nylon & Lace

Since 1971

2014 Lacey Ln. 32526 866-739-6274 (Toll Free)
(850) 682-6920 Fax: Same
E-Mail: margies@cyou
sew2000.com/sewwithmargies/
or www.sewwithmargies.com

Bernina Janome

Largest Independent Fabric Shop in Florida's Panhandle. Classes for all interests (garments to quilting) Fabrics include, Bridal, Party, Children, Knits, Quilt etc. Over 3000 bolts of fabric, over 700 book titles, quilting supplies.

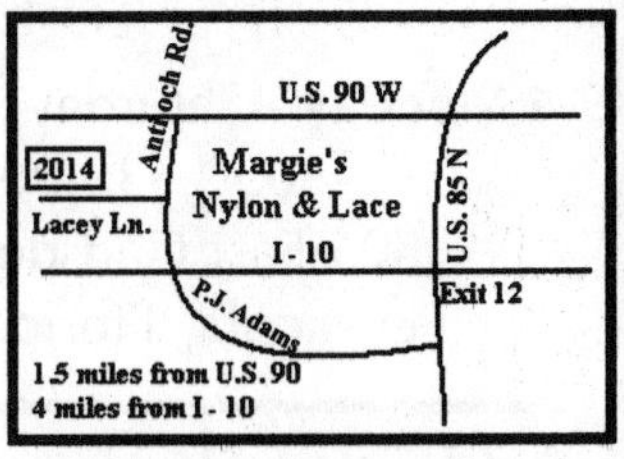

Mon - Sat 9am - 6pm

Crestview, FL #44

Niceville, FL #45

Mon - Sat 9:30 - 5

Terri Cloth, Inc.

93 John Sims Pkwy. 32578
(850) 678-7283
E-Mail: tccloth@aol.com
Owner: Terry Casey
Est: 1989 2200 sq.ft.

On the Florida Panhandle, we have the largest selection of 100% cotton from leading manufacturers. Notions, Books & Patterns.

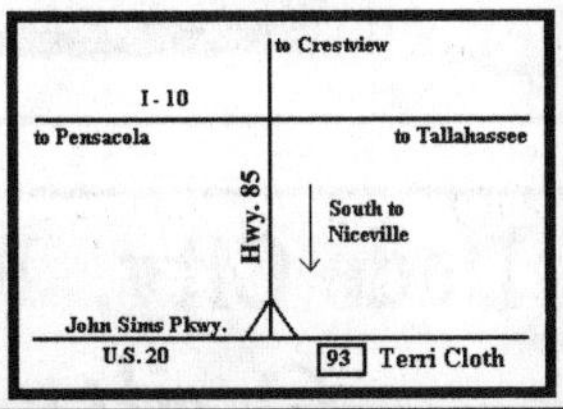

Panama City, FL #46

Quilting by the Bay

2303 Winona Drive
Panama City, FL 32405
(850) 215-7282
www.quiltingbythebay.com

Quilting by the Bay
Panama City, Florida

A wonderful selection of fabric, books, patterns and notions. Classes for all skill levels. Friendly, knowledgeable staff.

Monday through Saturday 10:00 AM to 6:00 PM
Tuesday 10:00 AM to 8:00 PM

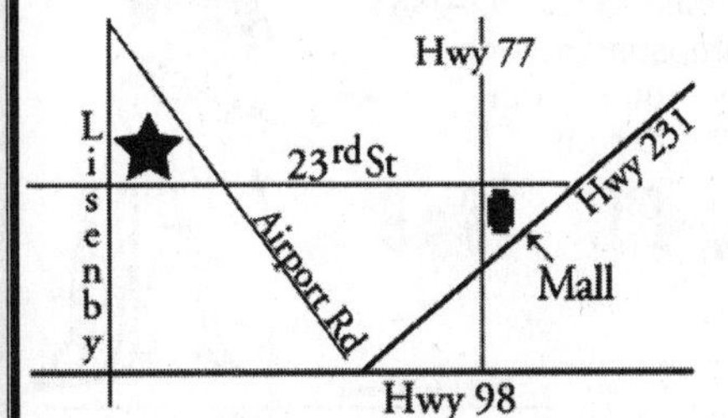

- *Just North of 23rd Street between Airport and Lisenby*
- *3 miles E of Hathaway Bridge*
- *3 miles W of PC Mall*

NEEDLES AND THREAD INC.

A QUILT SHOP

Port St. Joe, FL #47

Warm, Friendly family-like shop.

VON BOUINGTON
G. "SUSIE" PIPPIN

Fine Fabrics -- 100% Cotton -- Top Companies
All Notions -- Collector's Thimbles -- Books
Sewing Machines -- 1500 Bolts
Most Fabric $5.99 yd.

Mon - Fri 9 - 5:30
Sat 9 - 4

317 Williams Ave. 32456
(850) 227-9880
Fax: (850) 227-9846
quiltgals@gt.com.net

Pensacola, FL #48

Quilt Corner

. . . fine fabrics & notions

Quilt Corner, located in a 100 year old house, has all of your quilting needs. We have Dazor lamps, Dovo scissors, a unique quilting frame that will fit in a motor home or closet. We have silk batts and thread. We also have Bernina and Viking machines for purchase and to use in classes. Over 4,500 bolts of quality fabrics.

9-4 Monday - Saturday, Thursdays til 8
850 439 9080
805 East Gadsden Street
Pensacola, Florida 32501

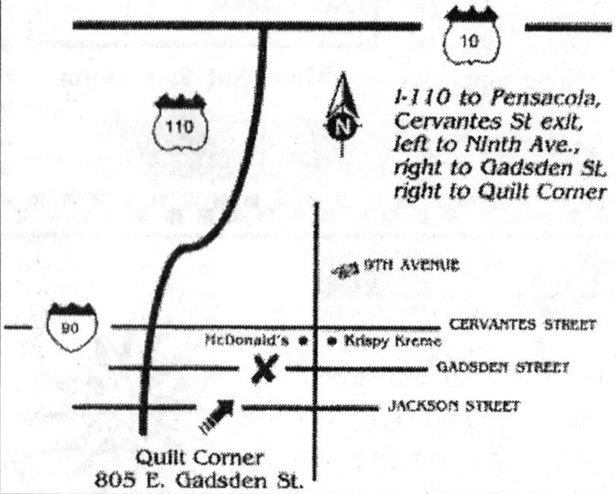

Tomorrow's Treasures

802 N. Suncoast Blvd. (Hwy. 19)
(352) 795-2600 Fax: (352) 795-0883
E-Mail: sew@tampabay.rr.com
Web Site: www.crquilts.com
Est: 1998 2600 sq.ft

Crystal River, FL #49

* Huge Classroom
* Warm & Personal Service
* Distinctive Designs
* Original Patterns
* Kits, Notions & Books
* Large Selection of Stencils
* Mail Order
* 4000 Bolts of the Finest 100% Cotton Quilting Fabrics
* Applique and Novelty Fabrics are our Specialty.
* Check out our website for the latest mystery quilt and free patterns.

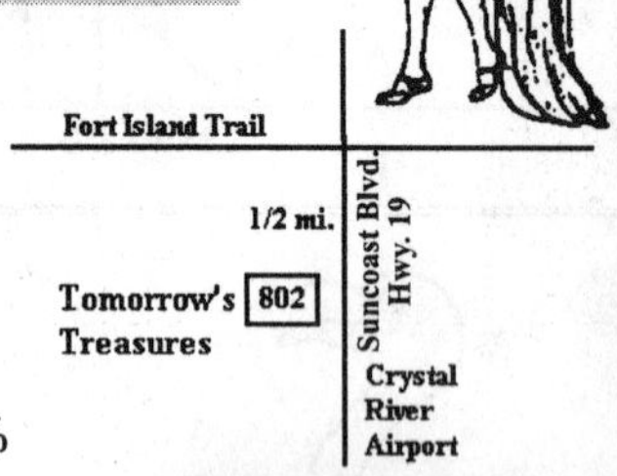

Mon - Sat 9 - 4
Tues 9 - 7
Open Sunday 1 - 4
Oct. thru April

Dade City, FL #50

Mon - Sat 10 - 5

Quilts Etc.

13230 South Hwy. 301 33525
(352) 567-0444 Fax: (352) 567-7255
Owners: Suzanne & Bill Stewart
Est: 1988 4000 sq.ft. 2000 Bolts

Fabric, Large Selection of Pre-Cut Fabrics & Kits, Quilting Supplies, Books, Patterns, and a Sale Porch.

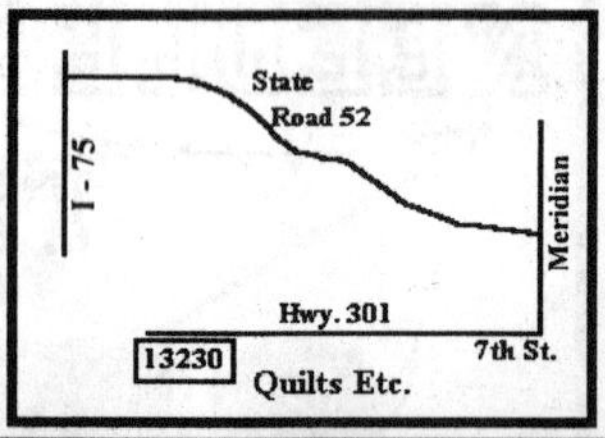

Hudson, FL #51

Tues - Sat 10 - 5
Tues, Thur, Fri 7 - 9 pm also

Quilt Til You Wilt & Sew What? Embroidery

9609 Fulton Ave. 34667
(727) 862-6141 Fax: (727) 868-4765
E-Mail: pipsqeak@gte.net
Owner: Pat Wilkinson
Est: 1998 1600 sq.ft.

Professional machine quilting. Quilt & Bear making classes, Supplies for both. Over 1000 bolts of fabric!! One room of embroidery, for all your professional embroidery needs.

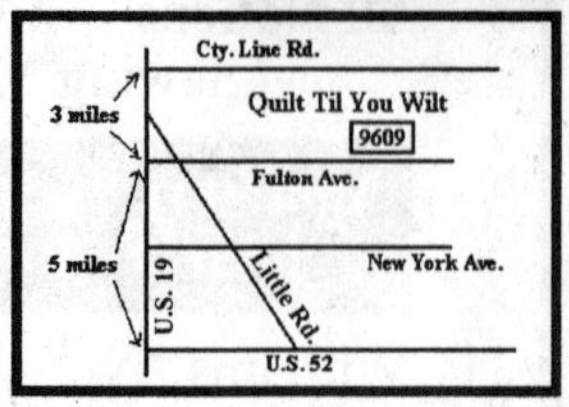

Dunedin, FL #52

RAINBOWS END QUILT SHOPPE

YOUR COMPLETE QUILT SHOPPE

941 BROADWAY STREET (ALT 19) 34698
(727) 733-8572 (800) 353-1928
WWW.RAINBOWS-END.COM
EST: 1982 6900 SQ.FT

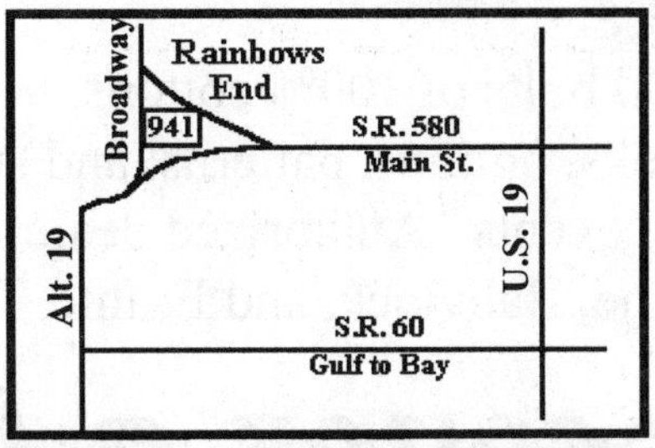

LARGEST QUILT SHOP IN FLORIDA
OVER 7000 BOLTS OF COTTON FABRIC
HUNDREDS OF BOOKS, NOTIONS, PATTERNS & STENCILS
QUILT, WALLHANGING & EMBROIDERY KITS
SILK & WIRE RIBBON -- BOOKS & PATTERNS
STOP & SEE OUR LARGE COLLECTION OF SAMPLES
OF PATTERNS, BOOKS & OUR CLASSES
A PFAFF & ELNA DEALER - SALES & SERVICE

MON - SAT 10 AM-5 PM & WED 10 AM - 8 PM

Country Quilts "N" Bears, Inc

1983 Drew Street 33765
(727) 461-4171 Est: 1986 3300 sq.ft.
Owners: Marilyn & John Humphries

Clearwater, FL #53

Country Store with a Christian Heart

Mon - Fri 9 - 5
Tues til 9
Sat 9 - 4

A fully stocked quilt shop —
3000 bolts of cotton fabrics.
Large selection of flannels.
Friendly Service.
Classes in quilting, country clothing, & miniature bears. Beginner bears, advanced and limited edition Teddy Bear classes taught by Francy Gordon. Mohair, luxury plush acrylic fur, glass eyes, joints and Bear accessories available.

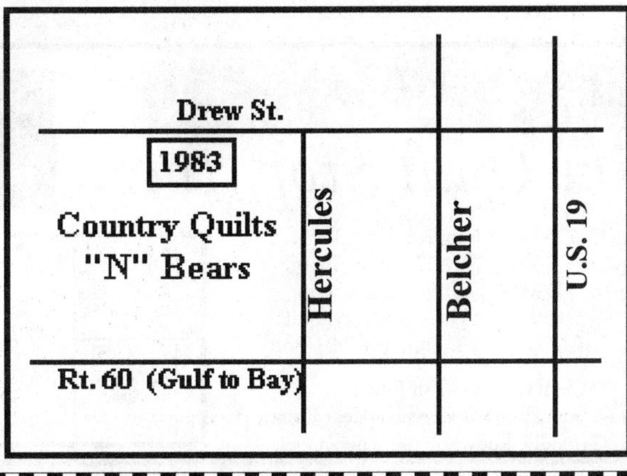

Winter Haven, FL #54

Call for directions
Just 25 minutes off I-4
near Cypress Gardens

AK Sew & Serge

1602 6th Street SE 33880
(863) 299-3080 or (800) 299-8096
Family Owned and Operated Since 1985

Mon - Fri
9 - 5:30
Sat 9 - 4

Over 6000 bolts of 100% cottons, heirloom fabrics, fashion and designer fabrics under one roof. Books, notions, patterns, and supplies. Call or stop in for our schedule of classes and special events. Authorized dealer for Viking, White, Elna, New Home, Singer, Pfaff, Janome, Babylock, and Esante. Your one stop source for all of your sewing needs.

Discover a Quilter's Paradise

Winter Haven, FL #55

Mon - Sat
9 - 5
Fri til 9

Heart to Heart
FABRICS & MORE
QUILTING AND SCRAPBOOK SHOP

102 Post Ave. 33880 (as of 7/02)
(863) 298-8185 fax: (863) 419-0479
Owners: Pat Brenchley & Patricia Roberts
Est: 2000 2000 sq.ft. 1800+ bolts.
Quilting & Scrapbooking Shop Specializing in 100% Cotton Fabrics, Sewing Machine Sales & Service. Acid & Lignin Free Archival Safe Papers, Stickers & Albums for Scrapbooks.

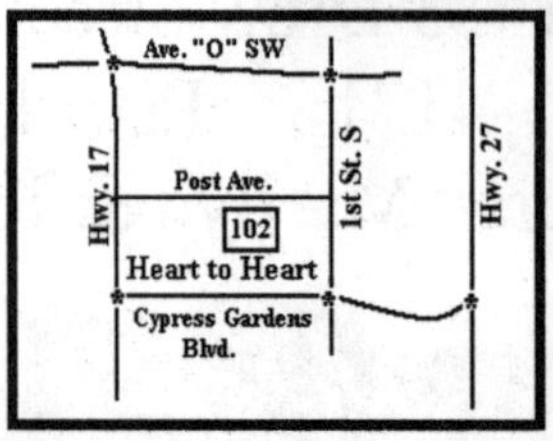

Largo, FL #56

Mon - Fri
10 - 5
Sat 10 - 4

The Quilt Stop, Inc.

7250 Ulmerton Rd. #D 33771
(727) 532-4566
E-Mail: QuiltStop@aol.com
Owners: Michael & Cheryl Solt
Est: 1997 1200 sq.ft. 1500+ Bolts

Over 1500 Bolts of Fine Fabrics.
Notions, Books. Classes - Year Round
Friendly, knowledgeable personnel.

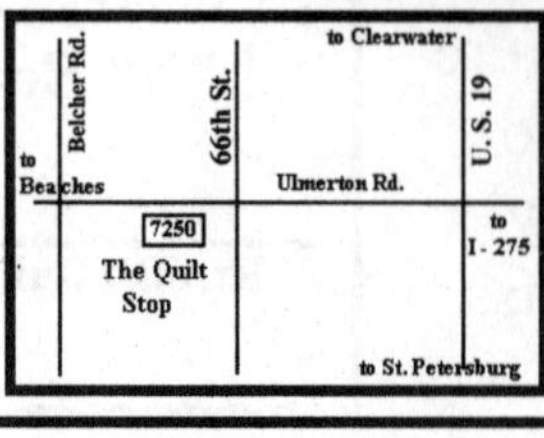

Granny's Trunk

4644 Cleveland
Heights Blvd. 33813
(863) 646-0074
Fax: (863) 646-4329
Owner: Pamela Bell
1500 sq.ft.

Mon - Fri 10 - 5
Sat 10 - 4

Over 2,000 Bolts of
100% Cotton Quilt Fabrics.
Quilt books, Patterns,
Notions.
Bernina & Brother Sewing
Machines.
Machine Embroidery
Supplies.

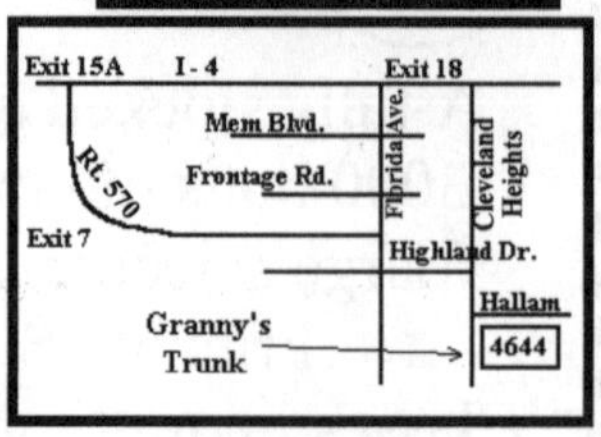

Lakeland, FL #57

Lakeland, FL #58

Mon - Fri 10 - 5
Sun (Oct-May) 10 - 3

The SugarBear Shoppe

2163 S. Combee Rd. 33801
(863) 665-1567
Fax: (863) 665-1699
E-Mail: shoppesugarbear@cs.com

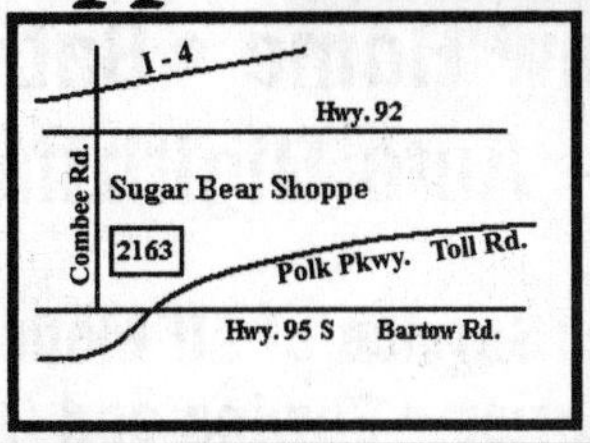

We are a small unique and personable shop with a lot going on and classes scheduled every day. We go the extra mile. Fabrics, Patterns, Books & Notions.

Quilters Haven & More

Ellenton, FL #59

Exceptional Fabric Selection, Knowledgeable & Friendly staff specializing in color coordination. Classes for all Skill Levels. Books, Notions & Patterns. Authorized Sales & Service of Husqvarna Viking Sewing Machines & Sergers. Free Lessons with any Machine Purchased.

Husqvarna VIKING

2418 U.S. Hwy. 301 N 34222
(941) 729-0511 Est: 1996
Owner: Barbara A. Raguso

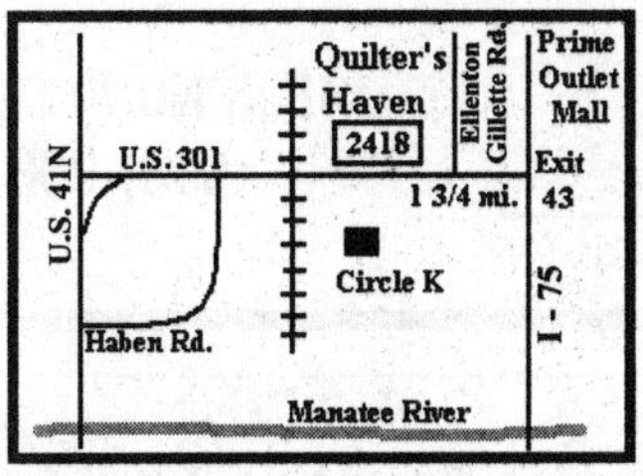

Mon - Fri 9:30 - 4
Summer Tues - Sat 9:30 - 4
Or by Appt.

Conveniently located off I - 75, Exit 43 (Ellenton) turn right on 301 (south), go approx. 1 3/4 miles. We are on right side (north) directly across from Circle K

Parrish, FL #60

Patches Galore, Inc.

Authorized BERNINA Dealer
Classes · Fabrics · Notions
Over 2000 Bolts
Classes in Quilting & Sewing

Mon - Fri 9 - 6
Sat 9 - 4

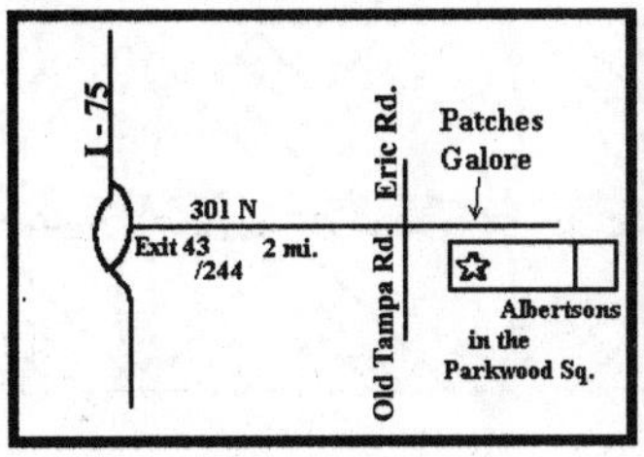

Owners: Lynn Briscoe & Lois Ankrom

www.patchesgaloreinc.com
E-mail: PATCHESART@aol.com

8915 US 301 North
Parrish, FL 34219
Located at Parkwood Square
941.776.5669
Fax 941.776.0742

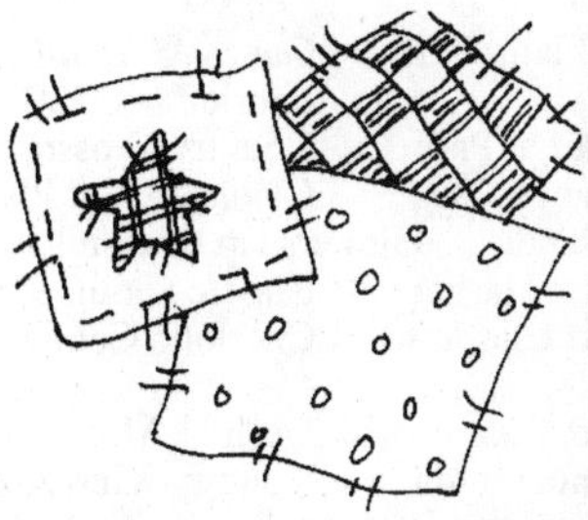

Tampa, FL #61

Mon 9:30 - 8
Tues - Fri 9:30 - 4:30
Sat 9:30 - 3

The Quilted Sampler

4109 S. Mac Dill Ave.
33611
(813) 831-8997

E-Mail: Qsampler@aol.com
Owners: Mischele Hart & Adrienne Tavares

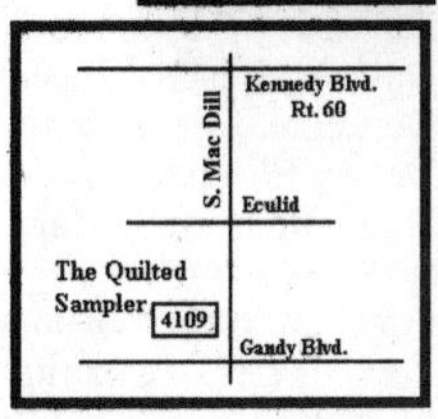

Tampa Bay Area's Premiere Quilt Shop Since 1984

Keep Me In Stitches
A Specialty Sewing Center

Tampa, FL #62 & 63

Authorized Dealers for

Janome/New Home • Baby Lock • Elna
Origins - Auto Digitizing Software

Service of all Models
Classes • Fabrics • Sewing and Quilting Supplies
Sewing Cabinets • Specialty Threads

Website: www.kmisinc.com
E-mail: keepmeinstitches@prodigy.net

Come visit us at either of our locations.
We're the friendly quilters!

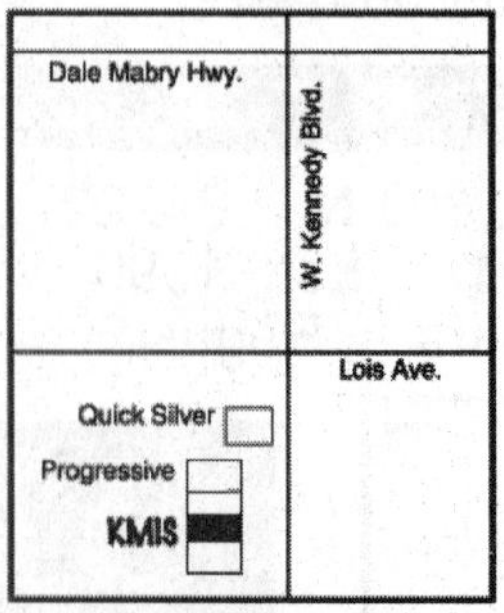

Store Hours Mon. - Sat. 9-5

4237 West Kennedy Blvd. Tampa, FL 33609
(813) 282-1526 • Fax 282-3655

14833 North Dale Mabry Hwy. Tampa, FL 33618
(813) 908-3889 • Fax (813) 908-3898

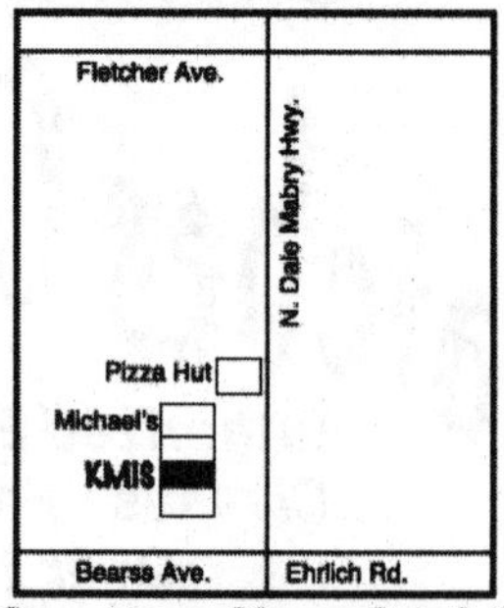

Store Hours Mon. - Sat. 9-5

Other Shops in Florida: We suggest calling first

Big Pine Key	Samantha's, 30883 Dolgado Ln.	305-872-2235
Boca Raton	Country Tyme Antiques, 93 NW 11th	561-391-7749
Crestview	Granny's Attic, 396 S. Main St.	904-682-3041
Dania	Designer Discount Fabrics, 1206 Stirling Rd.	954-923-4229
Davenport	Adventures in Quilts, 118 E. Bay St.	863-419-9267
Davie	Mary Beth's Quilting Patch, 6990 Griffin	954-797-7333
Daytona Beach	Pieces & Patches, 1425 Tomoka Farms	904-252-5588
De Leon Springs	Quilt Magic, 4475 Audubon Ave.	
Delray Beach	Nanny's Attic, 124 N. Swinton Ave.	561-278-8877
Dunnellon	Mary Glendenning Quilts, 8282 SW 204th Ct.	352-489-7120
Fort Lauderdale	Rita Marie's Inc., 1230 NE 38th St.	954-566-6074
Fort Myers	Simply Amish, 3541 Fowler St.	941-939-5119
Ft. Myers	Fabric Mart II, 6900 Daniels Pkwy. #15	941-482-5250
Gulf Breeze	Quilt Nest, 1450 Sterling Point Dr.	850-916-9319
Harbortown	Fabric Yarn & Sew Much More, 913 Gulf Breeze Pkwy.	850-932-1751
Hollywood	Ben Raymond Fabrics & Trimmings, 2050 Hollywood Blvd.	305-927-4011
Hudson	Pine Needles Fabric Quilt Shop, 8216 S.R. 52	727-819-9559
Inverness	Heckman's Country Quilts, 2780 E. Jupiter St.	352-341-0614
Jacksonville	Paula's Fine Fabrics, 4160 Southside	904-645-3363
Jacksonville	Alexa's Quilts & More, 8793 Chambore	904-641-9964
Key West	Key West Fashions, 201 Simonton St.	305-292-8951
Key West	Fabric World, 3210 N. Roosevelt Blvd.	305-294-1773
Kissimmee	Cheryl's Enchanted Quilting, 744 Country Woods Cir.	407-348-0182
Lake Worth	Sew 'N Tell, 2913 29th Ln.	561-642-4710
Lakeland	Fabric Warehouse, 3032 N. Florida Ave.	941-680-1325
Mossy Head	Calico Country Fabrics, P.O. Box 1280	904-461-2309
Mt. Dora	Madison Rose Quilts & Gifts, 431 N. Donnelly St.	352-735-9591
Oakland Park	Oakes & Acorns, 3700 NW 10th Ave.	954-630-0557
Ocala	Fabric Plus, 2391 S.W. College Rd.	352-351-8282
Orange Park	Country Crossroads, 799-3 Blanding	904-276-1011
Orange Park	Cleolas Art at Play, 906 Park Ave.	904-269-6517
Orlando	Gingersnap Station Limited, 2318 Edgewater	407-425-8811
Palm Harbor	Classic Cloth, 32680 U.S. Hwy. 19 N	813-785-6593
Port Charlotte	Charlotte County Sewing Center, 4200 Tamiami Trail	941-629-2202
Port Charlotte	Quilt N' More, 119 Tamiami Tr. #C	941-255-9330
Punta Gorda	Kountry Klub Kollectibles, 149 W. Marion Ave.	941-639-6139
Sarasota	Cooney's Collectible, 729 Indian Beach Circle	941-355-1843
South Daytona	Brian's, 333 Beville Rd.	904-760-6444
Southport	Estelle Fabrics, 7809 Gadsden Ave.	850-265-2078
St. Petersburg	Quilting Bee, 8842 4th St. N	727-217-9042
St. Petersburg	Just Quilted, 1490 51st Ave. NE	727-521-4373
St. Petersburg	Sewing Circle Fabrics, 408 33rd Ave. N.	727-823-7391
Tampa	Grand Ole Country Store, 8709 40th St. N.	813-980-6330
Tampa	Just By Chance, 6108 N. Central Ave.	813-234-1319
Tampa	Necchi Singer Sewing Centers, 104 Fletcher E	813-960-0377
Titusville	ABC Sewing Studio, 1915 Know McRea	407-267-8225
Titusville	Fabric Emporium, 3190 S. Hopkins Ave.	407-267-6080

17 Featured Shops

GEORGIA

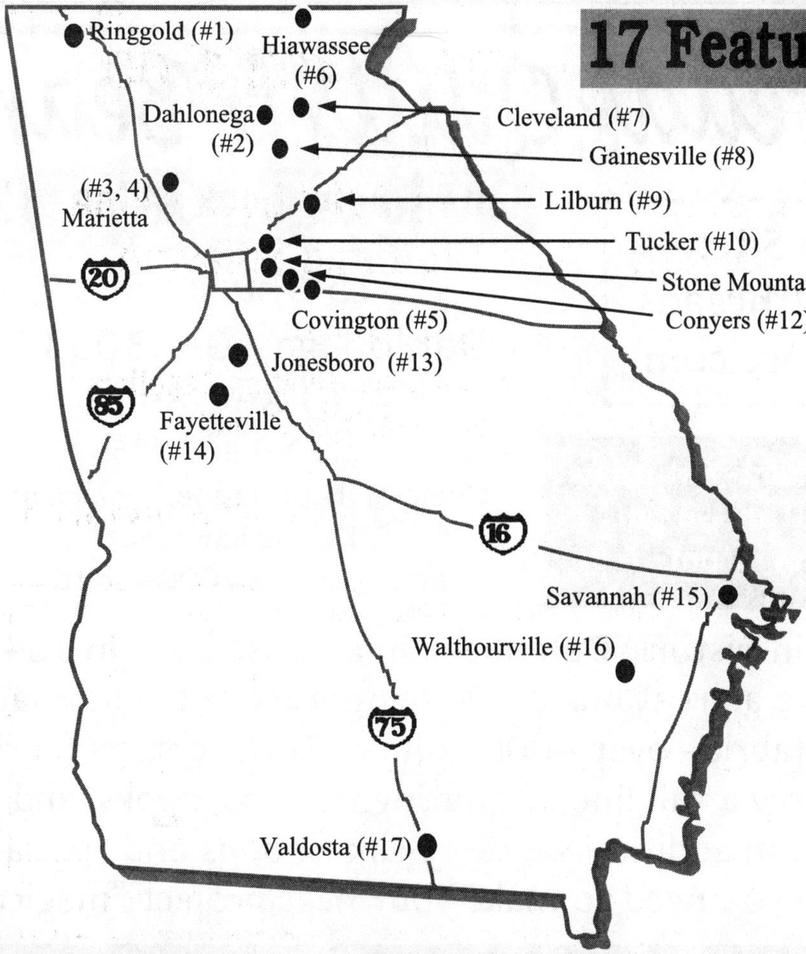

Sew Bee It

Tues, Wed, Fri
10am – 6pm.
Thurs 10am-9:30pm
Sat 10am-5pm.

MAKE OUR NEW QUILT SHOP your NEW REST STOP! Perfect for **SNOWBIRDS**- less than 1/4 mile off I-75. We have a couch and a TV w/ remote control for your travel companions who are…well, how should we put it, "different from us?" Come on down!

Sew Bee it — A Quilter's Garden

Coffee Bar * Clubs * Classes * Fun

Fabric*Books*Patterns*Notions

We keep it fresh and interesting. Our pallet of fabrics include:

- Batiks and ethnic prints
- The Entire Jinny Beyer's Quilter's Pallet
- Kaffe Fassett
- Thimbleberries
- Moda Marbles
- Kona Solids
- Reproductions

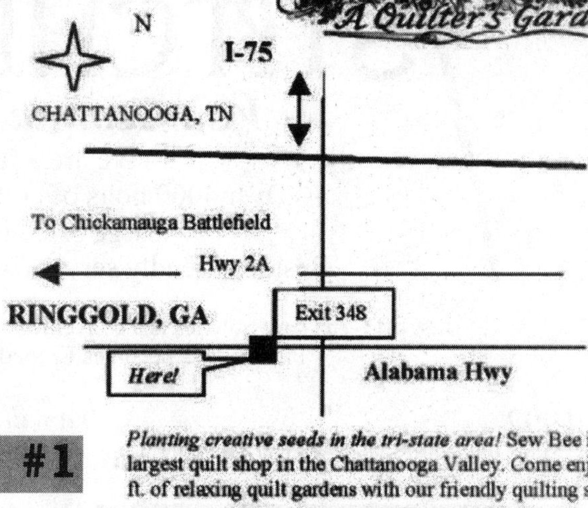

From I-75 Take Exit 348 and go west ¼ of a mile. We are on the left. Hwy 151 is Alabama Hwy.

Ringgold, GA #1

Planting creative seeds in the tri-state area! Sew Bee it is the largest quilt shop in the Chattanooga Valley. Come enjoy 3000 sq. ft. of relaxing quilt gardens with our friendly quilting staff.

www.Sew-Bee-It.com 706-937-9142 phone 706-937-9143 fax
Sew Bee It, 6103 Alabama Hwy. Ringgold GA, 30736

email pam@sew-bee-it.com

Magical Threads Quilts & Bears

Web Site:
Magicalthreads
quiltstore.com

Dahlonega, GA #2

315 Church St.
Dahlonega, GA 30533
(706) 867-8918
Fax: (706) 867-9253
Owners: Laurelanne Hackinson
& Kathie Lawrence
Est: 2001 2000+ sq.ft.

Monday - Saturday
10 am - 6 pm
Sunday 1 pm - 4 pm

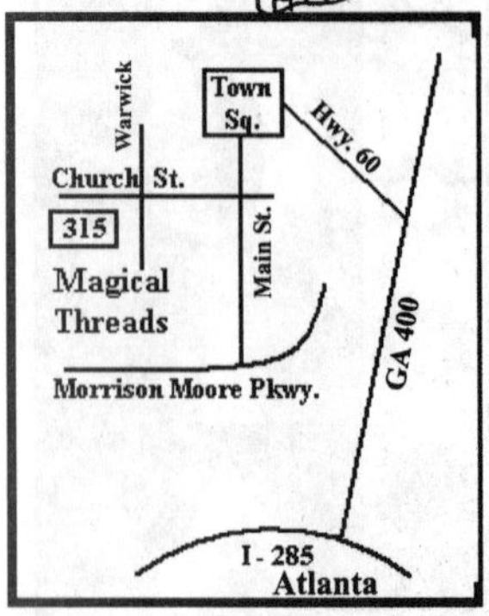

52 miles North of Atlanta

Located in historic Dahlonega in a house built in 1846. We have a great mix of contemporary & traditional quilting fabric - over 4000 bolts of 100% cotton fabric. We carry a full line of quilting notions, books, and patterns. In addition we carry silk ribbons and specialty yarns. All you need to make your next project "magical".

Marietta, GA #3

Tiny STITCHES

2520 E. Piedmont Rd.
Suite H 30062
(770) 565-1113

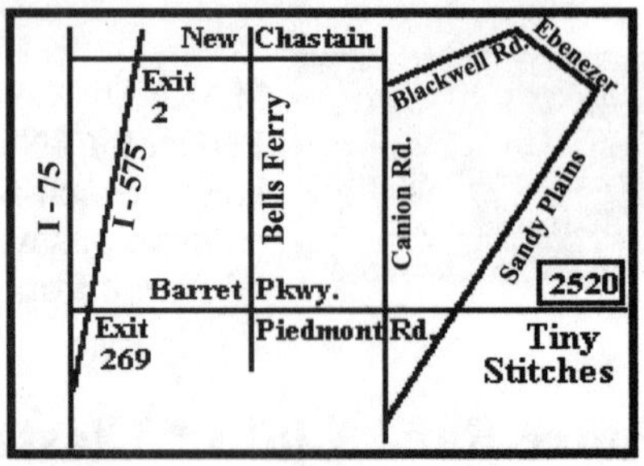

Visit Georgia's Largest Quilt Shop

We are a fully stocked quilt shop
— Over 4000 bolts of cotton fabrics — over 500 book titles —
Large selection of the newest notions
Besides friendly service we have classes in quilting & clothing.

Just off I-75, Tiny Stitches is a convenient stop for the traveling Quilter. Exit 269, east onto Barrett Pkwy. This becomes E. Piedmont, we are located at 2520 E. Piedmont.

Est: 1992

We will gladly do mail order.

Visit our website: www.tinystitches.com

Mon - Sat 9:30 - 5:30

est. 1986

Marietta, GA #4

Little Quilts®

1450-C Roswell Rd.
"Near Historic Marietta"
Phone: 770-578-6727
Fax: 770-509-9748
Email: littlequilts@mindspring.com

Mon - Sat
10 - 5

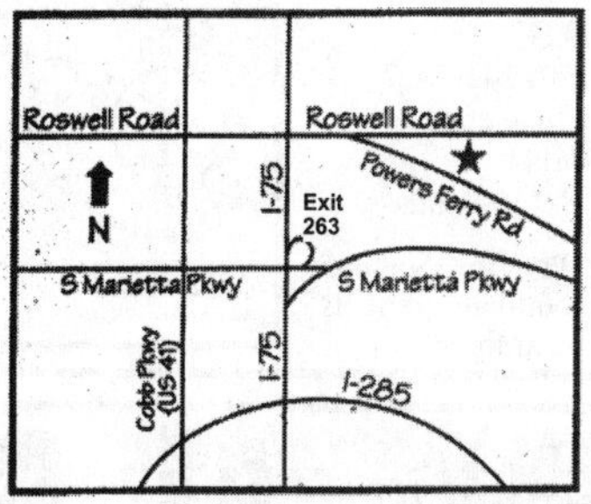

10 minutes from I-75 20 minutes N. of Atlanta

"Step Into Our World"

Featuring fabrics, books and patterns by Little Quilts

Our cozy shop is full of reproduction fabrics, rug hooking, stitchery, books, patterns, supplies, gifts and lots of inspiration!

Alice Berg * Mary Ellen Von Holt * Sylvia Johnson

AN OLD FASHIONED GENERAL STORE

PATRICK'S

Est. 1950
1176 Elm Street NE 30014-2406
(770) 786-3220
10,000 sq.ft. 3000+ bolts

100% Cotton Fabrics
Including
Homespuns, Flannels, &
Reproduction Fabrics.
100's of Quilt Patterns

Covington, GA #5

Monday - Saturday
8:30 - 6

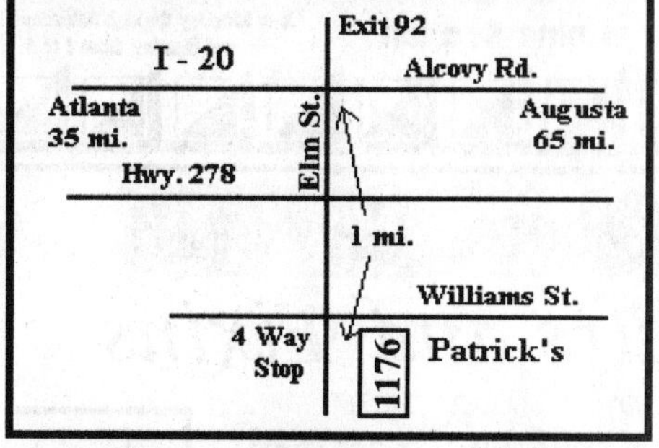

MasterCard VISA AMERICAN EXPRESS DISCOVER

Hiawassee, GA #6

Tues - Sat 10 - 4

Log Cabin Patchworks

35 S. Main St. 30546
(706) 896-7275
Web Site: www.LogCabinPatchworks-quilting.com
Est: 1980 600 sq.ft. 1200 Bolts

Set in a Log Cabin from the mid-1800's. We specialize in Thimbleberries, Homespuns, Flannels and Reproduction fabrics. Better Homes & Garden Quilt Sampler Shop 2002

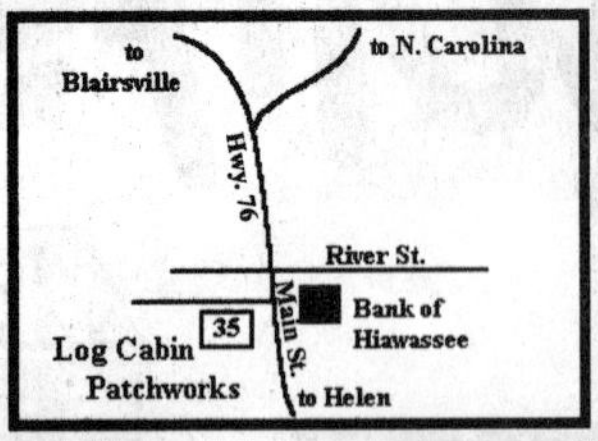

Cleveland, GA #7

Everyday 10 - 5

The Calico Barn

Rte. 384, 3599 Duncan Bridge Rd. 30528
(706) 865-9029
Owners: Grace Giebert & Jacqueline Stoner
Est. 1992

Machine quilting available. Over 1500 Bolts of Designer Fabrics, Patterns, Books, Stencils, and Quilting Supplies.

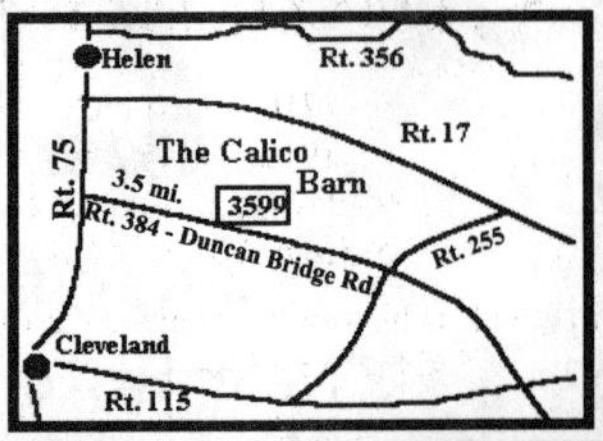

Gainesville, GA #8

Mon - Fri 10 - 5 Sat 10 - 4

Quilted Hearts Ltd.

2415 G Old Cornelia Hwy. 30507
(770) 536-3959 Fax: Same
Est: 1991 2500 sq.ft.
Owner: Sally Babcock

Located North of Atlanta, our shop has over 2000 Bolts of 100% cotton fabrics. We carry everything needed for quiltmaking, rug hooking, and knitting.

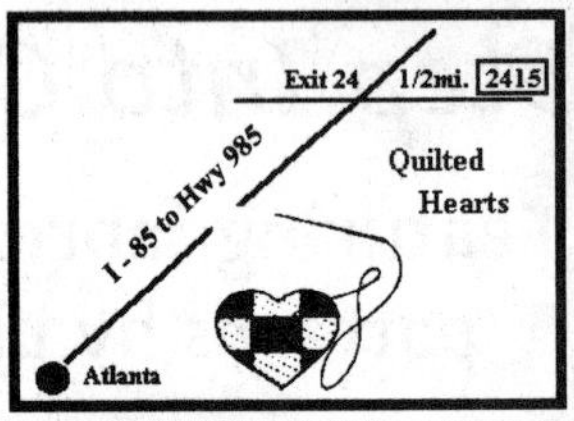

Lilburn, GA #9

Mon - Sat 10 - 5

Quilt Garden

92 Main St. 30047
(770) 923-2310 Fax: (770) 242-7362
E-Mail: GRBurkett@Juno.com
Owner: Gerry Burkett
Est: 1997 1000 sq.ft. 1100 bolts

100% Cotton fabrics, Books, Patterns, Notions, Kits, Classes. Two fun-filled quilter's retreats each year — call for info.

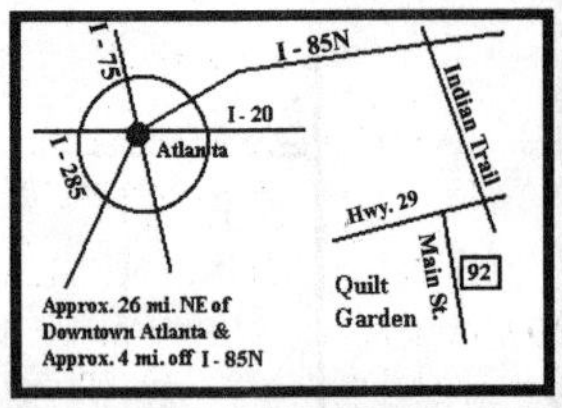

Tucker, GA #10

DREAM QUILTERS

2343 Main St-Tucker, Ga 30084
770-939-8034 or dreamq@bellsouth.net

We have fabric, food, fun, notions, books, patterns, classes, and a bobbin full of know-how. Only 2 miles from 285 East Come see us!

Open Monday through Saturday 10 to 5:30 and Sunday from 1 to 5

Stone Mountain, GA #11

Mon - Sat 10 - 5 Thur til 8

Village Quilt Shop

975 Main St. 30083
(770) 469-9883
Owner: Joyce P. Selin
Est: 1981 1200 sq.ft.

A "One-stop Quilt Shop"
Quilts -- Quilting Supplies -- Books
Fabrics -- Notions Class schedule Available.

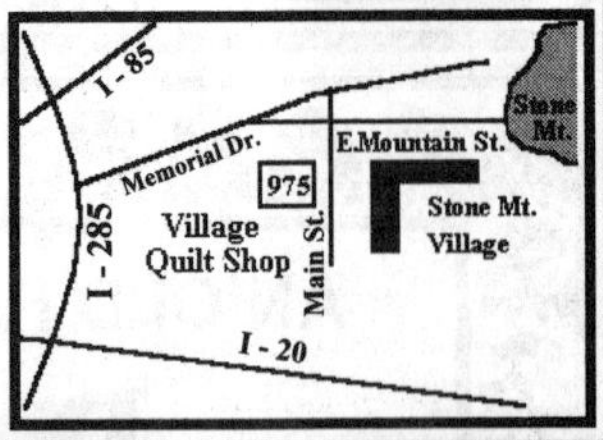

Conyers, GA #12

Mon - Sat 10 - 5 Thur til 7

QUILTING LINES

989 Green St. 30012
(770) 388-0789
Fax: (770) 388-0790
Web: www.quiltinglines.com
Owner: Patricia Lines Est: 1996

"Everything you need to make a quilt & more!" Quilting Classes, Sewing Classes, Doll Making & Silk Ribbon. elna sewing machines.

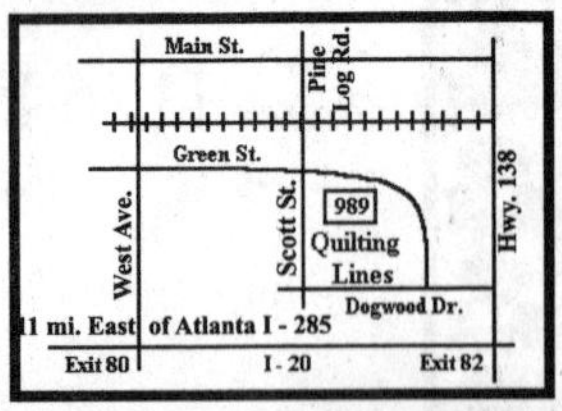

Jonesboro, GA #13

Mon - Sat 10 - 5

Quilts and Fixins

7986 N. Main St. 30236
(770) 472-0015 Fax: (770) 471-8822
E-Mail: Quiltsandfixins@aol.com
Est: 1998 5000 Bolts

100's of samples, books, patterns, notions. Many classes and gifts.

Exit 235 off I - 75 S. (Hwy 19&41-Tara Blvd.) Go S 3 mi, turn L onto Hwy 138. At next lite (N. Main) turn R. We're on the left.

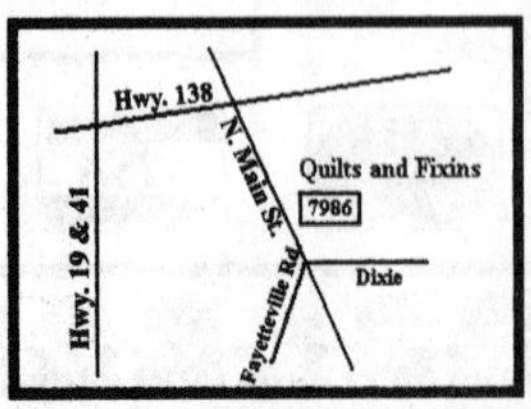

Fayetteville, GA #14

Mon - Sat 10 - 6

The Quilting Bee Shop and Gallery

355 N Jeff Davis Drive 30214
(678) 817-0602
Est: 2000 1300 sq. ft. 5000 Bolts

The Bee buzzes with 100% cotton fabric, books, patterns, & gifts. The Hive Gallery features local, & nationally known quilt artists.

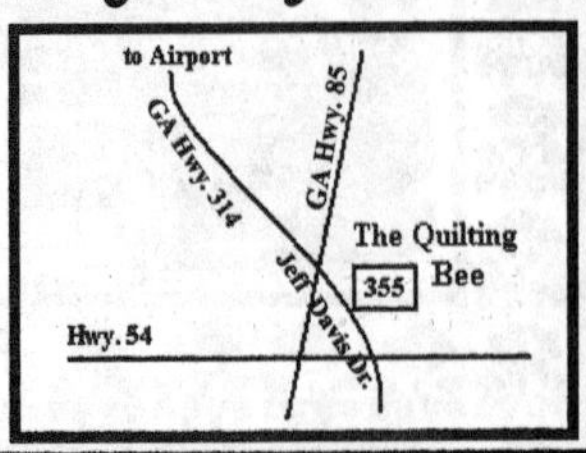

Savannah, GA #15

Colonial Quilts

Mon - Fri 10 - 6
Sat 10 - 4

11710 A Largo Dr.
(912) 925-0055
E-Mail: CQuilts11@aol.com
Savannah's Quilt Shop

Located in historic Savannah, we offer a wide array of fabric, notions, classes, books and patterns for quilting. Complete Jinny Beyer palette.

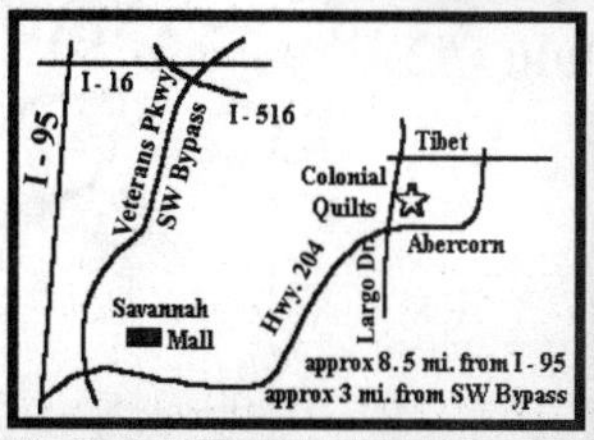

Walthourville, GA #16

MSA Variety Shop

Mon, Wed, Fri 10 - 6
Tues & Thurs 11 - 7
Sat 9 - 4

90 Sanders Road 31333
(912) 368-5335 Fax: Same
E-Mail: lockfam@coastalnow.com
Web Site: www.geocities.com/msa_variety
Owner: Lillian Lockett
Est: 2001 1200 sq. ft. 1200+ Bolts

100% cotton fabrics from the top manufacturers.
How to books, notions, classes.
Block of the month projects.

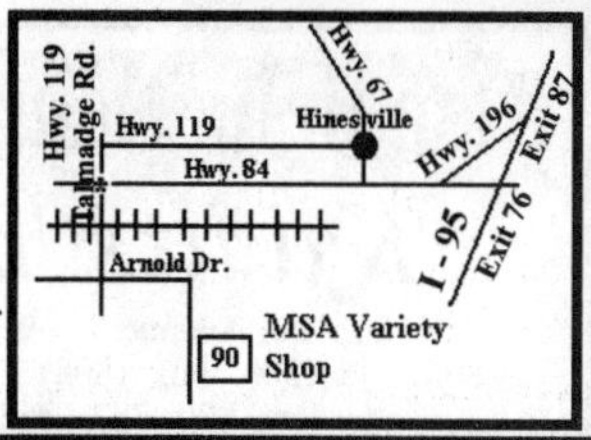

Valdosta, GA #17

The Quilted Peach

125 N. Paterson, Valdosta, GA 31601
(229) 293-9900 Toll Free (866) 747-0729
Fax: (229) 293-9292
E-Mail: info@thequiltedpeach.com
Web Site: www.thequiltedpeach.com
Owners: Kathy Dunigan (daughter) & JoAnn Hudgins (mother)
Est: 1997 1800 Bolts and Growing

Mon - Sat 10 - 5 2nd Sunday 2 - 5

Family business located in Valdosta's beautiful historic downtown. Shop specializes in "brights" -- batiks, Hoffmans, RJR, Jenny Beyer's Palette, Moda, Benartex -- you name it! Friendly and worth the trip to South Georgia

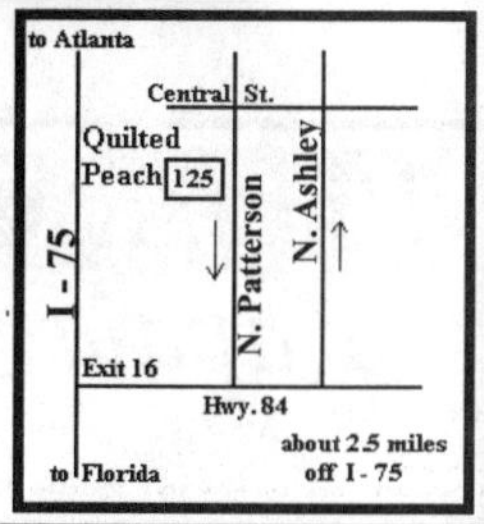

Other Shops in Georgia: We suggest calling first

Alpharetta	Southampton Quilts, 1920 Seven Seas Ct.	
Atlanta	Grannie Taught Us How, 1921 Peach Tree Rd. N.E.	404-351-2942
Augusta	Sewing Gallery, 362 Fury's Ferry Rd. #D	706-855-6479
Bainbridge	Janet's Fashion Fabrics, 124 E. Broughton St.	912-246-5674
Blairsville	Corn Crib, 101 Pat Haralson Memorial Dr. #C	706-745-3426
Blue Ridge	April Rose Quilts & Gifts, 662 E. Main St.	706-632-8494
Chickamauga	Chickamauga Country Store, 121 Gordon St.	706-375-5300
Columbus	Southern Sewing Center, 2507 Manchester Expy.	706-327-1231
Dahlonega	Amber Rose Quilts & Gifts, 105 Chestatee St. #E	706-864-5326
Helen	Rose Alpen Quilts & Gifts, 19 Chattahoochee St.	706-878-2179
Lafayette	Nine Patch Notions, 314 S. Duke St.	706-638-9970
Lumpkin	Westville Historical Handicrafts, Inc., PO Box 1850	912-838-6310
Macon	Patchwork Station, 4524 Forsyth Rd. #203	912-471-8288
St. Simons Island	Stepping Stones Quilts, 301 Skylane Rd., P.O. Box 21811	912-638-7128
Tucker	Quilts & Co., 2615 Mountain Ind. Blvd. #6	770-934-4224

HAWAII

4 Featured Shops

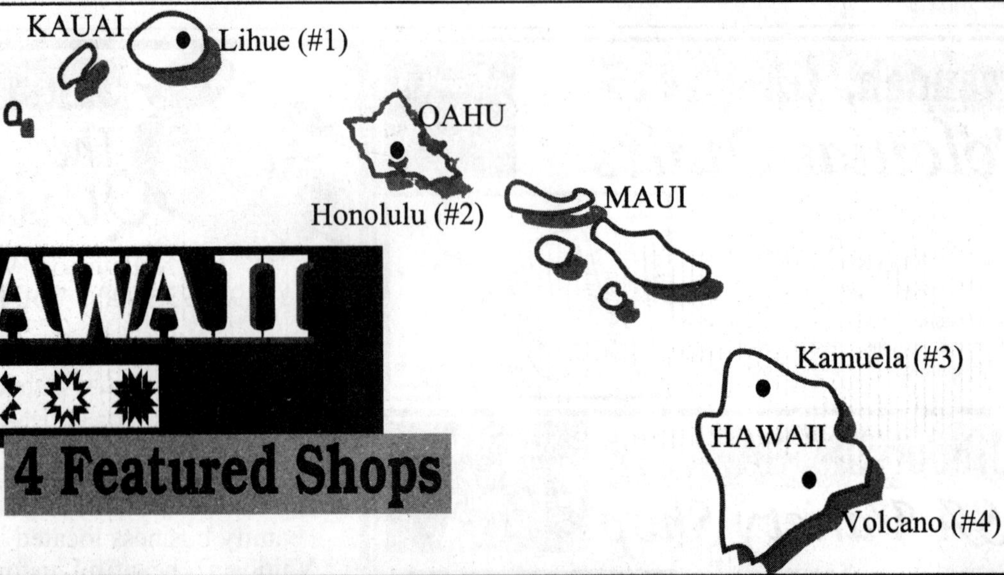

Lihue, Kauai, HI #1

Mon - Sat 9 - 5

Kapaia Stitchery

P.O. Box 1327 96766
3-3561 Kuhio Hwy.
(808) 245-2281 Fax: (808) 245-1772
E-Mail: kapaia@gte.net
Est: 1973 Visa, MC, Discover

We Love Quilting !
The best selection of Tropicals, Batiks, & Quality 100% Cottons for Quilting.

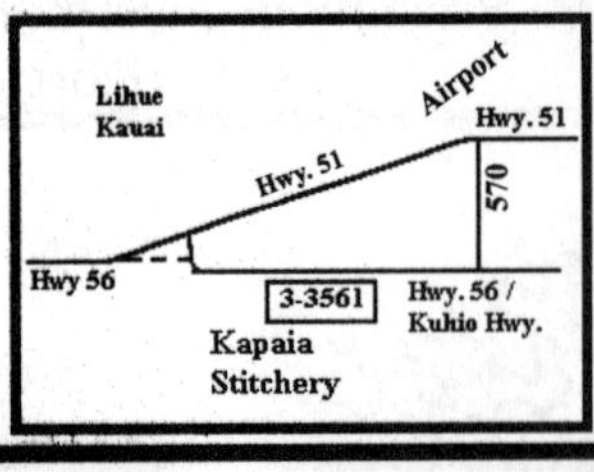

Honolulu, Oahu, HI #2

Mon - Fri 10 - 6
Sat 10 - 4

Kwilts 'n Koa

1126 12th Avenue 96816
(808) 735-2300 Fax: (808) 737-2300
Orders (800) 787-1855
E-Mail: KwiltsnKoa@hawaii.rr.com
Web Site: www.KwiltsnKoa.com
Owners: Kathy Tsark & Tsarkie
Catalog $10 yr.—4 issues
Est: 1991 650 sq.ft. 100+ bolts
Hawaiian quilting classes, patterns, kits / supplies; Hawaiian gifts & Koa wood.

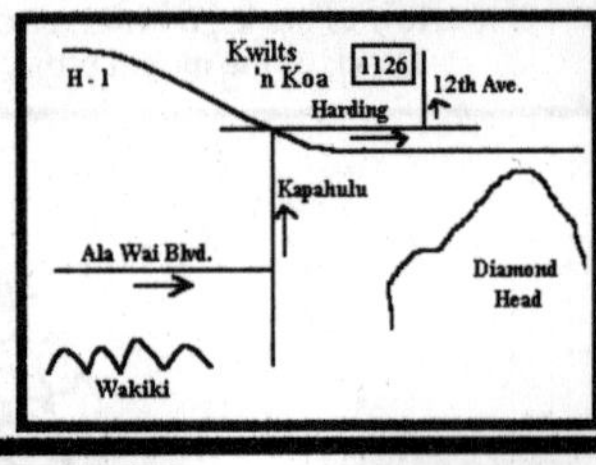

Kamuela, Hawaii, HI #3

Mon - Sat 9:30 - 4

Topstitch

Holomua Center, P.O. Box 2631 96743
(808) 885-4482
E-Mail: topstitch@lava.com
Owner: Ellie Erickson Est: 1978

A fine collection of cotton fabrics including tropical prints, quilting solids, and batiks. Needlecraft supplies and Hawaiian Quilts.

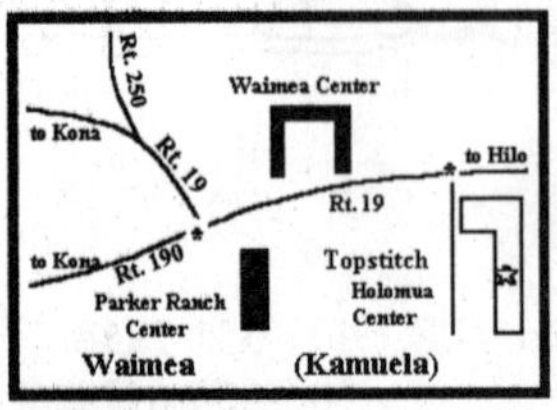

Volcano, Hawaii, HI #4

7 Days a Week 9:30 - 5:30

Kilauea Kreations

P.O. Box 959 96785
Old Volcano Hwy.
(808) 967-8090

Hawaiian Quilt Shop and local art.
Ready made to make you own.
Everything you need.
Fabric, Notions, Books, Kits

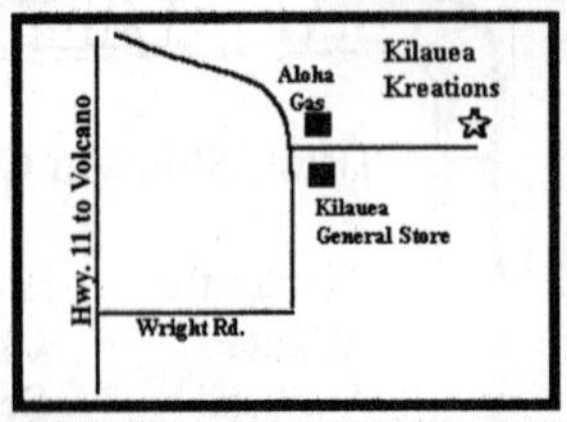

Other Shops in Hawaii: We suggest calling first

Aiea Homspun Harbor, 98-029 Hekaha St. #24 808-488-5844
Hilo Dragon Mama Fabrics, 266 Kamehameha Ave. 808-934-9081
Honolulu Bernina of Hawaii, 320 Ward Ave. #114 808-536-6931
Honolulu My Little Secret, 1050 Ala Moana Blvd. #B2 808-596-2990
Honolulu Little Hawaiian Quilt Shop, 2330 Kalahaua Ave. #201 808-924-8858
Honolulu Hawaiian Quilt Connection, 2525 Kalahaua # 220B 808-599-7766
Honolulu Kaimuki Dry Goods, 1144 10th Ave. 808-734-2141
Honolulu The Calico Cat, 1223 Koko Head Ave. 808-732-3998
Honolulu Quilts Hawaii, 2209 Young St.
Kahului Sew Special, 275 W. Kaahumanu 808-877-6128
Kailua-Kona Kona Kapa, P.O. Box 390136 808-326-7119
Kamuela Upcountry Quilters, P.O. Box 2631 808-885-7666
Kapaa Hawaii's Keepsakes, 484 Kuhio Hwy. 808-822-7963
Kealakekua Kimura's Fabrics, P.O. Box 435 808-322-3771
Kekaha Kauai Kwilts, 8689 Elepaio Rd. 808-337-2700
Lahaina Hawaii Quilt Company, 210 Nohea Kai #111 808-667-7660
Lahaina Ka Honu Gift Gallery, 277 Wili Ko Pl. #40 808-661-0173
Lahaina Totally Hawaiian, 1221 Honoapilani Hwy. #E5 808-667-2558
Paia Paia Mercantile, 2 Baldwin Ave. #B, PO Box 790883 808-579-6388
Wahiawa The Pineapple Patch, 64-1550 Kamehameha Hwy. 808-622-3494

IDAHO

15 Featured Shops

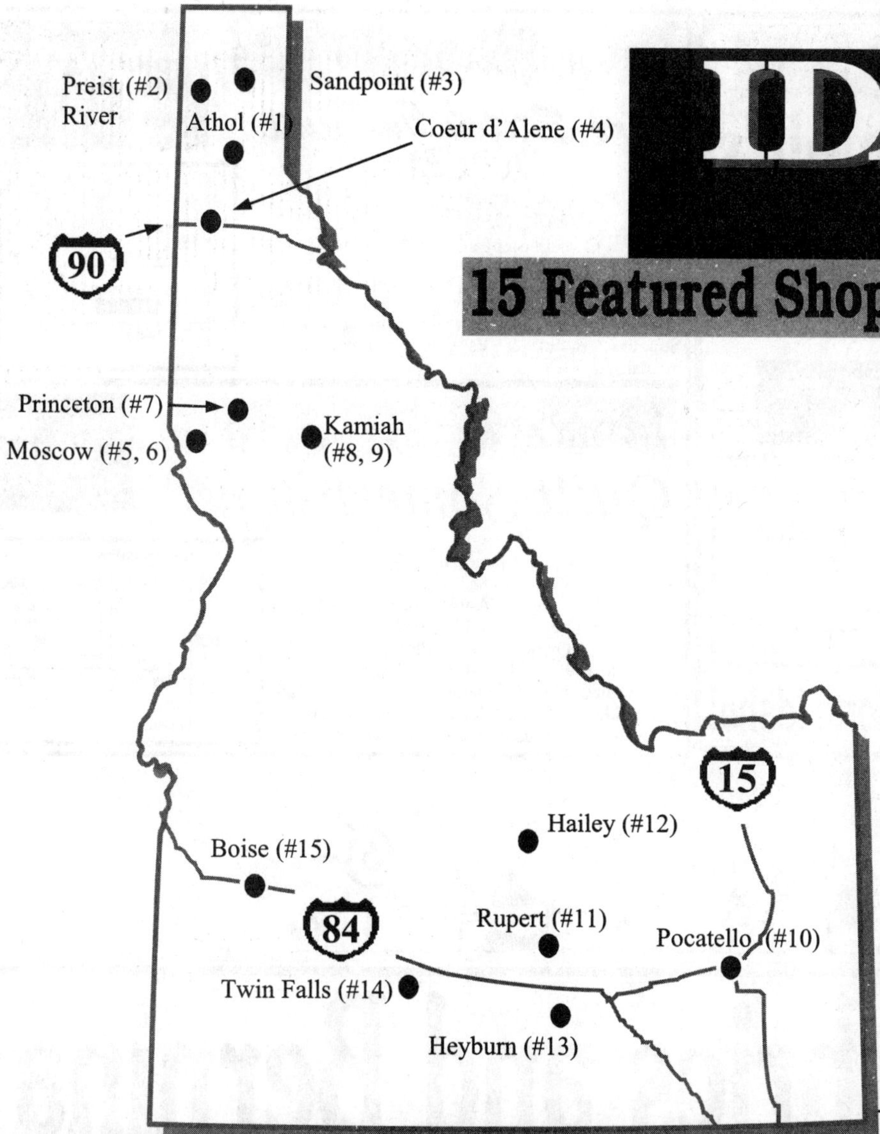

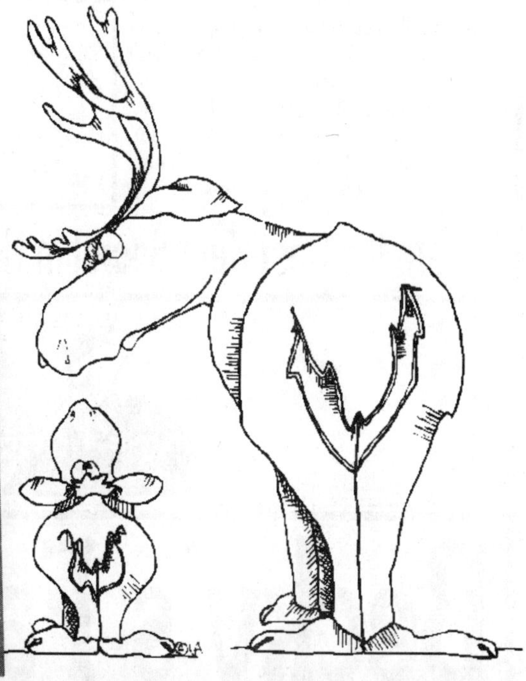

Sandpoint, ID #3

Granny Thimble's

1175 Fontaine Dr., Sandpoint, ID 83864
(208) 263-4875
E-Mail: chknlips@netw.com
Web Site: www.grannythimbles.com
Owner: Carol Kunzeman Est: 2001 1500 sq.ft.

Mon - Fri 10 - 6
Sat 10 - 4

If you are looking for a quaint little place to visit that will take you back in time where life was simpler, than come visit. We have over 2,000 bolts of fabric to choose from. We offer classes and help with all your projects and fabric needs. Come plan to sit and stay awhile and visit with us. We have the kettle on for tea and the cookies are in the oven just waiting to be shared with you!

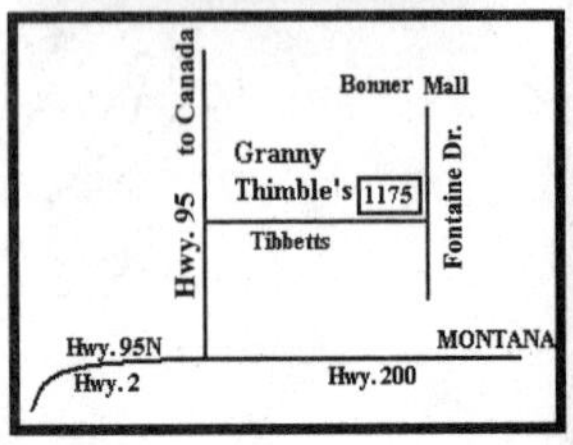

We are the Best Kept Secret in North Idaho!

Coeur d'Alene, ID #4

Mon - Fri 9:30 - 5:30
Sat 10 - 5
Sundays Mem. Day to Labor Day 12 - 4:30

A Stitch In Time Quilt Shop

7352 N. Government Way #G 83815
(208) 772-0560 Est: 1994
Owner: Stephanie Muehlhausen

Quilt Shop & Smocking & French handsewing Supplies. Bernina Sewing Machines—sales and service. Wide Selection of Quilting Fabrics, Supplies, Books & Patterns. Many classes available.

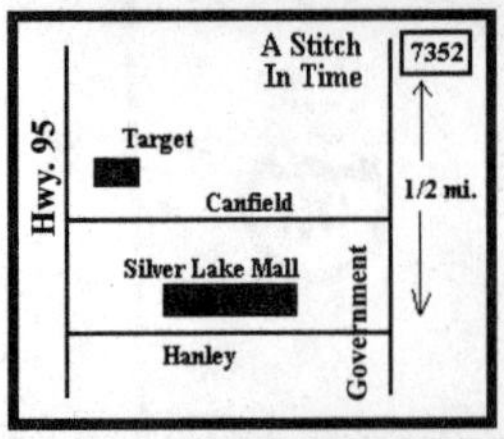

Moscow, ID #5

Mon - Sat 10 - 7
Sun 12 - 5

Quilt Something!

1420 S. Blaine St. 83843
(208) 883-4216
E-Mail: colleen@quiltsomething.com
Web Site: www.quiltsomething.com
Owner: Colleen Phillip
Est: 1996 3400 sq.ft. 2000+ Bolts
Full service shop. All major fabric houses including RJR, Benartex, Moda, Hoffman & more!
Located inside mall - many restaurants nearby.

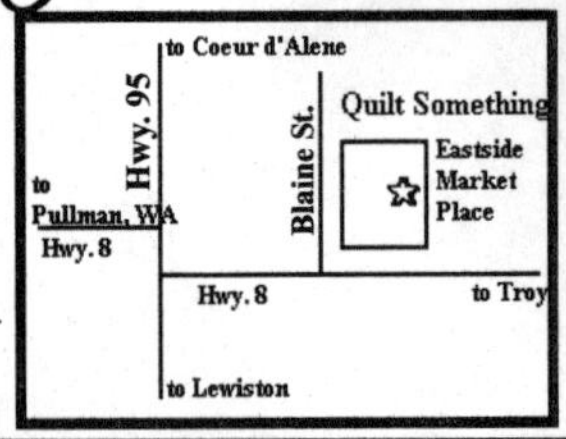

Becky's Fabrics and Bernina

410 West 3rd 83843 (208) 882-5224

Moscow, ID #6

Owner: Rebecca Keck
E-Mail: bernina@moscow.com
www.beckysfabrics.com
Est: 1992
Mail Order Available.

Mon - Sat 10 - 5

Nothing Sews Like A Bernina. Nothing.
BERNINA®

Becky's Fabrics is an authorized Bernina Dealership located in the heart of Moscow. We stock a complete line of Bernina sewing machines, sergers and accessories and have our own in-store technician available for service and repair on any Bernina machine. We also stock an assortment of quilting kits, a nice selection of books, patterns and notions. Our very friendly and knowledgeable staff is always ready to assist you with your sewing machine and quilting needs. As you are meandering through the rolling hills of the Palouse, stop by and say hello.

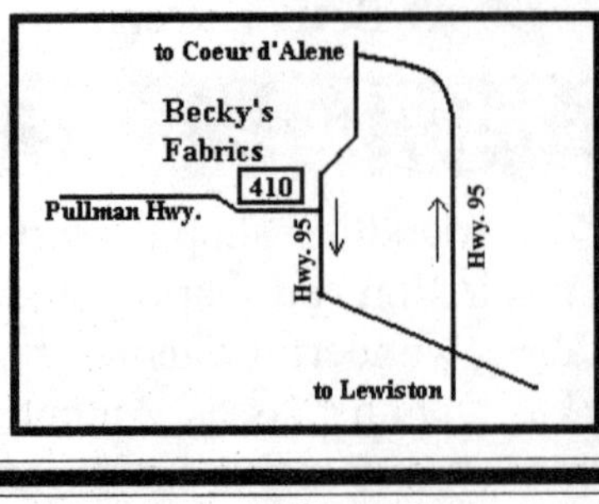

Princeton, ID #7

Tues - Sat 9 - 3 Or By Appt.

In The Pines Quilt Shop

1225 W. Hatter Creek Rd. 83857
(208) 875-0011
E-Mail: wjensen@turbonet.com
Owner: Wendy Jensen

A full line of quality quilting fabrics featuring Thimbleberries and Moda. Notions, books patterns and machine quilting.

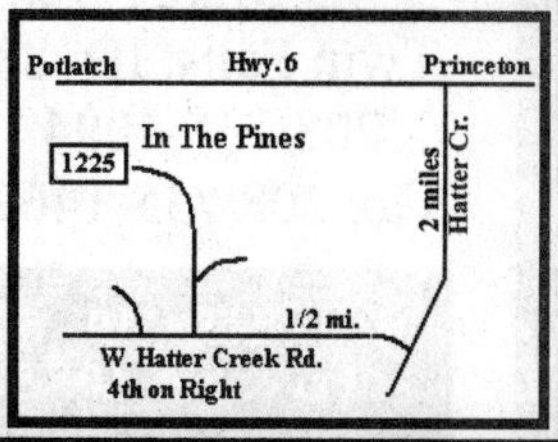

Kamiah, ID #8

Mon - Sat 10 - 5 Call first for B & B

Quilt House
BED & BREAKFAST and QUILT SHOP

HC 11, Box 142 83536
Toll free 877 QUILT BB (784-5822)
(208) 935-7668 Fax: (208) 935-7686
Owner: Elaine Hutchison

Directions: After going through Kamiah, cross bridge, take immediate left. This is the Woodland Rd., follow for 12 miles past the Woodland Friends Church. (12 miles, stay left) Take all 1st lefts after the church. (2 more miles to the Quilt House) Pass the Quilt House to the driveway.

Country mountain setting, 14 miles from Kamiah. Enjoy a week-end or week long quilt retreat in a beautiful 3 story log B&B with fabulous views. Sleeps up to 14.

Kamiah, ID #9

By Appt. Only

Kamiah Kustom Kwilting

P.O. Box 278 83536
(208) 935-0884
Est: 1992
E-Mail:
kamkuskw@camasnet.com
Owner: Joyce Anderson

A Machine Quilting Service!
Custom quilt finishing. Classes & quilting supplies available.

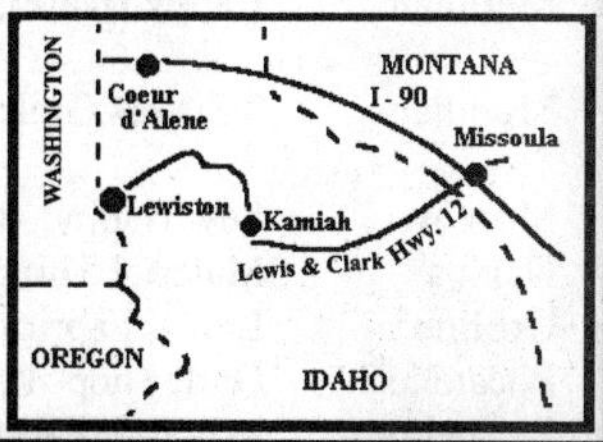

Rupert, ID #11

Mon - Fri 10 - 5:30 Sat 10 - 5

The Gathering Place

524 6th St. (On the Square) 83350
(208) 436-0455 Fax: (208) 436-9875
E-Mail: tgp@cyberhighway.net
Web Site: Coming Soon
Owners: Ron & Joyce Jensen
10,000 sq.ft. 5000+ Bolts

Idaho's largest quilt shop — 5000+ bolts of your favorite fabrics. Machine quilting. Fun Classes. Friendly Service. Country furniture, gifts & collectibles.

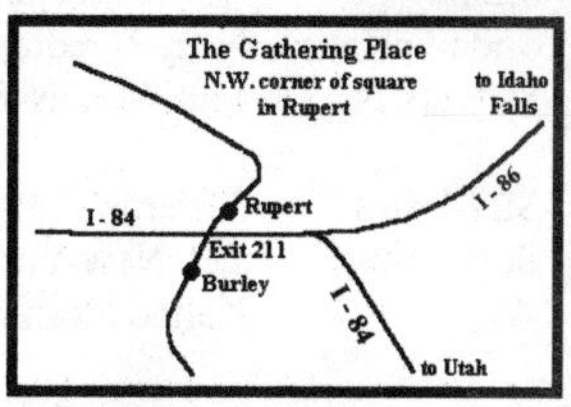

Pocatello, ID #10

Crafts & Frames

Sierra Pacific Crafts — Partners in Creativity

BENARTEX · HOFFMAN · MODA · MAYWOOD · KAUFMAN · RJR · SOUTH SEAS · SPIEGEL · NORTHCOTT MONARCH · KINGS ROAD · P&B COLOR SPECTRUM ·

THE AREA'S FINEST QUILT SHOP

We proudly feature Quilt Programs by:
Sharon Hultgren · Marti Michell
Jackie Robinson · Susan Garman
McKenna Ryan of
Pine Needles Art Quilt Kits
& Many More!

Look for our beautiful fabrics pre-cut and packaged for your convenience. Many of our patterns are exclusive to Sierra Pacific Craft stores and when in Idaho, **can only be found at Crafts & Frames in Pocatello.**

Stop in soon, we look forward to seeing you!

We glady ship anywhere!

1570 YELLOWSTONE
(208) 237-1014

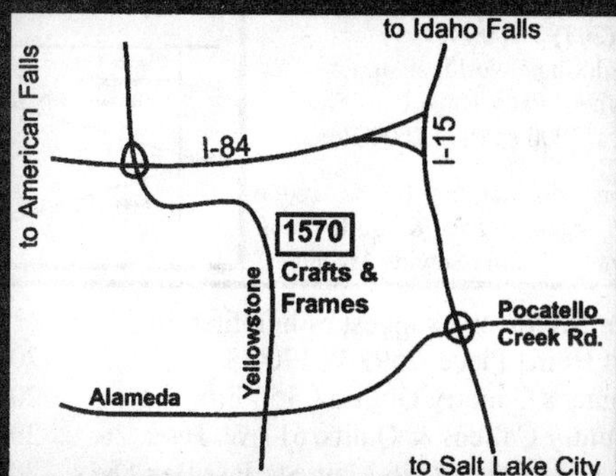

OPEN 7 DAYS A WEEK
M-F 9:30am-8pm SAT 9:30am-7pm SUN 11am-5pm
E-mail: crafts@ida.net
Owner: Emma Gebo Est. 1993

FABRIC, BOOKS & PATTERNS, NOTIONS

QUILTS THIS N' THAT

CLASSES, BERNINA MACHINES, GIFTS

9 E. Bullion 83333
(208) 788-1331

Mon - Sat 10 - 6
Sun 12 - 4

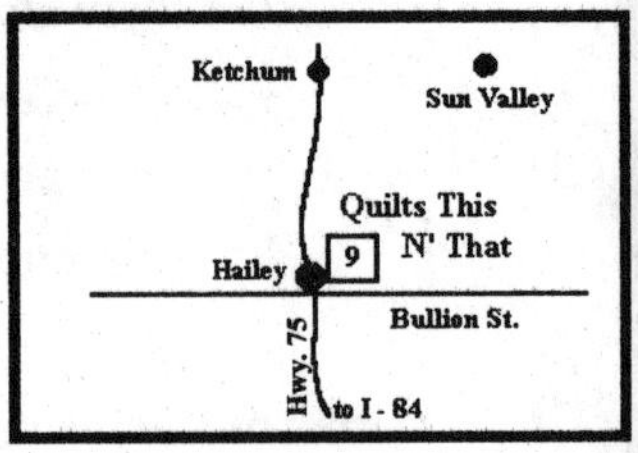

Fax: (208) 788-1868
E-Mail: lsullivan@sunvalley.net
Est: 1999 Over 1,000 bolts

Located in the Heart of the Scenic Wood River Valley, Just 12 miles from the famous Sun Valley Resort. We offer a unique collection of 100% Cotton Fabric from several manufacturers.

Hailey, ID #12

Heyburn, ID #13

Mon - Sat 10 - 6
Sunday by chance or Appt. please call

Carleen's fabrics & crafts, etc.

450 21st St. 83336
(208) 679-3573
Est: 1995
Mgr: Carleen Clayville
12-1500 Bolts

4000 sq.ft. of fabrics. Mainly Quilting Cottons. 65 - 70 shades of solids. Imported yarns, selected crafts. Bridal & better dress. Local consignment gifts & florals.
E-Mail: carleen@hereinidaho.com
Web Site: carleen.hereinidaho.com

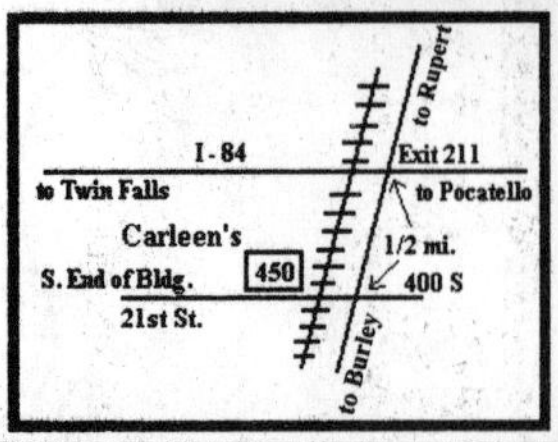

Stitchin' Time

129 Main Ave. W
Twin Falls, ID 83301
208/735-4094
Fax 208/735-1469

Owned by
Les & Cathy Reitz

E-Mail: stitchintime@onewest.net
www.stitchintime.ws
In downtown, where all the unique shops are.

Mon - Thur 10 - 5:30
Fri & Sat 10 - 5

Shop in a friendly, well-lit atmosphere. 5,000 sq. ft. store with over 2,500 bolts of quality 100% cotton. Loads of quilts on display to spur your imagination. Huge selection of Books, Patterns & Notions. Machine quilting available by Liz Mandelkow of Quilted for You.

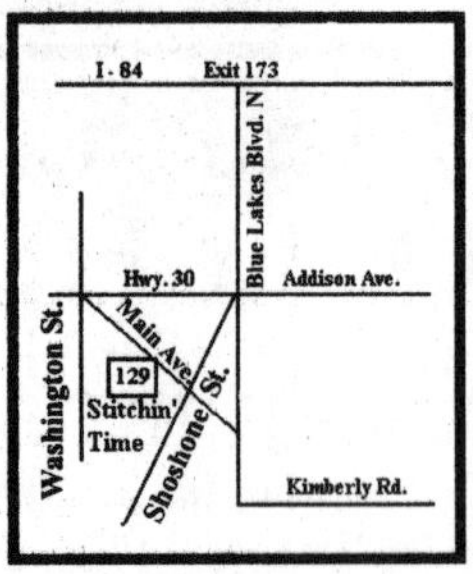

Metered Parking in front, Free Parking in back. Yes, there is a back door!

Twin Falls, ID #14

Boise, ID #15

Mon - Sat 10 - 6
Sun 12 - 5

The Quilt Crossing

5725 Fairview Avenue 83704
(208) 376-0087
E-Mail: qltxing@worldnet.att.net
Owner: Patty Hinkel
Est: 1987 3000 sq.ft. 2000 Bolts

Specializing in distinctive 100% cotton fabrics, classes, books, gifts & quilt / soft sculpture patterns. Bernina Sewing Machines.

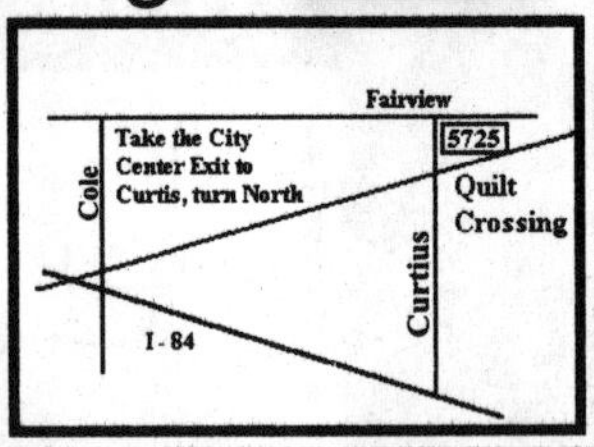

Other Shops in Idaho: We suggest calling first

Aberdeen	Old Home Place, 2597 W 1700 S	208-397-4335
Arimo	Tanner's Country Quilting, 150 Front St.	208-254-9384
Blackfoot	Country Calicos & Quilts, 617 W. Hwy. 26	208-684-5545
Bonners Ferry	Gini Knits, 7225 Main St., P.O.Box 854	208-267-5921
Caldwell	Francie's Fabrics, 7335 Pleasant View Dr.	208-454-1380
Caldwell	Quilt Ranch, 22780 Ballard Ln.	208-459-6609
Chubbuck	Mill End Fabric, 4415 E. Burnside Ave	208-238-1388
Clarkia	Joanne & Bucks Clothing Fabric & Photo, P.O. Box 1133	
Coeur d'Alene	Lyle's, 600 E. Best Ave.	208-765-9627
Eagle	Seams Etc., 124 E. State St.	208-939-8227
Grace	Fabulous Fabrics, P.O. Box E	208-425-3821
Grangeville	Melinda's Fabrics, 207 W. Main	208-983-0254
Idaho Falls	Quilts 'N' Things, 1375 E. 49th N	208-524-2439
Idaho Falls	Granny's Quilts, 390 N. Karey Ln.	208-522-0930
Idaho Falls	Quilted Daisy, 275 Cliff St.	208-523-6395
Lewiston	One Stop Stitches, 3115 6th St.	208-798-7317
McCall	Mountan Fabrics, 123 E. Lake	208-634-8450
Meridian	Happy Heart Quilting, 712 McGlinchey Ave.	208-888-4618
Meridian	2 Sisters Quilting Shoppe, 850 W. Franklin Rd.	208-887-4707
Moscow	Sew Happy, 408 S. Main St.	208-883-4932
Nampa	Material Things, 509 12th Ave. Rd.	208-461-4540
Orofino	Lura's Fabrics, 10494 Hwy. 12	208-476-7781
Pocatello	Quilt Shop, 119 S. Main	208-237-6619
Pocatello	Mill End Fabrics, 4415 E. Brunside	208-238-1388
Pocatello	The Fabric Center, 251 N. Main St.	208-232-3064
Preston	Fabric Farm & Quilts, 1173 S 1600 E	208-852-1419
Rexburg	The Quilt Barn, 2730 W 3800 S	208-356-6561
Rigby	Middleton's Cozy Quilts, 3904 E. 600 N	208-745-7120
Sandpoint	The Cotton Mill, 402 Cedar St.	208-263-0824
Shelley	Quilts Plus, 355 Meadowlark Dr.	208-357-1966
Soda Springs	Nifty Needle, 128 S. Main	208-547-2441
St. Maries	Mrs. Sew-N-Sew Quilt Shop, 1117 Main Ave. #1	208-245-6656
St. Maries	Patterns N More, 201 8th St.	208-245-8157
St. Maries	The New Yardstick, HC 2, Box 258	
Weiser	Kalico Korner, 455 State St.	208-549-0410

ILLINOIS

73 Featured Shops

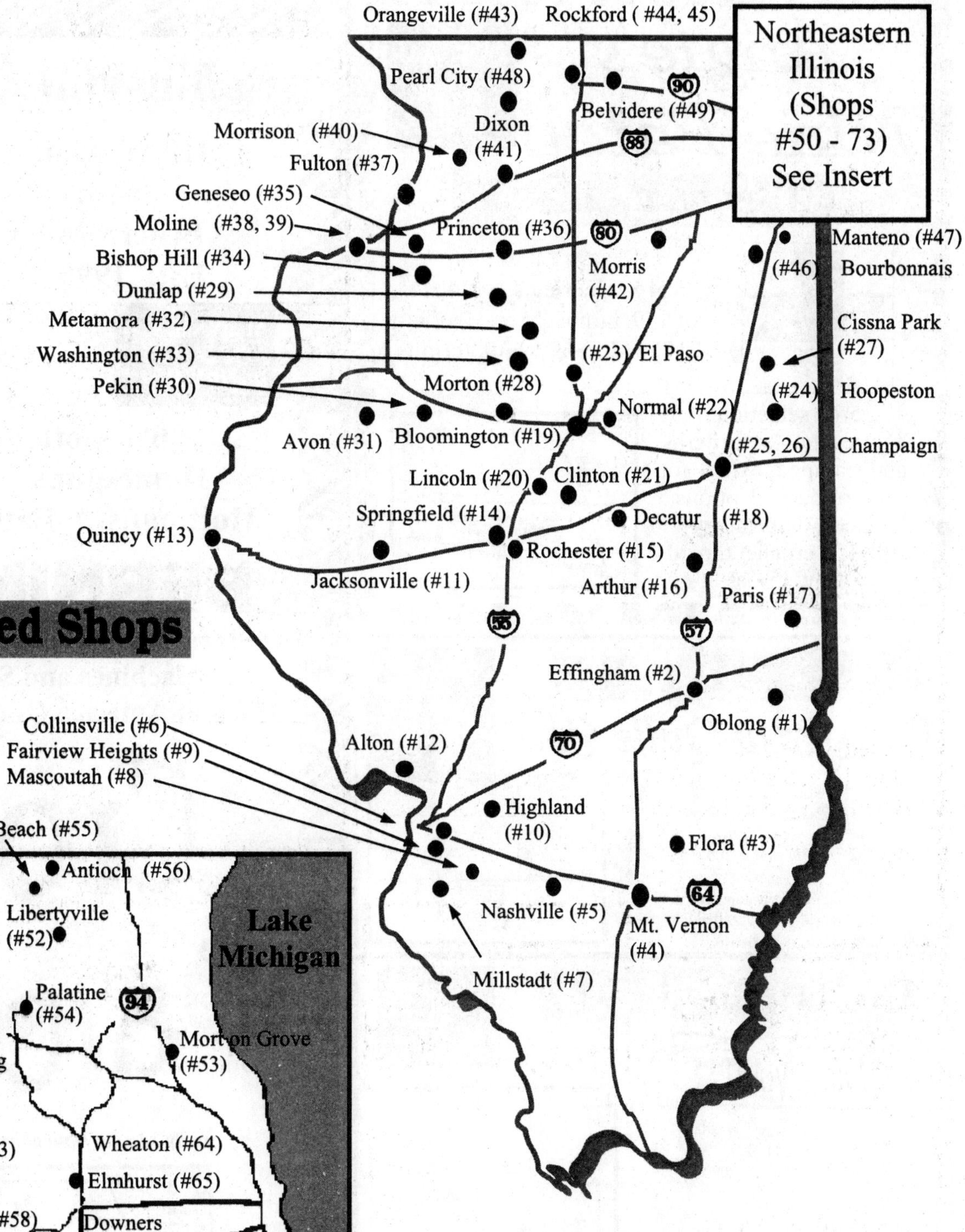

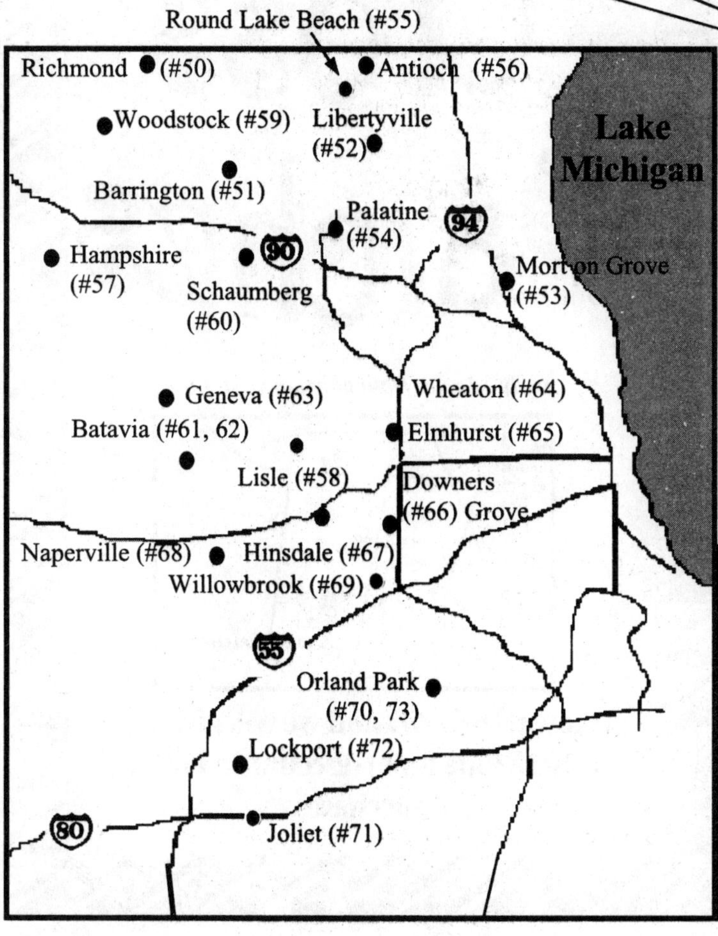

Angie's Nine Patch

Mon - Fri 9 - 5
Sat 9 - 3

Effingham, IL #2

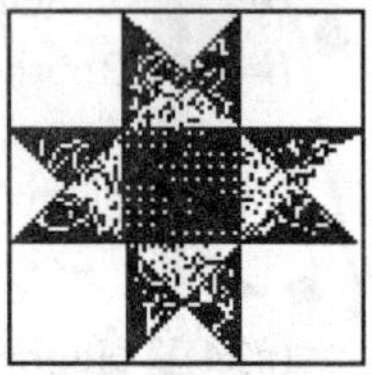

804 S. Henrietta 62401
Exit 159, turn right on Henrietta
(217) 347-9669 3000 Bolts

Large selection of fabrics, books, patterns and stamped textiles for embroidery. Notions, laces, embroidery flosses, crochet thread
Low Prices.

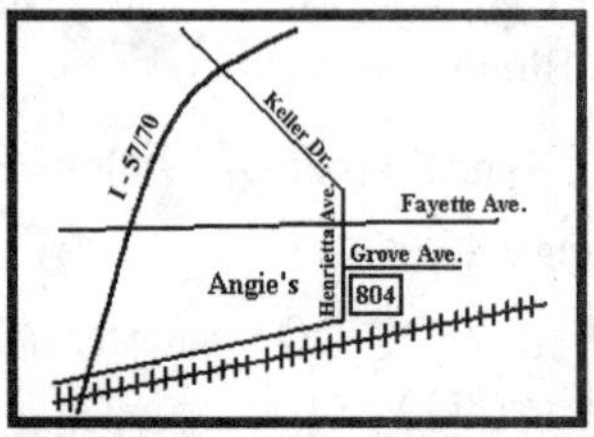

Flora, IL #3

Bear Paw Quilt Co.

Tues & Wed 9 - 5
Thur 9 - 8
Fri & Sat 9 - 5

117 W. North Ave. 62839
(618) 662-3391 Fax: Same
E-Mail: www.vern47@wworld.com
Est: 2002 3000 sq.ft. 2000+ Bolts

100% cotton fabrics from top companies and wool felt selected with quilters in mind. Books, patterns, notions, classes.

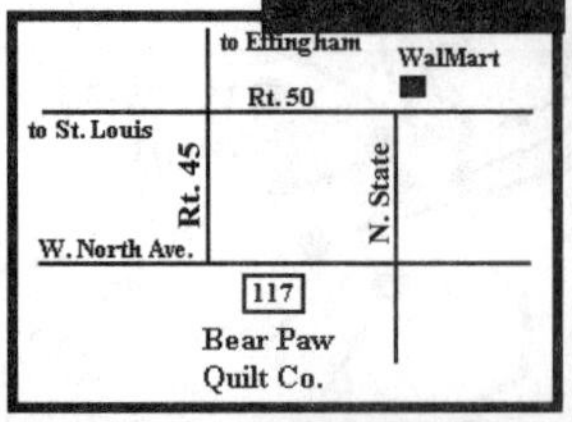

Mt. Vernon, IL #4

Mon - Fri 9:30 - 6
Sat 10 - 5

Mt. Vernon Sewing Mart

4112 Broadway 62864
(618) 244-5856
Owner: Dana Tabor 2000 sq.ft.

Fabrics, Quilting Supplies. Viking Sewing Machines & Sergers. Patterns, Books, Smocking Heirloom. Come & Browse.

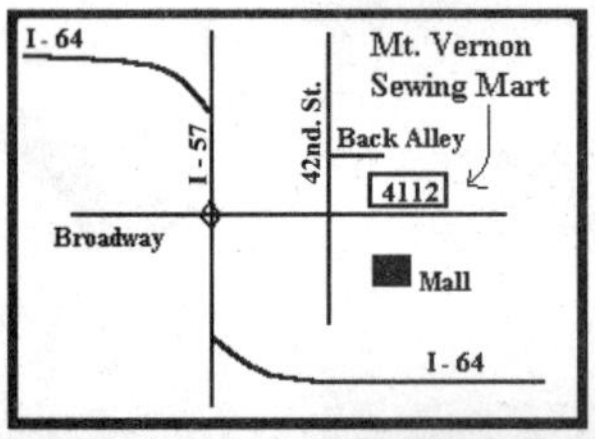

Nashville, IL #5

Mon - Thur 8 - 5:30
Fri 8 - 7
Sat 8 - 5

Lee's Quilting & Craft Center

212 E. St. Louis St. 62263
(618) 327-8898

Supplies for all your quilting needs. Over 1500 bolts of fabric. Over 600 quilting stencils. 114 quilt block designs to embroider.

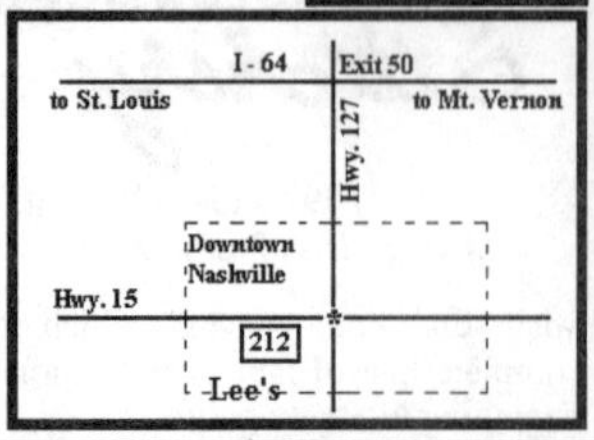

Collinsville, IL #6

110 W. Main St. 62234
(618) 345-3661
Owner: Mary Solomon
Est: 1990 4000 sq.ft.

Mon - Sat 9 - 4
Tues & Thur til 7:30

Over 3500 Bolts of 100% Cotton Fabrics
Homespuns * Modas
Hoffmans * Batiks * RJR

BERNINA®

Bernina Sewing & Embroidery Machines and Sergers & Horn of America Quilting Cabinets.

Cross Patches

Only 12 min. from downtown St. Louis

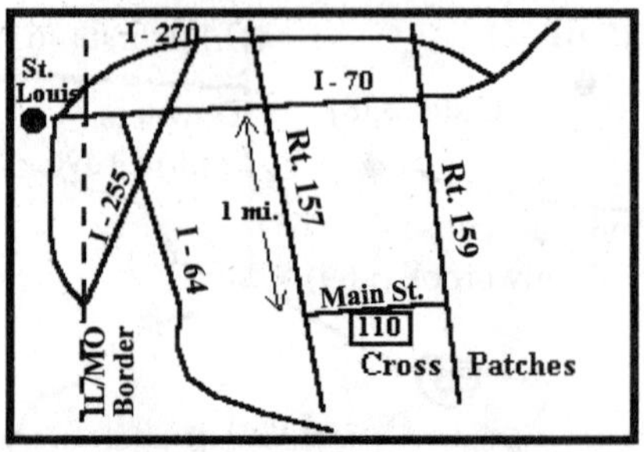

Show us this AD and we will give you a 10% (one time) discount on Fabric purchases.

Millstadt, IL #7

Mon - Fri 9 - 5
Sat 9 - 2

Quilts Unlimited

620 E. Washington 62260
(618) 476-3019
Est: 1969

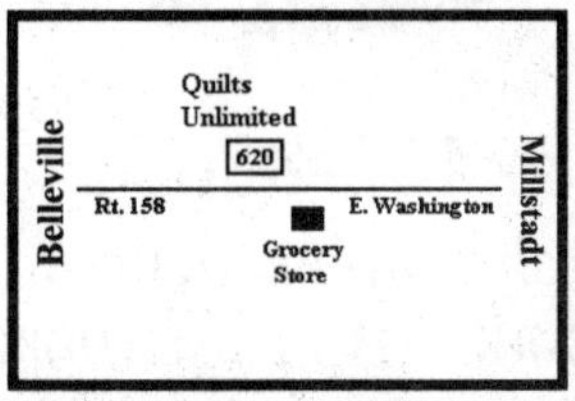

Custom Machine Quilting, Baby Quilts, Large Quilt Sales, "Magic Pillows", wall hangings, Quilt Stands, Shelves, Wood items, Crafts, Quilt top piecing.

Mascoutah, IL #8

Tues 2- 6
Wed - Fri 10 - 4
Sat 10 - 2

Patchwork Corner Crafts

200 N. Jefferson St.
62258
(618) 566-2652

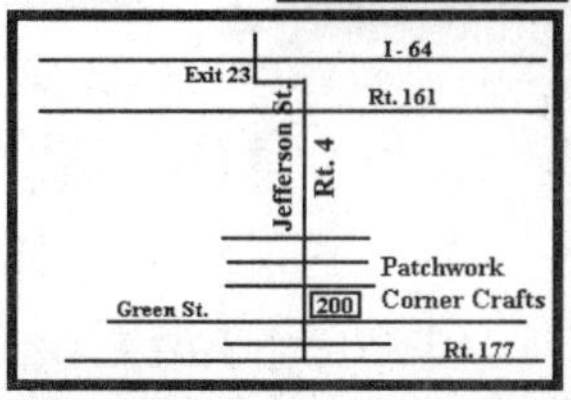

We have a large supply of quilting fabrics and supplies. We have pieced quilt tops, finished quilts and handmade crafts.

Since 1903

Jackman's Fabrics

www.jackmansfabrics.com

Superstore - Fairview Heights, Illinois

Quilting • Fashion • Bridal
Home Decorator Fabrics

baby lock Sergers, Embroidery & Sewing Machines
Only 15 minutes from downtown St. Louis

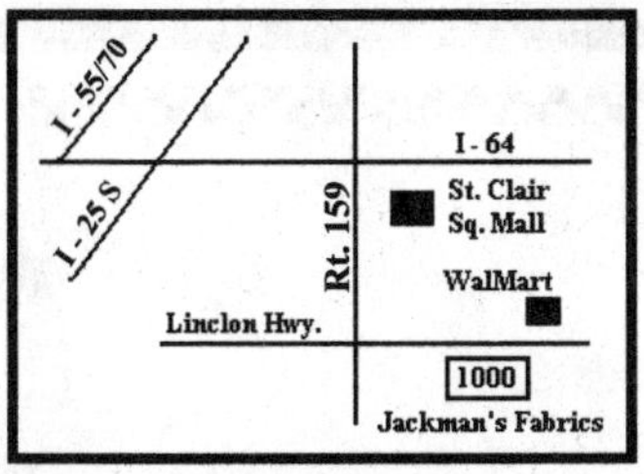

618-632-2700 • 1000 Lincoln Hwy., 62208
Mon. & Thurs. 10:00 - 9:00 • Tues., Wed., Fri. 10:00 - 6:00
Sat. 10:00 - 5:30 Sun. noon - 5:00

Fairview Heights, IL #9

Over 50,000 yards of quilting cottons!
Thimbleberries, Aunt Grace, Debbie Mumm, KP Kids, Hoffman, Timeless Treasures, RJR, Moda, Benartex, P&B, South Seas and more . . . including novelties, batiks, homespuns, flannels, broadcloths, wide sheetings, books, patterns & notions.

COME SEE US FOR ONE OF THE LARGEST AND NEWEST SELECTIONS OF COTTON FABICS IN THE MIDWEST.

Show us this ad and you will receive a 1 time 20% discount on your entire non-sale purchase.

Highland, IL #10

Mon - Fri 9 - 5
Sat 9 - 4

Rosemary's Fabric & Quilts

812 Ninth St. 62249
(618) 654-5045
E-Mail: seifried@hometel.com
Owner: Rosemary Seifried
Est: 1988

Largest Thimbleberries Selection in St. Louis Area.
Over 3000 Bolts of Fabric.
Everything a Quilter Needs!

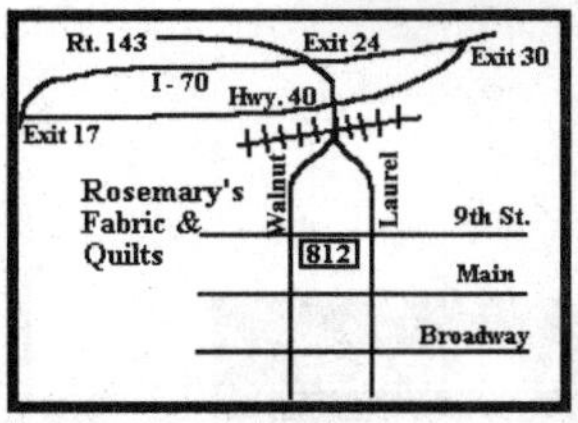

Jacksonville, IL #11

Mon 10 - 7
Tues - Fri 10 - 5
Sat 10 - 3

The Sewing Basket

1687 W. Morton Ave. 62650
(217) 243-5507
Owner: Marcia Cox

Quilt Shop with over 1000 bolts of 100% cotton fabrics & quilting supplies.

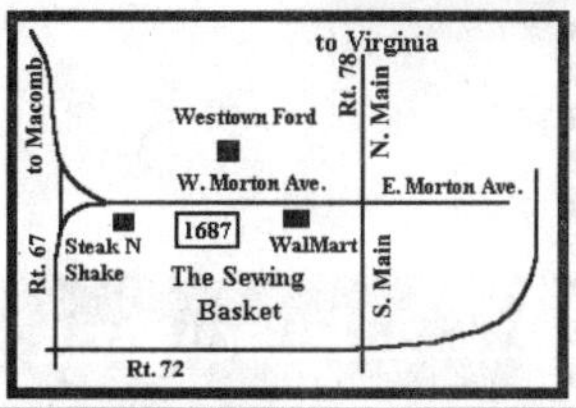

Alton, IL #12

PATCHWORK PLUS

Mon - Thur 9 - 5
Fri & Sat 9 - 4
Sun 12 - 4

108 W. Third St. 62002 (618) 462-8565

Fax: (618) 462-8565 E-Mail: patchplus@piasanet.com

Owner: Jan Coats Est: 1999 3600 sq.ft. 3000+ Bolts of 100% Cotton

Indulge your fabric craving in a relaxed atmosphere. Our knowledgeable and friendly staff can help you with color selection or any quilting problem you may have. Stop in and say "hello". Bring in your Quilters' Travel Companion book and receive a fat quarter free.

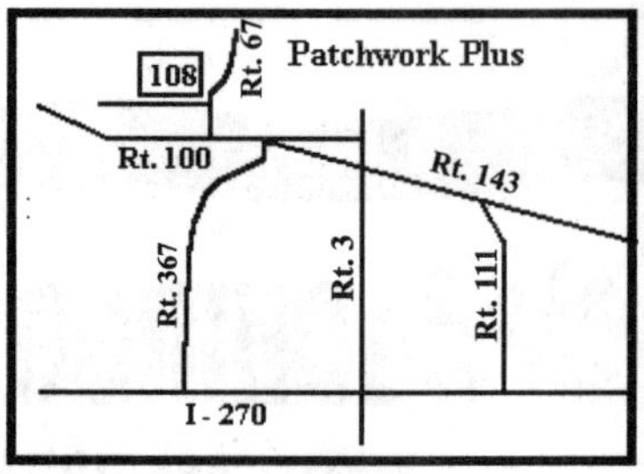

- We specialize in reproduction fabrics from 1800-1920.
  We have the largest selection of these fabrics in the St. Louis area.
- We have an Antique Quilt Club.
- We have the newest Block of the Month kits available.
- We also carry a complete line of embroidery thread including DMC and Krenik and counted cross-stitch supplies.
- We have a large classroom complete with sewing machines. Customize your own class with groups of 4 or more.

Custom Machine Quilting Also Available by:

All In Stitches—Kaye Sutton

2nd Floor of Patchwork Plus Tues - Thur 10 - 4 or by Appointment

Sew-4-Fun

Quilt Shop & Sewing Center

KEEPING THE WORLD SEWING

9 - 6 Mon - Fri
9 - 4 Saturday

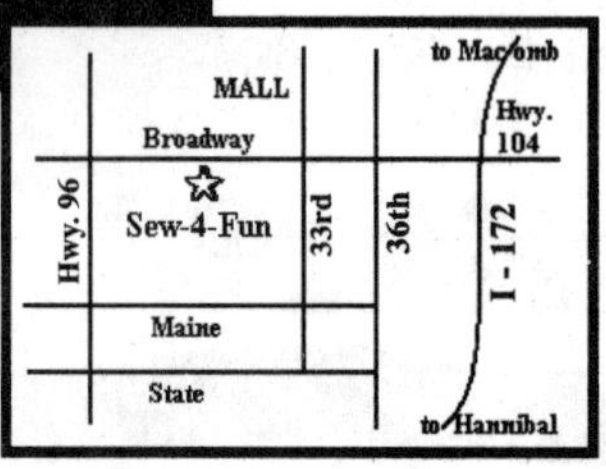

- **1000+ bolts of quilting cottons, and growing daily Benartex, Hoffman, Moda, P & B, In The Beginning and more.**
- **Heirloom Sewing and Smocking Supplies**
- **Great selection of books and patterns**
- **Husqvarna Viking and White brand Sewing Machines and Sergers**
- **Classes, Classes, and more classes -- Quilting, fashion, and Heirloom, Sewing and Serger Clubs**
- **Martha Pullen Gift of the Month Heirloom Club**
- **Block-of-the-Month**
- **Machine Repair Service**

Sew-4-Fun

3114 Broadway
Quincy, Illinois 62301
217-223-5498

Fax: 217-223-5546 E-Mail: Sew4fun@transedge.com

Authorized Husqvarna Viking Dealer

Quincy, IL #13

Quincy's First Sewing Room Offering Classes, Clubs, Sales and Service!"

Husqvarna VIKING

Mon - Fri 10 - 6
Sat 10 - 4

A great selection of quality 100% cotton fabrics, books, patterns and notions along with friendly customer service.

Springfield, IL #14

2765 W. Jefferson, Suite DD
62702
(217) 787-4251
Owner: Kathy Jennings

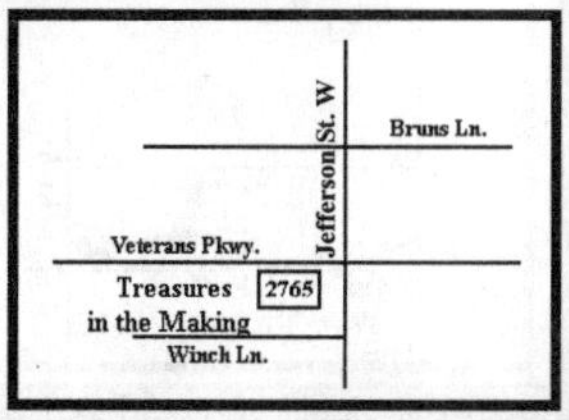

Mon - Fri
10 - 5
Thur til 8
Sat 10 - 4

peace & Applique

145 E. Main St.
P.O. Box 724 62563
Phone/Fax:
(217) 498-6771
Owner: Gretchen Quistgaard & Lois Weissberg
E-mail: quilter@peacenapplique.com
Web Site: www.peacenapplique.com

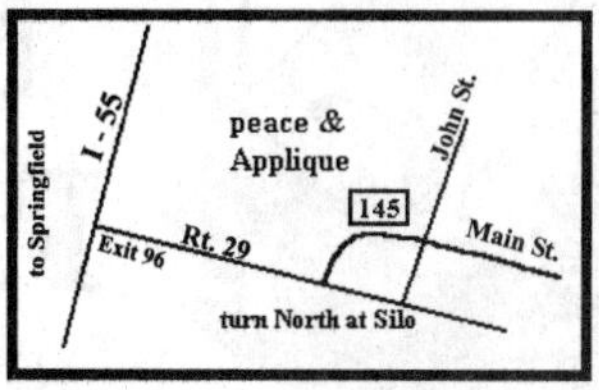

Visit our charming shop in an historic building with beautiful quilts hanging on the 12' brick walls. Over 3100 bolts of high quality cottons including Moda, Thimbleberries, Maywood, Kaufmann, with bright and rustic flannels, homespuns, and primitives. Many books & patterns. Classes for all interest and skill levels. Join us at the shop just 4 miles east of Springfield, by mail, or through our website.

Rochester, IL #15

"Every Day is a Great Day to peace & Applique"

Arthur, IL #16

Mon - Sat
8:30 - 5

Stitch & Sew Fabrics

220 S. Vine St. 61911
(217) 543-2287
Fax: (217) 543-2287
Est: 1994
E-Mail: stitchandsew@one-eleven.net
Owners: Sam & Dorothy Herschberger

Over 2000 Bolts of cotton including Hoffman, RJR, Fashion Fabrics and more Quilting Supplies, Books, Bulk Buttons. Authorized Elna

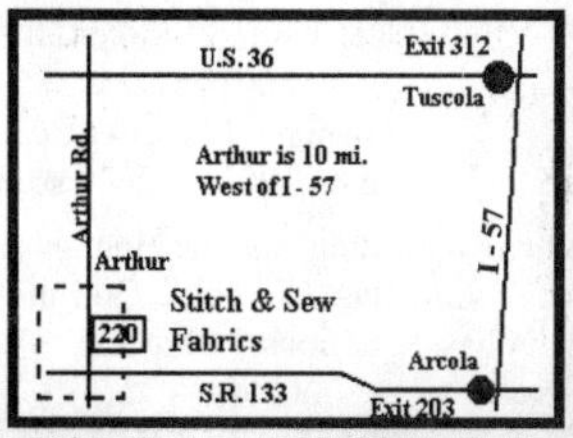

Decatur, IL #18

Mon - Sat
10 - 5

Quilt Patch

2885 N. Oakland Ave. 62526
(217) 872-1195
Owner: Doris Shookman

Opened in 2000. A Growing, Charming New Quilt Shop offering Quality Fabrics & Quilting Supplies, Customized Machine Quilting with Longarm. Plus Fun Quilting Classes.
Come Visit.

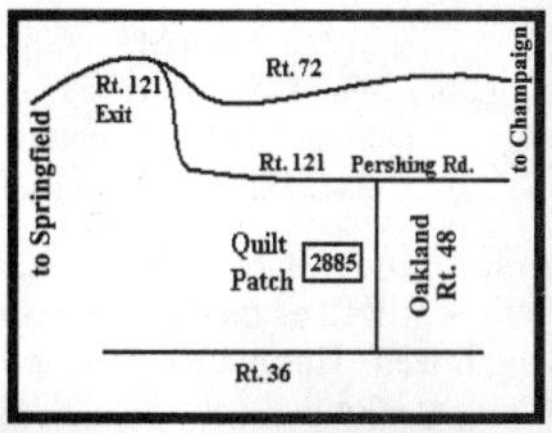

Bloomington, IL #19

Mon - Sat
10 - 5
Sun 12 - 4

The Treadle

2101 Eastland 61704
(309) 662-1733

Over 6000 Bolts of Calico Prints. Largest selection of quilt books, quilt patterns, craft patterns in central Illinois.

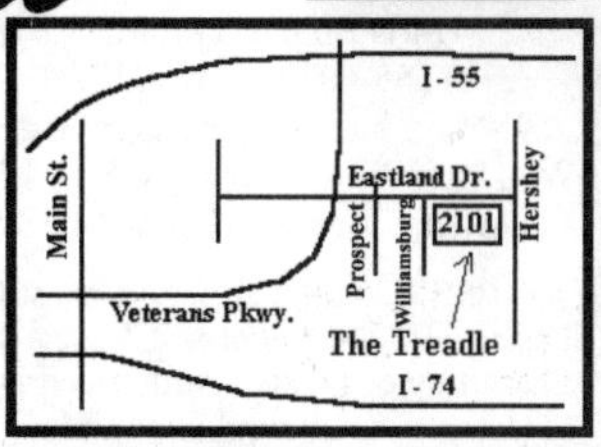

Paris, IL #17

Lori's Pins 'n Needles

Phone (217) 465-5541
Fax (217) 465-1043
Email: loris@comwares.net
Website: www.lorisviking.com

Husqvarna VIKING

"Quilting Headquarters"

- Over 3000 bolts of name brand 100% cotton fabrics
- Books, patterns and quilting tools
- Large classroom area—classes and demonstrations
- Authorized Husqvarna Viking Sewing Machine Sales and Service.

Monday - Thursday
9-6
Friday 9-8
Saturday 9-5

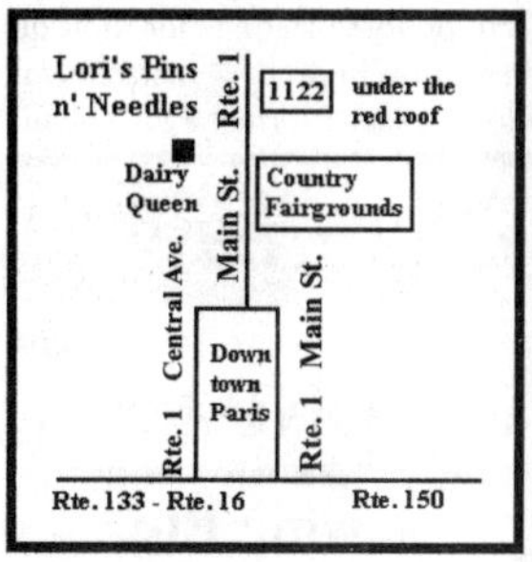

1122 N. Main St.
P.O. Box 815 61944

Lincoln, IL #20

Sew Many Friends

127 S. Kickapoo 62656
(217) 732-4527

email: ivykquilts@hotmail.com
Designers: Ivy Koritz & Sue Bidwell
Est: 2000 1200 sq.ft. 700 bolts & growing

Friendly, relaxed, well-lit atmosphere. Complete line of **supplies** for quiltmaking. **Machine quilting** services available. **Classes** for hand and machine quilting and construction, smocking, and clothing construction. Doll and clothing **patterns**. Needlework and yarn shop next door. 100% cotton fabrics from Hoffman, Moda, RJR, Maywood, SSI and more. **Bring this ad in for a free fat quarter**.

M & W 10 - 9
T, T, F, Sat 10 - 5

Quilting
*Sewing * Smocking*

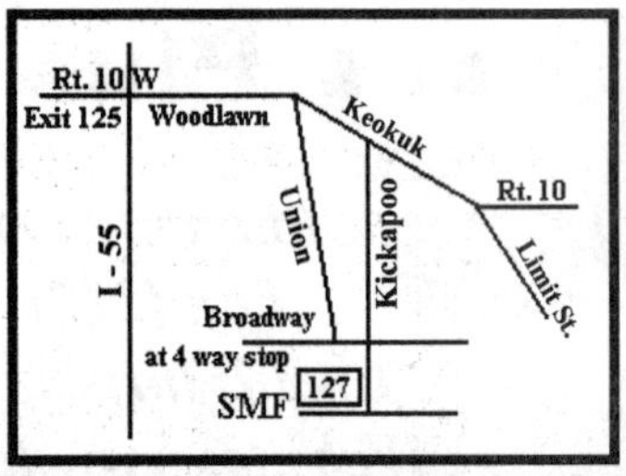

Quilters Delight

Mon, Thur, Fri 10 - 5:30
Tues & Wed 10 - 8:30
Sat 9 - 5

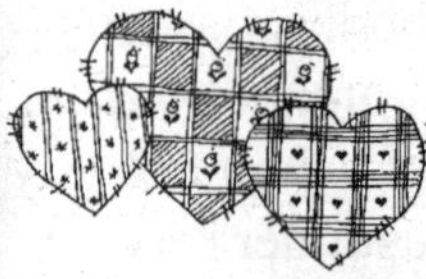

419 S. Walnut 61727
(217) 937-0159
E-Mail: smonkman@family-net.net
Owner: Shirley Jo Monkman

Clinton, IL #21

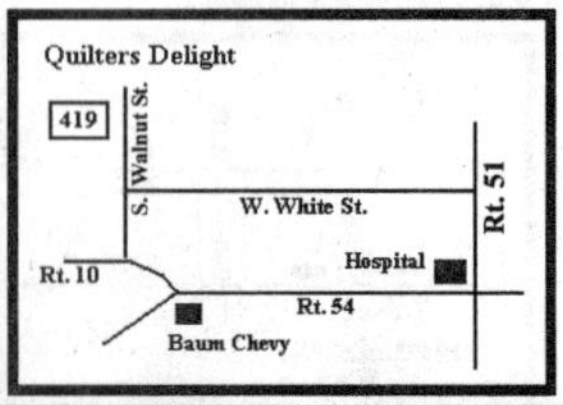

Fabrics, Batting, Sewing Notions, Needles and Threads, Books and Patterns, Classes and Much More.
"Blessed are the "Quilters" for they are life's piece makers."

Normal, IL #22

Sewing Studio

Mon - Fri 9:30 - 6
Sat 9:30 - 5
Sun 12 - 4

1503 E. College, Suite C 61761
(309) 452-7313
Owners: Margaret Couch
Est: 1983 2600 sq.ft.

Quality quilting and fashion fabrics. Quilting & sewing classes, books. Quilting & heirloom supplies & notions. Bernina / Viking / White Dealer

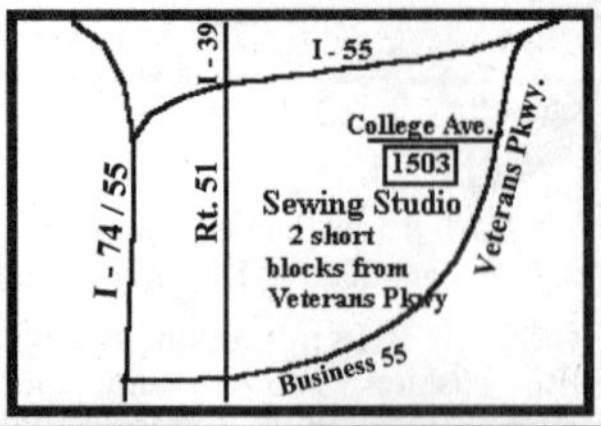

El Paso, IL #23

Karla's Country Quilt Shop

Tues 10 - 7
Wed - Sat 10 - 5

52 N. Elm St. 61738
(309) 527-8458
Owner: Karla R. Uphoff

100% cotton fabric, books, notions & gifts. Small town friendly with big town selection. Comfortable seating for non-quilters. Play area for children. Just 20 miles north of Bloomington/Normal and I-74 and I-55.

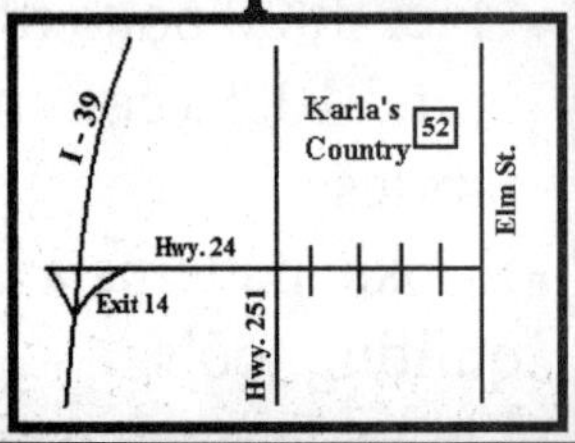

Hoopeston, IL #24

Sewing Boutique

Mon - Fri 9 - 5:30
Sat 9 - 3

222 E. Main St. 60942
(217) 283-7125 Fax: (217) 283-5580
E-Mail: sewbout@net66.com
Est: 1980 2200 sq.ft.

A full service fabric shop stocking fashion fabrics as well as quality cottons for quilting. Authorized Husqvarna Viking dealer.
Classes Galore!

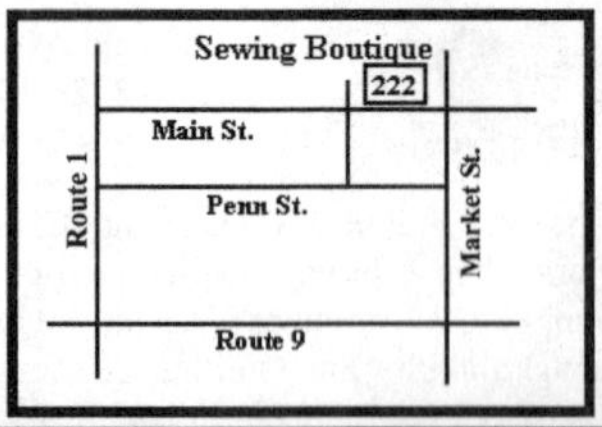

Champaign, IL #25

Mon 9:30 - 8
Tues - Sat 9:30 - 5:30

Londa's Sewing Etc.

404 S. Duncan 61821
(217) 352-2378
Fax: (217) 352-3389
Est: 1990
6000 sq.ft.

Owners: Londa & Charles Rohlfing

E-Mail: sewez45@aol.com
Web Site: www.londas-sewing.com

Top quality quilting and fashion fabrics. Sales & Service for brother, Pfaff, Singer & Elna. Wonderful classes and special events.
Come . . . browse.

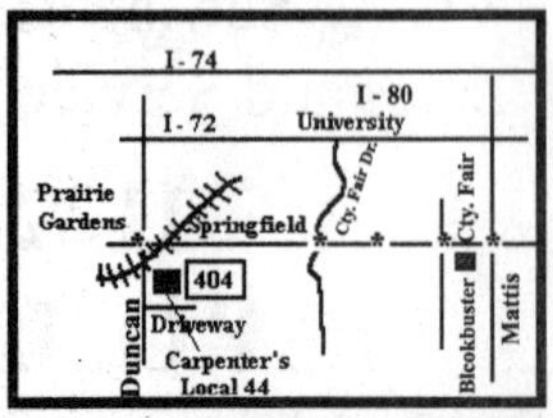

Champaign, IL #26

B & J Sewing Center

Mon - Fri 10 - 6:30
Sat 9 - 4

1914-D Round Barn Rd. 61821
(217) 355-6090 Fax: (217) 355-6036
E-Mail: bjsew2@msn.com Est: 1995
Web Site: www.bjsewing.com 1500 sq.ft.
Owners: Barbara & John Marcukaitis

Fine 100% Cotton Fabric, Notions, Quilting Supplies, Books, Patterns, Classes. Machine Quilting of Quilts. Authorized Dealer Husqvarna Viking Sewing Machines.

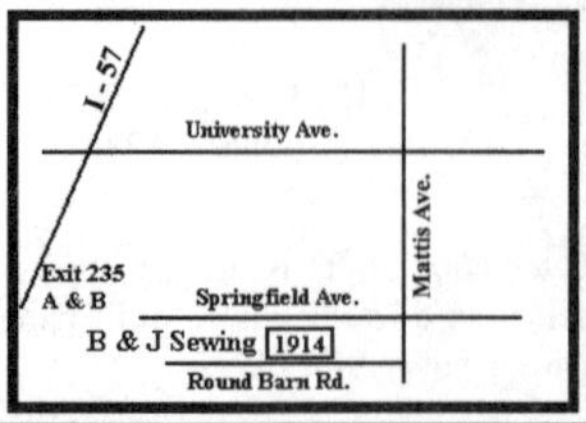

Prairieland Quilts

Unique selection of books, patterns, gift items, quilt frames, supplies and Janome sewing machines. Machine and hand quilting service available. Prairieland Quilts warehouses over 1500 patterns from over 50 quilt designers which is also available in our online store.

Mon - Fri 9 - 5
Sat 9 - 3

JANOME

107 N. 2nd. St. (Rt.49) 60924
(815) 457-2867 (800) 391-2867
Web Site: www.quilterswarehouse.com
Owner: Suzanne Bruns Est: 1993

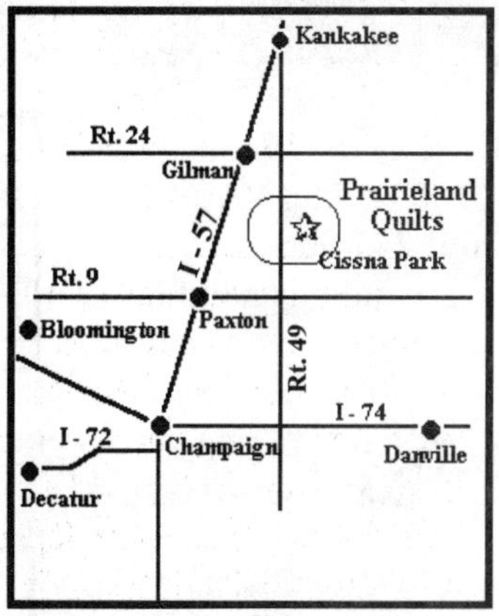

Cissna Park, IL #27

Bring your 'Travel Companion' with you and receive a one time 10% discount on your purchase.

The Quilt Corner

- Complete line of Quilting Fabrics
- Large selection of Batik and Flannel Fabrics
- Books, Patterns & Notions.
- Kits are our Specialty
- Complete line of Silk Ribbon
- We Offer a variety of Classes and Workshops

Mon - Thur 9:30 - 8 Fri - Sat 9:30-4:30

2037 S. Main St. 61550
(309) 263-7114
Owner: Karen Bailey
Est: 1988 5000 sq.ft. 4000 Bolts

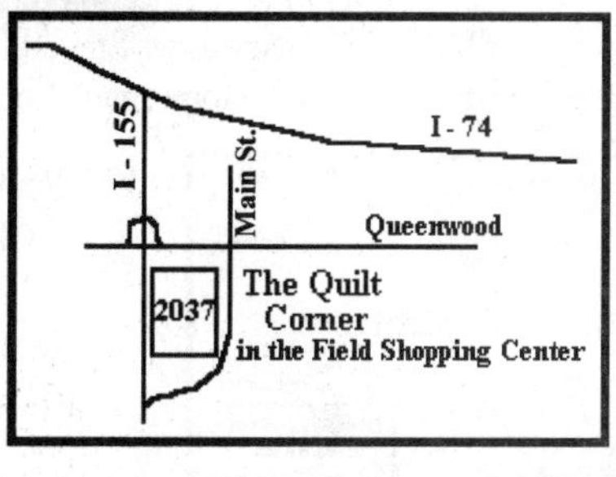

Morton, IL #28

Quilt & Sew Dreams

Two Great Locations!

Visit our Website:
www.quiltsewdreams.com

Mon 10 - 8
Tues - Fri 10 - 5
Sat 10 - 4

Dunlap, IL #29

"Lake of the Woods Plaza"
12200 N. Rte. 40 61525
(309) 243-9067
Email: quilt@npoint.net
Est: 1998

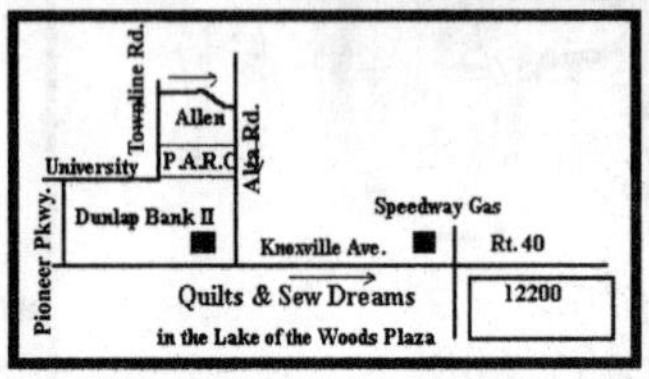

Just North of Peoria on Rte. 40.

Pekin, IL #30

In the "Derby Plaza"
1100 Derby St. 61554
(309) 347-2289
Email: qsdreams@mtco.com
Est: 2001

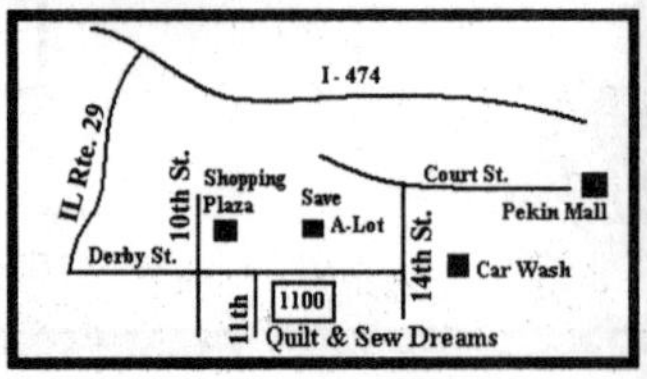

Full Service Quilt Shop & Husqvarna/Viking & White Dealership. Cozy Atmosphere with Friendly, Knowledgeable staff. Quality Cottons, Supplies, Service, Education & Inspiration.
Professional Machine Quilting Service

Avon, IL #31

The Clothesline Quilt Shop

Mon - Sat 10 - 5

102 N. Main, P.O. Box 122 61415
(309) 465-3850 E-Mail: Qultshop@avonil.net

Large selection of patterns, books, notions and 100% cotton quilt fabrics including Thimbleberries, Moda, and Hoffman.
We also custom machine quilt with a good selection for battings.

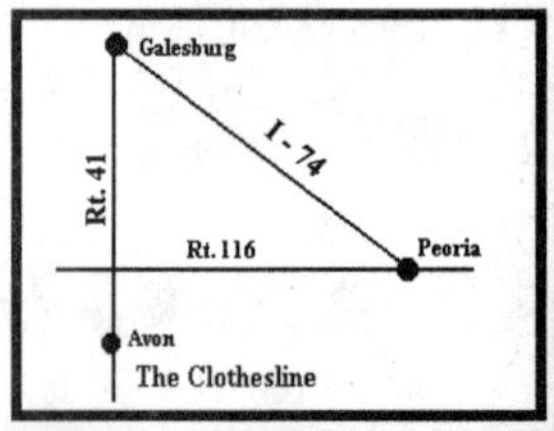

Metamora, IL #32

Mon 9:30 - 8
Tues - Fri 9:30 - 5
Sat 10 - 4

Cozy Corner Quilts & Sewing Center

101 W. Partridge St.
P.O. Box 409 61548
(309) 367-9303
Fax: (309) 367-9632
Web Site: www.cozycornersewing.com

Your Complete Quilt Shop! Over 2000 bolts of fabric.

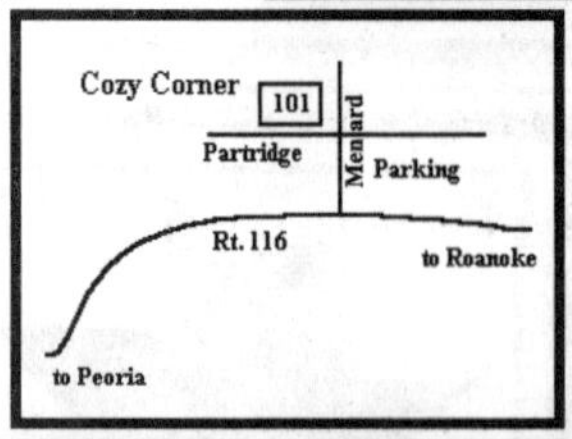

Washington, IL #33

Peg & Lil's Needle Patch

Mon 10 - 7
Tues - Fri 10 - 5
Sat 10 - 4

FABRICS - 1500 bolts 100% cottons
QUILTING - Large selection of Fabrics, Books, Patterns, Rotary tools, Stencils and Classes.
CRAFTERS - Patterns & Homespuns Lots of Samples on display.

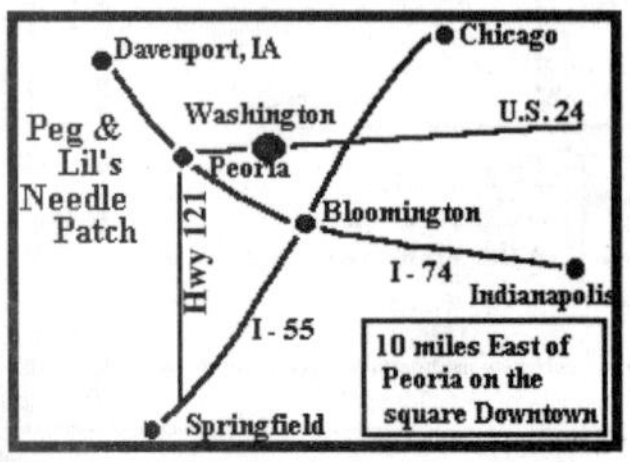

127 Peddlers Way 61571
(309) 444-7667
1400 sq.ft. Est: 1985
Owner: Lillian Cagle
Authorized Pfaff Sewing Machine Dealer

Bishop Hill, IL #34

7 Day a Week
10 - 5
April - Dec.

Village Smithy

309 N. Bishop Hill St. 61419
(309) 927-3851 Fax: (309) 937-5438
E-Mail: nelsonfarm@geneseo.net
Web Site: www.bishophill.com Est: 1984
Owner: Marilyn Nelson 2900 sq.ft. 600 Bolts

We feature vintage quilts, quilting supplies, fabrics, patterns, Antiques and Collectibles. Located in a charming historical village.

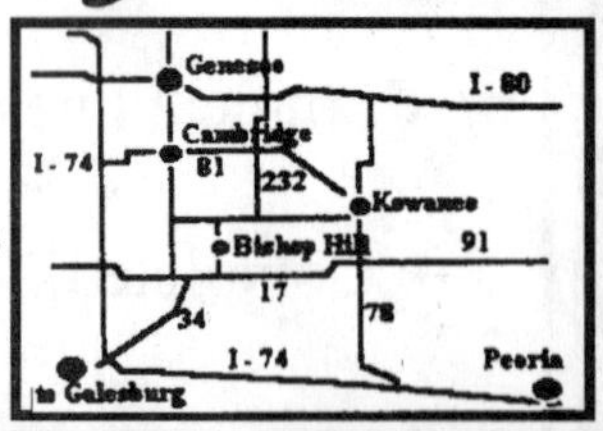

Geneseo, IL #35

Mon - Fri 10 - 5
Sat 10 - 4

Quilt Quarters

137 S. State St., Room 101 61254
(309) 944-2693 Est: 1992
E-Mail: quiltqtr@hotmail.com
Owners: Mike & Janette Dwyer

Satisfying Quilters and their needs. Come in and browse our fabric, patterns, books and inspiration. We are right above The Cellar in the Geneseo House "First floor, right door"

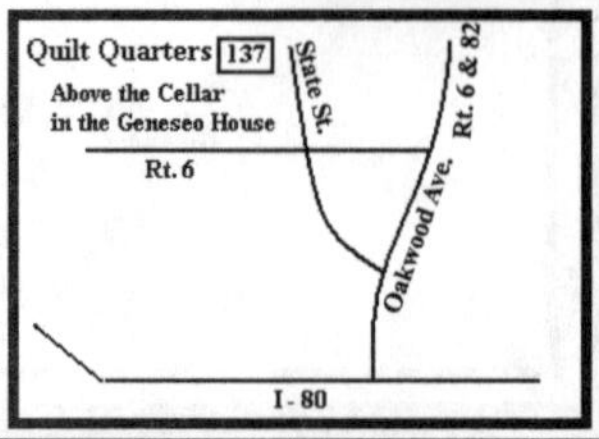

Princeton, IL #36

527 S. Main St. 61356
(815) 879-3739 (87 - WE - SEW)
E-Mail: quiltersgarden@yahoo.com Fax: (815) 879-3739
Owners: Beth Rosene & Carol Keller
Est: 2000 1700 sq.ft.

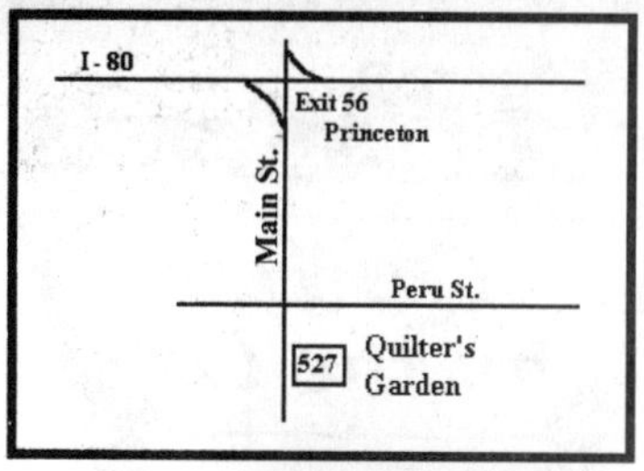

Quilter's Garden

Mon - Fri 10 - 5
Sat 10 - 4

Stroll our garden of quality fabrics, patterns, books and notions.
Over 2000 bolts of 100% cotton fabrics including Batiks
Cotton flannels,
Moda Marbles and Thimbleberries.
Classes at all skill levels.
Machine quilting
Block of the Month
Programs
Free parking in back

Bed and Breakfast sewing retreat center "Stairway to Stitchin" is available.
Home of zany quilt guild program, "A Visit from Aunt Sewsie."
Call or e-mail for details.

Featured in the American Patchwork & Quilting Shop Sampler 1998.

Fabric, Notions, Books, Patterns, Stencils, Machine Quilting, Classes.

Fulton, IL #37

1108 4th St. Fulton, IL 61252
(815) 589-2221

Hours: Tues - Sat 10 - 6 Sunday 12 - 4
Closed Mondays and Holidays

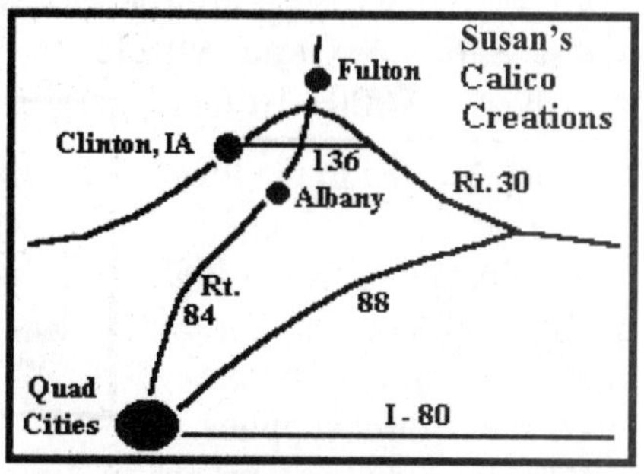

New Owner: Susan May
Est: 1986 4,000 sq.ft.

Moline, IL #38

3000+ bolts 100% cotton. Large assortment of Thimbleberries, Hoffman, Kaufman & Moda. Books, Patterns, Notions, & Bulk Buttons.

Mon - Fri 10 - 5
Sat 10 - 2
Call Ahead for Special Appt.

3201 - 23rd. Ave. 61265
(309) 762-9673 or
(800) 735-9673
E-Mail: quiltoz@mchsi.com
Owner: Harlene Rivelli
Est: 1987 2400 sq.ft.

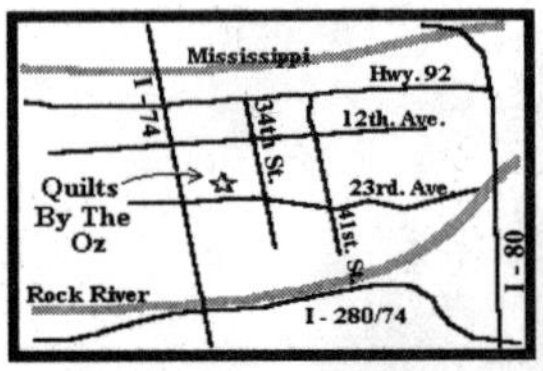

13 blocks east of I - 74

Moline, IL #39

M, T, Th, F 9:30 - 5
Wed 9:30 - 9
Sat 9:30 - 4

The Quilt Basket

2521 53rd St. 61265
(309) 764-1346
Owner: Ann Filiatreau
Est: 2002

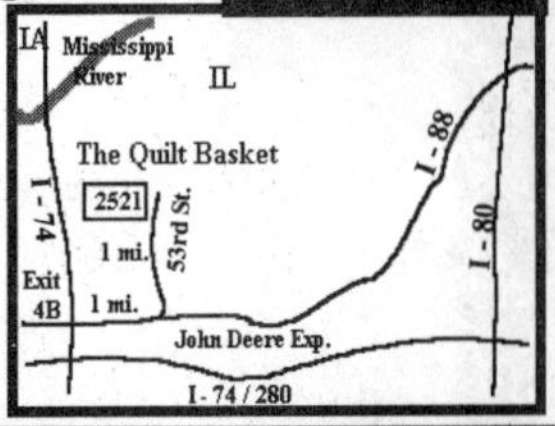

Machine quilting, Fabric, Notions, Books, Patterns, Quilt Classes, Basket Weaving, Classes. Large selection of Gift Items. Hand made wood items by local craftsmen.

Morrison, IL #40

Mon 12 - 9
Tues - Sat 10 - 5
Sun 12 - 3

CONstantly Stitching N' More

13690 Lincoln Road 61270
(815) 772-2833
Owner: Connie Barr
Est: 1992 5000 sq.ft.

Machine Quilting, Fabric, Notions, Books, Patterns, Quilt Classes. Basket Weaving Classes. Gift Items. Antiques.

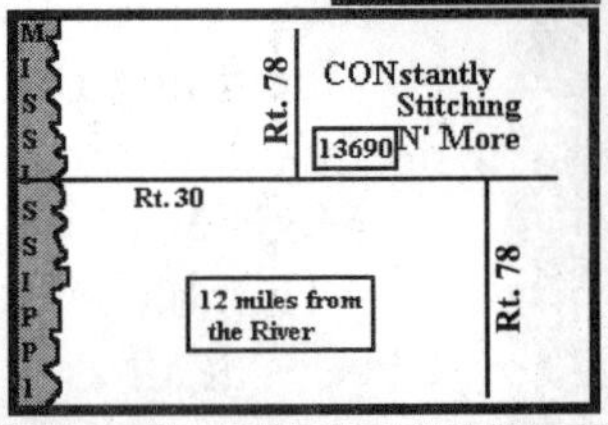

Dixon, IL #41

Tues - Fri 10 - 5
Sat 10 - 4

The Quilt Cellar

541 Penrose Road 61021
(815) 288-5594
Owner: Sue Ramage Est: 1992
Over 1500 Bolts including Homespun, flannels, Moda, Benartex & lots of reproduction fabrics. Quilting supplies and classes.

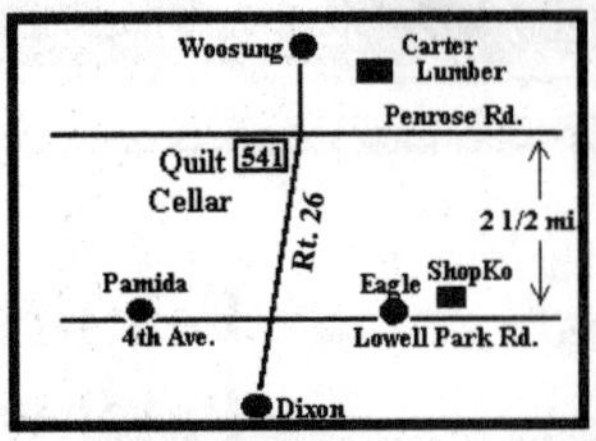

THE FABRIC CENTER
"A SEWING MACHINE SUPERSTORE"

A Quilters Dream

301 Liberty St. 60450 (815) 942-5715
fabctr@uti.com
Owner: Lonnie Booker
in nostalgic downtown

Morris, IL #42

- *Over 3,000 bolts of cotton fabric (discounted 20% off everyday)*
- *Largest selection of Hoffman fabrics in IL*
- *Also featuring Debbie Mumm, Moda, RJR, Concord, Mission Valley, Benartex, Hi-Fashion, Springs, Kaufman, P&B & more.*
- *Quilting notions, stencils, patterns and books and quilting frames.*
- *Brother & Janome New Home Dealer.*

Quilting Classes Avail. Year Round

Mon - Wed 9 - 5:30
Thur 9 - 7
Fri 9 - 5:30
Sat 9 - 5

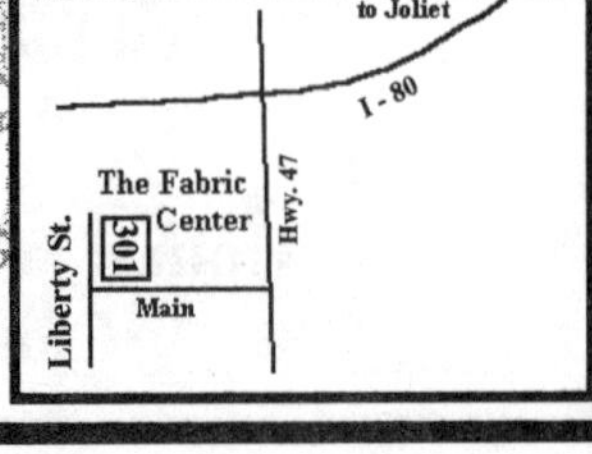

Orangeville, IL #43

Uniquely Yours Quilt Shop

12530 N. Oneco Rd. 61060
(815) 789-4344
Cell Phone (608) 558-5158
E-mail: gene.haffele@monroe.k12.wi.us
Owner: Sandy & Gene Haffele
Est: 1990 5000+ Bolts

Mon - Sat 9 - 5
Thur 9 - 8

New shop located in the lower level of our new home.
Over 2100 square feet of high quality 100% cotton fabric.
Large selection of books, patterns & quilt supplies.

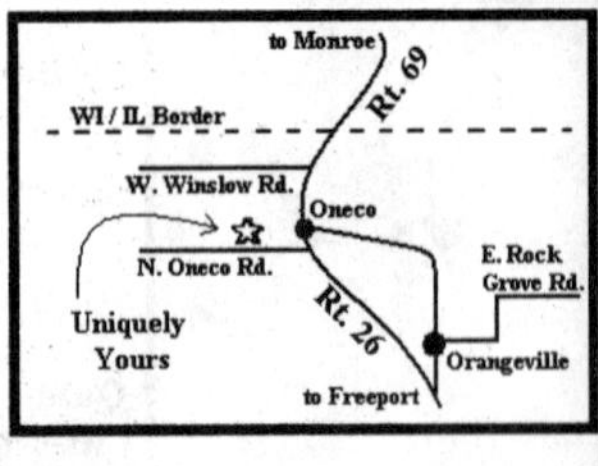

Country location, country charm, friendly, helpful staff.

Largest selection of Fabric in Stateline Area.

Rockford, IL #44

QUILTER'S GENERAL STORE INC.

6903 Harrison Ave. 61108
Toll Free: 877-548-4555 815-397-5160
Fax: 815-399-5025
E-Mail: farmquilts@aol.com
Web Site: www.quiltersgeneralstore.com
Owner: Jan Ragaller

Mon - Sat 10 - 5
Sun 12 - 4

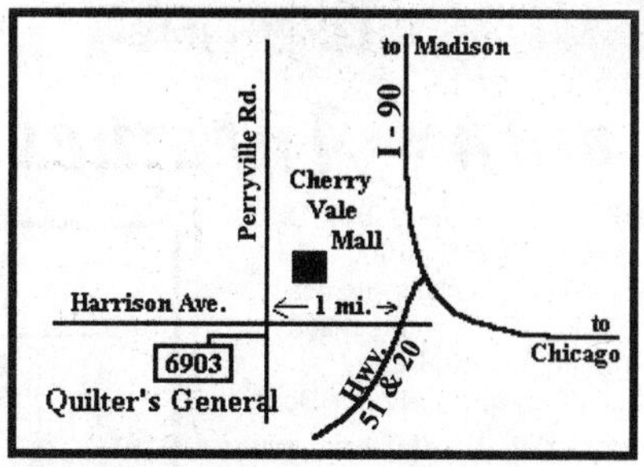

"Featured in American Patchwork and Quilting "Sampler 2001"

This "country in the city" shop boasts 2000+ bolts of cotton fabric, books, patterns, notions and a friendly, helpful staff of quilters. Located in a beautiful 1875 farm house. Classes for all levels. Newsletter and special orders upon request.

Rockford, IL #45

Quilter's Haven

Quilter's Haven carries a wide variety of 100% cotton fabrics, books, and patterns. In addition we carry supplies for rug hookers.
We offer a unique combination of classes and have several samples to inspire you!
Friendly, individual attention is what we are known for.

4616 E. State St. 61108
(815) 227-1659
Owners: Stephanie Gauerke
& Cathy Johnson
Est: 1995 1200 sq.ft.

Mon - Sat 10 - 4 Wed til 7

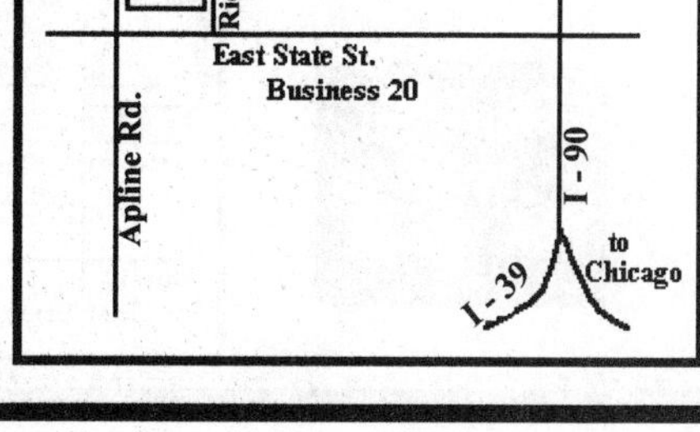

Bourbonnais, IL #46

Mon 9 - 8
Tues - Thur 9 - 6:30
Fri 9 - 6
Sat 9 - 4

B & J Sewing Center

616 S. Main St. 60914
(815) 937-9955 Fax: (815) 937-9566
E-Mail: bjsew@TheRamp.net Est: 1994
Web Site: www.bjsewing.com 3000 sq.ft.
Owners: Barbara & John Marcukaitis

Fine 100% Cotton Fabric, Notions, Quilting Supplies, Books, Patterns, Classes. Machine Quilting of Quilts. Authorized Dealer Husqvarna Viking Sewing Machines.

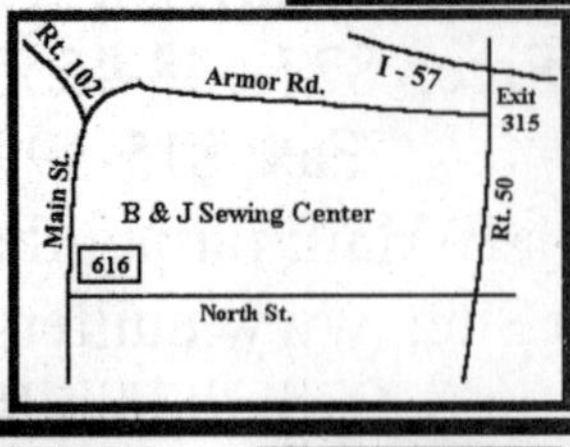

Manteno, IL #47

Mon - Fri 10 - 5
Thur til 8
Sat 10 - 3

Just Between Friends
Quilt Shoppe, Inc.

19 W. Division St. 60950
(815) 468-6050 Fax: (815) 468-6051
Owners: Jan Behm & Linda Michalek
Est: 1999 1200 sq.ft. 1000+ Bolts

Latest books, patterns, notions, fabric including large selection of Thimbleberries. Pfaff sewing machines. Friendly, personal service. 45 miles south of Chicago.

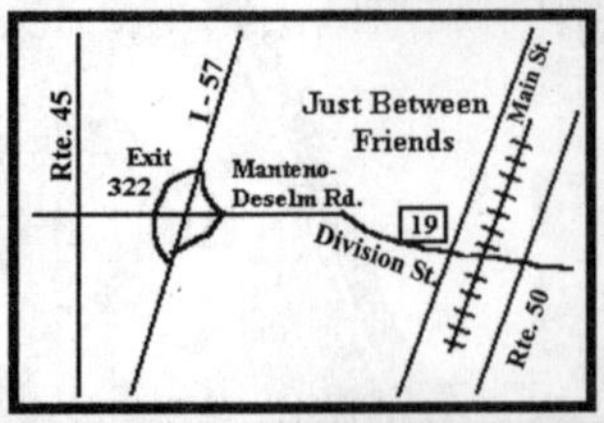

Pearl City, IL #48

Mon - Fri 11 - 7
Sat 10 - 5
Sun 11 - 5

Sew many Antiques

140 - 160 S. Main St., P.O. Box 55
(815) 443-2211 61062
E-Mail: sewmanya@aeroinc.net
Owners: Jill & Dave Kempel and Vicki & Dave Olsen
Est: 1992 4300 sq.ft. 1200+ Bolts

Filled with over 1200 bolts of fabric, patterns, books, gifts, and antiques. We offer classes, retreats & always a friendly welcome.

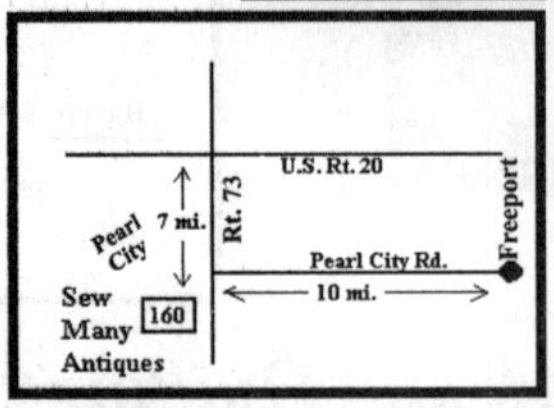

Belvidere, IL #49

Tues - Sat 10 - 5
Sun 11 - 4

All My Stitches

407 South State St. 61008
(815) 547-1099
E-Mail: AllMyStitches1@aol.com
Owner: Cindy Davison
Est: 2001 1200 sq.ft.

Collections of 100% cotton solids and prints from all the best manufacturers. Books, patterns, notions & classes. Husqvarna Viking dealer.

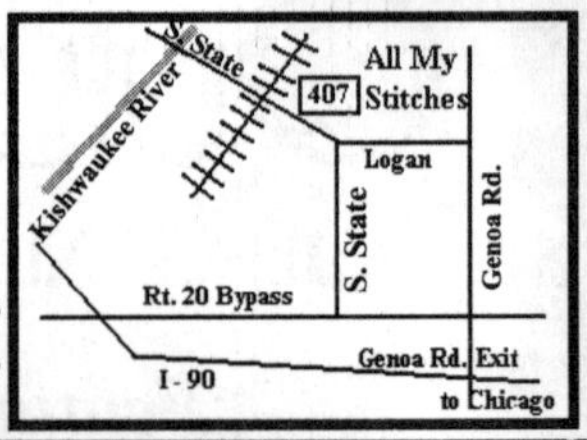

Sunshine and Shadow
Quilt Shoppe

5608 Broadway 60071
(815) 678-2603
Owner: Terri LaDuke
email: Terri@rsg.org
Est: 1991 2000 + Bolts
In Historic Richmond among Antique & Unique Shops

Richmond, IL #50

With new ownership we have doubled our selection of high quality fabrics. We carry the latest in books, patterns, and notions. We offer classes for all levels, along with a good selection of kits, and many samples to insprie you. Our friendly, knowledgeable staff looks forward to meeting you. Authorized Pfaff Dealer.

Mon - Sat 10 - 5
Sun 12 - 4

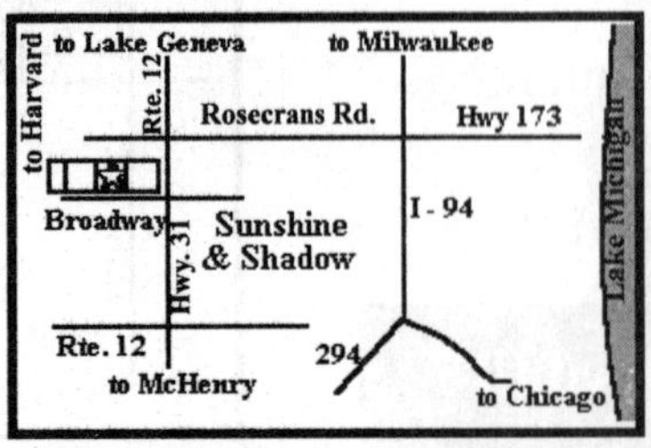

Barrington, IL #51

A Touch of Amish

130 Applebee St. 60010
(847) 381-0900
(888) 5-QUILTS (578-4587)
Owner: Lynn Rice
Est: 1986 2500 sq.ft.

Tues - Sat 10 - 4

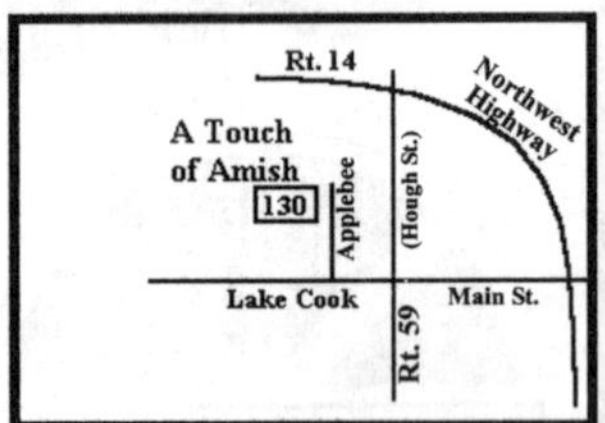

Wonderful fabrics, books, patterns, custom quilting, free weekly demonstrations, and always great service.

Libertyville, IL #52

LIBERTYVILLE Sewing CENTER

Mon - Thur 9 - 9
Fri & Sat 9 - 5

Large Selection of :
- Calicos featuring Hoffman.
- Quilting Supplies.
- Buttons
- Threads
- Sales & Service -All Makes & Models

When You're Ready for the Best® VIKING
Nothing Sews Like A Bernina. Nothing. BERNINA®
baby lock
brother

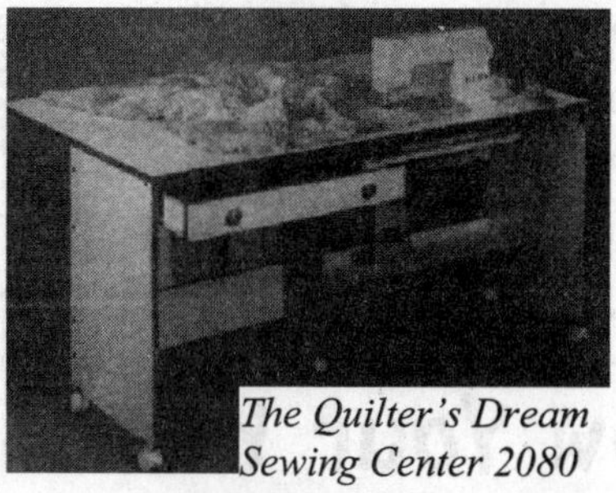

The Quilter's Dream Sewing Center 2080

326 Peterson Rd. 60048
(Brookside Shp. Ctr.)
(847) 367-0820
Est: 1982 5400 sq.ft.
Owners: Linda & Rick Mosier
E-Mail: Libertysew@aol.com
www.libertyvillesewing.com

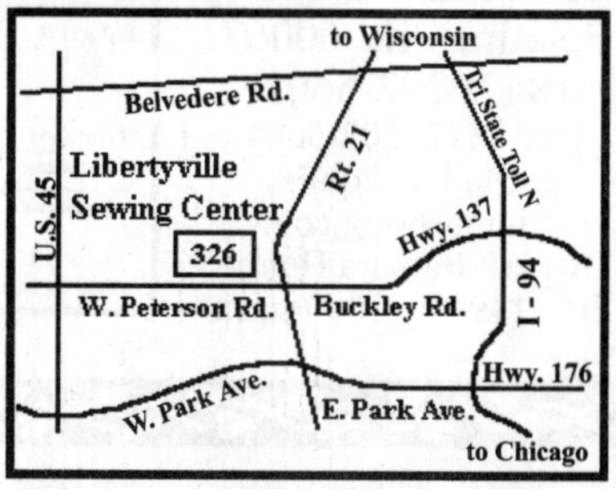

Exit Hwy. 137 from North or South
Exit Hwy. 21 from North only
Exit Hwy. 176 from South only

QUILTER'S PALETTE

6737 W. Dempster
Morton Grove, IL 60053
Phone: 847 . 663 . 8957
E-mail: qpalette@ameritech.net
4000 sq.ft. 3800+ bolts
Owner: Sharron Evans

*** Over 4,000 square feet of fabrics, * quilting and doll supplies.**

*** Many brands including Moda, Hoffman Batiks and reproduction fabrics, including 30's and Civil War.**

*** The Newest notions, latest techniques, * exhilarating classes and much, much more!**

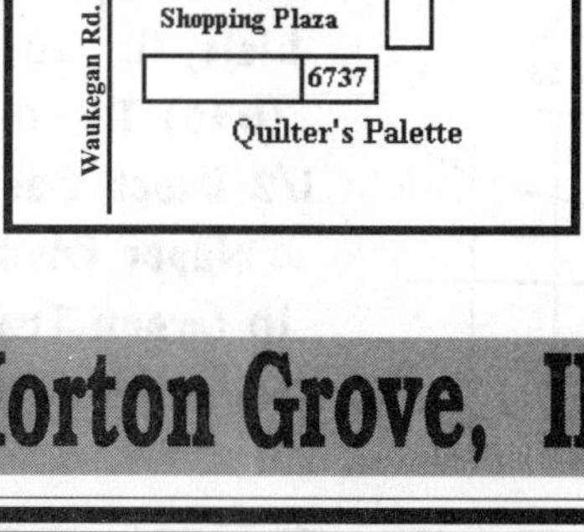

Sun 12 - 4 Mon & Thurs 10 - 8 pm Tues, Wed, Fri & Sat 10 - 5

Morton Grove, IL #53

Inspirations Everywhere!

Palatine, IL #54

Prints Charming II, Ltd.

Mon - Sat
10 - 5
T & Th til 8
Sun 12 - 4

Thousands of beautiful fabrics, challenging classes, newest notions, patterns & books, and friendly, competent staff. Only 5 minutes from Woodfield Shopping Area.

1905 S. Plum Grove Rd.
Palatine, IL 60067
(847) 202-5602
Fax: (847) 202-5604
E-Mail: pc2quilts
@mindspring.com
Owner: Barbara Hutton
Est: 1999 3000 sq.ft.

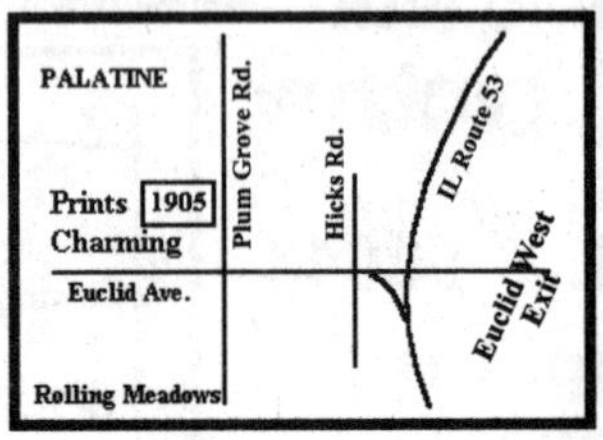

Round Lake Beach, IL #55

Sewing Source

M, W, F 10 - 6
T, Th 10 - 8
Sat 10 - 4
Sun 1:30 - 4

2213 N Route 83 60073
(847) 223-9009 Fax: (847) 223-8818
E-Mail: debbiesews@aol.com
Owner: Debbie Tomec
Est: 1995 3500 sq. ft. 1500 Bolts

We sell Janome and Pfaff sewing machines and carry a full line of quilting fabrics. Over 300 books and 400 patterns. Classes available.

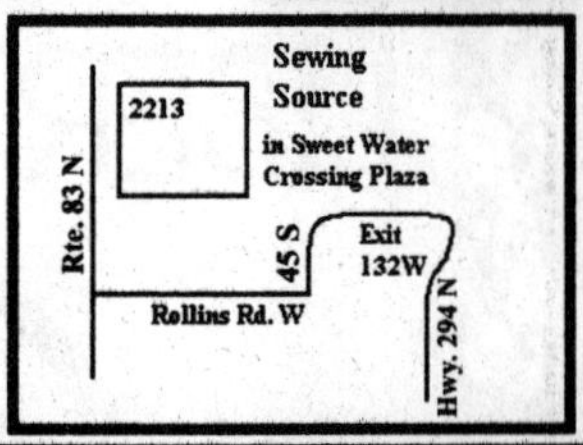

Antioch, IL #56

Quilter's Dream, Inc.

Mon, Fri, Sat
10 - 4
Tues & Thur
10 - 7
Sun 11 - 3

939 Main 60002
(847) 395-1459
Owners: Wendy Maston & Robin Kessell
Est: 1994 5000 sq.ft.

A complete line of Quilting Supplies & 100% cotton fabrics. A very unique town. We love visitors. Stop in & chat! Authorized ELNA Dealer.

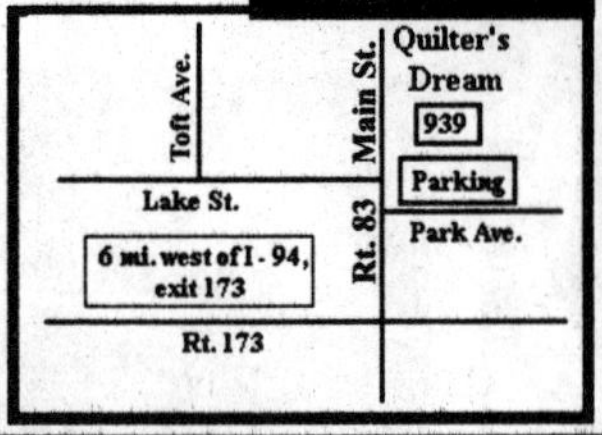

Judy's Quilt 'n' Sew

290 South State Street
In Downtown Hampshire, IL

#57

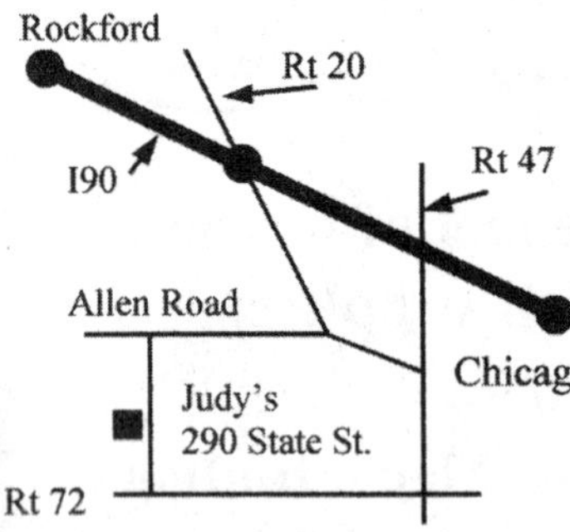

10 to 5 Mon-Fri, 10 to 3:30 Sat
12 to 3:00 Sunday

Traveling from Chicago, exit at route 47 South.
Traveling east exit route 20. Shop is 5 miles off I90.

Enjoy the charm of a quilt shop located in a beautifully restored 1905 Dutch colonial. With 1800 bolts of the latest fabrics, and quilt samples galore you'll quickly get swept up in the moment.

(847) 683-4739
www.FriendshipStar.com

Follow Your Heart

You can find us with a map but something
Inside will also know the way.
Our shop is filled with fabric that calls to you,
Inspires and rewards you for making the trip.
So come and touch...see...discover us!

Over 4,000 bolts of pure heaven
Books, Patterns, Classes and lots of fresh ideas.
Hours: Mon & Thurs 10-8
Tues, Wed, Fri 10-5
Sat 10-4 Sun 12-4

Lisle, IL #58

PIECEFUL HEART FABRICS

A new kind of quilting store.

2723 Maple Ave.
Lisle, IL 60532
(630) 718-0112
1/2 Block East of
Naper Blvd.
In Green Trails
Shopping Center

Woodstock, IL #59

Mon - Sat 9 - 5
Sun 12 - 4

The Quilt Studio, Inc.

180 Eastwood Dr. (Rt. 47) 60098
(815) 338-1212
Owner: Diane Webster
Est: 1994 2000 sq.ft

Fabric, Quilting Supplies. Ready-Made and Custom-Made Quilted Items.
Sewing Collectibles & Antique Quilts.
Quilt Racks & Handcrafts.

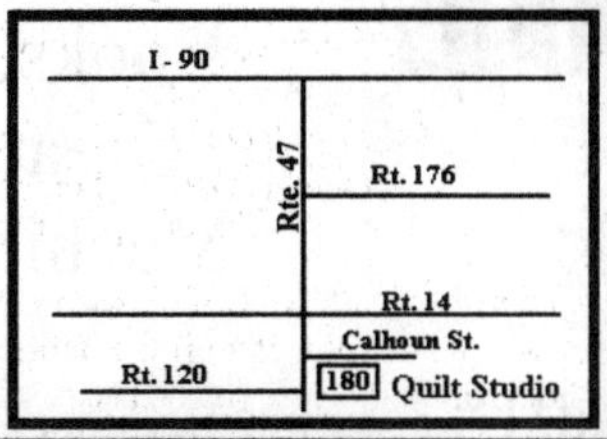

Schaumburg, IL #60

Mon - Sat 10 - 5
Closed Wed

Patches & Prints

634 S. Roselle Rd. 60193
(847) 524-4846 Fax: (847) 524-4847
E-Mail: PatchesPrints@aol.com
Web Site: www.patchesandprints.com
Owner: Susan Abraham
Est: 1999 1500 sq.ft. 1500 Bolts

Located NW of Chicago & known for its friendly and helpful staff, carrying fine cotton fabrics, quilting essentials and the "Handi-Quilter".

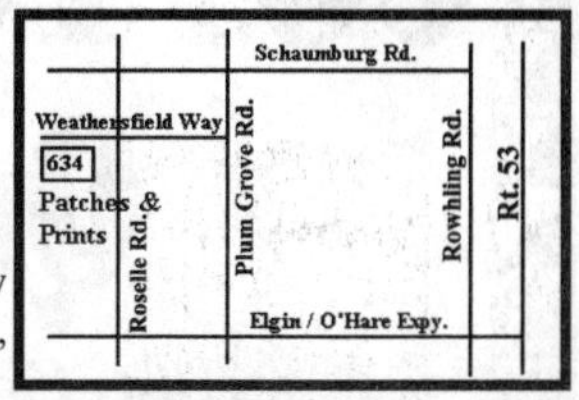

Batavia, IL #61

Windmill City Quilts

Owner:
Robin Saunders
'Quilt in a Day'
Certified Instructor

Always something On sale!

- Uniquely packages fabric collections
- Quilt Kits Galore
- Books and patterns
- Classes
- 2,400 Sq Ft
- 3,500+ Bolts
- Notions

Plenty of Parking. Comfy chair for Hubby

Mon, Wed, Fri, Sat 10 - 5
Tues & Thur 10 - 8 Sun 12 - 4

On the Fox River
Near Corner of Wilson & 25
Below Al's Creamery Restaurant

3 Webster Street
Batavia, IL 60510

(630) 482-2984
Fax: (630) 482-2985

email: robin@wcquilts.com
web: www.wcquilts.com

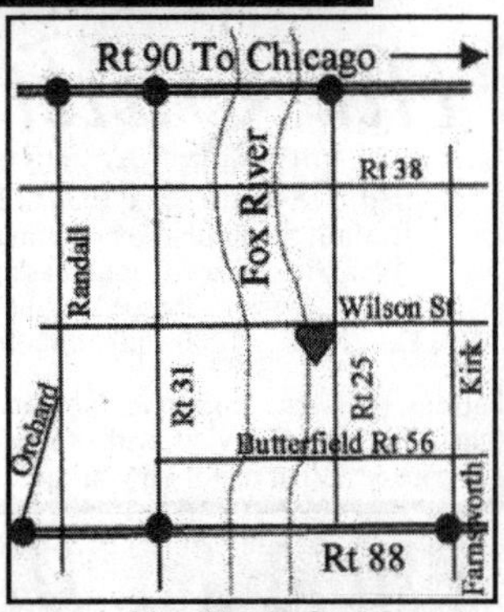

Map Not to Scale

Batavia, IL #62

QBU

Prairie Shop

1911 W. Wilson Street
Batavia, IL 60510
630-406-0237
Owner: Karen Lukac

Purveyors of fine quality quilting cottons, notions, books, beads and other goods for the discriminating fiber artist and jewelry artisan.
Over 3200 bolts of fabric & hundreds of beads from around the world!
Quilting & beading classes offered for all levels (weekends & Thursday evenings too)!

We'll be happy to send a current schedule of our class offerings with a SASE.
Watch for our website mid-2002!

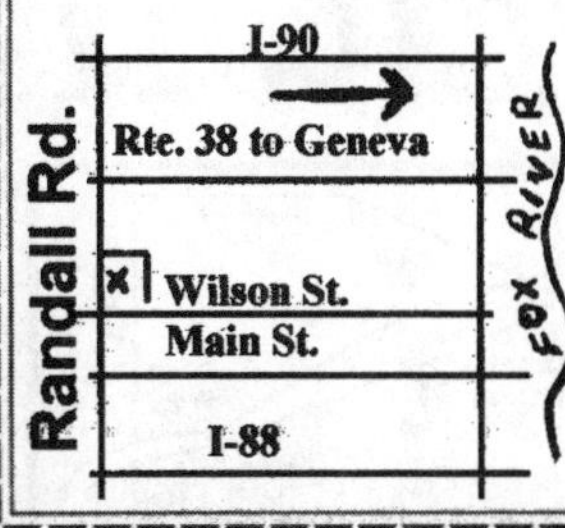

Mondays-Fridays 10 to 5
Thursdays 10 to 8
Sat. 10 to 4; Sun. 12 to 4

We are located at the NE corner of Randall & Wilson next to the Ace!

Geneva, IL #63

Mon - Fri 10 - 5
Sat 10 - 4

Quilted Fox

416 W. State St. (Rt. 38) 60134
(630) 232-4888
Owners: Herb & Gerri Buchholz
Est: 1978 2000 sq.ft.

We specialize in Princess Mirah Batiks
PFAFF Sewing Machines
Gammill Machine Quilting service and finishing of your pieced tops.

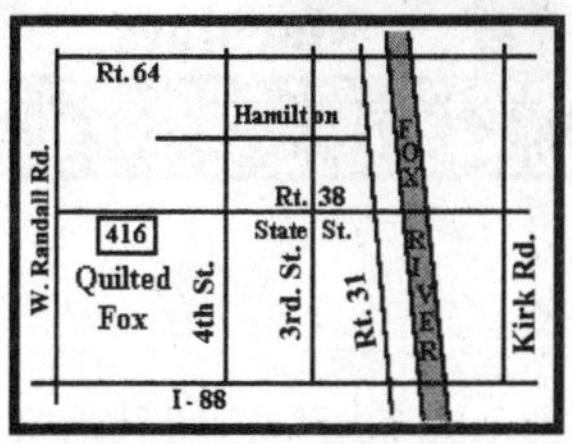

The COTTON COTTAGE Quilt Shop

1000 sq. ft. with 1500 bolts of 100% Cotton Fabrics. Books, Patterns, Notions. Great, friendly service. Machine Quilting Service Available.

1066 College Ave., Wheaton, IL 60187
(630) 668-6850
Fax: (630) 668-6825
E-mail: thecottoncottage@juno.com
Web Site: www.thecottoncottage.com
Owner: Charlene Hopeman Est: 2000

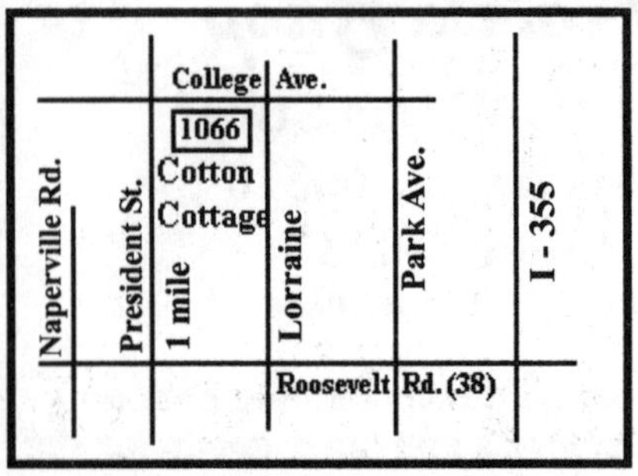

Wheaton, IL #64

Tues - Sat 10 - 4
Thurs 10 - 9

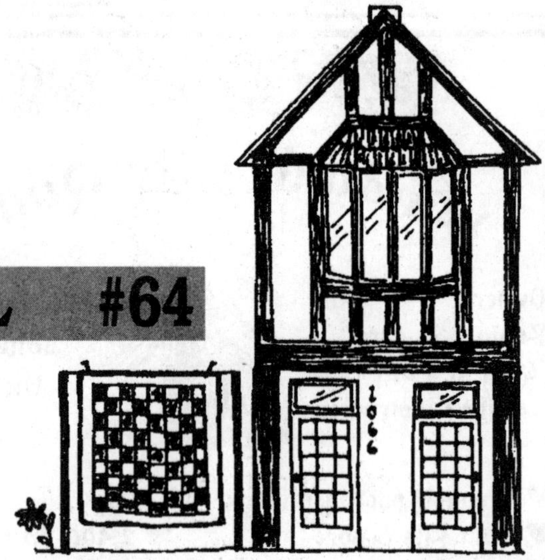

Elmhurst, IL #65

Fabrics Etc. II

We have 1200+ bolts for quilting and 1000+ bolts of knits & other fabrics. We have books, Stretch & Sew Patterns, Heirloom Laces & much more. Baby Lock & Janome Machines

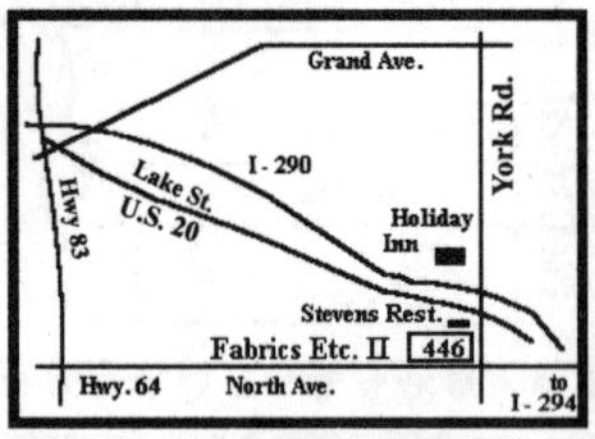

Mon - Sat 10 - 5

446 N. York Rd.
60126
(630) 279-1482
Est: 1995
2000 sq.ft.

Downers Grove, IL #66

Tues, Wed, Fri 10 - 5
Thur 10 - 9
Sat 10 - 3

The Quilt Basket

1012 Curtiss St. 60515
(630) 515-8820 Fax: (630) 724-1160
E-Mail: thequiltbasket@hotmail.com
Web Site: www.thequiltbasket.com
Owner: Renee Wright
Est: 1998 1200 sq.ft. 1200+ Bolts

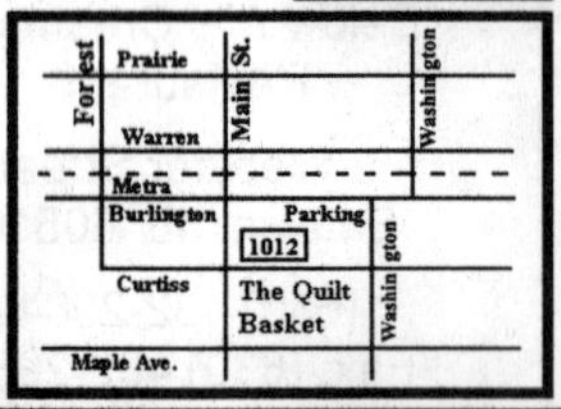

Fabrics, Classes, Books & Notions. Friendly Staff, Personal Service with years of quilting experience. Visit us for all your quilting needs.

Hinsdale, IL #67

Mon - Sat 10 - 5 or by Appt.

Tree House Quilts, Inc.

(of Interarts Gallery)

49 S. Washington St. 60521
(630) 455-6543 Fax: (630) 655-3098
Est: 1999

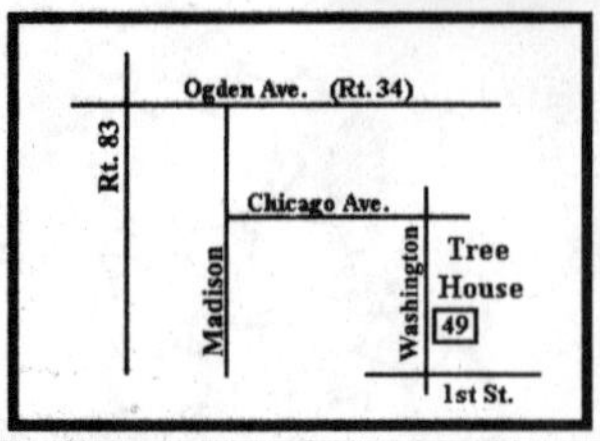

No fabrics only beautiful American made quilts, wallhangings, and unique hand-made items quilters love. See our vintage quilt windows.

Naperville, IL #68

790 Royal St. George Dr. #119
(630) 420-7050 60563
Owners: Beryl & Sarah Coulson
Est: 1981 4260 sq.ft.

Mon - Sat
10 - 5
Tues &
Thur til 9

Stitches N' Stuffing

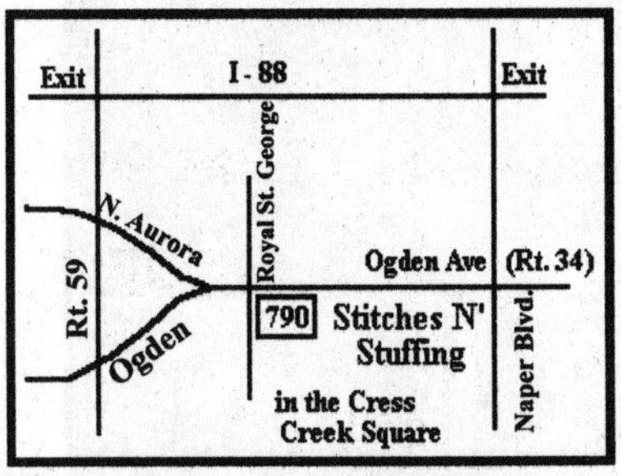

Facing Ogden Ave (Rt. 34)
In the Cross Creek Square

4000+ Cotton Fabrics, Homespuns,
Liberty of London. Patterns, Books, Notions.
Authorized Bernina sales/service
Smocking, Cross - Stitch, Heirloom Supplies.

Quilters & Crafters Heaven

Willowbrook, IL #69

7237 Kingery Rd. (Rt. 83), Willowbrook, IL 60527
630.321.9051 E-Mail: info@quiltfabric.com
Visit us for online shopping at: www.quiltfabric.com

quiltfabric.com

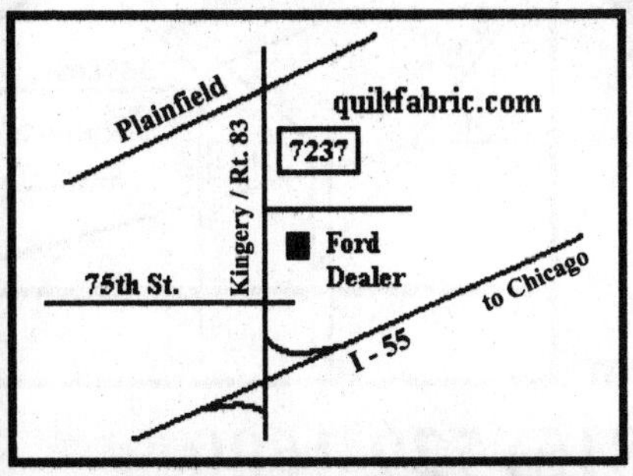

Tues, Wed,
Thur
9:30 - 5:30
Fri & Sat
9:30 - 4:30
Sun 12:30 - 4

Come in for some inspiration!
Bright, friendly atmosphere.
Kits, models, top quality fabrics,
patterns, books and notions.
PFAFF and Bernina authorized
dealer. Can't get here in person?
Shop online at our off-price store.

Threadneedle Street
"The Road to Creativity"

9925 W. 143rd Street
Orland Park, Illinois 60462
Phone: (708) 403-8490
E-mail: TNSTREET@aol.com

QUILTER'S TAKE THEIR FEET TO THREADNEEDLE STREET

Store Hours

Mon, Wed, Fri & Sat
10am to 5pm

Tues & Thurs
10am to 8pm

Sunday
Noon to 4pm

We are located in Historic Old Orland in a yellow Victorian house. We carry a substantial selection of 100% cotton fabrics, high-quality quilting supplies, clear and comprehensive sewing and quilting classes, and a large selection of books, patterns and kits. We provide knowledgeable service to our customers and are known for our helpful and friendly atmosphere. When you're in the area, this is a quilt shop stop not to be missed.

Creative Treasures
Annual Outdoor Quilt Show
Saturday of Labor Day Weekend

See you soon!
Nancy, Jeanne & Tammi

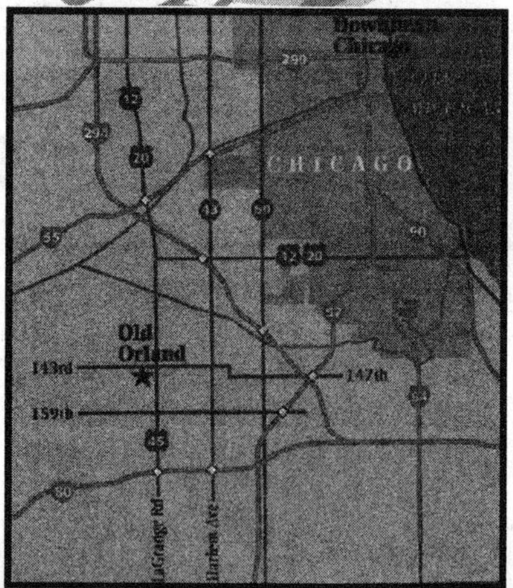

Orland Park, IL #70

Joliet, IL #71

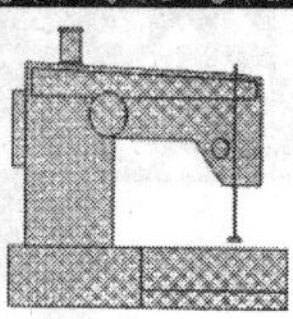

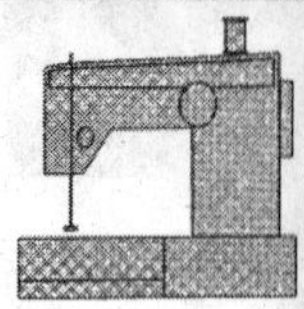

Roberts Sewing Center

The Lowest Prices in Illinois
Pfaff -- Singer -- Viking
Home & Industrial Machines

Roberts Sewing Center
A Quilter's Paradise

Bus Tours
Please Call Ahead
800-273-9111

5000 over bolts
of cotton fabric
highest quality—lowest prices

Mon - Sat 9:30 - 5:30
Tues & Thur 9:30 - 7:00
www.AQuiltersParadise.com

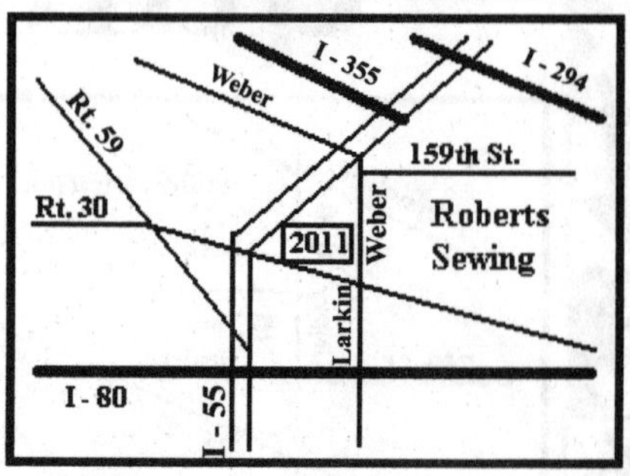

2011 S. Weber Rd. 60435 (815) 729-1600
Owner: Ken Roberts Est: 1930 4000 sq.ft.

Lockport, IL #72

Mon - Fri 10 - 5
Thur til 7
Sat 10 - 4

Thimbles

940 S. State St. 60441
(815) 836-8735 Fax: (815) 836-8761
E-Mail: MakeQuilts@aol.com
Owner: Tina Green

Located on Lockport's Historic State St.
1500 Bolts Fabric, Books, Patterns, Notions & Classes.

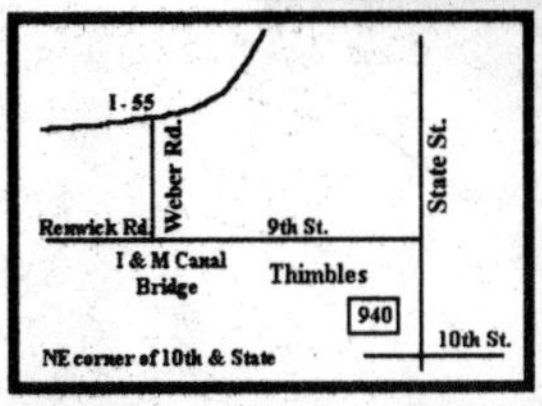

Quilters' Cotton Co.

Orland Park, IL #73

Est: 1988
2000 sq.ft.
Owners: Cheri Barrett, Kay McDonald & Laura Kincaid

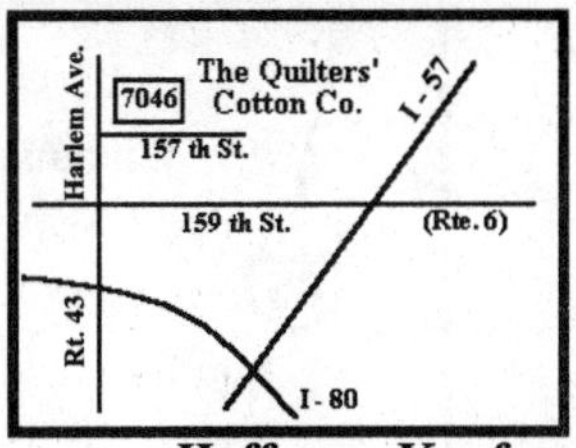

7046 West 157th Street 60462
(708) 614-7744

Mon & Wed 10 - 8
Tues, Thur, Fri 10 - 5
Sat 10 - 4

2500+ Bolts of 100% Cottons — Alexander Henry, Benartex, P&B, RJR, Hoffman, Kaufman, Marcus Brothers, Spiegel, Roberta Horton, Homespuns— Mission Valley, Red Wagon Flannels, 250+ Books, 150+ Pattern Companies, Great selection of notions, classes.

Other Shops in Illinois: We suggest calling first

Alton All in Stitches, 108 W. 3rd St. 618-462-1738
Antioch Hannah's Home Accents, 455 Lake 847-395-3355
Arlington Heights Linda Z's, 1030 E. Central 708-394-4590
Aroma Park Fabrics by D, 2974 S. Lowe Rd. 815-234-4700
Arthur Millers Dry Goods, 175 E 50 N
Arthur The Calico Workshop, 228 South Vine 217-543-2312
Arthur Melrose Quilts & Sewforth, R.R. #1, Box 133A 217-543-2844
Arthur Quilts & Crafts, R.R. 1 Box 185A 217-543-2702
Barrington Finn's Fabrics, 113 North Cook 708-381-5020
Benton J & J Fabric, 9093 Aden St. 618-439-6033
Butler Calico Quilts & Frames, RR #1 217-324-0478
Carpentersville Quiltmaster Inc., 1 S. Wisconsin St. 708-426-6741
Carpentersville Grist Mill Ends & Things, 39 E. Main St. 847-426-6455
Chicago The Art Institute of Chicago Dept. of Textiles Michigan Ave. 312-443-3696
Chicago Fishman's Fabrics, 1101 S. Desplaines 800-648-5161
Chicago Vogue Fabrics, 621 Roosevelt Rd. 312-829-2505
Crete Just Between Friends, 219 Milburn 708-672-5641
Crystal Lake Fabric Shop, 21 N. Williams 815-459-2084
Dunlap Quilt Crossing, P.O. Box 370 309-243-9028
Edwardsville Edwardsville Sewing Center, 110 N. Main St. 618-656-4272
Effingham Calico Shoppe, 1108 N. Merchant St. 217-342-6628
Elgin Mitches Stitches, 51 S. Grove Ave. 847-622-8399
Elmhurst Granny's Goodies Attic Shops, 116 N. York St. 630-834-0666
Fox River Grove Window Box Gardens, 38 Manchester Ct. 847-516-2496
Genoa Michelle's Creative Quilts, 241 S. Genoa St. 815-784-2316
Harvard Wood-N-Needle, 9320 Alden Rd. 815-648-4519
Hutsonville Apple Blossom Quilt Shop, St. Route 1 618-563-4388
Ipava Mildred's Quilt House, 6721 E. Quarter Rd. 309-753-8392
Liberty Pam's Quilt Shop, R.R. #1, Box 106 217-645-3871
Lombard The Sewing Room, 204 E. St. Charles 708-369-3228
Long Grove The Patchworks, 223 Robert Parker Coffin Rd. 847-634-0330
Macomb Aunt Kitty's Quilts & More, 121 N. Scotland St. 309-833-3907
Maquon Sew Ewenique, 314 Main St. 309-875-3335
Mattoon Fabrics N' More Inc., 817 S. 19th St. 217-234-4700
Milford Dixie Cloth Shop, 130 E. Jones 815-889-5349
Morton Grove Cotton Pickers Fabrics, Inc., 5926 Dempster St. 847-966-2907
Mt. Zion Stewart's Sewing Machines, Inc., 415 N. St. Hwy. 121 217-864-6142
Naperville Something Special, 815 Iris Ln. 630-416-3996
Odin Mary's Vogue Shop, 105 Green 618-775-8371
Olney Quilts & Clutter, 713 W. Main St. 618-395-0114
Pinckneyville Quilters Heaven, 1007 S. Main St. 618-357-5531
Pittsfield The Pin Cushion, 510 N. Jackson St. 217-285-6923
Princeton Old Times--Quilter Heaven, 954 N. Main 815-872-9841
Princeton All Things Quilted, 630 Timber Ridge Rd. 815-875-1296
Quincy Jean Lyle, P.O. Box 289 217-222-8910
Rantoul Needle & I, 126 E. Sangamon Ave. 217-892-2638
Rochester Debbie's Country Quilting, 2570 N. Walnut Rd. 217-498-9460
Rock Falls Heart Warmers, 10020 Buell Rd. 815-535-0305
Rockford Gingerbread & Calico, 4125 Charles St. 815-399-5194
Roscoe Home & Hearth Inc., 5496 Elevator Rd. 815-623-5353
Sycamore Made Just For You, 338 W. State St. 815-895-8122
Tinley Park Sew Creative, 15953 S. Harlem 708-429-6056
Washington Country Mile, 109 Washington Square 309-444-2137
Waterloo Warm Expressions, 1047 Gilmore Lake 618-939-3606
West Frankfort Calico Country Sewing Ctr., 310 S. Logan St. 618-932-2992
Wheaton Golden Threads, 2 S 373 Seneca Dr. 630-752-9770
Wheaton Craftique/Never Enough Knitting, 121 N. Main St. 630-221-1007
Woodstock Sewing Concepts, 100 Cass St. 815-338-7754
Wyanet Country Seams, 114 N. Walnut 815-699-7295

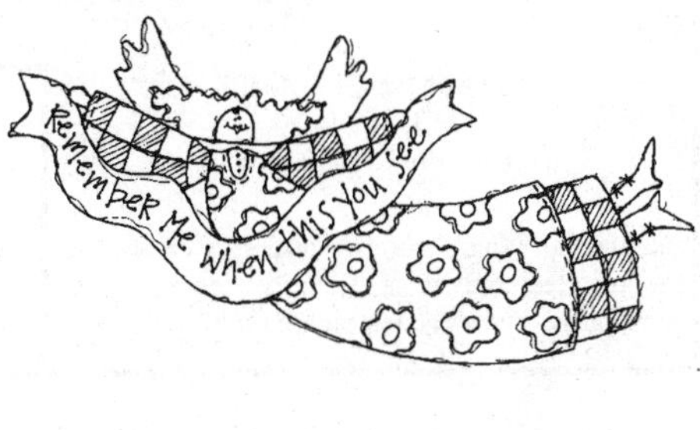

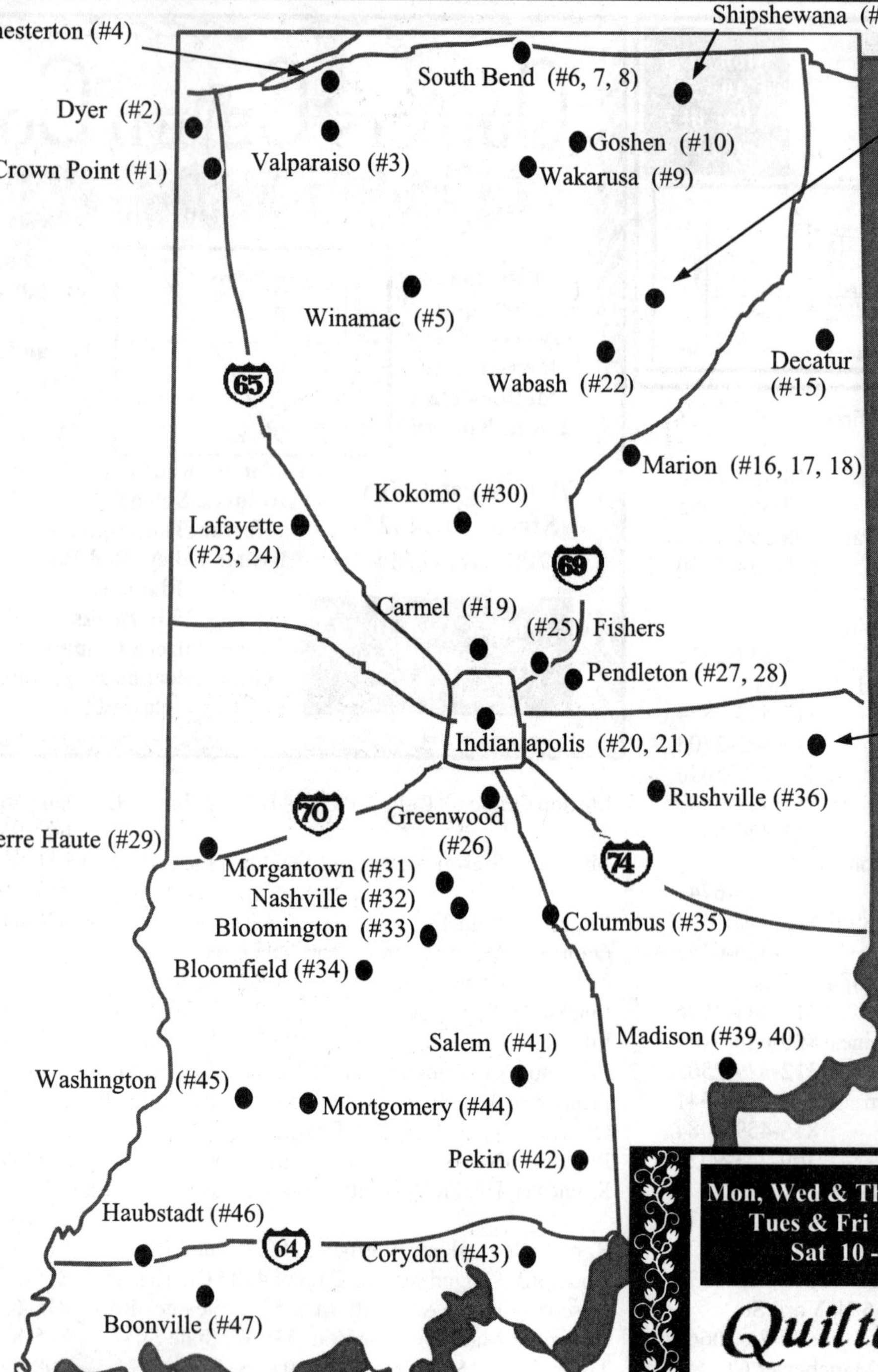

47 Featured Shops

INDIANA

Crown Point, IN #1

bits 'n pieces

Mon - Fri 10 - 6
Tues til 8
Sat 10 - 5

732 N. Main St. 46307
(219) 662-9030
Est: 1997 2000 sq.ft.

Quality quilting fabrics, notions, books & patterns featured in a friendly sewing room atmosphere. New classes each month. Join Us!

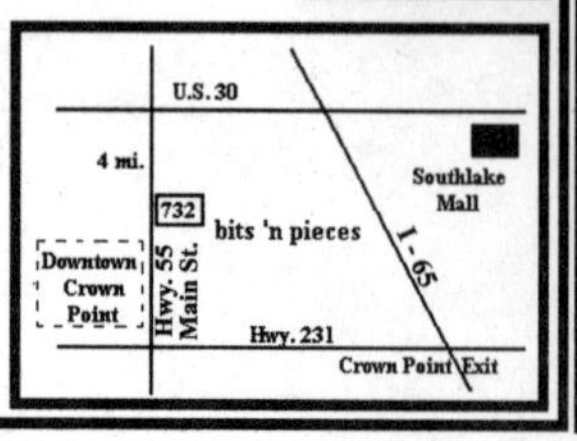

Mon, Wed & Thur 10 - 8:30
Tues & Fri 10 - 6:30
Sat 10 - 5:30

Quilter's Haven

Over 3,000 Bolts of 100% Cotton Fabrics. Large selection of Patterns, Books & Notions. All levels of Classes.

Sand Ridge Plaza (Rt. 30)
1060 Joliet St. 46311
(219) 322-4624
E-Mail:
QuiltHaven@aol.com
Owner: Judith Ann Bremer
Est: 1994 1800 sq.ft.

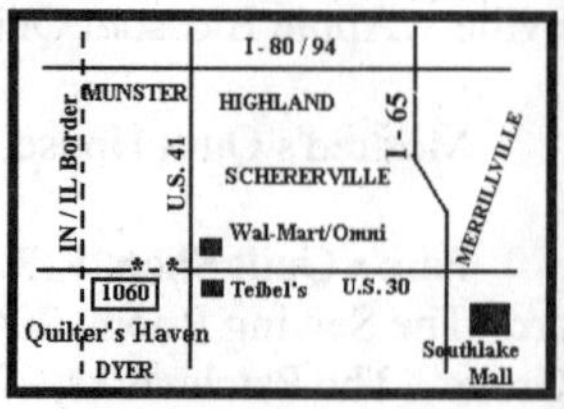

From the corner of U.S. 30 and U.S. 41: Go west on 30 to the second stop light. Turn left, immediately turn into Sand Ridge Plaza. Quilter's Haven is on the west end of the plaza.

Dyer, IN #2

Valparaiso, IN #3

Mon - Fri 10 - 5:30 Thur til 7 Sat 10 - 3

Needle & Thread

60 Jefferson 46383
(219) 462-4300 Est: 1990
Owner: Marlene Rock 1500 sq.ft.
1800 Bolts Free Newsletter

Visit our old Victorian house filled with everything for quilting, cross stitch, tatting, hardanger, & silk ribbon embroidery. Classes.

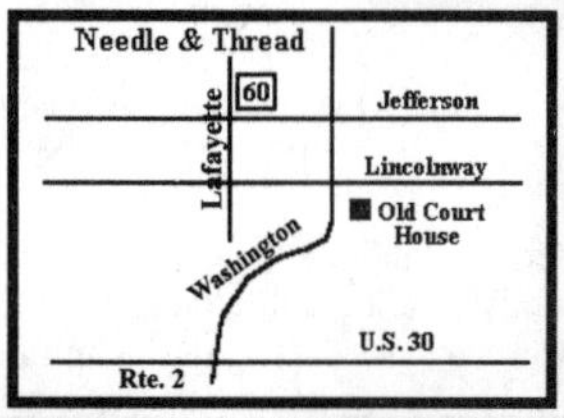

Winamac, IN #5

Tues - Fri 9 - 5 Sat 9 - 2

The Country Patch

125 W. Main St. 46996
(574) 946-7799 Est: 1992
Owner: Eddie Ploss & Gwen Thorgren

New and Unique Quilt Shop featuring 100% cotton 2000+ bolts.
Moda, RJR, Etc.

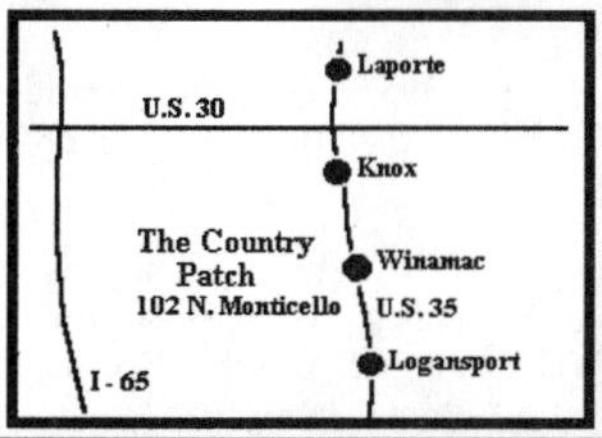

Crazy Eighths

Fabric, Friendship & Fun !!

1000 sq. ft. of 100% cotton fabrics, notions, books, & patterns in a renovated passenger train car.
Kits and gifts for quilters.

301 Grant Ave., Suite B
Chesterton, IN 46304
(219) 929-4511
Email: crazy.eighths@verizon.net
Web Site: www.crazyeighths.com
Owner: Ellen Maxwell
Est: 2002

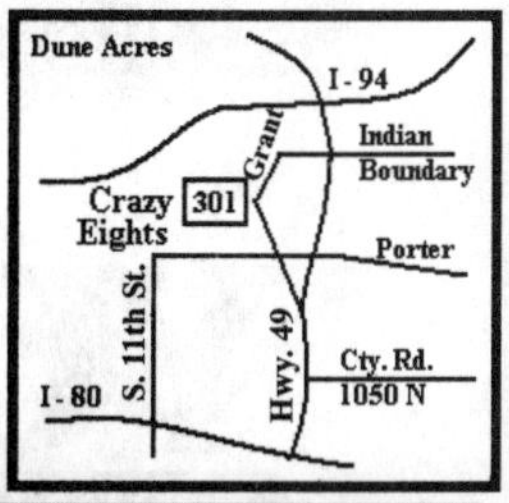

Tues - Fri 10 - 5 Sat 10 - 4

Chesterton, IN #4

#6 Erica's

Erica's Craft & Sewing Center

1320 N. Ironwood Dr.
South Bend IN 46615
574-233-3112 http://ericas.com

HOURS
Monday, Tuesday, Wednesday & Friday 9:30-5:30
Thursday 9:30-8:30
Saturday 9:00-4:00
Sunday 12:00-4:00

Fabrics by: Moda, Mumm's the Word, Teresa Kogut, Cheri Strole, RJR, P & B, Thimbleberries, Benartex, Hoffman, Balis, AE Nathan, and more, and more fabrics. Books, patterns, tools and more tools. Lots of samples and fabric packs. Bernina and Viking sewing machines and sergers. Minutes from the University of Notre Dame campus.

Visit our web site at http://www.ericas.com

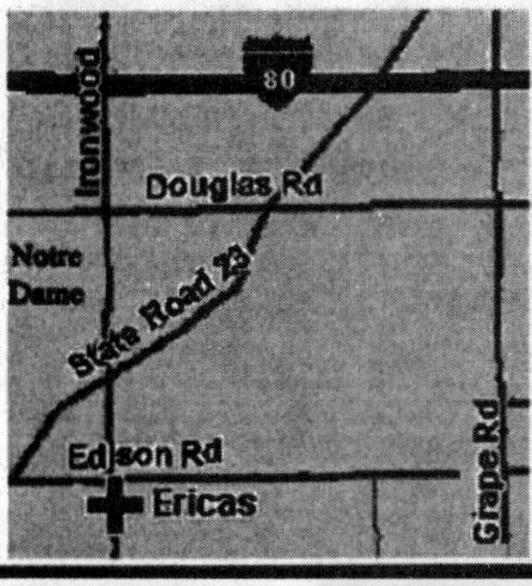

South Bend, IN #7

Mon - Sat 10 - 6 Thur til 8

Stitch 'N Time Fabrics

2305 Miami St. 46614
(574) 234-4314 Est: 1993
Fax: (574) 968-4314
E-Mail: stitchntime1@aol.com
www.stitchntimefabrics.com 3000+ Bolts
Owner: Valerie Strycker 3800 sq.ft.
Large Selection of Notions, Books & Patterns.
Singer, Juki & Pfaff sewing machines.
Service of all makes. Classes.

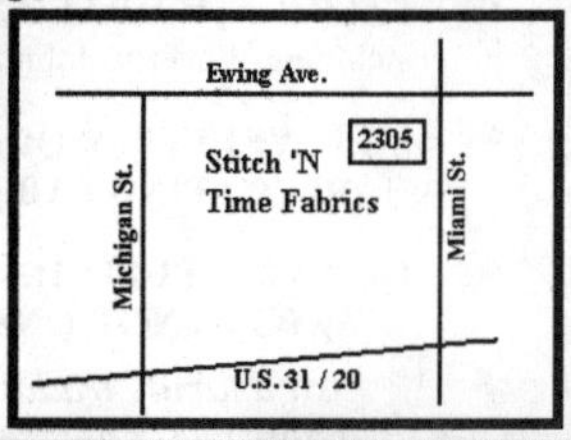

South Bend, IN #8

Mon - Sat 10 - 5 Or By Appt.

Heckaman's Quilts & Yarns

63028 U.S. 31 South 46614
(574) 291-3918

Quilts for Sale. Custom Orders Welcome
Let us Quilt your Heirlooms by Hand or Machine.
Hinterberg Quilt Frames. Beautiful Yarns. Ashford Spinning Wheels. Schacht Weaving Looms.

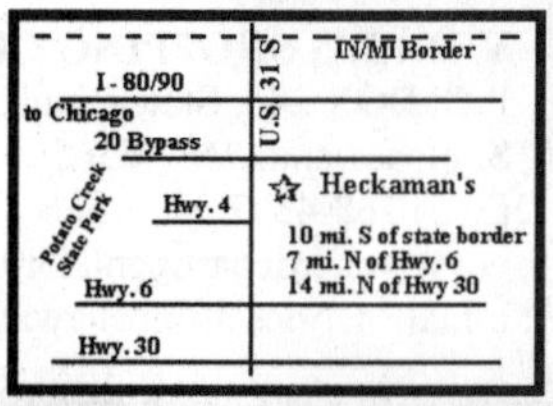

Wakarusa, IN #9

Mon 9 - 7 Tues - Fri 9 - 5 Sat 9 - 2

Jeanette's Fabric Boutique

105 S Elkhart St., P.O. Box 511 46573
(574) 862-4207 Fax: (574) 862-1637
E-Mail: jeanette@galaxyinternet.net
Web Site: www.jeanettesfabric.com
Owner: Jeanette Prenkert
Est: 1981 2500 sq. ft. 2000+ Bolts

Large selection quilting fabrics; many classes; personal help anytime; authorized Janome and Baby Lock dealer; unique store in a small town.

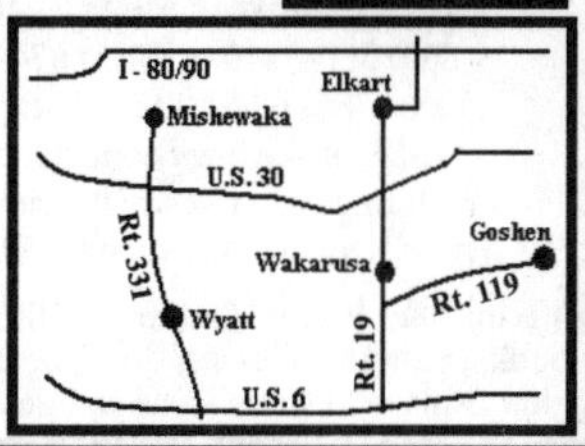

Goshen, IN #10

Mon - Fri 9 - 5:30 Sat 9 - 4

Meredith's Sewing Corner

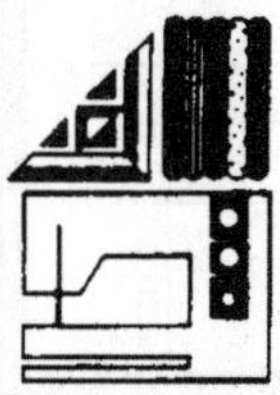

712 W. Lincoln Ave. 46526
(574) 533-3414

6000 square feet a full fabric store, needle crafts and Bernina Sewing Machines.
Wonderful displays.
Great prices.

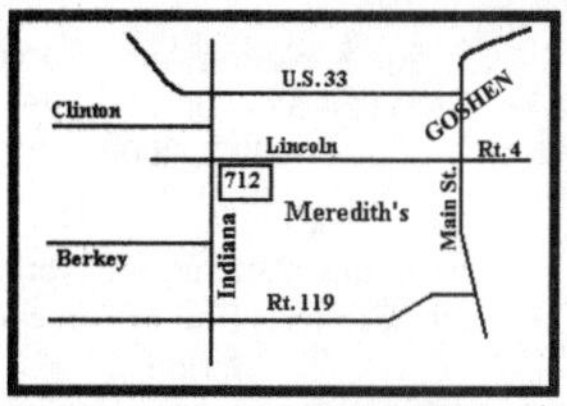

N. Manchester, IN #11

Tues - Fri 11 - 4
Sat 10 - 3

Creative Threads

229 E. Main St. 46962
(260) 982-1080
Owners: Jim & Shirley Mishler

We carry quality 100% cotton fabrics, quilt patterns, books & notions. Classes are available — Personal Service.

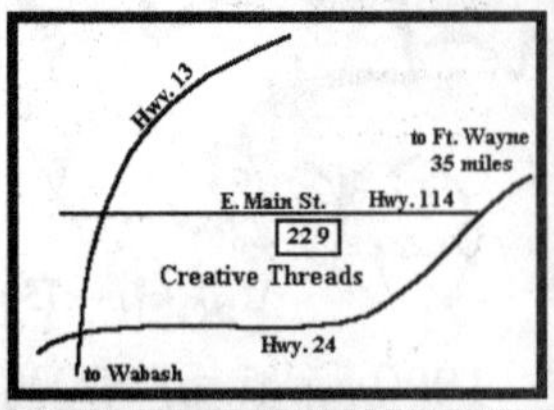

Shipshewana, IN #12

Mon - Sat 9:30 - 5

Rebecca Haarer Folk Arts and Antiques

165 Morton St. 46565
(219) 768-4787
Owner: Rebecca Haarer
Est: 1971 Free Brochure

Antique Quilts — gathered from this area. Amish Quilts, dolls, rockers, old fabrics, feed sacks, and stencils. Amish Quilt Lectures.

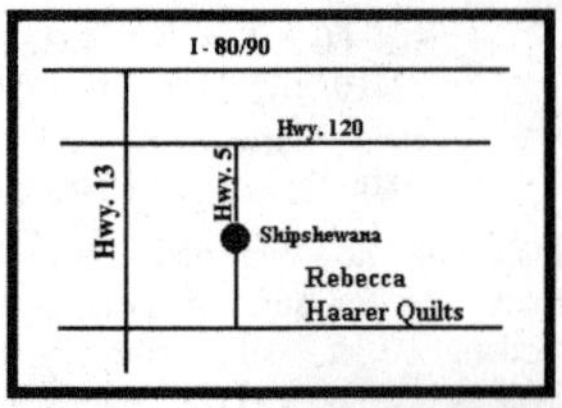

Shipshewana, IN #13

YODER DEPARTMENT STORE

"FIND THE BASIC AND THE UNUSUAL!"

- **OVER 12,000 BOLTS OF FABRIC with over 4,000 bolts of quilting type fabrics.** Brands include: Hoffman, Benartex, Concord, P & B, Marcus Bros., Peter Pan, Bali, Moda, RJR, V-I-P, Springs, Chanteclaire, Alaska hand dyed fabrics, homespuns, quilter's flannel and many more!
- **FASHION, BRIDAL AND HOME DECORATING FABRIC** (including Waverly, John Wolf & Robert Kauffman)
- **SILK, VELVET, WOOL, LINEN, DENIM, CALICO, AND MANY HARD-TO-FIND FABRICS**
- **QUILTING SUPPLIES AND BOOKS, PATTERNS, SEWING NOTIONS, TRIMS AND ACCESSORIES**

Visit a family tradition that still places friendly service, quality merchandise and value as their highest priority.

Open: 8:00 AM - 5:30 PM
Monday - Saturday, Closed Sunday
Will Mail Order Credit Cards Accepted.

YODER'S SHOPPING CENTER
P.O. BOX 245, State Road 5
Shipshewana, IN 46565
(260) 768-4887
www.yoderdepartmentstore.com
e-mail: fabrics@shipshewana.com

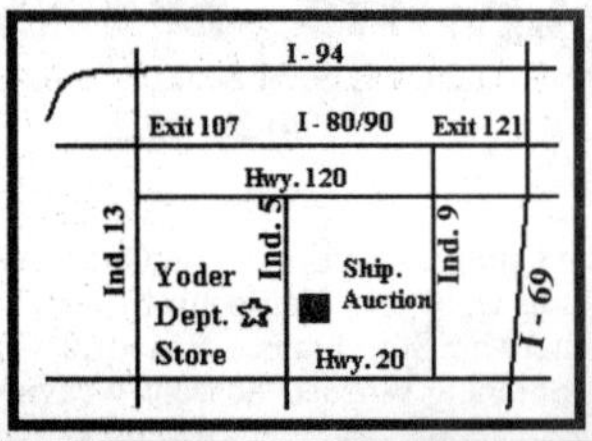

Shipshewana, IN #14

Mon - Fri 8 - 5
Sat 8 - 3

Spector's Store

305 S. Van Buren (Ind. 5)
P.O. Box 347 46565
(219) 768-4439

Full Line of Fabric and notions. Quilt and Craft supplies. Hand stitched, quilted items. Wallhangings & Quilts. Excellent Values on Solid & Printed fabrics.

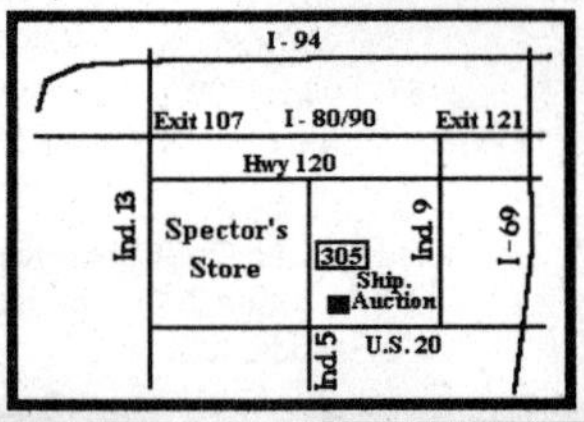

Decatur, IN #15

Tues - Fri 10 - 5
Sat 9 - 12

Country Creations

5342 N 400 W 46733
(260) 547-4535
E-Mail: fabrics2@onlyinternet.net
Owners: Bev and Gene Weber
Est: 1998 2500 sq.ft. 600+ Bolts

Cotton for quilting, supplies, books, patterns, classes.

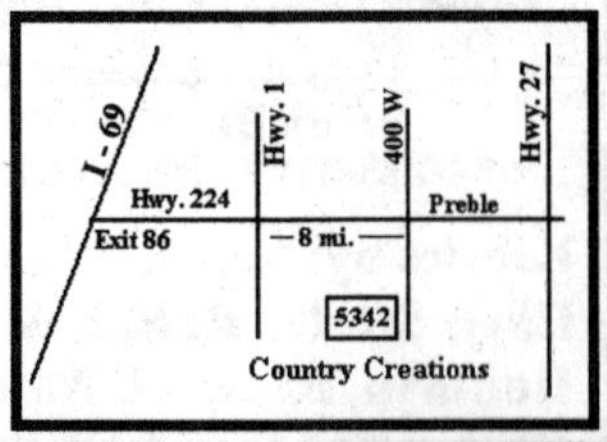

Marion, IN #16

Please Call First

The Quilters Hall of Fame

926 S. Washington, P.O. Box 681 46952
(765) 664-9333 Fax: Same

Annual Celebration featuring quilt shows, lectures, workshops and more. Third weekend in July! Call for schedule.
Renovation of Marie Webster Home is nearing completion. Plan to open in 2004
Web Site: www.quiltershalloffame.org
E-mail: quilters@comteck.com

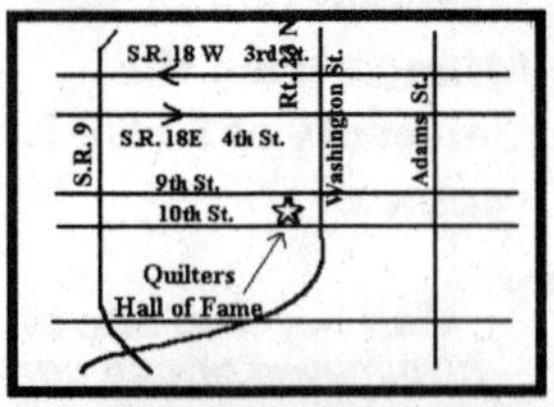

Marion, IN #17

Mon - Fri 10 - 5
Sat 10 - 2

Sunshine Fabrics

303 S. Norton Ave. 46952
(765) 664-8832 or (888) 664-8832
Est: 1997 2000 sq.ft.

Fabrics, Books, Patterns and Notions for the Quilter. Quilter's Hall of Fame located in Marion.

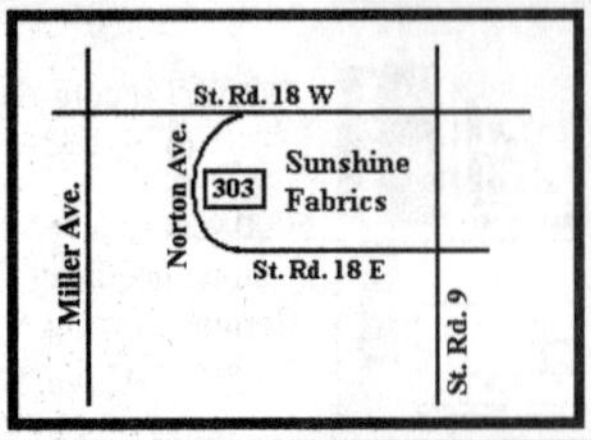

Marion, IN #18

Mon - Fri 10 - 6
Closed Wed
Sat 10 - 3

Sew Biz

3722 South Western Ave. 46953
(800) 500-3830 or (765) 674-6001
Fax: (765) 674-5992 Est: 1983
E-Mail: sewbiz@comteck.com
Web Site: www.sewbizmarion.com
Owner: Donelle McAdams 5000 sq.ft.

Viking & White Dealer. 100% cottons, books, patterns, classes, dolls, bears, bunnies, etc. A place to share ideas and get inspired.

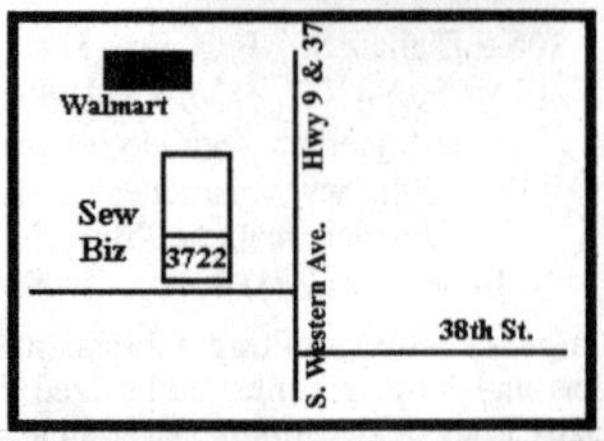

Quilt Quarters

2 Locations

12405 N. Meridian St.
(317) 844-3636 46032
Owner: Kaye England
Est: 1989
5000 sq.ft. 6000+ Bolts

Mon - Sat 10 - 5
Thur til 8:30

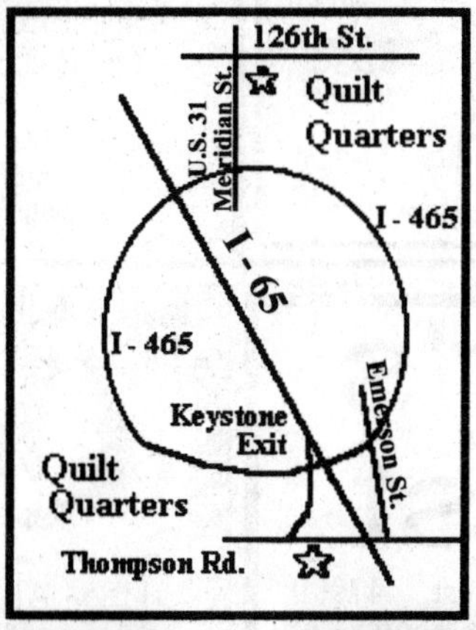

3137 E. Thompson Rd.
46227
(317) 791-1336
Est: 1995
5000 sq.ft. 4000+ Bolts

Mon - Sat 10 - 5
Thur til 8:30

Carmel, IN #19

Indianapolis, IN #20

Wonderful selection of traditional and non-traditional fabrics.
Bernina Sales and Service.
Patterns, Books, Notions, Stencils, Classes, Helpful Staff
WEB SITE: www.quiltquarters.com

Quilts Plus

1748 E. 86th Street Northview Mall 46240
(317) 844-2446 or (800) 840-2241
E-Mail: shop@quiltsplus.com
Web Site: www.quiltsplus.com
Owner: Jeanne Moosey
Est: 1977 3800 sq. ft. 3000 Bolts

Indianapolis, IN #21

Mon - Sat
10 - 5
Thurs til
8:30
Sun 12 - 4

- **We cater to all of your quilting needs**
- **Extensive Class Schedule**
- **Block of the Month Programs**
- **We ship anywhere!**

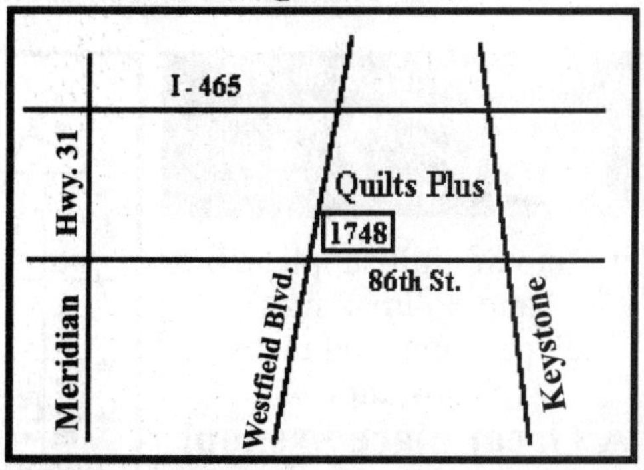

Wabash, IN #22

Mon - Fri 10 - 5:30
Sat 10 - 5

Nancy J's Fabrics

1604 South Wabash 46992
(260) 563-3505 Est: 1980
Owners: Nancy Jacoby & Miriam Peebles

The latest & greatest Fabrics. Books and Patterns for quilts, & dollmaking.
Plan to spend a day in Historic Wabash!

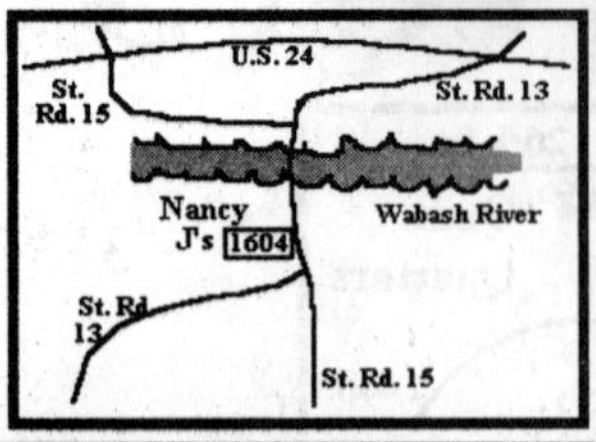

Lafayette, IN #23

Mon - Sat 9:30 - 5:30

The Paisley Pincushion

2101 Kossuth St. 47905
(765) 447-4996 Fax: (765) 447-7075
Est: 1995 2700 sq.ft. 3000 Bolts

Bernina Dealer & Quilt Store
With over 3000 bolts of fabric, books, patterns, notions, classes.

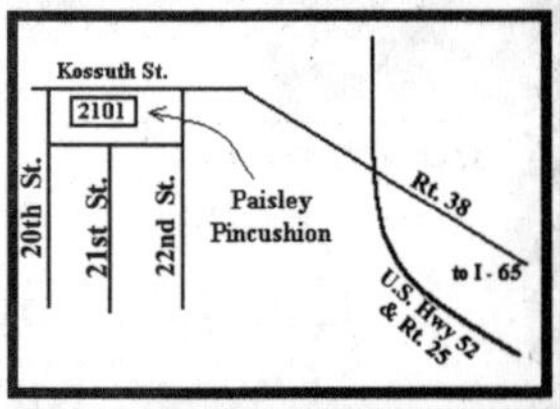

Quilter's Harvest

2307 State Road 25 West 47909
(765) 474-2057 Est: 1999 4000 sq.ft.
Web Site: www.quiltersharvestonline.com
Owners: Karen Löser & Stephen James

Quality 100% Cotton Fabrics
Quilting Supplies
Books & Patterns
Classes on quilting & wearable art
Block of the Months

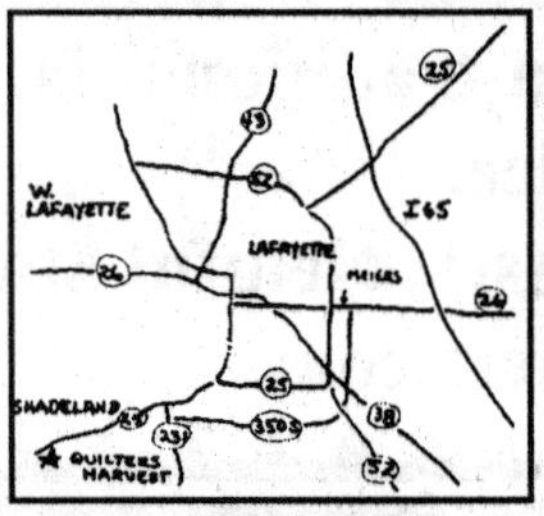

Mon - Sat 10 - 5
Thur til 7:30
Sun 11 - 3

Quilter's Harvest is located in an Historic 100+ year old brick Church, complete with a white picket fence & a beautiful stained glass window in the loft.

Lafayette, IN #24

Quiltmakers

11854 Allisonville Rd. 46038
(317) 585-5825
Fax: (317) 585-5826
E-Mail: shopquiltmakers@aol.com
Web Site: www.shopquiltmakers.com
Est: 1999 2400 sq.ft. 2000 Bolts

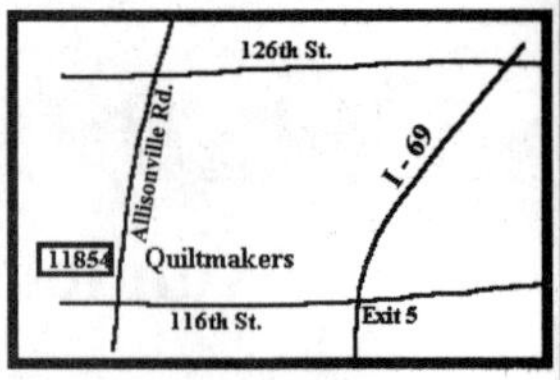

Fishers, IN #25

Find the latest fabrics from traditional to contemporary, homespun to hand-dyed here! Books, patterns and notions. Knowledgeable Staff.

Mon - Sat 10 - 5
Thur til 8:30 Sun 1- 4

Est: 1973

Greenwood, IN #26

4000 sq.ft.

The Back Door, Inc.

2503 Fairview Place #W 46142
(317) 882-2120
E-Mail: dttes@indy.net
Web Site: www.backdoorquilts.com
Owners: Linda Hale & Teri Dougherty

Mon - Thur 9:30 - 9
Fri 9:30-6 Sat 9:30 - 5
1st & 3rd Sundays Jan - Labor Day
All Sundays Labor Day to Christmas

Full line of quilt supplies, bear and dollmaking, tolepainting, and many, many samples.
A Great place to shop!

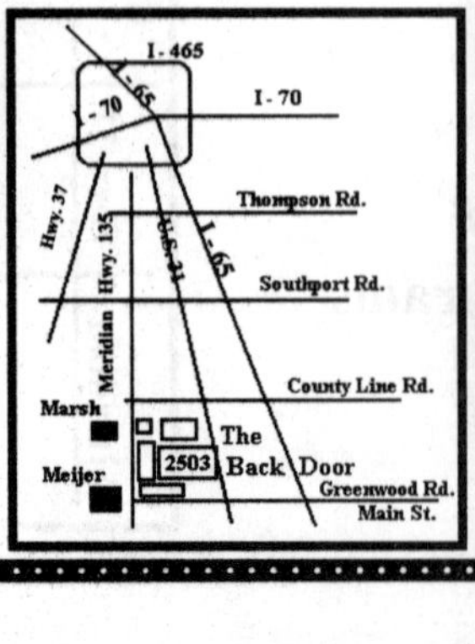

Pendleton, IN #27

Ruth's Legacy, Ltd.

104 W. High St. 46064
(765) 778-2488 Est: 1996 2200 sq.ft.

Mon - Sat 10 - 5
Sun 1 - 5

The very latest fabrics from Hoffman, Michael Miller, Kona Bay, Hi-Fashion & more. Classes, Patterns, Notions & Friendly Service. Over 35 different cat prints. Large selection of Batiks. Distinctive Gifts & Collectibles such as Just the Right Shoe, Lee Middleton Dolls and Shepherd's Dairy Soap plus Carol Wilson greeting cards & notepaper.

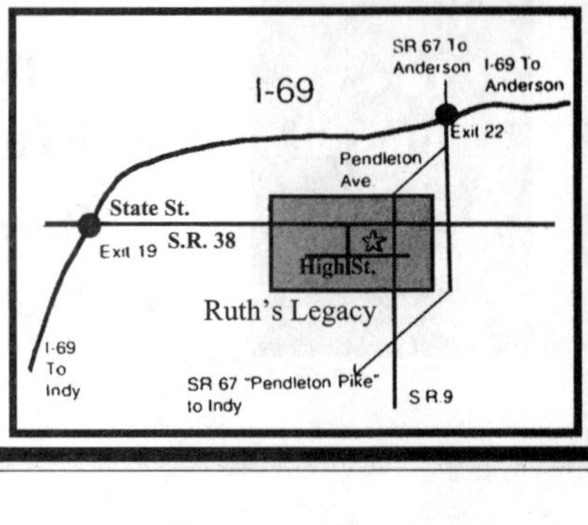

Pendleton, IN #28

Needle in the Haystack

Mail order Available
E-Mail nith@indy.net

132 West State St. (Hwy 38)
Pendleton, IN 46064
(765) 778-7936 (800) 779-7936
Owner: Tammy Vonderschmitt
Est: 1981 4000 sq.ft.

Mon - Sat 10 - 5
Sun 1 - 5

Fabric lines:

At Needle you will find:
Thimbleberries
Mumm's the Word
Moda
P & B
Marcus Brothers
In the Beginning
Homespuns
Flannels
Reproduction

Visit the Town Of Pendleton
There are great Antique Malls, unique Craft and Gift shops and wonderful Restaurants, come spend the day with us.

Heritage Craft Fair
Local Craft and Quilt Show
First weekend after Labor Day

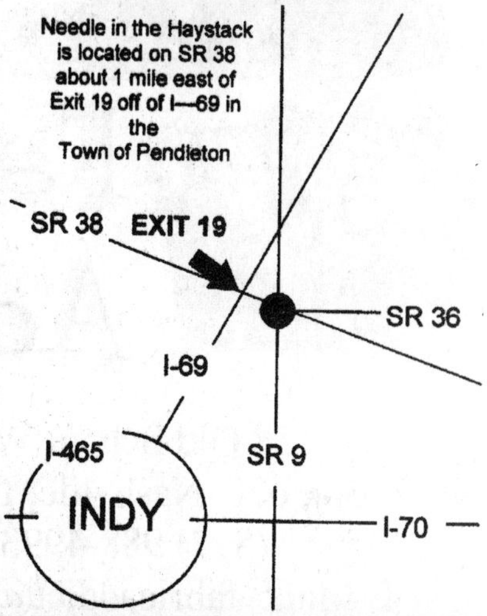

Quilts & More

1907 S. 3rd. St. (U.S. 41)
47802
(812) 232-0610
Owners: Basil & Chris Ave
Est: 1974

Mon - Fri
10 - 5
Sat 9 - 2

100% Cotton Fabrics, Quilting Patterns, Books,
Notions, Supplies, Quilting & Sewing Classes
Knowledgeable & Helpful Staff
Custom Monogramming
Sublimation and Screen Printing
Authorized Pfaff & Brother Dealer
Service on all makes sewing machines

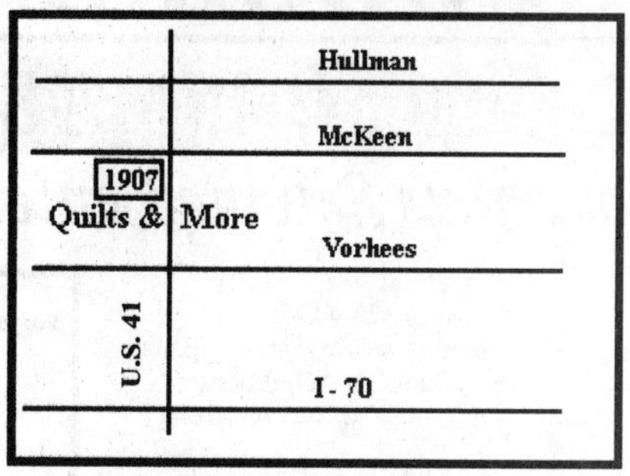

1 mile North of I - 70 on U.S. 41

Terre Haute, IN #29

Kokomo, IN #30

Mon - Fri 10 - 6
Sat 10 - 5
Sun 1 - 5

The Quilting Basket, LLC

439 E. Lincoln Rd. 46902
(765) 865-9269 Fax: Same
E-mail: jandr@netusa1.net
Web Site: www.thequiltingbasket.com
Owner: Joan Frazier
Est: 2001 1000 sq.ft.

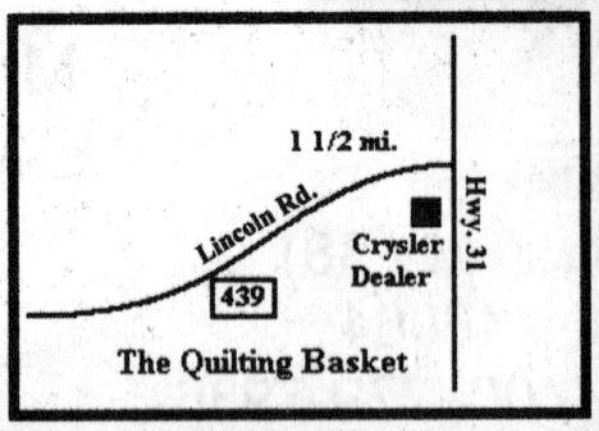

Friendly People. Lots of Variety--900 bolts of fabric. Gift Items, Notions, Books, Patterns, Classes

Morgantown, IN #31

Mon - Sat 10 - 5

Ady's Fabric & Notions

75 W. Washington St, P.O. Box 492 46160
(812) 597-0578 Fax: (812) 597-0593
E-Mail: lydiastout1@earthlink.net
Web Site: www.adysfabrics.com
Est: 2001 1500 Bolts

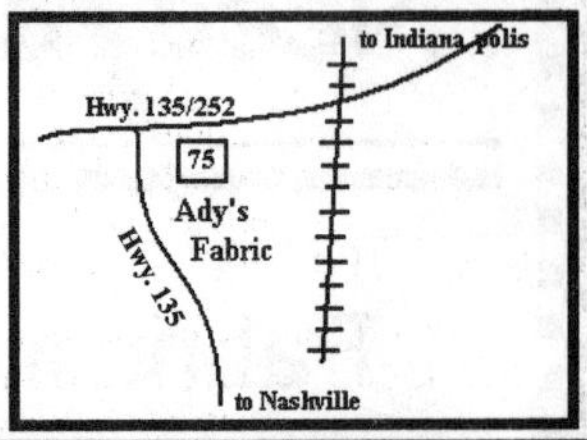

Large selection of 100% cotton fabrics. Complete line of notions, patterns & classes. Gifts for the Quilter. Scrapbooking supplies too.

Nashville, IN #32

Fabric Addict

158 Old School Way
P.O. Box 620, Nashville, IN 47448
(812) 988-4993
E-Mail: fabricaddict@cs.com
Web Site: www.fabricaddict.com
Owner: Mary Beth Woods

Quilting, doll & stitchery patterns. X-stitch, penny rug & rug hook. RJR, South Seas, P&B, Hoffman & homespuns, Flannels and more.

Call for Current Hours

Bloomington, IN #33

Just Around The Block

414 West 6th St.
Bloomington, IN
47404
(812) 333-1385
Owner: Nancy Hodson
Fax: (812) 339-2923
E-Mail:
Justaroundtheblock
@earthlink.net
Est: 2001
1900 sq.ft. 1800+ Bolts

Tues - Sat 10 - 5 Thur til 8

A complete, full service quilt shop carrying your favorite fabrics, books & notions. Classes too! Located in a newly restored 1902 House (Green & white), 2 1/2 Blocks West of County Courthouse Square.

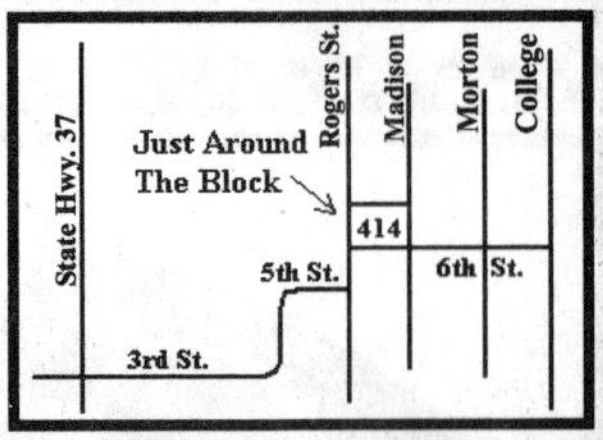

Bloomfield, IN #34

Mon - Sat 9 - 5:30

FABRIX

16 W. Main 47424
(812) 384-8044
E-Mail: fabrix@custom.net
Web Site: www.fabrixsewingcenter.com
Owners: Tina & Charles Allgood
Est: 1997 800+ Bolts

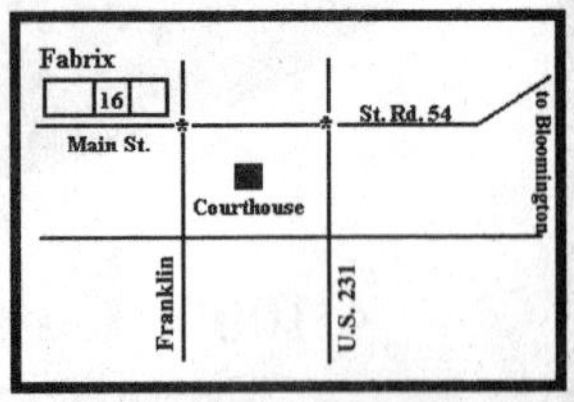

Quilt cottons and notions. Apparel and Bridal fabrics. Classes and private lessons. Authorized PFAFF dealer. Friendly support and a nice place to chat.

Columbus, IN #35

Mon - Thur 10 - 5
Fri 10 - 6
Sat 10 - 2

Columbus Sewing Center, Inc.

1735 Central Ave. 47201
(812) 372-4496
E-Mail: columbus_sewing@hotmail.com
Owner: Marilyn Achterberg
Est: 1974 1800 sq.ft. 900 Bolts

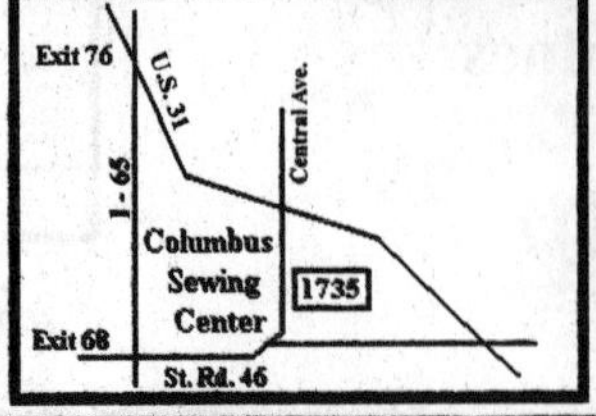

Located in a 100+ year old barn with personality! 100% cotton fabrics, books, patterns & more. Classes. Viking, White and Singer sales and service.

Rushville, IN #36

Mon - Sat 9 - 5
Wed 9 - 12

Country Quilt Barn

5026 W U.S. 52 46173
(765) 663-5882
Owners: Judy & Harold Bowling

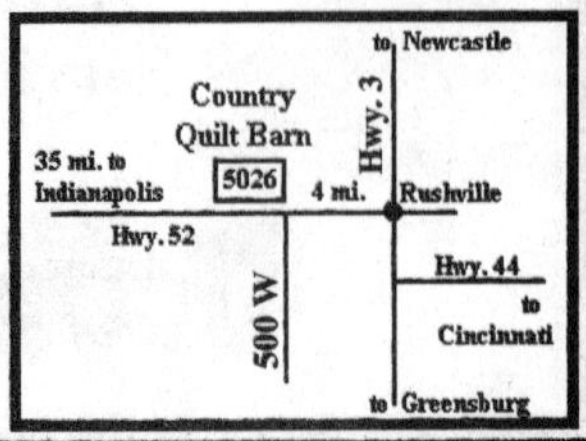

Good selection of Moda, Thimbleberries, Benartex, Springs, Mettler, Gutermann threads. Quilt classes, Patterns, Books, Stencils and Notions. Sewing Machine Repair.

Liberty, IN #37

Mon - Fri 9 - 5
Sat 9 - 3

Stitching Nook

41 W. Union St. 47353
(765) 458-6443
E-Mail: thenook@si-net.com
Web Site: www.stitchingnook.com
Owner: Diana Bruns
Est: 1982 800 Bolts

100% Cotton Fabrics, Quilting Notions, X-Stitch, Classes, Machine Sales, and Friendly Personal Attention.

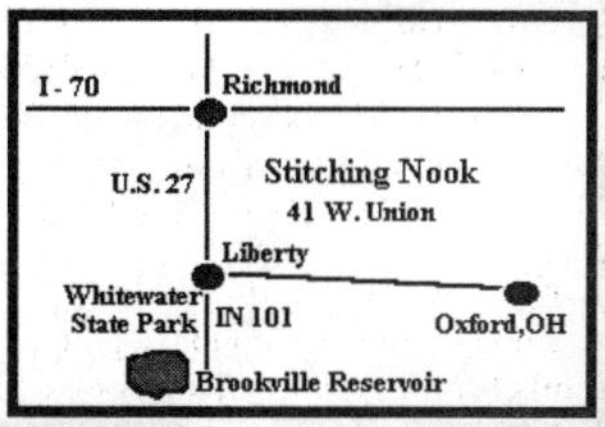

Liberty, IN #38

Pohlar Fabrics

Mon - Sat 9 - 5
Sun by Appt.

Over 2000 bolts of brand name 100% cotton fabrics, sewing & quilting notions, books, patterns and ready made gifts.
Machine Quilting. Exciting quilt classes!

6439 S. State Rd. 101 47353
(800) 357-3152 or
(765) 458-5466 fax also
E-mail: pfabrics@gte.net
Owners: Kenny & Rose Pohlar
Est: 1984 1150 sq.ft.

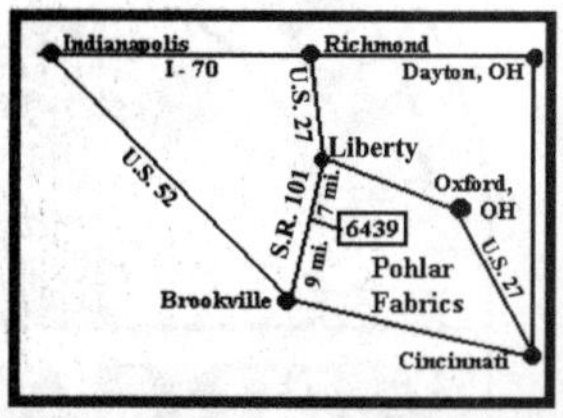

Madison, IN #39

Mon - Sat 9 - 5

L & L Yard Goods

1814 Taylor St. 47250
(812) 273-1041
Owner: Lenora C. Green
Est: 1986

Selection of Fabrics from Moda, Thimbleberries, Batiks from Hoffman, & other quality Homespuns & prints. Lots of wonderful Samples! Classes.

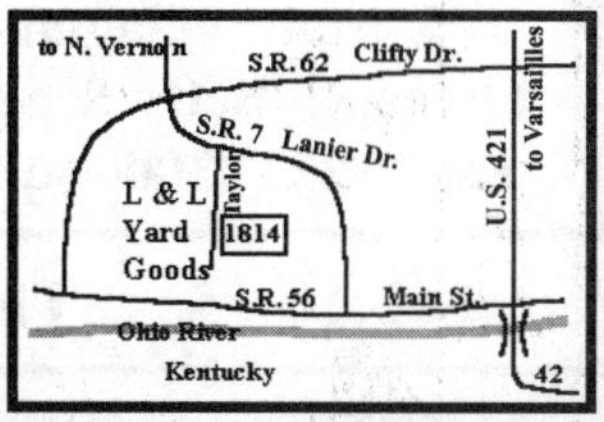

Madison, IN #40

Mon - Sat 10 - 5
Sun 1 - 5

Margie's Country Store

721 W. Main St. 47250
(812) 265-4429
Owner: Marjorie Webb
Est. 1970 900 Bolts

Quality fabrics, books, patterns. Many samples to inspire you. Gracious service. Large line of gifts and home decorations.

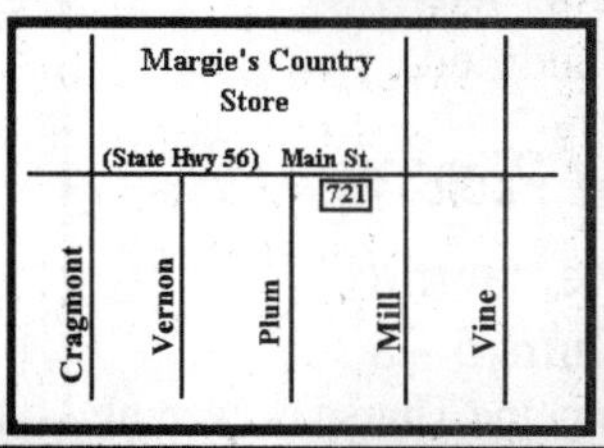

Salem, IN #41

Mon - Fri 9 - 5
Sat 9 - 3

The Quilted Cottage

203 E. Jackson St., Hwy. 60 47167
(812) 883-7577 Est: 2001
E-Mail: drygoods@blueriver.net
Web Site: www.salemquitedcottage.com
Owner: Susan Fleming & Connie Wright

Premium Cotton Fabrics, Notions, Books & Patterns, Professional Machine Quilting, Home & gift Items, Superior Service.

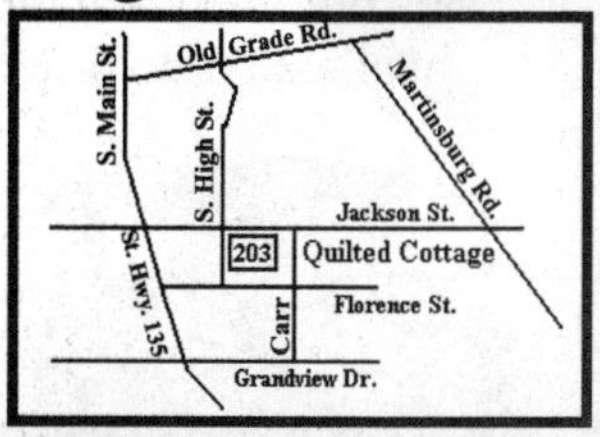

Pekin, IN #42

Mon - Fri 9 - 5
Sat 9 - 4

Quilt Corner

98 S. Shorts Corner Rd. 47165
(812) 967-4666
E-Mail: lorajn@wertc.net
Owner: Lora Nale Est: 1998 2000 Bolts

Large selection of Books, Patterns, Notions, Templates & Classes. Fabric includes Debbie Mumm, Thimbleberries, Moda, Fossil Fern, Hoffman, Flannels & More.

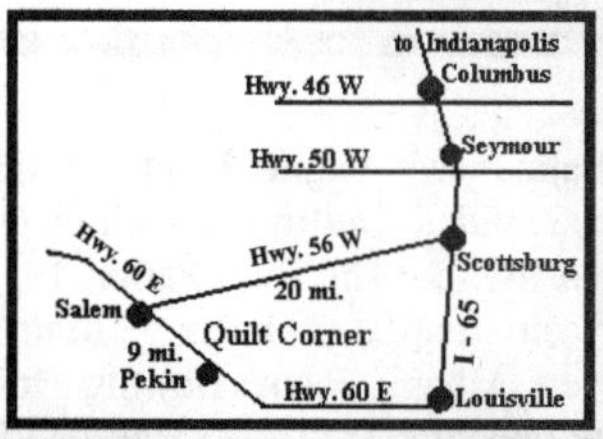

Corydon, IN #43

Quilters Garden

200 Elm St. 47112
(812) 738-1357 Fax: (812) 366-4846
E-Mail: betty@foxfirequilts.com
Web Site: www.foxfirequilts.com
Owner: Betty Warwick

Mon - Fri 10 - 5
Sat 10 - 4

Viking-Husqvarna Sewing Machines, Fabric, Quilting Supplies, Patterns, Classes, Books.

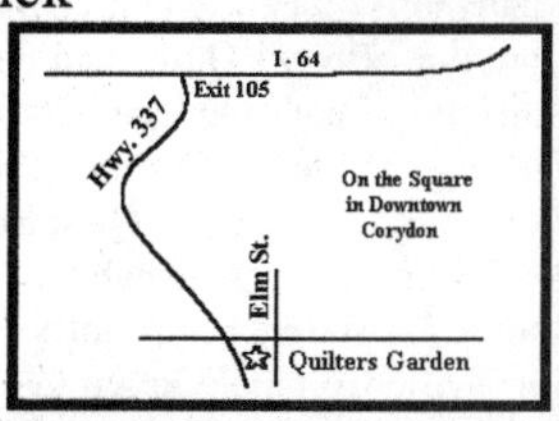

Montgomery, IN #44

Mon - Sat Daylight Hours

David V. Wagler's Quilts

R.R. 1 Box 73 450 E. 200 N.
(812) 486-3836 47558
Owners: David & Anna Wagler
Est: 1980 1900 sq.ft. 1500+ Bolts

Hand Made Quilts on display. Quilts made to order, applique, pieced, & wholecloth tops. 100% Cotton Fabrics, Stencils, Books, Patterns, Kits

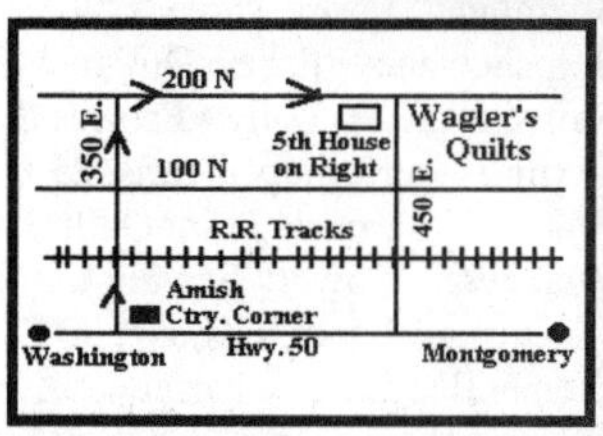

Washington, IN #45

Mon - Sat 10 - 5

The Stitching Post

400 East Main Street 47501
(812) 254-6063
Web Site: www.stitchingpostquilts.com
Owner: Mary Dell Memering
Est: 1986 1500 sq.ft.

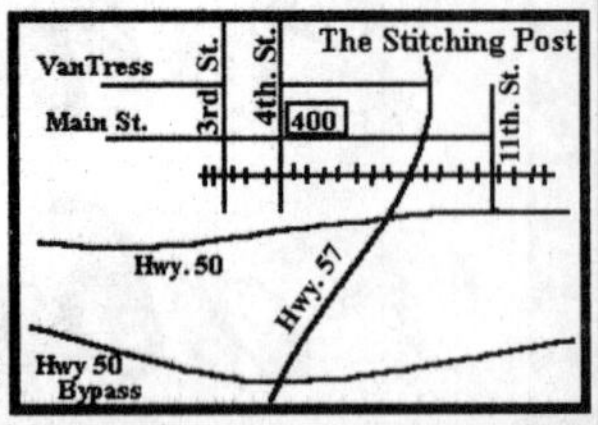

Southwest Indiana's largest selection of quality quilting fabrics--4000 bolts 100% cottons including Plaids & Hoffmans. Quilting supplies, notions, books, & patterns.

Haubstadt, IN #46

Tues 2 - 8 Fri & Sat 10 - 4

Quilts n' Bloom

R.R. #1, Box 53 47639
(812) 768-6009
Owners: Kathy & Rick Will

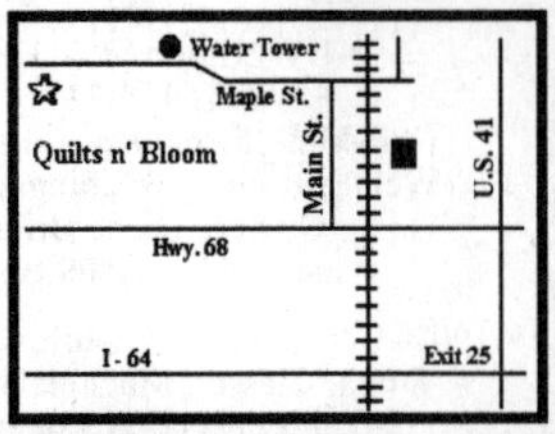

Quilting supplies, Books, Patterns, quality cotton Fabrics, Classes, Featherweight Parts & Service, Country Setting & Flower Garden.

Boonville, IN #47

THE VILLAGE MERCANTILE

123 S. 2nd. St. 47601 (812) 897-5687
E-Mail: villagmerc@aol.com
Owners: Betty & Steve Cummings
Est: 1992 3000 sq.ft. 6000+ bolts

Tues, Wed, Fri 10 - 5 Thurs 10 - 8 Sat 10 - 4

Turn of the century charm boasting a fantastic collection of 100% quilting cottons & homespuns. Hundreds of quilting books; patterns for quilts, critters & clothes; kits; silk ribbon supplies. Large selection of notions, stencils plus unique gifts for the quilt enthusiast. Be inspired by our many samples of wall hangings, clothing & critters. Kits available or to order on any project. Ongoing classes scheduled.

20 min. east of Evansville;
10 min. south of I - 64, exit 39
West side of the Historic Town Square

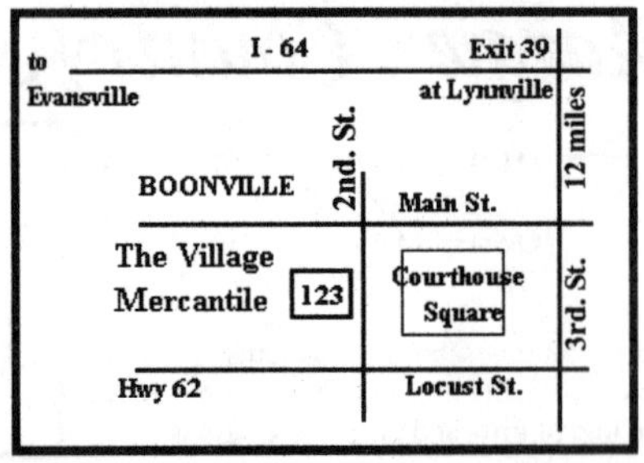

Victoria's Tea Room

2nd Floor, Village Mercantile
Tues - Sat 11 - 2 & Thurs 5 - 8

Plan to join us for a delightful lunch, or come Thursday evening for a specially planned and prepared dinner. Scrumptious homemade everything, specializing in soups, desserts, hot grilled sandwiches, pasta salads, breads, flavored coffees & teas. Our chicken and tuna salads are the best. Have you ever tasted a Tomato Pie?

Plan to spend the day with us - You won't be disappointed!

Other Shops in Indiana: We suggest calling first

Bedford	Quilts & More, 312 S St.	812-279-8593
Berne	Hilty's Dry Goods Store, Hwy. 27 N	
Brazil	Dorothy's Quilts & Crafts, R.R. # 17	812-446-5502
Brownstone	Quilt N Baskets, 209 S. Sugar St.	812-358-2338
Farmland	Quilts & Quilting, Cty. Rd. 600 W	765-468-7052
Frankfort	Mary's Crafts and Quilts, 52 W. Armstrong	765-659-3053
Goshen	Calico Point, 24810 County Rd. 40	219-862-4065
Grabill	Country Shops of Grabill, 13756 State	219-627-6315
Huntington	Patchwork Acres, 5279 W. River Rd.	219-356-1873
Indianapolis	Fabric Outlet, 3431 Kentucky Ave.	317-244-6007
Lynnville	Betty's Quilts and Fabrics, 244 West Third	812-922-3642
Madison	Joan's Quilts & Crafts, 115 E. Main St.	812-265-2349
Markle	Stitchin' Corner, 225 Lee St., P.O. Box 175	219-758-2217
Middlebury	Country Quilt Shoppe, 200 W. Warren	219-825-9309
Middlebury	Laura's Fabrics, 55140 G.R. 43	
Monroe	Wilmen's, Country Store, 421 E 100 S	
Morrisville	Colonial Outlet, 490 E. St. Clair	317-831-0026
Muncie	Country Designs, 705 Nebo Rd.--400 W	765-286-0505
Nappanee	Wagner Home Interiors, 1200 E. Market	219-773-2441
Nashville	Quilting Bee Gifts, 69 Franklin St. W	812-988-7496
Nashville	The Quilt Parlor, 1933 N. Orchard Hill Rd.	812-988-7373
Nashville	M C Quilts, 58 Main St. E #C	812-988-7778
New Albany	Jan's Sewing Things, 2223 E. Spring St.	812-945-8113
Noblesville	Arbuckle's Railroad Place, 1151 Vine	317-773-3915
Noblesville	World Class Sewing, 1150 South St.	317-776-2204
Odon	Hopes and Seams, 105 W. Main St.	812-636-4393
Pershing	Quilting & Variey Shop, 119 N. Market St.	765-478-1224
Rensselaer	From The Needles Point, 125 N. Front St.	219-866-5353
Salem	Craft Town, North Side of Public Square	812-883-6860
Seymour	Loose Threads, 205 S. Maple St.	812-524-2013
Shipshewana	Fabric Outlet, 440 S. Van Buren	219-768-4501
Shipshewana	Lolly's Fabrics & Quilt Shop, 228 W. Main	260-768-4703
Vernon	Heritage Crafts, 23 E. Brown St.	812-346-7933
Wanatah	Prairie Point Quilt Shoppe, 213 N. Main	219-733-2821
Warsaw	Lowery Sewing Center, 707 E. Winona Ave.	219-267-8631
Wheatfield	Fabric Cottage, 30 E. Grove St.	219-956-4171
Zionsville	Liberty Farmhouse, 25 Cedar St.	317-873-1776

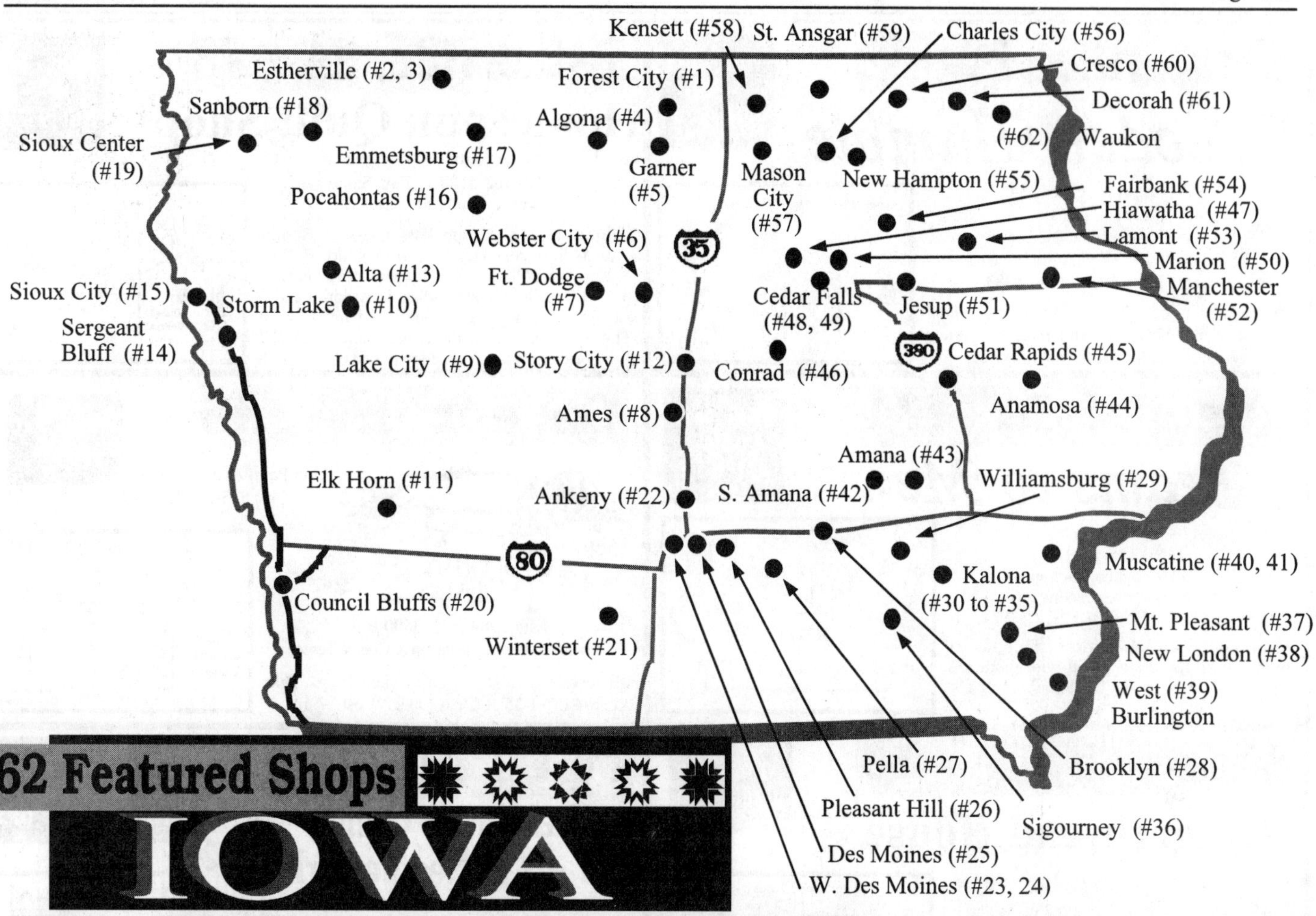

62 Featured Shops

IOWA

the Quilted Forest

Serving You:
9 am-5 pm
Mon.—Sat.
Thursday nights
Until 8 pm

Forest City, IA #1

We invite you to visit The Quilted Forest and discover what makes us special. We offer exceptional, friendly service, an incredible selection of fabric, notions, kits, and gifts for today's busy quilter. We offer classes, clubs, block of the month programs, mail order, quality machine quilting, original patterns, Bernina sewing machines, Horn of America, and Koala sewing tables, and much more. A Tea Room next door and other specialty shops nearby. Inspiration is our specialty, stop in soon for yours!

The Quilted Forest, 109 North Clark, Forest City, IA
1-641-585-2438 or 1-877-985-2438

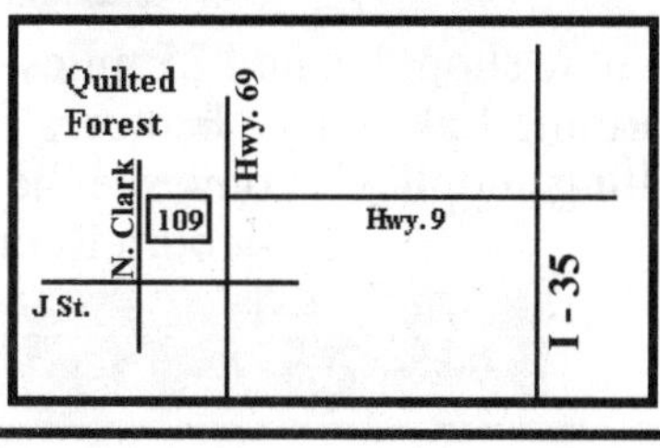

Owner: *Shelley Robson*
Established: 1998
Email: tqf@wctatel.net

Estherville, IA #2

Mon - Fri 9 - 5:30 Sat 9 - 4

Wooden Thimble

516 Central Ave. 51334
(712) 362-2561
E-Mail: woodenthimble@netscape.net
Web Site: www.woodenthimble.com
Owner: Mary Hart Est: 1983

Large selection of fabric, quilting, cross-stitch and craft supplies, books and patterns. Many hand made gifts and lots of friendly service.

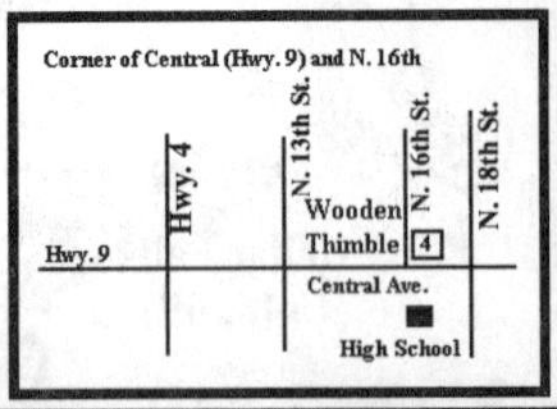

Estherville, IA #3

Mon - Fri 9 - 5 Sat 9 - 4

Homespun Quilt Shop

202 Central Ave. 51334
(712) 362-5100 Fax: Same
Owner: Candy Fredericksen

Quilting fabrics & supplies, Classes, Bernina Sales & Service. Thimbleberries Club, BOM's, $5.00 quilt block. Gifts including pottery, vintage lace, McCalls candles & Ardore candles (locally made soybean candle) and much more. "The quaint house on the corner" one block east of the bridge on the West edge of town.

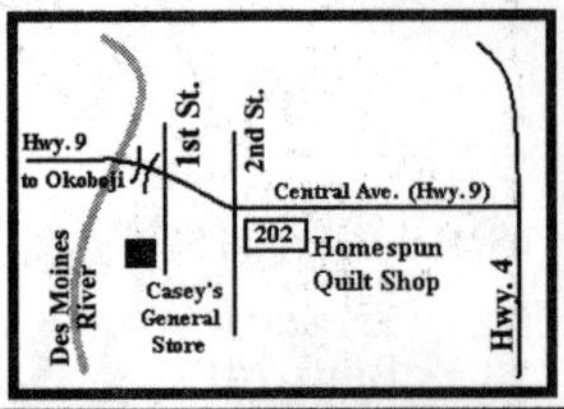

Algona, IA #4

Mon - Fri 9 - 5 Sat 9 - 3

Seams to Me

17 E. State 50511
(515) 295-5841
E-Mail: kboyken@ncn.net
Web Site: www.seamstome.com
Owner: Karen Boyken Est: 1987

Quality 100% cotton fabrics. Full line of notions & crafts. Walls filled with models & displays. Home of "Stitchin' Friends" patterns. Mail Order.

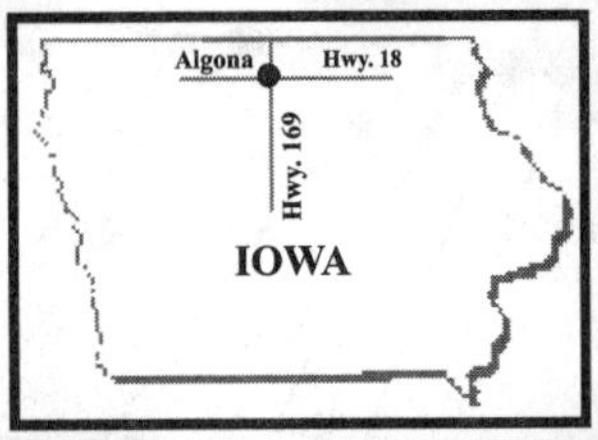

Garner, IA #5

Mon - Sat 9 - 5

2345 Palm Ave. 50438
(641) 923-3893

Est: 1984 3500 Bolts
Owners: Mary Etherington & Connie Tesene

Full service quilt shop in a chicken coop. Take Exit 194 off I-35 at Clear Lake. West 17 miles.

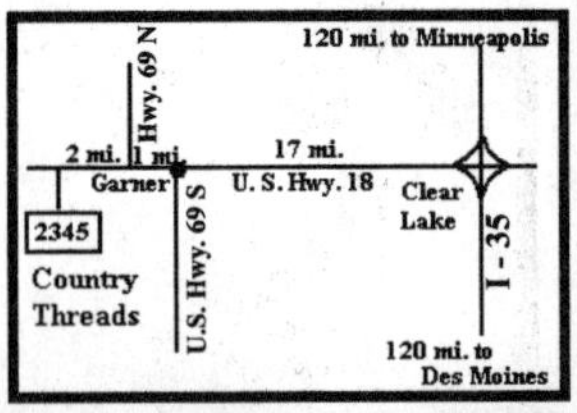

Webster City, IA #6

Mon - Sat 9:30 - 5:30

Gingerbread House

309 Bank St. 50595
(515) 832-1492
Fax: Same
Est: 1974 2000 Bolts

"as unique as you are"
CHECK US OUT
We are one of the most diversified stores around.

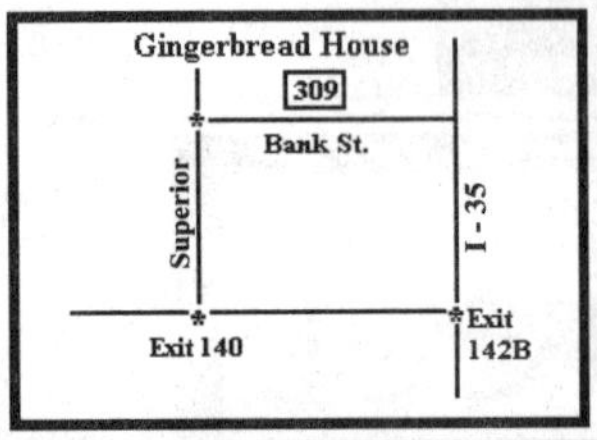

Fort Dodge, IA #7

Mon - Sat 10 - 5 Wed 12 - 5 Tues & Thur til 7

Grandma's Quilts, Crafts & Needlework

1422—1st. Ave. North 50501
(515) 955-1521
Owner: Mary Consier
Est: 1987 2000 sq.ft. Over 500 Bolts

In a House built in 1896 with a black wrought iron fence. We carry crafts, fabric, and lots of books and patterns. We also carry yarn. Pfaff Sewing Machines, Koala Cabinets & Ulmer Quilt Frames.

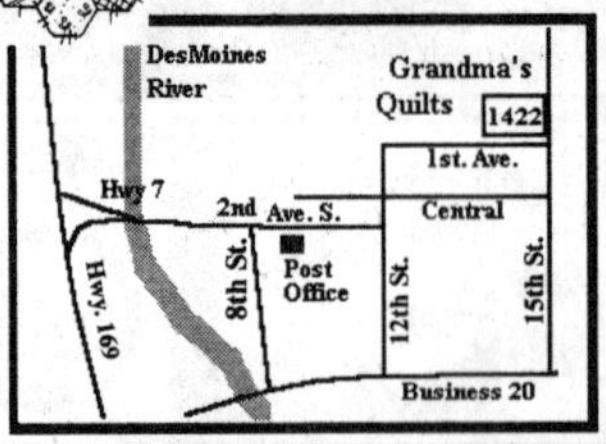

Ames, IA #8

Quilting Connection

Mon 10 - 8 Tues - Fri 10 - 5:30 Sat 10 - 5

323 5th St. 50010 (515) 233-3048
E-Mail: Jeanne@iaquilts.com Est: 1998
Web Site: www.iaquilts.com 2700 sq.ft
Owner: Jeanne Allen 3000+ Bolts

Husqvarna VIKING

Great selection of 100% cotton fabrics including Hoffman, Bali, RJR, Moda. Hundreds of books, patterns, & notions. Complete Line of Viking Sewing Machines.

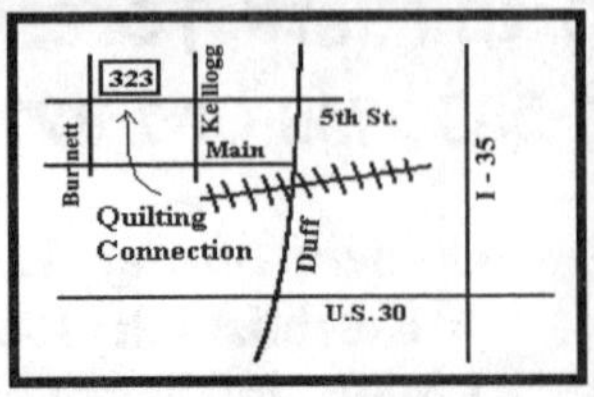

Moving to 238 Main St. (1 block south & 1 block east) in 2003.

Towne Square Quilt Shoppe

Mon - Fri 10 - 6 Sat 9 - 4

103 E. Main St.
Lake City, IA 51449
712-464-7477
tsqs@cal-net.net
Owner: Christi Savage
Est: 2001 1500 sq.ft.

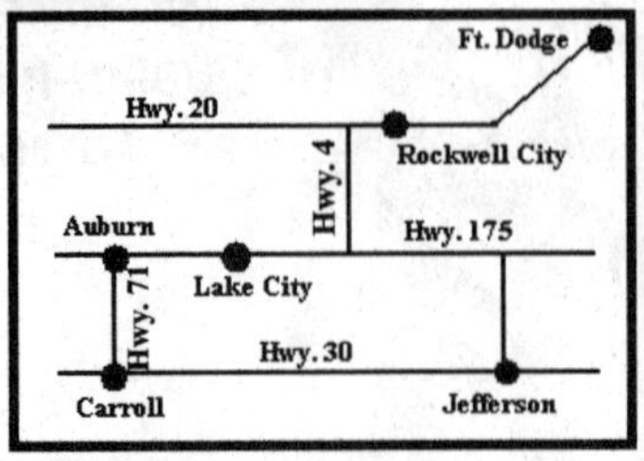

A new shop, located 25 miles NE of Carroll in Charming Lake City. Features fabric, patterns and quilting supplies. Come see the quilt block on the classroom floor.

Lake City, IA #9

Storm Lake, IA #10

One of a Kind Quilts

617 Lake Ave. Storm Lake, IA 50588
(712) 213-1050 Owner: Bettie Sproul
Est: Feb. 2002 3700 sq.ft. 3000+ Bolts

Not your ordinary quilt shoppe.
100% cotton fabrics, kits
Complete line of notions, Books,
Patterns & Classes
Many Great Gift Ideas
Batiks, Flannels, Moda, Plaids,
30's prints, Award Winning Teachers
Custom Machine Quilting

Mon - Fri 9 - 5:30
Thurs til 8
Sat 9 - 4 Sun 1 - 4

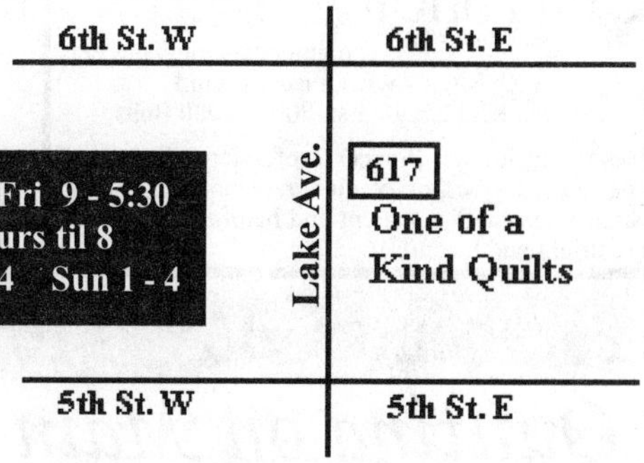

Elk Horn, IA #11

Prairie Star Quilts

4132 Main St.
Elk Horn IA 51531

712.764.7012
on the Web at www.prairiestarquilts.com

psquilts@metc.net

The Friendliest Quilt Shop You'll Ever Visit!

Everything for the Quilter
Over 2000 bolts,
Including 400 flannels
Kits, Kits, Kits
Reproductions
Wool Felt
Embroidery
Fast Mail Order
Custom Machine Quilting
Original patterns & books by 5 on staff designers
Quilt Retreats

Busses Welcome

Mon - Sat 10 - 5

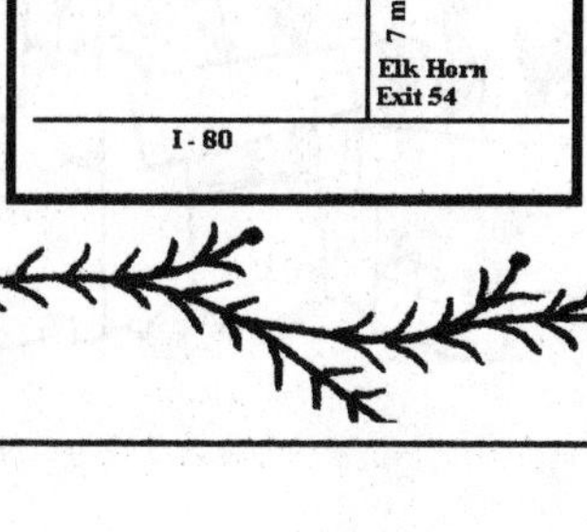

Selected by American Patchwork & Quilting Magazine as one of North America's 10 top Quilt Shops in 2002

Story City, IA #12

Mon - Sat 10 - 5

Quilters Corner

626 Broad St. 50248
(515) 733-2565
E-Mail: quilterscorner@excite.com
Owner: Diane Larson 1200 bolts

Fabric, notions, classes, custom hand quilting, guild member discount, mail order. Full Service store in Story City's historic business district.

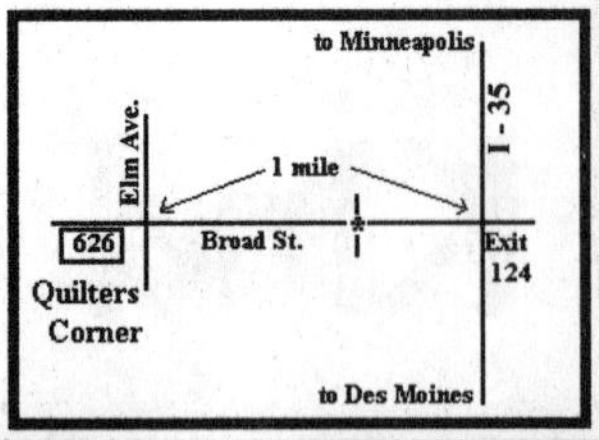

Alta, IA #13

Mon, Tue, Thur, Fri 9:30 - 5:30 Thur til 8 Sat 9:30 - 3

The Quilt Shoppe

206 S. Main 51002
(712) 284-2724
Owner: Pat Patten
Est: 1987 1200 sq.ft.

All cotton fabrics, books, patterns, notions, classes. Bus groups welcome. Personalized helpful service for all your quilting needs.

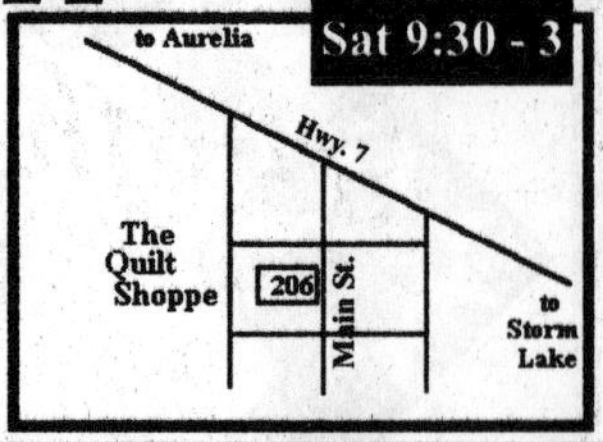

Sergeant Bluff, IA #14

Mon - Fri 10 - 6 Sat 10 - 5 Sun 12 - 5

My Quilt Shop is Your Quilt Shop

206 1st St.
P.O. Box 314 51054
(712) 943-9486
Fax: (712) 943-9487
E-Mail:
diamond3@longlines.net
Web Site: www.kimsquilts.com
Owner: Kim Gray Est: 2001 1000 Bolts

Nestled inside the Pioneer Professional Plaza, we specialize in the novice quilter. Our shop is light & airy, our staff is patient and helpful, our fabrics are bright and beautiful!

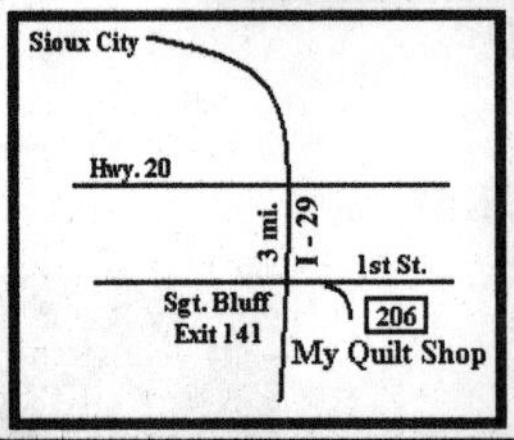

Heart & Hand Dry Goods Co.

Sioux City, IA #15

1551 Indian Hills Dr. #6 51104 (712) 258-3161
E-Mail: hrthand@aol.com Est: 1996
Web Site: www.heartandhand.com
Owners: Ann Brouillette & Lerlene Nevaril
2000 sq.ft. 1800 Bolts

Mon - Fri 10 - 5:30 Thurs til 6 Sat 10 - 5

We feature an antique-filled atmosphere that compliments the quilting fabrics, patterns & books, sewing notions, gift items and greeting cards. Mail orders, newsletter & machine quilting available.

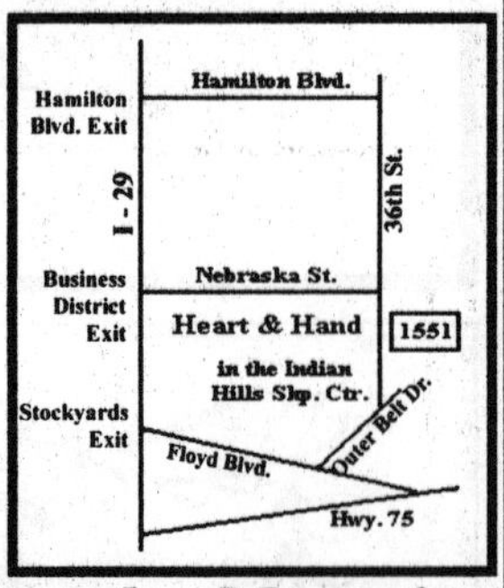

Featured in 1999 Quilt Sampler Magazine

Pocahontas, IA #16

Mon - Fri 9 - 5 Thur til 7 Sat 9 - 1

Quilting on Main

229 N. Main 50574
(712) 335-3969 Fax: (712) 335-3972
E-Mail: patches@evertek.net
Web Site: www.quiltingonmain.com
Owner: Bonnie Wood 2000 sq.ft.

Full line of fabrics, books, patterns & notions. Great selection of kits & fat quarters. Millennium Quilting Machine available for custom quilting.

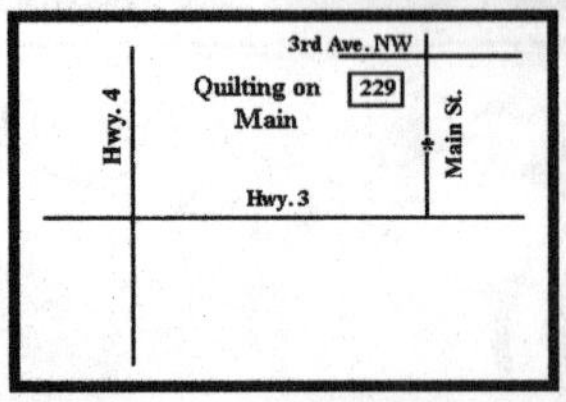

Emmetsburg, IA #17

Mon - Fri 9 - 5 Thur til 7 Sat til 4

Calico Cupboard

2201 Main St. 50536
(712) 852-2098
Owner: Deborah Hite
Est: 1981 2500 sq.ft. 700 Bolts

Large selection of quilting fabrics, notions, books, quilt & craft patterns and stencils. Great classes and friendly service !

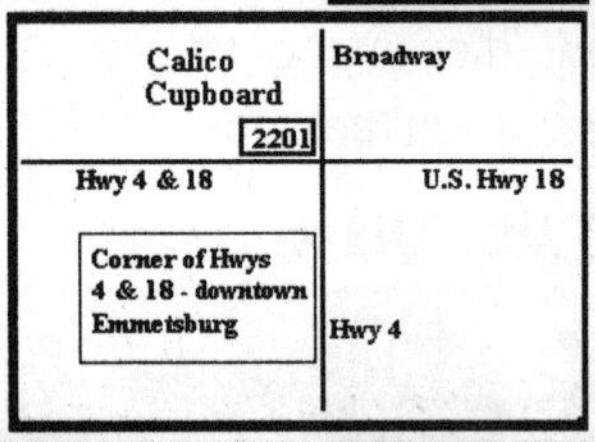

Sanborn, IA #18

Tues - Sat 10 - 5:30

Quilter's Coop

6063 - 280th St. 51248
(712) 736-2204
Owner: Judy Flanagan
Est: 1992 1280 sq.ft. 800 Bolts

Cotton Fabrics, Notions, Patterns & Books, Original Patterns, Country feel in an old Chicken Coop.

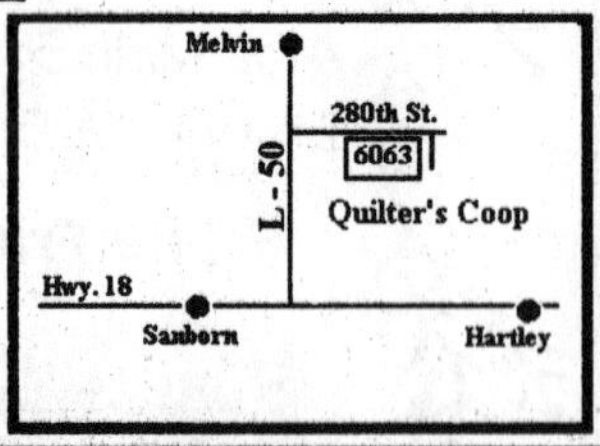

Sioux Center, IA #19

Mon - Sat 9 - 5:30 Thur til 9

Roelofs

24 3rd St. NW 51250
(712) 722-2611
Owner: Dixie Roelofs
Est: 1976 2000 sq.ft.

Quilting Fabrics & supplies; Fabric craft patterns and supplies; wall hanging kits; hemstitched flannel receiving blankets ready for crochet edge.

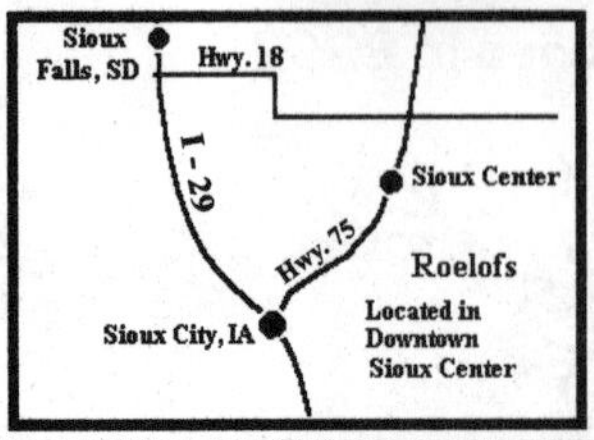

Council Bluffs, IA #20

Kanesville Quilting Gingham Goose

19851 Virginia Hills Rd. 51503
(877) 294-1009 or (712) 366-6003
E-Mail: quilt@kanesvillequilting.com
Web Site: www.kanesvillequilting.com
Owners: Mavis Hauser & Karen Krause
Est: 1990 3000 sq.ft.

Spacious, well lit shop, filled with 100% cotton fabrics, books, patterns, notions, and the latest magazines. We do machine quilting on your tops. Our friendly staff is always ready to assist you with your quilting needs.

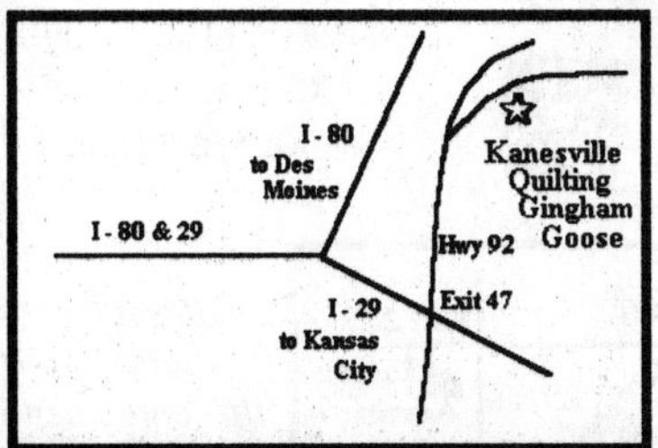

Mon - Fri 10 - 5:30 Sat 10 - 4

East on Hwy. 92

Winterset, IA #21

Mon - Sat 9 - 5

Quilting from the Heart

54 Court Ave. 50273 Est: 1998
(515) 462-3776 Fax: (515) 462-9435
E-Mail: qheart@dwx.com 2400+ Bolts
Web Site: www.quiltingfromtheheart.com
Owner: Cynthia Bortell 3000 sq.ft.

A Great Quilt Shop in the Heart of Madison County. A great selection of fabrics, notions, books, patterns & classes. You won't want to miss this shop!

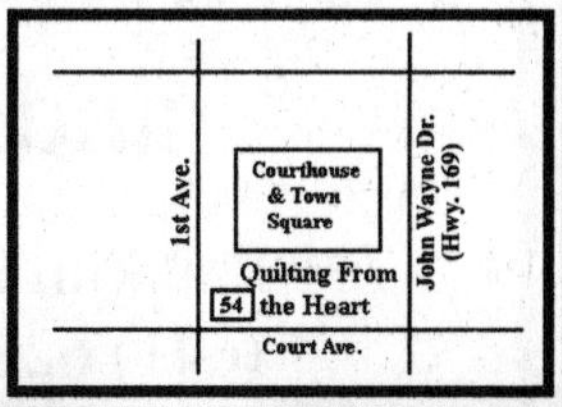

Ankeny, IA #22

Mon - Fri 10 - 5:30 Thur til 7 Sat 10 - 4

QUILTER'S HAVEN

305 S.W. Walnut St. 50021
(515) 964-2747 Fax: (515) 964-3472
E-Mail: bailey5@netins.net
Owner: Judy Larsen Est: 1985
Group Appts. Available

Clean & Bright Quilt Shop featuring 1800+ bolts of fabric & quilt books. We offer classes and a Thimbleberries' Club. Long Arm Quilting Service. **A Quilter's Dream!**

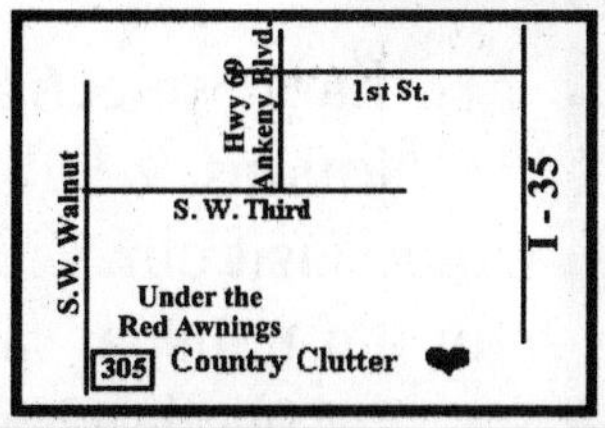

West Des Moines, IA #23

220 5th St. 50265
(515) 274-0660
E-Mail:
barbara@thequiltjunction.com
Web Site:
www.thequiltjunction.com
Over 2400 bolts of your favorite 100% cotton fabrics.

Mon - Sat 10 - 5 Sun 12 - 4 Thurs til 7 (close at 5pm on Thursdays Jan-April)

One stop shop for quilting supplies, accessories, notions, patterns, books, a large selection of buttons for quilts and crafts and a rainbow assortment of threads including variegated.
We also carry quilt bars and hangers to display your treasures.
Mail and phone orders welcome.
Dozens of samples on display.
Kits available for many items.

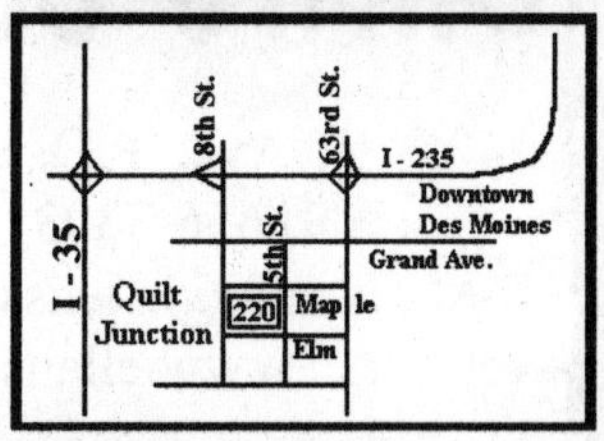

Located in historic Valley Junction

West Des Moines, IA #24

M -S 10 - 5 Thur 10 - 7 Sun 1 - 4

The Quilt Block

325 5th Street 50265
(515) 255-1010
Owner: Mary Miller
Est: 1987 3000 sq.ft. 2000 Bolts

Full line quilt supply store--fabrics, notions, books, patterns. Authorized Bernina dealer.

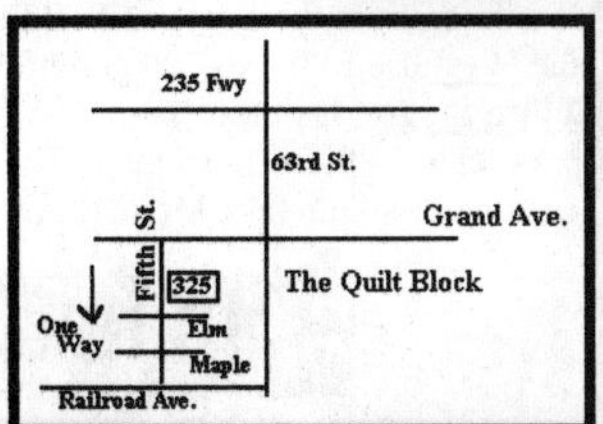

Des Moines, IA #25

Mon - Fri 10 - 5 Sat 10 - 4

Creative Sewing Center

3708 Ingersoll Ave. 50312
(515) 279-0019 Fax: (515) 279-2934
E-Mail: csew@earthlink.net
Web Site: www.creativesewingcenter.com
Owner: Lynda & Don Charleston
Est: 1992 2500 sq.ft. 1200 Bolts

Large Selection of Fabrics, Books, Patterns, & Notions. Horn Cabinets. Viking & White Sewing Machines & Sergers.

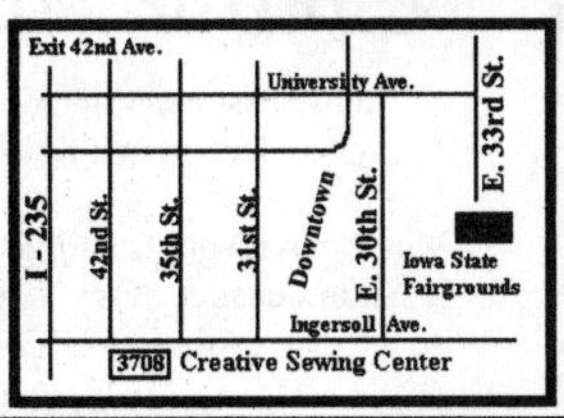

Pleasant Hill, IA #26

Mon - Sat 10 - 5:30 Thur til 7 Sun 12 - 4

Copper Creek Quilting

1225 Copper Creek Dr. #K 50327
(515) 299-5386 Est: 2000
E-Mail: mac@coppercreekquilting.com
Web Site: www.coppercreekquilting.com
Owner: Melissa Cisar 2300 sq.ft.

100% cotton fabrics. Large selection of flannel in plaids, brights, pastels & florals. Hundreds of books & patterns. Notions, Kits, classes & friendly staff. Home of the original PMS Night!

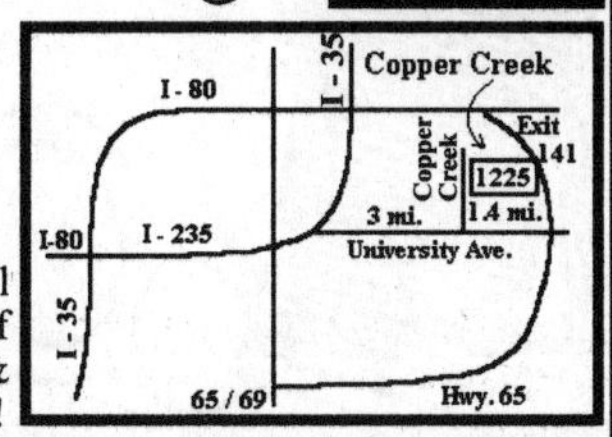

Pella, IA #27

Vande Lune Fabrics
and Quilt Shop

701 Franklin St. 50219
(641) 628-3350
Fax: (641) 628-8968
Located on the Southeast corner of Town Square
Est: 1972

Mon - Fri 9 - 5:30
Thur til 8
Sat 9 - 5

Large selection of the latest Books, Notions & Fabrics (over 3,000 bolts). Come visit our Vibrant Store. We are known for our unusual samples with available kits.
* Authorized Bernina Dealer. *

Pella Tulip Festival
May 2, 3, 4

PELLA
A touch of Holland

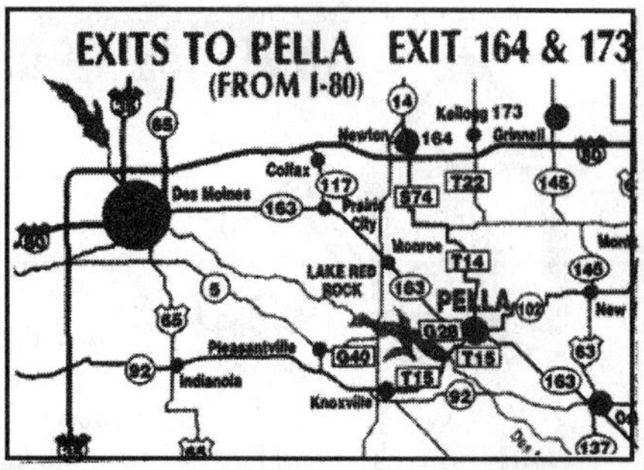

Brooklyn, IA #28

Mon - Sat 8 - 6

True Value

118 W. Front St.
52211
(888) 522-7712
Free Newsletter

12,000 yards of Quality Cotton Quilting Fabric (Debbie Mumm, Moda, Homespuns), Craft Patterns, Rubber Stamps, Silk Ribbon. Quilting & Craft Supplies. Lots of Models. Memory items & ideas.

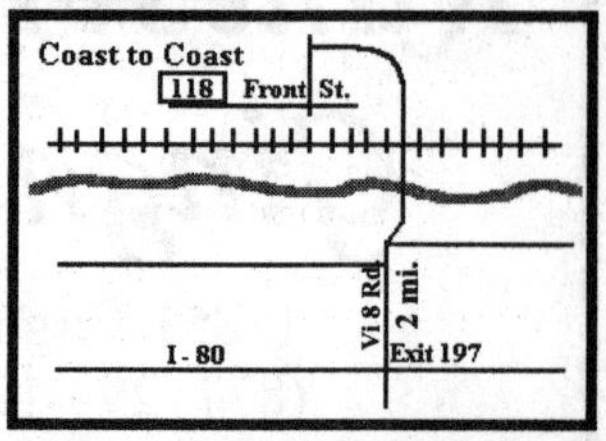

Rainbows & Calico Things

Wed - Sat 9 - 4
Other Times by Chance or Appt.

2811 240th St. 52361
(319) 668-1977
Owner: Barbara Wardenburg
E-Mail: barbaraw@avalon.net
Est: 1994 1100 sq.ft.
Web Site: www.avalon.net/~barbaraw/quiltshop.htm

Homespun Fabrics, Books, Patterns, Notions, Rulers - Olfa Products, Battings, Electric Quilt Software & a great selection of 100% Fine Cottons (1000 bolts) by Hoffman, P&B, Benartex, Moda, RJR, Marcus and more.

RAINBOWS & CALICO THINGS QUILT 2000 COLLECTOR PIN AVAILABLE HERE.

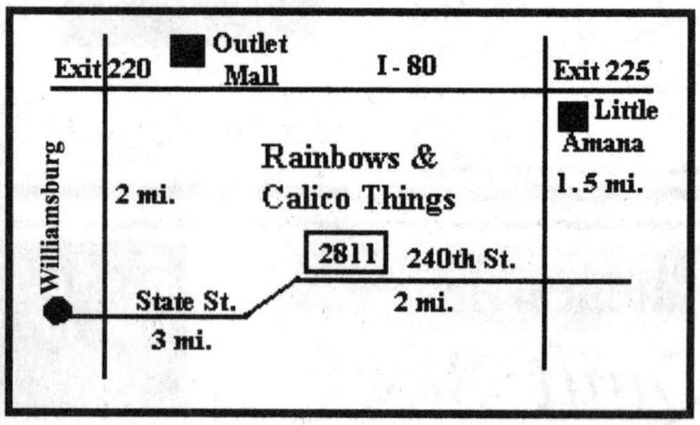

A unique shop located on a three generation farm just outside of historic Williamsburg, Iowa.

If coming from the **East** use I-80 Exit 225 follow map & signs. If coming from the **West** use I-80 Exit 220 go into Williamsburg. Turn east on **State St., (F-46)**, **240th St.** go 3½ miles. The Shop is located between the two exits on paved road parallel to I - 80 on Iowa map. This road also goes into Iowa City past the U of I Hospital/Stadium (aka Melrose Ave.)

Williamsburg, IA #29

Ellen's Sewing Center

405 "B" Ave., P.O. Box 252 52247
(319) 656-3303 Est: 1975
E-Mail: info@ellenssewingcenter.com
Web Site: www.ellenssewingcenter.com

Mon - Sat 8:30 - 5
Thur til 6

Kalona, IA #30

Large selection of Quilt Books, Quilt Supplies. Bernina Machines & Supplies.

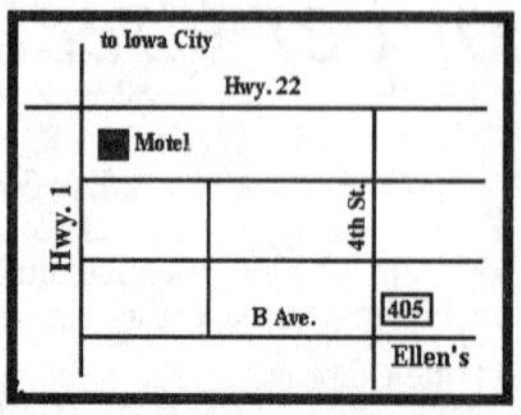

Kalona, IA #31

Summer 9:30 - 4
Winter 11 - 3

Kalona Historical Quilt & Textile Museum

In the Historic Village on D Ave.
Downtown Kalona

Museum with quilts dating 1830 - 1940
Shows change every 3 - 4 months
Admission $3

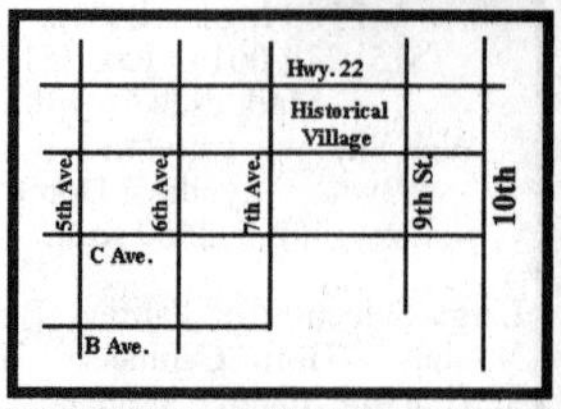

Kalona, IA #32

Mon - Fri 9 - 5
Sat 9 - 3
March - Oct
Sat 9 - 5

Stitch 'n Sew Cottage

207 4th St. P.O. Box 351
(319) 656-2923 52247 Est: 1981
Owners: Dorothy, Paul & Cande Schumann & Niva Burkholder

"Where Ma Saves Pa's Dough"

Fabrics, Notions, Quilting Supplies Pillow Forms, Embroidery Supplies, batting. 1000+ Bolts

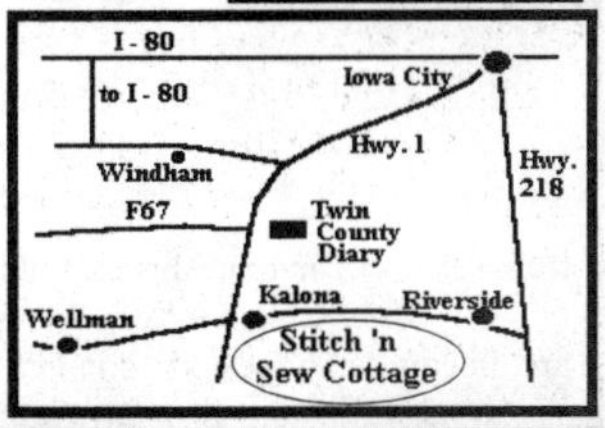

Kalona, IA #33

Mon - Sat
10 - 5

Woodin Wheel

515 "B" Ave. 52247
(319) 656-2240
Owner: Marilyn Woodin
Est: 1971

Over 300 New & Antique Quilts for Sale.

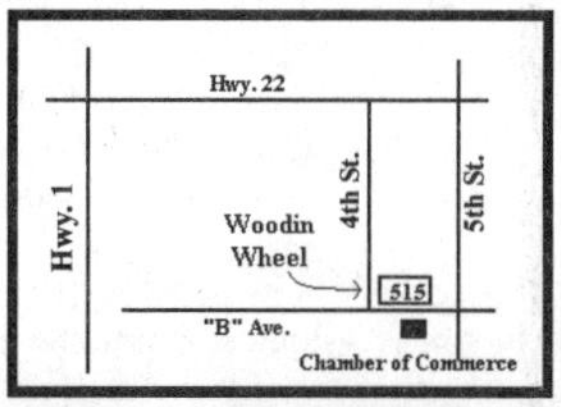

Kalona, IA #34

Mon - Sat
10 - 5

Willow Creek Collectibles

418 B Ave., P.O. Box 862 52247
(319) 656-3939
Owner: Juanita Troyer

NEW FLANNEL ROOM. 100% cotton flannels--specializing in homespuns. 100's of bolts of regular cotton fabrics. Huge selection of books & patterns for dolls, quilts, & stitchery with many models and quilts made up. Many quilt kits. Classes available.

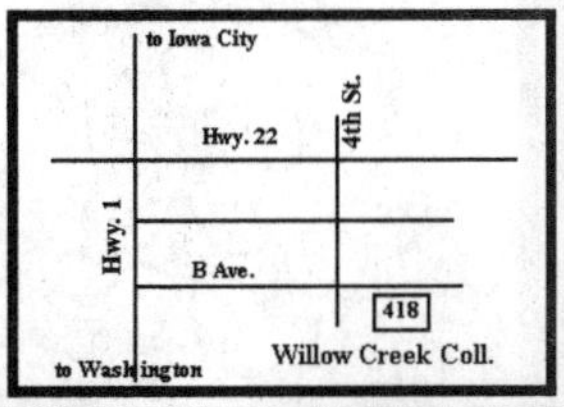

Kalona, IA #35

Mon - Sat 9 - 5
Evenings by Appt.

109 1st. St. Hwy 1 52247
(800) 233-4189 Est 1982

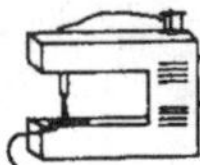

Stitches Galore

Owner: Linda Hiatt
Free Bi-Monthly Newsletter

Baby Lock, Elna & PFAFF Dealer.
Classes - Fabric - Buttons
Software - Brazilian Emb. Threads & More.

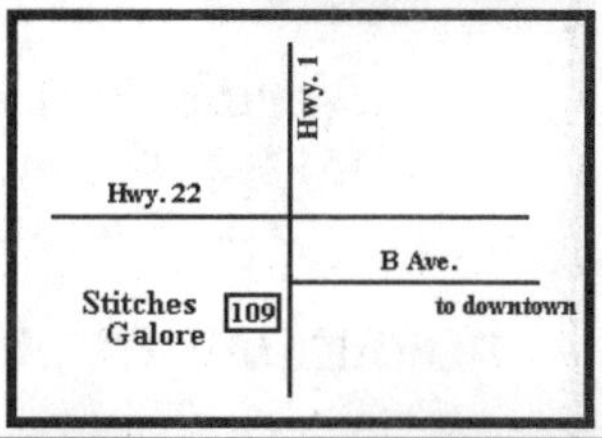

Sigourney, IA #36

Mon - Fri
9 - 4:30
Sat 9 - 12

In My Sewing Room

104 E Washington 52591
(641) 622-2212
Fax: (641) 622-2212
E-Mail: inmysewingroom@yahoo.com
Web Site: www.inmysewingroom.com
Owner: Adrian Gentry Est: 1990

Full service quilt shop; notions, books, homespuns, brights, batiks, reproduction prints, Husqvarna Viking dealer. Southeast Iowa's best kept secret.

Mt. Pleasant, IA #37

Mon - Fri
10 - 5
Thurs til 8
Sat 10 - 3

Quilters Paradise

120 N. Main St. 52641
(319) 385-1749
E-Mail:
paradise@interl.net
Owner: Cathy Hopkins
Est: 2001

Where Heaven is only a stitch away. Love, laughter & friends are always welcome. Offering quality cotton fabrics, books, patterns and notions.

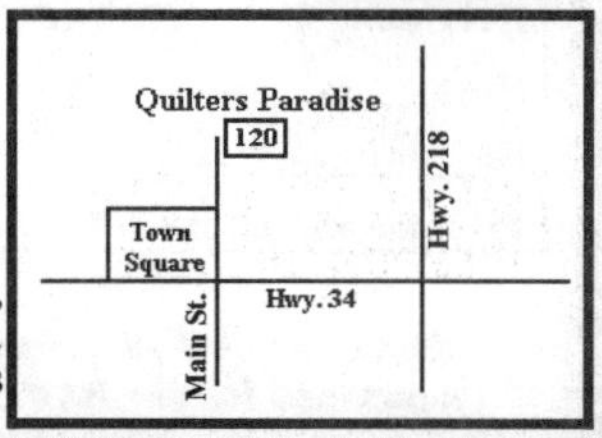

New London, IA #38

Tues - Fri
9 - 5
Sat 9 - 3

The Top Drawer

19472 162nd St. 52645
(319) 392-8142
Owner: Marlene Bennink

Located 3-1/4 miles north of Danville. Fabric, books, patterns, Block of the month kits, Craft Supplies. Mail Order Available.

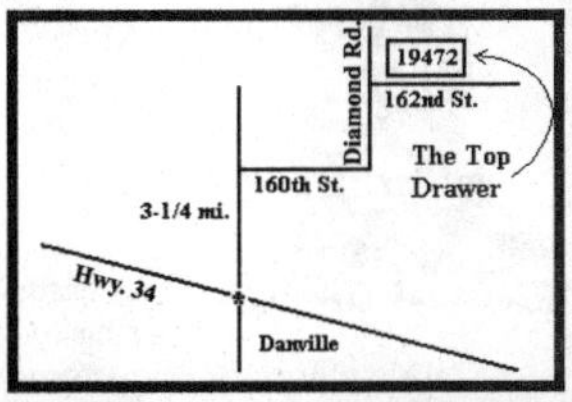

West Burlington, IA #39

Mon - Fri
10 - 5
Sat 10 - 3

Sandi's Sewing Connection

219 W. Mt. Pleasant St. 52655
(319) 752-2226 Fax: (319) 753-3096
E-Mail: sandigass@lisco.net
Web Site: www.sewingmachinedealers.com
Owner: Sandi Gass Est: 1991 1500 Bolts

Large selection of 100% cotton Fabric, Threads, Books, Patterns, Notions, Bernina Sewing Machines & Classes. Friendly & Helpful.

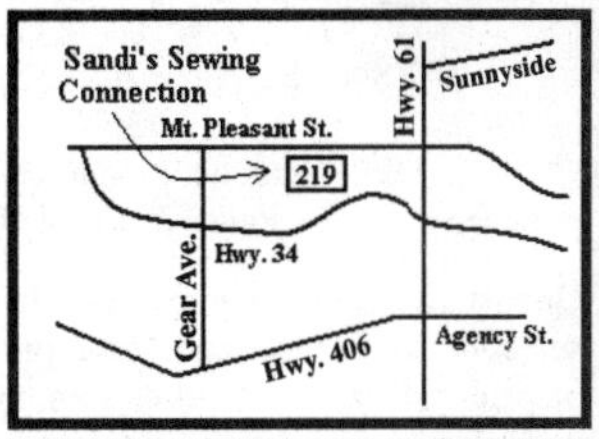

Est: 1996

The Cotton Shop

Mon - Fri 9 - 5
Sat 9 - 4

A hands-on store offering classes & support for quilters & crafters.
Over 2000 bolts of 100% cotton fabric. Wool felt and wools for rughooking. Now carrying cross-stitch patterns to compliment our great selection of books and patterns. Specializing in flannels.

Muscatine, IA #40

317 E 2nd St. 52761
(563) 262-5709
E-Mail:cottonshop@machlink.com
Web Site: www.cottonshoponline.com

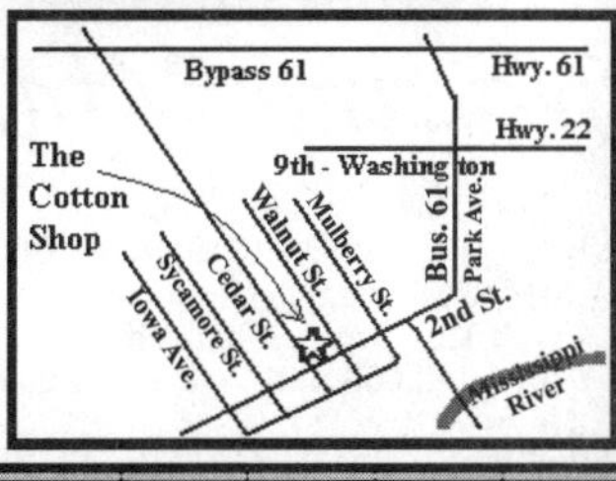

Muscatine, IA #41

Mon - Thur 9 - 5:30
Fri 9 - 8
Sat 9 - 5

Neal's Vacuum & Sewing Center

309 E. 2nd St. 52761
(563) 263-4543 or (800) 362-4543
Fax: (563) 263-7179 Est: 1951
E-Mail: nealssew@muscanet.com

Over 3000 bolts of fabric, books, patterns, and notions. Viking & White sewing machines and sergers. Lots of Personal Help!

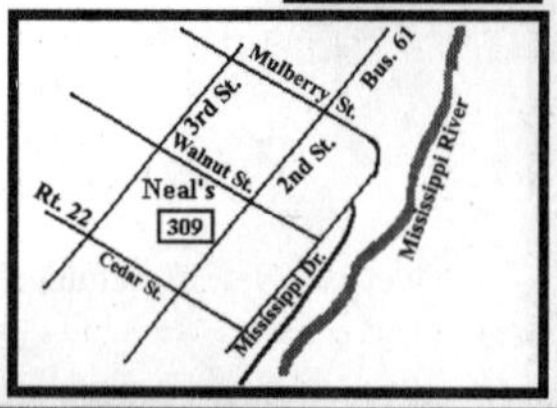

South Amana, IA #42

Mon - Sat 9:30 - 5
Sun 12 - 4

Fern Hill Gifts & Quilts

103 - 220th Trail 52334
(319) 622-3627 Fax: (319) 622-6120
e-mail: pasteph13@aol.com
Est: 1987 3400 sq.ft. 3000 Bolts

Relax & linger in our fabric loft with 3000 bolts of the latest fabrics. Antiques, architectural antiques, antique quilts, new quilts and wallhangings await your arrival.

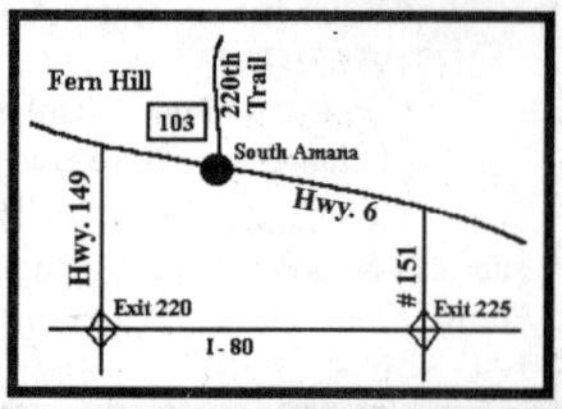

Amana, IA #43

Heritage Designs

Needlework & Quilting Supplies
4517- 220th Trail 52203 (319) 622-3887
Est. 1976 ~ 2000+ Bolts ~ 1200 sq. ft.

****OPEN DAILY**** Mon. thru Sat.10-5 & Sundays 11-4

Ten miles off I 80 on the main street in the historic village of Amana. An exclusive shop featuring supplies, and unique accessories and gifts for quilting & needlework. Find beautiful fabrics, books, craft patterns, notions, buttons, cross-stitch, tatting, & hardanger supplies.

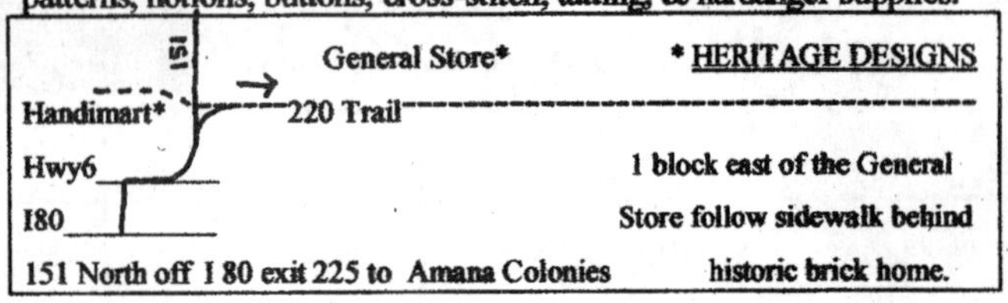

Hoffman - RJR - Moda - Benartex – Homespuns - Designer favorites.
Renowned for our fat quarter table & coordinated bundles!

The Quilt Basket

200 W. Main St. 52205
(319) 462-2222
Est: 2000 1500 Bolts

Mon - Fri 10 - 5
Tues til 7
Sat 10 - 3

Your Complete Quilt Store
A little off the beaten path,
but well worth the trip.

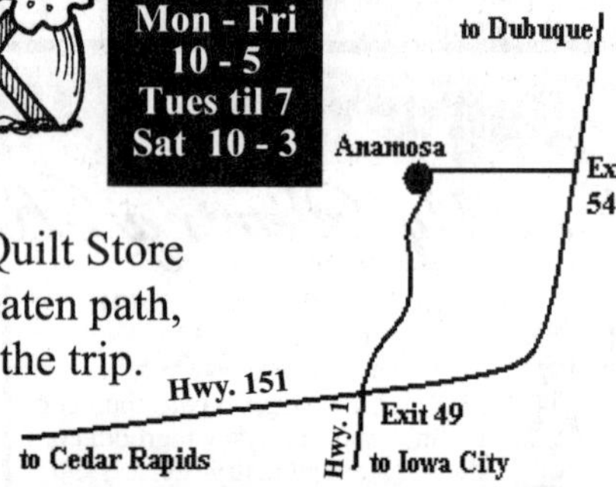

Anamosa, IA #44

Cedar Rapids, IA #45

Mon - Sat 10 - 5

The Keeping Room

2345A Blairs Ferry Rd. NE 52402
(319) 743-9929
Owner: Nancy Wagner Est: 2000

Charming shop featuring quality quilting fabrics and supplies. New fabrics arriving weekly: Moda, RJR, Nancy Crow, Hoffman, Bali, Benartex, Thimbleberries, & Peter Pan.

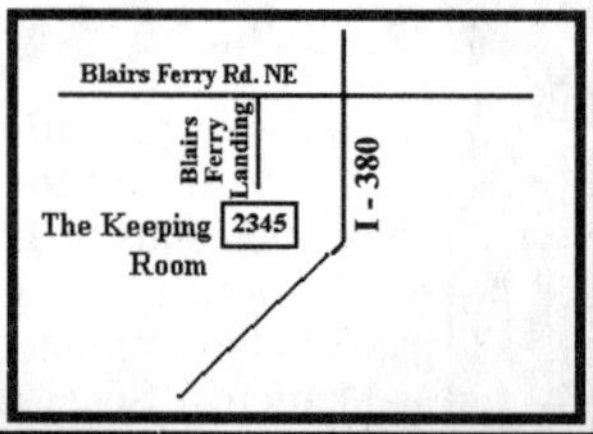

Conrad, IA #46

Mon - Sat 9:05 - 5:00

Conrad General Store

101 N. Main, P.O. Box 726
50621
(641) 366-2043 Fax: Same
E-mail: conradgs@adiis.net
Est: 1983 2500 sq.ft.

This century old general store has over 2500 bolts of fabric plus notions, patterns, and gifts. Machine quilting and classes offered.

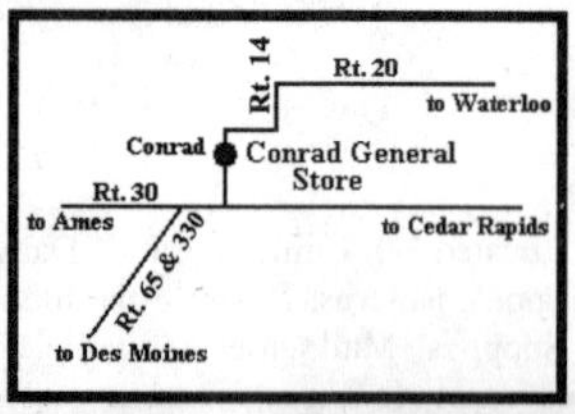

Hiawatha, IA #47

Mon - Fri 8 - 4

Nolting Mfg., Inc.

1265 Hawkeye Dr. 52233
(319) 378-0999 Fax: (319) 378-1026
E-Mail: nolting@nolting.com
Web Site: www.nolting.com
Est: 1987 12,000 sq.ft. Free Catalog

The original Longarm Quilting Machine Manufacturer. See machines being made. Try new and refurbished Longarms. Machine Quilting Shop, Patterns, Accessories.

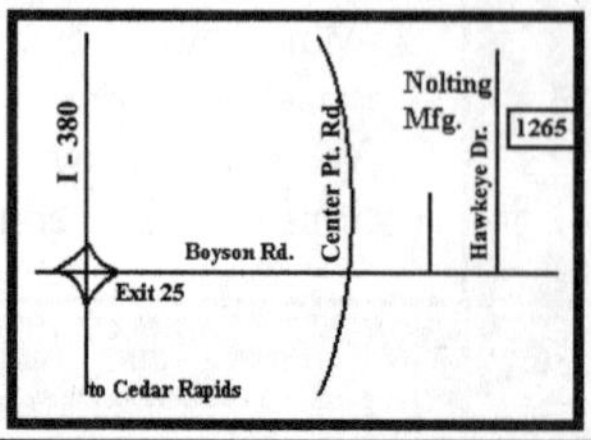

Cedar Falls, IA #48

Mon - Fri 10 - 5:30
Thur til 8
Sat 10 - 4

Crazy to Quilt

602 State St. Suite 2C, 50613
(319) 277-1360
E-Mail: jeanette@cedarnet.org
Owners: Jeni Moravec & Liz Wehrmacher

Quality quilting supplies and fabrics; large selection of flannels and homespuns; friendly, helpful staff; a variety of classes; special order welcome.

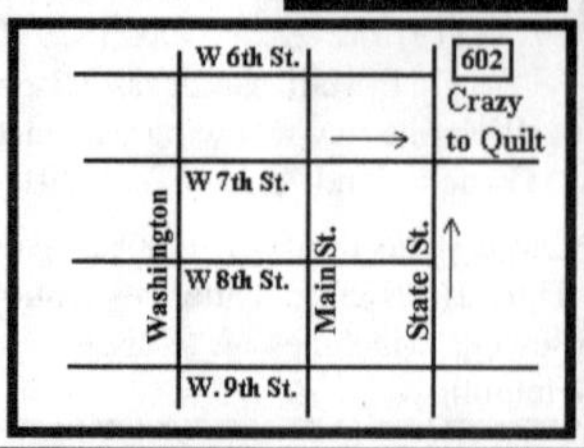

Tues - Sat
10 - 5

Cedar Falls, IA #49

212 Main St. 50613
(319) 277-8303 Est: 1993
Owners: Sara Bockenstedt
& Marsha Schoeder

Aunt Emma's Attic

A Quilter's Treasure Chest

**Full Service Shop.
Featuring—2000 Bolts of
100% Cotton Fabric
Large Supply of Notions,
Books, & Patterns
Mail Order Available.**

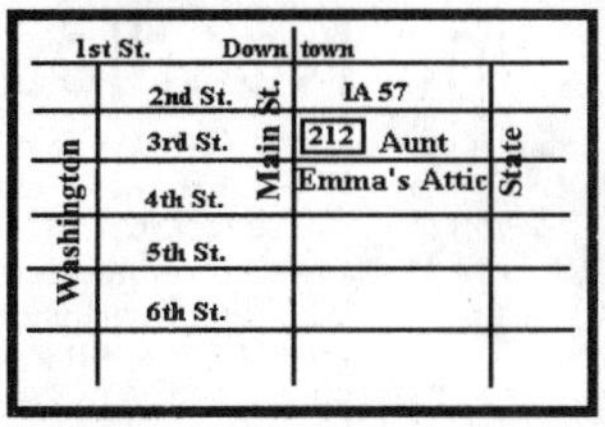

A GREAT QUILTING EXPERIENCE !

Marion, IA #50

Mon - Sat
10 - 5

Connie's Quilt Shop

785 8th Ave. 52302
(319) 373-9455
Owner: Connie Moyer
Est: 1992

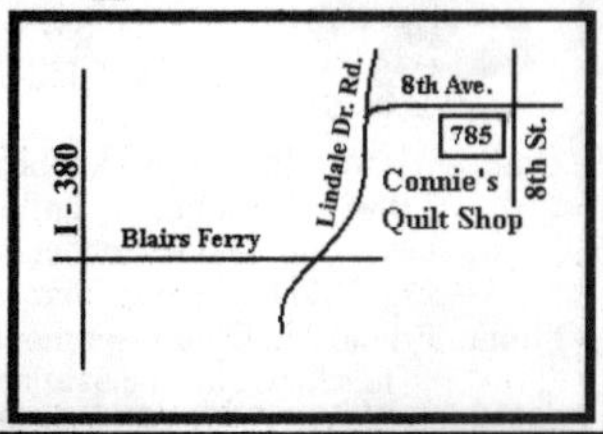

2000+ bolts of quality 100% cotton quilting fabrics. Large selection of books, patterns, & notions. Stop in & visit us!

Jesup, IA #51

Tues - Fri
2 - 8
or by Appt.

Merry's Stitchins

1923 Baker Rd. 50648
(319) 827-6703
E-Mail: merrys@jtt.net
Owner: Merry Backes 3000+ Bolts

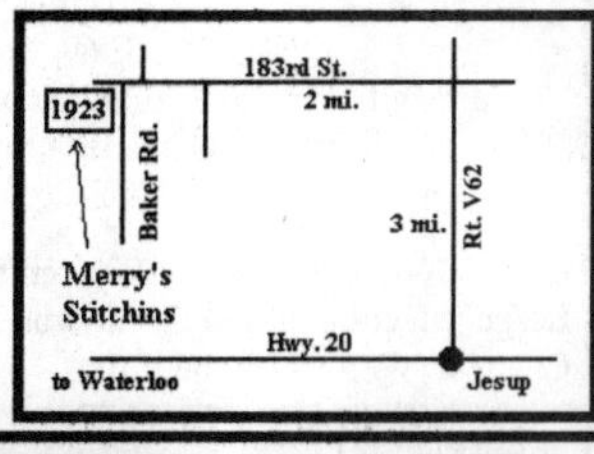

Custom machine quilting—Full line of thimbleberries & more. Quilting supplies. Oak quilt racks & Hangers.

The Quiltmaker's Shoppe

110 East Main St. Manchester, IA 52057
(563) 927-8017
Owner: Kathy Wilgenbusch

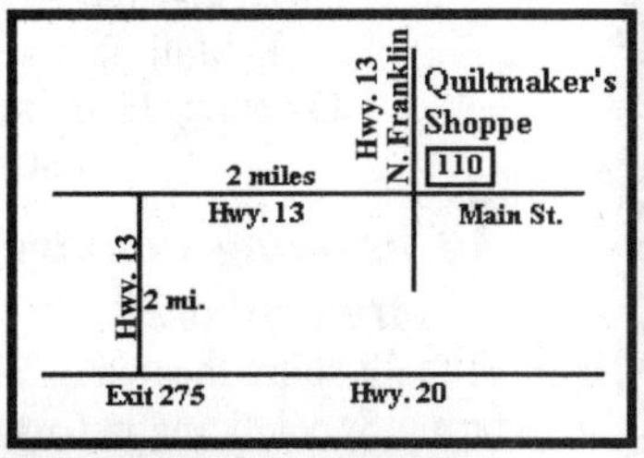

Tues - Fri 9 - 5
Thur til 8
Sat 9 - 4

Manchester, IA #52

We offer 100% cotton fabric from the top lines, the latest in books & patterns and a full line of notions. We also have kits, antique buttons and hand-crafted quilt racks & hangers. Come in and see what we have in store for you!

Lamont, IA #53

Mon - Fri
1 - 7
Sat 9 - 5

Quilter's Quarters

3290 150th St. 50650
(563) 924-2216 2500+ bolts
E-Mail: quiltersquarters@worldnet.att.net
Web Site: home.att.net/~quiltersquarters
Owners: Mark & Melinda Engelbrecht

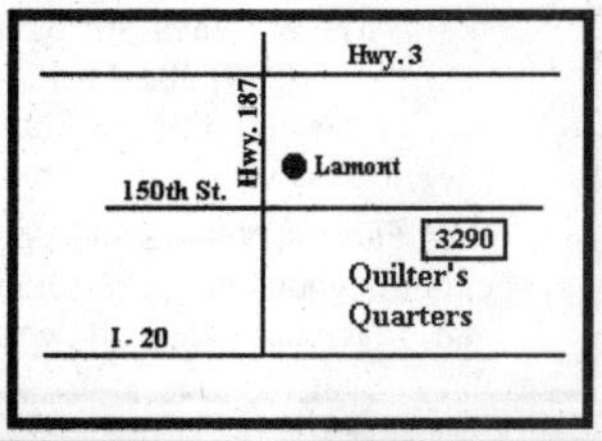

Quality Quilting fabrics and flannels, Books, Patterns, Supplies, Notions.

Fairbank, IA #54

Mon - Sat
9 - 5

Jo's Thread & Thimble

105 Grove St. 50629
(319) 635-2119
Owner: Jo Haberkamp
Est: 1974 2500 sq.ft.

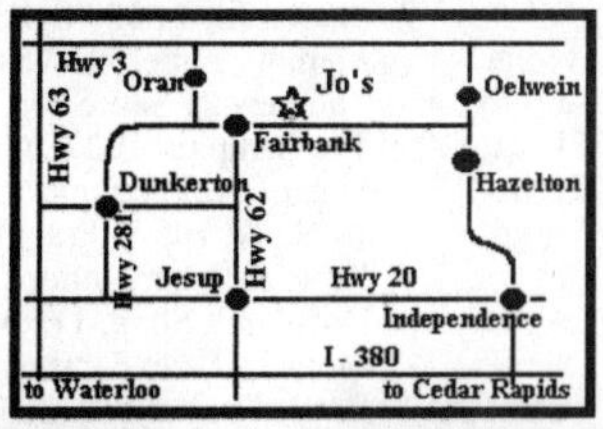

N.E. Iowa's finest quilt shop.
Very large selection of fabrics, notions, patterns, books, and quilting supplies.
Quilted Gift Items Also.

New Hampton, IA #55

Mon - Fri
9 - 5:30
Thurs til 8
Sat 9 - 5

Material Magic

22 E. Main 50659
(641) 394-2461

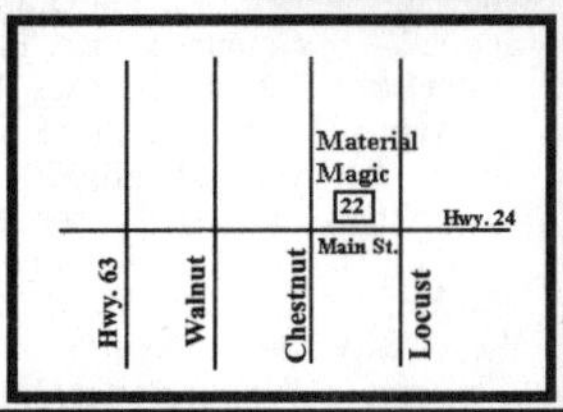

Large selection of 100% cotton fabrics, books, patterns & quilting supplies. Custom machine quilting. Hand-made crafts. Classes offered.

Charles City, IA #56

Mon - Fri
9 - 5:15
Sat 9 - 4

The Trading Store

209 N. Main St. 50616
(641) 330-4828
Owner: Edwin Benedict
Mgr: Shelby Zirbel

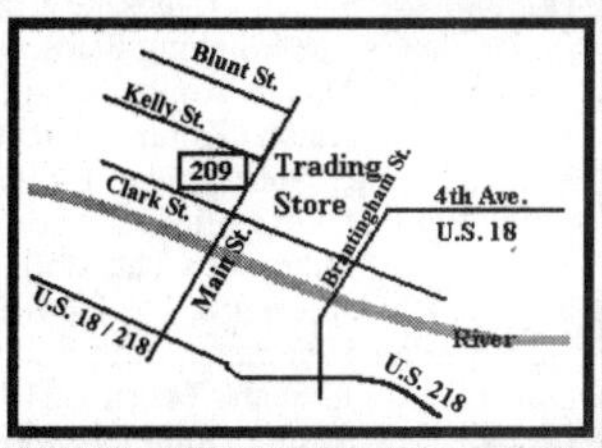

Sewing and quilting notions, exclusive patterns, ongoing classes, great fabric and time-tested value, all in a country-store style.

Mason City, IA #57

Mon - Fri 10 - 8
Sat 10 - 5

Beehive Quilt Shoppe

Willowbrook Mall
1631-4th St. SW #120 50401
(641) 422-1027

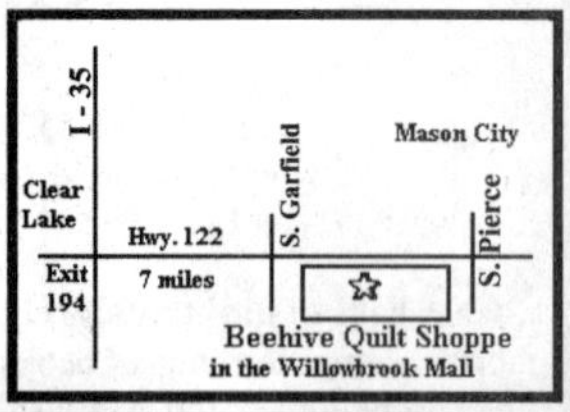

Quilter friendly shop in Willowbrook Mall with over 3,000 bolts of quality quilting fabrics, supplies, notion, books, patterns and daily classes. Thimbleberries Club and Debbie Mumm Friendship Club meet monthly. Custom machine quilting available.

Kensett, IA #58

Wed - Fri 10 - 5
Sat 10 - 3

Heart & Sew Quilts

908 Maple St. 50448
(641) 845-2234
Owner: Holly Adams

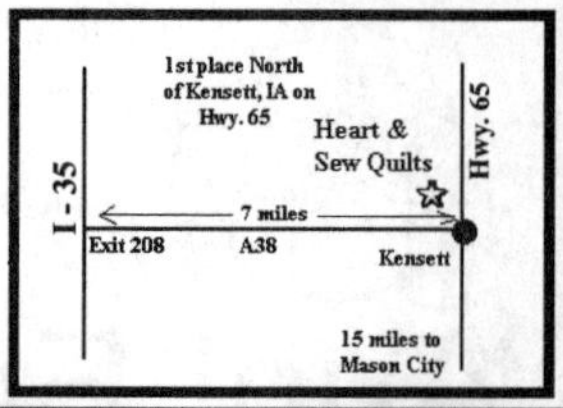

1895 Cottage in the country full of original, hand stitched Quilts of every size, (to warm your heart & home). Full size quilts, wall quilts, vests, santas and more.

St. Ansgar, IA #59

Mon - Sat 9 - 5

The Fabric Shoppe

230 W. 4th St., P.O. Box 17 50472
(641) 713-3669
E-Mail: Fabshop@omnitelcom.com
Owner: Pam Schaefer - Smith
Est: 1988 1900 sq.ft.

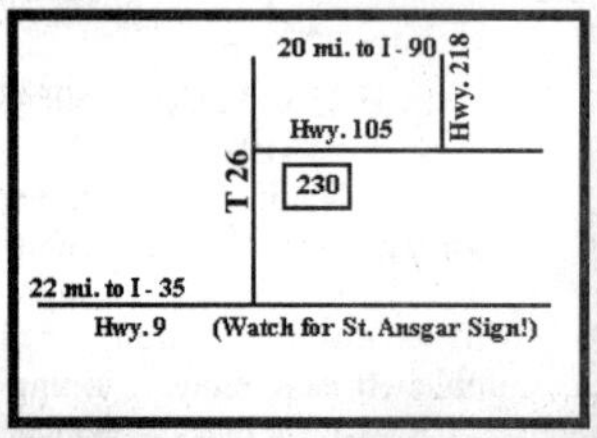

Over 3000 bolts quality 100% cotton fabrics. Large selection of books, patterns, & notions. Classes. Well worth the trip!

Cresco, IA #60

Mon - Fri 10 - 5
Thur til 8
Sat 10 - 4

Pine Needles Quilt Shop

105 2nd Ave. SW 52136
(563) 547-1212
Fax: (563) 547-4612
E-Mail: quilt@pineneedles.net
Web Site: www.pineneedles.net
Owner: Jill Reicks
Est: 1999 4000 sq.ft. 3000 Bolts

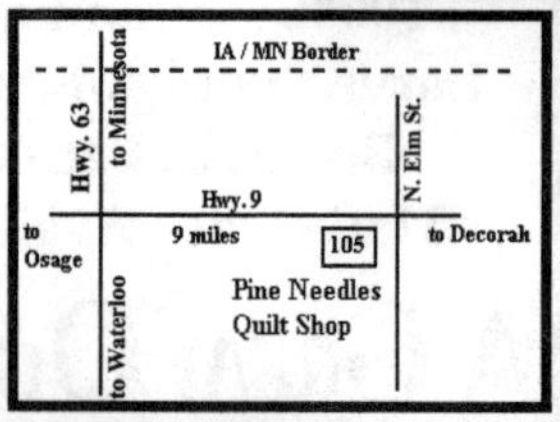

Spacious, well-lit atmosphere in a charming turn-of-the-century building. We offer full line of quilting supplies, classes, machine quilting and Bernina sewing machine dealership.

Decorah, IA #61

Mon - Fri 9 - 5
Thur til 9
Sat 9 - 4

The Sewing Basket, Inc.

519 W. Water St. 52101
(319) 382-4401
Owner: Darlene Frana

Quilting Fabrics, Notions and Books. Classes held throughout the year. Viking Sewing Machines Sales and Service.

Waukon, IA #62

Country Stitchin'

915 Hwy. 76 South, Waukon, IA 52172
(563) 535-7376 Fax: (563) 535-4325
E-Mail: jsnitker@acegroup.cc
Owners: Jane Snitker & Peg Mathis
Est: 1997

"A Charming Country Atmosphere"

Mon - Sat 9 - 5

Unique Quilt shop, located on a 4½ acre farm. Specializing in Custom HAND Quilting.
Many samples on display.
All samples are for sale.
Quilt Tops--several to choose from
Quilt Classes Year Round
Large selection of fabrics, books, patterns & notions.

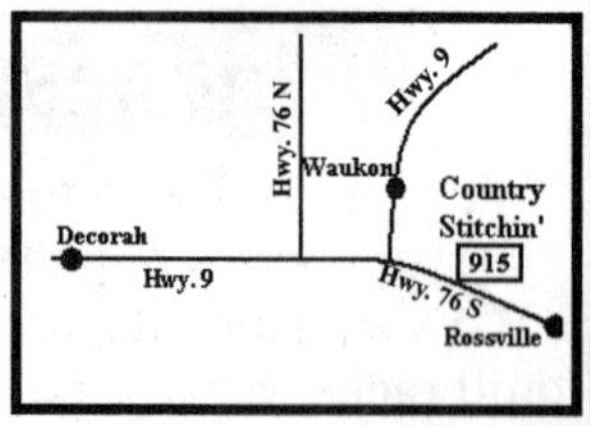

Other Shops in Iowa: We suggest calling first

Albia	Prairie Point Shoppe, 508 N. 10th St.	641-932-3866
Altoona	Back Door Fabrics, 106 2nd St. S.E.	515-967-2321
Ames	Fairlight Quilts, 400 Main St. #1	515-233-4959
Anamosa	Cristy's Design Quilting & Crafts, 307 S. Davis	319-462-2398
Ankeny	Time to Quilt, 913 NE 28th St.	515-964-4135
Audubon	Sweet Williams, 409 S. Park Pl.	712-563-3443
Bellevue	Shared Ideas, 128 S. Riverview Dr.	319-872-4915
Boone	Memory Lane, 715 Carroll St.	515-432-3222
Burlington	The Sew 'N Sew Shop, 3206 Division	319-752-5733
Chariton	The Sampler, 102 S. Grand	515-774-2116
Colfax	Sugar Creek Sampler, 11627 N. 19th Ave. W	
Corydon	J's Nook, 105 S. Franklin	515-872-2709
Creston	Knits & Other Notions, 209 W. Montgomery	515-782-8874
Danbury	Dots Quilt Shop, 115 Main St.	712-883-2495
Denison	Memory Lane Fabrics, 28 N. Main St.	712-263-8383
Des Moines	Bartlett's Quilts, 820 35th St.	515-255-1362
Eldorado	Eldorado Store, 29014 State St., P.O. Box 1	319-422-3097
Exira	Twigs Country Classics, 112 W. Washington	712-268-2622
Fairfield	The Sewing Room, 59 W. Broadway	641-472-7540
Fayette	Country House Cottons, P.O. Box 375	319-425-4384
Fort Madison	Catricia's Needles 'N Brushes, 713 Avenue G	319-372-9270
Griswold	Quilting Party, 442 Main St.	712-778-2332
Hawkeye	Karol's Quilting, 103 E. Main St.	563-427-3736
Humbolt	Janice's Keepsake Krafts, 19 6th St. S	515-332-5683
Indianola	The Stitching Place, 127 N Buxtun	515-961-5162
Kalona	Yoders Antiques, Gifts & Quilts, 432 B Ave.	319-656-3880
Kalona	Kalona Kountry Kreations, 2134 560th St. S.W.	319-656-5366
Kalona	Country Livin', 1369 Hwy. 1	319-656-3773
Lineville	Quilt Loft, 304 W. 3rd St.	641-876-2265
Monona	Suhdrons's The Mall, 120 W. Center	319-539-2135
Nevada	Julieann's, 1024 6th St.	515-382-5819
New Market	Helen's Quilting Boutique, R.R. #1, Box 228	712-585-3678
Oelwein	Louann's Fabrics, 21 E. Charles	319-283-5165
Onawa	Susie's Quilts-N-More, 904 Iowa Ave.	712-423-9625
Osage	Nolt Quilts, 3416 Orchard Ln.	641-732-1463
Panora	Quilting Market, 317 W. Market St.	515-755-2118
Parkersburg	The Stitchery, 903 Muller	319-346-1691
Postville	Sudron's Fabrics, 138 W. Greene, Box 225	319-864-3919
Quasqueton	It's Material, 203 S. 7th St.	319-934-3126
Red Oak	Quilting on the Square, R.R. #3, Box 39	712-623-3884
Rudd	Laughing Lady Quilt Shop, 416 Chickasaw St.	515-395-2638
Shenandoah	Quilt Basket, 624 W. Sheridan Ave.	712-246-1365
Spencer	Beehive, 404 Grand Ave.	712-262-3918
St. Olaf	Country Calico, R.R. #1, Gunder Rd.	319-783-2445
Storm Lake	Country Stitches, 1122 N. Lake Ave.	712-732-5419
Strawberry Point	Keppler Krafts, 35536 Hwy. 13 N	319-933-6069
Terril	Dodge Crafts, 200 N. 4th St.	712-853-6159
Volga Crazy	Little Quilt Shop, 510 Washington St.	319-767-4125
Walnut	Old Time Quilting Shop, 218 Antique City Dr.	712-784-3664
Waukon	The Homestead, 920 2nd. St. NW	319-568-2336
West Des Moines	Donna's Dolls, 234 5th St.	515-274-2522
Winterset	Fons & Porter Quilt Supply, 115 N. John Wayne Dr.	515-462-1020

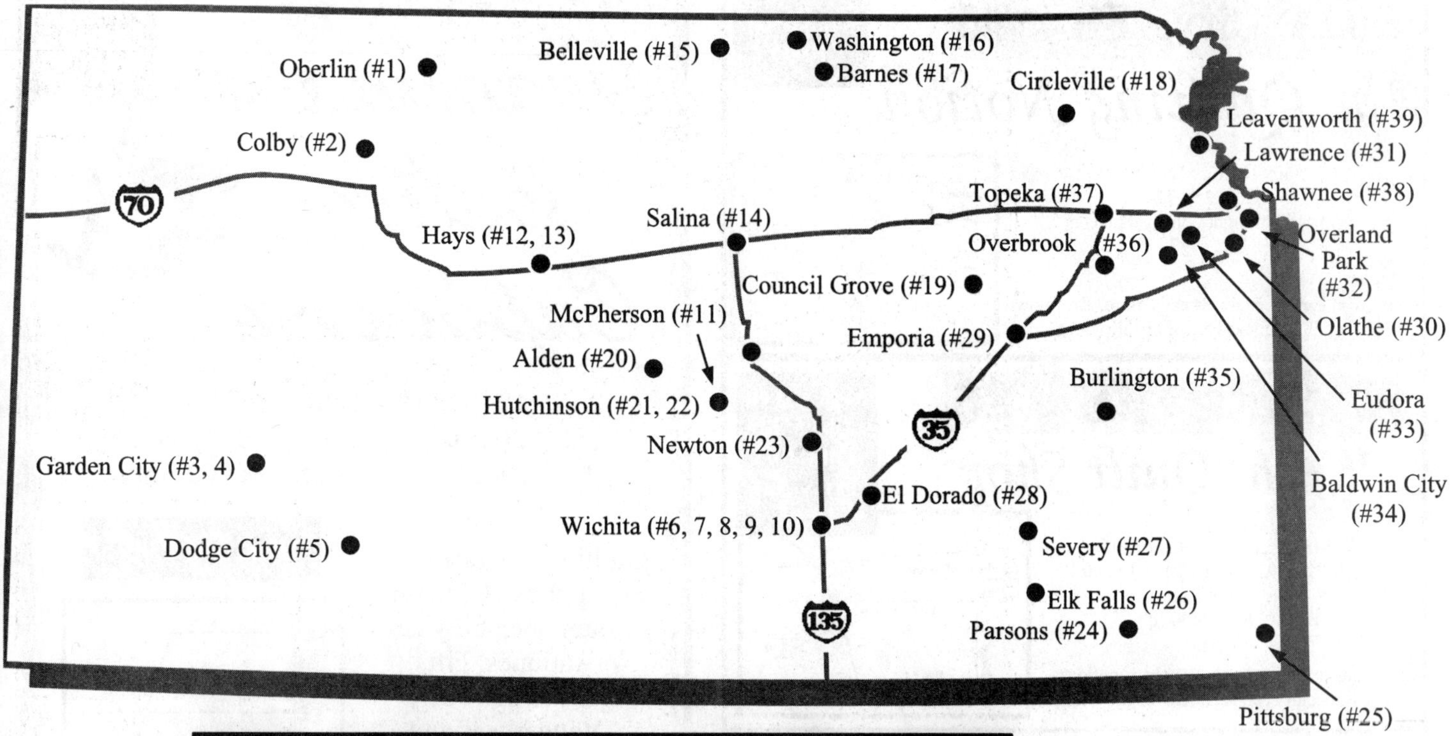

KANSAS

39 Featured Shops

Oberlin, KS #1

Mon - Sat 9:30 - 5

Carrousel Quilt & Gift Shop

141 S. Penn 67749
(785) 475-3666
E-Mail: angienjoe@networksplus.net
Web Site: coming soon
Owner: Angela Weller

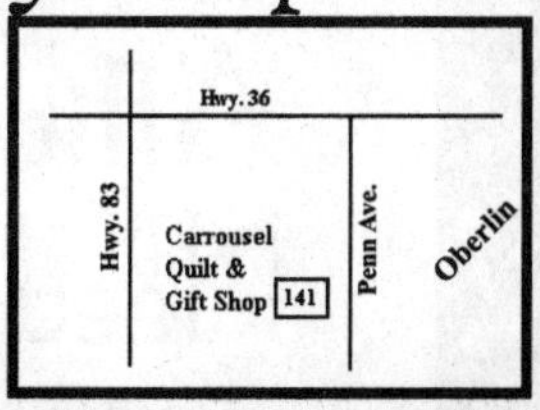

Hundreds of bolts of fabric, classes, notions, patterns, books, antiques & framing.

Colby, KS #2

Mon - Sat 9 - 5

Quilt Cabin

160 E. 2nd 67701
(785) 462-3375
Est: 1988

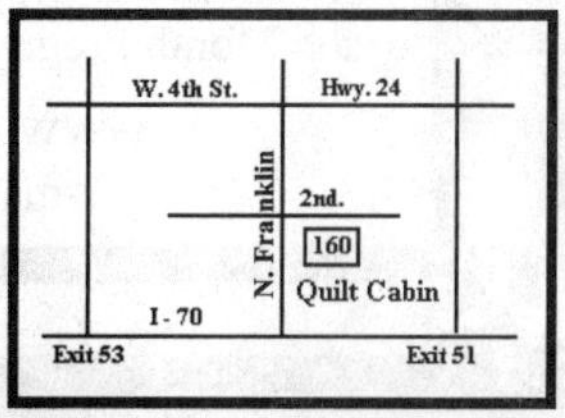

Good Selection of quality 100% cotton fabrics. Books, patterns, notions and classes. Decorator fabrics. Custom window treatments. Janome Sewing Machine Sales & Service.

Garden City, KS #3

Mon - Sat 9 - 5:30 Sun 1 - 5

Bar K Fabrics

401 N. Main 67846
(620) 275-7689
Owner: Barbara Fillmore
Est: 1988 2200 sq.ft. 1200+ Bolts

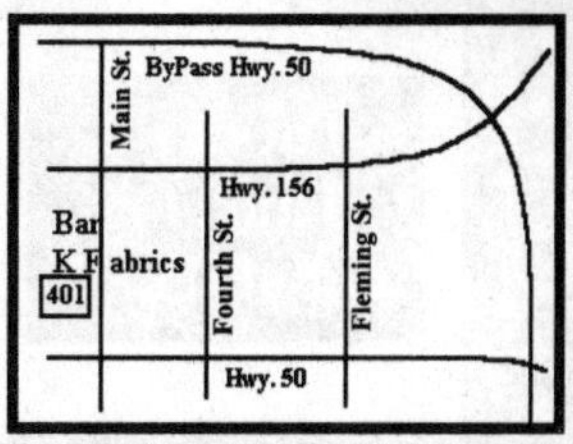

Great selection of quilt and fashion fabrics, sewing and quilting notions. We offer fun classes, service and sales of machines and vacuums.

Garden City, KS #4

Mon - Fri 9:30 - 5:30 Sat 10 - 5

The Quilt Rack

321 N. Main 67846
(316) 275-8786
E-Mail: jmac@gcnet.com
Web Site: www.gcnet.com/quilts
Owner: Jeaninne McCarthy
Quilting and all the Extras!
Threads! Threads! Threads!
Cross-Stitch, Hardanger, Needlepoint
Silk Ribbon Embroidery
Elna & Singer sewing machines and sergers.

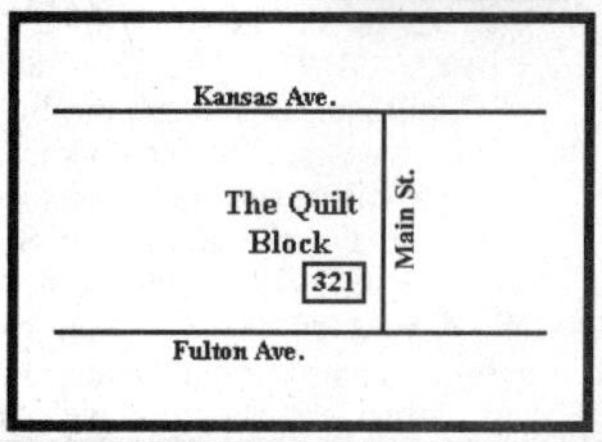

Dodge City, KS #5

Mon - Sat 10 - 5

The Quilting Notion

509 N. 2nd 67801
(620) 225-9777
E-Mail: quiltingnotion@yahoo.com
Est: 1997

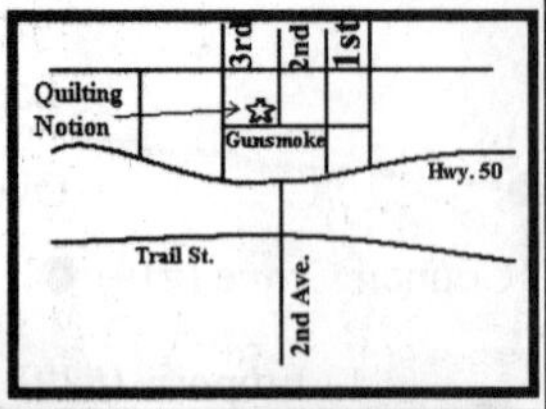

Located in Eckles Main Street Centre, Downtown Dodge City, 1 ½ blocks east of historic Boot Hill.

Wichita, KS #6

**Mon - Wed 10 - 5:30
Thur til 8
Fri & Sat 10 - 5**

Kechi Quilt Shop

7348 W 21st N #106 67205
(316) 773-0338 or (877) 744-8500
Owner: Janet Robinson
Est: 1996 2400 sq.ft.

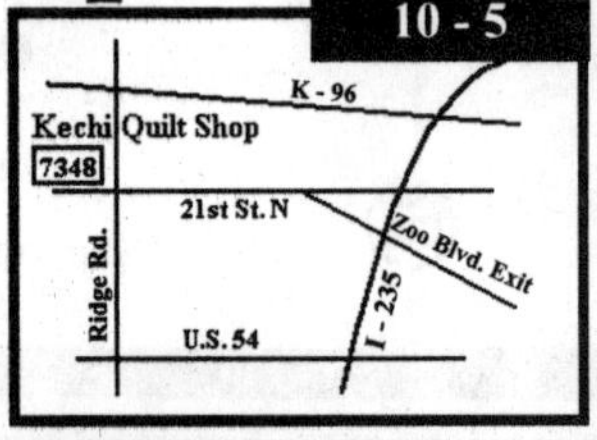

Cottons, stencils, books, patterns, notions, classes, special events, Blocks-of-the-Month.

Gramma's Calico Cupboard

1945 S. Hydraulic 67211
(316) 264-0274 Owner: Betty Webb
Est: 1982 3500 sq.ft. 6000 Bolts

Mon - Sat 9:30 - 5

Quilting & Craft fabric & supplies. Christmas room open all year. Antiques, gifts including Muffy Vanderbear and handmade rag dolls.

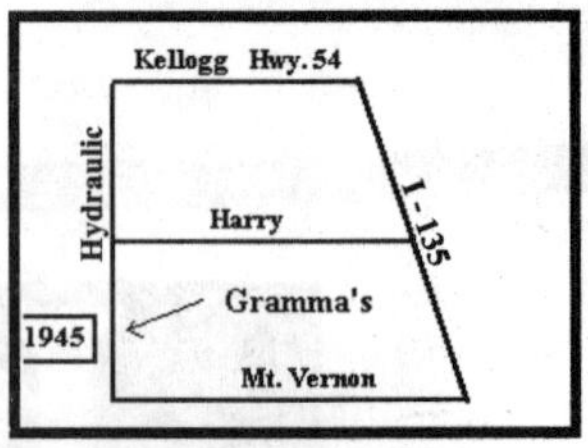

Wichita, KS #7

Wichita, KS #8

Prairie Quilts

**Mon - Fri 9 - 6
Sat 9 - 5:30**

1010 S. Oliver (Parklane Shopping Center)
(316) 684-5855 67218
Owner: Shirley Binder
Est: 1996 1300 sq.ft. 3000+ Bolts

Complete Selection of Quilting Supplies. Fabrics, Books, Patterns, Notions & Classes. Ask About our Block of the Month Program.

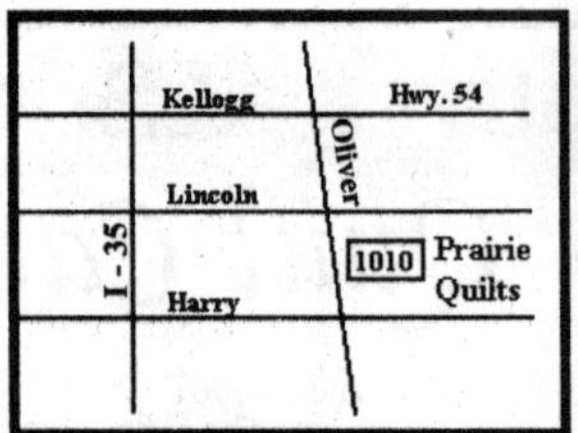

www.prairiequilts.com
e-mail: sbinder@fn.net

Wichita, KS #9

**1717 Briggs St. 67203
(316) 265-4646 Est: 1997**

Attic Heirlooms Needlleart Shop

Teacher & supplies of needlearts. Silk ribbon, wired ribbon, tatting, buttons, beads, charms, crazy quilting & embellishments galore. Silk prints, Books & Patterns.

**Tues 1 - 8
Thur, Fri & Sat 11 - 5**

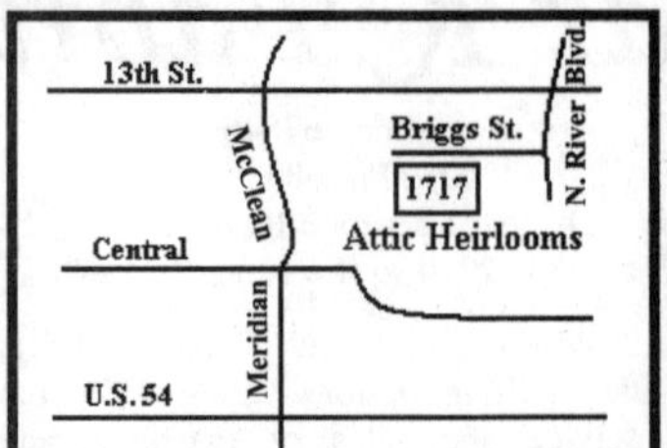

Wichita, KS #10

**Mon - Fri 9:30 - 6
Sat 9:30 - 5**

The Sewing Center

2101 W. 21st St. 67203
(316) 832-0819 Fax: (316) 838-8341
E-Mail: kansassewbiz@prodigy.net
Web Site: www.sew2000.com/kansassewbiz/
or www.kansassewbiz.ogdomains.com
Owners: Charley & Beverly Seyfert
Est: 1977 5000 sq.ft.

Quilting & Fashion Fabrics - Notions - Books Classes - Singer & Elna Dealer for Sales & Service. A one stop shop that welcomes all.

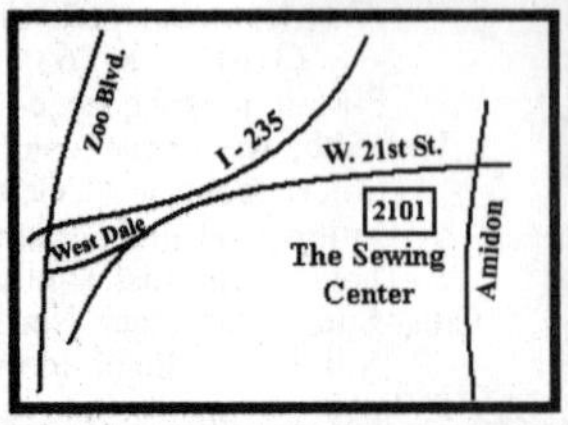

McPherson, KS #11

Mon - Fri 9 - 6 Thur til 8 Sat 9 - 5

101 N. Main, McPherson, KS 67460
(620) 241-5257
Toll Free 1-800-QUILTER

The Button Hole

FABRICS • NOTIONS • GIFTS

Step into Victorian Elegance.
Quilter's heaven, 100% cotton fabrics, books, patterns, and notions. Cross stitch and fine gifts from Brighton Jewelry & Accessories. Vera Bradley Bags, Crabtree & Evelyn Herman Dodge Bone China, and much more. Enjoy a variety of coffees, teas and pies & pastries in The Hearth Room located in "The Button Hole" where you can always "Expect the Unexpected."

Web Site: www.thebuttonhole.net

Email: sales@thebuttonhole.net
Fax: (620) 241-5234
Owner: Evelyn Birkhead
Est: 1996 10,000 sq.ft. 15,000 Bolts

Pfaff and Brother Sewing Center

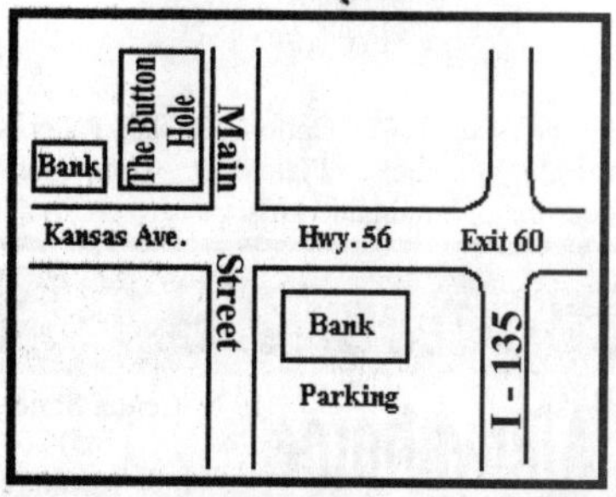

Hays, KS #12

Quilt Cottage Co. & Cross Stitch, Too!

Mon - Fri 10 - 5:30 Sat 10 - 3

2504 Vine (corner of Centennial and Vine) 67601

(785) 625-0080

Est: 1994 3000 sq.ft. 2500 Bolts
Owners: Debbie Huebner & Kari Schultz

Top quality quilting fabrics.
The area's finest selection of books, patterns and notions.
Cross-stitch fabrics, patterns & DMC floss.

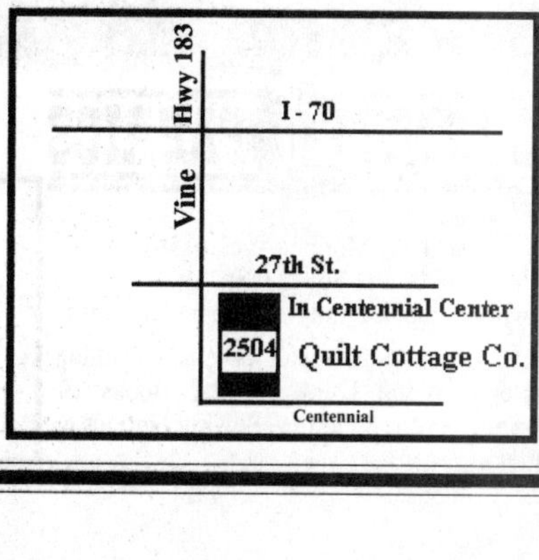

Hays, KS #13

Mon - Fri 9:30 - 5:30 Sat 9:30 - 5

Fabric Gallery

1010 Main, (Downtown Hays) 67601
(785) 625-8122
Owner: Diane Werth
Est: 1995 2500 sq.ft. 2000 Bolts

Large selection of fashion & quilting fabrics & notions. Elna Sewing Machines & Sergers.

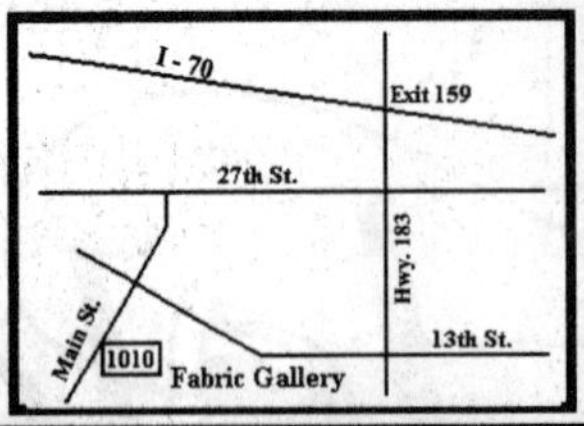

Salina, KS #14

Mon - Fri 9:30 - 5:30 Sat 9:30 - 5

Quilting Bee

120 S. Santa Fe 67401
(785) 823-9376
Fax:
(785) 823-7628
Owner: Sherril Bieberly
Est: 1979 4000 sq.ft.

Come visit out full line quilt shop!
We feature Kansas Troubles quilters fabrics, books & patterns plus a large selection of other fabrics including Moda, Thimbleberries, flannels, homespuns & felted wool. Lots of kits.

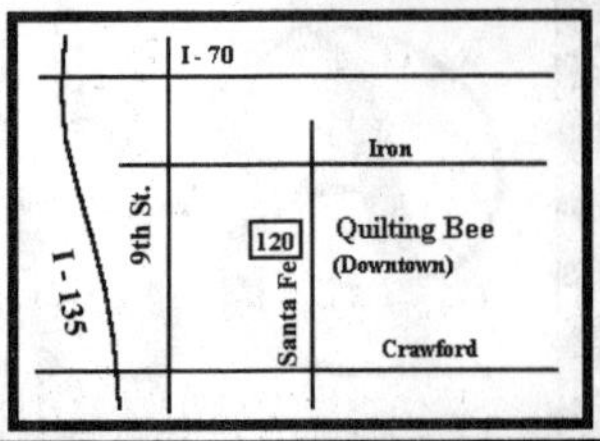

Belleville, KS #15

Mon - Fri 9 - 5:30 Sat 9 - 5

Sew Country

1834 M St. 66935
(785) 527-2332 Fax: Same
Owner: Sheila Cornett
Est: 1992

1200+ bolts of 100% Cotton, Books, Patterns, Notions. Flannels, Plaids & Homespuns. Unique line of handmade gifts.

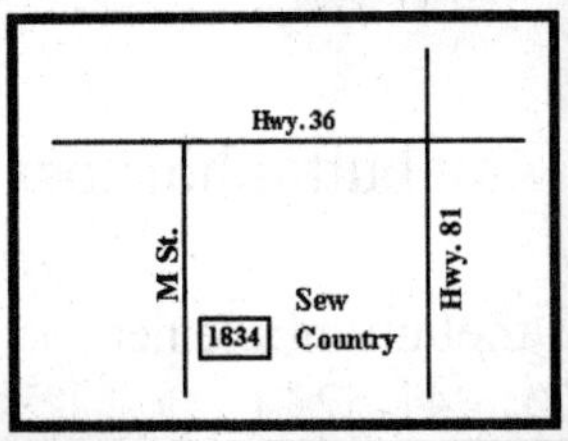

Washington, KS #16

Tues - Sat 10 - 5:30

Honeysuckle Fabrics

311 "C" Street 66968
(785) 325-3432
E-Mail: honeyfabrics@yahoo.com
Owner: Terry & Ruth Bailey
Est: 2002 2500 sq. ft.

Wonderful selection of 100% cotton fabrics, books, patterns and notions. Classes and the friendliest staff around.

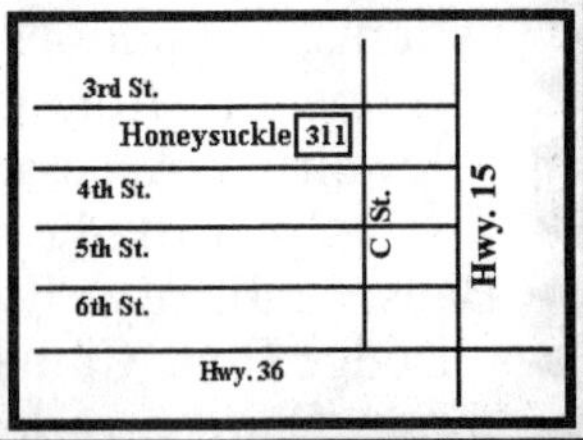

Barnes, KS #17

Mon - Sat 10 - 4 Sun & evenings by appt.

Downhome Quilting

10 N. Center Street, Box 22 66933
(785) 763-4400
E-Mail: drebesnj@jbntelco.com
Web Site: www.barnesmercantile.com
Owner:
Norma Drebes

Machine Quilting, Binding & Finishing on Quilts. Embroidered Cross Stitch & Pieced tops and Finished Quilts for Sale.

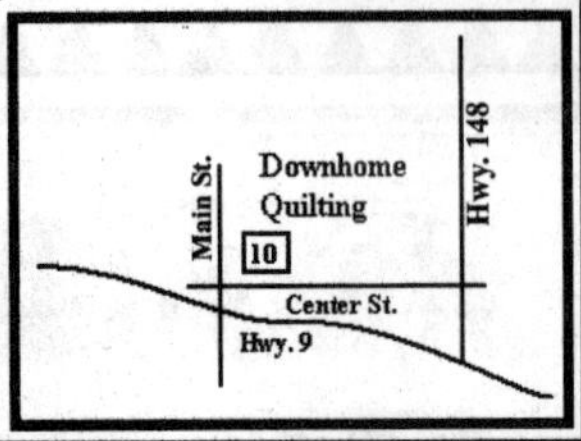

Circleville, KS #18

Thur, Fri Sat 10 - 6 Sun 10 - 2

Circleville Corner Fabrics

301 Grant 66416
(785) 924-3355
Web Site: www.geocities.com/circlefabrics
Est: 2000 2500 sq.ft. 1000 Bolts

Over 1000 bolts and growing! 100% cotton fabrics of numerous popular designers. Large store in a small town. Unique fabrics, wonderful patterns and books.

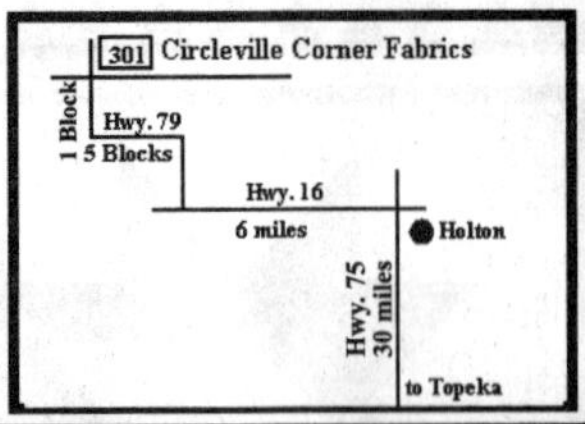

Council Grove, KS #19

Tues - Fri 10 - 5 Sat 10 - 4

Prairie Pieces

200 W. Main St. 66846
(620) 767-6628
E-Mail: twoquilt@cgtelco.net
Owner: Toni Steere
Est: 1990 3000+ Bolts

Full line quilt shop. Hoffman, Moda and other fabric lines. Renown for our Fat Quarters. Gift items and antiques. Small town service with a smile.

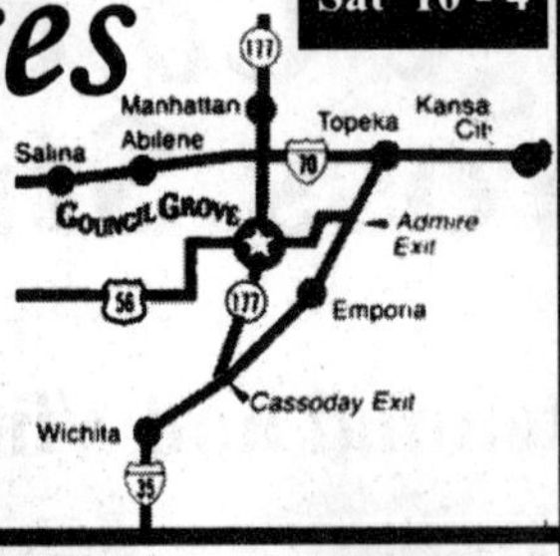

Alden, KS #20

Mon - Sat 10 - 4:30

Prairie Flower Crafts

205 Pioneer St. 67512-0158
(800) 527-3997
E-Mail: PrFlrCraft@aol.com
Owner: Sara Fair Sleeper
Est: 1970 5370 sq.ft.
27 years collecting cotton fabric for quilts.
Large selection of RJR, Thimbleberries, Hoffman, South Sea Imports, Clothworks, Timeless Treasure, P&B Fabrics, Benartex, Liberty of London, Etc.

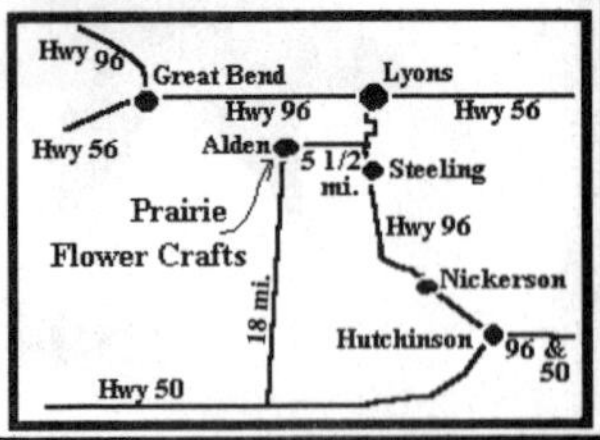

Hutchinson, KS #21

Mon - Sat 9 - 5:30

Country Fabrics

6411 W. Morgan Ave. 67501
(620) 662-3681 Est: 1977
Owners: Janet, Randy, & Leland Headings

100% Cotton Solids and calicos. Quilting Notions, Wood Quilt Frames, Books, & Batting. Fashion Fabrics, Sewing Notions & Patterns.

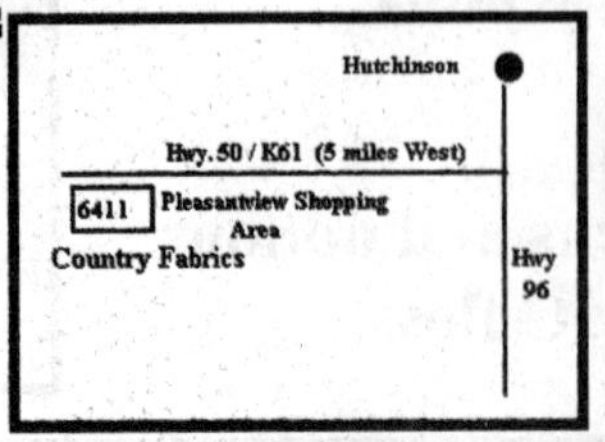

Hutchinson, KS #22

COTTONWOOD QUILTS

Owner: Becky Lomasney

fine fabrics, notions & gifts

Mon - Sat 9:30 - 5

126 N. Main 67501
(630) 662-2245

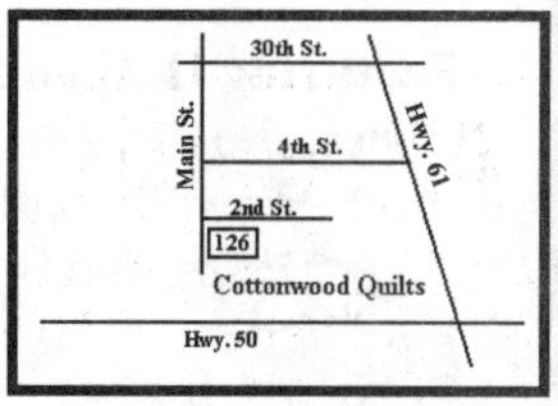

We happily do special orders and Mail Orders.
3000+ bolts. Many Block of the Month Programs.
We've recently doubled our space: RJR Thimbleberries, Moda, P&B, Clothworks, Benartex, Kona Bay, Maywood, Hoffman, 30's Reproductions, Primitives.
Thimbleberries Club Shop. Experienced, friendly personnel.

Newton, KS #23

Charlotte's Sew Natural

UNIQUE FABRICS FOR QUILTING & FASHION

The BEST source for

Fabrics • Patterns • Buttons
Trims • Notions • Classes

710 N. Main 67114 (316) 284-2547
Owner: Charlotte Wolfe

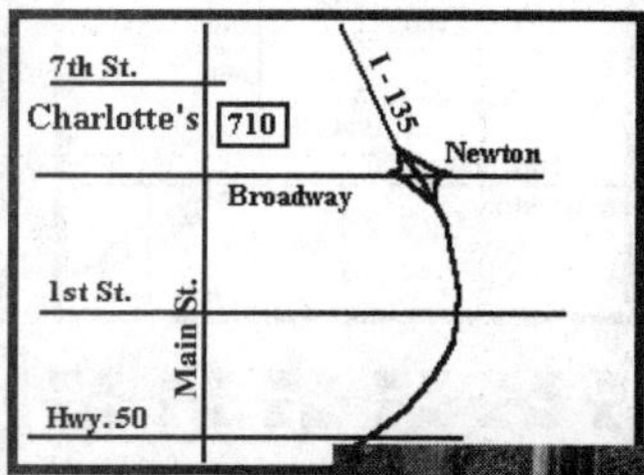

www.sewnatural.net

"Fuzzy Wuzzy Couch Quilt"
Collect all of Charlotte's original patterns!

Mon - Fri 9:30 - 5:30
Thur til 8
Sat 9:30 - 5

Historic Downtown

Newton, Kansas

Need'L Network

Parsons, KS #24

- Over 3,000 bolts of 100% Cotton Fabric
- Wool & chenille by the yard
- 100's of books and patterns
- Custom Machine Quilting
- Mail Order Welcome

1777 E. Hwy. 400
(67357
(316) 421-5006
E-Mail:
dieker@terraworld.net
Web Site:
www.needlnetwork.com
Owner: Rhonda Dieker

Mon - Fri 10 - 5
Sat 9 - 4

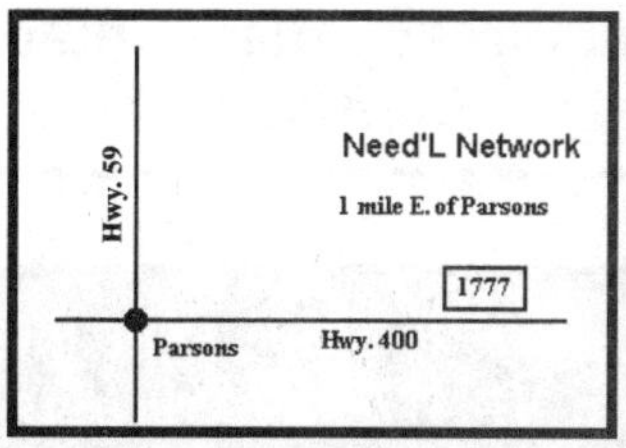

Largest Quilt Store in SE Kansas

Pittsburg, KS #25

Three Women & A Blanket, Inc.

Mon - Fri 10 - 6
Sat 10 - 3

913 N. Broadway 66762
(620) 231-6083 Fax: (620) 231-1675
E-mail: threewomen&ablanket@wequilt.com
Owners: Debi Rankin, Debbie Walker, & Ginger McElwee
Est: 2001 3600 sq.ft. 1500+ Bolts

Bright, airy shop with great variety of fabrics, notions, classes, books, patterns and consigned gift items. Stop in for a unique quilting experience. Group programs available.

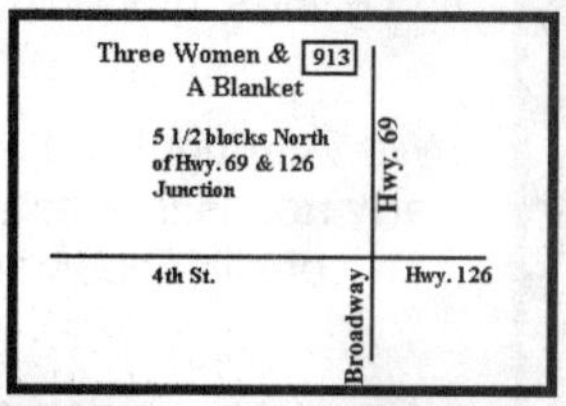

Elk Falls, KS #26

Quilts & More

Tues - Fri 10 - 5:30
Sat 10 - 4

Located in a "Living Ghost Town"
in the Heart of the Kansas Ozarks
105 N. 10th, P.O. Box 23 67345
(620) 329-4440 Owner: Edie Baker
E-Mail: quiltsandmore@sktc.net

Custom machine quilting, cotton fabrics, patterns, notions, & more. We specialize in novelty long arm quilting.

Needle In A Haystack

Severy, KS #27

R.R. #1, Box 174 67137
(620) 736-2942
Fax: (620) 736-2222
Owner: Lois Klepper
Est: 1991 3000 Bolts

Mon & Wed - Sat 9 - 5
Sun 1 - 5
Summer Hrs. 7 day a week

Fabric - Books - Notions
Machine Quilting
Handcrafted items for sale.

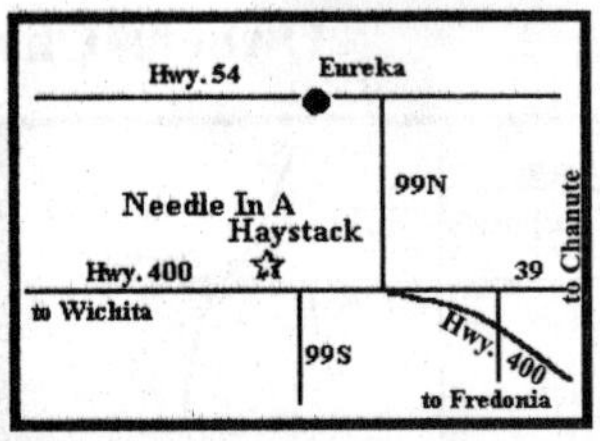

El Dorado, KS #28

Mon - Fri 10 - 5:30
Sat 9 - 5:30

Sew N Sew

(316) 320-7600 309 S. Vine 67042
Est: 1992 Owner: Karen Hayes
E-mail: sewnsew@powwwer.net
Web Site: www.karenssewnsew.com

Featuring Hoffman, P&B, Moda, and other fine fabrics. Books, notions, classes and an abundance of fun! We will gladly ship products

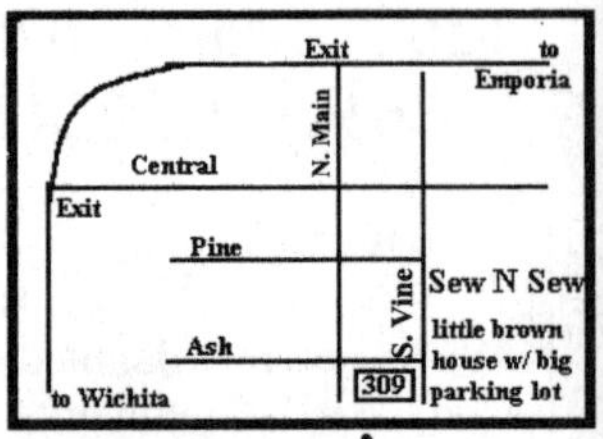

Come See Us !

Fabric Corner

Est: 1992
Owner: Colleen Janssen

627 Commercial - Emporia, Kansas
(620) 342-3040

Emporia, KS #29

Dreams can come true! Ours did when we moved to a spacious turn-of-the-century building we spent nearly a year refurbishing. Photographs can't begin to capture the inviting atmosphere, but try to imagine 14 ft. tall ornate tin ceilings, 6,500 sq.ft. of original hardwood floors, adorned with several thousand bolts of fabric from all the most popular quilting designers and manufacturers.

We thoroughly enjoy visiting with quilters from around the country and sharing creative ideas. For those in your party not as interested in quilting, we have a great selection of fashion fabrics as well as the most wonderful array of silk ribbon supplies and books, plus there's lots of room to just sit and relax.

We are in the heart of downtown with a variety of shops nearby.

Comprehensive Sewing Center

- Authorized BERNINA dealer.
- Books, quilt frames, applique and craft patterns
- Greatest selection of notions in the area

Mention This Ad and Receive 10% off except our already discounted Berninas.

Mon - Fri 9 - 5:30 Sat 9 - 5
Sun 1 - 4 *(call to verify)*

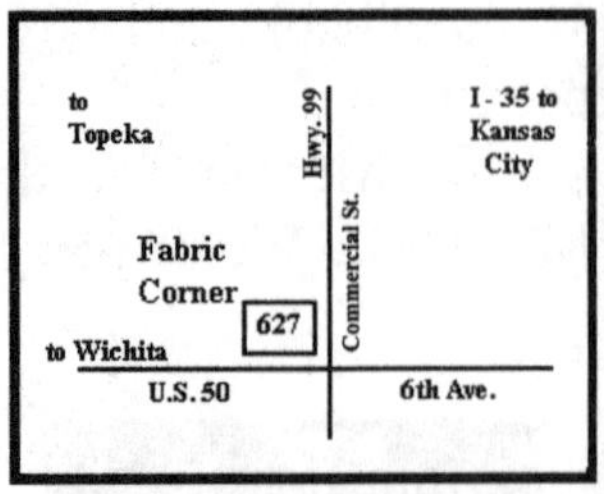

Emporia is located at the intersection of I - 35 and the Kansas Trpk (I - 335). Also, Hwy. 50 (6th Ave.) and Hwy. 99 (Commercial St.) intersect less than a block from our store.

Quilters' Haven

Fabric ✦ *Quilting Supplies* ✦ *Classes*

2,000+ Bolts of Moda, Maywood, Hoffman, Kauffman, Clothworks, South Seas, Bali, Balson-Hercules, Timeless Treasures, Kona Bay, RJR, and more. Large selection of batiks, flannels, children's fabrics, wool kits, patterns and stencils, plus helpful friendly service.

120-B So.
Clairborne Rd.
Olathe, Kansas
66062
(913)764-8600

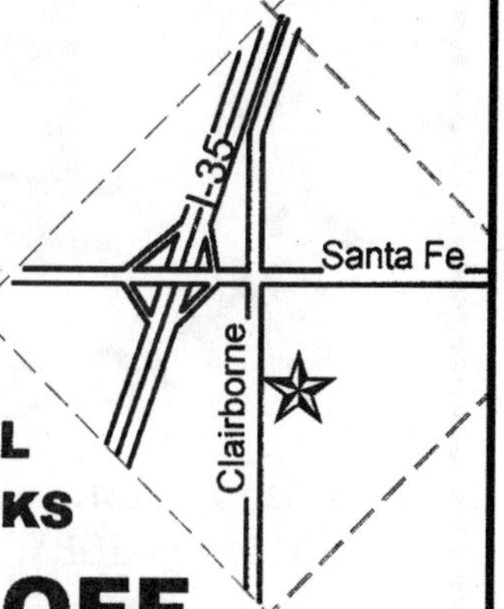

Quilter's Choice
PFAFF
Sewing Machines

Mon. - Sat.
9:30 to 5:30
Thurs. 9:30 to 8:00
quiltershaven.com

ALL BOOKS
20% OFF
EVERY DAY!

Olathe, KS #30

Stitch On Needlework Shop

Mon - Sat 10 - 5:30 Thur until 8 pm Sunday 1 - 4

926 Massachusetts St., Lawrence, KS 66044
785-842-1101 stchon@aol.com
Est. 1976 3,000 sq.ft. 2500+ bolts of 100% Cotton

Batiks, Flannels, Homespuns, 1930's. Large selection of books, patterns and Models. Counted Cross Stitch and fun buttons. Large gift selection of Department 56, Radko, Old World Christmas, Yankee, Aromatique, Smokers, Nutcrackers and Much, Much more.

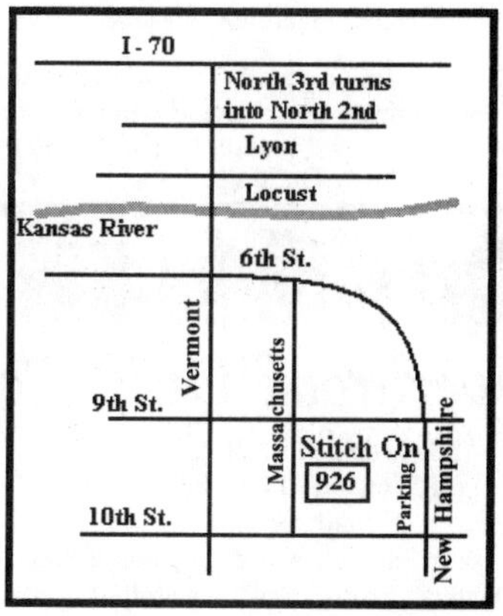

Lawrence, KS #31

Overland Park, KS #32

Harper's Fabric & Quilt Co.

7917 Santa Fe Dr. 66204
(913) 648-2SEW
Toll-Free
(877) 780-2SEW
E-Mail: harpersfab@aol.com
Owner: Elaine Johnson
Est: 1969

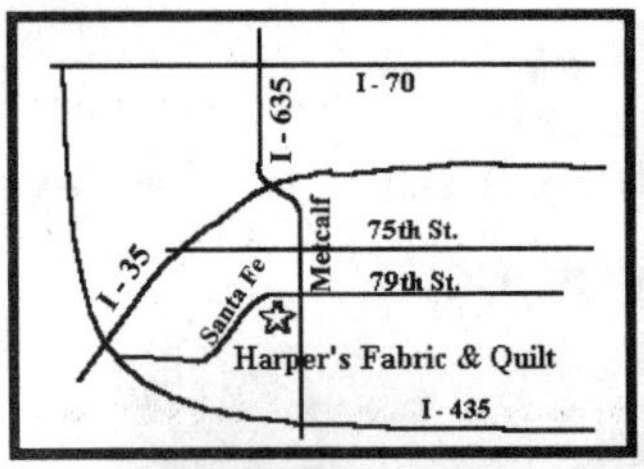

Mon - Fri 10 - 6
Sat 10 - 5

Large Selection of Brand Name 100% Cottons, Flannels, Kids Prints, Reproduction and Novelties. Books, Quilting Supplies & Notions Classes, Seminars and Workshops. Premier Husqvarna Viking Sewing Machines.

Husqvarna VIKING

Quilts on Display

Quilting Bits & Pieces

2200+ bolts of quality fabrics with corresponding fat quarters, BOM's, classes, redwork, notions, books & patterns, kits and machine quilting.

Eudora, KS #33

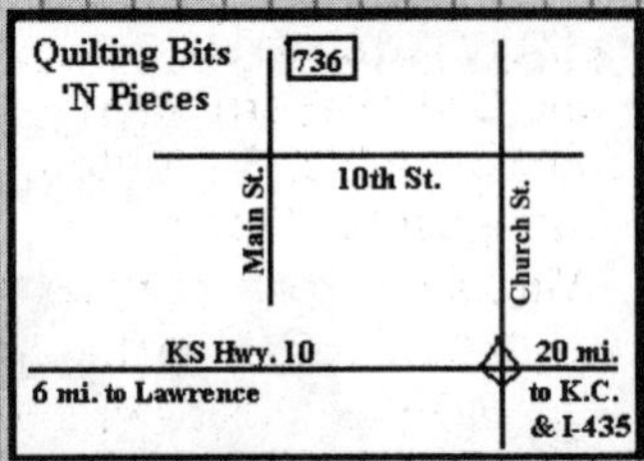

M, W, F, S 9:30 - 5 T & Th 9:30 - 7

Website: www.eudoraks.com
Est: 1997
e-mail: bitsnpieces@sunflower.com

736 Main St. 66025 (785) 542-2080

Baldwin City, KS #34

Mon - Sat 9:30 - 5
Tues til 6

Quilters' Paradise

713 8th St. 66006
(785) 594-3477 Est: 1986
E-Mail: qparadis@eudoramail.com
Web Site: www.grapevine.net/~qparadis
Owner: Sharon A. Vesecky

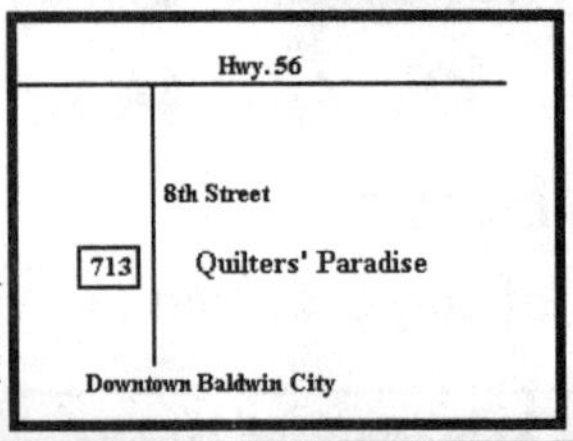

Quilting supplies, books, patterns, fabric—Hoffman, Jinny Beyer, Debbie Mumm, Springs, Concord, Maywood Studio, Moda. Needlework supplies. Machine Quilting.

Burlington, KS #35

Mon - Fri 10 - 5:30
Sat 10 - 3
Sun by Appt.

Silver Threads & Golden Needles

321 Neosho 66839
Owner: Jerry Anne Hoyt
(620) 364-8233
Est: 1985 2000 sq.ft.

Quilters Discount Fabrics, Patterns, Notions, Crafts, Gift Items, Quilting Supplies & Craft Patterns.

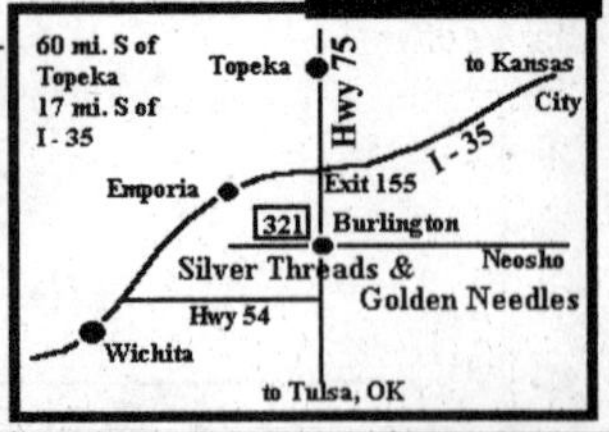

Overbrook, KS #36

Tue - Sat 10 - 5

Overbrook Quilt Connection

500 Maple P.O. Box 50 66524
(785) 665-7841 or (888) 665-7841
E-Mail: oqc@sftnet.org
Web Site: www.overbrookquilts.com
Owners: Roxane Fawl & Carolyn Meerian
Est: 1994 4300 sq.ft.

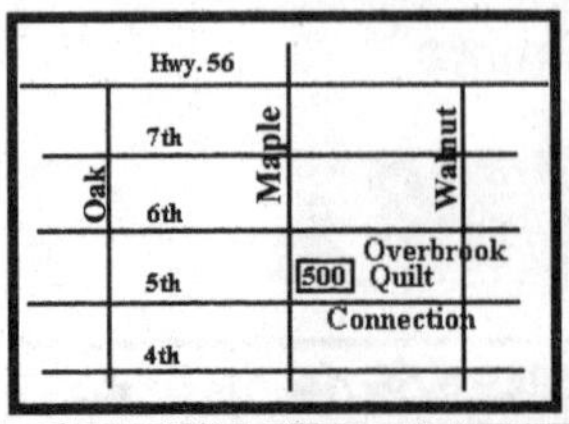

2000 bolt inventory, books, patterns, notions, classes. Mailorder. Free flier.

Topeka, KS #37

Mon - Fri 10 - 5
Thur til 7
Sat 10 - 3

Stitchin Traditions Quilt Shop

3005 SW Topeka Blvd.
66611
(785) 266-4130

E-Mail: stitchintraditions@kscable.com
Est: 1997 1600 sq.ft. 750+ Bolts
Full service quilt shop serving Topeka and the surrounding area. We offer a large selection of fabric, books, patterns, notions and classes.

Shawnee, KS #38

Prairie Point

Fabrics, Quilting Supplies & Classes

- Great selection of the best new fabrics including flannels, novelty prints, ethnic designs, country homespuns and prints, contemporary jewel tones, 1930's and Civil War era reproduction prints, Bali Batiks, Japanese and more!
- Wide assortment of notions
- >1,000 books and patterns
- Many cotton, polyester and wool battings from which to choose
- Classes at all levels

Store Hours:
Mon - Thurs 10:00 - 8:30
Fri & Sat 10:00 - 5:00
Sunday 1:00 - 5:00

Stop in for a visit. With so many inspirational samples, you're bound to find a project you just can't resist!

Located in Suburban Kansas City
7341 Quivira Rd.
Shawnee, KS 66216
(913) 268-3333
Toll Free (888) 268-5606

Web Site:
www.prairiepoint.com
email:
PrairiePTQuilts@aol.com

Leavenworth, KS #39

The Quilter's Quarters

Mon, Tues, Thurs, Fri, Sat 9:30 - 5:30
Wed 12 - 8

Minutes from Kansas City, The Quilter's Quarters is dedicated to providing the best possible customer service in the friendliest atmosphere. Quilters will truly find a home in our civil war vintage building where the surroundings may be antique, but the fabric and ideas are cutting edge. Unlike a fabric museum, our merchandise is constantly being updated. You will find our large selection of fabrics, notions, books, kits, plus new and antique quilts just outside the front gate of historic Fort Leavenworth. Featured in 2 books-- "Kansas City Quilt Maker Portraits & Patterns" and "Kansas City Scrap Book" by Terri Atkinson.

219 Delaware
Leavenworth, KS 66048
(913) 651-6510
www.quiltersqtrs.com
Owner: Jerry Ann Stube

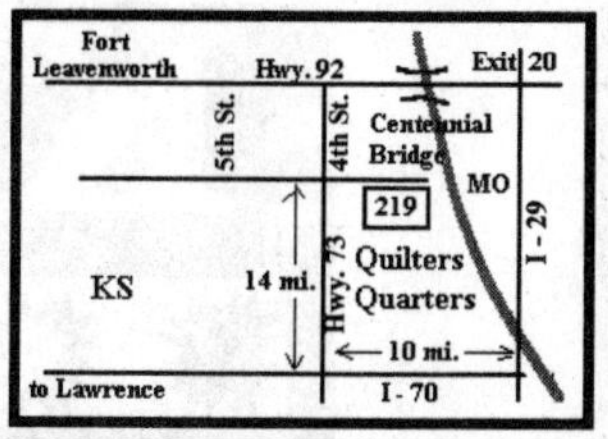

Other Shops in Kansas: We suggest calling first

Admire Heart of the Prairie, 3902 Hwy. 99 Rd. R 316-528-3564
Anthony Pride of the Prairie Quilt Shoppe, 131 W. Main St. 316-842-5945
Clay Center Clione's Collections, 709 5th St. 913-632-3839
Clearwater Ginny's Quilts, Box 64 316-584-2554
Elk Falls Old Church Quilts & More, 10th & Osage St. 316-374-2226
Emporia Quilts & Yardage Plus, 7 E. 6th Ave. 316-343-3850
Emporia Carol's Quilting, 511 S. Exchange St. 620-343-9197
Galva The Quilt Barn, 221 E. Hwy. 56 316-654-3400
Holton Sunflower Quilting, 403 New York 785-364-5177
Independence Quilt 'N Things, 115 S. Penn 316-331-5548
Kansas City Jessie's Quilting, 3316 N 131st. 913-721-1364
La Crosse Patchwork Parlor, 812 Main St. 913-222-3536
Lakin Patchwork Garden, 404 W. Hwy. 50 620-355-1441
Lawrence Sarah's Fabrics, 925 Massachusetts 913-842-6198
Manhattan Ideas Unlimited Quilt Shop, 523 South 17th 785-539-6759
Manhattan Weisner's Sew Unique, 314 Poyntz Ave. 913-776-6100
Minneola Quilts-N-More, 101 Olive St. 620-885-4500
Norton The Sewing Box, 128 S. State 913-877-3821
Oakley Quilt Shop, 423 Hudson Ave. 785-672-3870
Osage City Calico Cupboard, 513 Market 785-528-4861
Osawatomie Calico Quilts and Crafts, 400 Pacific Ave. 913-755-6495
Ottawa Chris' Corner, 229 S. Main St. 913-242-1922
Oxford Variety Shoppe, 106 S. Summer St. 316-455-3698
Seneca Picture This, 420 Main St. 913-336-3296
Shawnee Mission Bernina-Pfaff Sewing Center, 7251 W. 97th 913-371-6400
Topeka The Sunflower Seed, 4004 SW Hunton 785-228-0588
Topeka Bennett's Sewing Center, 2125 N. Kansas Ave. 785-232-9117
Topeka Cozy Craft Corner, 915 NE Hilltop 785-234-9293
Valley Falls Dodie's, 421 Broadway St. 785-945-6646
Wichita The Picket Fence, 141 N. Rock Island St. 316-262-7774
Winfield The Sewing Basket, 211 E. 9th Ave. 316-221-4517

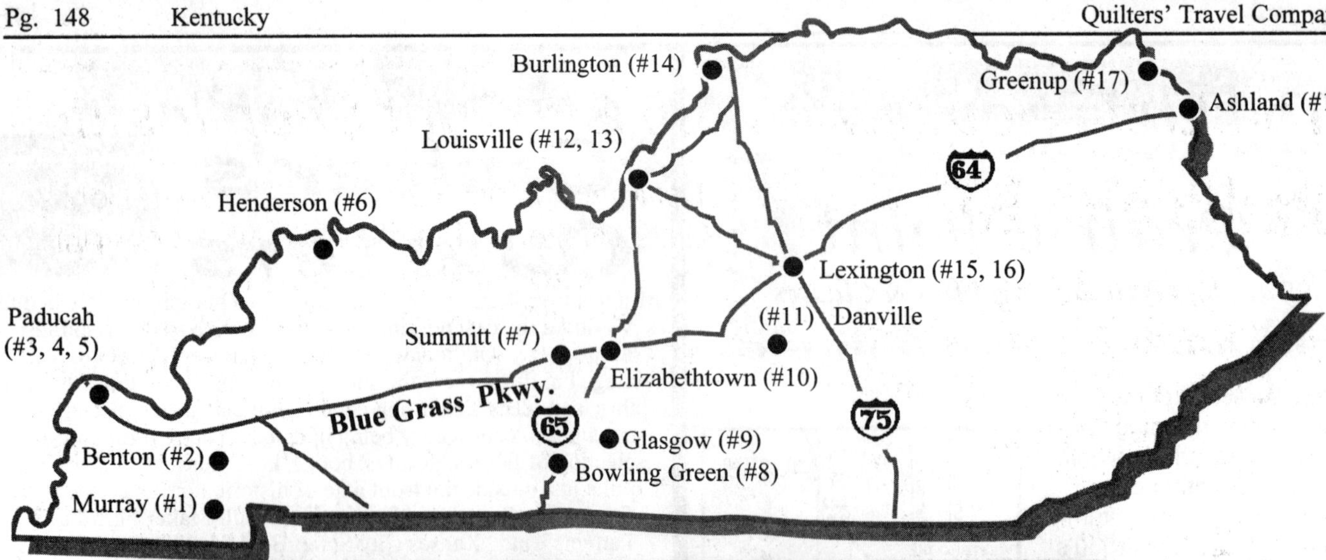

KENTUCKY

18 Featured Shops

Paducah: Quilt City U.S.A.

Elizabethtown, KY #10

Mon by Chance
Tues 3 - 9, Wed 9 - 6,
Thur 9 - 9, Fri 9 - 6
Sat 9 - 3
Sun Closed

Uniquely Yours Quilt Shop

2973 Rineyville Rd. 42701
(270) 766-1456
E-mail: uniquelyquilts@aol.com
Owner: Mary Sennott

Over 2000 bolts of 100% Cotton Fabrics. Books, patterns, notions and classes. Friendly, professional advice. Quilts for sale.

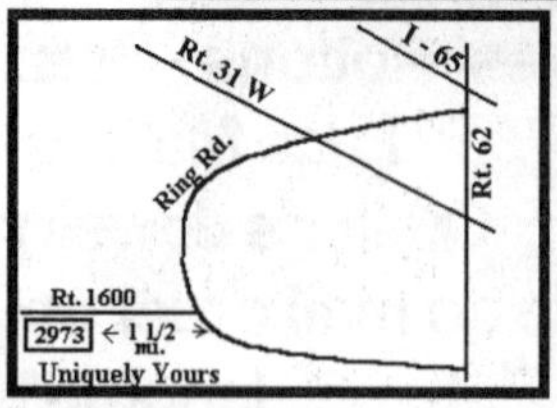

Danville, KY #11

Mon - Sat
10 - 6

World Wide Fabrics

104 Man O'War Blvd. 40422
(606) 236-1175
Owners: Earl & Jean Steinhauer
Est: 1976 4000 sq.ft.

Authorized Bernina Dealer
Calico Cottons Quilting Books and Supplies
Bridal Fabrics and accessories. Complete line of Notions, Drapery & Upholstery.

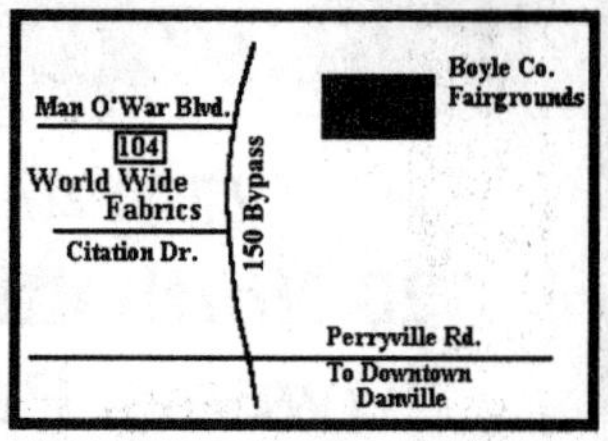

Louisville, KY #12

Mon - Sat
9:30 - 5
Tues &
Thur til 7

Forget-Me-Not Quilt Shoppe

2116 S. Preston St. 40217
(502) 638-0630
E-Mail: dhamfanci@aol.com
Owners: Darlene Hamilton & Jeni Siebel
Est: 2001

100% cotton fabrics, Quilting Supplies, Books, Patterns, Classes.
Authorized Janome Dealer.

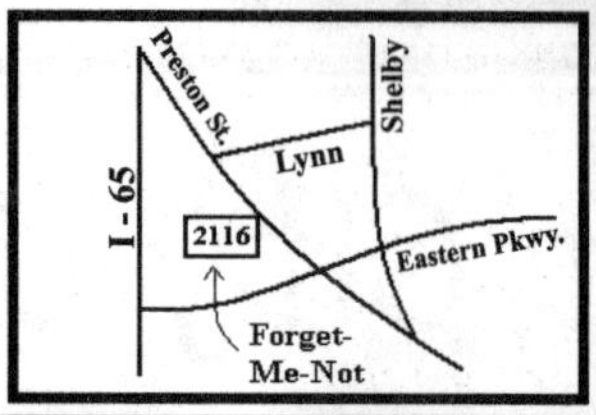

Louisville, KY #13

Happy Heart Quilt Shop

Mon - Fri 10 - 5 Sat 10 - 4

7913 3rd. St. Rd. 40214
(502) 363-1171
Owner: Yvonne Fritze
Est: 1985
3500 sq. ft.

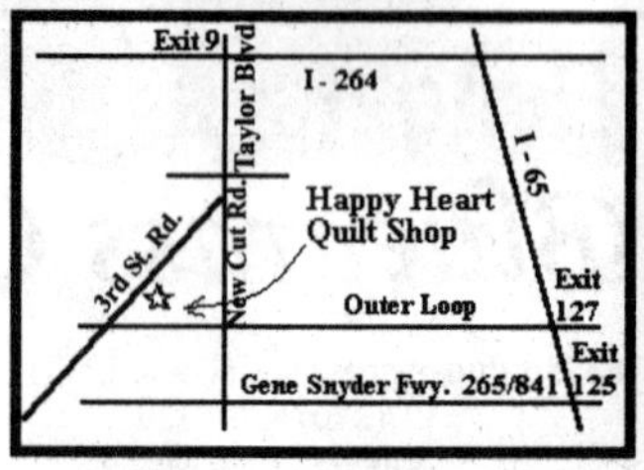

Happy Heart Quilt Shop is located ten minutes from I - 264, exit 9; or I - 65 exit 127, Kentucky Fair & Exposition Center and Louisville International Airport. There is a vast array of fabrics, 4000 bolts, in most major fabric lines, hundreds of books, patterns, stencils and notions in 3500 square feet of shopping space.
Quilt kits are available—applique, cross-stitch, whole cloth, and pieced blocks. Merchandise is displayed on spacious shelving and antique pieces.
Special features for customers include newsletters, classes, retreats, sales, demonstrations and problem solving.
We also have two day-long bus trips to the AQS Show in Paducah each year. We are well known for our friendly service and our love of quilting.

Burlington, KY #14

Mon - Sat
10 - 6
April - Oct
3rd Sun 12 - 5

Cabin Arts

5878 N. Jefferson St. 41005
(859) 586-8021
E-mail: cabinarts@nkol.net
Web Site: www.nkol.net/cabinarts/
Owner: Linda Whittenburg
Est: 1992 1300 sq.ft. 4000 Bolts

Quality Quilt Fabrics plus notions, books & more. Local Handcrafted Treasures. Classes Available. Located in historic district in 1850's Log Cabin.

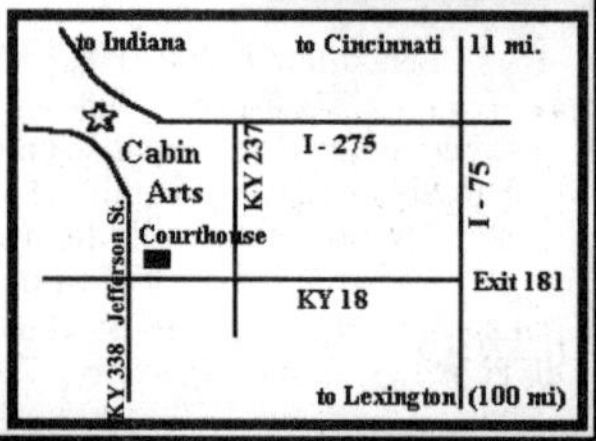

Lexington, KY #15

Mon - Sat
10 - 5:30
Thur til 7

Corner Quilt Shop

153 Patchen Dr. #67 40517
(859) 268-7467
Owner: Teresa Fritz

Large selection 100% cotton fabrics, books, notions, classes. Call and watch for new location in fall of 2002.

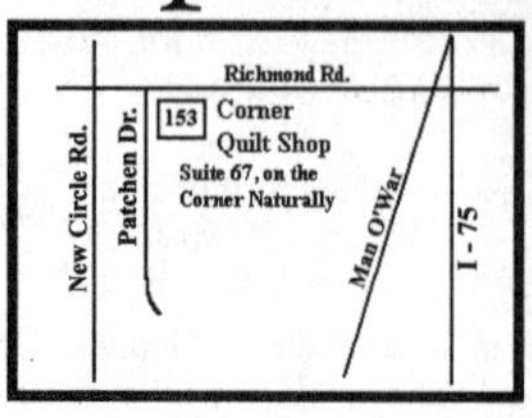

Lexington, KY #16

QUILTER'S SQUARE

140 MOORE DRIVE, LEXINGTON, KY 40503
(859) 278-5010 or fax at (859) 278-0274

Don't miss this one!

Twenty years in the business and getting better every year! When traveling on Interstates 64 or 75 through Kentucky, Quilter's Square is located just a few miles off the Interstate in the ♥ of the BLUEGRASS.

Friendly Service
Exceptional Selection of FABRIC, BOOKS, PATTERNS, NOTIONS, & GIFT ITEMS

Authorized BERNINA Dealer & Service
Hours: Mon.-Fri. 10-6
Thursday 10-9
Sat. 10-5:30

New Circle Rd. (Circle 4) to Nicholasville Rd. to Moore Dr. (behind Wendy's)
QUILTER'S SQUARE
140 MOORE DRIVE

Visit us at:
quilterssquare.biz

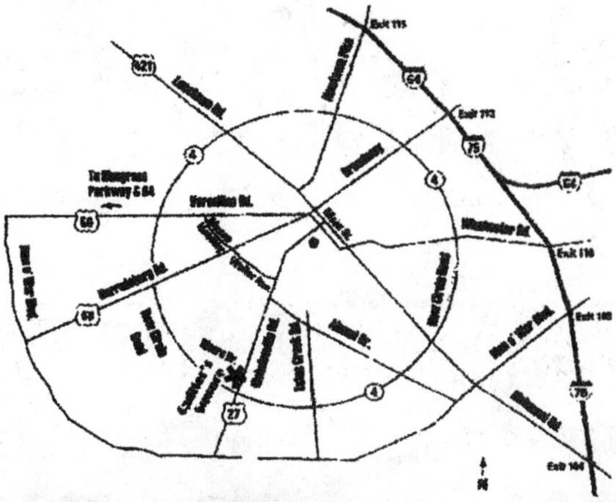

Other Shops in Kentucky: We suggest calling first

Albany	Quilters Hideaway, 114 S. Washington St.	606-387-6675
Allensville	Grandma's Cupboard, 5760 Russellville Rd., Hwy 79	502-483-2461
Barbourville	Kno Discount Fabric, Hwy. 229 & 25 E	606-546-9362
Berea	Quilt Shop, 102 Center St.	859-986-1239
Boaz	Quilting Kaleidoscope, 8510 Old Mayfield Rd.	270-534-4808
Bowling Green	Singer Sewing Center, 575 Campbell Ln.	502-842-2434
Corbin	The Kentucky Quilt Co., 1878 Cumberland Falls	606-523-4393
Dawson Springs	Junction House, 10315 Nortonville Rd.	502-797-3572
Dry Ridge	The Quilt Box, P.O. Box 9 Warsaw Rd.	606-824-4007
East Bernstadt	Harris' Fabric Shop, 5506 U.S. Hwy. 25 N	606-843-7336
East Bernstadt	Quilting B, 1870 E. Hwy. 30	606-843-2803
Edmonton	Marilyn's, 108 River Rd.	270-432-0334
Frankfort	Wilma's Linens & Lace, 202 W. Broadway St.	502-223-1976
Glasgow	D & M Quilting Shop, 20 Flint Knob Rd.	270-678-2568
Grand Rivers	Rocky Hollow Quilts, 136 Chandler Ct.	270-362-2651
Harrodsburg	Farmhouse Treasures, 2784 Louisville Rd.	859-734-7001
Hueysville	Quilt Shop, 738 Saltlick Rd.	606-358-9490
London	Sexton's Fabrics, 2435 N. Laurel Rd.	606-843-6610
Louisa	Sewing Cottage, R.R. # 4, Box 1530	606-638-3102
Louisville	Baer Fabrics, 515 E. Market St.	502-569-7016
Louisville	Kentucky Art & Craft Gallery, 609 W. Main	502-589-0102
Louisville	The Smocking Shop, 3829 Staebler Ave.	502-893-3503
Magnolia	Bits and Pieces Fabric Shop, 7396 N. Jackson Hwy	502-528-2487
Magnolia	The Jewel Box, 10075 N. Jackson Hwy.	502-528-3087
Morgantown	Embry's Crafts & Fabrics, 225 Rochester St.	270-526-2681
Mt. Vernon	Heritage Crafts, Hwy. 461	606-256-9077
Murray	The Busy Bee's Custom Quilt Shop, Route #2	502-753-5347
Murray	Murray Sewing Center, 942A S. 12th St.	502-753-5323
New Castle	Quilt Stitchin, P.O. Box 387	502-845-4987
Paducah	Web of Thread, 1410 Broadway	502-575-9700
Paducah	Hancock Fabrics, 3841 Hinkleville Rd.	502-443-4410
Paducah	Sewing Center of Paducah, 842 Joe Clifton Dr.	502-442-1661
Paducah	Michael Stewart Antiques 136 Lone Oak Rd.	502-441-7222
Paducah	English's Sewing Machines, 7001 Benton Rd.	502-898-7301
Perryville	I Love Quilts, 334 Buell St.	606-236-8800
Philpot	The Quilting Place, 6845 Milton Rd.	502-729-2290
Philpot	Sew Much More, 6481 Ditto Rd.	270-926-8886
Pineville	Kathy's Needle & Thread P.O. Box 118 Route #2	606-337-6753

Greenup, KY #17

Mon 9 - 6
Tues - Fri 9 - 5
Sat 9 - 4

Lil's Fabrics

2035 Ashland Rd. 41144
(606) 473-3869
Owner: Lillian McKenzie

Over 1400 bolts of name brand fabrics.
Notions, Books, Patterns, Gifts and Classes.
Always with a friendly smile.

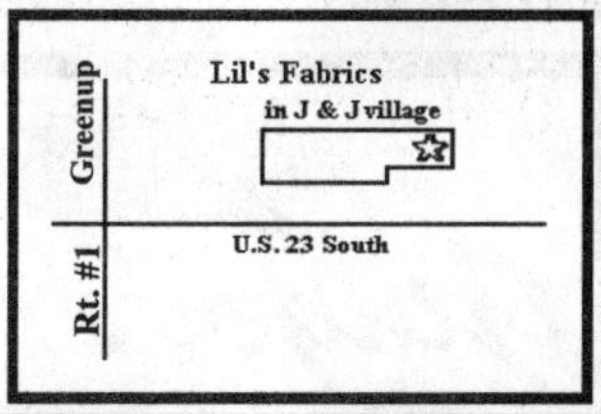

Ashland, KY #18

Mon - Fri 10 - 5
Closed Wed
Sat 10 - 12

Craft Attic Quilt Shop

2027 Hoods Creek Pike 41102
(606) 325-1212
E-Mail: dmag999893@aol.com
Owner: Donnie Maggard
Est: 1982 1500 sq.ft. 1000 Bolts

100% Cotton Fabrics.
Full Line of Quilting Supplies.
Books , Stencils , Classes

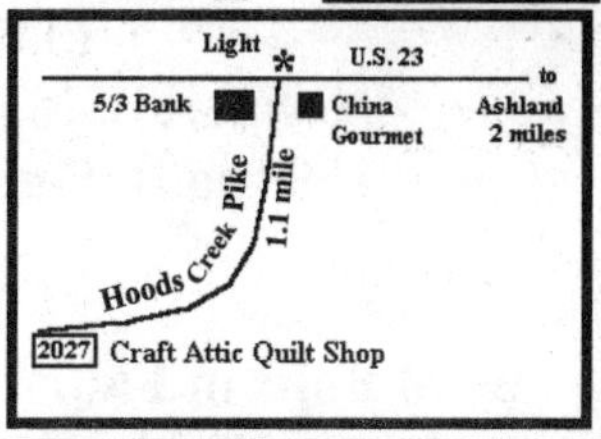

Renfro Valley	O Shep Originals, Hwy. 25	606-256-5018
Rockfield	Country Quilts, 1586 Blue Level Providence Rd.	270-782-9526
Russell	Quilting Connection, 401 Belfonte	606-836-9920
Russell Springs	Norma's Quilts, 2288 S. Hwy. 76	270-866-4330
Russellville	Kountry Korner, 100 Cumberland Cir.	270-726-2003
Salyersville	Quilting Shop, 664 E. Mountain Parkway	606-349-1303
Whitesburg	Cozy Corner, 210 E. Main St.	606-633-9637

LOUISIANA

13 Featured Shops

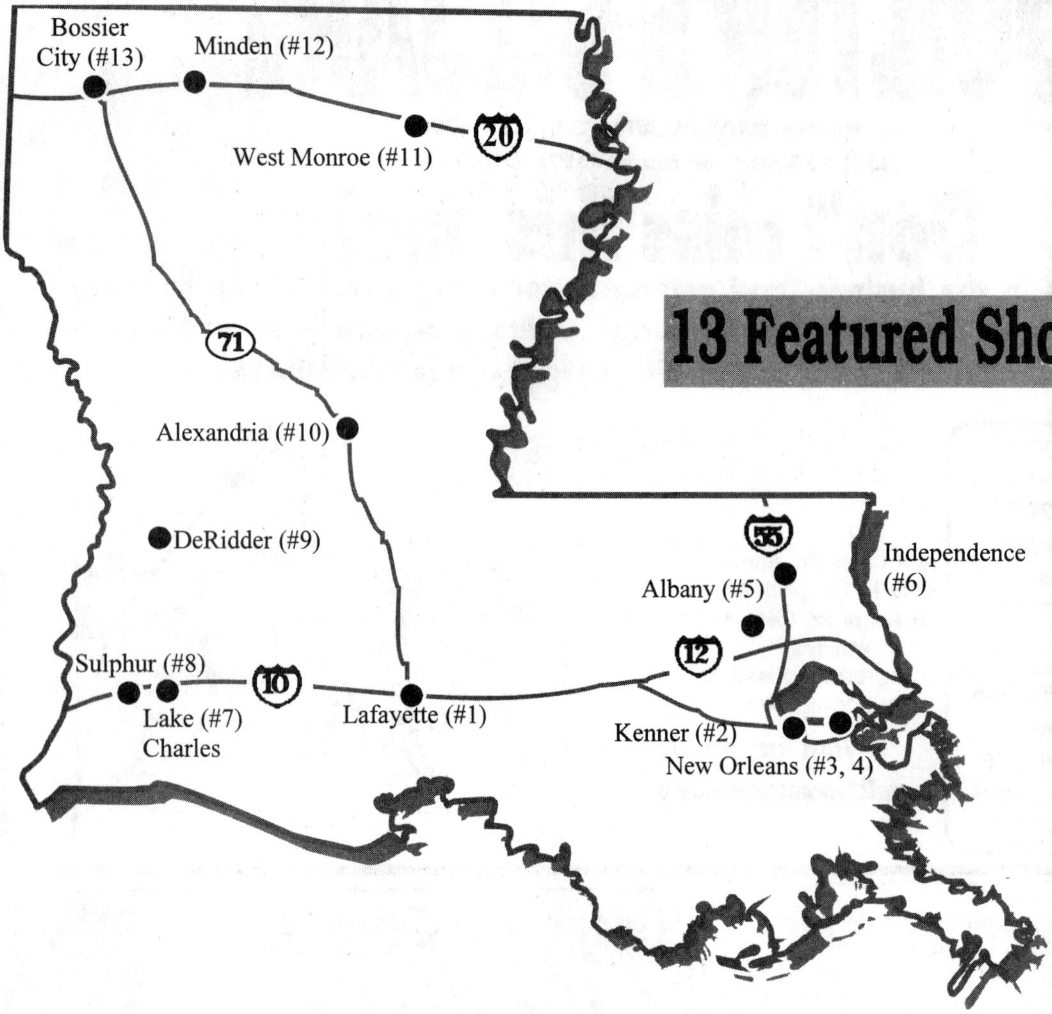

Lafayette, LA #1

Ginger's Needleworks

Open: Mon, Tues, Thur, Fri 10 - 5
Sat 10 - 3 Closed Wed & Sun

1001 East Gloria Switch Road 70507
(337) 232-7847
Owner: Ginger Moore Est:1984
1600 sq.ft. Quilting 200 sq.ft. Yarns

3000 Bolts of Fabrics
Lots of Notions
Patterns & Books

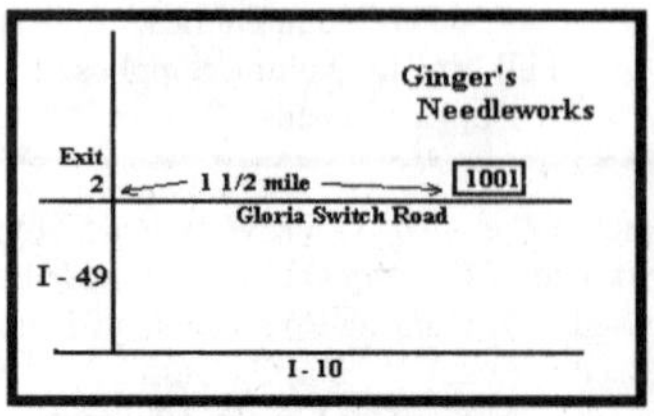

Visit our mailorder web catalog at: www.quiltknit.com

Kenner, LA #2

Mon - Sat 10 - 5

Scrap-Happy Quilter

2546 Williams Blvd. 70062
(504) 463-0094 Fax: Same
Owner Janice Andrews
Est: 1997 1400 sq.ft. 2000+ Bolts

Bright, Cheery Full Service Shop 5 minutes from New Orleans International Airport.

New Orleans, LA #3

7 Days A Week 9 - 6

Quilt Shop in New Orleans

816 Decatur St. 70116
(504) 522-0835
Web Site: www.quilt-shop-nola.com
Owners: Janelle & Richard Garrett

We offer a variety of hand-quilted items; patchwork quilts, pillow covers and clothing. Our clothing is of exquisite traditional or contemporary design that is very unique.

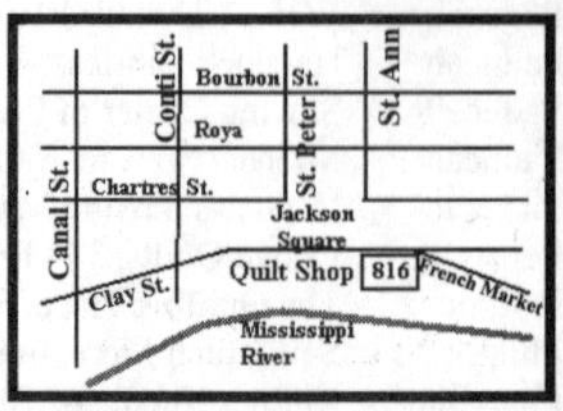

New Orleans, LA #4

(800) 453-6998

Quilt Cottage

Mon - Sat
10 - 5

801 Nashville Avenue 70115 (504) 895-3791

Owners:
Carol Schiaffino
& Jeanne Lincks
Est: 1981 2000 sq.ft.

Your Complete Quilt Shop !

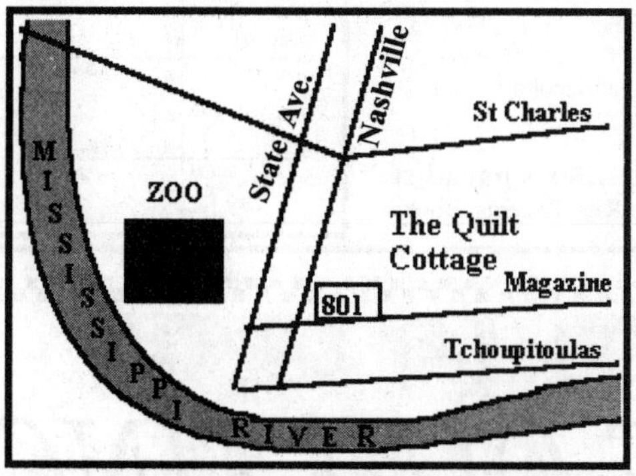

Room full of 100% cotton fabric. Over 1500 Bolts. The latest books, notions, & Patterns. New, Antique, Custom made quilts. Repair. Our own Mardi Gras Fat Quarter Packets, Patterns and Bolts of Mardi Gras fabrics are stocked year 'round.

Send us your name and address and we'll send you our free newsletter three times per year.

Albany, LA #5

The Quilt Shop

Mon - Fri
10 - 5
Sat 10 - 3

29937 S. Montpelier Ave., P.O. Box 1716, Albany, LA 70711
225/209-2097 225/209-2096 FAX quilter@I-55.com E-MAIL
Owners: Judy Jensen & Rhoda Jordan
Est: 2001 3000 sq.ft. Over 1500 Bolts of 100% Cotton

"pursuing the heavenly art of quiltmaking"

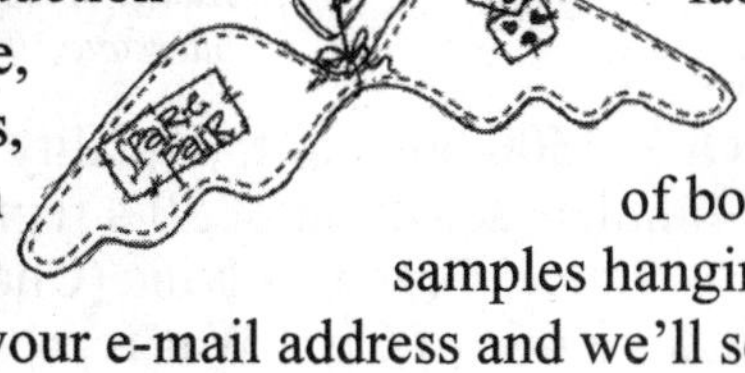

Specializing in pre-Civil War, Civil War, post-Civil War reproduction fabrics, as well as Aunt Grace, Thimbleberries, flannels, and redwork. Huge selection of books and patterns with over 100 samples hanging from our walls.
Send us your e-mail address and we'll send you our newsletter!

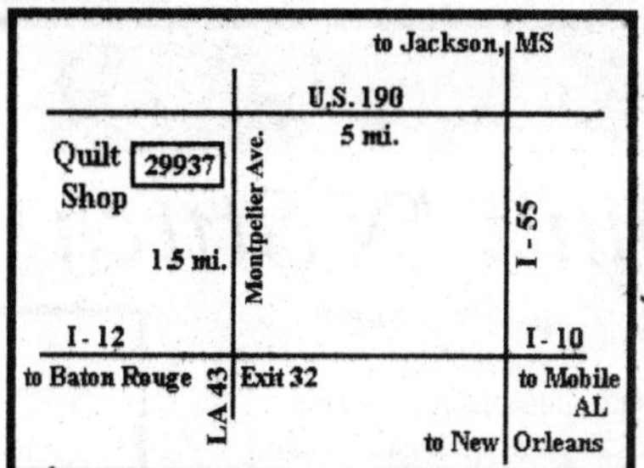

Independence, LA #6

Mama's Quilt Shop

15111 Catfish Farm Road
70443
985-878-6396
Email: mamasquiltshop@yahoo.com

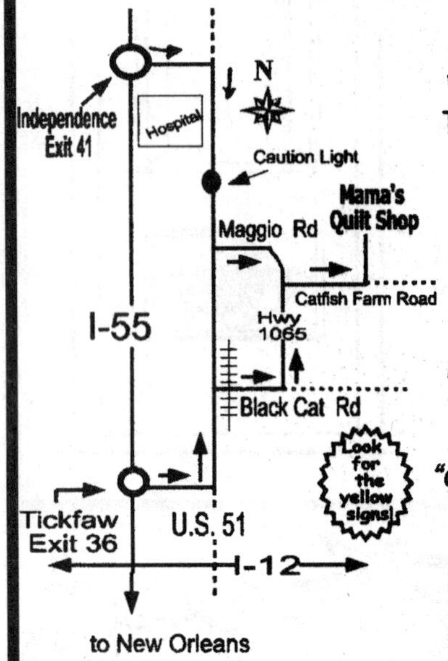

Our fabric lines include Civil War and 30's reproductions, Thimbleberries, Jinny Beyers, RJR, Benartex, Marcus Brothers, Timeless Treasures, and many, many more. **Best prices around!**

Fabrics, notions, books, classes, and lots of inspiration at the "quilt shop in the country."

Hours: 9 am -5 pm Mon-Sat

Lake Charles, LA #7

Mon - Fri 10 - 5 Sat 10 - 3

Heartstrings Quilts & More

3113 Ryan St. #4 70601
(337) 497-1200

Quilters one-stop shopping! A great line of quilting fabrics, notions, books, patterns, threads, batting, BOM's, classes, Bees & clubs.

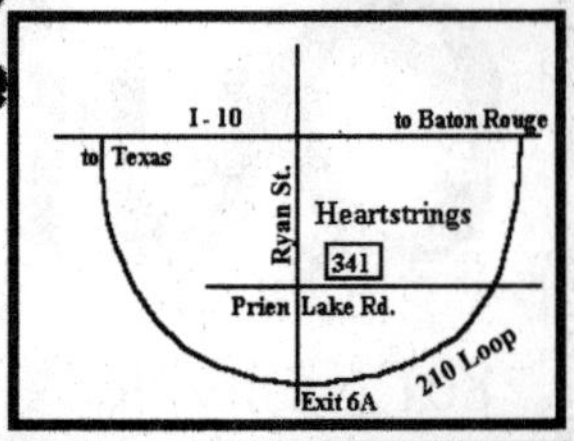

Sulphur, LA #8

Mon - Fri 9:30 - 5 Sat 10 - 3

Mary Ann's Fabric Cottage

1017 S. Beglis Pkwy. 70663
(337) 528-9190 Fax: (337) 528-9195
E-Mail: maryann@fabriccottage.com
Web Site: www.fabriccottage.com
Est: 1994

"Your one-stop quilter's paradise."
Quilt Fabrics, Quilt Kits, Patterns, Books

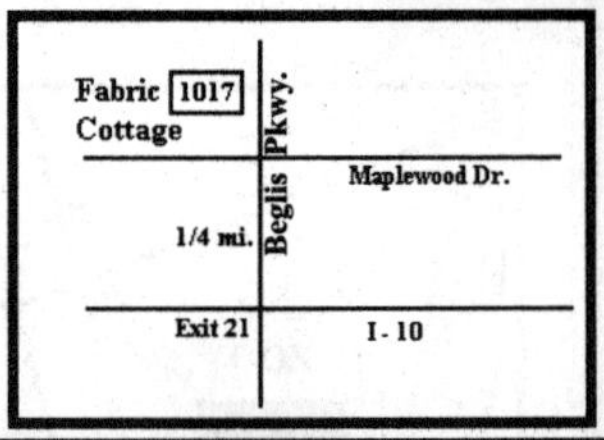

DeRidder, LA #9

THE QUILTING ROOM

113 S. Washington Ave.
DeRidder, Louisiana 70634
(337) 462-4944
E-Mail: srich1@mindspring.com
Owner: Sandra Rich

Tues - Fri 9:30 - 5:30 Sat 10 - 5

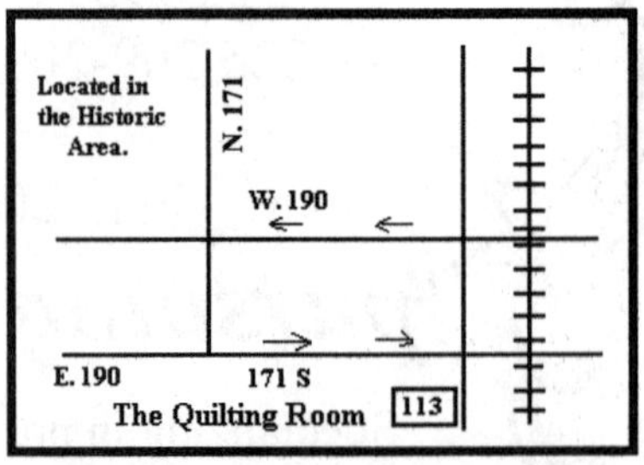

DeRidder is located 45 miles north of Interstate 10 on US Highway 171.

Over 2500 bolts of top quality 100% cottons
Complete selection of 30's reproduction Aunt Grace, Granny's Nine (Chanteclaire).
Large line of Civil War reproduction prints
Great selection of books, patterns, and notions
Janome Sewing machine dealer.
Friendly, personal service is our key to success.

Alexandria, LA #10

Mon - Fri 9 - 5 Sat 9-2

Red Roof Quilt Shop

5412 Masonic Drive 71301
(318) 443-1589
Quilts110@cox-internet.com
Owners: Faye Dantzler

We cater to quilters. 100% Cotton fabrics, from top companies with a wide selection of books & notions. Custom made quilts too.

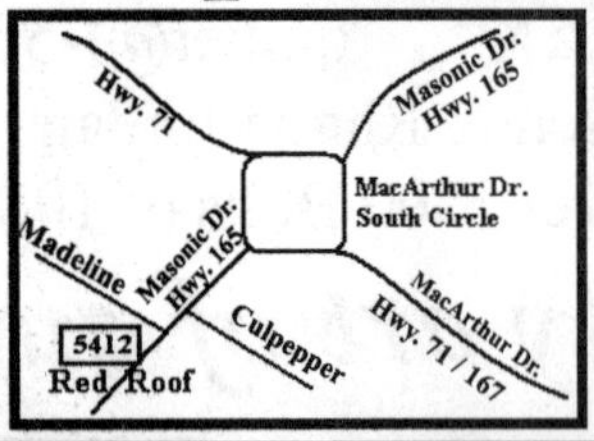

West Monroe, LA #11

Mon - Fri 9 - 5 Sat 10 - 4

Quilt 'N Stitch

6049 Cypress St. 71291
(318) 396-6020
E-Mail: qultstch@bayou.com
Web Site: www.quiltnstitch.com
2000+ Bolts

The store is located in a house where antiques nestle among the many fabrics, books, and notions. Authorized Bernina Dealer

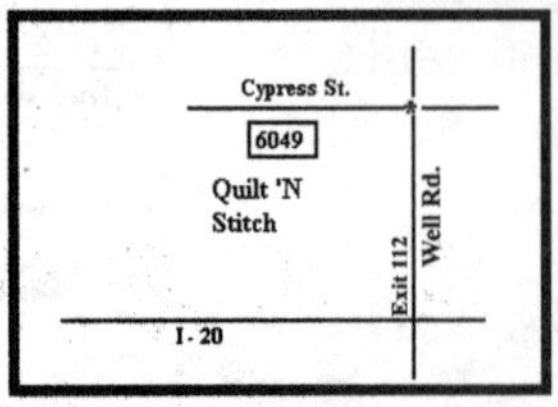

Minden, LA #12

Tues - Fri 10 - 5
Sat 10 - 2

The Little Country Quilt Shop

534 Old Arcadia Rd. 71055
(318) 377-2462
Owner: Nona Sale
Est: 1983

We have approx. 1500 bolts. All the latest books, patterns, & supplies. Also a variety of classes. Plus we have old and new quilts for sale. Please drop by for our group meeting on the second Thursday of the month 9 - 4.

From I - 20 take Exit 49. Go North 3½ miles to the 2nd traffic light. Turn right & stay in exit lane for 1/4 mile. Lane turns into Old Arcadia Rd. Shop is 1 mile on left.

Bossier City, LA #13

Mon - Sat 10 - 6

Fabric Boutique

Heart of Bossier Shopping Ctr.
1701 Old Minden Rd. 71111
Toll Free (877) SEW-ASAP (739-2727)
(318) 742-0047 Fax: (318) 742-5934
Owner: Shirley C. Warren
Est: 1972

Unique combination of classes, quilting supplies & fabrics. Authorized Bernina, Sewing Machine dealer.

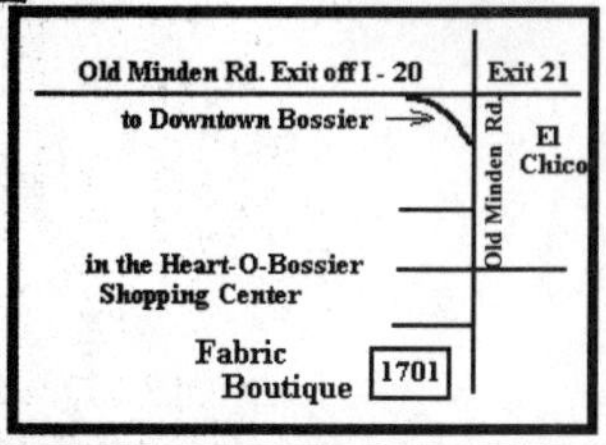

Other Shops in Louisiana: We suggest calling first

Covington	Annie's Sewing Center, 2256 Phillip Dr.	985-867-8067
Gibson	Alice & Lee's Quilts & Crafts, 6233 Bayou Black Dr., P.O. Box 858	504-575-2389
Houma	Jo's Cloth Cottage, 205-C Bayou Gardens Blvd.	504-879-4602
Metairie	The Quilting Bee, 3537 18th St. #15	504-456-2304
Metairie	Alder Sewing & Vacuum Center, 4441 Veteran	504-866-8050
New Iberia	Quilts & Things, 1610 Freyou Rd.	318-367-7772
Ruston	Louisiana Quilt N More, 1800 Trade Dr.	318-768-2662
Shreveport	Needlepoint Shop, 6505 Line Ave. #43	318-865-7878
Westlake	Quilt Shop, 910 Sampson St.	337-497-1885

Notes

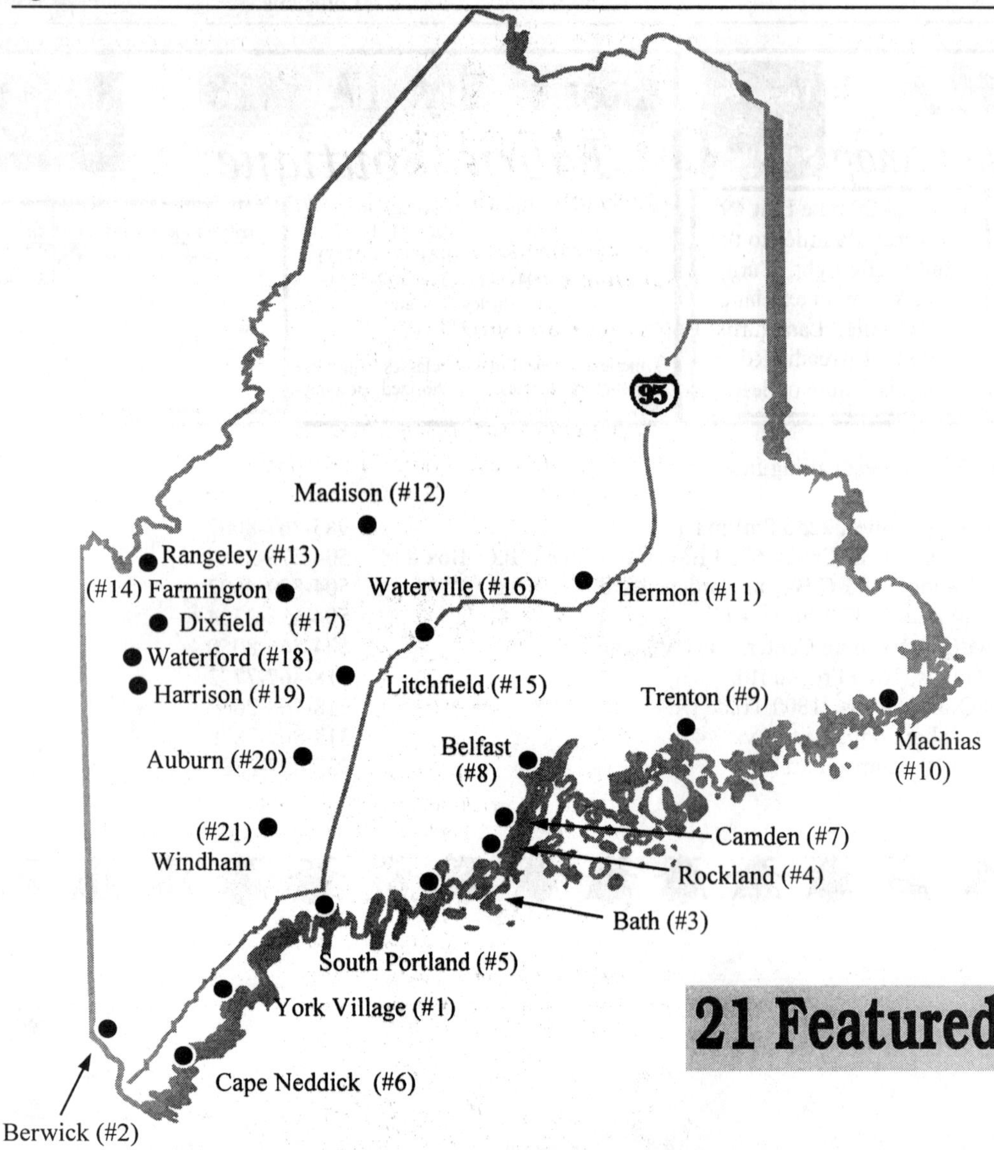

MAINE

21 Featured Shops

York Village, ME #1

May 1 - Oct 30
Mon - Sat 10 - 5
Sun 12 - 5
Winter Thur, Fri, Sat 10 - 4
by chance or Appt.

Rocky Mountain Quilts

130 York St. (Rt. 1A) 03909
(800) 762-5940 or (207) 363-6800
Web Site: www.rockymountainquilts.com

For Sale: Over 400 Antique Quilts, Tops & Blocks plus Vintage Fabrics (1770 - 1950).
Restoration and washing.

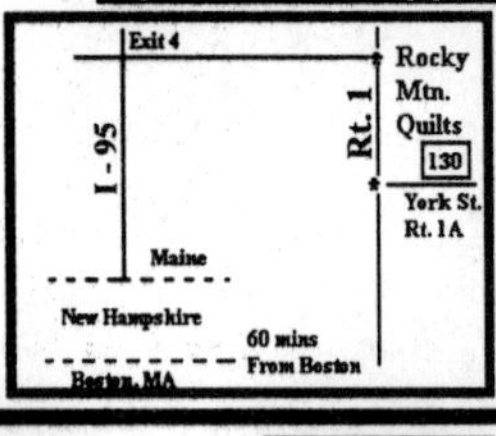

Berwick, ME #2

Wed - Sat 10 - 5
Sun 1 - 5

Cottage Herbs

372 Diamond Hill Rd. 03901
(207) 698-5507
Owner: Nancy Riley Est: 1980

Large Selection of Homespuns and Country Fabrics. Many Books, Patterns, Notions
Quiltmaking ★ Dollmaking ★ Dried Arrangements ★ Classes Avail. ★ Baskets, etc.
★Specializing in Dried Flowers

DIRECTIONS:
(We're easy to find)
Just Follow the signs on Route 9 in Berwick

Bath, ME #3

Tues - Sat 10 - 5

Mariner's Compass Quilt Shop

11 Centre St. 04530
(207) 443-2900
Owner: Amanda B. Ulmer

"Guiding Quilters to the City of Ships"
Offering "quilter's grade" 100% cotton fabrics, books, patterns, quilting notions and classes for all ages, including children. PFAFF Machines.

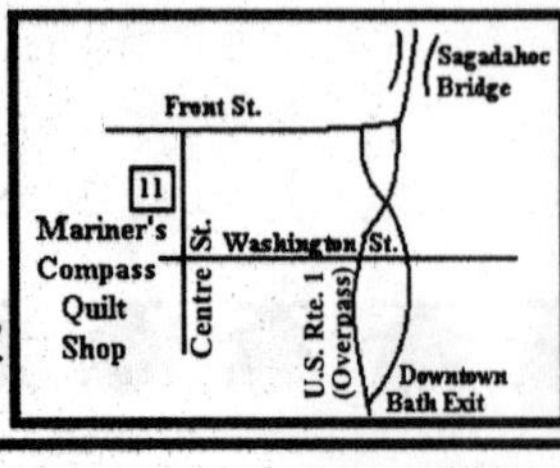

Rockland, ME #4

Mon - Sat 9 - 6
Sun 12 - 5

Fabric Bonanza

195 Park St., Rt. 1 04841
(207) 594-2555 Fax: (207) 594-2556
E-Mail: info@fabfabrics.com
Web Site: www.fabfabrics.com
Owners: Joel & Barbara Fishman
Est: 1976 8000 sq.ft. 2500 Bolts

Over 2500 bolts of 100% cotton top quality quilting fabric, supplies, books and patterns.
Located on Route 1 in Mid-Coast Maine.

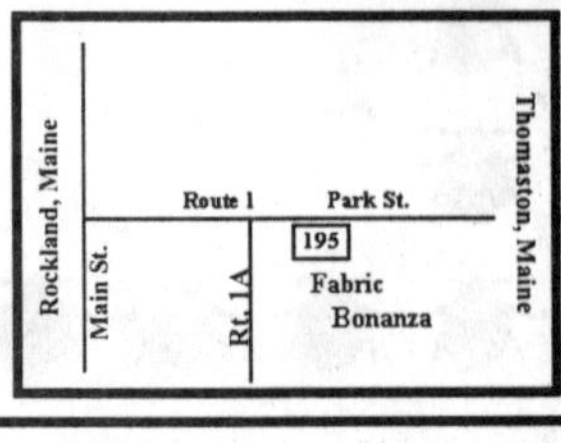

EVERYTHING QUILTERS NEED

PineTree Quiltworks is a full service quilt shop that also offers quilting supplies via mail order catalog.

When you visit Maine, visit PineTree. Only a few minutes from I-295, Pine Tree's a great place to stock up on vacation quilting supplies.

Store Hours:
Mon - Fri
10 - 4:30
Tues til 8:30
Sat 10 - 2

fabric, of course • 100% cotton sewing & quilting thread • machine quilting supplies synthetic & natural-fiber batts • hoops & hoops on stands • measuring tools & rulers value viewers • design mirrors • basting systems • pencils & markers • note cards rippers • clippers • snippers • scissors • fabric care products, including Retayne, Synthrapol, Orvus Quilt Soap and Conservator's Choice™ acid-free tissue paper • paper foundations • patterns . . . and interested quilters who'll answer questions & help with fabric selection

PineTree Quiltworks

South Portland, ME #5

585 Broadway 04106
Shop: (207) 799-9535 Mail Order: (207) 799-7357
E-mail us: pinetree@quiltworks.com
Web Site: www.quiltworks.com

DIRECTIONS

From I - 295: Take exit 6A to Forest Avenue South. Bear right off the exit; follow signs to Route 77. You'll be on State Street; bear right at the bottom of the hill and cross the bridge into South Portland. You'll be on Broadway. Watch on your left; PineTree is immediately after Dunkin Donut and Biddeford Savings Bank before you reach the first set of lights. LOOKING FORWARD TO SEEING YOU!

Knight's

A Working Quilt and Gift Shop

1901 US Route One
03902
(207) 361-2500
Fax: (207) 361-2501
quilts@cybertours.com

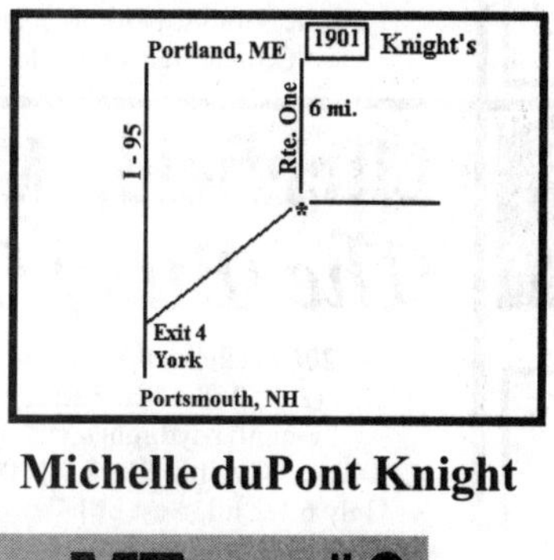

Michelle duPont Knight

We are open year round
Mon-Sat 10-5
Sunday 12-5

Cape Neddick, ME #6

Pull up in front of a New England cape with a porch waiting for you to sit a spell, and you know you're in for a treat. The moment you walk in the door, you'll realize that we're not your ordinary quilt shop.

We have over 3000 bolts of top-name fabrics like Hoffman, RJR, and Alexander Henry, so the shop is always a feast for the eye. We have over 500 books and patterns, notions, and samples to inspire you. But you'll remember our service long after you've made your purchase. Our knowledgeable staff will walk you through each aspect of your project. You can also choose from our many classes to try something new, or to perfect the skills you have.

In addition to wonderful quilt supplies, we have a wide assortment of New England gifts, original dried floral arrangements, and artwork from right here in York.

Knight's is a friendly place where each new customer is treated like an old friend.

Camden, ME #7

Mon - Sat 10 - 5

QUILTERS COTTAGE

75 Union St.
04843
(207) 236-2933
Fax: Same
E-Mail: Quiltcttge@aol.com
Owner: Martha McSweeney Brower

Maine made quilts and pillows. Oil Cloths; Kona Cotton Solids; Cotton Prints; Applique Supplies; Books; Kits; Patterns; Notions; etc.

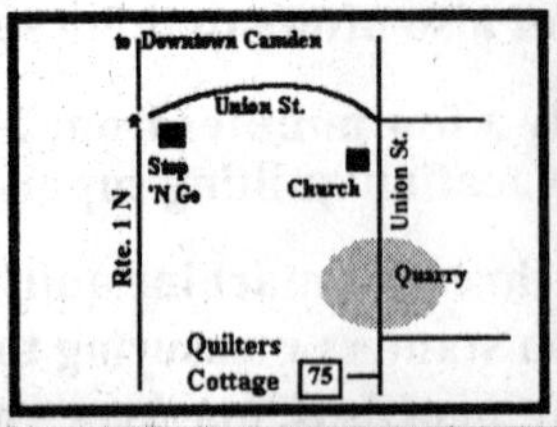

Belfast, ME #8

Nancy's Sewing Center

The "BIG" Little Quilt Shop in Belfast

216 Belmont Ave. 04915
(207) 338-1205
Owner: Nancy E. Black
Est: 1984 1200 sq.ft.
E-Mail: quiltfab@mint.net

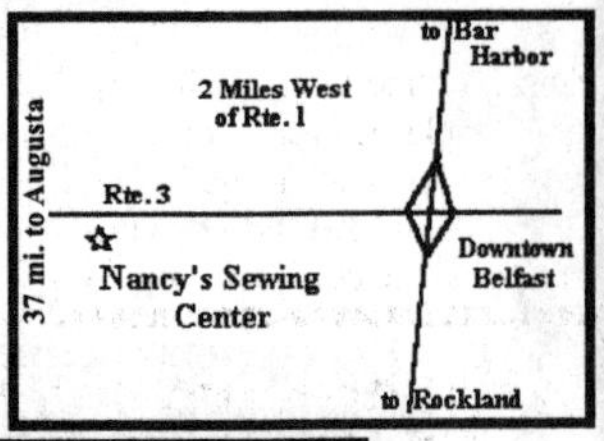

Mon - Fri 9 - 5 Weekends 10 - 4

1500 Bolts of 100% cotton top quality quilting fabrics, quilting supplies, books, patterns, threads, Machine Quilting, Quilt Show every October
www.nancyssewingcenter.com

Trenton, ME #9

Mon - Fri 9:30 - 6 Sat 9:30 - 5

Sewing by the Sea, Inc.

11 Periwinkle Lane 04605
(207) 664-2558 Fax: (207) 664-2560
E-Mail: sewing@midmaine.com
2000 sq.ft.

Downeast Maine's Sewing Resource
Quilt Cottons, Polartec™, Kwik Sew Patterns, Maine themed kits. Pfaff Dealer.

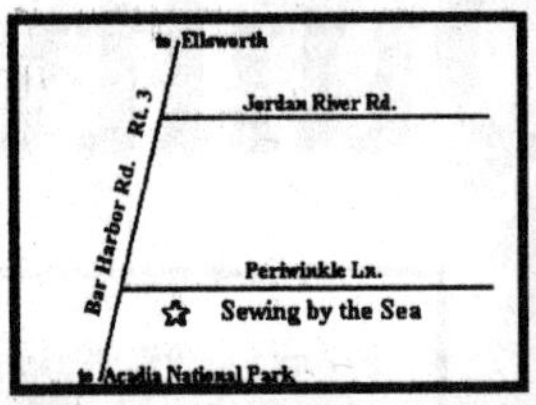

Machias, ME #10

Tues - Sat 10 - 4

Gingham Fabrics

Route 1 East
Mail: Box 286, Cutler, ME 04626
(207) 255-8238
Owner: Linda M. Throckmorton
Est: 1977 1700 sq.ft.

Eastern most quilt shop in the USA. Look for the geodesic dome midway between Ellsworth and Calais.

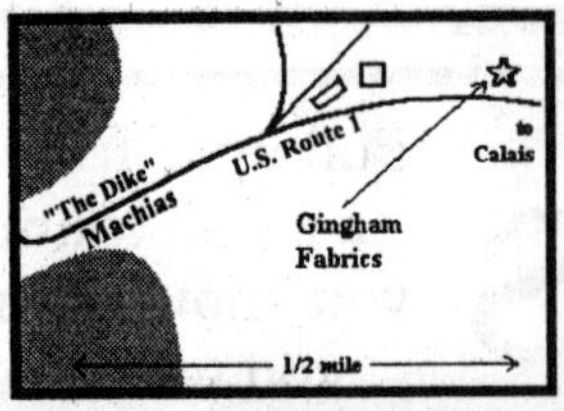

Hermon, ME #11

Call for Hours

"David's Wife", A Quilt Shop

Coldbrook Rd. 04401
(207) 848-7222

We occupy white farm buildings in a lovely country setting, but it is only a few miles from Bangor. Fabric lines include RJR, Bali's by Island Batik, Princess Mirah and Hoffman. Northcott including the State Flower Collection, Benartex and many others. Books and patterns, both new and popular, are in stock. Classes, clubs and workshops year round.

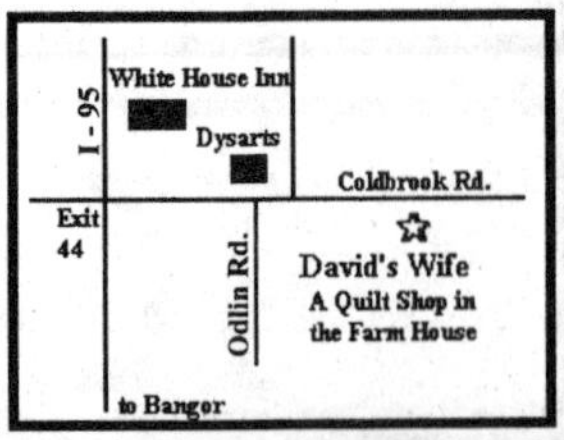

Madison, ME #12

Mon - Fri 9 - 6 Sat 9 - 5 Sun 12 - 5

The Fabric Garden

413 Wilton Rd. 04950
(207) 474-9628
Web Site: www.fabricgarden.com
Owner: Michaela Murphy
Est: 1978 2400 sq.ft.

The store for all your sewing and quilting needs. Name brand fabrics, books, patterns & notions. Janome sewing machines sales and service. "A Quilters must stop shop!"

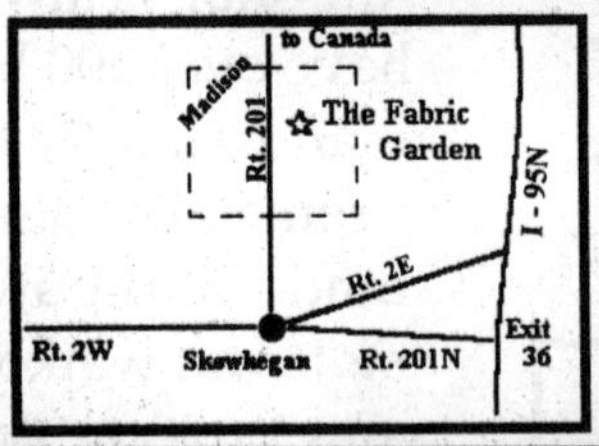

Rangeley, ME #13

Tues - Sat 10 - 5

Threads Galore Quilt Shop

27 Pleasant St., P.O. Box 219 04970
(207) 864-5752 Est: 1996
E-Mail: thrdsglr@netscape.net
Owners: Carol & Dan Perkins

Hand guided Machine quilting.
Fabric, Books, Notions, Classes.
Quilted items for sale.

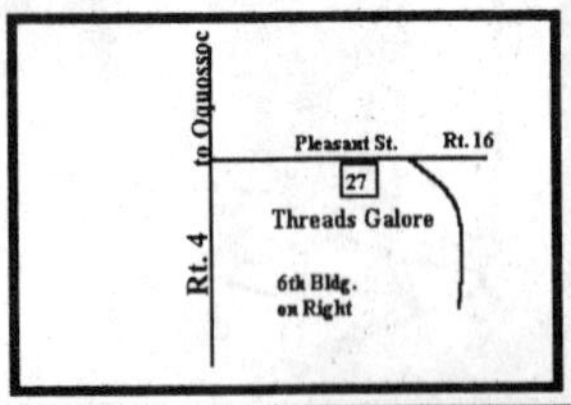

Farmington, ME #14

Mon - Sat 9 - 5 Sun 11 - 3

Fabric Inn

R.R. #4, Box 5057 04938
(207) 778-4288
Est: 1976 2000 sq.ft.

The store for all your sewing and quilting needs. Name brand fabrics, books, patterns & notions. New Home sewing machines sales and service.

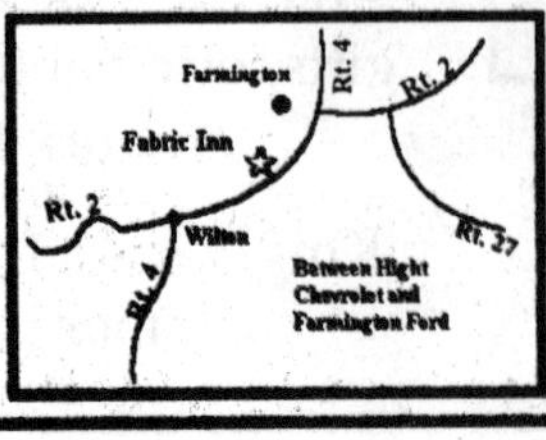

Litchfield, ME #15

Mon - Sat 10 - 4 Sun by chance

The Busy Thimble

2040 Hallowell Rd. 04350
(207) 268-4581 Est: 1990
e-mail: bsythmbl@ctel.net
Owner: Cynthia Black 1000 sq.ft.
Only 6 1/2 mi. west of I - 95, Exit 28

More than 1500 bolts of antique reproduction fabric and homespuns.
Complete Library & Notions galore!

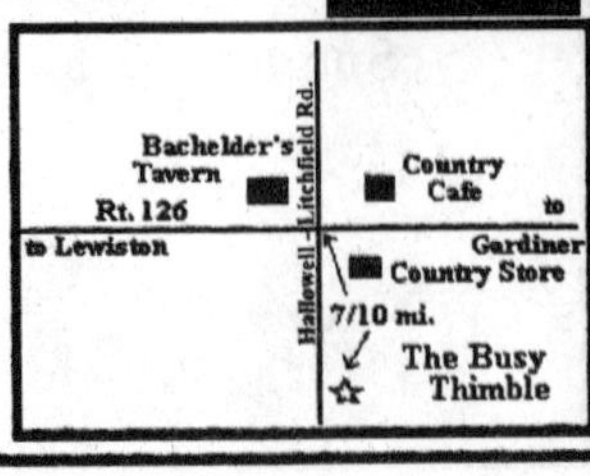

Waterville, ME #16

Tues - Sat 10 - 5

Cherie's Quilting Loft

10 Railroad Sq. 04901
(207) 873-9606
E-Mail: quilting@midmaine.com
Owner: Cherie Millett

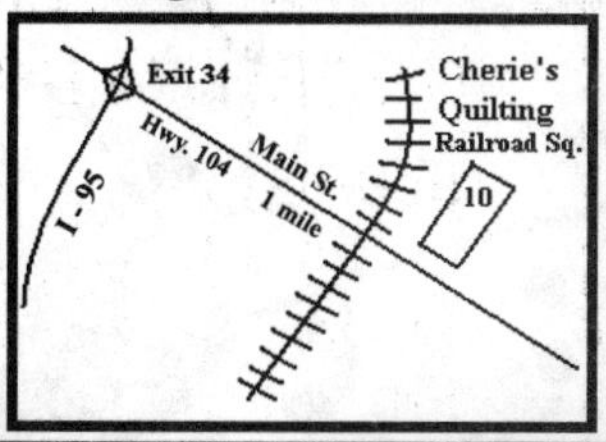

Your non-traditional quilt shop, specializing in tools, books & classes of the latest techniques. Professional machine quilting, quilted items for sale. Sales of Pfaff sewing & embroidery machines. Sales & Education of Handi-Quilter

Dixfield, ME #17

**Tues 9:30-8
Wed - Fri 9:30 - 5
Sat 9:30 - 1**

Log Cabin Craftworks

31 Main St. on U.S. Route 2 04224
Phone/fax: (207) 562-8816
Owner: Norine Clarke
Est: 1981 550 bolts 2500 sq. ft.

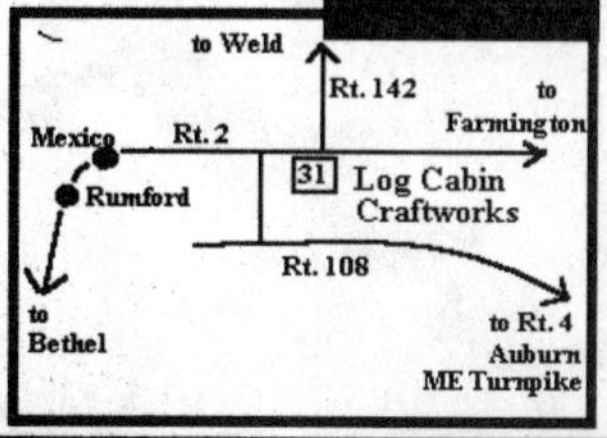

Located in the foothills of Western Maine for over 20 years, we offer supplies for quilting, counted cross stitch, rubber stamping, scrapbooking, painting crafts and more.

Waterford, ME #18

**Mon - Sat 9:30 - 6
Sun 10 - 5**

Kedar Quilts

Rt. 35, Box 61 04088
(207) 583-6182 Fax: (207) 583-6424
E-Mail: kedarburn@cyberlours.com Est: 1989
Web Site: members.aol.com/kedar01
Owner: Margaret Gibson 1000 Bolts

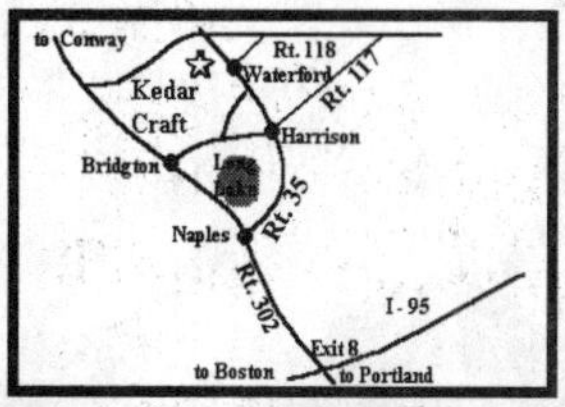

Fine 100% Cotton Fabrics, Notions, Classes, Books. FOR SALE: New Quilts, Wallhangings and much more. Quilt Weekends and Retreats. Located at Kedarburn Inn.

Harrison, ME #19

Wed - Sat 10 - 4

Home Sweet Home Quilts

Rt. 117, 15 Main St., P.O. Box 221 04040
(207) 583-0914
E-Mail: theugos@megalink.net
Owner: Beth Ugosoli
New larger showroom

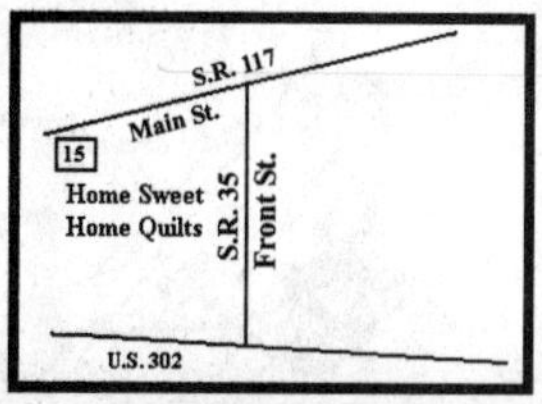

100% top quality cotton fabric, books, patterns, notions, gifts, classes; antique and new quilts for sale.

Auburn, ME #20

**Mon - Fri 10 - 6
Sat 10 - 4**

Quiltessentials

909 Minot Ave. 04210
(207) 784-4486 Est: 1994
Web Site: www.quilt-essentials.com

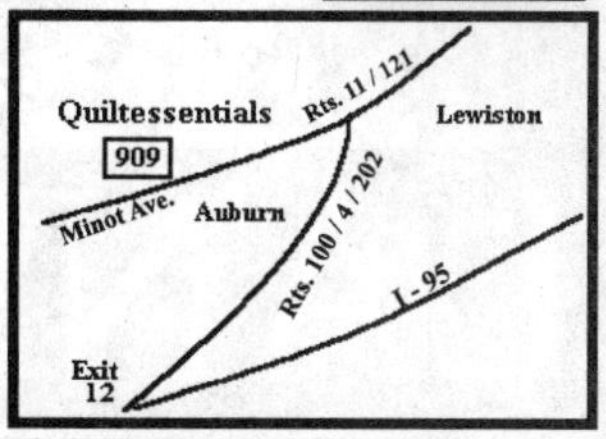

Full line of Quilt and Basket Making supplies & classes. Unique selection of 100% cotton fabrics, books & notions. Handmade Baskets including quilting baskets. Yarn & Knitting Supplies.

Windham, ME #21

**Mon - Fri 9:30-4:30
Tues til 8
Sat 9:30-4
Sun 11 - 3**

Calico Basket Quilt Shop

31 Page Road 04062
(207) 892-5606
E-Mail: CalicoBasketQlt@aol.com
Owner: JoAnne Hill
Est: 1982 1300 sq.ft.

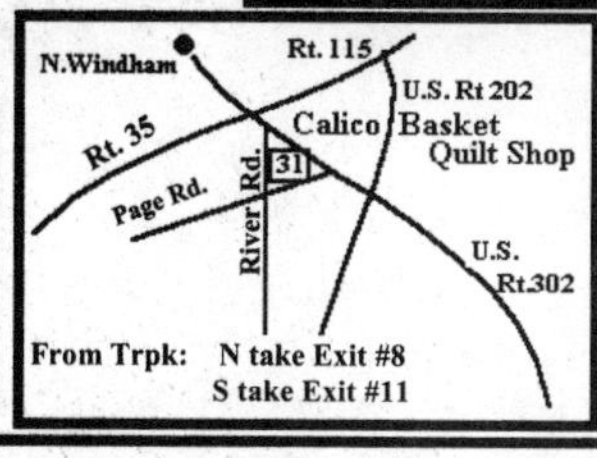

Over 5000 Top Quality Fabrics. The Latest Books, Notions, Craft Patterns, and Quilting Supplies.

Other Shops in Maine: We suggest calling first

Freeport	Quilt & Needlecrafts, 22 Main St. R.R. #1	207-865-3224
Harrison	Jan's Golden Needle, 24 Zakelo Rd.	207-583-2654
Jefferson	Country Creations, Route 32, P.O. Box 949	207-549-7424
Kennebunk	Mainely Quilts, 108 Summer St.	207-985-4250
Lincoln	Dot's Fabric Shop, 184 Main St.	207-794-2945
Lisbon Falls	Anne Virginia Quilt Co., 13 Union St.	207-353-3079
Lisbon Falls	Mill Fabric Center, 2 Ridge	207-353-8421
New Harbor	Duck's, 2634 Bristol Rd.	207-677-3741
Newcastle	Alewives Fabrics, R.R. #1, Box 480	207-563-5002
Newport	Robyn's Nest Fabrics, Rt. 7	207-368-2419
North Edgecomb	On BoardRoute, 27 Booth Bay Rd.	207-882-7536
Pittsfield	Quilter's Dream, 9 Easy St.	207-938-3524
Saco	Patchwork Boutique Quilt Shop, 304 Beach St.	207-284-7287
Sidney	Mystic Maine Quilts, Middle Rd.	207-547-4331
Wiscasset	The Marston House, P.O. Box 517	207-882-6010

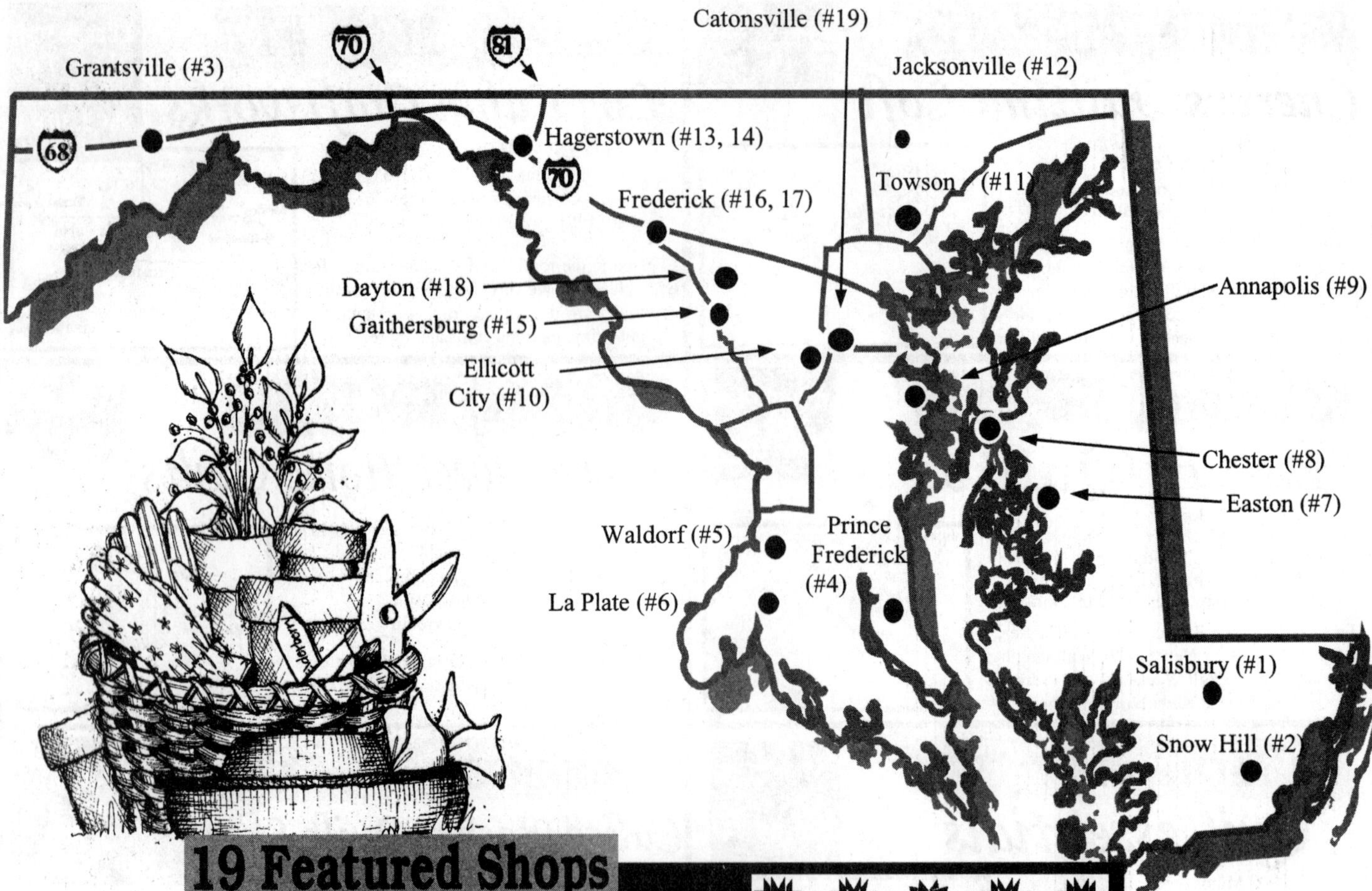

19 Featured Shops

MARYLAND

Salisbury, MD #1

Mon - Sat 10 - 6

Jenny's Sewing Studio

311 Civic Ave. 21804
(410) 543-1212
E-Mail: jenny@shore.intercom.net
Web-Site: www.jennys-sewing-studio.com
Owner: Jennifer Friedel
Est: 1982 3200 sq.ft.

Full service quilt shop & sewing machine dealer. (New Home, Singer, Babylock, Janome) Over 2000 bolts of fabric and approx. 20 classes offered.

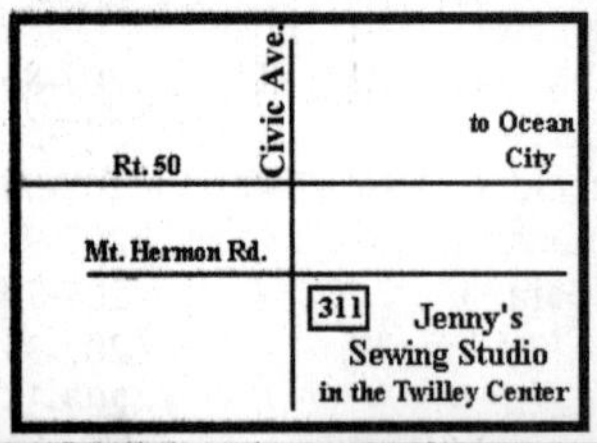

Snow Hill, MD #2

Tues - Sat 10 - 5

The Fine Needle

121 South Dr. 21863
(410) 632-0772 Fax: (410) 632-0150
E-Mail: quilts@fineneedle.com
Web Site: www.fineneedle.com
Owners: Ingrid Claflin & Stacy Mitchell

Fine fabric, fine gifts, and friendly service. Special one day summer seminars for the traveling quilter.

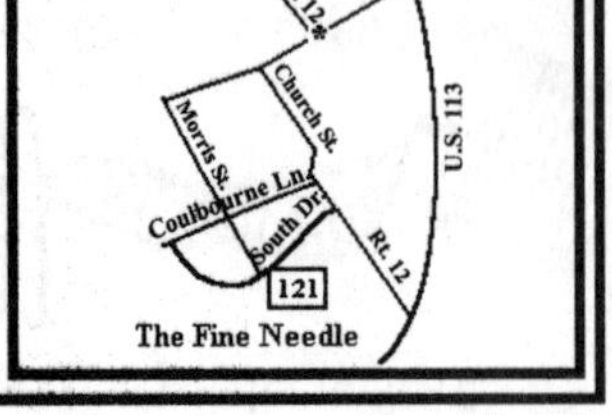

Grantsville, MD #3

Mon - Sat 9 - 5

Four Seasons Stitchery

P.O. Box 218 116 Main St. 21536
(301) 895-5958
Owner: Jane Benson
Est: 1985

Most Complete Quilting Shop in the Tri-State area. Over 1000 bolts all cotton fabrics. Books, Notions & Cross Stitch Supplies.

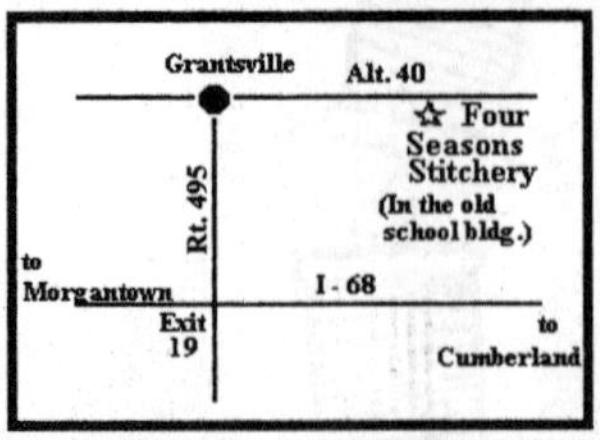

Prince Frederick, MD #4

Calvert Quilt Shoppe

Mon - Thur
9 - 6
Fri to 7
Sat 9 - 4

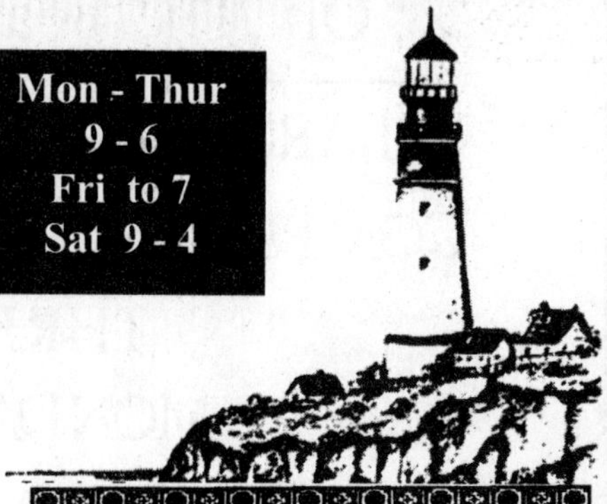

MD Rt. 4 at 20 Industry Lane 20678
(410) 535-0576 Fax: (410) 535-1197
E-Mail: marti@softhome.net
Est: 1966 5000+ Bolts

We carry major manufacturers of Quilting Products.
100% Cotton, Name Brand Fabrics, Notions, Quilting Classes.
Janome Sewing Machine Sales and Service.

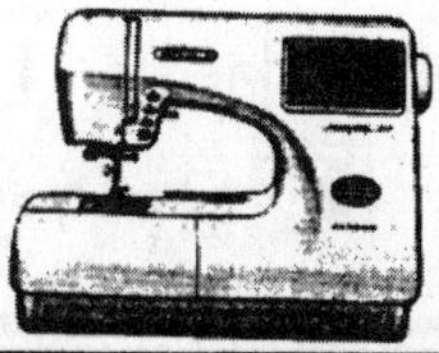

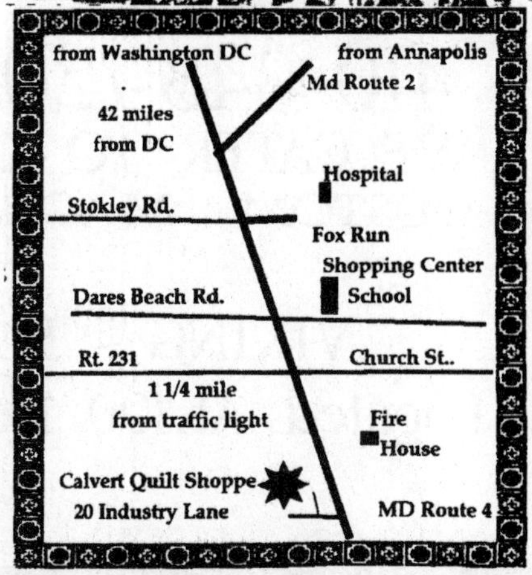

Waldorf, MD #5

Mon - Sat
10 - 5
Thur til 8
(1st Sun each month Sept 1 to May 1)

Cheasapeake Bay Quilting

12096 Ell Ln., Bus. Rt. 5 20602
(301) 638-5300 or (877) 227-1354
E-Mail: cbquilting@cs.com
Owner: Nancy Gorski

Located in historic southern Maryland - a friendly shop offering a full complement of quilting fabric, notions, books, patterns & classes.

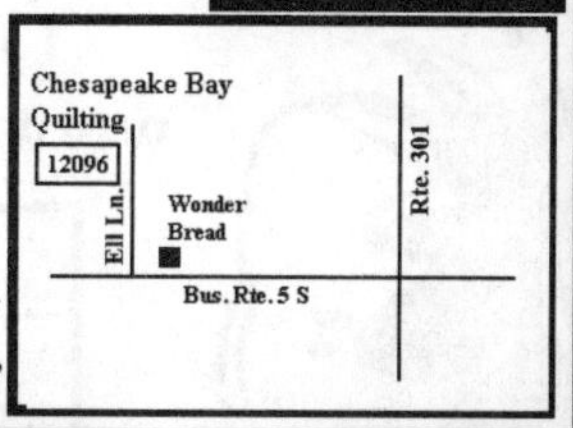

Easton, MD #7

Mon - Sat
10 - 5

Lilies of the Field
101 Marlboro Ave.
Easton Plaza
Easton, MD 21601
410-822-9117

Web Site: www.sew 2000.com/lilies-field
Owner: Regina Chapman

Fine Fabrics, notions, trims, books and classes for the discriminating woman who sews.

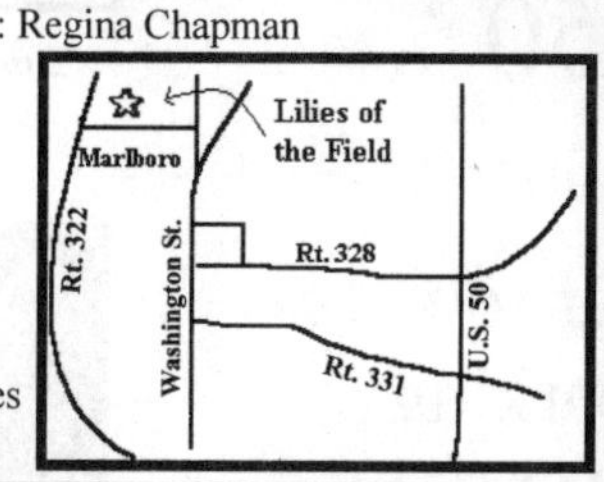

La Plata, MD #6

"Potomac Square"
9375 Chesapeake St. #113 20646
(301) 392-9575

"Feel at Home" at My Sew-N-Room. Over 1000 bolts of fabric from the major suppliers and designers. We have an excellent selection of books, notions, and patterns. Block of the Month's and Kits are Available. We have completed quilts for purchase.

Tues 10 - 8
Wed - Fri 10 - 6
Sat 10 - 4

Fax: (301) 392-9576
Owners:
Patricia & Gary Foster
E-mail:
shop@mysewnroom.com

Visit Us at: www.mysewnroom.com

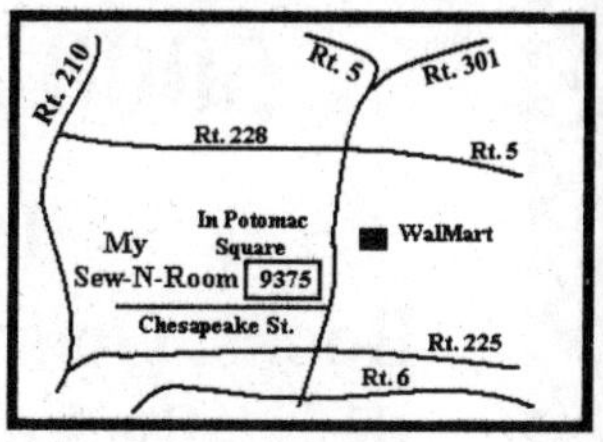

Peggy's Sewing Center LTD.

On The Beautiful Eastern Shore Of Maryland

LARGE SELECTION OF 100% COTTON FABRIC
COMPLETE LINE OF NOTIONS & QUILT SUPPLIES
THREADS & MORE THREADS
MONDAY thru FRIDAY 10AM~6PM
SAT 10AM~4PM

410~643~7202
WE CATER TO QUILTERS
CUSTOM MACHINE QUILTING AVAILABLE

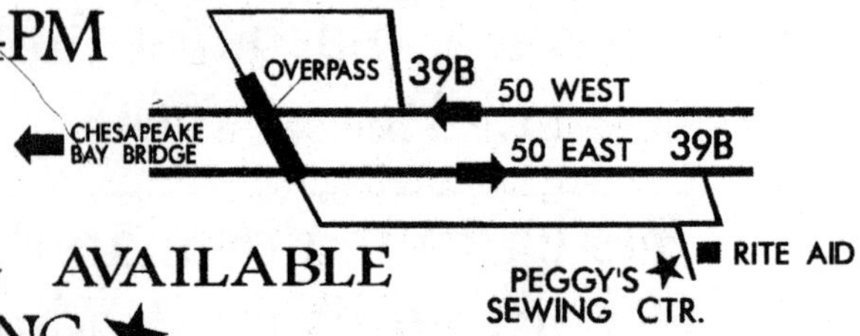

★ FEATURING ★
VIKING ~ ELNA ~ JANOME ~ SEWING MACHINES
Located At 100 Helfenbein Lane Suite 110 Chester Md 21619

Chester, MD #8

Cottonseed Glory

Est: 1978

Annapolis, MD #9

4 Annapolis St. 21401
(410) 263-3897
Owner: Pat Steiner
www.cottonseedglory.com

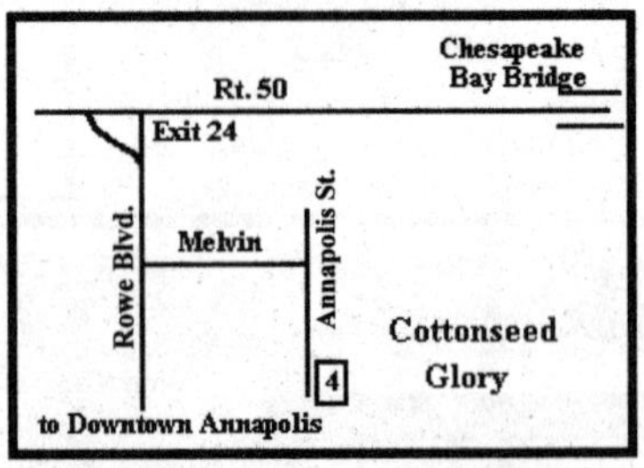

1/2 miles from U.S. Naval Academy & Historic area of Annapolis

5000 bolts from over 50 manufacturers.

Books, Gourmet Notions, Classes year round
Friendly, knowledgeable help, free parking.
PATTERNS, PATTERNS, PATTERNS!

Mon - Sat 10 - 5
Sundays 1 - 4
(No Sun hours June - Aug)

Visit Both Locations

BEAR'S PAW FABRICS

Towson, MD #11

8812 Orchard Tree Lane 21286
(410) 321-6730
(800) 761-2202
695 to Exit 29B (Loch Raven Blvd.)
-right on Joppa Rd.
-right on Orchard Tree Lane
-5th store on left

Ellicott City, MD #10

8659 Baltimore National Pike (Rt. 40)
(410) 480-2875 21043
(888) 877-4898
695 to Exit 15B (Route 40 W)
-Rt. 40 West to Ridge Rd (Howard Cty)
-U-turn at Ridge
-Store immediately on right

FINE SELECTION OF QUILTING FABRICS, NOTIONS, PATTERNS, BOOKS AND BUTTONS.

Just a pretty country drive north of Baltimore!

Stitches Etc, Inc.

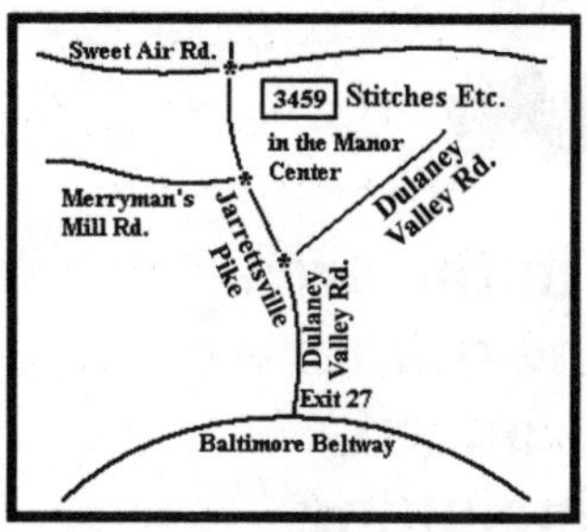

Jacksonville, MD #12

Manor Shopping Center
3459 Sweet Air Rd.
(Mail: P.O. Box 266,
Phoenix, MD 21131)
410-667-9522

Store hours;
Tuesday - Friday
11:00 am--5:30 pm
Saturday
11 am--4 pm
Evening hours by appointment for your convenience!

3,000 bolts of quality quilting fabrics, specializing in novelties, 1930's and civil war reproductions.
A THANGLES shop--
stocking all sizes and patterns.
Authorized Janome, Elna, and Singer sales and service.

Wilson Sew & Vac, *Your Favorite Quilt Shop*, offers:

- Over 1,000 bolts of fine, quality fabrics by suppliers including Thimbleberries, RJR, Moda, Hoffman and many more
- A large selection of books and patterns
- Finished quilts, wallhangings with fabric kits available

Hagerstown, MD #13

WILSON Sew & Vac *Your Favorite Quilt Shop.*

21680 Leitersburg Pike
Hagerstown, MD 21742 (301) 790-3526

STORE HOURS: Mon., Tues., Thurs., & Fri. 9 a.m. - 5 p.m. • Sat. 9 a.m. - 2 p.m. • Wed. CLOSED

Hagerstown, MD #14

Traditions at the White Swan

Authorized Bernina Dealer

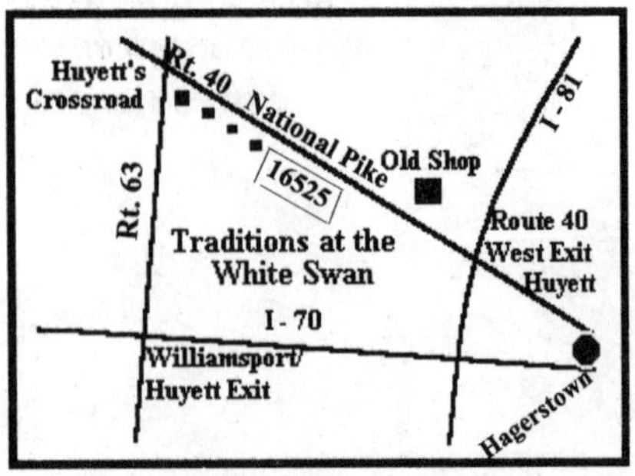

3½ miles West of town

Largest Quilt Shop in the area with everything for the quilter— beginner thru advanced.
2500 bolts of fabric including— Hoffman, RJR, P&B, Benartex, Marcus Brothers & Mums the Word.
Notions, Books, Patterns, Stencils, & Classes

June - Aug
Tues - Sat 10 - 5
Sept - May
Mon - Sat 10 - 5
Sun 1 - 5

16525 National Pike 21740
(301) 733-9130 Est: 1985
Owners: Dick & Wendy Shank 1700 sq.ft.

Gaithersburg, MD #15

Mon - Sat 10 - 6
Sun 12 - 5
Class Eve.

15926 Luanne Dr. 20877
(301) 527-0598 Est: 1995 2500 sq.ft.
Owners: Susan & Gary McLaughlin

CAPITAL QUILTS

Great selection of high quality fabric and a full range of necessities and niceties for the quilter. The largest selection of books in the area, we feature patterns by local artists. We're proud of our many classes. Service is friendly & helpful. Bring in your 'Problem Pieces'. Easy Access by Public Trans.

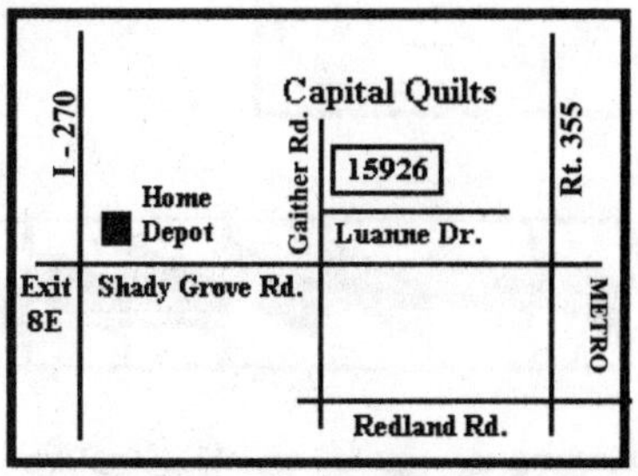

We Are Very Easy to Find!

Needles & Pins

FREDERICK MARYLAND'S PREMIER QUILTING, STITCHERY AND DOLLMAKING SHOP

An independent shop specializing in top-quality fabrics, including flannels and reproduction prints.

We have the region's largest selection of patterns for a wide variety of cloth and whimsical dolls, Santas, snowmen, animals, quilts, wallhangings, clothing and stitchery.

Many models on display!

www.needles-n-pins.com

310 East Church Street
Frederick, Maryland 21701

Open 7 Days a Week

Call for shop hours and directions!

301-695-7199
1-877-695-7199
Toll free

Kunin Felts and Hobbs' Battings

Books, Notions, Stencils, and Kits

Individual Instruction Available

10% Guild and ASG Discounts Everyday

Hundreds of Holiday Patterns and Accessory Items

Homespun Towels in many patterns for decorating

Frederick, MD #16

Frederick, MD #17

Sisto's Sewing & Quilting

Mon - Sat 10 - 6
Mon & Thur 10 - 8

1911 N. Market 21701
(301) 695-0643 Fax: (301) 695-1653
E-Mail: sistosquilting@erols.com
Owner: Linda M. Sisto
5,200 sq.ft. 5,000+ Bolts

Fabrics, Patterns, Books, Notions. Brand names: RJR, Hoffman, Moda, Kauffman. Authorized dealer for Bernina, Brother, Janome and Singer Sewing Machines.

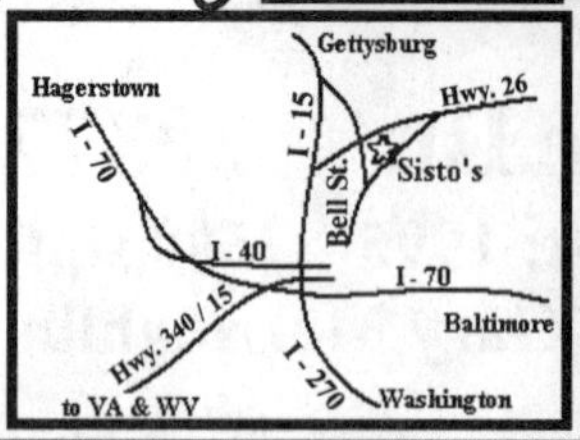

Dayton, MD #18

4714 Linthicum Rd. 21036
(410) 531-5723 or (877) GO-QUILT
E-mail: diane@thequiltblock.com
Web Site: www.thequiltblock.com
Owner: Diane Janoske Est: 1995

The Quilt Block

Mon - Sat 10 - 5
Tues & Thur Til 8

- Friendly, knowledgeable staff
- Classes (2 classrooms)
- 200+ Books, Patterns
- Notions wall
- 1800+ bolts
- Free Newsletter
- Multiple Block of Month Programs
- Mail Order Available
- Longarm Machine Quilting Service Avail.

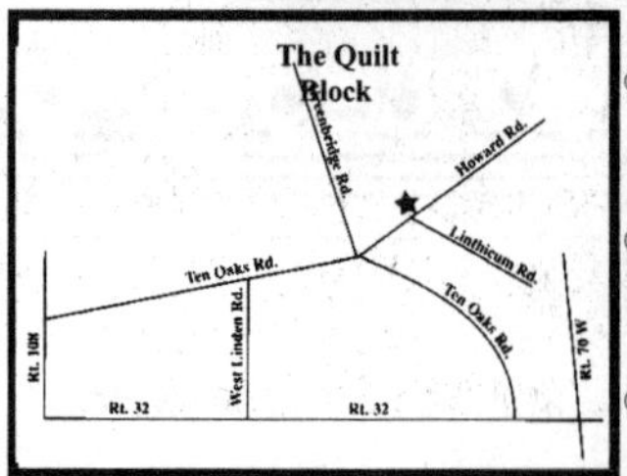

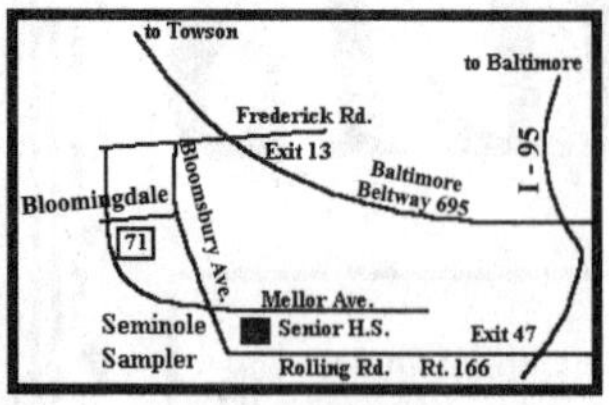

- Fine Cotton Fabrics
- Quilting Books and Patterns
- Quilting and Sewing Notions
- Batting and Supplies
- Unique Block of the Month Patterns
- Wearable Art Patterns
- Classes for Every Level

SEMINOLE SAMPLER

71 Mellor Ave. 21228
(410) 788-1720
E-Mail: seminolesampler@erols.com
Web Site: www.seminolesampler.com

Mon & Thur: 10 - 8
Tue, Wed, Fri, Sat: 10 - 5
Sun: 1 - 5

3600+ sq.ft. of quilt store featuring more than 4000 bolts of fine cotton fabrics; especially known for extensive collections of solid color, batik, contemporary and oriental fabrics. Excellent offering of books and patterns, notions and supplies. Regularly scheduled classes in every aspect of quilting, for all levels of experience. Service oriented staff cheerfully willing to assist with all quilt project needs. Guild discount on Mondays.

Catonsville, MD #19

Other Shops in Maryland: We suggest calling first

Baltimore Blanks, 6709 A Whitestone Rd.
Baltimore Harbor Quilting, 3500 Parkdale Ave. 410-462-4022
Baltimore Baltimore Museum of Art / Textile Gallery Art Museum 301-396-6266
Bethesda Amish Quilts, 7910 Kentbury Dr. 301-656-1644
Boonsboro Old School Fabrics, 230 Potomac 301-432-6195
Easton American Pennyroyal, 5 N. Harrison St. 410-822-5030
Flintstone Cathy's Country Quilts, 12712 Murleys Branch Rd. NE 301-478-2589
Fruitland The Dusty Attic, 301 S. Division St. 410-546-1656
Fulton Quilt Studio, Inc., P.O. Box 243 301-490-3544
Harwood Sunflower Hill Dyers, 510 Polling House 301-261-5790
New Market American Quilts & Coverlets, 18 E. Main St.
Oakland Not Just Quilts, 210 E. Alder St.
Pocomoke City D & E Fabrics, 1527 Ocean Hwy. 410-957-2337
Potomac Stella Rubin Antiques, 12300 Glen Rd. 301-948-4187
Rockville Anna Marie's Fashion Fabrics, 2011 Veirs Mill Rd. 301-762-8491
Rockville G Street Fabrics, 11854 Rockville Pike 301-231-8998
Upper Marlboro Stitches & Sew On, 9020 Trumps Hill Rd. 301-627-2990

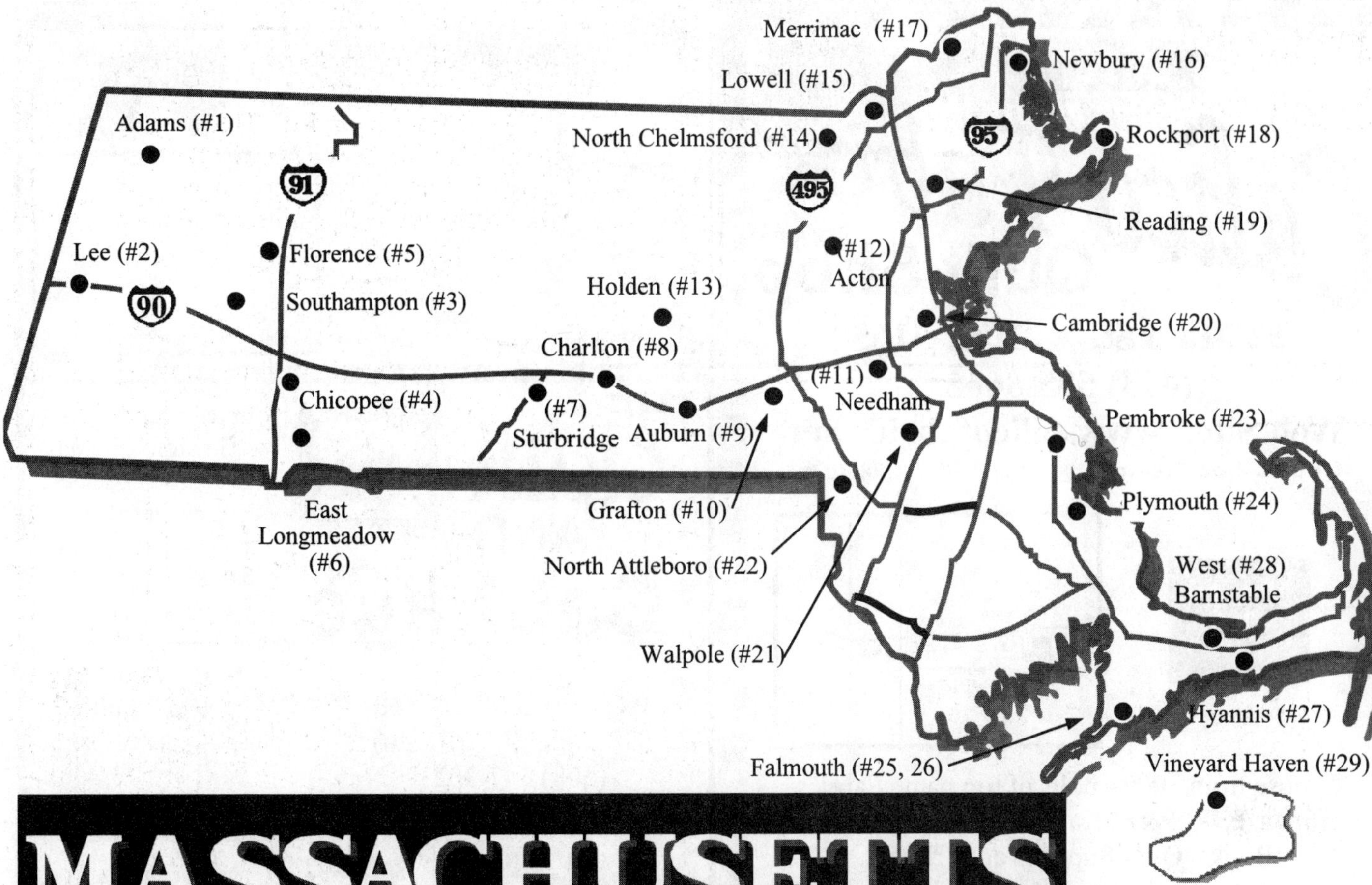

MASSACHUSETTS

29 Featured Shops

Adams, MA #1

Mon - Sat 10 - 5 Thur til 9

A Stitch in Time

21 B Park St. 01220
(413) 743-7174
E-Mail: a_stitchintime@yahoo.com
Est: 1996

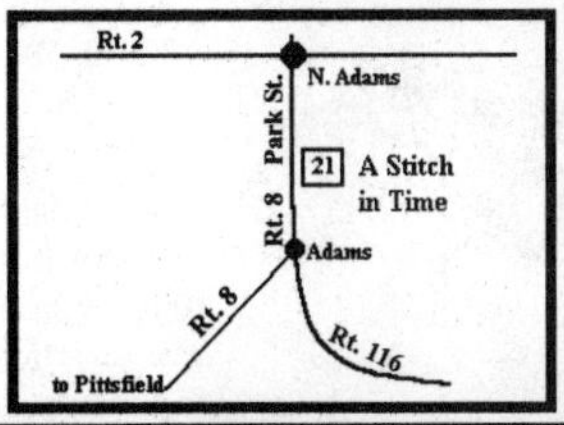

Great selection of 100% Cotton Fabrics "To Die For". Quilting Supplies, Books, Gifts and Quilts. Variety of Yarns, Patterns and Needles.

Lee, MA #2

Mon - Sat 10 - 6 Sun 12 - 6

Pumpkin Patch

58 W. Center St. (Rt. 20)
(413) 243-1635 01238
Owners: Susan & Dan Sullivan
Est: 1985 800 sq.ft.

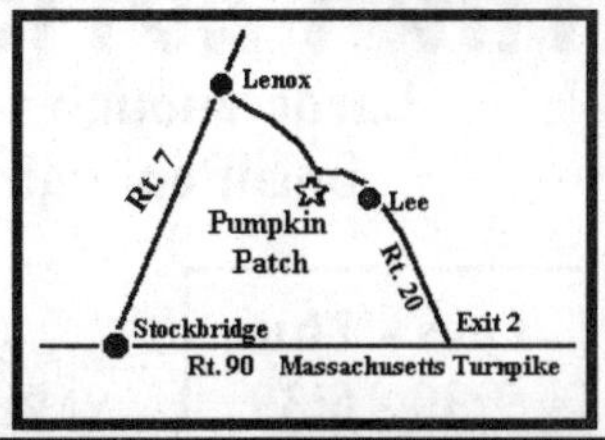

Located in the beautiful Berkshires!
Cotton fabrics, books, patterns, etc. . . .
Classes, machine quilting . . . .
Bernina Sewing Machines

Southampton, MA #3

Tues - Thur 10 - 8 Fri & Sat 10 - 4 Sun noon - 5

Southampton Quilts

162 College Hwy. 01073
(413) 529-9641
Owners:
Maureen Mason & Nancy Aurnhammer

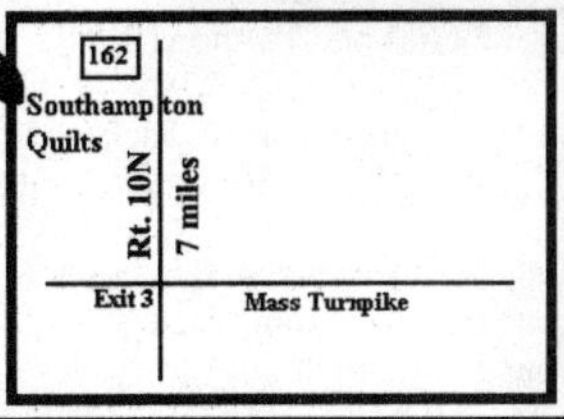

E-Mail: nm@southamptonquilts.com
Web Site: www.southamptonquilts.com
We are a quaint, cozy shop dedicated to all quilters. Easy to get to, friendly welcoming atmosphere.

Chicopee, MA #4

Tues 10 - 4 Wed & Thurs 10-4 & 5:30-8 Sat 10 - 3

Bayberry Quilt & Gift Shoppe

137 Sheridan St. 01020
(413) 592-9653
Web Site: www.bayberryquilts.com
Owner: Laura J. Knapp Est: 1999

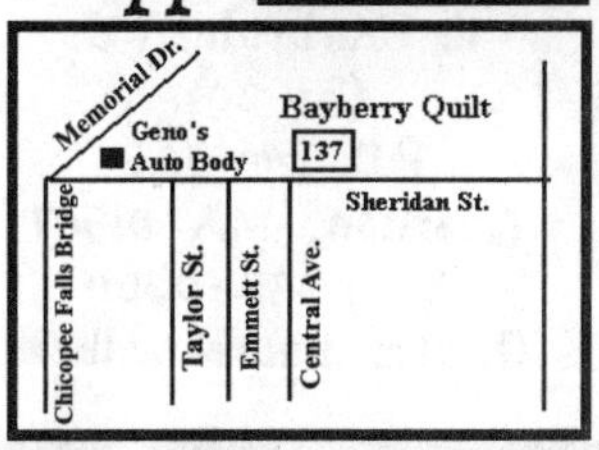

Full line of quilting fabrics, supplies, books & patterns displayed in a 9 room Victorian farm house. Handcrafted gifts, quilts and more. Unique Shop.

Florence, MA #5

Calico Fabric Quilt Shop

52 Main St. 01062-3165
(413) 585-8665
Web Site: www.calicofabric.com
Owner: Joan Trecartin Est: 1980 1000 sq.ft.

Mon - Fri 10 - 5
Sat 10 - 3

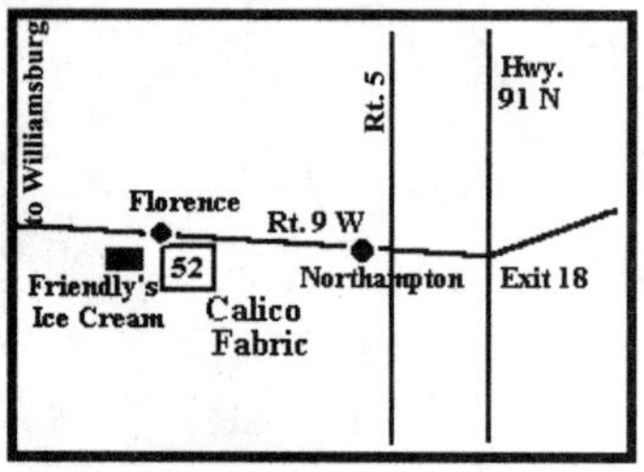

Choose from 3000+ bolts of top name Fabrics.
Hoffman, RJR, P&B, Kaufman, Moda, Kona Bay.
Books, Quilt Supplies and Classes.
Handicapped Accessible

Largest Quilt Shop in the Area!

East Longmeadow, MA #6

Mon - Thur 10 - 9
Fri & Sat 10 - 5
Closed Mondays in July & Aug.

Thimbleworks

Sewing Machine Center

56 Shaker Rd. 01028
(413) 525-4789

Great selection of 100% cotton Fabrics, Books, Patterns & Quilting Supplies. Authorized Pfaff dealer.

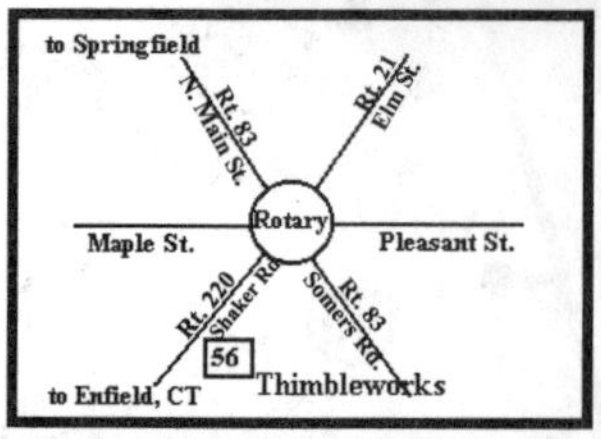

THE Quilt AND Cabbage

P.O. Box 534 01566
538 Main St. (Rt. 20)
(508) 347-3023

Enter a relaxing & warm atmosphere of 1000 bolts - select cottons, homespun, flannels, fleece. Best array of books, patterns, stencils. Custom sweatshirts & quilted items. Leave with inspiration, treasures & a smile!

Sturbridge, MA #7

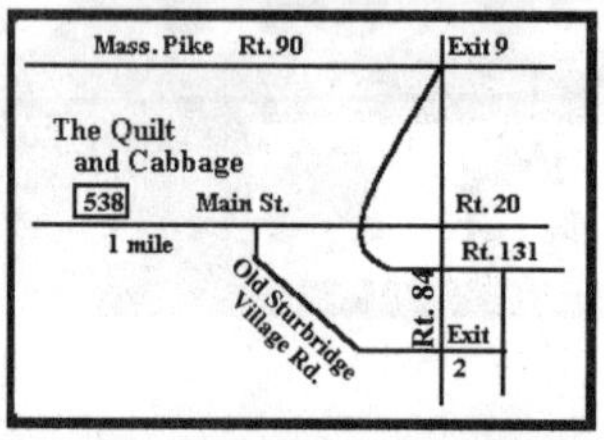

Mon & Wed - Sat 9:30 - 4:30
Sun 11 - 4
Closed Tues

Est: 1991

Charlton, MA #8

The Fabric Stash, Inc.

Large enough for a good selection,
Small enough for good service.

Tues - Thur 9:30 - 6:30
Fri 9:30 - 8
Sat 9:30 - 5
Sun 12:30 - 4

FABRICS for: quilting, clothing, home decorating
YARN, NOTIONS and BUTTONS
CLASSES in: quilting, knitting and sewing.
LONG ARM QUILTING $16. PER SQ. YD.
Edge to edge, stippling or swirls and loops

16 Sturbridge Rd.
(Rt. 20)
P.O. Box 705
Charlton, MA 01507
(508) 248-0600
Owner: Laurel Wilber

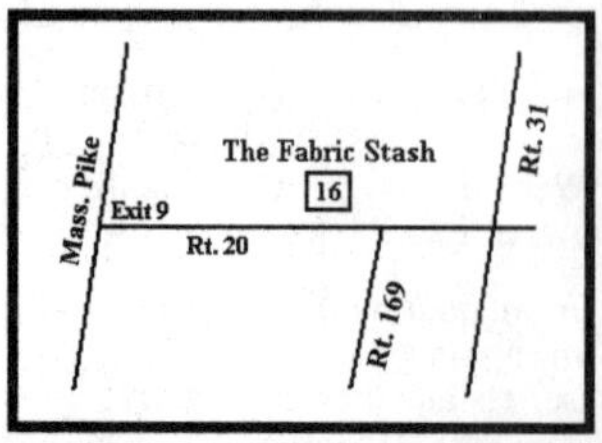

Auburn, MA #9

Mon - Wed 10 - 8
Thur - Sat 10 - 5
(Oct-May)
Sun 12 - 3

Appletree Fabrics

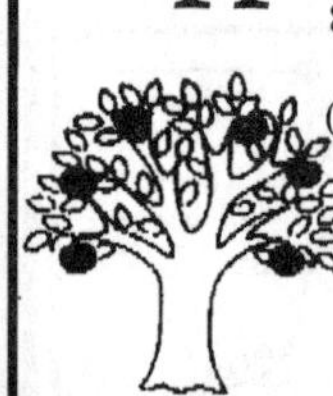

850 Southbridge St. 01501
Rts 12/20, Westside Plaza
(508) 832-5562 Est: 1991
Owner: Lois Therrien

Over 2500 bolts of beautiful cotton prints, solids & homespuns. Large selection of books & patterns. Classes.

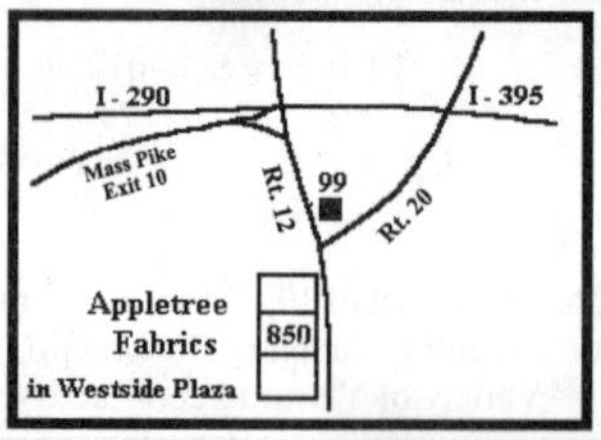

Grafton, MA #10

Tues - Sat 10 - 5
Sun 12 - 5

Calico & Co.

2 Grafton Common (Rear) 01519
(508) 839-5990
Owner: Joanne & Richard Erenius
Est: 1984 1000 sq.ft. 800 Bolts

Helpful & Friendly Service & Supplies for your every Quilting need. Classes to inspire your creativity.

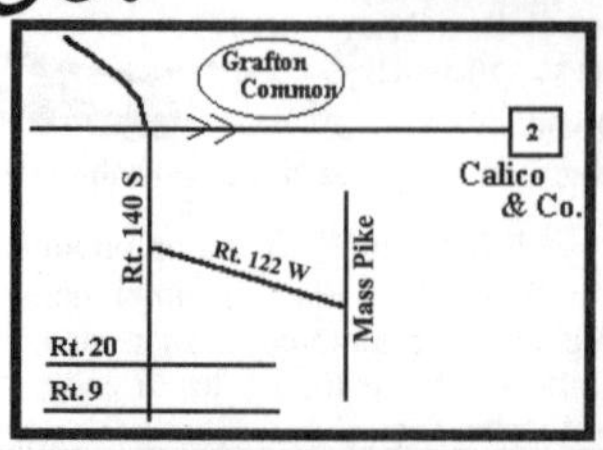

The Button Box Quilt Shop

Needham, MA #11

974 Great Plain Ave., Route #135 02492
781-449-1810 Toll Free 866-iQUILT2 (866-478-4582)
E-Mail: buttonbox@gis.net Est: 1995
Owner: Catherine Gentile 2800 sq.ft. 4000 Bolts
Web Site: www.buttonboxquiltshop.com

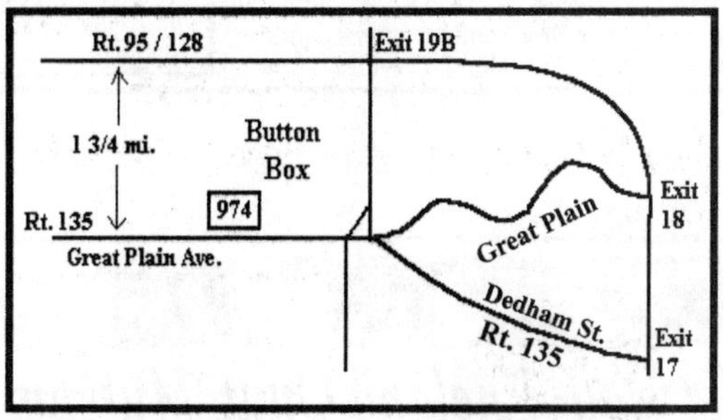

Mon - Sat 9:30 - 5:30
Wed & Thur til 8
Sundays 12 - 5
Sept. thru June

Documentary/Vintage Reproduction and Contemporary Fabrics our Specialty.

Beautiful Japanese Sateens.

The Best Button Shop in Massachusetts.

PFAFF

Authorized Dealer for Pfaff Sewing Machines

Ralph Jordan's

... your Quilt Destination

Everything for your Special Quilting Projects from beginning to end . . . and More.

Over Two Thousand 100% Cotton Prints: Plaids & Solids by Hoffman, RJR, South Seas, Concord, Moda, P&B, Peter Pan, Alexander Henry, Spiegel, Momen House, Benartex, Quilters Only and Hi-Fashion.

A complete selection of quilting books, patterns, templates, stencils, scissors, rotary cutters, mats, hoops and much, much more.

We also offer over 80 classes in quilting and crafts for beginner to advanced students.

Acton, MA #12

254 Great Rd. Rt. 2A
Goulds' Plaza 01720
(978) 263-0606

Tues, Wed, Thur
9:30 - 9:00
Mon, Fri, Sat 9:30 - 5:30
Sunday 12:00 - 5:00

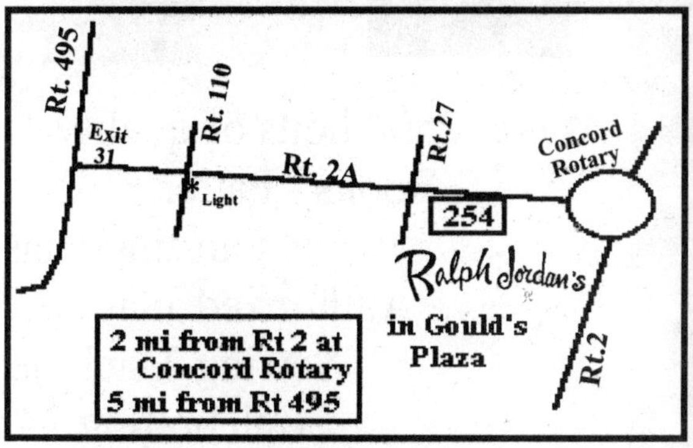

We honor All Quilt Guild Membership cards for 10% off quilt fabric, books and notions. (AQS, NEQG, and EQA included!)

Holden, MA #13

Wed - Sat
10 - 4:30
Thur til 8
June to Aug
Closed Sat

Betsey's Sewing Connection & Quilt Shop

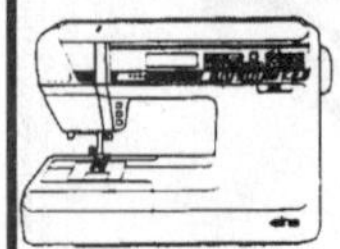

1085A Main St. 01520
(508) 829-6411
E-Mail: betseysquiltshop@yahoo.com
Owner: Betsey Berry
Est: 1973

28 years sharing sewing & quilting knowledge. Excellent cotton fabrics, quilting notions, books. Elna sales & service.

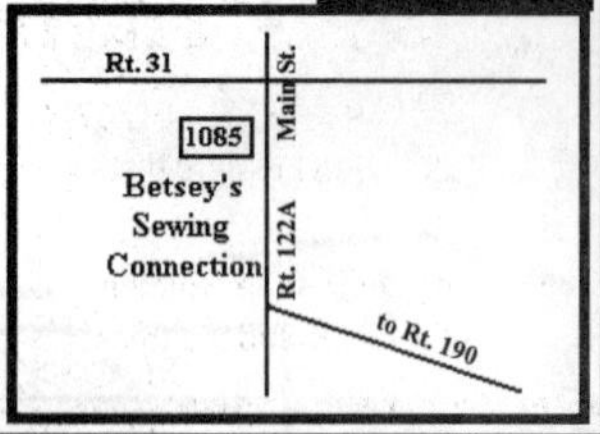

N. Chelmsford, MA #14

Mon - Sat
9:30 - 5
Thurs til 8:30

Mill Girl Quilts

345 North Rd. 01863
(978) 251-8118 Fax: (978) 251-9807
E-Mail: millgirl@ix.netcom.com
Web Site: millgirl.home.netcom.com
Owner: Susan Dillinger
Est: 2000 1800 sq. ft.

Friendly, service-oriented staff. Close by New England Quilt Museum. Over 2400 bolts, books, patterns, notions, classes, machine quilting service.

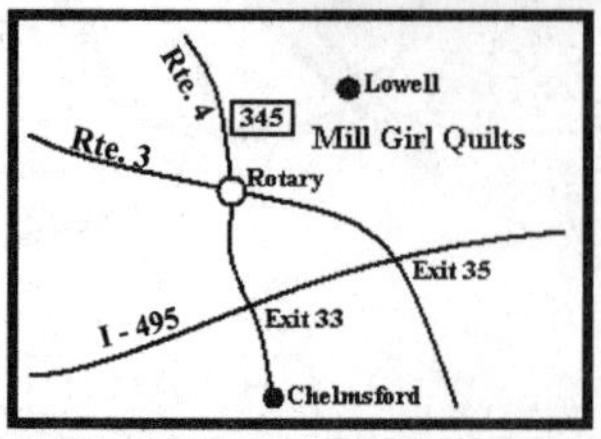

Lowell, MA #15

Tues - Sat
10 - 4
Sun May - Nov 12 - 4

The New England Quilt Museum

18 Shattuck St. 01852
(978) 452-4207
Free to Members (Weekdays Only)
Adm: $4, $3 Seniors & Students

Directly across from the National Park Visitor Center. From Boston's North Station trains are served by a bus every 15 minutes.

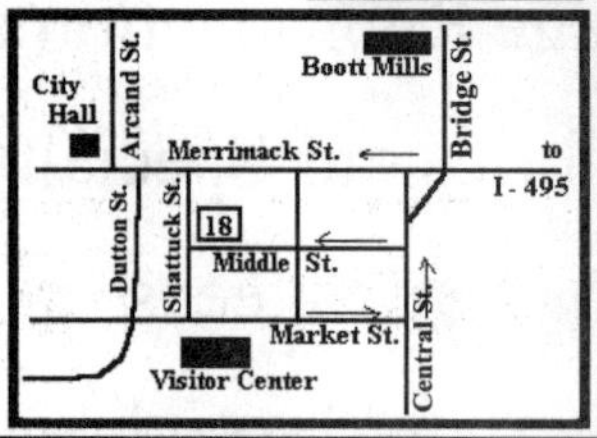

Newbury, MA #16

Tues - Sat
9:30 - 4:30

The Crazy Ladies at The Quilted Acorn Shoppe

72 Newburyport Tpk. (Rt. 1) 01951
(978) 462-0974 Est: 1983
Schedule of Classes & Sales
Web Site: www.QuiltedAcorn.com
Owners: Cynthia Erekson & Sandra Schauer
Unique combination of Quilting, Folk Art Painting and Stenciling: supplies and classes. We specialize in Homespuns & Antique Reproduction Fabrics.
Doll Patterns & Gail Wilson Kits.

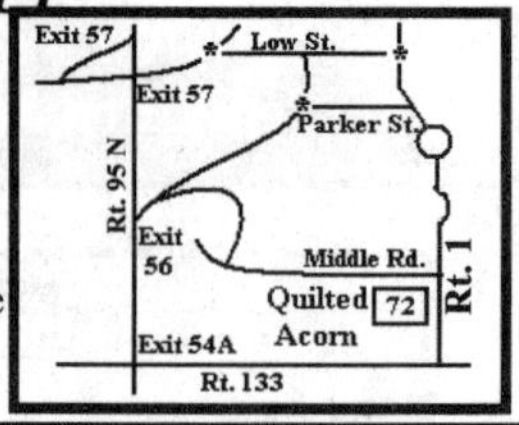

Red Barn Sewing & Yarn Center

116 W. Main St. Rte. 110 01860 (978) 346-9292
email redbarn@greennet.net
Owners: Helen Gosselin & Linda Ouellette
Est: 1978 2000 sq.ft.

Mon - Fri
9 - 5
Sat 9 - 4

Merrimac, MA #17

Over 2500 bolts of quality 100% cotton fabrics,
Books - Patterns - Notions - Yarns
Quilting Classes
Authorized Janome/New Home
Sewing Machine Dealer
Celebrating 24 years

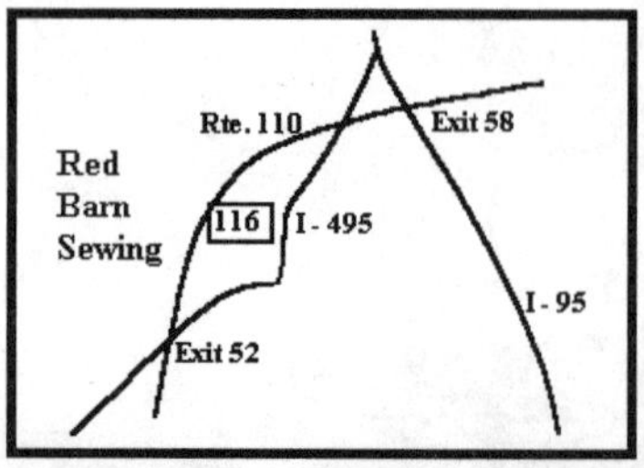

Rockport, MA #18

By Chance or Appt.

Rockport Quilt Shoppe

2 Ocean Ave. 01966
(978) 546-1001
or (800) 456-0892
Fax: (978) 546-2193
E-Mail: gdwhite@shore.net
Owner: Gloria White

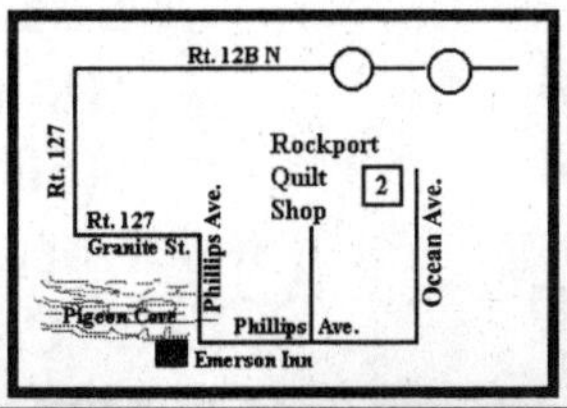

Antique Quilts—Large Stock on Hand. Vintage Linens. Textile Restoration. Custom Work. Decorative Accessories.

Reading, MA #19

Tues - Fri 9:30 - 5 Thur til 7 Sat 9:30 - 4

Mary Rose's Quilts & Treasures

159 Ash St. 01867
(781) 942-9497

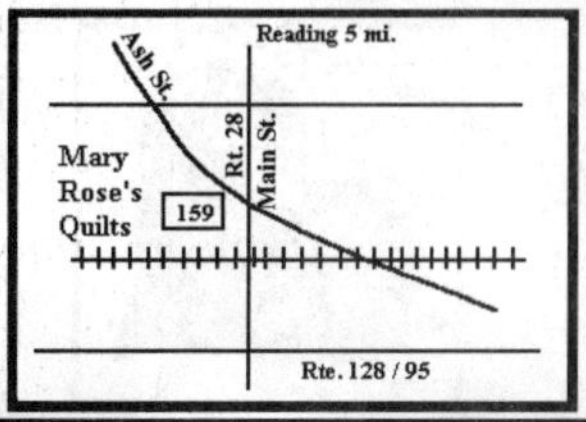

Small cozy quilt shop with a lot of supplies, fabrics & hidden treasures.

Cambridge, MA #20

Mon - Sat 10 - 6 Thurs 10-7 Sun 12 - 5

Cambridge Quilt Shop

95 Blanchard Rd. 02138
(617) 492-3279
Owners: Margaret Lawler, Lynn Gorst, & Shannon Krasnov
Est: 1996 1100 sq.ft.

Our shop maintains 1200 bolts of fabric and over 400 current quilt books, plus the latest in quilting supplies and classes!

Email: quilters@cambridgequilts.com Web: www.cambridgequilts.com

Walpole, MA #21

Please Call for Hours

All About Quilts

958 Main St. 02081
(508) 668-0145
Web Site: www.allaboutquilts.com
Owner: Linda & Mike Publicover

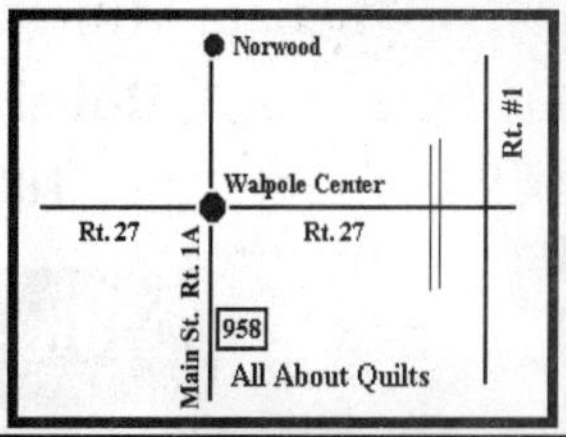

Quilting fabric, supplies, classes for all levels. Day, Night and Weekend Marathons.

North Attleboro, MA #22

Mon - Sat 10 - 6

Quilter's Stash

560 Kelley Blvd. Rte. 152 02760
(508) 699-3010
E-Mail: Qstash@msn.com
Web Site: www.quilters-stash.com
Owners: Sue Kassler & Jean Hall

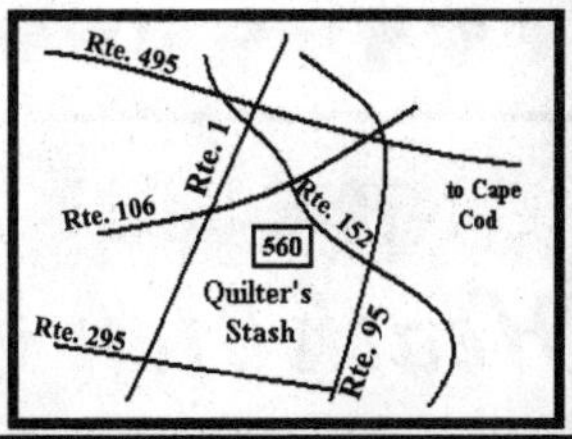

A fabulous selection of fabric, plus notions, quilt-related gifts, antique quilts, tops, and linens -- and classes for all skill levels.
1.5 miles E of Rte. 1 -- 3 miles W of Rte. 495

Pembroke, MA #23

Mon - Sat 10 - 5:15 Sun 12 - 5 Thur Eves.

Tumbleweed

158 Center St. 02359
(781) 293-6400
Est: 1973 1000 sq.ft.

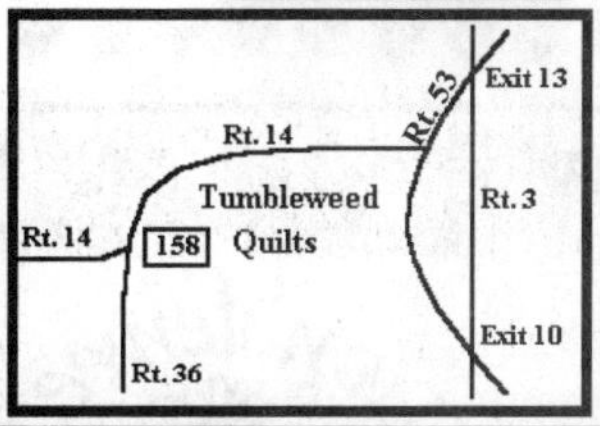

Large selection of fabrics, hundreds of books, notions, batting & more. In a pre-civil war house. Classroom in barn.

Plymouth, MA #24

Mon - Sat 9 - 4:30

Sew Crazy

5 Main St. Extension Rt. 3A
(508) 747-3019 02360
Owner: Dottie Krueger
Est: 1977

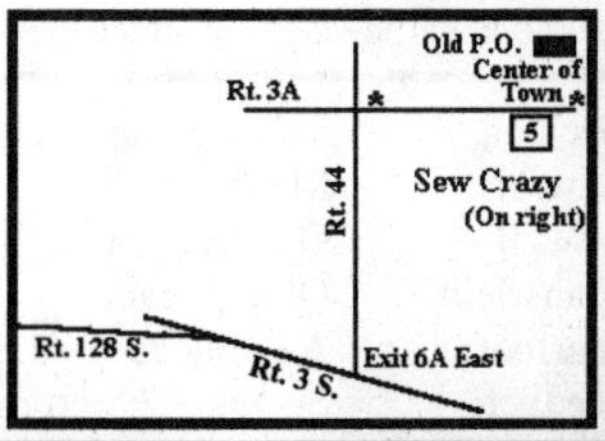

Elna, Pfaff, & New Home Sewing Machines. Over 900 bolts of fabric and more coming. Notions & Lots of Patterns.

Falmouth, MA #26

Mon - Fri 10 - 5:30 Sat 10 - 4

Sit n Stitch

Bernina Corner

690 Main St. 02540
(508) 540-9188 Fax: Same
E-Mail: Imaquilt8@aol.com
Est: 1997

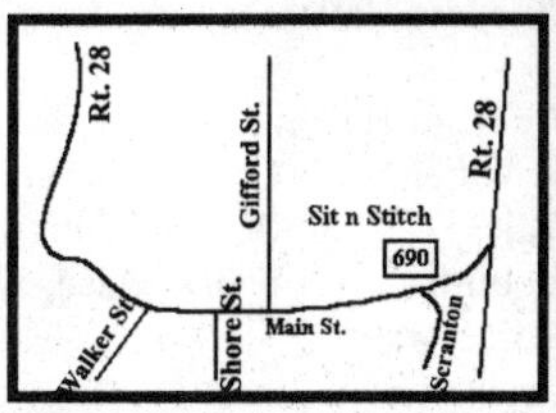

100% cotton quilting fabric. Patterns, books & notions. Full line of Bernina Sewing & Embroidery Machines. Classes.

Falmouth, MA #25

Common Thread Quilts

Offering Fabric • Quilt Supplies • Classes

97 Davis Straits Rd. (Rt. 28)
Falmouth, MA 02540
(508) 495-4400 Fax: (508) 495-4401
E-mail: ComThreadQuilts@aol.com
www.CommonThreadQuilts.com
Owner: Linda McCarthy
Est: 1998

Open Year Round

Featuring a Barn full of inspiration! Offering both Quilts for Sale and Kits to make your own Cape Cod Memories.

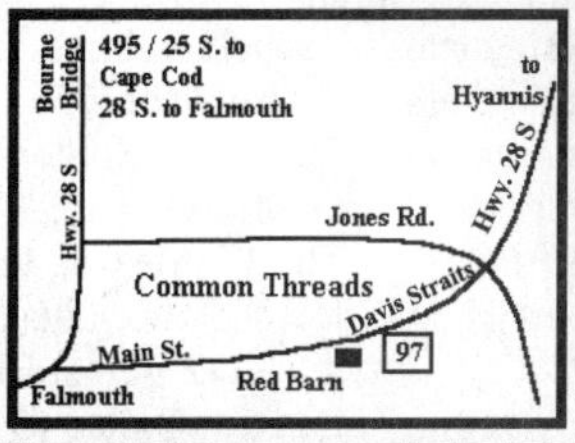

Largest Quilt Shop on Cape Cod

Heartbeat Quilts

765 Main St. 02601
(800) 393-8050
(508) 771-0011
www.heartbeatquilts.com
Est: 1987 3500 sq.ft.
Owner: Helen Weinman

Hyannis, MA #27

6000+ Fabric Bolts: (Hoffman, RJR, P&B, Moda, Michael Miller, Hi-Fashion, Maywood, Kona Bay, Cherrywood, Robert Kaufman, Northcott, & Nancy Crow)
1000+ Books & Patterns

Mon - Sat 10 - 6 Sun 12 - 4

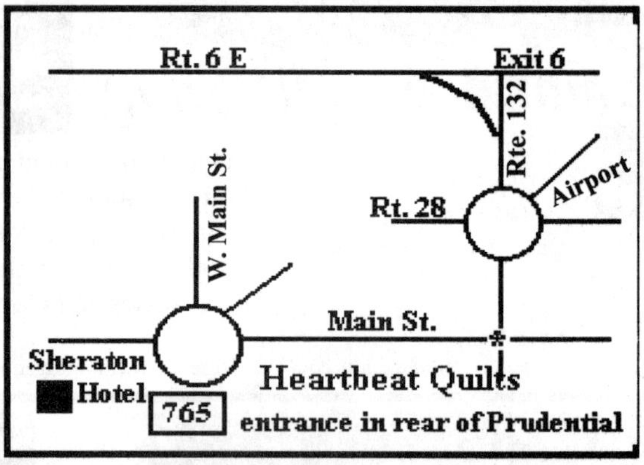

Embellishments, Fancy Threads, Silk Ribbon, Buttons, Fancy Velvets. Workshops Free Newsletter *Mailorder*

6000+ Bolts of Fabric

West Barnstable, MA #28

Mon - Sat 10 - 5:30
Sun 12 - 5
Thur Eves.

Tumbleweed™

Corner of Rt. 6A & Rt. 132
(781) 362-8700 02668
Est: 1985 3200 sq.ft.

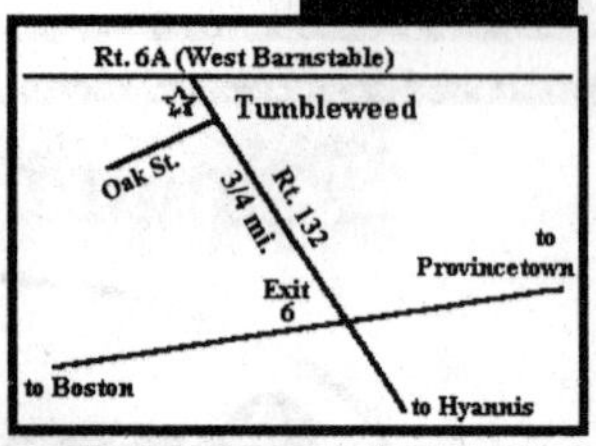

Wonderful fabric gathered from the best mills for quilts, clothing and home decoration where the contemporary mixes with the traditional.

Vineyard Haven, MA #29

Mon - Sat 10 - 5
Wed til 6

Heath Hen Quilt Shop

79 Beach Rd. Tisbury Market Pl. 02568
(508) 693-6730
E-Mail: lbenson@geoserve.net
Owner: Lynne A. Benson
Est: 1985 1000 sq. ft.

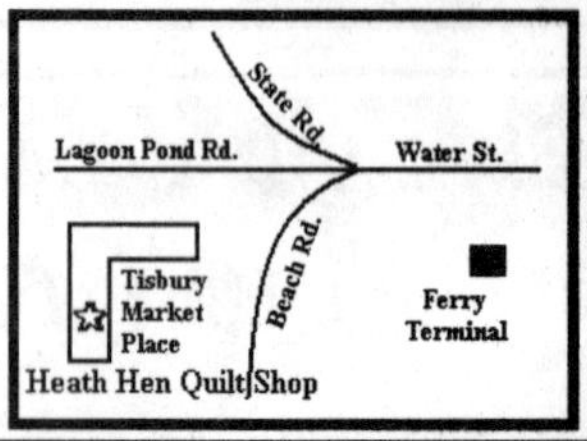

Located .4 mile from steamship dock. Full line of quilting fabrics, exquisite yarns, notions, books, Bernina sewing machines and classes.

Other Shops in Massachusetts: We suggest calling first

Dracut	Snip N Stitch Quilt Shop, 395 Textile Ave.	978-674-0137
Arlington	Fabric Corner, 783 Massachusetts Ave.	781-643-4040
Bellingham	Quilt Center, 373 Center St.	508-876-9955
Brewster	The Yankee Craftsman, 230 Route 6A W	508-385-4758
Brimfield	Lion Ent., Little Alum Pond Rd.	413-245-7799
Cambridge	Sew Low Discount Fabrics, 473 Cambridge St.	
Dorchester	Ross Common Quilts, 15 Fairfax St.	617-436-5848
East Brookfield	Calico Crib Quilt Shoppe, 108 Howe St.	508-867-7389
Easthampton	Christina's Cottage Quilting, 116 Cottage	413-529-1060
Falmouth	Fabric Corner, 12 Spring Bars Rd.	508-548-6482
Fiskdale	Colonial Crafts, 479 Main St.	508-347-3061
Framingham	Rachel's Fabrics, 337 Worchester Rd.	508-872-1141
Framingham	Fabric Place, 136 Howard St.	508-872-4888
Franklin	Franklin Mill Store, 305 Union St.	508-528-3301
Gloucester	Quilted Gallery, 77 Rocky Neck	978-283-7978
Greenfield	The Textile Co., Inc., Power Sq.	413-773-7516
Greenfield	Bear's Paw Quilts & Country Crafts 1182 Bernardston Rd.	413-773-9876
Hingham	Purrfect Quilts, 13 Amber Rd.	781-749-2423
Ipswich	Loom N' Shuttle, 190 High St.	508-356-5551
Lawrence	Malden Mills, 46 Stafford St.	978-685-6341
Lowell	Quilters Corner, 308 Trotting Park	978-441-9225
Mansfield	Quiltessential, 2 Woodland Way	508-339-2292
Marlboro	A Quilter's Garden, 33 Main St.	508-485-5481
Medway	Sisters, 97 Summer	508-533-7407
New Bedford	Julie's Fabric Barn, 166 Rivet St	508-995-7477
Rehoboth	The Store on 44, 224 Winthrop St.	508-252-5640
Salem	Marketplace Quilts, 139 North St.	978-740-3890
South Hadley	The Calico Shop, 40 Searle Rd.	413-536-3245
South Hamilton	Cranberry Quilters, 161 Bay Rd.	508-468-3871
Springfield	Osgood Textile Co., 30 Magaziner Pl.	413-737-6488
Vineyard Haven	Eve Stone & Son Antiques, Ltd., RDF 527	508-693-0396
Vineyard Haven	Beas Fabrics, State Rd., P.O. Box 1296	
Wakefield	Cottage Quilting, 70 Greenwood	781-244-6906
Wales	Ilona's Whim, 10 Stafford Rd.	413-245-3827
Woburn	Fabric Place, 300 Mishawun Rd.	781-938-8787
Worcester	Shirley's Sewing Center Inc., 452 W. Boylston St.	508-853-8757

For the Upper Peninsula Shops #72-82 See Insert
Calumet (#78)
Ontonagon (#82)
Ironwood (#81)
Sault Ste. Marie (#76)
Paradise (#77)
Marquette (#79, 80)
Iron Mountain (#74)
Norway (#75)
Escanaba (#73)
Menominee (#72)
75
UPPER PENINSULA
Bellaire (#2)
75
Cedar (#1)
Grayling (#3)
Williamsburg (#5)
Traverse City (#4)
Beulah (#8)
Manistee (#6)
Cadillac (#7)
East Tawas(#12)
West Branch (#10, 11)
Au Gres(#13)
Custer (#9)
Gladwin (#14)
75
Midland (#15, 16)
Bay City (#69, 70)
Saginaw (#71)
Davison (#64, 65)
Whitehall (#21)
Greenville (#17)
Burton (#63)
Port Huron (#66)
Clinton Twp. (#53)
Norton Shores (#22)
Comstock Park (#18)
Imlay City (#61)
Lapeer (#62)
Jenison (#24)
Grand Rapids (#19, 20)
Flushing (#68)
Portland (#23)
Richmond (#60)
Sterling Heights (#67)
Zeeland (#25)
Bath (#41)
Fenton (#51, 52)
Troy (#56)
Holland (#26)
Hastings (#27)
Charlotte (#40)
St. Clair Shore (#59)
Kalamazoo (#29, 30)
Southgate (#55)
Battle Creek (#28)
Mason (#43)
Berkley (#57, 58)
South Haven (#31)
Wayne (#45)
Lansing (#42)
Jackson (#37)
White Lake (#50)
94
East Lansing (#36)
Belleville (#54)
69
Tecumseh (#38)
(#32, 33) St. Joseph
Benton Harbor (#35)
Ypsilanti (#44)
(#34)
Stevensville
Livonia (#49)
Ann Arbor (#46)
Monroe (#48)
MICHIGAN
Plymouth (#47)
Howell (#39)
82 Featured Shops

Cedar, MI #1

Quality Quilt Fabric
★
Redwork Patterns & Supplies
★
Patterns
★
Books

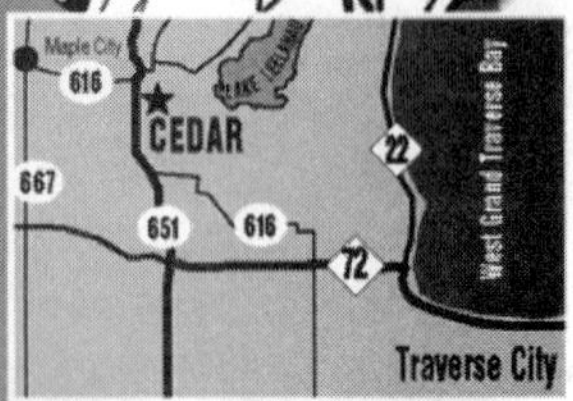

Liberty Quilt Shop
9027 S. Kasson • Cedar, MI 49621
Downtown Cedar
(231) 228-6689
Monday - Saturday 10:00 - 5:30

Bellaire, MI #2

Mon - Fri 10 - 6
Thur til 8
Sat 10 - 5

Cousin's Quilt & Needlework Shop

222 N. Bridge St. 49615
(231) 533-4661 Est: 2001
E-Mail: hartwig@torchlake.com
Web Site: cousinsquiltandneedlework.com
Owners: Carmen Hartwig & Jayme Makowski
We may be small but we are overflowing with ideas. Moda's, Bali batiks, and Flannels. Cross stitch and specialty Fibers.

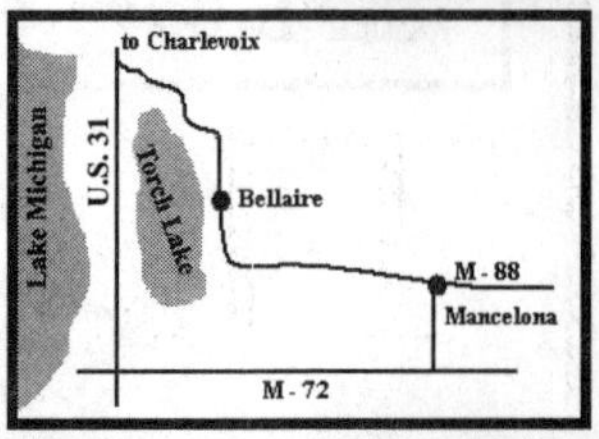

Grayling, MI #3

Mon - Sat 10 - 5

The Icehouse Quilt Shop

509 Norway Street 49738
(989) 348-4821
E-mail: icehouse@freeway.net
Web Site: www.theicehousequiltshop.com
Owner: Ali Baynham Est: 1980

A unique shop for the person seeking quality in quilting, gifts, and gourmet food. Visit our Christmas Lodge. We've added a Bed & Breakfast, too! B&B Phone (989) 348-6630

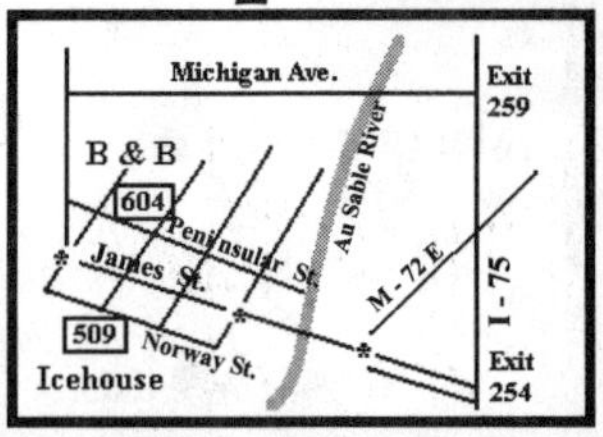

Traverse City, MI #4

Mon - Thur 9:30 - 8
Fri & Sat 9:30 - 5:30

Sewing Depot

1425-C S. Airport Rd. W 49686
(231) 946-2554 or (800) 432-9288
E-Mail: stitch@coslink.net 7000+ sq.ft.

"One place...all your sewing resources."
Quality sewing and embroidery machines, software, and cabinets. Great selection of classes, books, patterns and beautiful fabrics!

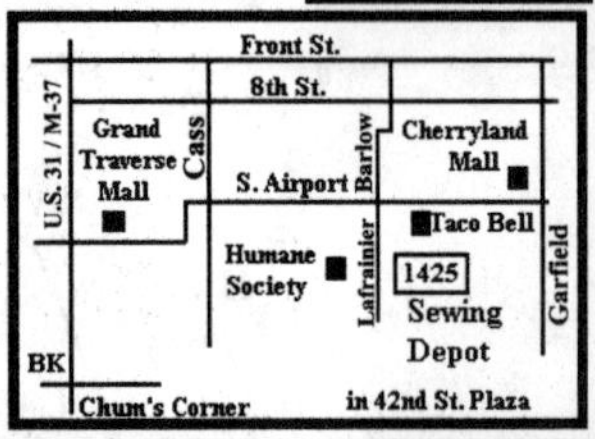

Williamsburg, MI #5

Mon - Sat 10 - 5:30
Sun 12 - 5:30

Cranberry Christmas & Country Store

3997 M 72 East 49690
(231) 938-5944 Est: 1994 600+ Bolts
E-Mail: cranberrychristmas@yahoo.com
Web Site: www.cranberrychristmas.com
Growing inventory of 100% cotton fabrics & homespuns, patterns & stitcheries set amongst primitive antiques, gift & food items.

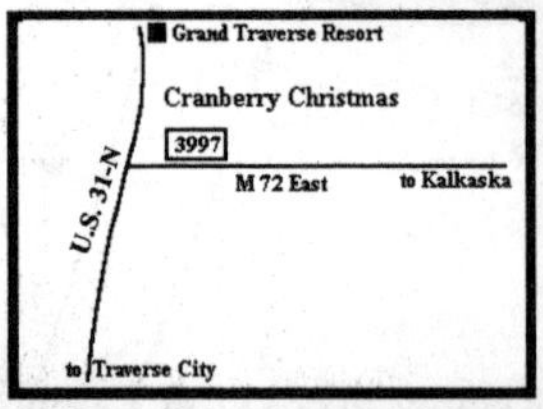

Cadillac, MI #7

Mon - Sat 9:30 - 5:30

Julie Ann Fabrics

109 S. Mitchell 49601
(616) 775-8301
Owners: Gerald & Ruth Britton
Est: 1973 2000+ Bolts

Great selection of quilting fabrics, books, patterns, notions. Classes. Pfaff & Janome sewing machines & sergers sales & service.

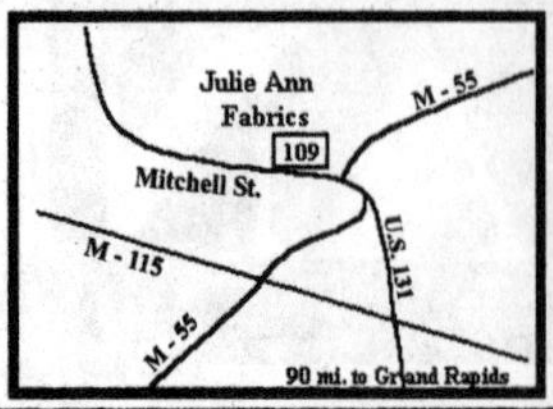

Manistee, MI #6

The Quilted Heart

607 Parkdale (North U.S. 31) 49660
(231) 723-7069
Owner: Judy Dunlap Est: 1989

- Fabrics, books, patterns & quilting supplies
- Our specialty—KITS for quilts and clothing
- Classes
- Friendly, helpful staff
- Gifts & collectibles
- Mail Order
- Inspiration and Ideas in every room

Mon - Sat 10 - 5

E-Mail:
judy@thequiltedheart

Visit our on-line catalog at:
www.thequilted heart.com

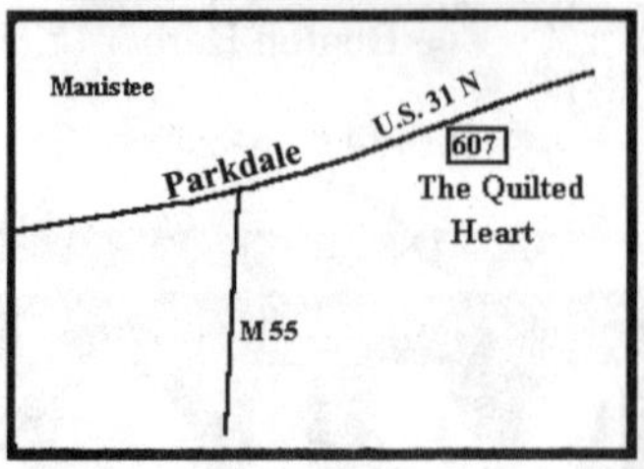

Unique Setting in an old Farmhouse
"The biggest little quilt shop in Michigan"

Quilts By The Lake

(231) 882-4024
194 South Benzie Blvd.
P.O. Box 615, Beulah, MI 49617
Owner: Rebecca Zerfas
Est: 1980 2500 sq.ft. 2000+ Bolts

MAKE SURE AND VISIT US WHILE IN THE AREA. WE'VE BEEN TOLD THAT WE'RE WORTH THE TRIP!

Beulah, MI #8

We specialize in quality quilting supplies. You'll find a large variety of fabrics, books, patterns, notions and quilting kits. Classes are held for all skill levels. Let our friendly knowledgeable staff help you with your next project.

Some of the fabric lines that we carry:
Moda • Hoffman • Benartex • P&B • Kona Bay
In The Beginning • RJR • Alaska Dyeworks • Bali
Momen House • Seven Islands • Marcus Bros.

Mon - Sat 10 - 5 Call for Ext. Summer Hrs.

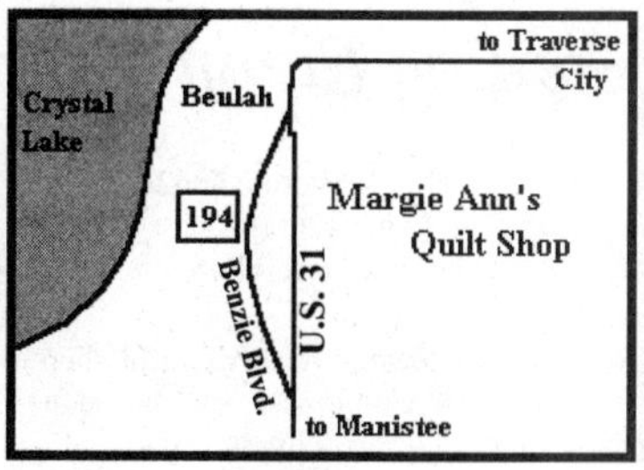

We also have a wonderful Gift Department
Quilts • Woven Rugs • Lang Graphics
Folk Art • Pottery • Baskets
Hand Blown Glass • Scandinavian Books & Gifts
Dale of Norway Sweaters

Custer, MI #9

1200+ bolts of 100% cotton fabric plus patterns, books and notions all located in a 100 year old brick farm house

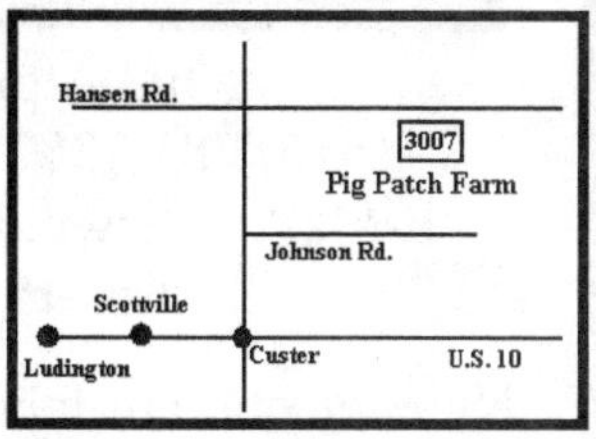

Mon - Sat 10 - 5

3007 E. Hansen Rd. 49405
(231) 757-2812
E-Mail: pigpatch@t-one.net
Web Site: www.pigpatchfarm.com
Owner: Sue Riffle Est: 1998

West Branch, MI #10

Crocker's Attic

Winter Hrs. Vary May thru Dec. Mon - Thur 11 - 4 Fri & Sat 10 - 5

3156 W. M-55 48661
(989) 345-1780 Est: 1993
E-Mail: crocker@voyager.net
Owner: Jolee Crocker 600+ Bolts

Primitive home furnishing and gift shop featuring Moda, Indo, Aunt Gracies and Homespuns. Specializing in Reproduction Fabrics, Thimbleberry prints and more.

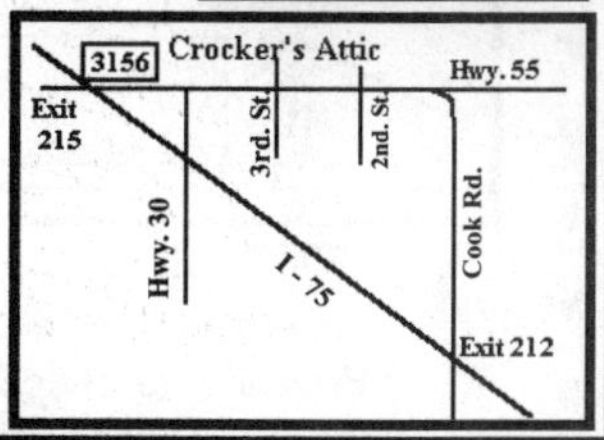

West Branch, MI #11

Button Hole

Mon - Fri 9 - 6 Sat 9 - 5

218 West Houghton 48661
(989) 345-0431
Web Site: www.buttonholeshop.com
Owner: Darlene Jones
Est: 1981 3300 sq.ft.

We have Everything for the Quilter ! ! Located in a Victorian, downtown West Branch on Business Loop I - 75

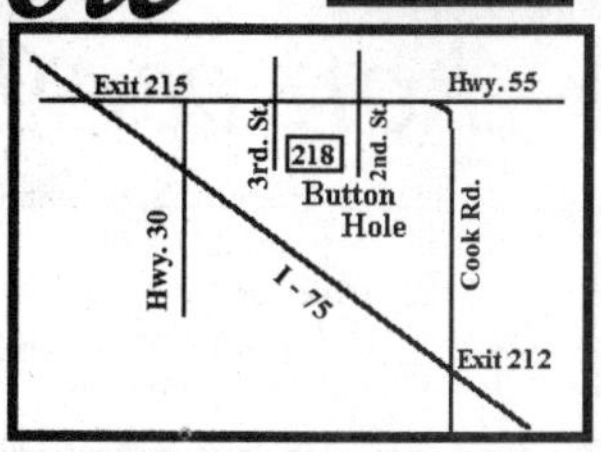

East Tawas, MI #12

Mon - Sat 10 - 5
Summer Sun 11 - 4

Cotton Patch Quilt Shop

306 Newman St. 48730
(877) 362-6779 or (989) 362-6779
E-Mail: ctnpatch@alpena.cc.mi.us
Web Site: www.cottonpatchfabrics.com
Owner: Doni Butzin
Est: 1996 3000 sq.ft. 3000+ Bolts
Full Service Quilt Shop.
Block of the Month Clubs.
Machine Quilting Services.

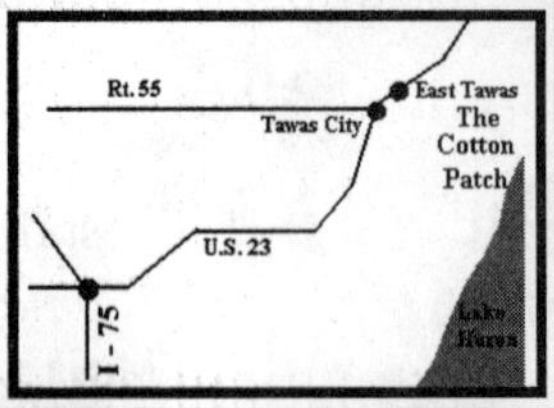

Au Gres, MI #13

Tues - Fri 10 - 4:30
Sat 10 - 12

Bayview Calicos

3631 E. Huron (U.S. 23) 48703
(517) 876-6933
Owner: Evelyn Griffore
Est: 1988

Quilt fabric and supplies. Classes.
Christmas year round.
"Where Friendly Quilters Meet"

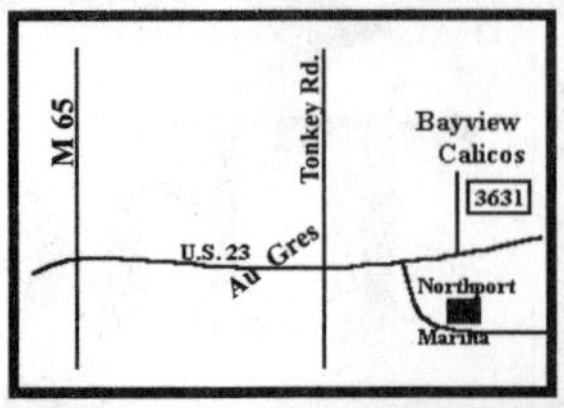

Gladwin, MI #14

Tues - Sat 10 - 4

The Log Cabin Fabric Shoppe

1902 Lakeshore 48624
(517) 426-1422
Owner: Cherie Thornton

We are now located in a beautiful shop in the country. Come visit our brand new barn full of quilting delights.

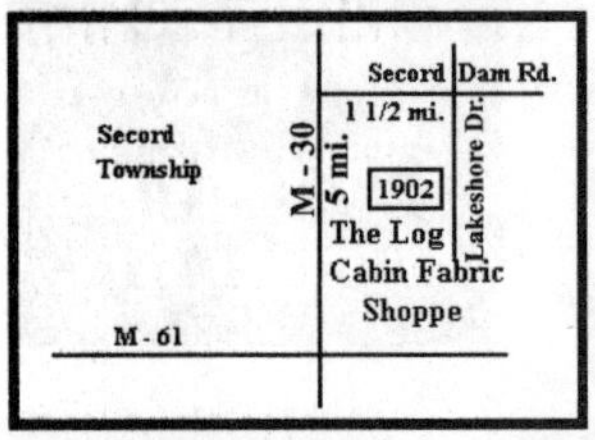

Midland, MI #15

Mon - Thur 9:30 - 6
Fri & Sat 9:30 - 5

Quilted Giraffe

713 Ashman St. #2 48640
Across from Erb Lumber
(989) 837-2666
E-Mail: qgiraffe@aol.com
Est: 1996 1400 sq.ft.

Large selection of 100% quality cottons, supplies, and classes. A year-round mini quilt show. Fun, Friendly and Knowledgeable Staff.

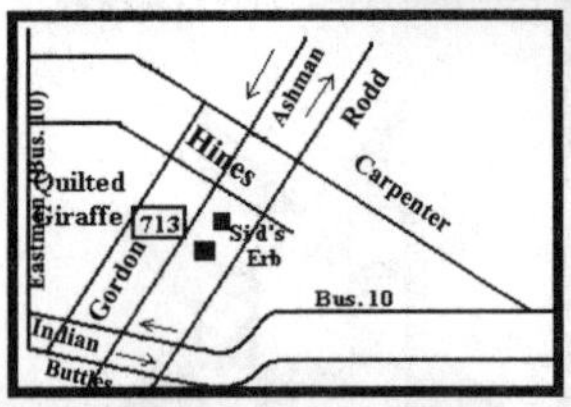

MATERIAL MART

Your Complete Quilting Supply Source

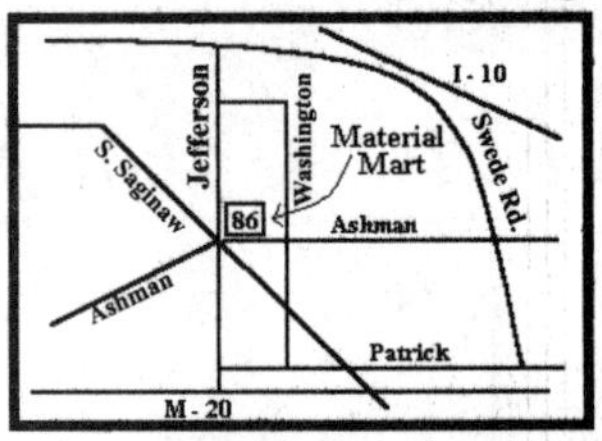

86 Ashman Circle 48640
(517) 835-8761
Fax: (517) 835-9820
E-Mail: matrlmart@aol.com
Web Site: www.materialmart@husqvarna.com
Est: 1971 4100 sq.ft.

Over 3000 bolts of top designer fabrics,
latest notions & quilt books.
Friendly, knowledgeable staff.
Professional Machine Quilting

Mon - Fri 9:30 - 9
Sat 9:30 - 5
Sun 12 - 5

Midland, MI #16

Greenville, MI #17

Mon - Fri 10 - 6
Sat 10 - 2

Forever Fabrics

214 S. Franklin St. 48838
(616) 225-8486
E-Mail: o1sewandsew@chartermi.net
Owners: Sheila Crawford & Judy Jensen
Est: 2002

Relax as you enjoy our great selection of quilting fabrics, notions & books. Customer Service is our #1 goal.

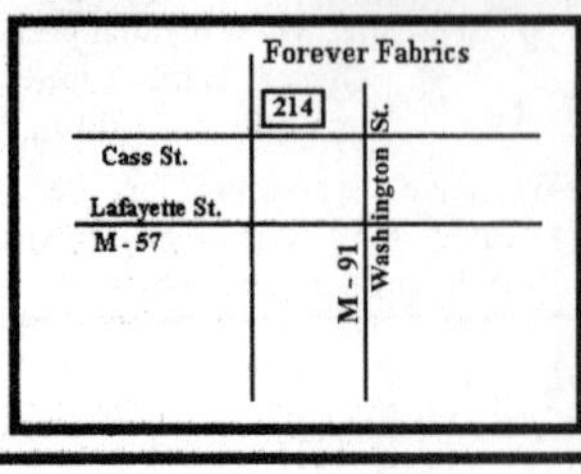

Comstock Park, MI #18

Attic Window Quilt Shop

Est: 1997
1200 sq.ft.

Mon 10 - 8
Tues - Fri 10 - 5:30
Sat 10 - 3

5307 Alpine NW 49321
(616) 785-3357 Fax: (616) 785-3358
E-Mail: atticwindowquiltshop@altbi.com
Owner: Sally Johnson

Nice selection of fabric, books, patterns, and notions. Specializing in reproduction fabrics 1800's - 1940's Special order and hard-to-find items. Classes, mail order and more.

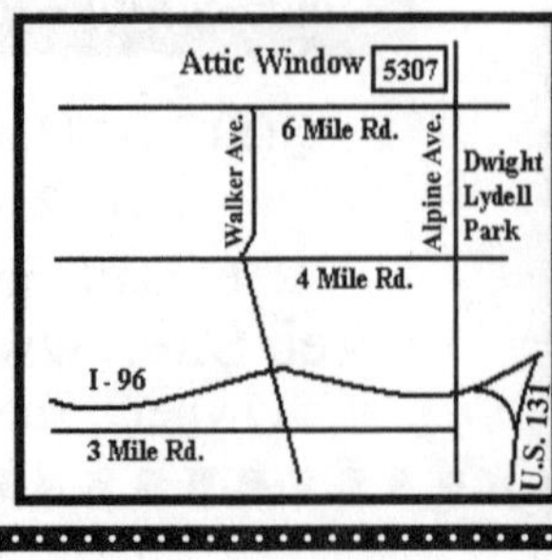

Grand Rapids, MI #19

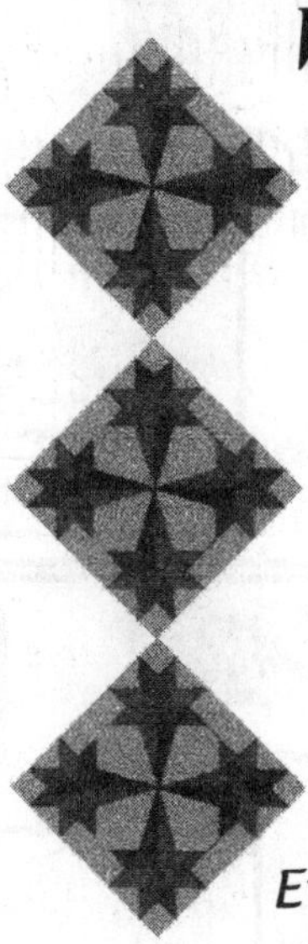

West Michigan's "grandest" quilt shop!

Grand Quilt Co.

5290 Alpine Ave. N.W. (M-37)
Comstock Park, MI 49321
(Just three miles north of Grand Rapids)

(616) 647-1120 E-mail: grquiltco@aol.com
Owner: Lori Verbrugge
Est: 1997 4500 sq. ft.
4,000+ bolts of 100% cotton fabric!

Ask how to join The Material Girls, our bi-monthly fat quarter club!

Every quilting goodie a quilter's heart desires in a friendly, comtemporary atmosphere. Ask to receive our quarterly 16-page newsletter, filled with fun classes, new product info and special store events!

Weekdays 10 - 9
Saturdays 10 - 5
Closed Sundays

Take I-96 to Alpine Ave. exit (Exit 30). Go North 3 miles. Grand Quilt Co. is just beyond the traffic signal at 6 Mile and Alpine.

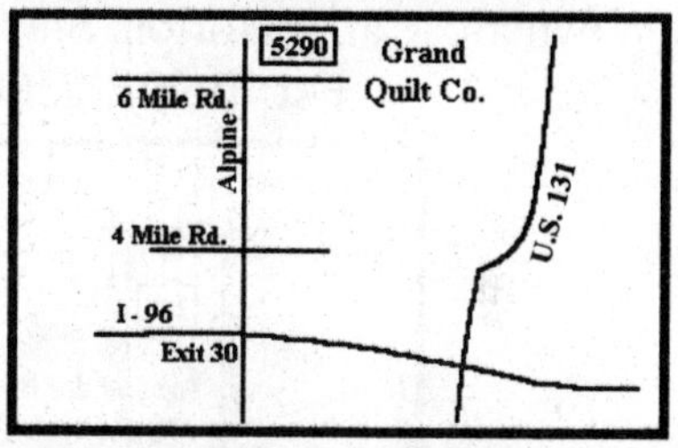

Sewing & Quilting Center

SMITH OWEN

SALES • SERVICE • CLASSES

Western Michigan's largest Quilt Shop

Check on the latest in books, notions, and patterns. Many Quilts and wall hangings on display in our showroom.

4051 Plainfield NE
Grand Rapids, MI 49525
(616) 361-5484
www.smithowensew.com

Hours

Mon & Thur	9 - 8
Tues, Wed, Fri	9 - 5
Sat	10 - 3

Get off I-96 at Plainfield exit #33. Go north 2 miles. Smith-Owen is on the left across from Kentucky Fried Chicken.

Check out our different quilting models of sewing machines.

- **Viking Quilt Designer**
- **Pfaff QuiltStyle**
- **Juki Quilter**

Grand Rapids, MI #20

Whitehall, MI #21

Mon - Sat 10 - 5

103 E. Colby St. 49461
(231) 894-2164

Two floors of unique and original merchandise. The finest quality quilting fabrics and notions.

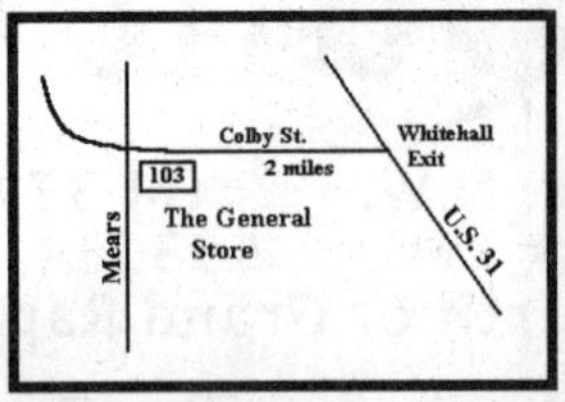

Norton Shores, MI #22

Mon - Sat 11 - 6
Sun 12 - 6

Stitched Heart

in the Airport Antique Mall
4206 Grand Haven Rd.
(231) 798-3318
Owners: Sue Steinhauer & Mike Chaban

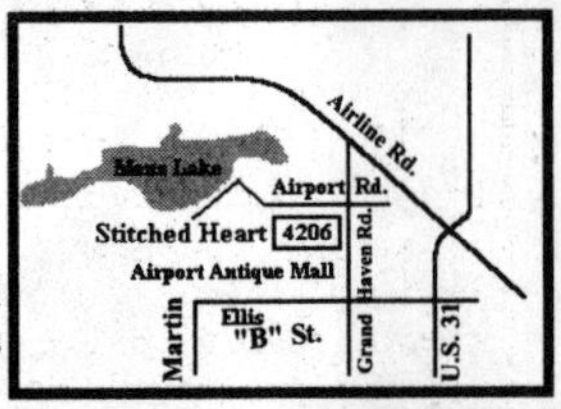

New & Used Quilting Supplies - Quilts - Wall Hangings - Wearable Art - Vests - Fine Antiques Collectables - Fat Quarters - No Bolts of Fabric

Portland, MI #23

Around the Block Quilt Shop

120 Maple St. 48875
(517) 647-5430
E-mail: Aroundtheblock@mvcc.com
Owners: Cathy Norton, Steve & Cathy McCann
Est: 1999 2500 sq.ft.

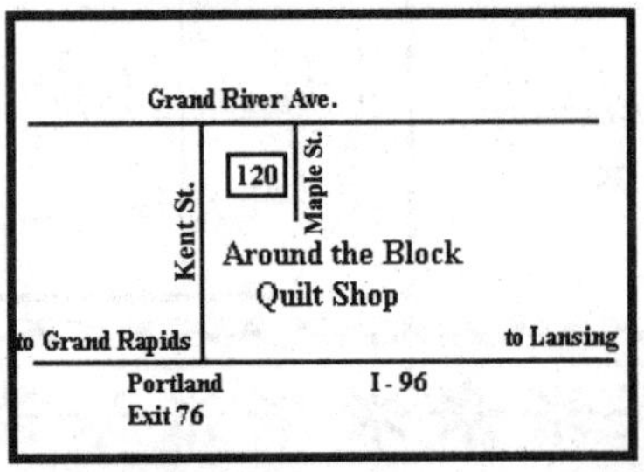

Website: sew2000.com/aroundtheblock

100% Cotton Fabrics by Hoffman, Benartex, Thimbleberries, Debbie Mumm & RJR.
Classes, Books, Patterns, & Notions.
Machine Embroidery Supplies from OESD
Lansing Area Bernina Dealer.
Machine Service—All Brands.
Machine Quilting Available

Mon, Wed, Fri, Sat 10 - 6
Tues & Thurs 10 - 8

Jenison, MI #24

Mon - Sat 9:30 - 9

Country Needleworks

584 Chicago Dr. 49428
(616) 457-9410 Est: 1981
Owners: Cheryl Van Haitsma & Barb Langerak

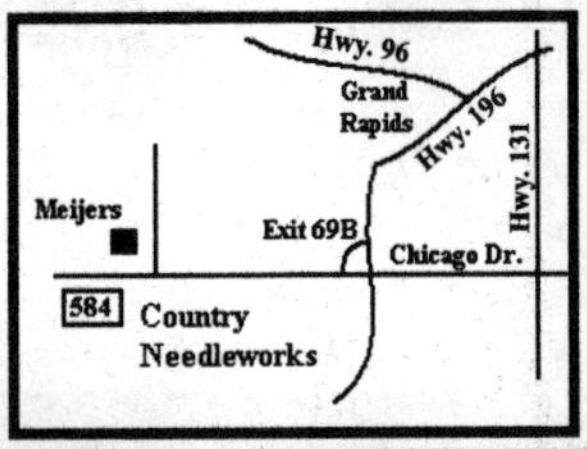

Your complete needlework shop carrying: quilt fabric & accessories, cross-stitch supplies, scrapbooking supplies, largest stamping center in West Michigan. Giftware.

Zeeland, MI #25

Mon - Fri 9 - 5:30
Fri til 8
Sat 9 - 2

It's Stitching Time

150 E. Main 49464
(616) 772-5525

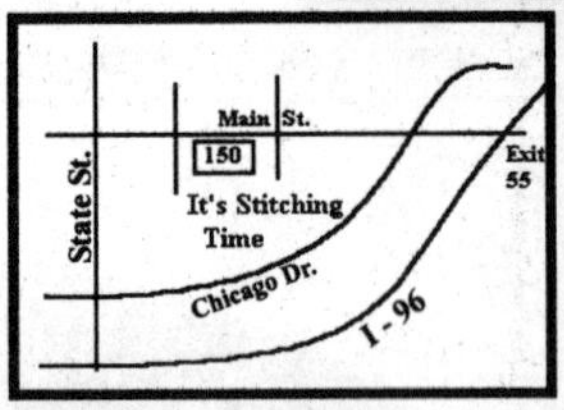

Complete Needlework and Quilt Shop.
Over 350 Quilt Books.
Lots of patterns, fabric, rulers.
A Quilter's Dream Shop.

Holland, MI #26

Mon - Sat 9 - 9

Field's FABRICS

www.fieldsfabrics.com

281 East 8th 49423
(616) 392-4806

Owner: Jack Veldman
Est: 1953
12,000 sq.ft.

Packed with Fabrics !
10,000+ Bolts
Many Unique Prints.

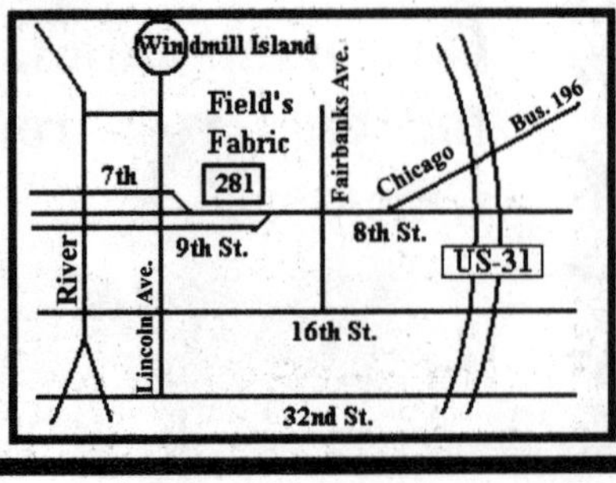

Hastings, MI #27

Mon - Thur 8 - 5:30
Fri 8 - 7
Sat 9 - 5:30

Sisters Fabrics

218 E. State St. 49058
(616) 945-9673

Large selection of calico, books, patterns, quilting supplies, fleece, dress fabrics, JHB and Streamline buttons, etc.

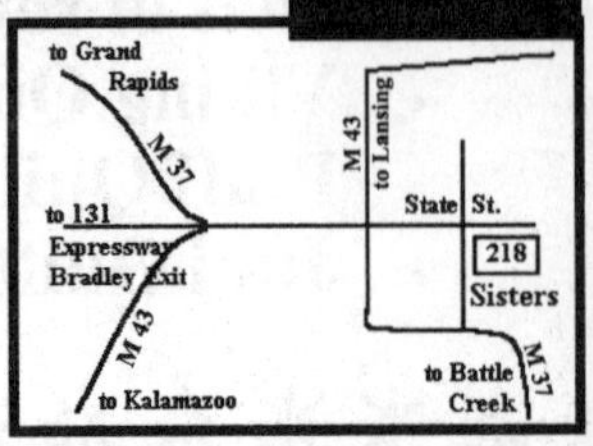

Battle Creek, MI #28

Tues - Fri 10 - 5
Sat 10 - 1

The Quiltery

1540 East Columbia Ave. 49104
(616) 965-2116
Est: 1981 2500 sq.ft.
Owner: Lynne Evans

HUGE selection of quality 100% cottons by Hoffman, RJR, Jinny Beyer, Benartex, Roberta Horton, and others; notions, books, and patterns. Call for a free newsletter listing classes & sales.

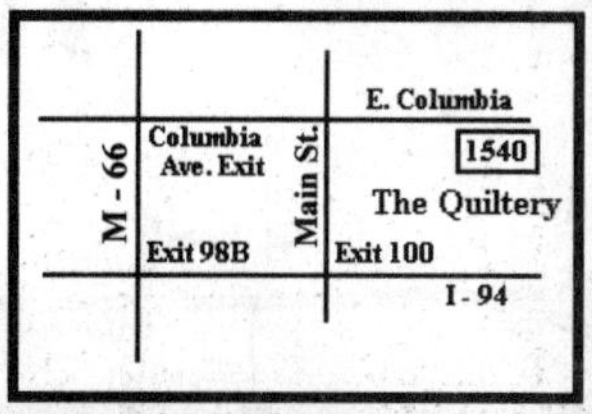

Kalamazoo, MI #29

Mon - Fri 9 - 5:30
Wed til 7
Sat 9 - 4

Viking Sewing Center

5401 Portage Rd. 49002
(616) 342-5808
Owners: Phil & Julie Rotzien
2500 sq.ft.

1000+ bolts of 100% cotton fabric. Quilting, heirloom, garment and specialty sewing classes. Viking & White sewing machine sales & service.

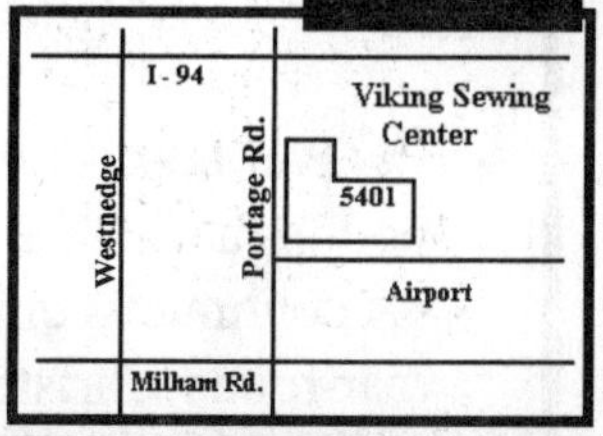

Kalamazoo, MI #30

Quilts Plus

Mon - Fri 10 - 6
Thur til 8:30
Sat 10 - 4

- Fabrics
- Classes
- Quilting Supplies
- Books & Patterns
- Hoops
- Blocks of the Month
- Quilt Kits & Fabric Packs
- Hinterberg & Ulmer Quilt Frames
- Gifts
- Samples Galore

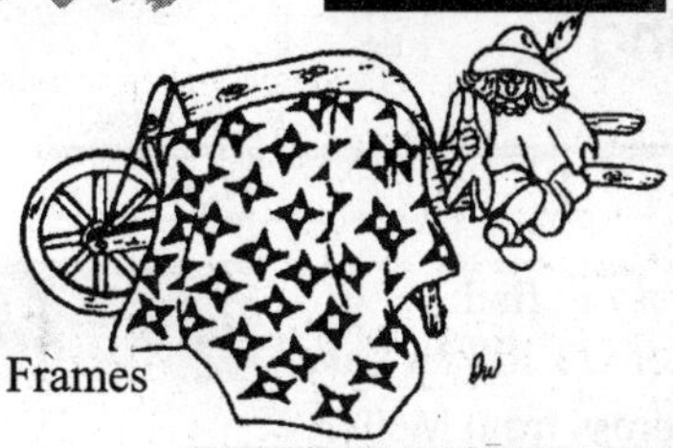

4644 W. Main
Kalamazoo, MI 49006
Tel: (616) 383-1790
Fax: (616) 383-2182
E-mail: quiltspluskazoo@hotmail.com
Owner: Kathleen Edwards Est: 1996

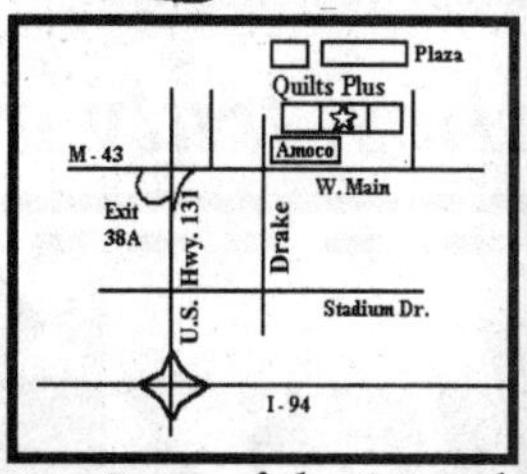

20% off--Empty a Bolt--Last Business Day of the Month

South Haven, MI #31

Sept - May
Sat 8 - 5, Sun 1 - 4
Weekdays by Appt.
June - Aug
Mon - Fri 10 - 5
Sat 8 - 5, Sun 1 - 4

Calico Creations

70325 16th Ave. 49090
(616) 637-5558
E-Mail: CALICO@cybersol.com
Owner: Cornelia Miller

Quilt supply shop; SW Michigan Largest Supply of Quilt Books. Offers Classes: basic, traditional hand piecing & quilting to advanced machine piecing & quilting. Large supply of quilting fabrics & notions along with gifts for quilters.

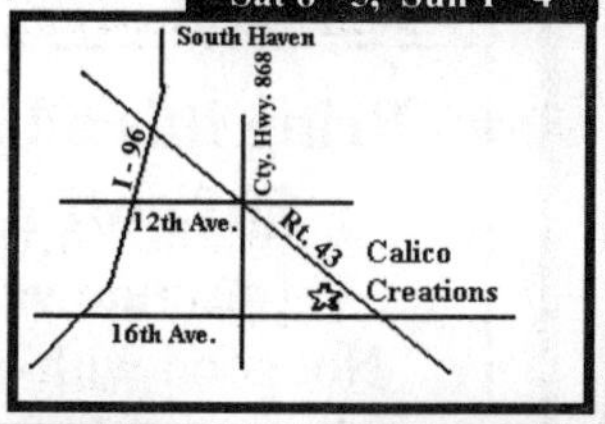

St. Joseph, MI #32

Call for Appt.

Eileen's Design Studio

4503 Bacon School Rd. 49085
(616) 429-1876 Fax: Same
E-mail: eds@parrett.net
Web Site: www.eileensdesignstudio.com
Owner: Eileen Chapman
Est: 1993 2000 sq.ft. Free Catalog

Tour a "working studio", located in the barn behind Eileen's 130-year-old home. Eileen's patterns, books and fabric kits are available.

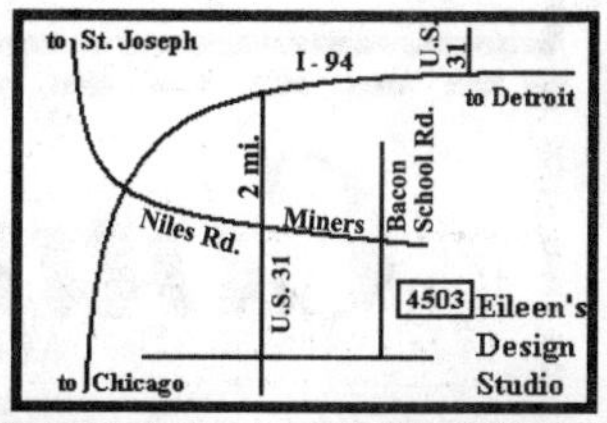

Loving Stitches

Est: 1996

QUILT SHOP LLC

WWW.LSQUILTSHOP.COM

Owner: Holly Martin

Over 3000 100% cotton fabrics to choose from!!
Patterns, Books, Supplies
See our perennial garden in season.

7291 Red Arrow Hwy.
49127
(269) 465-3795

WWW.LSQUILTSHOP.COM

e-mail:
HOLLY@LSQUILTSHOP.COM
HEATHER@LSQUILTSHOP.COM

Mon. Thru Fri. 10-5
Sat. 10-3

Stevensville, MI #34

St. Joseph, MI #33

Mon - Sat 10 - 5:30

The Silver Needle

415 State St. 49085
(616) 982-8521
Owners: Sherry Krause & Joyce Patrick
Est: 1998

Located in the lovely lakefront town of St. Joseph, we carry bright, bold fabrics, patterns, books, notions & Quilt Magics. We also have some prepackaged kits.

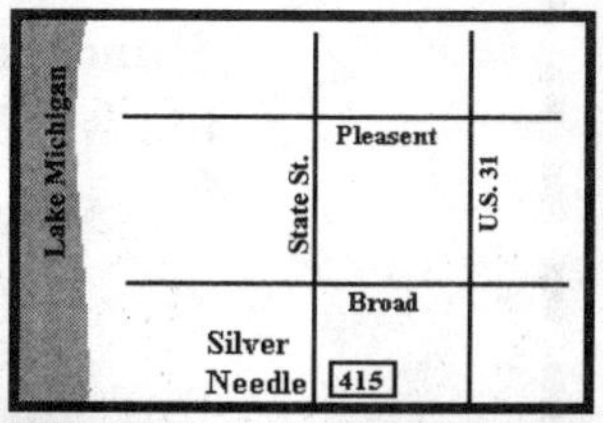

Benton Harbor, MI #35

Tues - Fri 10 - 5
Sat 10 - 4

Carol's Quilt Cottage

1985 Zoschke Rd. 49022
(616) 849-4065
Owner: Carol Frosolone
Est: 1997

Available will be a wide variety of notions, patterns, books, quality 100% cotton fabric, and many gift ideas. Full service quilt shop. Lectures & workshops on Hawaiian quilting.

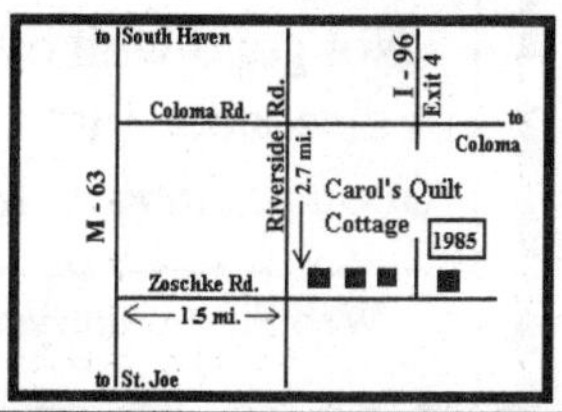

Country Stitches

America's Largest Quilt Shop is a Quilter's Heaven!

- Over 6000 bolts of 100% cotton fabric line the shelves.
- A continuous quilt show and year-round Christmas displays offer ideas and inspiration.
- Friendly, knowledgeable staff are trained and ready to help with your creative project.

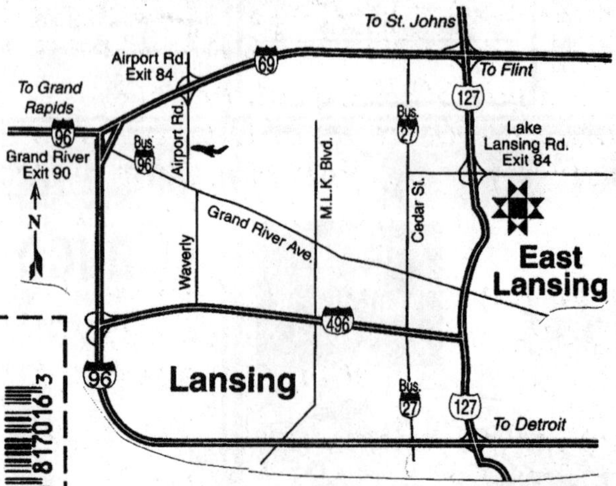

Hours:
Monday - Friday
9:30 am - 9:00 pm
Saturday
9:30 am - 6:00 pm
Sunday - Closed

Call **517-351-2416** or **1-800-572-2031** for more information

Bring this ad and receive 50% off any item
(maxium value $25.)
Not good with other specials or discounts. Instock items only.
Good at East Lansing location only.

We're easy to find:
One block east of US 127 on Lake Lansing Rd. across from Meijer

East Lansing, MI #36

Web Site: countrystitches.com

Treat yourself to Country Stitches, truly a unique quilt shop.

Country Stitches

America's Largest Quilt Shop

SECRET STASH ROOM with over 200 bolts 1/2 off! Hundreds of items 1/2 off!

Thousands of bolts of 100% cotton fabric line the shelves.

Hours:
Monday - Friday
9:30 am - 9:00 pm
Saturday
9:30 am - 6:00 pm
Sunday
12 pm - 5:00 pm

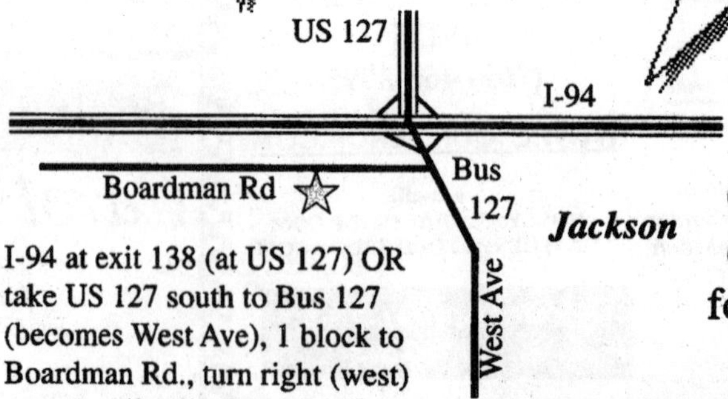

Bring this ad and receive 50% off any item
(maxium value $25.)
Not good with other specials or discounts. Instock items only.
Good at Jackson location only.

Web Site: countrystitches.com

I-94 at exit 138 (at US 127) OR take US 127 south to Bus 127 (becomes West Ave), 1 block to Boardman Rd., turn right (west) approx. 1/2 mile. Just past Lowe's. 1965 Boardman Road.

Call **517-782-7100** or **1-800-782-3830** for more information

Jackson, MI #37

The Quilt Patch

HOURS
Monday, Wednesday & Friday
10:00 am - 5:00 pm
Tuesday & Thursday
10:00 am - 8:00 pm
Saturday
10:00 am - 4:00 pm
Sunday
Noon - 4:00 pm

Enjoy 3000 Sq. Ft. of Quilter's Paradise
Packed with 4000 Bolts of Quality -- 100% Cotton Fabrics
From all the Top Designers, Plus Hundreds of Books, Patterns & Notions
Learn from Experienced Quilters

We offer a Variety of Classes & Workshops
Featuring all the latest and Traditional
Quilting Techiques. Something for everyone!

123 W. Chicago Blvd., Tecumseh, MI 49286

517-423-0053

WEBSITE: thequiltpatch.com

Tecumseh, MI #38

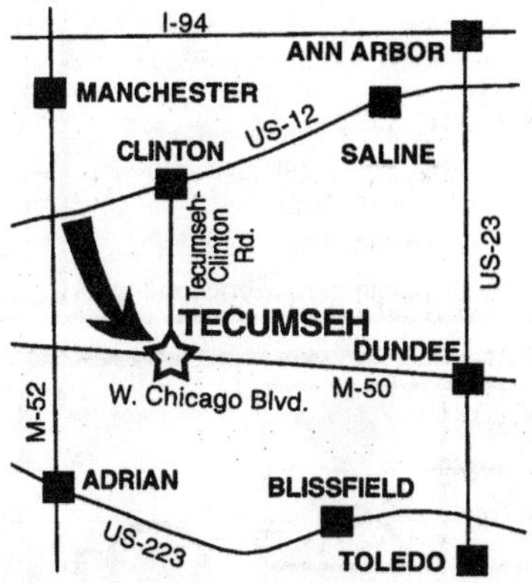

The Stitchery

Howell, MI #39

1129 E. Grand River Ave. 48843
(517) 548-1731
E-Mail: stitchry@ismi.net
Owner: Susan Reid
Est: 1980 4000 sq.ft.
New Home / Janome Dealer

100% Cotton Prints including Hoffman, RJR, Moda, Marcus, Peter Pan, Northcutt's "Quilt for a Cure", Kona Bay, Kona Cottons, South Seas, Thimbleberries, Benartex, Flannels, Alma Lynne, Clothworks & RJR. 108" Quilt Back Prints.

Heirloom Sewing Supplies, Wools for rug Hooking & Primitives, plus many Books, Supplies, Notions & Classes

Mon - Fri 9 - 6
Sat 9 - 4
Call for Quilt Guild Outings Special Discounts

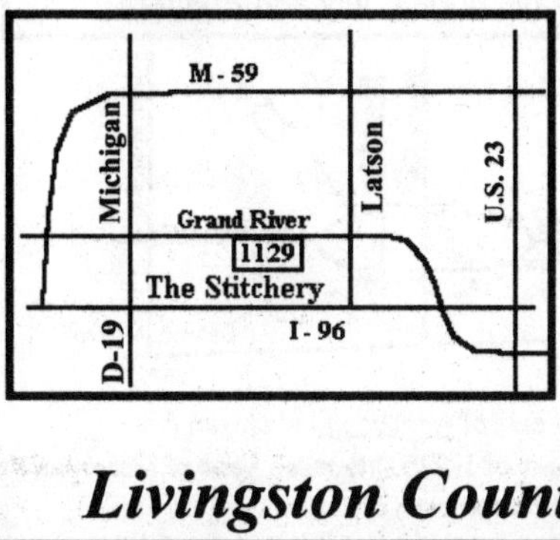

Website: www.thestitcheryonline.com

Livingston County's Largest Quilt Shop & Sewing Machine Center

Charlotte, MI #40

Mon - Sat 10 - 5:30

Hen House of Charlotte

211 S. Cochran 48813
(517) 543-6454
Owner: Nancy Conn
Est: 1974

A craft shop specializing in quality materials including 100% cotton and homespun fabrics, Stenciling, X-Stitch, Tole Painting and Basket Supplies

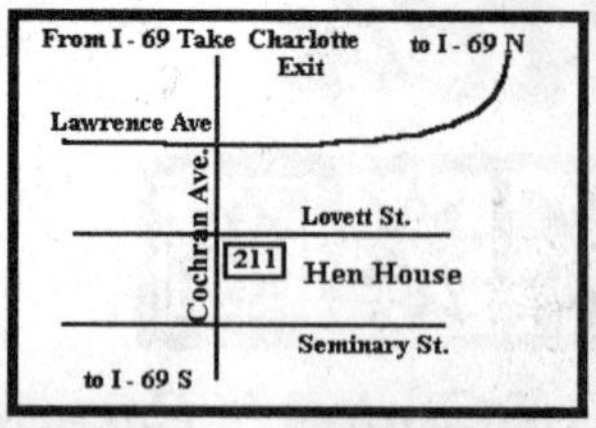

Bath, MI #41

**Tues 10 - 7
Wed & Thur 10 - 6
Fri 10 - 5
Sat 10 - 4**

Quilting Memories

13630 B. Main St. 48808
(517) 641-6522
Owner: Dorothy Mills
Est: 1994 1500 sq.ft.

Complete supplies for quilters. Silk Ribbon, Brazilian Embroidery. Offer weekend and evening classes. Great assortment of quilters cottons.

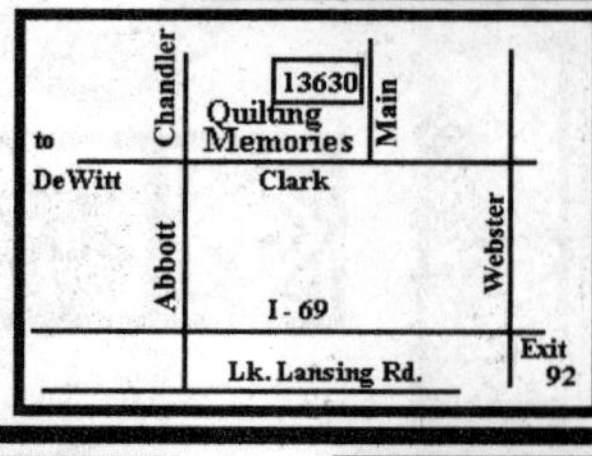

Lansing, MI #42

**Mon - Thurs 10 - 9
Fri & Sat 10 - 6**

The Quilt Depot

323-B S. Waverly Rd. 48917
(517) 323-3090 (888) 809-9323
Fax: (517) 323-3313
E-Mail: tqdepot@thequiltdepot.com
Web Site: www.thequiltdepot.com
Owner: Patti Parmenter
Est: 1998 1450 sq.ft. 1500 Bolts.

The friendly shop with great fabrics and fun!

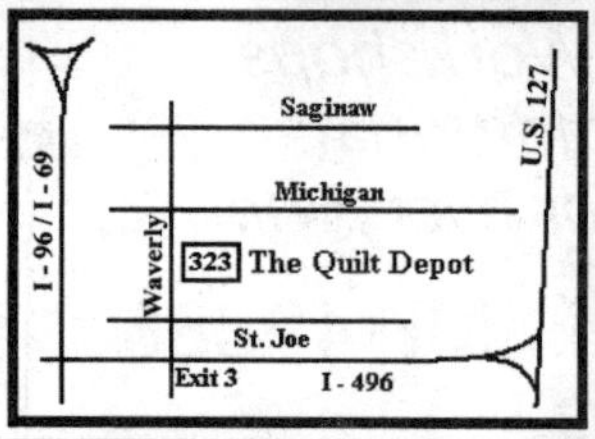

Mason, MI #43

**Mon - Fri 9 - 8
Sat 9 - 5:30
Sun 12 - 5**

Kean's Store Co.

406 S. Jefferson St. 48854
(517) 676-5144

Large selection of quality quilting fabrics, bear supplies, mohair, quilt books, patterns, books, & notions.
Bring a friend, spend the day, lots to see!

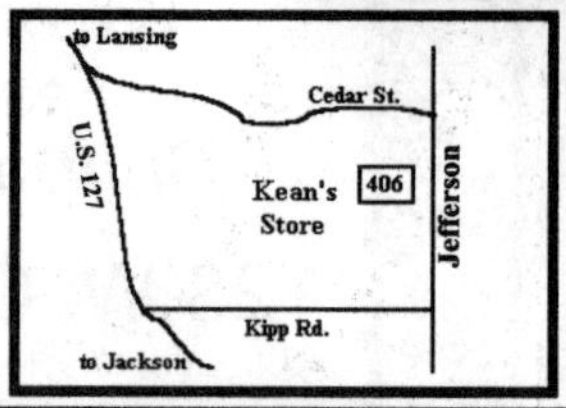

The Quilting Season

5150 W. Michigan Ave.
Ypsilanti, MI 48197
(734) 528-1740 Fax: Same
Web Site www.quiltingseason.com
Est: 2001 1800 sq.ft.

Ypsilanti, MI #44

1500 Quilting Fabrics that Enchant and Inspire

RJR Fabrics, Moda Fabrics, Hoffman California, Benartex, Bali Fabrics & more.

Quilting Books, Patterns, Supplies and Classes

Located 3/4 mile East of US-23 on US12 in the big red barn at Schmidt's Antiques.

**Tues - Sat 9:30 - 5
Sun 12 - 5**

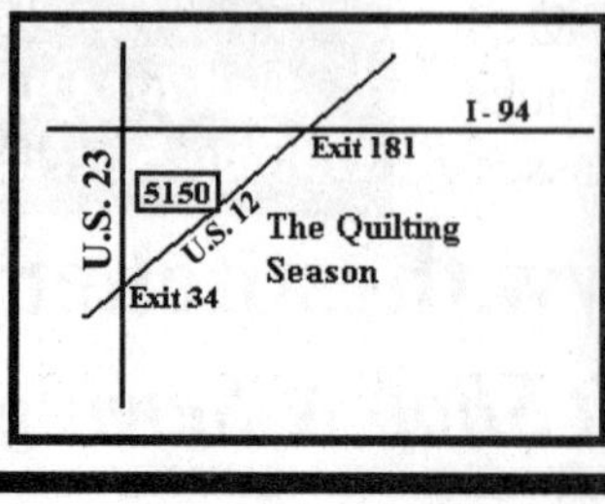

Bits 'n Pieces

34629 W. Michigan Ave.
Wayne, MI 48184
(734) 641-4970 **#45**

Est. 1981

www.bitsnpieces.net

Cotton Fabrics

Quilting Supplies

Books • Patterns • Kits • Block-of-the-Month

BERNINA Sewing Machines

Sales • Service • Repair

Mon - Sat 10 - 5 Tues & Thurs 'til 7
(closed Mondays during July and August)

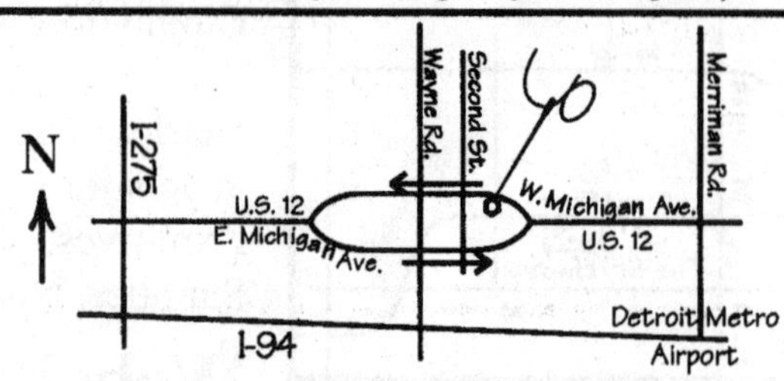

On the south side of Westbound Michigan Ave.
Approximately 3½ miles east of I-275, 1 ½ miles west of Merriman Rd. and 4 miles north of I-94.

#46 Viking Sewing Center of Ann Arbor

Sew Exciting! at Viking Sewing Center of Ann Arbor

5235 Jackson Rd.
Ann Arbor, MI 48103
734-761-3094
800-252-0829
www.vikingsewing.com

Store Hours
M - F 10am - 6pm
Sat 10am - 4pm
Evening Hours by appointment

Exit 169 off I-94

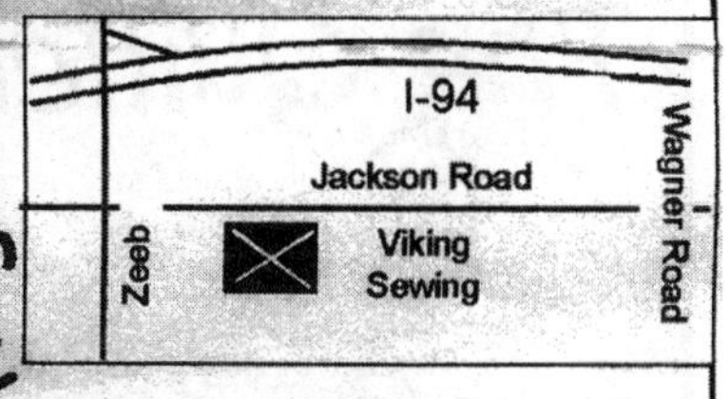

Why run around in circles when we have ... 6,000 bolts of fantastic fabrics for all of your sewing needs? - hard to find sewing accessories - classes, books ... patterns galore - software for quilting and embroidery - expert repair on all makes and models - used machine reconditioning - sewing machines and sergers for every budget - top quality furniture for your sewing room - award winning authroized sales and service - Husqvarna Viking and White sewing machines with a complete try before you buy showroom! Why shop anywhere else?

Plymouth, MI #47

QuiltWorks

580 Forest Avenue #4 48170
(734) 207-8708
E-Mail: thequiltworks@worldnet.att.net
Web Site: www.thequiltworks.com

Your place for contemporary cotton fabrics for quilting and clothing. Let our friendly, knowledgeable staff help you make your project come to life. Books, patterns, books, notions, classes...complete quilting supplies for the novice to the expert.

Large selection of Hoffman batiks

Mon - Sat
10 - 5

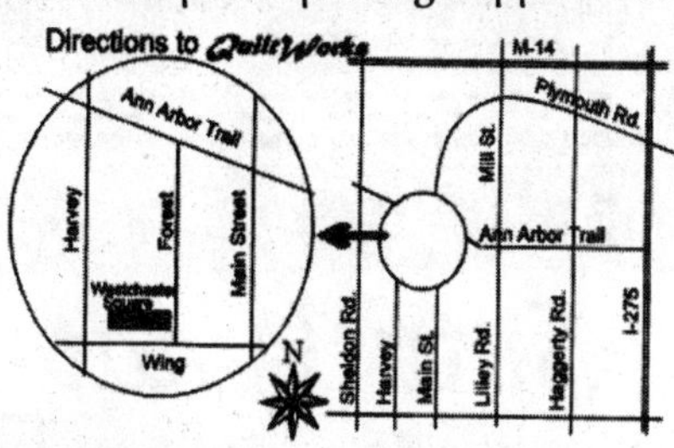

Monroe, MI #48

Kinder's Corner

Mon, Tues, Wed 10 - 6
Thur 10 - 7
Fri 10 - 5
Sat 10 - 4

4531 W. Dunbar 48161
Phone/Fax (734) 457-9111
E-Mail: info@cattalesquilts.com
Web Site: www.cattalesquilts.com
Est: 1999 2000sq.ft.

Full service Quilt Shop.

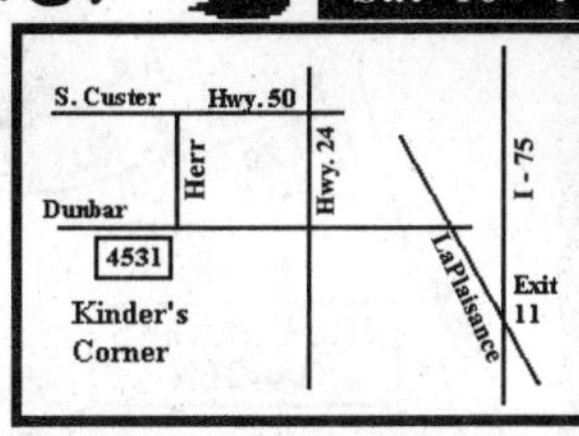

Livonia, MI #49

Please Call for an Appt.

Creative Quilting

36749 Angeline Cir. 48150
(734) 425-6385
Owner: Jean Coleman Est: 1990

The Finishing Touch

A MACHINE QUILTING SERVICE

Custom machine quilting. Quilts accepted from UPS and U.S.P.S. Design choices by mutual agreement per letter or phone. Call for a flyer.

White Lake, MI #50

Tues - Fri 10 - 5
Sat 10 - 4

More Than Quilting

9135 Highland Rd #7 (M-59)
Mail: P.O. Box 541,
Highland 48387
(248) 698-3020
Owners: Carolyn Anderson & Wanda Gregory

Quality fabrics and yarns, patterns, books, notions, buttons and more. Classes in knitting, crocheting and quilting. Personalized service!

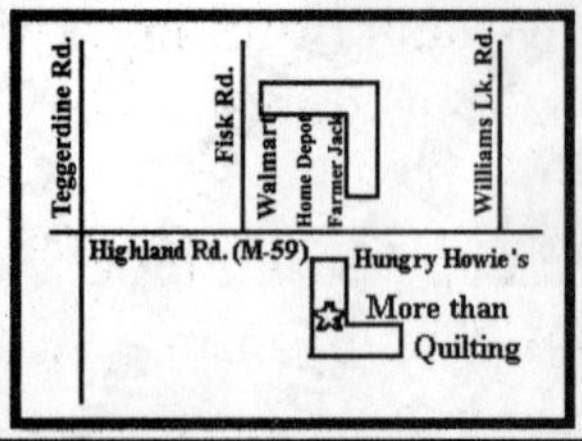

Fenton, MI #51

Tues - Fri 10 - 6
Sat 9:30 - 4

The Cotton Gin
Quilt Shop & Yarn Basket

1535 N. Leroy 48430
(810) 714-6004
Owner: Hope Vergin

Fabric, Books, Yarn, Notions, Classes & Machine Quilt Service.

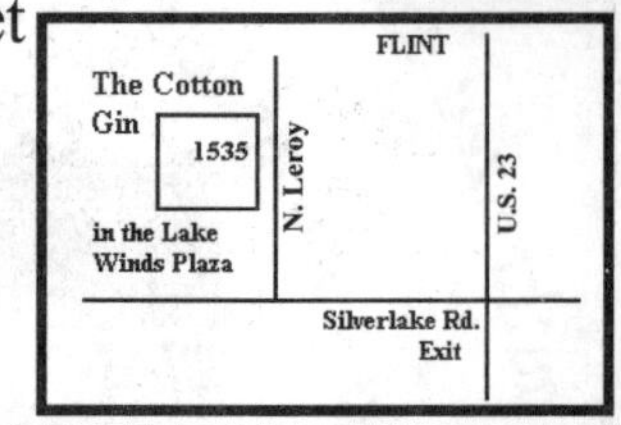

Fenton, MI #52

The Quilters Garden

Mon, Tue, Wed, Fri 9:30 - 6
Thursday 9:30 - 8:30
Sat 9:30 - 4

Providing a variety of high quality 100% cotton quilting fabric, books, patterns, quilting supplies and classes.

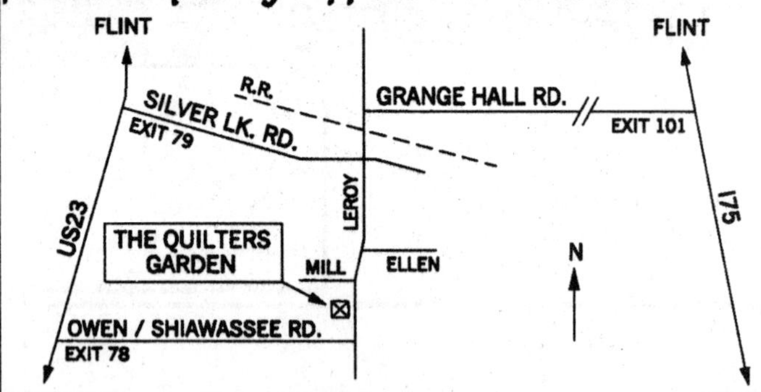

302-1/2 S. Leroy, Fenton, MI 48430
810-629-0331
quilt@thequiltersgarden.com
www.thequiltersgarden.com

QUILTER'S CORNER

36743 Garfield Rd.
Clinton Twp., MI 48035
Ph. (586) 790-8292
Fax (586) 790-8293

M & F 9 TO 5; T-W-Th 9 to 8; Sat 10 to 4; Sun Closed

Friendly, fun staff!! Great selection of 100% cotton fabrics (incl. Flannels & homespuns), wide range of colors of nonwoven wool felts, books, patterns, notions, classes to suit everyone!

Host shop for Thimbleberries Quilt Club.

GIFT CERTIFICATES
VISA - MASTERCARD - DISCOVER

Take I - 94 to Exit 236. West on Metro Pkwy. 4 miles to Garfield Rd.

On SW corner (near bank) in Hitching Post Shopping Center.

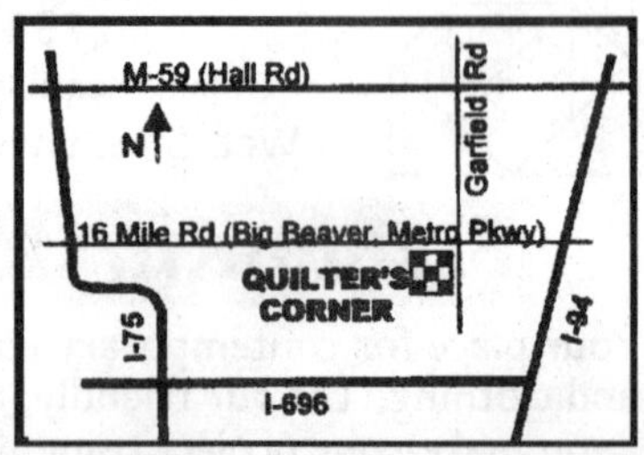

Clinton Twp, MI #53

Belleville, MI #54

Mon - Sat 10 - 6
Sun by Appt.

Threads 'n Treasures Quilt Shop

129 South St. 48111
(734) 697-9376 Fax: Same
E-Mail: katking@provide.net
Owner: Kay Atkins Est: 1996

25% off all 1500 bolts everyday when you buy ½ yard or more per cut. Overall machine quilting. Custom quilts, classes.

Southgate, MI #55

Mon - Fri 10 - 6
Sat 10 - 3

Sew What

13736 Fort St. 48195
(734) 281-1344 Fax: Same
E-Mail: sewwhat59@aol.com
Est: 1997 1400 sq.ft. 1000+ bolts

100% cotton fabrics from Hoffman, Benartex, Thimbleberries, Mumm's the Word, Moda and more. Quilting supplies, books & patterns. Special orders welcome.

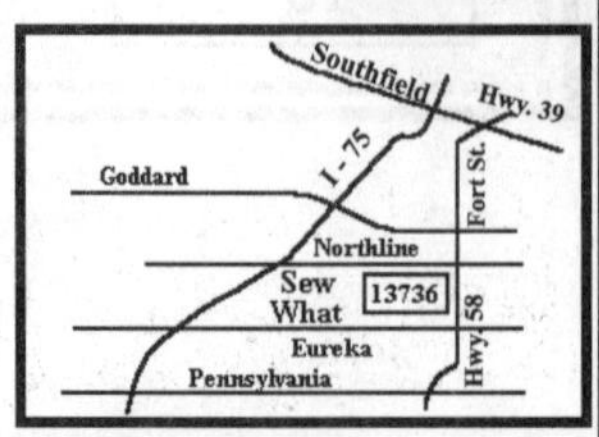

The Quilted Goose

Custom Machine Quilting Services

The Quilted Goose offers custom machine quilting services. Excellent quilter with design imagination can make the most of your creation. We offer four levels of quilting, from simple all-over designs to heirloom quality quilting. Your quilts will be treated with loving care in our smoke-free studio.

Be sure to ask for a copy of our brochure **"What Our Customers Have to Say About The Quilted Goose"** and find out what our customers already know!

Let us help you get your quilt tops out of the storage closet and onto a bed or a wall! **Call or email today for current turn-around time or to request a copy of our free brochure.**

Troy, MI #56

The Quilted Goose

646 East Long Lake Road, Troy, MI 48085
248-740-8867
248-740-8869 FAX
Email: info@thequiltedgoose.com
www.thequiltedgoose.com

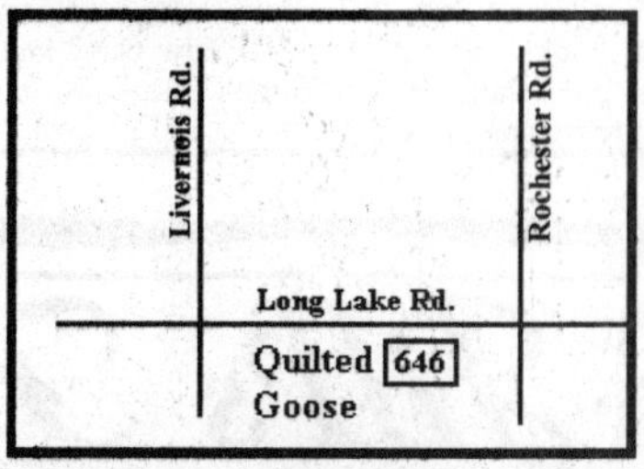

Linda M. Thielfoldt, Designer
Hours By Appointment - please call.
Member of IMQA

Berkley, MI #57

Mon - Fri 10 - 6:30
Wed til 9
Sat 10 - 5
Sun 12 - 3

Guildcrafters

QUILT SHOP

2790 West Twelve Mile Road
248-541-8545
Web: Guildcrafters.com

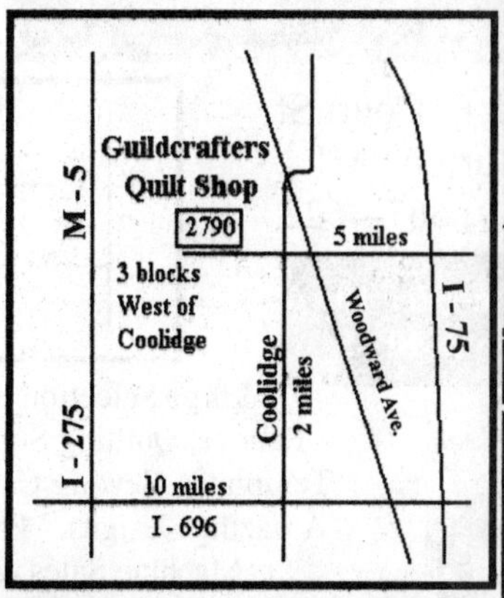

20 Years in Business 1982-2002

Owners: Jo & Nanci Merecki

5000 Bolts

Cottons, Large Flannel Section, Reproductions, Wools, Bright Novelty Fabrics, Books & Patterns
Largest supply of quilt merchandise in the area

Berkley, MI #58

By Appt.

Cheryl's Heirloom Quilting

(248) 544-1113
Owner: Cheryl Mathe—designer

Please Call for Directions

Experienced long-arm machine quilting.
100's of designs or custom design available.
Excellent service. Call for information.

St. Clair Shore, MI #59

Mon, Tues, Fri 10 - 6
Thur 10 - 9
Sat 10 - 4

The Quilters Patch

31384 Harper 48082
(586) 293-1999
Owner: Beverly Maxvill
Est: 1981 1200 sq.ft.

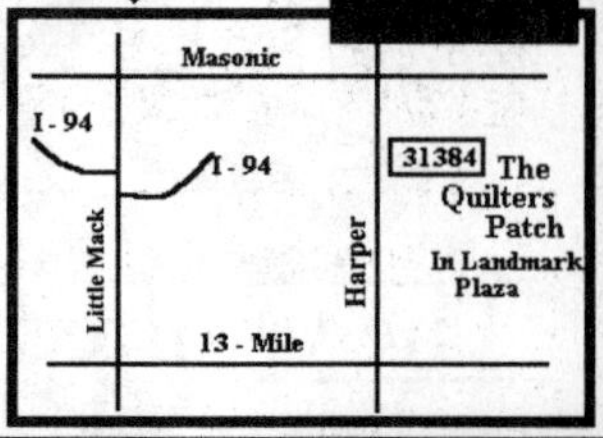

Victorian Block of the Month as seen in "Keepsake Catalog" and many original designs available for Quilts & Blocks. Fabrics-Notions-Books.

Richmond, MI #60

Tues - Thur 10 - 5
Fri 10 - 7
Sat 10 - 4

Sew Together

69295 Main St. 48062
(586) 727-1555
E-Mail: quilting@massnet1.net
www.geocities.com/sewtogetherquiltshop
Owners: Gina Kaszynski & Susan Weinert

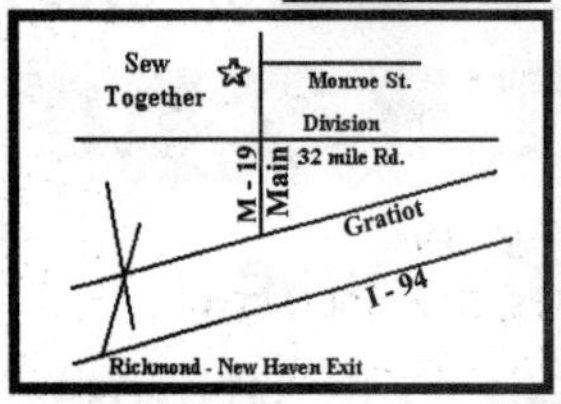

A large variety of cotton fabrics, many different threads and embellishments. Huge assortment of books and patterns. We now carry knitting supplies and have some gorgeous yarns. Inquire about our doll club.

Imlay City, MI #61

Mon - Fri 9:30 - 5:15
Sat 9:30 - 5

The Pincushion

113 East Third Street 48444
(810) 724-7065
2 Miles North of I - 69 & M-53
Owner: Joyce Schihl
Est: 1971

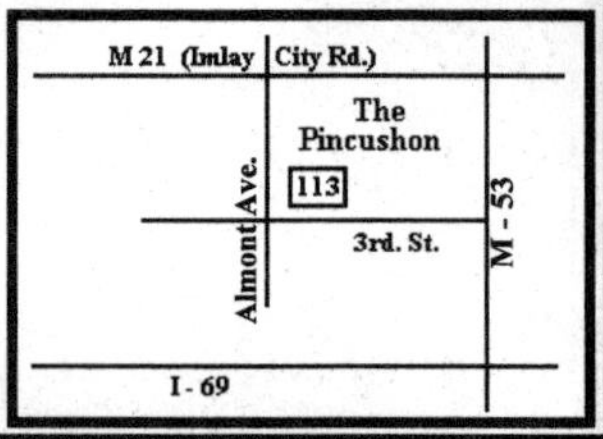

Everything For The Quilter.
Quality Quilting Fabric & Supplies. An Extensive Book Inventory. Small town Friendly service. Our customers are our friends.

Jill's Fabrics
& Costume Rental

Two Great Locations!

Lapeer, MI #62

2268 N Lapeer Rd.
Lapeer, MI 48446
(810) 667-4025

Mon - Sat 10 - 5

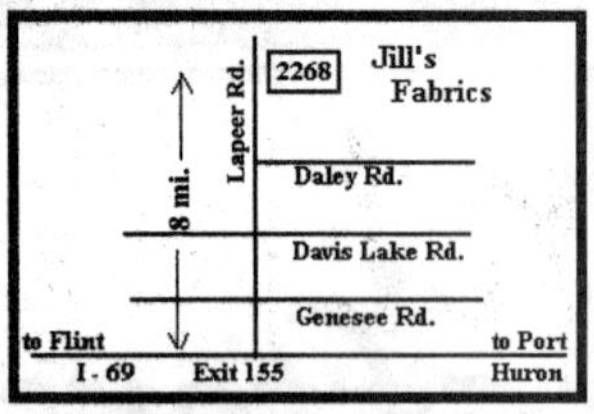

Visit our Web Site at: **www.jillsfabrics.com**
E-Mail: jills@tir.com Fax: (810) 667-4622
Owner: Jill Hurd

Burton, MI #63

4163 E. Court St.
Burton, MI
(810) 667-4622

Mon - Fri 10 - 6
Sat 10 - 5

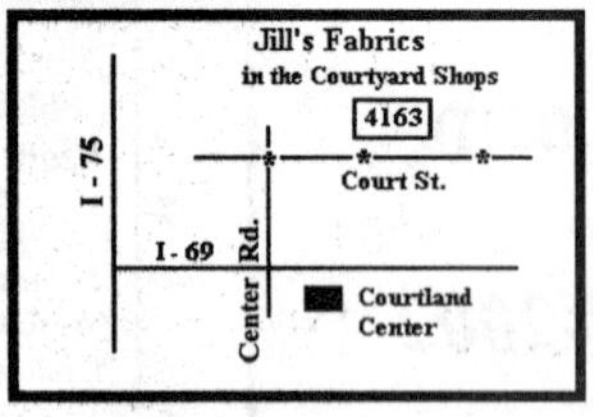

Large Selection of 100% Cotton Fabrics, Quilting Supplies, Books, Templates, Sewing Cabinets, Classes, Amazing Designs. Pfaff, & Brother Machine Sales & Service.
Costume Rentals (Lapeer Only)
We pride ourselves on customer service.

Davison, MI #64

Linda's Country Quilt Shop

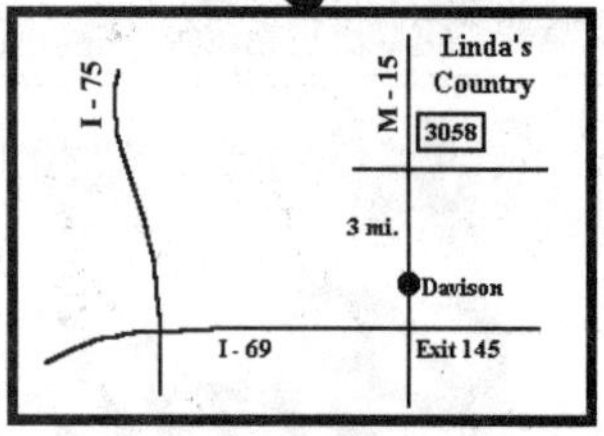

3058 N. State Rd. Unit F
M - 15 48423
(810) 658-9051
Owner: Linda Jacobsen
Est: 1998
2500 sq.ft. 2200 Bolts

We are a country store with a large variety of traditional fabrics by RJR, Thimbleberries, Moda, South Seas, Benartex, P&B Fabrics, Timeless Treasures, Michael Miller and more.

Mon - Sat 9 - 5

Davison Fabrics

Thousands of Fabric Bolts Including:
Benartex ❖ Thimbleberries ❖ Kaufman
RJR ❖ Hoffman ❖ Spiegel ❖ Roberta Horton
Free Spirit ❖ South Seas ❖ Debbie Mumm
Timeless Treasures ❖ In the Beginning
Indo US ❖ Monarch ❖ Maywood ❖ P & B
Theresa Kogut ❖ Fasco ❖ Hi Fashion
Bali ❖ Spechler-Vogel ❖ And Many More!

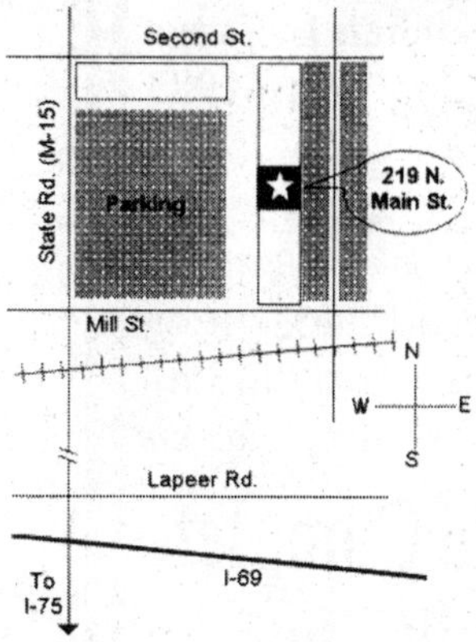

Authorized Sales & Service
Commercial & Residential
We Service All Brands

Largest Selection of Craft Patterns in the State

Davison, MI #65

219 N. Main Street
Downtown Davison
(810) 653-2641
info@davisonfabrics.com

Est. 1944
Owners: Greg & Ramona Nolan
Over 6000 square feet

Hours:
Mondays - Saturdays
9 a.m. - 5:30 p.m.

Over 400 classes annually
100's of Book Titles
100's of Quilting Stencils
Hobbs & Quilters Dream Batting
Quilting Frames and Hoops
Olfa, Creative Grid, Omni Grid
and Fiskar Rulers & Rotary Tools
Quilting & Sewing Gifts
Wonderful Selection of Buttons
Heirloom & Smocking Supplies
Many of those Hard to Find Notions

Port Huron, MI #66

Sew Elegant

Quilt Shoppe

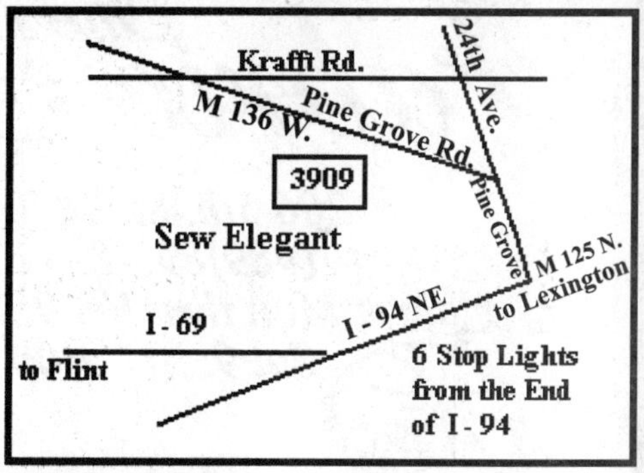

VAST SELECTION OF BOOKS, PATTERNS AND SEWING NOTIONS FOR QUILTERS.

3909 Pine Grove Rd. 48059
(810) 982-6556
Fax: (810) 982-6996
E-Mail: elsew@aol.com
Web-Site: www.sewelegant.com
Owner: Linda Anderson
Est:1986 4880 sq.ft.

PFAFF MACHINES
SALES & SERVICE

Mon - Sat
10 - 5:30
Sun 12 - 4:30

Eastern Michigan's Largest Quilt Shop!
Our Shop is full of 100% cotton Fabrics--
over 8,000 bolts

Sterling Heights, MI #67

4090 17 Mile Road 48310
(586) 979-7422

Quilt-n Friends

Gretchen L. Tatge
Est: 1983

1500 bolts of 100% Cotton Fabrics
Notions ... Books ... Patterns
Gifts ... Machine Quilting
Newsletter every 2 months ... Friendly Staff
Classes Year Round ... Michigan's Finest Teachers

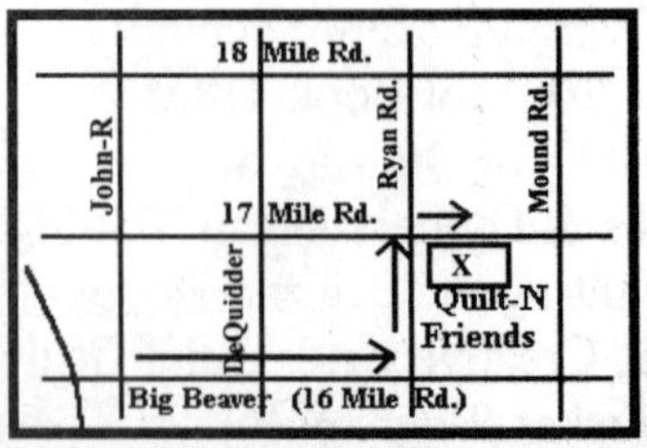

"The Complete Quilt Shop"

Mon - Fri 9 - 5 Sat 9 - 3
Mon & Thurs Eve til 8:30

Flushing, MI #68

Mon - Sat 10 - 5
Sun 1 - 4

100% Cotton fabrics.
Quilting books & patterns.
Notions.
Lots of classes.
Warm and personal service.
Quaint setting.

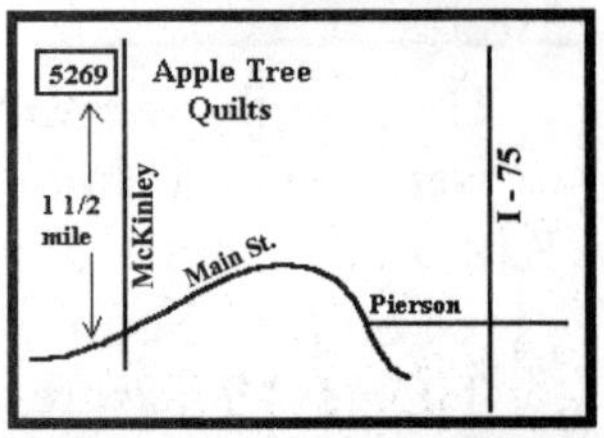

APPLE TREE QUILTS

5269 McKinley Rd. 48433
(810) 659- 4190
Owner: Judie Martin
Est: 1996
2000 sq.ft. 1000+ Bolts

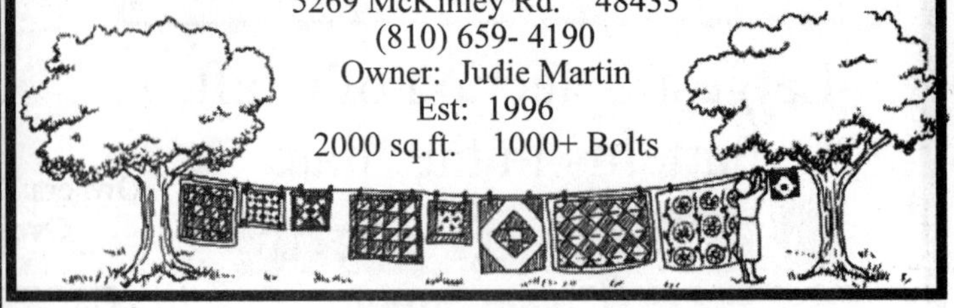

Bay City, MI #69

The Fabric Fair

206 5th. St. 48708
(989)893-8971
Hours: Mon thru Fri 9:30 - 7:00
Sat 9:30 - 5:00

Nothing Sews Like A Bernina. Nothing.
BERNINA®

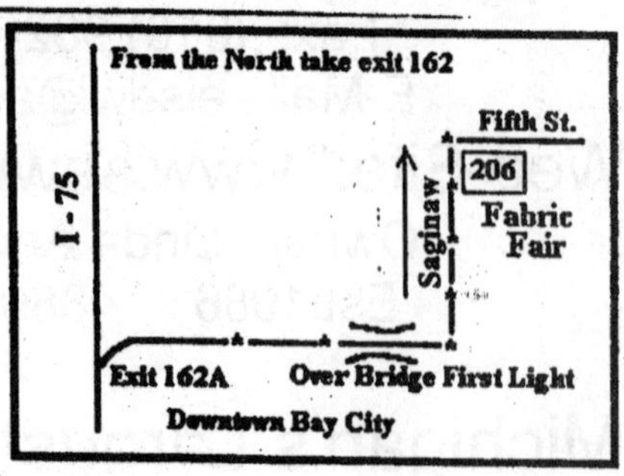

Come visit our unique 110yr. old newly remodeled building.
A Fabric Store since 1955.
10,000+ Bolts 7000 sq. ft.
Owner: Cecelia Wieland

- *Quilters cotton, notions and frames*
- *Bridal, Formal and Special Occasion*
- *Quality Woolens, Knits & Ribbing*
- *Linen, Tencel, Silk & UltraSuede*
- *Heirloom Fabric and Laces*
- *Polar Fleece, Berber & Flannel*
- *Homespuns and Tapestries*
- *Tricot, Swim and Dancewear Fabric*
- *Ceramic Buttons and Pins*
- *Stretch and Sew & Burda Patterns*
- *Silver Cloth,Linen Toweling, Ticking*

Bay City, MI #70

Mon 12 - 9
Tues - Fri 10 - 6
Sat 10 - 2

Snail's Trail Quilt Shop

214 S. Henry 48706
(517) 895-9003
Fax: (517) 894-2549
E-Mail: trail214@famvid.com
Owners: Pat LaRoche & Kathy Baker

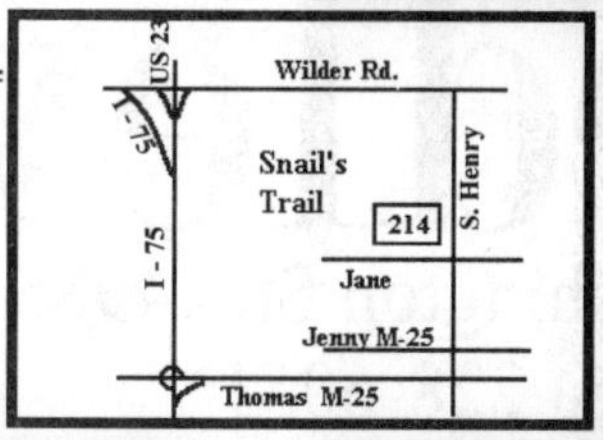

Fabrics including Hoffman & South Seas. Crafters, you'll love our Button Crock! Large Selection of Patterns. Classes. Featuring wearable art.

Saginaw, MI #71

Mon - Sat 9 - 4
Thur til 7

The Fabric Stash

3541 State St. 48602
(989) 790-9317
Owners: Karen Butler & Joanne Schaeding

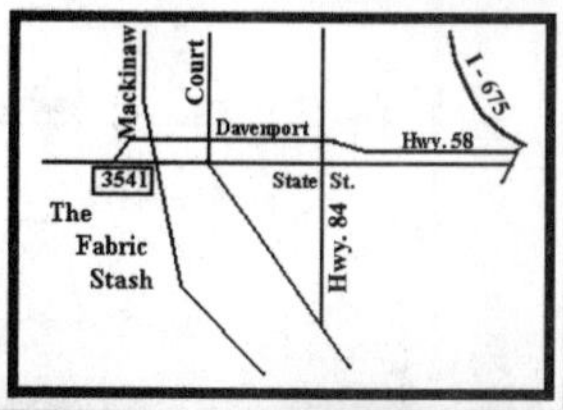

Fine cotton fabrics, books, notions, supplies and classes for quilting. Unique kits and blocks-of-the-month.

Menominee, MI #72

Mon - Fri 9:30 - 5:30
Thur til 8
Sat 10 - 4
Sun 1 - 4

Quilter's Haven, Ltd.

707 1st St. 49858
(906) 864-3078
E-Mail: qhaven@webcntrl.com
Owner: Chris Caselton
Est: 1996 2000 sq.ft. 1800 Bolts

A friendly quaint quilt shop along the beautiful shore of Lake Michigan. Notions, books, patterns galore!! Bernina Sewing Machine Dealer

Escanaba, MI #73

Mon - Fri 10 - 5
Sat & Sun by Appt.

Quilts 'n Stuff by Glenna

608 S. 14th St. 49829
(906) 786-3436 Fax: (906) 789-1483
E-Mail: garkens@quiltsnstuff.net
Web Site: www.quiltsnstuff.net
Owner: Glenna Arkens Est: 1992

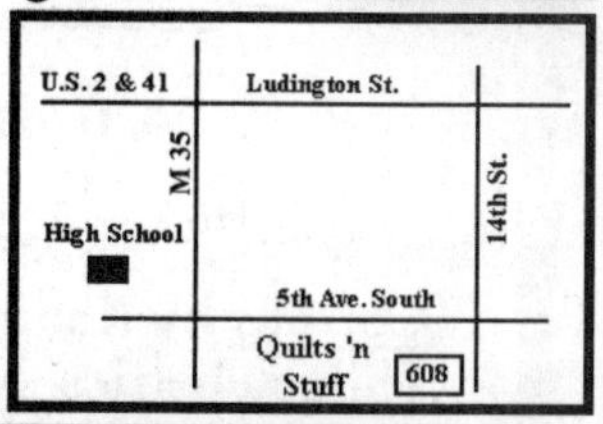

Featuring: quilting fabric (lots of batiks), silk ribbon, applique patterns, Upper Peninsula & floral art quilts.

Iron Mountain, MI #74

Mon - Fri 10 - 5
Sat 10 - 2

From the Heart

211 E. Hughitt St. 49801
(906) 779-1864 Est: 1997
E-Mail: heart@up.lib.mi.us
Owner: Susan Kangas

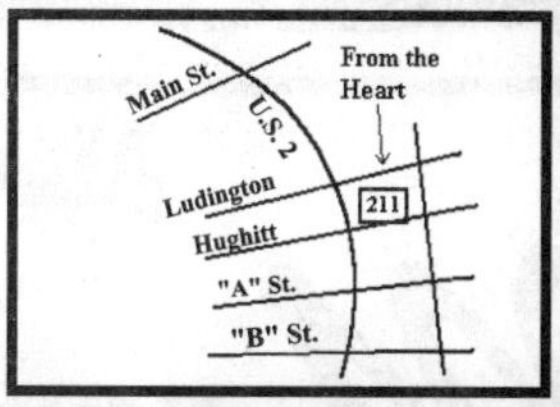

Small, friendly shop with fine quality fabrics, books, patterns, supplies, yarn and knitwear. Classes.

Norway, MI #75

Jeri's Quilt Patch

703 Brown St. U.S. 2 49870 (906) 563-9620
Web Site: www.geocities.com/jerisquiltpatch

Mon - Sat 10 - 5

Yearly Quilt Show & Fabric Sale
2002 JQP Quilt Show Aug 24 - Sept 2
2003 JQP Quilt Show Aug 23 - Sept 1
2004 JQP Quilt Show Aug 28 - Sept 6

Unique Quilt Shop, 100% Cotton Fabric, Quilting Supplies plus Antiques & Gifts. Featuring Antique Linens, Fabric, Quilts & Quilt Tops.

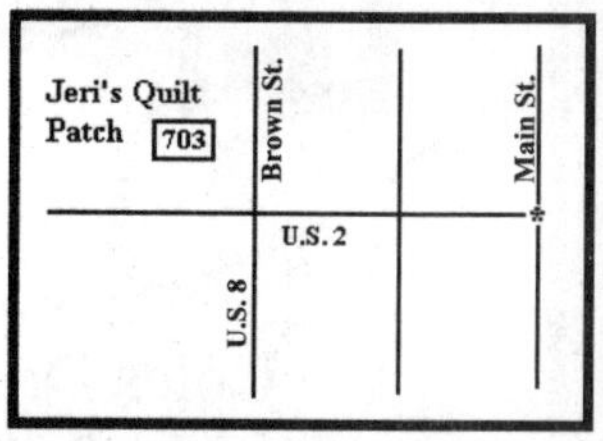

Quilter's Special-Fat Quarters only $1.00 ea.

Sault Ste. Marie, MI #76

May 1 - Oct 15
Mon - Fri 9 - 5
Sat 9 - 3
Oct 16 - Apr 30
Tues - Sat 9 - 5

Gloria's Happy Hooker

Quilting & Needlecraft Supplies

M - 129 (2733 Ashmun St.) 49783
(906) 635-9937
Owner: Gloria Larke

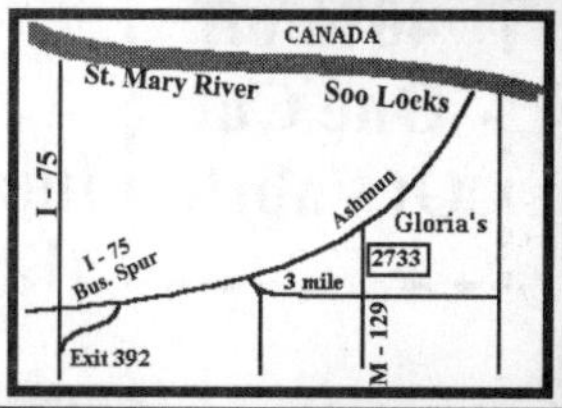

Quilting Fabric including RJR, Hoffman, Moda. Yarn, counted cross-stitched, needlepoint books & supplies. Home of the Famous Soo Locks.

Paradise, MI #77

Open 7 Days
Summer 10-7
Winter 10 - 5

Village Fabrics & Crafts

32702 W. Hwy. M-123 P.O. Box 254
(906) 492-3803 49768
www.VillageFabricsAndCrafts.com
E-Mail: villagefab@sault.com
Owner: Vicki Hallaxs Est: 1986

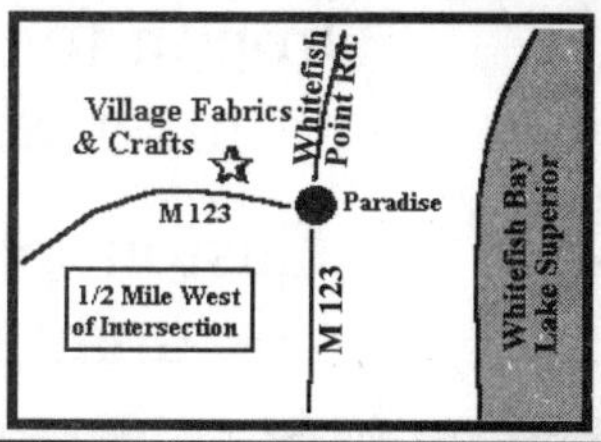

Quilting, knitting, crocheting, counted cross stitch, silk ribbon embroidery, unique needlearts, hundreds of books and patterns—many of local attractions. Gifts

Calumet, MI #78

Mon - Sat 10 - 5
May 1 — Dec 31

Traditions

Between Hancock & Calumet
51950 U.S. #41 49913
(906) 482-8674 Est: 1993
E-Mail: ceskola@pasty.com
Web Site: www.traditions-shop.com
Owners: Barb Heinonen, Carol Eskola
Carole Ryynanen & Sue Pietila

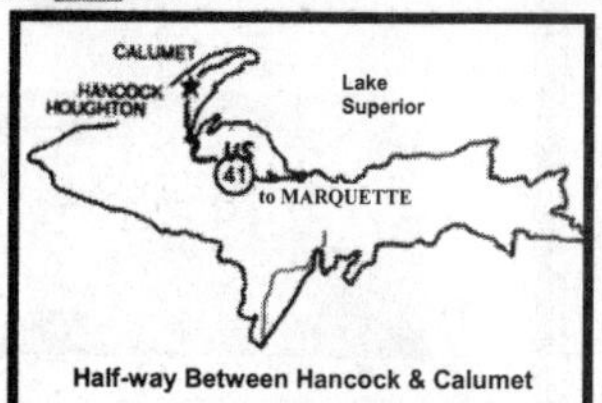

Books, fabrics & supplies for Quilting plus local art, florals, smocking, dolls and baskets.

Marquette, MI #79

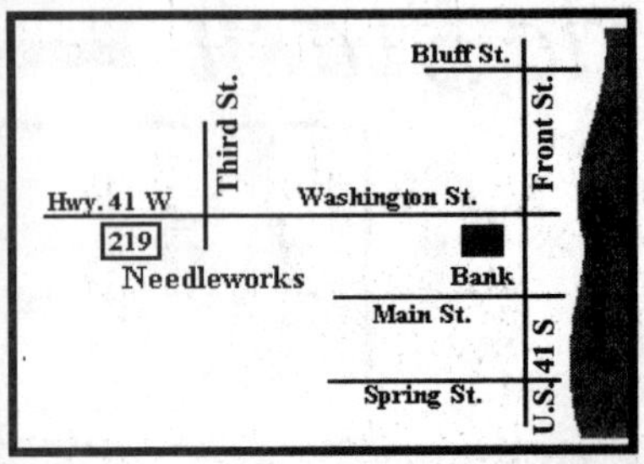

Needleworks

219 W. Washington St. 49855
(906) 228-6051
Owners: Sherrie Jaqua & Family

Mon - Sat 10 - 6
Fri til 9
May - Dec Sun 12 - 4

A unique shop combining Quilting & Knitting, Weaving & Spinning for the northcountry fiber art enthusiast. FEATURING:

<u>Cottons</u> by Kaufman, Hoffman, Moda, P&B, Debbie Mumm, Jinny Beyer, Thimbleberries, Northcott & David Textiles. 100% wool yarns-grown locally.

Unique buttons • Kwik Sew patterns • Australian quilting magazines • Classes
Large Selection of Quilting, Weaving, Knitting & Spinning Books.

Thimbleberries
Cottons $5.99
Flannels $7.99

A fun shop to visit! Lots of Professional Help!

Marquette, MI #80

Quilting by Lake Superior

Merricks

dba Ben Franklin

40% off One Cut Of Fabric

3,000 Bolts of Fabric
Including 100% cottons and flannels from top designers

Fleece, Upholstery, Yarn

Also gift items, notions, kits and books

Long Arm Gammil Quilting Machine

Drop in for a cup of coffee and meet with new friends.

Custom picture framing and matting is offered.

100 Coles Dr., Marquette, MI 49855
(906) 226-9613 Fax: (906) 226-8004
Jwm2180@yahoo.com
Owners: Jim & Sarah Martin
Est: 1963 6,000 sq.ft. 3,000 Bolts

Mon - Thur 9 - 6
Fri 9 - 7 Sat 9 - 5
Sun 12 - 4

BERNINA

Ironwood, MI #81

Visit us at: www.fabricpatch.com

The Fabric Patch

121 N. Lowell St. 49938
(906) 932-5260 Fax: (906) 932-5004
E-Mail: fabric@portup.com Est: 1981

Mail Order Available.

Quilting, Rubber Stamping and Craft Headquarters of the North.
Largest Selection in Michigan's Upper Peninsula and Northern Wisconsin.

Choose from over 3500 Bolts of Quilting Fabrics Huge Selection of Quilting Books and Craft Patterns.
Ongoing Block of the Month Kits
Call or Stop In for Details

Authorized Dealer for Husqvarna Viking and White Sewing Machines & Sergers.

Mon - Thur 9:30 - 5
Fri 9:30 - 6
Sat 9:30 - 4

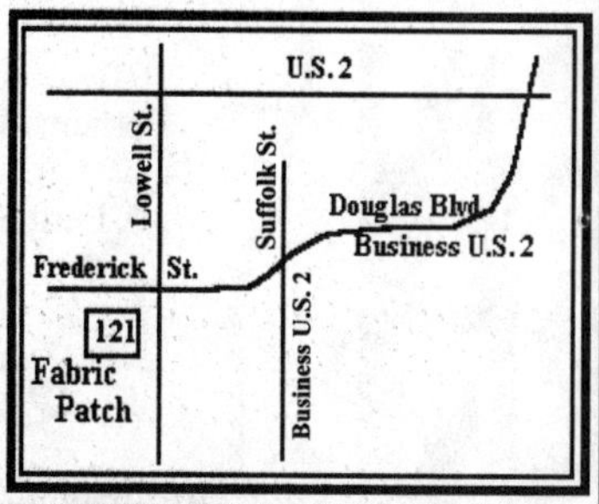

Ontonagon, MI #82

Quilter's Closet

Mon - Fri 11 - 5:30
Sat 11 - 4

409 Lake St. 49953
(906) 884-2225
Est: 2001
Owner: Laura D. LaHaie

Fabrics, Sewing Notions, Yarns & Notions, Craft Kits & Supplies, Craft Books, Teas & Spices.

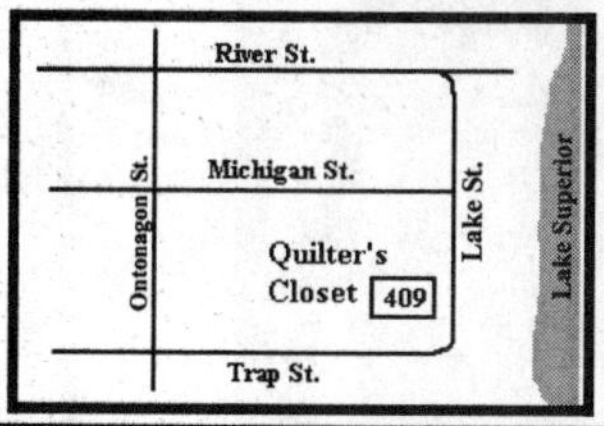

Other Shops in Michigan: We suggest calling first

Beaverton	Lelia's Place, 1333 McKimmy Dr.	517-435-3275
Belleville	Sue's Quilt Shop, 48120 Harris Rd.	313-461-6540
Boyne City	Bayne River Quilt Co., 221 1/2 S. Lake St.	231-582-6970
Brethren	Studio North, 5630 Farnsworth Rd.	616-477-5679
Brighton	Hickory Hill, 1113 S. Hacker Rd.	810-220-4455
Brown City	Ann's Fabric Shop, 5044 Bailey Rd.	810-346-3237
Caledonia	Rainbow's End Yarn, Craft & Variety, 9343 Cherry Valley Ave.	616-891-1106
Caledonia	Needle Ittle Quilting, 9563 Kraft Ave. SE	616-891-8912
Caro	Quilt Talk, 209 N. State St.	517-673-7994
Caro	Ruby's Yarn & Fabric, 3 N. Almer	517-673-3062
Chassell	Einerlei Shop, 422 Wilson Memorial Dr.	906-523-4612
Croswell	Wanda's Fabric Shop, 61 N. Howard Ave.	810-679-3482
Dearborn	Lace, Quilts N' Roses, 3728 Monroe St.	313-792-8804
Farwell	Elm Creek Ltd., 2609 W. Surrey Rd.	989-588-6061
Flint	Bizzy Bee Quilts 1149 Pickwick Pl.	810-233-3982
Flushing	Innovative Imprints 10264 Beecher Rd.	810-659-9606
Frankenmuth	Frankenmuth Woolen Mills, 570 S. Main St.	517-652-8121
Gowen	Loving Stitches, 3168 Johnson Rd.	616-984-6321
Grand Haven	The Wooden Spool Quilts & Antiques, 210 Washington	616-844-0884
Grand Rapids	The Daisy Den Stitchery, 2210 Rosewood SE	616-245-2994
Hillsdale	Laurie's Farmhouse Quilting, 6551 Cambria Rd.	517-357-4478
Lambertville	Village Fabrics & Crafts, 8019 Summerfield Rd.	313-856-5350
Lapeer	Lapeer Fabrics, 110 W. Park	810-667-9098
Macomb	Hearthstone Quilts, 23404 Harrellson St.	810-598-5936
Mason	Yards of Fabric, 116 E. Ash	517-676-2973
Milford	Quilter's Shoppe, 4458 Country View Ln.	
Mio	The Fabric Shoppe, 432 E. Kittle Rd.	none
Mohawk	Phyl's Fabrics, 1020 N. Ahameek St., P.O. Box 229	906-337-0567
Montrose	Country Novelties, 14274 Marshall Rd.	313-639-2430
Munith	Patchwork, Inc., 11970 Hannewald Rd.	517-596-2501
Munsing	Mama Bear's Den, 206 E. Superior St.	906-387-1570
Muskegon	Great Lakes Quilting & Crafts, 1712 McLaughlin	231-773-5095
New Era	Needle Nook4708 1st St.	231-861-4077
Novi	Banks Vacuum Corp., 43039 Grand River	810-347-7655
Omer	Quilt Patch Antiques, 429 E. Center St.	517-653-2332
Oscoda	Loose Threads, 208 S. State St.	989-739-7115
Parma	Unique Quilts, 128 E. Main St.	517-531-3843
Perrinton	Calico Cupboard, 4625 MacArthur	517-236-7728
Petoskey	Calico Crafts, 1691 Spring P.O. Box 2390	616-347-1511
Port Huron	Mary Maxim, Inc., 2001 Holland Ave.	810-987-2000
Portland	Quilters Gallery, 1419 E. Grand River	517-647-7716
Prudenville	Chris' Fabrics, 960 W. Houghton Lake Dr.	517-366-4790
Reading	Kathryn's Country Fabrics, 7911 S. Edon Rd. M-49	517-268-5815
Riverdale	Sheila's Fabrics, 11995 W. Monroe Rd.	517-833-7835
Rockford	Material Girls, 8321 Atlanta Dr. NE	616-866-3721
Roscommon	Grandma's Quilts, 306 Smiths Blvd.	517-821-7041
Saranac	Candy Corner Emporium, 7129 Bliss Rd.	616-527-1170
South Lyon	The Artcraft Shop, P.O. Box 276	810-437-3830
Traverse City	Abbey Rose, 3200 S. Airport Rd. W	231-947-8270
Traverse City	BJ's Cozy Quilts, Etc., 1425 S. Airport Rd.	616-922-6766
Traverse City	Boyd's and Sew Much More, 966 S. Airport	616-946-4011
Trenary	Nimble Thimble Shop, Highway 41	906-446-3529
Walled Lake	Grandma Honey's Quilts, 1925 Shankin Dr.	248-624-4677
Washington	Creative Corner, 66800 Van Dyke Rd.	810-752-7444
Yale	Sew 'N Sew, 1 N. Main St.	

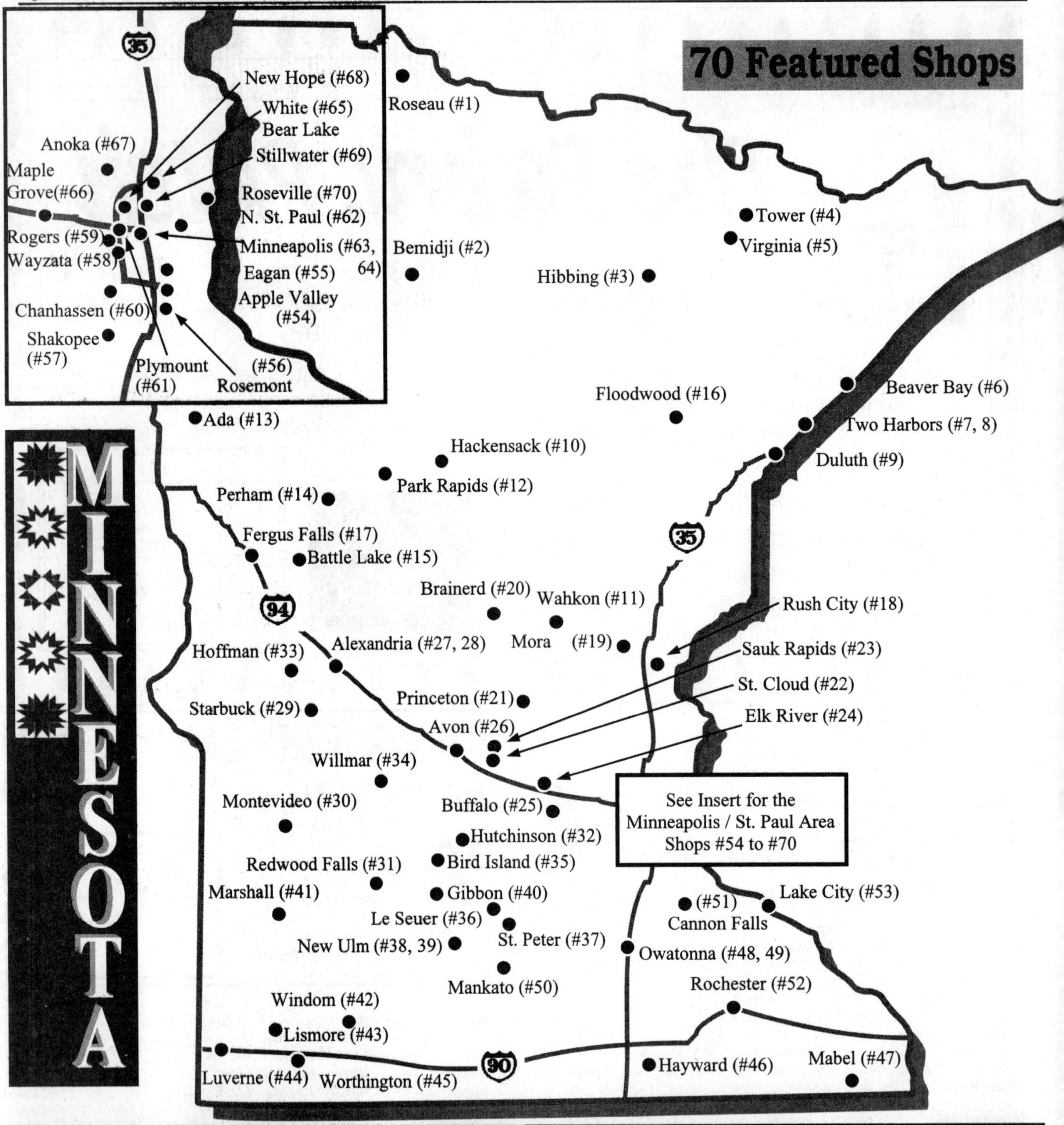

Roseau, MN #1

Mon - Sat 10 - 5:30

Quilt S'More

Quilt Like CRAZY!

114 2nd St. NE 56751
(218) 463-3867 Fax: Same
E-Mail: aemagnusson@wiktel.com
Owner: Judy Magnusson

We offer Fabrics, Notions, Machines and Classes Year Round

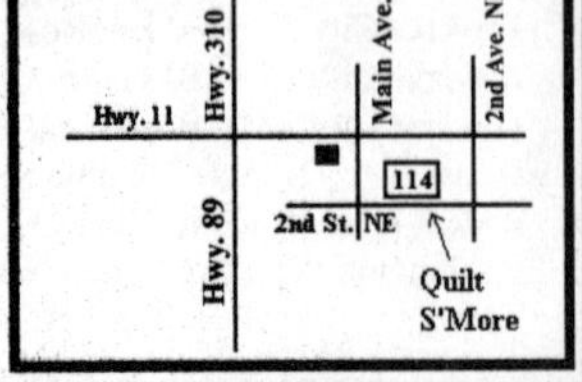

Bemidji, MN #2

Tues - Fri 10 - 5 Sat 10 - 3

Willow Wood Quilt Shop

23621 Cty. Rd.9 56601
(218) 759-2310

Tucked in the woods 6 miles south of Bemidji, Willow Wood has quality cottons, patterns, supplies, gifts and antiques. Classes.

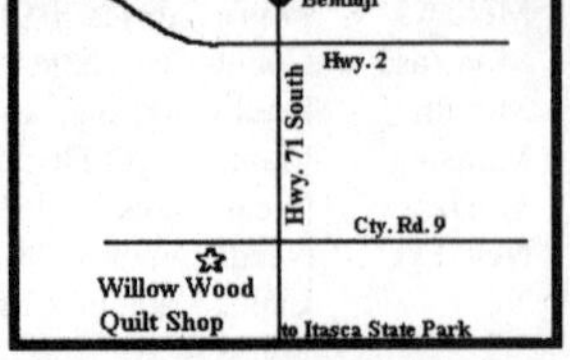

Hibbing, MN #3

Mon - Fri 9 - 5
Sat 9 - 2

PINS-N-NEEDLES

314 E. Howard St. 55746
(218) 262-5531
E-Mail: pins@cpinternet.com
Owner: Jean Stimac
Est: 1993

Over 2000 bolts of fabric, supplies, books, patterns, needlework & yarn for all your quilting & hand work needs.

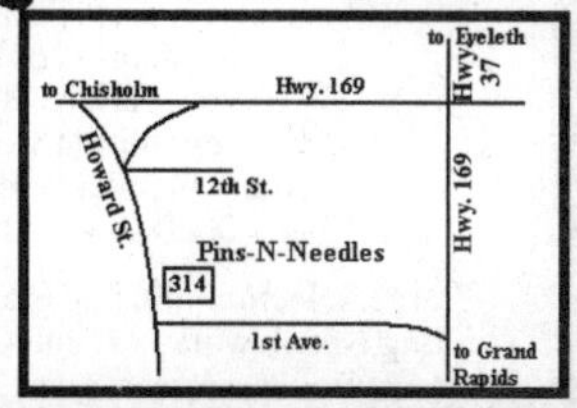

Tower, MN #4

Tues 10 - 6
Wed - Sat 10 - 5

North Country Quilts

504 Main St. 55790
(218) 753-4600
E-Mail: northcountryquilts@yahoo.com
Web Site: www.lakevermilion.cc
Owners: Dan & Corrine Hill

Full service shop. Fabric, books, patterns, notions, classes and machine quilting. Personal attention with a smile is our specialty.

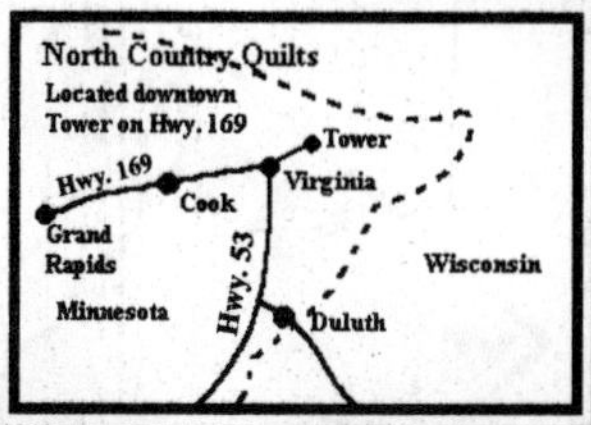

Virginia, MN #5

Mon - Sat 9 - 5
Thur til 8
Summer: Sat 9 - 2

Pinberries

406 Chestnut St. 55792
(218) 741-8446
Owners: Betsy Nelson & Sheril Prebeg

Take a beautiful drive "Up North" to Virginia and Pinberries. We have a friendly Northwoods atmosphere and a wonderful assortment of cozy flannels, homespuns and 100% cotton fabrics. While you're here, take a minute to enjoy our unique gift shop!

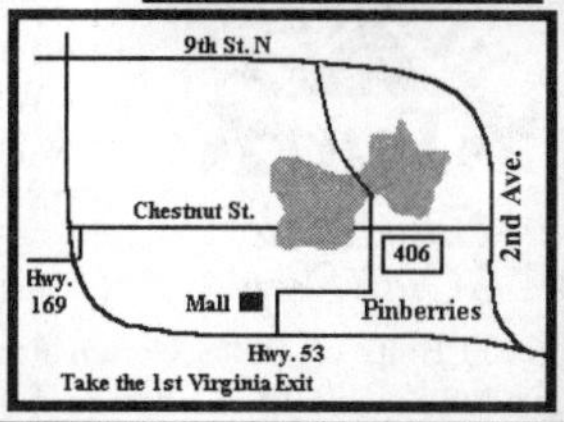

Beaver Bay, MN #6

Mon - Sat 10 - 4
Sun 12 - 4

Quilt Corner

Beaver Bay Mini Mall, P.O. Box 304
(218) 226-6406
Owner: Roxanne Johnson
Est: 1990 800 sq.ft.

Over 2000 Bolts of Cotton Fabric. Books, Notions, Patterns, & Stencils. Many Quilts for sale. Gifts too.

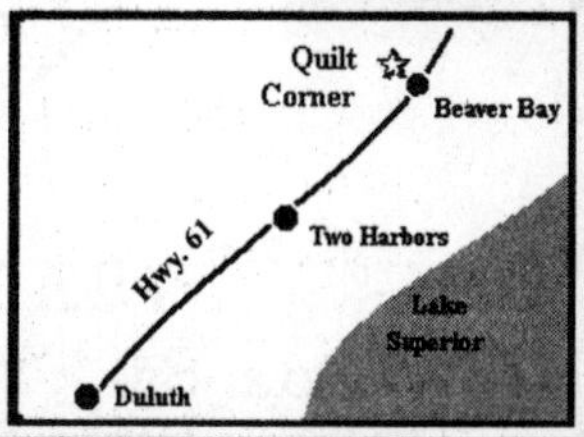

Two Harbors, MN #7

Mon 12 - 8
Tues - Sat 10 - 5
Sun 11 - 4

Quilter's Cabin

3067 E. Castle Danger Rd. 55611
(218) 834-4303
Owner: Debbie Lind Est: 2002

Fabric, supplies, patterns, gifts and quilts for sale. Located 12 miles north of Two Harbors on Lake Superior.

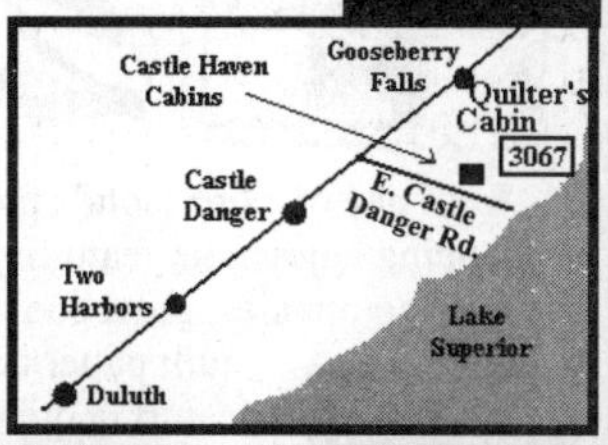

Two Harbors, MN #8

Mon - Fri 9 - 5
Sat 9 - 3

WINGS BY THE BAY

601 First Ave. 55616
(218) 834-5111
E-Mail: jwings@lakenet.com
Owners: Jerry & Char Wing

Unique Quilt Shop with Fabric, Books, Notions & Classes. Hallmark cards, gifts, Russell Stover candies, Souvenir tees, sweatshirts and sundries.

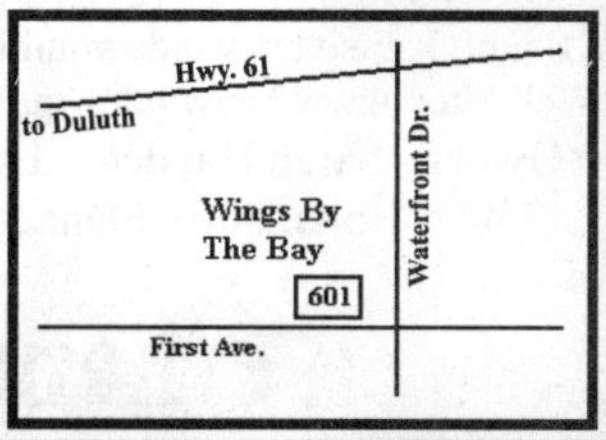

Duluth, MN #9

Mon 10 - 8
Tues - Fri 10 - 5
Sat 10 - 4

Creations Unlimited

319 N. Central Ave. 55807
(218) 628-2900
Owners: Kim & Terry Wells Est: 1997

A Quilt Junkies Haven filled with fabrics, books, patterns, & quilting supplies. Beautiful samples line our walls to inspire your creativity.

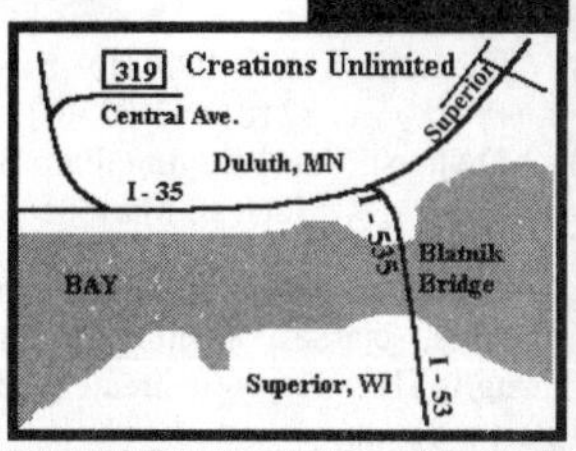

Piecemakers Quilt Shop

313 State Highway 371 South
Hackensack, MN 56452
218.675.6271
Established: 1984

Visit our Web Site!
www.cottontales.net
Email: quiltr@uslink.net

Owners: Mary & Pam Curo

Hackensack, MN #10

Home of Cotton Tales Patterns!

Inspiration is our Specialty!
Come in and be inspired!

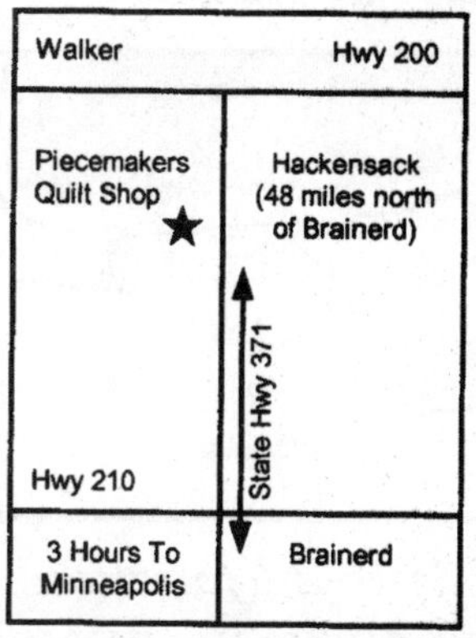

Open Daily
for your convenience
* except Sunday in Dec. & Jan.

Store Hours:
March-October 10-5
November-February 10-4

Mail Order Available
Block of the Month
Newsletter• Quilt Kits!
Classes, Workshops & Retreats
All your quilting needs

Marlyn's Quilting Nook
Wahkon MN

185 North Main
P.O. Box 85 Wahkon, MN 56386
(320) 495-3800
Email: fishy@mlec2.net

Supplies, Classes . . .
and Sew much more!

Come Join the Fun
1 Little Town . . . 9 Great shops
Something for everyone

Located on the south shore
Of beautiful Lake Mille Lacs

Look for the large "1918" brick building on the West side of Hwy 27

Wahkon, MN #11

Daily
10 - 6

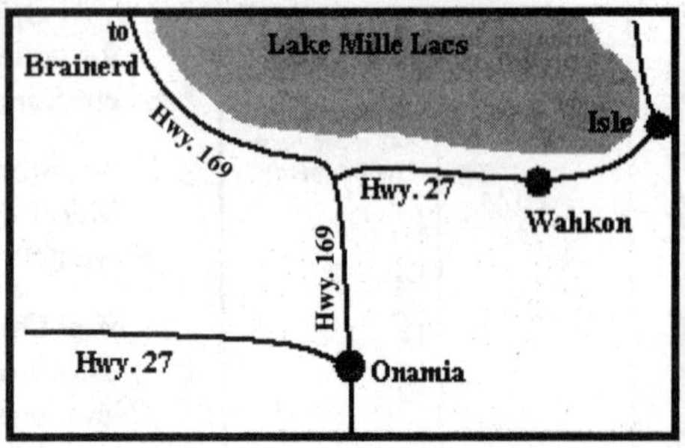

Six miles East of 169/27 junction
Five miles West of 47/27 junction

Park Rapids, MN #12

Mon - Sat
9 - 5

Monika's

210 S. Main 56470
(218) 237-3896 Fax: (218) 732-3821
E-Mail: dwilkins@wcta.net
Owner: Monika Wilkins
Est: 1984 5000 sq.ft. 3000 Bolts

Large Selection of name brand Fabrics, Quilting Needlework, Art and Craft Supplies, Patterns, Books, classes, gifts. Heritage Lace Showcase store.

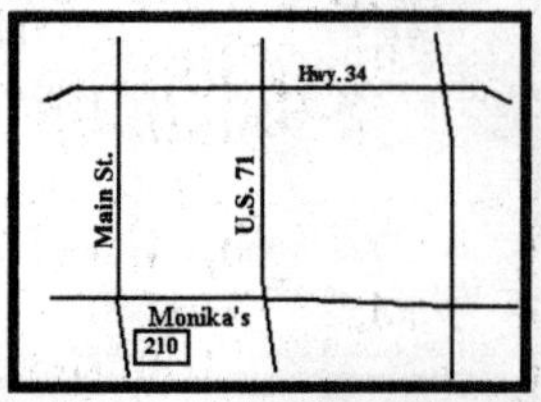

Ada, MN #13

Mon - Fri
9 - 5:30
Sat 9 - 3

Just For Fun
Gifts, Fabric & Quilt Shop

101 W. Main St., P.O. Box 221 56510
(218) 784-3568 Fax: (218) 784-2123
E-Mail:
justforfun@loretel.net
Web Site:
www.justforfun.biz
Owner: Patricia A. Olson
Est: 1997

3500 Bolts of 100% Cotton Fabrics, 100's of Notions, Patterns & Books. Lots of Samples and Kits. Nestled in a lovely 1900's home.

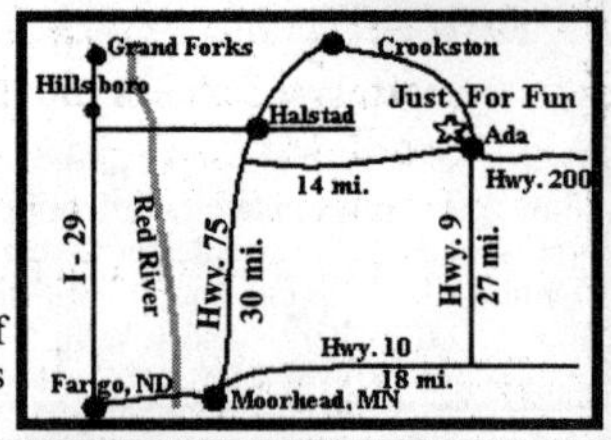

Bay Window Quilt Shop

Visit one of Minnesota's premier quilt shops! Enjoy two levels of shopping enjoyment featuring a huge selection of quality fabrics from over 30 companies, great books, patterns, notions, and our own in-house quilt pattern designer. Don't miss our new gift shop featuring quilts for sale & antiques! Classes. Custom Quilting. Terrific Service! Thimbleberries Quilt Club, Redwork Club, Fun Club, Book Club, and Thimbleberries Quilt Club by Mail.

Mon - Fri
9 - 5:30
Sat 9 - 4

116 2nd Ave. SW 56573
(888) 346-7275 or (218) 346-7272
Email: katie@baywindowquiltshop.com
Web Site: www.baywindowquiltshop.com
Owner: Sarah Hayden Est: 1989
3500+ Bolts, 800+ Flannels Bolts

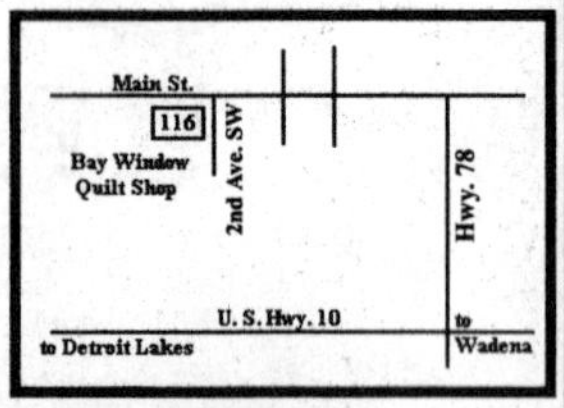

Perham, MN #14

Battle Lake, MN #15

Mon - Sat
9 - 5

B's Quilt Shop

122 Lake Ave. S, P.O. Box 516 56515
(218) 862-2230
Owners: Carol Boyum, Pam Boyum & MarJean Martelle

Machine & custom quilting, fabrics, notions, patterns, classes, memory quilts, computer design. Helping you create your quilt from start to finish.

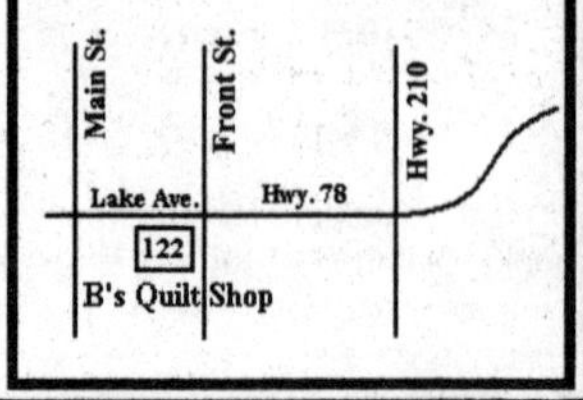

Floodwood, MN #16

Hingeley Road Quilting

Mon - Thur 10 - 5
Fri 10 - 7
Sat 9 - 5
Mem. Day thru Thanksgiving
Sun 11 - 5

Top Quality Quilt Fabric

Moda	Benartex	Maywood Studios
RJR	Clothworks	Timeless Treasures
P&B	Free Spirit	Michael Miller
Hoffman	Northcott	In the Beginning
SSI	Thimbleberries	Alexander Henry

Block of the month kits & patterns

We carry the entire line of:
Hoffman Bali Handpaints - 100 plus colors
Moda Marbles - 120 plus colors
Benartex Fossil Ferns - 150 colors plus the new Flannel Fossils summer 2002

Guilds/groups and buses welcome anytime

Quarterly Newsletter

11284 Hwy. 2
Floodwood, MN 55736
218-476-3139
Opened December 2000
1800 Bolts & growing
HingeleyRoadQuilting@msn.com

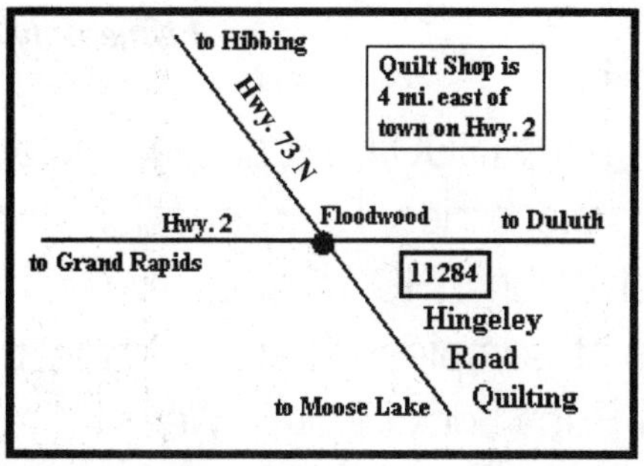

Quilt Supplies:
Notions/thread
Books
Patterns
Ott Lights
Batting

Large Suppply of Original Kits

Australian Patchwork - Quilting Magazine
Full-line of quilter's computer products

Thimbleberries Club
Primrose Gradation
State Flower Fabrics.

We have a 10,000 Bolt Attitude! www.quickquiltkits.com

Rush City, MN #18

Fabrics Fashions and More

Mon - Fri 9 - 5
Sat 9 - 4

485 S. Dana, Box 21 55069
(320) 358-3693 Est: 1995
E-Mail: Jthorn@ecenet.com
Web Site: www.communityshowcase.net
Owner: Virginia Thorn 1900 sq.ft.

Well worth the stop! Fabrics, Books, Notions & more. Home of PFAFF Integrated Dual Feed. Authorized PFAFF Sales & Service.

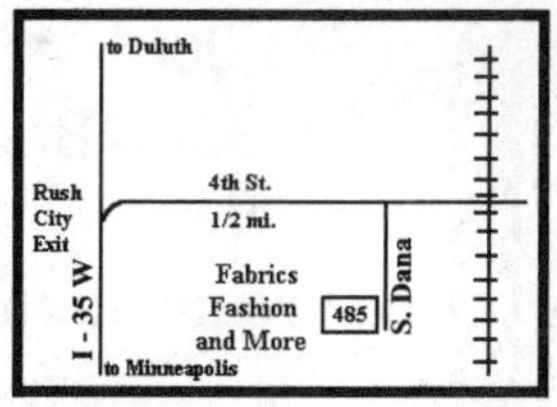

Quilters Cottage

PFAFF

316 N. Tower Rd. 56537
(218) 739-9652
Fax: (218) 739-0722
quilters@prtel.com
Owner: Jolene Miller
Est: 1988 2000 Bolts

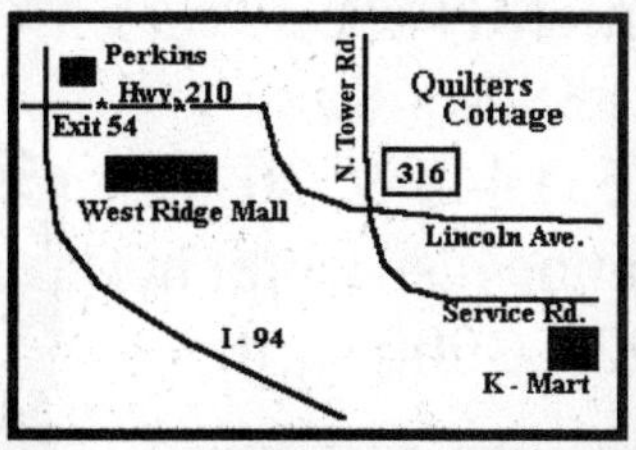

Mon, Tues, Wed & Fri 10 - 5
Thur 10 - 6:30
Sat 10 - 3

Your one stop quilt shop. We supply everything but the time.

Fergus Falls, MN #17

Mora, MN #19

Mon - Fri 9 - 5
Sat 9 - 4

Miss Fannie Turgeon's
MEMORIES in CLOTH

206 W. Forest 55051
(320) 679-4842 or
(800) 859-3591

Owner:
Donna Gilbert
Fax: 679-3357

E-Mail: dbos@misfannieturgeons.com
Antique reproduction dolls & handstitched samplers. Great fabrics, books, patterns, antiques and a great retail shop.

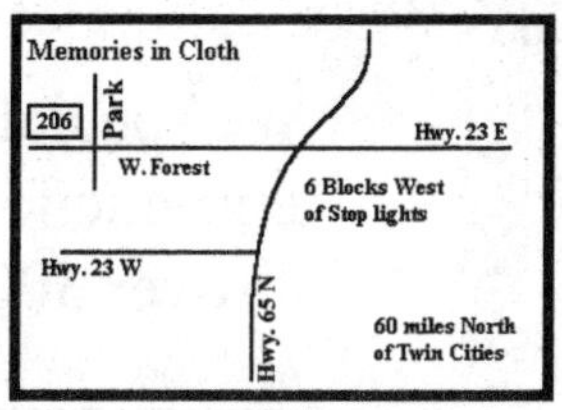

Est: 1971

Brainerd, MN #20

909 S. 6th St. 56401
(218) 829-7273 or (888) 441-7273

Country Fabrics, Quilts, & Collectibles

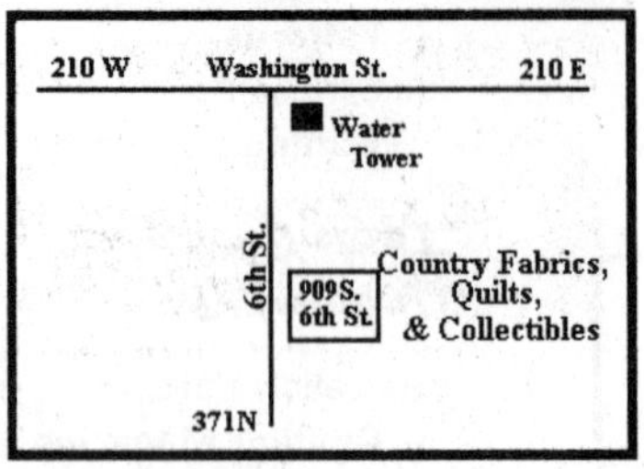

Show us this coupon and receive 10% off your purchase. 1 time only.

Mon - Fri 9:30 - 5:30
Sat 9:30 - 5

Our 1800 Mercantile is filled with over 5000 calicoes by the leading designers: Moda, Thimbleberries, Reproduction Prints, Batiks by Hoffman and much more. Check out our large selection of 100% wool for rug hookers and primitive appliqué. Our store is filled with 100's of samples. There is something to inspire everyone. We are your authorized Elna & Baby Lock dealer. We service all brands of machines and sergers. If you're not into quilting--visit our quaint 2nd floor. It's filled with unique gifts and antiques.

Princeton, MN #21

Country Treasures Quilt Shop

Hundreds of Books
1,000's of Fat Quarters
3500 Bolts of Fabric

Frequent buyers cards / no expiration
Free Newsletter
Lots of Samples for Sale

Come See --
Dyanne & Shirley with over 50 years of combined quilting know-how.

We specialize in 1930's Reproduction Fabrics with over 300 in Stock.

105 Rum River Dr.
Princeton, MN 55371
(763) 389-0680
Fax: (763) 444-9530
E-Mail: ldyanne@sherbtel.net
Est: 1992 3000 sq.ft.

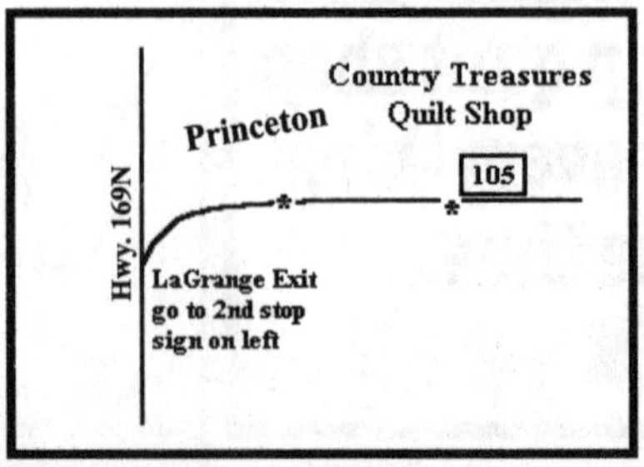

Mon - Fri 9:30 - 5:30
Thur til 7 Sat 9:30 - 4

"The Quilt Shop for Every Quilter"

St. Cloud, MN #22

Gruber's QUILT SHOP

in "Waite Park"
304 4th Ave. NE 56387
(320) 259-4360
www.grubersquiltshop.com
Owner: Sue Poser

Selected one of the top 10 Quilt Shops in North America 2001 by American Patchwork & Quilting Magazine.

Mon, Wed, Fri 9 - 7
Tues, Thur, Sat 9 - 6
Sun 12 - 5

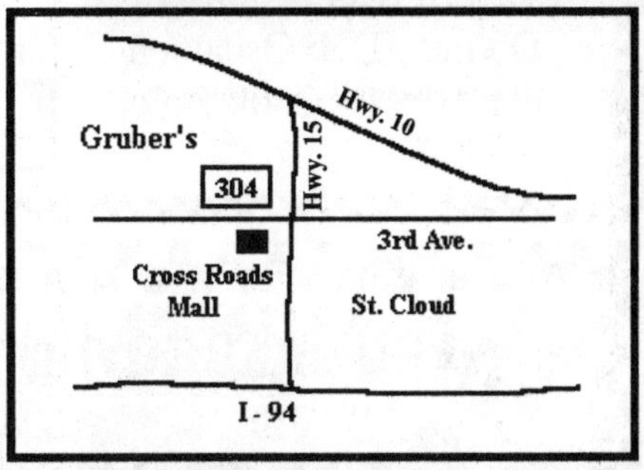

6,000 plus 100% cotton Fabrics, 200 plus Patterns, 100's of Book titles from the greatest companies available to quilters, to entice you, and feature samples in our shop on the way to or from everywhere in Minnesota.

Sauk Rapids, MN #23

Bound---in---Stitches
Quilt Village

2078 - 45th Street N.E.
Sauk Rapids, MN 56379
Phone: (320) 255-9021
Owners: Michelle & Wayne Johnson

Store Hours:
Tuesday - Friday
10 a. m. - 6 p. m.
Saturday
9 a. m. - 3 p. m.

Home of "Peaceable Hand Dyes" and Bound-in-Stitches patterns

MasterCard & Visa Accepted

Directions: From St. Cloud, take Hwy. 15 North. Exit right on County Road 29 East. At stop sign, turn left on County Road. 1. Go one mile. Turn right on County Road 15. Continue east for 1/2 mile. Quilt Shop is located on the right.

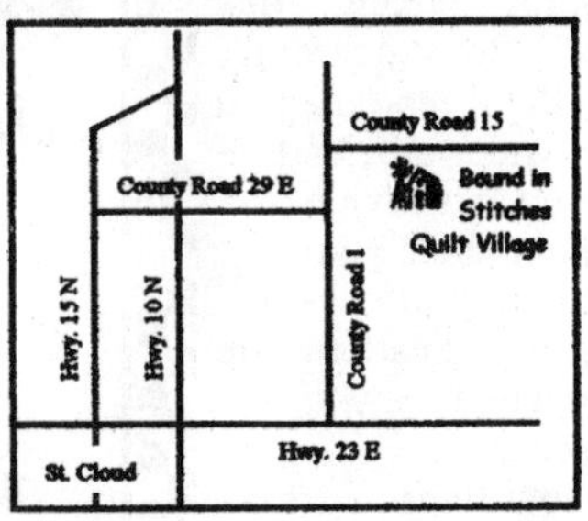

Quality Quilting Supplies

- 100% Cotton Print Fabrics- Moda, Hoffman, Bali, Thimbleberries, South Seas, Nancy Crow & more
- Hand Dyed Fabrics
- Books & Patterns
- Quilting Notions
- Kits
- Block of the Months
- Classes year round
- Quilting Giftware
- Friendly, Knowledgeable Staff
- Specializing in Color Expertise
- Many Samples on Display
- Unique & Relaxed Country Setting
- Ample Parking for RV's and Buses!

Visit us on the web at: www.bound-in-stitches.com

Elk River, MN #24

Cottage Quilts & Fabrics

We are located in the lower level of the "Back to the 50's" Restaurant.

Large selection of 100% cottons, quilting supplies, notions, patterns, books and classes. "Come Quilt With Us!"

Mon - Fri 10 - 5
Thur til 7:30
Sat 10 - 4
Sun 12 - 4

17325 Hwy. 10 55330
(763) 241-1490
Owner: Deb Oscarson
Est: 1994 2500 Bolts

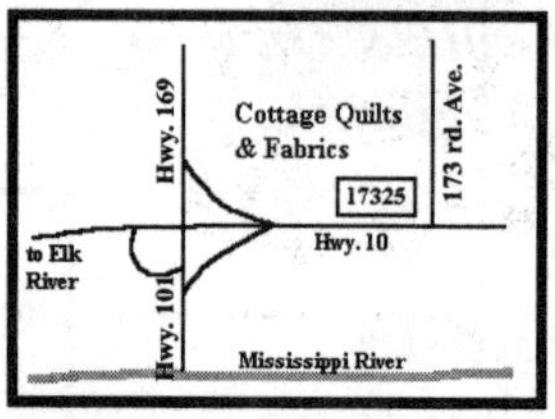

Buffalo, MN #25

Lady of the Lake Quilts & Fabrics

Mon - Sat 10 - 5
Thur til 7

One West Division St. 55313
(763) 682-1990
Owner: Karen Sargent
Est: 1997 1400 sq.ft.

Hundreds of Yards of Cottons, also Books, Notions, and Gifts.

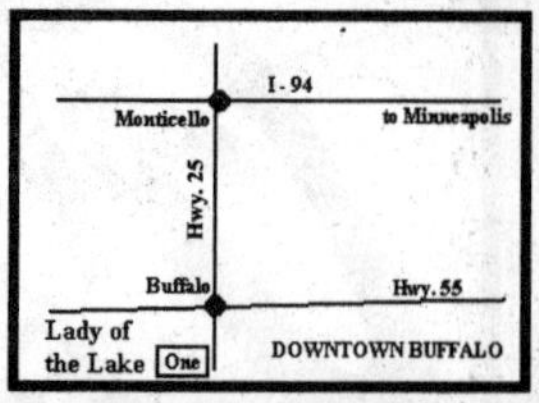

Avon, MN #26

Aunt Annie's Quilts & Silks

Visit our newly expanded shop.
Over 2400 sq.ft. of well lit shopping & classroom area.
3000+ bolts of fabrics including African, Bali, Japanese, Australian, Hoffman, Kaufman, RJR, Moda, Kona Bay, Momen House, Monarch, Alexander Henry, Nancy Crow, hand-dyed & painted and many others. Fine woolens, silks, rayons & flannels.
Inspiring samples & displays.
Local & international books and magazines.

Known for color assistance, enticing & unique fabrics, knowledgeable & helpful staff. Fabrics chosen by working artists for creative quilters and sewers.

Tour groups welcome.

Mon - Fri 9 - 6
Sat 9 - 4

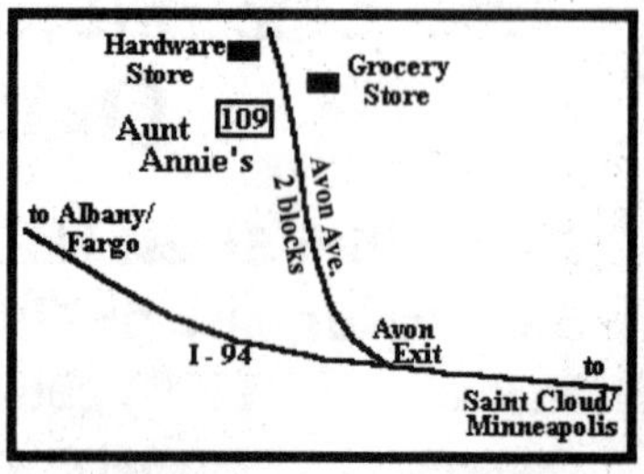

109 Avon Ave. S, P.O. Box 359 56310
(320) 356-1061
Owners: Lucy Senstad & Sue Kelly

Alexandria, MN #27

The Common Threads Quilt Shop, Inc.

Mon - Fri 10 - 5
Thur til 6
Sat 10 - 3

109 15th Ave. E 56308
(320) 763-6771

"BLESSED ARE THE QUILTERS FOR THEY SHALL BE CALLED PIECEMAKERS"

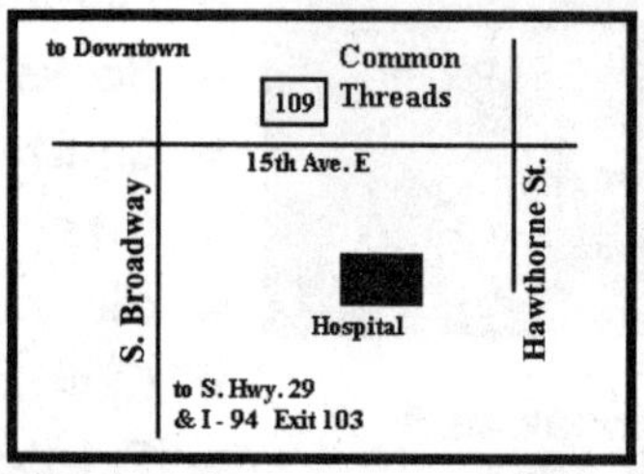

We specialize in 100% quality cotton fabrics made by leading designers, the newest quilting books, unique patterns, specialty quilting notions, primitive wool rug hooking, gifts and classes starting at the "beginner" level. Browse through our "garden" of inspiring samples and displays, reproduction prints, homespuns and flannels and meet with our friendly and knowledgeable staff. Free inspiration and advice is always available. We would be happy to help you coordinate fabrics for your projects and make up kits on request. Ongoing "Block of the Month" kits and patterns are also available. Stop in with a friend, spend time with kindred spirits, and experience the common thread running through our lives.

Alexandria, MN #28

Alexandria Stitchin' Post

Tues - Fri 9:30 - 5
Sat 10 - 3

110 5th Ave W 56308
(320) 763-3400 Fax: Same
E-Mail: jkennedy@gctel.com
Owners: Terilyn Kennedy & Jane McCrery
Est: 1996 1100 sq.ft.

A "Must See" Shop Featuring Janome Sewing Machines, Quilting Supplies, Dolls & Accessories. Over 1000 Bolts of Contemporary & Heirloom Fabrics plus Laces.

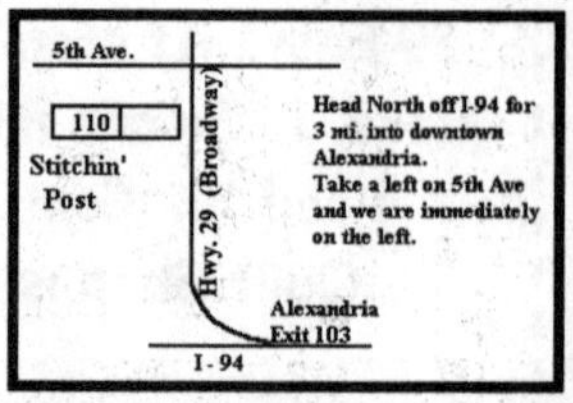

Starbuck, MN #29

Quilting from the Heartland®

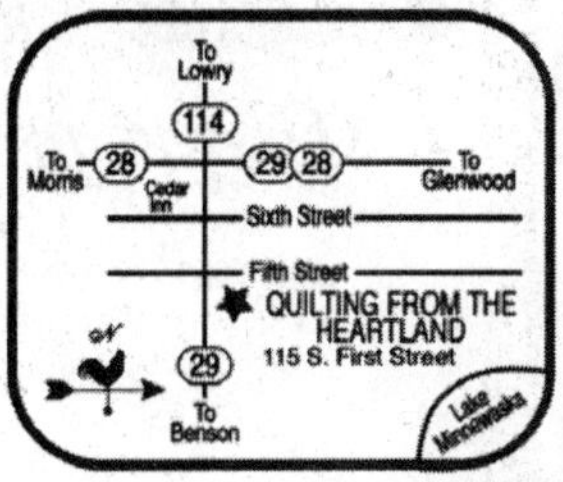

101 East Fifth Street
Starbuck, MN 56381

320-239-4044
320-239-4049 FAX
800-637-2541

STORE HOURS
Mon-Fri 9AM-5PM
Sat 10AM-2PM

QUILTING SUPPLIES ♥ FABRIC ♥ GIFTS ♥ CLASSES ♥ MACHINE QUILTING ♥ HUSQVARNA VIKING SEWING MACHINES

Heartland Quilt Company

STORE HOURS
Mon-Fri 10AM-5PM
Thurs 10AM-7PM
Sat 10AM-3PM

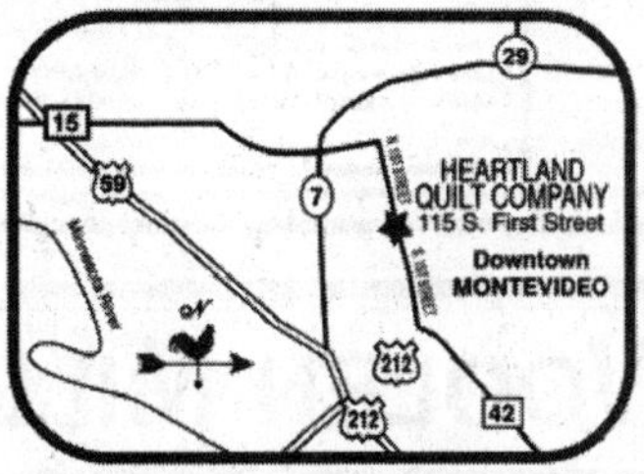

115 South First Street
Montevideo, MN 56265

320-269-9660
Phone & Fax

Montevideo, MN #30

Two Locations ~ 800-624-4001

Redwood Falls, MN #31

141 E. 2nd Street • Redwood Falls, Mn. • 507-637-5221

Selected in the premier issue of American Patchwork Quilting Sampler Magazine as one of the top ten shops in North America

Hours: Mon.-Fri. 9:00 a.m. - 5:00 p.m. • Thurs. 9:00 a.m. - 8:00 p.m. • Sat. 9:00 a.m. - 4:00 p.m.

Hutchinson, MN #32

7 N. Main Street • Hutchinson, Mn. • 320-234-7298

Located in the same building as the Thimbleberries design studio.

Hours: Mon. 9:00 a.m. - 8:00 p.m. • Tues.-Fri. 9:00 a.m. - 5:00 p.m. • Sat. 9:00 a.m. - 4:00 p.m.

MAIN STREET COTTON SHOP™

FREE FULL COLOR CATALOG

Mail Order Available 24 Hours a Day!

Hoffman, MN #33

Mon - Fri 9 - 12 & 1 - 5 Sats by Appt.

Nuts & Bolts Quilt Shop

213 First St. N 56339
(320) 986-2447
E-Mail: jccbsjg@runestone.net
Owner: Cindy Gulbrandson Est: 1996

A friendly small town quilt shop specializing in custom machine quilting. We carry 100% cotton fabrics, notions, patterns, books, gifts, and are always willing to help with your project.

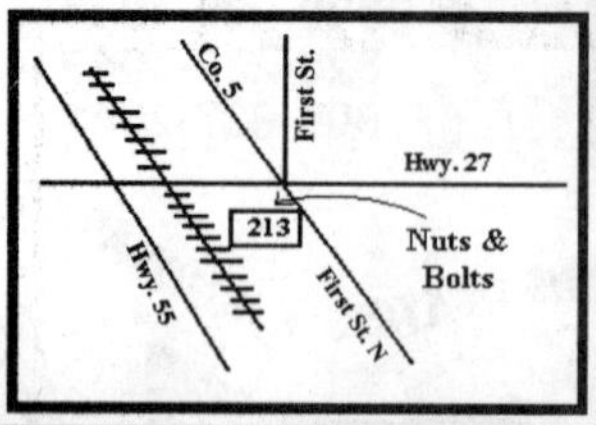

Willmar, MN #34

Mon - Fri 9:30 - 5 Sat 10 - 2

Darlin Quilts

6691 Hwy. 71 NE 56201
(320) 235-7576
Owner: Lin Grinde

Machine Quilting, Fabrics, Patterns & Classes.
5 miles North of Willmar on Hwy. 71

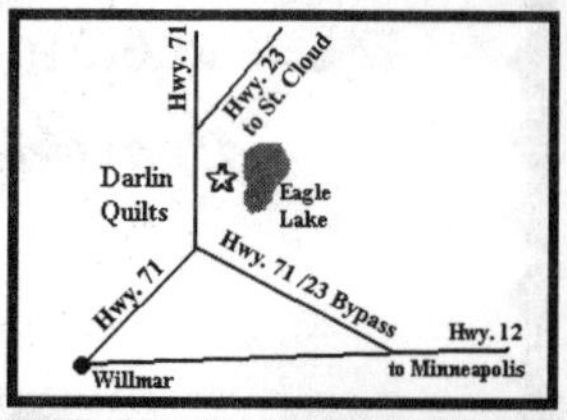

Bird Island, MN #35

Mon - Fri 9 - 5 Sat 9 - 3

GATHERING FRIENDS Quilt Shop

101 S. Main, P.O. Box 189 55310
E-Mail: gfriends@willmar.com
www.gatheringfriendsquiltshop.com
(320) 365-4670
Owners:
Deb Jacobs &
Kathy Squibb
Est: 1998 2500 bolts

Large selection of 100% cotton fabrics & flannels, gift items and quilting kits. Custom-made oak quilt racks.

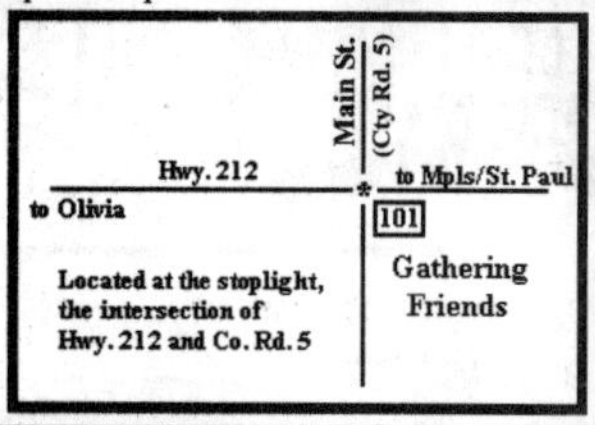

Le Sueur, MN #36

Mon - Fri 8 - 7 Sat 8 - 5:30 Sun 8 - 1

Le Sueur Variety & Sewing

209 Valleygreen Sq. 56058
(507) 665-6303
Fax: (507) 665-6006

Sewing Machines & Repairs, Custom Embroidery, Quilt Supplies, Custom Framing, Expanded Fabric Department, Craft Supplies & Pet Supplies

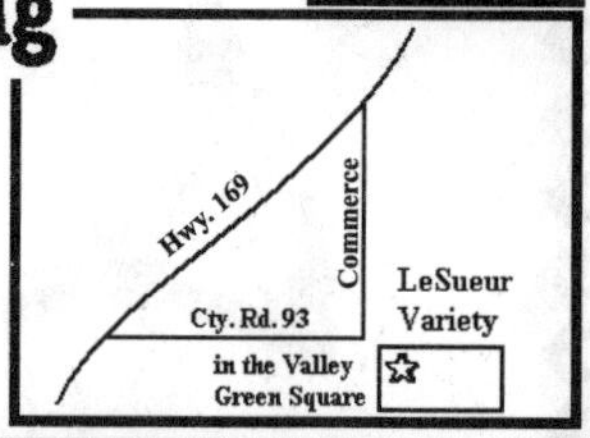

ST. PETER WOOLEN MILL

Mary Lue's Yarn & Quilt Shop

101 W. Broadway 56082
(507) 934-3734
Fax: (507) 934-9040
E-Mail: spwoolen@prairie.lakes.com
Web Site: www.woolenmill.com
Est: 1867 6400 sq.ft.
1000 Bolts Free Catalog

Mon - Fri 9 - 5:30 Thur til 8 Sat 9 - 5

Large selection of fabrics, yarns, gifts, knitting & sewing machines, and quilting supplies.

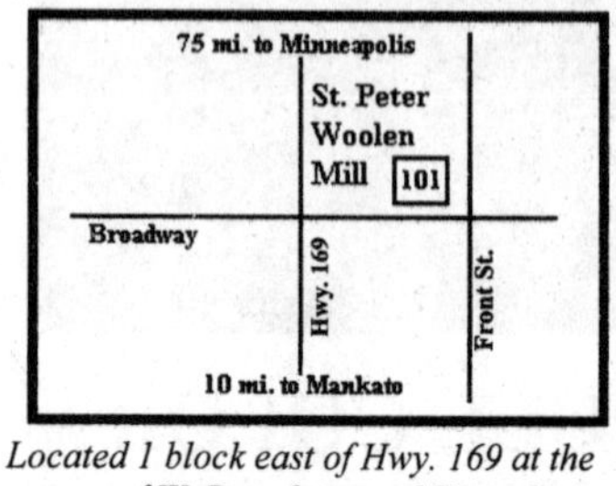

Located 1 block east of Hwy. 169 at the corner of W. Broadway and Front St. in downtown St. Peter, MN

Custom wool carding since 1867. Manufacturers of NATURE'S COMFORT wool batting.

"LIKE QUILTING THROUGH AIR"

St. Peter, MN #37

MUGGS Fabric & Bridal

Owner: Margaret (Muggs) Meyer

Mon - Fri 9:30 - 8 Sat 9:30 - 5 Sun 12 - 4

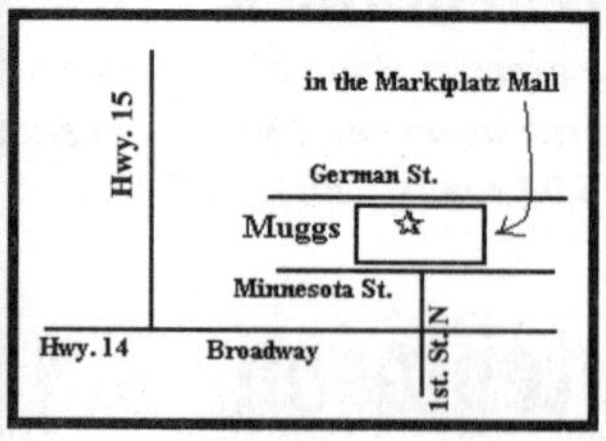

101 N. German
Marktplatz Mall
56073
(507) 359-1515
Fax: (507) 359-1405
3000 sq.ft.

New Ulm, MN #38

- **Quality Fabrics**

▼Maywood▼RJR▼Debbie Mumm▼Hoffman▼B&P

- **Quilting Books • Tools • Notions**
- **Quilts For Sale**
- **Featuring**

PFAFF Sewing Machines

Expert Advice always gladly given

Marshall, MN #41

Mon - Fri 9:30 - 6
Thur til 9
Sat 9:30 - 5

Fabrics Plus

237 W. Main 56258
(507) 537-0835 Fax: (507) 537-1320
E-mail: elaine@fabricsplus.com
Web Site: www.fabricsplus.com
Owner: M. Elaine Nyquist
Est: 1985 2500 sq.ft.

Southwest Minnesota's finest fabric selection. Over 3500 bolts of cottons for quilting plus fashion, home decor. Sewing Machines Also.

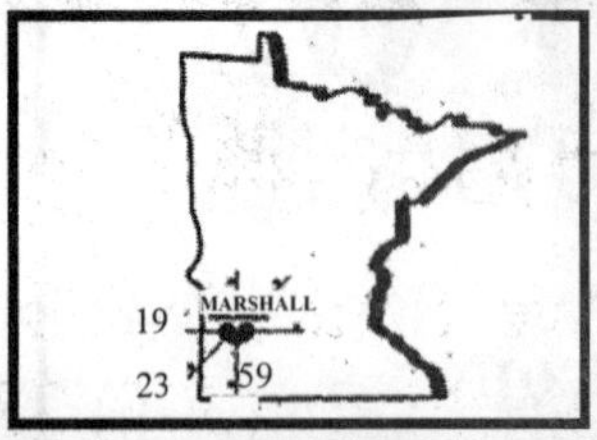

Windom, MN #42

Mon 9 - 6:30
Tues - Fri 9 - 5
Sat 9 - 3

Prairie Quilting

1293 Hale Place 56101
(507) 831-2740
E-Mail: jrkp@rconnect.com
Owner: Kay Peterson

Unique Quilt Shop location next to feed store. Great selection of 100% cotton fabrics, books, patterns, and notions. Quilts for sale.

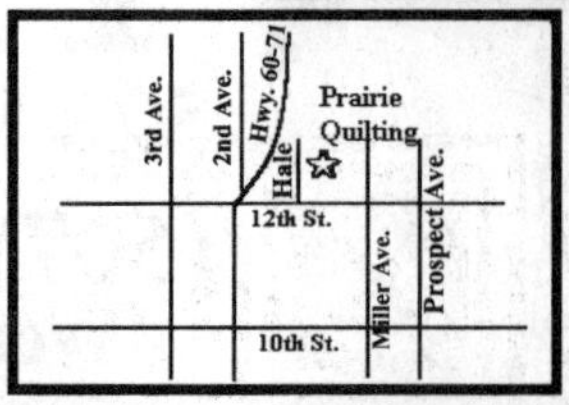

Lismore, MN #43

Jan - April
Tues - Sat 9 - 5
May - Dec
Tues - Sat 9 - 5
Sun 12 - 5

Country Hearts

12405 State Hwy. 91 56155
(507) 472-8707 Est: 1998
E-Mail: Chearts@frontiernet.net
Owner: Karon Nagel 2600 sq.ft.

Quilting Fabrics, Notions, Patterns, Books and many samples. Quaint Country Shop. Many handcrafted wood items.

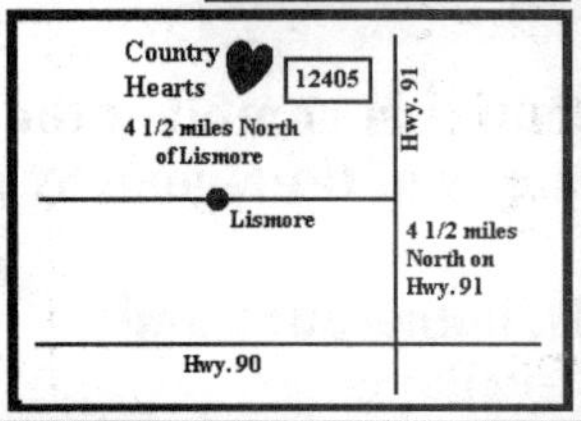

Luverne, MN #44

Mon - Sat 9 - 5
Thur til 8

The Sewing Basket

204 E. Main
R.R. #1, Box 175 56156
(507) 283-9769
E-Mail: sewing@ideasign.com
Owner: Barbara Bork

Your full service Quilt Shop!

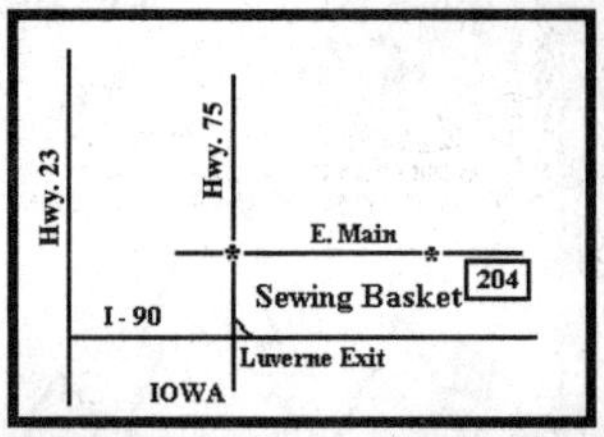

Worthington, MN #45

Mon - Thur 9 - 5:30
Fri 9 - 9
Sat 9 - 4

1820 Oxford St. 56187
(507) 372-2707
Owner: Zuby Jansen
Est. 1982 3600 sq.ft.

CRAFTY CORNER Quilt & Sewing Shoppe

We sell 100% cotton fabrics.
3850 bolts in stock.
Many Patterns Bernina Sewing Machine sales & Service. Quilting Supplies!
Singer Featherweights in stock

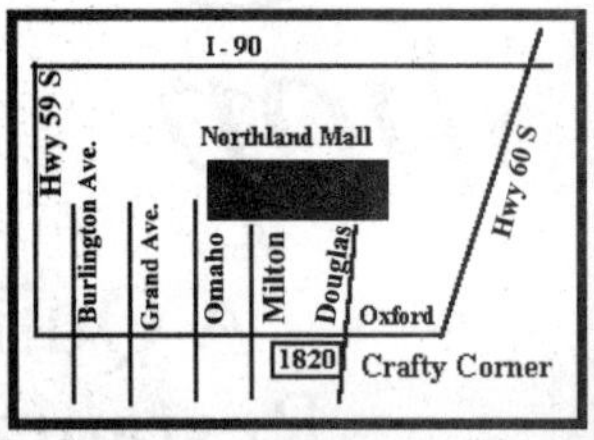

Hayward, MN #46

Mon - Fri 10 - 5
Sat 10 - 3

Calico Hutch

100 W. Front St., P.O. Box 482 56043
(507) 377-1163
E-Mail: quilts@clear.lakes.com
Web Site: www.calicohutch.com
Est: 1982 1000 sq.ft. 1000+ Bolts

100% Cotton, Flannels, Books, Patterns & Kits. Day or night classes. Help with color coordination. Lots of Samples.

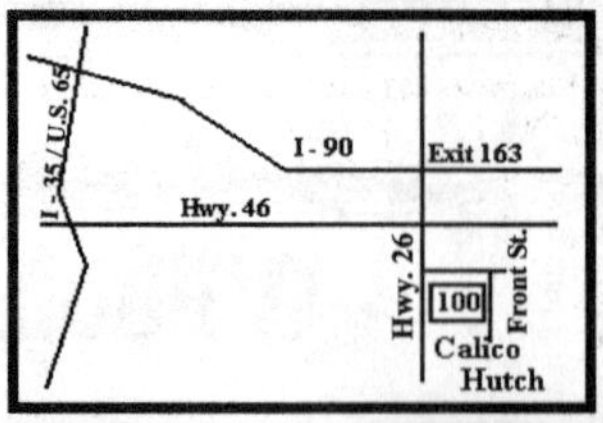

Mabel, MN #47

Mon - Sat 8:30 - 5
Sun 1 - 5

Quilter's Heaven & Gifts

121 N. Main St., P.O. Box 66 55954
(507) 493-5666 Est: 1996 3000 sq.ft.
Owner: Cheryl Gjere-Aberg 1500+ Bolts

Look for the Yellow Building!
Cotton Fabrics, Books & Patterns, Notions, Classes, Machine Quilting, Newsletter.

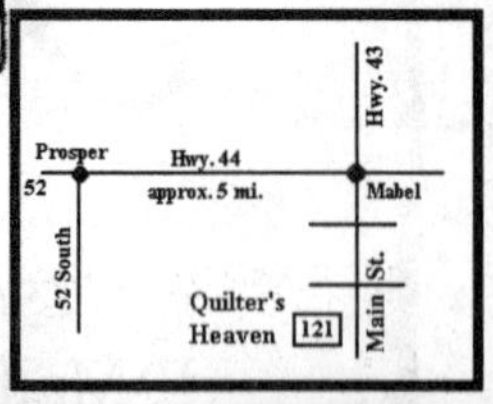

Owatonna, MN #48

Mon - Fri 9 - 6
Sat 9 - 4:30

The Cotton Patch

110 W. Broadway 55060
(507) 451-5979 Est: 1993 1500 Bolts
Web Site: www.thecottonpatchquilts.com
Owners: Cathy Torrey & Laura Wertwijn

Spacious, well-lit shop staffed by helpful, experience quilters. An abundance of quality 100% cotton fabric & supplies for all your quilting needs. Located on downtown's charming Central Park, just 1 mile off I - 35 and 5 minutes from Cabela's.

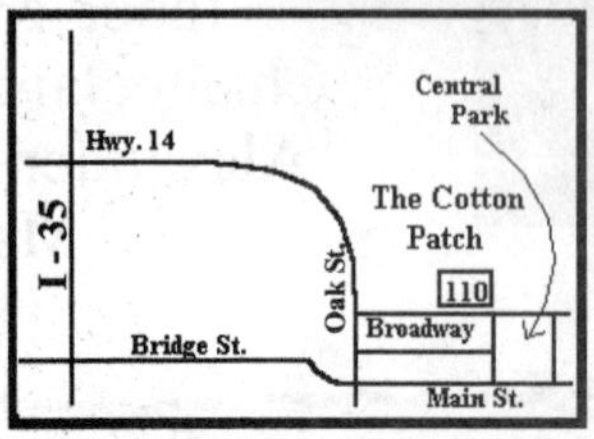

Owatonna, MN #49

Tues & Thur 1 - 5:30
Wed, Fri, Sat 10 - 5:30

The Doll House

740 S. Oak Ave.
55060
(507) 451-6642
Owner:
Jeanne Voll
Est: 1971 800 sq.ft.

New & Vintage Debbie Mumm Fabrics, Thousands of Patterns, Yarns & Collectible Dolls

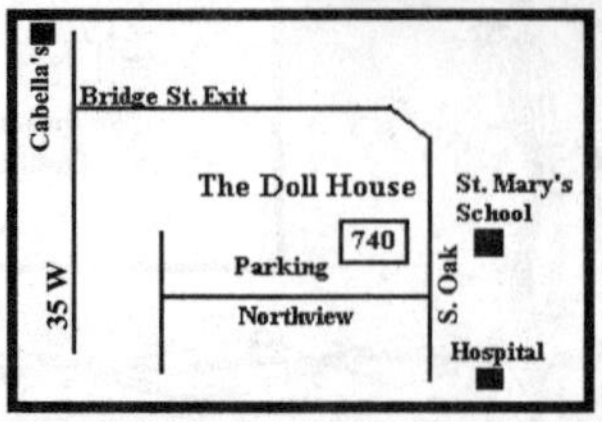

The Quilter's Mercantile

Mankato, MN #50

1400 Madison Ave. Suite #314, Mankato, MN 56001
Phone/Fax: (507) 385-7777
Web Site: www.quiltersmerc.com
E-Mail: quiltersmerc@aol.com

Mon - Sat 9 - 5
Tues & Thur til 8
Sun 1 - 5

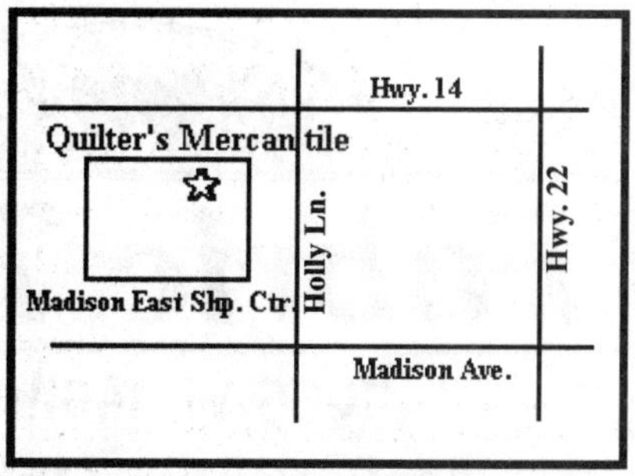

Lots of Books, Patterns and Notions.
Come and visit our antique filled shop where inspiration abounds. We carry a full line of 100% cotton dry goods for the traditional and contemporary quilters; from batiks to homespuns, there's something for everyone.

Take Hwy. 14 to Hwy. 22 South. Go to Madison Ave. - Turn Right - Go about 1 Mile West to the Madison East Shopping Center. We are located in the mall.

Create a treasured heirloom for someone you love or for your own home.

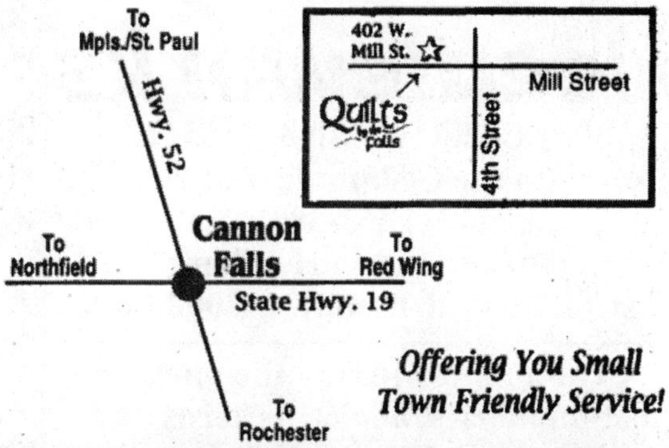

Offering You Small Town Friendly Service!

Cannon Falls, MN #51

402 W. Mill St. 55009
(507) 263-2528 or (888) 899-2528
www.cannon.net/~quilts
e-mail - quilts@cannon.net
Owners: Marilou & Larry Welt

1999 *QUILT SAMPLER* FEATURED SHOP

Mon - Sat 9 - 5 Thur 9 - 8

3500+ bolts of quality quilting fabrics & homespuns
100's of books & patterns
16 feet of notions
Gifts - classes
100's of models for inspiration

Free Inspiration & Advice Always Available

Quilts by the falls

Rochester, MN #52

Mon - Fri 10 - 6
Sat 10 - 5

Just A Little Something

304 6th St. SW 55902
(507) 288-7172
E-Mail: quiltsandminis@aol.com
Owner: Crystal D. Monson Est: 1996

Great Selection of Quality Fabrics. Books, Patterns, Notions. Old Fashioned, Friendly Service. We will help you with your projects. Quilting Classes.

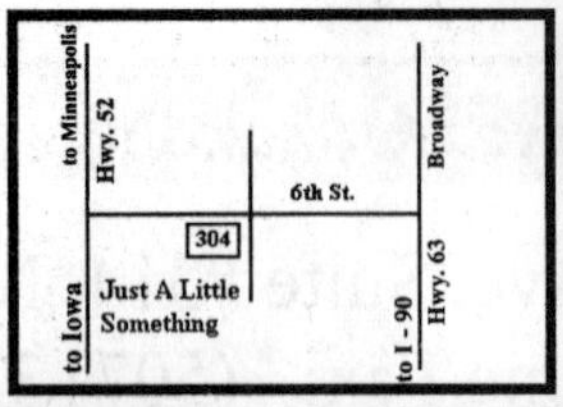

Lake City, MN #53

RATHER BEE QUILTING

116 S. Washington
55041
(651) 345-3958
Owners: Janet Bruce & Judy Rutz
Est: 1998

Mon - Fri 9 - 5
Thurs til 6
Sat 9 - 4

Known for beautiful fabrics, innovative classes and friendly, knowledgeable help.

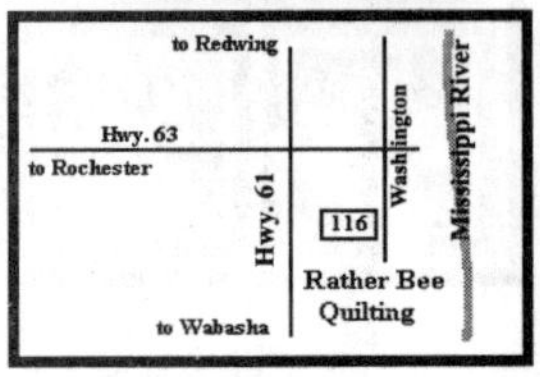

"Where all the pieces come together!"

Apple Valley, MN #54

Fabric Town

7655 W. 148th St.,
Apple Valley, MN 55124
952 / 432-1827 • 1-800-475-2137
E-Mail: fabrictown@aol.com
Web Site: www.fabrictown.com
Owner: Barbara Sherman — Est. 1981

Mon. - Fri. 10 - 8:30
Sat. 10 - 5
Sun. 12 - 5

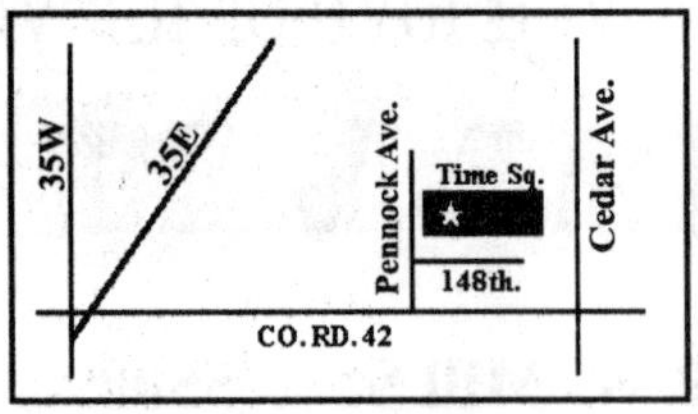

Our <u>3,000 sq.ft.</u> store features:
5,000 BOLTS OF 100% COTTON,
BOOKS, PATTERNS, KITS,
HUNDREDS OF SAMPLES
LOOKING FOR SOMETHING? WE SHIP!
Our friendly, knowledgeable staff is looking forward to meeting you!

Eagan, MN #55

Country Needleworks

3924 Cedarvale Blvd. 55122
(in the Cedarvale Mall)
(651) 452-8891
Owner: Susan Herzberg
Est: 1989 2000 sq.ft. 2000 Bolts

A Quilt Shop offering the finest in cotton fabrics, books, patterns and quilting supplies.
Classes & Gift Certificates Available.

Mon - Fri 9:30 - 8:30
Sat 9:30 - 5

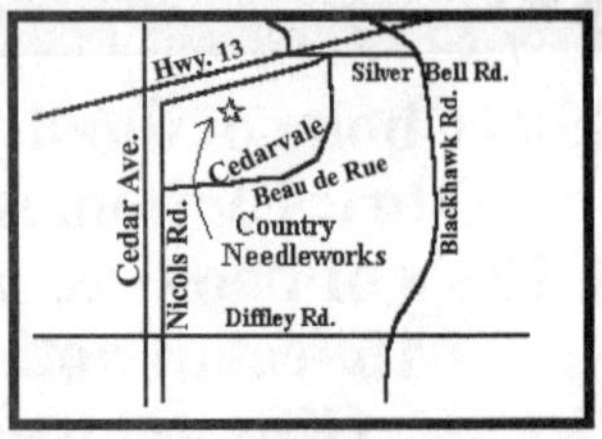

Located just 3 miles south of the Mall of America at the intersection of Hwy. 13 and MN 77.

Rosemount, MN #56

Tues - Fri 10 - 9
Sat 10 - 6
Sun 12 - 5

Quilter's Haven

14680 S. Robert Tr. 55068
(651) 322-7071 Fax: (651) 322-4994
E-Mail: Quilthav@frontiernet.net
Owners: Kathy Watson & Jean Graham
Est: 2002 1500 sq.ft. 750+ Bolts

Visit our quaint 100+ year house, 5 rooms full of new fabrics, patterns & notions. European country florals, brights, & children's prints.

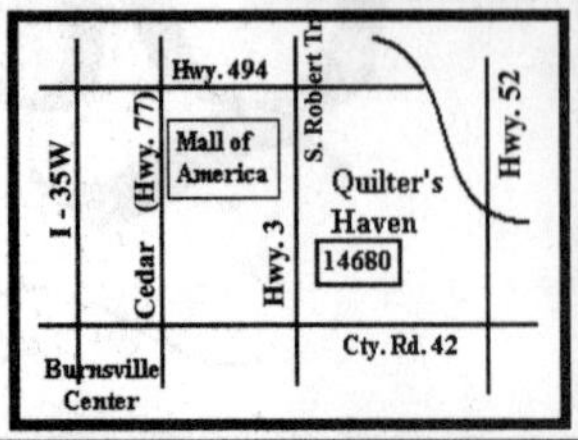

Shakopee, MN #57

EAGLE CREEK QUILT SHOP

333 2nd Ave. W, Shakopee, MN 55379
(952) 233-3774
Fax: (952) 233-5540
Owners: Lori Gillick & Becky Kelso
2300 sq.ft. 2500 Bolts

Located in an enchanting turn of the century railroad depot, our shop features hundreds of plaids, homespuns and flannels as well as complete lines of 1800's - 1930's reproduction fabrics.
You'll find wonderful samples to inspire you and many kits to entice you.
Conveniently located two miles west of Valley Fair on Hwy. 101, just 20 min. from the Mall of America.

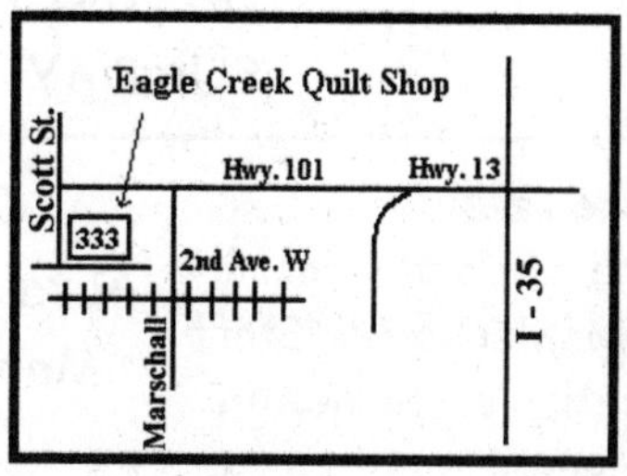

www.eaglecreekquiltshop.com

Mon 10 - 5 Tues 10 - 8 Wed - Sat 10 - 5

Wayzata, MN #58

... Eclectic collection of fabrics — from traditional to contemporary
... 2000+ bolts of cotton fabric
... 300+ book titles, large selection of patterns
... Quilting tools and supplies
... Kits, bundles and fat quarters
... Handi Quilter, Classes year round
... Friendly, knowledgeable staff

W A Y Z A T A
Quilting Emporium

927 East Lake Street 55391
(952) 475-2138
Owners: Deb Buchholz & Wendy Fedie
Est: 1980 1650 sq.ft.

Mon - Thurs 9 - 8:30 Fri & Sat 9 - 5

www.wayzataquilting.com

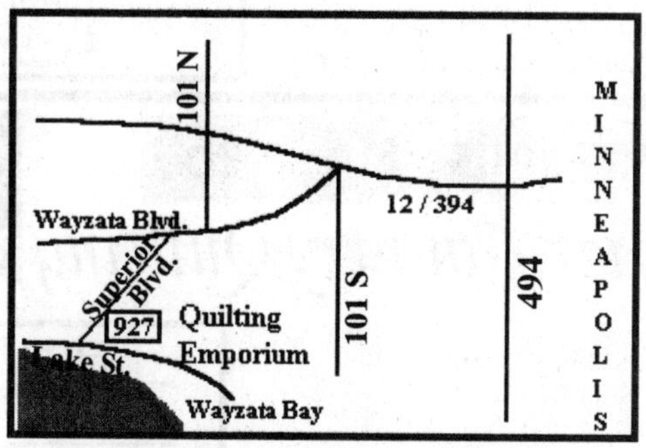

Twenty minutes west of Minneapolis — over 2000 bolts of cotton —

A complete quilt shop !

Quilted Treasures OF ROGERS

QUILTING SUPPLIES * COTTON FABRICS * CLASSES * KITS

Rogers, MN #59

14178 Northdale Blvd.
Rogers, MN 55374
(763) 428-1952

SHOP HOURS:
M, W, F 10 - 6
T, Th 10 - 9
SATURDAY 10 - 4
SUNDAY 12:30 - 4

- 2000 square feet
- 4000+ bolts of Cotton Fabric
- Friendly, Knowledgeable Staff
- Large selection of Minnesota based Designers
- Samples Galore
- Hundreds of fat quarters
- We specialize in Kits
- Seasonal Retreats and Workshops
- Frequent Buyer Cards

Owners:
Rita Kroening &
Mary Wilberg

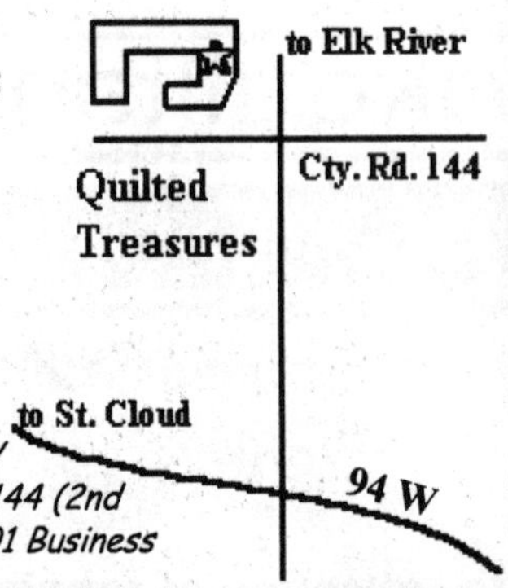

Located just one mile North of 94 W on Hwy. 101. Turn West on Cty. Rd. 144 (2nd stoplight) and turn North into the 101 Business complex. The shop faces 101.

The Sampler

a quilt shop and more.....

535 W. 78th St., Box 532
Chanhassen, MN 55317
(952) 934-5307
E-Mail: sampler@pconline.com
Web Site: www.the-sampler.com
Owner: Karol Plocher
Est: 1977 2650 Sq.ft.

An "exciting" shop to visit if you're Minnesota bound, our diverse fabric selection helps you to create fabulous quilts! See entire line of Kaffe Fassett, huge selection of Bali Batiks, Japanese, African & more. Lots of kits, fat quarter bundles, BOM's, gifts, classes, mail order plus a creative & talented staff!!

Mon & Wed 9:30 - 6:30
Tues & Thur 9:30 - 8:30
Fri & Sat 9:30 - 5:30
Sun 12 - 4:30

Chanhassen, MN #60

Directions:

Take Highway 494 to Highway 5 West - go to Great Plains Blvd (Chanhassen exit) — turn Rt. — Follow street around Chanhassen Dinner Theater to first left.

Plymouth, MN #61

Mon - Sat 9:30 - 6:30

SnuggleBug, A Quilt Shop

3900 Vinewood Ln. N, Suite 9 55441
in Cottonwood Plaza
(763) 557-8656
E-Mail: snugglebugaquilt@qwest.net
Owner: Alexis Lair
Est: 2001 1500 sq. ft.

Beautiful Batiks and Vibrant Brites.
Books, Patterns, Notions & Classroom.

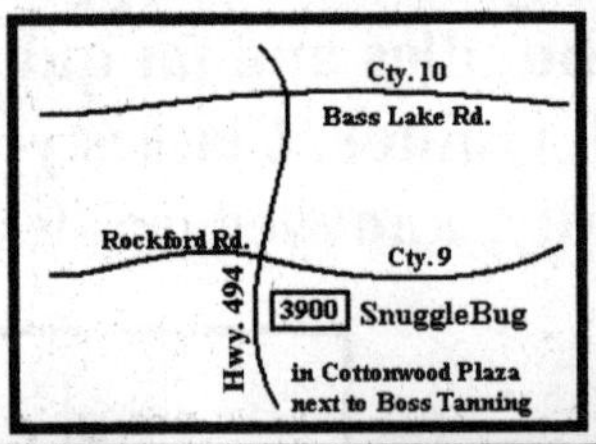

North St. Paul, MN #62

Mon - Fri 10 - 5
Sat 10 - 3

Rosebud's Cottage

2580 Seventh Ave. 55109
(651) 426-1885 Fax: (651) 426-1879
Owner: Roseann Meehan Kermes
Est: 1997 2700 sq.ft.

Specializing in the primitive look for quilters, rughookers, stitchers and painters. Nationally acclaimed bus tours. Primitive gifts & goodies!

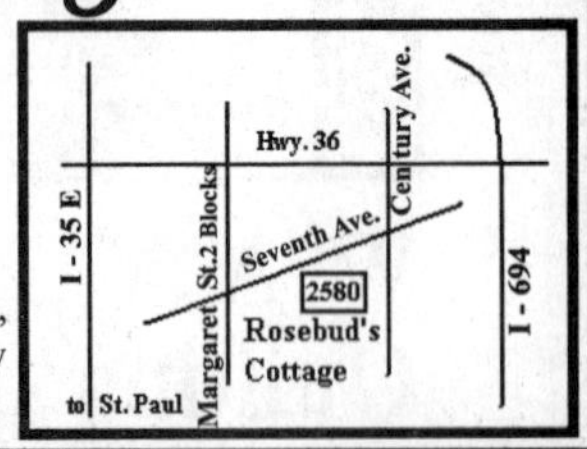

Minneapolis, MN #63

Mon - Sat 10 - 5
Sun 12 - 4

Eydie's Country Quilting

2822 W. 43rd St. 55410
(612) 929-0645

Thousands of bolts of 100% cotton fabrics from flannels to batiks. Specializing in reproduction fabrics. Supplies, books, patterns, classes. Only 15 minutes from the Mall of America.

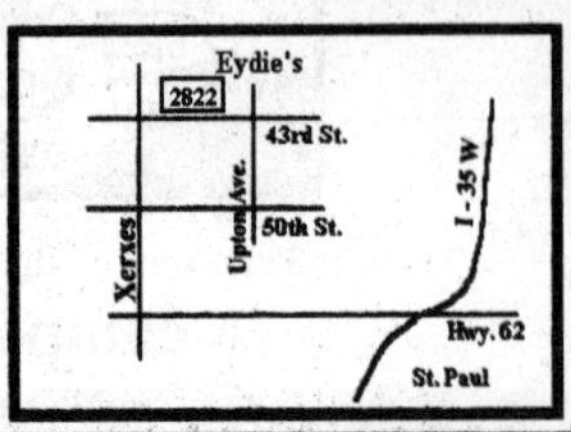

Minneapolis, MN #64

Mon - Sat 9:30 - 5

Glad Creations, Inc.

3400 Bloomington Ave. S 55407
(612) 724-1079 Fax: (612) 276-0275
E-Mail: nancy@gladcreationsquilts.com
Web Site: www.gladcreationsquilts.com
Est: 1976 1500 sq.ft. 3000 Bolts

Great selection of fabrics, books and quilting supplies. Original line of patterns for rotary cut machine pieced quilts.

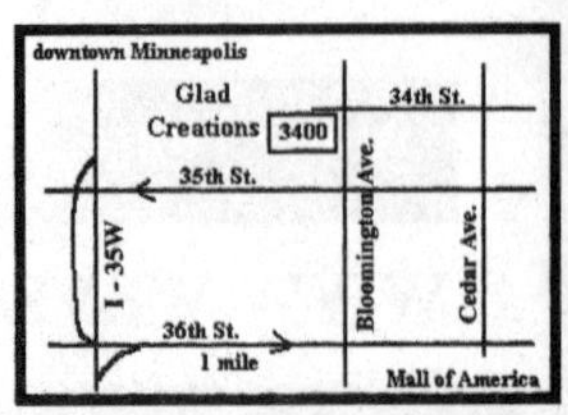

White Bear Lake, MN #65

Bear Patch Quilting Co.

2001 TOP TEN QUILT SHOP

A Quilter's Heaven filled with 100% cotton fabrics, patterns, books, notions, and samples to inspire your creativity. Bear Patch also offers a large selection of wool and rug hooking supplies. Year round classes. Lots of samples and great ideas.

651-429-1039
2199 Fourth St. 55110
e-mail: bearpqc@aol.com
Est: May 1997
4600 sq.ft. 3500+ Bolts

Mon - Fri 9 - 9
Sat 9 - 5
Sun 12 - 4

St. Paul's Authorized Bernina Dealer serving the Twin Cities.

Nothing Sews Like A Bernina. Nothing.

BERNINA®

Join us for:
Patchwork Thursdays,
and Redwork Embroidery Club

www.bearpatchquilting.com

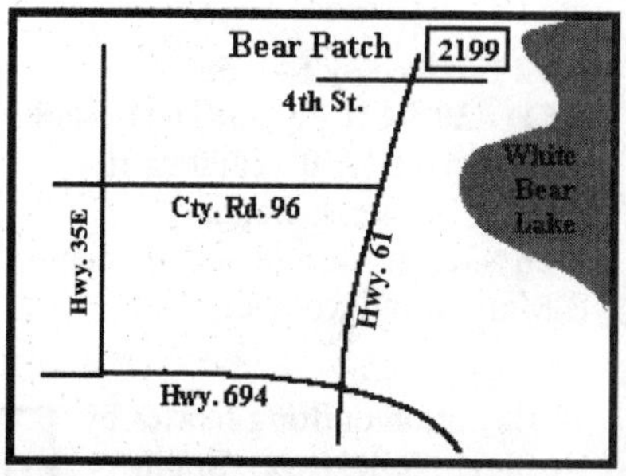

The Quilter's Basket

Maple Grove, MN #66

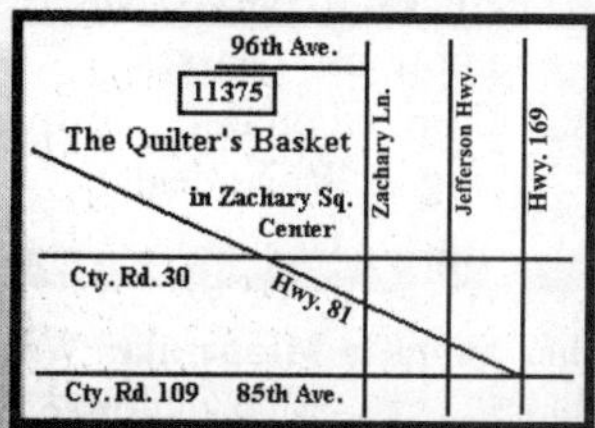

3rd Saturday of Each Month
"Pick-A-Chip Saturday"
Save 10,15, or 20%!

Zachery Square Shopping Center
11375 96th Ave. N 55369
(763) 493-5577
E-Mail: tqb97@aol.com
Est: 1997 1700 sq.ft. 3000 Bolts

- Cotton Fabrics
- Quilting Books
- Reed
- Gift Items
- Quilting & Basket Notions

Monthly Specials

Store Hours:
Mon-Th 9:30 am - 8:30 pm
Fri-Sat 9:30 am - 5:30

www.TheQuiltersBasket.com

Anoka, MN #67

Mon - Sat 10 - 5
Sun 12 - 4
Call First

The Quilt Essentials Shop

241 Van Buren St. #1 55303
(763) 433-9133 Fax: (763) 506-9991
Owner: Julie Anderson
Est: 1999 1250 sq.ft. 1200 bolts

100% cotton fabrics, books, patterns, quilting supplies, gifts, stencils and classes. We are 2 blocks north of Main street on 3rd & Van Buren

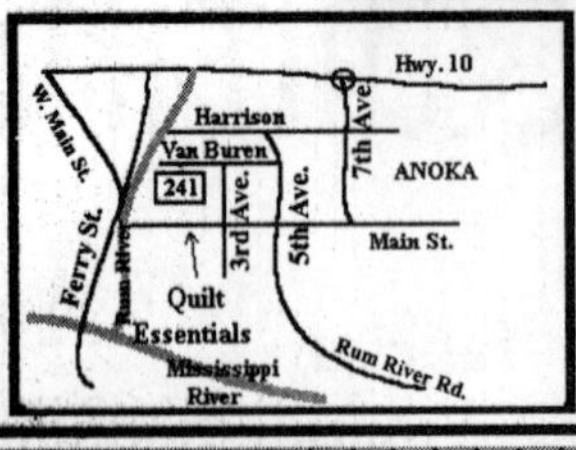

New Hope, MN #68

Mon - Sat 9:30 - 6

Quilts, Comforts & Tea, Inc.

6028 W. Broadway 55428
(763) 536-0512
E-Mail: joleigh@mcleodusa.net
Owners: Gerald & Leigh Gleason
Est: 1999 2900 sq.ft. 1000 Bolts

We have a Gammill Quilting machine. We offer classes on the quilting machine. You may then rent the machine. Only place in Twin Cities that you can rent a Gammill Quilting Machine. 10% off fabric purchase when you mention QTC.

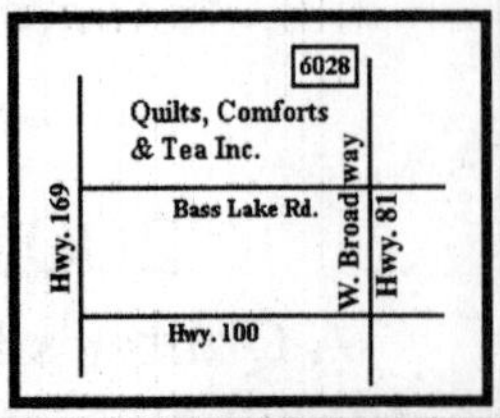

Stillwater, MN #69

AND SEW ON

1672 S. Greeley St. 55082
(651) 430-9441 or (888) 641-5408
Established 1990 2000 sq.ft.
Owner: Deborah Gangnon
Web Site: www.and-sew-on.com
E-Mail: aso@woldnet.att.net

Mon & Wed 9:30 - 6:00
Tue & Thur 9:30 - 8:00
Fri 9:30 - 5:00
Sat 9:30 - 4:00

Located in historic Stillwater

100% cotton quilting fabrics by Hoffman, RJR, R&B, South Seas and more...
The latest in books, patterns and notions. Classes.
Authorized premier Husqvarna Viking & White dealer.

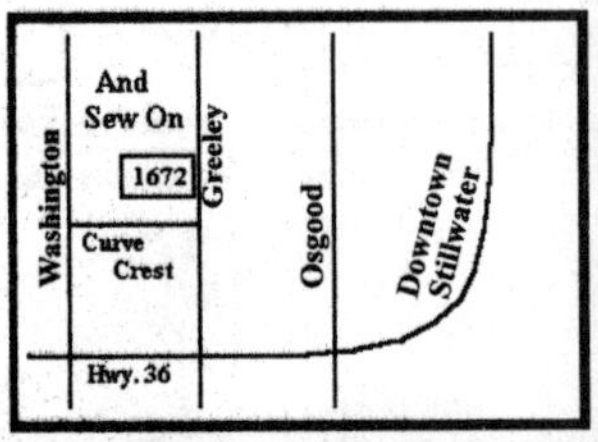

Roseville, MN #70

Mon - Sat 10 - 5:30
Tues & Thur til 8

Colorful Quilts & Textiles

"Located in the Hamline Shopping Center"
2817 N. Hamline Ave. 55113
(651) 628-9664
Web Site: www.colorfulquiltsandtextiles.com

Unique contemporary fabrics for innovative quilts & wearables. Also books, classes, dyes, & fabric paints. Cities' largest selection of hand-dyed fabrics. Personalized service & inspiration.

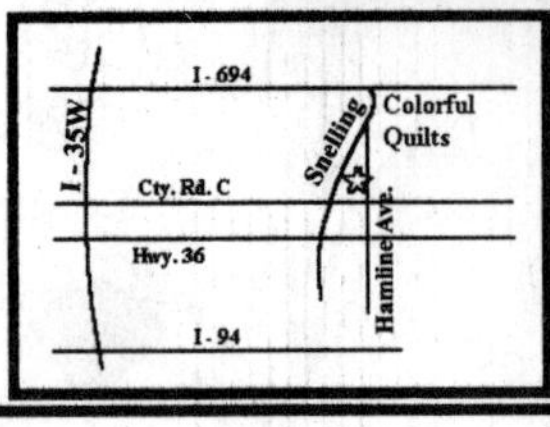

Other Shops in Minnesota: We suggest calling first

Afton	Afton Quiltworks, 3192 St. Croix Trail S	651-436-4065
Albert Lea	Lady of the Lake Quilts, 520 Park Ave.	507-373-6045
Alexandria	The Quilt Shop, 1903 Cty. Rd. 22 W	320-763-7177
Austin	Creations From the Heart, 400 N. Main St.	507-433-5551
Bagley	Gram's House Of Quilts, RT 2 Box 55A	218-694-3000
Baxter	Tangled Threads, 149 Norway Dr. N	218-828-3087
Chanhassen	QuiltSMART, West 96th St.	612-445-5737
Cottage Grove	Cottage Quilting, 8074 Jody Ave. S	612-458-8507
Crookston	Veronica's Quilt Haven, 303 S. Main St.	218-281-5374
Deer River	Needle Nook, 37584 County Road 129	218-246-2794
Duluth	The Quilting Shoppe, 2033 Woodland Ave.	218-724-4855
Emily	Carladdie Craft, R.R. 3, Box 158	218-763-2544
Fairmont	Wood-N-Needle, 84 Downtown Plz.	507-238-5411
Farmington	Homemade Stitches, 3731 Upper 204th St. W	612-460-6213
Felton	Lori's Quilt Factory, R.R. #1, Box 138	218-494-3911
Hollandale	The Seed Room, 100 Central Ave. N	507-889-6351
Howard Lake	Piece Makers Quilt Shoppe, 809 6th Ave.	320-543-3107
Le Sueur	River Bobbin, 119 S. 5th St.	507-665-4057
Madelia	Ma's Cupboard, 17 W. Main St.	507-642-3457
Menahga	Lorraine's Quilting, 214 1st St. NE	218-564-4047
Merrifield	K Dee Quilt Shop, 21755 Cty. Rd. 3	218-833-0176
Minneapolis	Northwind Quilts, 3133 35th Ave. S	612-729-1777
Minneapolis	Hearts & Ivy Collection, 3112 W 28th St.	952-925-6997
Minneapolis	The Quilt Works 1055 E. 79th St.	312-588-5345
Minneapolis	Bernina Sewing Center, 10550 France S	952-888-5100
Mountain Lake	Quilts & More, 1104 6th Ave.	507-427-2728
New London	Quilt Cupboard, 18 Main St.	320-354-2977
Northfield	Jacobsen's, 419 Division St.	507-645-4672
Oklee	Country Stitch 'N, 204 Main St.	218-796-5744
Oklee	The Oklee Quilt Shop, 128 S. Main St.	218-796-5151
Park Rapids	Miss Molly's Mercantile, 105 Lake Ave.	218-732-6537
Pelican Rapids	Calico Cupboard, 25 1st Ave. NW	218-863-4681
Perham	Quilt It by the Bay, 116 2nd Ave. SW	218-346-7399
Randall	Sew Casual, 525 Pacific Ave.	320-749-2326
Ray	Quilters Corner, 4794 Town Rd. 180	218-346-2299
Richmond	Pine Cellar, Hwy 23	320-597-3267
Rochester	Quilts Galore, 357 Elton Hills Dr. NW	507-288-2220
Sauk Centre	Water's Edge Creations, 455 Leko Dr.	320-352-6322
Sleepy Eye	Pine Needle Quilting, 32189 Cty. Rd. 29	218-728-6950
Sleepy Eye	Prairieville Quilting, R.R. #3, Box 115	507-794-2466
St. Charles	Yoder's Quilts, Rt. 1, Box 76	None
St. Charles	Amish Market Sq., I - 90 & Hwy 74	507-932-5907
St. Cloud	Granny's Legacy, 25284 Lake Rd.	320-251-5397
St. James	Stitch-A-Quilt, 806 1st Ave. S	507-375-7757
St. Paul	Crossroads Shoppe, 619 Grand Ave.	651-225-4467
St. Paul	Moose Country Quilting, 1293 Portland	651-646-5218
St. Paul	Treadle Yard Goods, 1338 Grand Ave.	651-698-9690
Staples	Quilting Memories, 216 2nd Ave. N.E.	218-894-1776
Staples	4 P's in a Pod, 8419 72nd St. SW	218-397-2527
Thief River Falls	Annette's Fabrics, 212 E. 3rd St.	218-681-3501
Thief River Falls	Quiltingly Yours, 212 Parkview St.	218-681-6780
Truman	Quilting Thimble, 105 E 6th St	
Walnut Grove	Plum Creek Patchwork, Rt. 2, Box 95	
Wells	The Creative Needle, 135 S. Broadway	507-553-3195
West Concord	Pieces Be With You, 54336 237th Ave.	507-356-4255
Winona	The Cinderella Shoppe, Mankato Ave.	507-452-9175
Zimmerman	Cindy's Stitches, 28503 127th St.	612-856-3704

Pass Christian, MS #1

Tues - Fri 10 - 5 Sat 10 - 4

Peacemakers Quilt Shop

106 W. Second St. 39571
(228) 452-1221
E-Mail: pcmakers@bellsouth.net
Web Site: www.peacemakersquiltshop.com
Owner: Michelle Hammons
Est: 1998 2400 sq.ft. 2000 Bolts

We carry a great selection of 100% cotton fabrics. Classes galore! Books, patterns, notions. Located in historic old downtown Pass Christian, MS. Turn North at the Harbor.

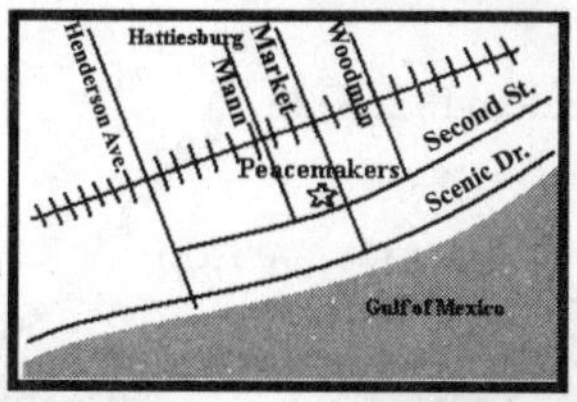

Vicksburg, MS #2

Mon - Sat 9 - 5:30

Stitch-N-Frame

2222 S. Frontage Rd., Suite D 39180
(601) 634-0243 Fax: (601) 634-0287
E-Mail: kmccoy@vicksburg.com
Web Site: www.stitch-n-frame.net
Owner: Kay McCoy Est: 1983 2800 sq.ft.

Home of Ulmer Quilt frames. Anywear Shoes. Over 4000 bolts plus all the supplies you'll need. Join our on-line newsletter to get our "Thursday Specials". Numerous Blocks of the Month. Toll free # (877) 634-1462

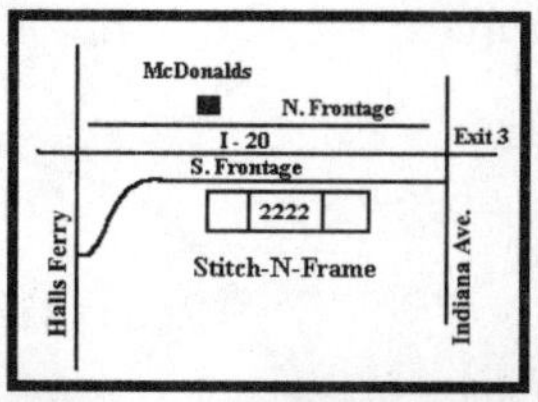

Tupelo, MS #3

Mon - Sat 10 - 5:30

Heirlooms Forever

3112 Cliff Gookin Blvd. 38801
(662) 842-4275 or (800) 840-4275
Fax: (662) 842-2284 Est: 1983
E-Mail: kathy@sews.com 7000 sq.ft.
Web Site: www.sews.com

Over 1500 bolts of fabrics, quilting supplies, books, notions, threads, Bernina, Brother, Pfaff & Viking Machines Sales & Service. Helpful & Friendly.

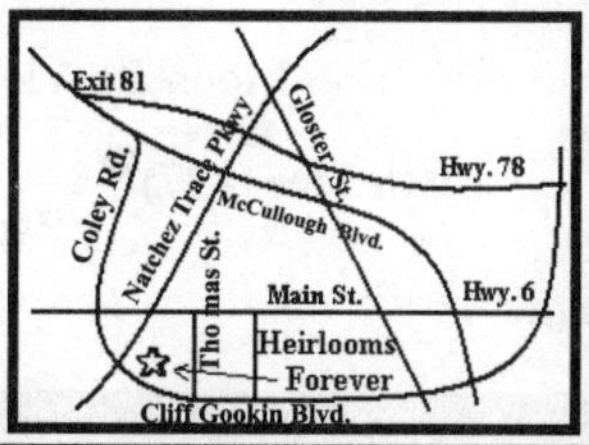

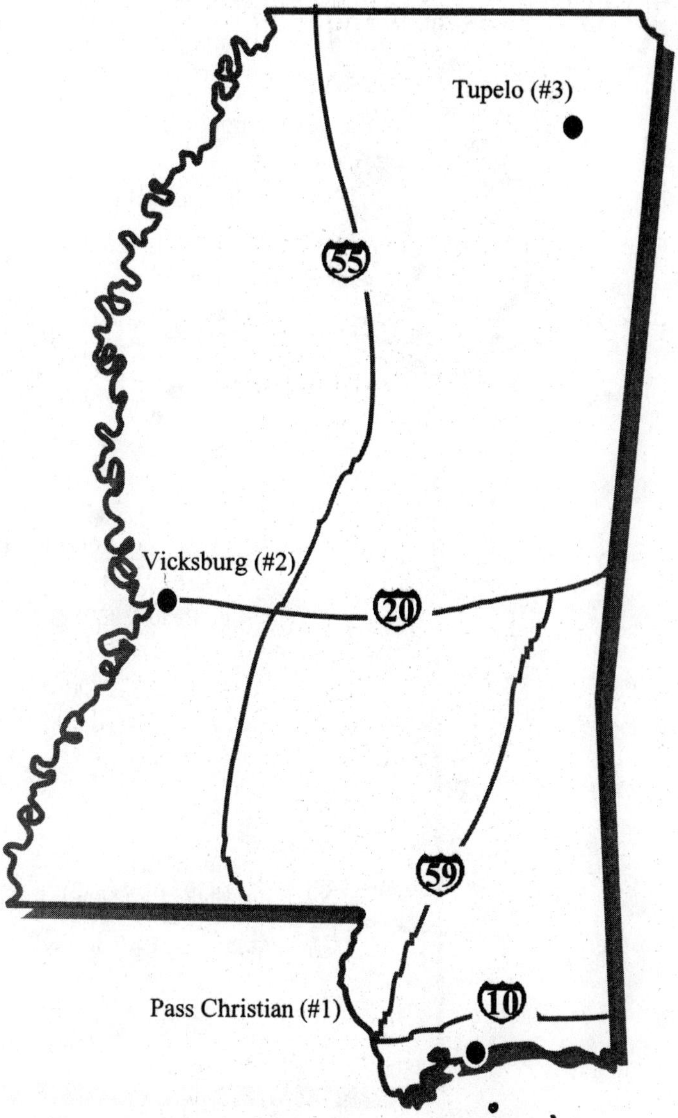

3 Featured Shops

MISSISSIPPI

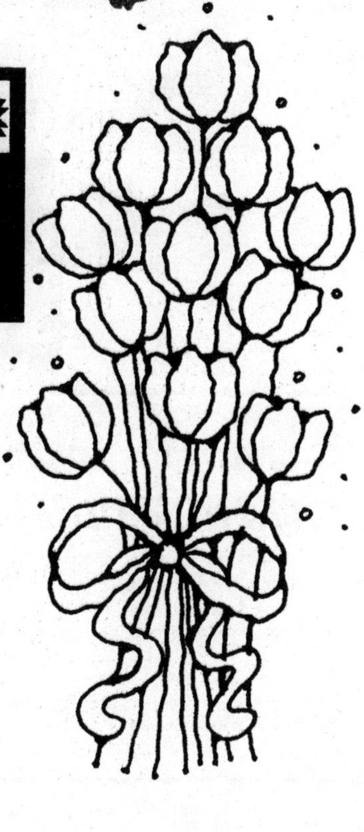

Other Shops in Mississippi: We suggest calling first

Bay St. Louis	Old Books & Curiosities, 126 Main St.	601-467-9791
Booneville	Quilt Gallery, 1114 Hwy. 30	601-728-3302
Brookhaven	Melanie's Fabric, 128 W. Monticello St.	601-833-4608
Brookhaven	Dry Goods Shop, 127 S. Jackson St.	601-833-3253
Houston	Sara's Fabrics, 467 E. Madison St.	601-456-5987
Maben	Springer's Dry Goods, 124 Highway 15	601-263-8144
Meridian	The Craft Cottage, 2034 40th St	601-482-2821
Sarah	Quilts & Crafts by Barbara, 1130 Truslow Rd.	662-349-6590
Summit	Wards Linen Outlet, 814 Robb St.	601-276-3348

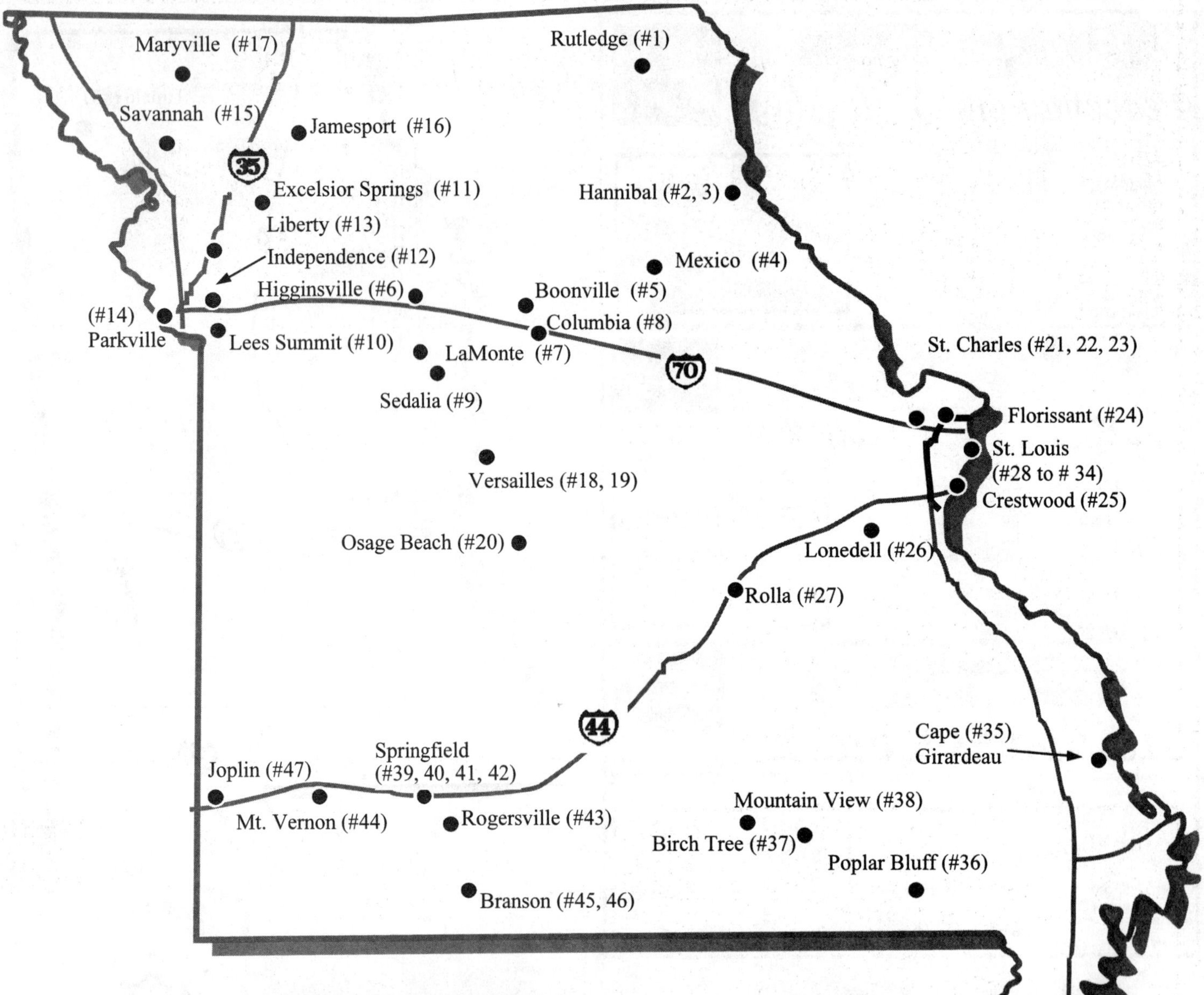

47 Featured Shops

MISSOURI

Rutledge, MO #1

Mon - Sat
8 - 5

Zimmerman's Store

Main St., Box 1 63563
(660) 883-5766 Est: 1974
Owners: Paul & Lydia Zimmerman
Mgr: Ellanor Zimmerman

2000 bolts of 100% cotton fabrics at reasonable prices. Batting, quilt patterns & books, sewing notions, hand quilted quilts, pillows, aprons etc.

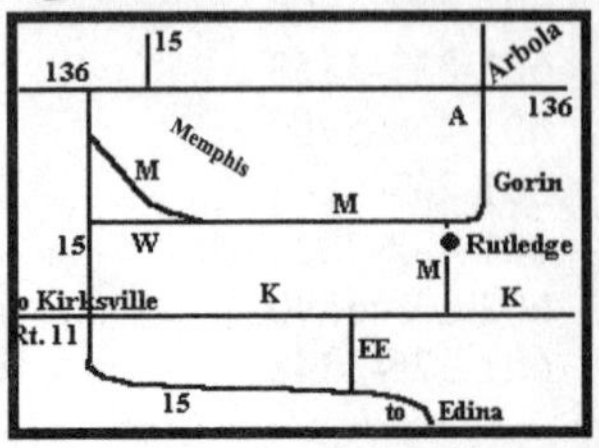

Hannibal, MO #2

Mon - Sat
9:30 - 5
Sun 11 - 5

Quilts 'n Treasures

219 N. Main 63401
(573) 248-1607
Owner: Joyce Riggs Est: 1995

Quilts custom made for you and for sale.
Other quilted items.
Christmas and Holiday gifts. Plus Classes.

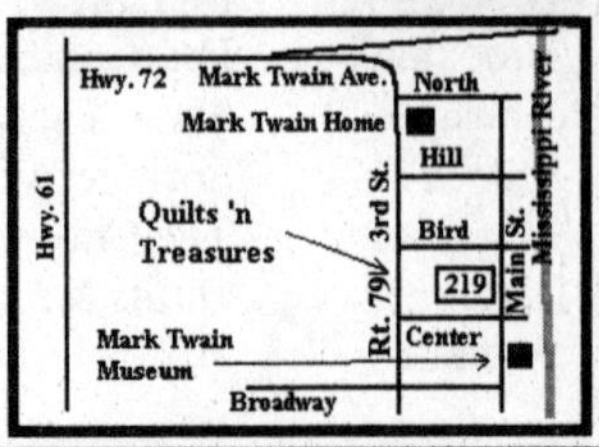

Hannibal, MO #3

Hickory Stick
Quilt & Gift Shop

326 N. Main
Hannibal, MO 63401
(573) 221-4538
Fax: (573) 248-0396
–Open Daily–

Extensive Collection Of Redwork

Web Site: www.hickory stitckquiltsetc.com

Located across from Mark Twain's Home

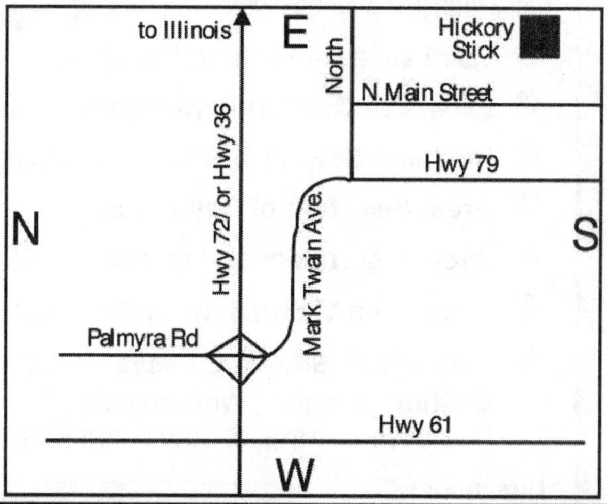

- Quilting Supplies
- 2500 Bolts fabrics
- Books & Patterns
- Primitive Stitchery
- Stamped Embroidery Kits & floss
- Unique Buttons
- Wholecloth Quilt Tops
- Department 56 Villages, Houses and accessories
- English Ironstone Table Settings
- Florals & Wall Decor
- Lamps
- Fine Linens
- April Cornell
- Locally Made Quilts

Mexico, MO #4

Mon - Sat 9 - 5

Sticky Wicket

111 N. Jefferson St. 65265
(573) 581-6262
Web Site: www.stickywicketquilt.com
Owner: Mona Leonard
Est: 1998 2000+ sq.ft. 900+ Bolts

Quality cotton fabric, Thimbleberries, Moda, Mumm, homespuns and more. Quilt supplies, craft gift items, gifts, candles and more. Classes.

Mexico exit off I-70, Highway 54 North (East) to first Mexico exit. Straight on S. Clark to Jackson. Right on Jackson to N. Jefferson, turn left, ½ block on right.

Boonville, MO #5

Mon - Sat 9 - 5

The Fabric Shop

511 E. Spring 65233
(660) 882-5113 Est: 1994
E-Mail: LTKFRED@Socket.net 800 Bolts
Owner: Cheri Friedrich 2400 sq.ft.

I have fabric in stock for Quilts and Crafts. Patterns, Notions, Quilting Supplies & Frames Gifts. Embroidery Room. Machine Quilting

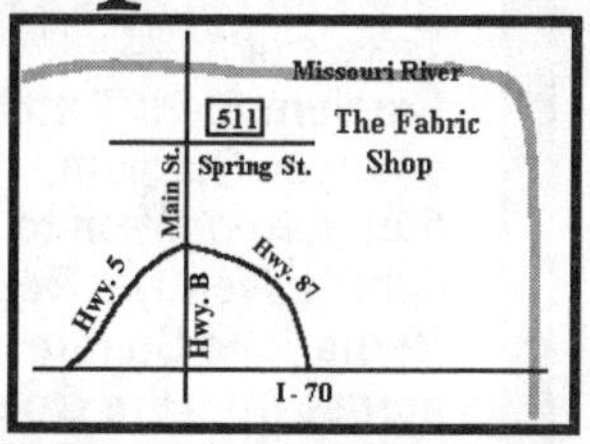

Higginsville, MO #6

Mon - Fri 9:30 - 6 Thur til 8 Sat 10 - 4

Quilter's Harvest

1913 Main St. 64037
(660) 584-3399
E-Mail: quilter@ctcis.net
Web Site: www.quiltersharvest.com
Owners: Pam Fisher & Donna Campbell
Est: 2000 1300 sq.ft. 1300+ Bolts

Everything a quilter needs! Quality fabrics, notions, kits, books and patterns. We also have finished quilts. Always ready to help with friendly service.

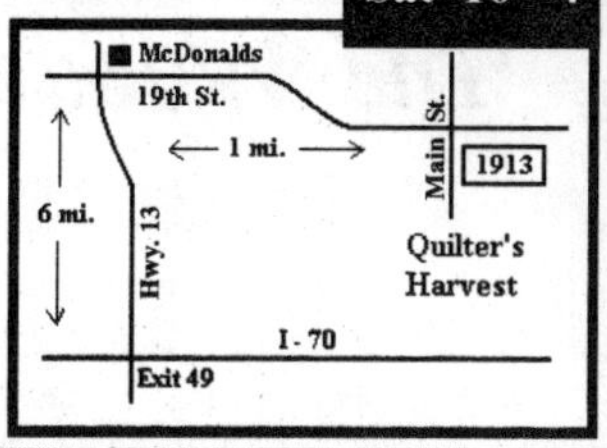

LaMonte, MO #7

Mon - Fri 9 - 5 Closed Th & Sun Sat 9:30 - 2:30

Jan & Angie's Country Connection

Hwy. 50 &
Pleasant Green Rd.
P.O. Box 98 65337

(660) 347-5150 Fax: Same
Est: 1998 1500+ Bolts

Large selection of quilting and fashion fabrics with great prices. Notions, books, patterns, gifts, and cards. Friendly Service!

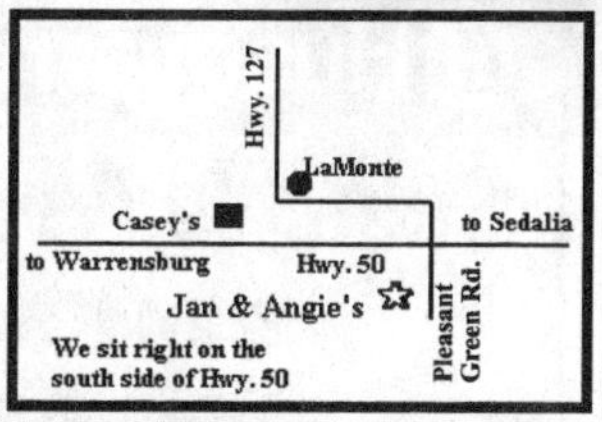

Silks & More Fine Fabrics and Viking Center

Come Quilt with Us....

Visit Silks & More on your next trip to the Midwest. We're sew much more than just a fabric store.

- 5,000 sq. ft. of Quilting Paradise
- Extensive Quilting Department
- Heirloom Sewing & Smocking Supplies
- Great Selection of Quilting Books
- Wide Assortment of Patterns & Notions
- Husqvarna Viking Sewing Machines
- Lots of Fun Sewing Classes including Quilting, Fashion, Wearable Art, Heirloom Sewing, & Sew Much More!

Directions:

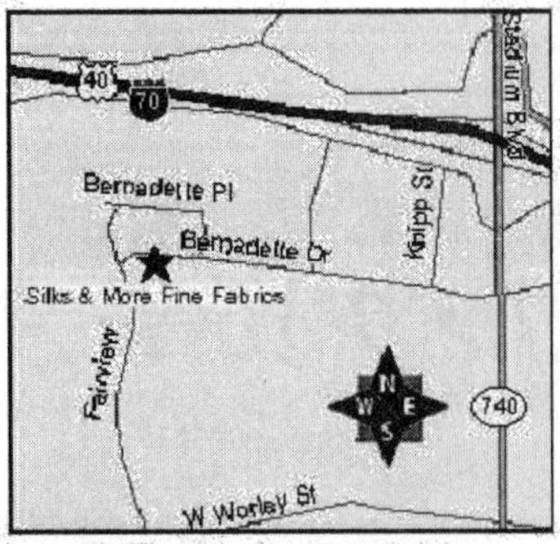

Silks & More Fine Fabrics is located in the heart of Missouri quilting country half way between St. Louis and Kansas City on Interstate 70. Take exit #124 - Stadium Blvd. Turn south on Stadium, then turn right on to Bernadette Dr. (second stop light at Wendy's Restaurant). We are located in Bernadette Square, a shopping center on your right, across from the Columbia Mall.

We also now have four additional Viking Centers located inside these JoAnns Fabrics Centers:

Affton, MO	St. Charles, MO
Ferguson, MO	and in Columbia, MO

Web Site: SilksNMore.com
Email: sewing@silksnmore.com
Established 1985

10 - 7 Mon - Thr
10 - 5 Fri & Sat

Husqvarna VIKING

SILKS & MORE FINE FABRICS

2541 Bernadette Dr.
Columbia, MO 65203 **#8**

573-446-2655 1-800-269-2655

Sedalia, MO #9

Mon - Fri 9 - 5
Sat 9 - 4

D & T Quilt Shop

3620 S. Marshall 65301
(660) 826-4788 Fax: (660) 826-4788
E-Mail: dandt@murlin.com
Owner: Theresa Gerber
Est: 1991 1200 sq.ft.

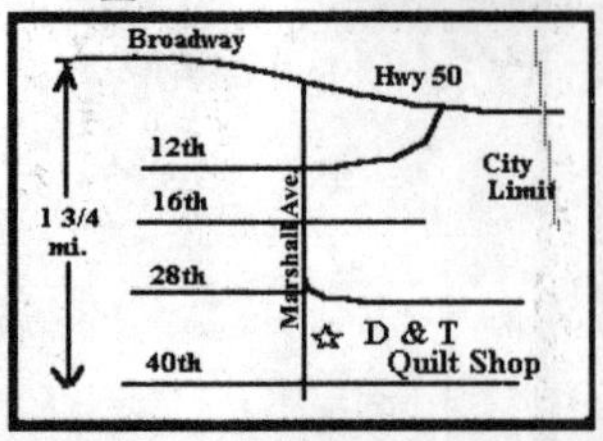

Fabrics, Notions, Embroidery Blocks, Classes. 4500+ Bolts. Buttons by the Lb. $4.99. Happy to ship orders. Hand & Machine Quilting. We'll also sew your tops together. Friendly Country Atmosphere

---

QUILTER'S STATION

Fabrics
Quilting Supplies

824 SW Blue Parkway
Lee's Summit, MO 64063

(816) 525-8955
E-Mail quiltersstation@prodigy.net
Web. www.quiltsstation.com

Toll Free 1-866-649-8024

Over 3500 bolts of the latest in fabrics including, Benartex, Moda, Hoffman, RJR, Kona Bay and others. As well as a large selection of books, patterns, and notions. Classes available.

Lees Summit, MO #10

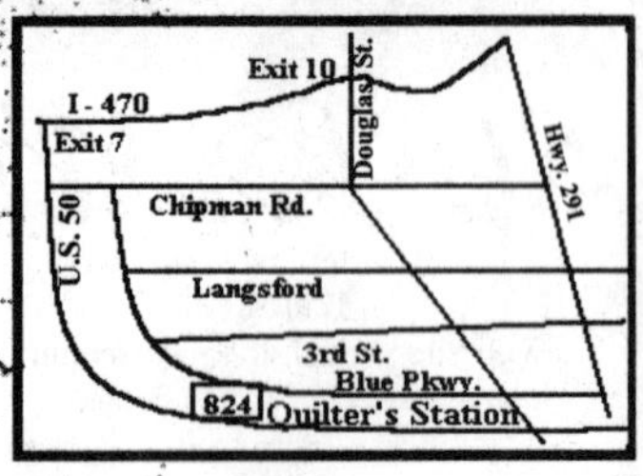

Mon, Tues, Wed 9:30 - 5:30
Thur 9:30 - 8
Fri 9:30 - 5
Sat 9:30 - 3

Excelsior Springs, MO #11

Tues - Sat 10 - 5

The Wooden Spool

233 E. Broadway 64024
(816) 637-2567
Owner: Jamie Fondren

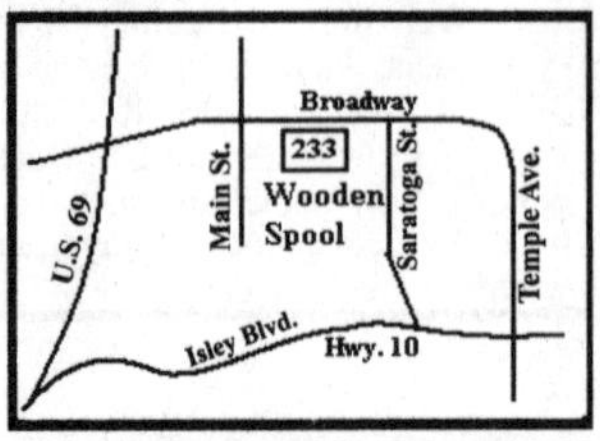

Great quilt shop opened in May 2002 in our newly renovated turn of the century building. For all of your quilting needs: Fabric, Notions, Books, Patterns, Kits and Classes.

Independence, MO #12

RUSTIC YEARNINGS

17601 A East 40 Hwy. Colonnade Shopping Center 64055
(816) 373-2423 E-Mail: rusticy@aol.com
Est: 1993 8500 sq.ft. 5000+ Bolts
Website: www.rusticyearnings.com

Large Selection of Books, Notions, Patterns & Fabrics for Quilting and Crafting. Also unique Home Accessories & Gifts plus P. Buckley Moss Gallery.

Open 7 Days

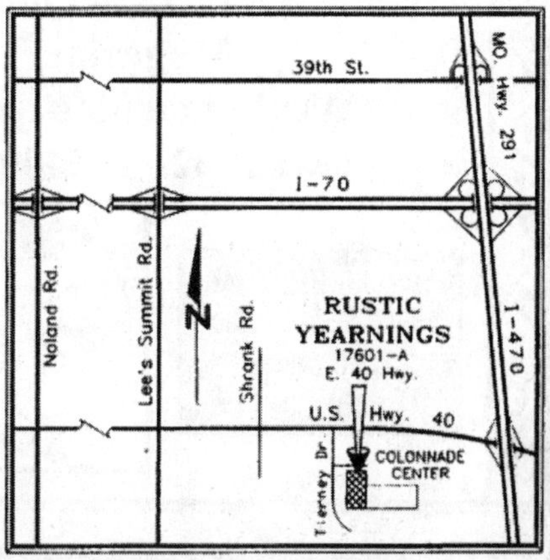

LIBERTY QUILT SHOP

Hours: 10am - 5pm
Open until 7
Mon. & Thur.
Closed Sunday

Liberty, MO #13

131 S. Water
Liberty, MO 64068
816-781-7966
Email: LibertyQlt@aol.com
Website: www.LibertyQuiltShop.com

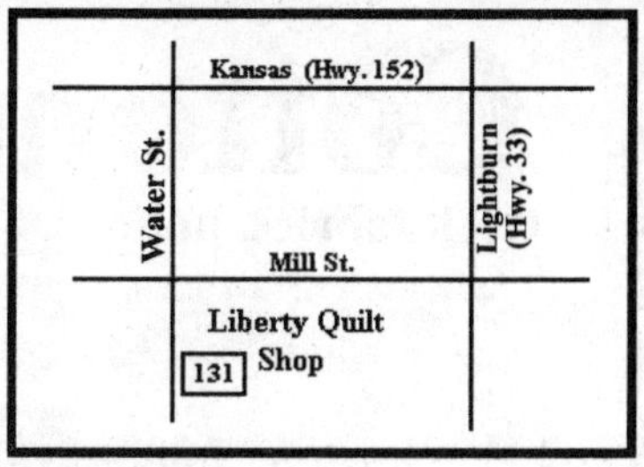

Located in historic Corbin Mill Place -- a perfect day trip setting! Have lunch and shop in Liberty -- home of several antique and gift shops. We stock the finest quality of 100% cotton fabrics and a wide selection of books, patterns and notions. Our specialty is primitive and reproduction style. Our high ceilings are the perfect setting for an ongoing quilt show. Featured in 1998 issue of Quilt Sampler magazine as a favorite shop. Come in and meet our friendly and knowledgeable staff.

Parkville, MO #14

Peddler's Wagon

Everything a quilter needs plus friendly smiles and expert help.
Huge Collection of Models
***Featured in 1996 Quilt Sampler Magazine ***
We do machine quilting
Est: 1982 3400 sq.ft.

Hours:
10 - 5 Tues. - Sat.
Extended Holiday hours

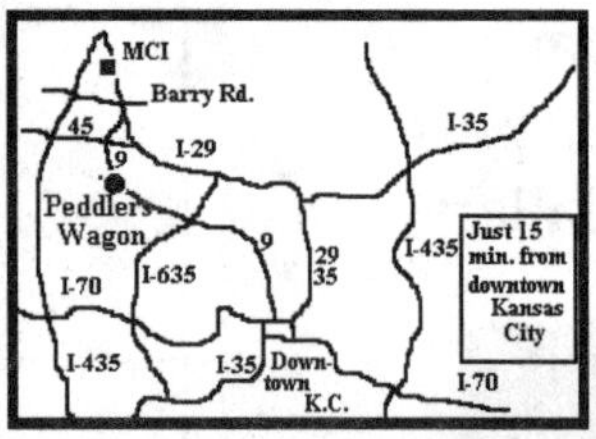

115 Main Parkville, MO 64152
816-741-0225

Savannah, MO #15

Mon - Fri 9 - 5
Tues til 9
Sat 9 - 4

Wild Hare Quilt Shop

420 Court St. 64485
(816) 324-4053
E-Mail: topstitch@ponyexpress.net
Owner: Melanie Rouse

Fabrics, Books, Patterns, Notions, Classes

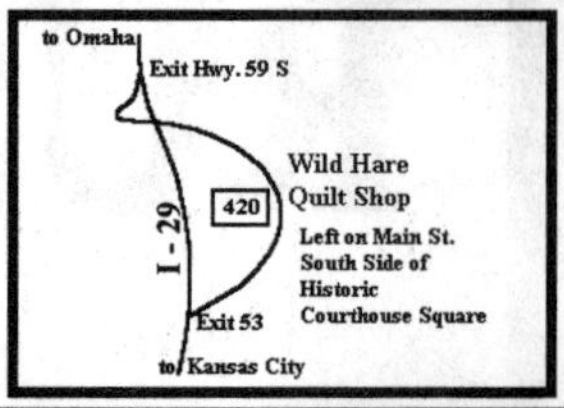

Jamesport, MO #16

Mon - Sat 9 - 5
Closed Thur

Fabric Barn

21914 St. Hwy. 190 64648
No Phone

Large selection (approx. 1900 bolts) of 100% cotton prints, books, patterns, templates and notions. We carry 160+ bolts of thimbleberries fabric and patterns.

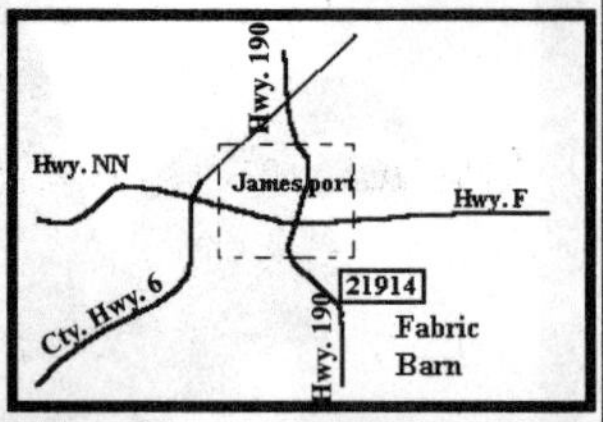

Maryville, MO #17

Mon - Fri 10 - 5:30
Sat 10 - 4:30

Thimble 'n Thread

1312 S. Main St. 64468
(660) 562-4955
Owner: Patty Bagby
Est: 1994 1400 sq.ft. 1500 Bolts

Area's largest selection of quilting books, patterns, fabric. Enjoy charming displays, friendly helpful service. Classes. Bernina Machines. Custom quilting service.

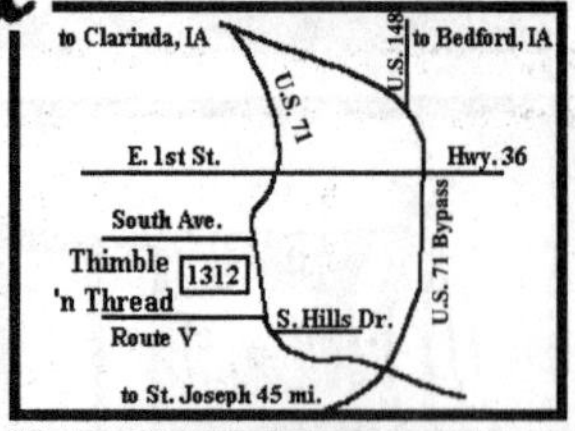

Linda's Cottonpatch

Owner: Linda Petty

Quilt fabrics, notions, books & patterns.

Versailles, MO #18

502 W. Newton 65084
T, Th, F 10 - 5:30 Sat 9 - 1
(573) 378-6191
Toll free
(877) 633-3440
Fax: (573) 378-5289
Est: 1993 2400 sq.ft.
lspetty@laurie.net
www.sewquilts.com

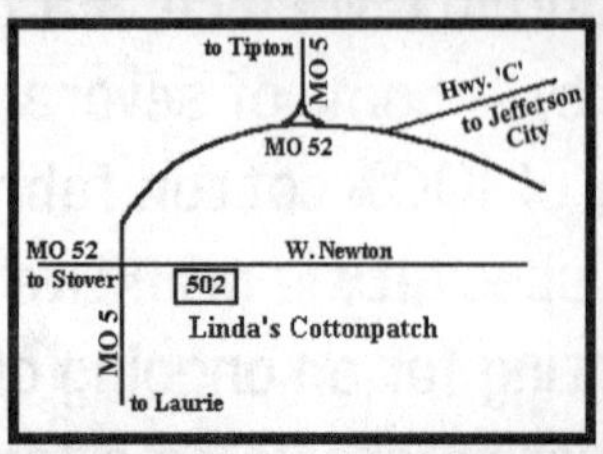

Husqvarna VIKING

Versailles, MO #19

Mon - Sat 9 - 5

Clark's Fabrics

813 N. Newton 65084
West Vue Shopping Center
Hwy 5 & 52 W. Est: 1964
(573) 378-5696 1800 sq.ft. 1700 Bolts
Owner: Kirk Chapman

Great selection of all types of fabric, including quilting, clothing and home decorating.

Buttons, Buttons, Buttons !

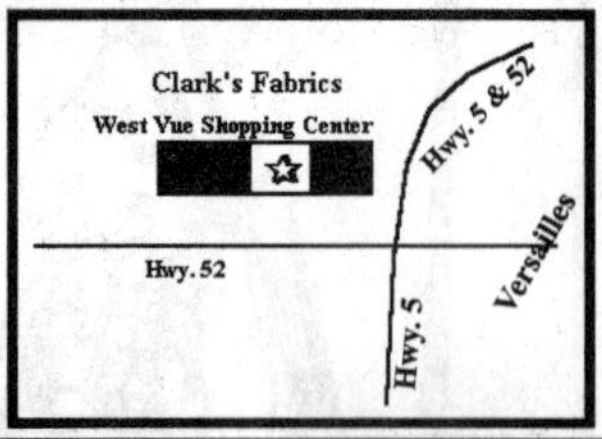

Osage Beach, MO #20

Mon - Fri 10 - 5
Sat 10 - 4

Quilter's Cove

Sewing & Embroidery

1040 Main St. 65065
(573) 302-9923 Est: 2002
E-Mail: Quilterscove1@aol.com

Fabrics - Notions - Books - Patterns. Machine Embroidery Supplies. Sewing & Embroidery Machines. Offering a variety of classes.

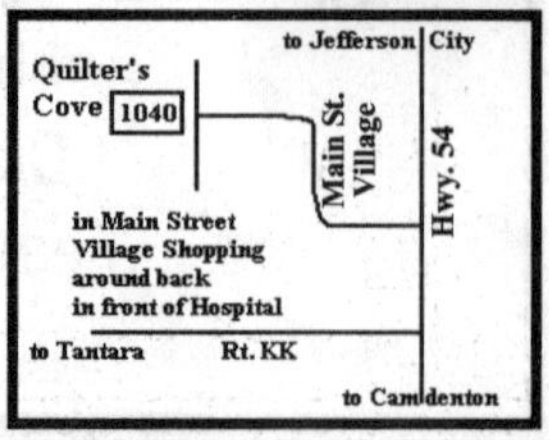

Patches Etc. Quilt Shop

Visit us at: www.patches3.com

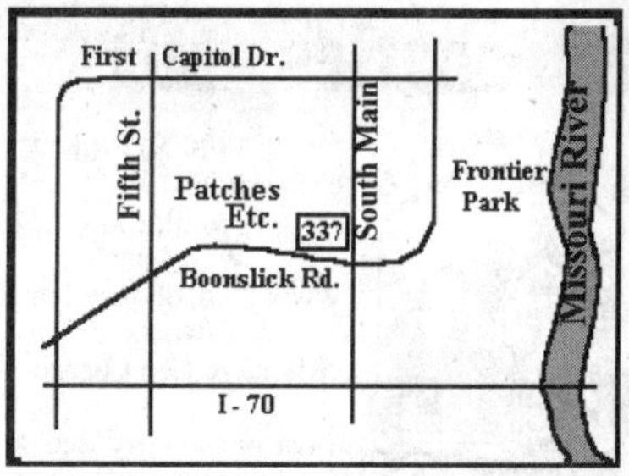

Quilts, Fabric and Patterns -- Home of 'Redwork'.

Mon - Sat 9:30 - 5
Sun 11 - 5

337 South Main 63301
(314) 946-6004
Owner: Ann Watkins-Hazelwood
Est: 1979 1500 Bolts
E-mail: 3patches@prodigy.net

Voted one of the 10 Best Quilt Shops in the 1st edition of Better Homes and Gardens Quilt Magazine.

Historic St. Charles, MO #21

Certified appraisals by Ann Watkins-Hazelwood.
Also visit our Craft Center and Button Shoppe.

St. Charles, MO #22

"Out of the scraps of my life God has made a beautiful quilt."

Kalico Patch

412 Boone's Lick Rd. 63301
636-946-9520
kalicopatch@aol.com
Web Site: Coming Soon
Owner: Karel Owens
Fabric: 5,000 bolts and more arriving weekly. Classes, bears and quilt racks. Custom orders welcomed. Machine quilting available.

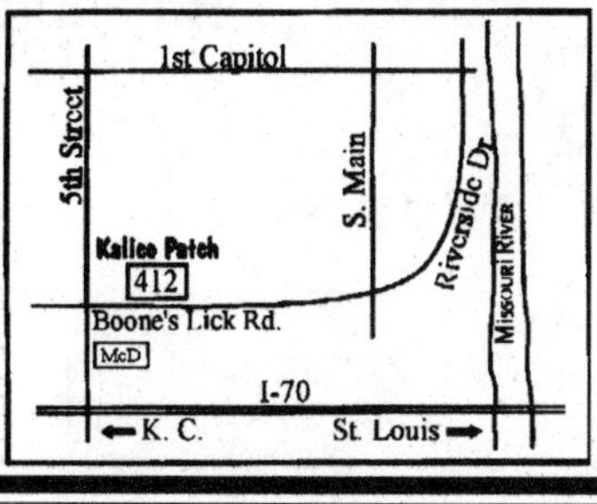

We are a convenient stop for traveling quilters. Our shop is just off I - 70. To accommodate our travelers we offer half-day quilting classes. Please send a SASE for a schedule of our classes. If you are planning a bus tour to the St. Charles area, we will schedule special classes for your quilt group. On your first visit to our store, bring this ad for a 15% discount on fabric and books. In addition, if it happens to be your birthday, bring proof and this ad for a 20% discount.

St. Charles, MO #23

Open 7 Days a Week

1309 N. Fifth St. 63301
(636) 946-0619 Fax: (636) 940-7134
E-Mail: rhonaloc@aol.com
Web Site:
www.lococohouse.com
Owners
Rhona & Leo Lococo

A warm and cozy Bed & Breakfast where Quilters can sew, eat and have lots of fun. Quilt Shop Tours available.

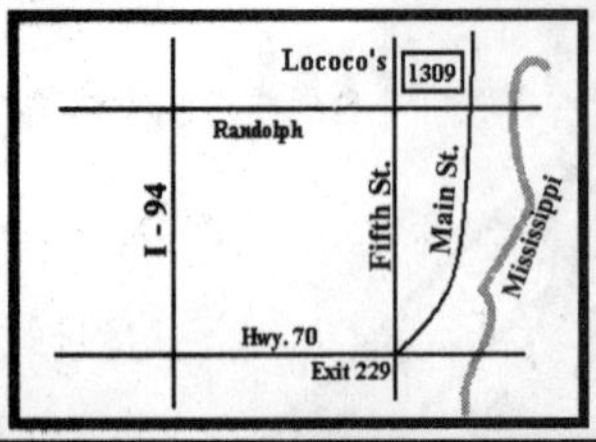

Florissant, MO #24

Mon - Sat 10 - 4 Wed til 8

Helen's Hen House

180 Dunn Rd. 63031
(314) 837-7661
Owners: Helen Argent & Joan Nicolay
Est: 1978 1350 sq.ft.

Over 2000 Bolts. Specializing in homespuns & reproduction fabrics. Complete line of quilting supplies, patterns & Books.
Exit #26B from I-270. Exit #9C from I-70.

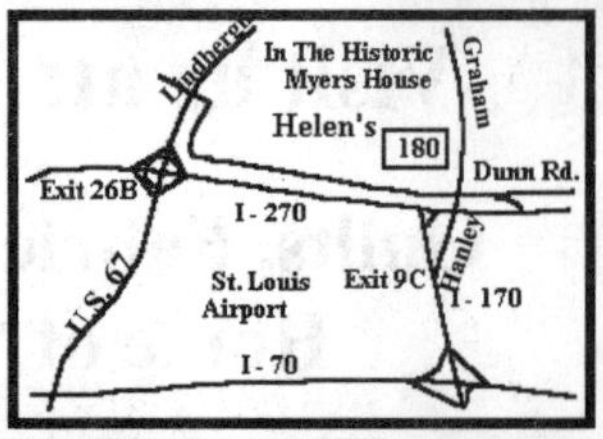

Crestwood, MO #25

Mon - Fri 9:30 - 5:30 Sat 9:30 - 4:30 Class Eves.

Quilt 'N' Stitch

9109 Watson Rd. 63126
(314) 961-0909 or (888) 681-0909
e-mail: qltnstitch@aol.com
Web Site: www.quiltnstitch.net
Owner: Connie Ewbank
Est: 1992 2400 sq.ft. 2000 Bolts

Large selection of fabrics - Christmas, homespuns, contemporary. Books, patterns, notions, classes. Also counted cross stitch.

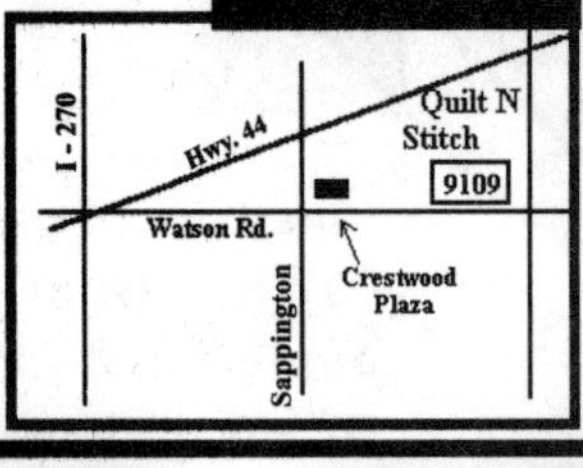

Lonedell, MO #26

Please Call First

Quilt-A-Lot Fabrics

112 Seven Springs Ct. 63060
(636) 629-8106
E-Mail: quiltalotmo@yahoo.com
Web Site: www.quiltalot.com
Est: 1998

Visit our web site, call for mail order or look for us at quilt shows. Cotton Fabric, Stencils, Notions, Quilt Blocks by Fairway Needlecrafts and Beginner Quilt Kits.

We have fabrics and supplies in our home while we're looking for a new shop. Please call for directions and hours or visit us on the web.

Rolla, MO #27

Mon - Fri 9 - 6 Sat 9 - 5

Fabrics Unlimited

13795 U.S. 63 S 65401
(573) 364-5245
Owner: Betty I. Lewis 1600 sq.ft.
2500 total bolts, 1100+ quilt fabric

Quilting Fabrics, Notions, Batting, Quilt Books. Machine Quilting. Machine Binding. Our main business is quilt supplies.

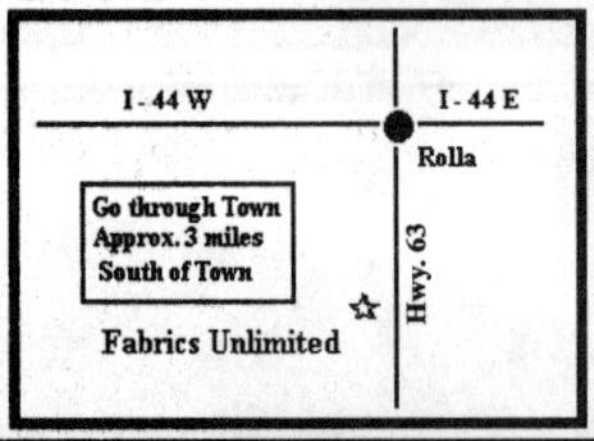

St. Louis, MO #28

Mon - Thur 10 - 9 Fri & Sat 10 - 5 Sun: By Appt

The Sign of the Turtle

5223 Gravois 63116
(314) 351-5550 Est: 1975
Owners: Ann & Bill Hofmann
1600 sq.ft. 300 Bolts 50 Solids

St. Louis Area's Quilting Headquarters!
By the Bevo

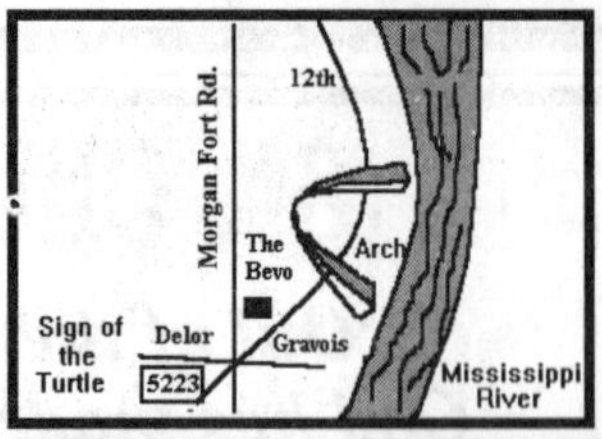

St. Louis, MO #29

M, W 9:30 - 5 T, Th 9:30 - 7 Fri & Sat 9:30 - 4:30

THE QUILTED FOX

SELECTED AS ONE OF THE TOP TEN FEATURED SHOPS 2001 QUILT SAMPLER MAGAZINE BY BETTER HOMES AND GARDENS

4000 bolts of unique quilting fabrics
International, Oriental, African and more
Fox Fabric club for the out-of-towner

Easy Access off & on the highway
Mail Orders always welcome

10403 Clayton Rd. 63131
(314) 993-1181
Established 1994; 2500 sq. ft.
E-Mail: info@quiltedfox.com
Web Site: www.quiltedfox.com
Owner: Louise L. Georgia

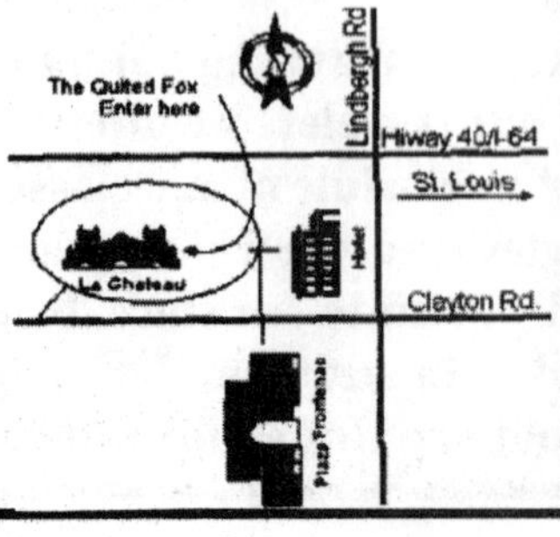

St. Louis, MO #30

Tues - Sat By Appt.

Treasured Keepsakes

1771 Parker Rd. 63138
(314) 741-4018
(800) 300-6316
Est: 1998 Catalog $2

We have a large selection of stamped embroidery. Pearl Cotton. Hand & Machine quilting also special order quilts.

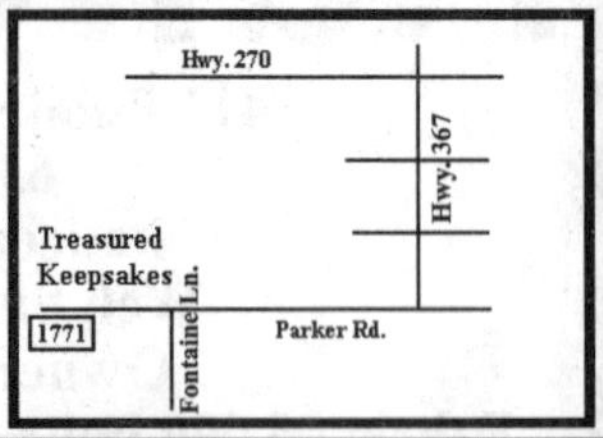

St. Louis, MO #31

Free Brochure

QUILTERS' EXPRESS TOURS

491 Maymont Dr. 63011
(636) 230-9179
E-Mail: Lbanner@igateway.net
Web Site: www.quilterstours.com
Owner: Sharon Banner

Group Tours to quilt shops in St. Louis, Mo.
Bus tours.
Rent-A- Tour Guide.
Self-guided map tours.

St. Louis, MO #32

Sew Busy, Ltd.

13228 Tesson Ferry Rd.
St. Louis, Mo. 63128
1-314-842-8885
1-800-643-8885
Email Sewbusyltd@aol.com
Web Site www.sewbusyltd.com
Owner - Linda Kwentus

1700 plus bolts - all 100% top quality cottons
Books, patterns, notions and classes.

Our specialty is PhotoTransfer

OUR #1 PRIORITY IS CUSTOMER SERVICE!

Monday thru Friday 10 - 5
Saturday 10 - 4

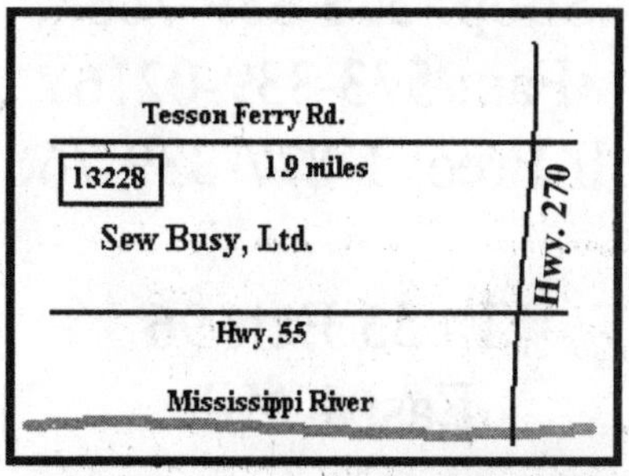

Jackman's Fabrics

SINCE 1903

www.jackmansfabrics.com

Over 50,000 yards of quilting cottons!

Thimbleberries, Aunt Grace, Debbie Mumm, KP Kids, Hoffman, Timeless Treasures, RJR, Moda, Benartex, P&B, South Seas and more . . . including novelties, batiks, homespuns, flannels, broadcloths, wide sheetings, books, patterns & notions.

618-632-2700 • 1000 Lincoln Hwy., 62208
Mon. & Thurs. 10:00 - 9:00 • Tues., Wed., Fri. 10:00 - 6:00
Sat. 10:00 - 5:30 Sun. noon - 5:00

Show us this ad and you will receive a 1 time 20% discount on your entire non-sale purchase.

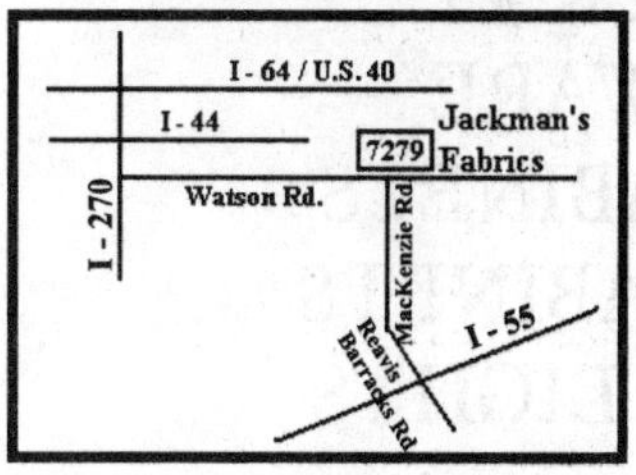

7279 Watson Rd., Mackenzie Pt. Plaza
St. Louis, MO 63119
314-352-7979
Mon. & Thur. 10:00-9:00
Tues., Wed., Fri. 10:00-6:00
Sat. 10:00-5:30 • Sun. noon-5:00

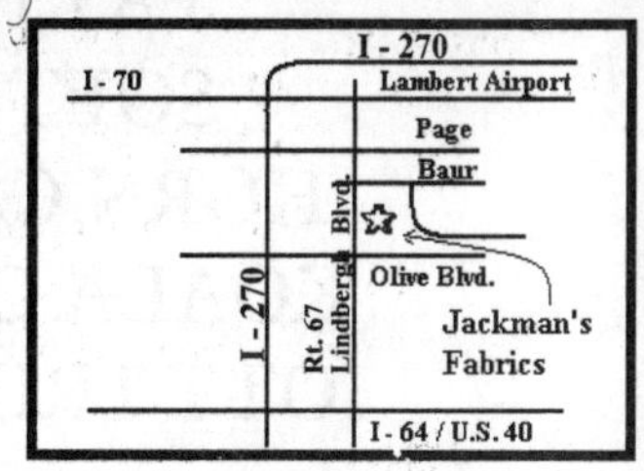

1234 North Lindbergh
St. Louis, MO 63132
314-994-1060
Mon. & Thur. 9:30-9:00
Tues., Wed., Fri. 9:30-6:00
Sat. 9:30-5:30 • Sun. noon-5:00

St. Louis, MO #33 & 34

Quilting by the Mississippi River

The SEWING BASKET

2504 William St.
Cape Girardeau, MO 63703-5763

Shop: 573-339-7667
Fax: 573-339-0216
Toll Free: 1-877-339-7667

I - 55 Exit 96
East 1 Mile

HOURS:
Mon. - Fri. 9:30 a.m. - 5:30 p.m.
Sat. 9:30 a.m. - 4:00 p.m.

PFAFF · BERNINA
HUSQVARNA · VIKING

Fabrics
Notions
Books
PATTERNS
SOFTWARE
HORN CABINETS
KOALA CABINETS
OTT-TRU LIGHTS

Guild Field Trips Welcome

Cape Girardeau, MO #35

Poplar Bluff, MO #36

8:30 - 5:30
Except Fri.
close @ 5

Quilters Craft Shop

1302 South 11th 63901
(573) 785-6514
Owner: Mary L. Hoeinghaus
Est: 1984 800 sq.ft. 500 Bolts

100% cottons, books & Patterns specialize in Quilts, quilt racks and many other crafts. Machine Quilting.

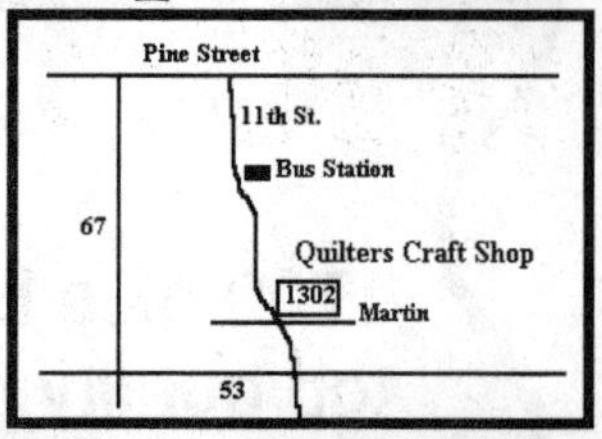

Birch Tree, MO #37

Tues - Sat 9 - 5

The Hideaway Quilt Shop

3217 W. 1st St.
P.O. Box 57 65438
(573) 292-1008

Name brand fabrics.
Ready made quilts, too.
Love to share quilting stories.
Come spend an hour or two.

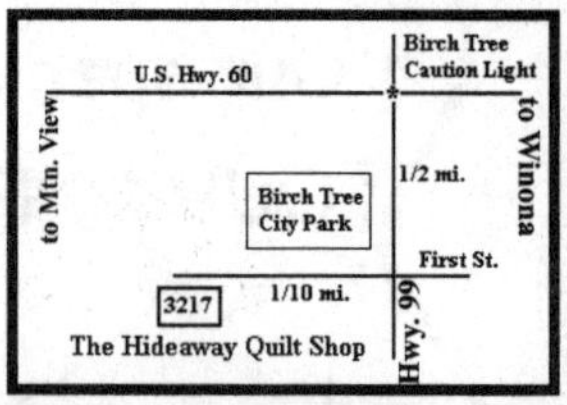

Calico Cupboard

116 Oak St., P.O. Box 1296 65548
(417) 934-6330
dgodsy@socket.net
Darlene Godsy

Mon - Fri 10 - 5 Sat 10 - 3

5000 bolts of fabrics, lots of patterns, books and notions. We have a toy sewing machine museum with over 300 toys. Also featherweights for sale including parts for the featherweights.
Plus friendly Ozark service.

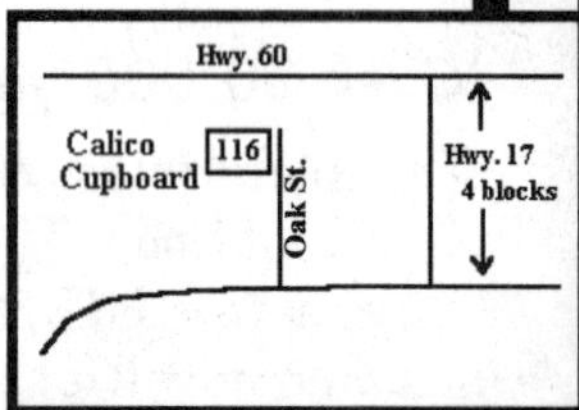

Mountain View, MO #38

Springfield, MO #39

Tues - Fri
9:30 - 5:30
Sat 10 - 4

The Quilt Shoppe

2762 South Campbell 65807
(417) 883-1355
Owners: Rosalie Carey & Gilda Young
Est: 1978 2100 sq.ft.

100% cotton fabrics(1500 prints, 300 solids), 200 stencils, books, patterns, notions, Q-Snap frames, Hinterberg frames.
"Down the street from Bass Pro"

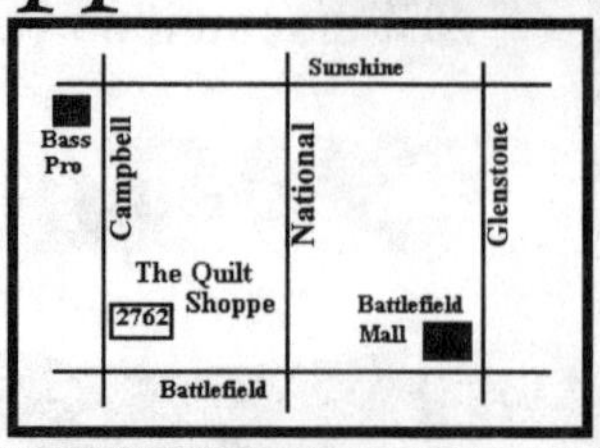

Springfield, MO #40

Merrily We Quilt Along

- Unbelievable number of books!
- Large selection of 100% cotton and 100% wool fabrics.
- Classes for all levels of quilters.
- Bring in your book for a 10% discount.

2942 E. Sunshine St.
Springfield, MO 65804
(417) 890-9000
Fax: (417) 890-9131
Email:
merrily@merrilywequiltalong.com
Owner: Merrily Parker
Est: 2001 2800 sq.ft. 2000+ Bolts

Mon - Fri 10 - 5 Tues 10 - 7 Sat 10 - 4

Web Site: www.merrilywequiltalong.com

We are the "Sunshine Store"

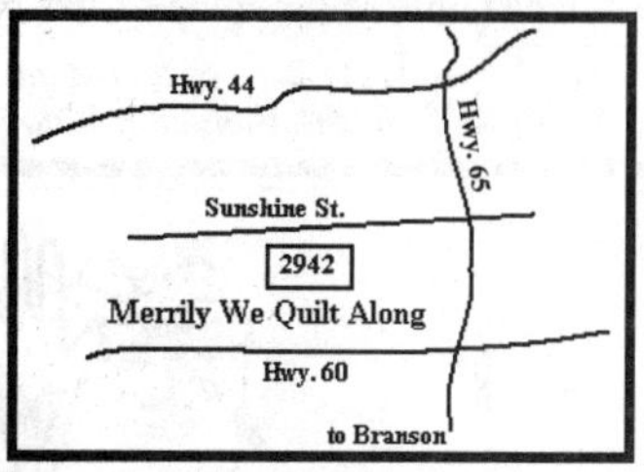

THE QUILT SAMPLER, INC.

www.quiltsampler.com

1802A South Glenstone • "On The Plaza" • Springfield, MO 65804

Mon -Fri: 10 - 5 • Thurs: 10 - 8 (winter hours 10 - 7) •Sat: 10 - 4 • Sun: 12:30 - 4

(417) 886-5750 • Toll Free 1-877-453-3773 • E-mail: Qltsampler@aol.com

Est. 1994 • 5500 sq. feet • Cristen Powell, owner

- *5000+ bolts of quality cotton fabrics including a large selection of flannels*
- *Books, Patterns, Notions, and more!*
- *Block of the Months • Kits -- Bed Quilts, Wallhangings and Wearables*
- PFAFF® *Dealership and Featherweight Sewing Machines*
- *Friendly, knowledgable staff*

"WHERE FRIENDS AND FABRIC MEET!"

Springfield, MO #41

Springfield, MO #42

Mon - Sat 9 - 5

COUNTRY SAMPLER QUILT SHOP

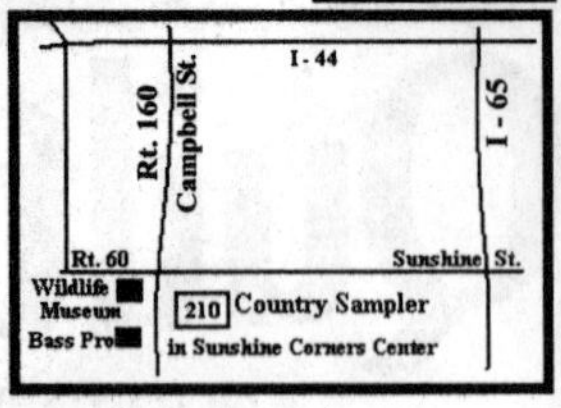

"We specialize in making memories!"

Fabrics, notions, quilts, collectibles, gifts & more

A featured shop in the Quilt Sampler 2000!

210 W. Sunshine, Springfield, MO 65807
Across from Bass Pro & the World of Wildlife Museum!
Formerly Located in Republic, MO

417-732-4848 or toll free 1-888-867-8424
E-mail: ctrysmplr@aol.com Website: countrysamplerquilts.com

Enjoy our general store atmosphere & friendly conversation while having a bottle of the coldest Coke in town—and they're still a dime!

Be sure and visit our new sister store in the Victorian Village in Branson, MO

Rogersville, MO #43

Mon - Fri 10 - 5
Sat 10 - 4

Quilt'in Time Quilt Shoppe

123 Johnstown Dr. 65742
(417) 753-7373
E-Mail: quiltintime@msn.com

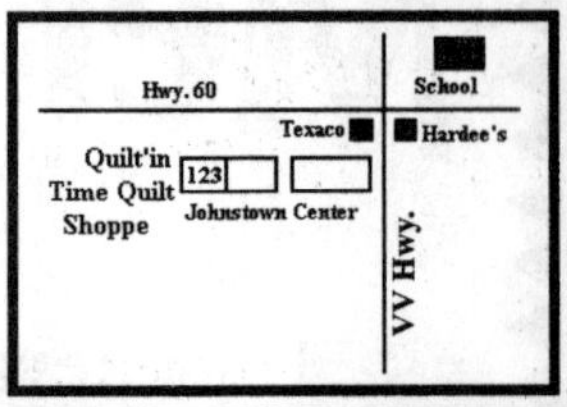

Fabric, notions, patterns, classes, custom quilting with Gammil quilt machine in store. Creating timeless treasures that last for generations. At the stop light at 60 and VV turn south, first shopping center to the west is Johnstown Center.

Mt. Vernon, MO #44

Mon - Sat 9 - 5:30
Sun 1 - 5

Turner's Calico Country
& Ben Franklin

207 E. Dallas 65712
(417) 466-3401
E-Mail: info@calico-country.com

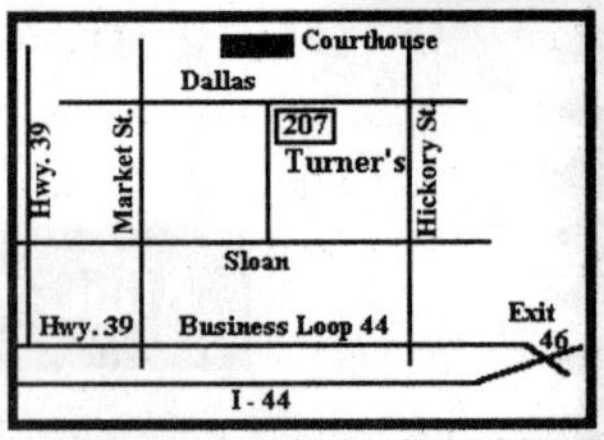

Quilt Show Everyday, 1000's of Calicos, Quilting Supplies, 100's of Sewing & Craft Patterns, Old Time Candy Case, Fresh Homemade Fudge, Ozark-Made Oak Baskets, Fenton and Collectibles.

Of all the 'shows' in Branson our shop is the best one!!

Quilts & Quilts

1137 West Hwy. 76 65616
in Branson Heights Shopping Ctr.
(417) 334-3243
Owner: Marlys Michaelson Est: 1981 8,000 sq.ft.

Branson, MO #45

Summer
8 - 7 Mon - Sat
9 - 6 Sun
Winter
9 - 5 Mon - Sat
10 - 4 Sun

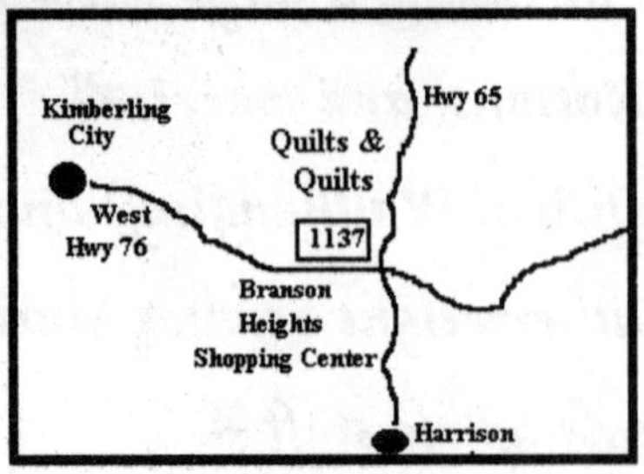

PATTERNS FOR CRAFTS AND QUILTS. Extensive collection of patterns for quilts, applique, and clothing (including the entire Eleanor Burns line) and much more. GREAT line of FAST and EASY "iron-on" projects.

COLOR AND FABRIC MAKE THE QUILT and we love to offer our years of experience in selecting the "perfect" combination so you end up with the "perfect" quilt.

OVER 500 BOOK TITLES - if we don't have it - we can order it and ship it to you.

FABRICS TO DIE FOR - Huge collection of Aunt Gracies, Modas, Hoffmans, Flannels, & State Flower Fabrics.

GREAT SELECTION OF GIFT ITEMS

Lots & Lots of Models--It's a Quilt Show Everyday

Branson, MO #46

Mon - Sat 9 - 6

COUNTRY SAMPLER QUILT SHOP

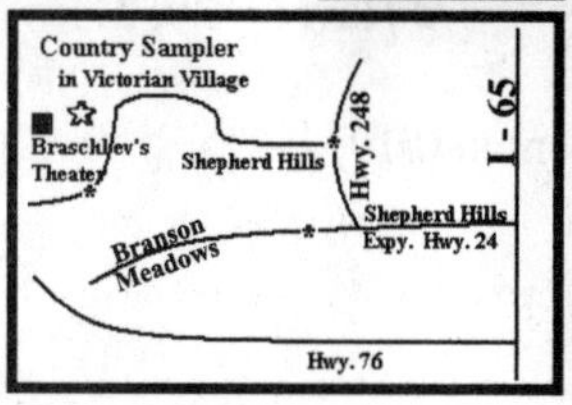

"We specialize in making memories!"

Fabrics, Notions, Quilts, Gifts, Collectibles,
House Wares, Vera Bradley, & more.

3044 Shepherd of the Hills Exp. -- Victorian Village
Just two block east of Shoji Tabuchi Theatre

417-336-5090 or toll free 1-888-867-8424
E-mail: ctrysmplr@aol.com Website: countrysamplerquilts.com

An eclectic collection of modern to primitive and
fun to fabulous in a wonderfully unique setting!

Be sure and visit our sister store across from Bass Pro in Springfield

Joplin, MO #47

Mon - Fri 9 - 6
Sat 9 - 4

Sew Neat

1603 E. 20th 64804
(417) 782-4242
Owner: Brenda Orban

Quilt fabric & supplies, sewing supplies.
Quilt Classes, beginner & advanced.
Heirloom & craft classes.
Many items not available anywhere else.
Come visit our qualified staff.

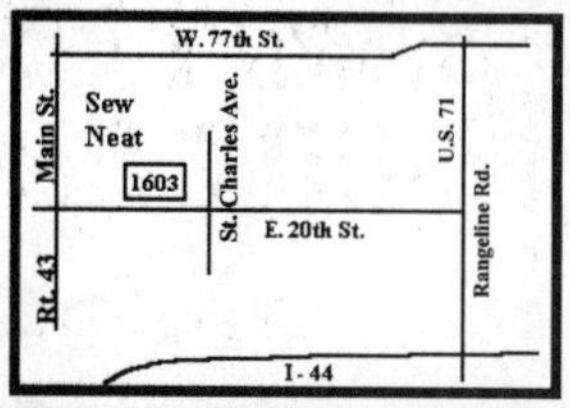

Other Shops in Missouri: We suggest calling first

Appleton City	AC Sewing Supply, 116 E. 4th St.	
Arbela	Laura's Quilts, Rt. 2, R.R. #1, Box 204	816-945-3970
Ballwin	In Stitches, 14664 Manchester Rd.	314-394-4471
Beaufort	Quilt N Time Quilt Station, 4149 Hwy. 50, R.R. #1	573-484-3120
Bismarck	Dogwood Mountain Quilt Shop, 1567 Loughboro Rd.	573-734-2336
Branson	Ozark Mountain Quilts, 101 N. Bus. Hwy. 65	417-332-1484
Branson	Quilt Cottage, 122 Skyview Dr.	417-339-3445
Branson	Amish Country Store, 3100 N. Gretna Rd.	417-334-6523
Branson	Carolina Mills Factory Outlet, 3617 W. Hwy. 76, P.O. Box V	417-334-2291
Branson	I Love Quilts, 100 Pat Nash Dr. Bldg. #15	417-332-0122
Branson	Ivy Rose Quilts & Gifts, 118 W. Main St.	417-337-7585
Branson	Log Cabin Quilts, 3612 Shepard of the Hills	417-335-4236
Branson	Ozark Mountain Quilt Co., 3562 Shepherd Hill Expy.	417-336-6294
Branson	Quilts & Such, 300 Tanger Blvd. #311	417-337-8881
Branson	The Cotton Patch Quilt Shop, 2420 W. Hwy. 76	417-334-2040
Branson	Rosebrier Quilts and Gifts, 117 E. Main St.	417-336-3436
Branson	Orphanage Dolls & Pretties, 102 W. Main St.	417-334-2990
Brookfield	Grandma's Hope Chest, 207 1/2 N. Main St.	660-258-7665
Cape Girardeau	Quilting Shop, 134 Dena Ln.	573-335-0761
Carthage	Treetop Quilts, 429 Poplar St.	417-358-2604
Centerview	Country Cottage Fabrics, 537 SW BB Hwy.	660-747-5368
Columbia	Friends Together Antiques, 4038 E. Broadway	573-442-6759
Craig	Fabrics Unique, Rt. 1	816-683-5757
Deepwater	Mary Jane's Fabrics, 947 SE 901st Rd.	
Doniphan	Nor-Star Quilts, Rt 8 Box 7372	573-996-5249
Ellington	Pin Cushion, 104 Hwy. 106	573-663-2921
Eminence	Barb's Quilts, 203 Main St. #A	573-226-3418
Farmington	Becky's Quilts & Supplies, 1007 Sainte Genevieve Ave.	573-756-3353
Fredericktown	Carolina Fabric Center, 323 N Chamber	573-783-2222
Hannibal	Yore Quilts, 403 Broadway 573-221-2480	
Hopkins	Young's Craft & Sewing, 415 E. Barnard St.	660-778-3272
Independence	Kenley's Quilting, 420 S. Main #200	816-461-1767
Jamesport	Rolling Hills Store, 24777 Hwy. 190	no phone
Jamesport	Leona's Amish Shop, Rt. 2	816-684-6628
Jamesport	Ropp's Country Variety, Rt. 2, Box 173	no phone
Jamesport	The Garden Cottage Shop, 21870 Hwy. 190	no phone
Jamesport	Sherwood Quilt & Crafts, 1091 Hwy. U	no phone
Jefferson City	Meadow Ridge Train Depot, 5824 Meadow Ridge Dr.	573-395-4910
Jefferson City	Ben Franklin Store, 1803 Missouri Blvd.	573-635-1233
Kirksville	Kaye's Fabrics, RR 3 Box 102	816-665-0123
Kirkwood	Dixie's Vintage Quilts, 825 N. Kirkwood Rd.	314-965-8589
Laquey	Country Bumpkin Enterprises, Hwy. AA, Bldg. 28151	573-765-4479
Lebanon	H & H Fabric and Quilt Center, 326 W. Commercial St.	417-532-2378
Linn	Quilts & More, 205 E. Main St.	573-897-0355
Marshall	Betty Sue O'Dell, 466 S. Odell	816-886-3663
Nevada	Mary's, 111 W. Walnut	417-667-3151
Oak Grove	Phanora's Variety, 1560 S. Broadway St.	816-625-8531
Osage Beach	Quilts & Things, 1040 Main St. Village	573-348-4146
Osage Beach	Crossroads II, Stone Crest Mall	573-348-2002
Osceola	Quilts and Crafts, 312 Second St.	417-646-7746
Ozark	Country Quilter, P.O. Box 685	417-581-0910
Ozark	Quilting & Sewing Paradise, 901 W. Jackson	417-581-0443
Palmyra	Rosebrook Creations, 116 W. Jefferson St.	573-769-3504
Potosi	Quilter's Corner, 201 E. High St.	573-438-6718
Potosi	Busy Bee Quilt Shop & Florist, 103 Fissell St.	573-438-8660
Rocheport	Micki's Fabric & Yarn Shop, 10300 W. Sontag	573-446-8085
Rolla	Uniquely Yours, 404 E. St. Rt. 72	573-364-2070
Schell City	Wild Flower, 107 W. 1st St.	417-432-3202
Springfield	I Love Quilts, 1844 E. Arlington Dr.	
Springfield	Crafters Delight, 2717 W. Kearney St.	417-866-4184
Springfield	Patchwork Corner, 702 E. Commercial St.	417-866-6160
Springfield	Seams Like Yesterday, 4542 S. Delaware Ave.	417-883-4424
St. James	Wanda's Machine Quilting, 17772 St. Rd. U	573-265-7071
St. Louis	Eunice Farmer Fabrics, 9814 Clayton Rd.	314-997-1531
St. Louis	Thimble & Thread, 2629 Yeager Rd.	
St. Peters	The Quilter's Block, 124 Lake Ridge Dr.	314-281-8903
Ste. Genevieve	Monia's Unlimited, 316 Market	573-883-7874
Steelville	Yadkin Creek Mercantile & Quilt, 115 W. Main St.	573-775-5514
Tunica	Brick-Bracks & Quilts Etc., 2981 Grand Casino Pkwy. S #C	662-363-1444
Varsailles	Pleasant Valley Quilts, 14912 Hopewell Rd.	573-378-6151
Versailles	Excelsior Fabrics, 19346 Excelsior Rd.	
Vienna	GS Fabric and Gifts, Hwy. 42 W.	314-422-3500
Warrensburg	Traci's Crafts & Gifts, 319 N. Holden St.	816-429-6844
Warsaw	Wooden Wagon 242 W. Main,	660-438-6400
Weston	Missouri River Quilt Co., 519 Main St. #A	816-640-5308

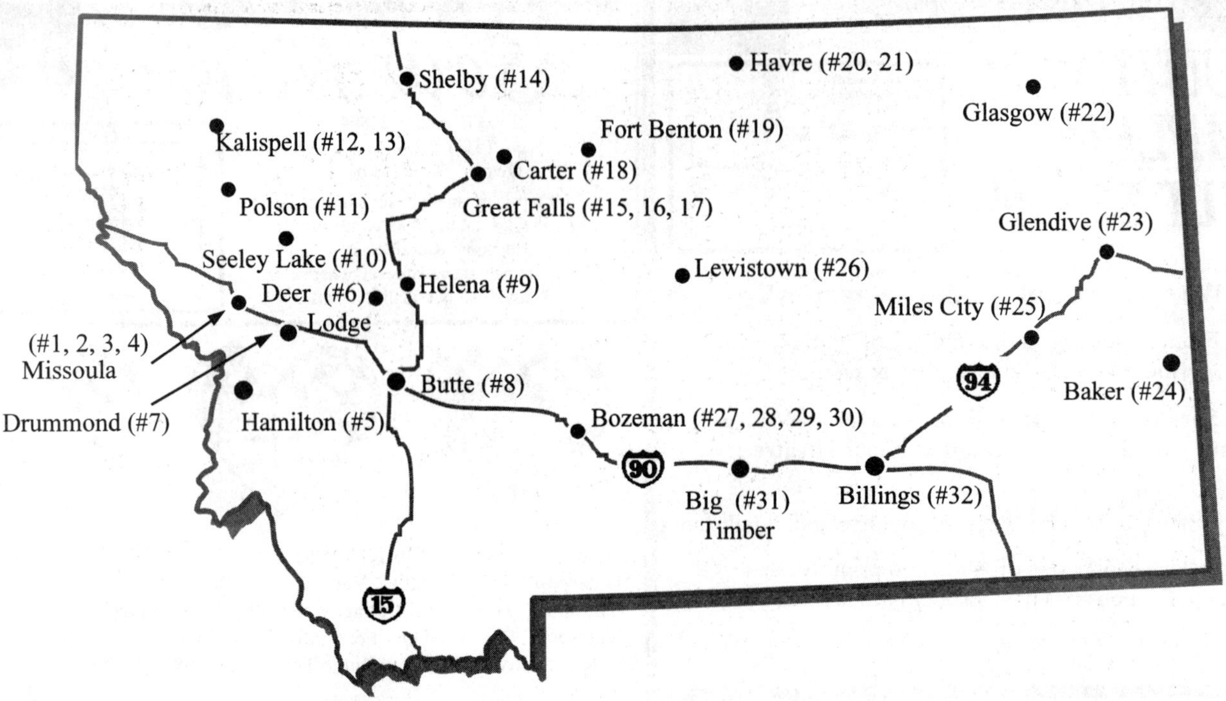

32 Featured Shops

MONTANA

Bernina Center

Mon - Fri 10 - 5:30
Sat 10 - 4

1900 W. Broadway 59808
(406) 728-2119
Fax: (406) 728-3394
E-Mail: sharonmm@marsweb.com
Web Site: ww.sewingmachinedealers.com/berninacenter
Est: 1986 4250 sq.ft. 1500+ Bolts

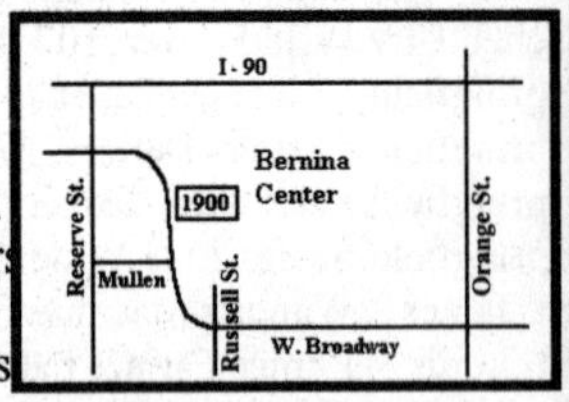

Quilting Fabrics specializing in Batiks, Orientals, Flowers, & Childrens. Complete line of Fossil Ferns, Fleece, Books, Patterns & Notions. Full line Bernina Dealer.

Missoula, MT #1

Missoula, MT #2

Tues - Fri 11 - 5
Sat 10 - 4

Berry Patch Quilts

3800 Russell St. #130 59803
at Russell Square
(406) 542-6644
Fax:
(406) 542-6650
Est: 2002
13550 sq.ft.
E-Mail: berrypatchquilts@msn.com
Owners: Sheila McIntosh & Louise Yamasaki

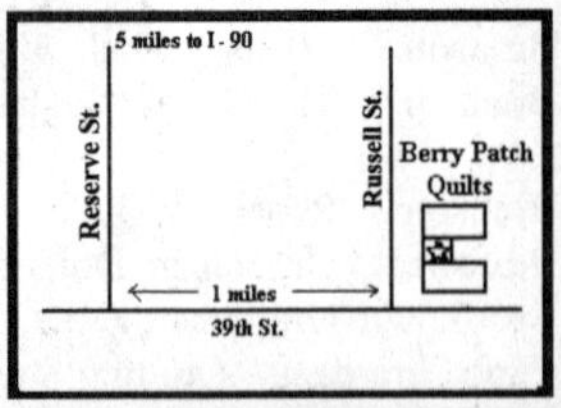

Our cozy shop offers friendly hometown service. Call ahead and we'll accommodate your travel plans. Looking forward to meeting you.

Missoula, MT #3

Mon - Sat 10 - 5

Country Friends Quilt & Gift Shop

1519 Cooper St. 59802
(406) 728-7816
E-Mail: info@countryfriendsquilts.com
Web Site: www.countryfriendsquilts.com
Est: 1988 1800 packed sq.ft.
Owners: JoAnn Farley & Earlene Cusker

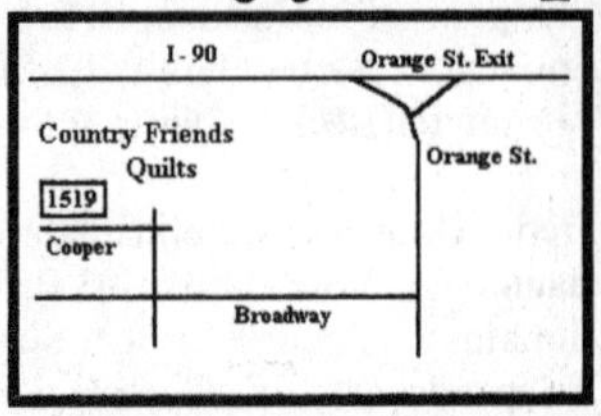

Specializing in Traditional, Primitive & Americana! Fabrics all 100% Cotton.

Missoula, MT #4

Timeless Treasures Quilt Shop

Located in the Towne Court at Reserve St.

2412 River Rd. 59804
(406) 542-6566 Fax: (406) 327-0742

www. ttqsmontana.com

E-mail: quilts@montana.com

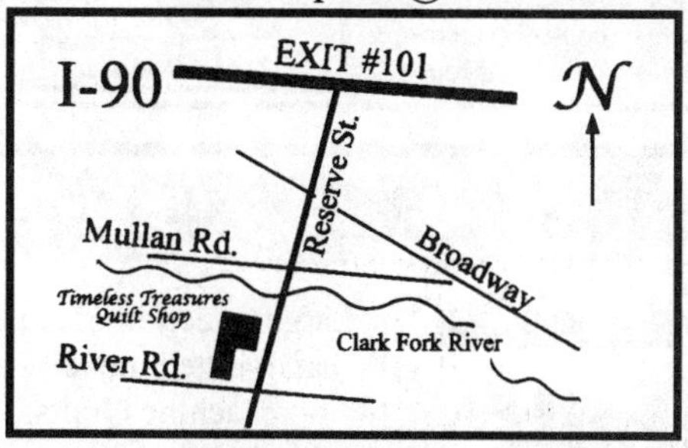

*** Featuring Fine Cotton Fabrics ***
*** Books, Patterns, Notions & Classes ***
*** Quilts for Sale ***

Custom Hand-Guided Machine Quilting
Bring your finished quilt tops along - we'll quilt them and then ship them back to you!

Mon - Fri 10 - 6
Sat 10 - 4

PROFESSIONAL MEMBERSHIPS:
International Machine Quilter's Association
American Quilter's Society
Missoula Quilter's Guild
Bitterroot Quilter's Guild

Hamilton, MT #5

THE FABRIC SHOP AND QUILTS

410 N. 1st
59840
(406) 363-3471
E-Mail: rcrb@cybernetl.com
Owner: Rosalie Reinbold
Est: 1972
3500 sq.ft.

"EVERYTHING FOR THE QUILTER"
Large selection of all the Best Cotton Fabrics, Flannels, Books, Patterns and Quilting Supplies. Year around Classes for all levels. Friendly, Helpful Staff. Thimbleberries BOM and Club. Kits, Quilts for Sale, Mail Order.

Mon - Sat 9:30 - 5:30

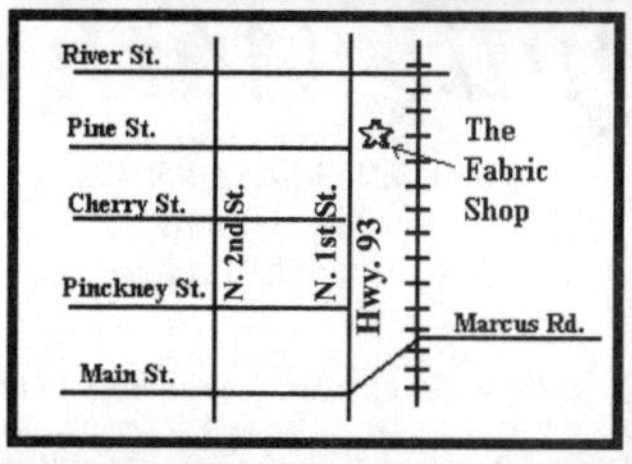

Deer Lodge, MT #6

Quilters Corner, Etc.

Mon - Fri 9 - 6
Sat 9 - 5

401 Main St. 59722
(406) 846-3096
Fax: (406) 846-2298
E-Mail: donnamaccpt@aol.com
Web Site: www.quiltsinmontana.com
Owner: Donna McCarthy 3500 Bolts

A bank built in 1912 is the home of 3000 Bolts of fabric, patterns, books and quilting ideas.

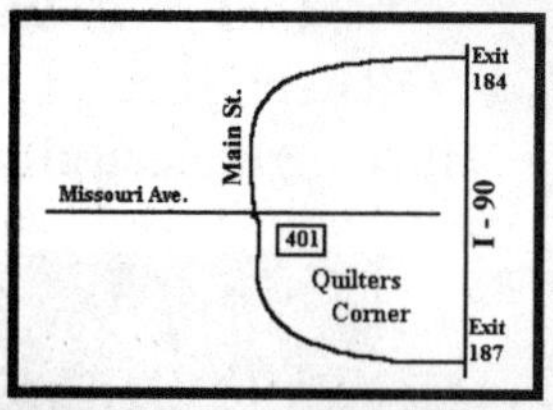

Drummond, MT #7

Mon - Sat 10 - 5

Cotton Patch Quilt Shoppe

38 Front St. 59832
(406) 288-3297
Owners: Monica Prince & Mary Ellen & Maretta McGowan
Est: 1999 1800 sq.ft.

1500 Bolts of 100% cotton fabric. Specializing in Western, Wildlife and Floral Fabric. Books, Notions, & Patterns. Friendly, personal service.

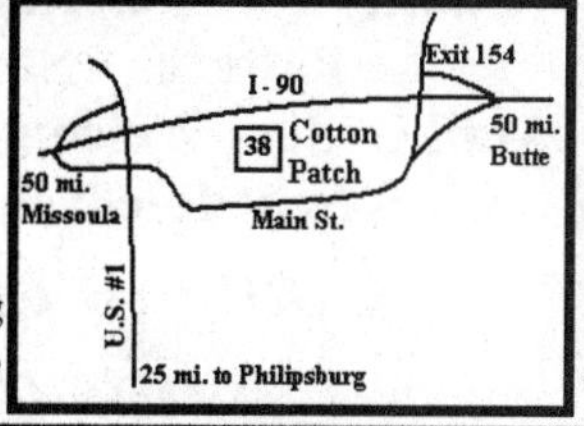

Butte, MT #8

Mon - Sat 10 - 5:30
Sat 10 - 4

the Silver Thimble Inc.

3104 Busch St. 59701
(406) 494-1633
E-Mail: Lstanhope@prodigy.net

Quilting cottons, specialty fabrics, tools, notions, patterns & more. Authorized Husqvarna Viking Dealer.

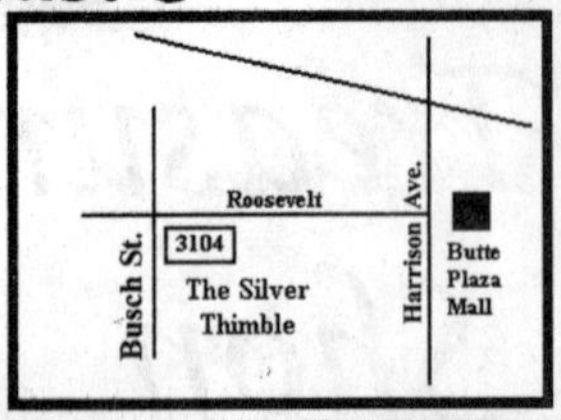

Helena, MT #9

Mon - Fri 10 - 5:30
Sat 10 - 5
Summer Sat til 4

Sue's Sewing Palace Bernina

1112 Helena Ave. 59601
(406) 443-5724 Fax: Same
E-Mail: syannone@initco.net
www.suessewingpalace.com
Owner: Sue Yannone

Largest in-town selection of quality 100% cottons, specializing in batiks and brights, threads, patterns, books & classes. Award winning Bernina dealer.

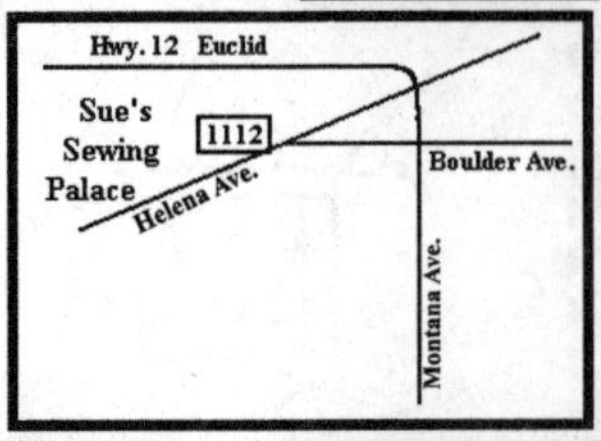

Seeley Lake, MT #10

Mon - Sat 10 - 5:30
Sun 12 - 4

Deer Country Quilts

Bison & Bear Trading Center, Hwy. 83
(P.O. Box 808) 59868
(406) 677-2730 Fax: (406) 677-2885
Web Site: www.deercountryquilts.com
Owner: Penny Copps
Est: 1996 2300 sq.ft. 3000 Bolts

Stitch a memory in the beautiful Seeley-Swan Valley. Fabric, Classes, Notions—Everything you need including inspiration.

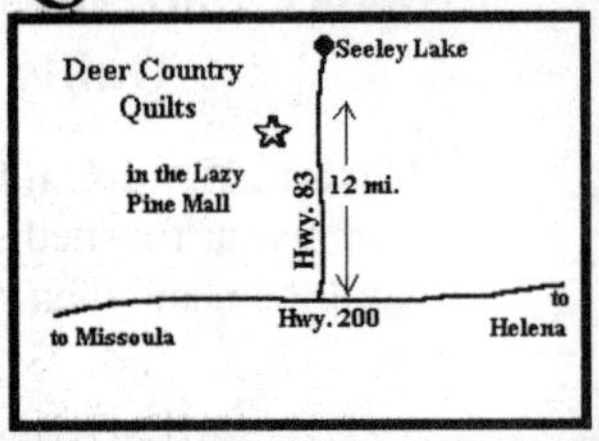

Polson, MT #11

Mon - Sat 9:30 - 5:30

All In Stitches

210 Main St. 59860
(406) 883-3643
E-Mail: aistitch@digisys.com
Est: 2000 2000 sq. ft. 2000 Bolts

All In Stitches carries a wide selection of batiks, orientals, brights, books, patterns & kits. We offer a variety of classes year round.

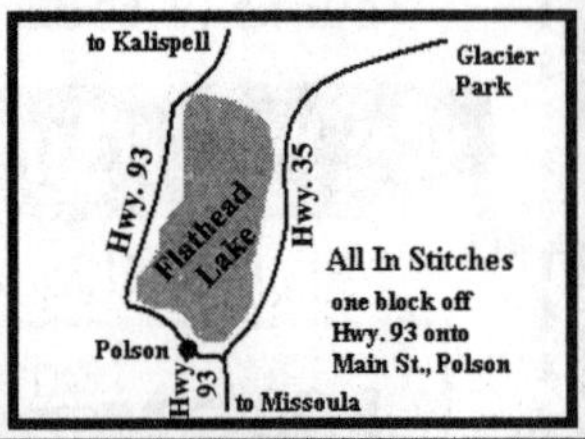

Kalispell, MT #12

Glacier Quilts

2960 Hwy. 2 East
P.O. Box 7274 59901
(406) 257-6966
Owner: Susan Gilman
info@glacierquilts.com

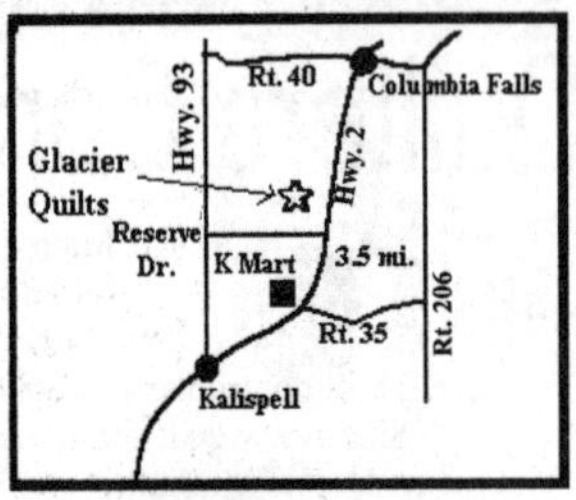

Mon - Fri 10 - 5:30
Sat 10 - 4

Authorized Elna Dealer

elna

www.glacierquilts.com

Quality 100% Cotton Fabrics - Flannels - Books - Patterns - Notions - Quilts - Classes
Mail Orders Welcome / Online Ordering Available
Class Schedule/Newsletter available on request.

Come in and check out the quilts on the ceiling!

Kalispell, MT #13

Quilt Gallery

Quilts • Fabrics • Supplies
Unique Patterns • Gifts •
Lessons

Large selection of antique, handquilted, novelty and machine Quilts.
Mail Orders Welcome
Owner: Joan P. Hodgeboom
Est: 1983 4700 sq.ft.

1710 Hwy. 93 S. 59901
(406) 257-5799
Next to Diamond Lil Inn

Mon - Fri 9:30 - 5:30
Sat 9:30 - 5

Selected by American Patchwork & Quilting magazine readers as one of the Top 10 quilt shops in the nation.

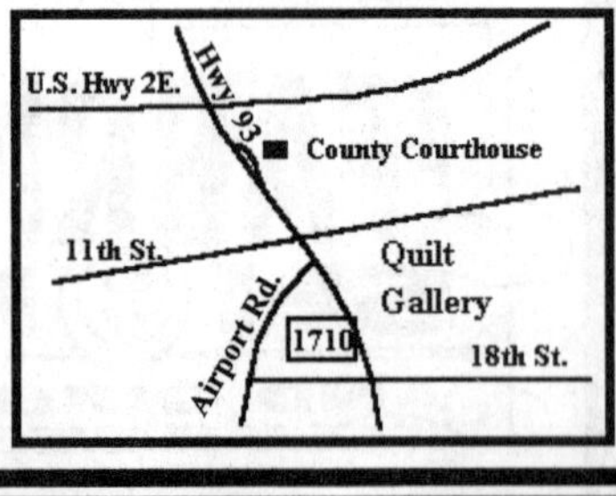

Shelby, MT #14

Mon - Fri 9:30 - 5
Sat 10 - 4

Quilt With Class

860 Oilfield Ave. 59474
(406) 434-5801
(800) 474-5801 (MT only)

Large variety of classes. Friendly, personalized service. Excellent selection of finest fabrics, notions, books. Phone orders welcome. Will mail anywhere.

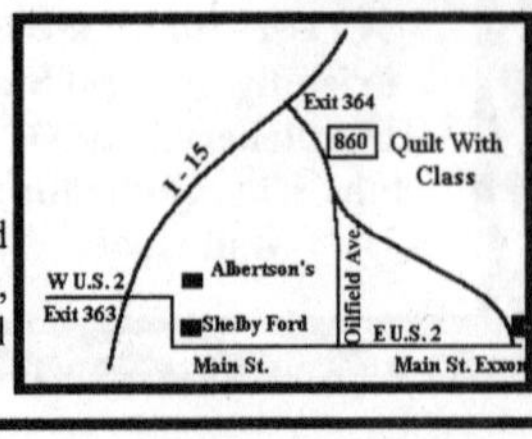

Great Falls, MT #15

Mon - Fri 10 - 6
Sat 10 - 5
Sun 11 - 4

The Quilt-A-Way

222 13th St. S 59401
(406) 453-2788
E-Mail: quiltawy@mt.net
Owner: Toni Echart

We are a Full-Service Quilt Shop. Over 2500 bolts of 100% designer Cottons. Friendly, expert staff.

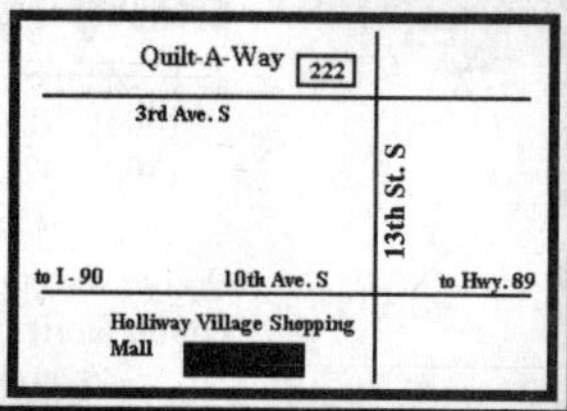

Great Falls, MT #16

Mon - Fri 10 - 5:30
Sat 9 - 4:30

Big Sky Quilts

202 2nd Ave. S #3 59405
(406) 727-1757 Fax: (406) 965-3671
E-Mail: jw@bigskyquilts.com
Web Site: www.bigskyquilts.com
Est: 1999
1200 sq.ft. 900 Bolts

Fantastic cotton fabrics, flannels, lots of kits, books and classes with individual attention and plenty of fun quarters. Hand-guided custom machine quilting at a reasonable price. Authorized sales & service for Elna sewing machines.

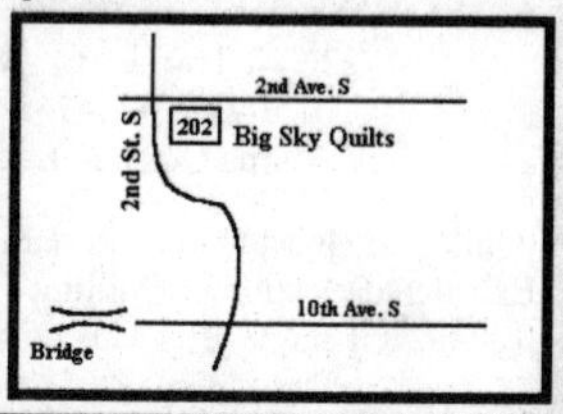

Great Falls, MT #17

Mon - Sat 10 - 6

Bernina Silver Thimble

1323 9th Ave. S 59405
in the Payne Financial Group Inc. Bldg.
(406) 452-7222
E-Mail: silverthimble@myexcel.com
Owner: Debra & Scott Royce Est: 2001

Bernina sewing machines, accessories. Many patterns & books, decorative threads and unique notions.

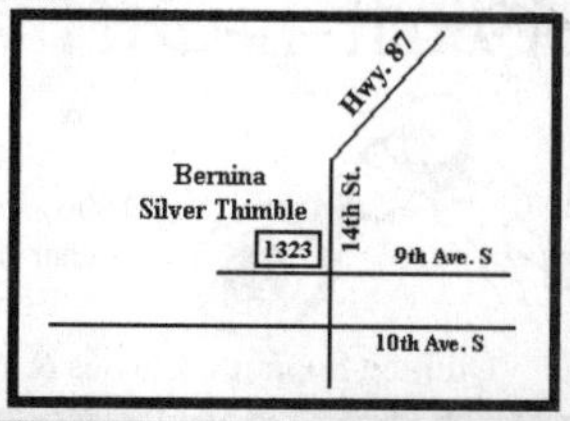

Carter, MT #18

The Quilting Hen

www.quiltinghen.com
1156 Buck Bridge Rd. Carter, MT 59420
(406) 734-5297

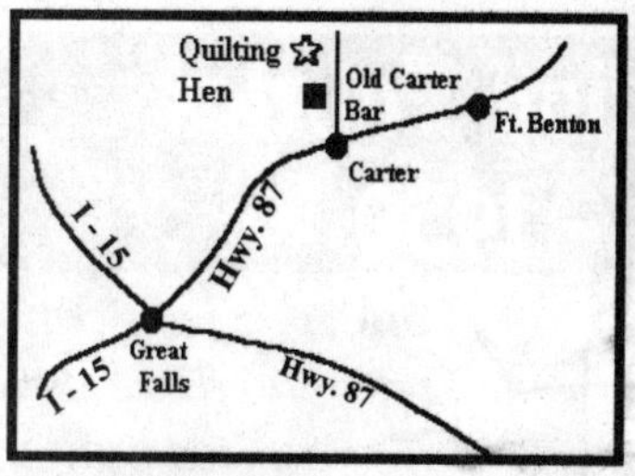

One Mile behind The Old Carter Bar

Tues - Sat 9 - 5

Area's Largest Quilting Fabric Store.
Feature Article (And the Cover!) In Sewing Professional Magazine.
Only 23 miles North of Great Falls, MT
Annual Outdoor Quilt Show held every June.

We also sell and service PFAFF in Great Falls and Bozeman. In Great Falls Call (406) 799-7556
In Bozeman Call (406) 556-8100

A Traditional Quilt Store on the Farm

Fort Benton, MT #19

Wed, Thur, Fri 12 - 7
Sat 10 - 5
Sun 11 - 4

"Bless My Buttons" Quilting and More...

1514 Front St. Box 1420 59442
(406) 622-5150
Owners: Paulette Albers, Maggie Onstad & Gini Onstad

Step into our 'little piece of heaven' and discover the endless possibilities with fabrics, threads, patterns, classes, gifts and more.

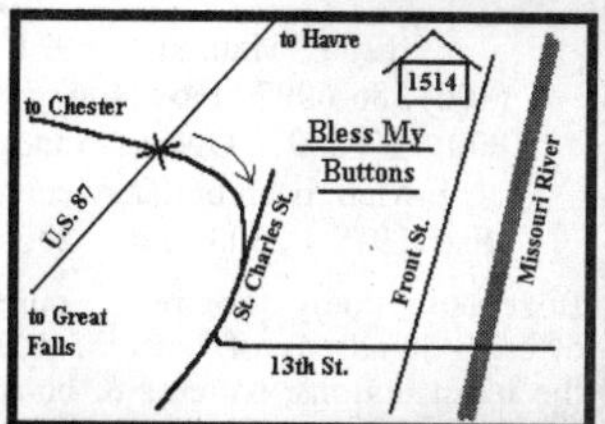

Havre, MT #20

Mon - Sat 9:30 - 5:30
Eves During Classes

The Silver Thimble

104 3rd Ave. 59501
(406) 265-4531 Est: 1981
E-Mail: silverthimbl@havre.nt.us
Owner: Brandy Carlson, Linda Howerton, & Carol Minick
3500 sq.ft.

Full line of fabrics for quilting & wearables, Bernina machines, latest books & patterns, unique notions. Classes available.

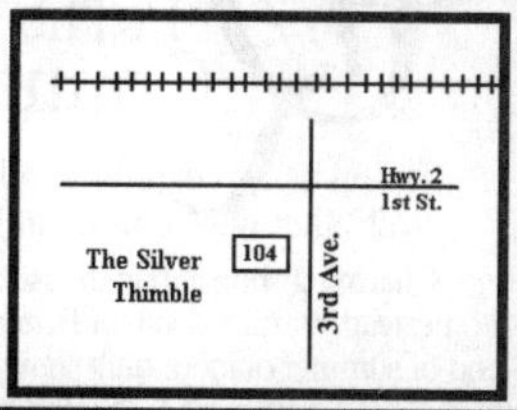

Havre, MT #21

Mon - Fri 10 - 5:30
Sat 10 - 5

The Crazy Quilters

126 Third Ave.
59501
(406) 265-7212

1400 bolts of fabric - batiks, Thimbleberries, Kaffe Fasselte wools and wool felts and much more. Books, patterns & notions too.

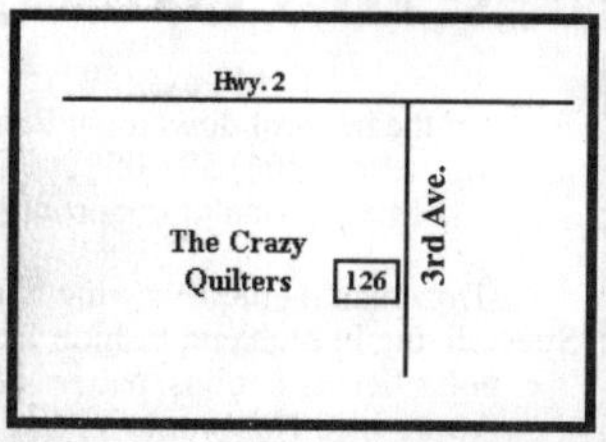

Glasgow, MT #22

Mon - Sat 9:30 - 5:30

The Plaid Square

513 1st Ave. S 59230
(406) 228-9665 Est: 1999
E-Mail: della@nemontel.net
Owner: Della Berg 1500 sq.ft. 1200+ Bolts

Full line quilting shop in Eastern Montana. From reproductions to flannels, homespun plaids to hand-dyed batiks. PFAFF dealer.

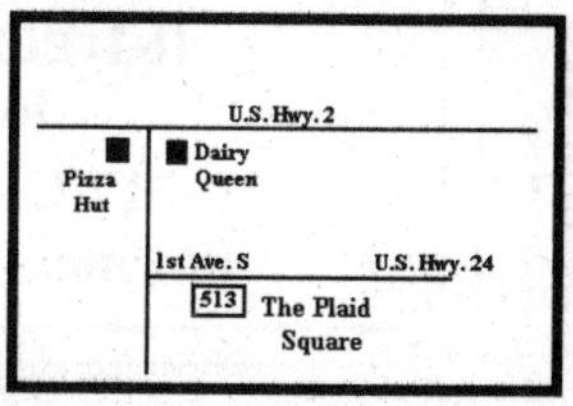

Glendive, MT #23

Mon - Sat 10 - 5

The Enchanted Room

222 W. Towne St. 59330
(406) 365-4745
Owners: Myrna Quale & Laura Gluecker

Quilt Shop located in Restored Historic Home. Excellent Selection of Quilting Fabric, books, & notions. Unique gifts, Custom Floral, Home Decorating accessories.

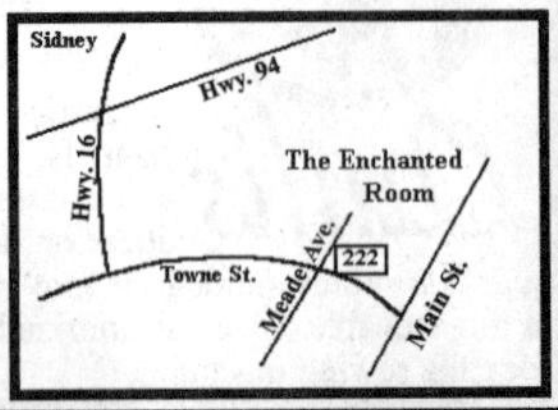

Baker, MT #24

Mon - Sat 9:30 - 5

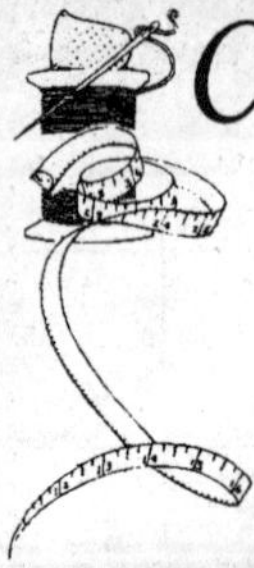

Creative Stitches

baby lock

23 S. Main St. 59313
(406) 778-2122
(800) 542-2122
Est: 1990

Large selection of 100% cotton fabrics, quilt books & notions.

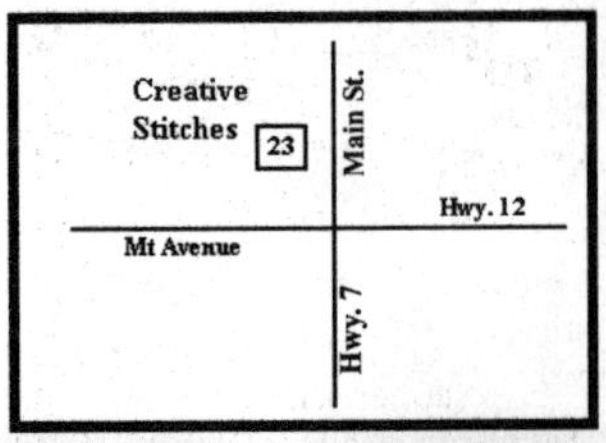

Miles City, MT #25

Mon - Sat 9 - 5:30

Copper Thimble Fabrics & Quilts

709 Main St. 59301
(406) 232-7226
Fax: (406) 232-7226
Est: 1980
7000 sq.ft.
E-Mail: cprthmbl@midrivers.com 1000+ Bolts
Owners: Gayle Muggli, Vicki Hamilton, and Linda Losinski

Quality fabrics — Hoffman, Henry, Benartex & more. Books, patterns, notions, gifts. Viking dealer. Commercial quilting. Eastern Montana's largest quilt store.

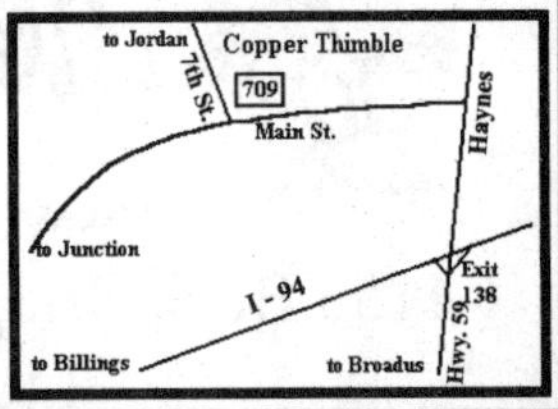

Lewistown, MT #26

Mon - Sat 9:30 - 5

Gingerbear Quilt-n-Gift Shop

305 W. Virginia St.
59457
(406) 538-2847
Owner: LaVerna Conard

Quilting Supplies, Classes & Patterns.

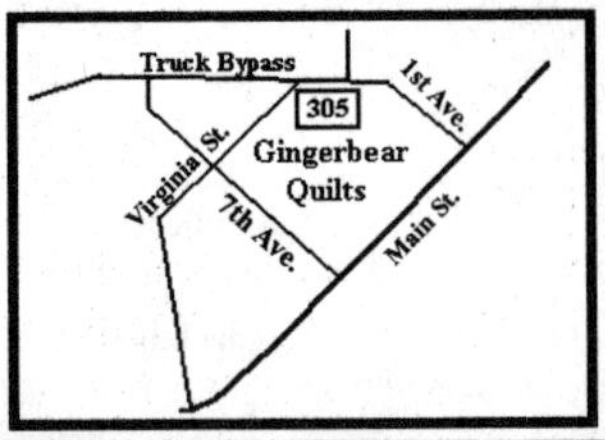

Reproduction Fabrics
❋ 1775 - 1950 ❋

Patchworks
ReproductionFabrics.com

Your source of cotton reproduction fabrics for quilters. Authentic fabric reproductions, 1775 - 1950, including natural indigo-dyed prints.

Bozeman, MT #27

9 - 3 pm Monday - Friday

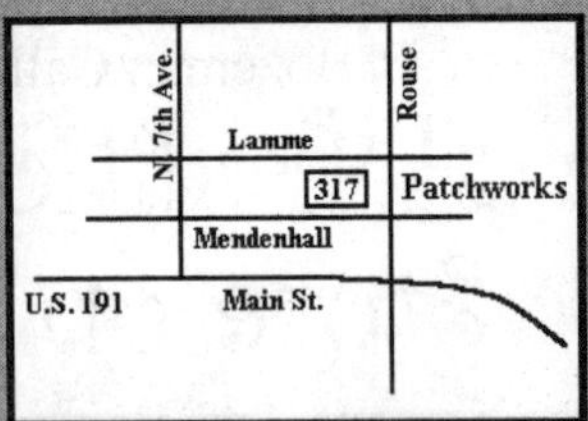

Visit Our Website:
www.reproductionfabrics.com
Email: staff@reproductionfabrics.com
Toll-free: 1-888-728-2495
406-586-1775
317 E. Mendenhall #D
Bozeman, Montana 59715

Bozeman, MT #28

Mon - Sat 9:30 - 5:30

Bear Comforts

126 E. Main St. 59715
(406) 586-6097 Fax: (406) 586-5239
(800) 757-6097 Owner: Sandy Taylor
E-Mail: bearcomf@avicom.net
Est: 1977 2500 sq.ft. 2000 Bolts

Bozeman's only complete quilting store offering hundreds of bolts of 100% cotton, the latest notions, patterns & books for your selection. Custom machine quilting services.

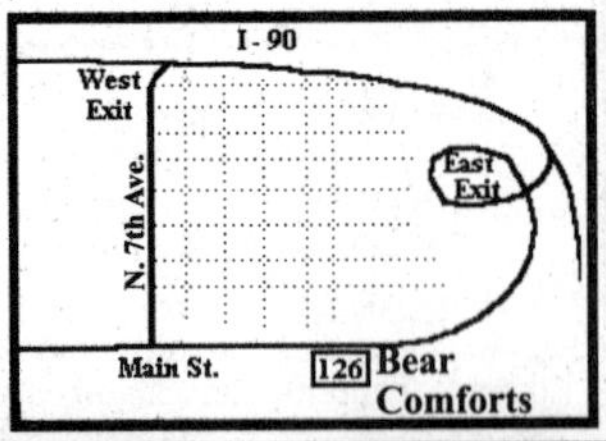

Bozeman, MT #29

Mon - Sat 11 - 4 Wed til 9 Thurs til 6

Quilting In The Country

5100 S. 19th Rd. 59718
(406) 587-8216
Owner: Jane Quinn
E-Mail: jquinn@quiltinginthecountry.com
Web Site: www.quiltinginthecountry.com

Charming shop in bunkhouse on 120 year old homestead. 3 miles south of Bozeman. Classes. Free end of summer outdoor quilt show. Featured in "Quilt Sampler" & "Simply Quilts".

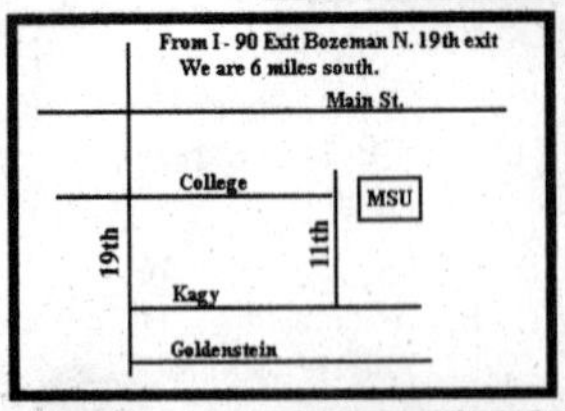

Bozeman, MT #30

Mon - Sat 10 - 5:30 Sat 10 - 4

the Silver Thimble Inc.

11 E. Main 59715
In the heart of downtown Bozeman
(406) 587-0531
E-Mail: Lstanhope@prodigy.net

Bozeman's unique sewing boutique! Specializing in high end fashion fabric, cottons, polar fleece, notions, patterns & more. Authorized Husqvarna Viking Dealer.

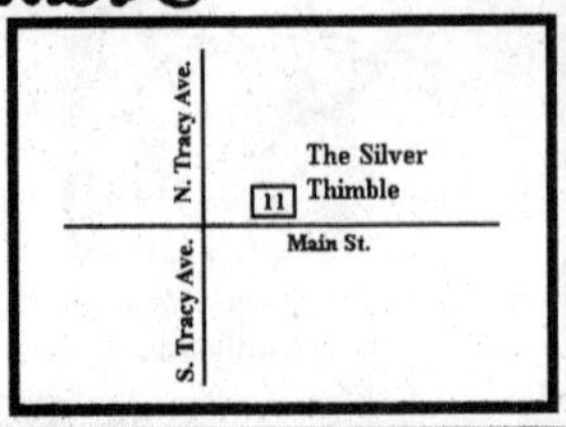

Big Timber, MT #31

Mon - Sat
10 - 6

LITTLE TIMBER QUILTS

108 McLeod P.O. Box 1630 59011
(406) 932-6078 Fax: (406) 932-5511

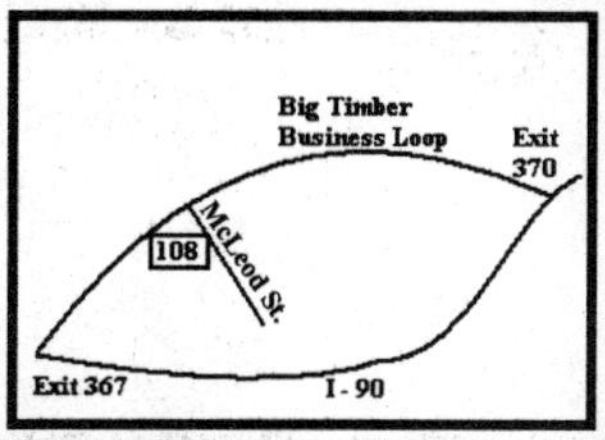

Owner: Susie Mosness
Est: 2001 3500 sq.ft.
Small town store with big ideas, great flannels, batiks and cottons.
Home of Janome Memory Craft machines.

Billings, MT #32

Mon - Sat
9:30 - 5:30

Bernina Sewing Center

1505 Rehberg Ln. 59102
(406) 656-4999
Owners: Frank & Doris Holzer
900 Bolts

Authorized Bernina Dealer.
Quilting books, patterns, supplies.
100% cotton calicos & solids.
Classes. Friendly & helpful

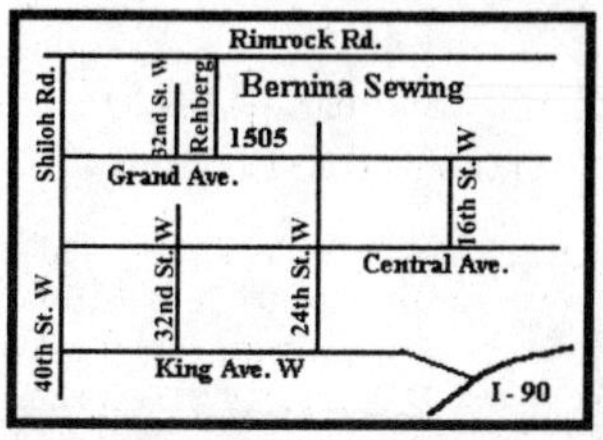

Other Shops in Montana: We suggest calling first

Arlee	Montana Stars, 898 Hi Frances Rd.	406-726-3116
Bigfork	Pine Needles, 8250 Mt. Hwy. 35, P.O. Box 2379	406-837-0423
Bigfork	Lynn's hip hop Shop, 1847 Hwy. 209	406-837-6634
Billings	Grand Quilts, 1827 Grand Ave. #1	406-256-8338
Billings	Pin Cushion, 2646 Grand Ave. #9	406-652-6328
Billings	Fiberworks, 1310 24th St. W.	406-656-6663
Billings	The Craft Depot, 740 Constitution	406-256-7701
Billings	Flynn Quilt Frame Co., 1000 Shiloh Overpass Rd.	406-656-8986
Bozeman	Museum of the Rockies, 600 W. Kagy Blvd.	406-994-2251
Broadus	Fabric to Fashion, 106 Crane Ave.	406-436-2963
Chinook	Country Quilts & Fabrics, 16 Clear Creek Heights	406-357-2891
Circle	Circle of Threads, 117 W. Main St.	406-485-3332
Dillon	Crafty Quilter, 104 N. Montana St.	406-683-5884
Drummond	Quilter's Rose, 282 Airport Rd.	
Great Falls	The Wild Hare Quilt Shopp, 900 2nd St. S #1	406-727-1757
Helena	Scraps of Heaven, 828 N. Rodney St.	406-443-5724
Helena	Quilting Memories, 1335 Valley Speedway Rd.	406-458-3755
Laurel	Ben Franklin Store, 13 Colorado Ave.	406-628-7124
Lewistown	Megahertz, 223 W. Main St.	406-538-8531
Libby	Quilters' Cottage, 910 Main St.	406-293-6306
Livingston	Fish Tales 102 N. F St.	406-222-0844
Philipsburg	Pickle Dish Quilt Shop, 130 E. Broadway	406-859-3750
Ronan	Ribbons, Star and Wing, 1319 U.S. Hwy 93 S	406-676-8265
Scobey	Bev's Sewing Center, 123 Main St.	406-487-2841
Shelby	The Creative Needle, 225 Main St.	406-434-7106
Stevensville	Seams Beautiful, 317 Main St.	406-777-0016
Twin Bridges	Mary R. Originals, 204 South Main	406-684-5878
West Yellowstone	Busy Bee Fabrics, PO Box 839	406-646-7752

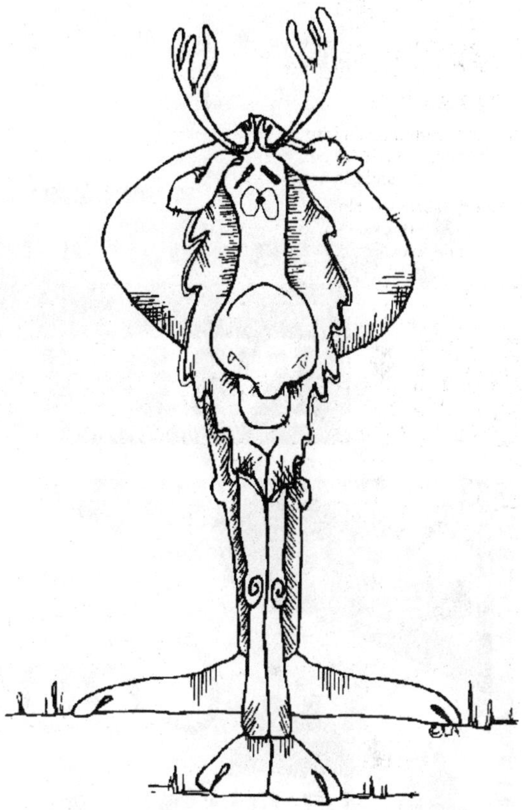

Notes

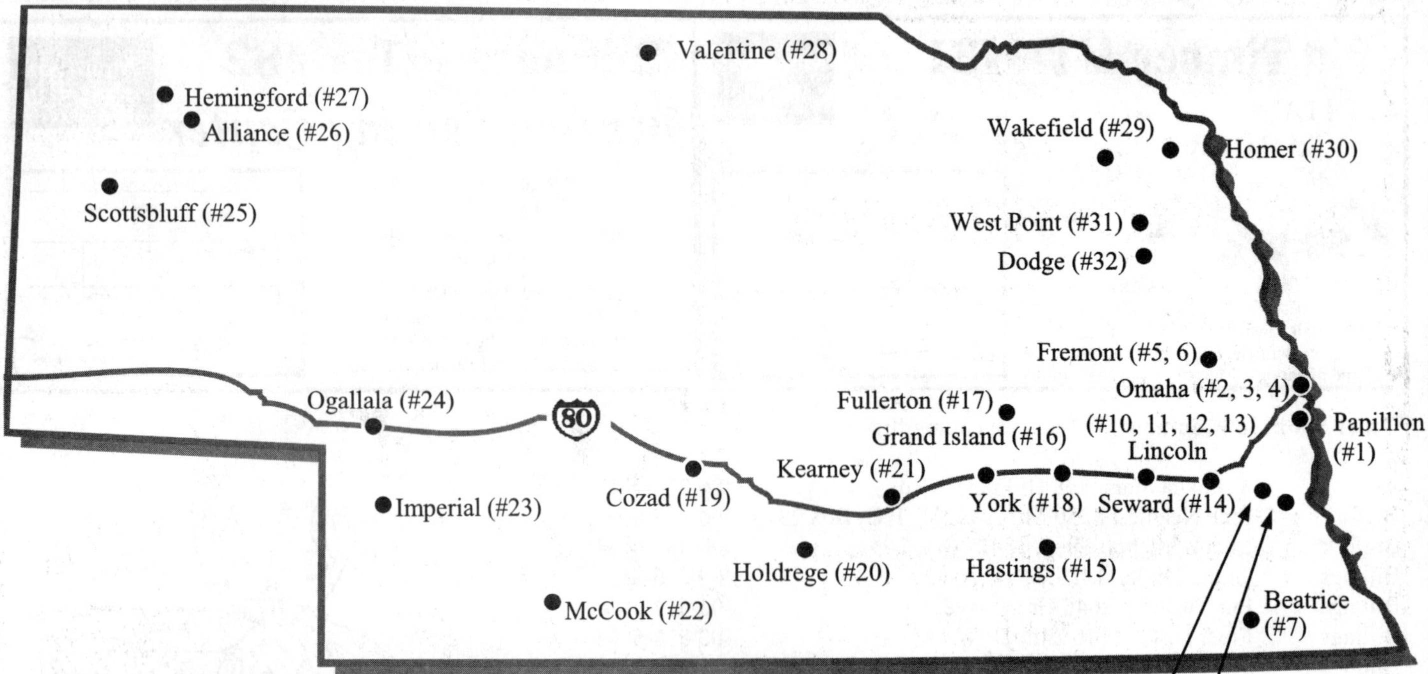

32 Featured Shops

NEBRASKA

Two Locations
in the Omaha Area

Country Sampler

Mon - Sat 10:00 - 5:30
Thurs til 8:00 Sun 12:00 - 5:00

Omaha, NE #2

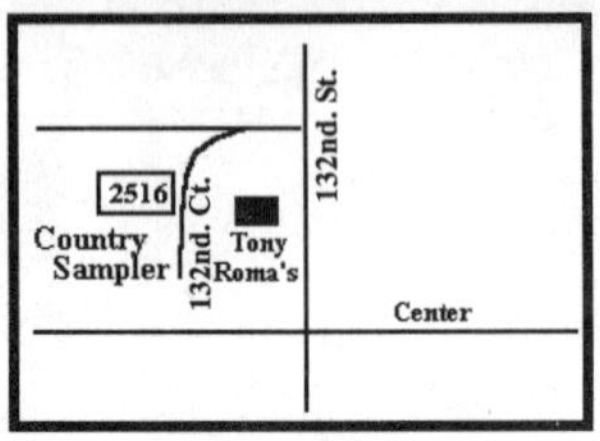

2516 S. 132nd Ct.
Omaha, NE 68144
(402) 333-6131
Est: 1990 3400 sq.ft.

Papillion, NE #1

841 Tara Plaza
Papillion, NE 68046
(402) 537-9515
Est: 1998 3100 sq.ft.

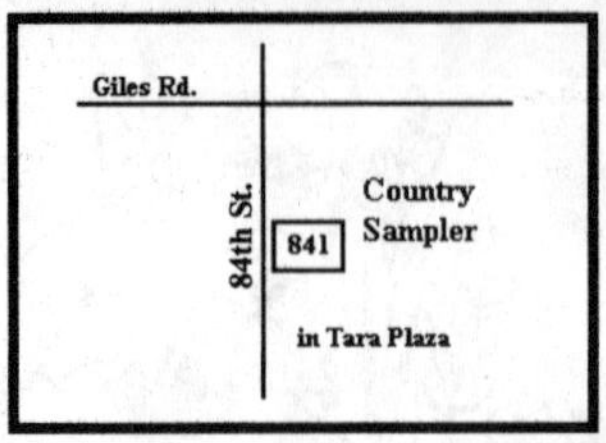

Owner: Deb Cizek

Come and see why **Country Sampler** was selected as a featured shop in the Better Homes & Gardens Quilt Sampler Magazine for 2002! Over 2,000 bolts of 100% cottons, flannels and homespuns! Tons of kits, patterns and books, block of the months, stitcheries, and rug hooking supplies.

Omaha, NE #3

David M. Mangelsen's®

3457 S. 84th St. 68124
Westgate Plaza
(402) 391-6225
Fax: (402) 391-4659
Est: 1961 37,000 sq.ft.

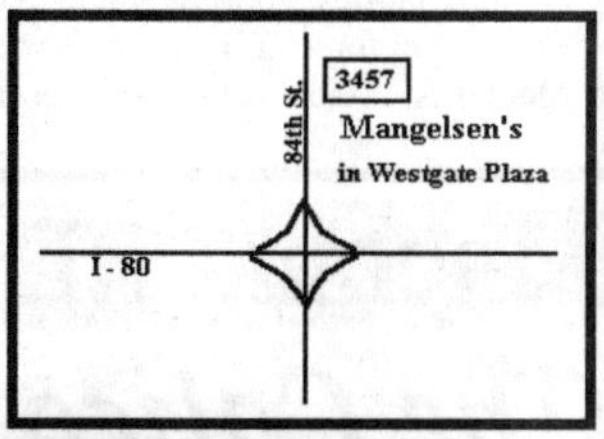

Mon - Fri 9 - 9 Sat 9 - 8 Sun 12 - 5

The store where you shop for FUN !
A Quilter's dream.
Fabric, Patterns, Books, Notions, Crafts, Floral, Party Goods and More !

Omaha, NE #4

Mon - Sat 9:30 - 5:30
Thur til 8
1st Sun 12 - 5

Log Cabin Quilt Shop

2809 South 125 Avenue #283 68144
In Westwood Plaza
E-Mail: sue@logcabinquilts.com
Web Site: www.logcabinquilts.com
(402) 333-5212
Est: 1980 1700 sq.ft.

Complete line of books, patterns, fabrics, and notions for quilters.
Service with a smile !

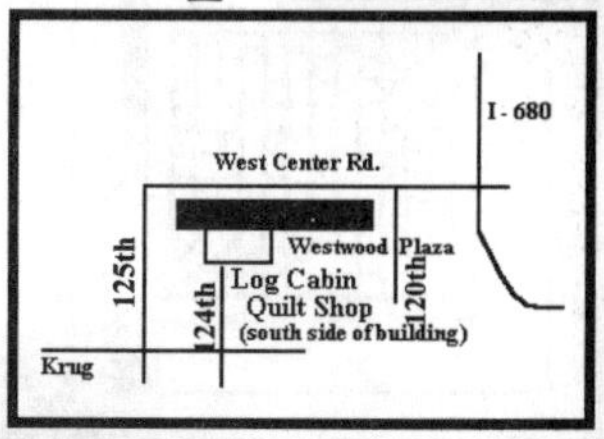

COUNTRY TRADITIONS

Est: 1997
4400 sq.ft.
2500+ Bolts

Come Visit Our Wide Selection of:
Country, Homespun and Reproduction Fabrics, Quilting Supplies & Classes. Folk Art Craft Patterns and Books, Homespun Crafts, Gifts & Collectibles all in a setting of a wonderful Historic Brick Bldg.

413 N. Main 68025
(402) 721-7752

Mon - Fri 10 - 5:30
Thur til 8
Sat 10 - 5

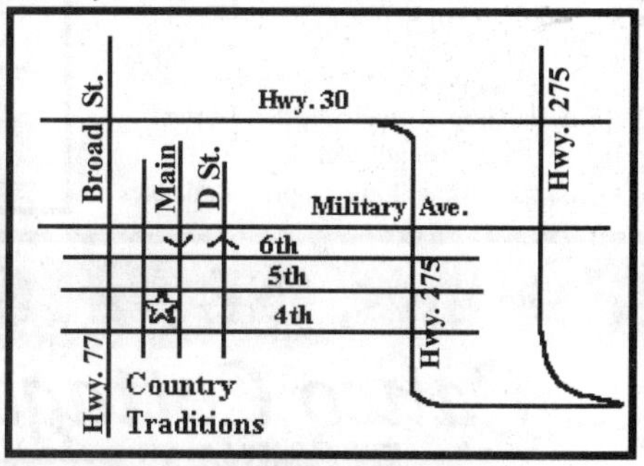

Fremont, NE #5

Visa and Master Card Accepted.
Mail Orders always Welcome.
Email: CntryTraditions@aol.com

Fremont, NE #6

Mon - Fri 10 - 6
Sat 10 - 5

SUNSHINE STITCHES

2625 N. Broad St. 68025
(402) 727-9233
Web Site: www.sunshinestitches.com
Owner: Monica Morrison

We will add sunshine to your life!
Quilting Supplies, Fabric & Notions
Classes, Sewing Machine Sales & Service.

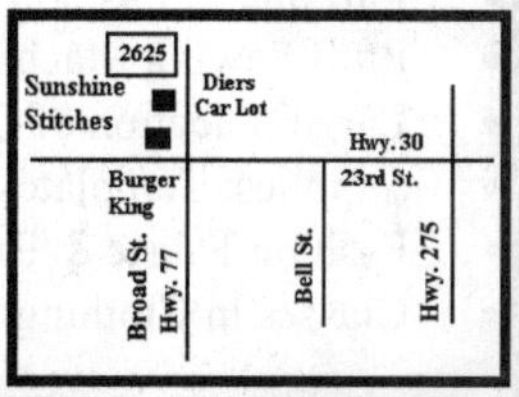

Beatrice, NE #7

Mon - Sat 10 - 5
Thur til 6:30

Loper's Sewing & Embroidery Workroom

311 Court St. 68310
(402) 223-3108
Web Site: www.loperfabrics.com
E-Mail: loperfabrics@beatricene.com

2nd largest Bernina dealer in Nebraska. Specializing in embroidery software, threads, stabilizers and sewing workroom accessories. Large selection of thread for machine quilting, machine embroidery & serging.

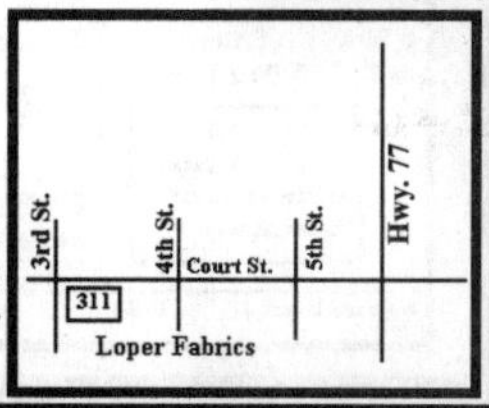

Syracuse, NE #8

Mon - Fri 9 - 5
Sat 9 - 4

COMMON THREADS

325 5th St. 68446
(402) 269-2235
Owners: Julie & David Zahn
commonthreads@alltel.net
Est: 1997 1800 sq.ft. 800 Bolts

Nice selection of 100% Cotton fabrics, books, patterns & gifts.
Located in a restored 1890's Bank Building!

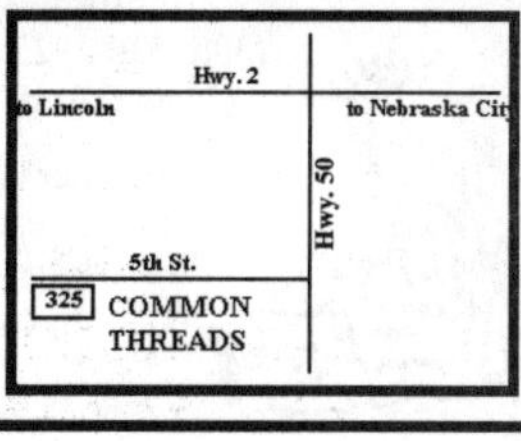

Palmyra, NE #9

Owner:
Gloria Hall
Est: 1989
600 sq.ft.
Price List Avail.
(800) 284-8574

By Appt.

Grandma's Quilts

296 N. 10th Rd.
68418
(402) 780-5773

We have over 100 quilts dating from 1870's to 1960's Vintage Fabric, Tops, Blocks, Feed Sacks & Old Linens.

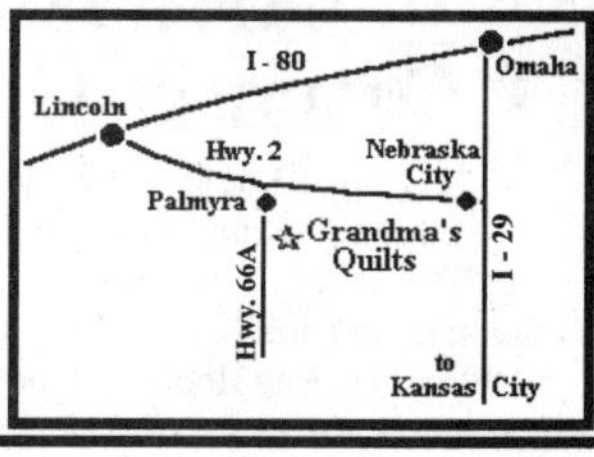

E-Mail: grandma@grandmasquilts.com
Web Site: www.grandmasquilts.com

THE BACK PORCH

Classic Needle Arts
2710 N 48th St. 68507
(402) 465-0000
Owner: Deb Fick
Est: 2001 4600 sq.ft.

Lincoln, NE #10

- Fabric
- Patterns & Books
- Smiles
- Notions
- Perle cotton
- For the crazy quilter--specialty threads, ribbons, & lace.
- Cross stitch patterns & books.
- Weeks & Sampler Threads.

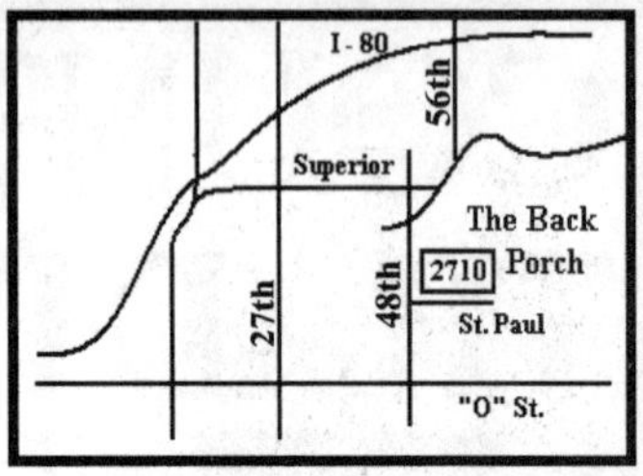

Mon - Sat 10 - 5

Lincoln, NE #11

Mon - Sat 10 - 5:30

Hooper Creek Sewing & Quilting

110 S. 56th St. 68510
(402) 488-2766 Est: 1999

Quilting fabrics, notions, and patterns. Dealership for Pfaff and Elna Sewing Machines. Machine Quilting Service.

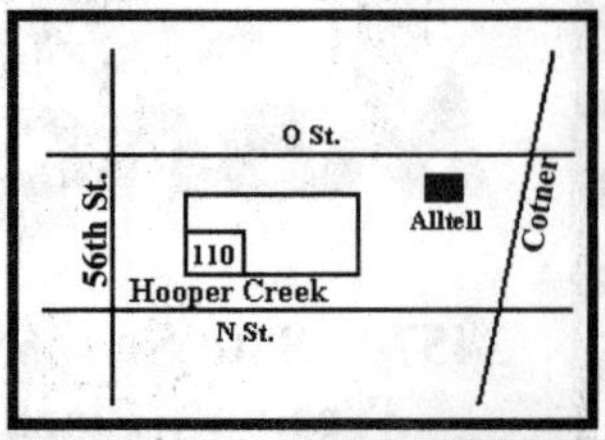

Lincoln, NE #12

Mon - Sat 10 - 5 Sun 1 - 4

The Calico House

5221 S. 48th 68516
In Sutter Place Mall
(402) 489-1067 Fax: (402) 489-1067
Est: 1974 2300 sq. ft. 1500 Bolts

Friendly, Experienced Staff. We love plaids & flannels. Always the Latest Fabrics and the Greatest Patterns.

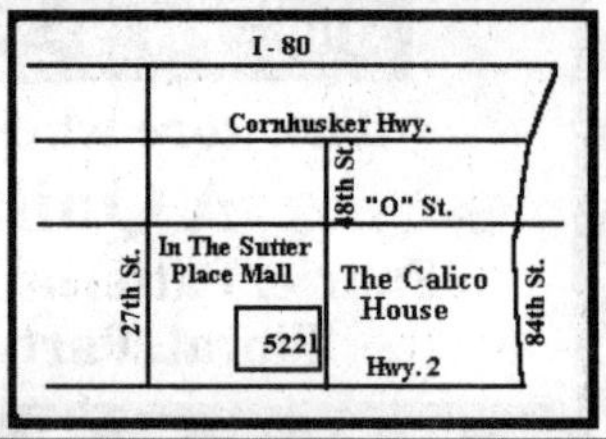

Lincoln, NE #13

Mon - Sat 10 - 5 Sun 1 - 4

Creative Hands

5220 S. 48th St. 68516
(402) 483-1538

Specializing in quality cotton fabrics and friendly service.
Books, patterns, quilting supplies available.

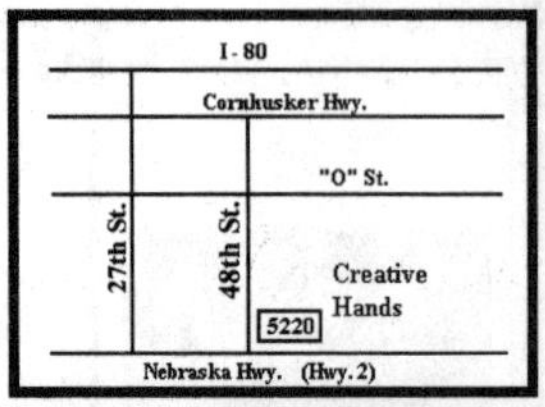

Hastings, NE #15

Mon - Fri 9:30 - 5:30 Sat 9:30 - 5

Calico Cottage

BERNINA

NEW LOCATION

731 West 2nd 68901
(402) 461-6767
Everything for the Quilter!

Over 1000 bolts Cotton Fabric. Quilting Notions, Books, Patterns, Classes. Authorized Bernina Dealer.

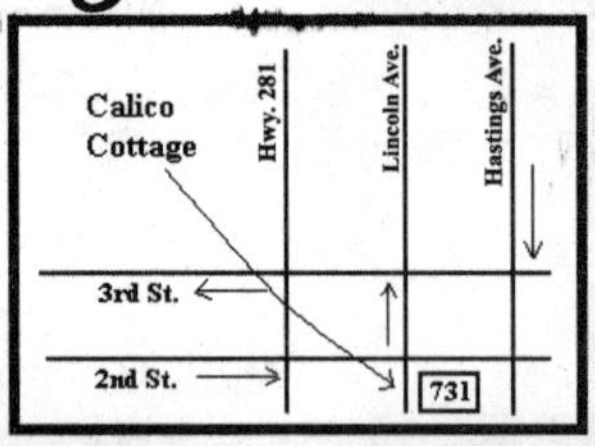

One of Nebraska's most Complete Sewing Centers!

- Full line of Fashion & Quilt Patterns
- Pfaff Sewing Machines & Sergers
- Large Selection of Quilt Fabrics & Books
- Supplies: Templates, Frames, Needles, Etc.
- Fashion Fabric & Bridal Specialties
- Classes in Clothing Construction & Quilt Making

636 Seward St. 68434 Owner: Marian Fosler Est: 1970
Hrs: Mon -Sat 9 - 5:30 Thurs til 9 Sun 1 - 4

Seward, NE #14

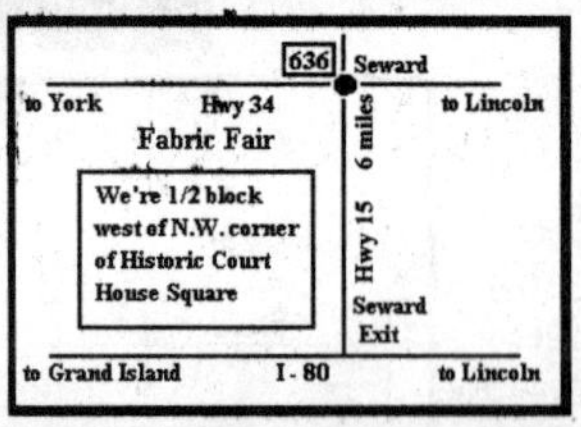

(402) 643-4760
fabric fair

Grand Island, NE #16

Mon - Fri 10 - 5:30 Sat 10 - 4

The Platte River Quilting Co.

205 N. Locust St.
68801

(308) 382-5535 Est: 1978
Machine Quilting Over 1000 Bolts

Quilting Supplies Bear Making Supplies
Primitive Rug Hooking Supplies.

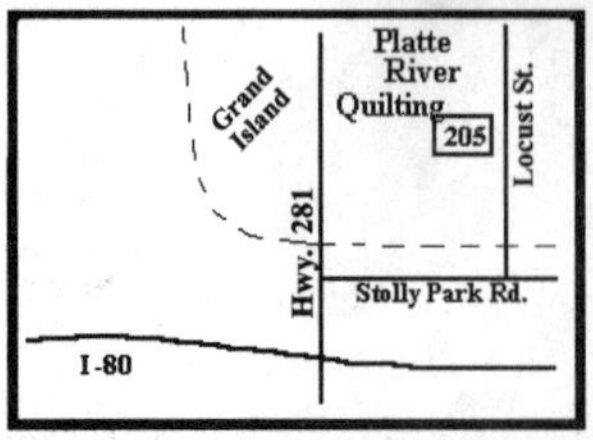

Fullerton, NE #17

Mon - Fri 9 - 5 Sat 9 - 12

Calico Annie's Quilt Shop

210 Broadway 68638
(308) 536-2925 Est: 1999
Owner: Anne Wemhoff

Bolt after bolt of the newest fabrics nestled in a turn-of-the-century hardware store. 40 miles north of I - 80 exit 332 onto Hwy. 14

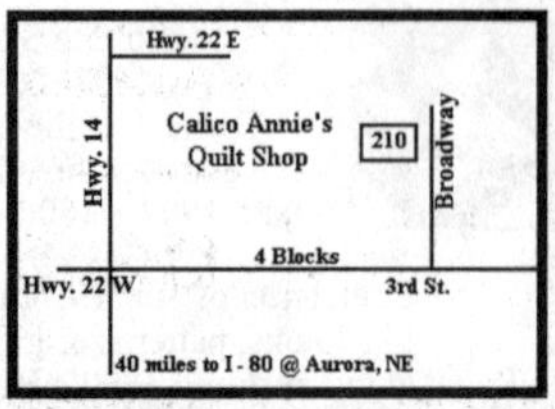

Countryside Fabrics

York, NE #18

718 Lincoln Ave. 68467
Phone & Fax (402) 362-5737
countrysidefabrics@alltel.net
Owners: Ed & Lola Schall
Est: 1970 4000 sq.ft.

- Over 3000 Bolts of Quilting Fabric
- Complete line of Quilting Supplies, Books, Patterns and Notions
- National, State & Local Trunk Show, Seminars, & Special Programs. Block of the Month & Mystery Quilts by Mail
- Year-round Classes. State recognized Designers/ Instructors on staff
- Local Quilt Artists featured each month on display
- Fashion, Bridal & Special Occasion Fabrics
- FREE newsletter on request
- Authorized Bernina Sewing Machines, Sergers, and Emboridery Systems Dealer
- Mail Orders welcome!

Mon - Fri
9:30 - 5:30
Thursdays
til 9:00 pm
Sat 9am - 5pm

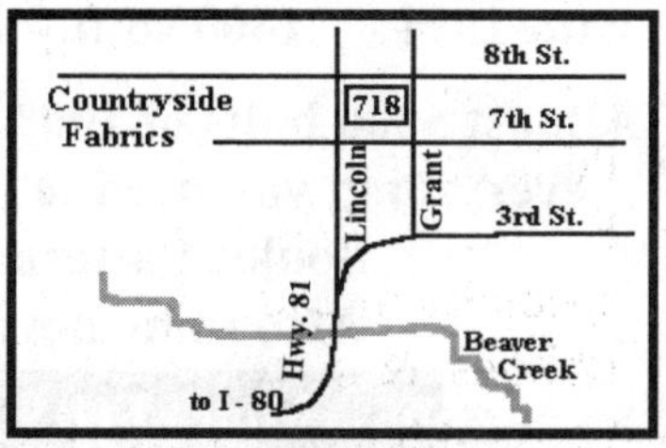

York's One-Stop Fabric Center

BERNINA — ONLY FIVE MINUTES OFF HWY 80/81 JCT. IN DOWNTOWN YORK

Use your... VISA ... MasterCard ... DISCOVER ...BERNINA CREDIT Cards

Prairie Point Junction

124 East 8th, Box 184
Cozad, NE 69130
308-784-2010
E-mail: prairiepointjunction@yahoo.com

Cozad, NE #19

Let our displays inspire!

Hours:
Mon - Fri
10-5
Saturday
10-4

Over 2000 bolts of 100% cotton fabrics specializing in flannels, brushed cottons, and homespuns.
Just minutes off I-80.

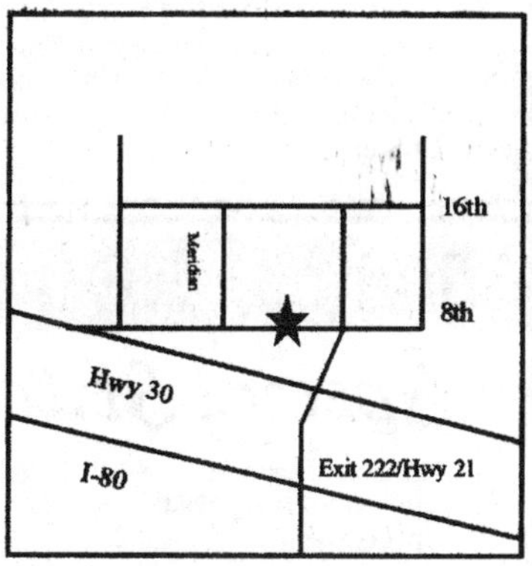

We Love Mail Order!

Mastercard, Visa, and Discover Accepted

- Hundreds of books, patterns, notions, kits
- Primitive Embroidery patterns and fabrics
- Over 30 colors of Wool Felt
- Original Pattern Designs

Visit us on the web at www.prairiepointjunction.com

Quilter's Delight

Holdrege, NE #20

323 West Ave. 68949
(308) 995-2728
E-mail: quilter@atcjet.net
Owner: Janet Kugler
Est: 1991 1400 sq.ft.

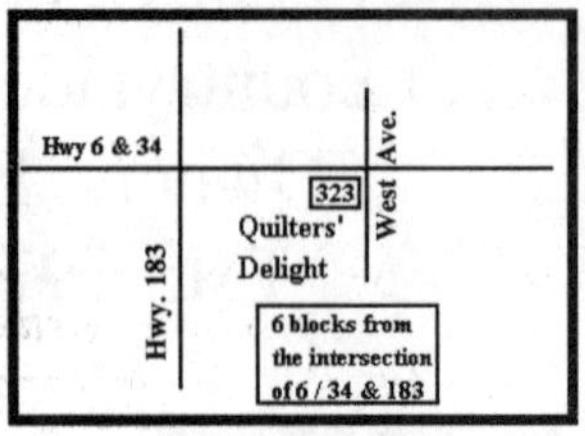

Almost 5000 bolts of 100% Cotton fabric. Plus everything you need to finish your project: Books, Patterns, Notions. Also some novelty items.

Mon - Fri 9:30 - 5:30
Thurs til 8 Sat 9:30 - 5

Kearney, NE #21

Mon - Fri 9:30 - 5:30
Sat 10 - 4

Quilter's Trunk

2114 Central Ave. 68847
(308) 236-6286
Fax: (308) 236-6156

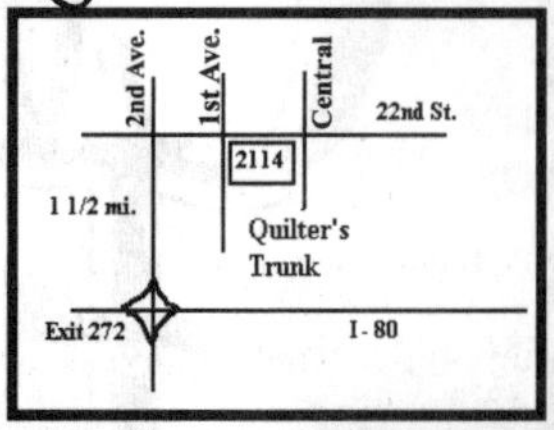

100% Cotton Fabrics — Quilting Supplies
Bernina Sewing Machines and Service.
Primitive Gift Items and Candles.

McCook, NE #22

Mon - Sat 9:30 - 5:30
Thur til 8

Sew Little Time

213 Norris Ave. 69001
(308) 345-4572

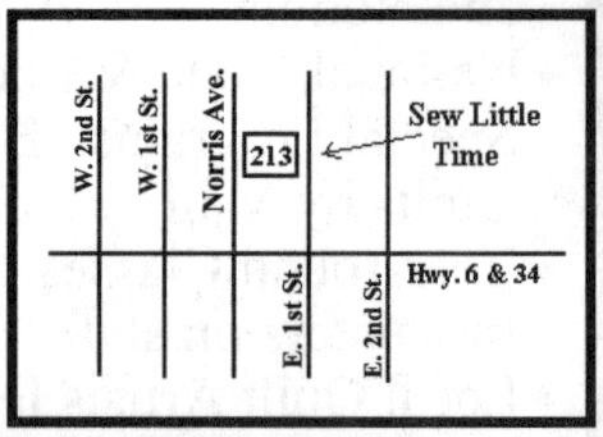

Quilting books, notions, patterns, 100% cotton fabrics. Great Displays. Smocking plates and supplies.

Imperial, NE #23

Mon - Fri 9 - 5:30
Sat 9 - 5

PRIOR'S AND SEW FORTH

525 Broadway,
P.O. Box 668 69033
(308) 882-4354
Owner: Lila V. Prior

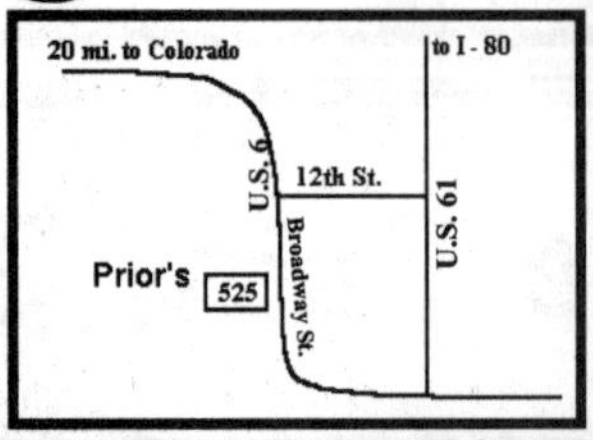

Fabrics — quilting (4000+ Bolts) and fashion; all top quality. All your quilting supplies and other sewing notions.

Silver Thimble Sewing Center

108 N. Spruce 69153
(308) 284-6838
Fax: (308) 284-8945
Owner: Julie Peterson
Est: 1988 2500 sq.ft.

Show us this ad and Receive a Free Gift.

Mon - Sat 9 - 5:30
Thur til 8

Ogallala, NE #24

3000+ Bolts of Cottons, Quilt Fabrics and Supplies. Books, Notions, Batting, Classes.
Pfaff Sewing Machine Sales and Service.
Full line fabric store.

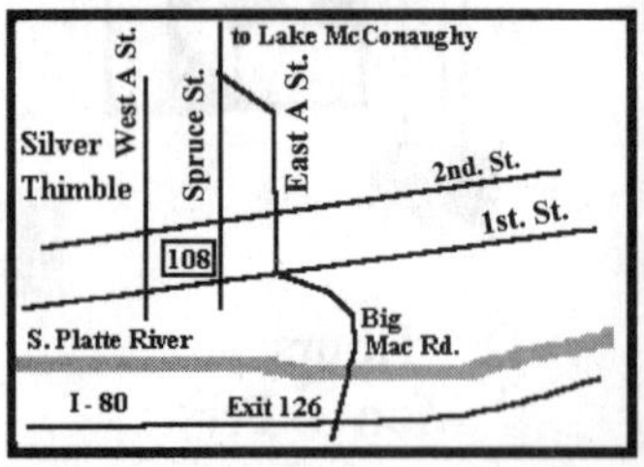

Less than 5 min. off I - 80

Scottsbluff, NE #25

Tues - Fri 10 - 5
Sat 10 - 4

Prairie Pines Quilt Shop

70756 County Rd. 20 69361
(308) 632-8668

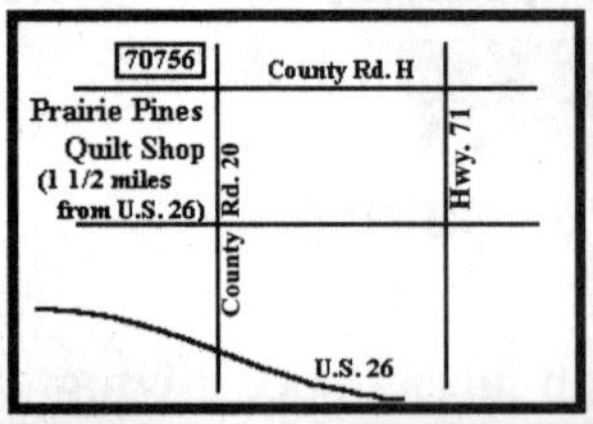

Supplies and classes for Quilting and Cross-Stitch. Including 2000 bolts of 100% cotton fabrics. Authorized Bernina & New Home Sales & service.

Alliance, NE #26

Mon - Sat 9 - 5:30

Special Stitches

402 Box Butte Ave. 69301
9(308) 762-3784
E-Mail: rthiems@aol.com
Web Site: www.specialstitches.com
Owner: Deb Thiems Est: 1987

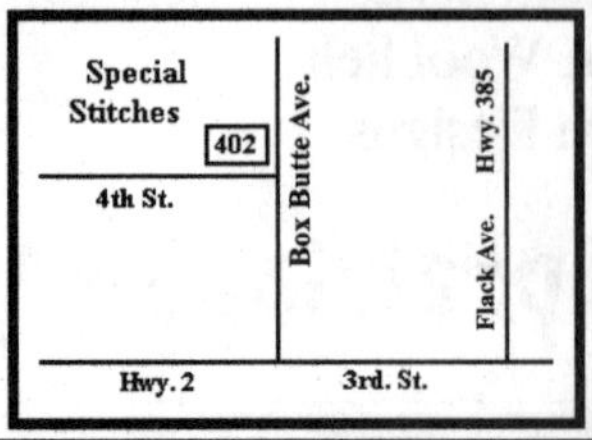

Quilting Supplies, Counted Cross Stitch, Machine Quilting, Viking Sewing Machines & Sergers.

Hemingford, NE #27

Mon - Sat 10 - 5

PAT'S CREATIVE

7355 Gage Rd. 69348
(308) 487-3999 Fax: Same
E-Mail: dsbuskirk@bbc.net
Owners: Pat - Sonya - Toni
Est: 1975 2700 sq.ft. 2500 Bolts

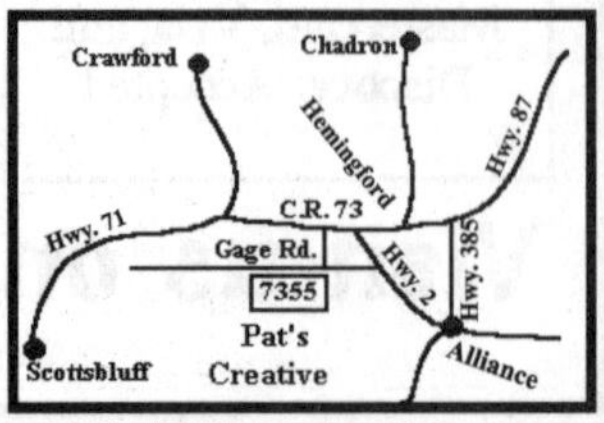

Over 1500 quilting cottons - 200 flannels fashion fabrics - books, patterns, threads, notions - Bernina - Janome.
YOUR 1 STOP SEWING SHOP

Valentine, NE #28

Mon - Sat 9 - 6

The Gallery

226 N. Main 69201
(402) 376-3834
E-Mail: gallery@inebraska.net
Owner: Mary Mulligan Est: 1988

A unique Boutique and Quilt Shop, featuring over 1500 bolts of fabrics, quilt books, patterns & supplies. We also have Western Art & gifts.

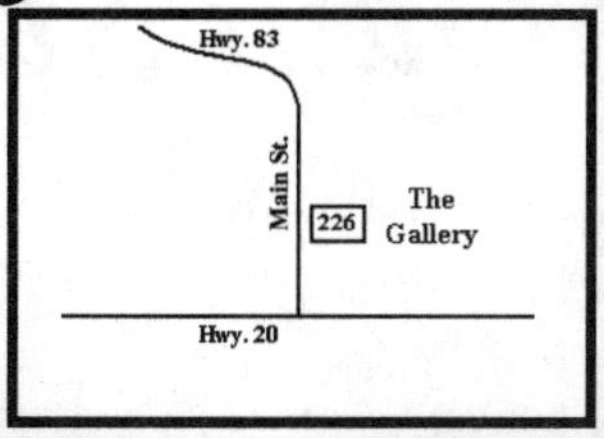

Wakefield, NE #29

Mon - Fri 8 - 5:30 Sat 10 - 3

The Quilt Shop

301 Main St., P.O. Box 88 68784
(402) 287-2325 Fax: (402) 287-2130
E-Mail: quiltshop@thenetpages.com
Web Site: www.thenetpages.com/quiltshop/

Custom & Ready made quilts - Block of the Month - Lessons - Fabric - Books - Notions. Machine & hand Quilting - machine embroidery

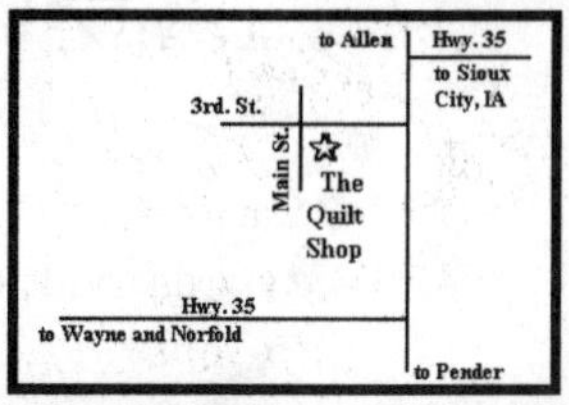

Homer, NE #30

Wed - Sat 10 - 5

A Wish & A Prayer

102 S. First St., P.O. Box 453 68030
(402) 698-2221 Fax: (402) 698-2337
E-Mail: brblia@pionet.net Est: 1994
Owners: Barb Lauritsen & Jody Rohde

"By the hand & from the heart"
Quality 100% cotton fabrics, kits, B.O.M.'s
Personal, knowledgeable, friendly service our specialty.

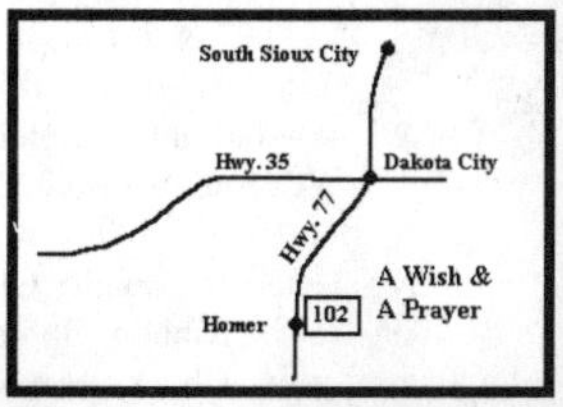

West Point, NE #31

Mon - Fri 9:30 - 5 Thur til 7 Sat 9 - 2

Creative Notions

107 N. Main St. 68788
(402) 372-2004

• Cotton Fabrics • Books & Patterns •
• Woods • Ceramics •
• Quilting Supplies • Craft Patterns •

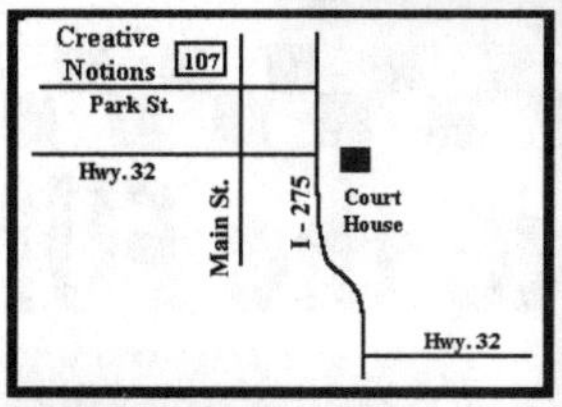

Selected by Better Homes & Gardens American Patchwork & Quilting as one of the Top Ten Quilt Shops in North America.

Dodge, NE #32

VOGIES Quilts & Treasures

Mon - Sat 9 - 5:30

Over 3000 bolts of quilting fabrics.
Hundreds of Books, Patterns, and samples on display. Unique Giftware.
Mail Orders Welcome. Visa & Mastercard accepted.

Check us out on the web:
www.vogies.com
153 Oak St., P.O. Box 367
Dodge, NE 68633-0367
(402) 693-2230
E-mail: vogies@tvsonline.net
Owner: Dave & June Vogltance

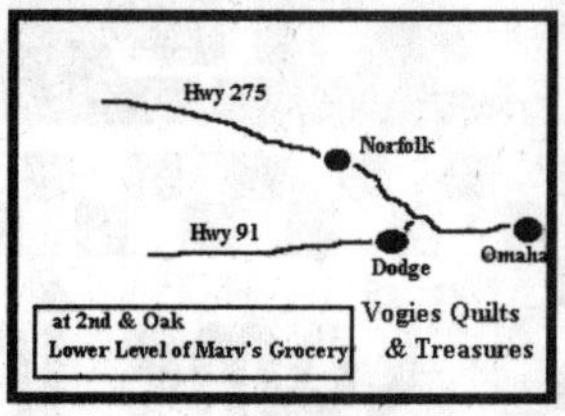

Everyday is a "Quilt Show" at Vogies!

Other Shops in Nebraska: We suggest calling first

Alliance	Prairie Creations, 5611 Madison Rd	308-762-8365
Alliance	Quilting Memories & Creations, 1629 Buchfinck Ave.	308-762-2893
Aurora	Pieceful Dreams, 2121 P St.	402-694-2900
Aurora	The Sewing Basket, 906 S "O" Rd.	402-694-3795
Bayard	Wildflower Sewing & Crafts, 316 Main St.	308-586-2528
Beemer	Marilyn's Tea Room & Quilt Room, 417 E. 3rd St.	402-528-3282
Bellevue	Country Corner, 1323 Harrison St	402-731-8707
Columbus	Sew - What, 3411 21st St.	402-563-3900
Fairbury	Quilt Patch, 412 4th St	402-729-6607
Fremont	Sue's Custom Quilting, 849 N "L" St.	402-727-7322
Hastings	Vintage Treasures, 1308 Highland Dr.	402-463-3620
Heming Ford	Pat's Creative Stitchery, RR #1 Box 47	308-487-3999
Kearney	Quilt Blocks Etc., P.O. Box 63	308-236-8973
Lincoln	Sew Creative, 5221 S. 48th St.	402-489-6262
Lincoln	Karens Country Fabric, 5500 Old Cheney Rd Suite 9	402-421-6151
Maywood	Forever's Treasures, 207 S. Cherry St.	308-362-4921
North Platte	Jo's Stitchery & Quilt Shop, 408 N. Chestnut St.	308-532-3225
Omaha	OK Sewing & Vacuum, 928 S. 72nd St.	402-397-5007
Omaha	Bernina Sewing Centers, 3407 S. 84th St.	402-392-0430
Omaha	Quilting B's, 6342 Lafayette	402-551-9181
Papillion	Quilt Boutique, 546 N. Washington St.	402-339-6984
Plainview	Kountry Keepsakes, 408 Locust, R.R. #2, Box 191	
Red Cloud	Sewing Box, 422 N. Webster St.	402-746-3592
Wayne	Just Sew, 512 E. 7th	402-375-4697

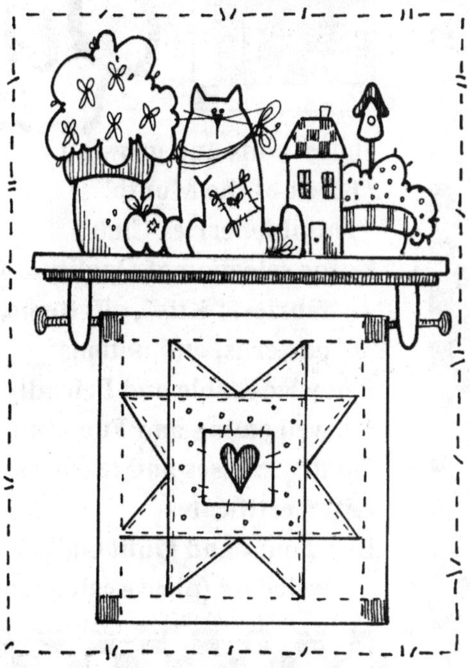

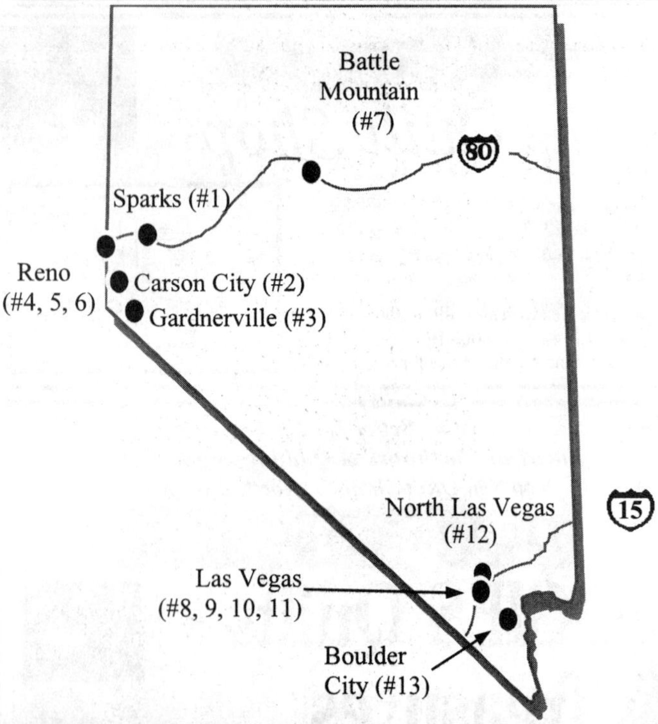

Sparks, NV #1

Mon - Sat 10 - 4

Quilt Stop

101 15th St. 89431
(775) 355-3233
Owner: Joan Carroll 6000 Bolts

100% Cotton Fabric, Classes, Books, Patterns, Notions, Quilts on Display. Also mail order. Call for info.

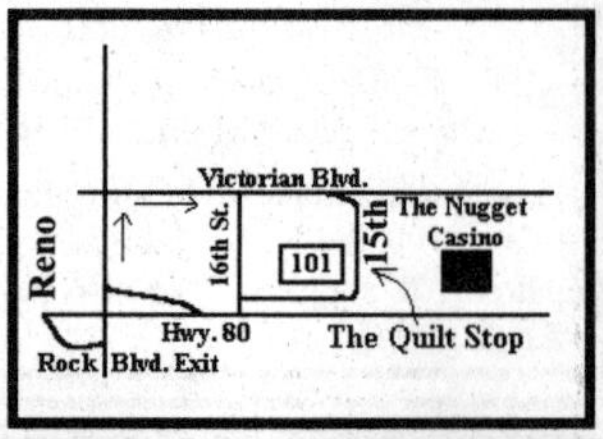

Carson City, NV #2

Mon - Sat 9:30 - 5:30

CLOTH COTTAGE

602 N. Curry St. 89703
(775) 841-9191 or (877) 964-9191
E-Mail: info@clothcottage.com
Web Site: www.clothcottage.com
Est: 1996 2400 sq.ft. 1000+ Bolts
Carefully selected, top quality Quilting Fabrics, Notions, Books, Ribbon, Home Decorating Anitques & gifts. Check my website for show schedules. ½ block off 395 behind State Museum.

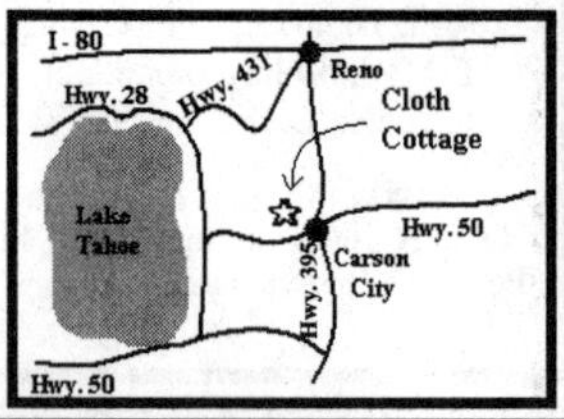

NEVADA

13 Featured Shops

"Come in and experience the FUN with us !!!"

The Quilt House

Gardnerville, NV #3

1363 #6 Hwy. 395,
P.O. Box 70 89410
(775) 782-8845
Fax: (775) 782-7823
Owners: Gary & Janet Pierce

Est: 1999

- **3000+ bolts and growing**
- **"Block of the Month"**
- **"Thimbleberries Club"**
- **Large selection of Quality 100% cotton fabrics, "Kits", gift items, books, patterns, and notions**
- **Knowledgeable and Friendly staff and welcoming and Fun atmosphere.**
- **Quality classes and teachers**
- **Gift Certificates**
- **Bus Tours and Quilt Guilds welcome (please call ahead)**

We will be moving into our NEW BUILDING (2 blocks away) in Sept./Oct. 2002 Phone # the same

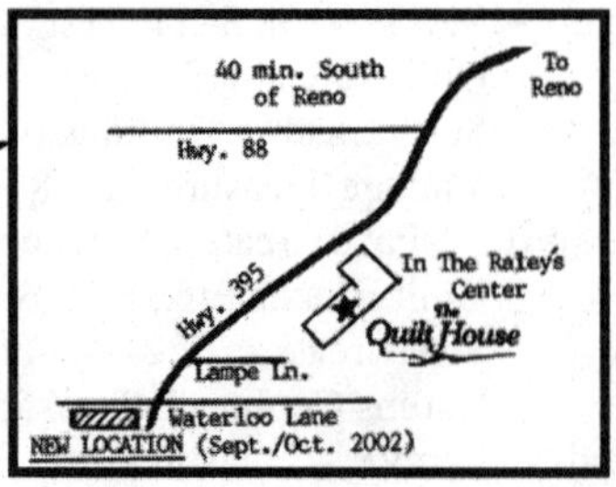

Hours: Monday - Friday 10am - 5pm
Saturday 10am - 4pm
closed Sunday

Visa and Mastercard accepted
Mail Order Available

Reno, NV #4

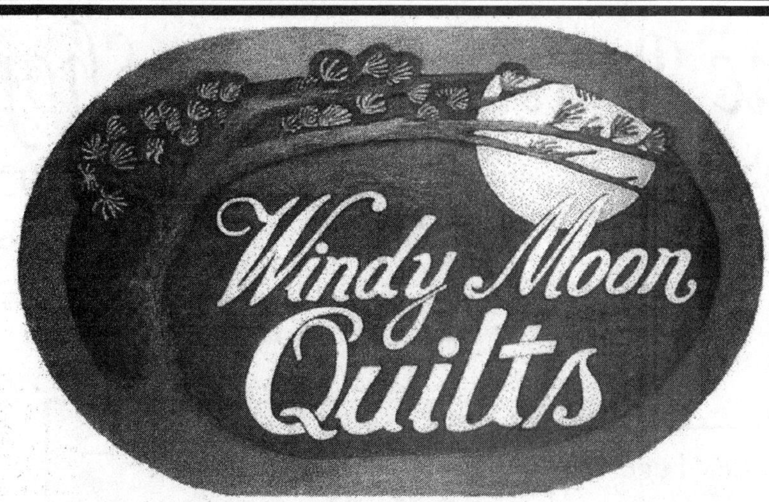

440 Spokane Street 89512

6,000 sq. ft. of fabric, books, notions, patterns, classes, gifts, and quilting help.

All the Quilter's Needs

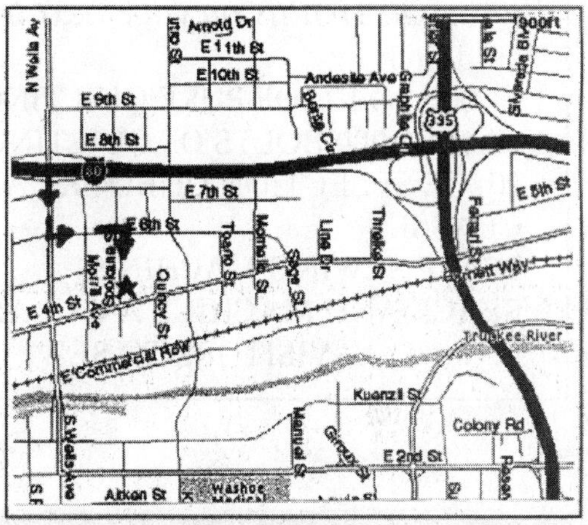

"Biggest little Quilt Shop in the West"

Visit, Call or Fax
Monday - Saturday 10 - 6
Sunday 11 - 5
(775) 323-4777 or (800) 622-8082
FAX (775) 323-4790

Shop on Line ➡ ***www.windymoonquilts.com***

Reno, NV #5

Mon - Sat
9:30 - 5:30

Sierra Sewing

4145 S. Virginia St. 89502
(775) 823-9700
Owner: Lee Levin

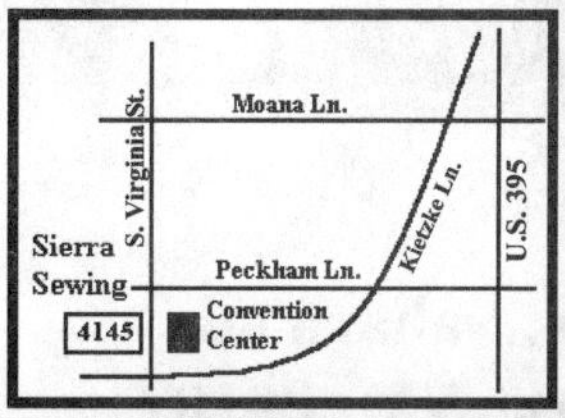

Great Quilt Fabrics and all the latest notions and Viking, Pfaff & White Machines.

Reno, NV #6

Mon - Fri 10 - 5:30
Sat 10 - 5
Sun Oct - Dec
11 - 4

Needle In A Haystack

970 W. 7th St. 89503
(775) 323-8587 Fax: (775) 323-8562
E-Mail: Mitzi@the-needle.com
Web Site: www.the-needle.com
Est: 1993 2200 sq.ft. 3000+ Bolts

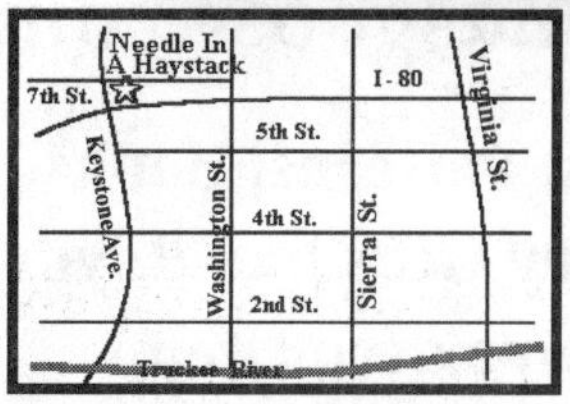

Nestled in this old Victorian Home are bolts & bolts of fabric, surrounded by patterns and handcrafted gifts.

Thimbles 'n Quilts

175 S. Scott St. 89820
(775) 635-3110
gloriad@desertlinc.com
Owners: Janet Himelspach & Gloria Derby

Mon - Fri
10 - 6
Sat 10 - 5

Battle Mountain, NV #7

Fabrics, patterns, books, specialty threads, classes and notions.

Travelers — Bring in this ad for a 10% discount

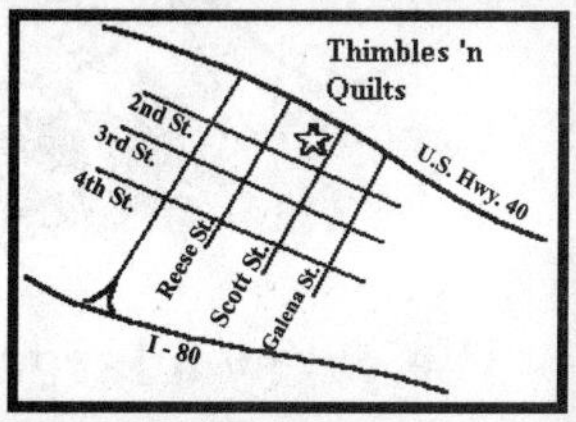

Fabric Boutique Quilt Shop

4465 W. Charleston, Las Vegas, NV 89102
www.fabricboutique.com (702) 878-0068

Owners: Helen Clapp, Ev Dahl

Be sure to visit us on your next trip to Las Vegas!
You'll find:
- 11,000 SQ.FT. OF PURE QUILTING HEAVEN
- OVER 5,000 BOLTS OF QUILTING COTTONS
- HUGE SELECTION OF BOOKS AND PATTERNS
- CLASSES
- PFAFF SEWING MACHINES
- SPACE AND MACHINE AVAILABLE FOR VISITORS TO SEW!

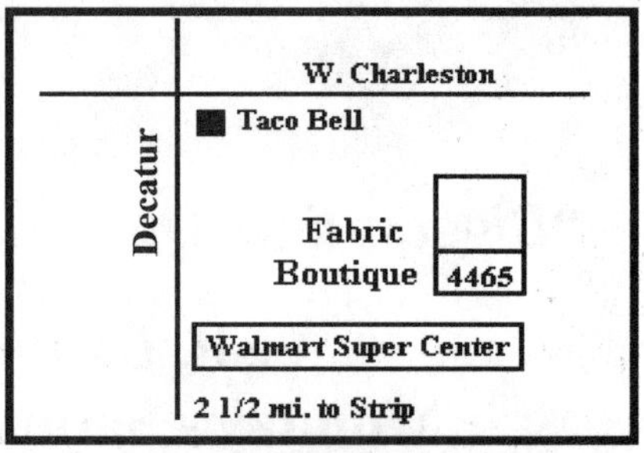

Las Vegas, NV #8

Open 7 Days A Week

Est: 1993

The Christmas Goose

5,000 sq.ft.

Las Vegas, NV #9

4750 W. Sahara #6
Las Vegas, NV 89102
(702) 877-1158
E-Mail: Cmasgoose@aol.com
Owner: Jeanette Sherrick

www.Christmasgoose.com

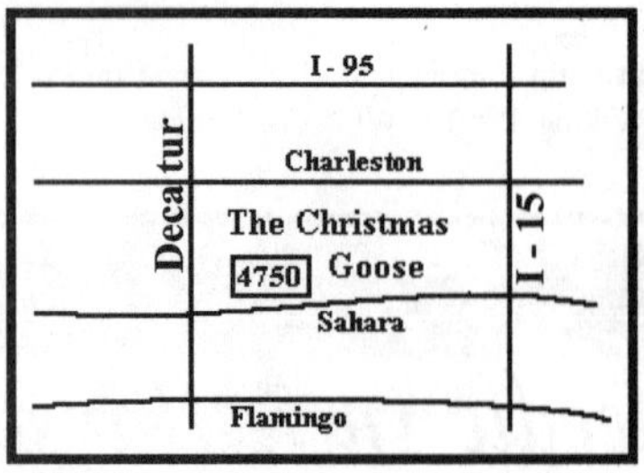

We carry a large selection of cotton fabrics, Patterns, Books, Notions and Quilting Supplies. Plus Country Gifts like Boyds Bears, Yankee Candles, Williraye and home décor items.

Mon - Sat 10 - 6
Sun 12 - 4

Nancy's Quilt Shop

3290 N. Buffalo Dr. 89129
(702) 839-2779

Las Vegas, NV #10

Las Vegas' newest quilt shop! Quality cotton fabric including Moda Marbles, batiks, flannels; WoolFelt®; redwork, patterns, notions, books, DMC floss, gifts and classes. Special arrangements for visiting quilt groups.

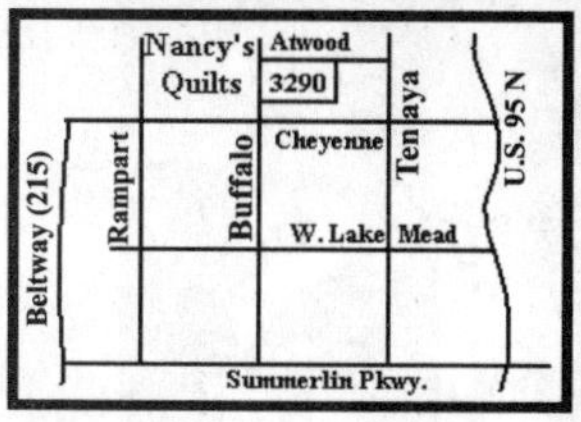

Mon - Sat 9 - 6

Owners: Nancy & Mark Laussade Est: 2002
nancy@nancysquiltshop.com 3,700 sq.ft.
www.nancysquiltshop.com

Las Vegas, NV #11

Mon - Fri 10 - 5 Sat 10 - 4

Pieceful Pleasures Quilt Shop

2381 E. Windmill Ln. #13
89123
(702) 263-8170
E-Mail: info@piecefulpleasures.com
Web Site: www.piecefulpleasures.com
Owner: Marsha Chappell

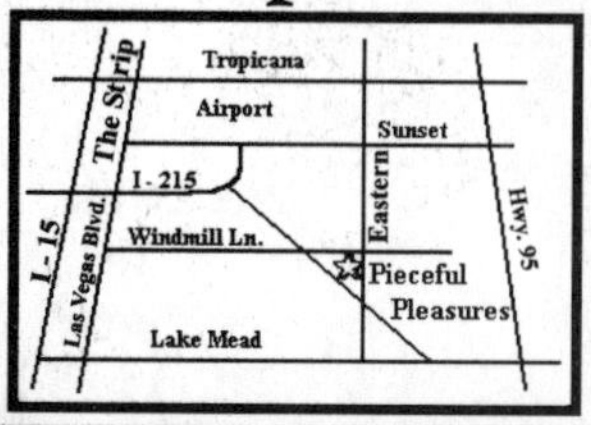

fabric - patterns - books - notions - classes for all ages. Just 2 mi. S of airport at SW corner of Windmill & Eastern .8 mi. E of 215.

N. Las Vegas, NV #12

Mon - Fri 10 - 5 Sat 10 - 4

Uncommon Threads

2575 E. Craig Rd., Suite H 89030
(702) 399-3175
Fax: (702) 399-6668
Owner: Ronnie Hobbs
Est: 2000

2000 square feet of over 2000 bolts of 100% Cotton Fabrics, Notions, Books & Patterns. Classes available. 1/2 mile west of I-15 on Craig Road.

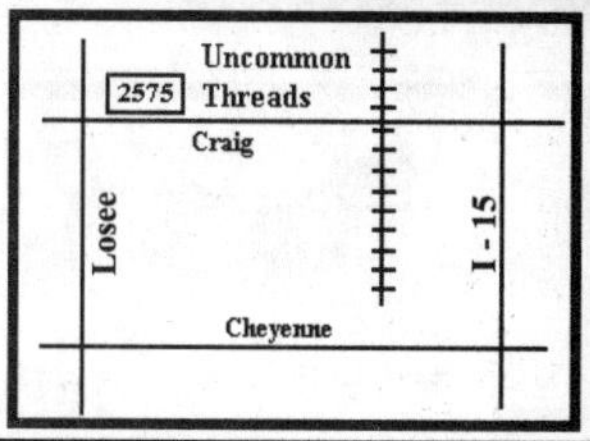

fiddlesticks

quilts and other works of heart

Tues - Sat 10 - 5:30

(702) 293-2979
Owner: Nanci Bowen
Email: fiddlesticksquilts@msn.com
Web Site: www.fiddlesticksquilts.com

Located in Historic Old Town... come visit a gentler time and treat your senses. We have a unique selection of quilt fabrics, books and notions, all carefully chosen with our customers in mind. Among our favorites are warm Moda plaids and all kinds of vintage prints, bark cloth, linens and velvets. You'll find antiques, gifts and one-of-a-kind treasures made by local craftspeople as well as many classes taught by these artists. More than just a fabric store, we specialize in new ideas and personal customer service. Come stretch your creativity and let us spoil you... the tea kettle is always on!

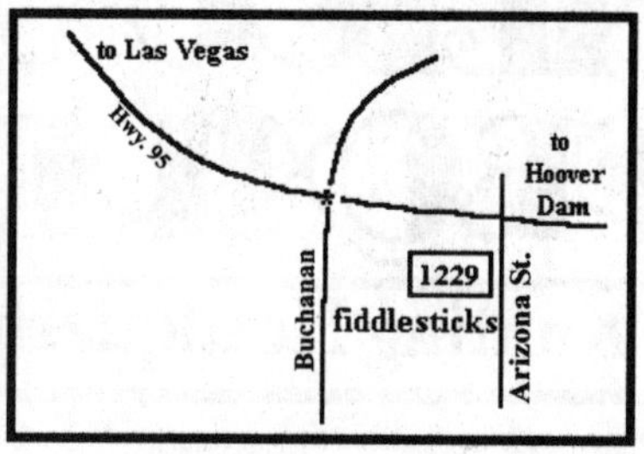

1229 Arizona St. 89005

Boulder City, NV #13

Other Shops in Nevada: We suggest calling first

Boulder City	Blue Dahlia Quiltworks, 540 Avenue B #A 702-294-0708
Carson City	Quilts Country Charm, 3659 Green Acres Dr. 702-882-2745
Fallon	Workman's Farms Crafts & Nursery 4990 Reno Hwy. 702-867-3716
Las Vegas	Quilts in the Attic, 4465 W. Charleston Blvd. 702-880-4558
Las Vegas	Maudie's Antique Cottage, 3310 E. Charleston 702-457-4379
Minden	TRS Designs, 1731 Westwood Dr. 775-782-6179
Pahrump	I Can Make That …., 111 S. Frontage Rd. 775-727-0994
Reno	Sew-N-Such, 3702 S Virginia St #G8 775-825-6677
Winnemucca	Those Moody Girls, 4695 Weatherby Dr. 775-625-2711

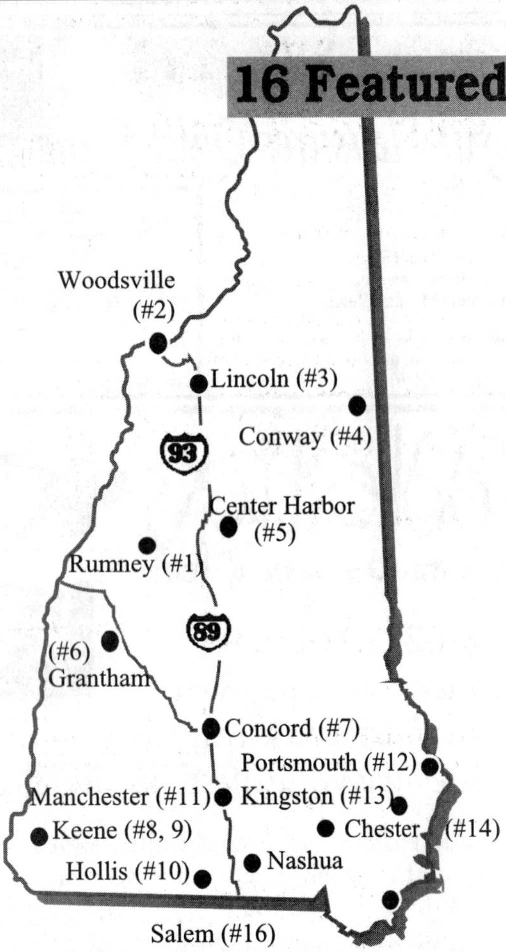

NEW HAMPSHIRE

CALICO CUPBOARD

Quilting & Knitting Headquarters

Rumney, NH #1

Main Street 03266
(800) 348-9567 or (603) 786-9567
E-Mail: info@calicocupboard.com
Web Site: www.calicocupboard.com
Est: 1978 2000 sq.ft.
Owners: Joe & Nancy Kolb

A Delightful Experience

In A Quaint New England Village

- **Super collection of the newest quilting fabrics.**
- **Terrific selection of cozy flannels and bright, whimsical kids' prints.**
- **Outstanding variety of quilting books.**
- **Warm atmosphere and friendly service.**

Mon - Sat 9:30 - 5:30
Sun 9:30 - 5
Closed April

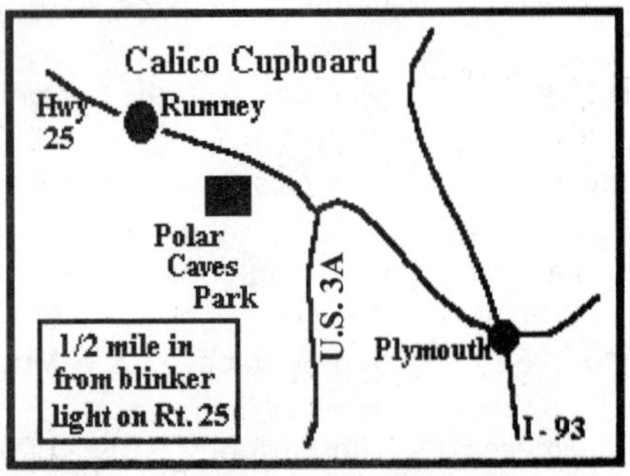

We're Worth the Trip!

Woodsville, NH #2

Tues - Sat 9:30 - 5 Fri til 6

Seams Sew Easy Fabric Shoppe

65 Central St. 03785
(603) 747-3054
Owners: Chris & Lloyd Steeves

A complete fabric store featuring a large selection of quilting fabrics and supplies. Quality Paton's yarns.

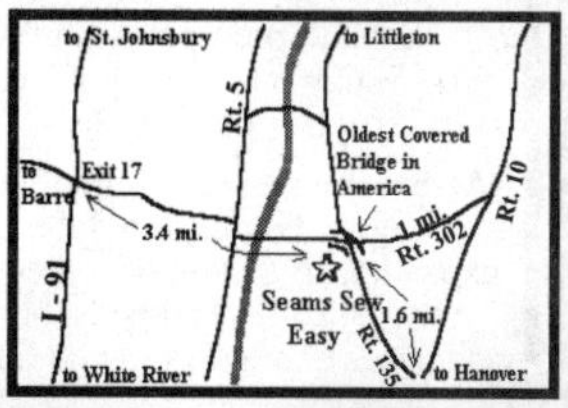

Lincoln, NH #3

10 - 5 Daily Extended Hrs July - Oct

Pinestead Quilts

Main St. 03251
(603) 745-8640
Owner: Kathleen Achorn Sherburn
Est: 1980

A personal quilt shop where your projects interest us. Quilting, knitting, cross-stitch & craft supplies. Fabrics, books, patterns, kits. Ready-made quilts, wallhangings & crafts.

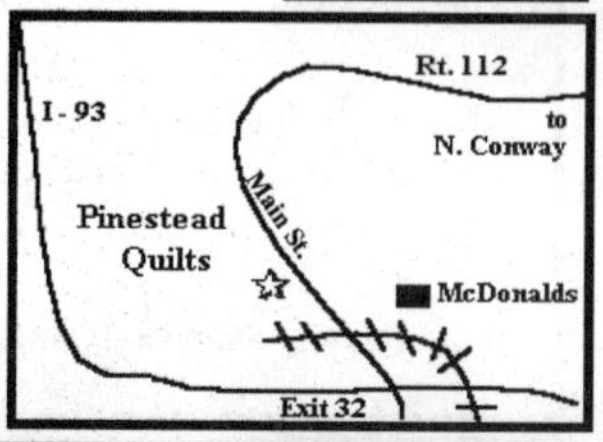

Conway, NH #4

Mon - Sat 9 - 5:00 Sun 10-4

THE QUILT SHOP AT VAC N SEW

Over 2000 Bolts of Cottons
All at Discounted Prices
Books, Patterns, Elna, PFAFF

Rt. 16 Next to Family Dollar
Toll Free 888-447-3470
www.quiltshopnh.com

Center Harbor, NH #5

Mon - Sat 9 - 6 Sun 9 - 5 Extended Summer hrs.

Keepsake Quilting

In Senters Marketplace
Route 25B P.O. Box 1618 03226
(603) 253-4026
Est: 1988 Free 128 pg. Catalog

America's largest quilt shop with over 10,000 bolts of cotton! Hundreds of finished Quilts.
Don't miss it. It's a Quilter's Paradise!

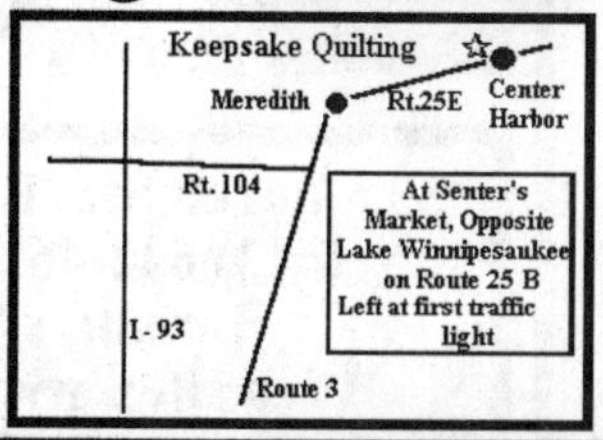

Grantham, NH #6

Mon - Fri 9:30 - 5 Sat 9:30 - 3

Sunshine Carousel Quilt Shop

Sawyer Brook Plaza, Route 10 03753
(603) 863-5754
E-mail: scqs@srnet.com
Web Site: www.scqs.com
Owner: Elaine Pillsbury
Est: 1990 5000 sq.ft.
3000+ Bolts

Full Service Quilt Shop
"Let us help you make a memory!"

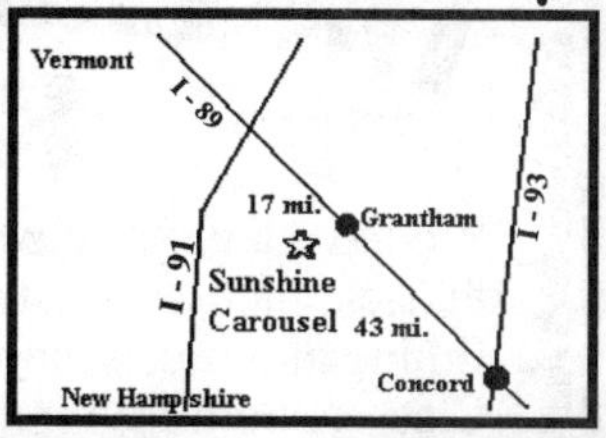

Concord, NH #7

Mon - Sat 10 - 5 June, July, Aug Mon-Fri 10 - 5 Sat 10 - 1

Golden Gese Quilt Shop

22 Liberty St. 03301
(603) 228-5540
Owner: Nancy Gesen
Est: 1987 1200 sq.ft. 2000 Bolts

100% Cotton Fabric, Books, Patterns, Notions & Classes. Helpful Assistance.

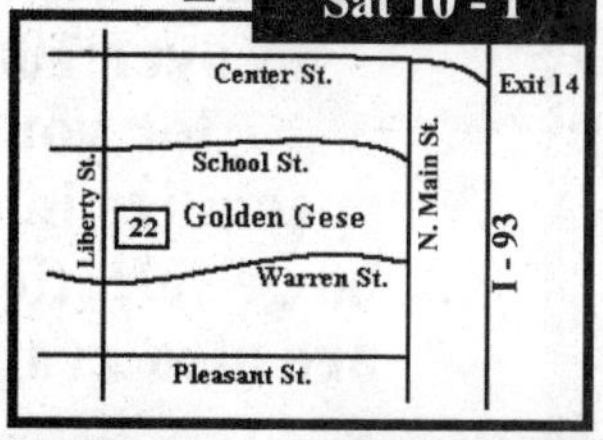

Keene, NH #8

Mon - Fri 10 - 5:30 Sat 10 - 4

The Moses House

423 Winchester St. 03431
Phone/Fax: (603) 352-2312
E-Mail: info@themoseshouse.com
Web Site: www.themoseshouse.com
Owners: Fran & Russ Moline
Est: 1987 1800 sq.ft.

The best quilting fabrics, books, patterns, and supplies. Many reproduction fabrics. Redwork. Quilting frames on display. NOLTING Longarm Quilting Machine dealer.

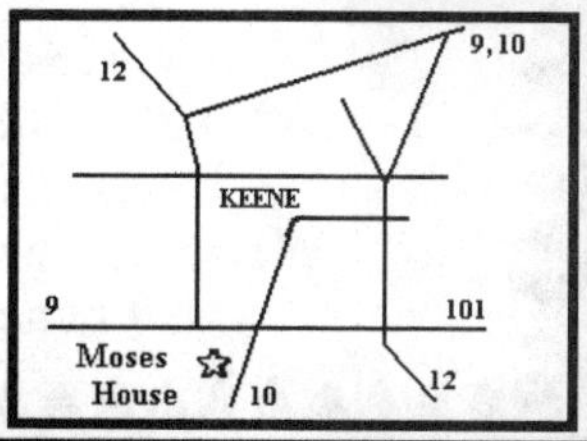

Hollis, NH #10

Tues - Sat 10 - 5

Quiltopia

Hollis Village Marketplace 03049
(603) 465-9119
E-Mail: jdamon@quiltopia.com
Web Site: www.quiltopia.com
Owner: Judy Damon
Est: 1999 1000 sq. ft. 1200 Bolts.

Colorful fabrics from top manufacturers, including Balis, brights, orientals. Oceans of notions, plus books, patterns, stencils. Friendly, helpful service & expert advice.

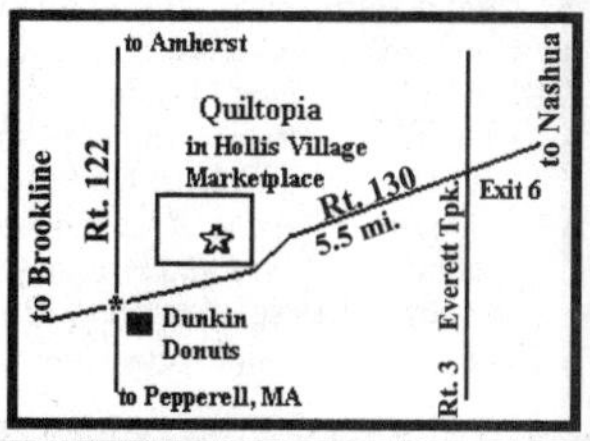

Keene, NH #9

Mon - Sat 9:30 - 5:30 Fri til 8

NEW ENGLAND FABRICS

– & Decorating Center –

Tremendous Selection of Beautiful Fabrics for:

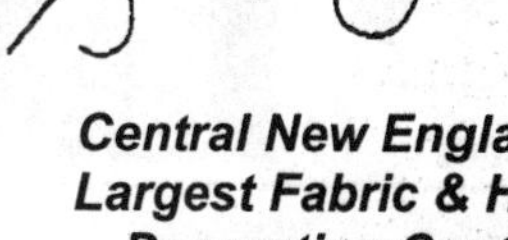

- Quilting • Apparel • Bridal
- Draperies • Slipcovers
- Upholstery & More!

Plus Yarn & Sewing Machines

Central New England's Largest Fabric & Home Decorating Center!

55 Ralston St., Keene, NH 03431
(603) 352-8683
www.nefabrics.com

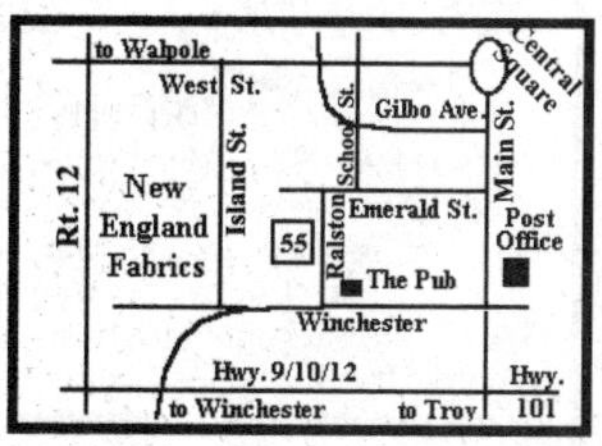

Manchester, NH #11

Mon - Fri 9:30 - 4
Thur til 6
Sat 9:30 - 2

The Chestnut Quilter

76 Lowell St. 03101
(603) 647-8458
E-Mail: chestnutquilter@hotmail.com

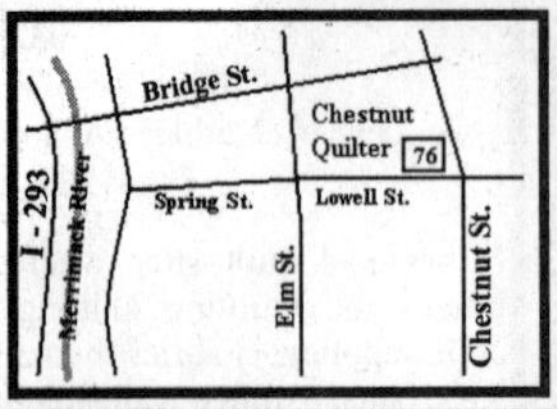

Fine Quilting Supplies, Quilting Classes

Portsmouth, NH #12

Mon - Sat 9:30 - 5:30
Sun 12 - 5

Portsmouth Fabric Co.

112 Penhallow Street 03801
(603) 436-6343 Fax: (603) 430-2943
E-Mail: pfc@portsmouthfabric.com
Web Site: www.portsmouth.com Est: 1979
1100 sq. ft. 6000 Bolts Online Catalog

An exceptional selection of natural fiber and designer fabrics, fine laces and silks. An expanded collection of contemporary quilting cottons, batiks and ikats, buttons, fiber art magazines and books. Swiss Bernina machines.

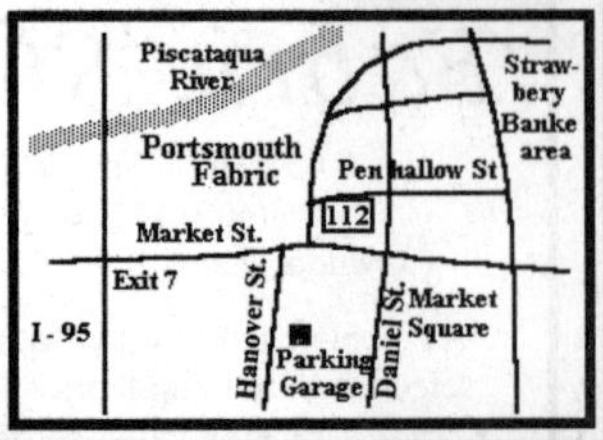

Silver Thimble Quilt Shop

53 Church St., Box 86 Kingston, NH 03848
(603) 642-4615 Fax: (603) 642-4386
Email: silverthimble@ttlc.net
Web site: www.silverthimblequilt.com
Store Hours:
Monday through Saturday
9:00 am - 5:00 pm

Silver Thimble Quilt Shop offers over 1000 bolts of fabric for you to choose from. We specialize in elegant florals and Bali's. A large selection of books and patterns are also available. Stop in today!!

Kingston, NH #13

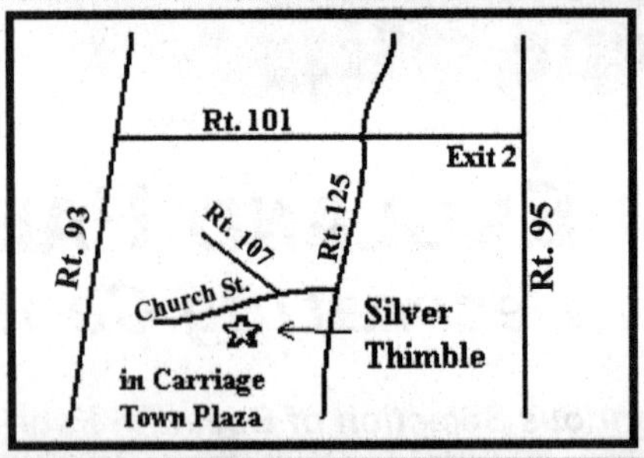

Chester, NH #14

Tues - Sat 9:30 - 4
Thur til 8

The Village Quilter

184 Raymond Rd., Rt. 102 03036
(603) 887-5957
E-Mail: staff@theVillageQuilter.com
Web Site: www.thevillagequilter.com
Owners: Deborah Wamsley & Christine Doherty
Est: 1999 1500 sq.ft. 1000 Bolts

An olde New England Quilt Shoppe featuring a great selection of flannels, homespun and traditional quilting fabrics.

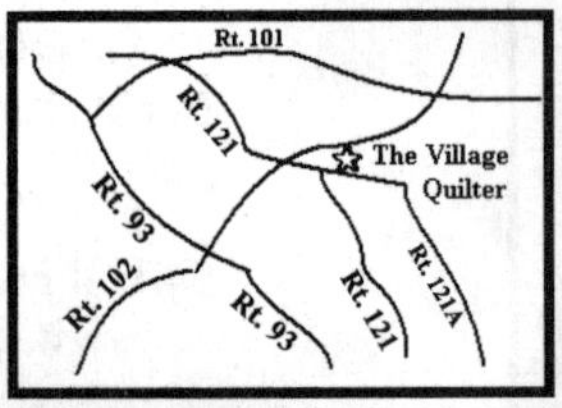

Nashua, NH #15

The Little Quilt Shop

We have a great selection of fine quality 100% cotton fabrics: including Thimbleberries, Moda, Thirties, Kids, Ethnic and much more.
Classes, notions, threads, machines and 100's of books and patterns.

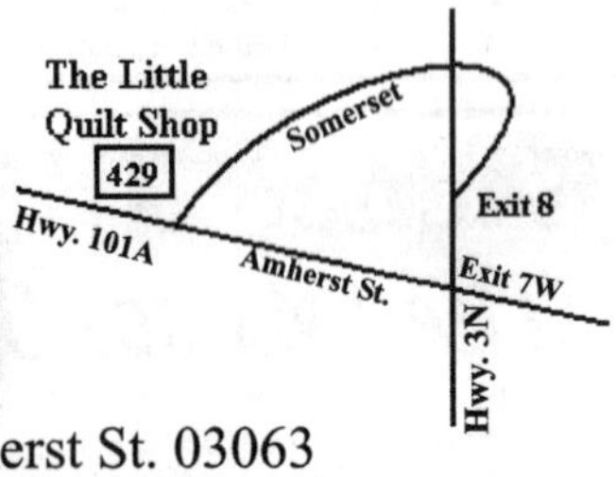

Mon - Sat 9:30 - 5:30
Tues til 9

429 Amherst St. 03063
(603) 886-6084 Fax: (603) 886-6085
E-mail: info@fatquarters.com
Web Site: www.thelittlequiltshop.com
Owner: Shirley Collins

Salem, NH #16

Mon - Fri 10 - 5
Wed til 7
Sept - May
Sat 10 - 4

Audreys *Sewing Studio and Vacuum Center*

26 Ermer Rd. (Rt. 111) 03079
(603) 898-0777 Fax: (603) 894-6933
Audrey@audreys.com www.audreys.com
Owner: Audrey Gordon Mgr: Sue Walch
Est: 1987 5000 sq.ft.

We feature a large variety of sewing and embroidery machines, unlimited lessons, 100% cottons, Books and patterns, Quilting classes & cabinets.

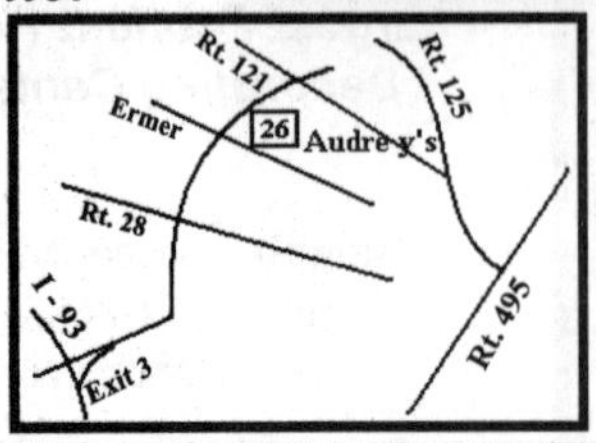

Other Shops in New Hampshire: We suggest calling first

Andover	Wilcox Farm Quilts, Rt. 11, 322 Main St.	603-735-5891
Bedford	Saginaw Quilted Apple, 99 Powder Hill Rd.	
Bedford	Martin's House of Cloth, 4 Ridgewood Rd.	603-669-4127
Bedford	The Patchworks, 133 Bedford Center Rd.	603-472-3002
Center Barnstead	Barn Door Quilting, 665 Barn Door Gap Rd	603-269-3480
Concord	Bittersweet Fabric Shop, 8 Cottage St.	603-753-4920
Derry	Ben Franklin, 121 W. Broadway	603-432-2650
Exeter	Fabrications by Annette, 140 Epping Rd #5	603-772-5200
Guild	The Dorr Mill Store, P.O. Box 88	800-846-3677
Hillsboro	Apple Tree Fabrics, 70 Old Drift Way	603-478-5552
Nashua	Covered Bridge Quilting Shop, 449 Amherst St.	603-889-0765
Sanbornville	Needleworks, 126 Witchtrot Rd	603-788-2965
Tamworth	Patchwork House, Rt. 16	603-367-9269

16 Featured Shops

New Jersey

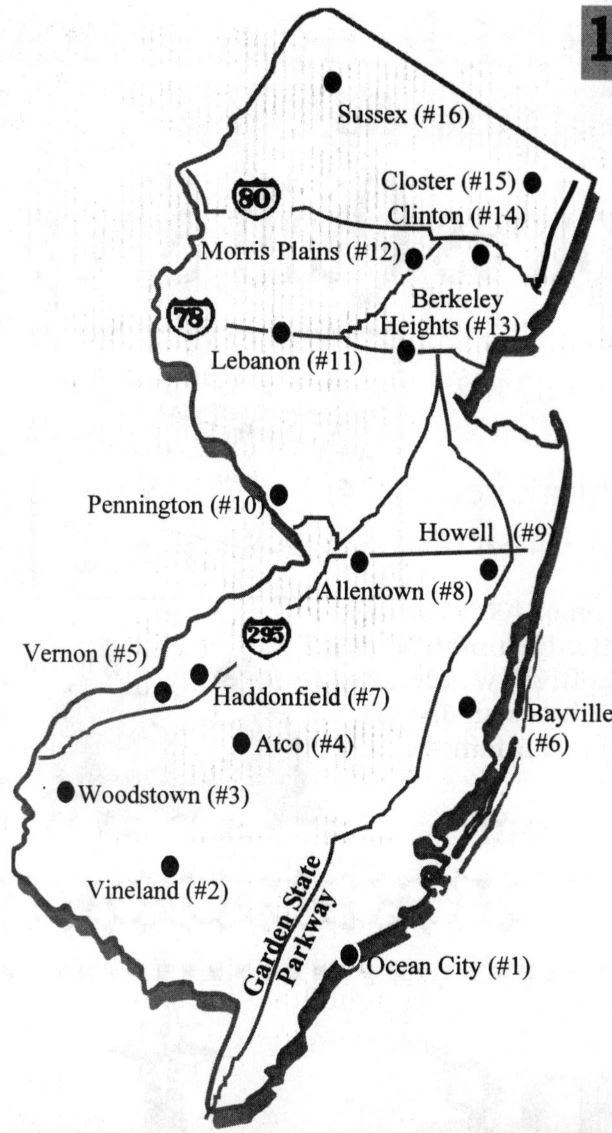

Ocean City, NJ #1

Calico 'N Cotton

715 Asbury Ave. 08226

(609) 399-7166

Owner: Holly Flanders

Est: 1990 1900 sq.ft.

Summer
Mon - Fri 10 - 5
Sat 10 - 5
Sun 12 - 4

Winter
Mon - Sat 10 - 5
Sun 12 - 4

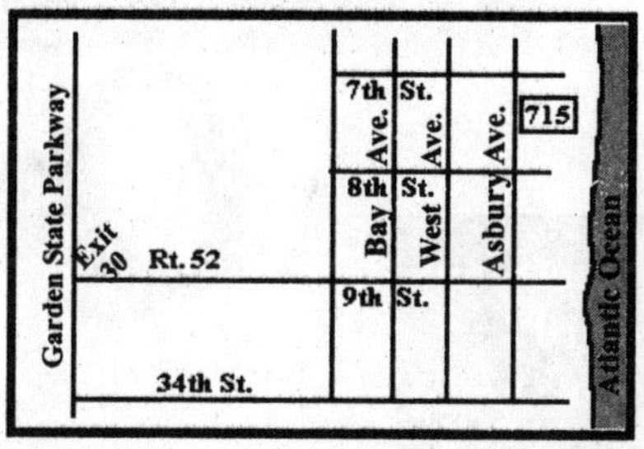

1500 Bolts of 100% Cotton

Classes ◆ Books ◆ Notions

Craft Patterns ◆ Gifts

Vineland, NJ #2

The Pin Cushion

Mon - Fri 9:30 - 6
Thur til 8
Sat 9:30 - 5:30

36 Landis Ave. 08360
(856) 692-5460
Est: 1972 4000 sq.ft.
2000 Bolts (Quilt Prints)

Dress, Bridal, Quilt Fabrics.
Notions, Patterns & Accessories.

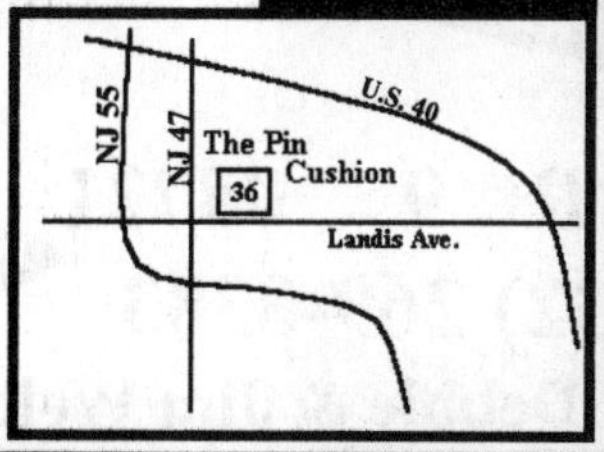

Woodstown, NJ #3

Tues - Fri 10 - 4
Sat 10 - 3

4 S. Main St. 08098
(856) 769-9901

Pieceful Stitches
A Quilt Shop

Owner:
Kristine DeJohn

This quilt shop is filled with classes, fabric, books, & patterns topped off with lots of laughter. A great day out. Woodstown is a wonderful small home town.

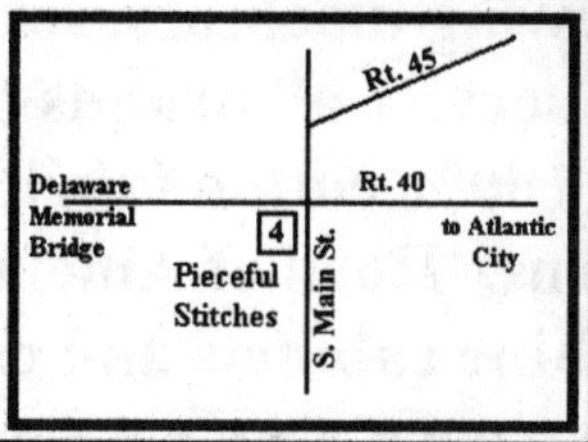

Atco, NJ #4

T, W, Th 10 - 5
Fri 12 - 7
Sat 10 - 3

Quilted Treasures Inc.

416 Raritan Ave. 08004
(856) 768-2222
Owner: Lynn Hannigan

Small but growing Quilt Shop offering quilting Fabric, Lessons and Supplies.

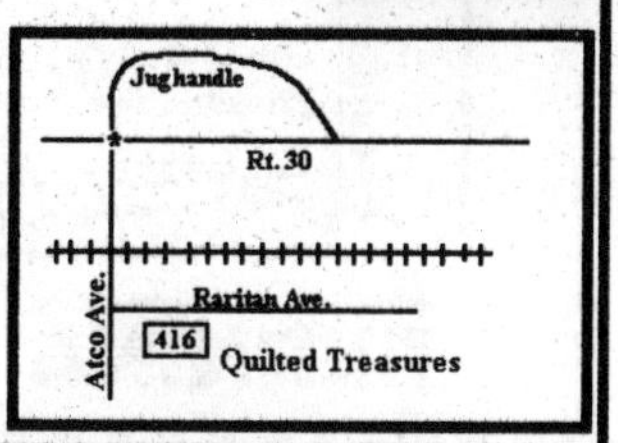

Est: 2001

Vernon, NJ #5

Pieceful Choices Quilt Shop

Tues & Wed 10 - 5
Thurs 10 - 8
Fri 10 - 7
Sat 10 - 4
Sun 11 - 2

99 Route 94, Vernon, NJ 07462
(973) 823-9297
E-mail: moestuf@earthlink.net
Owners: Maureen & Jon Lasslett

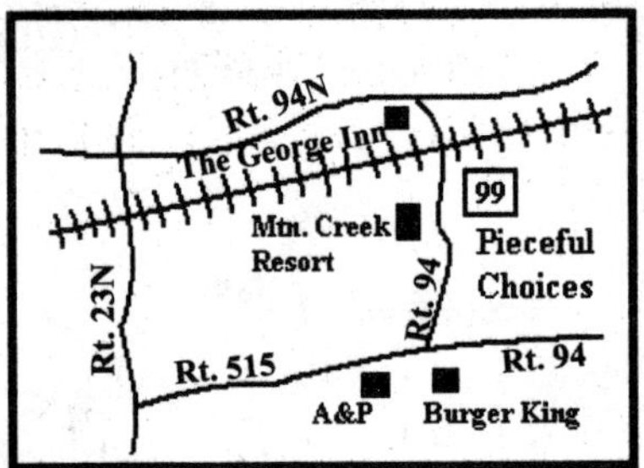

A country quilt shop with a beautiful selection of 100% cottons, books, notions, patterns, kits and quilter's gifts. "Thimbleberries Corner", custom made quilt hangers & "primitive" woodcrafts. Vintage linens, quilts for sale, and lots of antiques on display. Classes & delightful gatherings. Come browse our famous "Fat Quarter Wall".

www.piecefulchoices.com

Bayville, NJ #6

Quilting Possibilities

Tues - Sat
10 - 5
Sun 12 - 4

500 Rt. 9 08721
(732) 269-8383

Owners: Debbie & Jim Welch
E-Mail: qps@quiltingposs.com

Est: 1994
3300 sq.ft.

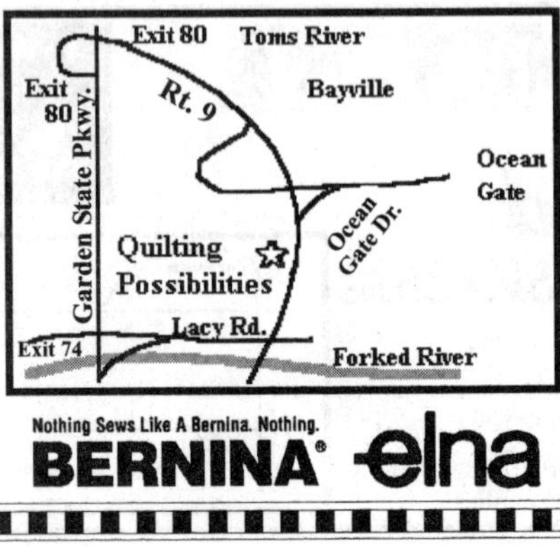

Nothing Sews Like A Bernina. Nothing.
BERNINA® elna

Web Site: www.quiltingposs.com

We are an authorized Bernina and Elna dealer, and carry a full line of sewing machines, sergers, and supplies. We repair and service all brands of sewing machines. Name Brand 100% cotton fabric (4000+ bolts), books, notions, patterns. Horn of American and Koala Sewing machine cabinets and cutting tables.

Haddonfield, NJ #7

The Little Shop

Mon - Sat 10 - 5
Sun 12:30 - 4
Class Nights 7 - 9

143 Kings Hwy. East 08033
(856) 429-7573 Est: 1960
Owner: Deborah Hagy Hansen 1700 sq.ft.

10 minutes from Philadelphia. Quality cotton fabric. Instruction & Gifts. All the latest books & notions.

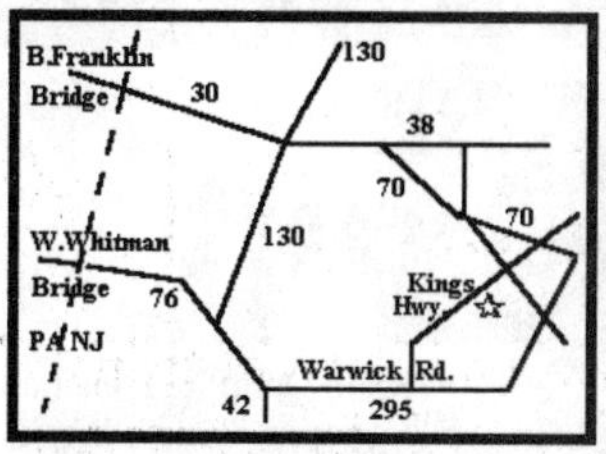

Visit our website at: "Littlequiltshop.com"
e-mail us at: LSQUILTS@aol.com

Allentown, NJ #8

Quilter's Barn

Tues - Sat
9:30 - 4
Thur til 7:30
Sun 12 - 5
Closed Sun July & Aug

34 South Main St.
P.O. Box 295 08501
(609) 259-2504 Est: 1975
qbpatti@aol.com
www.Quiltersbarn.com

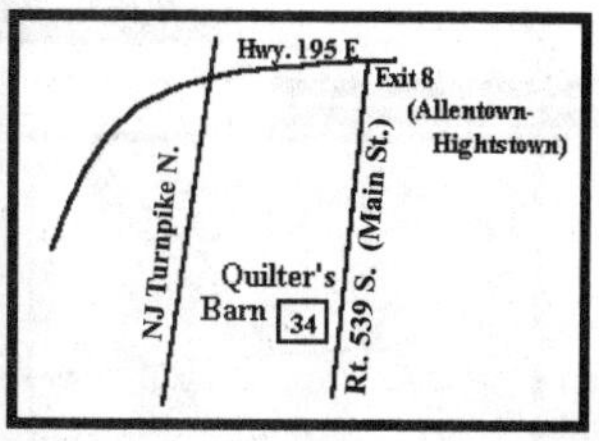

Over 1,500 bolts of fabric, Books
Patterns Notions
Batting Classes
Blocks of the Month
Friendly personal service

Howell, NJ #9

Beary Unique Quilt Shoppe

Tues - Sat 10 - 4
Sun 12 - 3

4134 Route 9 South in Howell Plaza
(732) 905-5445
E-Mail: BearyUniqueQS@aol.com
Web Site: www.bearyuniquequiltshop.com
Owner: Rebecca Szabo
Est: 2000 1100 sq.ft. 500+ Bolts
A Quilt Shop Just for You!
The finest quilting cottons and supplies. A 500 sq.ft. classroom and bear/dollmaking supplies!

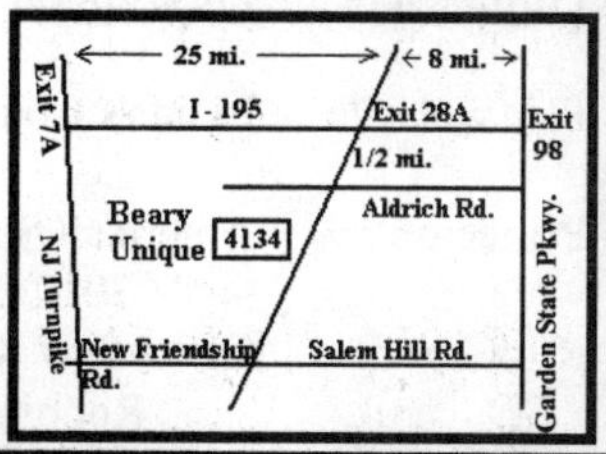

Pennington, NJ #10

Pennington Quilt Works

Mon - Thur 10 - 5
Fri 10 - 7
Sat 10 - 4
Sun 12 - 4

Pennytown Shopping Village
Route 31 North
(609) 466-5722
E-Mail: pqworks@aol.com
Owner: Jan Crane Est: 1996

Wonderful selection of fabrics, books and supplies. All the basics, but always something new. Fun Classes. Warm expert service.

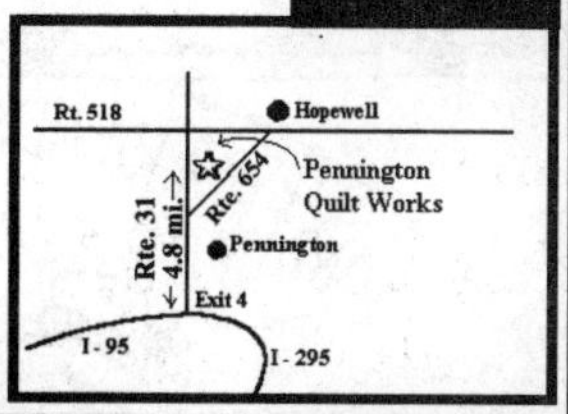

Lebanon, NJ #11

Budding Star Quilts

Mon - Sat 10 - 5:30
Sun 1 - 4

Rt. 22 E, Lebanon Plaza 08833
(908) 236-7676
Web Site: www.buddingstarquilts.com
Owner: Kathy Verser Est: 1987 2000+ Bolts

We Specialize in Kits for all Levels!

Thimbleberries Club

Over 2000 Bolts 100% Cotton Fabric.
Large selection of flannels.
Classes. We carry all current Thimbleberries Fabrics and products.

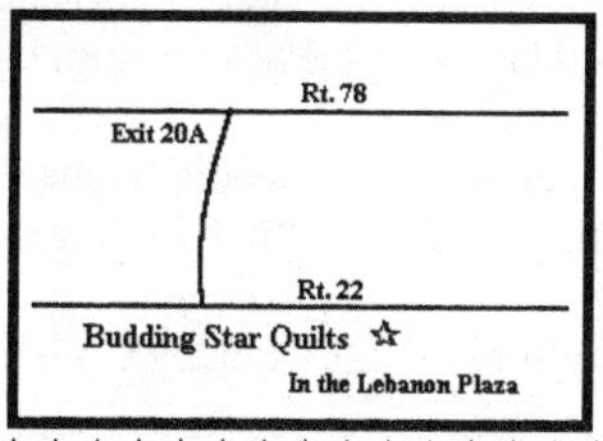

Morris Plains, NJ #12

Aardvark & C.

Mon - Sat 10 - 7

748 Speedwell Ave. 07950
(973) 539-9033
Owner: Sally Alworth
Est: 1987 3400 sq.ft. 3000 Bolts

Great selection of fabrics, books, notions and classes. Also cross stitch, lace and ribbons. 30 minutes from NYC.

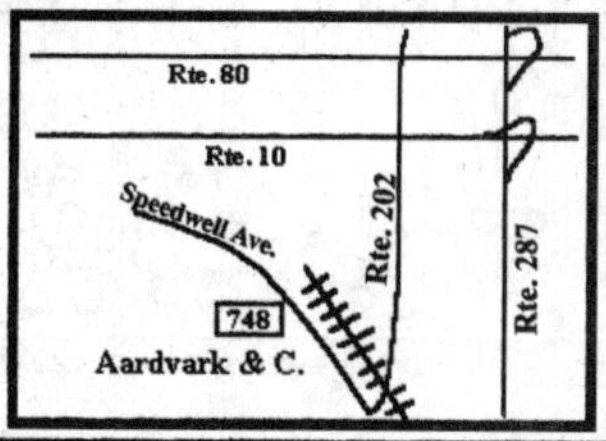

Berkeley Heights, NJ #13

Quilt Connection

Tues - Fri 10 - 5
Thur til 9
Sat 10 - 4
Sun 12 - 4

Fabulous selection of fine cottons including Alexander Henry, Hoffman Batiks, P&B, & Kaufman. Classes, notions, books & patterns. Gift Items especially for quilters. Janome dealership.

432F Springfield Ave. 07922
(908) 286-0200
Fax: (908) 286-1100
Owner: Sally Davis
Est: 1998
1400 sq.ft. 3000+ bolts

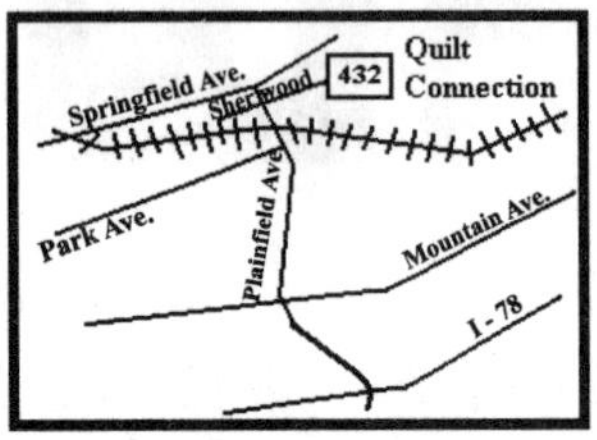

Web Site: www.njquiltconnection.com

Clinton, NJ #14

Kindred Quilts

Mon - Sat 10 - 5
Thur til 7:30
Sun 12 - 4

21 E. Main St. 08809
(908) 730-8896
E-Mail: kindredquilts@att.net
Web Site: www.kindredquilts.com
Owner: Toby Preston
Est: 1999 1500 sq.ft.

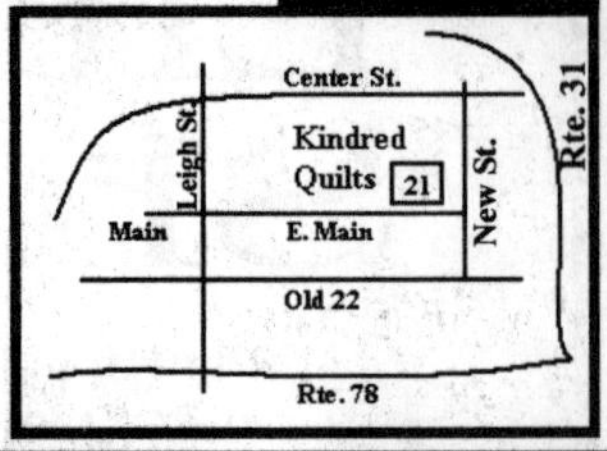

2,000 bolts of 100% cotton fabric, notions, primitive stitcheries, hand-dyed fabrics, as well as wool-felt for penny rugs.

Closter, NJ #15

Quilt Plus

Mon - Fri 10 - 6
Sat 10 - 5

223 Closter Dock Rd. 07624
(201) 767-0506
Fax: (201) 767-1781

E-Mail: QuiltPlus@mail.com
Owner: Connie Woo

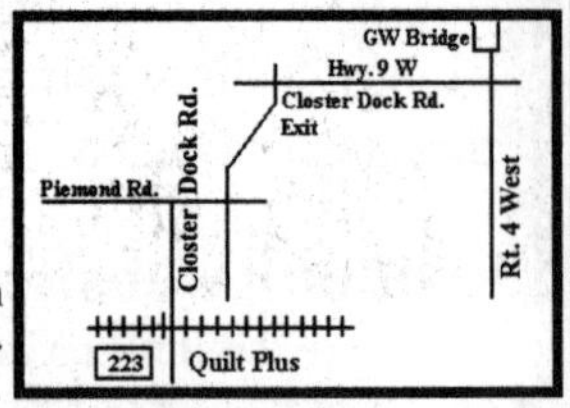

Only quilt Shop in Bergen County! Selected High Quality Fabrics. Unique Japanese Fabrics. Sashiko Books & Patterns. Special Bag Supplies.

Sussex, NJ #16

Ben Franklin®

Mon - Sat 9 - 9
Sun 10-5

455 Rt. 23, A & P Plaza 07461
(973) 875-7444 Fax: (973) 875-1500
E-Mail: BenFranklin45@aol.com

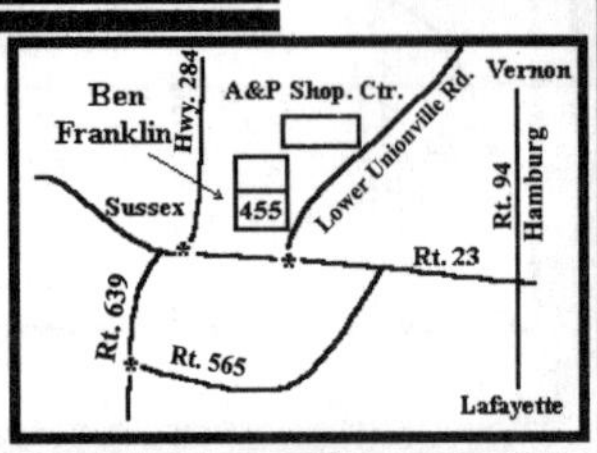

1700+ Bolts 100% cotton - Hoffman, South Seas, etc. 2000+ ribbons, laces, & trims. Full line Kunin felt, gifts, framing, special orders. Large Craft Department.

Other Shops In New Jersey: We suggest calling first

Bedminster	Lamington General Store, 285 Lamington Rd. 523 Rt.	908-439-2034
Blairstown	Needle Niche, 28 Main St.	908-362-8773
Bridgeton	Broad Meadows Country Fabrics 100 Mary Elmer Dr.	856-451-2433
Browns Mills	Pastimes, 13 Trenton Rd	609-893-3311
Cape May Courthouse	Quilted Gull, 1909 N. Rt. 9	609-624-1630
Delran	Simply Stitches, 263 Southview Dr.	
Denville	Bows, Bits & Stitches, 9 Broadway	
Elmer	The Fabric Place, 160 Dutch Row Rd.	609-358-7375
Elmer	Mothers & Daughters Quilting, 131 Elmer St.	856-358-6113
Forked River	Country Sisters, 110 N. Main	609-693-7224
Hackensack	Julia's Fabrics, 137 Main St.	201-487-4110
Hightstown	Pat's Custom Crafts, 100 Harron Ave.	609-448-5441
Hopatcong	Needle Niche, P.O. Box 592	973-398-8412
Lakewood	Stitch N'Sew Center, 123 E County Line Rd	732-363-2220
Medford	Country Collection, 109 Route 70	609-654-1414
Mercerville	Sew DiffRent, 528 Hwy 33	609-586-1440
Milford	Azimoon Fabrics, 246 Hickory Corner Rd.	908-996-3062
North Plainfield	Fabric Land, 855 Rte. 22	908-755-4700
Phillipsburg	Prescription Quilts, 105 Cty Rd. 519	908-995-9650
Pleasantville	Lynda's Country Corner, 39 E. Verona Ave.	609-645-2058
Princeton	American Sewing & Vacuum Center 301 N. Harrison St.	609-921-2205
Rio Grande	Olsen Sew & Vac Center, 1121 Rt. 47 S. Robbins Nest Plaza	609-886-5510
Scotch Plains	Cozy Corner Creations Quilt Shop 425 Park Ave.	908-322-8480
Somerville	Millstone Workshop, 1393 Main St.	908-874-3649
Westfield	Village Curtains, 509 Central	908-789-2555

NEW MEXICO

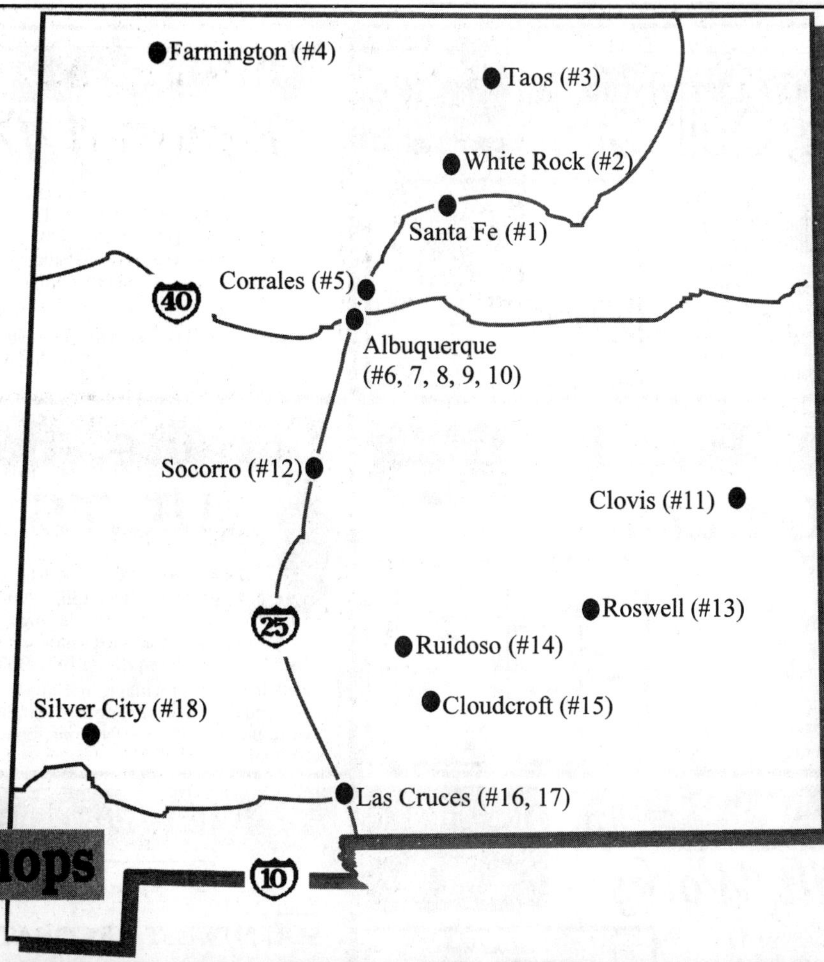

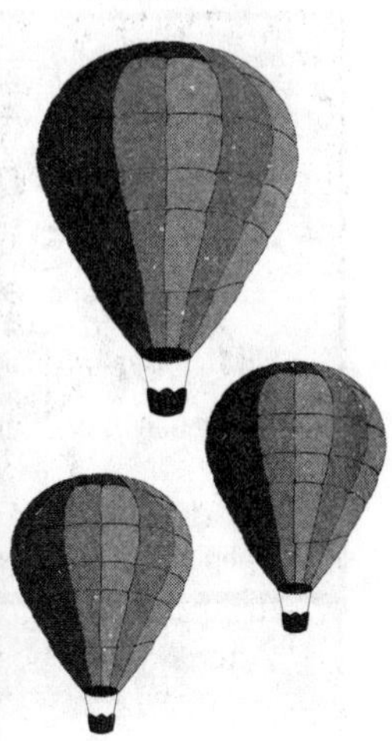

18 Featured Shops

Santa Fe Quilting, Inc.

3018-A Cielo Court, Santa Fe, NM 87507
(505) 473-3747
Fax: (505) 995-0257 E-Mail: allen14w@cybermesa.com
Owners: Mary McCusker & Allen Winchester
Est: 2000 2000 sq.ft. 3000 Bolts

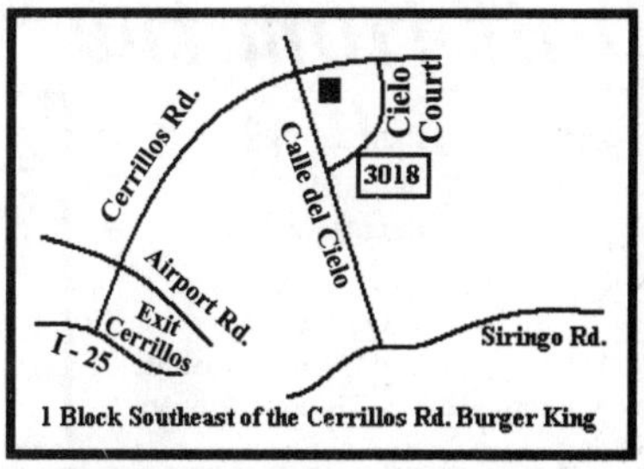

Mon - Sat 10 - 5:30 Thur til 9 Sun 2 - 5

Bright cottons, including a wide selection of Batiks. Cottons from Japan. Oriental and Southwest Fabrics and Patterns. Sashiko Supplies, Numerous Flannels. Books & Time Saving Notions. Block of the Month Kits & Classes. Sewing Machines available for classroom use by travelers. Fabrics from most major fabric companies are available in our store.

Santa Fe, NM #1

White Rock, NM #2

Tues - Fri 10 - 5:30
Sat 10 - 4:30

PANDY'S Quilt Store

13 Sherwood Blvd. 87544
(505) 672-2004 Est: 1999
E-Mail: pandy@pandysquiltstore.com
Web Site: www.pandysquiltstore.com
Owner: Pandy Lolos 1600 sq.ft. 1200 Bolts

We carry brights, batiks, marbles and oriental fabrics plus PFAFF sewing machines.

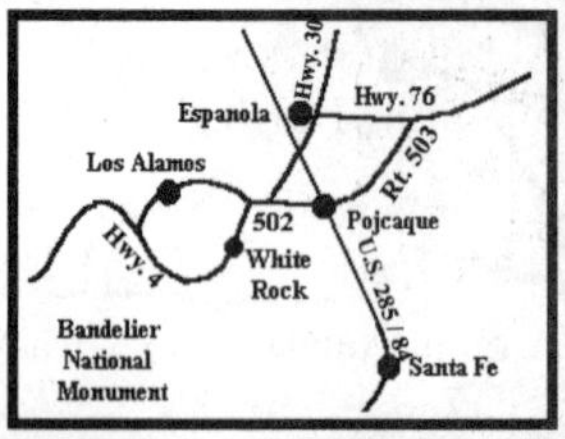

Taos, NM #3

Mon - Sat 10:30 - 5:30
Sun 12 - 4

Taos Adobe

102 Teresina Lane 87571
(505) 751-3219 Fax: Same
E-Mail: taostogs@taosnet.com
Owners: Peter & Jan O'Donohue

Features Quilts, southwestern and juvenile fabrics in 100% cotton and hard to find prints.

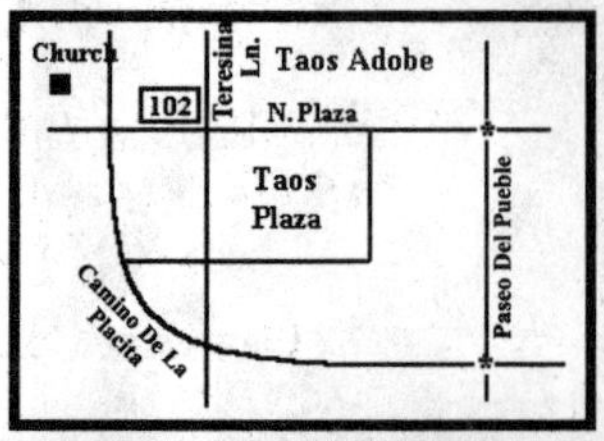

Farmington, NM #4

Open Tues - Sat

Quilt Garden

2501 E. 20th St., Suite 7 87401
(505) 325-2116
Owner: Judy Schlotterback
Est: 1997
1400 sq. ft. 1500-1800 Bolts.

Let us help you with your quilting ideas. Fabrics, notions, books, patterns to inspire and stimulate quilters of all levels.

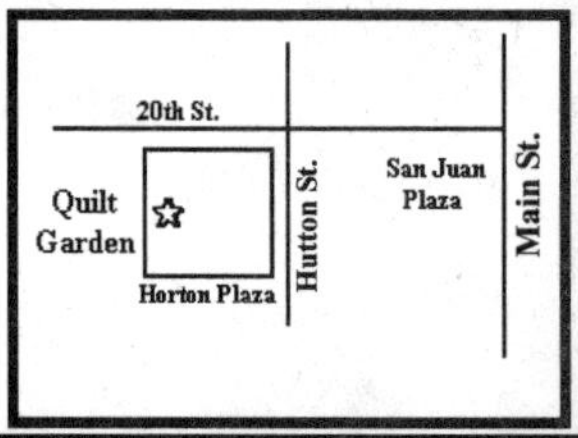

Corrales, NM #5

Mon - Fri 10 - 5:30
Sat 10 - 5
Sun 12 - 4

QUILTS OLE'

4908 Corrales Rd. 87048
(505) 890-9416 Fax: (505) 890-9451
Web Site www.quiltsole.com
Owner: Cathy Gormley
Est: 2000 1500 sq.ft. 1400+ Bolts

Located in a quaint village, northwest of Albuquerque. Specializing in brights, batiks & unusual prints. Notions, books, classes too!

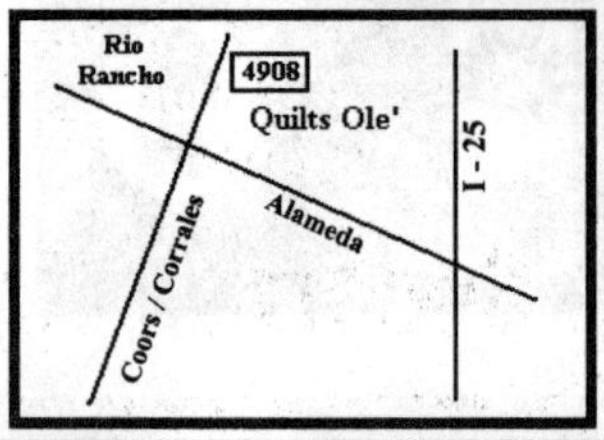

Albuquerque, NM #6

Mon - Fri 9 - 6
Sat 9 - 5
Sun 2 - 5

The Quilt Works

11117 Menaul N.E. 87112
(505) 298-8210
E-Mail: quilt@thuntek.net
Web Site: www.quiltworksabq.com
Est: 1985 1750 sq.ft.
Owner: Shirley Brabson

We have over 3000 bolts of cotton fabric. We're Friendly and Helpful !

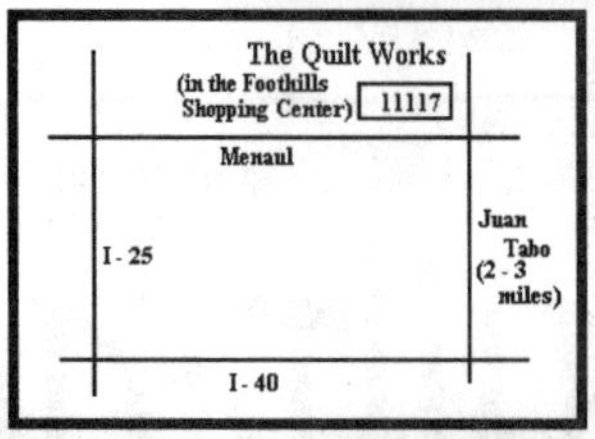

Albuquerque, NM #7

Mon - Sat 9 - 5
Sun By Appt.

SOUTHWEST DECORATIVES

5711 Carmel Ave. NE, Ste. B 87113
(505) 821-7400 Fax: (505) 821-6556
E-Mail: swd@swdecoratives.com
Web Site: www.swdecoratives.com
Owner: Mary-Jo McCarthy
Est: 2001 3700 sq.ft. 1800 Bolts

Beautiful Southwest theme fabrics, patterns and lots more! Catalog $3

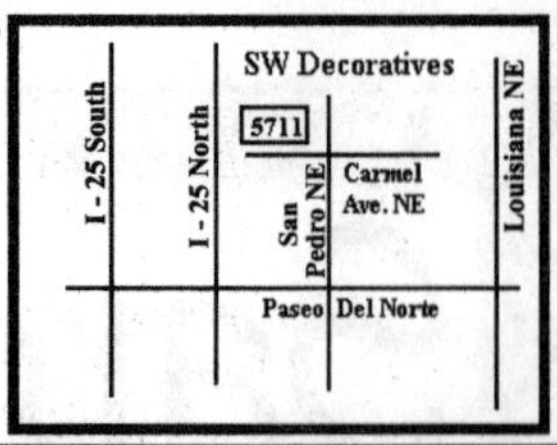

Albuquerque, NM #8

Mon - Sat 10 - 5
Sun 2 - 5

Quilt from the ♥

417 Tramway NE #1 87123
(505) 292-8560
Owner: Leta Brazell

A Full Service Quilt Shop !
Quilts for Sale, Custom Quilts, Finishing, Classes, Fabric, Books, Notions & More.

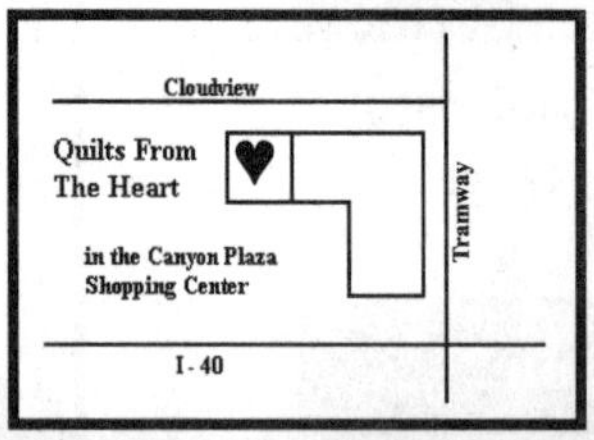

Albuquerque, NM #9

Mon - Thur 9 - 8
Fri & Sat 9 - 5
Sun 12 - 5

Ann Silva's Bernina Sewing Center

3101 Menaul NE 87107
(505) 881-5253 Fax: (505) 881-3127
E-Mail: silvainc@nmia.com Est: 1980
Web Site: www.annsilvasbernina.com
Owner: Ann Silva 6600 sq.ft. 1500+ Bolts

Top ranking Bernina dealership. We carry a complete line of Bernina accessories. Specializing in Southwestern fabrics, patterns, books, threads & more!

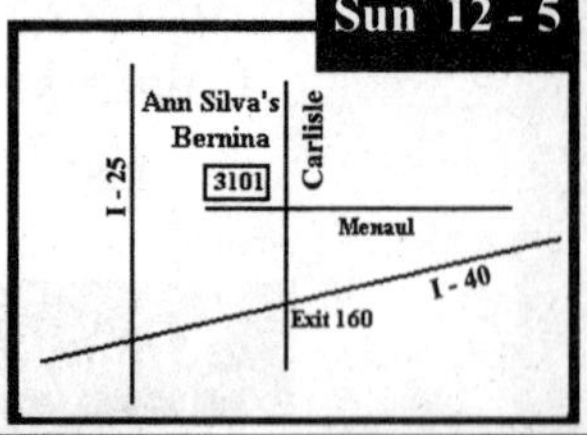

Albuquerque, NM #10

Mon - Fri 10 - 6
Sat 10 - 5
Sun 12 - 5

A Quilter's Affaire Inc.

12500 Montgomery 87111
(505) 292-8925
Owner: Kathy Heger
Est: 1994
2500 sq.ft.

Featuring over 1500 bolts of fabric, notions, books, & patterns for quilting and crafting. Classes Too!

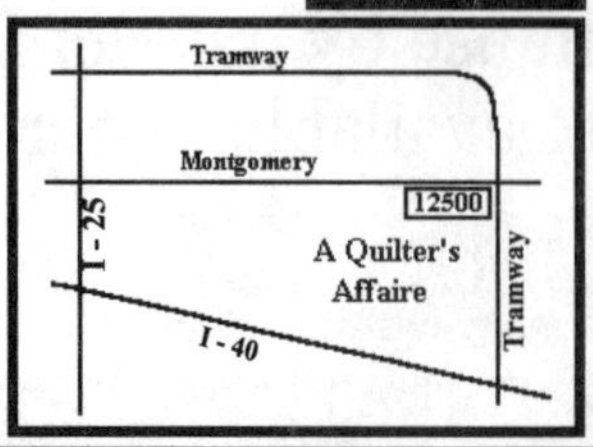

Clovis, NM #11

Mon - Sat 10 -5

The Patchwork House

519 Main St. 88101
(505) 769-8072
E-Mail: judym@plateautel.net
Owner: Judy Matthews

Best Selection of Quality Quilting Fabrics, Books, Patterns, Notions for 100 miles. Classes and custom Quilting Service Avail.

Bobbie's Bobbin

108 N. California St. 87801
(505) 838-0001 Fax: (505) 838-1094
E-Mail: bbobbin@zianet.com
Owners: Bobbie & Gary Stendel

Custom embroidery, Sensational Fabrics, Quilters Supplies, Notions, Books, Beads and Sewing Machine Service/Repair.
"Best Little Sewing Store in Socorro!"

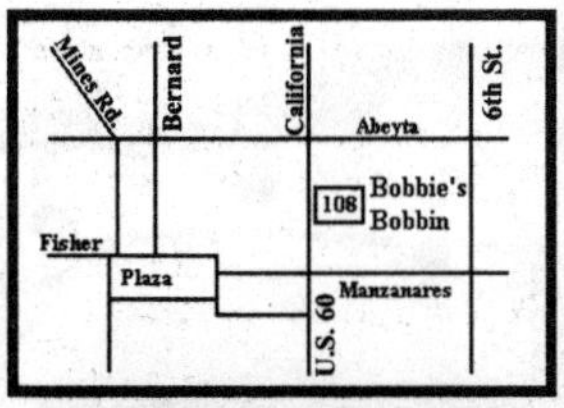

Mon - Sat 10 - 6

Socorro, NM #12

Roswell, NM #13

Mon - Fri 10 - 5 Sat 10 - 3

Calico Cow Quilt Shop

318 N. Main 88201
(505) 623-8647 Est: 2001
E-Mail: Carolynnoling@aol.com
Owner: Carolyn Pollard Noling

Cotton Fabrics, Flannels, Notions, Books & Patterns.

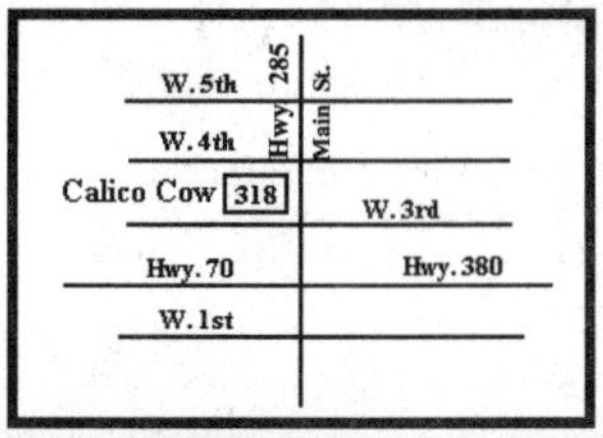

Ruidoso, NM #14

Ruth Ann's Originals

Fabrics, Books, Patterns, Quilting Supplies, Quilts
May - Sept. we have 5 great teachers for lessons. Original Designed Clothing from Ladybugs.

Mon - Sat 10 - 5 May 1 - Oct 15 Sundays 10 - 3

2511 Sudderth 88345
(505) 257-0568
Fax: Same
Ruth Ann Crumpton
Est: 1996 1500 sq.ft.
500 Bolts + Hand Dyed Fabrics

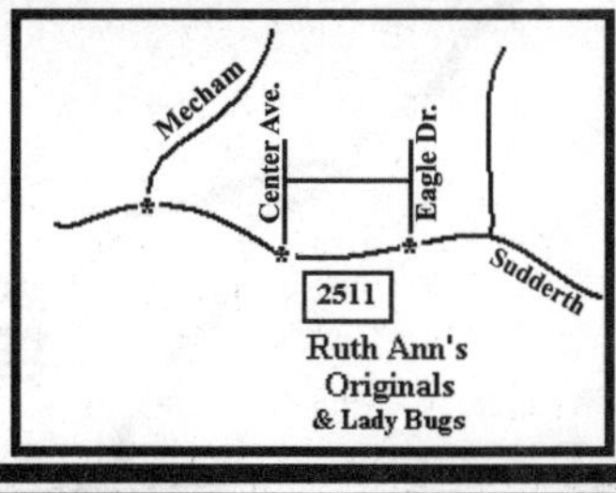

Cloudcroft, NM #15

Daily 10 - 5

The Scrap Basket

Located in Pine Stump Mall
300 Burro, P.O. Box 478 88317
(505) 682-1468
E-Mail: pdrake@pvtnetworks.net
Web Site: www.pvtnetworks.net/~pdrake

Small shop in a mountain village.
Retail Quilts, Fabric, Supplies, Related Gifts, Books & Patterns & Classes

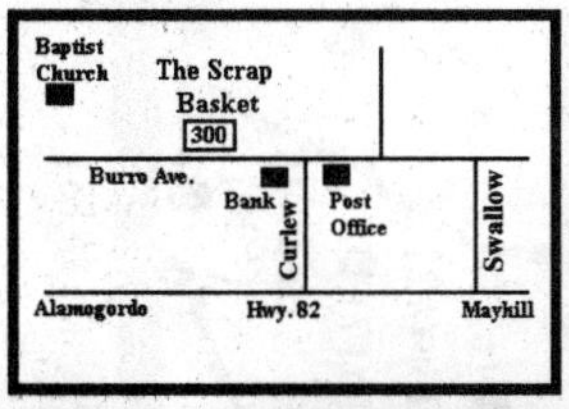

Las Cruces, NM #16

Sun - Fri 12 - 5 Sat 9 - 5

Soft Creations

207 Avenida de Mesilla 88005
(505) 525-8155
E-Mail: tinadal@zianet.com
Owner: Tina Dalcour
Est: 1996 2000+ sq.ft.

Come for inspiration, ideas and the greatest place to buy supplies and fabric!

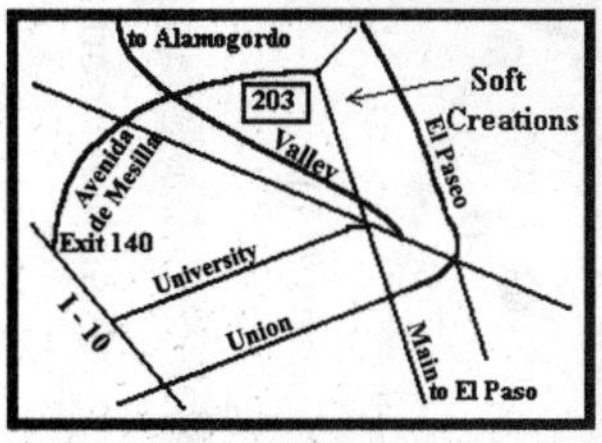

Las Cruces, NM #17

Mon - Sat 10 - 5

Desert Threads Quilt Shop

151 S. Solano, Suite G 88001
(505) 524-3473
Fax: (505) 524-3493
E-Mail: desertthreads@cs.com
Web Site: www.desertthreads.com
Owners: Nancy Elkin & Laura Michalik
Est: 1997 1700 sq.ft.

Centrally located in Las Cruces we have the area's largest selection of southwest fabric, patterns and kits. Classes. Elna Machines.

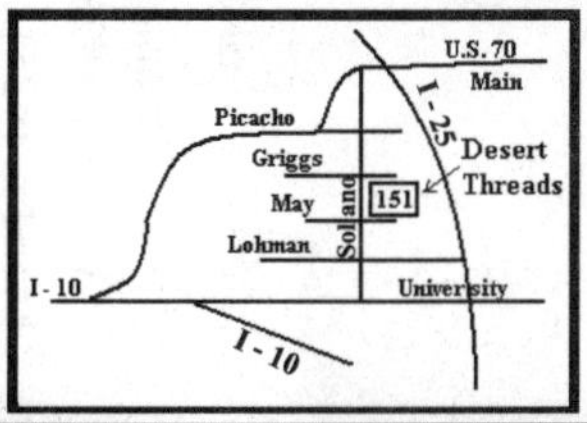

Other Shops in New Mexico: We suggest calling first

Albuquerque	Quiltiques, 6040 Aspen Ave. NE	505-266-7276
Angel Fire	Forever Treasures, 13 Halo Pines Ter., PO Box 63	505-377-1125
Belen	Bar NM Square, P.O. Box 975	
Carlsbad	Chrisden Craft, 1316 W. Mermod St.	505-885-0789
Chama	Little Foot Ltd., P.O. Box 1027	505-756-1412
Farmington	Quilted Threads, 5501 Evergreen Dr.	505-325-4490
Farmington	Apple Barn, 5991 Hwy. 64	505-632-9631
Lincoln	Lincolnworks, PO Box 32	505-653-4693
Los Cruces	Karen's Creative Fabrics, 1424 Missouri Ave.	505-541-0854
Raton	Quilter's Keepsakes, 104 Pecos Ave.	505-445-2092
Santa Fe	Moxie, 205 W. San Francisco St.	505-986-9265
Santa Fe	The Bedroom, 304 Catron St.	505-984-0207
Taos	Yukio's, 226 Pasio Del Puello Norte, P.O. Box 3123	505-758-2269

Silver City, NM #18

Mon - Sat 9 - 5

Thunder Creek Quilt Company

1330 N. Hudson St. 88061
(505) 538-2284 or (800) 376-4201
Owners: Cindy Ugarte & Nancy Coryell
Est: 1995 700+ Bolts

Specializing in Southwestern Fabrics & Patterns. Cotton Fabric. Notions, Sulky & Gutermann Threads. Gingher Scissors. Classes. Gifts.

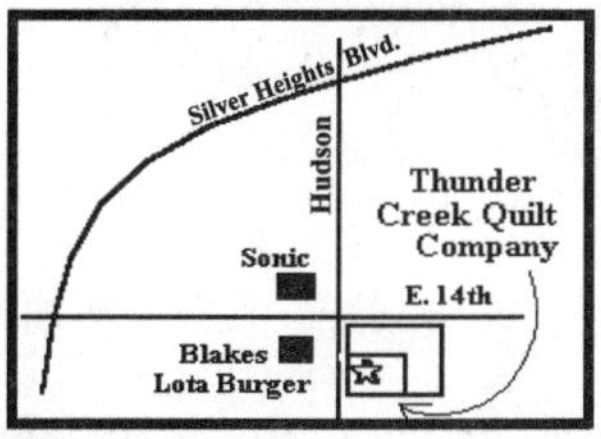

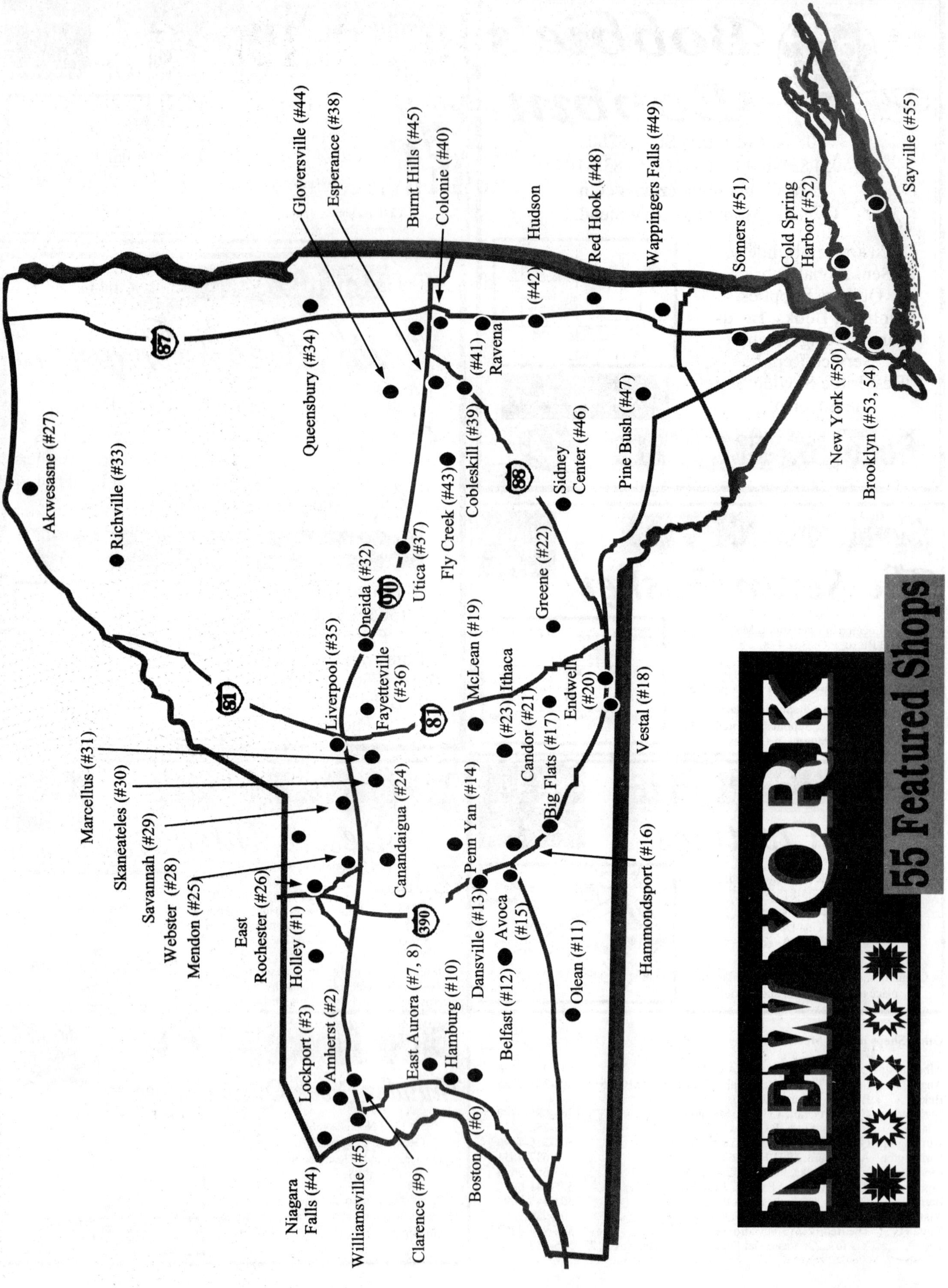
NEW YORK
55 Featured Shops
Niagara Falls (#4)
Williamsville (#5)
Clarence (#9)
Boston (#6)
Lockport (#3)
Amherst (#2)
East Aurora (#7, 8)
Hamburg (#10)
Belfast (#12)
Olean (#11)
Holley (#1)
East Rochester (#26)
Mendon (#25)
Webster (#28)
Savannah (#29)
Skaneateles (#30)
Marcellus (#31)
Dansville (#13)
Avoca (#15)
Hammondsport (#16)
Canandaigua (#24)
Penn Yan (#14)
Big Flats (#17)
Candor (#21)
(#23)
Vestal (#18)
Endwell (#20)
Ithaca
McLean (#19)
Liverpool (#35)
Fayetteville (#36)
Oneida (#32)
Greene (#22)
Utica (#37)
Fly Creek (#43)
Sidney Center (#46)
Cobleskill (#39)
Akwesasne (#27)
Richville (#33)
Queensbury (#34)
Gloversville (#44)
Esperance (#38)
Burnt Hills (#45)
Colonie (#40)
(#41) Ravena
Hudson
(#42)
Red Hook (#48)
Pine Bush (#47)
Wappingers Falls (#49)
Somers (#51)
Cold Spring Harbor (#52)
New York (#50)
Brooklyn (#53, 54)
Sayville (#55)
81
87
88
90
390

Apple Country Quilt Shop & Café

Authorized Gammill Quilting Systems Dealer

Remember us on your next road trip!
51 State St. (Route 31 on the curve)
Holley, NY 14470
1-585-638-5262
Toll free 1-866-340-6100
www.applecountryquilts.com

Tues - Sat 10 - 4

Holley, NY #1

Apple Country Quilt Shop & Café has so much more to offer. Now boasting over 1500 bolts of the best quilters cottons, notions, books, quilting classes and long arm classes. You can also take a test drive on a new Gammill Quilting Machine. Only 20 minutes off the New York State Thruway exit 48 coming from the west or 35 minutes west of Rochester. Visit us on the web at www.applecountryquilts.com from there you can access a map, send us an email or see what we have in store in the up coming months including classes, sales, dinner specials and the like!

Our Café is open during shop hours and for dinners Friday & Saturday 4:30 - 7:30 pm After you have completely indulged yourselves in quilting goodies stop in at the Apple Country Café for a delectable lunch. Homemade soups, sandwiches and our Chef Vicki's specials of the week. Then how about one of our many totally Homemade desserts, all done right here in house by our own pastry chef Carol. Everything from Crème Brule to our always favorite bread puddings.

Amherst, NY #2

Visit Us At: www.
threadsoftimesewing.com

Threads of Time

Mon - Fri 10 - 9
Sat 10 - 5

Northtown Plaza,
3125 Sheridan Dr. 14226
(716) 837-1372
Email - tot@buffnet.net
Owners: Mari Wojcik & Jeanette Rogers

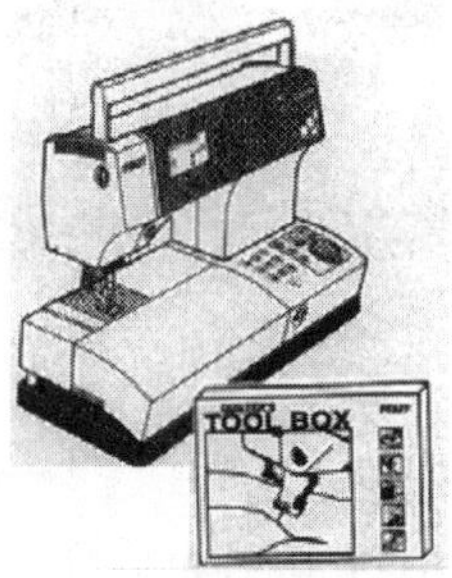

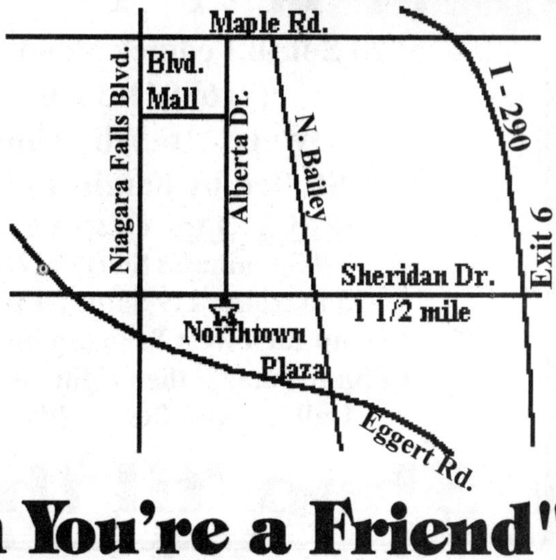

We carry over 3500 of bolts of fine cotton fabrics for all your quilt dreams.
Classes, books, patterns, a great variety of threads, notions & . . . lots of ideas.
PFAFF Authorized Sales & Service

"If You're a Quilter -- Then You're a Friend"

Lockport, NY #3

5410 Stone Rd. 14094
(716) 433-5377
Owner: Judith Farnham
Est: 1982

Pine Grove Workshop

Mon - Sat 10 - 4:30

2000 Bolts 100% Cotton
Old and New Quilts
Hundreds of Books, Patterns, & Notions
Classes—Spring Seminar

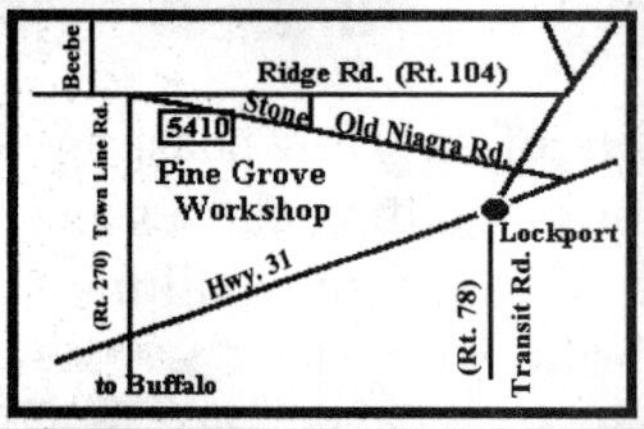

Niagara Falls, NY #4

Tues 10 - 2:30
Wed & Fri 10 - 8:30
Thur 10 - 4:30
Sat 10 - 3

Quiltmakers & Friends

4716 Military Rd. 14304
(716) 297-4067
Owner: Florence M. Rhodes

Hundreds of bolts — 100% cotton fabrics. Large selection of quilt books, notions, patterns & gifts. Classes offered.

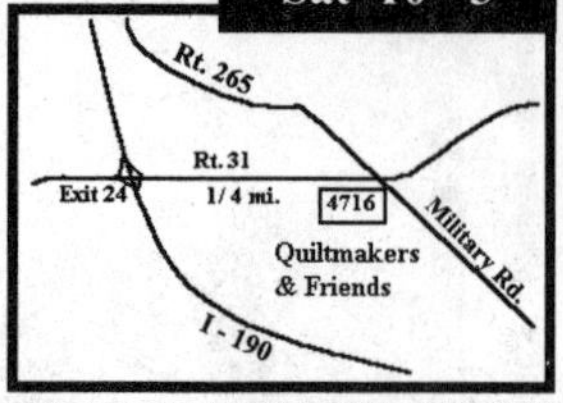

Williamsville, NY #5

Tues & Wed 10 - 8
Thur - Sat 10 - 5

Sew What?

6816 Main Street 14221
(716) 632-8801
Owner: Ann Shaw
Est: 1990 1500 Bolts 1900 sq.ft.

Large selection of unique and unusual quilting fabrics, the newest books and notions. Quilting classes and professional quilting service available.

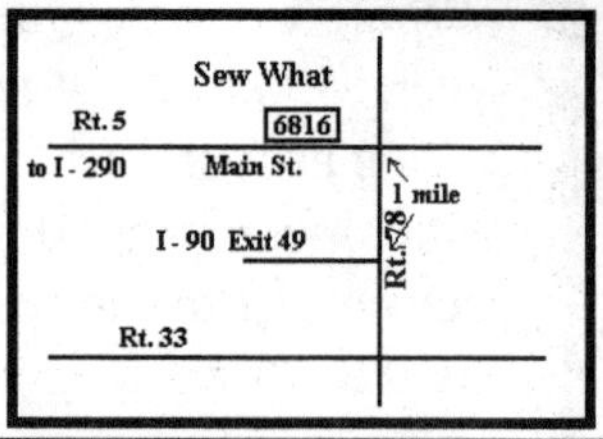

Boston, NY #6

est. 1989
3600 sq.ft.

Tues - Sat 11 - 5
Tues & Thurs evenings til 7
Closed Sun & Mon

The Quilt FARM

"WORTH THE DRIVE"
The Answer to a Quilter's Prayers in God's Country

5623 South Feddick Road 14025
(716) 941-3140
Owner: Isabell Schmit
Staffed by Family and Friends

DIRECTIONS: (a scenic country drive 30 minutes South of Buffalo)
I - 90 to Route 219 South, Exit at Rice Road
Off exit ramp turn west & go (up hill) to first intersection, left on Zimmerman, then right on South Feddick Road
Call for specifics . . . It's a challenge.

A barnful of quilters supplies:
- **... 3,000+ bolts of 100% cotton**
- **... large selection of notions**
- **... elna sewing machines**
- **... 450+ books & patterns plus kits**
- **... Finished and Custom order Quilts**
- **... Origin of "Quilt Farm" Patterns**
- **... Classes**

"Shop 'til the Cows come home."

East Aurora, NY #7

THE CARRIAGE QUILT SHOPPE

593 Main St (By the Viaduct)
East Aurora, NY 14052
(716) 655-4561

- Amish Carriage in shoppe
- Amish quilts
- Amish Mustache Rugs
- Amish Gifts

Machine Quilting Service in Shoppe!

Readymade Quilts
Custom Order Quilts
100% Cotton Fabrics
Books
Patterns
Notions
Classes in the Loft

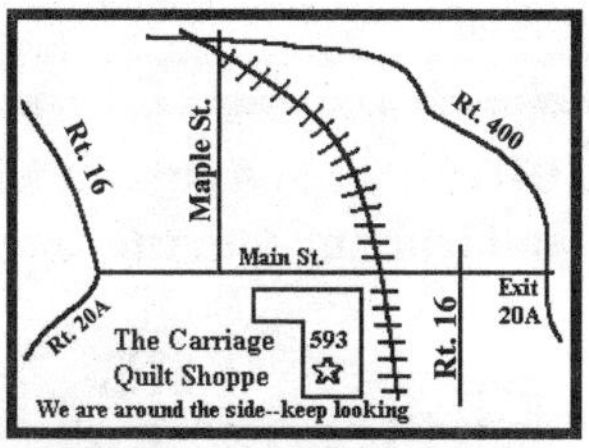

-call for summer hours!

Mon - Fri 10 - 6
Wed 9 - 5 Sat 9 - 4

East Aurora, NY #8

659 Main St. 14052
(716) 652-2811
Fax: (716) 652-2863
Est: 1978 3500 sq.ft.

Clarence, NY #9

10750 Main St. 14031
(716) 759-8081
Fax: (716) 759-1715
Est: 1996
3000 sq.ft.

Aurora Sewing Center

Mon 10 - 8
Thur 10 - 9
Tues, Wed, Fri 10 - 5:30
Sat 10 - 4

Owners: Regis Boire & Barb Perry
www.Aurorasewingcenter.com
E-Mail Questions ASCBARB@aol.com

Stop in and visit our shops — You'll be pleasantly surprised!

- *We have over a 1000 Bolts of fabric to choose from.*
- *Thousands of book titles, quilting, sewing, applique & more.*
- *The latest in craft, quilting, & applique patterns — with lots of displayed samples!*
- *Look-in on our classroom activities — we have over 90 different classes offered each semester.*
- *Bernina sewing machines, sales and service.*
- *Service of all makes and models*
- *Large display of Horn cabinets.*

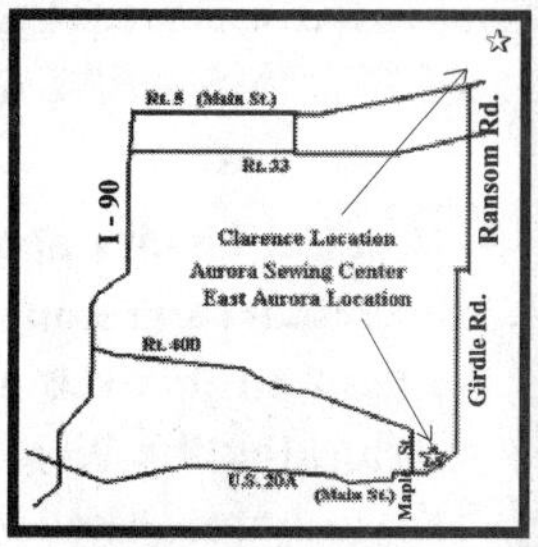

BERNINA®

2 Great Locations ! !

Hamburg, NY #10

Tues - Fri 10 - 5
Thur til 9
Sat 10 - 4

Creative Needleworks

21 Main St. 14075
(716) 646-3013
Toll Free: (866) Stitch'n
E-Mail: cneedleinc@aol.com
Owner: Jane Macchioni Est: 1998

Inspiration abounds for both quilters and cross stitchers in this cozy shop. Friendly, knowledgeable staff welcome your visit!

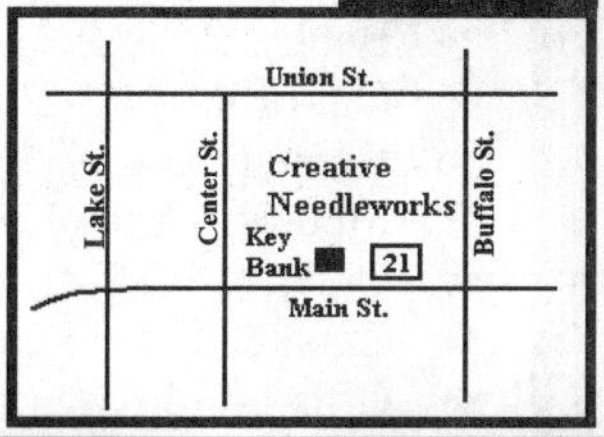

Olean, NY #11

Mon - Thur 10 - 6
Fri 10 - 8
Sat 10 - 4

Pine Tree Quilt Shop

138 N. Union Street 14760
(716) 372-0495
E-Mail: irish10@froggernet.com
Owner: Kathleen Wiley
Est: 2000 1200 sq.ft. 1200 Bolts.

In the heart of the enchanted mountains. A unique shop carrying 100% cotton, books, patterns and gifts.

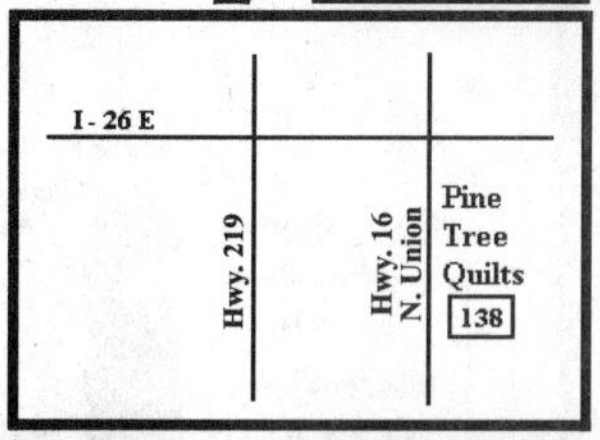

Belfast, NY #12

Mon - Fri 10 - 5
Sat 10 - 4

Quilts and Other Legacies

41 Main St. 14711
(585) 365-2493 Fax: (585) 365-2491
E-Mail: qwbouldin@wnyweb.net
Owner: Gail Wightman-Bouldin
Est: 1998 3200 sq.ft.

Cotton fabrics and supplies quilters love. Wonderful displays of Genesee Traditions Sewing and quilting furniture. Local goods & country hospitality

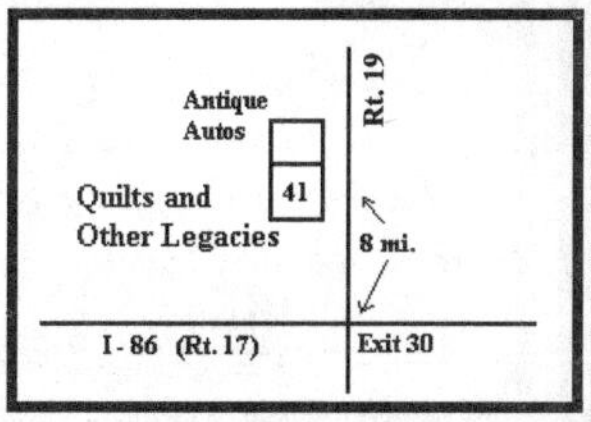

Dansville, NY #13

Mon - Fri 9:30 - 5:30
Sat 9:30 - 5

Material Rewards

10160 Sandy Hill Rd. 14437
(585) 335-2050
E-Mail: quilts@materialrewards.com
Web Site: www.materialrewards.com

2500 bolts of 100% cottons, books, notions, patterns.

ALL THE CREATIVE COMFORTS FOR QUILTERS

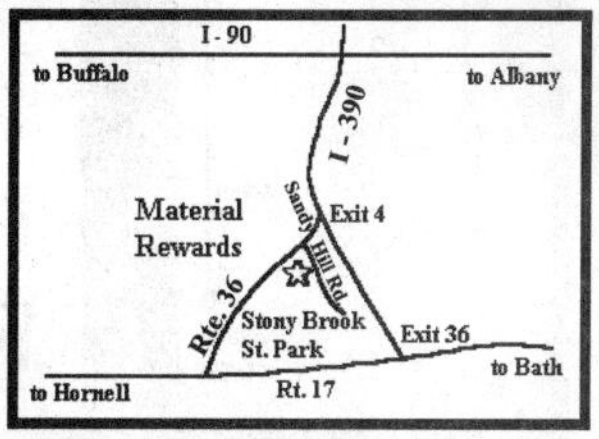

Weaver-View Farms

Amish Country Store

1190 Earls Hills Road · Penn Yan, NY 14527

Open Year 'Round -- Closed Sundays & Religious Holidays

1-315-781-2571

www.weaverviewfarms.com

75+ HANDSTITCHED QUILTS • HOMESPUNS
QUALITY COTTONS • FURNITURE • BOOKS
PATTERNS • FAT QUARTERS • HOMEMADE FOODS

Magical history abounds in the Finger Lakes region, never more so than on this 128 acre farm overlooking the West Shore of Seneca Lake. The 14-room farmhouse is open year 'round with a collection of useful old-fashioned wares and one-of-a-kind country gifts...

Our Amish quilts are made by friends and family. Coordinate your quilt with our selection of specialty fabrics. Homespun aprons, tablerunners & handquilted pillows, Gingham dresses & bonnets for little girls. Oak & iron quilt hangers.

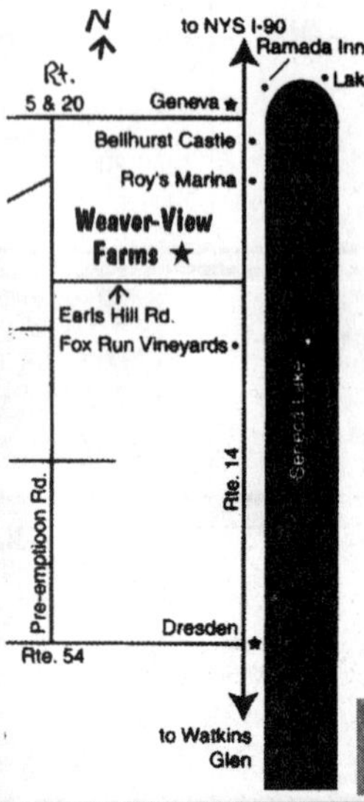

This map shows only major routes.

From Rochester & North:
Take 1 - 90 to the Geneva exit (exit 42) or follow Routes 5 & 20 into Geneva. Follow Route 14 South along Seneca Lake, approximately 7 miles. Watch for sign on right. Turn right onto Earls Hill Road, farm is on the right.

From Elmira & South:
Follow Route 14 North through Watkins Glen, along Seneca Lake, approximately 28 miles. Watch for signs on the left, turn left onto Earls Hill Road, farm is on the right.

Penn Yan, NY #14

Avoca, NY #15

By Appt. Please

Cottonseed Quilting Co.

9 Charlesworth Ave., P.O. Box 360 14809
(607) 566-9264
E-Mail: qlt@infoblvd.net
Owner: Susan Haneline

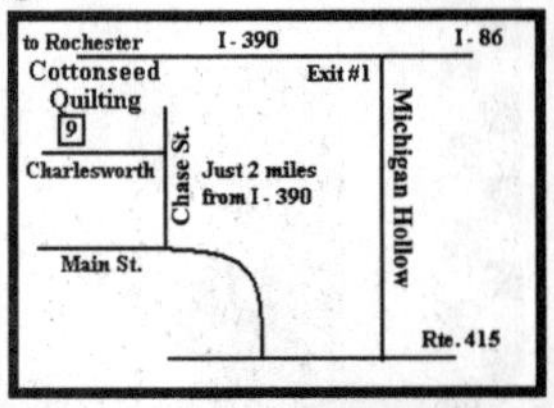

Excellence in Individualized Machine Quilting. Extensive selection of patterns & thread colors. Free Brochure on request. APQS Millennium. Every 5th quilt is half price!

Hammondsport, NY #16

**Mon - Sat 10 - 5
Sun 11 - 4**

Lake Country Patchwork

67 Shether St.
P.O. Box 332 14840
(607) 569-3530 Est: 1996
Owner: Candace Hosier

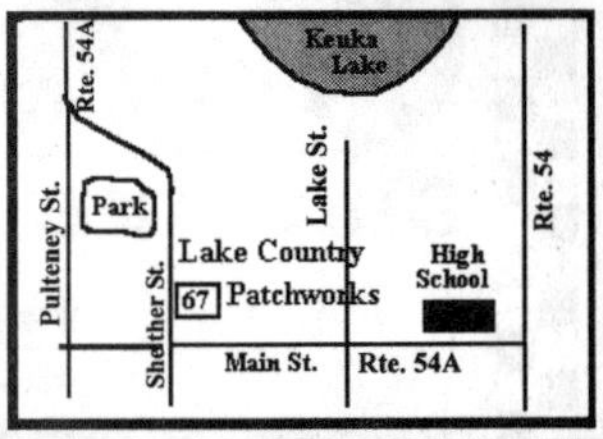

Let the natural beauty of the Finger Lakes inspire your next quilt. We have 100% cotton fabrics, quilting supplies and books. Quilts & gift items.

Come . . . and enjoy a unique shopping experience in the ambiance of our renovated 19th century country church

18 Canal St.
14814
(607) 562-7596
Owner: Jody Kravec
Est: 1986
4500 sq.ft.

- The Finest 100% Cotton Fabrics Available, Quilting Books, Notions, Gadgets & Gifts
- Out-of-the-Ordinary Patterns for Dolls, Quilted Clothing & Home Decor
- Models & Samples to Inspire Creativity
- Quilts & Wallhangings for Sale
- Counted Cross Stitch Patterns, Threads & accessories
- Gifts—Dolls, Santas, Hand-made Gifts
- Christmas Throughout the Year

**Mon - Sat 10 - 5
Thur til 8
(Sept. thru Dec.)**

The Village Sampler is easily accessible from Exit 49, Route 17 / I-86

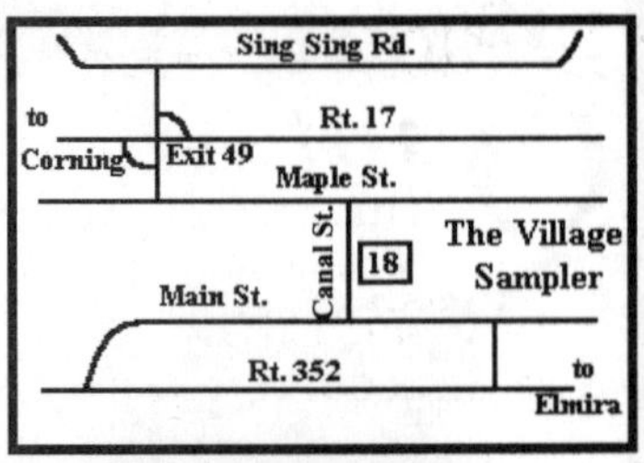

Big Flats, NY #17

Vestal, NY #18

Grandmother's Thimble

Quilt & Fabric Shop

Mon-Wed & Fri 10 - 5:30
Thur 10 - 7
Sat 10 - 4

3036 Old Vestal Rd., Vestal, NY 13850
(607) 797-7022 www.grandmothersthimble.net
E-mail: gthimble@stny.rr.com Fax: (607) 797-7022
Owner: Justine A. Layman Est: 2001 3,000 sq.ft.

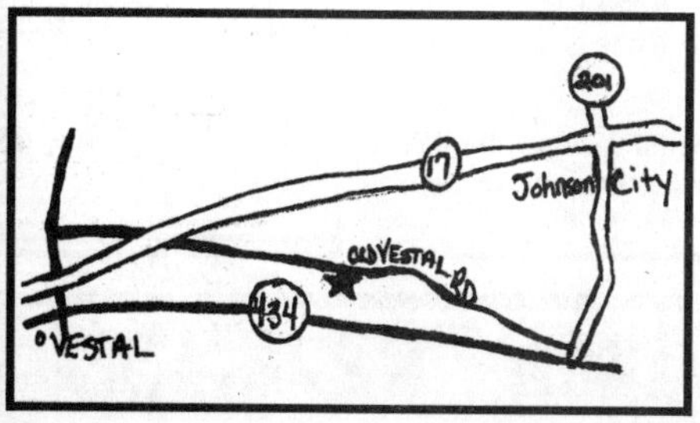

Over 1000 bolts of 100% cotton fabric!

Books, Notions, Bernina Sewing Machines & Access.

Many classes from beginner to advanced

Courteous Staff ready to help with your Quilting Needs.

McLean, NY #19

P.O. Box 430, 3 Stevens Rd. 13102
Phone: (607) 838 - 3095
Owner: Clara Travis

Featured in Patchwork and Quilting Ideas Magazine, Winter '97 Issue

Patchwork & Pies

Quilting Gadgets, Gismos and Gottahaves
Bus Tours and Quilt Guilds welcome but do call ahead
*100% cotton fabrics *Notions * Books
* Patterns * Gifts

Tuesday - Friday 10 - 5:00
& Saturday 10 - 4:00
Closed between Christmas and New Years.
Please call for other special holiday hours.
Fax: (607) 838-0108
E-Mail claratravis@compuserve.com
Web Site:
www.patchworkandpies.com

We are located in an old country store at the five crossroads in the historic village of McLean, NY. Come and browse through one of New York State's most unique quilt stores and enjoy home made pie, sweet rolls and coffee before returning to the lovely scenery of the beautiful Finger Lakes. Ten minutes from Interstate 81 and Route 13.

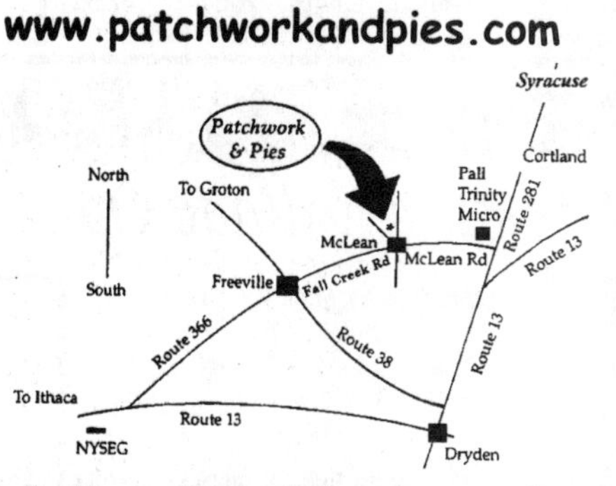

On I - 81: coming South from Syracuse, Exit 12 coming North from Binghamton, Exit 10

Endwell, NY #20

Mon - Fri 9 - 5:30
Sat 9 - 1

Sew Much More

2723 East Main St. 13760
(607) 748-8340
Owner: Nancy Valenta
Est: 1990 2400 sq.ft.

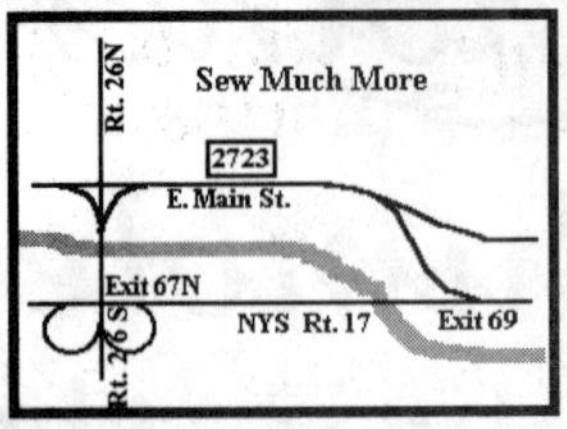

Over 4000 bolts of 100% cottons. Heirloom sewing, specialty threads, books and patterns galore. A delightful experience for your palette. HUSQVARNA VIKING Authorized Dealer.

Pucky Huddle Delight

Est. 2002

1800 sq. ft. of 100% Cotton fabrics, battings, quilting supplies, fat quarters, notions, patterns, books, classes, quilts, gifts and collectables.

Between Owego and Ithaca
12 miles from NYS Rte. 17

Delight-ful Discounts for Quilt Guild Cards

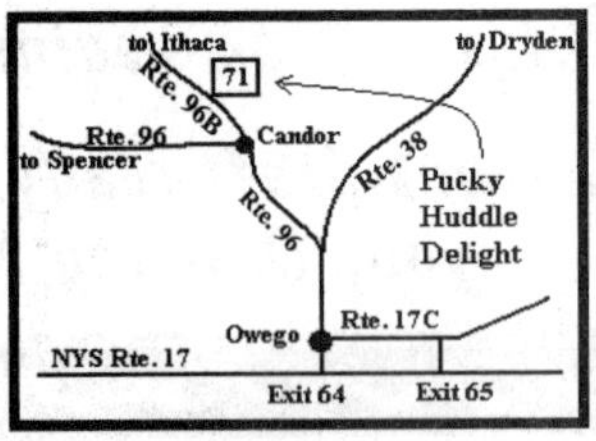

Tues - Sat: 11 am - 8 pm
Sun: 11 am - 6 pm

Owner: Jennifer L. Kopcho
Email: PuckyHuddleDelight@clarityconnect.com
Telephone: (607) 659-7PHD Fax: (607) 659-7744
71 Owego Road (NYS Rte 96B) 13743

Candor, NY #21

Greene, NY #22

M, T by appt.
W - F 10 - 6
Sat 10 - 4
Sun 1 - 4

Creative Threads

604 Jackson Hill Rd 13778
(607) 656-8883
2000+ Bolts

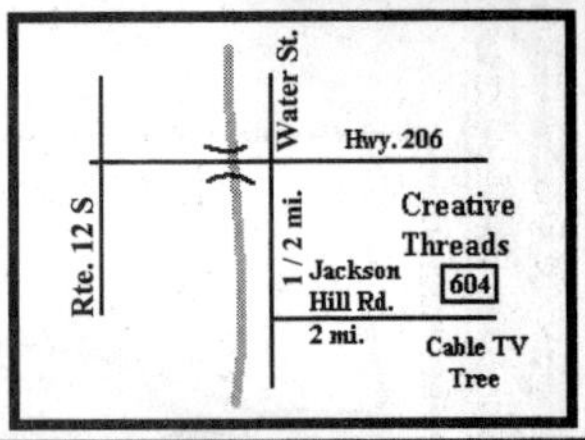

Friendly, family run quilt shop. Brother & Elna dealer & service center. Full service quilt shop and custom machine quilting.

Ithaca, NY #23

Quilters Corner

Ithaca New York

200 Pleasant Grove Rd. 14850
(607) 266-0850
E-Mail: quilters@e-quilterscorner.com
Web Site: www.e-quilterscorner.com
Owners: Katie Barnaby,
Sherry Haefele, Cyndi Slothower,
Linda Van Nederynen & Merrie Wilent
Est: 1995 3500 Bolts

A diverse collection of exciting fabric selected by five wild women. Huge book selection, patterns, notions, and gifts. Authorized Pfaff & Janome dealer. Bus tours welcome, please call ahead so we can be fully staffed for you. Special promotions and projects available on our web site. Gallery of constantly changing quilts for inspiration. New York's headquarters for Bali batiks. Block of the month quilts and kits with our original beautiful fabric packs.

Mon - Fri 10 - 6
Sat 10 - 5 Sun 1 - 4

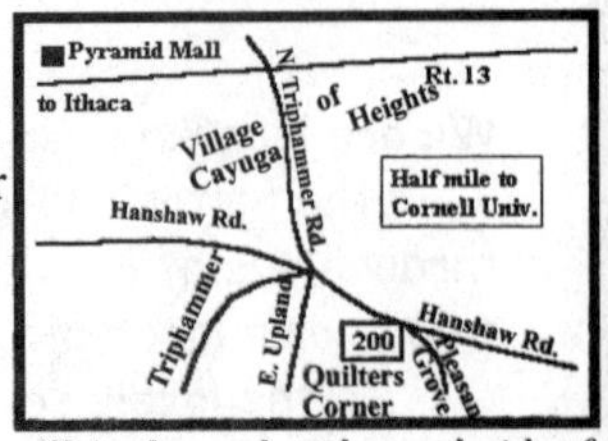

We're located on the north side of Ithaca at Community Corners.

Canandaigua, NY #24

Mon - Fri 10 - 5
Sat 10 - 4

FABRICS, etc.

71 S. Main St. 14424
(585) 394-6350 Fax: (585) 394-6533
E-Mail: fabrics@frontiernet.net
Web Site: www.fabricsetc.com
Owner: Mary Hoffman
Est: 1993 1500 sq.ft.

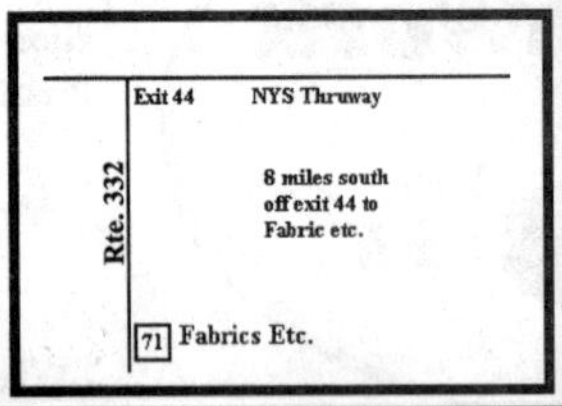

In the heart of the beautiful Finger Lakes. Quilt supplies, Fashion fabrics, patterns, books, classes & much more. Pfaff & Babylock.

Mendon, NY #25

Mon - Fri 10 - 5
Sat 10 - 4

Mendon Village Quilt Shop

1350 Pittsford-Mendon Rd. 14506
(585) 624-3130
Owners: Linda Liljequist
& Dorothy Lindblom

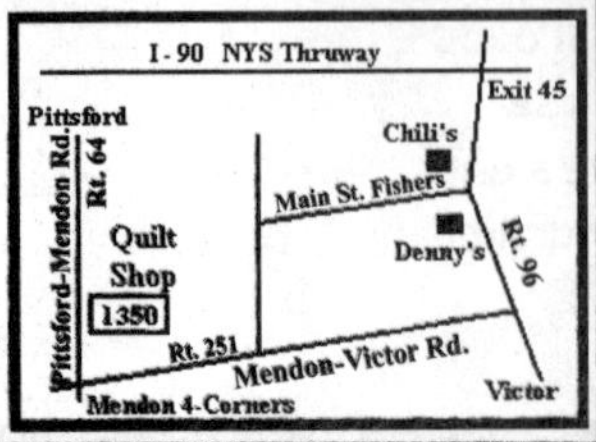

A hands-on shop with quality fabrics, quilting supplies, gifts, classes and knowledgeable staff offering friendly service and support.

Webster, NY #28

PAM'S SEWING SHOPPE

182 North Avenue
Webster, NY 14580
585-872-2080

Fax: 585-872-9728
Est: 1994 2000 sq.ft.
Pamssewingshoppe@aol.com
Owners: Pam Doell & Melissa Morgante

Mon - Thurs 10 - 6
Fri & Sat 10 - 4
Call for Evening Hours

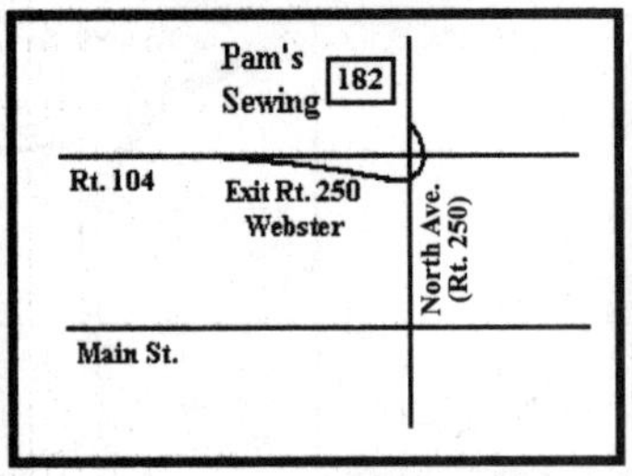

2500+ bolts of quilting cottons, flannels, heirloom fabrics and laces. We also have a large assortment of books, patterns, and notions for quilting and heirloom sewing. Free seminars for quilt guilds and tour groups. Call for details.

Savannah, NY #29

Mon - Sat 9 - 5
Thur & Fri til 8

Springlake Market & Fabrics

4219 Yates Rd. 13146
(315) 594-8485
Owner: Arlene Zimmerman

One of a Kind Store!

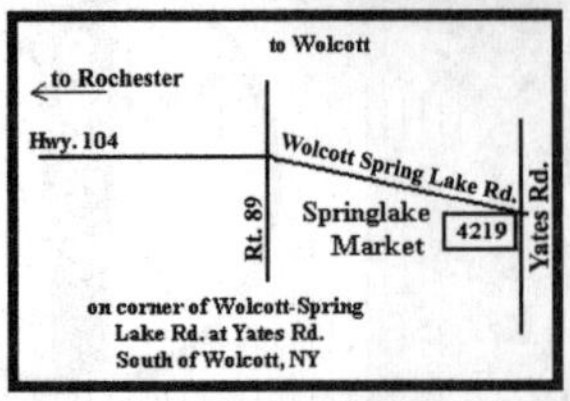

Great selection ... name brand fabrics unbeatable prices ... with a dutch country flair ... notions ... books ... crafts.

Skaneateles, NY #30

Patchwork Plus

36 Jordan Street 13152
(315) 685-6979
Owner: Judi West Est: 1987

4000 bolts of 100% cottons, books, notions, patterns;
Bernina Sewing Machines;
Plus friendly service in Skaneateles;
Gateway to the Finger Lakes

Mon - Sat 10 - 4

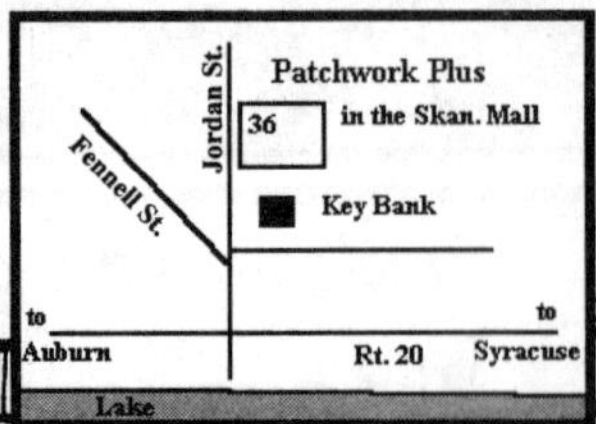

Marcellus, NY #31

Mon - Sat 10 - 4 Or by Appt.

The Quilting Shoppe

2162 Lawrence Rd. 13108
(315) 673-1126
Owner: Elaine Lyon
Est: 1983 1800 sq.ft. 1800+ Bolts

MACHINE QUILTING SERVICE
Custom Made Quilts. Quilted Jackets
Quilts for Sale.

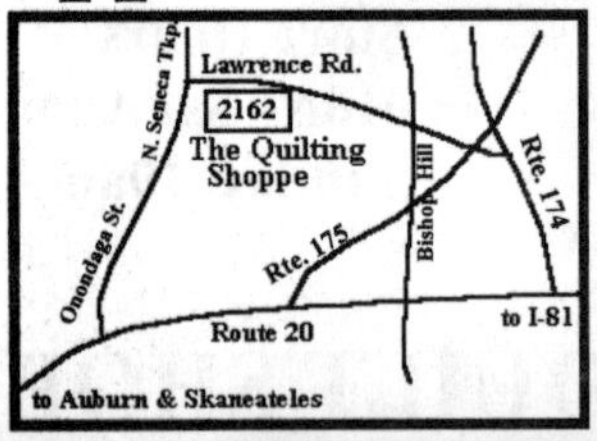

Oneida, NY #32

Mon - Sat 10 - 5 Thur til 8

Cottons Etc.

228 Genesee Street 13421
(315) 363-6834 Est: 1980
Owner: Paula Schultz 1700 sq.ft.
Swatch Set $2 and LSASE.
e-mail: cottons@ny.tds.net

Our motto is "You Can Never Have Too Much Fabric!" A Pot-pourri of Quilting & Fashion Fabrics, Notions, Books & Patterns. Ask for free gift!

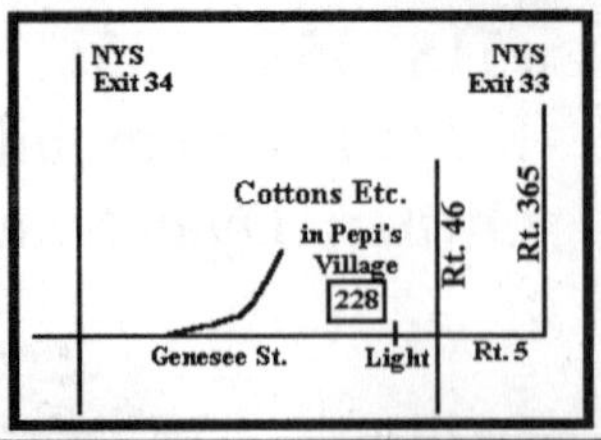

Richville, NY #33

Tues & Thur 4 - 9
Wed & Sat 10 - 4
and whenever we are home, closed Sat June & July

Fabric Arts

20 Phelps Rd., P.O. Box 349 13681
(315) 287-2145
E-Mail: fabricrt@northnet.org
Web Site: www.sew2000.com/fabricarts
Owners: Norb & Dorothy Hall
Est: 1985 2500 sq.ft.
Machine Quilting Services, Fabrics, Books, Notions, Classes, Sewing Machines— for all your quilting needs see us.

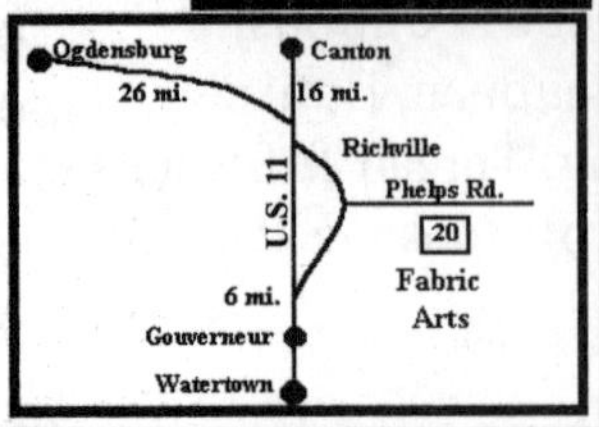

Queensbury, NY #34

Mon - Sat 10 - 5
Sun 12 - 4

The Quilting Bee

974 Rt. 9 12804
(518) 792-0845
Owner: Pat Strain
Est: 1987 1500 sq.ft. 3300+ Bolts

Cotton fabrics include designer's calicos & solids, books, patterns & notions.
Banner flag supplies, Gifts and Quilts.
Bernina Dealer.

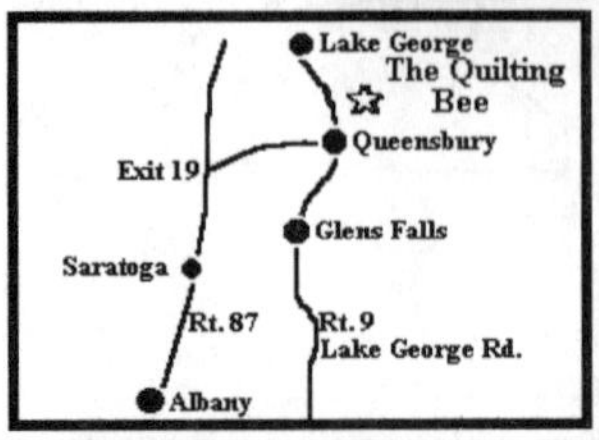

Liverpool, NY #35

Chickadee Fabrics

526 Old Liverpool Road • Liverpool, New York 13088 • 315/453-4059

Central New York's Premier Quilt Shop

Fabrics, Books, Notions, Classes, and Quilt restoration. Staffed by knowledgeable quilters

1865 square feet with over 2500 bolts of fabric and 2 dedicated classrooms

Featuring fabrics by Hoffman, P&B Textiles, Kona Bay, RJR, and many others.

Books by That Patchwork Place, C&T Publishing, and Quilt Digest Press.

Over 100 classes offered per year with day, night, Saturday, custom, and private classes

Easily accessible from both interstate highways.

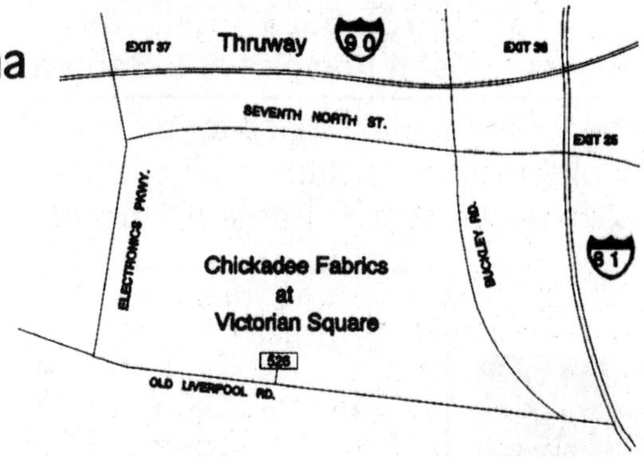

Store Hours: Mon - Sat 10:00 - 5:00

Calico Gals

Fayetteville, NY #36

all kinds of fun stuff for quiltin' and stitchin'

Barbara Huntington & Janet Lutz: Owners

Located in the Canal Barn at
7070 Cedar Bay Road in Fayetteville.
Featuring quality quilting cottons,
cozy flannels, books, patterns and notions
in a cozy, rustic atmosphere.

The Barn Shops are open 10:00 - 5:00 Mon. thru Sat.
315-445-0617

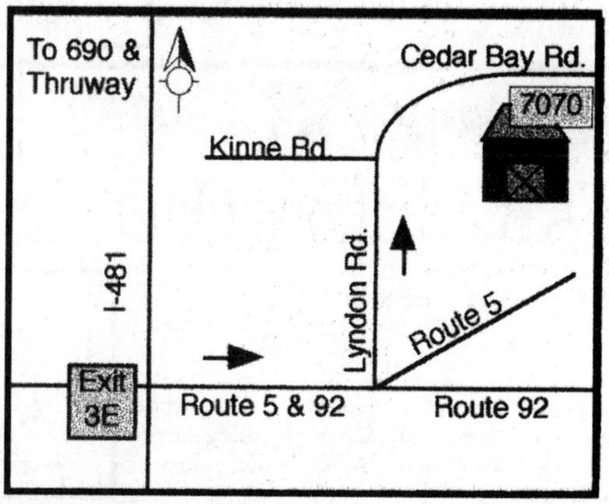

Utica, NY #37

Tiger Lily Quilt Co.

2336 West Whitesboro St. 13502
(315) 735-5328 Est: 1991
Owners: Susan Kowalczyk & Sandra Jones

A shop with unusual fabrics for quilting & sewing. Books, notions, patterns, gifts, classes and newsletter. Bernina Affiliate.

**Mon - Fri 9:30 - 5:30
Sat 10 - 4**

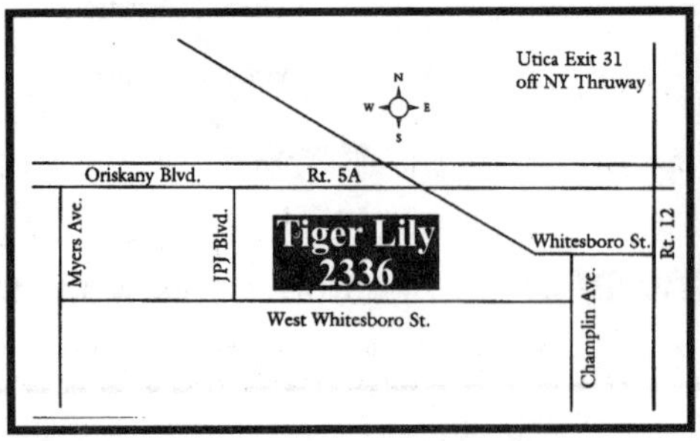

Directions to Tiger Lily: Thruway Exit #31, follow signs to Route 12, then to Route 12 South. Exit at 5A West (Oriskany Blvd.) and proceed through 3 lights. Turn left at JPJ Blvd. Immediately after 3rd light.

Esperance, NY #38

By Appt. Only

Hickory Hill Quilts

P.O. Box 273 12066
(888) 817-6577
Web Site: www.hickoryhillquilts.com
Owner: John & Kris Driessen

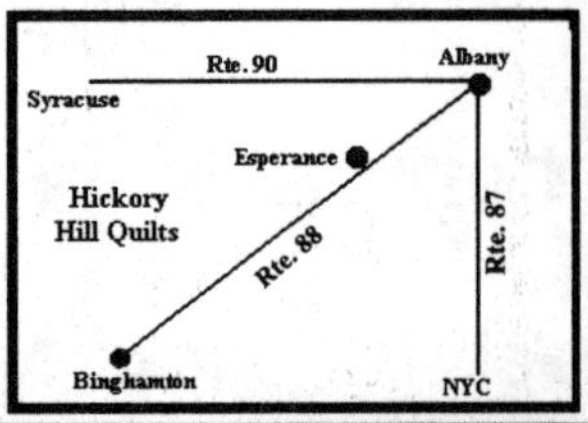

Hickory Hill Quilts offers antique quilts, vintage and reproduction fabric, quilt heritage books and Quilters Dream Cotton Batting. Visit us on the Web.

Cobleskill, NY #39

**Mon - Sat 9 - 6
Thur til 8
Sun 11 - 5**

The Yardstick

115 Plaza Ln., Suite 8 12043
(518) 234-2179 Est: 1975
E-Mail: yardstic@telenet.net
Web Site: www.yardstickny.com
Owner: Merilyn Ludwig 2500 sq.ft.

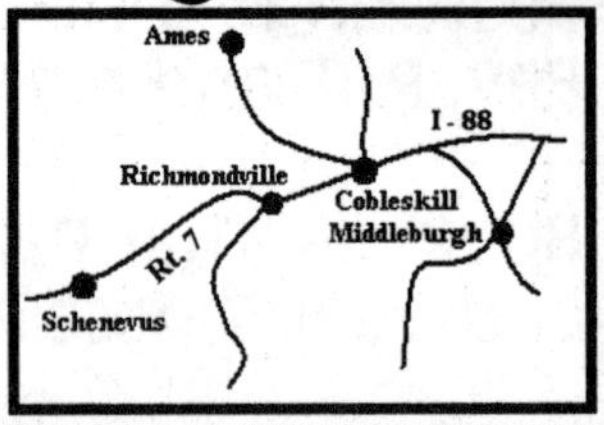

Husqvarna Viking sewing machines sales & service. Over 2000 bolts of 100% cotton fabrics, books, notions, patterns, & classes. Friendly Knowledgeable Staff.

Flying Geese Fabrics

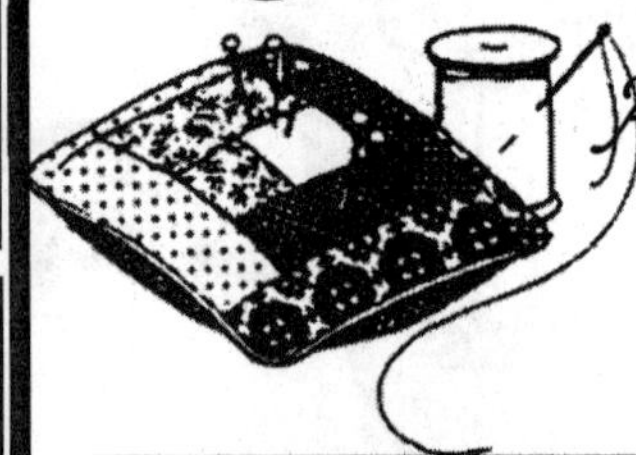

A Quilter's Delight!

Fine Quilting Fabrics
Designer Prints
The Newest Books,
Patterns & Notions
Quilting Classes
*Gifts * Gift Certificates*
Blocks of the Month
Free Newsletter

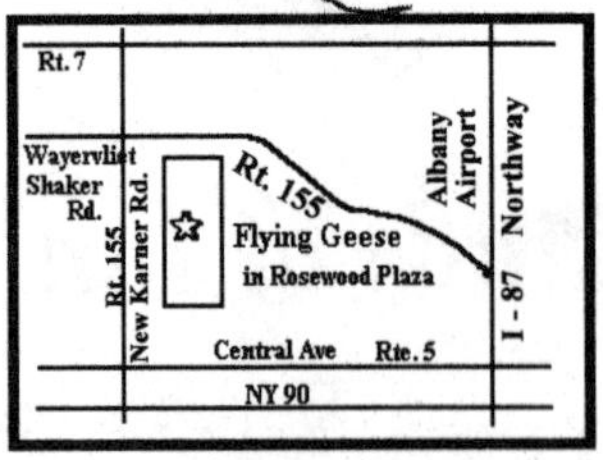

Just 2 miles West of I - 87—Exit 4, 155 West

Colonie, NY #40

Rosewood Plaza 501 New Karner Rd. 12205
(518) 456-8885 Est: 1996 2000 Bolts
E-Mail: flyinggeesequilts@yahoo.com
Owners: Donnie Brownsey,
Tara Conlon & Joanne Skudder.

Mon - Fri 10 - 5 Thur 10 - 8 Sat 10 - 4

Ravena, NY #41

**Tue 10 - 9
Wed - Fri 10 - 5
Sat 10 - 4**

Log Cabin Fabrics

702 Starr Rd. 12143
(518) 767-9236
Owner: Londa VanDerzee
Est: 1987

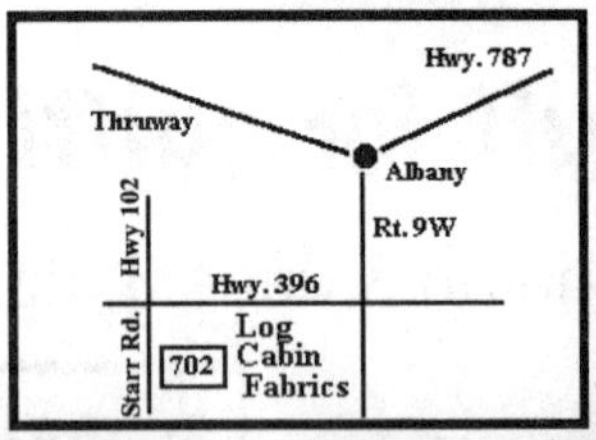

Visit a country quilt shop, 15 minutes south of Albany. Over 1200 bolts, classes, books & patterns.

Hudson, NY #42

**Thur - Mon
9:30 - 5:30
Sun 12 - 5**

FABRICations Quilt Shop

558 Warren St. 12534
(518) 822-0772

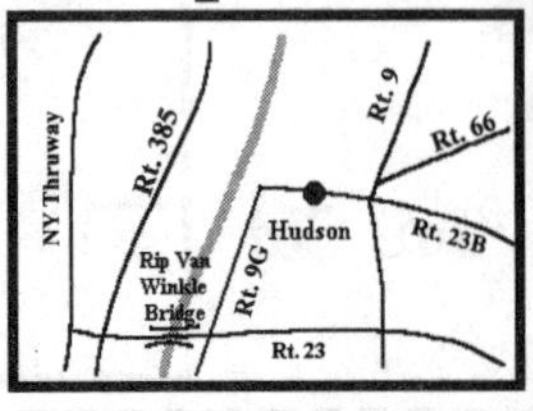

Over 3000 bolts of 100% cotton quilting fabric, featuring international & contemporary fabrics along with traditional. Books, notions, supplies & Classes.

Fly Creek, NY #43

3 miles North of Cooperstown, NY

Heartworks
Quilts and Fabrics

Open Year Round
Mon - Sat
10 - 5

6237 St. Hwy. 28, P.O. Box 148 13337
Owners: Margaret & Jim Wolff
(607) 547-2501
E-Mail: hrtworks@telenet.net

Est: 1989

Original Design Block of the Month

A real country quilt shop with over **3000 bolts of Fine Cotton Fabrics** and Cotton Flannel Fabrics, Batting, Books, Stencils and a full line of notions. One-of-a-kind **full size quilts** (made here in NY,USA), quilt repair, custom design of quilts for interior decorators, and hand quilting of your quilt tops.

Authorized dealer for **Elna** Sewing Machines.

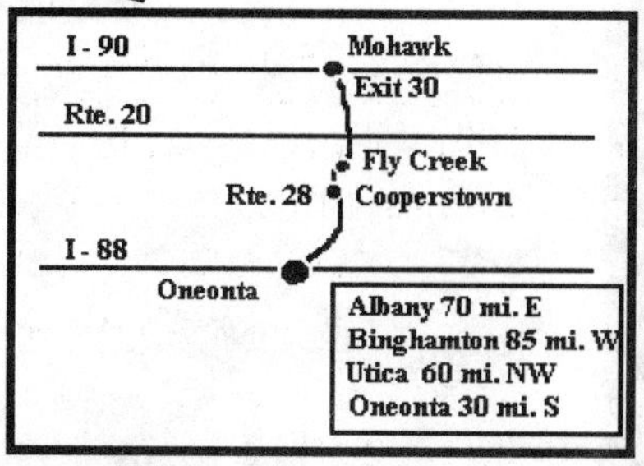

Between visits to our shop, please visit us on the world wide web at:
www.heartworksquilts.com
featuring our applique kits & is updated monthly

Gloversville, NY #44

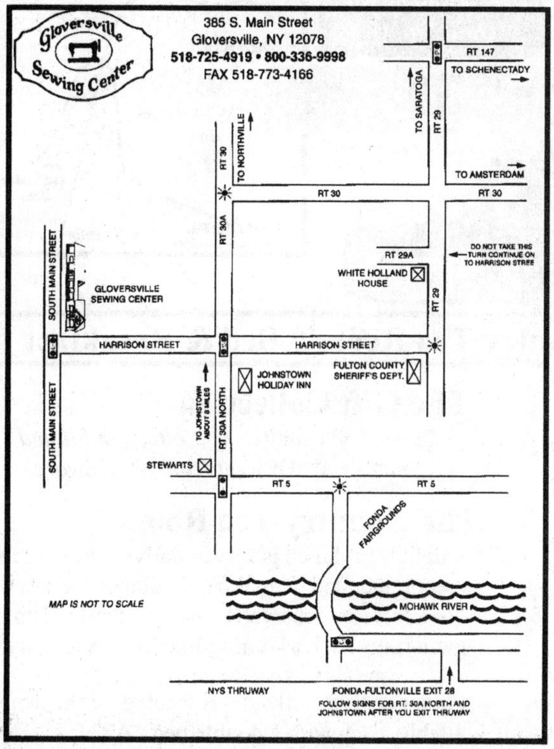

Gloversville Sewing Center

385 S. Main St. 12078
(518) 725-4919 or
(800) 336-9998
Fax: (518) 773-4166
Web Site:
www.gloversville sewingcenter.com
Owners: Diana & John Marshall
Est: 1981 4600 sq.ft.
3000+ Bolts

Area's Largest Selection of
Quilting Books & Patterns

Over 3000 Broadcloths in Stock

Large Assortment of
Decorative Threads
Silk Ribbons
Specialty Needles
Sewing Machine Attachments

Specializing in Sales & Service of
Bernina Brother

Mon - Fri 9 - 5:30
Thur til 8 Sat 9 - 5

Burnt Hills, NY #45

Nine-Patch Fabrics

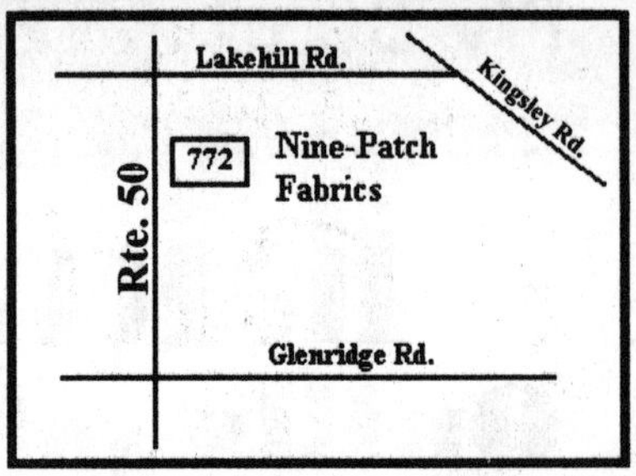

Located on Route 50. 1/3 miles south of Lakehill Road in the Shopping Plaza on your left 5 miles North of Glenridge Road in Scotia.

We specialize in Batiks and Flannels with a Large Selection of other Prints by Top Manufacturers.

Mon-Fri 10-6 Tues 10-8 Sat 10-4

772 Route 50,
Burnt Hills, NY 12027
518-399-1999
Mary Hoover Est. 1999

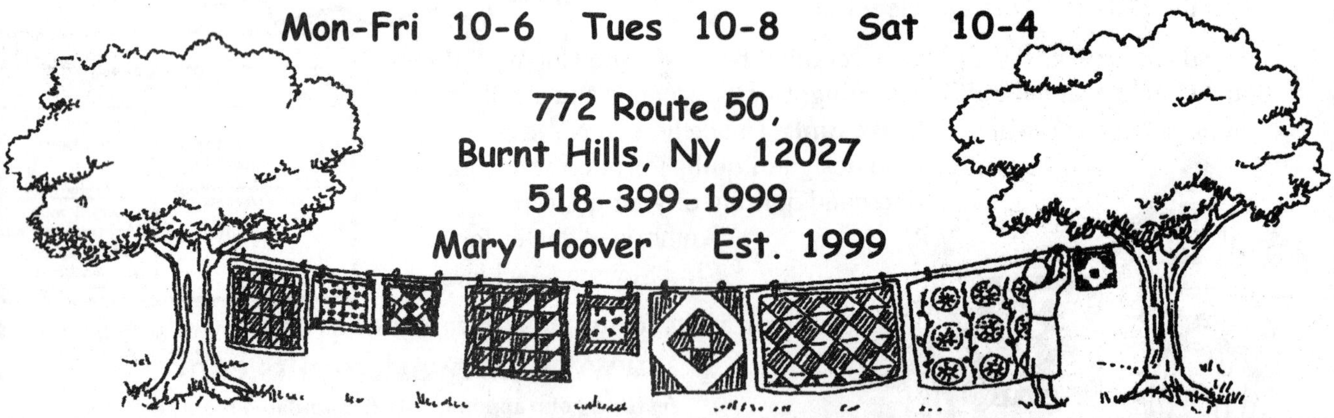

The Fieldstone House

Hours: 7 days a week 11 - 5
Closed Occasionally for Quilt Shows

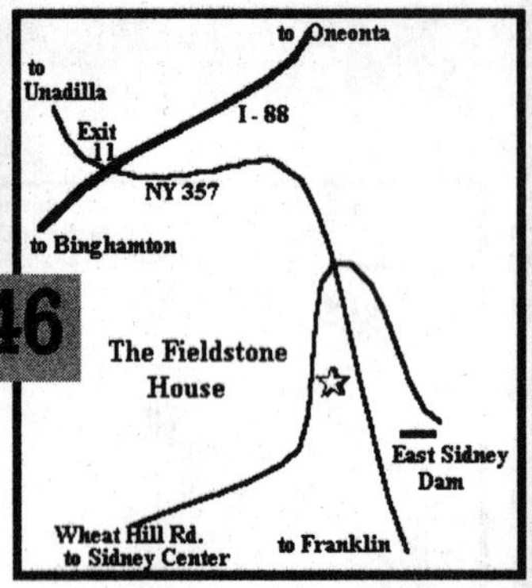

Sidney Center, NY #46

1884 Wheat Hill Rd. 13839
(607) 369-9177
e-mail: fieldstonehouse@mkl.com
www.fieldstonehouse.com
Proprietors: Jane & Allan Kirby

***Featuring a:* Fabric Shop * Gift Collection * Country Tea Room * Bed & Breakfast**

The Fabric Shop

Three rooms are filled to capacity with more than 12,000 bolts

Alexander Henry • Benartex • Concord • Bali Fabrications Debbie Mumm • Clothworks • Hoffman • Kaufman • Moda • Marcus Brothers • Maywood Studio • Northcott • P&B • Peter Pan • Red Wagon RJR • Roberta Horton • Nancy Crow • Timeless Treasures ... and more.

Books, Threads, Needles, Muslin, Battings, Templates, Buttons, Cutting Tools, Flannels, Cross-Stitch Patterns/Fabric, Clothing Patterns

The Gift Collection

Baskets ❖ Candles ❖ Pottery ❖ Stuffed Animals ❖ Wrought Iron ❖ Tinware

The Country Tea Room

A delightful lunch is served daily; reservations recommended. Breakfast & dinner are also available by reservation only. Small group gatherings such as quilt guilds are a specialty.

The Bed and Breakfast The Kirby Homestead, a fieldstone house in a quiet country hill side, is located on the same property approximately one-half mile from the shop. Four comfortable rooms are available, each with a double bed. A full breakfast is served to guests at the Country Tea Room. This is the perfect location for a quilting retreat!

Pine Bush, NY #47

Quilter's Attic

Route 302, Pine Bush, NY 12566
845-744-5888

2000 Bolts of Fabric
Large Selection of Books, Patterns & Notions
Lots of Quilt Kits
Wool and Stitchery Kits
Primitive Kits
Rug Hooking Kits
Large Classroom
Blocks of the months
Horn Cabinet Dealer
Koala Cabinet Dealer
Pfaff Sewing Machines
Yearly Retreats

New Customers: Bring in this ad for a FREE GIFT!

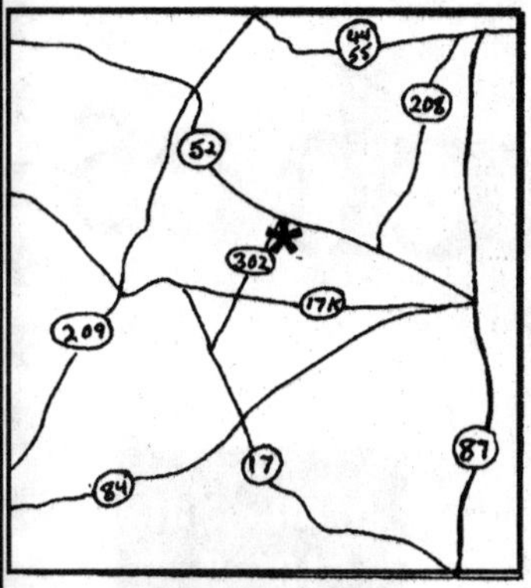

Our friendly and knowledgeable staff look forward to meeting you. Bus tours welcome, please call ahead.

Est. 1994
Owners: Kathy & Wayne Joray

Packed full of Samples to inspire you! Q.A. is located in a wonderful old Victorian. There's always something new going on at "The Attic"!

Just Minutes from Major Highways

From Route 17: Exit 119 (Route 302N) to Pine Bush. 10 miles on right.

From Route 84: Exit 8 (Route 52W) 15 miles to Pine Bush. Left on Rt. 302—1/10th mile on left.

Shop Hours:
Tuesday—Saturday 10:00-4:00
Sundays 1:00-4:00
Closed holidays—please call ahead.

Visit our on-line shop quiltersattic.com

Red Hook, NY #48

Tues - Fri 10 - 5
Sat 10 - 4:30

The Village Fabric Shoppe

33 W. Market St. 12571
(845) 758-8541 Fax: (845) 758-4334
Web Site: www.villagefabricshoppe.com
Est: 1981

We specialize in fine, quilting fabrics - Hoffman, P&B, Thimbleberries & More - year round classes, supplies, books, patterns, gifts, kits - Friendly Service.

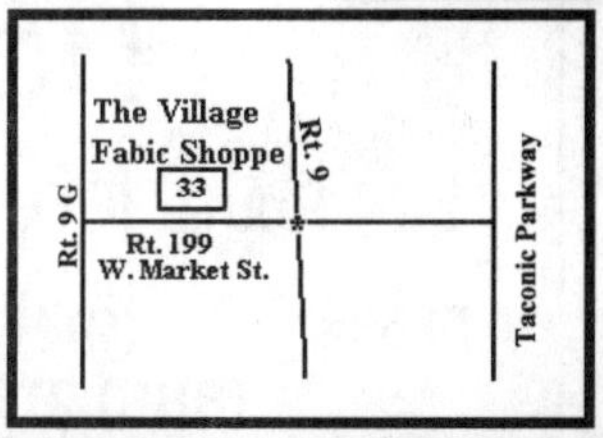

Wappingers Falls, NY #49

Tues, Wed, Fri 10 - 5
Thur 10 - 8
Sat 10 - 4
Sun 12 - 4

Quilt Basket

Cambridge Commons #4
939 Route 376 12590
(845) 227-7606
Visit our Online Catalog:
www.quiltbasket.com
Owners: Cathy & Allan Anderson
Est: 1989 1800 sq.ft. 3000 Bolts

All Fabrics, & Books Discounted.

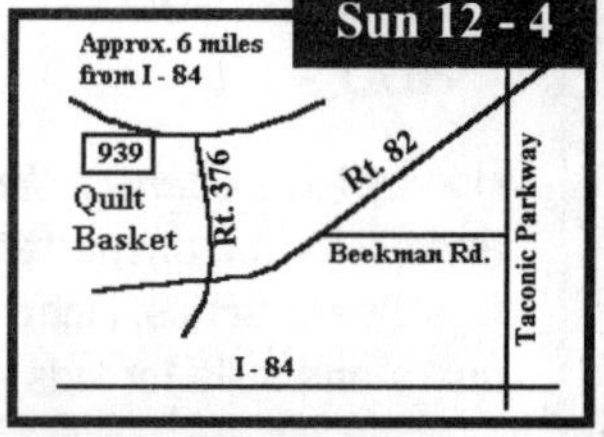

New York, NY #50

Tues - Fri 11 - 7
Sat 10 - 6
Sun 11 - 5

157 West 24th St. 10011
(212) 807-0390
Fax: (212) 807-9451
E-Mail: info@cityquilter.com

THE CITY QUILTER

Outstanding selection of 100% Cotton Fabrics.
Gifts, books, patterns, notions and classes.
Bernina machines and accessories.

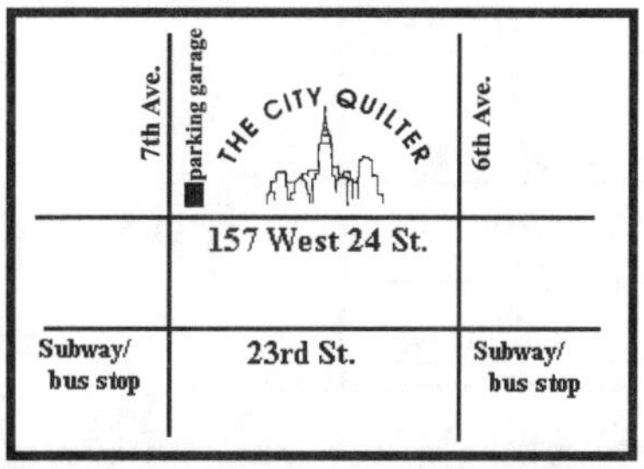

Owner:
Cathy Izzo

Somers, NY #51

The Country Quilter

344 Route 100, Somers, NY 10589

The quilt shop in the historic district of the Hamlet of Somers, with a friendly, knowledgeable staff ready to help you!

Phone: (914) 277-4820
(888) 277-7780
Fax: (914) 277-8604
Email:
qtc@countryquilter.com
Owner: Claire Oehler
Opened: 1990
1800 sq.ft.

Mon to Sat
9:30 - 5:30
Thurs 'til 9

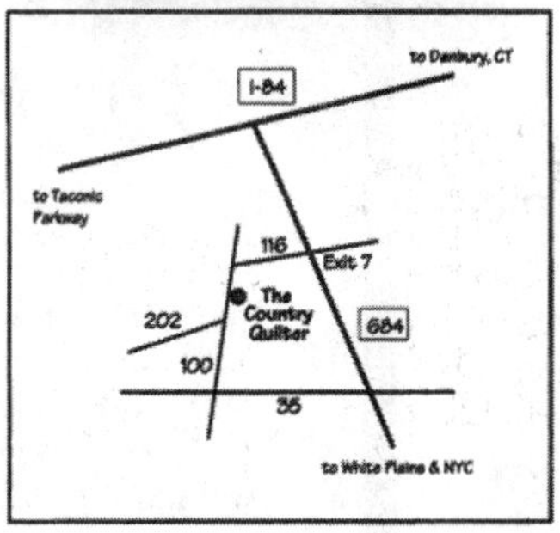

Home of *The Country Quilter* patterns and books ... Transportation series, Southwest series, Lighthouse series, & quilts and dolls for kids of all ages!

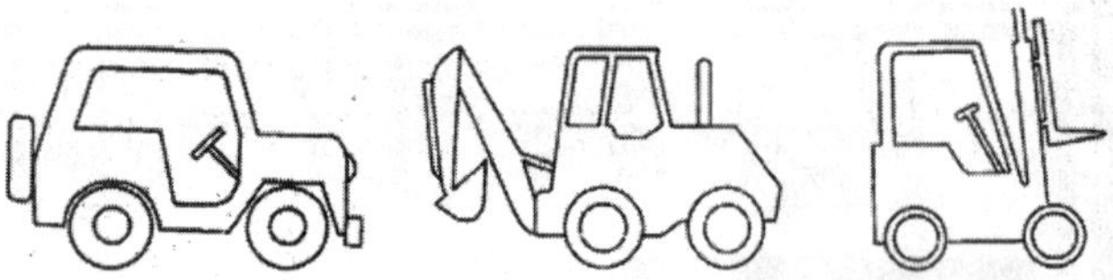

Quality Quilting Supplies

Over 2500 Bolts of 100% Cotton Fabrics
Over 900 Book Titles
Basic as well as Unusual Notions
100s of Patterns
Great Selection of Crazy Quilting Supplies
Everything for the Cloth Dollmaker
100s of Quilt Stencils
Quilting Classes Year-Round
Gifts for Quilters and Quilt Lovers
Fast Mail Order Service
Come in and meet our Friendly, Helpful Staff!

Visit us on the web at:
www.countryquilter.com

Sentimental Stitches

The latest in 100%
Cotton Fabrics and
Quilting Supplies.
Notions — Books
Classes
1800 sq.ft.

Mon - Sat
10 - 5
Sun
12 - 5

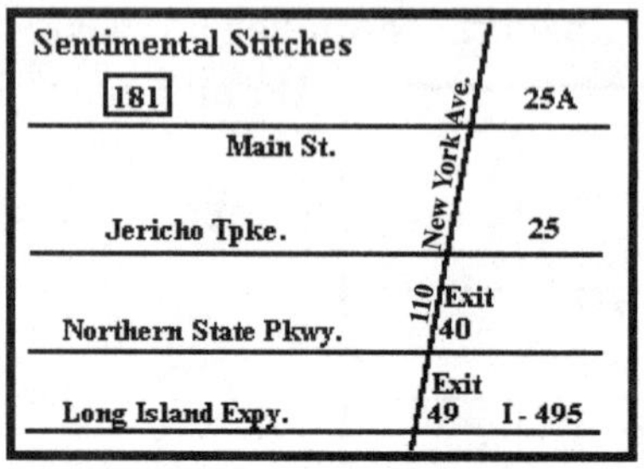

Cold Spring Harbor, NY #52

181 Main St. 11724 (631) 692-4145
Owner: Norma Gaeta Est: 1981

Brooklyn, NY #53

By Appt. Only

SEW BEARY SPECIAL

1025 E. 28th St. 11210
(718) 951-3973
Est: 1993
Owner:
Marcie Brenner

A Shoppe for Quilters! Large selection of 100% cotton Fabrics, Books, Patterns, Tools, Supplies, Battings, Gifts & Classes

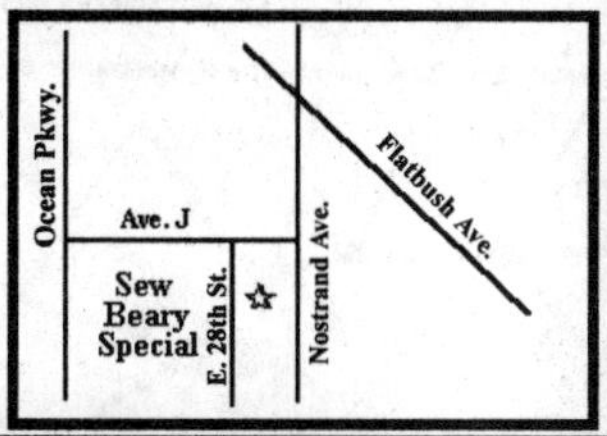

Brooklyn, NY #54

SEW BROOKLYN

Jewel-like color packed store. Quilting cottons, embellishments, books, notions, ribbons, yarns, classes. Landmarked neighborhood / great restaurants cafes / museum / botanic gardens.

Mon - Fri 10 - 7
Sat 10 - 6
Sun 11 - 5

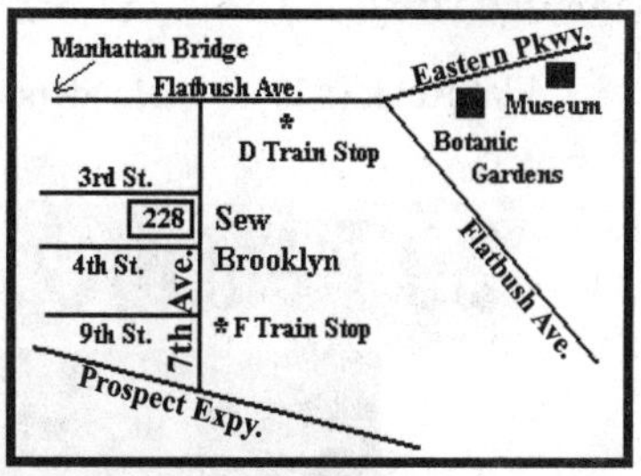

www.sewbrooklyn.com

228 7th Ave. 11215
(718) 499-7383

Fax: (718) 499-7263 700 Bolts
Owners: Jari Anderson & Elaine Smith

Sayville, NY #55

PATCHWORKS Quilting GALLERY

Mon - Fri 10 - 6
Sat 10 - 5
Sun 12 - 4

A Complete Quilt Shop featuring Pfaff Sewing Machines, the latest 100% cotton fabrics, notions, books, patterns and classes.

www.patchworks.com

122 Main St. 11782
(800) 647-5596
Est: 1979 2000 sq.ft.
2000 Bolts
Owner: Carolyn Bachsmith

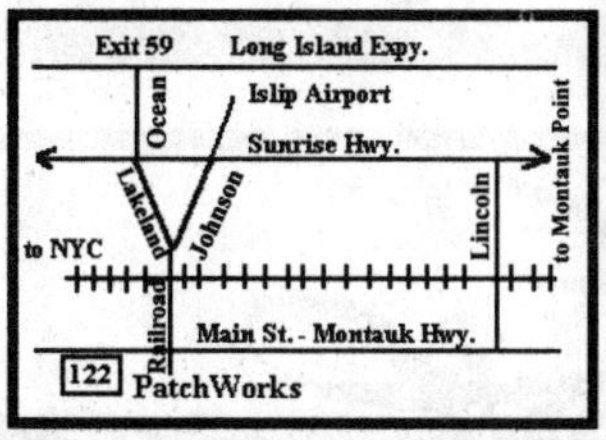

Other Shops in New York: We suggest calling first

Albany	The Sewing Store, 265 Osborne Rd.	518-482-9088
Altona	Maw & Paw's Fabrics, 4954 Military Tpke.	518-236-5762
Amherst	Amherst Museum, 3755 Tonawanda Creek Rd.	716-689-1440
Apalachin	The Churn Dash, 4538 State Route 434	607-625-2630
Auburn	Finger Lakes Quilting, 11 Melrose Rd.	
Averill Park	Quilt Lady, Rt. 43	518-674-0913
Baldwin	Sue's Fabric World, P.O. Box 383	914-855-0196
Brockport	Country Treasures, 27 Market St.	716-637-5148
Brooklyn	Sew Materialistic, 1310 Coney Island Ave.	718-338-6104
Cazenovia	Cazenovia Quilt Shop, 45 Albany St.	315-655-8500
Clayton	Patchwork North, 425 James St.	
Croghan	Fabric Hutch, Main St.	315-346-6360
Croton-on-Hudson	Pinwheels, 416 Albany Post Rd	914-271-1045
Dundee	The Fabric Shop, 8 Main St.	607-243-7052
East Aurora	Vidler's, 690 Main St.	716-652-0481
Endicott	Quiltwerks, 400 Lillian Ave.	607-785-5179
Floral Park	Patchwork Patch, 32 Hemlock St.	516-326-0774
Fredonia	Mauzy's Sewing Center, 40 E. Main St.	716-672-2242
Ft. Edward	Cajon Creations, 147 Broadway	518-746-1647
Fulton	Herron's Fabric Center, 121 Cayuga St.	315-592-4031
Gilbertsville	Gilbert Block Quilt Shop, 9 Commerical St.	607-783-2872
Glen Head	Calico Square, Inc., 14 Meadow Ln	516-676-5577
Greenwood Lake	It's About Time, 274 Pine Hill Rd.	914-477-0066
Hamilton	The Pin Cushion, 37 Milford	315-824-5410
Hartsdale	Hartsdale Fabrics, 275 S. Central Ave.	914-428-7780
Hillsdale	Labors of Love, P.O. Box 352	518-325-6486
Hillsdale	K & K Quilted's, Rt. 23	518-325-4502
Huntington	Homespun Quilting, 18 Austin Ln.	631-757-3029
Hurleyville	Chris-Sans Nubian Quilt House, Meyerhoff	914-434-6667
Ithaca	Homespun Boutique, 314 E. State St.	607-277-0954
Malden Bridge	Quilts & Antiques, Box 118	518-766-4759
Manhasset	The Watermelon Patch, 500 Plandome Rd.	516-365-6166
Maryland	Smitty's Stitchery, 208 Lake Shore Dr. N	607-433-5292
Monsey	Patchwork Sampler, 7 Fieldcrest St.	914-357-1011
Mt. Kisco	Pins and Needles, 161 Main St.	914-666-0824
New York	Quilts Plus, 86 Forsyth	212-334-0123
New York	The Quilted Corner, 120 4th Ave.	212-505-6568
New York	Susan Parrish Antiques, 390 Bleecker St.	212-645-5020
New York	B&J Fabrics, 263 W. 40th St.	212-354-8150
New York	Paron Fabrics, 56 W. 57th	212-247-6451
New York	Woodard & Greenstein Antiques, 506 E. 74th St.	212-988-2906
New York	Hirschl & Adler Folk, 21 East 70th St.	212-988-3655
New York	Judith & James Milne Inc. , 06 E. 74th. St.	212-472-0107
New York	The Gazebo of New York, 114 E. 57th St.	212-935-1041
New York	Laura Fisher Antique Quilts1050 2nd. Ave. #57	212-838-2596
New York	Museum of American Folk Art, 61 W. 62nd. St.	212-977-7170
New York	Down Quilt Shop, 518 Columbus Ave.	212-496-8980
New York	Janos & Associates, 110 East End Ave.	212-988-0407
Norwich	Kinsley Creations, 8 Pleasant St.	607-334-9989
Norwood	Quiltin' Bee, 1140 River Rd.	315-353-4687
Norwood	Martha Drologio, 1140 River Rd.	
Penfield	Teddy's Threads, 11 Colonial Dr.	716-381-4987
Penn Yan	The Quilt Room, 1860 Hoyt Rd.	315-536-5964
Plainview	Melani's Moods Ltd., 14 Manetto Hill Mall	516-935-4644
Port Chester	Nimble Thimble, 509 N. Main St.	914-934-2934
Port Jefferson	Stitchin Time, Inc., 326 Main St.	516-928-4544
Port Jervis	Fabrics Center, 57 Front St.	914-856-2122
Poughkeepsie	Krakower Fabrics, 646 South Rd.	914-462-4157
Pulaski	Fahnestock Fabrics, 4865 N. Jefferson St.	315-298-4411
Rochester	Fabrics and Findings, Inc. 50 Anderson Ave.	716-461-2820
Rochester	Made on the Park, 357 Linden St.	716-271-4212
Rochester	Jackie Lynn's Fabric Center, 471 Ridge Rd. E	716-336-9280
Rockville Center	Bramson House, 5 Nassau	516-764-5006
Roslyn	Arbor House, 22 Arbor Lane	516-538-0009
Saratoga Springs	Quilt Essentials, 454 Broadway	518-489-2229
Seneca Falls	Country Quilting Shoppe, 3600 Rt. 89	
South Dayton	Block in the Square Quilt Shop, 30 Maple St.	716-988-3013
St. James	Corner Cupboard, 367 Lake Ave.	516-584-7288
Stanley	Tobin's Quilt Factory, 3331 Cty. Rd. 20	716-526-6120
Watertown	Judy Quick Quilting, 27081 Cty. Rte. 160	315-788-7349
West Oneonta	Country Fabrics, HCR Box 620	607-432-9726

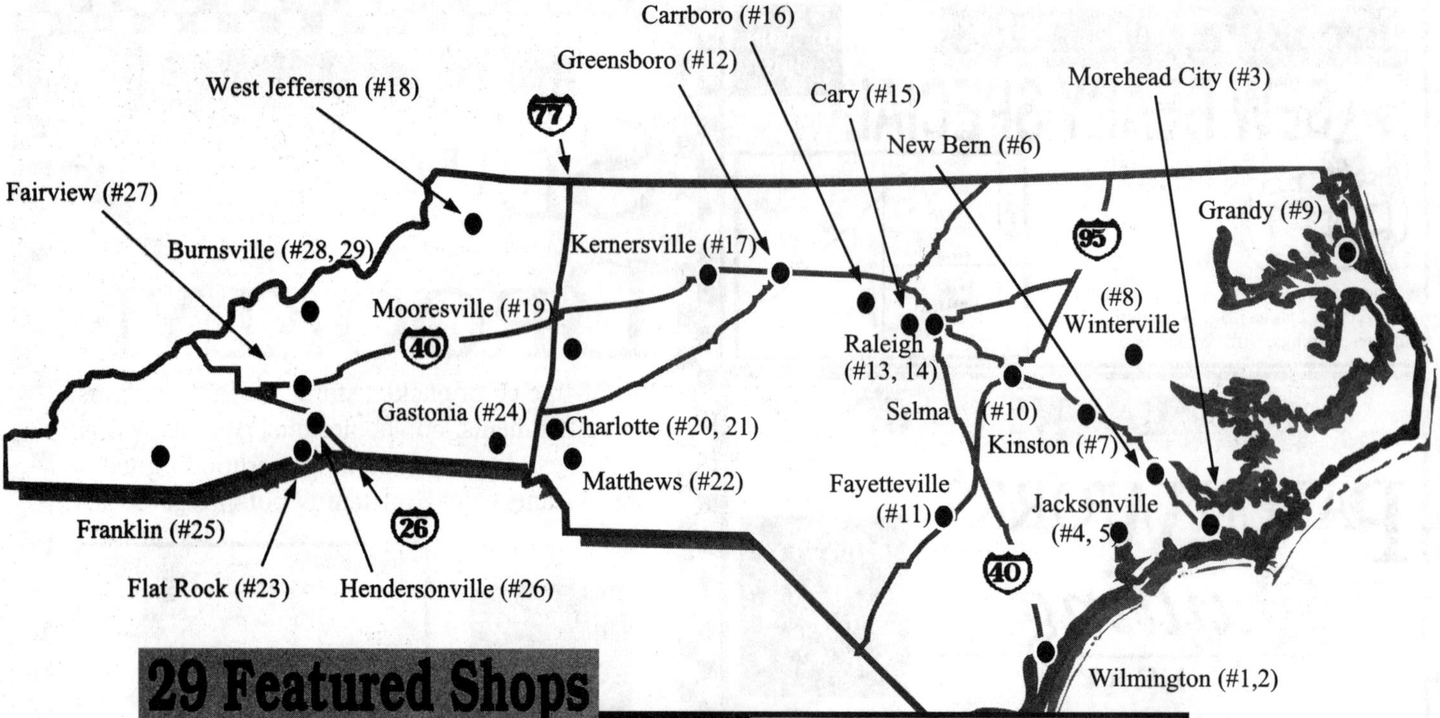

29 Featured Shops

NORTH CAROLINA

Quilter's Heaven

Fabrics, Supplies, and Classes. PFAFF Sewing Center

Fabric—Over 1500 Bolts
Hoffman, Alexander Henry, Robert Kaufman, P&B, and Moda
Books —100 Titles and More
Notions—Great Variety of Threads
Mettler, Cotty, Luny, Mez Alcazar, Sulky, Finishing Touch
Classes—All Skill Levels

Mon - Sat 10 - 5

Wilmington, NC #1

4403 Park Ave 28403 (910) 395-0200
Owners: Mary Sneeden Est: 1991 2200 sq.ft.

Wilmington, NC #2

Mon - Fri 10 - 5 Sat 10 - 3

Sewing Circle

5751 Oleander Dr. #5 28403
(910) 387-9399
E-Mail: FRANSSC@aol.com
Web Site: www.franssewingcircle.com
Owner: Fran Kertesz

Husqvarna Viking Sewing Machines. Unique selection of quilt fabrics, fashion fabrics, patterns, books, buttons and notions. Quilt Kits - made to order and ours.

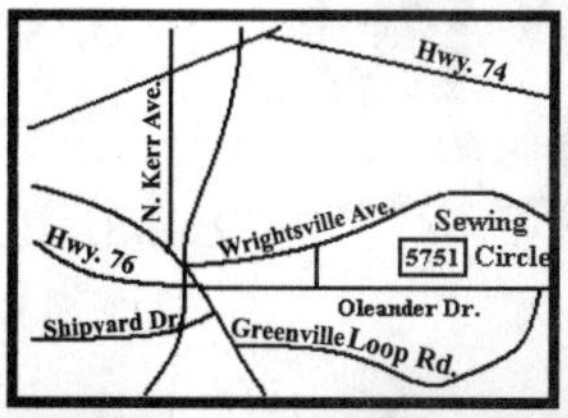

Morehead City, NC #3

Tues - Sat 9:30 - 5

Sew It Seams

104 N. 7th St. 28557
(252) 247-2114
Owner: Lillian Lawrence

Personal Service and Southern Hospitality. Great Selection of 100% cotton fabrics, books, patterns, notions and classes.

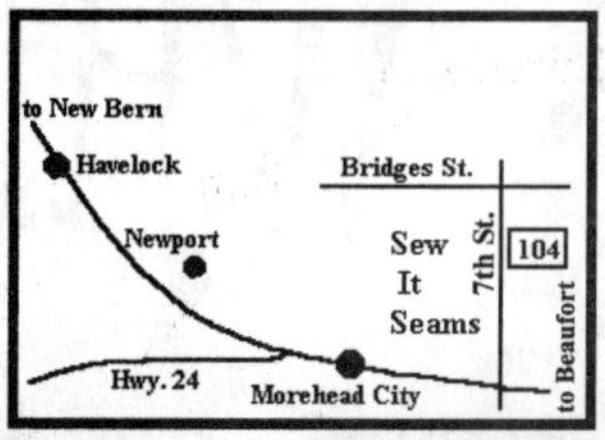

Jacksonville, NC #4

Tues - Fri 10 - 5 Sat 10 - 4

The Cotton Patch Quilt Shoppe

112 Phillips Rd. (Hwy. 17) 28540
(910) 938-1395
Fax: (910) 938-7543
Owner: Sharon C. Turner
Est: 1993
2750 sq.ft. 6000 Bolts

Large selection Fabrics, Books & Patterns, Notions, Ceramic Buttons, Classes. "A Really Great Quilt Store."

Jacksonville, NC #5

Tues - Fri 10 - 4 Sat 10 - 2

The Country Collection

2864 Wilmington Hwy (Hwy 17 S) 28540
(910) 347-1960 Fax: Same
E-Mail: countrycollection@ec.rr.com
Owner: Frances Cauley
Est: 1994 1800+ sq. ft. 2000+ Bolts

100% cotton designer fabrics. Books, patterns, notions & classes. Jinny Beyer & Thimbleberries Quilt kits. Pfantastic Pfaff sewing machines. Friendly professional guidance. Mail order.

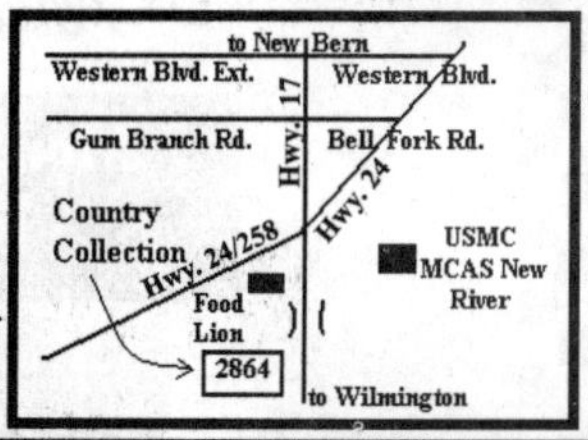

New Bern, NC #6

Mon - Sat 10 - 5:30 Thur til 7

The Quilt & Stained Glass Co., Inc.

319 Middle St. 28560
(252) 635-1054
Owner: Rich & Donna Daniels
2000+ Bolts

Quilt, Stained Glass and Jewelry Supplies - Classes - Custom Designs Unique Gifts

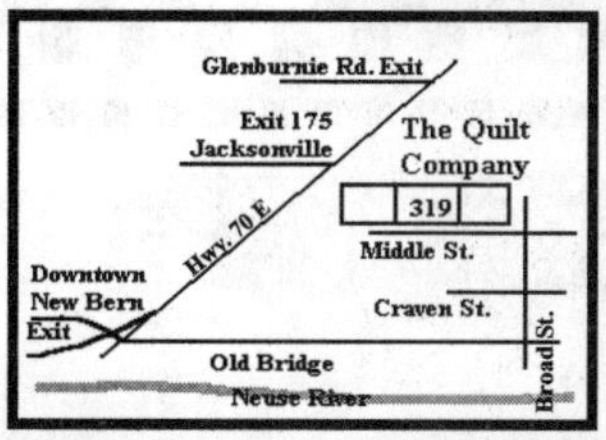

Kinston, NC #7

Tues - Fri 10 - 4 Sat 10 - 2

The Country Collection

1685 Highway 258 North 28504
(252) 522-3521 Fax: (252) 522-3521
E-Mail: countrycollection@ec.rr.com
Owner: Frances Cauley
Est: 1999 1500 sq. ft. 1500+ Bolts

100% cotton designer fabrics. Books, patterns, notions & classes. Jinny Beyer & Thimbleberries Quilt kits. Pfantastic Pfaff sewing machines. Friendly professional guidance. Mail order.

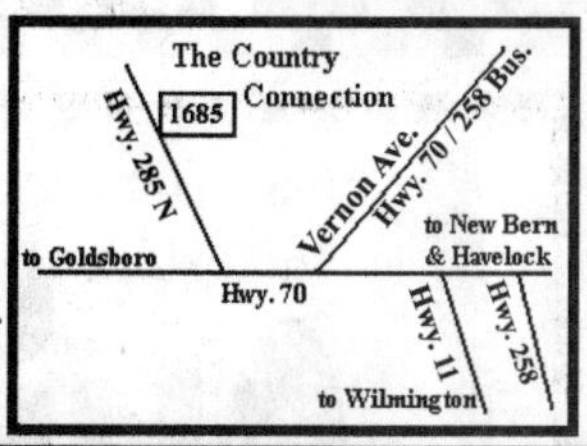

Winterville, NC #8

Mon - Fri 11 - 6 Sat 10 - 3

QUILT SHOP

2423 Winter Village Shp. Ctr. E 28590
(252) 321-2262
E-Mail: tmgquilts@aol.com
Owner: Wanda Conklin Est: 1997

Machine Quilting, reasonable rate and fast service. Quilts old & new, 100% cotton fabric & notions, frames and hoops plus much more.

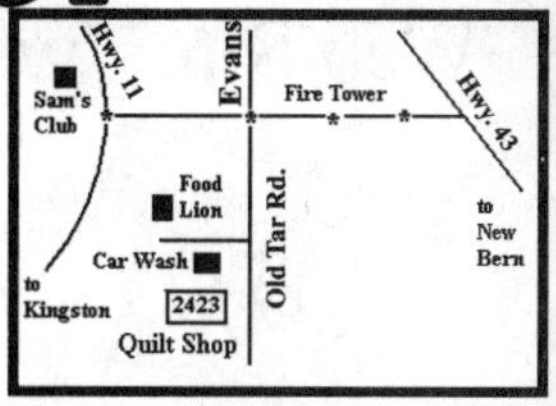

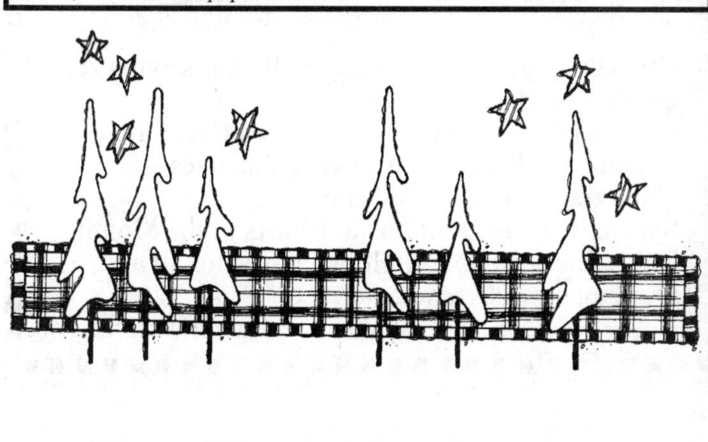

Grandy, NC #9

Quilt Shoppe

Cindy Holland
Est: 2001

Mon - Sat 10 - 5

6599 Caratoke Hwy.
Grandy, NC 27939
252-453-8944
Fax:
252-232-3415
E-Mail:
jandcholland
@yahoo.com

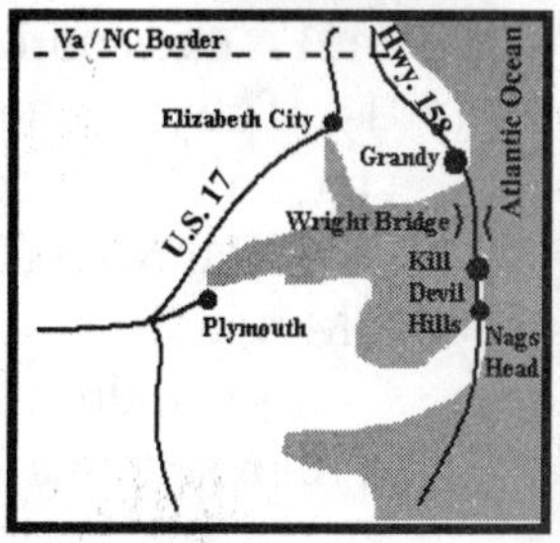

Specializing in brights, batiks, nautical and tropical. Featuring the latest in books and patterns. Stop by on your way to the Outer Banks of North Carolina, 12 miles north of the Wright Memorial Bridge.

Selma, NC #10

WHISTLE STOP

Quilt Shop

A destination for quilters & friends.

Bolts & Bolts of Fabric

Mon - Sat 10:00 - 5:00 Closed Wed
1st Sunday of each Month 1 - 4

104 E. Anderson Street,
Selma, NC 27576
919/975-0404

Email: conniewalker@mindspring.com
Connie Walker, Owner
Est: 2001
1100 sq.ft. 2400+ Bolts

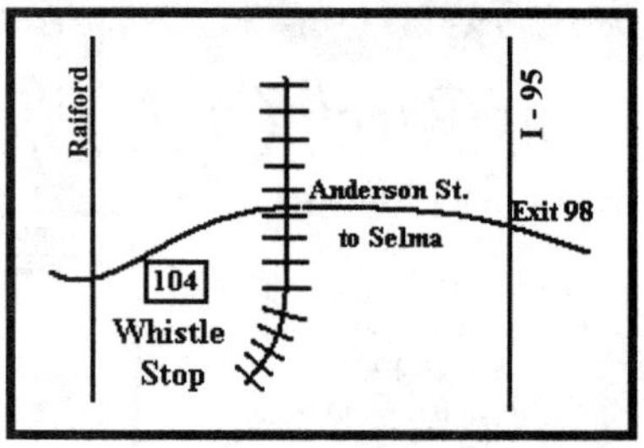

Conveniently located just ½ mile off I - 95, exit 98.

Over 2400 bolts of 100% designer cottons, books, patterns, notions & more including batiks, homespuns, novelties, 30s & Civil War reproductions. Kits are our specialty!
Plan a trip to the Whistle Stop and discover Uptown Selma, home to over 20 shops and more than 100 antique dealers -- all within walking distance!

Fayetteville, NC #11

Est: 1996
3600 sq.ft.

Loving Stitches

150 Andrews Rd. 28311
Andrews Commons
Shopping Center
(910) 630-3912
E-Mail: quilts4u@lovingstitches.net

Web Site: www.lovingstitches.net

From I-95 take exit 46A toward Fayetteville. Stay on this Hwy. until it ends on Ramsey St. (401). Then turn left and you'll pass a VA Hospital (R), Wal Mart (L), & Methodist College (R) to Andrews Rd. We're in strip mall on the left.

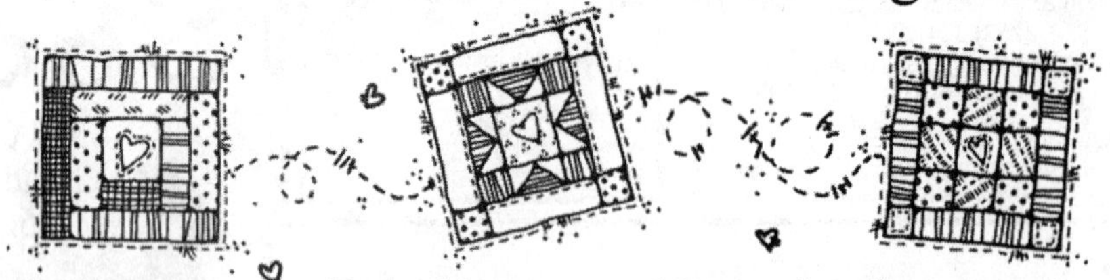

Mon & Wed - Sat 10 - 6
Tues 12 - 6

- Everything you could want for all your sewing & quilting needs
- Over 4000 bolts of current 100% cotton fabrics
- Repairs on all brands of sewing machines
- Authorized BERNINA dealer
- Specially made Quilt kits & Blocks of the Month
- Enjoyable sewing & quilting classes for all ages
- Quilting services available
- Busses Welcome! Call ahead and we'll wait for you.

Nothing Sews Like A Bernina. Nothing.
BERNINA®

12 Randy's Quilt Shop

2417-C Lawndale Drive, Greensboro, N.C. 27408

Over 8500 bolts of fabric

Thousands of Batiks

Notions, Books
& Patterns

Classes from
Beginner
To Advanced

Professional,
Knowledgeable Staff
Years of Experience in all
aspects of Quiltmaking

Authorized Bernina Dealer

Store Hours
Mon—Sat
10-6
Sun– 1-6

Tel– 336-545-5558
Fax- 336-545-5805
E-mail rsilv60128@aol.com

www.randysquiltshop.com

Owner: Randy Silvers

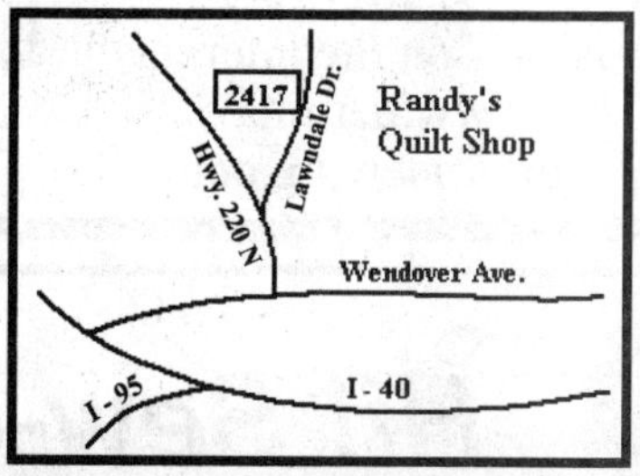

Raleigh, NC #13

Archangel Fabrics

1612 N. Market Dr. 27609
(919) 790-7792
Fax: (919) 790-1834
E-Mail: archangelfabrics@mindspring.com
Owner: Sandy McKenzie
Est: 1995 2500 sq.ft.
Web Site: www.archangelfabrics.com

Mon - Sat 10 - 5

Over 4000 bolts 100% designer cottons, classes,
supplies, gifts, notions, books & patterns.
Machine quilting service available.

Raleigh, NC #14

Bernina World of Sewing

3500 bolts of 100% cotton fabric. Authorized Bernina Dealer. Wide variety of specialty patterns, threads, notions and sewing accessories. Large selection of sewing cabinets and work tables.

"Come Visit Us and be a part of the excitement"

Mon - Sat 10 - 5
Thur til 7

6013 Glenwood Ave. 27612
(919) 782-2945
Visit Us on the internet:
www.bernina
worldofsewing.com

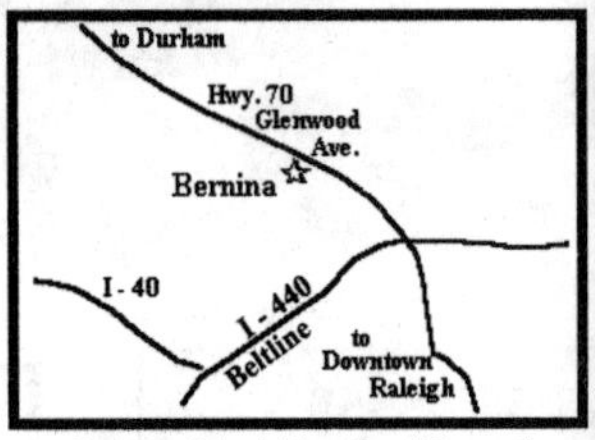

Located 1- 1/4 miles West of Crabtree Valley Mall on Hwy. 70 in Oak Park Shopping Center.

Cary, NC #15

Mon - Fri 10 - 6
Sat 10 - 5

Etc. Crafts

226 E. Chatham St. 27511
(919) 467-7636
Owner: Jean Petersen

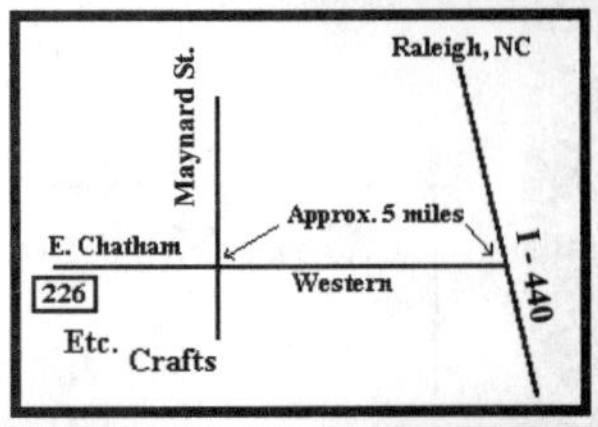

Large selection of 100% Cotton Quilting Fabrics. Books and Notions.

Carrboro, NC #16

Mon - Sat 10 - 6
Sun 1 - 4

Thimble Pleasures

205 W. Main St. 27510
(919) 968-6050
E-Mail: thimblepleasures@mindspring.com
Web Site: www.thimblepleasures.com
Owner: Julie Holbrook
Est: 1993 2000 sq.ft.

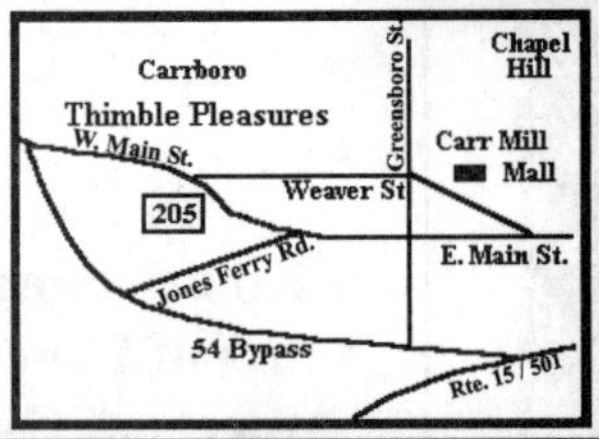

Over 3000 Bolts of 100% Cotton Designer Fabrics. Books, Patterns, Notions. Wide variety of classes. Quarterly Newsletter.

Hi! Sew-Ciety

YOUR COMPLETE SEWING CENTER

&

QUILTING PEACE BY PIECE

Perfectly located in Kernersville, NC, THE HEART OF THE PIEDMONT TRIAD.

Visit us at our **redesigned** 3000 sq.ft. shop, with loads of **fabrics**, patterns, books, templates, supplies and best of all a **knowledgable** and **friendly staff**. Come on by and chat about your latest projects, see our large selection of quilting fabrics with a southern touch, and our line of wonderful machines.

Easily accessible from either Interstate 40

I-40 BUSINESS TO EXIT 15, NC HWY 66
Turn right towards High Point, go one block to Plaza 66 South on Right

I-40 East or West TO EXIT 203, NC HWY 66
Turn toward Kernersville, go approx 1.5 miles to Plaza 66 South on left.

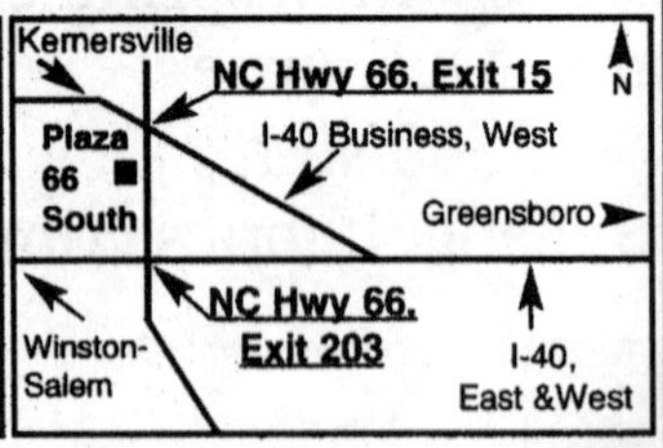

Open Mon-Fri 9 to 6 & Sat 9 to 3

Plaza 66 South Shopping Center
806-R NC Hwy 66 South
Kernersville, NC 27284
336-993-1500 or 336-993-7770

#17

West Jefferson, NC #18

Mon - Fri 10 - 5
Dec - March
Tues - Sat 10 - 5

The Quilt Gathering

103 S. Jefferson Ave. 28694
(336) 246-5655 Est: 1999
E-Mail: quilt-gathering@fastransit.net
Owner: Gail Patrissi 2000 sq.ft.

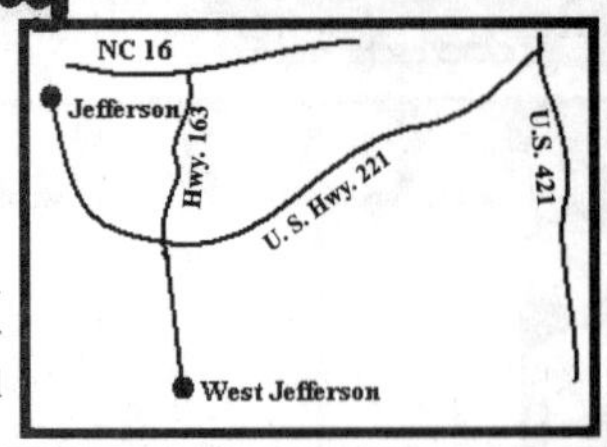

We're name droppers: Jinny Beyer, Thimbleberry, Princess Mirah: just a few of our fabulous fabrics. Notions, buttons, and patterns too!

Mooresville, NC #19

Tues - Sat 10 - 6

Opening Spring/Summer 2002

Quilters Loft Company

188 N. Main St.
28117
(704) 662-8660
Owner: Erica Ransom

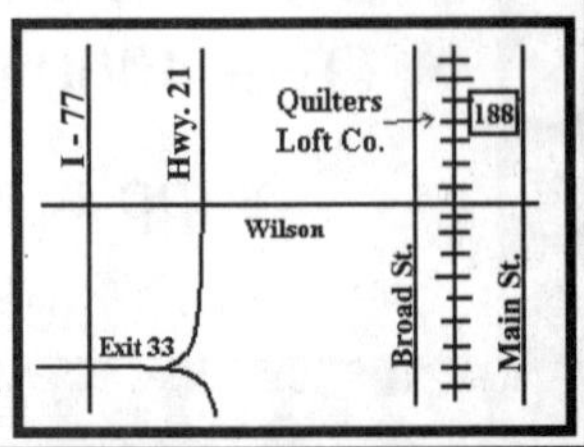

Fabrics, patterns, books, notions, classes.
Corner of Main & Moore Sts 1906 Bank Bldg.
Entrance on Moore-upstairs.

Charlotte, NC #20

Mon - Sat 10 - 4:30

Quilter's Gallery

901 South Kings Dr. Suite # 135
(704) 376-2531 28204
Owner: Patti Cline & Cindy Page
Est: 1981 2000 sq.ft. 2000+ Bolts

Cotton Fabrics--Traditional and unusual prints, Batiks, and Homespuns. Wide range of books and patterns. German Mohair & Teddy Bear Supplies. French Heirloom Sewing Supplies. Buttons and trims.

Charlotte, NC #21

Mon - Fri 10 - 5:30 Sat 10 - 4

The Sewing Bird

4247-B Park Rd 28209
(704) 676-0076 Fax: (704) 676-0179
E-Mail: sewinbird@aol.com
Web Site: www.sewingbird.com
Owner: Anne Schout
Est: 1990 2500 sq. ft. 1200+ Bolts

Great selection of fabrics from around the world not your average quilting cottons. Notions, patterns, books, friendly service. JANOME

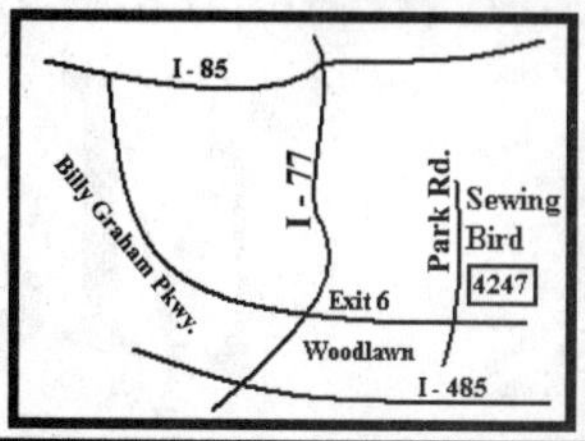

Matthews, NC #22

Mon - Thur 10 - 4:30 Fri & Sat 10 - 4

QUILT PATCH FABRICS

1017 Stallings Rd. 28104 (704) 821-7554
Web Site: www.quiltpatchfabrics.com
Owners: Charlotte Harkey, Bryan Gregory, Janice Cooper Est: 1996
Full color range of 100% cotton fabrics (2000+ bolts), books & patterns, notions, hand & machine technique classes, machine quilting service available.

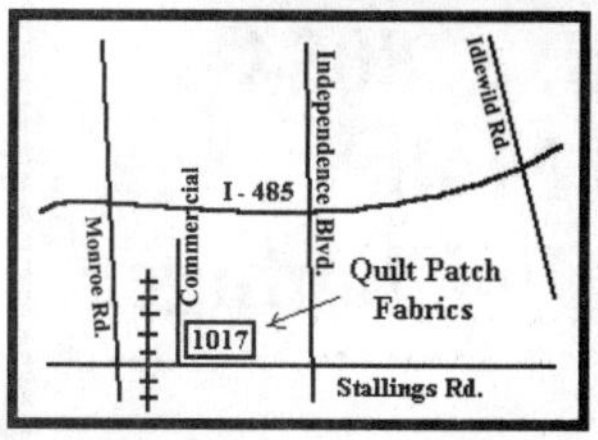

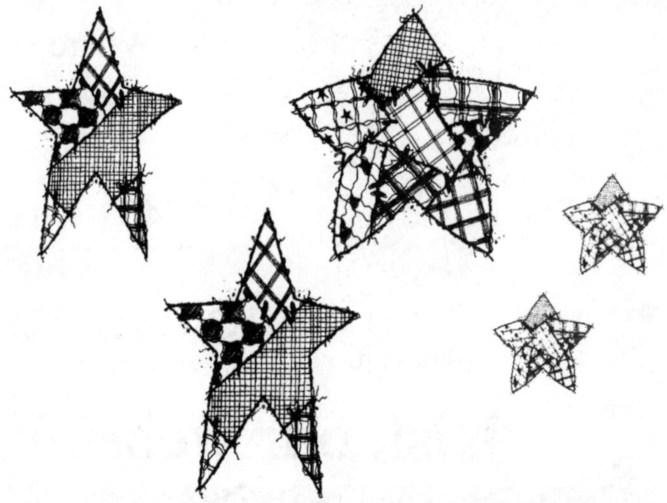

The Quilting Corner, Inc.

Route 4, Box 55A, McMurray Rd.
Flat Rock, NC 28731 (828) 698-7125
Website: www.quiltingcorner.com

Hours:
MWFS 10 - 5
T & Th 10 - 7
Sun 1 - 5

2000 sq.ft. of pure Quilting Heaven!

Visit the Western North Carolina Mountains and our cozy log cabin.
We carry only the best fabrics, books, newest notions and patterns.
Or join us for a class taught by one of our professional teachers.
We carry Vicking sewing machines and the Handi Quilter Frame.
We are also the proud owners of the TQC Stylus designed for the Handi Quilter Frame.

Exit #22 (Upward Rd.) on I - 26 in the Log Cabin next to the Dish Barn.

I - 26 West: turn right off of Exit #22 ramp. Turn Left on McMurray Rd.

I - 26 East: turn left off of Exit #22 ramp. Turn Left after the light - making sure you do not get back on the expressway. (McMurray Rd.)

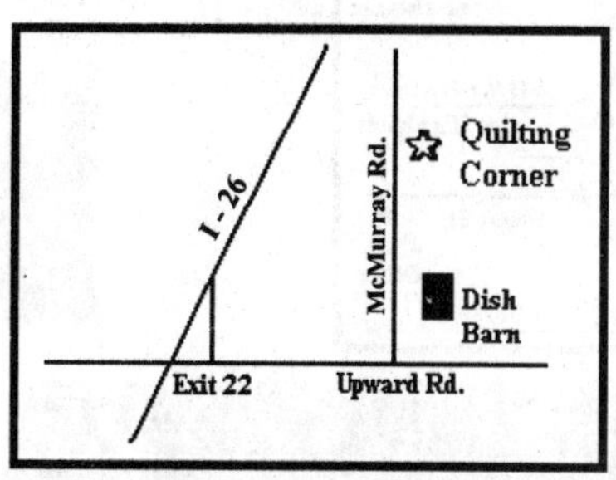

Flat Rock, NC #23

Gastonia, NC #24

(800) 627-9567

Mary Jo's Cloth Store

Mon - Sat 9 - 5:45
Mon & Thur til 8:45

"The Place" for investment sewers.
Where variety is the greatest. Prices are the lowest and large quantities can be found.

401 Cox Rd. 28054
Gaston Mall
Owner: Mary Jo Cloninger

Est: 1951
32,000 sq.ft.

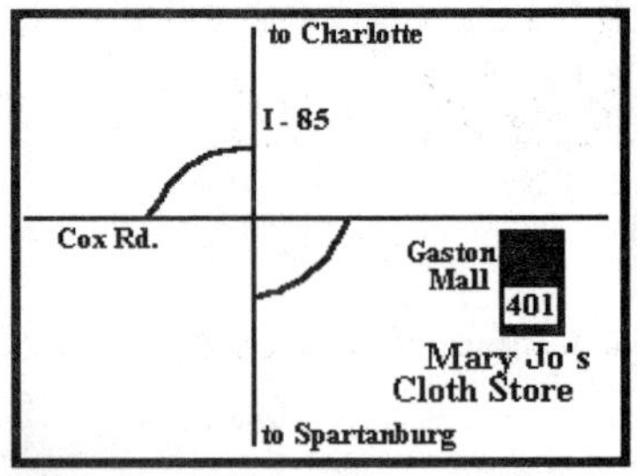

visit our website: www.maryjos.com

Ann's Needle & Hook Depot

"The Fun Place To Be"

495 Depot St. 28734
(828) 524-9626
Fax: (828) 524-9040
E-Mail: warrens@dnet.net
Owner: Ann Warren

PFAFF

• Competitive Prices Ask For A Demo

- Quilting Fabrics—Homespuns, Wool, Cottons, Batiks, Bear Fur
- Notions
- Rug Hooking
- Patterns & Books
- Wearable Arts / Classes
- Lots of Sample Models
- **Unique Gifts**
- Jewelry-Snowmen, Cats, Bears, Roosters, Lamps, Folk Art, Primitives

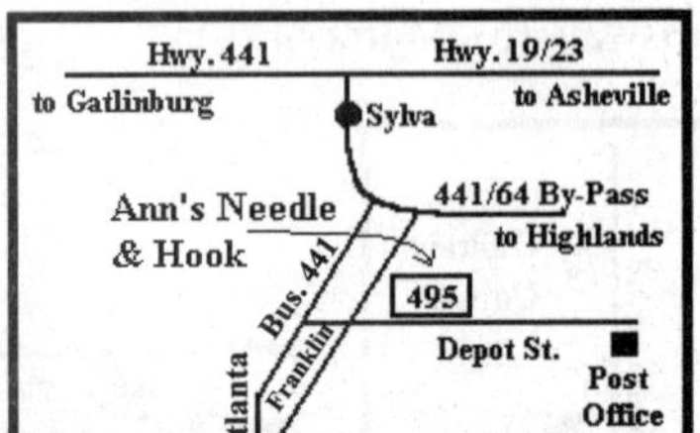

Mon - Fri
9 - 5
Sat 10 - 4

Franklin, NC #25

Hendersonville, NC #26

M, T, Th, F 10 - 5
Wed 10 - 2
Sat 10 - 4

Village Quilt Company

117 W. Barnwell St. 28792
(828) 692-8200
E-Mail: Villagequiltco@aol.com
Owner: Randi Lowery Est: 1999

Your Personal Quilt Shop
Cottons, Flannels, Homespuns, Quilting Supplies
Books * Patterns * Classes
Procion dyes * Setacolor fabric paints

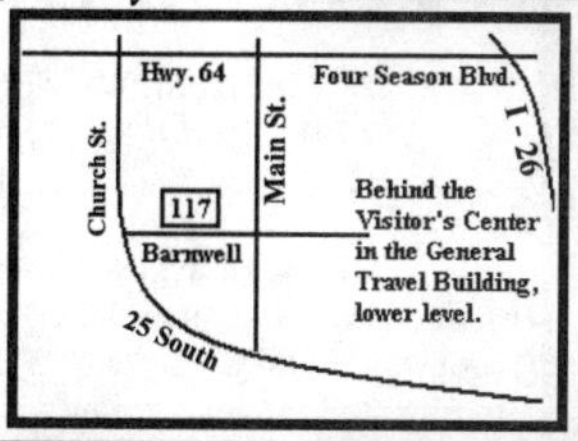

Fairview, NC #27

Mon - Thur 1:30 - 5:30
Sat 10 - 4

Quilt Bow-Tik Shoppe

1346 Charlotte Hwy. (Hwy. 74) 28730
(828) 628-9505
E-Mail: Quiltbowtik@cs.com
Est: 2001

Fabric, books, patterns, Gutermann Threads, Quilters Dream Batting.

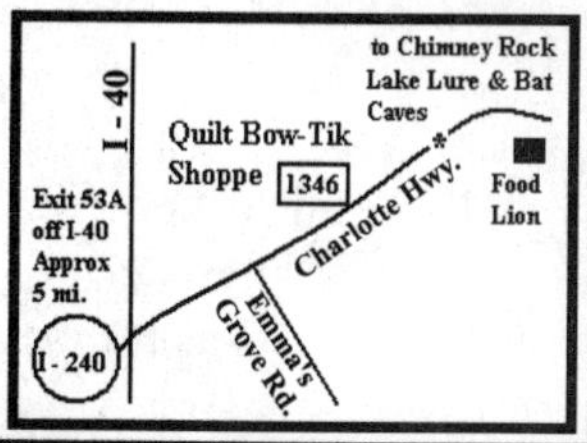

Burnsville, NC #28

Mon - Fri 9 - 5
Sat 9 - 4

The Country Peddler

3 Town Square 28714
(828) 682-7810
Owners: Barbara & Tommy Pittman
Est: 1980

Great selection of quilts, fabrics, & notions. Custom quilts made to order. Quilted and fabric gifts.

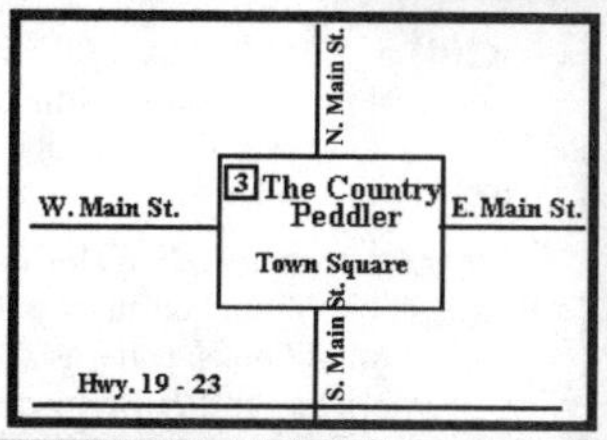

needle • me • this

2000 square feet of Fabrics with a Flair
Not your everyday Cottons Notions
Books Patterns Classes Friendly Service.
Authorized Dealer for
Janome Memory Craft 10,000, light weight
Jem Gold and all models in between.

Mon - Fri 9:30 - 5:00
Sat 9:30 - 3:00

Look for the Blue Building with the Yellow Awnings.

Burnsville, NC #29

112 W. Main St. 28714
(828) 682-9462
Fax: (828) 682-9462
Owner: Carol McCroskey
Est: 1987
2000 sq.ft. 2000 Bolts

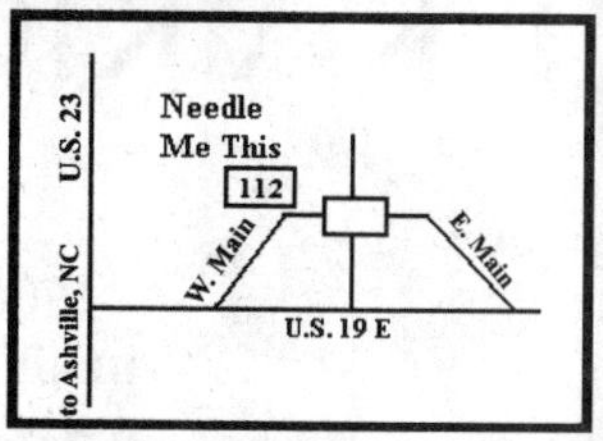

Other Shops in North Carolina: We suggest calling first

Asheville Street Fair, 42 Battery Park Ave. 704-253-0836
Asheville Folk Art Center, P.O. Box 9545 704-298-7928
Ashville Waechter's Silk Shop, 94 Charlotte St. 828-252-2131
Black Mountain Marti's Patchwork Cottage, 206 Sutton Ave. 828-669-9005
Burnsville Young's Fabrics, Crafts & Antiques, 724 S. Main St. 704-682-6633
Carrboro Mulberry Silks, 200 N. Greensboro St. #B6 919-942-7455
Chapel Hill Cotton Boll Creative Sewing Center, 91 S. Elliott Rd. 919-942-9661
Cherokee Quilt and Comfort Gallery, Acquoni Rd. 704-497-4103
Elizabeth City Quilts & More, 505 E. Church St. 252-338-9500
Fayetteville Magnolia Station, 623 Wakefield Dr. 910-867-2170
Fayetteville Crafts, Frames & Things, Inc., 108 Owen Dr. 910-485-4833
Fletcher Carolina Fabric Outlet, 6024 Hendersonville Rd. 704-684-0801
Franklin Maco Crafts, 2846 Georgia Rd. 828-524-7878
Franklin Sharon's Quilt Shoppe, 39 Palmer St. Cir 828-524-3046
Franklin Sew Creative, 91 Highlands Rd.
Franklin La Poma & La Poma, P.O. Box 777 828-524-5114
Goldston Calico Quilt Antiques, Belview Ave. 919-898-4998
Greensboro Log Cabin Craftshop, 5435 N. Church St. 336-282-7331
Greensboro Quilts 'N Silks, 3000 Lawndale Dr. 336-286-1288
Highlands Azure Rose Quilts & Gifts, 344 Main St. 828-526-8280
Highlands Highlands Emporium, 375 Main St. 828-526-1660
Morehead City Quilt Cottage, 905 Arendell St. 252-726-1505
New Bern New Bern Fabric Center, 1218 S. Glenburnie Rd. 252-633-4780
Newland Brenda Kay Crafts, Rt. 4, Box 489
Newton Phyllis' Crafts, 19 N. College Ave. 704-464-7770
Pfafftown South Fork Cloth Shop, P.O. Box 95 919-765-0640
Raleigh Carolina Sew N Vac Center, 6320-111 Capital Blvd. 919-873-1981
Rockingham Cozy Comfort, 515 E. Broad Ave. 910-410-0102
Spindale The Mitchell Fabrics, 400 Spindale St. 800-870-5312
Waynesville W K Fabrics, 2348 Russ Ave. 828-456-3250

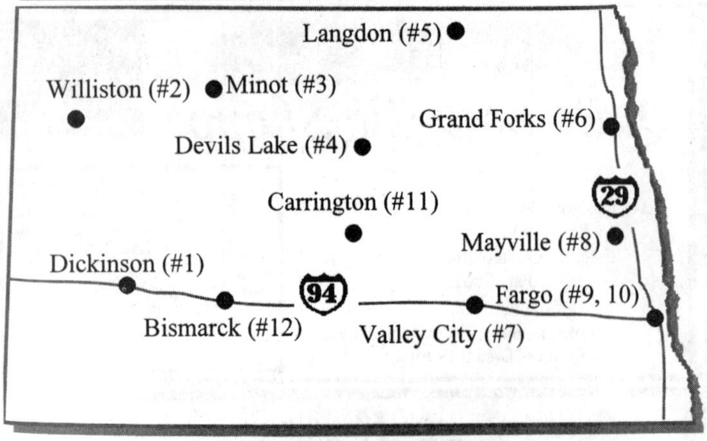

12 Featured Shops

NORTH DAKOTA

Dickinson, ND #1

Mon - Sat 9:30 - 5:30

Bernina Sew and So

38 1st St. W 58601
(701) 225-1408 7200 sq.ft.
Owners: Bev Haas & Betty Volesky

Dakota's Largest Fabric Store.

Mail order and newsletter available upon request. Quilt, Bridal, Fashion Fabrics. Bernina and Janome Dealer.

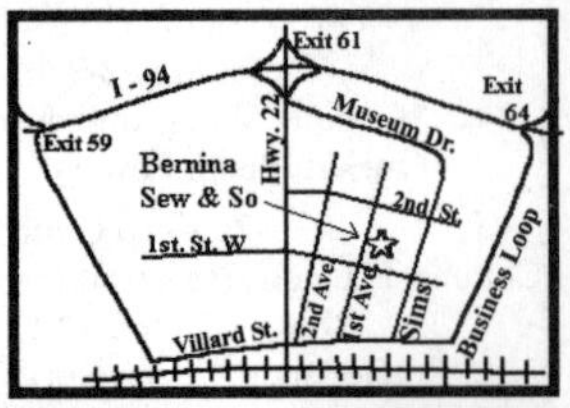

Williston, ND #2

Mon - Fri 10 - 5:30 Sat 10 - 4

Sylvia's Quilt & Sew

16 East Broadway 58801
(701) 572-0718 Fax: (701) 572-7018
E-Mail: sewquilt@citlink.net
Owners: Sylvia Paulson
Est: 1988 4000+ Bolts 600+ Books

100% cottons including Hoffman, Moda, RJR, Debbie Mumm & many others. Large selection of books, patterns & notions. Authorized Pfaff & Bernina Dealer.

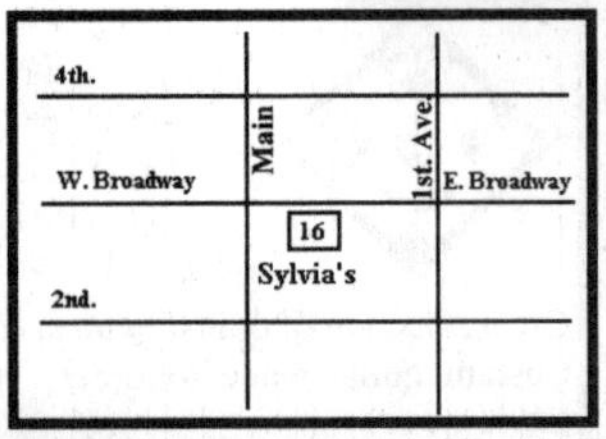

Minot, ND #3

PRAIRIE ROSE QUILT SHOP

(701) 852-2835
1500 53rd Ave. SW 58701
prairierosequilt@hotmail.com
www.prairierosequiltshop.com

Owner: Carmen R. Haugen
Est: 1998 1750 sq.ft.
2500 Bolts

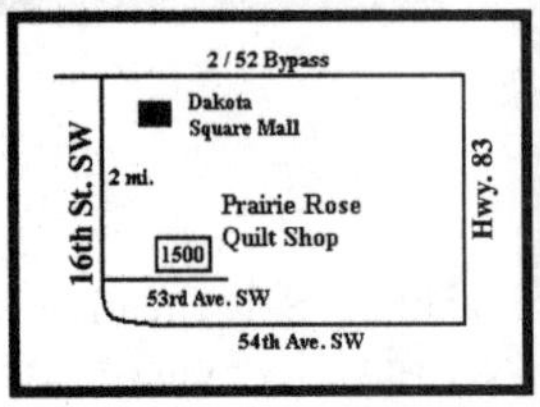

Mon - Fri 10 - 5 Sat 10 - 2

Full service quilt shop offering quality quilting fabric and machine quilting. Specializing in florals, plaids, batiks, flannels & wool.

Devils Lake, ND #4

Mon - Sat 9:30 - 5:30 Thur til 9

Lone Star Quilting

316 4th St. 58301
(701) 662-3634
Owner: Barb Simons
Est: 1996

Featuring freestyle meandering, custom designs; extensive thread palette; binding service and always one on one friendly service. Lets complete your work of Art!

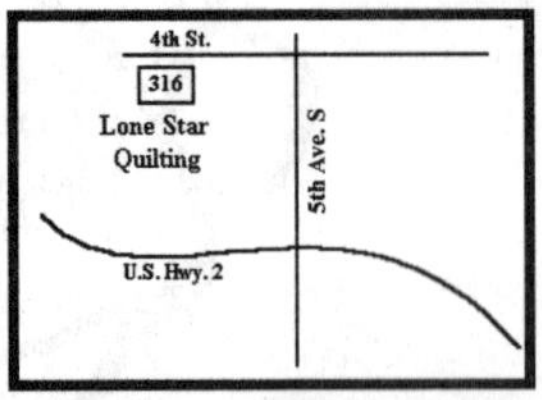

Langdon, ND #5

Mon - Sat 9:30 - 5:30

Homespun

802 3rd St. 58249
(701) 256-2609

E-Mail: barbkr@utma.com
Owner: Barbara Kruk

Quality Quilting fabrics, books, patterns, notions and quilting classes. Bernina Sales. Friendly, Knowledgeable staff.

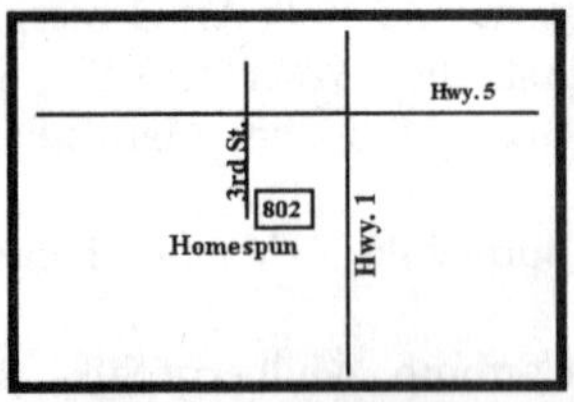

Grand Forks, ND #6

Tues - Fri 10 - 5 Sat 10 - 4

Quilted Rabbit

8 S. 3rd St. 58201
(701) 772-7173
Owner: Tes Weekesmurphy
Est: 1994

Gifts, Collectibles, Custom Machine Quilting & More
"A little out of the way, but a little out of the ordinary!"

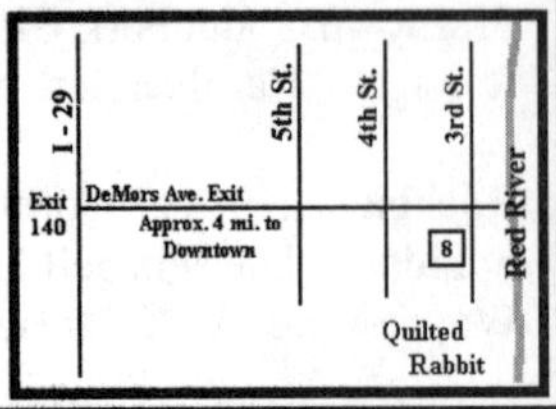

Valley City, ND #7

Mon - Sat 9:30 - 5:30

Cotton Patch Treasures

330 Central Ave. N 58072
(701) 845-4926
Owner: Georgia Manstrom
Est: 1993 2100 sq.ft.

Distinctive gifts such as Boyds Bears. Fabrics, classes, Books, Patterns, Quilting Supplies. Pfaff Sewing Machine Dealer.

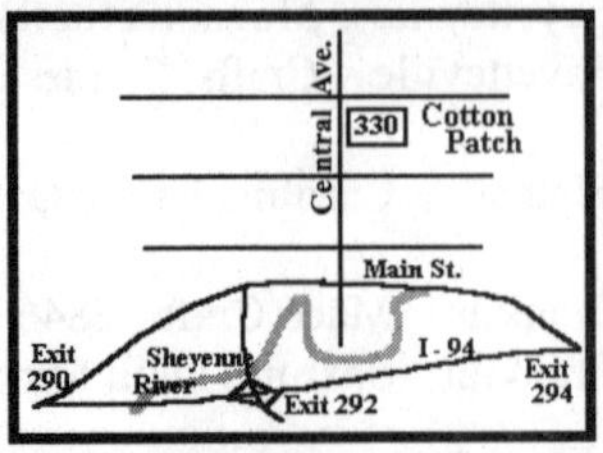

Mayville, ND #8

Faye's Henhouse Quilts

Mon - Sat
9 - 5:30
Tues til 9

37 Center Ave. North, Mayville, ND 58257
(701) 786-3790
Website: www.fayesquiltshop.com
Owner: Faye Grandalen
Est: 1996 3200 sq.ft. 3000+ Bolts

Fine cotton fabrics, quilting supplies, books, patterns, notions, and custom machine quilting, classes, gift items, and quilt racks.

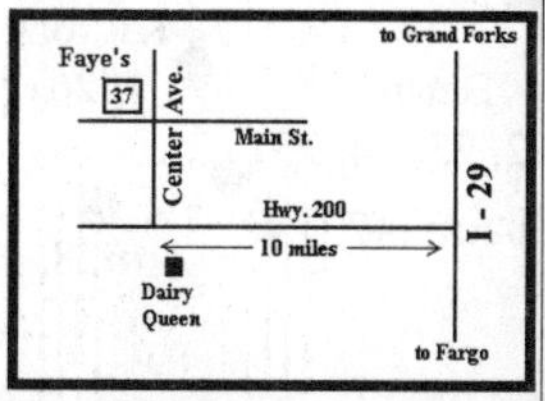

Rae-Bon Quilt & Sewing Center

4325 13th Ave. SW #5
Fargo, ND 58103
(701) 433-7203
email: raesew@aol.com
Fax: (701) 433-7204
Est: 1995 2700 sq.ft.

Fargo, ND #9

Over 2000 bolts of 100% cottons, heirloom fabrics . . . many cozy flannels. We offer classes, an extensive selection of threads, many books, patterns and handy notions.

Mon 10 - 8
Tues - Fri
10 - 5:30
Sat 10 - 4

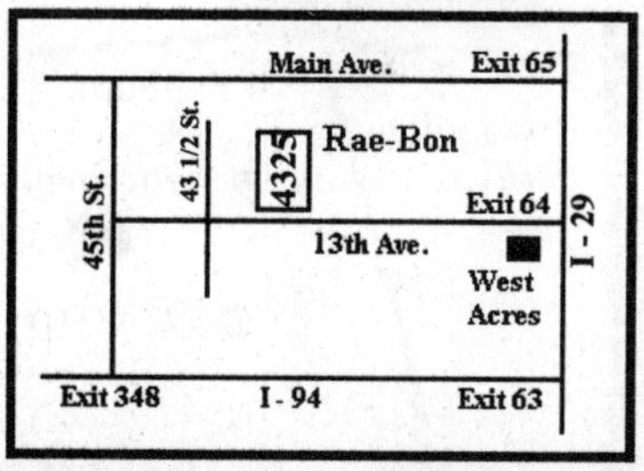

Owner: Tanya Zink
dfabqult@daktel.com

Designer Fabrics & Quilting Supplies

2 Great Shops !!

Carrington, ND #11

929 Main St. 58421
(701) 652-3535
Fax: (701) 652-3528
Est: 1992

Mon - Sat 10 - 5

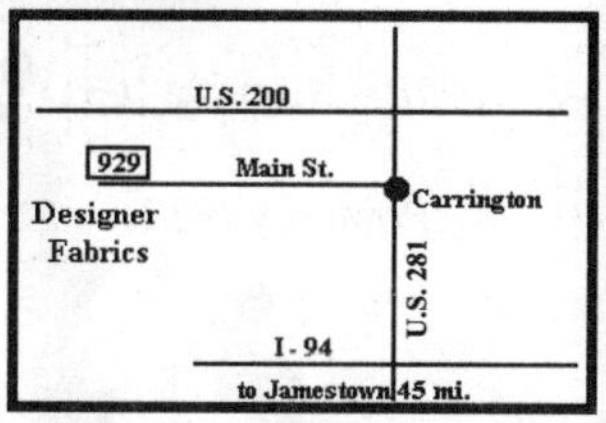

Complete quilt shop located in a historical building, specializing in traditional quilting. Many books, patterns, notions & classes. Friendly, helpful staff.

Fargo, ND #10

745D 45th St. SW 58103
(701) 277-1899
Fax: (701) 277-1897

Mon - Fri 10 - 8
Sat 10 - 5

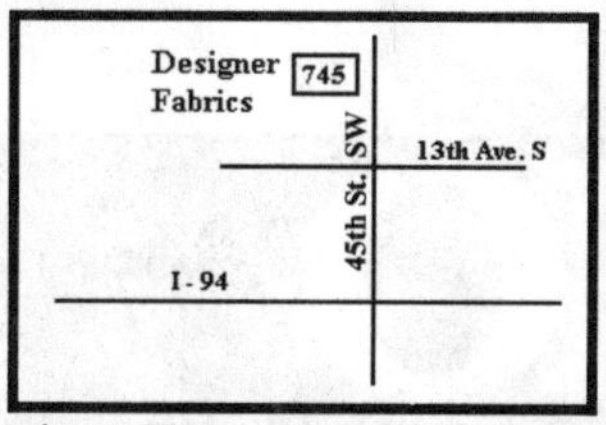

Come and visit our second location. Here you will find a warm friendly atmosphere filled with thousands of bolts of cotton fabrics, quilting supplies, Bernina sewing machines and Horn cabinets. Our knowledgeable, friendly staff will assist you with all your quilting, sewing and embroidery needs.

Bismarck, ND #12

The Quilt Shoppe

Mon 10 - 8
Tues - Fri
10 - 5:30
Sat 9:30 - 5:30

Inside J & R Vacuum & Sewing
223 E. Main 58501
(701) 258-5619
(800) 371-5515
Owners: Jim & Rene Barnhardt

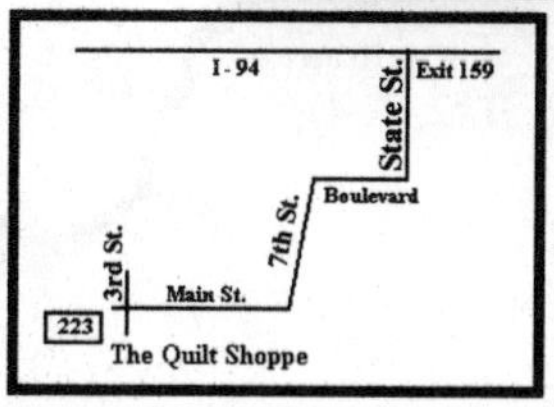

Quilt Supplies, classes, name brand 100% cotton quilting fabrics, books, patterns, notions, cabinets, PFAFF & Viking sewing machines.

Other Shops in North Dakota: We suggest calling first

Fargo	Quilter's Quarters, 604 Main Ave.	701-235-6525
Minot	Carol's Etc., 112 S. Main St.	701-839-6183
New Town	Polly's Quilts, P.O. Box 218	701-627-3885
Northwood	From The Heart, 22 44th St.	701-587-6019
Wahpenton	Pin Cushion Quilt Shop, 500 Dakota Ave.	701-642-9757
Williston	Quiltmakins, 12542 Hwy. 1804	701-774-3315
Willow City	Ye Olde Sew & So, 365 Main St.	701-366-4372

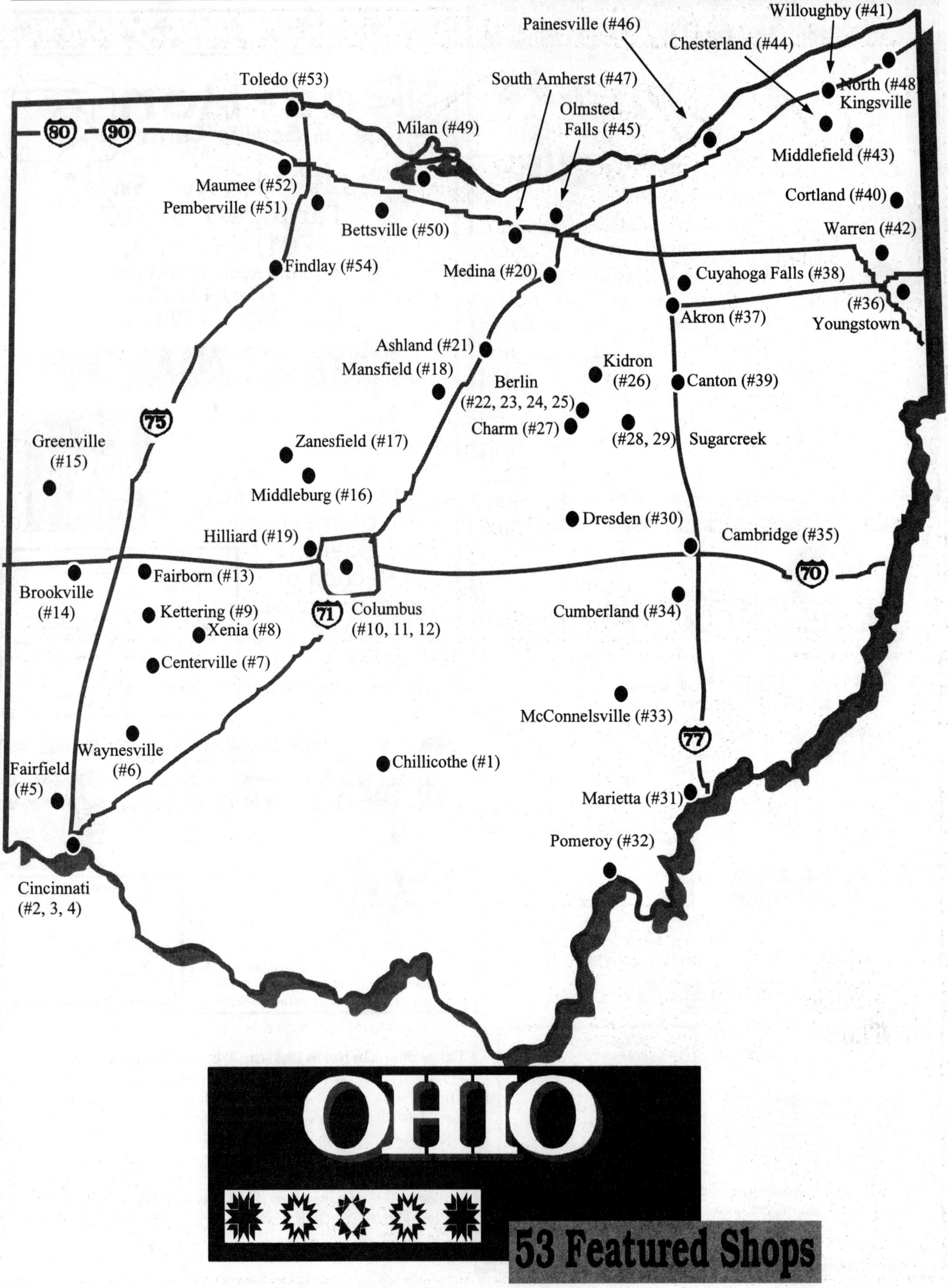

OHIO

53 Featured Shops

Creations SEWCLEVER Quilt Shop

192 S Paint St.
Chillicothe, OH 45601
(740) 775-1957 or toll free
1-888-SEW CLVR
Fax: (740) 773-2390
E-Mail: Sewclver@bright.net

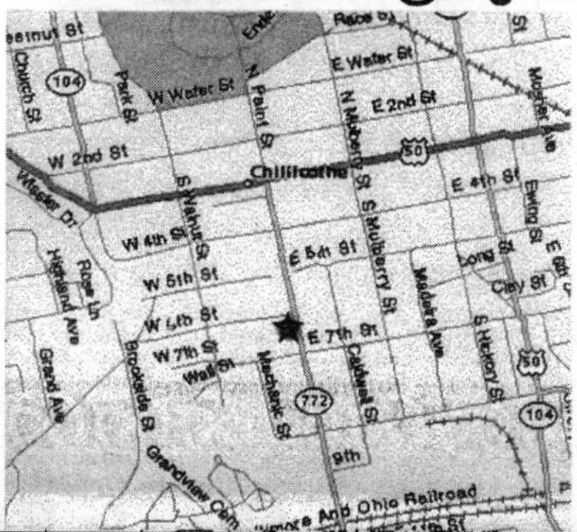

Creations SewClever is a friendly, full-line quilt shop found in a beautiful 1800's Greek Revival home in the historic district of downtown Chillicothe, OH. Call, write, or e-mail us for class schedules, or a free newsletter.

- Machine Quilting Services
- Janome Sewing Machines
- Kits
- Fine Fabrics
- Classes

MON. - SAT. 10 AM - 5PM

Chillicothe, OH #1

www.creationssewclever.com

Best Friends Quilt Shoppe

Fabric, classes, supplies, and *friendly* advice for all your quilting projects! Come visit Today!

M-F 10-9
Sat 10-5
Sun 12-4

More than 2500 bolts of Designer Quilting Fabric

400+ FLANNELS!
1930's Repro's
Debbie Mumm

KITS– Quilts, Purses and more...
Fat Quarters of EVERY Fabric
Quilting Books & Software

Cincinnati, OH #2

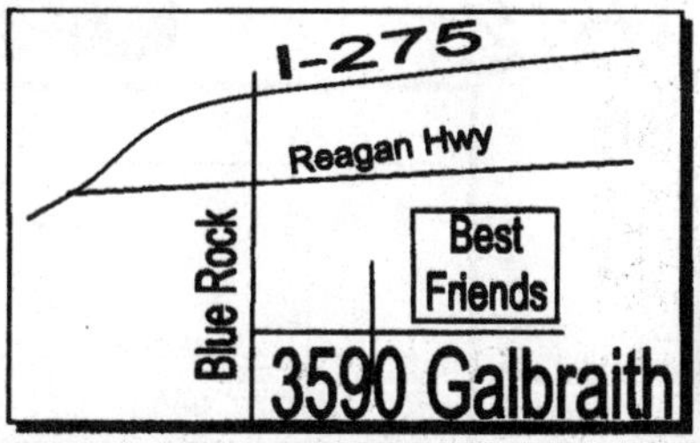

(513)385-2200
email:qshoppe@cinci.rr.com
3590 W. Galbraith Rd Cincinnati OH 45239

Easy access from I-275 on Cincy's West Side!

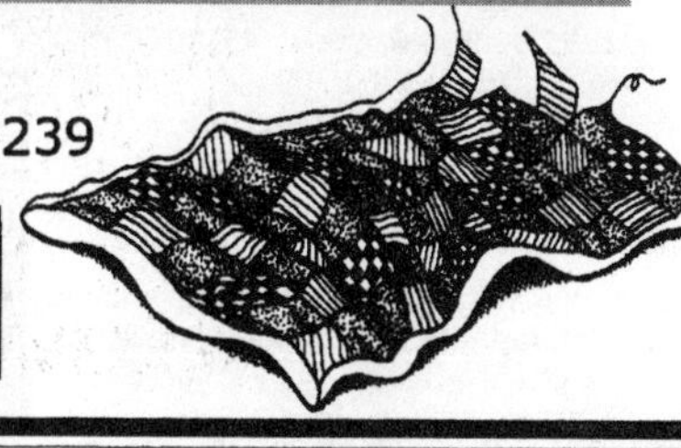

Cincinnati, OH #3

Creative Cottage
Quilting & Cross Stitch

6934 Miami Ave. 45243 in "Madeira"
(513) 271-2028
Owner: Marie Tsacalis
Est: 1988 3300 sq.ft.
15 min. from downtown Cincinnati

QUILTING - Large selection of books, patterns, stencils & tools.
FABRIC - 1500+ bolts of exciting cotton plus large selection of homespun and flannels.
CROSS STITCH - Huge selection of cross stitch books, fabrics, exciting fibers and notions.
CLASSES AND WORKSHOPS AND LOTS OF FUN, FUN, FUN...

Mon - Sat 9:30 - 5:30
Wed til 8:30
Sun 1 - 4

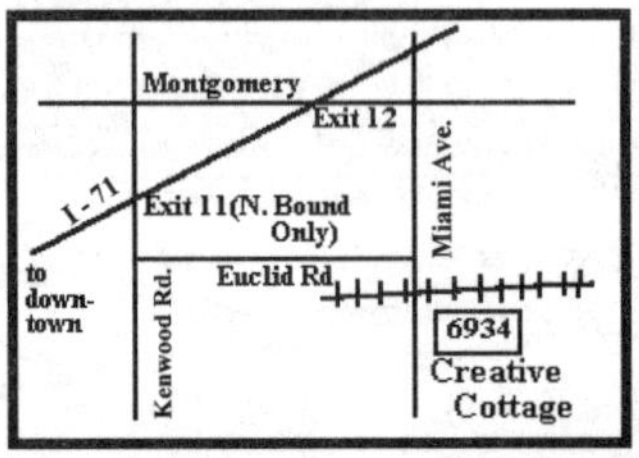

Cincinnati, OH #4

Victorian Quilt Shop

Mon - Thur 10 - 8
Fri & Sat 10 - 5

8556 Beechmont Ave. 45255
(513) 474-9355
Est: 1998 3800 sq.ft.

We stock 4500 bolts of designer cotton fabric, including Hoffman, Moda, P&B, Thimbleberries, Northcott, Bali, Maywood, RJR, Benartex, Kona Bay, etc.
We offer supplies, books, stencils, notions, classes, various discounts, unique gift items, specialty threads, glass beads, and imported heirloom fabrics, laces & supplies.

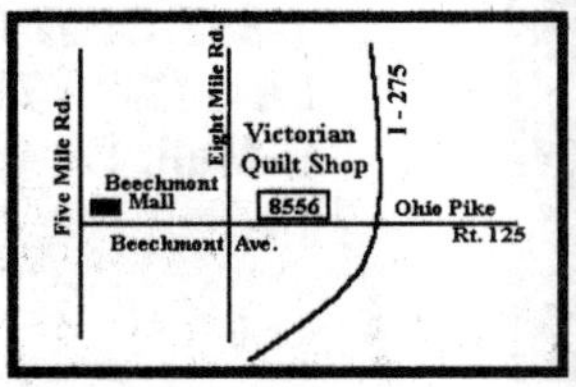

Fairfield, OH #5

Stitches 'n Such

Mon, Tues, Thur 10 - 7
Wed, Fri, Sat 10 - 4

702 Nilles Road 45014
(513) 829-2999
Web Site: www.stitchesnsuch.com
located 5 miles north of Cincinnati

Fabric, fabric, fabric - over 2,000 bolts including homespuns, flannels, fleece, wool. Patterns, books, notions. We also carry rug hooking supplies.

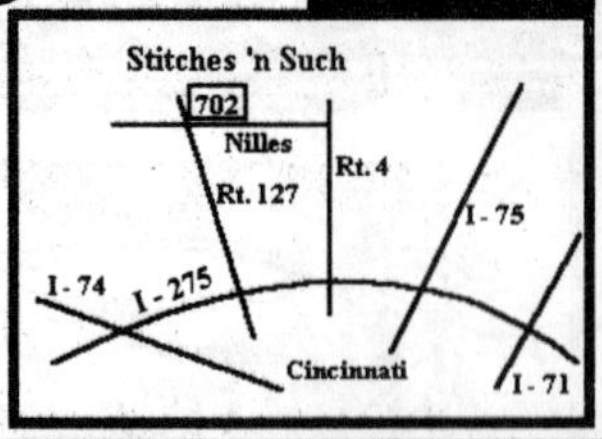

Waynesville, OH #6

Mon - Sat 10 - 5
Thur til 8
Sun 12 - 5

Fabric Shack

99 S. Marvin Ln. & Miami St. 45068
(513) 897-0092 Fax: (513) 897-7176
E-Mail: info@fabricshack.com
Web Site: www.fabricshack.com
Owner: Maxine Young
Est: 1986 3000 sq.ft. 7000+ Bolts

The ultimate quilt shop . . .
All the fabrics, colors, designers, the biggest in the midwest . . .
Notions, patterns, and books too!

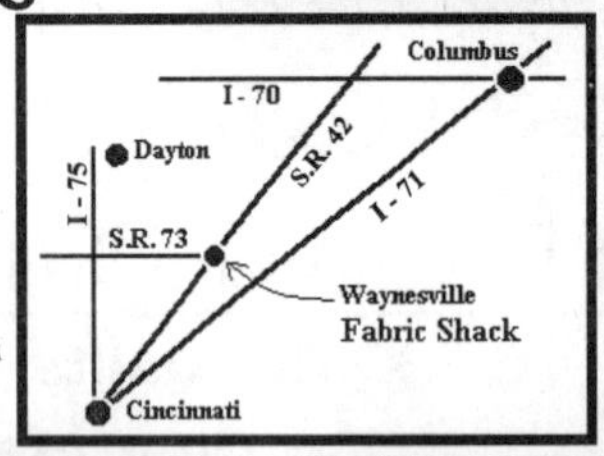

Centerville, OH #7

Sew-A-Lot

Mon - Thur 10 - 8
Fri & Sat 10 - 5

232 N. Main St. 45459
(937) 433-7474 Fax: (937) 433-0757
E-Mail: sewalot@erinet.com
Owner: Debbie Bernhard
Est: 1982 3500 sq.ft. 2500 Bolts

Sales & Service of Pfaff & Elna machines.
Great selection of 100% cotton fabrics, patterns, books & machine threads. Classes.
Historic building built in 1874.

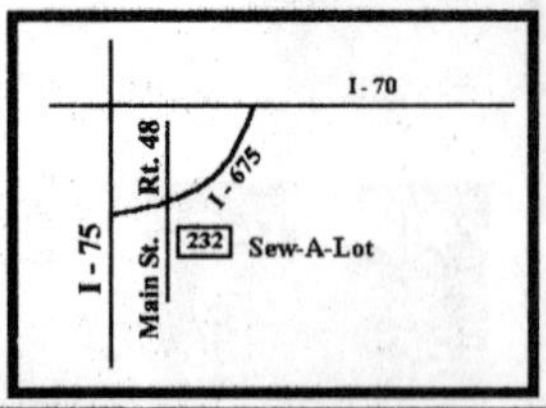

Xenia, OH #8

Mon 12 - 8
T, Th, F 10 - 4
Sat 10 - 2

Unique Stitches Machine Quilting & Fabric

1295 Bellbrook Ave. 45385
(937) 376-0363
E-Mail: usquilts@aol.com
Web Site: www.uniquestitches.com
Owner: Marian Gebele
Est: 1997 3000 sq.ft. 1000 Bolts

A small, but unique quilt shop. Professional machine quilting, binding, photo transfer, repair. Custom made quilts, decorator bedspreads, shams, dust ruffles.

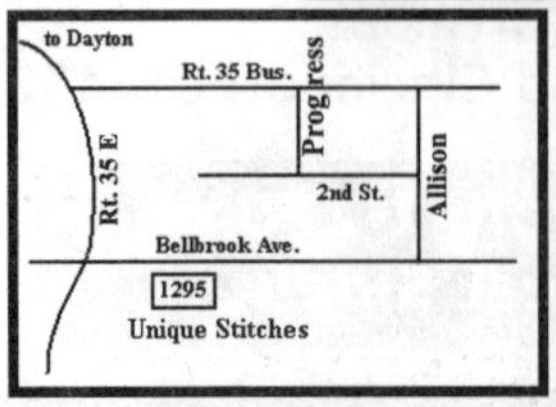

Kettering, OH #9

Sew Biz

Mon - Fri 10 - 6
Sat 10 - 4

2280 E. Dorothy Ln. 45420
(937) 299-3391
E-Mail: tww_sb@dayton99.com
Owners: Linda Adams, Jacie Rinne & Mary Miller
Est: 1959 5000 sq.ft.

Books, Patterns. Quilting and Heirloom Supplies. Classes — Hand and Machine. Bernina Machines and Service.

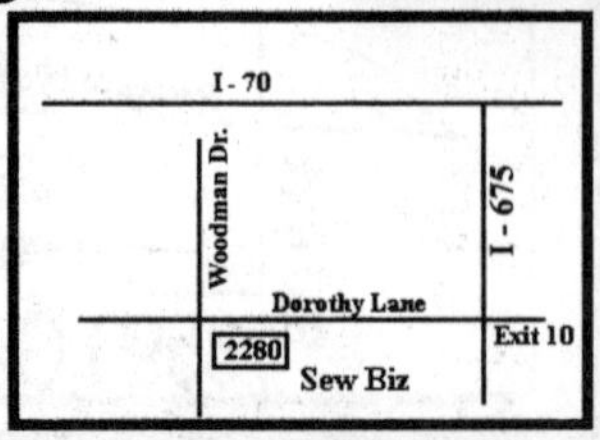

The Glass Thimble

3434 N. High St. 43214
(614) 267-9566 Fax: (614) 447-2440
E-Mail: baquilter@aol.com
Owners: Bev & Gary Young
Est: 1979 5800 sq.ft.

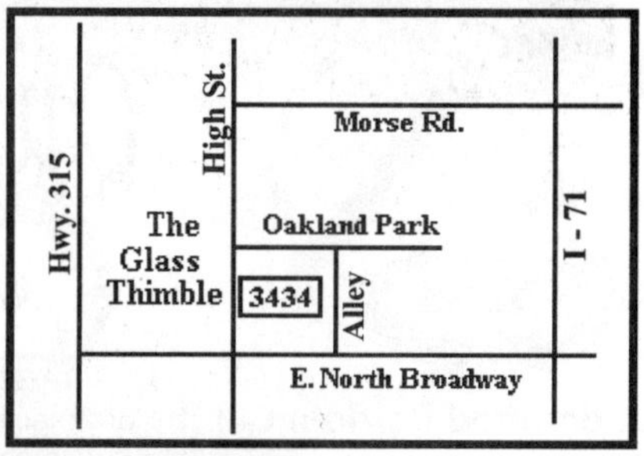

Columbus, OH #10

The Complete Quilt Shop . . . .
Over 6000 bolts of cotton Fabrics,
lots of books & patterns plus
stained glass supplies.
We love quilting and it shows.

Mon & Wed
10 - 6
Tues & Thur
10 - 8
Fri & Sat 10 - 5

Come Shop with us On-Line: www.glassthimble.com

QUILT BEGINNINGS

A Friendly Place to Shop

Columbus, OH #11

Bright, airy quilt shop with over 3500 bolts. Our staff loves to help with any quilt project.

(614) 237-1322

Mon & Wed 10-6
Tues & Thur 10-8
Fri & Sat 10-5

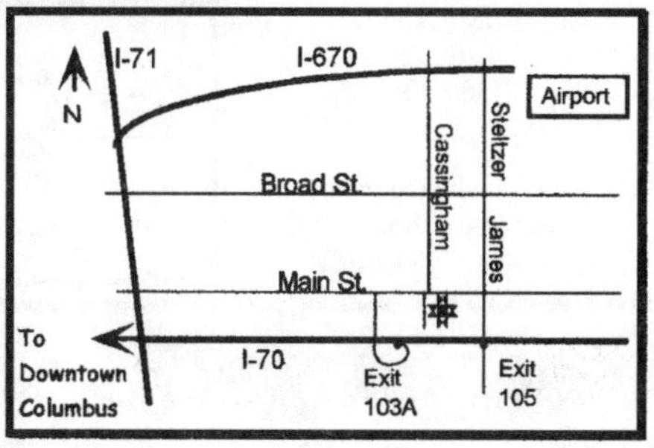

2525 E. Main St. 43209
5 minutes from airport.
4 miles from downtown.

www.quiltbeginnings.com Est. 1998 Authorized PFAFF dealer

WE MAKE & SELL OUR ORIGINAL PRODUCTS

Shop established June 1979

MOTHER Gay Dell-Howard **DAUGHTER** Pati Shambaugh

QUILT TEACHERS DESIGNING FOR QUILTERS

Handcrafted Heirloom Hoops!

NEW *Quilter's Jewels* 12"~$30.00 The newest in the Cinch Hoop Family

- *Cinch Hoop* The First Patented Cinch Hoop on the Market! MAPLE 14"~$50 18"~$55 CHERRY 14"~$60 18"~$65
- *Hoop-de-Deux* The best border hoop on the market! 12"~$40 16"~$45 20"~$50 24"~$55
- *Emma Sings* The first quilters' songbook $20

- Hand piece **accurate** hexagon or 60° diamond design in HALF the time!
- Durable, great for take along projects!
- Method preferred by English quilters...and *they* know what's proper.
- Sold over 80,000 pcs. in first year, 96!

The key: Pati's technique (taught since '90) combined with the soft flexible plastic.

Accept only the original!

1" Hexagons (50/pkg.)
1½" Hexagons (40/pkg.)
1½" 60° Diamonds (60/pkg.)
all $12.50/pkg. w/ $1.50 s&h (Ohio add 75¢ tax)
AND Tec~Spec patterns for Quilt Patis

Helen's Hoops *Picking Up the Pieces*
911 City Park Avenue, Columbus, Ohio 43206
phone: (614) 443-9988 fax: (614) 443-9798
e-mail: QLTPATI97@aol.com

Columbus, OH #12

Fairborn, OH #13

Tues, Wed, Fri, & Sat 10 - 4
Mon & Thur 10 - 8

Daisy Barrel, Inc.

19 West Main Street 45324
(937) 879-0111
Web Site: www.daisybarrel.com
Owners: Marjorie, Sandy, Judy, Phyllis, & Gretchen
Est: 1972 5000 sq.ft. 4000+ Bolts

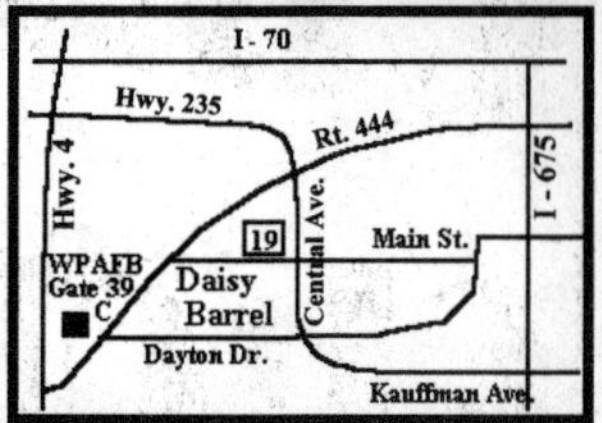

We specialize in best quality materials for the quilter, cross-stitcher, teddy bear maker, (including mohair) and stenciler. Our experienced staff will be glad to help.

Brookville, OH #14

Relocating at Press Time in the Brookville/Englewood, Ohio area Call (888) 275-5777 for directions from I-70 and I-75, approx. 25 mi. from Indiana

Quilts N' Things

www.quiltsnthings.com

Owner: Joanne Zirkle
Est: 1984

Finest Cottons, Oriental Prints, Notions, Books, Stencils, Finished Quilts, Wallhangings, Gifts, Classes. Machine Quilting
Bus and Guild Tours Welcome

Mon - Fri 9:30 - 7:00
Thur til 8:30 Sat 9:30 - 4:00

Greenville, OH #15

Mon - Fri 9:30 - 5:30
Sat 10 - 4

The Fabric Gallery

413 S. Broadway 45331
(937) 547-9126 Fax: (937) 547-9127
Est: 1999 1300+ Bolts

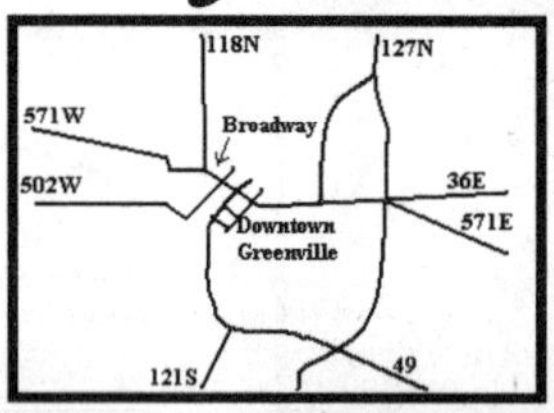

Quality quilting fabrics including homespuns and flannels. Also garment fabrics, patterns, notions, uniquely displayed. Classes offered.

Middleburg, OH #16

Tues - Sat 10 - 5
Sun & Mon by Appt.

Sweet Mountain Quiltery

6079 C. R. 158, P.O. Box 31 43336
(937) 666-2085
E-Mail: swtmtnquiltery@2access.net
Owner: Jill Hardman Est: 1997

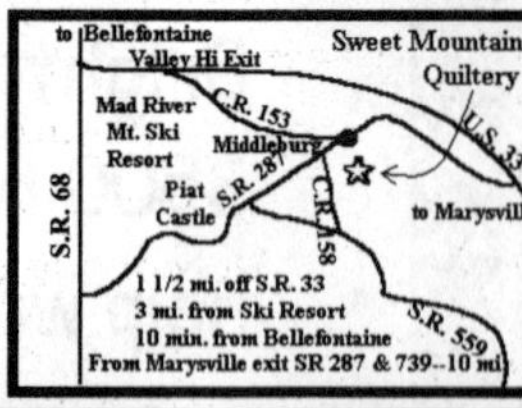

Fabrics by Moda, Hoffman, Thimbleberries, RJR, P&B, Kona Bay, Clothworks and many more. Books, Patterns, Accessories, Quilts, Classes. Custom piecing & hand quilting available. Hinterberg Hoops & Frames. Ott lites. Personal Assistance — Free!

Zanesfield, OH #17

Wed, Fri & Sat 10 - 6
Tues & Thur 12 - 6

Mad River Quilt Company

4830 Cty. Rd. 10 43360
(937) 593-7758
Owner: Noma Fidago
Est: 1998 1500 sq.ft.

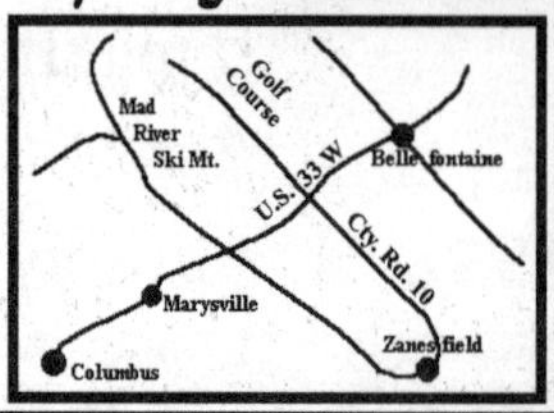

We carry the finest 100% cotton fabrics for all your quilting needs. Feature 1000 sq.ft. classroom with NQA certified instructor.

Mansfield, OH #18

Mon - Thur 10 - 5:30
Fri & Sat 10 - 4

Quilt Connection

415 Park Ave. W 44906
(419) 522-2330 Est: 1980
E-Mail: quiltwthus@aol.com
Web Site: www.quiltconnectionoh.com
Owner: Janet Williams 1200 sq.ft.

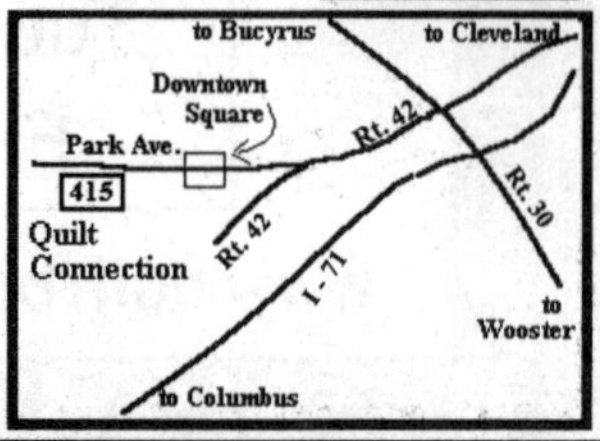

Visit us for quality products & personal, friendly service!
Fabrics, Quilt & Sewing Supplies, Bernina Sewing Machines. Classes.

Quilt Pox Shoppe & More

Owner:
Karen Sue Weiler

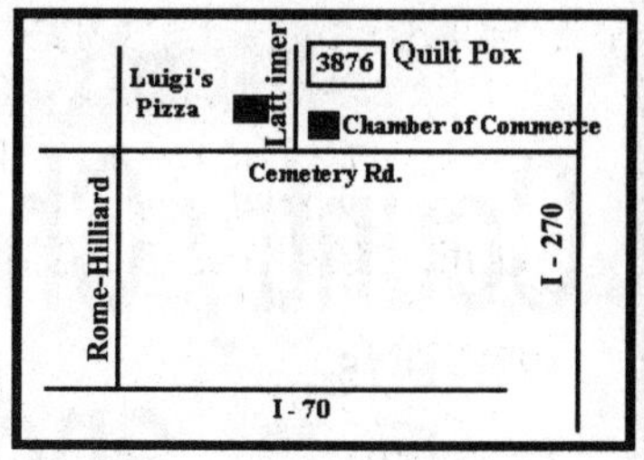

Hilliard, OH #19

Summer Hrs 6/21 - 9/30
Mon - Sat 10 - 5
Winter Hrs 10/1 - 6/20
Mon - Sat 10 - 5
Tues & Thur til 8

3876 Lattimer St. 43026
(614) 771-0657
3700 sq.ft. 3500+ Bolts
www.quiltpoxshop.com

We carry Hinterberg frames & hoops. Custom Machine Quilting. Janome Sewing Machines. Notions.

Proverbs, 31:22 N.I.V.
She makes coverings for her bed.

Bus tours: By appt. only please.
Plus: We have a child's play area for your little ones and two reclining easy chairs and color T.V. for those who are with you that have not been infected with "*Quilt Pox*" yet.

Medina's Quilting Bee

Friendly, knowledgeable service. Thimbleberries and Moda Headquarters!
Quality fabrics including RJR, Hoffman, P&B, Clothworks, Benartex & more.
Great selection of books, patterns and notions. Rug hooking supplies including hand dyed wool, kits and Rigby cutters.
Classes and workshops for the beginner thru the advanced.
Member of the Northern Ohio Quilt Shop Hop last week of September-Call for details
Free newsletter by mail or E-mail

Located in Historic downtown Medina.

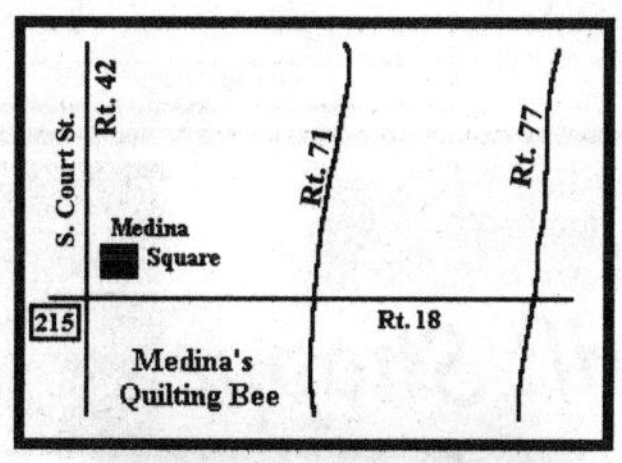

Medina, OH #20

215 S. Court St. 44256
(330 764-3333
E-Mail: qbee@nobleknights.com
Owner: Linda McCauley
Est: 1997

Mon - Sat 10 - 5
Thur til 7
Sun 12 - 4

Bring this ad and receive 50% off any item. (maximum value $15). *Not good with other discounts*
EXPIRES May 2004

www.medinasquiltingbee.com

Ashland, OH #21

Country Charm Fabrics and Sew Crazy

Est: 1975

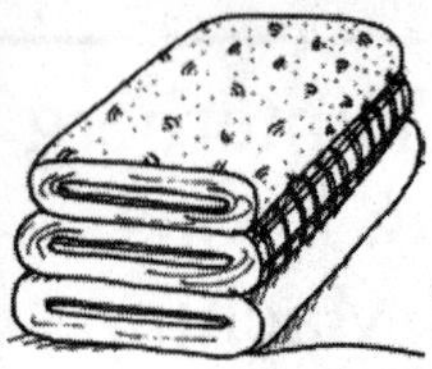

1422 Township Road 593 44805
Country Charm—(419) 281-2341
Sew Crazy—(419) 281-9422
Owners: Cindy Doggett & George Finley
E-Mail: countrycharmfabrics@yahoo.com

Husqvarna VIKING

Mon, Tues, Thur, Fri 10 - 5
Sat 10 - 4
Closed Sun & Wed

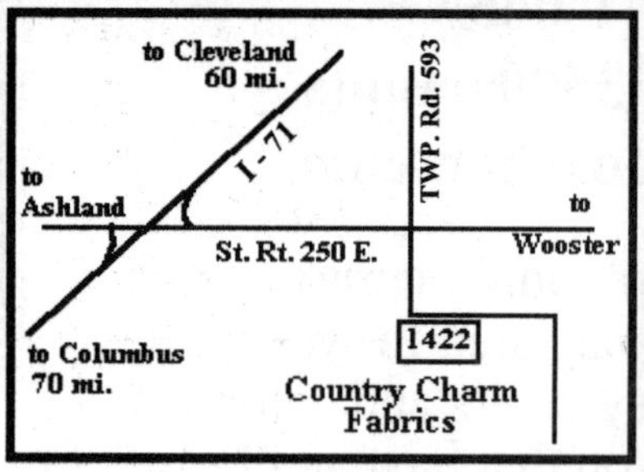

A Complete array of Quilting fabrics from the best mills in America. Notions, Quilt Frames, Classes, and all of the essentials for the Quilting Enthusiast.
Viking Dealer Sewing Machines & Serger Repair

Berlin, OH #22

Mon - Sat 10 - 6

Country Craft Cupboard

P.O. Box 419, 4813 E. Main St.
(330) 893-3163 44610
Owner: Karen Lamp
Est: 1984 3500 sq.ft. 1000 Bolts

1000 bolts of specialty fabrics, plus craft supplies, rug hooking & more!! Hundreds of patterns! Lots of models! In an old country store.

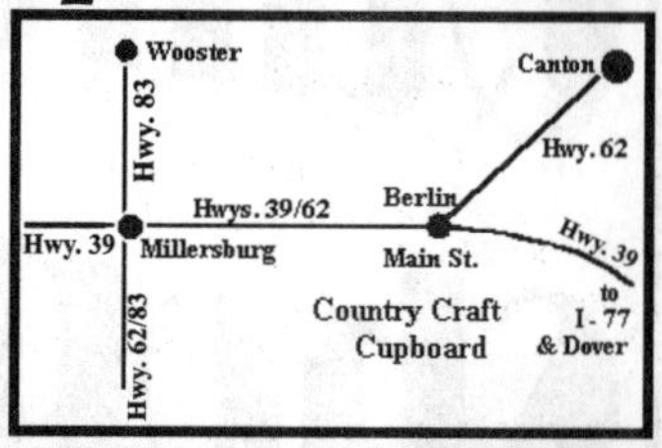

Berlin, OH #23

Mon - Fri 8 - 8
Sat 8 - 6

Spector's Plain & Fancy

German Village Shopping Center
Oak St. 44610
(330) 893-3935

Full Line of Fabrics, Notion, Quilt & Craft Supplies & Patterns. Excellent Values on solid & Printed Fabrics.

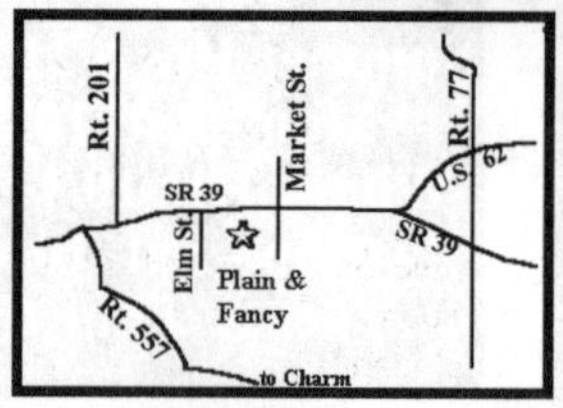

Gramma Fannie's Quilt Barn

Mon - Fri 10 - 5
Sat 10 - 6

Visit our unique shop specializing in:

- our own line of patterns & kits
- custom order quilts
- top of the line quilt fabrics
- books
- stencils.

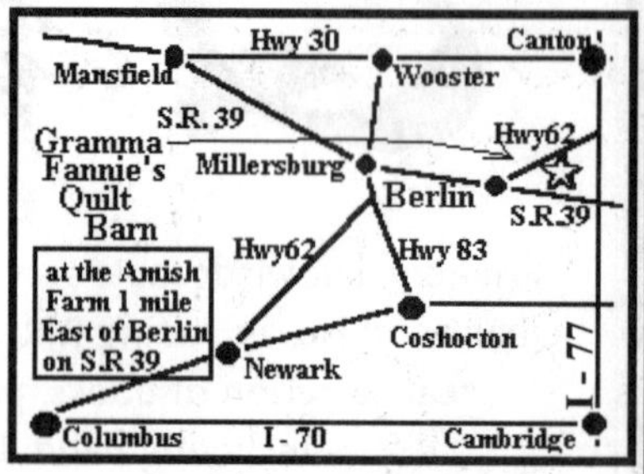

Located at Schrock's Amish Farm and Home
4363 State Route 39
P.O. Box 270
44610
(330) 893-3232
Call about our Annual Quilt Show
Est: 1991
1 mile east of Berlin

www.amish-r-us.com

Berlin, OH #24

Berlin, OH #25

Mon - Sat 9 - 5

Helping Hands Quilt Shop

4818 St. Rt. 39, Main St., P.O. Box 183
(330) 893-2233 44610
Fax: (330) 893-8004 Est: 1975
Web Site: www.amishheartland.com

Hundreds of handmade crafts and quilts. All your fabric and quilting supplies. Quilt museum with video and Christmas room. Two buildings.

Kidron, OH #26

Mon - Sat 9:30 - 5
closed major holidays

Hearthside Quilt Shoppe

13110 Emerson Rd. Box 222 44636
(330) 857-4004 Est: 1990
E-mail: hearthsidequilts@aol.com
Owners: Clifford & Lena Lehman
2400 sq.ft. Mgr. Cheryl Gerber

Amish and Swiss Mennonite Quilts, Wall Hangings made in our area. Large selection to choose from. Custom orders welcome! Free Brochure.

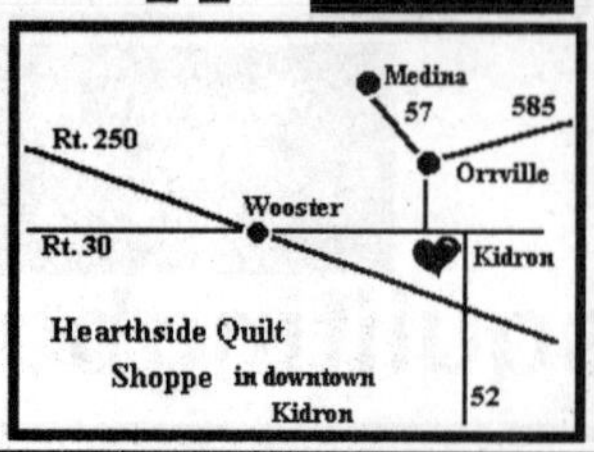

Charm, OH #27

Mon - Sat 8 - 5

Miller's Dry Goods

4500 S.R. 557 Est: 1965
Mail—Millersburg, OH 44654
(330) 893-9899
Owners: The Miller Family
Also—a whole barn full of quilts.

Over 8,000 bolts of fabric, including outlet in basement. Beautiful selection of local handmade Quilts, Wall Hangings, Rugs, Tablerunners, etc. Also Quilt books, patterns, stencils and lots of notions.

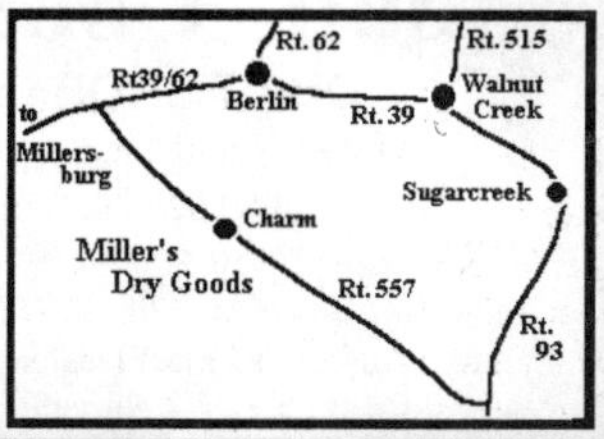

Sugarcreek, OH #28

Mon - Sat 8:30 - 5 Fri til 8

Spector's Store

122 E. Main 44681
(330) 852-2113
Mgr: Mary Mullet

Full Line of Fabric and notions. Quilt and Craft supplies. Excellent Values on Solid & Printed fabrics.

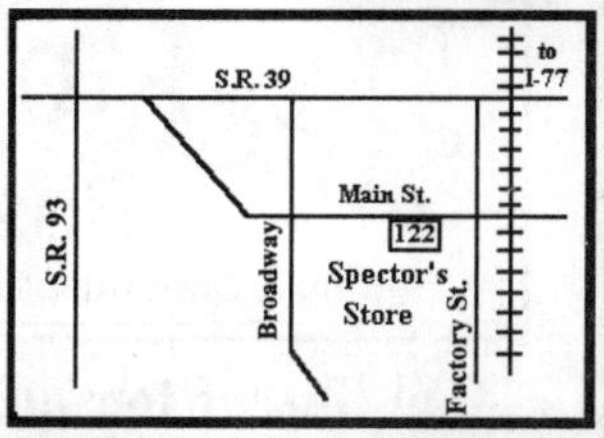

Sugarcreek, OH #29

Mon - Sat 9 - 5

Swiss Village Quilts and Crafts

113 S. Broadway P.O. Box 514 44681
(330) 852-4855
Owners: Aden & Anna Hochstetler
Est: 1982 1250 sq.ft. Free Brochure

Quality, local-made Quilts, Wallhangings and related items. Wooden toys Etc. Most items made locally by Amish
Special orders gladly Accepted.

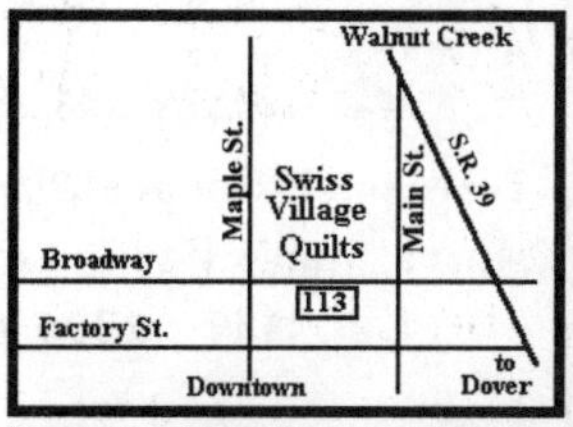

Quilt Bee

Mon - Sat 10 - 5

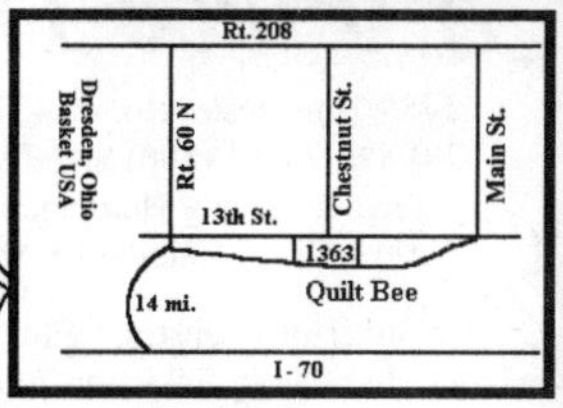

1363 Chestnut St. 43821
(740) 754-2261 or (888) 223-5450
Owners: Marilyn & Ken Swope
Est: 1991 800 Bolts

Beautiful selection of quality fabrics. Basket weaves and prints. Custom made jumpers, vests, jackets. Quilt supplies.

Dresden, OH #30

Basket Village U.S.A.

Marietta, OH #31

Townsquare Fabrics
& Quilt Shop

#7 Tiber Way 45750
(877) 373-6150 (toll free)
Owner: Effie Townsend
Est: 1985
E-Mail: townsquare@bigfoot.com

Mon - Sat 10 - 5

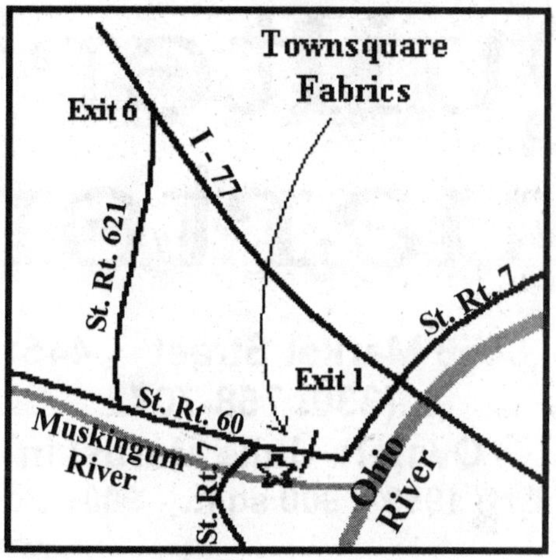

Cotton Fabric	Stencils
Quilting Supplies	Batting
Patterns	Books

New Larger Showroom
Authorized Bernina® Dealer

Pomeroy, OH #32

Mon - Sat 9 - 5

The Fabric Shop

110 W. Main St. 45769
(740) 992-2284 Fax: (740) 992-4189
E-Mail: fabricshop@eurekanet.com
Web Site: www.eurekanet.com/~fabricshop
Owner: Becky Anderson Est: 1959

We specialize in Quilting fabric and supplies. Singer Sewing Machine Dealer. Located on the beautiful Ohio River in historic Pomeroy, OH.

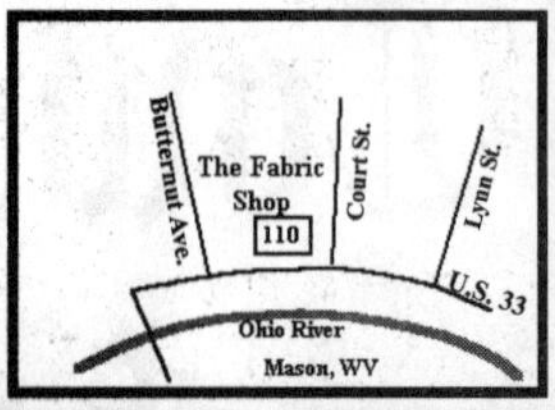

McConnelsville, OH #33

Mon - Sat 9 - 5

SEW N SEW QUILT SHOP

32 E. Main St. 43756
(740) 962-6206
Web Site: www.sewnsewohio.com
Est: 1988

Authorized Pfaff Dealer, Quilt Fabrics & Supplies

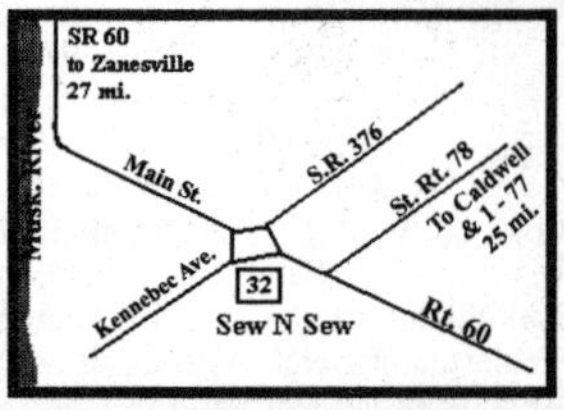

Cumberland, OH #34

Tues - Fri 11 - 5 Sat 11 - 4

Cumberland Quilt Shop

424 Main St., P.O. Box 73 43732
(740) 638-2626 Fax: (740) 962-4276
E-mail: quiltshop@msn.com
www.cumberlandquiltshop.com
Owners: Rita & Phil Lawrence

Top quality 100% cotton quilt Fabric, Books, Patterns, Notions & Classes. Custom Machine Quilting. Located in the historic Cumberland Bank Building. Est: 1996

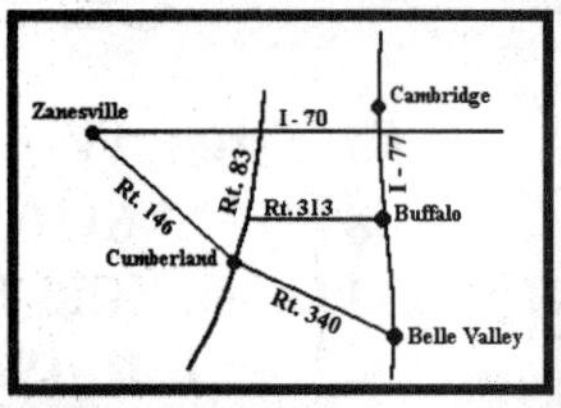

Cambridge, OH #35

The Stitchin' Post

Sewing & Craft Supplies

Mon - Sat 10 - 6

1996 E. Wheeling Ave. 43725
(740) 435-9590

Full line of top quality quilting fabrics from RJR, Mumm, Thimbleberries, Benartex, Hoffman to mention a few. Notions & Books Galore. Also available needlepoint, rubber stamping and scrapbook supplies.

Fax: (740) 432-7340
E-Mail:stitchinpost@jadeinc.com
Owners: Hallie Ray & Linda Britten
Est: 1999 2800 sq.ft.

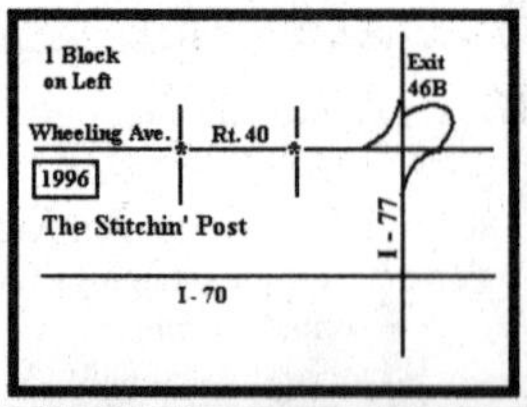

Quilter's Quarters

8458 Market Street 44512
(330) 758-7072
Owner: Julie Maruskin
Est: 1989 900 sq.ft. 900+ Bolts

We carry quilting supplies, fabrics, tools, books and patterns.

Youngstown, OH #36

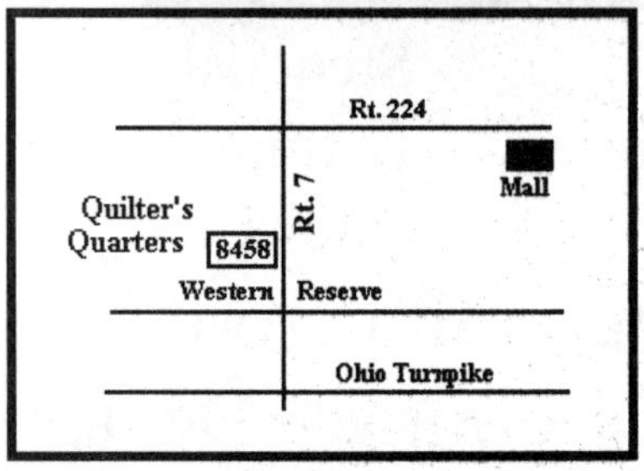

Mon - Fri 11 - 5
Sat 11 - 4
Closed Tues & Sun

Akron, OH #37

Mon-Thur 10 - 6 Fri & Sat 10 - 5 Sun 12 - 4

A Piece In Time

5485 Manchester Rd. 44319
(330) 882-9626 (800) SANDY98
Owner: Sandy Heminger
6000 sq.ft. Catalog LSASE

Truly Wonderful Fabrics, Elna Sewing Machines, Incredible Selection of Books & Notions & (Nation wide) Exquisite Custom Machine Quilting.

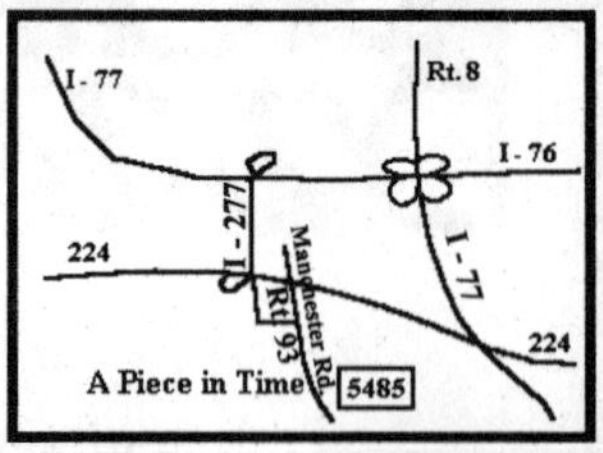

Cuyahoga Falls, OH #38

Mon - Thur 10 - 9 Fri & Sat 10 - 4

Stitch, Piece 'n Purl

2018 State Rd. 44223
(330) 928-9097

Welcome to Northeastern Ohio's most complete shop featuring Calico, quilting supplies, quilt frames, Knitting yarns, Needlework and Needlework supplies.

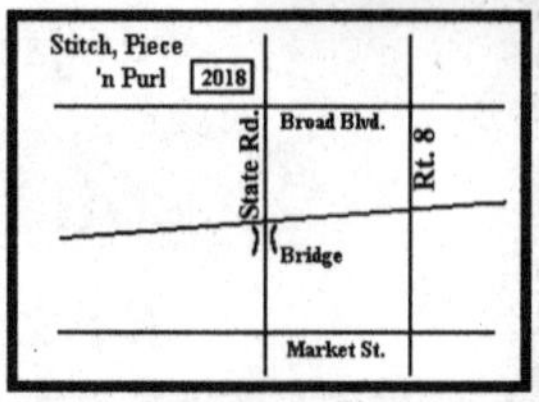

Quality Sewing & Quilting Supplies

PINE TREE QUILT SHOPPE

Classes on Quilting & Sewing

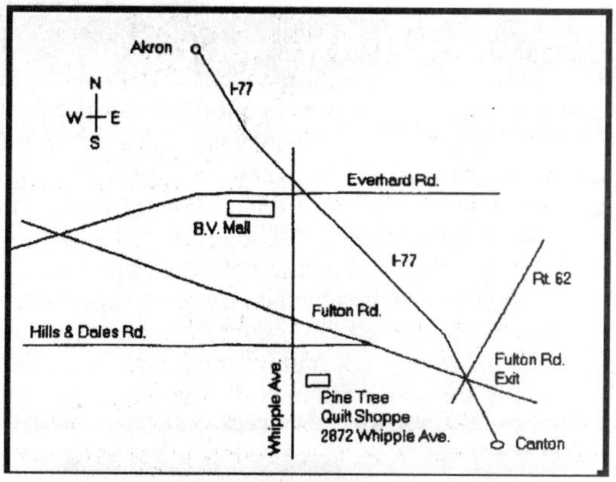

2872 Whipple Ave.
Canton, OH 44708
(330) 477-4877
E-mail:
pinetreequilt@aol.com

Tues 9:30 - 8
Wed - Fri
9:30 - 4:30
Sat 10 - 4

Canton, OH #39

Cortland, OH #40

Designers Two

Fabrics & Sewing Machines

284 W. Main St. 44410
Phone & Fax 330-638-3737
1-800-732-8932
design2@onecom.com www.d2quiltshop.com
Owner: Peg Viole Est: 1989

Mon - Fri 10 - 5
Sat 10 - 2

Hoffman fabrics galore! Elegant Maywood backgrounds. Great priced Moda's, cozy flannels, the Favorite quilting patterns, unusual notions, trims from New York's finest cutting rooms, heirloom, silk ribbon and more! Our shop is stuffed to the brim & well worth the trip!

----Guild member discounts----

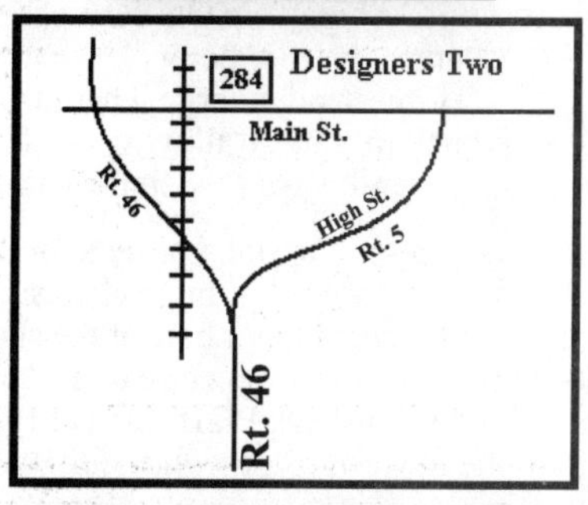

Willoughby, OH #41

ERIE STREET QUILTS

Located on Clark Avenue at the corner of Second St.
38025 Second St., #102
Willoughby, OH 44094
(440) 953-1340
e-mail esf4134@aol.com
Owner: Mary Huey Est: 1979
Web Site: www.eriestreetquilts.com

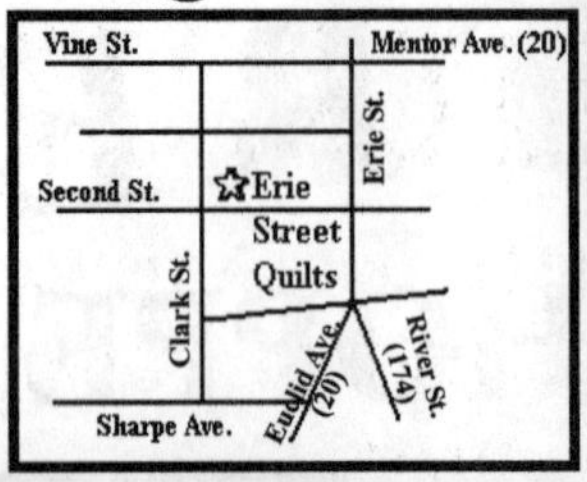

Mon & Thur 10 - 8 Tues, Wed & Fri 10 -6 Sat 10 - 5

We offer a unique selection of cotton fabrics along with books, patterns, and supplies in a cozy new location. Classes are available year round in basic quilt making skills, working with color, and developing creativity. Several groups meet on a monthly basis at the shop for fellowship and skill building. The shop is one of the founding members of the annual Northern Ohio Shop Hop which is the last week of September. With 23 years serving Northeast Ohio quilt makers, we have built up a gold mine of experience and information. We hope you will stop in for a visit the next time you are in our area!

Warren, OH #42

Mon & Thurs 10 - 8
Tues, Wed, Fri 10 - 5
Sat 10 - 3

A Quilting Asylum

179 Folsom NW 44483
(330) 847-6711
E-Mail: qasylum@netdotcom.com
1000+ Bolts

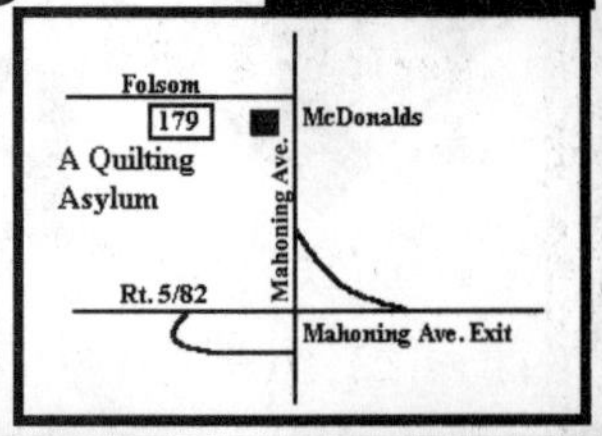

Pfaff Sewing Machines, machine quilting service, major lines of fabrics, notions, books, patterns, quilt frames, plus antiques & gift shop.

Middlefield, OH #43

Mon - Fri 10 - 5
Sat 10 - 4

Iona's Quilt Shop

15864 Nauvdo Rd 44062
(440) 632-9410
E-Mail: ionaquilts@simcon.net
Owner: Iona Eden
Est: 1998 1500 sq. ft. 900 Bolts

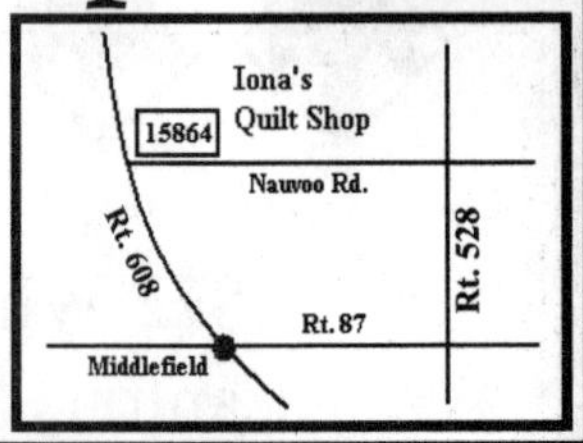

Fabrics, Notions, Quilts, Wallhangings, Books, Patterns, Classes, Will take Special Orders.

For Fabric Lovers, By Fabric Lovers

Olmsted Falls, OH #45

ABIGAYLE'S QUILTERY

8096 Columbia Rd. 44138 (440) 235-7446
E-Mail: shop@abigayles.com
Web Site: www.abigayles.com
Owners: Beverly Morris & Nancy Bryant
Est: 1999 3000+ Bolts

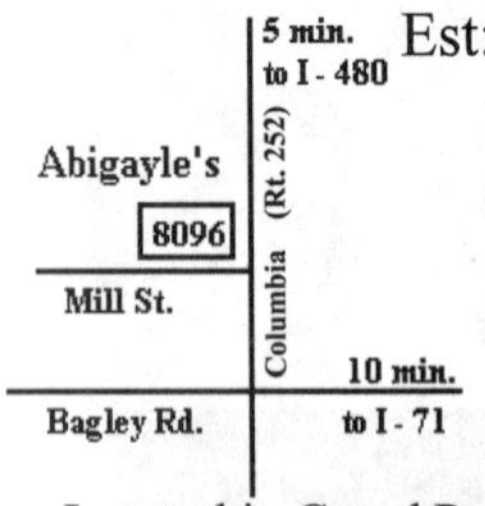

Mon - Sat 10 - 6
Thur til 8 Sun 12 - 5

Located in Grand Pacific Junction in Historic Olmsted Falls, Ohio, Abigayle's Quiltery occupies the Simmerer Homestead; a large, charming Victorian home. Step back in time & allow yourself to stroll along the brick walkways & visit the surrounding shops.

At Abigayle's we take pride in our great selection of ever-changing samples, huge class schedule, many fun and interesting clubs, both here at the shop and by mail. We host several quilt shows, feature almost constant trunk shows and have books, patterns, Pfaff, Elna & Baby Lock sewing machines and the newest, most wonderful 100% cotton fabrics around.

Remembrances

12570 Chillicothe Rd. 44026
(440) 729-1650
Owner: Cheryl Pedersen
Est: 1984 1200 sq.ft.
Visit our Web Site At:
www.shopremembrances.com

Chesterland, OH #44

Cotton Fabrics, Notions, Books.
Classes: quilting & dollmaking.
We specialize in Redwork and Reproduction Fabrics.

Mon - Sat 10 - 5

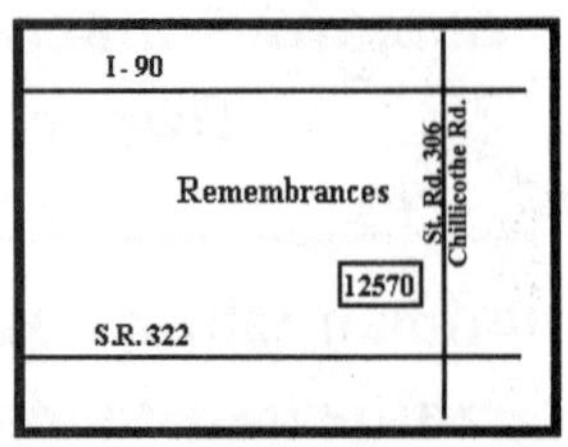

Named one of the top ten Quilt Shops by American Patchwork & Quilting Quilt Sampler for 2002

Painesville, OH #46

Tues - Fri 10 - 5
Sat 10 - 4
Last Sun 12 - 3

Parlour Quilts, Inc.

Top Quality 100% Cotton Fabrics, Classes, books, patterns, notions, batting & quilting needs. Located in a cozy, quaint historic building in downtown Painesville. The best kept secret of northern Ohio, established in 1998, having the most friendly workers, giving personal attention if needed.

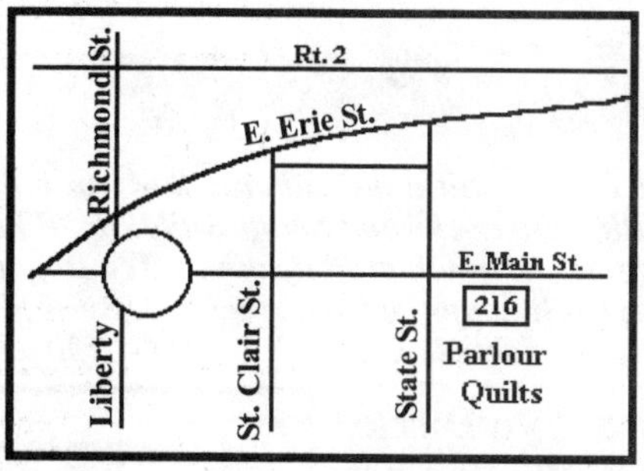

216 E. Main St. 44077
(440) 357-0055
E-Mail: pqi@ncweb.com
Owner: Suzanne K. Kane
1400 sq.ft. 1600 Bolts

Authorized BERNINA and HORN of America Dealer

QUILTS & KREATIONS

South Amherst, OH #47

101 E. Main St. 44001
Phone / Fax (440) 986-4132
E-Mail: quiltskreations@centurytel.net
Owner: Sandra Whitaker

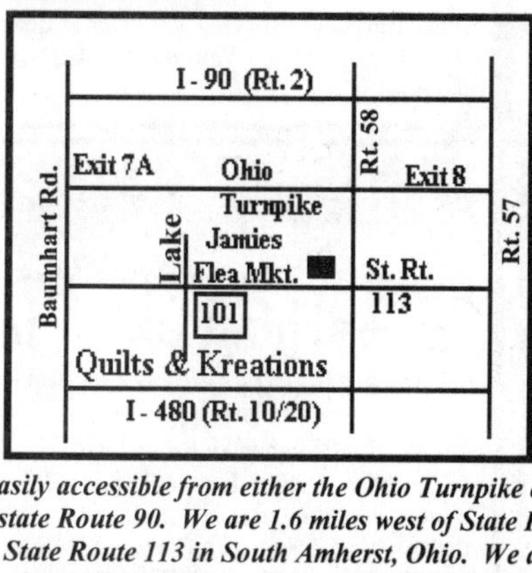

Easily accessible from either the Ohio Turnpike or Interstate Route 90. We are 1.6 miles west of State Route 58 on State Route 113 in South Amherst, Ohio. We are on the southeast corner of the street at the light.

QUILTS & KREATIONS was established in 1980 and we have grown in size throughout the years. We offer you over 3600 sq.ft. of shopping area in our 100+ year old building. There are over 4000 bolts of designer fabric to choose from. We stock the area's largest selection of 100% cotton fabrics, patterns, books, and unique craft patterns. We are Lorain County's only authorized Bernina Dealer and Lorain County's most complete quilt shop.

BERNINA®

Mon - Sat 10 - 5 Thur til 7

North Kingsville, OH #48

Mon - Fri 10 - 6
Sat 10 - 4:30

Quilt Depot

2736 E. Center 44068
(440) 224-3255
Owner: Leanna Rodabaugh 2000 Bolts

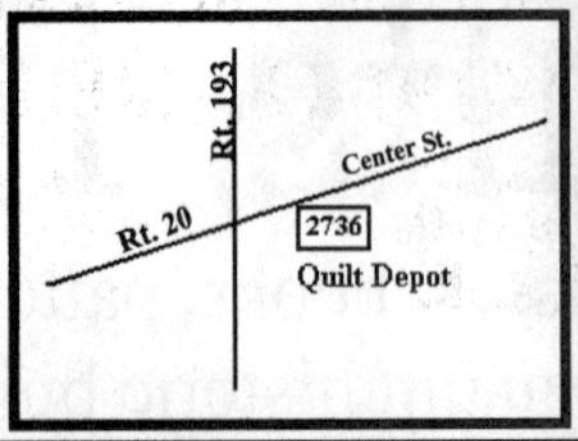

100% Cottons Books, Patterns, Notions, & Classes

Gingersnap Junction Quilt Shop

Shop for Fabrics, Antiques, Florals, Crafts, Boyd & Ganz Bears, and much, much more!

Classes, Classes, Classes...Call for a quilt class schedule, or visit our website at www.gingersnapjunction.net We offer a large selection of over 1,000 bolts of fabric, patterns and quilt books, with every accessory you'll ever need. If we don't have it, we'll get it!!!

Milan, OH #49

All this is presented in a beautiful old building that was built in 1835, formerly called the Lockwood Smith Building. While you are shopping, enjoy lunch at Pollyanna's Tea Room, featuring tea from Daily soups, salads, quiche, desserts plus scones are the choice each day. Lunch 11 AM - 2:30 pm

Owners: Mary & Lyn Dircks
jean@gingersnapjunction.net
Est: 2001 Catalog $12.95
6,000 sq.ft.

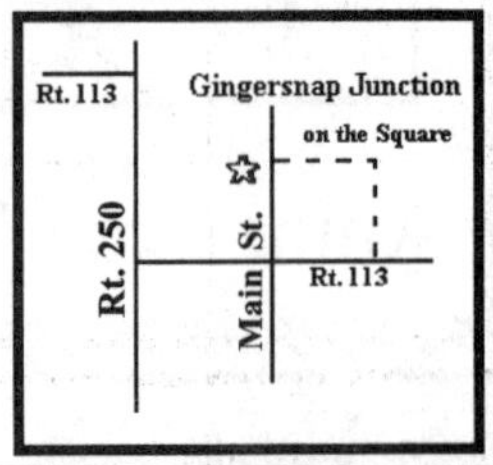

One Main Street on the Square, Milan, OH 44846
(419) 499-9411

Stop in Tues thru Sat 9 AM - 5 PM

THE DOOR MOUSE

Over 12,000 bolts of cotton, patterns, and quilting supplies in a barn setting. Featuring quilts and many handcrafted memories, legends and heirlooms which capture the beauty and simplicity of rural life. Join our friendly staff for classes in the corn crib.

Mail Orders Welcome. We accept Visa/MC & Discover

5047 W. SR 12
P.O. Box 455 44815
(419) 986-5667
E-Mail:
doormouse@nwonline.net
Web Site: www.thedoormouse.com
Owner: Mary Ann Sorg

Mon - Sat 10 - 5
Wed til 8
Last Sunday of each month 12 - 5

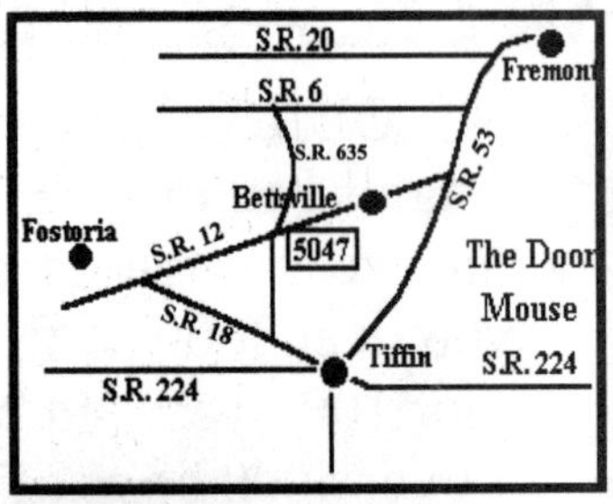

Est: 1979 3600 sq.ft.

Bettsville, OH #50

Pemberville, OH #51

Mon - Fri 10 - 3 & 6 - 9
Sat 10 - 3
Sun 12 - 3

Quilt Makers

208 E. Front St. 43450
(419) 287-0221
Owners: Judy Seifert & Judy Kaminski
Est: 2002 1000 sq.ft.

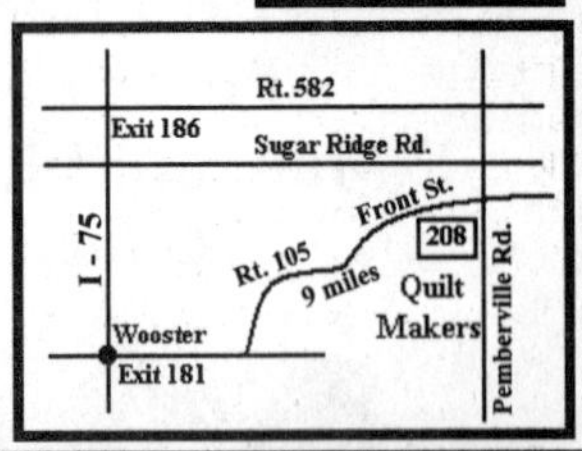

Small warm atmosphere. We cater to quilters with Quality Fabrics, Patterns, Books, Notions, and classes.

Maumee, OH #52

Mon - Sat 10 - 4
Tues eve 7 - 9

The Quilt Foundry

234 W. Wayne 43537
(419) 893-5703
Owners: Mary Beham, Margaret Okuley, Peg Sawyer, Gretchen Schultz
Est: 1981 1000 sq.ft.

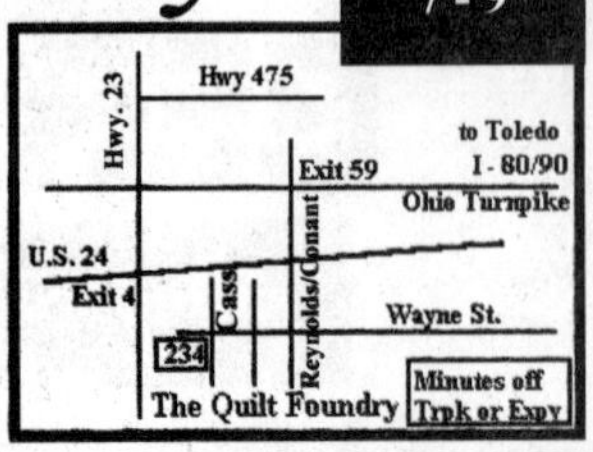

The Quilt Foundry offers friendly, personalized service in your search for wonderful fabric, supplies, books and classes.

Toledo, OH #53

Mon - Sat 10 - 5
Thur 10 - 8

something extra inc.

a country needlework shop
with a passion for primitive

3310 Glanzman Rd. 43614
(419) 385-7299 Fax: (419) 385-8570

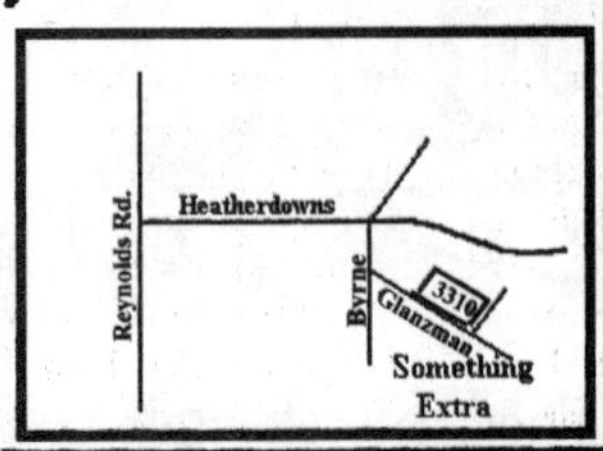

Counted cross stitch, Primitive stitch embroidery, Custom Framing, Applique & Quilting, Moda Fabrics, Wool Rug Hooking, Over-dyed wool, Antiques, Gifts, classes and so much more! MC and Visa accepted.

Findlay, OH #54

ohio farm house

Monday thru Saturday
9:30 - 5:00
Open 12:00 - 4:00 Sundays
in November and December
(419) 422-5031

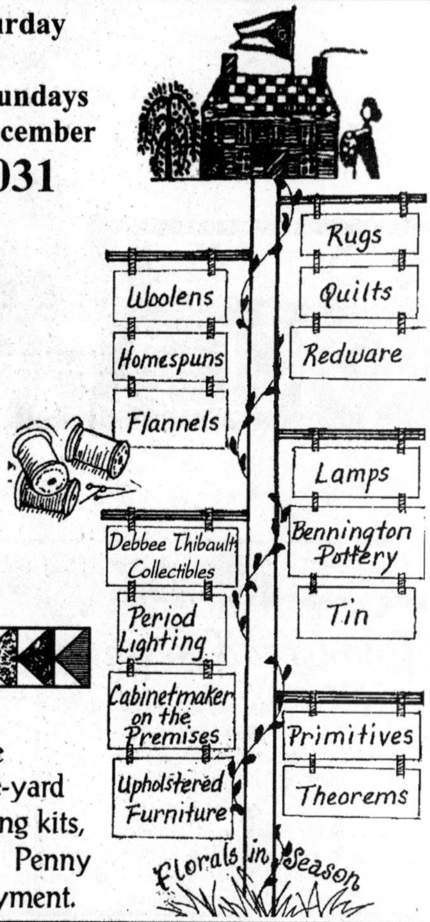

Larry and Darlene Hammond, Proprietors

A Quilter's Delight...
Great selection of "Fat Quarters" and Bolts and Bolts of Homespun Fabrics. Featuring the primitive look of Moda, Brannock & Patek designs, plus many Civil War reproduction fabrics. Boasting a large selection of flannels and coordinating fabrics. During your visit, browse through our offerings of primitive pieced quilts, matching bedding ensembles, pillows, clothing and much more!

16056 Rt. 224 E., Findlay, Ohio 45840

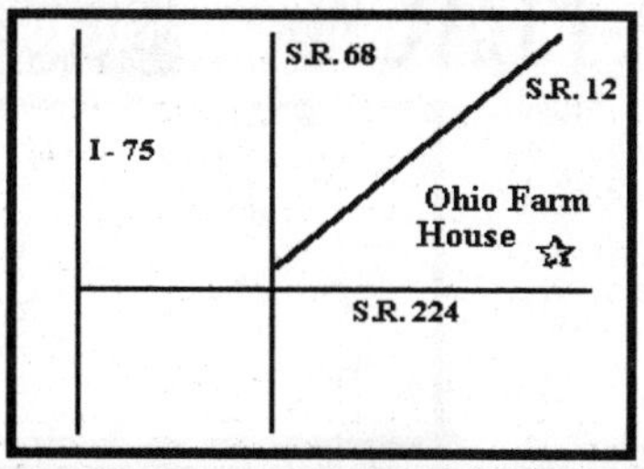

* Woolens and Etc *
Hand-dyed and Felted Wool available
Fat Quarters, Fat Eighths, Stripped or by-the-yard
Choose from our primitive woolen rug hooking kits, cutters, dyes, project books, frames and hoops. Penny rugs and other project samples for your enjoyment.

Other Shops in Ohio: We suggest calling first

Anna	Dishong Country Store, P.O. Box 257	513-394-3283
Archbold	Sauder's Farm & Craft Village, 22611 State Rt. 2	419-446-2541
Athens	Quilt Shop, 9629 Oxley Rd.	740-592-3874
Athens	Dairy Barn Arts Center, 8000 Dairy Ln.	740-592-4981
Barberton	Quilting by B.J. & Friends, 166 14th St. NW	330-825-2296
Beavercreek	Unique Stitches, 3206 Shetland Rd.	937-429-0894
Bellefontaine	Coblentz Crafts and Fabrics, 5451 C.R. 25	513-468-2081
Berlin	Zinck's in Berlin, 115 E. Main St., P.O. Box 153	330-893-2071
Burbank	Land of Canaan Quilts, 122 W. Easton Rd.	330-893-3028
Canton	The Sewing Basket, 1525 Navarre Rd. SW	330-456-9538
Canton	Schoolhouse Quilt Shoppe, 2872 Whipple Ave. N.W.	330-477-4767
Centerville	Stitching Post, 101 E. Alex Bell Rd. #176	937-436-9200
Chillecothe	The Cross Patch, 14 W. Water St.	614-774-4104
Cincinnati	St. Theresa Textile Trove, 1329 Main St.	513-333-0399
Cincinnati	Zellerwood Originals, 824 Loda Dr.	513-752-3763
Cleveland	Rafael's, 2342 Professor Ave.	216-241-2210
Cleveland	Sew Cozy, 2553 Queenston Rd.	216-321-7654
Cleveland	Pat's Quilted Treasures, 10043 Hunting Dr.	440-546-1458
Columbiana	Heart of the Country, 14895 South Ave. #14	330-482-5001
Columbus	Quilts--Michael Council, 130 Buttles Ave.	614-229-9099
Columbus	Plantation Quilts, 2363 Somersworth Dr.	614-252-5552
Cuyahoga Falls	Stow Needlecraft, 191 Van Doren Dr.	216-688-6145
Dayton	Quilting Books & Patterns, 10670 Willow Brook Rd.	937-885-6189
Delta	Tender Loving Care, 219 Main St.	419-822-5861
Dover	Country Mouse, 202 W 3rd St.	216-343-1313
Dresden	American Harvest Dry Goods, 617 Main St.	740-754-3622
Dublin	Wall to Wall Quilts, 5325 Indian Hill Rd.	614-889-0118
Gallipolis	Maynard's Quilt Fabric & Craft, 1192 Jackson Pike	740-441-9060
Greenville	J & J Fabric Notions, 1856 Ross St.	937-548-3776
Greenville	Extra Special Products, 5339 State Route 571 E.	513-548-9388
Hartville	Yankee Barn 1120 W. Maple St.	216-877-6507
Hebron	Heavy Metal Quilting, 140 E. Main St., P.O. Box 53	740-929-3940
Hilliard	Snippy Stitcher, 3550 River Landings Blvd.	614-777-9442
Jackson	Guhl's Country Store, 120 #C Twin Oaks Dr.	614-286-5271
Kenton	Ye Olde Schoolhouse, 10389 CR 190	419-675-1652
Kidron	Cozy Corner Quilt Shop, 4776 Kidron Rd.	330-857-0441
Lancaster	Prairie Rose Quilting House, 463 Buckingham Ln.	614-654-1922
Lancaster	The Farmer's Country Store, E. 6th Ave.	614-654-4853
Lebanon	Oh Susannah, 6 S. Broadway	513-932-8246
Lima	Country Side Stitch & Sew Shop, 1207 North McClure Rd.	419-649-1391
Louisville	Empty Spools, 10087 Reeder Ave.	
Loveland	Lady Bug Quilt Shoppe, 1464 Highway 28	513-575-0110
Mansfield	Quilts for You, 2456 Bell Rd.	419-884-1497
Mansfield	Bev's Fabric Shop, 466 Melody Lane	419-589-3276
Middlefield	Country Touch, 16881 Peters Rd.	216-632-5537
Millersburg	Land of Canaan Quilts, 3340 St. Rt. 39	330-893-3028
Millersburg	Katie's Quilts & Wall Hangings, 7635 St. Rt. 241	
Millersport	Quilter's Retreat, 2595 Canal Dr., Box 667	740-467-2366
Minerva	Calico Grandma's, 616 Valley St.	216-868-6937
Mogadore	Heritage Quilt Shop, 558 Etter Rd.	330-628-6269
Mount Vernon	Jordan's Quilt Shop, 16 S. Main St.	740-393-7463
Mt. Hope	Lone Star Quilts, 7700 CR 77, Box 32	none
Newark	Jerry's Fabrics, 37 S. 3rd St.	614-349-7195
North Canton	Village Classics, 151 Spruce Dr. NW	330-499-2606
North Olmsted	Sew Much Fun, 25343 Lorain Rd.	440-734-6690
North Olmsted	Hoops N' Hollers Quilt Fabric & Gift Shop, 24888 Lorain Rd.	216-779-4700
Oberlin	Gingko Gallery & Studio, 19 S. Main St.	440-774-3117
Perrysburg	Ribbonry, 119 Louisiana Ave.	419-872-0073
Plain City	The Fabric Shoppe, 9872 U.S. Route 42 S.	614-873-4123
Portsmouth	Homespun Treasures, 319 Chillicothe St.	740-353-8426
Portsmouth	Seams Like Yesterday, 325 Front St.	740-355-2009
Portsmouth	Clara's Sewing Center & Fabric Shop, 2227 6th	614-354-1881
Protorville	D & B Quilt Shop, 6971 St. Rt. 775	740-886-8730
Salineville	The Attic, 16060 Spring Valley Rd.	
Shiloh	Country Fabrics, 1991 Shatzer Rd.	419-896-3785
Sidney	BJ Fabrics, 1126-B Michigan St.	
Springboro	Sally's Quilts and Gifts, 250 S. Main St.	513-748-1992
Stow	Karol's Quilts, 4874 Stow Rd.	330-688-1201
Upper Arlington	Fabric Farms, 3590 Riverside Dr.	614-451-9300
Wadsworth	The Fabric Peddler, 139 College St.	330-336-1101
Walnut Creek	The Farmer's Wife, 4952 Walnut St.	216-893-3168
Washington Court House	Lewis St. Crafts, 625 Lewis St.	614-335-2272
Wooster	Quilting Elf, 2592 Varian Rd.	330-262-7426
Worthington	Quilted Threads, 871 Troon Trl.	614-847-5857

17 Featured Shops

OKLAHOMA

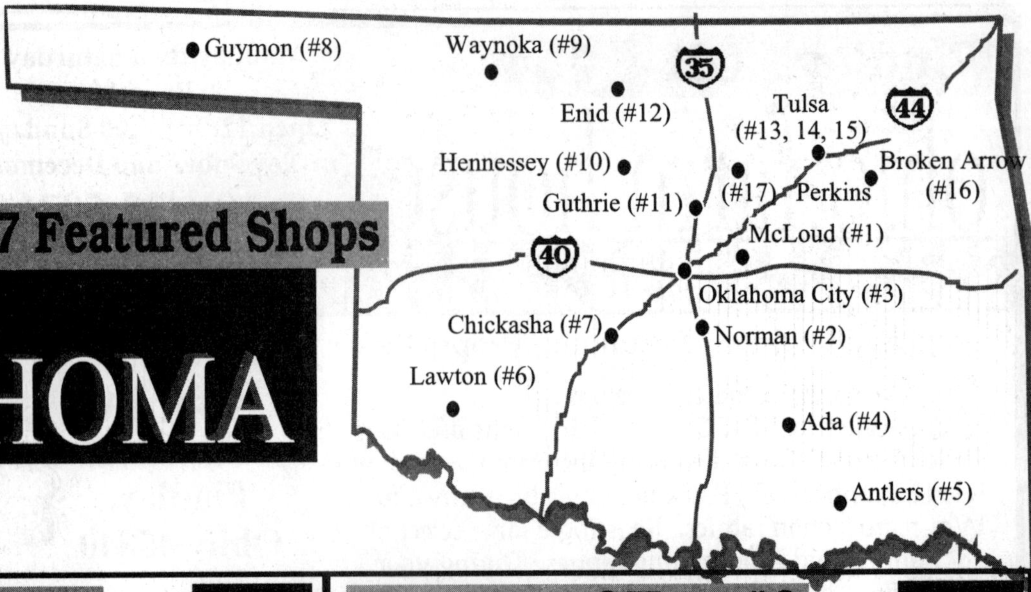

McLoud, OK #1

Flexible Call Before coming

Homestead Sewing Cottage

801 N State Hwy 102, PO Box 888 74851
(405) 964-6887
E-Mail: sitnwhittlebill@juno.com
Owners: Bill & Wanzalle Beck
Est: 2001

See hay fields, pecan trees, North Canadian River bottom, farm animals, & Kickapoo Indian headquarters. Singer dealer w/quilting notions, thread & custom embroidery, supplies.

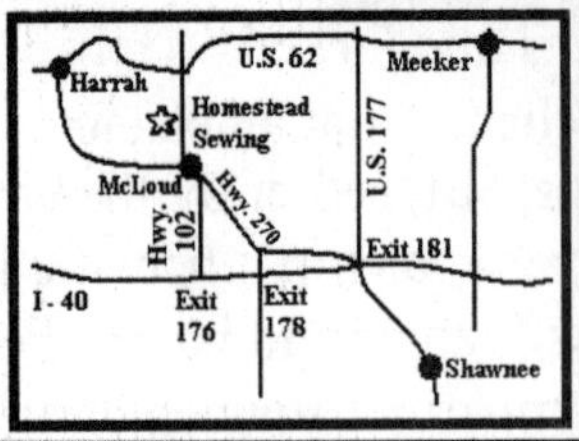

Norman, OK #2

Mon - Fri 10 - 5 Tues til 7 Sat 10 - 4

PATCHWORK PLACE

924 24th Ave. SW 73069
(405) 321-4569
E-Mail: store@patchworksinc.com
Web Site: patchworksinc.com
Owners: Anne Gaines & Nancy Baysinger

Fabrics - Books - Tools
Patterns for Quilting

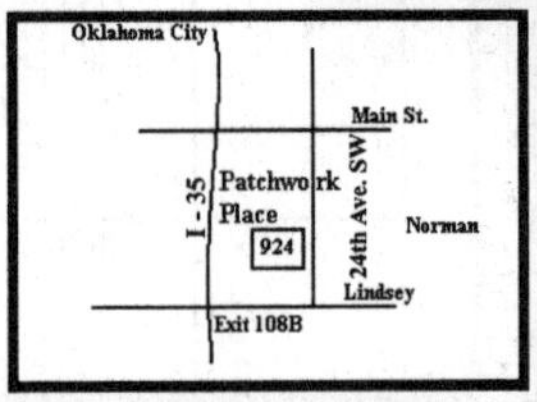

Oklahoma City, OK #3

Oklahoma QUILTWORKS

9323 N. Pennsylvania 73120 (405) 842-4778
Barbara Stanfield & Carole Jo Evans Est: 1988 2400 sq.ft.

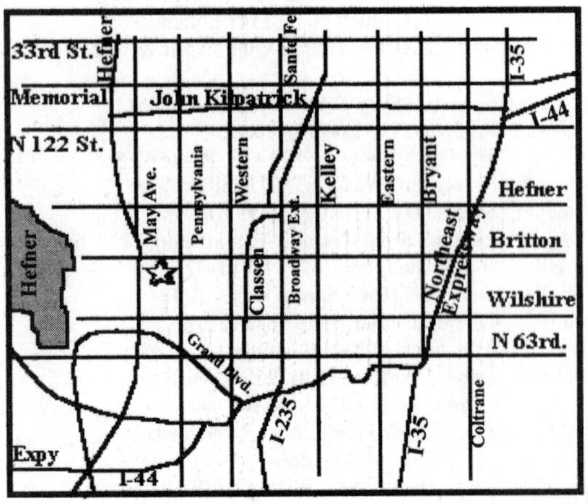

3500+ bolts of Cotton Fabric
500+ Quilting Book Titles

Mon - Fri 10 - 5
Thur til 8 Sat 10 - 3

Visit us on the Web at
www.okquiltworks.com
or e-mail us at: quilters@okquiltworks.com

Ada, OK #4

Mon - Fri 9:30 - 5
Sat 9:30 - 4

Quilters Heaven, Inc.

107 W. Main St. 74820
(580) 310-0596 Fax: (580) 310-0597
E-Mail: quilter@adacomp.net
Est: 1996 4000 sq.ft. 1000+ Bolts

Large selection of 100% cotton fabrics. Patterns, books, notions and gifts. Janome sewing machines, custom machine quilting. Mail orders welcome.

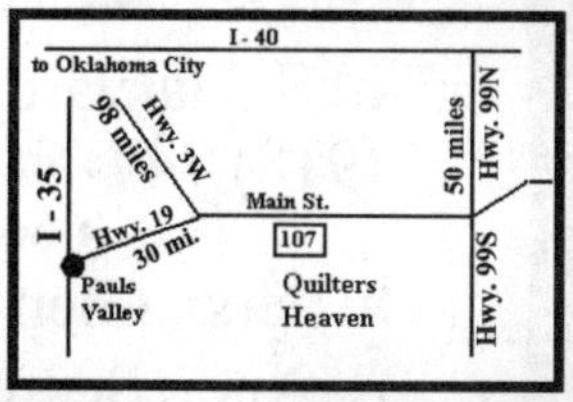

Antlers, OK #5

Mon - Fri 9 - 6
Sat 9 - 4
Evenings s by Appt.

Betsy's Quilts

HC 83, Box 870, P.O. Box 947 74523
(580) 298-5821 Fax: Same
(888) 817-5821 Est: 1994
Owner: Betty Hairfield 3600 sq.ft.

Over 1000 Bolts of Name Brand Fabrics.
Books, Patterns, Notions.
Quilts & Quillows for Sale.
Machine Quilting Pattern or Outlined.

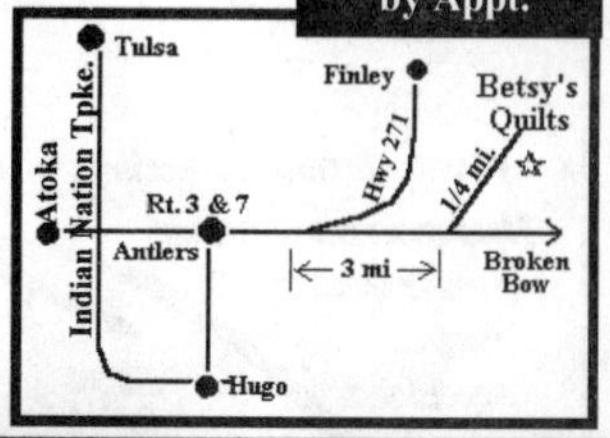

Lawton, OK #6

Mon - Fri 10:30 - 5
Tues til 8
Sun 1 - 5

Morning Star Quilt Works

1010 SW "E" Ave. 73501 (580) 248-9200
Owners: Carola Whicker & Bobbie Sowers

We have 1500 bolts of fabric, quilting and tapestry notions, books, patterns, a large selection of pre-worked needlepoint with coordinating thread and yarns, classes and gifts.

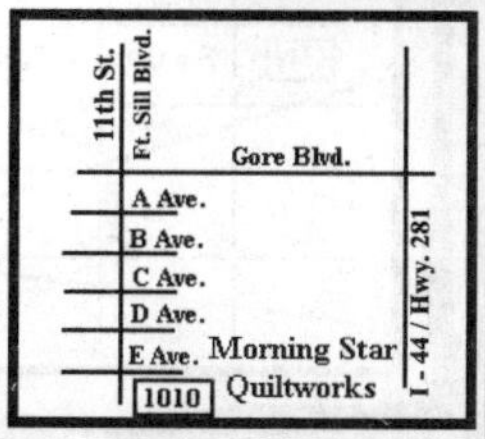

Chickasha, OK #7

Please Call Ahead for Hours

Becky's Stitch in Time

2227 Carolina 73018
(405) 224-0332 Fax: (405) 222-3983
E-Mail: Isellem4u2@aol.com
Owner: Noel & Becky Lambert

We carry a full line of flannels, reproductions and homespuns. Lines include P&B, Benartex, Michael Miller & More.

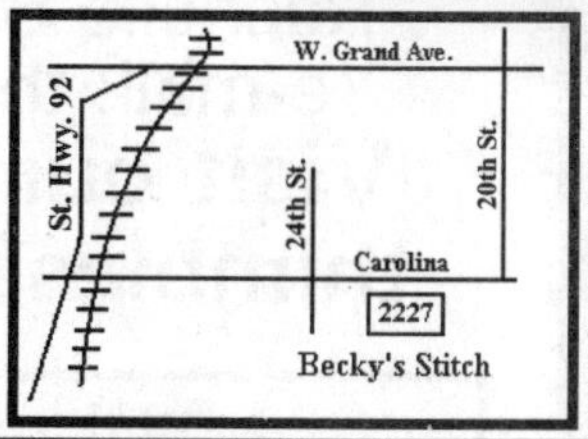

Guymon, OK #8

Mon 5 - 8
2nd Sat 10 - 5
or by Appt.

Cheryl's Quilt Corner

1608 N. Ellison 73942
(580) 338-3677 Owner: Cheryl Ashpaugh
E-Mail: cherylas@ptsi.net
Web Site: www.cherylsquiltcorner.com

A growing shop meeting your quilting needs with a warm home atmosphere. Custom machine quilting, 100% top quality cotton fabrics, books, patterns, notions & battings. Classes by request.

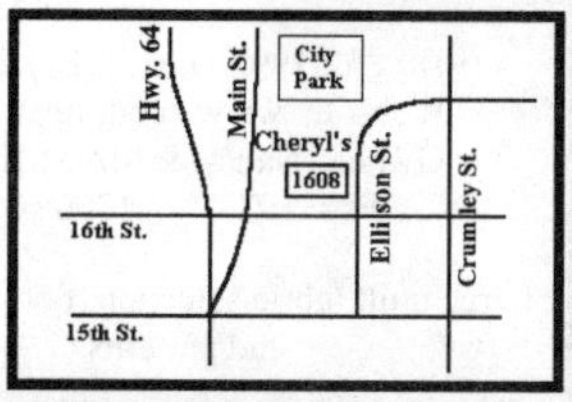

Quilter's Depot

Connie Allen • Nadine Hayes

200 S. Main 73860
(800) 903-7762
(580) 824-0400
Fax: (580) 824-0401 Depot@Pldi.net

Tuesday - Saturday 10:00 AM - 5:00 PM

Waynoka, OK #9

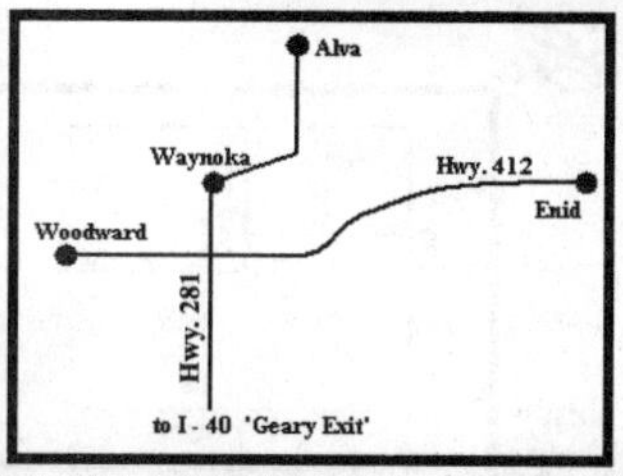

An Uptown Quilt Shop in a small town.
2,000 bolts of brand name fabrics, Patterns, supplies and notions with an "At Home" atmosphere.

Hennessey, OK #10

Prairie Quilt

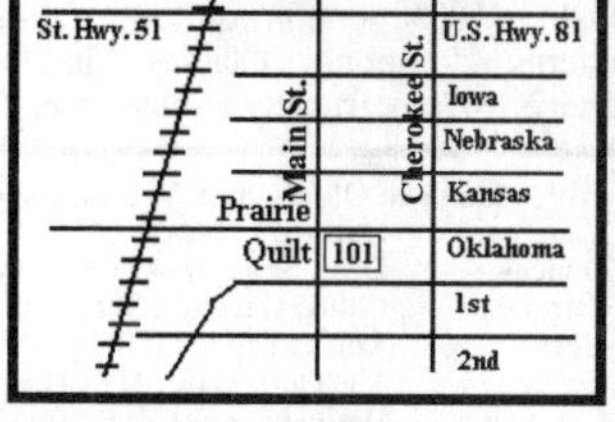

Prairie Quilt is the producer of the Oklahoma City Winter Quilt Show held the third weekend of January each year.

Step back in time in this delightful shop located beside the Gardens Edge tea room. Large selection of 100% cotton fabrics, notions, books, and patterns.

101 S. Main St., Hennessey, OK 73742
(405) 853-6801 Fax: (405) 853-4548
E-Mail: randa@prairiequilt.com
Website: www.prairiequilt.com
Est: 2001 5,000 sq.ft. 3,500 Bolts

Mon - Fri 9 - 5
Sat 9 - 1

Guthrie, OK #11

Mon - Sat 10 - 6

Extra Special

109 S. Division St. 73044
(405) 282-1144 Est: 1991
E-Mail: laurah@extraspecialfabric.com
Web Site: www.extraspecialfabric.com
Owner: Laurah Kilbourn 1000 Bolts

Specializing in Western fabrics, Southwest, Novelty, Calico, Faux Fur, Fleece, Barkcloth. Fashion to quilting. Clothing; Western Victorian; broomstick skirts decorated T-shirts.

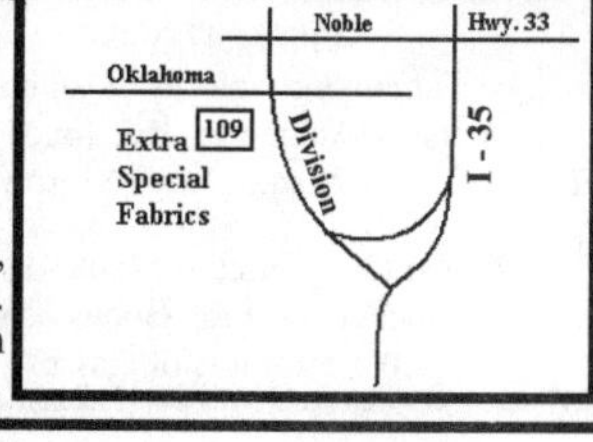

Thimbles & Threads

100% cottons notions classes books patterns
gifts, stitcheries, buttons
Husqvarna Viking
- sewing machines
- sergers
- accessories

Enid, OK #12

121 N. Grand 73701
580-234-3306
Rachelle Burleson, Proprietor
e-mail: thimbles@enid.com
Visit our website: www.
thimblesandthreads.com

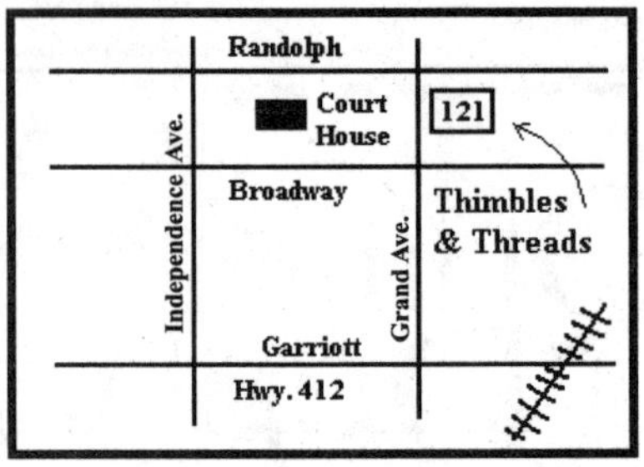

Mon - Fri
10 - 5
Sat 10 - 3

Northwest Oklahoma's
Premiere Quilt Shoppe!

Tulsa, OK #13

The Quilters' Nook

1740 S. Harvard 74112
(918) 747-NOOK
(6665)
Owners: Glen Jones
& Anne Seereiter
Est: 1987 6000 sq.ft.

Mon - Fri
9:30 - 5:30
Sat 9:30 - 4:30

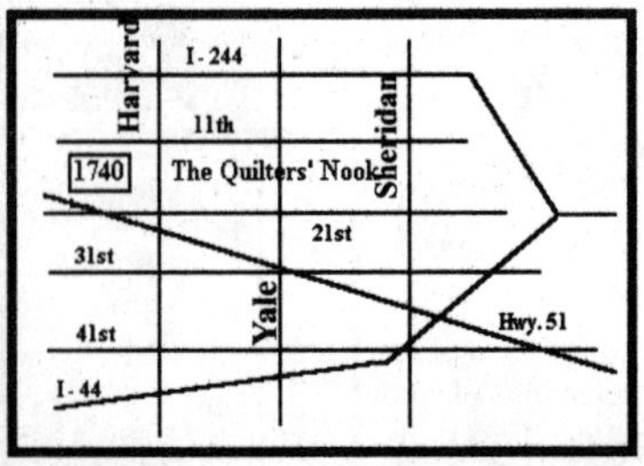

Fabric - Always 100% Cottons (2500+ bolts).
Notions - To ease tasks.
Patterns & Books - For inspiration & instruction (400+ titles).
FRIENDLY SERVICE !

Tulsa, OK #14

Mon - Fri
10 - 5:30
Tues til 7
Sat 10 - 5

Cotton Patch

8250 East 71st St. 74133
(918) 252-1995 Fax: (981) 294-9542
Web site: www.ecottonpatch.com
Owner: Nancy & Mike Mullman
Est: 1977 1200 sq.ft.

Large quilt fabric selection, books, notions, and patterns.

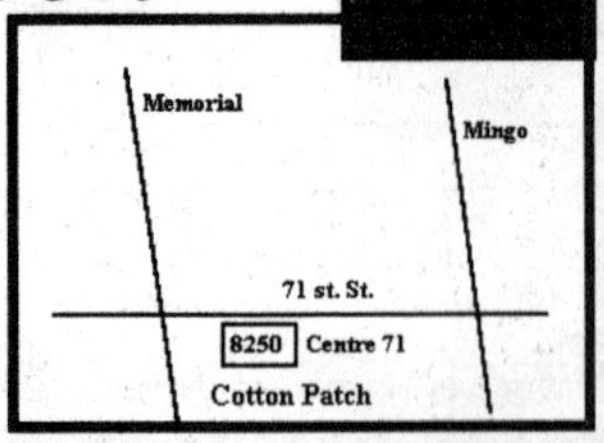

Tulsa, OK #15

Mon - Sat
10 - 4

Nora's Quilts, Etc.

8130-B S. Lewis 74137-1207
Located at the Plaza
(918) 298-0271
Owner: Nora N. Cope
Est: 2001 1350 sq.ft.

A complete Quilt Shop - Heirloom Quilts, Fabric - Classes - Notions & Books-Patterns-Rug Hooking

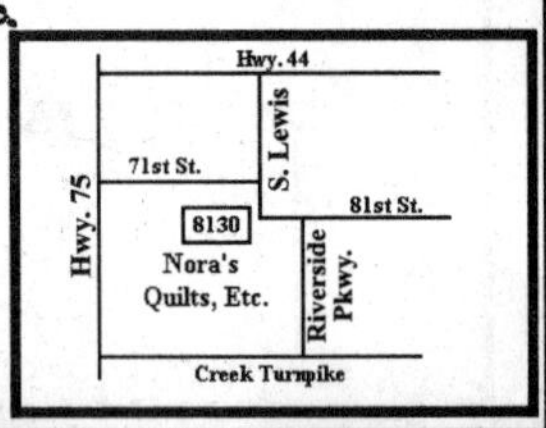

Broken Arrow, OK #16

Mon - Thur
9 - 6
Fri 9 - 5
Sat 10 - 4

The Quilted Thimble

825 N. Aspen 74012
(918) 259-1077 Fax: (918) 251-6852
E-Mail: QuiltedT@aol.com
Web Site: www.QuiltedThimble.com
Owner: Marilyn Shoalmire & Linda McMurray
Est: 1998 2400 sq.ft.

Quality 100% cotton quilting fabrics, books, patterns & notions. Classes. In-shop quilting service. Warm, friendly atmosphere. Tours!

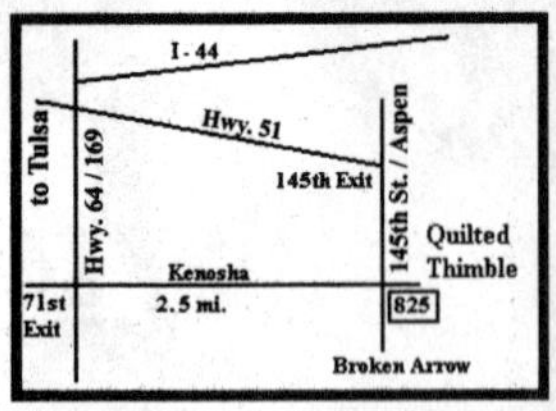

Perkins, OK #17

Mon - Fri
10 - 5;30
Thur til 8
Sat 10 - 4

The Quilting Post

411 N. Main, P.O. Box 1109 74059
(405) 547-8300
E-mail: Granniesew@aol.com
Owners: Darlene Leach & Joyce Rigsby
Est: 2001 1500 sq.ft. 700 & growing Bolts

100% Cotton Fabrics -- Moda - Hoffman - Thimbleberries, Etc. Books. Notions.
We offer lots of classes.

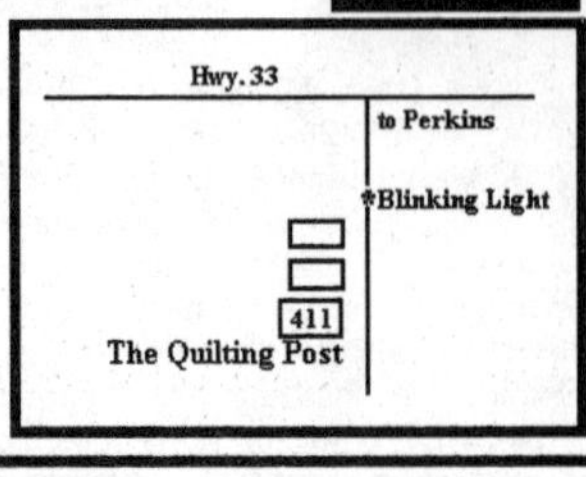

Other Shops in Oklahoma: We suggest calling first

Claremore	Quilting Classics, 14352 E. 480 Rd. #A	918-341-2919
Duncan	Deb's Sew Biz, 427 S. Hwy. 81	580-255-2843
Fargo	Calico Gal Quilt Shop, 121 1st St.	405-698-2440
Gore	Round Top Quilt Shop, Ray Fine Dr. Box 217	918-489-5652
Grove	The Quilt Shop, 2112 U.S. Hwy. 59 N	918-786-2046
Guymon	Heritage Quilts, 1907 Blue Sage Dr.	405-338-1402
Harrah	Martin Fabric Shop, 1960 N. Church Ave.	405-454-2960
Heavener	Stitching Time, 506 E. 1st St.	918-653-3081
Henryetta	Tiger Mountain Quilt Barn, Box 296A Route 2	918-466-3244
Jenks	Victorian Charm Quilt Shoppe, 225 E. Main St.	918-298-9090
Lawton	Hilltop Fabrics, PO Box 169 8202 W. Lee RR #4	405-536-5776
Mangum	Busy Bee, 120 E. Lincoln St.	580-782-3805
Miami	Seay's, 224 "E" St. SW	918-540-0741
Mustang	Nimble Thimble, 500 N. Financial Ter. #A	405-376-5595
Nowata	Shrum's Country Quilters, 520 E. Cherokee Ave.	918-273-3393
Oakwood	J & J's Quilting Place, R.R. #2, Box 28	405-891-3575
Ponca City	Linda's Creative Sewing, 111 N. 4th St.	405-762-6694
Shawnee	Sue's Sewing Shoppe, 2301 North Kickapoo	405-273-4600

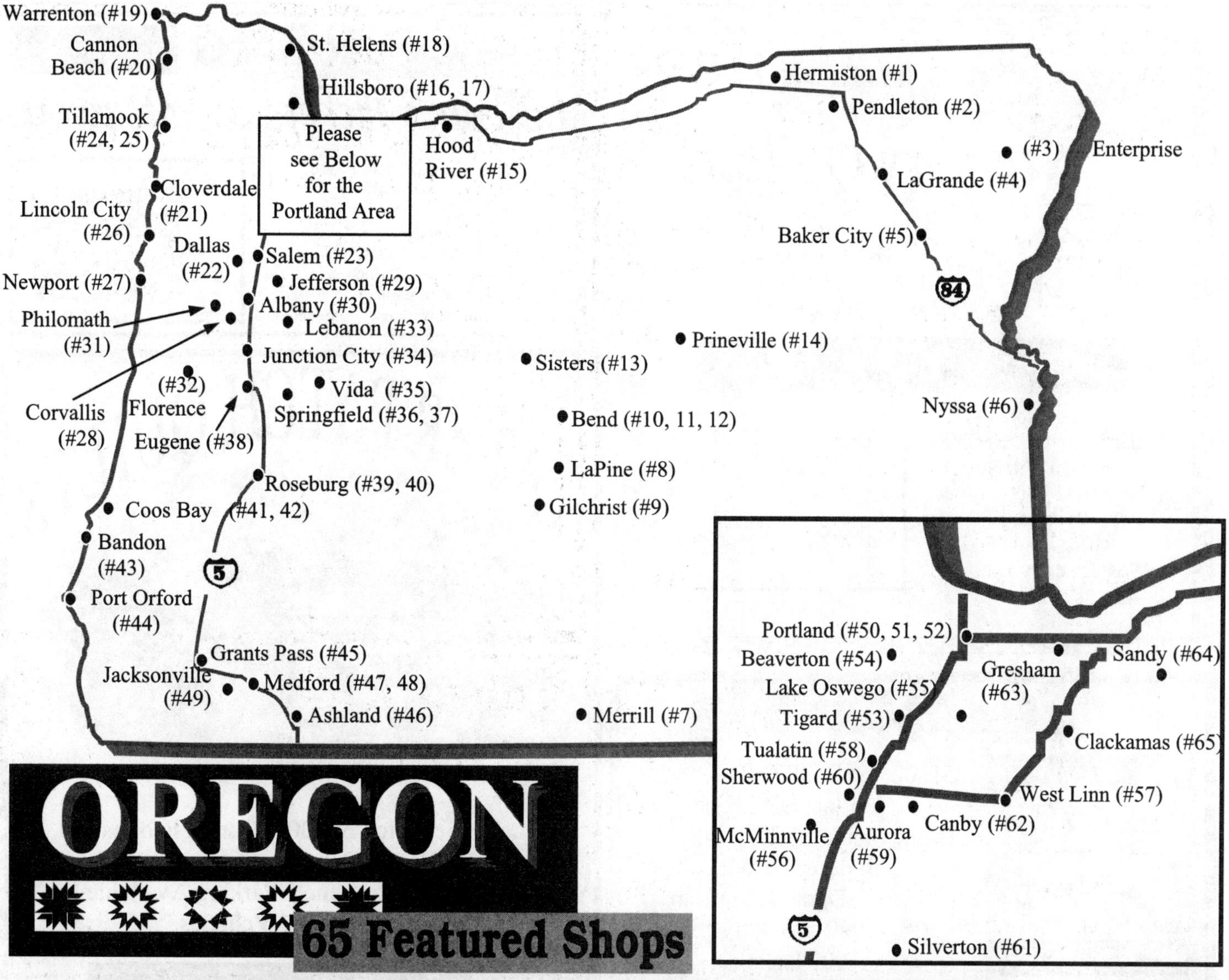

OREGON

65 Featured Shops

Hermiston, OR #1

Tues - Sat 10 - 5

Country Loveables Quilt Shop

148 E. Main 97838
(541) 567-2726
Owner: Judy K. Robinson

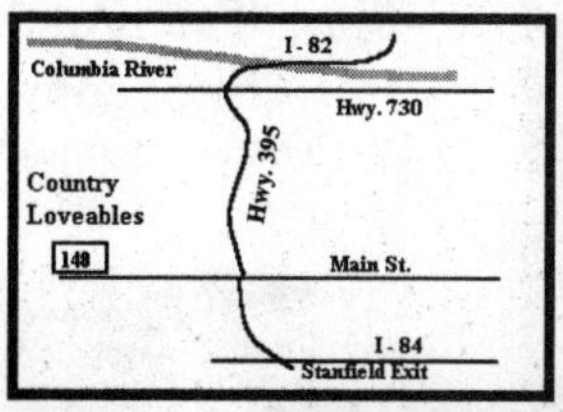

1000 bolts of Fabric: Moda - P&B
South Seas - Maywood - Kona Bay - Hoffman
Books, Patterns, Notions, Classes

Pendleton, OR #2

Mon - Fri 10 - 6
Sat 10 - 2

the Quilt House

1005 SW Frazer 97801
(541) 276-2128
Owner: Anita James
Est: 1997
2200 sq.ft.
1500+ Bolts

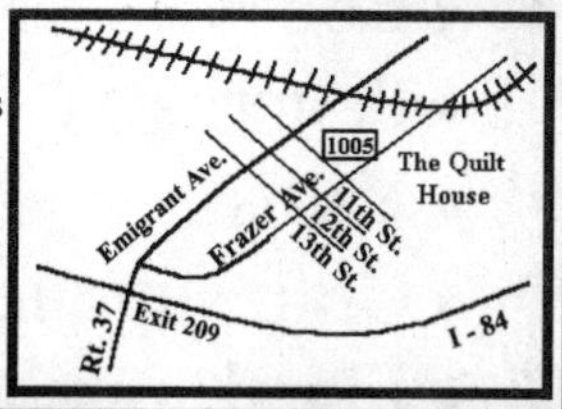

100% cotton quilting fabric. Books, Patterns, Notions and Classes. Stitchery patterns. DMC
Web Site: www.thequilthouseweb.com

Enterprise, OR #3

Tues - Fri 11 - 5
Sat 11 - 4

The UnCommon Thread

115 N River 97828
(541) 426-3089 or (877) 434-6623
E-Mail: grappler@uci.net
Est: 1997

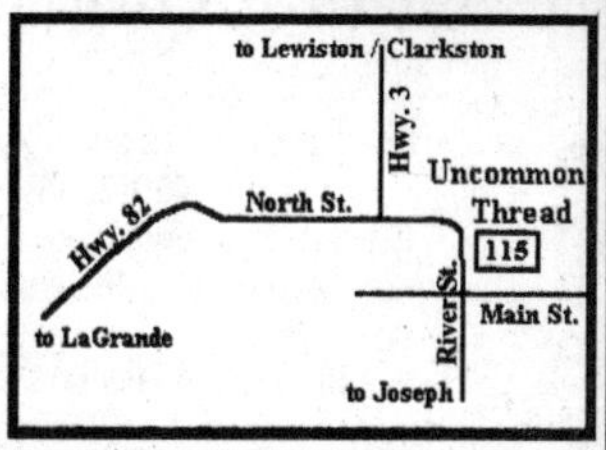

Specializing in natural fibers & friendly advice. We offer quilting fabrics, books, patterns & notions, yarn, spinning fibers, classes & unique rugs, hats, etc.

La Grande, OR #4

Mon - Fri 10 - 5
Sat 10 - 4

Quilt Therapy

1101A Washington 97850
(541) 663-1817
Fax: (541) 663-9728
Est: 2001 1600 sq.ft.
Owner: Faith Hohstadt
& Joanne Mahoney
E-Mail: quilttherapy@eoni.com
Web Site: www.eoni.com/~quilttherapy

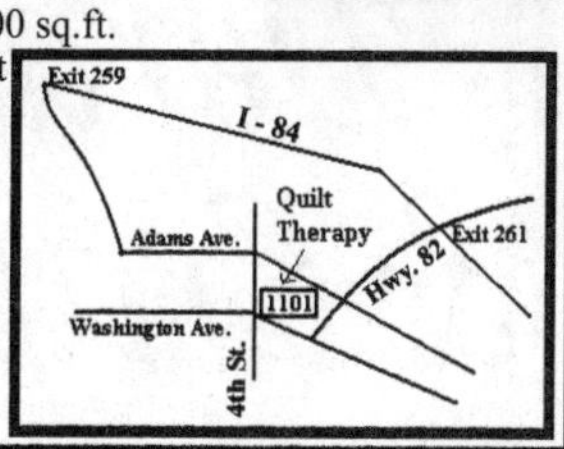

Everything for your quilting addiction! Batiks, orientals, reproductions, gifts, notions, quilt racks, BOM, classes and More!! Books, patterns, consignments and helpful advice.

Baker City, OR #5

Kountry Quilters

2658 10th St. 97814
(541) 523-0500
Fax: (541) 523-8565
Owner: Ruth Pedersen

Mon - Fri 10 - 6 Sat 10 - 5 Sun 12 - 5

Quilting Fabrics—Benartex, Batiks, Hoffman, Kaufman, Timeless Treasures. 1800+ Bolts Books, Patterns, Notions, Gifts. PFAFF. We also carry knitting supplies.

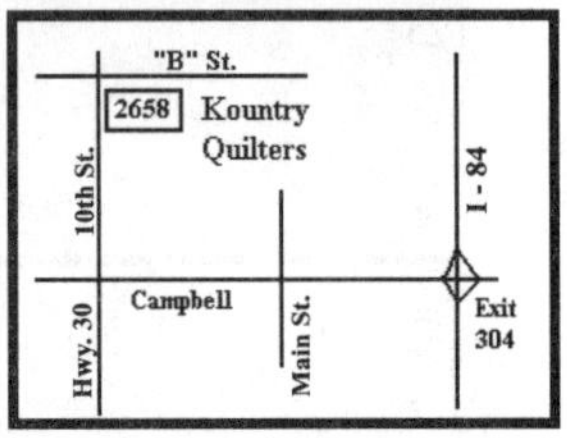

Nyssa, OR #6

Mon - Sat 10 - 6

Marilynn's Pickets & Patchwork

118 Main St. 97913
(541) 372-5336

3000 Bolts
Books, Patterns, Classes, Gifts.
Best Selection of flannels in Eastern OR & Western ID.
Friendly, helpful "down home" atmosphere!

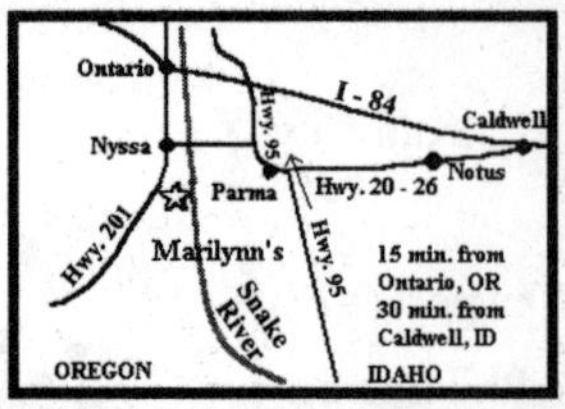

TATER PATCH QUILTS

Large Selection of 100% Cotton Fabrics and Flannels. Books, Patterns, Notions and Classes. "On the Road to Reno" Parking Available for Recreational Vehicles.

Mon - Fri 10 - 5 Sat 10 - 4

14141 Falvey Rd. 97633
(541) 798-5955
E-Mail: TaterPatchQuilts@aol.com
Est: 1996 2100 sq.ft.

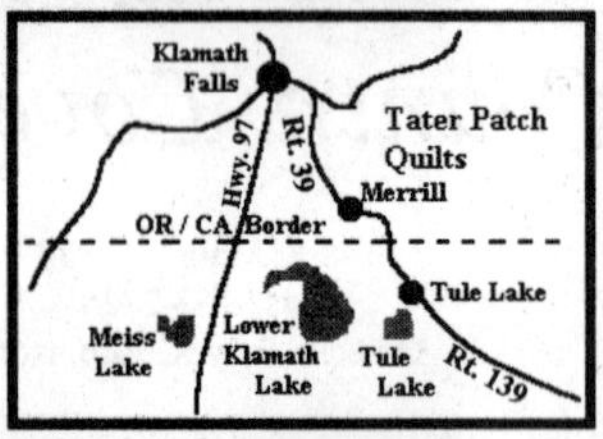

Merrill, OR #7

LaPine, OR #8

51602 1st St., P.O. Box 807,
LaPine, OR 97739
Phone / Fax: (541) 536-2360
E-Mail: deramc@aol.com
Owner: Dera McMurrian
Est: 1999 3,000 sq.ft.
1900 Bolts

- Quilting fabrics
- Notions
- Books
- Patterns
- Yarns
- Craft supplies
- Floral supplies
- Classes
- Much more.

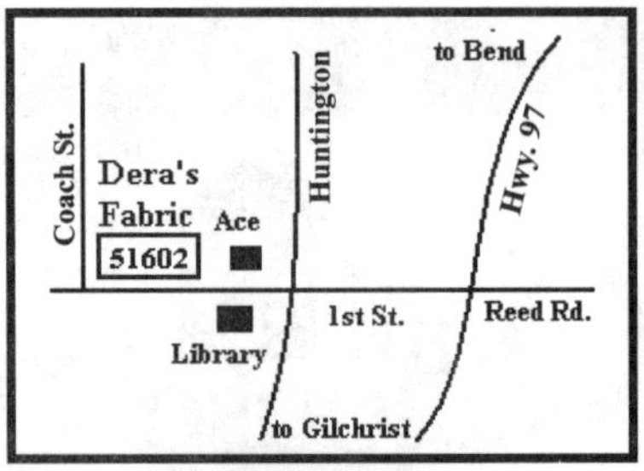

Mon - Fri 9 - 5 Sat 10 - 4

Dera's Fabric & Craft Supplies

Gilchrist, OR #9

Tues - Fri 10 - 5:30 Sat 12 - 4 Longer in July

Pinetown Quilting Adventures

P.O. Box 320, 71 Michigan Ave. 97737
(541) 433-2435
E-Mail: Pinetown@coinet.com
Owner: Cynthia Buell

Always Something special to be found.
Visit us on your trip to the Sister's Quilt Show.

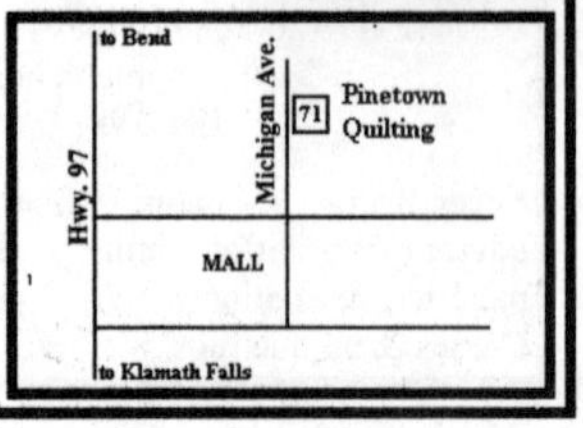

Bend, OR #10

Mon - Fri 10 - 5:30
Sat 10 - 4:30

Mountain Country Mercantile
fabric

1568 NW Newport Ave. 97701
(541) 382-5984
6500 square feet of fabric, mostly calico - flannel - wool. 6000-7000 bolts of fabric.

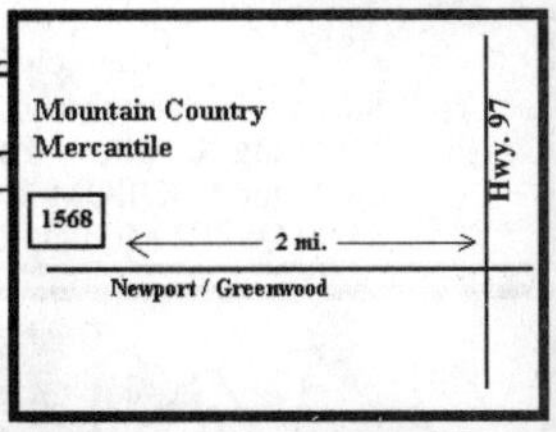

Bend, OR #11

Sew Many Quilts
So Little Time

The quilt shop that combines a charming personality, the friendliest atmosphere and a great selection of fabrics, books, patterns, notions, antiques and unique gifts.

You don't want to miss our shop!!

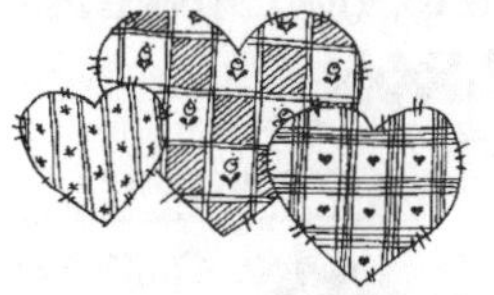

Mon - Sat 9:30 - 6
Sun 11 - 4

541-385-7166

Opening 2002 - call for directions

Owners: Gail Ransdall & Sharon Lang
E-Mail: mslang@coinet.com

Bend, OR #12

Mon - Sat 9:30 - 5:30
Sun 12 - 4

BJ's Quilt Basket and Bernina Center

20225 Badger Rd. 97702
(541) 383-4310 Fax: (541) 383-2484
Owner:
Barbara Schreiner
Est: 1992
5400 sq.ft. 3500 Bolts
E-Mail: barb@bjsquiltbasket.com
Web Site: www.bjsquiltbasket.com
Top Quality fabrics, 600 book titles, patterns, notions, classes, fat quarters, fabric packets, mail order. July Festival of Classes

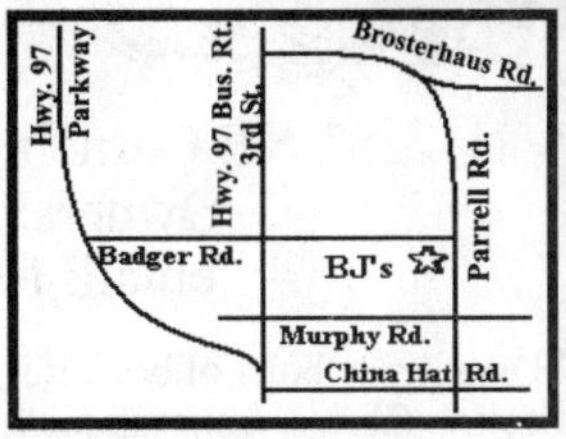

STITCHIN' POST

Established 1975~Jean Wells

Sisters, OR #13

Where originality and inspirational ideas capture the quilter:

Exclusive Stitchin' Post designed Block-of-the-Month Clubs:
Pieceful Village • Quilted Glory • Seasons in the Pines • Call of the Wild

Fabric Finders Swatch Club
Gifts for Quilters and Gardeners
7000+ bolts of cotton fabrics
Original patterns designed by the Stitchin' Post Staff

***Home of* The Sisters Outdoor Quilt Show™**
July 13, 2002 • July 12, 2003
(Always the Second Saturday in July)

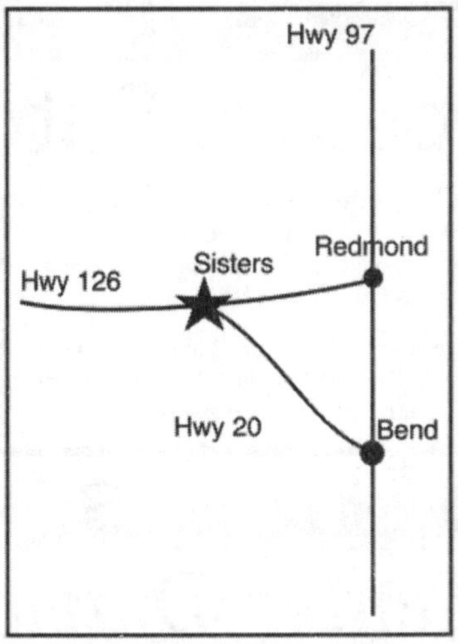

Hours: Mon-Sat 9 - 5
Sun 10 - 5

Shop online or come visit one of the finest quilt shops in America.

311 W. Cascade/PO Box 280, Sisters, OR 97759 • (541)549-6061 • Fax (541) 549-1922
e-mail: stitchin@empnet.com • www.stitchinpost.com

Prineville, OR #14

Mon - Fri 9:30 - 5:30
Sat 10 - 4
Oct - May Mon til 7

Prairie Girls' Quilt Shop, LLC

970 NW Third St. 97754
(541) 416-2004 Fax: (541) 447-3052
E-Mail: prairiegirls@coinet.com
Web Site: www.e-prairiegirls.com
Est: 2000 2100 sq.ft. 1600 Bolts

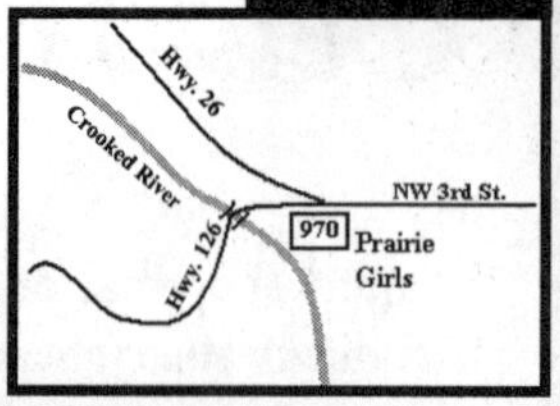

Customer service oriented quilt shop, specializing in classic western, flannels, homespun, batiks, & 30's fabrics. Quilting supplies, books & patterns.

Hood River, OR #15

Mon - Sat 10 - 4
Thur til 6

Every Thread Counts E.T.C.

1215 "C" Street 97031
(541) 386-5044
Est: 1987
Owner: Ann Zuehlke
E-Mail: etc@gorge.net
Web Site: www.everythreadcounts.com
Quilting Supplies * Fabric
Newsletter * BOEOM * Classes
$5.00 Quilt * Monthly Clubs

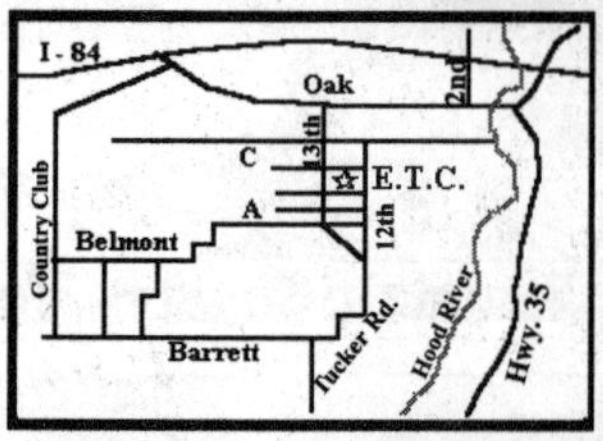

MAINSTREET CLOTH & MERCANTILE

WHERE THERE IS "ALWAYS SOMETHING NEW"!

We have a vast array of fabrics. Fine English lawns, Flannels and everything in between.
See our 2nd Shop too--
MainStreet Embellishments
Ribbons, Buttons, beads, Rubber Stamps, Paper Arts and more.

Quilt Sampler Top Ten Shop 2002

Owner: Toni Lynn
Est: 1996
2 Stores - 4300 sq.ft.
2500 Bolts

Home of: MAINSTREET PATTERN COMPANY "ART FROM THE HEART"

231 E. Main St.
Hillsboro, OR 97123
503-849-1891
Mon - Fri 10 - 5:30
Sat 10 - 5
www.mainstreetcloth.com

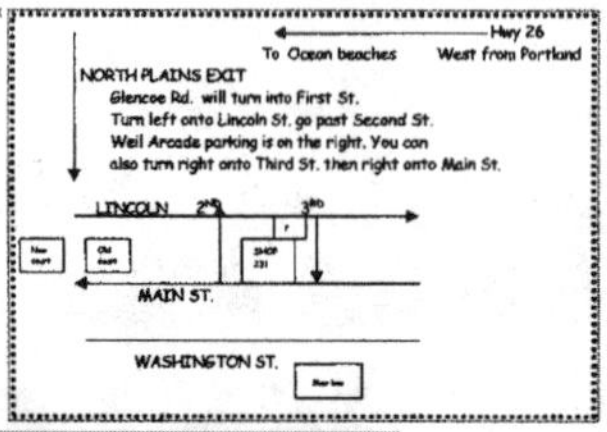

Hillsboro, OR #16

Hillsboro, OR #17

Furever Friends Quilt Shop

2257 NE Cornell Rd. 97124 (503) 640-1907
Owners: Don & Nola Aman
email: ffquiltshop@aol.com

Mon 12 - 7
T, W, Th 10 - 7
Fri 10 - 6
Sat 10 - 4

Over 1,500 bolts of beautiful, high quality, 100% cotton fabrics, from unique to traditional: Batiks, Watercolors, 30's & 40's Reproductions, Florals, Landscapes, Kids & Bugs, Brights and Flannels... Over 300 Quilt Book Titles. Classes almost every afternoon & most evenings. (Gather 2 to 6 people & we'll have a class, beginners & beyond!) Quilt tools & individual help always available. Photo T-shirts & Photo-Quilts our specialty since 1988! Professional Machine Quilting (& Machine Binding) service also available. Thanks for letting us serve you!

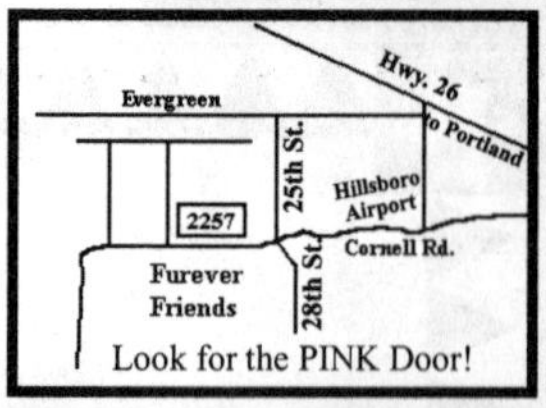

St. Helens, OR #18

Mon - Fri 9:30 - 6
Sat 9:30 - 5

Fibers & Stitches

58093 Columbia Hwy. 97053
(503) 397-5536 Fax: (503) 397-5536
E-Mail: swidmer@columbia-center.org
Owner: Sue Widmer

Large selection of Cotton Fabrics, Books, Patterns & Quilting Notions. X-stitch patterns, fabric, notions also available.

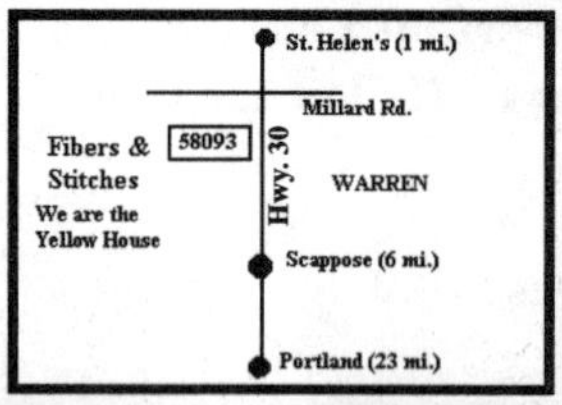

Warrenton, OR #19

Mon -Thurs 10 - 5
Fri - Sat 10 - 6
Sun 10 - 4

Northwest Stitchin's

926 E. Harbor St. 97146
(503) 861-0107
Fax: (503) 861-0165
E-Mail: quilter@northweststitchins.com
Web Site: www.northweststitchins.com

Quality 100% Cotton Quilting Fabrics, Notions, Patterns and Books. We maintain a large Selection of BOM's, Kits and Classes.

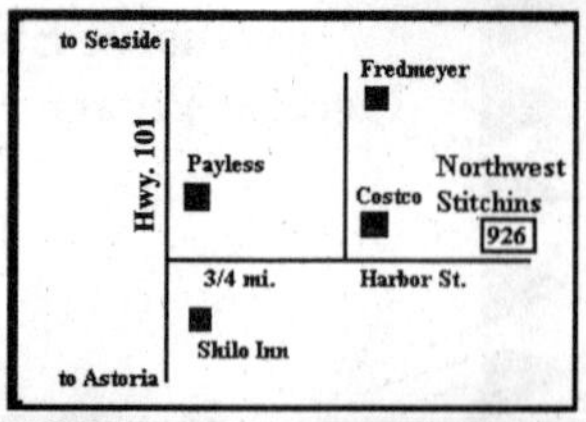

Cannon Beach, OR #20

7 Days a Week 10 - 5

Center Diamond

1065 S. Hemlock 97110
(503) 436-0833 Fax: (503) 436-2540
E-Mail: Bonniewa@aol.com
Web-Site: www.centerdiamond.com
Owners: Julie & Bonnie Walker
Est: 1994 1500 sq.ft. 2000+ Bolts

Over 2000 bolts of the most gorgeous 100% cotton fabrics. Books, patterns, notions & gifts. Located 1 block from the beach.

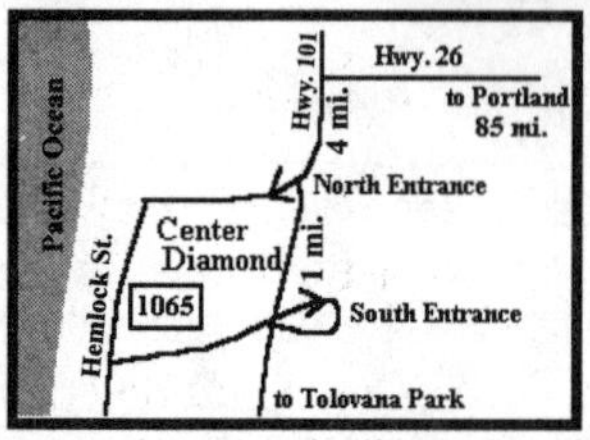

Cloverdale, OR #21

Mon - Sat 10 - 5

B J's Fabrics & Quilts

38105 Hwy. 101 S, P.O. Box 215 97112
(503) 392-6195 Est: 1997
E-Mail: BJsfabricsquilts@wcn.net
Owner: Barbara Lewis
Over 2000 bolts of fabric. Hwy. 101 from the North-2 miles south of Cloverdale, turn left past the 90 mile marker, then left again at the 2nd driveway. Hwy. 101 from the South-¼ mile from the Pacific City Turn-off, turn right after BJ's Fabrics & Quilts state sign, L 2nd driveway.

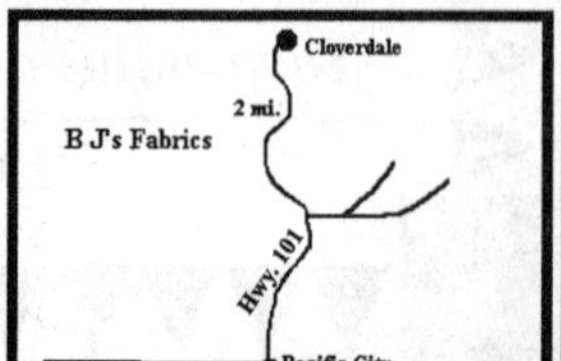

Rachel Greco, Owner

Grandma's Attic Sewing Emporium, Inc.

- 100% cotton fabrics for Quilting/Sewing
- Patterns, Books, Notions and More!
- Block of the Month/Fabric Clubs by Mail
- Send for FREE catalog!

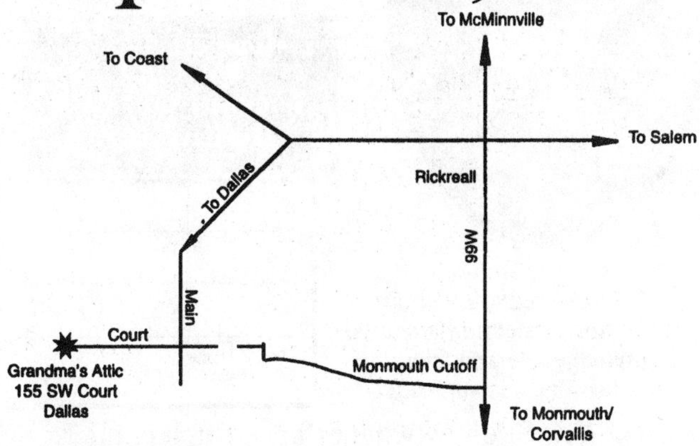

Dallas, OR #22

167 SW Court St. 97338
Est: 1995 4400 sq.ft.
2000+ Bolts

Mon - Fri 9:30 - 5:30
Sat 10 - 5
Sun 12 - 4

(503) 623-0451 Fax: (503) 623-6523
E-Mail: GrandmasAttic@compuserve.com
Web: www.GrandmasAtticQuilting.com

GREENBAUM'S Quilted Forest

240 Commercial St. N.E. 97301

Salem, OR #23

We carry the largest selection of calico, books, quilting supplies and shop samples in the area, displayed in a historic building with high ceilings to give you a quilt show every time you walk in.

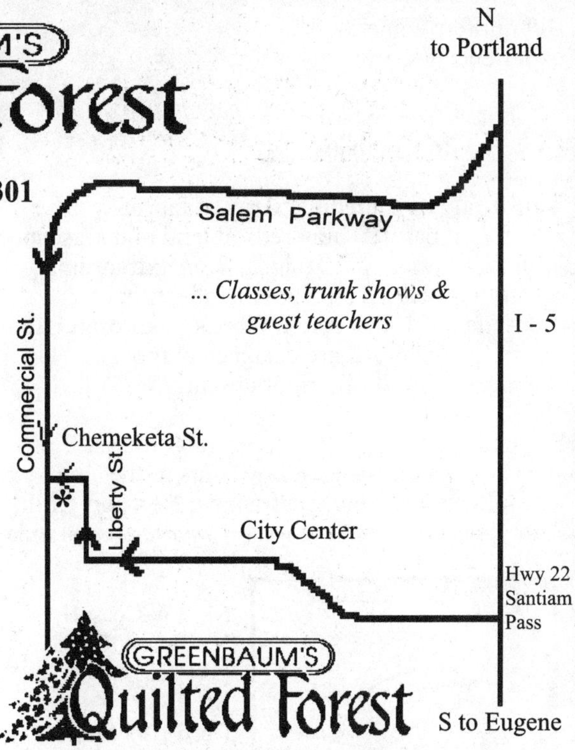

(503) 363-7973 **Toll Free (877) 700-2233**

3000 square feet, with a large selection of Hoffman, Batiks, and reproduction (1860's & 1930's) fabrics.

sylvia@quiltedforest.com
Website: www.quiltedforest.com

Hours: Mon - Fri - Sat 9:30 - 5:30
Tues, Wed, Thur 9:30 - 8 Sun 12 - 5

Established 1900 as a General Store

Jane's Fabric Patch

Tillamook, OR #24

1110 Main Ave. 97141
(503) 842-9392
E-mail: fabric@pacific.com
Owner: Jane Wise
Est: 1981 4000+ Bolts

Mon - Fri 9 - 5:30
Sat 10 - 4
Summer - Sundays & Holidays 11 - 3

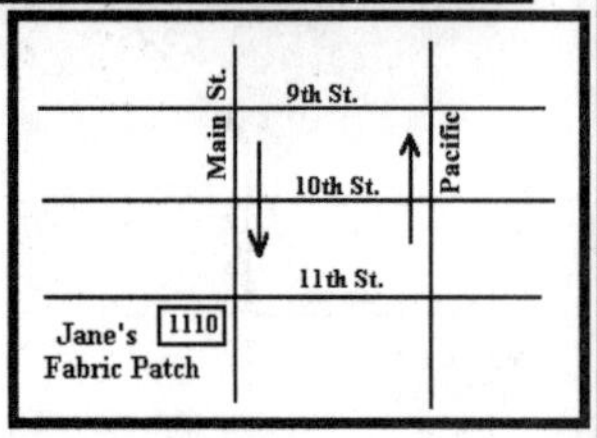

Coastal Retreat.
Multi-faceted Quilt shop.
Large fabric selection, creative, knowledgeable and friendly ideas and assistance.

Web Site: www.janesfabricpatch.com

Tillamook, OR #25

Tues - Sat 10 - 4
Sun 12 - 4
Closed Sun Nov - Feb

LATIMER QUILT & TEXTILE CENTER

2105 Wilson River Loop 97141
(503) 842-8622
E-Mail: latimertextile@oregoncoast.com
Web: www.oregoncoast.com/latimertextile

An active textile museum, dedicated to the preservation and promotion of the textile arts...weaving, spinning, quilting, history, research, education and exhibits.
Exhibits change every four to eight weeks.

We are located one block east of Shilo Inn off Hwy. 101

Lincoln City, OR #26

Mon - Sat 10 - 5:30
Sun 11 - 5

Seams Sew Right Quilt Shoppe

3203 SW Hwy. 101 97367
(541) 994-6946 Fax: (541) 994-6919
E-Mail: Chrisnquilts@aol.com
Owner: Chris Murrell Est: 2001 2200 sq.ft.

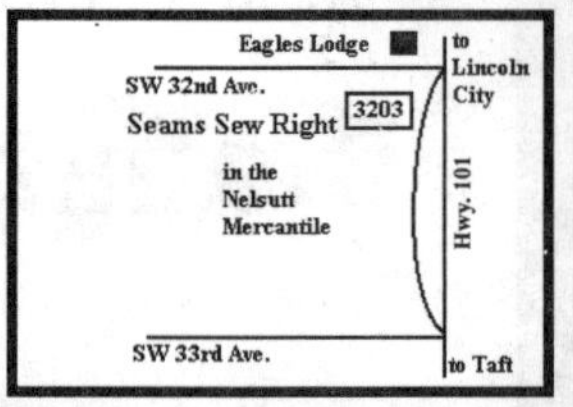

A friendly Quilt Shop in a historic mercantile. Full line of 100% Cottons, Notions, Books & Patterns on the beautiful Oregon Coast.

Newport, OR #27

In Newport, Oregon most visitors come to see the beauty of the coast, the aquarium, the lighthouses, the migrating whales…

But quilters come to experience the real beauty of the Coast, the fabrics at Newport Quilt & Gift Company!

NEWPORT QUILT & GIFT COMPANY

You'll find an incredible array of fabrics you've never seen before: hundreds of land and seascape fabrics, architectural designs, & an extraordinary selection of batiks among our collection of thousands of 100% cotton fabrics. Our original fabrics and patterns are designed at the Newport Quilt Studio right upstairs.

So send the family off to the regular tourist sites and plan to spend a few hours at the #1 quilter's sightseeing attraction, Newport Quilt! And visit our website at *www.newportquilt.com* today.

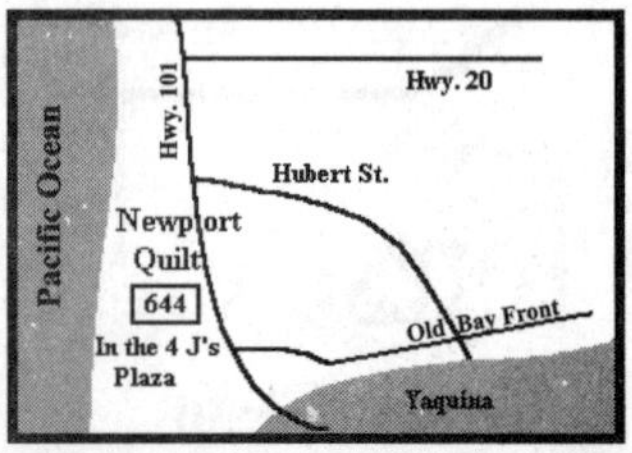

644 SW Coast Hwy
Newport, OR 97365
(541) 265-3492
Est. 1989
Open 10-5 Mon-Sat
Owner Julie Golimowski

NEWPORT QUILT & GIFT COMPANY
www.newportquilt.com

Corvallis, OR #28

Mon - Sat 9:30 - 5:30

Quiltwork Patches

209 S.W. 2nd St. 97333
(541) 752-4820
Owner: Jessy Yorgey
Est: 1979 650 sq.ft. 1800 Bolts

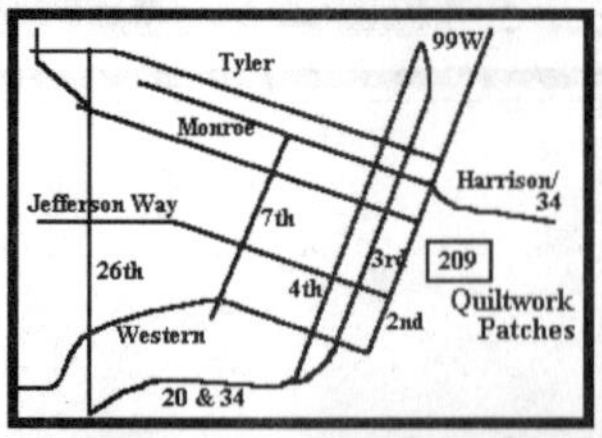

Over 1800 bolts of fine quality fabrics, plus a large selection of Quilter's tools and books. Free Brochure

Jefferson, OR #29

Mon - Fri 9:30 - 7:30
Sat 9 - 6
Sun 12 - 5

The Grateful Thread

115 S. 2nd St.
P.O. Box 1290 97352
(541) 327-3333

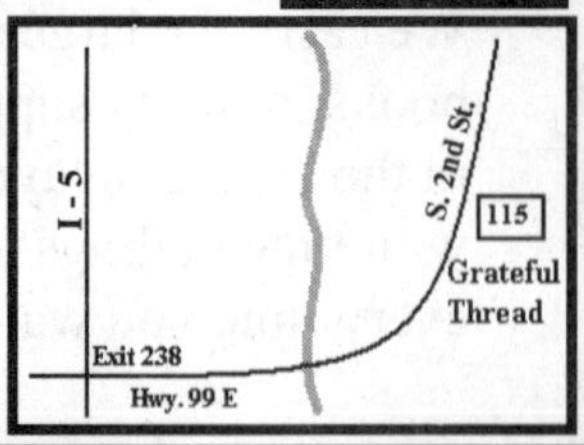

Fabrics that Rock! 100% cotton prints & solids. Books, notions, classes and handcrafted items. Friendly, personal service. Open 7 day a week.

Albany, OR #30

Mon - Sat 10 - 5

The Quilt Loft

126 Ferry SW 97321
(541) 928-7242
Fax: (541) 917-0058
E-Mail: robertsd@peak.org
Owner: Karen Roberts Est: 1996

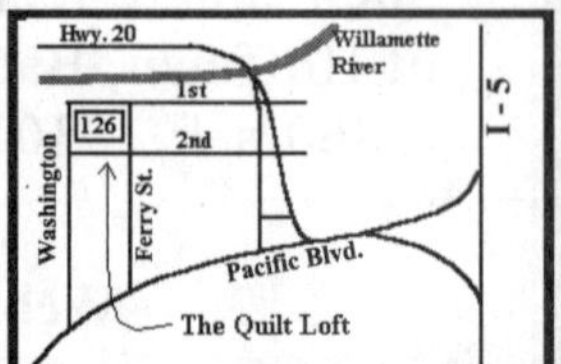

Quilts, Classes, Supplies and Gifts in historic downtown Albany.

JanniLou Creations

1243 Main P.O. box 333
Philomath, OR 97370-0333
(541) 929-3795; fax (541) 929-3597

JanniLou CREATIONS

QUILT SHOP

Philomath, OR #31

- Great Patterns, books, notions & more.
- Absolutely beginning to advance classes
- Mail order catalog $1

Next time you're in Philomath, drop by to see us "on location" at the old Waucomah movie theater building.

Mon, Wed, Fri and Sat, 9:30a-5:30p
Tues & Thurs 9:30a-9:00p

Admit One ...or many!

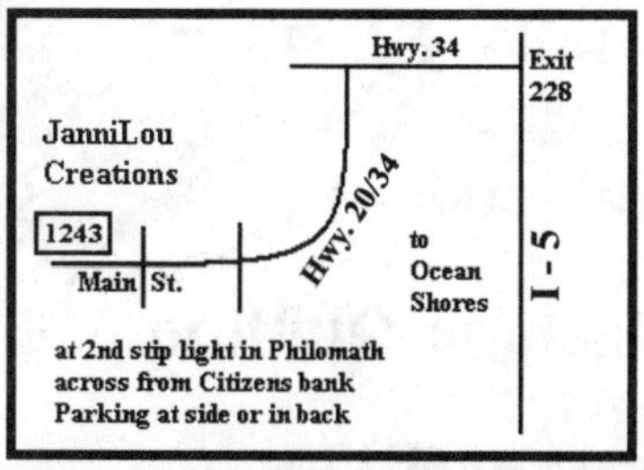

Florence, OR #32

Mon - Sat 10 - 5

Jodi's Quilts & Fabrics

5045 Hwy. 101 97439
(541) 997-3293 Fax: (541) 997-3573
E-Mail: Jodi@Presys.com
Owners: John & Jodi Ringen

100% Cotton Fabrics, Notions, Doll Making Supplies, Great Selection of Books, Embellishments for Crazy Quilts, Friendly, Helpful Service. Classes Too.

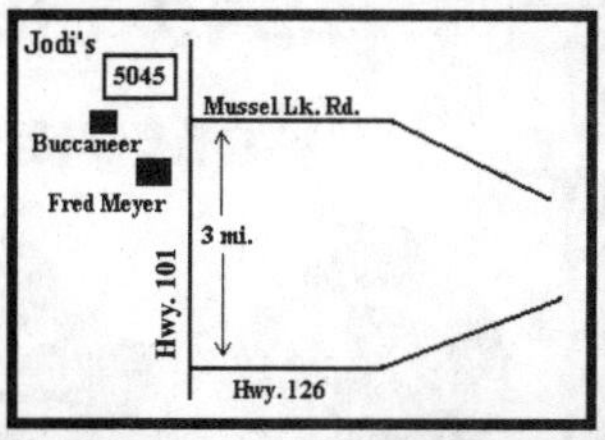

Lebanon, OR #33

Tues - Fri 10 - 5:30
Sat 10 - 4

STRAWBERRY PATCHES Quilt Shop

824 Main St. 97355
(541) 258-4075
E-Mail: sueberry@proaxis.com

Web Site: www.strawberrypatchquilts.com
Owner: Sue Davis

Toll Free (888) 610-7779

I'm either the 1st or Last Quilt Shop Fix as you cross over the Santiam Pass on Hwy. 20

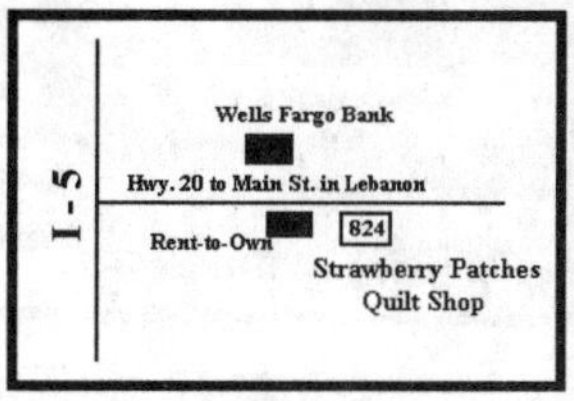

Quilter's Junction

595 Ivy St. (Hwy. 99) 97448 (541) 998-2289

Mon - Fri 10 - 5 Thur til 8 Sun 1 - 5

Toll Free: (877) 998-2289
Complete line of Fabric, Notions, Books, & Patterns.
Quilts & Gifts.
e-mail: quilt@quiltersjunction.com

Web Site:www.quiltersjunction.com

Junction City, OR #34

Vida, OR #35

Wed - Sun 10 - 5

FOXFIRE FARM Quilt and Gift Shoppe

49209 McKenzie Hwy. 97488
(541) 822-1011
E-Mail: KKrions@aol.com
Owner: Kathie Hoffman

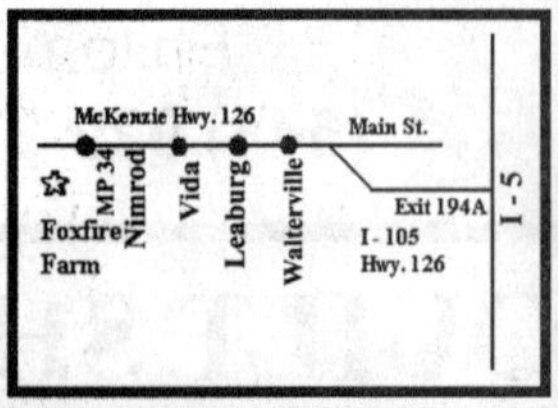

Fabric (Full line of Moda Marbles) Books
Patterns - Notions - Classes - Block of Month
Custom Machine Quilting

Springfield, OR #36

4227-C Main St. 97478
(541) 746-3256
Est: 1993 1400 sq.ft.
Owner: Joan Karagavoorian

Something to Crow About

Mon - Sat 10 - 5:30
Sun 12:30 - 5

Over 3,000 Bolts of Cottons, Flannels, Homespuns, Wools, Thimbleberries and Mumm's The Word Fabrics.
Patterns, Craft Supplies & Gifts.
Call about Thimbleberries Club and Girl Gang.

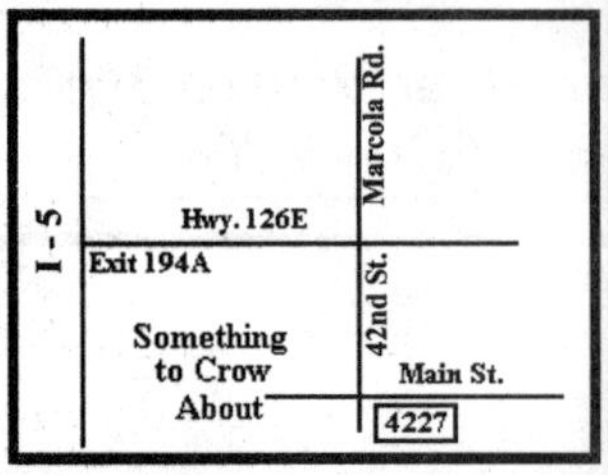

Classes: Quilting & Doll making.

Springfield, OR #37

Mon - Fri 9:30 - 9
Sat 9:30 - 6
Sun 11 - 6

Ben Franklin Craft & Frame Shop

1028 Harlow Rd. 97477
(541) 726-2641
Fax: (541) 726-2643
Est: 1990 11,000 sq.ft.

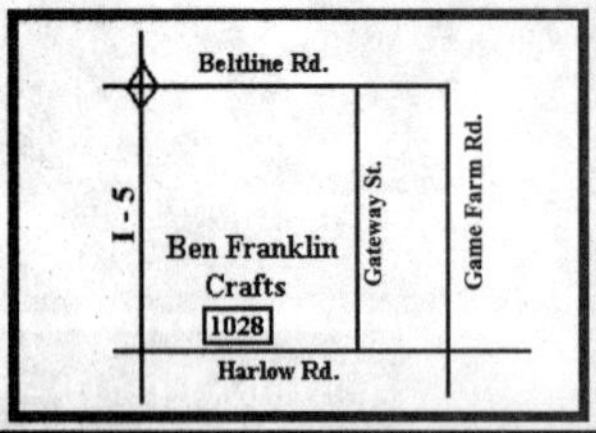

A full service Craft store with a great fabric department featuring quality quilt fabrics, books, patterns, batting and quilting notions.

Eugene, OR #38

Mon - Fri 10 - 5:30
Sat 10 - 5

Aunt B's Fabrics

447 W. 11th Avenue 97401
(541) 343-9296

100% Cotton Fabrics, flannels, books, notions, batting and classes. Large selection of craft and stitchery patterns.

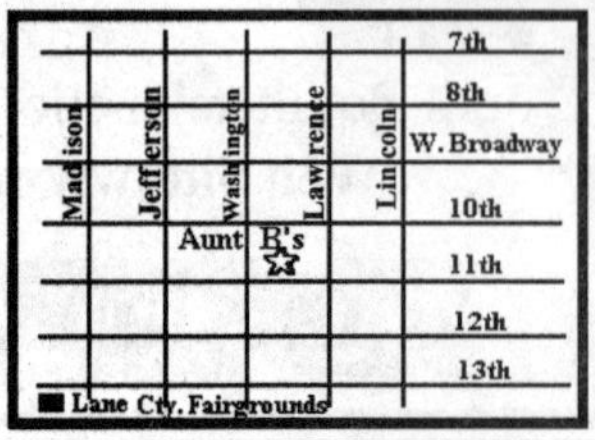

Seams Like Old Times Quilt Studio

- 100% Cotton Fabrics
- Quilting Books
- Quilting Supplies
- Custom Machine Quilting

10% Discount w/Ad Excluding BERNINA®

BERNINA® Sales & Service

Mon-Fri 10-6 Sat 10-5
541-672-5396
2240 Stewart Parkway
Roseburg, OR 97470

Est 1994

Exit #127 of I-5 head west on Stewart Parkway
We're across from Subway

Roseburg, OR #39

PLAZA SEWING CENTER

A QUILTER'S HAVEN

**We have a full line of high quality fabrics for the quilter.
Over 3,000 prints and over 200 solids.
A great selection of quilt and craft patterns and books.
Also a great selection of aids, notions and threads.
GREAT PRICES!**

Mon. - Fri. 9:30 - 6
Sat. 9:30 - 5:30
Sun. 11-5

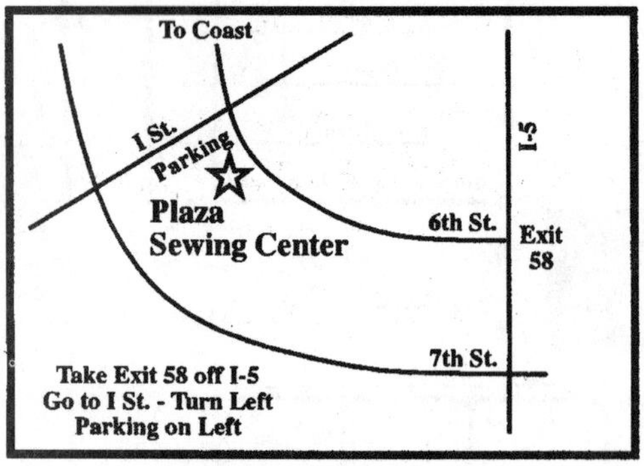

Only 8 Minutes From Freeway

**311 SE 6th St. Golden Rule Plaza 97526
(541) 479-5757
Owners: Rick & Mary Chapman
Est: 1967 5000 sq. ft.**

Grants Pass, OR #45

QuiltZ

Ashland, OR #46

Located in beautiful Ashland Oregon.
Home of the Oregon Shakespeare Festival.

***EVERYTHING* for the Quilter .....**
Huge selection of the finest cotton fabrics
Over 2500 Bolts
Batiks, Orientals, 30's Reproductions,
Theme Prints, Brights, Children's Prints,
Complete selection of Moda Marbles
Friendly & Knowledgeable Staff
Tax Free Shopping!

QuiltZ HOURS:
Monday - Saturday 10 to 5
Sunday – Noon to 4
(Closed Sundays in Winter)

QuiltZ has......
Color of the Month
20% off
*Different Color
Every Month!*

DIRECTIONS TO QUILTZ

From I-5 North use Exit 19
From I-5 South use Exit 11
Follow signs to Shakespeare.
QuiltZ is 2 blocks from
Shakespeare on Main Street.

QuiltZ
293 East Main, Ashland, Oregon
(541) 488-1650 FAX (541) 488-0751

Medford, OR #47

Mon - Sat 10 - 6
Sun 11 - 5

Grandma Dee's

Fabrics, Quilts & Stitchery, Inc.

4918 Crater Lake Ave. 97501
(541) 608-2874 Fax: (541) 608-2961
E-Mail: varneracres@charter.net
Owner: Deanna M. Varner Est: 2002

Beautiful fabrics from Kona Bay, Batiks, Hoffman and RJR. Specialty items, patterns, catalogs and more. Tremendous amounts of bus parking!

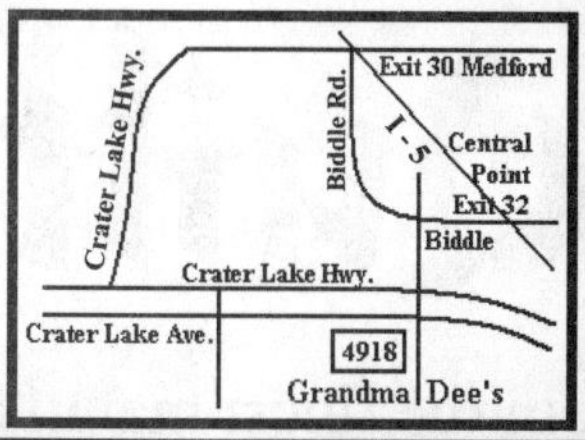

Jacksonville, OR #49

Mon - Sat 10 - 5
Sun 11 - 4

Country Quilts & Crafts

110 5th St., P.O. Box 405 97530
(541) 899-1972 or (877) 409-5466
E-Mail: countryquilt@msn.com
Web Site: www.countryquilts.com
Owners: Marge Wall
Est: 1988 650 Sq.ft.

Over 100 quilts both hand and machine.
Fine Fabrics and Quilts, Quilts, Quilts ! !

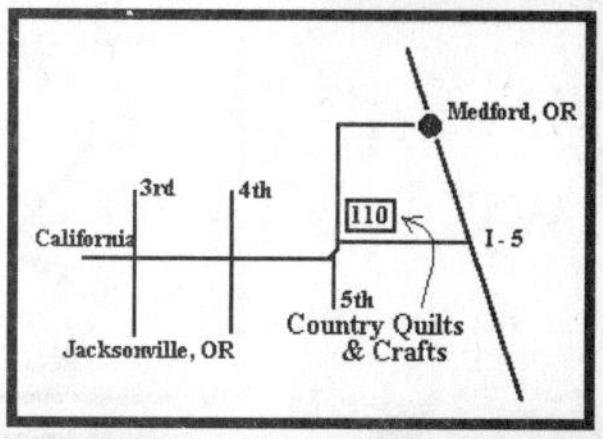

Portland, OR #50

Tues-Sat 10 - 4

Patchwork Peddlers

4107 NE Tillamook
(503) 287-5987 97212
Owner: Gail Pope
Est: 1977 1200 sq.ft.

Largest selection of quilt books in the Northwest; 1200 bolts of 100% cotton fabric.

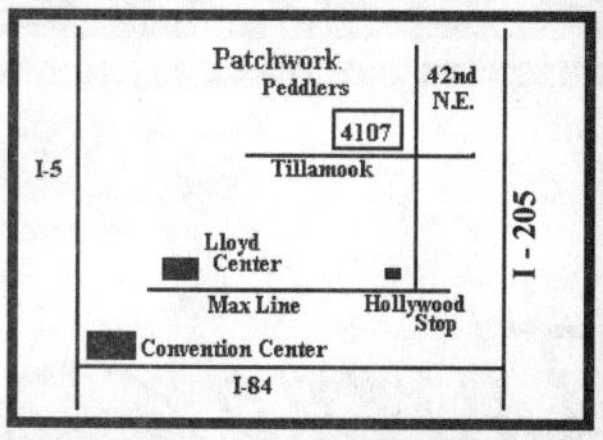

Portland, OR #51

Mon - Fri 10 - 6
Sun 1 - 5

Daisy Kingdom

134 NW Davis St. 97209
(503) 222-9033 Fax: (503) 274-2827
Web Site: www.daisykingdom.com

"Where imagination creates the unusual."
Quilting, home décor, bridal, gifts, dress goods.
Authorized Bernina Dealer.

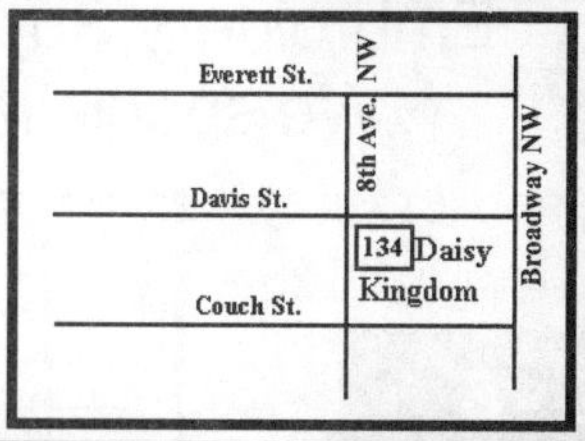

Tigard, OR #53

Mon - Sat 9:30 - 5:30
Sun 11 - 5

Fanno Creek Calicos

12192 SW Scholls Ferry Rd. 97223
(503) 579-7977 Fax: (503) 590-4537
E-Mail: fannocreek@netzero.net
Web Site: www.fannocreekcalicos.com
Owner: Susan Baxter
Est: 2000 2000 sq.ft. 1500+ Bolts

Southwest Portland's Premier Quilt Shop supplying quilters with the latest fabric, notions, books & classes. "We'll keep you in stitches."

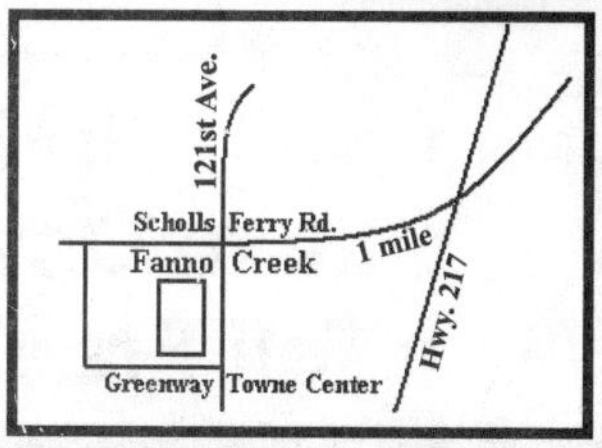

1000+ bolts of Hoffman, Kona Bay, South Seas, Maywood and Moda.

Medford, OR #48

CALICO JUNCTION

1310 - C Center Dr. 97501 (541) 770-8001
Owner: Vickie Kiser
Est: 1977 1500 sq.ft. 1000 Bolts

Mon - Sat 10 - 6 Sun 12 - 5

Fat Quarter Sale Every Sept. 25th 25 fat quarters for $25

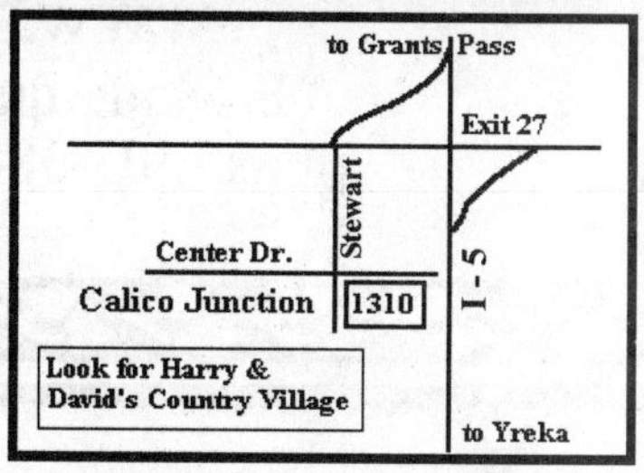

Southern Oregon's Largest Pattern Selection

FIBERS IN MOTION

7855 SW Capitol Hwy.
Portland, OR 97219
503-977-2758

Mon - Fri 10 - 6
Sat 10 - 5

Portland, OR #52

Fax: 503-977-2762
fibersinmotion@aol.com
Owner: LuAnn Rukke
Est: 2002 1800 sq.ft.

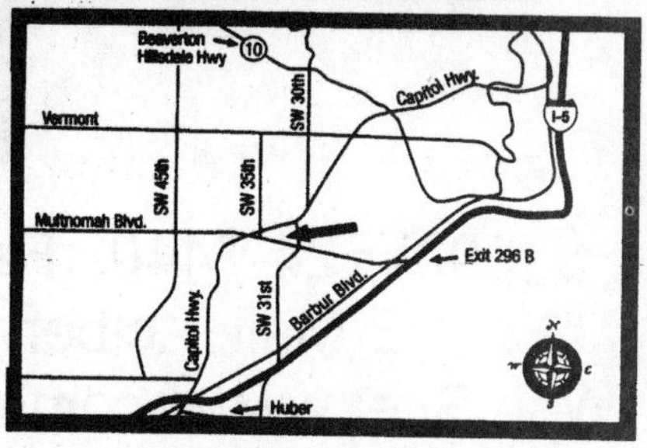

Portland's newest Quilt & Wearable Art fabric store. Located in historic Multnomah Village. Celebrate your creativity… fabrics, buttons, notions, books, gifts & classes. All designed to inspire the artist within.

Beaverton, OR #54

StoryQuilts.com

Large selection of 100% cotton fabrics from the finest manufacturers along with books, notions, classes, quilt kits and block of the month programs.

Mon, Wed, Fri 9:30 - 5:30
Tues, Thur 9:30 - 8:30
Sat 10:00 - 5:00 Sun 1:00 - 4:00

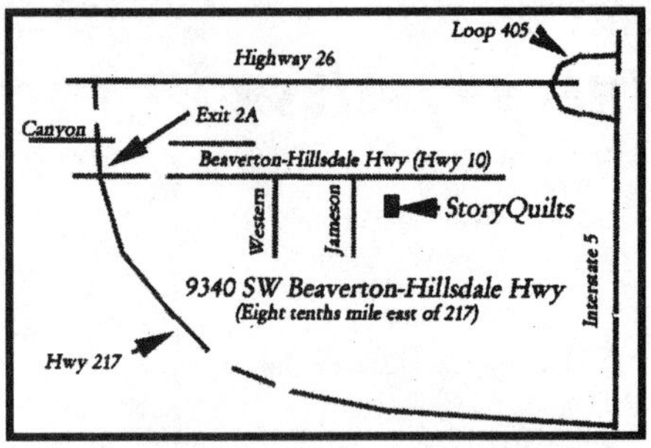

9340 SW Beaverton-Hillsdale Hwy.
503-384-0185
www.storyquilts.com
E-Mail: quilter@storyquilts.com
Fax: 503-384-0613 2650 sq.ft.

Directions: Take exit 2A from hwy. 217. Go East on Beaverton-Hillsdale (hwy. 10) approximately 0.8 miles. StoryQuilts is just East of Jameson (stop light) on the right.

Lake Oswego, OR #55

A Common Thread

Owned and operated by women who sew

Portland's #1 Bernina dealer. Quilting and Fashion Fabrics, Books, Notions, Patterns, Embroidery Supplies, Unusual threads. We specialize in Customer Service.

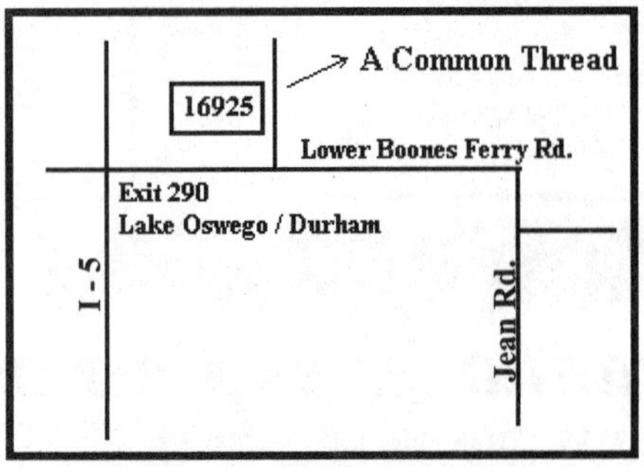

Mon - Fri 9:30 - 6
Sat 10 - 5 Sun 12 - 5

(503) 624-7440 Fax: (503) 670-9860
E-Mail: Actbernina@aol.com
Web Site: www.acommonthreadfabrics.com
Owner: Laura Dickson
Est: 1999 4300 sq.ft. 3000+ Bolts

16925 SW 65th
Lake Oswego, OR 97035
Toll Free: 1-877-915-6789

McMinnville, OR #56

BOERSMA'S

It's SEW Much Better!

203 E. 3rd St. 97128
(503) 472-4611 (800) VAC-SEWS
Website: www.boersmas.com
E-mail: jack@boersmas.com
Owners: Jack & Michelle Boersma
Est: 1935
Located in Historic Downtown
20,000 sq.ft. 9000 Bolts

Mon - Thur	8:30 - 6
Fri	8:30 - 7
Sat	9 - 5

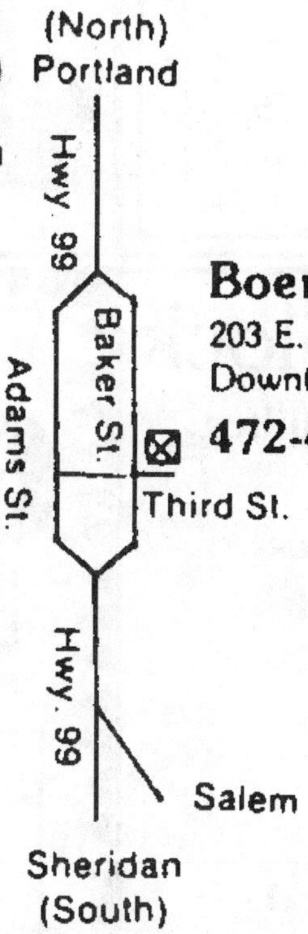

Boersma's
203 E. 3rd St.
Downtown
472-4611

Gammill Quilting Systems

- ♥ Sales & Service
- ♥ Hands-on Training
- ♥ Set-Up & Delivery
- ♥ Classes
- ♥ In-store Machine Rental

- ♥ Fine 100% Cottons
- ♥ Quilt Books
- ♥ Notions
- ♥ Classes
- ♥ Collectibles & Gift Items

Sewing Machine Sales & Service
Experienced Staff

West Linn, OR #57

The Quilt Shoppe

1795 Willamette Falls Dr.
West Linn, Oregon 97068
503•722•7430

Come See Us
4500 plus bolts of fabric
We have more space for
fabric, a great classroom
and easy access from
Stafford Rd. or
Interstate 205

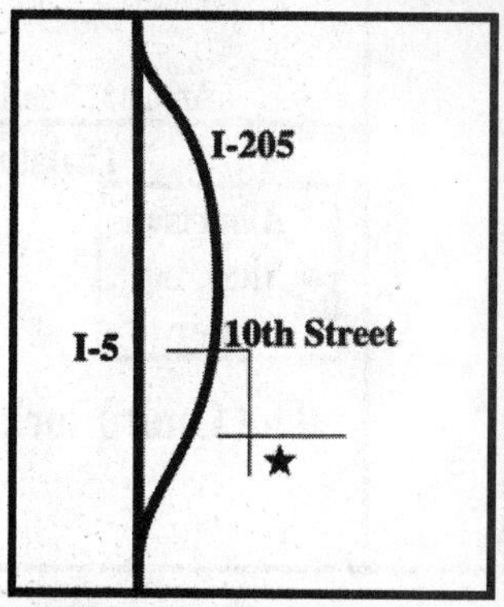

From I - 205: Take the 10th Street Exit, Go West on Willamette Falls Dr., Go three blocks, We're on the left.

Mon - Fri 9:30 - 5:30
Sat 10 - 5 Sun 11 - 5

We pride ourselves in friendly customer service"

Tualatin, OR #58

Mon - Fri 10 - 6
Sat 10 - 5
Sun 11 - 4

The Yard Sale

8355 SW Warm Springs St. 97062
(503) 691-8031
Owner: Shellie O'Donnell
Est: 2000 1200 sq.ft.

1000+ Bolts of 100% Cotton Fabric, Books, Notions, & Classes. Flannels, 30's Reproductions, Batiks & More. Stop By, We'd Love to Meet You.

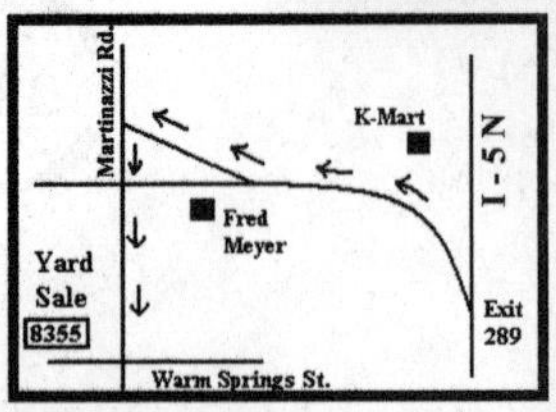

Aurora, OR #59

Tues - Sat 11 - 5
Sun 12 - 5

Jacob's House
Quilt Shop

21641 Main St. NE
97002
(503) 678-3078
Owner: Karen Stephens

Specializing in vintage, reproduction, & homespun fabrics for all your quilting needs. Located in Historic Jacob Miley House.

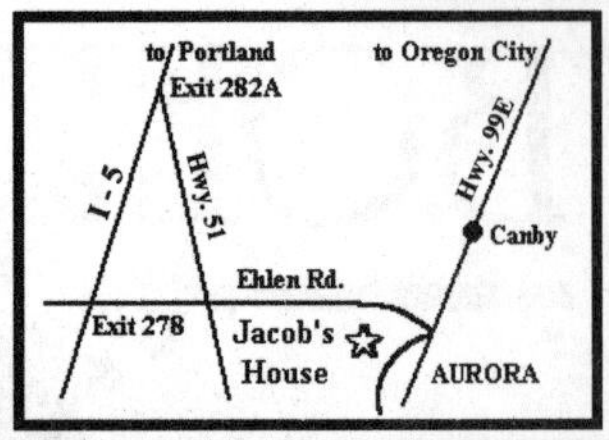

The Quilt Block
Everything for the Quilter...

Sherwood, OR #60

16064 SW Tualatin-Sherwood Rd. 97140
(503) 625-1040
E-mail: Quilt.block@verizon.net
Owner: Julie Fugate
Est: 1995 2400 sq.ft. 2500 Bolts

Mon - Fri 10 - 6 Sat 10 - 5 Sun 12 - 4

Colorful and varied selection of fabric, kits, books, notions and patterns. Classes for every level. Long-arm quilting machine available for rent. Authorized Husqvarna-Viking Dealer
www.thequiltblocknw.com

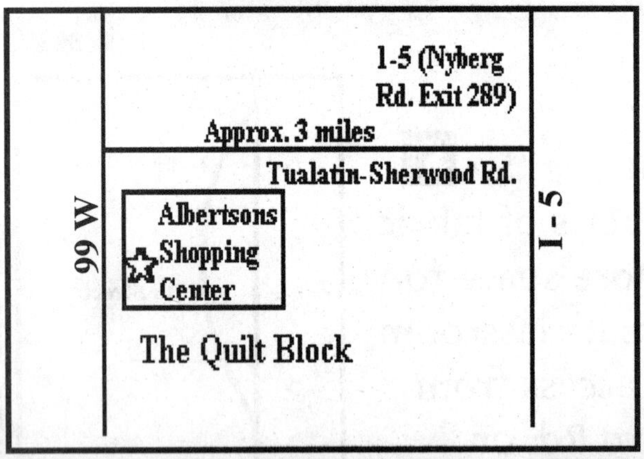

Canby, OR #62

Country Dry Goods

Mon - Fri 10 - 5
Sat 10 - 4:30

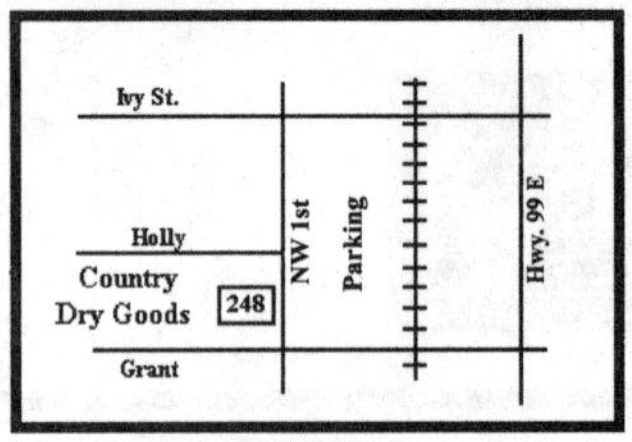

248 NW 1st Ave.
97013
(503) 263-3563
Est: 1987 2000 sq.ft.
Owner: Linda Peck

DEDICATED TO THE QUILTER AND WOULD BE QUILTER.
We carry the latest books, patterns and 100% cotton fabrics.

Gresham, OR #63

KATIE'S QUILT SHOPPE

336 N. Main St. 97030
(503) 491-1077
lloriquilts@verizon.net
www.quiltersfabrics.com

Located in the Historic Shopping District. This unique little shoppe offers distinct fabrics, books, notions, machine quilting, and, of course, classes.

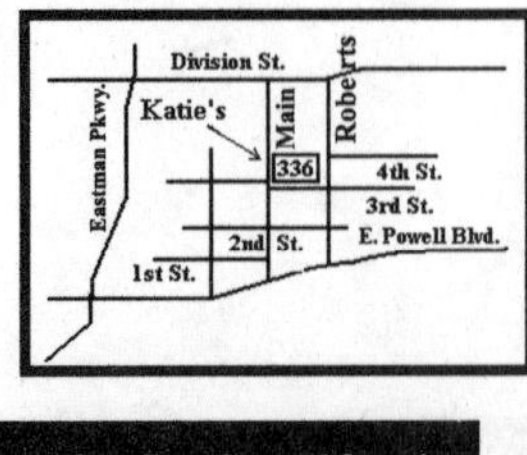

Mon 10 - 4 Tues - Sat 10 - 5 Sun 12 - 4

Silverton, OR #61

Mon - Sat 10 - 5:30

Window Box Quilts

106 N. First 97381
(503) 873-5015
E-Mail: windowbox.quilts@verizon.net
Owner: Melia Ragone
Est: 1999 1500 sq.ft.

Quaint shop in Historic Silverton. Beautiful fabrics featuring reproductions of the 1800s and more recent. Warm friendly customer service.

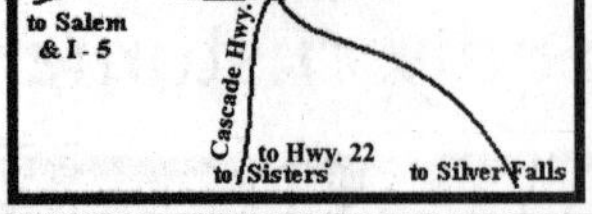

PARADISE Quilts & Fabrics #64

38821 Proctor Blvd. • Sandy, OR 97055
503-668-3106
e-mail: paradisequilts@effectnet.com

Fabric • Notions • Patterns
Fat Quarters • Books • Classes

JoAnn Dries, Owner
Tuesday - Saturday 9-6
Sunday 11-4

Machine Quilting Service Now Available.... by Dennis Dries

Clackamas, OR #65

The Quilting B

• 15410 SE 94th • Clackamas, OR 97015 • 503.656.2999
Come visit us Monday-Saturday
10:00 am -5:00 pm
205 South - take exit 13
205 North - take exit 12
call for further directions!

Fabric
Books
Classes
Patterns
Gift items
Folk art pottery

Other Shops in Oregon: We suggest calling first

Aurora Mohler House 1865, 21317 Hwy. 99E NE 503-678-7799
Aurora Quilt Plus, P.O. Box 186 503-678-2124
Beaverton Mill End Retail Store, 4955 NW Western Ave. 503-646-3000
Bend Mo Quilts, 22875 E. Hwy. 20 541-389-2574
Bend Amish House, 2620 NE Hwy. 20 #230 541-388-4651
Brookings Country Keepsakes, P.O. Box 4012 541-469-6117
Brownsville Troyer's Stitches, 898 W. Bishop 541-466-5323
Canyonville J & J Fabric and Crafts, 413 SE Main St. 541-839-4319
Coos Bay Linda's Crafts & Quilts, 63425 Jerome 541-751-8118
Corvallis Sewing Plus/Country Calico, 6120 S.W. Country Club 541-758-3323
Cottage Grove Pandora's Box, 517 Main
Eugene The Quilt Patch, 23 E. 28th St. 541-484-1925
Florence Laurel Street Fabrics, 208 Laurel St. 541-997-7038
Gold Beach Patchworks Studio, 33066 Nesika 541-247-8626
Grants Pass Tribal Creations, 111 NE "A" St. 541-472-1658
Grants Pass Jordan's, 1100 NW Regent Dr. 541-476-0214
Grants Pass Quilt Country, 2175 NW Vine St. 541-479-2700
Gresham Craft Warehouse, 604 Eastman Pkwy. 503-661-0574
Lake Oswego The Pine Needle, 429 First St. 503-635-1353
Lake Oswego Bernina Sew n' Vac & Fabric Chalet, 16925 SW 65th Ave. 503-624-7440
Lake Oswego Quilter's Quest, 18305 Timbergrove Ct. 503-620-2572
Lincoln City Sew Tech & Technique, 1315 SW Hwy. 101 541-996-9696
McMinnville Sew Much More!, 416 NE 3rd St. 503-435-1701
Milwaukee Mill End Store, 9701 S.E. McLoughlin Blvd. 503-786-1234
Newberg Threads and More, 602 B E. 1st 503-538-3577
Newberg Itchin' to Stitch, 3809 Coffey Ln.
Oakland Cathy's Quilts & Crafts, 322 Oakwood Dr. 541-459-9774
Portland Amish Quilt Shop, 5331 S.W. Macadem 503-223-2693
Portland Josephine's Dry Goods, 921 SW Morrison 503-224-4202
Portland Alyen Creations, 1851 SE Locust Ave. 503-236-2968
Portland A Quilted Kitchen, 9938 SW Terwilliger 503-245-5158
Portland Scarborough Flair, 4442 N. E. 131 Pl. 503-254-3882
Portland Fabric Depot, 700 SE 122nd Ave. 503-252-9530
Prineville Pioneer Quilts, 5210 NE Lark Ln 541-447-4549
Reedsport Quilt Shop, 679 W. Alder Pl. 541-271-2616
Salem Salem Bernina, 2661-A Commercial St. SE 503-362-8523
Salem Ruth's Quilt Tops & More, 2651 Brooks Ave. NE 503-485-5330
Salem Heartland Quilts, 4939 Countryside NE 541-962-5374
Springfield Jean Marie's Fabrics, 637 Main St. 541-746-0433
Sublimity Needles & Thread, 246 NE Starr St. 503-769-1336
Sublimity Country Classics, 480 S. Center 503-769-4645
Sunriver The Whimsy Goose, P.O. Box 3888 541-593-7650
Sweet Home Seamingly Creative, 1245 Main St. 541-367-8934
Talent McQuilts, 117 N. Pacific Hwy. 541-535-2573
Tigard Calico Corners, 9120 SW Hall Blvd. 503-624-7218
Wheeler Creative Fabrics, 475 Nehalem Blvd., P.O. Box 303 503-368-5900
Yoncalla Quilt Connections, 8542 Hayhurst Rd.

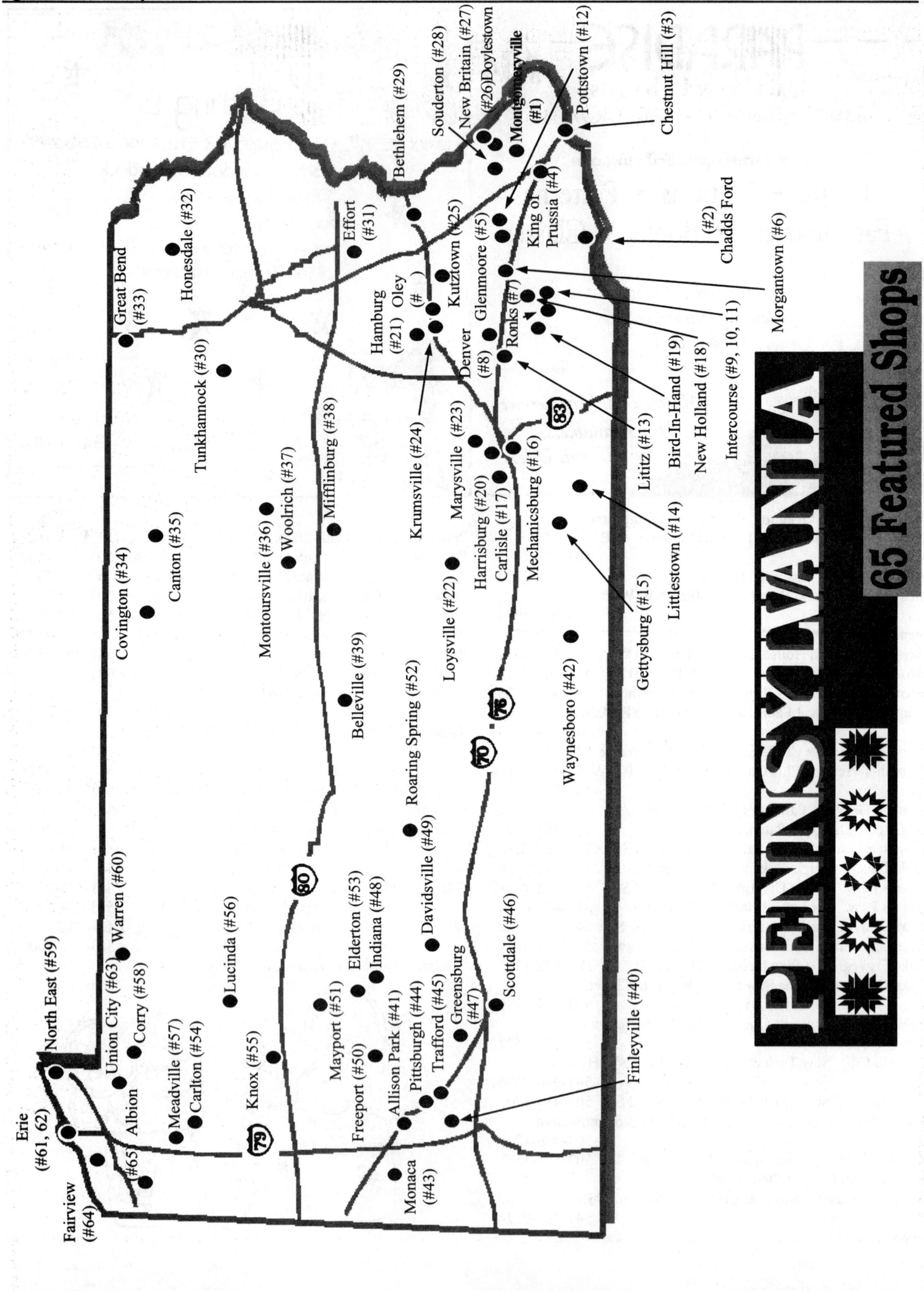
PENNSYLVANIA
65 Featured Shops
Erie (#61, 62)
Fairview (#64)
(#65)
North East (#59)
Union City (#63)
Albion
Corry (#58)
Warren (#60)
Meadville (#57)
Carlton (#54)
Knox (#55)
Lucinda (#56)
Freeport (#50)
Mayport (#51)
Elderton (#53)
Indiana (#48)
Allison Park (#41)
Pittsburgh (#44)
Trafford (#45)
Greensburg (#47)
Monaca (#43)
Finleyville (#40)
Scottdale (#46)
Davidsville (#49)
Roaring Spring (#52)
Belleville (#39)
Mifflinburg (#38)
Montoursville (#36)
Woolrich (#37)
Covington (#34)
Canton (#35)
Tunkhannock (#30)
Great Bend (#33)
Honesdale (#32)
Effort (#31)
Bethlehem (#29)
Souderton (#28)
New Britain (#27)
(#26)Doylestown
Montgomeryville (#1)
Pottstown (#12)
Chestnut Hill (#3)
King of Prussia (#4)
(#2) Chadds Ford
Morgantown (#6)
Glenmoore (#5)
Kutztown (#25)
Oley (#)
Hamburg (#21)
Krumsville (#24)
Denver (#8)
Ronks (#7)
Intercourse (#9, 10, 11)
New Holland (#18)
Bird-In-Hand (#19)
Lititz (#13)
Marysville (#23)
Harrisburg (#20)
Carlisle (#17)
Mechanicsburg (#16)
Loysville (#22)
Littlestown (#14)
Gettysburg (#15)
Waynesboro (#42)
79
80
70
76
83

The Country Quilt Shop

Largest quilt shop in PA!

Located just 20 miles northeast of Philadelphia

515 Stump Road, Montgomeryville, PA 18936 (215) 855-5554

where memories are handmade!

- Largest selection of
  - *Homespuns*
  - *Batiks*
  - *Reproductions*
- Something for everyone
  - *Wool*
  - *Primitive*
  - *Rug Hooking*
  - *Crazy Quilts*
  - *Fancy Threads*
  - *Embellishments*

An assortment of over 4500 bolts of the finest 100% cotton fabrics— Hoffman, RJR, Moda, P&B, Thimbleberries & more! A large complete display of books, patterns, tools & notions.

Featured in Quilt Sampler as one of the top 10 shops in the country

Visit us at www.countryquiltshop.com

Buses and Tour Groups Welcome!

- Block of the Months
- Classes for all levels
- Experienced & Courteous Staff
- Annual Quilter's Retreat
- Samples Galore
- Online and Mail Orders welcome

Montgomeryville, PA #1

Owners Joe & Renee Fallon
Est. 1987 3600 sq. ft.

Mon, Fri, Sat	Tues, Wed, Thur	Sunday
10am - 5pm	10am - 9pm	1pm - 5pm

A Patch of Country

Chadds Ford, PA #2

22 Olde Ridge Village 19317
(610) 459-8993

Mon - Sat 10 - 5
Thurs til 8
Sun 12 - 5

1983 - 2003 Celebrating 20 Years of Excellence

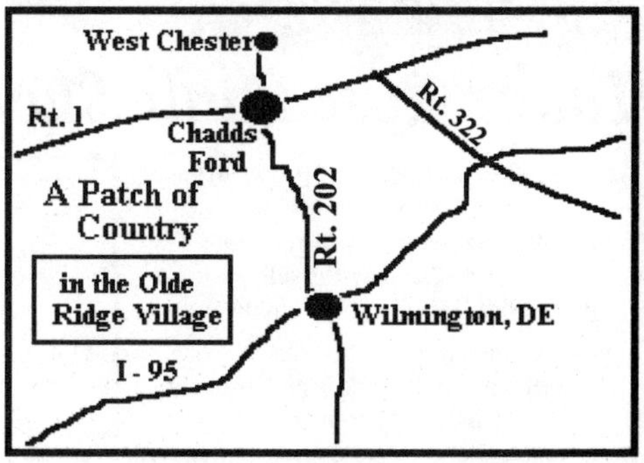

Owner: Karen Reed
Est: 1983 2200 sq.ft.

- Block of the Month Programs for hand, machine or applique techniques
- Highest Quality Cottons & Quilter's Tools
- 250+ Book Titles, Patterns
- Staffed exclusively by Friendly, Knowledgeable Quilters
- Special Order & Mail Order Services Available
- Year-round classes for all skill levels with full student support.

Located 1 mile south of Route 1 on Route 202. Within half an hour of the New Jersey & Maryland state lines. 1 mile north of the Delaware state line. Minutes from Brandywine River Museum, Winterthur Museum, Longwood Gardens, Brandywine Battlefield State Park and Valley Forge.

Chestnut Hill, PA #3

Byrne Fabrics

We specialize in natural Fibers --
wool, cotton, linen, silk
Large selection of buttons and ribbons.
Bernina and Brother authorized dealer.

Mon - Sat 10 - 6
Wed til 8 Sun 12 - 4

8434 Germantown Ave.
Philadelphia, PA 19118
215-247-3485 or 888-302-9411
E-Mail: byrne@brynesewing.com

Fax: 215-753-7006
Est: 1979
1500 sq.ft.
Owners:
Debbie & Mike
Byrne

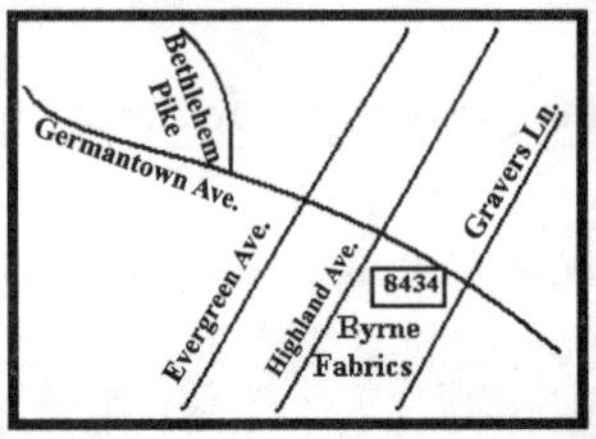

www.byrnesewing.com

King of Prussia, PA #4

Steve's Sewing & Vacuum Center

Valley Forge Shopping Centre, Rte 202
156 West Dekalb 19406
(610) 768-9453 Fax: (610) 337-2622
E-Mail: steves@stevessewandvac.com
Web Site: www.stevessewandvac.com
Owners: Steve & Karen Chubin
Est: 1992 7000 sq.ft. 2000+ Bolts

Mon - Fri 10 - 9
Sat 10 - 5 Sun 12 - 5

Sewing Machines • Sergers • Vacuums
Quilting Supplies • Fabrics • Sewing Notions
Accessories • Furniture • Lessons • Classes

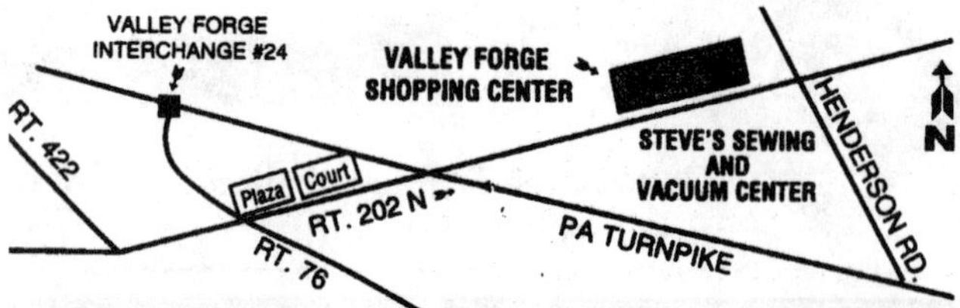

Directions: from Rt. 76 or PA Turnpike; Take Route 202 (Dekalb Pike) North past King of Prussia Plaza and Court. Turn left into Valley Forge Shopping Center (approx 1-1/2 miles). Steve's is in lower level.

SINGER baby lock BERNINA ORECK
EUREKA ROYAL DIRT DEVIL

Glenmoore, PA #5

Mon - Sat 10 - 5
Wed til 8
Sun 12 - 4

Tudor Rose Quilt Shop

Ludwig's Village, Rt. 100 & 401
(610) 458-5255 19343
Web Site: www.tudorrose.com
Owner: Jane Russell
Est: 1990 1200 sq.ft. 2000+ Bolts

100% cotton fabrics. Plus silks & wools. Everything a quilter needs plus friendly smiles, expert help.

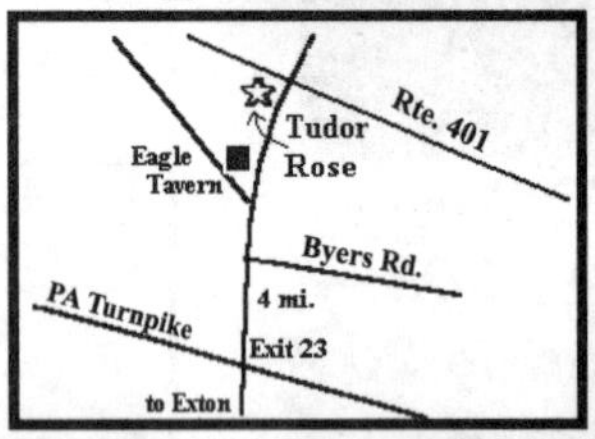

Morgantown, PA #6

Mon - Fri
9 - 9
Sat 9 - 5

Hayloft Fabrics

R.D. #1, Box 505 19543
(610) 286-5045

One Stop Fabric Shop!
We carry a huge selection of beautiful dress and quilt fabrics. Batting, Notions, and Yarn.

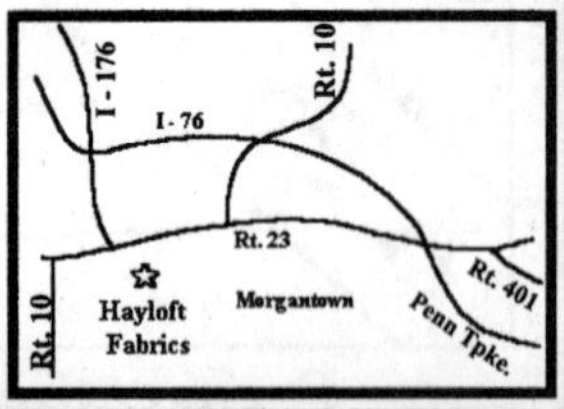

Ronks, PA #7

Mon - Thur
9 - 6
Fri 9 - 8
Sat 9 - 7

Dutchland Quilt Patch

2851 Lincoln Hwy. E 17572
(717) 687-0534
Web Site: www.Dutchlandquilts.com
Visa, MC, & Disccover Welcome

One of Lancaster County's Largest Fabric Shops. Large selection of Quilts (Over 350 in stock) and crafts.

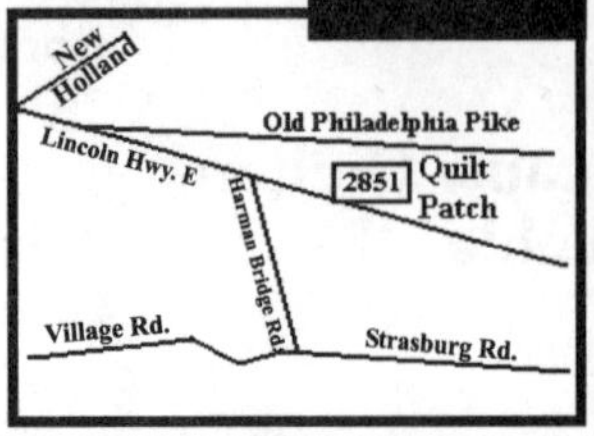

Denver, PA #8

Mon, Tues &
Fri 8:30 - 8:30
Wed, Thur &
Sat 8:30 - 5

Burkholder's Fabrics

2155 W. Rt. 897 17517
(717) 336-6692
Owners: Eugene Martin
Est: 1972 3000 sq.ft.

Sewing notions, quilt supplies, lace, fabrics, including VIP, Debbie Mumm, Springmaid, Concord, Hoffman, Peter Pan, knits & more.
We accept all major credit cards.

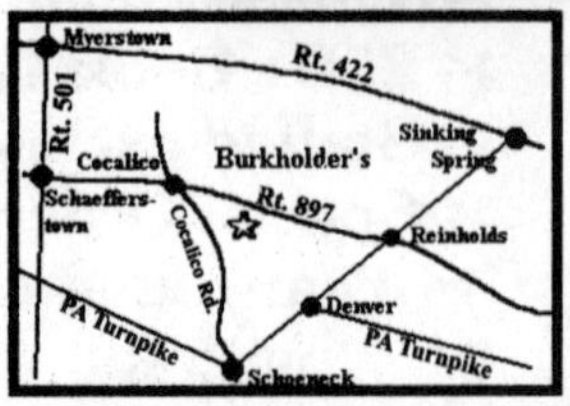

BRUBAKER'S SEWING CENTER

"Discover the FUN of Sewing!"

Since 1934

- Pfaff, Janome and Brother Sewing Machines
- Amish Custom Cabinets
- Fabrics and notions
- Classes and clubs
- Specialty Sewing Machines
- Friendly, helpful staff
- Parking for Cars and Buggies
- A fun place to stop and shop!

You can also visit us at:
www.BrubakersSewing.com
Or email at: Brubakers34@hotmail.com

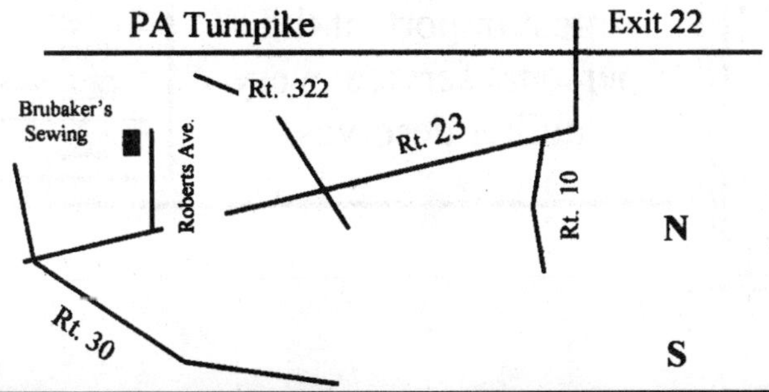

Owners: Amy & Glenn Smith

New Holland, PA #18

20 North Roberts Avenue
(12 miles from the PA Turnpike)

1-800-466-7315

Store Hours:
Mon. thru Friday 8-5:30
Thursday 8-8
Saturday 8-3
Closed Sunday

From PA Turnpike, take exit 22. Follow 10 south to Main St. Turn right, this is Rt. 23. Follow Rt. 23 west into New Holland. Turn right on Roberts Avenue. Brubaker's is on the left.

From Lancaster, take Rt. 30 to Rt. 23 east
Follow Rt. 23 into New Holland
Turn left on Roberts Ave.

Bird-In-Hand Country Store

2679-B Old Philadelphia Pike Bird-In-Hand, PA. 17505
717-393-5321

From The Usual To The Unique At Amazing Prices...

Patterns / Quilting Templates
Books / Notions / Fat Quarters
Amish Made and Antique
Quilts, Wallhangings and More !

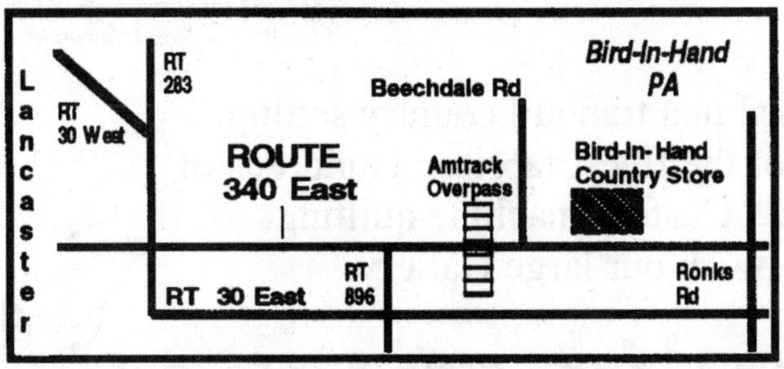

Bird-in-Hand, PA #19

**Moda Hoffman Kona Bay Maywood
Marcus Bros Momen House Benartex
Westminister Fibers RJR Mission Valley
N.Crow Clothworks Bali Fabrics SSI
David Textiles Hi-Fashion Northcott P&B
R.Kaufman Timeless Treasures
Rose & Hubble Liberty Concord
Makower Etc.
Homespuns Batiks Wools
Japanese Sateens and More!**

"A Quilter's Paradise In The Heart Of Amish Country"

Purveyor Of Fine Fabrics & Amish Quilts

Harrisburg, PA #20

**Mon - Fri 10 - 6
Sat 10 - 4**

QUILTERS GATHERING

5490 Derry St. 17111
(866) 287-7495
(717) 564-4828
Fax: (717) 564-4837
E-Mail: pam@quiltersgathering
Web Site: www.quiltersgathering.com
Owner: Pam Balek Kraft
A contemporary quilt shop !!!
Also wools, crazy quilting supplies, heirloom embroidery supplies, and Long-Arm quilting

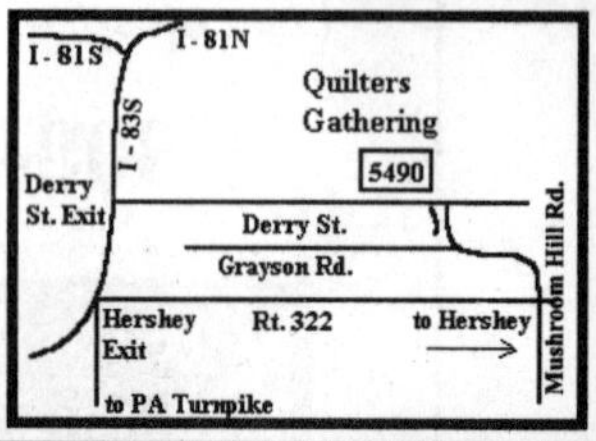

Hamburg, PA #21

260 N. 4th St. 19526
(610) 562-7173
E-Mail: HapSew@cs.com
Owner: Jean Boyd
Est: 1990 1000 sq.ft.

Happy Sewing Room

We offer beautiful cotton fabrics, quilting supplies, patterns, books, sewing machines, classes & most important the personal service every quilter deserves.

**Tues - Fri 9:30 - 6
Sat 9:30 - 12**

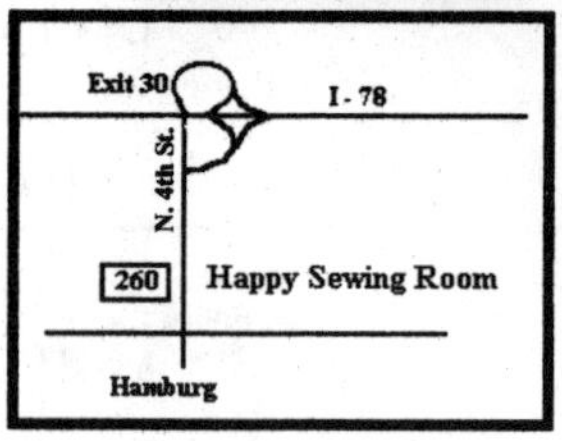

Loysville, PA #22

Wise Dry Goods

**Mon, Thur Fri, Sat 9 - 5
Wed 9 - 9**

R.R. #1, Box 274-C 17047
(717) 789-4308
Est: 1993 2600 sq.ft. 1400 Bolts

Fabrics, Notions, Cross Stitch Embroidery
Located out in the Country!

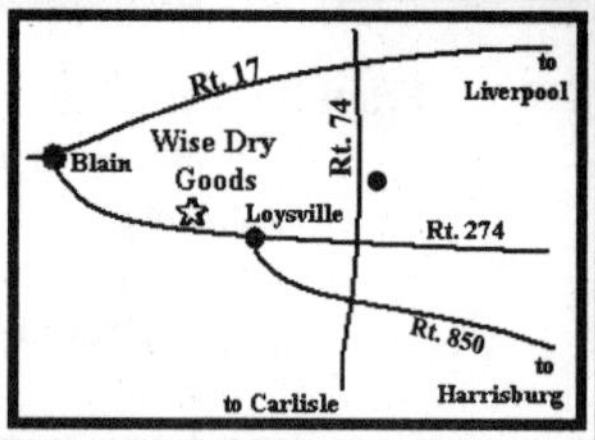

Marysville, PA #23

**1975 Valley Rd.
Marysville, PA 17053
Phone / Fax: (717) 957-4225
Email: Jbac1@aol.com
Website: www.smilespinners.com
Owners: Cathy L. Queitzsch & Joel L. Bacon
Est: 2000 3000 sq.ft.**

**Mon - Thur 10 -6
Fri 10 - 8 Sat 10 - 4
Sun 1 - 4**

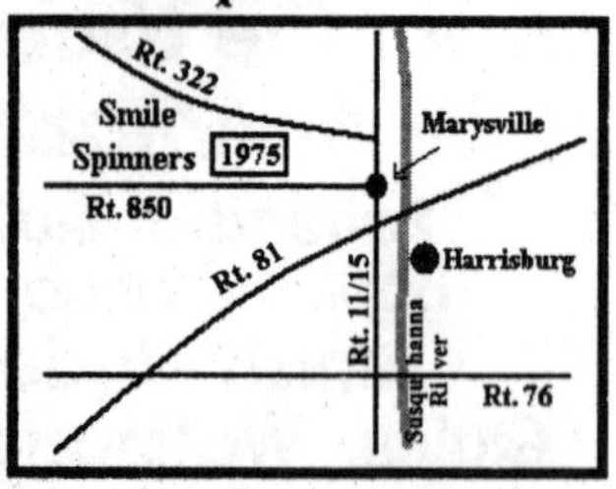

Located near Harrisburg, PA Just 4 mi. West of Marysville on Rt. 850

A full service Quilt Shop located in a tranquil country setting. Gorgeous 2000+ bolt collection of the finest fabrics. Hundreds of books, Notions, and Patterns. Custom machine quilting. Ever changing Quilt Show in our large Gallery.

We'll have you in stitches

Krumsville, PA #24

Hours Vary Please call First

Critter Pattern Works

592 Old Rt. 22 19534
(610) 756-3381 Fax: (610) 756-3382
E-Mail: info@critterpat.com
Web Site: www.critterpat.com
Owner: Debora Konchinsky
Est: 1989 Catalog $3

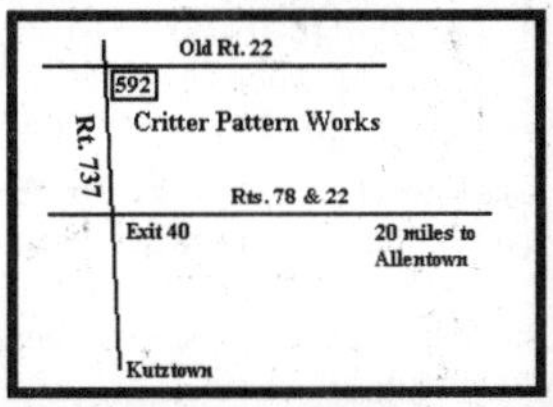

We design machine applique quilt patterns and offer 4 day Quilt Camps throughout the year, teaching our animal themed patterns.

Kutztown, PA #25

Mon & Tues 9 - 5 Wed - Fri 9 - 8 Sat 9 - 4

Wooden Bridge Drygoods

195 Deysher Rd.
19530
(610) 683-7159
Fax: (610) 683-6595

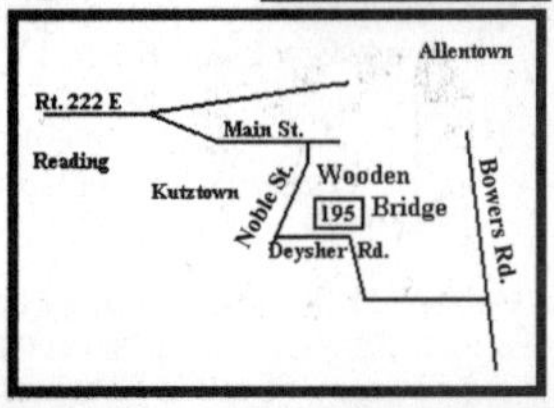

Fabrics, quilting supplies, notions, Kwik-Sew patterns, quilt books, quilt tops. If you can't find it ask for it and we'll try to find it.

Doylestown, PA #26

Byrne Sewing Connection

We specialize in natural Fibers -- cotton, linen, silk, batiste, heirloom laces
Large selection of specialty threads.
Bernina and Brother authorized dealer.

Mon - Sat 10 - 6
T, W, Th til 8 Sun 12 - 4

422 E. Butler Ave.
New Britain, PA 18901
215-230-9411 or 888-302-9411
E-Mail: byrne@brynesewing.com

Fax: 215-230-0378
Est: 1979
4500 sq.ft.
Owners:
Debbie & Mike Byrne

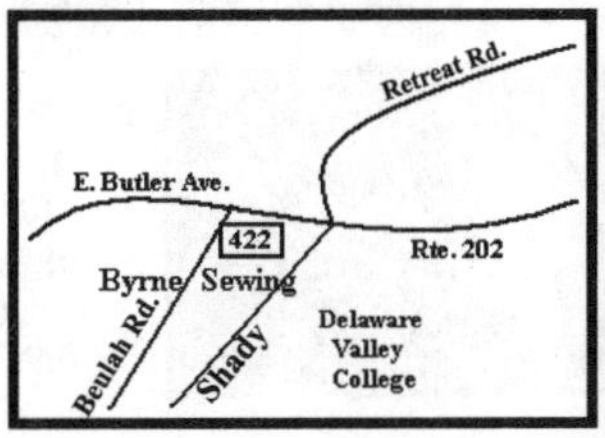

www.byrnesewing.com

New Britain, PA #27

Tues - Sat 10 - 5

Hentown Country Store

326 W. Butler Ave. 18901
(215) 345-8286 Est: 1962
Owner: Midge Smith 2500 sq.ft.
Newsletter Avail. 500+ Bolts

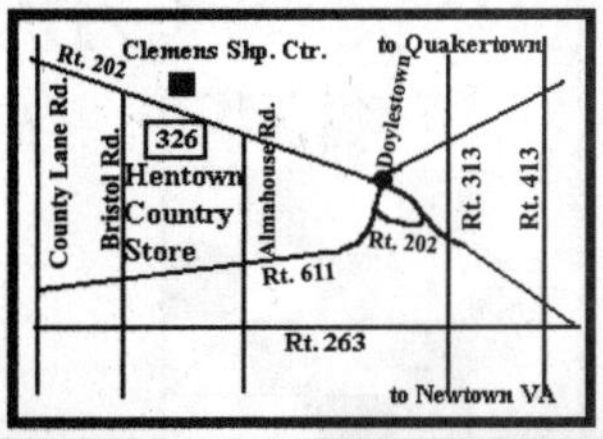

100% Cotton Fabric, Homespun. Very Large (7000+) selection of Craft & Quilt Patterns. Teddy Bear Making Supplies. Handmade Folkart.

Souderton, PA #28

Mon- Thurs 9 - 9 Fri 9-6 Sat 9 - 5

The Souder Store

357 Main St. 18964
(215) 723-2017 or (877) 870-8150
E-Mail: souderfabricshop@netcarrier.com
Est: 1922

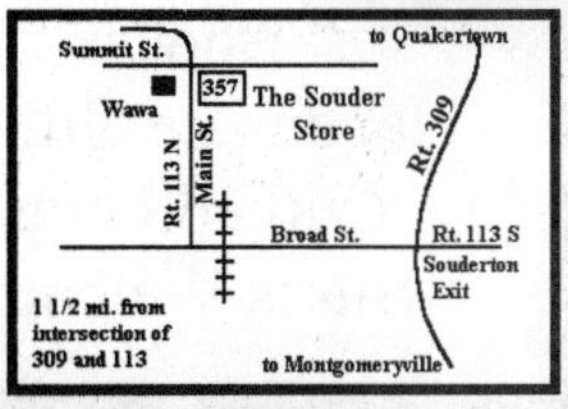

Extensive collection of 100% cotton quilting fabrics and supplies. Large selection of bridal fabrics, silks, wools and dress goods.

Bethlehem, PA #29

Mon - Fri 10 - 4 Sat by Appt.

Schlosser Quality Quilt Frames

25 Club Avenue 18018
(610) 758-8488 Fax: (610) 317-9613
E-mail: sqqf@tidalwave.com Est: 1989
Owner: Herbert Schlosser

Fabric--Notions--Books--Patterns
Frames for both quilters and needleworkers.
Antique Quilts. Singer Featherweights.
Notions for Cross Stitchers.

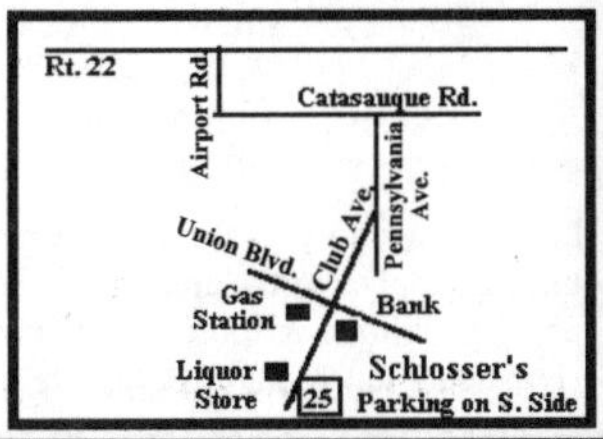

Tunkhannock, PA #30

Endless Mountains Quiltworks Inc.

Tues - Sat 10 - 6 Sun 1 - 5

158 W. Tioga St. 18657
(570) 836-7575
Fax: (570) 996-5145
EMQ2001@epix.net
www.emquiltworks.com
Owner: Jeannette Goeringer Kitlan
Est: 2001 1200 sq.ft.

We nourish the quilter's heart, hands and soul with over 2000 bolts of beautiful cotton fabric, classes, books and gifts. Books 20% off everyday.

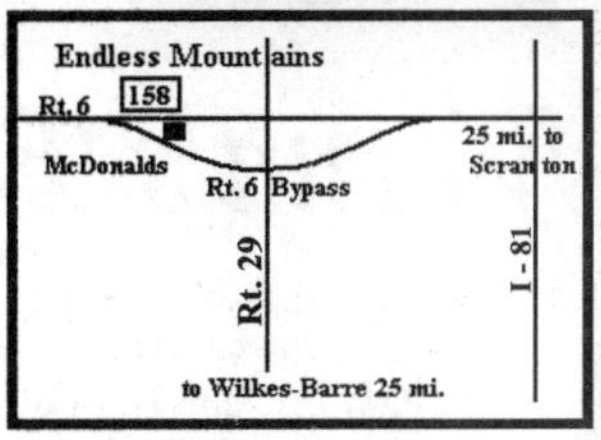

Located on Bus. Rt. 6 West across from McDonald's in Tunkhannock, PA., the gateway to the Endless Mountains of northeastern PA

Effort, PA #31

7 Days a Week 10 - 5

The Country Quilterie

Carriage House Square
R.R. #3, Box 2482, Route 115 N, 18330
(570) 620-9707
E-Mail: makwant@noln.com
Owner: Maryann Kwant
Est: 1989 1500 sq.ft. 2500 Bolts

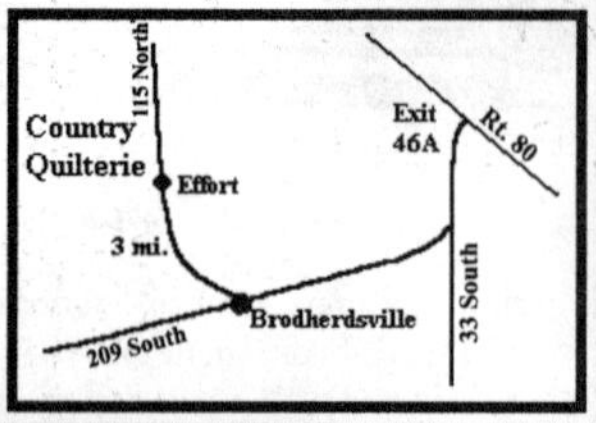

Over 2500 Bolts of Quilting Fabric, Books, Notions, Supplies. Largest selection of Quilts in the Poconos. Quilted Accessories and Gifts.

Honesdale, PA #32

Tues - Sat 10 - 5

The Mountain Quiltworks

R.R. #4, Box 4111 18431
(570) 253-9510
Owner: Amy R. Dunn
250+ Bolts 1100 sq.ft

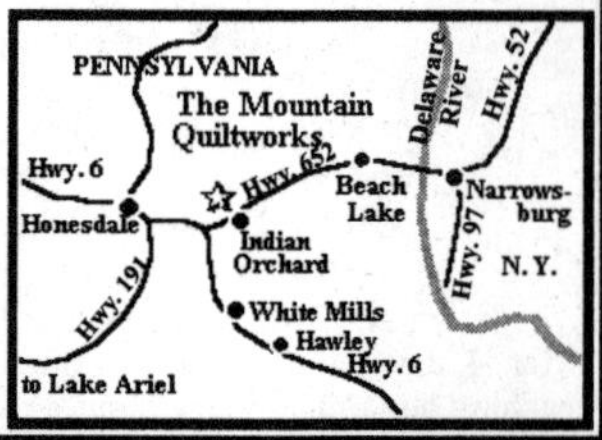

Custom Hand-Quilting our Specialty! Find everything you need to create tomorrow's heirlooms. From various source books, stencils & patterns too of course, top quality cotton fabrics.

Great Bend, PA #33

Sisters Choice Quilt Shop

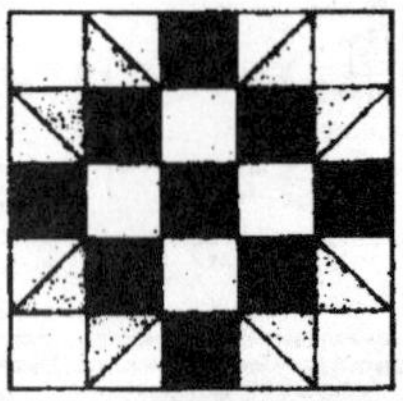

P.O. Box 772, Randolph Rd.
Great Bend, PA 18821
(570) 879-4196 Est: 1991
Email - barmondi@epix.net
Owner: Bettie Armondi

Tues - Fri 10 - 4 Sat 10 - 2

100% Cotton Fabric,
Books.
Handmade Gifts &
Quilted Items.
Buses Welcome

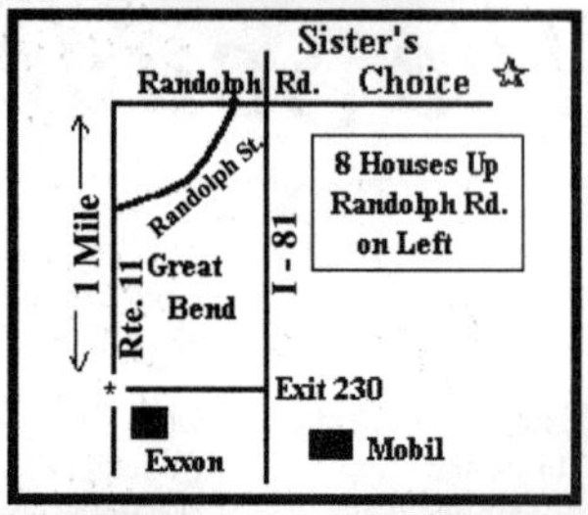

Covington, PA #34

Tues - Fri 10 - 5 Sat 10 - 3

Williams Quilt N Craft Supply

1 Main St. 16917 (570) 659-5079
Owner: Joyce Williams

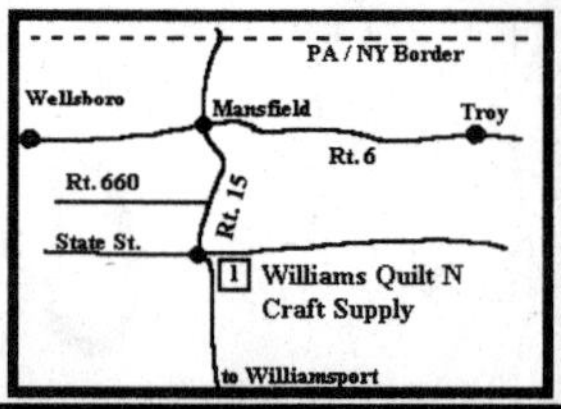

1200+ bolts of 100% cotton fabric. Hoffman, Moda, RJR, P&B, Benartex & Many more.
All your quilting supplies.
15% off fabric with a guild membership card.

Canton, PA #35

Tues - Sat 10 - 5

The Weathervane Quilt Shop

R.R. #2, Box 26, Rt. 14 17724
(570) 673-4944 Fax: 297-3074
E-Mail: nortsned@epix.net
Owner: Nancy Swatsworth
Est: 1996 3000 sq.ft.

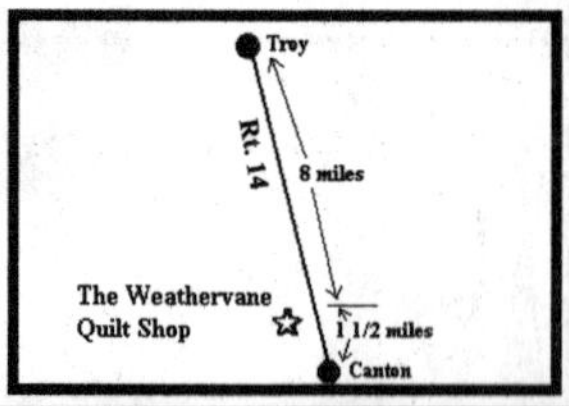

1000+ Bolts of 100% fine cotton fabrics, books, patterns, notions. Lovely handmade gifts. Featherweight Singer Sewing machines.

Montoursville, PA #36

Tues, Wed, Thur 10 - 5 Fri 10 - 7 Sat 10 - 3

Our Gathering Place

936 Plaza Dr. Savoy Plaza 17754
(570) 368-1130
Owner: Chris Kroboth 4000 Bolts

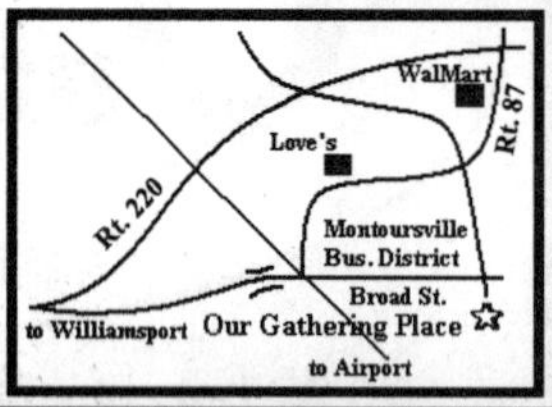

Fine cotton fabrics and quilting supplies.
Many books and patterns plus classes.
Come Gather, share & enjoy!
Montoursville is located about 5 mi. E of Williamsport off I - 180 / U.S. 220

Woolrich, PA #37

Open Everyday

Woolrich SINCE 1830

Park Ave., P.O. Box 130
17779
(570) 769-7401
Fax: (570) 769-7832

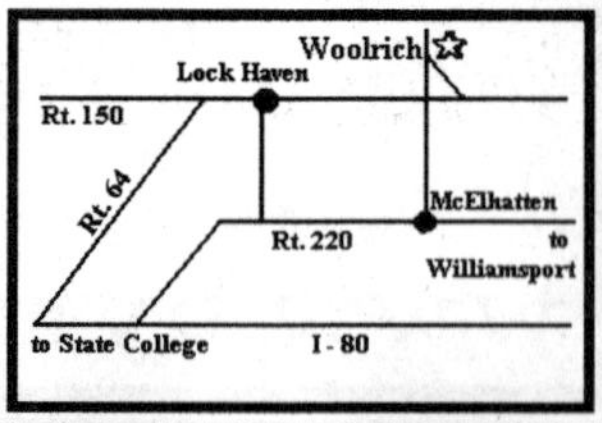

The Store for Outdoor People. Sportswear & Outerwear for Men & Women. Large Selection of Quilters Cottons, Mill End of Wool for Braiding Rugs or Making Garments.

Mifflinburg, PA #38

Mon, Tues, Thurs, Fri 9 - 9 Wed & Sat 9 - 5

Verna's Fabrics

RR 4, Box 175A 17844
(570) 966-2350
Owner: Verna H. Duke

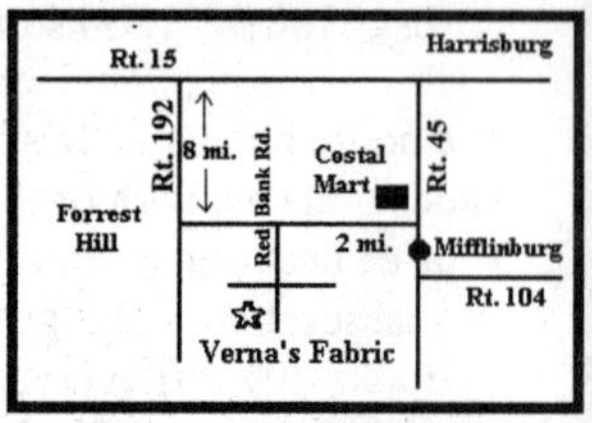

Fabrics — Books — Patterns

Belleville, PA #39

Mon - Sat 9 - 5

A.M. Buchanan Dry Goods

Newly Remodeled!

2459 S.R. 655 17004
(717) 483-6428
Owner: Anna M. Buchanan
Est: 1983 1700 sq.ft. 2050 sq.ft.

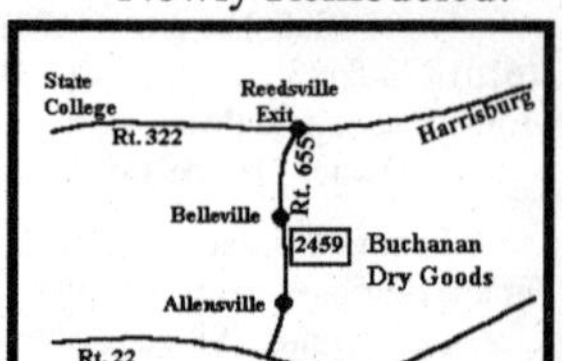

Largest selection of fabrics, patterns, books & quilting supplies in the area. Hand made Quilts, hangings, Pillows & more. Great Gifts in stock. Located 2 mi. south of Belleville on Rt. 655

Finleyville, PA #40

Quilters Corner

6101-1 Route 88 Finleyville, PA 15332
1-724-348-8010
www.quilterscorner-pa.com

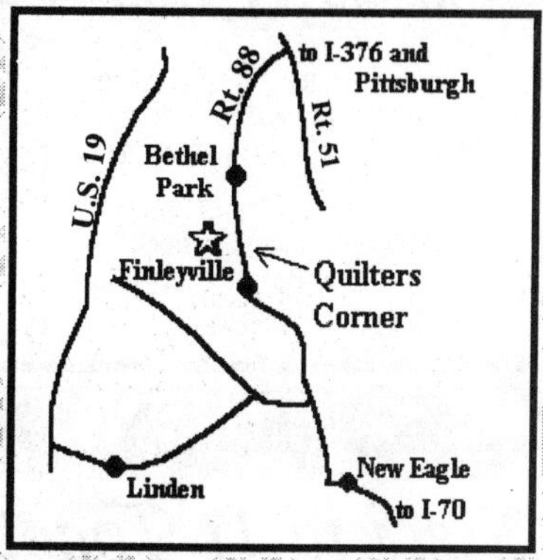

Enter the exciting world of quilting...

- ***Explore our extensive selection of both traditional and contemporary cotton fabrics with over 4000 bolts to browse.***
- ***Consult with our friendly, knowledgeable staff.***
- ***Choose from a variety of "Block of the Month" selections.***
- ***Classes for all skill levels from beginner to advanced***
- ***Books, Patterns, Notions ~ We will be happy to order anything you need!***

Est: 1989 with over 3750 sq. ft.
Mary Beth Hartnett- Owner

Shop Hours:
Monday- Saturday 10:00 am-5:00 pm
Thursday evening till 9:00 pm

We are your premier quilt shop in South-Western Pennsylvania.

Allison Park, PA #41

3940 Middle Rd. 15101
(412) 487-9532
Fax: (412) 487-9581
e-mail: quilt@nauticom.net
Owner: Karen Montgomery
Est: 1994 3500 sq.ft.

Mon - Sat
9:30 - 5
Mon & Thur
til 9

THE QUILT COMPANY

Pittsburgh's Largest Quilt Shop!

Featuring 100% cottons, books, and original patterns.
Quilting Supplies & Notions.
Featured by American Patchwork & Quilting as
one of the top 10 shops in the Country for 1997.

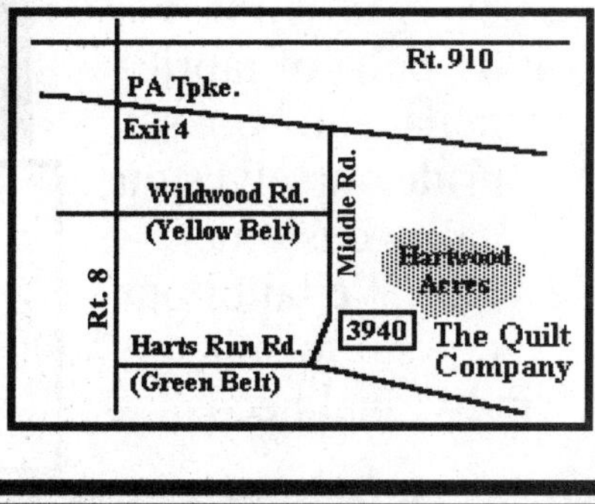

Waynesboro, PA #42

Mon & Fri 8 - 8
Tues - Thur 8 - 5
Sat 8 - 4

Benedict's Country Store

6305 Marsh Rd. 17268
(717) 762-6788
Est: 1980 2200 sq.ft. 3000 Bolts

Over 3000 Bolts Fabric in stock.
Large selection Quilt Books, Patterns and Quilting Supplies.

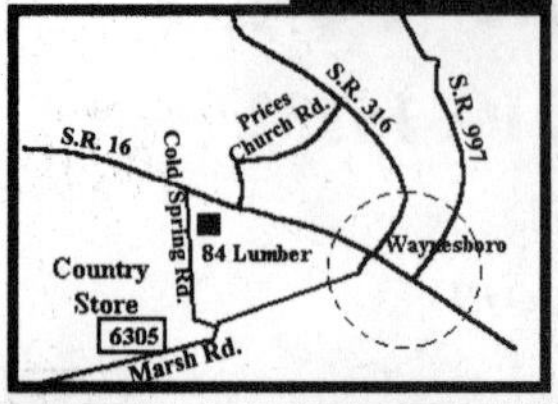

Monaca, PA #43

Mon - Sat 10 - 4

The Quilt Basket

1116 Pennsylvania 15061
(724) 775-7774
Owner: M. Maxine Holmes
Est: 1984

The Quilt Basket is a complete quilt shop offering lots of classes & all the supplies: i.e. fabrics, patterns, books, and notions.

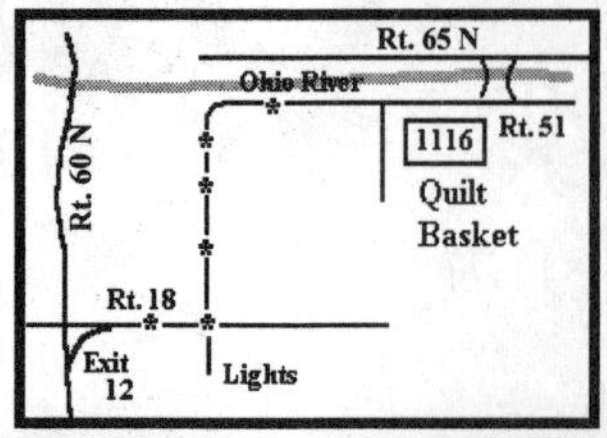

Pittsburgh, PA #44

Mon - Sat 10 - 5
Thur til 8

Piecing It Together

3458 Babcock Blvd. 15237
(412) 364-2440
E-Mail: piecngit@fyi.net
Web Site: www.fyi.net/~piecngit
Owners: Johanna Blanarik
Est: 1986 1200 sq.ft.

Complete line of quilting supplies, 100% cotton fabrics, books, notions, patterns, and classes. Lots of samples. Personal, friendly.

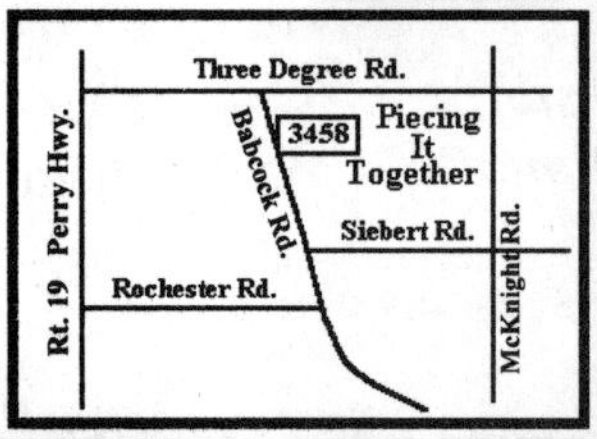

Trafford, PA #45

Wed - Sat 10 - 3

The Quilter's Shop

329 Cavitt Ave. 15085
(412) 856-6088
Web Site: www.quiltershop.com

100% Cotton Fabrics, Quilting Supplies, Books, Classes and great Service.
Exit 6 off PA Turnpike.

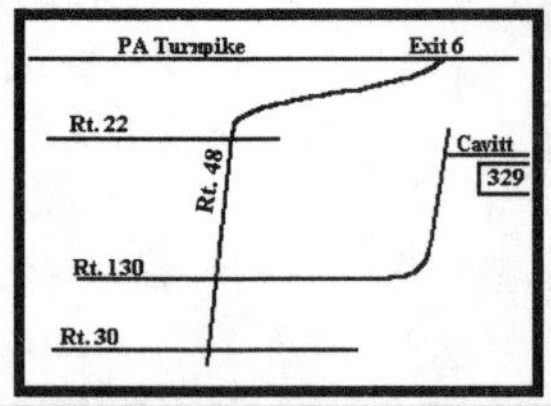

Scottdale, PA #46

Tues - Sat 10:30 - 5

Kate & Becca's Quilt Patch

West Overton Village, 1045 Frick Rd. 15683
(724) 887-4160
Web Site: www.quiltpatchetc.com
Owners: Kate Hepler & Becca Flack

Calico Prints, Stencils, Quilt Books, Templates, Quilt Kits. Selection of Handmade Quilts—Contemporary and Traditional. Done by craftspeople who do only the finest work. Gifts for all occasions.

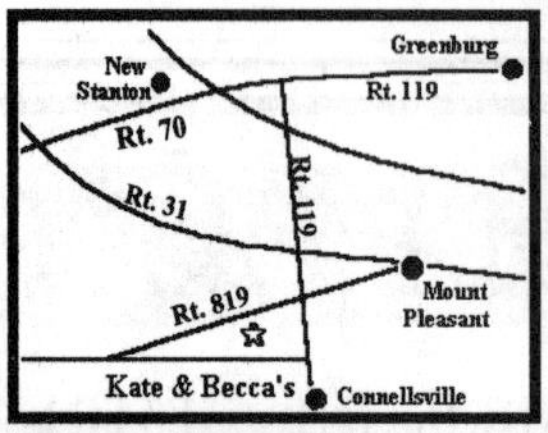

The Stitch In Time Shoppe

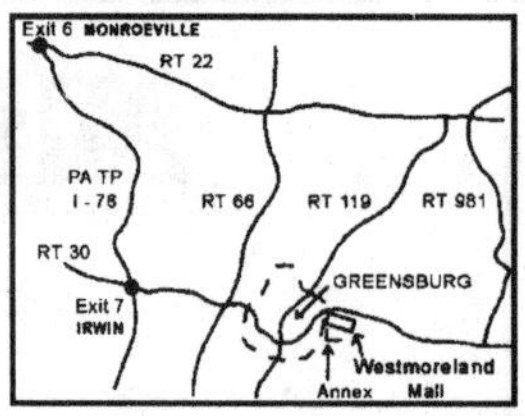

Mon - Wed - Fri 10:00 am - 8:00 pm
Tues - Thurs - Sat 10:00 am - 7:00 pm
Sunday Noon - 5:00 pm

100% cotton quilting fabrics, name brands, classes, books. Pfaff, Brother, Elna Sales & Service. Located directly behind Westmoreland Mall

Greensburg, PA #47

#12 Westmoreland Mall Annex 15601
(724) 836-0611

Indiana, PA #48

Daffodil Cottage Quilt Shop

533 Philadelphia St.
Indiana, PA 15701
(724) 465-4990

1400+ bolts of fabric, stencils, and books. We pride ourselves on quality customer service. We tailor our classes to suit individual needs.

Mon 10 - 8
Tues - Sat 10 - 5

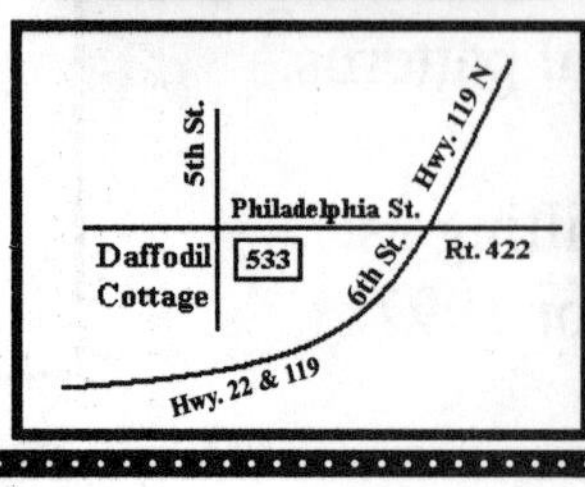

Davidsville, PA #49

Tues - Fri 9 - 4
Sat 9 - 3

Darlene's Quilts & More

110 N. Main St., Jackson Square 15928
(814) 479-2581
Owner: Darlene Kleinman
Est: 1998 300+ Bolts

Good selection of 100% cotton fabric, notions, stencils & patterns. Helpful staff.
Free Classes. A little bit of everything.

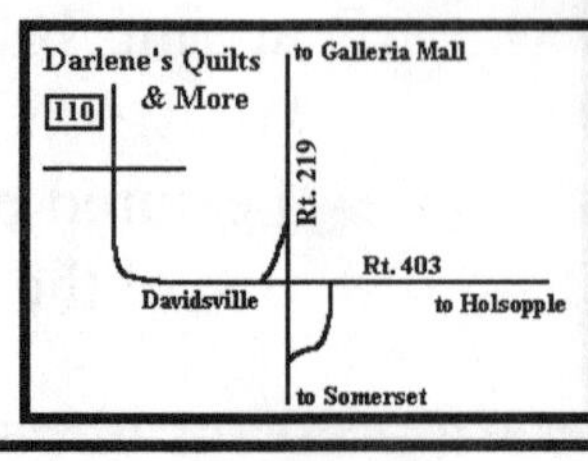

Patches, Pretties, 'n Lace

2000+ Bolts of Fabric

Books • Patterns • Notions
Classes • Seminars • Workshops

Authorized
elna Sewing Systems Dealer

We feature the following fabrics:
• Hoffmans • Bali Handprints • RJR Thimbleberries
• Moda • Andover • Concord • South Sea • HSF Flannels
• Red Wagon Cottons and other Homespuns

SPECIAL CLASSES for GROUPS
We will organize a special class for a group of four or more friends & neighbors!

Complete Moda Marble Collection along with numerous other complete Designer Collections

HORN SEWING CABINETS
— In Stock & On Display —

Visit our **OTT Lighting Center** *featuring*
Portable Lamps, Table Lamps, Floor Lamps, Screw in Bulbs and 2 & 4 Foot Tubes

WE HAVE SPECTRAVISION LIGHTING

In Stock and on Display are 22" & 29" Hoops as well as the Homestead and Classic Frames and Quilt Display Racks

Check Out Our "Hoop Combo Special"
One Stand, 22" & 29" Hoops And Both Half Hoop Adapters

EdMar *Brazilian DimensionalEmbroidery Floss, Kits, Books and Classes*

Tues. thru Sat. 10 - 4
Other Times by Appointment
Closed Sun. & Mon.

#50

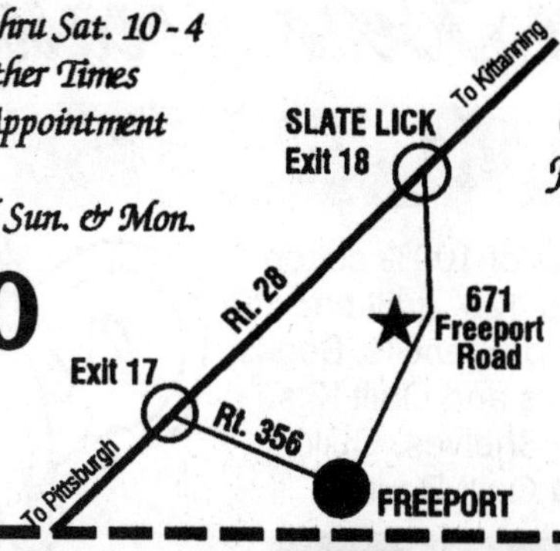

671 Freeport Road
Freeport, PA 16229
724-295-2800

Fax: 724-295-2828
E-Mail: ppnl@nb.net

BRING THIS AD IN FOR A 10% DISCOUNT ON FABRICS & BOOKS
Expires May 31, 2004

Husqvarna VIKING

MAYPORT COTTONS & Quilt Shop

68 Paradise Rd. 16240
(814) 365-2212
Owner: Patty Toy
Est: 1999

Mon & Fri 10 - 5
Tues & Thur 10 - 8
Sat 10 - 3

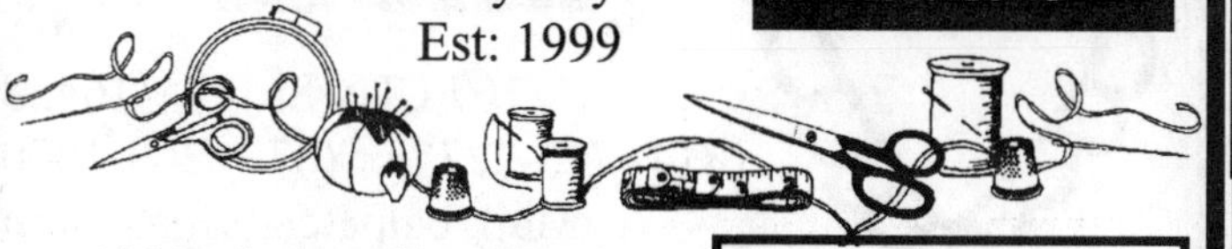

1000+ bolts of beautiful 100% cottons, mettler thread, lots of books, patterns, & notions. Full variety of classes.

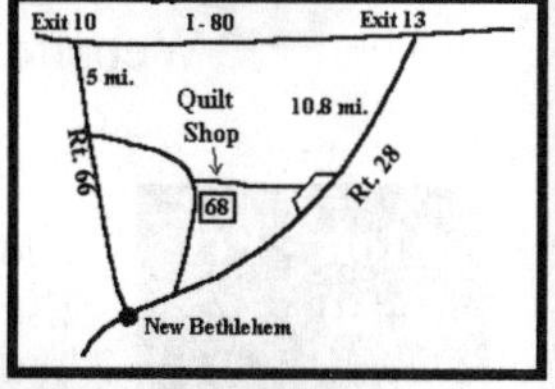

Mayport, PA #51

Roaring Spring, PA #52

Country Beefers

Mon - Fri 9:30 - 4:30
Saturdays
May - Sept 10 - 2
Oct - Apr 10 - 4

RD #1, Box 495 16673
(814) 224-4818 Est: 1981
Owners: Louann Ferraro & Betty Beegle

Cotton fabrics, homespuns, books, craft patterns, notions, stencils. Also locally made gift items, appliqued clothing and Yankee Candles.

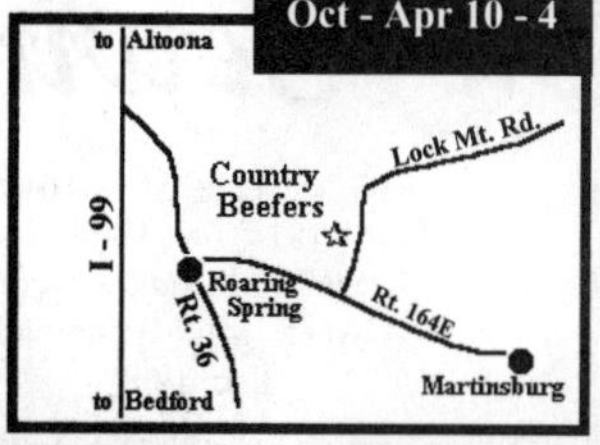

Elderton, PA #53

Judys' Sewing Center

M, T, TH, F 10 - 5
Wed 12 - 8
Sat 10 - 3

Rte. 422, P.O. Box 178 15736
(724) 354-3360 Fax: (724) 354-3145
E-Mail: judyssew@ptdprolog.net
Web Site: www.judyssew.com
Owners: Judy Hicks & Judy Kimmel
Est: 2000 1700 sq.ft.
1800 Bolts 100% Cotton Fabric. Heirloom Supplies. Books, Patterns, Notions, Threads, Stencils. Husqvarna Viking Sales-Service. Friendly Service. Fun Classes.

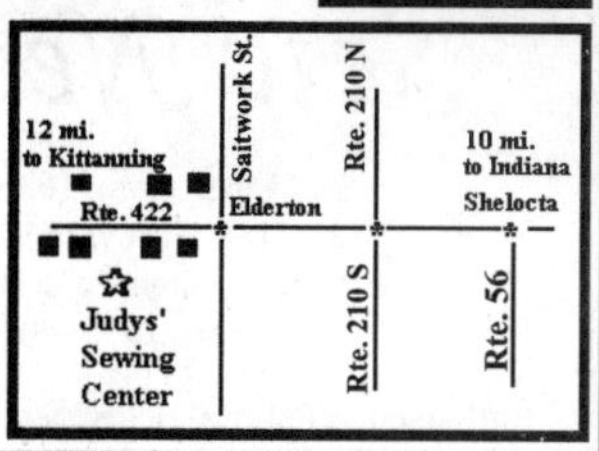

Carlton, PA #54

Mon - Sat
9:30 - 5

Homespun Treasures Quilt Shoppe

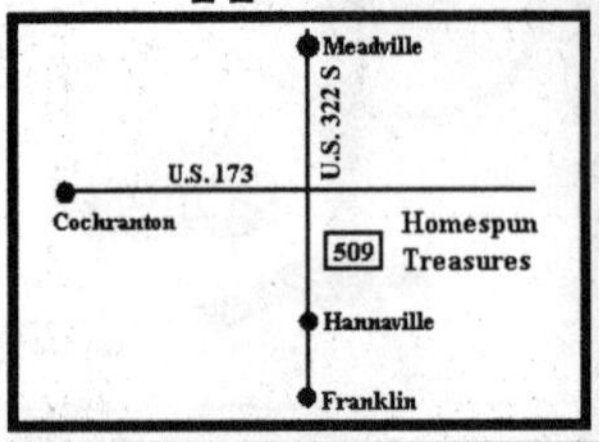

509 U.S. 322 16311
(814) 425-2889
E-Mail: quiltLov@toolcity.net
Owner: Gail M. Baker

Located between Meadville & Franklin, PA. Large selection of Fabric & Books & Notions. Classes Available. Always looking to see your work. Bring it in and share.

Knox, PA #55

Est: 1987

Countryside Crafts & Countryside Quilts

Owners:
Jolinda Tharan (Crafts)
& Sally Byers (Quilts)
6361 Canoe Ripple Rd.
Knox, PA 16232
Exit 7 from I - 80
(814) 797-2434

Mon - Sat 10 - 4:30
Sun 1 - 4:30

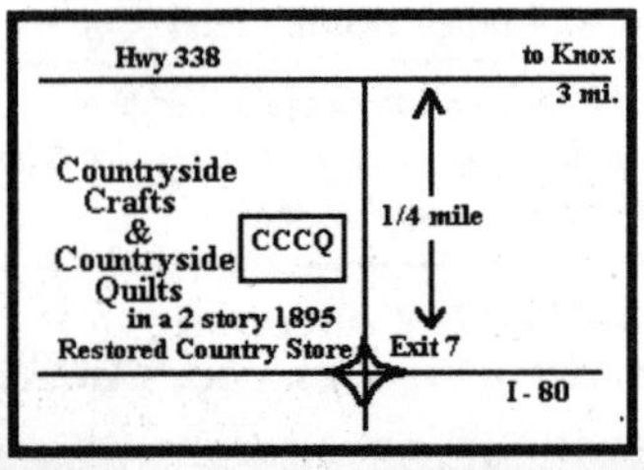

In the heart of Clarion County.
We are the area's Largest and Most Unique Country gift, craft and Quilting supply shop.
With 100% Cottons, Books, Quilting Patterns and the area's largest supply of craft patterns.
Homespuns and flannels.
Handmade Country Clothing. Free Newsletter.

Country Bear Creations

Lucinda, PA #56

Over 500 bolts of 100% cotton fabric 90", 108" & 120" quilt backing.
Large selection of Stencils, Books, Patterns, Tools and Quilt Kits.
Custom Made Shelves, Quilting Frames & Quilt Racks.

Mon - Sat 9:30 - 5:30

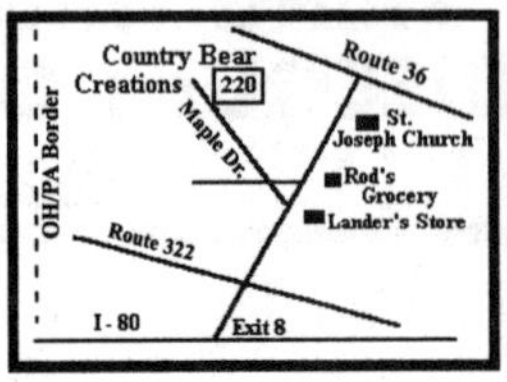

220 Maple Drive 16235
(814) 226-8893
Owners: Keith & Sharon Kennedy
Mail Orders Welcome
MC Visa Discover Am Exp.
E-Mail: cbear@csonline.net
Web Site: www.countryheirloomsquiltdesigns.com

Meadville, PA #57

Mon - Fri
10 - 6
Sat 10 - 3

The Quilt Square

Dunham Rd. (William Bainbridge Tech. Ctr.)
(814) 333-4383 16335
Owner: Becky VanKleeck
Est: 1981

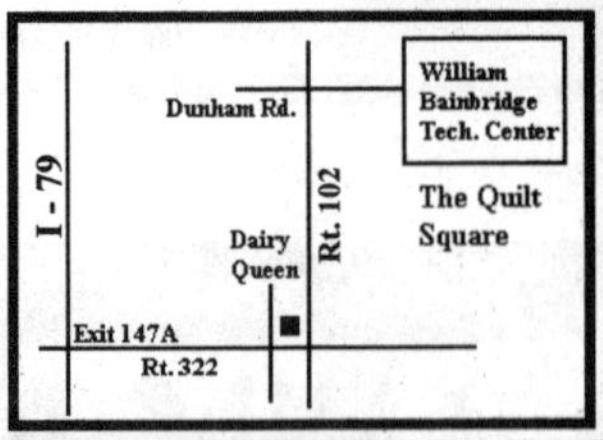

2000 bolts. A staff that loves to see your show & tell. 10% off when you have us sign this ad. Sewing machines excluded.
2 1/4 miles from I - 79

Corry, PA #58

Tues 10 - 7
Wed - Fri
10 - 5
Sat 10 - 3

My Sewing Room

109 N. Center St. 16407
(814) 664-9424
E-Mail: MSR@tbscc.com
Owner: Miki Hammond
Est: 1999

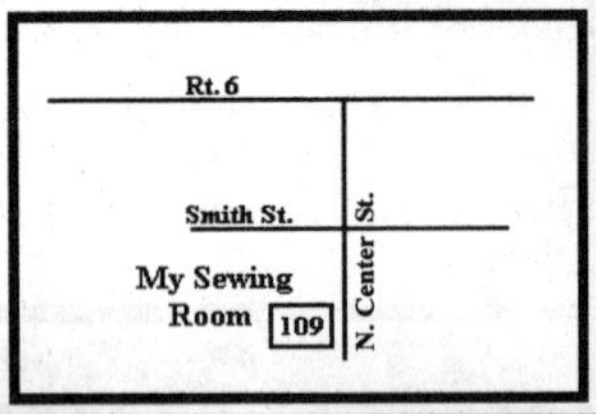

Great selection of quilts, fabrics & notions. We always have something new and creative going on.

North East, PA #59

CALICO PATCH Quilt Shop

107 Clay St. #3 16428
(814) 725-2275 or (877) 260-1000
E-Mail: calpatchqs@aol.com
Website: www.calicopatchquiltshop.com

Mon - Fri
10 - 5
Sat 10 - 4

Owner:
Joy Reich
Est: 1998
1600 sq.ft.
1400+ Bolts

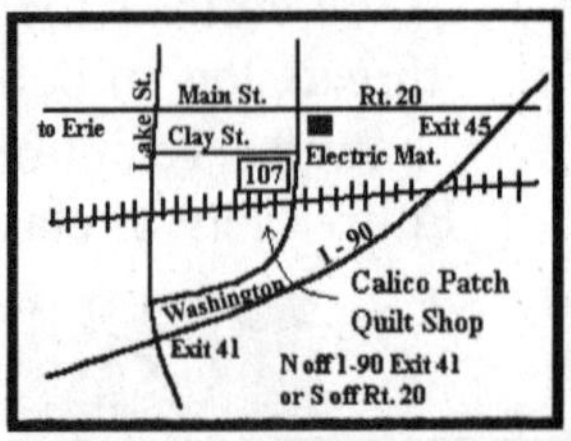

Books - Notions - Classes and the largest selection of Thimbleberries Fabric in the Tri-state area.
Mail Order - Guild discount.

Warren, PA #60

Mon - Fri
10 - 5:30
Sat 10 - 4

Sew Necessary

209 Liberty St. 16365
(814) 723-3188 Fax: (814) 723-3192
Owner: Karen Eggleston
Est: 1995

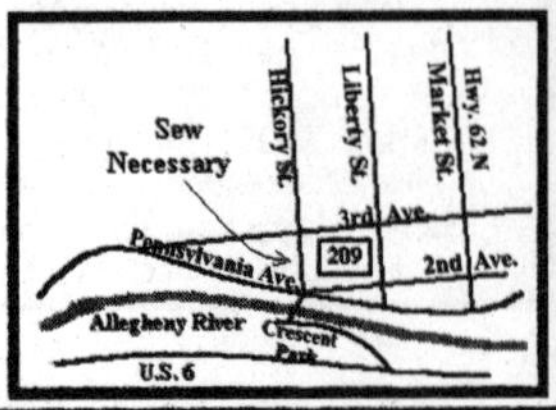

100% Cotton Fabrics! Check out our classes. Books, patterns, notions, quilting supplies, yarns and cross-stitch supplies.

Union City, PA #63

Tues - Sat 10 - 5

The Sewing Loft

40 N. Main St. 16438
(814) 438-9007 or (877) 9SEWING
Owners: Judy Heintz, Juanita Johnson, Jean Grzejka, & Kathy Hamilton

Over 800 bolts of 100% cotton from top designers. Samples, classes, friendly service and the coffee is always on.

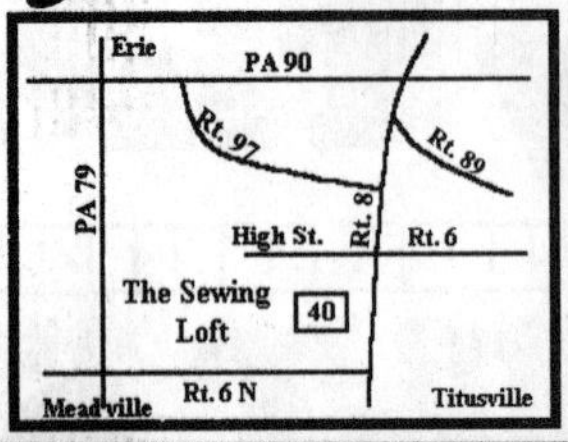

Fairview, PA #64

Thursday 10 - 3 and by Appt. or chance.

International Fabric Collection

7870 W. Ridge Rd. #8 16415
(800) 462-3891
E-Mail: info@intfab.com 1500 sq.ft.
Web Site: www.intfab.com
Owner: Dorothy Brown Est: 1987

Cottons from Japan, Italy, Holland, Africa. Yukata, mud cloth, Kente cloth, Liberty of London. Unusual Books & Patterns. Sashiko Supplies.

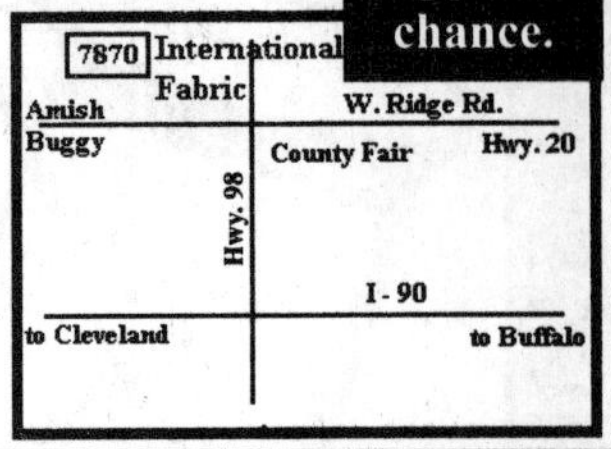

Albion, PA #65

Tues - Sat 10 - 4 Thur til 8

The Quilt Parlor

14250 Tracy Rd. 16401
(814) 756-5062 Fax: (814) 756-5069
E-Mail: quiltparlor@hotmail.net
Owners: Timothy & Megen Bell
Est: 1995 1000 sq.ft. 1000 Bolts

Quaint little Quilt Shop in the country. Specializing in antique quilts and custom machine quilting. 10 minutes from I - 90.

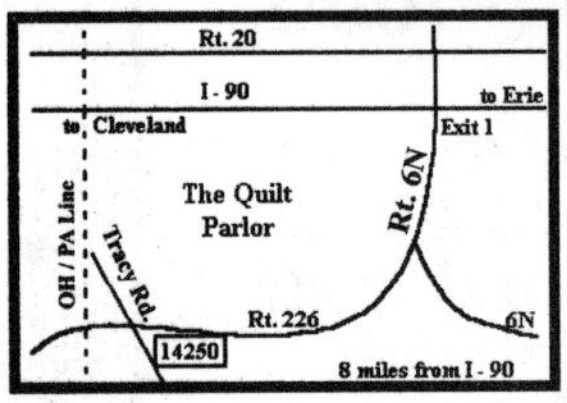

City	Store Name Store Address	Phone
Ackermanville	The Village Barn, 1547 Mill Rd.	610-588-3127
Allentown	Tucker Yarn Co., 950 Hamilton Mall	610-434-1846
Allentown	Julie's Sewing Basket, 1870 Briarcliff Ter.	610-434-7600
Allentown	Quiltery, 2030 Whitehall Ave.	610-439-8948
Allentown	L & M Fabrics, 4713 W. Tilghman St.	610-530-1601
Altoona	Ben Franklin Crafts, 120 Park Hills Plaza	814-944-7788
Altoona	Moore Stitches, 1635 E. Pleasant Valley Blvd.	814-943-2977
Altoona	R Quilt Shop, 2700 Windwood Rd.	814-942-2606
Annville	Hershey's Quilt Shop, 112 W. Main St.	717-867-8484
Belleville	Mercer & Bratt Amish Quilts, 234 W. Main St.	717-935-2327
Bellevue	The Quilted Cottage, 690 Lincoln Ave.	412-734-5141
Bethlehem	Fabric Mart of Bethlehem, 2485 Willow Park	610-866-3400
Bethlehem	Hancock Fabrics #158, 3813 Nazareth Pike	610-691-9325
Bethlehem	Creative Quilting Workshop, 415 High St.	610-868-0376
Bird in Hand	Quilt Barn, 207 N. Harvest Rd.	717-656-9495
Bird in Hand	Fisher's Hand Made Quilts, 2713-A Old Philadelphia Pk	717-392-5440
Bird in Hand	Sylvia Petersheim Quilts, 2544 Old Philadelphia Pike	717-392-6404
Bird-in-Hand	Lapp's Dry Goods, 3137 Old Philadelphia Pike	None
Camp Hill	Country Patchwork, 1603 Carlisle Rd.	717-761-2586
Canton	Four Hands Fabric Shop, 158 N. Center St.	570-673-5280
Clarks-Summit	Carriage Barn Antiques, 1550 Fairview	717-587-5405
Columbia	Sew Nice Too, 515 Chestnut St.	717-684-0896
Connoquenessing	Added Touch, 1366 Evans City Rd.	412-789-7019
Dallas	Back Mountain Quiltworks, 52 Mill St.	717-675-4018
Denver	Garman's Quilts, 175 W. Church St.	717-336-6381
Denver	Sauder's Fabrics, 681 S. Muddycreek Rd.	717-336-2664
Doylestown	Sew Smart Fabrics, 53 W. State St.	215-345-7990
Elkland	Golden Thimble, 114 W. Main St.	814-258-5677
Ephrata	Grandma's Quilt Shop, 202 Martindale	717-768-7060
Equinunk	Janos Quilt Shop, P.O. Box 246	717-224-6008
Frederick	Quilted Heirlooms, 2015 Hoffmansville Rd.	610-754-1980
Gap	M & N Hand Made Quilts, 270 Octorara Trail	717-768-8673
Gipsy	Village Variety Store, 33 Main St.	814-845-7503
Glenside	Granny's Sewing Den, 243 Keswick Ave.	215-885-4959
Goodville	Obie's Country Store, 1585 Main St.	717-445-4616
Greenville	Sew Much To Do, 170 Main St.	724-588-2248
Harborcreek	Millie's Quilt Thimble, 3229 Davison Rd.	814-898-2978
Haverton	Quilting Cottage, 1910 Darby Rd.	610-449-3241
Huntingdon	Petunia Patchwork, 3050 Emmett Ave.	814-643-5048
Intercourse	Village Quilts, 3519 Old Philadelphia Pike	717-768-0783
Intercourse	The Country Market at Intercourse, P.O. Box 555 3504 Old Philadelphia Pike	717-768-8058
Intercourse	Nancy's Corner, 3503 Old Philadelphia Pike	717-768-8790
Jennerstown	My Front Porch, 1654 E. Pitt St.	814-629-5414
Kutztown	Sugar Creek Quilt Co., 2753 New Smithville	610-285-0368
Lancaster	Sawtooth, 57 Deer Ford Dr.	717-295-3961
Lancaster	Pennsylvania Farm Museum, 2451 Kissel Hill	717-569-0401
Lancaster	Strawberry Patch, 112 Willow Valley Square	717-464-2224
Lebanon	Tom's Quilts, 15 E. High St.	717-279-6262
Leola	Riehl's Quilts & Crafts, 247 E. Eby Rd.	717-656-0697
Leola	Country Lane Quilts, 221 S. Groffdale Rd.	717-656-8476
Lower Burrell	L and K Cottage Quilts 3176 Oregon Dr.	724-334-8599
Mahanoy City	Chesko Fabrics, 301 E. Centre	717-773-0140
Mansfield	Lucia's Fabric & Craft Shop, Rte. 15 S	717-662-7024
Mechanicsburg	Quaint Quilts, 500 Cocklin St.	717-766-7166
Midland	Create A Stitch, 17 7th St.	724-643-4833
Mifflinburg	Mary Koons Quilts, 408 Chestnut St.	717-966-0341
Milford	Haybarn Gift & Quilting Shop, 167 Arbutus Ln., P.O. Box 134	
Montoursville	Stere Sewing Machine Center, 1116 S. Broad St.	717-368-8819
Mt. Joy	Amish Quilts of Lancaster County, 2123 Milton Grove Rd.	717-653-9121
New Brighton	Amy Baughman's Sewing Center, 472 Constitution Blvd.	724-846-8140
New Brighton	Boyde's Country Stitch, 81 E. Inman Dr.	412-846-4175
New Holland	Cedar Lane Dry Goods, 204 Orlan Rd.	717-354-0030
New Wilmington	The Quilting Bee, 126 S. Market St.	724-946-8566
Northampton	Dave Iron's Antiques, 223 Covered Bridge Rd.	610-262-9335
Oley	Ladyfingers Sewing Studio, 6375 Oley Trpk.	610-689-0068
Philadelphia	A&J Fabrics, 752 S. 4th St.	215-592-7011
Pittston	Edelstein's Fabrics, R.R. 141 South Main	717-655-1930
Punxsutawney	Lydia's Quilt Shop, R.D.7, Box 113	814-938-5533
Quarryville	Good's Store, 333 W. 4th St.	786-9028
Rebersburg	Brush Valley Dry Goods, Star Route, Box 33	None
Ronks	Family Farm Quilt, 3511 W. Newport Rd.	717-768-8375
Ronks	Amish Country Traditions, 227 A Hartman Bridge Rd.	717-687-9270
Saltsburg	Patchwork at Heart, 219 Point St.	412-639-8441
Sayre	Mary's General Store, 927 W. Lockhart	717-888-2320
Sayre	The Stitching Post, 206 Desmond	717-888-8037
Scranton	Scranton Fabric Center, 737 Oak St.	570-346-0721
Sharpsville	Shaffer's Countryside Quilting, 2741 Winner	724-962-9394
Trafford	Quilting Needle, 418 Cavitt Ave.	412-380-8003
Verona	Ages Ago Antiques, 722 Allegheny River	412-828-9800
Volant	Quilted Collectibles, Main St.	412-533-3863
Wellsboro	Gammie's Attic, RD 6, Box 128	717-724-6151
West Chester	Gone to Pieces Quilt Shop, 62 East Street	610-399-8535
Wilkes Barre	Touch of Eyelet, 1006 Wyoming Ave.	717-283-3048
Willow Grove	Yours, Mine & Ours Sewing, 219 Easton	215-659-3347
Wyoming	Quilts to Treasure, 886 Shoemaker Ave.	717-693-1299

RHODE ISLAND

6 Featured Shops

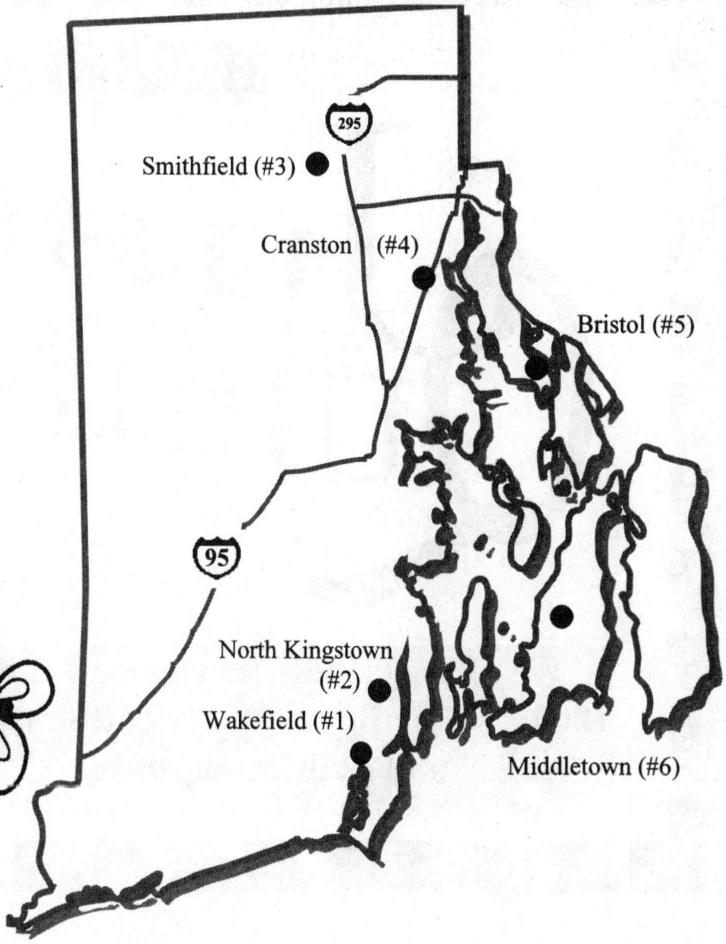

Wakefield, RI #1

Tues - Sat 10 - 5

Folk Art Quilts

269 Main St. 02879
(401) 789-5985
Owners: Evie Cherms & Mary Loftes

100% Cottons—Moda, Hoffman, P&B, Benartex and More. Quilting supplies, notions & patterns.

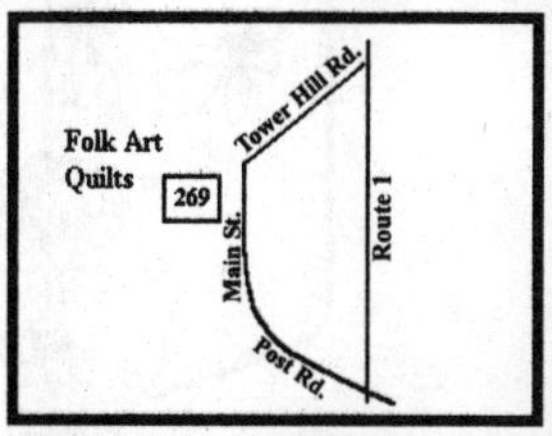

North Kingstown, RI #2

Mon - Sat 10 - 5
Sun 12 - 5
Jan & Feb Daily 12 - 5

Quilt Loft at Wickford Place

1340 Tower Hill Rd. 02852
(401) 294-4177 Fax: Same
Web Site: www.wickfordplaceinc.com
Est: 1994 9000 sq.ft. 400+ Bolts

Bolts, Fat Quarters, Books, Patterns, Thread, Quilting Supplies, Quilts, Wallhangings. Also finished crafts and hand made furniture.

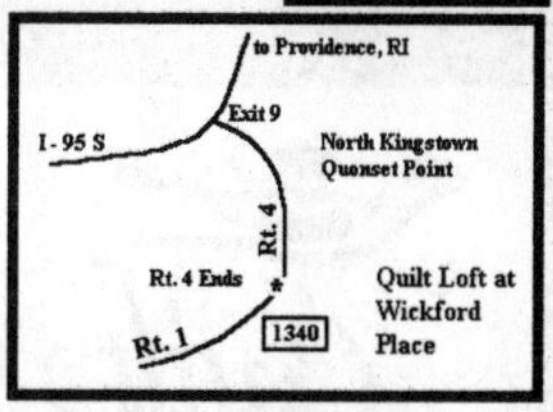

Smithfield, RI #3

Tues - Sat 10 - 5 Wed til 8

Quilter's Market

20 Cedar Swamp Rd. 02917
(401) 233-3949
Owner: Lynda Young

Over 1200 bolts of 100% cotton fabric. Books, Patterns and Notions totally devoted to Quilting. Classes and Private Lessons.

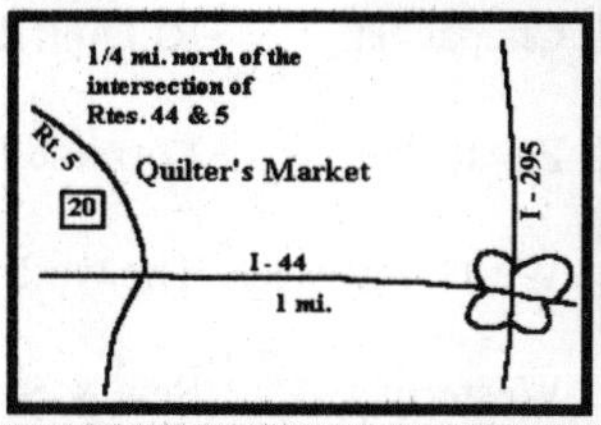

Cranston, RI #4

Mon - Fri 10 - 5:30
Sat 10 - 5
Closed Summer Mondays

Blaine's Sewing Machine Ctr.

1280 Oaklawn Ave. 02920
(401) 463-8824 Fax: (401) 463-8140
E-Mail: blainesewing@worldnet.att.net
www.sewingmachinedealers.com/blainesewing
Owner: Natalie Delaney

Blaine sewing celebrates 50 years of serving New England. Family-operated business, we carry Bernina, Janome-New Home, Elna, Babylock Sewing Machines and Sergers. Software for all brands of machines. Full line sewing supplies, cabinets, and machine travel bags.

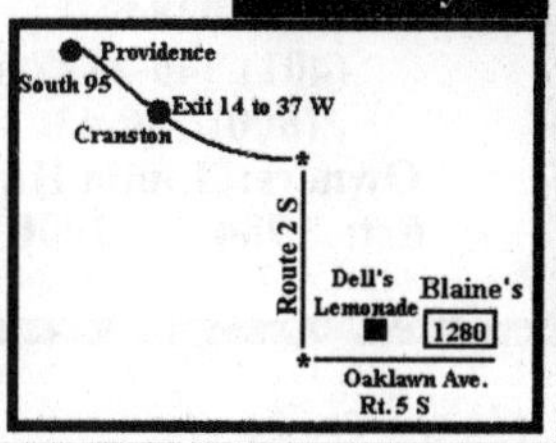

Bristol, RI #5

Tues - Sat
10 - 5

Est: 1998

Just Quilts

576 Metacom Ave.
Bristol, RI 02809
(401) 254-1240
Web Site: www.justquilting.com

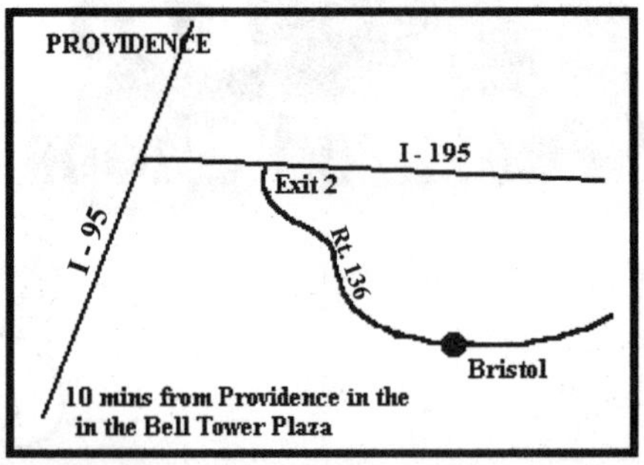

We offer friendly service and carry 1000+ bolts of fine quality cotton fabrics and quilting supplies.

Rhode Island's largest selection of Quilting Fabrics.
Hoffman, Henry's etc.
Books, Sterling Thimbles, Classes & Workshops, Quilts & Gifts

Quilt Artisan

Mon - Fri
11 - 5
Sat
11 - 4

Middletown, RI #6

747 Aquidneck Avenue
02842
(401) 846-2127 or
(800) 736-4364
Owners: Linda Hilliard
Est: 1984 2000 sq.ft.

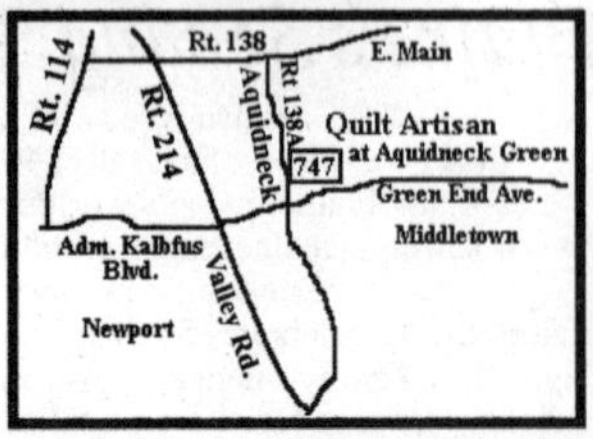

Other Shops in Rhode Island: We suggest calling first

Chepachet	RI Quilt Co., 9 Putnam Heights Rd. 401-567-8544
Pawtucket	Lorraine Fabrics, 593 Mineral Spring Ave. 401-722-9500
West Greenwich	The Quilt Shoppe, 74 Nooseneck Hill Rd. 401-397-4040
Westerly	Sew & Sew, 271 Post Rd. 401-322-9194

10 Featured Shops

SOUTH CAROLINA

Quilter's Heaven

Fabrics, Supplies, and Classes. PFAFF Sewing Center

Fabric—Over 1500 Bolts
Hoffman, Alexander Henry, Robert Kaufman, P&B and Moda
Books —100 Titles and More
Notions—Great Variety of Threads
Mettler, Cotty, Luny, Mez Alcazar, Sulky, Finishing Touch
Classes—All Skill Levels

Mon - Sat 10 - 5

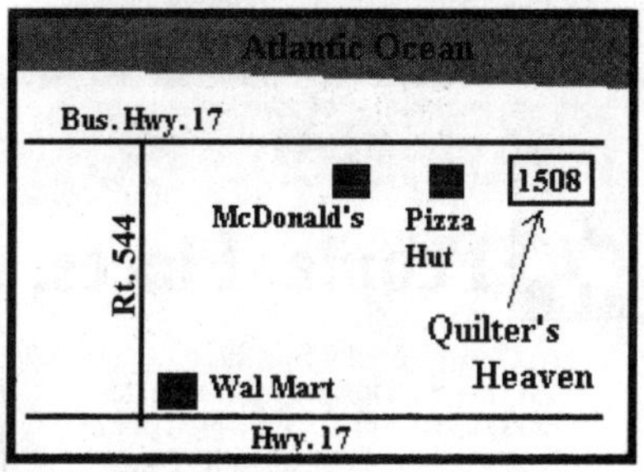

Surfside Beach, SC #1

1508 Hwy. 17 N 29575 (843) 477-1611
Owners: Mary Sneeden Est: 1994 2000 sq.ft.

Island Threads

A Quilt Shoppe

10225 Ocean Hwy. 17
Pawleys Plaza Unit #372
P.O. Box 616 29585
843-235-3725
E-mail: ithreads@sccoast.net
Fax: 843-235-3723

Mon - Sat 10 - 5

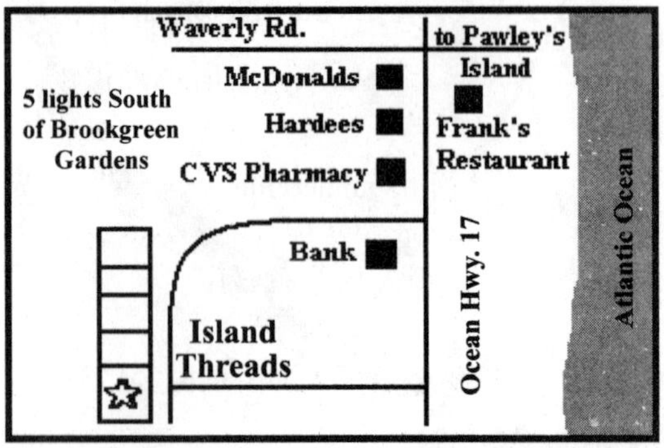

From North 5th Lt. from Brookgreen Gardens
South 1st Lt. from Pawleys Island @ South Causeway

- 100% Cotton Fabrics - over 1800 Bolts
- Thimbleberries Club
- Professional Staff for Assistance
- Many Books and Patterns
- Day and Evening Classes
- Notions - Buttons - Threads (Cotty, Sylco, Mettler, Sulky)
- Custom Embroidery Service
- Newsletter & Mail Orders

"Bringing Ideas to Reality"

Owners: Pat & Rhett Roman
Est: 1998 1500 sq.ft.

Pawleys Island, SC #1

Conway, SC #3

Mon - Fri 10 - 6 Sat 10 - 3

Sew Many Common Threads

2290 Hwy. 544 29526
(843) 347-6000
E-Mail: sew@sccoast.net
Web Site: www.commonthreads.com
Est: 1996 2500 sq.ft.

fabrics, patterns, books, notions, classes
Husqvarna Viking Dealer.

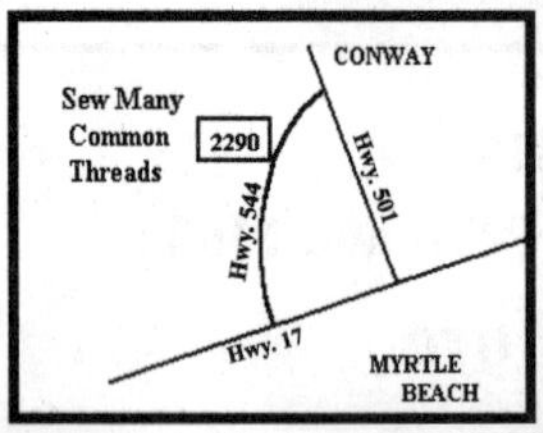

Summerville, SC #4

Mon - Fri 10 - 5:30 Sat 10 - 5

People, Places, & Quilts

129 West Richardson Ave. 29483
In Cauthen's old Hardware Store
(843) 871-8872 Free Newsletter
E-Mail: email@ppquilts.com
Web Site: www.ppquilts.com
Owner: Diane F. Wilson Est: 1990

A full service quilt shop with folk art ~ specializing in reproduction fabrics. Selected by Better Homes & Gardens Quilt Sampler as one of the top 10 shops in America.

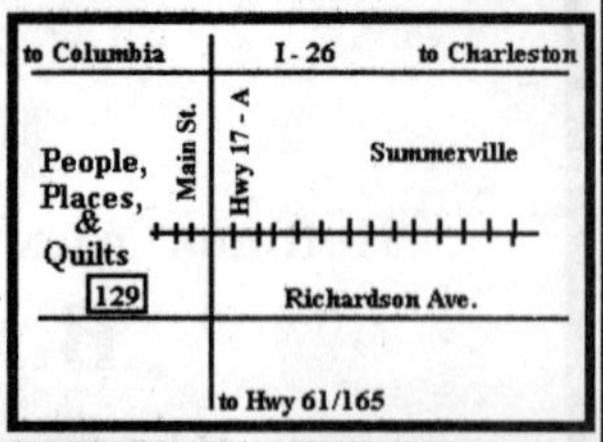

Charleston, SC #5

Mon - Sat 10 - 5

People, Places, & Quilts

1 Henrietta St. 29403
In Historic Downtown Charleston
(843) 937-9333 Free Newsletter
E-Mail: email@ppquilts.com
Web Site: www.ppquilts.com

A full service quilt shop with folk art ~ specializing in reproduction fabrics. Selected by Better Homes & Gardens Quilt Sampler as one of the top 10 shops in America.

1 block off Marion Square within walking distance of the Museum, Visitors Center and Aquarium

Bluffton, SC #6

Mon - Sat 11 - 5

Belfair Towne Village 103 Towne Dr. 29910
(843) 815-7878
E-Mail: crossstitchjunct@aol.com

Cross Stitch Junction

Owners:
Geri Rihn &
Cheryl Walter
Est: 2000
1400 sq.ft.

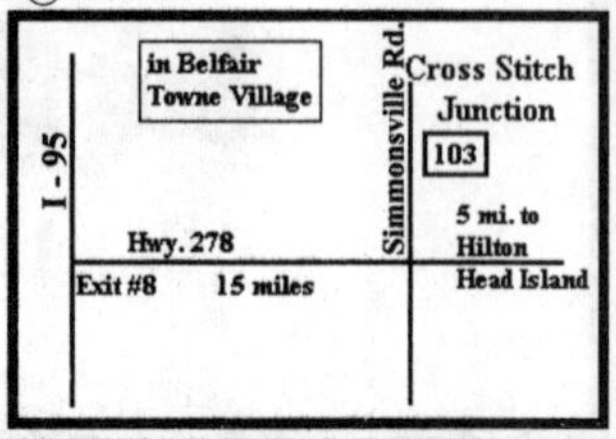

"Quilting and Cross Stitch Boutique"
Reproduction Samplers & Designer Charts.
Classes · Finest Cottons · Exquisite Linens
Specialty Threads · Supplies · 2000+ Bolts

For all your quilting needs . . . and wants.

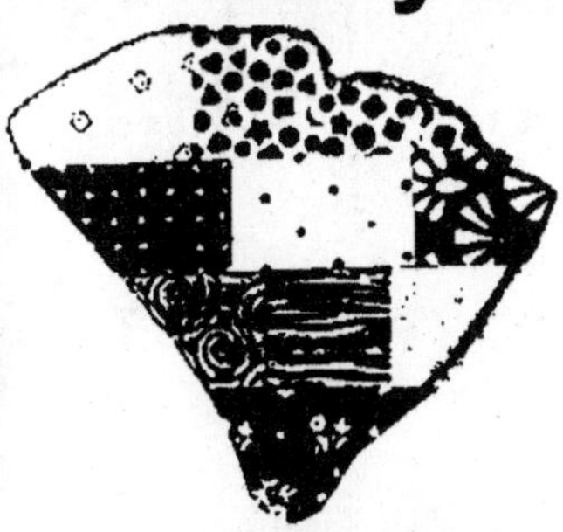

CAROLINA QUILTMAKER

Always the newest in books and fabrics. Custom machine quilting service.
Bring us your antique or new tops for quilting. Customer service our specialty.

Tues 10 - 7 Wed - Sat 10 - 5

2716 Devine St. 29205 (803) 931-0900
Owners: Ellen Simon & Leonard Damond
Est: 1996 1500 sq.ft. 1000 Bolts

Columbia, SC #7

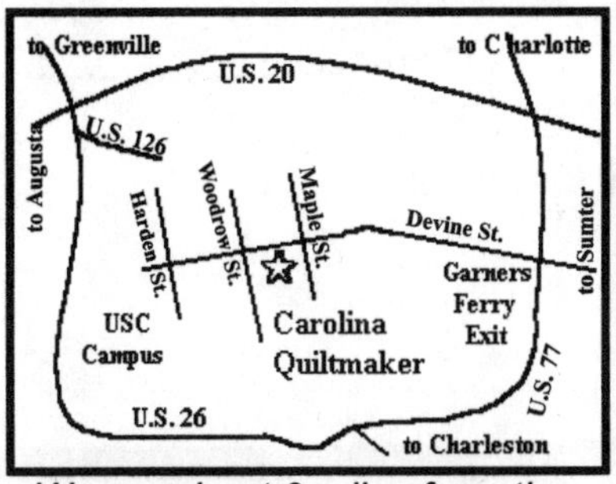

We are about 6 miles from the Garners Ferry Exit off U.S. 77

Little Mountain, SC #8

Mon - Fri 9:30 - 5 Sat 10 - 4

Little Mountain Quilt Shop

834 Main St. In Historical District of
Little Mountain 29075
(803) 932-0504
Owner: Kathryn M. Gertz

100% Cotton Fabrics -- Large selection of Books, Patterns, Notions, Classes Morning / Evening and friendly atmosphere.

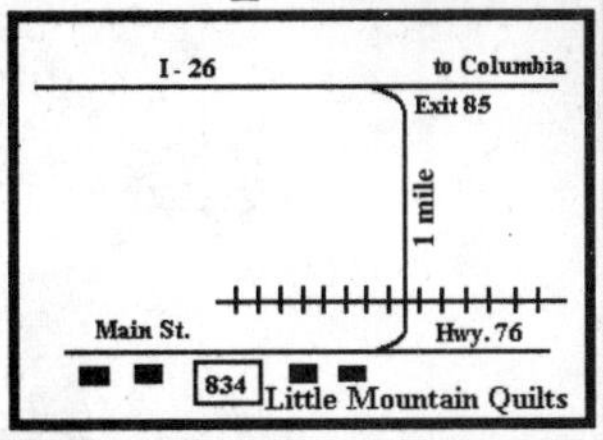

Greenville, SC #9

Mon - Fri 10:00 - 5:45 Sat 10 - 5

Viking Says Sew'n Quilt

1296 Woodruff Rd. 29607
In Shops of Merovan
Web Site: www.heirloomsandcomforts.net
Est: 2001 1400 sq.ft. 1200+ Bolts

Greenville's most complete quilt shop-- Fabrics - Books - Patterns - Notions - Classes - Machines - Heirloom Sewing - Easy on/off I-85 & I-385 Husqvarna/Viking Dealer

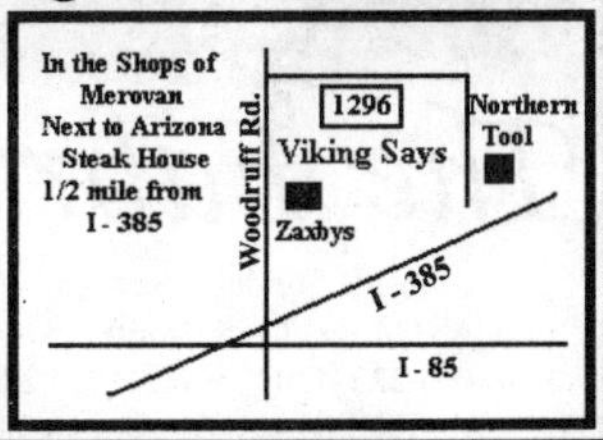

Other Shops in South Carolina: We suggest calling first

Anderson	Ninety-Six Fabrics, 910 Bypass 28 S	864-26-6674
Beaufort	Patches of the Heart, 3016 Ashwood Cir.	803-522-3303
Beaufort	Creative Stitches, P.O. Box 4843	803-524-1892
Charleston	Margiotta's Sewing Machine Co., 874 Orleans Rd.	803-766-3621
Columbia	South Carolina Folk Art Archive, University of South Carolina	803-777-7251
Florence	Needle Niche, 518 W. Palmetto St.	843-678-9373
Greenville	Classic Keepsakes, 626 Congaree Rd.	864-288-0273
Myrtle Beach	Oak Street Fabrics, 504-C 27th Ave. N.	843-448-8021
Reevesville	Quilt House, 6841 Johnston Ave.	803-563-3890
Richburg	Quilt Therapy, 120 Weaver Dr.	803-329-2638
Salem	Calico House, 22 Cardinal Point	
Seneca	Ninety-Six Fabrics, 227 Market St.	864-882-3370
Sumter	Crafty Needle Shop, 600 Bultman Dr. #1B	803-775-9393

Central, SC #10

Mon - Fri 9:30 - 5:30 Sat 9 - 4

Heirlooms & Comforts

104 Madden Bridge Rd. 29630
(864) 639-9507
Web Site: www.heirloomsandcomforts.net
Est: 1984 2000 sq.ft. 1800 Bolts

Upstate's most complete quilt shop--Fabrics - Books - Patterns - Notions - Classes - Machines - Heirlooms Sewing - In a friendly atmosphere. Husqvarna/Viking Dealer.

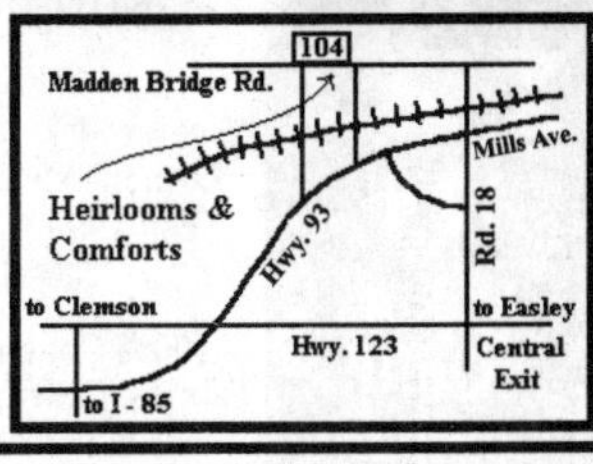

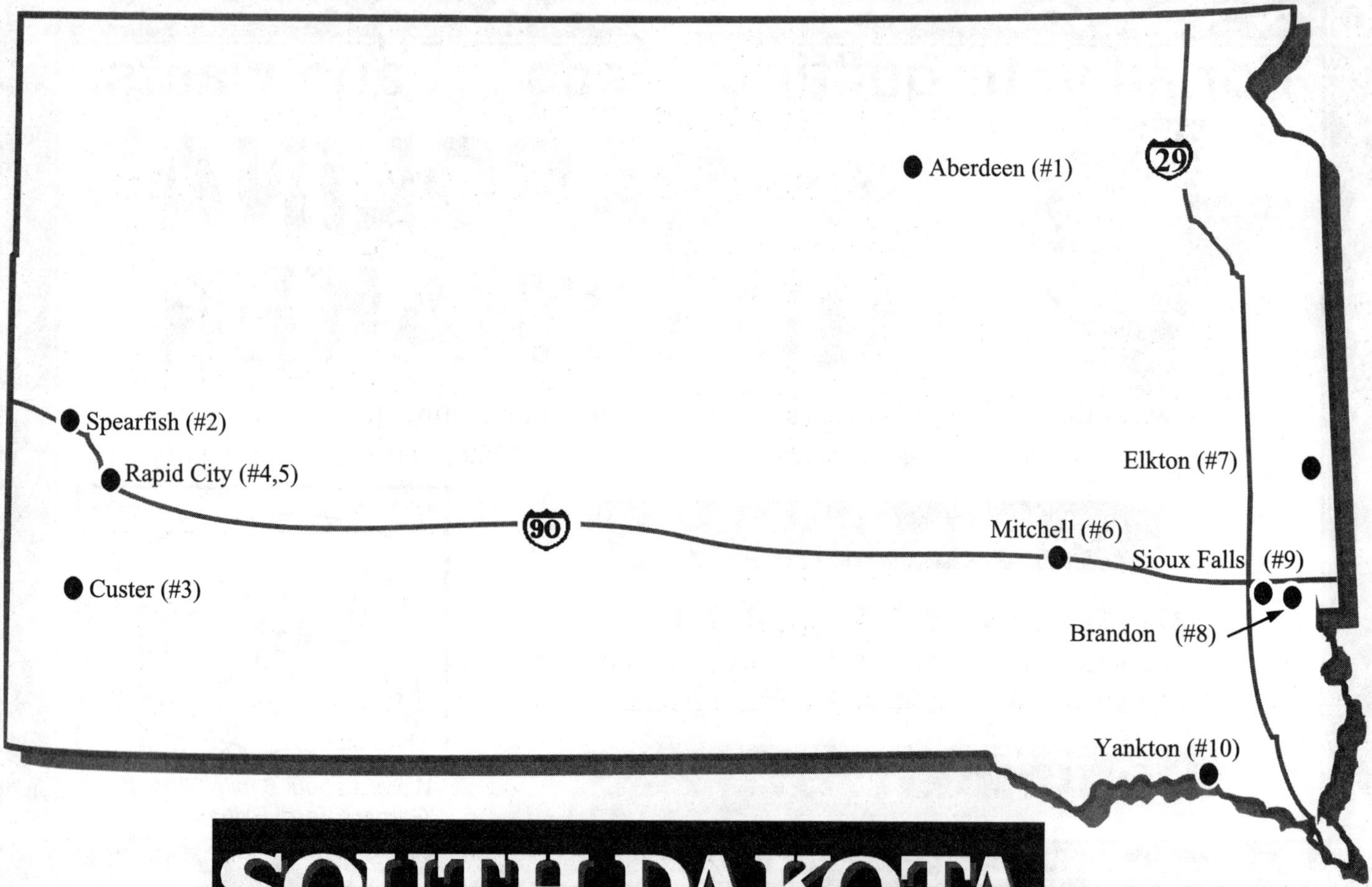

SOUTH DAKOTA

10 Featured Shops

Aberdeen, SD #1

Mon - Sat 9 - 5:30
Sat 9 - 4

The Fabric Bin

inside Sander's Sew -N- Vac
111 & 113 S. Main 57401
(605) 225-4203 Fax: (605) 225-6707
E-Mail: sewvac@mdex.net
Est: 1945 5000 sq.ft.

Offering Sewing Machine Sales & Service, classes, notions and quality cotton fabrics from Moda, Thimbleberries, Hoffman, RJR, Benartex

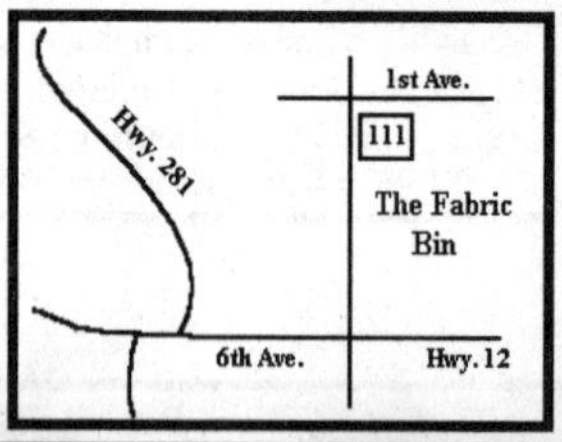

Spearfish, SD #2

Mon - Fri 9 - 5
Sat 9 - 4

Dakota Quilt Company

1004 Main St. 57783
(605) 642-2939 or (877) 642-2939

Web Site:
www.dakotaquilt.com
Owner: Melodee Nelson
Est: 1998 1300 sq.ft.
1000 Bolts

100% Cotton Quilting Fabrics, Patterns & Books, Machine Quilting, Dakota-made Quilts.

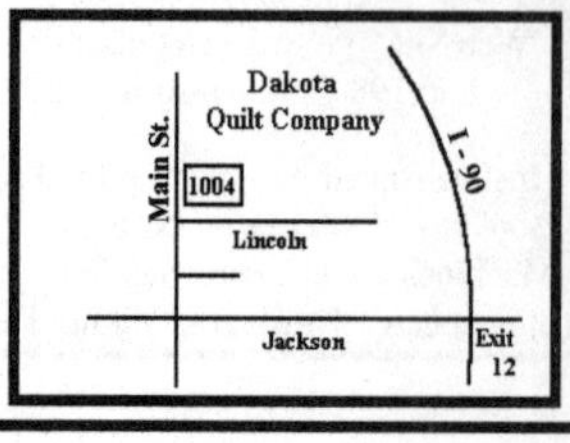

Custer, SD #3

Mon - Sat 9 - 5

The Quilt Shop

325 Mt. Rushmore Rd. 57730
(605) 673-3606

Quilting fabric and supplies.
Next to the Dairy Queen.

When Visiting the Black Hills Come Visit Us!
We Are Located 25 Miles from Mt. Rushmore

Thimble Cottage Quilt Shop And Boutique

OPEN
Mon. - Fri.
9:00 - 5:00
Saturday
10:00 - 4:00

1201 Mt. Rushmore Rd.
Rapid City, SD 57701
(605) 341-6569
www.thimblecottage.com

Filled with the Best Quilting Fabrics, Books, Notions, Gifts and Patterns Including Pearl Louise Design Originals!

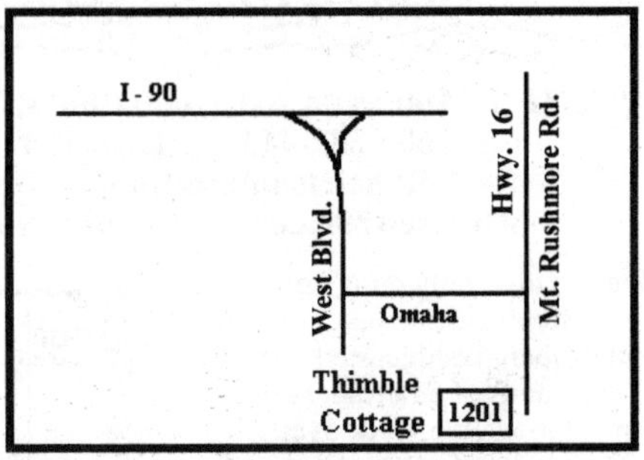

Rapid City, SD #4

Quilt Connection Etc.

Rapid City, SD #5

2050 West Main, Suite #4 57702
(605) 355-0178
E-Mail: quiltetc@dtgnet.com
Owner: Joan Schaff 2000 sq.ft. 3000+ Bolts

Monday - Friday 9 - 8 Saturday 9 - 5

"THE FUN SHOP"
featuring the finest quilting fabrics, books, and notions available. Viking sewing machines and accessories.

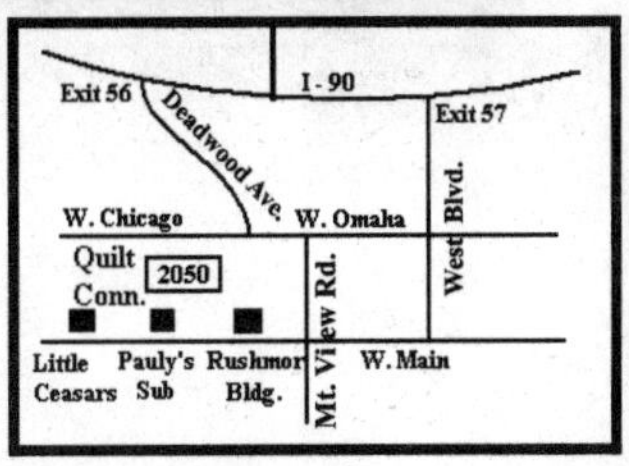

Mitchell, SD #6

Mon - Sat
9 - 5:30

The Pin Cushion

320 North Main Street
(605) 996-0947 Fax: (605) 996-0017
E-Mail: pincushion@santel.net
Owner: Carma Popp
Est: 1987 2000 sq.ft.

100% cottons, Books, and Patterns. Classes. Friendly, helpful staff. Authorized Pfaff Dealer

PFAFF

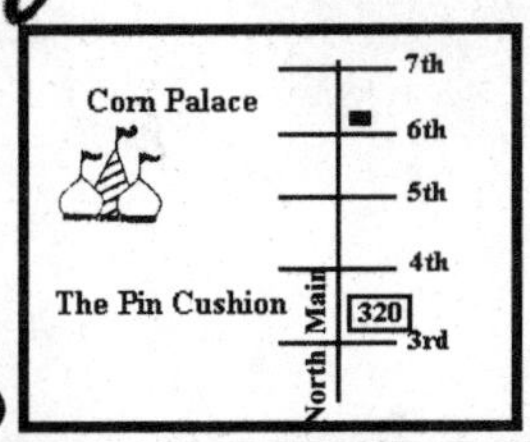

Elkton, SD #7

Mon - Fri
9 - 5
Thur til 9
Sat 9 - 4

Ivy Lane Quilts & "Stuff"

502 E. North Dr. 57026
(605) 542-2051 Fax: (605) 542-2052
E-Mail: ivylane@itctel.com
Owners: Linda Louder & Bev Lytle.
Free Newsletter Est: 1998 2000 sq.ft.

Moda, RJR, Benartex, Hoffman, SSI, P&B, Kona Bay. Outstanding books, patterns, notions & class offerings. Authorized Pfaff dealer, machine quilting. 1st in customer service.

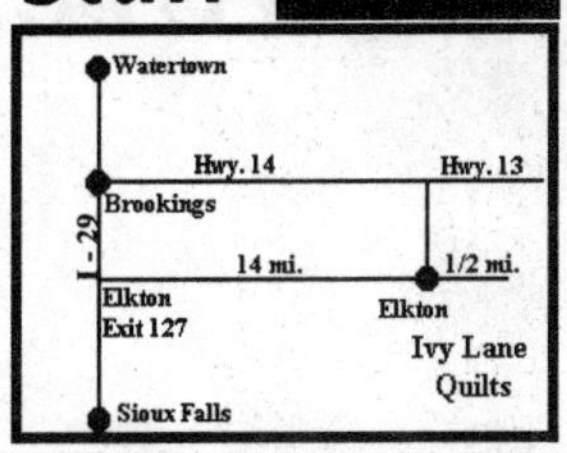

Brandon, SD #8

Mon - Fri 9:30 - 5
Sat 9:30 - 3

Quilted Memories

600 N. Splitrock Blvd. 57005
(605) 582-7411
Owner: Jeff & Twyla Voldseth
Est: 1997 1000+ Bolts

Great 100% cotton fabrics, patterns & books, lot of classes to choose from, quality notions, gifts. Right off I - 90 Interstate.

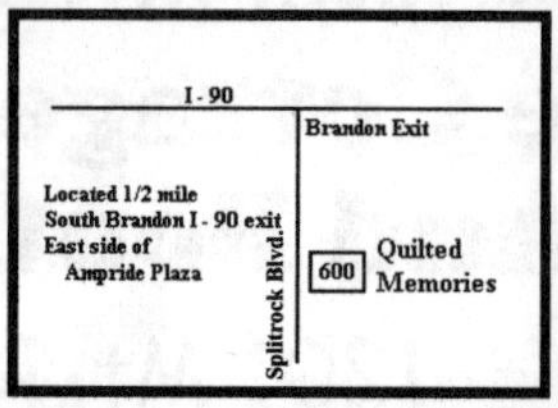

Sioux Falls, SD #9

Heirloom Creations

2131 S. Minnesota Ave., Sioux Falls, SD 57105
605-332-4435 Est: 1989
E-Mail: heirloomcreation@qwest.net
www.sew200.com/heirloom_creations

Sioux Falls' only quilt store, Bernina dealer and embroidery headquarters for all brands of embroidery machines. We stock over 5,000 bolts of cotton fabric and flannels and feature our own exclusive original quilt patterns and quilt kits.

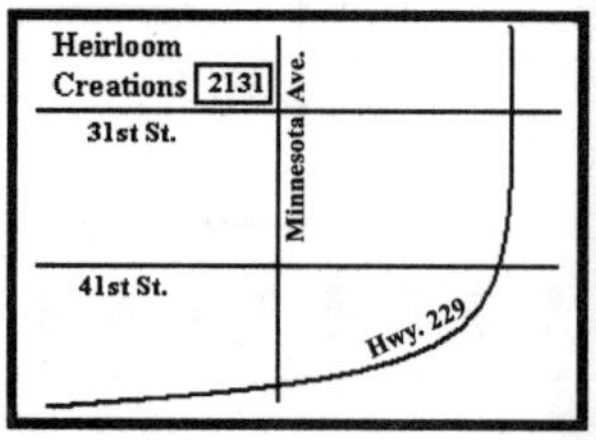

Hours: M-F 9:30-5:30, TH 9:30-8:00, Sat 9:30-4:00

BERNINA

Yankton, SD #9

Four Seasons

909 Broadway #4 57078
(605) 665-3406
Visit Us On-Line at:
www.fourseasonsfabric.com
E-mail: fourseasonsfabric@msn.com
Owners: Misty & Jon Nockels

A great array of cottons, books, patterns, notions and other quilting goodies plus apparel fabrics and super classes!
Authorized Bernina Dealer
Machine Embroidery Supplies

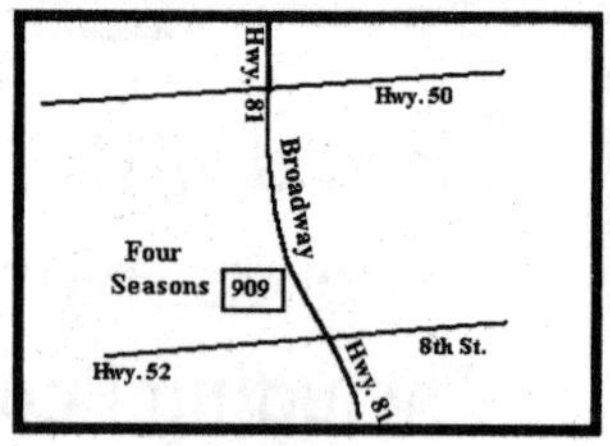

Mon - Fri
10 - 5:30
Thur til 8
Sat 10 - 5

Other Shops in North Dakota: We suggest calling first

Elk Point	Prairie Point Quilters, 412 W. Main St.	605-356-3540
Gregory	Quilt Stitchery, 515 Main St.	605-835-9050
Hartford	Sewing Treasures, 305 Colton Rd.	605-528-7140
Newell	Quilting in the Country, R.R. #1, Box 11	605-456-2822
Pierre	Bears Den Quilts, 3451 Bond Pl.	605-224-4423
Prairie City	Strictly Country, 103 S. Main St.	605-866-4484
Stickney	Needle Nook, Main St.	605-732-4310
Trent	Olive's Mercantile, R.R. #1, Box 31	605-428-4147
Winner	The Sewing B, 225 S. Main St.	605-842-0802

Notes

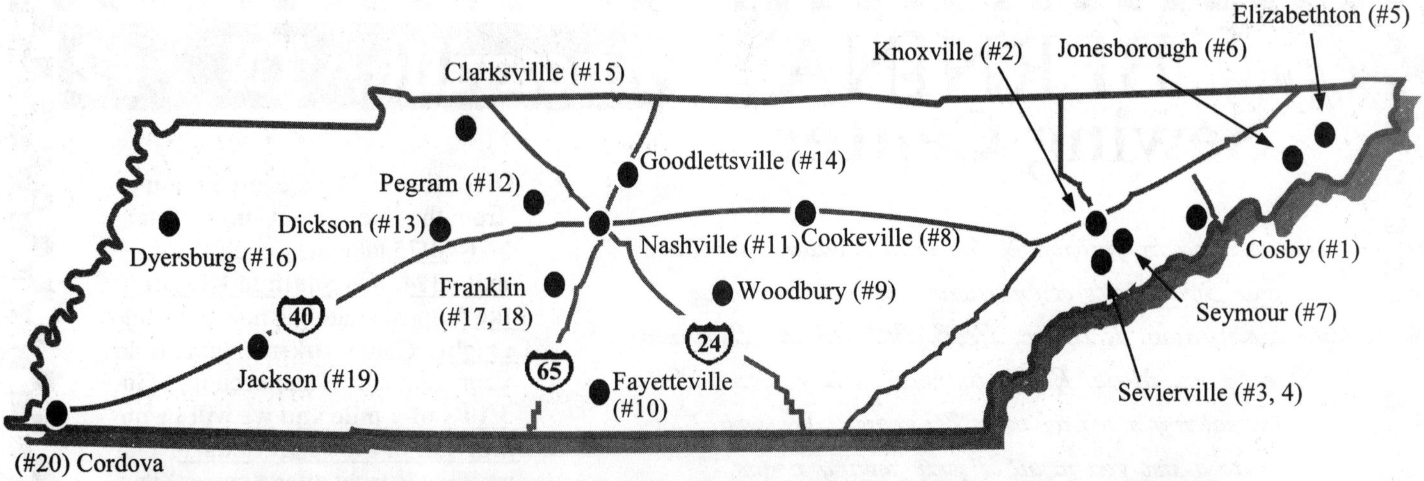

TENNESSEE

20 Featured Shops

Holloway's Country Home

3892 Cosby Highway (Scenic Hwy. 321)
(just 19 miles from Gatlinburg)
(423) 487-3866
e-mail: jamahol@mindSpring.com
Web Site: www.HollowaysQuilts.com
Owners: Maria & John Holloway

Cosby, TN #1

HAND QUILTED WITH AMERICAN PRIDE

Uniquely designed quilts, wall hangings.

THE LARGEST SELECTION OF FINE VINTAGE QUILTS IN THE AREA!

Be sure to visit Our House Next door

- **Fabrics, quilt kits, and supplies**
- **Needlecraft Kits**
- **Quilted Vests and Jackets**
- **Ponchos**

Call or email us about our Quilt Retreats

If you are a collector of American Quilts or other American hand crafts, visit us in our historical log building in the quiet country atmosphere of the small Tennessee community of Cosby.

Send for your autographed copy of Maria Holloway's new book. "WINDOWS OF MY WORLD" Pictures & stories of her favorite quilts plus over 200 recipes for the gourmet. Hard back version $16.95 + $2.00 shipping

Daily 9:00 - 5:00
Closed Sundays

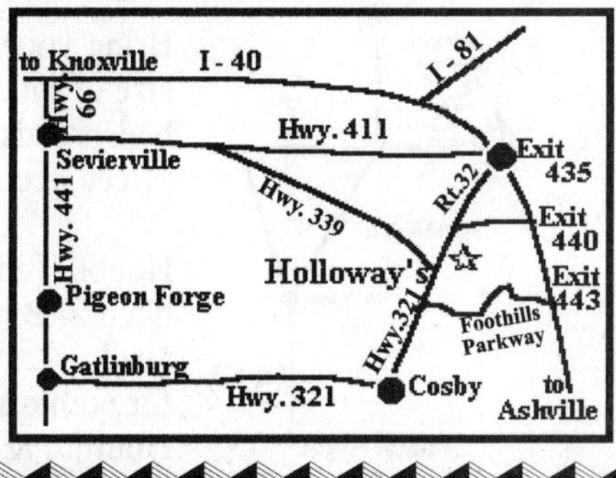

Gina's BERNINA Sewing Center

Knoxville, TN #2

Specializing in quilting & heirloom sewing. We have over 3000 bolts of top quality brands including Robert Kaufman, Hoffman, P&B, Bali, In the Beginning, Free Spirit, Moda, RJR, etc. Gina's has been a full service sewing store for over 20 years. We would love to assist you in all of your sewing needs.

Call for our extensive class schedule.

Gina's is the place for all your Bernina needs.

Directions: We are just 5 minutes from the interstate. Coming from **I-40/75** take the Lovell Road **exit #374**. **Go South to Kingston Pike** (approximately 1 mile) and **take a right**. (Landmark= Walgreens on your right at this intersection). **Go 3/10's of a mile and we will be on your left in Farragut Square**. Our building is right after a nursery that changes names every few months (currently Saplings) So don't count on the name but it hasn't disappeared completely yet!
Follow these directions & you'll make it!

10816 Kingston Pike
Knoxville, TN 37922
(865) 966-5941 or
Toll free 1-877-236-1291

Join us on the web at ginasbernina.com

Store Hours
Monday-Friday 9:30-5:00
Saturday 9:30-4:00

Sevierville, TN #3

MACHINE QUILTIN' BY IVA

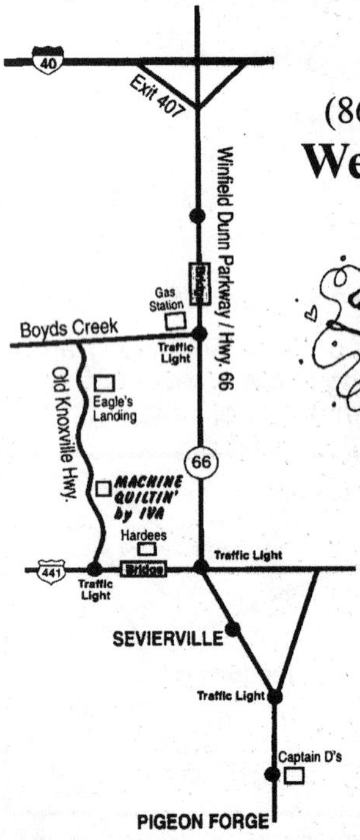

1020 Old Knoxville Hwy. 37862
(865) 428-8008 Fax: (865) 908-8483
Web Site: www.IvasQuilts.com

Mon - Fri
9 - 5:30
Sat 10 - 4:30

CUSTOM QUILTING

Bring your quilt top by for pricing or call with size of top. Quilting also available for bedspreads, comforters and shams. Quilting priced according to size of top.

Hobbs Heirloom, Hobbs Cotton and Warm & Natural Batting in Stock for all your quilting needs. Large assortment of patterns and books for both quilting and clothing. Assortment of Quilting & Sewing Notions.

FABRIC FOR ALL SEWING NEEDS

Debbie Mumm • Peter Pan
Springmaid • K.P. Kids
Northcott • Maywood
Mission Valley • Benartex • P&B
Fabri-Quilt • Cute As A Button
Moda • Jinny Beyer • RJR
Thimble Berries • Alaska Dieworks
Kona Bay • Hoffman • Bali
Large Assortment of Homespuns
Over 3500 Bolts of the Best

SEWING & QUILTING NOTIONS

Threads • Sulky Embroidery/Bobbin/
Sliver Metler Metrosene • Metler Quilting
Pearl Cotton • Thimbles
Hand Sewing/Machine Needles
Buttons • Rotary Cutters
Cutting Mats • Replacement Blades

the
CHERRY PIT
QUILTING SUPPLIES • FABRICS • PATTERNS

115 Bruce Street
IN HISTORIC DOWNTOWN
SEVIERVILLE, TN 37862

www.quiltingatthecherrypit.com
email Tcherrypit@aol.com

+3000 plus bolts of fabric +classes +extensive selection of books and patterns +kits +boms +250 plus models +3600 sq.ft. show rooms.

Owners: Jane & George Washington

Open
Mon - Fri
9:30 - 5:00
Sat
Every 2nd Sat
9:30 - 1:00
Phone
865-453-4062

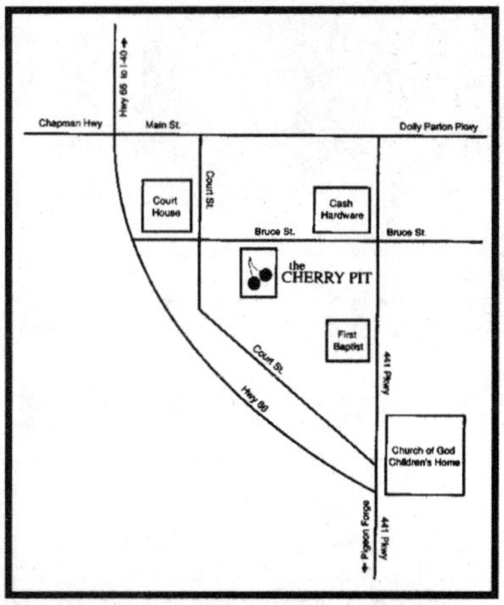

Sevierville, TN #4

Elizabethton, TN #5

Mon - Sat
9:30 - 5:30

Yates Remnant Shop

510 E. Elk Ave. 37643
(423) 542-9251
Owner: Kay Wood
Est: 1962

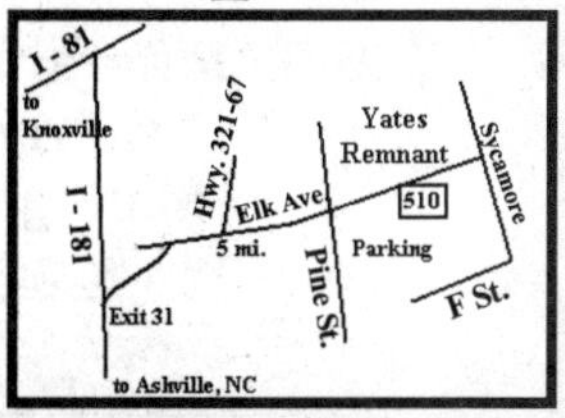

Full Line Fabrics — Quilt — Bridal — Upholstery — Large Assortment Lace Trims. User Friendly — Special Orders.

Sewing Bee

112 E. Jackson Blvd., Hwy. 11-E 37659
(423) 753-7399 Est: 1994

Jonesborough, TN #6

Located in Tennessee's Oldest Town

Tues - Fri 10 - 5
Sat 10 - 3

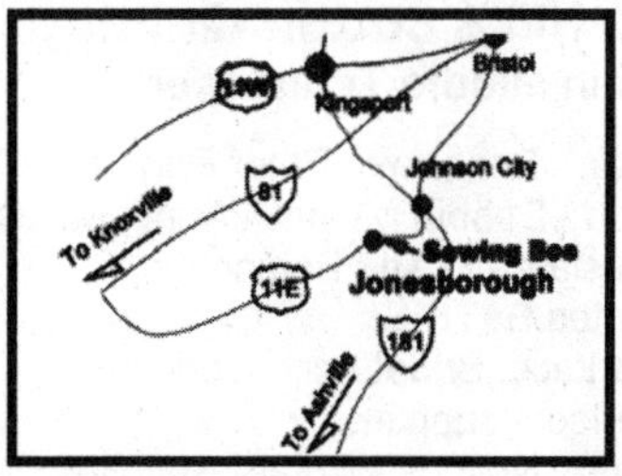

Quilting Fabrics and Notions.
Authorized Pfaff dealer.
Books, patterns & gift items.

Authorized Pfaff Dealer

Seymour, TN #7

Quilts By Wilma

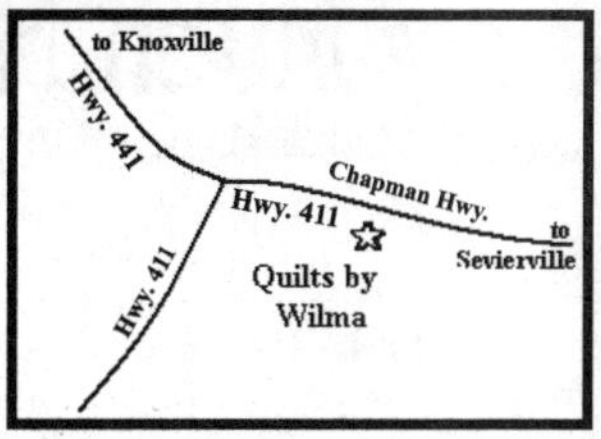

13029 Chapman Hwy. 37865 (865) 453-8555
Owner: Wilma Prebor
Est: 1976 3500 sq.ft.

Daily 9 - 6
Call for
Winter Hours

Hundreds of quilting tools, books, stencils, patterns and designer fabric. Over 300 locally made Quilts.

If You Need It, We've Got It

Glenda's Fabrics & the Quilter

735 S. Jefferson Ave. (931) 528-2734

"A Premier Quilt Shop"

eMail glenda@charter.net

www.glendasfabrics.com

Cookeville, TN #8

9 AM - 5 PM Mon. - Sat

Glenda's is conveniently located 3/4 miles north of I-40 (Exit I-40 at Exit 287—Jefferson Ave.) Glenda's Fabrics is in the Jefferson Square Shopping Plaza next to Life Shoes.

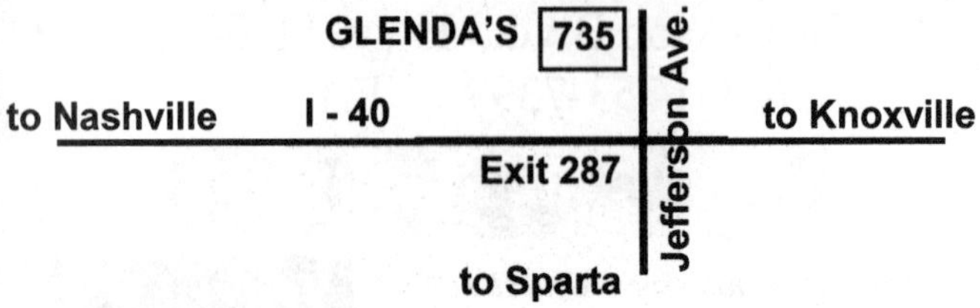

Largest Selection of 100% cotton Quilting Fabrics & Supplies in Middle Tennessee

Featuring: Kaufman - Hoffman - Benartex - Peter Pan - RJR
Timeless Treasures - Maywood - Debbie Mumm - Aunt Gracie
Moda marbles, dots & stars - In The Beginning
Hand Painted BATIKS
Imported Silks, Satins & Lace, Bridal Accessories.
Children heirloom supplies
Books - Templates - Needles - Notions - Rotary Supplies
Quilting frames & Hoops

VISA MasterCard AMERICAN EXPRESS

Woodbury, TN #9

**Mon - Fri 9 - 5
Sat 9 - 2**

Cloth Shop

227 W. Main St. 37190
(615) 563-5201
Owners: Arthur & Margie Petty
1600+ sq.ft. 1000+ Bolts

100% Cotton Fabrics • Quilting Supplies
Batting • Books • Notions • Cluny Lace

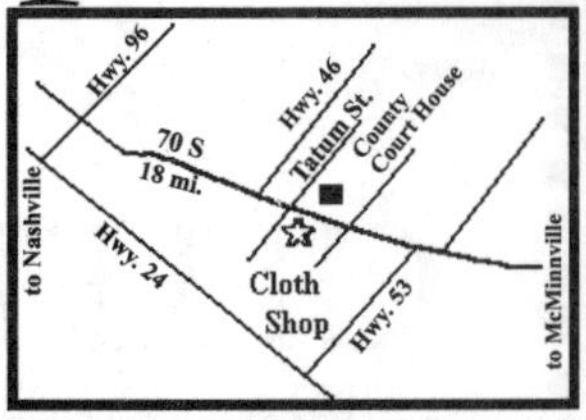

Fayetteville, TN #10

103 East Market St. (On the Square)
Fayetteville, TN 37334
(931) 433-1886
E-Mail: bhook@tnweb.com
Web Site: www.hookedonquilting.com
Owner: Betty C. Hook
Est: 1998 3800 sq.ft. 2500 Bolts

Hooked On Quilting

We cater to quilters and those who love quilts. 100% cottons from well known manufacturers, notions, books and patterns. We machine quilt, sell quilts--new and antique and do custom work for our customers.

**Mon - Sat
10 - 4:30**

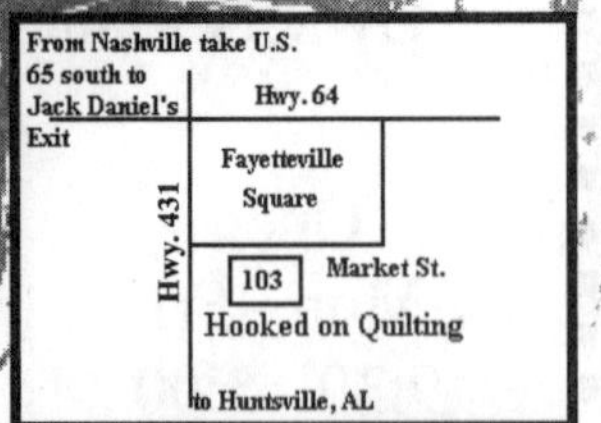

Nashville, TN #11

**Mon - Fri 10 - 4:30
Sat 10 - 3**

Sew Much More
Specialty Quilting Shoppe

195 Thompson Ln. 37211
(615) 332-7970
E-Mail: sewmuchmore@juno.com
Est: 1994 1400 sq.ft. 1200+ Bolts

Friendly, courteous staff. Great selection of fabrics, notions, books, patterns and Janome machines. Classes to fit your schedule all set in a quaint little old house.

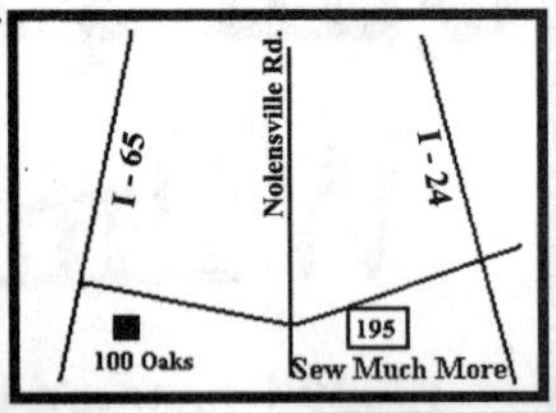

Pegram, TN #12

Mon - Sat 9 - 5

Harpeth Clock & Quilt Co.

462 Hwy. 70 37143
(615) 646-0938 Fax: (615) 646-5702
Web Site: www.harpethclock.com

100% cotton Fabrics, Notions, Books, Patterns, & Battings. Quilts for sale. Quilters on site to help you. Just 20 min. W of Nashville

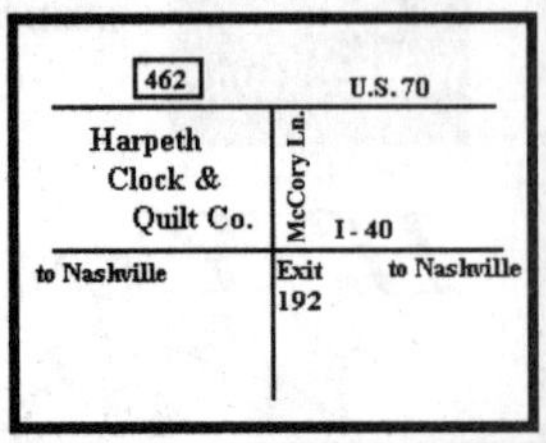

Dickson, TN #13

**Tues - Fri 10 - 5
Thur till 8
Sat 10 - 4**

The Sewing Bug
& Quilt Shoppe

105 B Center Ave. 37055
(615) 740-0078 Fax: (615) 740-0078
E-Mail: sewbusy363@aol.com
Owner: Vickie Dalton
Est: 2001 1200 sq. ft.

Whimsical shop in an old Victorian house. Always fresh coffee, tea. Sitting area for husbands. Also heirloom fabrics & laces.

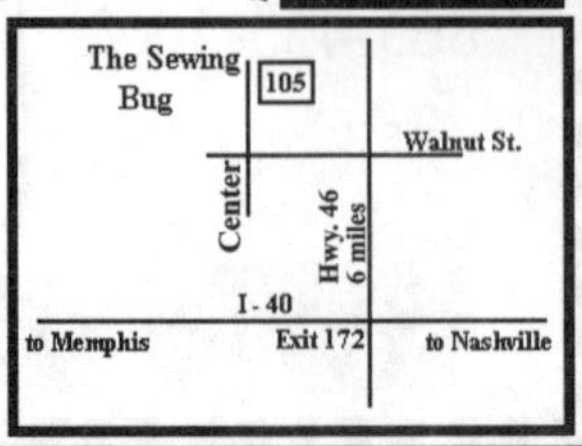

Goodlettsville, TN #14

Quilter's Attic

126 N. Main St. 37072
(14 Miles North of
Downtown Nashville)

(615) 859-5603

Established 1987

Mon - Fri 9 - 4
Thurs til 8 Sat 10 - 4

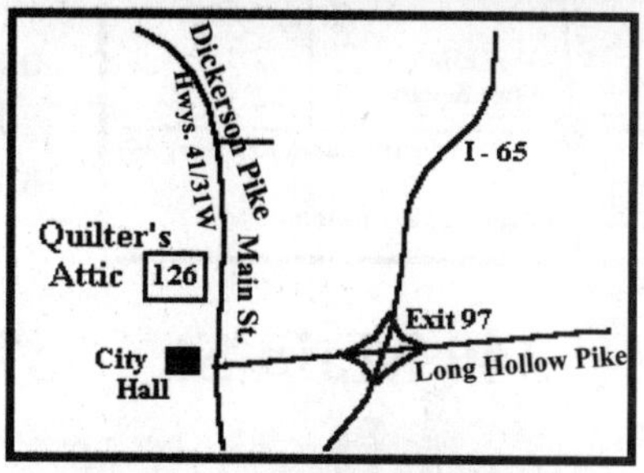

Easy Access From I - 65

One stop shopping for quilters and bear makers...
Classes, fabric, books, patterns and notions...
Set in the midst of an antique community...
4500 sq.ft. Over 3000 Bolts
Owners: Jean Shaw, Connie Stowers & Betsy Ross

Clarksville, TN #15

Country Quilting

1953 Madison St.
37043
(In the Tradewinds
South Shopping Center)
(931) 551-3650
E-Mail: CQuiltn@aol.com
2 Web Sites: www.Clarksville.com
or www.CountryQuilting.com

Mon - Fri
10 - 5
Sat 10 - 4

Smocking & Heirloom
Sewing Fabrics, Notions,
Gifts, Books, Patterns,
Classes, Workshops,
Seminars.
Authorized Bernina Dealer

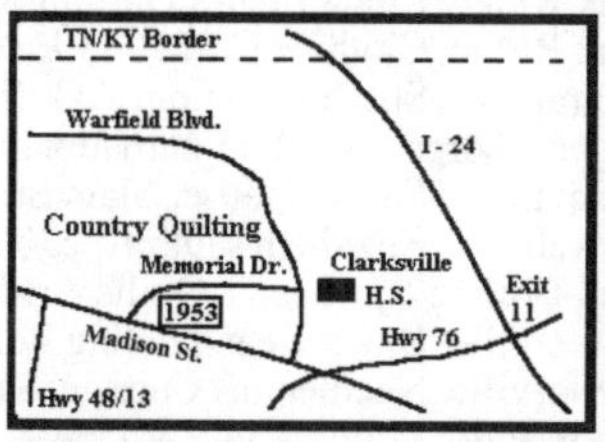

Dyersburg, TN #16

Sew Many Ideas

100 D. Community Park Rd. 38024
(731) 286-4721 Fax: (731) 285-7151
Web Site: www.sewmanyideas.com
Est: 1988 2400 sq.ft.
Owners: Trish & Mark Brown

Mon - Sat 9 - 5 Tues til 8

Gold Standard Bernina Dealer
Full line of Bernina machines
in stock. 100% Cotton Fabrics.
Moda, Thimbleberries, Jinny
Beyer and more!
Quilting notions, patterns,
books & embroidery supplies.

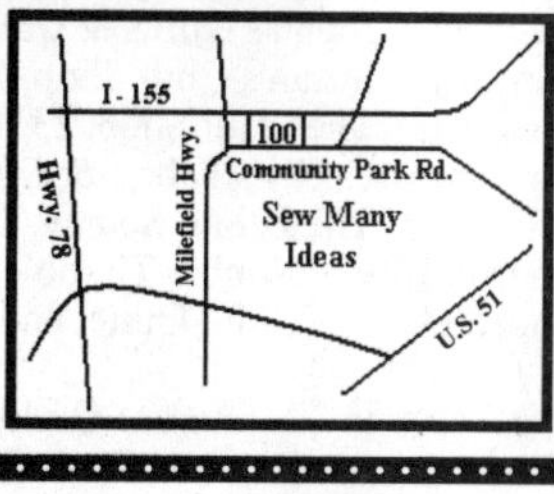

Patchwork Palace

"Antique Salvations"

Largest Selection of Vintage Quilts in the Southern States — 200 to 300 in stock.
Also Vintage Linens & Aprons
We carry a full line of Handcrafts made from Antique Linens & Quilts.

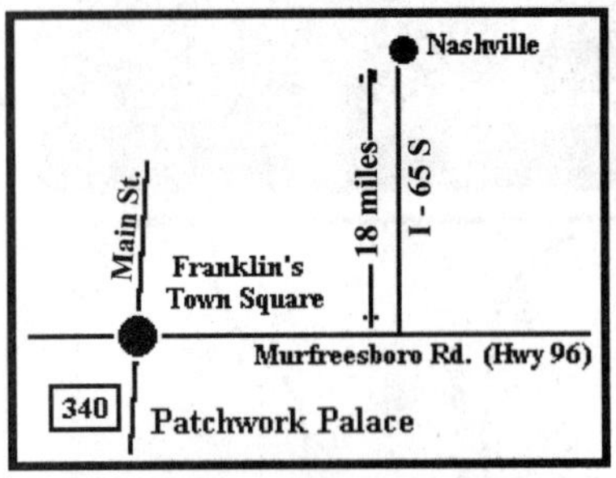

Antiques
Bears - Angels
Pillows - Dolls
Most are one-of-a-kind designed & made by local Artisans

340 Main St. 37064

Franklin, TN #17

(615) 790-1382
Fax:
(615) 790-1106

Collectibles
The Boyd's Collection
Debbee Thibault Folkart
Ganz Cottage Collectibles

Franklin, TN #18

Mon - Sat 9:30 - 5

Stitchers Garden

413 Main St. 37064
(615) 790-0603
E-Mail: myra@stitchersgarden.com
Web Site: www.stitchersgarden.com
Owner: Myra Nickolaus
Est: 1988 3000 sq.ft.

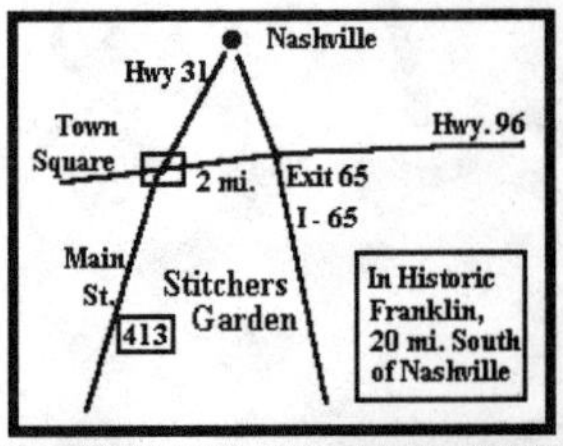

Middle Tennessee's Most Complete Quilting Shop! Over 8000 bolts of all cotton fabrics, complete Jinny Beyer palette, Q-Snap frames, stencils, books, templates, patterns, and classes.

Jackson, TN #19

Mon - Fri 10 - 5:30
Sat 10 - 4

Cherry Lane Quilt Shoppe

24-D Federal Dr. 38305
(731) 661-0666
Fax: (731) 661-9669
E-Mail: cherrylanequilts@aol.com
Web Site: Coming Soon
Owner: Pam Cole Est: 2001 1700 sq.ft.

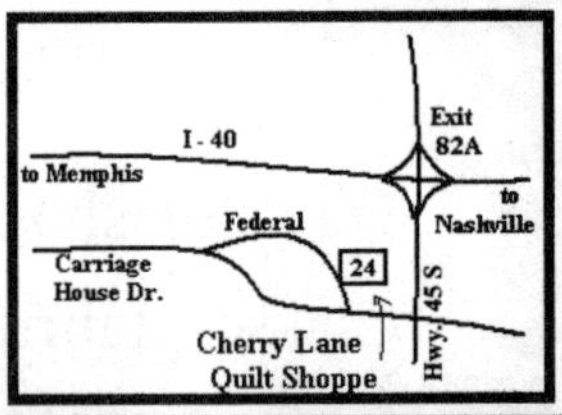

Friendly happy people work and shop here. Cherry Lane isn't a street, it's a destination for all quilt lovers. Right off I - 40!

Cordova, TN #20

Mon - Sat 10 - 6

QuiltSmiths

8553 Macon Rd. #102 38018
(901) 624-9985 Fax: (901) 624-9974
E-Mail: qltsmith@bellsouth.net
Web Site: www.QuiltSmiths.com
Owners: Michael & Rita Smith
Est: 1999 1550 sq.ft. 2500 Bolts

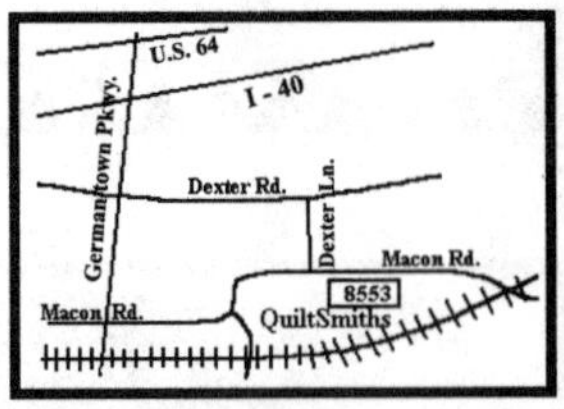

Best lines of fabric. Large selection of batiks, children's prints, 1930's prints, Moda, Hoffman, Kona Bay-all your favorites! Classes, notions, friendly service.

Other Shops in Tennessee: We suggest calling first

Athens	The Cotton Patch Quilt Shop, 154 County Rd. 653	423-745-1914
Bell Buckle	Bingham's, 3 Webb Rd. E	615-389-6908
Benton	The Quilting Shop, 411 Highway N.	423-338-4072
Brentwood	Sew Much More, 7 Brentwood Ct.	615-376-9761
Chattanooga	Ann's Quilt Shop, 3609 Ringgold Rd.	423-698-8000
Cleveland	Lofty Creative Fabrics, 54 Mouse Creek Rd. NW	423-478-5815
Cleveland	The Sewing Connection, 118 Stewart Rd	423-479-8468
Columbia	Miss Ellie's, 390 Bear Creek Pk.	931-381-4028
Columbia	Piececorps, 2514 Sowell Mill Pike	931-381-4769
Cookeville	Parrott's Fabric House, 396 Short St.	931-526-1788
Cookeville	Country Patchworks, 134 S. Willow Ave.	931-526-7276
Corssville	Fairyland Fabrics, 3315 Lantana Rd.	931-788-2453
Decatur	Decatur Quilting, 856 Goodfield Rd.	423-334-2949
Decherd	Country Quilting & Stitchery, 101 Noles St.	931-968-0048
Elizabethtown	Ida's Place, 874 Gap Creek Rd.	423-542-0999
Gatlinburg	Quilts & Such, 918 Pkwy.	865-430-9340
Gatlinburg	Victorian Eye 611 Parkway #C3	865-436-0805
Greenback	Joann's Quilts & Crafts, 1254 Cloyds Church	423-856-6246
Grimsley	Susan's Quilt Shop, 5300 S. York Hwy.	931-863-3446
Harriman	The Quilt Shop, 2310 S. Roane St.	423-882-9700
Harrogate	Cosby's Fabric & Crafts, 662 Patterson Rd.	423-869-5599
Jackson	The Fabric Source, 1090 U.S. Hwy. 45 Bypass	901-668-1877
Johnson City	Nimble Thimble, 2230 N. Roan St.	423-282-1075
Johnson City	CMQ Outlet and Sewing Center, 1600 E. Jackson St.	423-753-9220
Jonesborough	Tennessee Quilts, 123 E. Main St.	423-753-6644
Kingsport	Ramblin Rose, 216 Colonial Heights Rd.	423-239-7408
Knoxville	Grainery, 12010 Prater Ln.	865-675-5153
Maryville	Family Tree Antiques, 1065 Regent Circle	423-984-2166
Maryville	Dorothy's, 433 Lee Lambert Rd.	423-983-4969
McMinnville	B & B Fabrics & Quilting, 303 Red Rd.	931-473-7469
McMinnville	B & J Quilt Shop, 1202 Sparta St.	931-473-8141
Memphis	Cloth Connections, 3724 Summer Ave.	901-458-7129
Memphis	Stitches Inc., 5498 Poplar Ave.	901-681-9276
Monterey	Reba's Flower Shop, 104 E. Commercial Ave.	931-839-2113
Murfreesboro	Quilt Connection, 1009 Memorial Blvd.	615-867-0210
Murfreesboro	AAA Silver Threads, 1447 Kensington Dr.	615-890-7551
Nashville	B Quilted, 2435 Cabin Hill Rd.	615-883-5143
Nashville	Children's Corner, 3814 Cleghorn Ave.	615-292-1746
Nashville	Rostitchery, 500 5th Ave. N #910	615-226-8797
Nashville	Fine Antique Quilts, 401 Hunt Club Rd.	615-373-4759
Norris	Museum of Appalachia, P.O. Box 359	423-494-7680
Oak Ridge	The Quilting Corner, 37 E. Tennessee Ave.	423-483-7778
Oak Ridge	Linda Evan's Quilting Loft, 119 E. Irving Ln.	423-220-9096
Oak Ridge	Cloth 'N Craft, 333 E. Main St. #508	865-425-0486
Pegram	Stitchin Station, P.O. Box 212	615-797-9477
Pigeon Forge	Quilts International, 2662 Teaster Ln.	423-429-2772
Pikeville	Fabric House, Main St. PO Box 607	423-447-6195
Powell	Elizabeth's Quilts, 2302 Bull Run Valley Rd.	865-947-5766
Red Boiling Springs	Quilts & More, 3606 Carthage Rd.	615-699-3776
Sevierville	Black Bear Trading Post, 832 Parkway	423-428-5649
Sevierville	Needlecraft Cottage, 3103 Laurelwood Way	423-428-7044
Sevierville	Edith's Cloth & Crafts, 2267 Shinbone Rd.	
Smithville	Becky's Fabrics & More, 105 W. Main St.	615-597-8521
Sparta	Aunt Bonnie's Quilts, 138 Scott Town Rd.	931-738-4750
Sparta	Peggy's Sew-Shop, 16 E. Bockman Way	931-836-2888
Union City	Stitchin Post, 611 S. 1st St.	901-885-1800

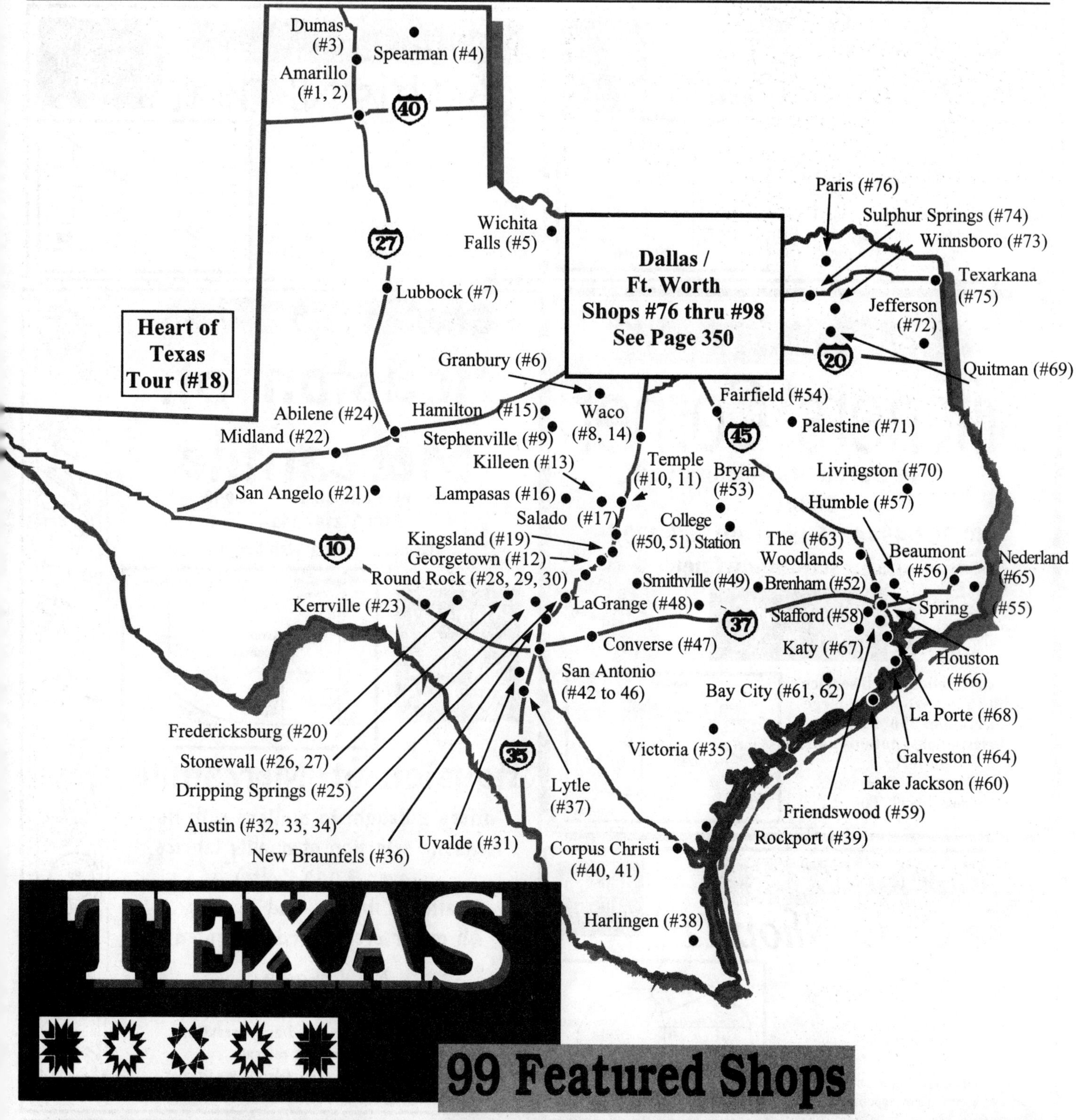

TEXAS

99 Featured Shops

Amarillo, TX #1

Mon - Sat 10 - 5

Old 66 Quilts & More

3614 W. 6th Ave. 79106
(806) 373-7777
E-Mail: aliceama@arn.net
Web Site: www.old66quilts.com
Owner: Alice Grant
Est: 1996 7500 sq.ft. 2000 Bolts

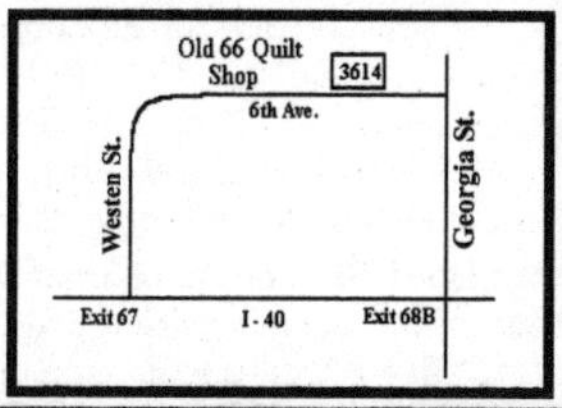

Quilt Shop located on Historic Route 66. Quilting supplies, fabric, notions, books and long arm quilting supplies. Route 66 Fabric.

Amarillo, TX #2

Mon - Sat 9:30 - 5:30

Get the Red Carpet Treatment at

R & R Quilts and More

4332 Teckla Blvd. 79109-5422
(806) 359-6235
Owner: Millie Riggs
E-Mail: rrquilts@amaonline.com
Web Site: www.rrquilts.com

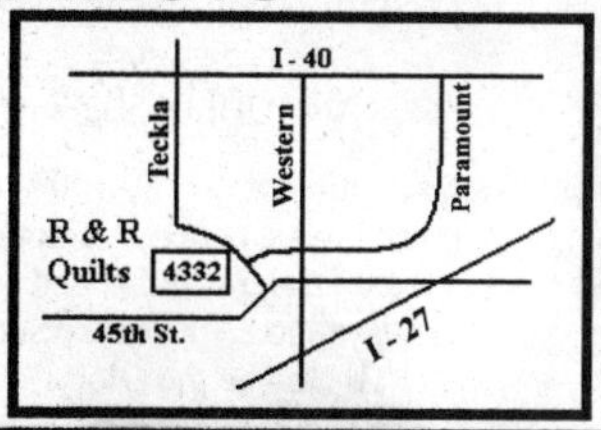

Over 4500 Bolts of 100% cotton fabrics. Classes, Supplies, Books and Patterns.

Dumas, TX #3

Mon - Fri 10 - 6
Sat 10 - 4

Down Home Quilts

102 E. 7th, Suite A 79029
(806) 934-4041 Fax: (806) 934-4042
E-Mail: downhomequilts@nts-online.net
Onwers: Carol Gillingham & Helen King
Est: 2001 1800 sq.ft. 1100 Bolts

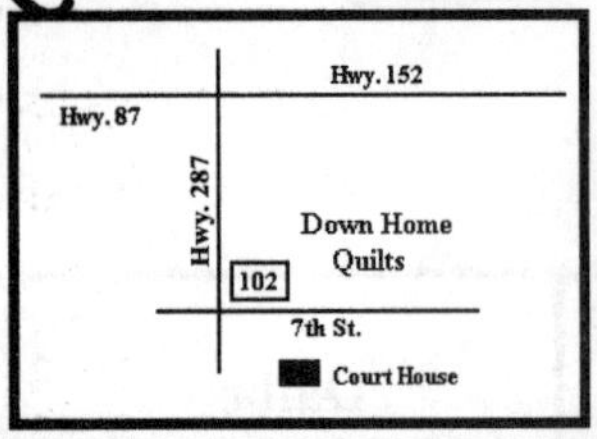

Quilt kits for those on the go. Fabric, batting & notions for those planning their own. And Custom Quilting to help you finish your project.

Spearman, TX #4

Mon - Fri 9:30 - 5:30
Sat 9:30 - 5

Jo's This N' That

214 Main 79081
(806) 659-3999
Owner: Joan Farr

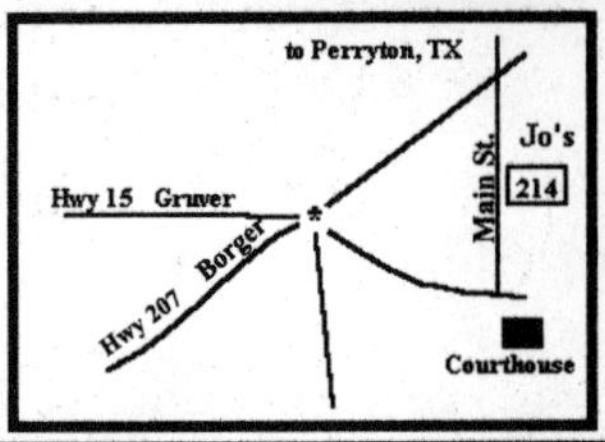

We are a Traditional Quilt Shop.
Also machine Quilting & Monogramming.

Wichita Falls, TX #5

Stitchers' Corner

900 Van Buren St., Wichita Falls 76301

940-767-4944 Fax: (940) 767-4706

E-mail: scquilt@wf.net

Tues - Fri 10 - 5
Sat 10 - 3

"Texas friendly" full service quilt shop. We have a large selection of 100% cotton fabrics, books, notions and patterns.
PFAFF sales & service.
Cross Stitch Too!

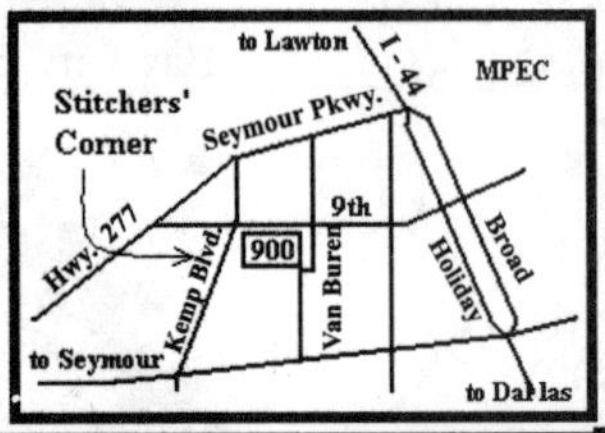

Granbury, TX #6

Houston St. Mercantile

126 N. Houston St. 76048
(817) 279-0425
Owner: Glenda Westbrook

Mon - Fri 10 - 5
Sat 10 - 6
Sun 12 - 5

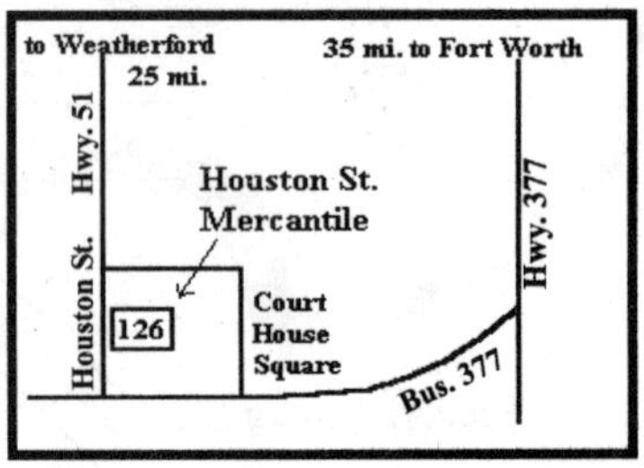

Houston St. Mercantile
offers a delight to quilters with its fantastic selection of quality fabrics, (over 3,000 Bolts) patterns, books, and classes.
All major credit cards accepted.

Also of interest is
The Quilt Inn of Granbury,
a quaint and historic Bed and Breakfast especially for quilt retreats.
For information call owner, Glenda Westbrook
817-279-0425, email-houstonstmerc@itexas.net

Lubbock, TX #7

Mon - Sat 10 - 5

The Quilt Shop II

4525 50th St. 79414
(In the Sunshine Sq. Shopping Center)
(806) 793-2485
Owner: Lunann Burke
Est 1979

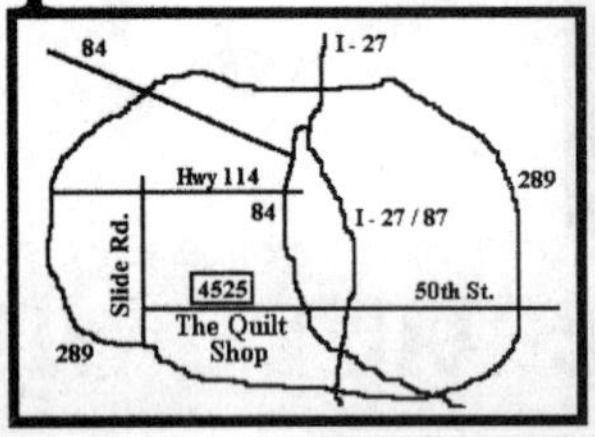

We have 1500 bolts of cotton, books, supplies & classes. Appraisals by appointment.

Waco, TX #8

Mon - Fri 10 - 5:30
Sat 10 - 4

Nancy's Quilt Block

1412 N. Valley Mills Dr. #220 76710
(254) 776-4989
E-Mail: NANQUBLOCK@prodigy.net

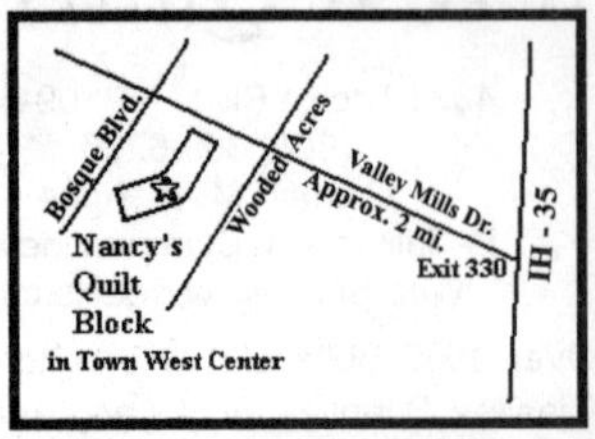

Good selection of quality 100% cotton fabrics, books, patterns & notions.
Authorized Dealer of Pfaff and Viking.
Classes available. Friendly Service.
"To God be the Glory."

Stephenville, TX #9

Mon - Sat 9 - 6

The Flying Needle

1495 W. South Loop
76401 Est: 1971
(254) 965-7577 or (877) FNEEDLE
E-mail: Theflyingneeedle@ht.comp
Web Site: www.Theflyingneedle.net

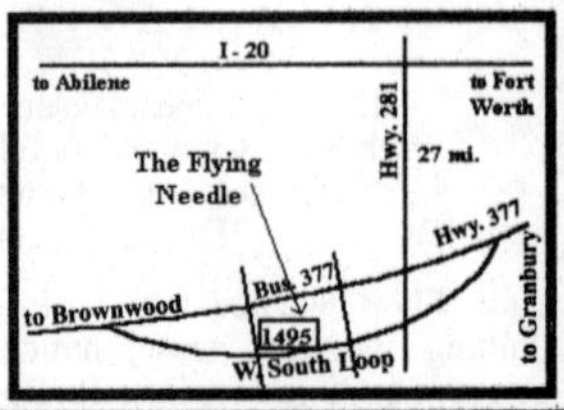

2300+ Bolts of Cotton from Dozens of Manufacturers, Notions New and Old, Hundreds of Books, Patterns and Supplies.

#10

A Stitch in Time

In the historic Governor Ferguson Home
518 North 7th & French, Temple, Texas
Owner: Karen Summers
Licensed Pullen/Viking Instructor
Phone 1-254-774-9990 • e-mail: astitchintime@sbcglobal.net

We offer creative inspiration and:

- Moda
- Timeless Treasures
- Hoffman
- E.E.Schenck/Maywood
- Jinny Beyer
- Maggie Walker Designs
- Thimbleberries
- Kaffe Fassett Fabrics
- Felts & Homespuns

Come recharge your creative batteries in Central Texas newest full line Quilt Shop. Explore a restored former Texas Governor's home, see the latest fabrics and patterns, find unique jewelry, browse among beautifully restored antiques, learn a new skill, or just relax with a cup of coffee.

From the North take Exit 303 (N. 3rd Street), follow 3rd Steet 1.9 miles to French, then 2 blocks right on French.

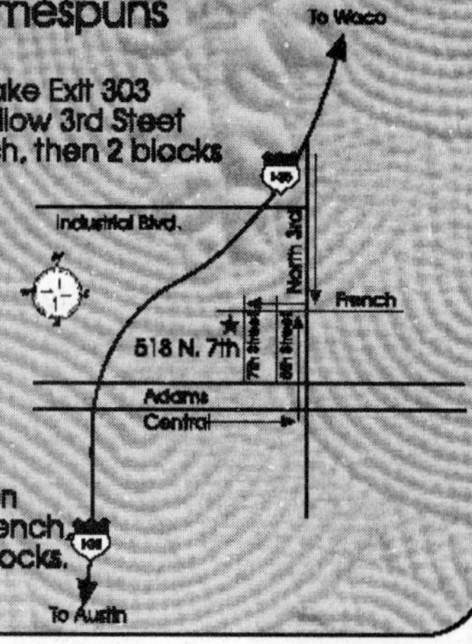

From the South take Exit 301, (Central Ave.) .9 mile to 3rd, then left 6 blocks to French, and then left 2 blocks.

You will also find everything for Heirloom Sewing:

- silks
- handkerchief linen
- nelona
- lace
- heirloom cotton
- lace insertion

The Sewing Machine & Quilt Stores

Mon - Fri 10 - 6
Sat 10 - 5
Or Call, We'll be happy to stay late.

Quilting & Sewing Machine Classes.
Notions & Books & Patterns
Authorized Dealer for Bernina, Janome & Brother Machines
20 years experience in repairing all brands.
Help in choosing a commercial quilting machine.
Kid's Camp: Kids come and learn to sew!

Waco, TX #14

5900 Bosque 76710
(254) 772-2887

Temple, TX #11

1719 W. Ave "M" 76504
(254) 774-9797 or
(800) 506-9797

Killeen, TX #13

1002 E. Elms #113 76542
(254) 616-2200

Georgetown, TX #12

3010 Williams Dr. 78628
(512) 863-9201

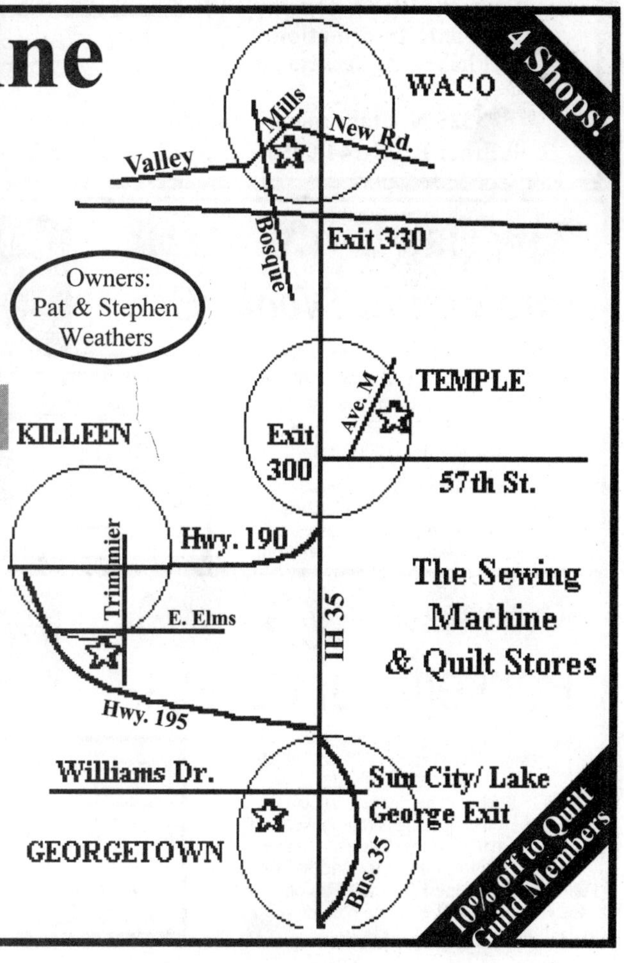

Hamilton, TX #15

Tues - Fri 9 - 5
Sat 9 - 3

One More Stitch

210 E. Pierson St. 76531
(254) 386-8874
E-Mail:
onemorestitch@htcomp.net
Est: 2001 1700 sq.ft.

Quilt Fabric - Batting - Notions - Classes
A unique shop in an Old Meat Processing Plant.

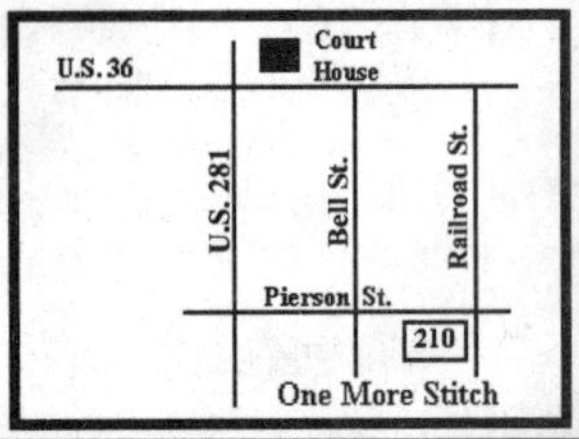

Lampasas, TX #16

Tues - Sat 10 - 4

M.J.'s Fabrics, Fashions, and Quilts

410 E. 3rd St. 76550
(512) 556-8879
Est: 1989 3000 sq.ft.

Top of the line fabrics.
Unique Patterns. Friendly Clerks.
Info on places of interest in the area.
Knitting and Needlepoint Supplies.

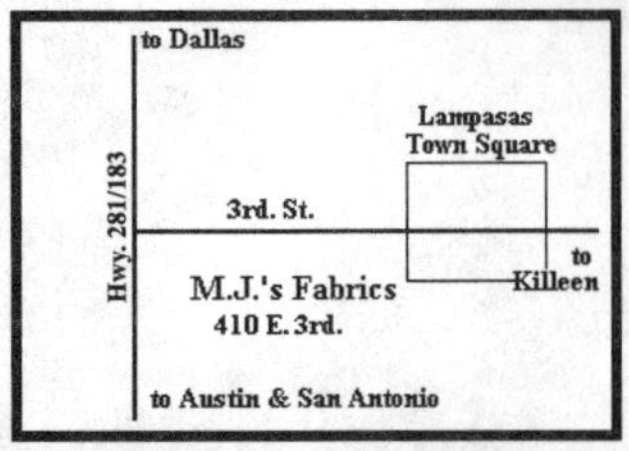

Salado, TX #17

The Sewing Basket

Mon-Fri
10 to 5
Sat 10 to 5:30
Closed Sundays

100% Cotton Fabrics - ideal for quilting
Books and Patterns
Quilting Tools & Sewing Notions
Mettler and YLI Thread
Classes - Classes - Classes
Pfaff Sewing Machines

End-of-the-Bolt Sale
On the first Thursday, Friday, and Sat of the month, buy what's left on the bolt - ANY BOLT - and take 30% off !

Fabric Card
Purchase $200 in merchandise and get $20 fabric free !!

Visit our Web Site for up-to-date Information
www.TheSewingBasket.com

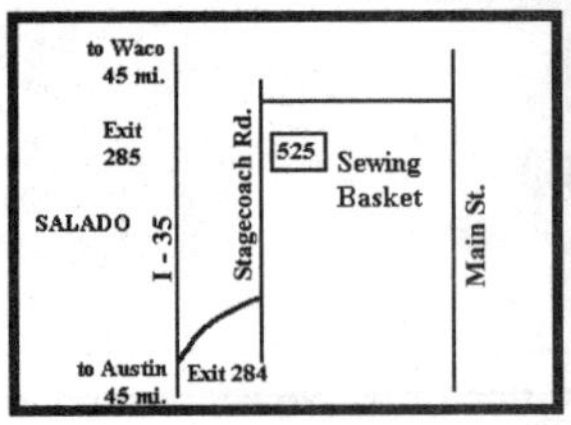

Off I-35, between exit 284 & 285

525 N. Stagecoach Salado, TX 76571
Toll Free: 1-877-244-0450 254-947-5423 Est: 1998

Central Texas Tour #18

Heart of Texas Shop Hop

Over 20 stores thru the Heart of Texas
Jan 5 - Feb 8

For more information call:
254-774-9797

E-Mail:
hot45shophop@msn.com

Kingsland, TX #19

Mon - Fri 9 - 5
Thur 9 - 6
Sat 9 - 4

Barb's Quilt Nook, Etc.

120 Dan St. P.O. Box 868 78639
(915) 388-5225 Fax: (915) 388-3999
E-Mail: barbsew@moment.net
Owners: Barbara & Jon Selby
Est: 2001 1000 sq.ft.

All Your Quilting Needs!
100% Cotton Fabrics - Books 20% off
Patterns - Notions - Classes
Come, We would Love to Meet You!

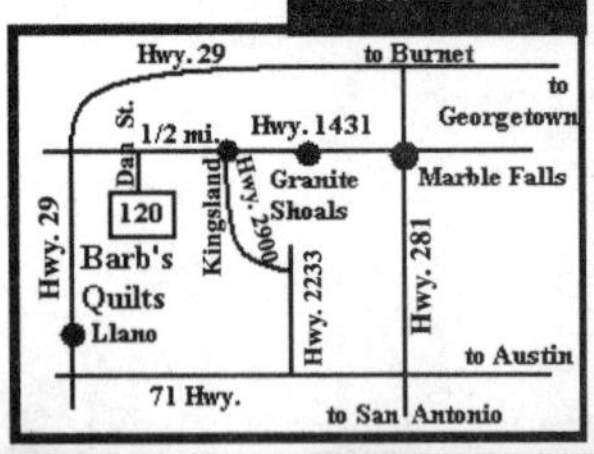

Fredericksburg, TX #20

Mon - Sat 10 - 5:30

Pocketful of Poseys

311 East Highway St. 78624
(830) 990-4140 or (877) 427-6739
Fax: (830) 990-8221
E-Mail: Claurent@KTC.com
Web Site: www.geocities.com/pocketfulofposeys
Owner: Cynthia Laurent-Conner
Est: 1999 3600 sq.ft. 1500+ Bolts
Full line of Quilting Fabrics & Notions, Books & Patterns, Threads & Buttons plus more. Located in the hill country.

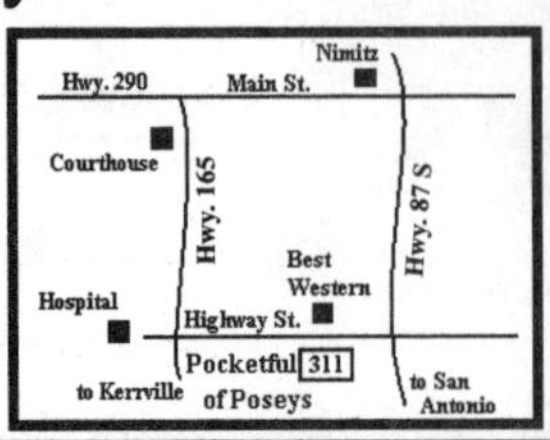

The Quilt Connection

Come visit the friendliest quilt shop in West Texas! We offer a large selection of 100% cotton fabrics from all of your favorite brands, as well as books, patterns and notions. We are a full service Gold Standard Bernina sewing machine dealer.

Fax: (915) 942-6768
quiltconnection@aol.com
Janet Moran & Angie Stripe
Est: 1997 2500 sq.ft.

Mon - Fri 10 - 5
Sat 9 - 4

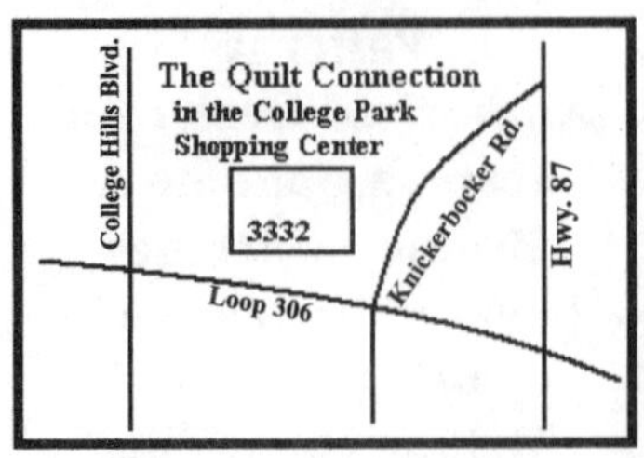

3332 W. Loop 306, San Angelo, TX 76904
(915) 223-8334

San Angelo, TX #21

Needle Nook

Midland, TX #22

3211 W. Wadley 79705
#16B Imperial Shopping Ctr.
(915) 694-9331
(800) 843-6962
Fax: (915) 694-1682
Owner: Suzanne Garman
Est: 1975 3000 sq.ft. 2500 Bolts

Mon - Fri
10 - 5:30
Sat 10 - 4

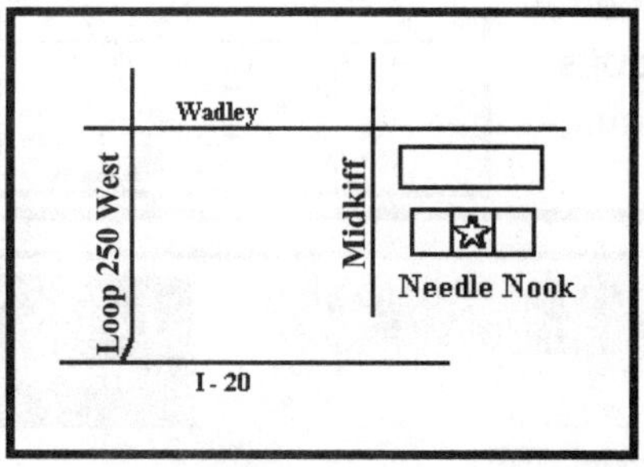

Everything a Quilter Needs

Wonderful fabric selection, Quilting Books & Patterns,
Wearable Art, Full line of Sulky & Mettler Threads,
Machine & Hand Quilting Classes, Stencils, Silk Ribbon,
Quilting Notions & Custom Machine Quilting

Creations

Great Stuff for the Quilter and Sewing Enthusiast

Kerrville, TX #23

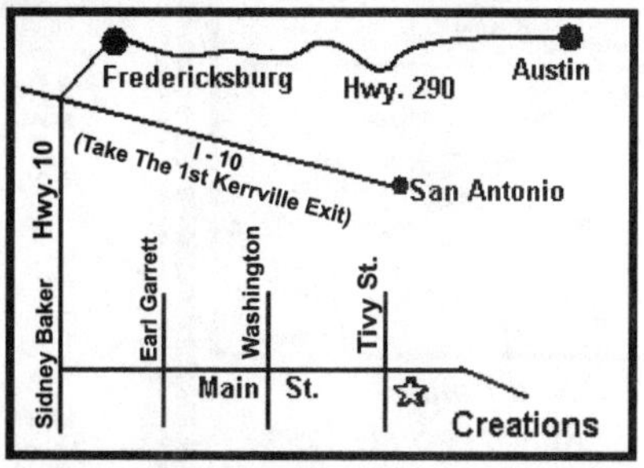

CREATIONS
1013 E. MAIN
KERRVILLE
830-896-8088
Est: 1978

COTTONS, WASHABLE LINEN & BALI RAYONS
BROTHER EMBROIDERY MACHINES
SERVING COFFEE AND FROZEN CAPPUCCINO
GIFTS AND ACCESSORIES *HORN CABINETS* *E-SHOPPING*
ELNA SEWING MACHINES & SERGERS
FEATURED IN '96 EDITION OF QUILT SAMPLER

MON.--SAT. 9:30--5:30
SUNDAY 12:30--4:00

www.creations-online.com
e-mail: creation@hilconet.com

Abilene, TX #24

Mon - Fri 9:30 - 5:30
Sat 9:30 - 5

Patchwork Garden Quilt Shop

3161 S. 23rd, Suite 9 79606
(915) 698-5544 Fax: (915) 698-6468
E-Mail: edjd@bitstreet.com
Owner: Jeanne Davis Est: 2002

We offer a selection of fabrics including Moda, Hoffman, Maywood, RJR, and Benartex: as well as a wide selection of books, notions, and patterns including the original needlework designs of the owner DBA PidderPatterns.

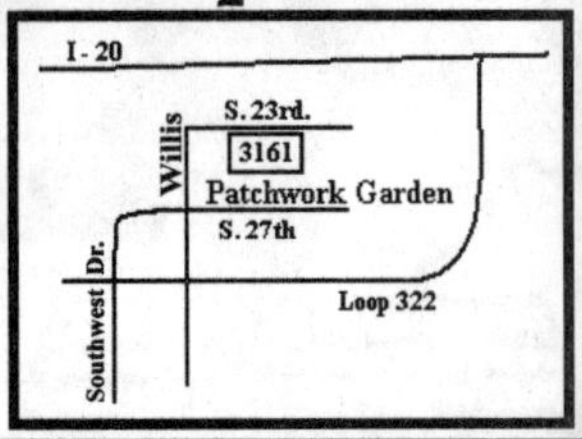

Dripping Springs, TX #25

Peacemakers

301 Mercer St., P.O. Box 1023
Dripping Springs, TX 78620
(512) 858-0272
PeacemakersNewsFlash@msn.com
Owners: G.B. & Jote Khalsa
Est: 1996 1500+ Bolts

Mon - Sat 10:30 - 5

Peacemakers is the Texas Hill Country's best source for beautiful 100% cotton quilting fabrics, books, Pfaff Sewing Machines

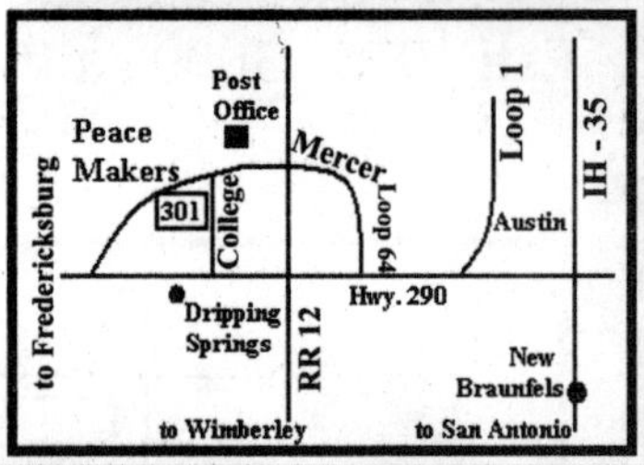

Stonewall, TX #26

Tues - Sat 10 - 4:30

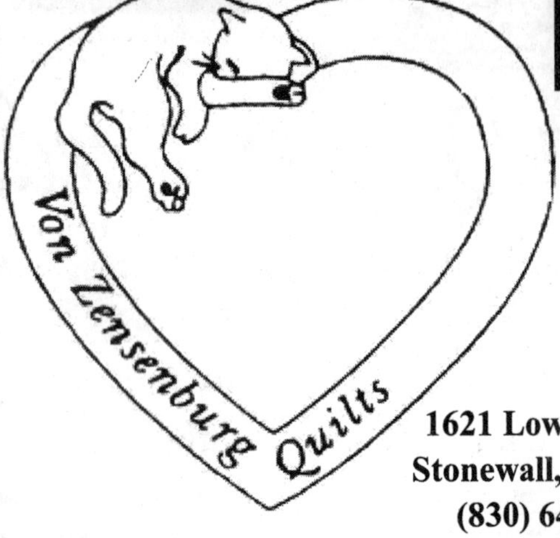

1621 Lower Albert
Stonewall, TX 78671
(830) 644-2554
Fax: (830) 644-2894

Website: www.VonZensenburgQuilts.com
E-Mail: Lzensen@ktc.com
Owners: Lorraine Zensen & Jim Fridley
Est: 1999 2000 sq.ft. 1500 Bolts

Full Line of Fabric, Notions, Books & Patterns. Classes. Quilters' B&B above Quilt Shop

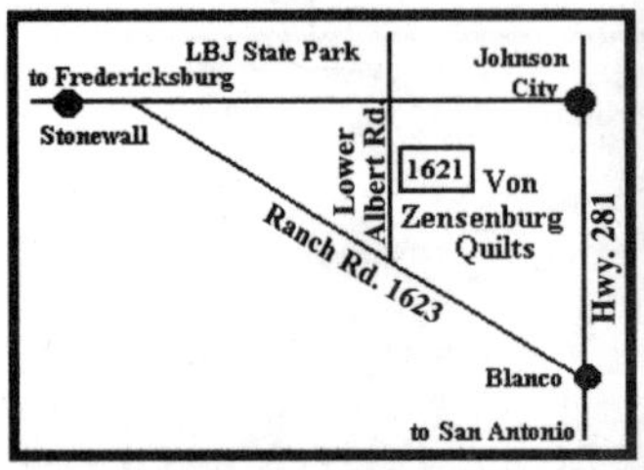

Located 1 mile east of LBJ Ranch & State Park

Stonewall, TX #27

Quilters' B & B

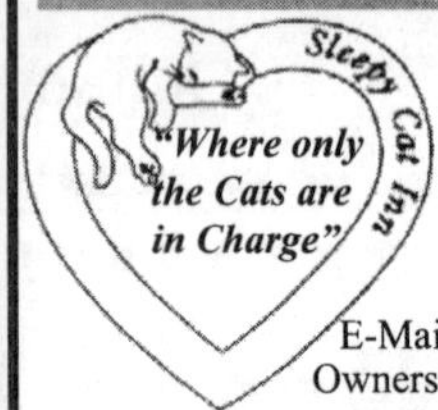

1621 Lower Albert Rd. 78671
(830) 644-2554
Fax:
(830) 644-2894
E-Mail: zensen@ktc.com
Owners: Lorraine Zensen & Jim Fridley
Web Site: www.SleepyCatInnTexas.com
Quilters' Bed & Breakfast above Von Zensenburg Quilts

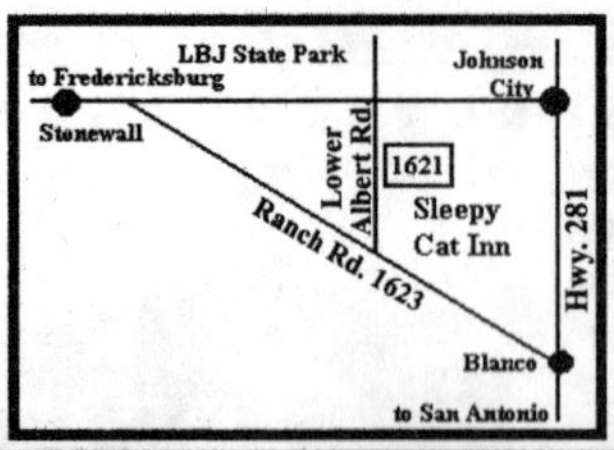

Roundrock, TX #28

Mon - Fri 9 - 6
Sat 9 - 5

Austin Sewing Machines

2000 S. IH 35, Suite C-1 78681
(512) 310-7349
Fax: (512) 310-7465
E-Mail: oldbob@texas.net
Web Site: austinsewing.com
Est: 1953 2800 sq.ft.

Over 2,000 Bolts of Current Fabrics. Husqvarna Viking & PFAFF Sewing Machines, also Janome Sales & Service -- also vacuums

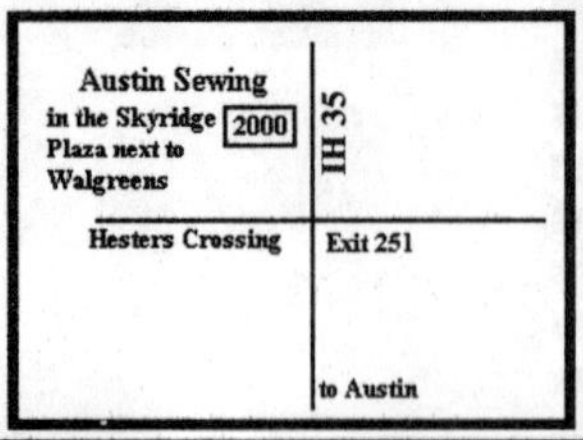

Round Rock, TX #29

Evenings & Weekends By Appointment

Kim's Quilts

1501 Lawnmont #414 78664
(512) 248-8858
E-Mail: kim@kims-quilts.com
Web Site: www.kims-quilts.com
Owner: Kim Jones Est: 1998

Custom quilt studio. Excellent quality, affordable prices. Hand-tied * 100% cotton fabric * hypo-allergenic batting. See quilts, books, fabric & crafts in stock on my website.

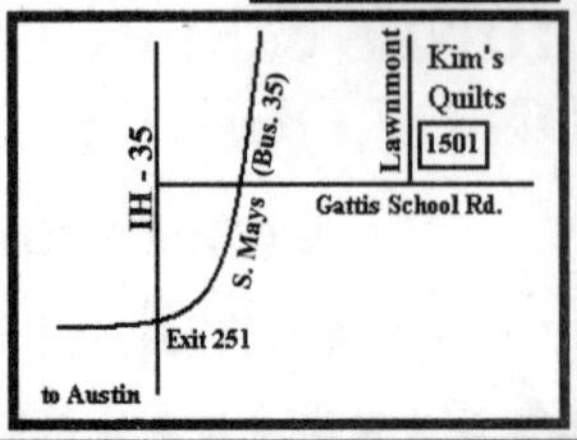

Round Rock, TX #30

Tues - Sat 10 - 5

Mini Stitches

208 W. Bagdad Ave. #7 78664
Corner of Brown & Bagdad
(512) 255-8545
Owner: Carol Kussmaul Est: 1994

Fulfill your creative destiny with our select fabrics, patterns, classes, and personalized assistance. Silk Ribbon also available.

Uvalde, TX #31

Tues & Fri 10 - 4

Wren's Nest

800 S. Getty St. 78801
(830) 279-0330 Fax: (830) 278-7530
E-Mail: wrennest@the-i.net
Owner: Wren Leinweber
Est: 2001 900 sq.ft.

Small Shop with big Heart.
Fabrics, Books, Cross Stitch, Cotton Threads, and Notions.

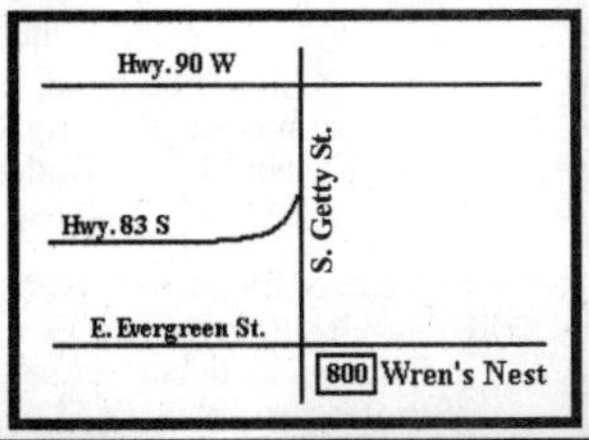

Austin, TX #32

Mon - Fri 10 - 6 Tues til 8 Sat 10 - 5

Honey Bee QUILT STORE

10401 Anderson Mill Rd. #107
78750
(512) 257-1269
www.honeybee quiltstore.com
Owners: Dianne Ferguson, Maryann Westerberg & Carolyn Thompson

Honey Bee Quilt Store is a new quilt store located in far northwest Austin. We opened with 1,200 bolts and are adding to our inventory all the time.

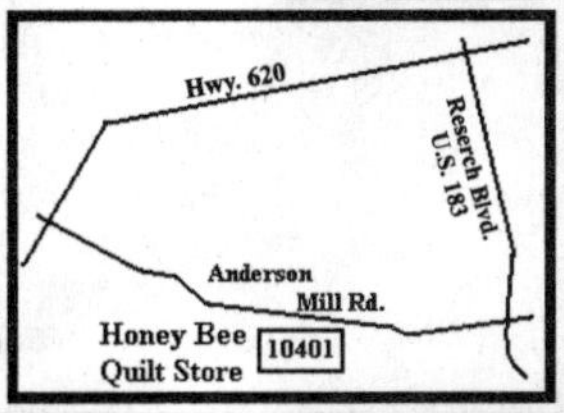

Austin, TX #33

Mon - Sat 10 - 5 Thur til 8

The Quilt Store, Inc.

2700 W. Anderson, #301 78757
(512) 453-1145
www.quiltstore.com

More than 5,000 bolts of 100% fabric plus much more.

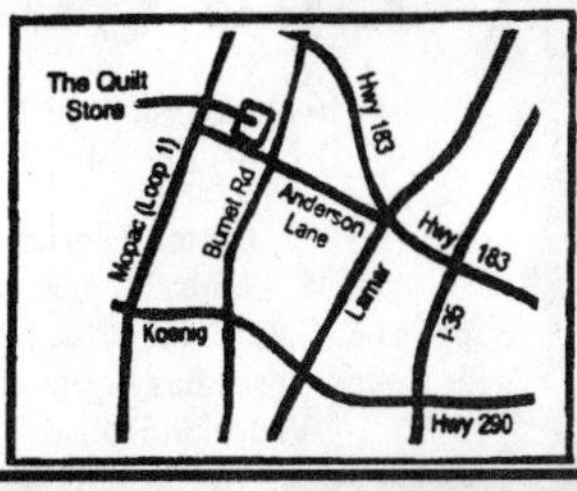

Austin, TX #34

Mon - Sat 9 - 6

Ginger's Needlearts & Framing

5322 Cameron Rd. 78723
(512) 454-5344
or (800) 982-8444

Fax: (512) 454-1489
Est: 1985 4000 sq.ft. 2000+ Bolts
Since our buying philosophy is, "When in doubt, buy it all.", our shop is packed with cross stitch and quilting.

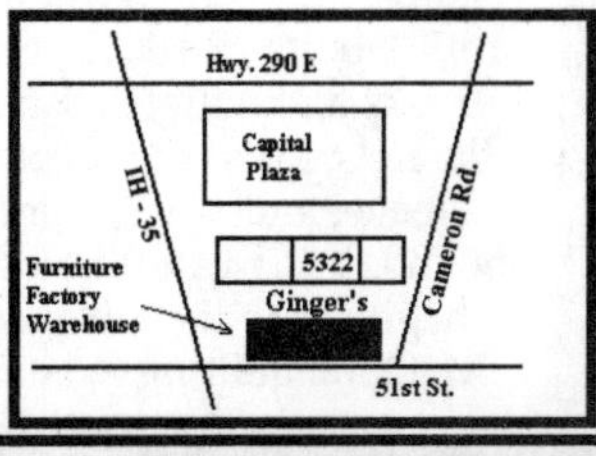

Victoria, TX #35

Mon - Fri 10 - 5 Sat 10 - 2

Quilters Patch

205 North Star, Suite Q 77904
(361) 578-0380 or (866) 578-0380
E-Mail: qpatch@tisd.net
Web Site: www.quilterspatch.com
Owners: Karen Leach & Sherry Ware
Est: 1995 2000 sq.ft. 4000 Bolts

Bolts of Cotton Fabric, Hoffman, Moda, RJR, Aunt Graces, Kaufman, Hi-Fashion, Batiks, P&B, & Kona Bay. Located off Hwy. 77

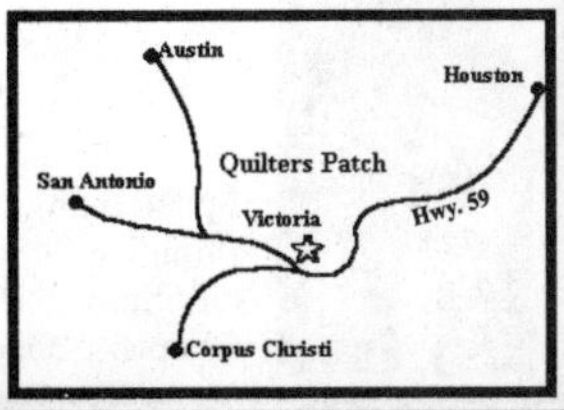

Millstream Cottons

Large selection of top name 100% cotton fabrics. Quilting supplies, books, patterns, notions, kits & classes.

471-A Main Plaza 78130
(830) 620-1382 Fax: (830) 620-1387
E-Mail: millstream@compuvision.net
Owner: Sally Shimek
Est: 1997 2000 sq.ft.

Mon - Fri 9:30 - 5 Sat 10 - 4

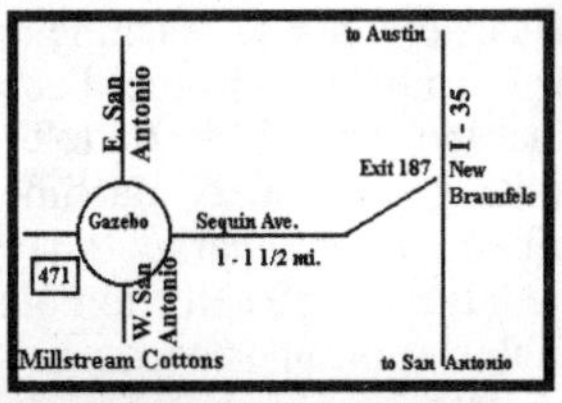

New Braunfels, TX #36

Lytle, TX #37

Mon - Sat 9 - 6

Kalico & Keepsakes

14945 Main St., P.O. Box 329 78052
(830) 772-4721
Owner: Dee Cromer
Est: 1997 2300 sq.ft.

Full line quality Fabric and Notions.
Classes — day, night and Saturdays.
Professional finishing on Gammill Machine.
Our Customers are soon Friends.

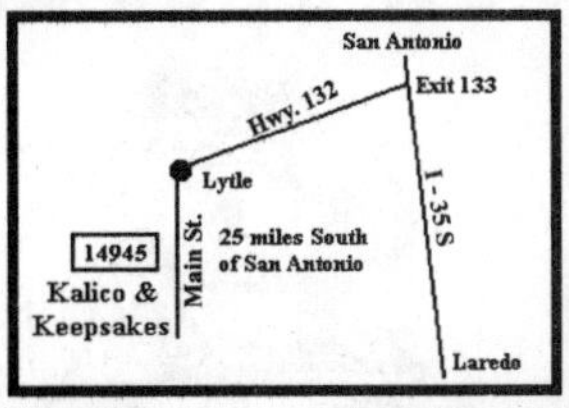

Harlingen, TX #38

Mon - Sat 9:30 - 5:30

Scaiefs Fabrics

810 S. Dixieland Rd. 78552
(956) 425-4082 or (800) 221-1-SEW
E-Mail: scaiefs@aol.com
Web Site: www.sew2000.com/scaiefsfabrics
Est: 1978

Home of Bernina, New Home, Pfaff, Pacesetter by Brother. A fabulous assortment of good quilting cottons - color sorted. Plus threads, cutters, mats, templates, patterns, books, and sewing machine accessories.

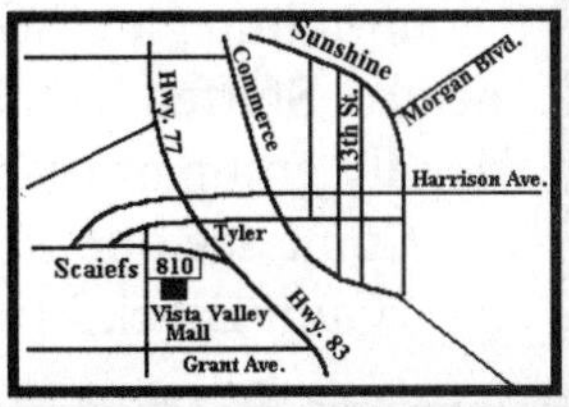

Rockport, TX #39

Mon - Fri 10 - 5 Sat 10 - 4

Golden Needles & Quilts

701 N. Allen 78382
(361) 729-7873 Fax: Same
E-Mail: KTSTAN@aol.com
Web Site: www.quiltscapes.com
Owner: Kay Stanley
Est: 1989 2800 sq.ft. 2000+ Bolts

Original Blocks of the Month & Patterns.
100% cotton fabrics, books, notions.
Custom Machine Quilting.

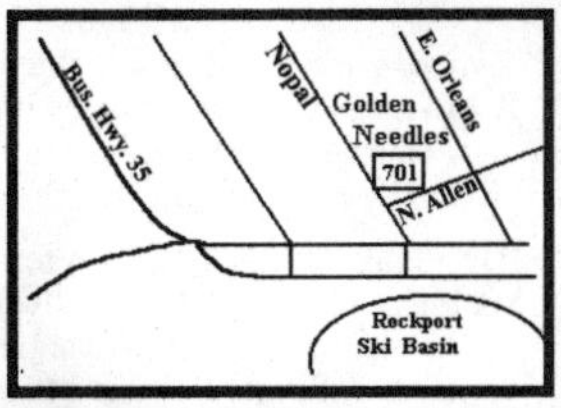

Corpus Christi, TX #40

Divine Quilters Quilting Fabric and Classes

Tues - Fri 10 - 5:30 Sat 10 - 4

11229 Leopard St. 78410
(361) 241-8155 Fax: (361) 241-8199
E-mail: lariains@aol.com
Owners: Lari Ainsworth & Dubby Pemberton
Est: 2001 1400+ sq.ft. 1500+ Bolts

Quaint little store boasting of 1500+ bolts of 100% cottons, books and notions. Batiks, flannels, 30's reproductions, fleece, and novelty prints abound. Classes offered for the beginner to the advanced. Machine quilting available.

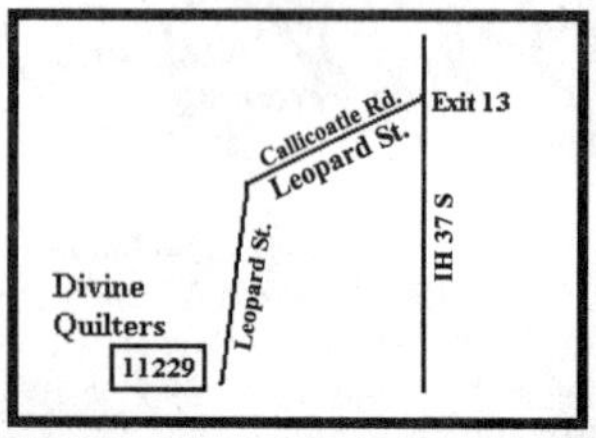

Corpus Christi, TX #41

Mon - Fri 10 - 6 Sat 10 - 5

The Quilt Cottage

5433 S. Staples 78411
(361) 985-0908
Web Site: www.thequiltcottage.com
Owner: Lynda Butler
Est: 1994 1600 sq.ft.

A very warm & friendly shop. We have over 2000 bolts all cotton fabric. Loads of Books, Patterns, Notions, Classes, etc. Professional Machine Quilting

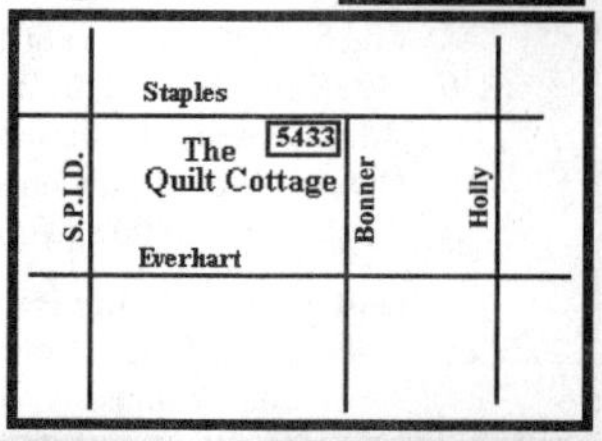

San Antonio, TX #42

Tue - Sat 10 - 5 Tue & Thur til 7

Las Colchas

110 Ogden St. 78212
(210) 223-2405

100% Cotton Fabrics - checks, plaids, Homespuns. Supplies & Classes Patterns, Books, Kits. Year Round Christmas Room all in a cozy Victorian House.

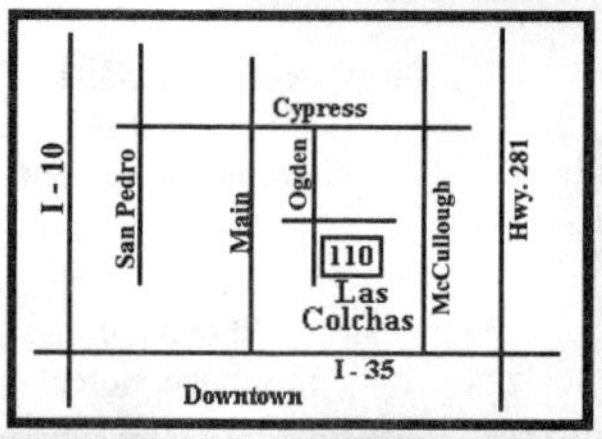

Creative Sewing Center- Bernina

11777 West Ave. at Blanco Rd. 78216
(210) 344-0791 or toll free 877-331-7862
berninasat@aol.com Terry & Vince Soll

Mon - Sat 9:30 - 6:00 Sun Noon - 5

Come visit us when you are in the San Antonio area. Bus tours welcome and handicap parking right in front. There are 8000 square feet filled with beautiful quilting and natural fiber fabrics from unusual novelty prints to the complete color range of Moda Marbles. Large selection of rulers, quilting accessories and books. We carry the largest selection of threads in the area—from machine embellishment to quilting & fiber arts. Heirloom lace, trims and fabrics including floral batiste. Sales, service and machine instruction for Bernina and Brother Pacesetter. Machines from $199.00 to the most exciting embroidery machines and software on the market today. We have a large selection of sewing machine notions, accessories and cabinets.

San Antonio, TX #43

San Antonio, TX #44

Mon - Sat 10 - 6 Sun 12 - 6

Plain Jane's

555 Bitters Rd. 78216
(210) 496-5436

Specializing in Country Primitive Folk Art and Hand did Stuff. Patterns, quilts, Samplers, dolls.

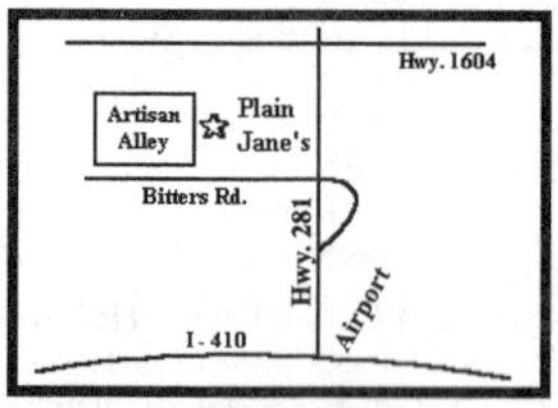

San Antonio, TX #45

Sew Special Quilts - Bernina

The Market at Leon Springs
24165 IH 10 West #421, 78257
(210) 698-6076
Owners: Laurie Mangold
Est: 1987 2600 sq.ft. 1800 Bolts

Mon - Sat 9 - 5 Thur til 8 Sun 12 - 5

A full service shop for all of your quilting and wearable needs. Staffed by a helpful, friendly group of crazy ladies. Come see our unique "Quilt Block Floor".

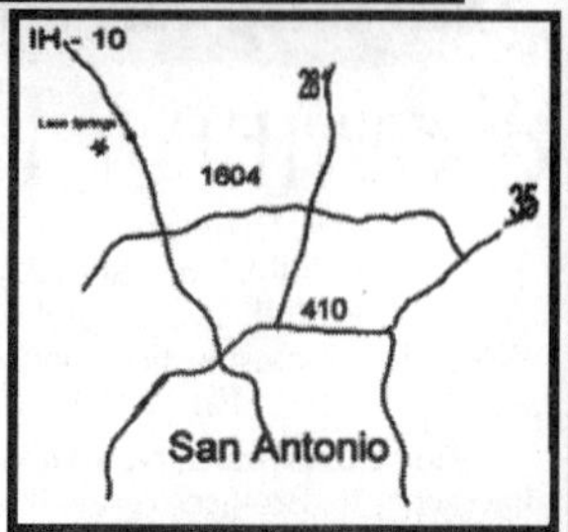

Exit 550 from Boerne
Exit 551 from San Antonio

San Antonio, TX #46

Mon - Fri 9:30 - 5:30 Sat 9:30 - 3

Seventh Heaven

6706 N. New Braunfels 78209
(210) 882-9980
Owner: Dixie Bradbury & Shelby Bonner
E-Mail: quilts@seventhheavenquilts.com
Web Site: seventhheavenquilts.com
Est: 1990 3600 sq.ft. 2000+ Bolts

Heavenly delight 100% Cotton Fabrics, Supplies. Thimbleberries, RJR, P&B, and Moda. Patterns, Books and more. Elna & Singer Sewing Machines.

Converse, TX #47

Tues - Fri 1 - 5
Sat 10 - 3

General Store/Quilt Studio

305 S. Seguin 78109
(210) 659-7278
Owners: Rosalie & Les Bourland
Est: 1985 2094 sq.ft.

600 Bolts 100% Cotton Fabric, Books, Patterns, Quilt Frames, Batting and other supplies. Quilt Classes.

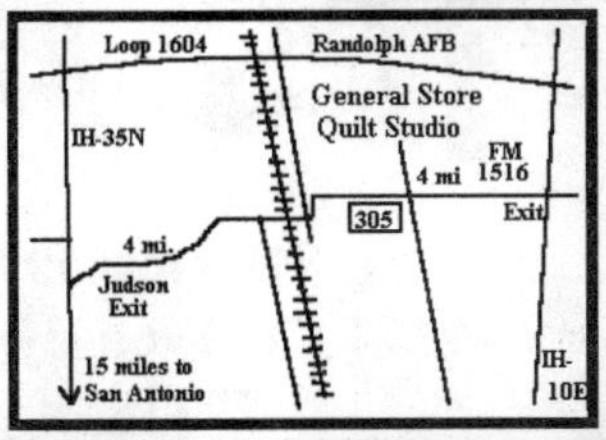

La Grange, TX #48

Tues - Sat 9 - 5:30

the Quilters' Cottage

239 N. Madison 78945
(979) 968-8804
E-Mail: quilters@cvtv.net
Fax: (979) 968-6131

Featuring Easy-Does-It Foundation Pieced Miniature Patterns by Patchwork Plus. Quality Cotton Fabric, Books, Patterns, Notions, Classes and Pfaff Sewing Machines.

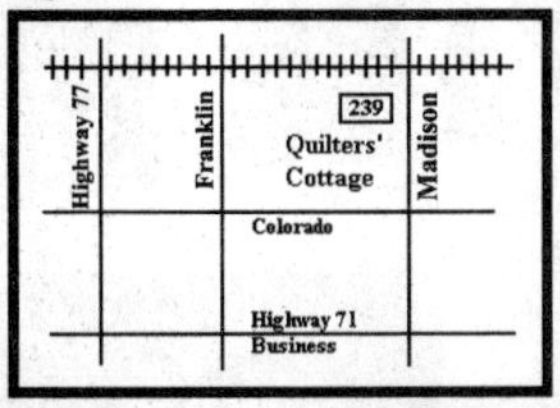

Smithville, TX #49

Tues - Sat 10 - 5
Sun 1 - 5

Stitchin' Time Quilt Shop

206 Main St. 78957
(512) 237-5255
E-Mail: Stitchintime@smithsys.net
Owner: Brenda Knode
Est: 1999 2000 sq.ft.

Located along the Colorado River convenient to San Antonio, Houston and Austin. Large selection of books, redwork patterns & fabric.

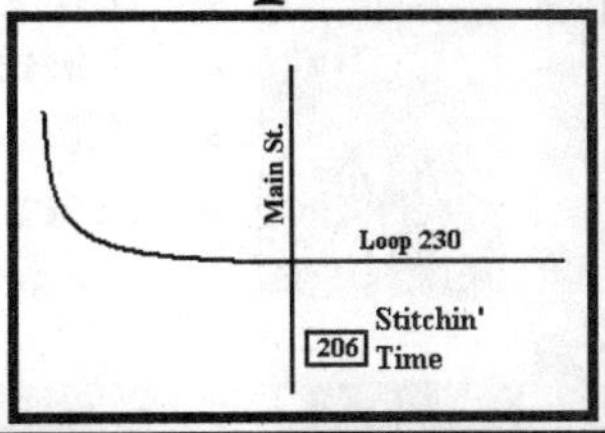

College Station, TX #50

Mon - Sat 10 - 6

Pruitt's Fabric and Quilt Shop

318 George Bush Dr. 77840
(409) 693-9357 Fax: (409) 696-6264
E-Mail: pruitt@cy-net.net Est: 1946

Everything A Quilter Needs
Large selection of vibrant colored cottons (5000+ Bolts), quilting books, patterns, & supplies, plus Silk, Wool, Linen, Velvet, Ultra Suede, Bridal Laces and Trims. Special Orders Welcome.

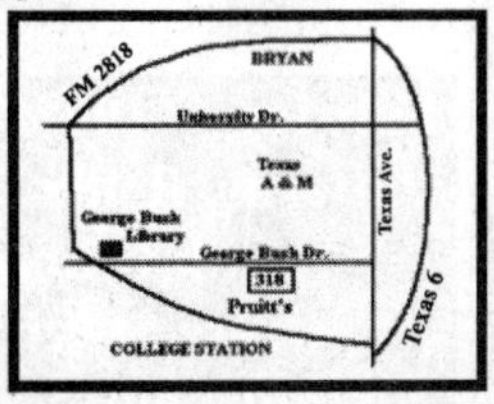

College Station, TX #51

By Appt. Only

Dyeing To Be Different

14 Ranchero Rd. 77845
(979) 776-8632
E-Mail: smjjd@myriad.net
Web Site: Coming Soon
Owners: Sandra Melville,
Connie Currin & Judy Ross

We specialize in one-of-a-kind assorted and custom hand-dyed fabrics and wearable art.

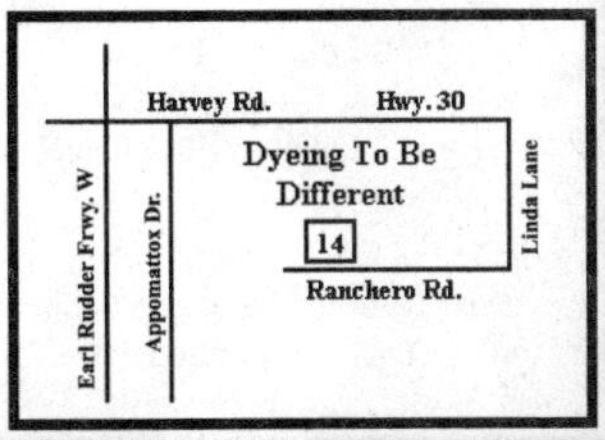

Brenham, TX #52

Stitch Haven

For Those Who Love Quilting Needlework and Fine Fabrics

Tues - Fri 10 - 5:30
Sat 10 - 3

Featuring Cotton Fabrics and Supplies for Quilting, Wearable Art, Smocking, and Silk Ribbon Embroidery

1600 S. Day St. 77833
(979) 836-3200
Fax: 979-836-3355
Web Site: www.stitchhaven.com

Bryan, TX #53

Tues - Fri 10 - 5:30
Sat 10 - 4

Polly's Quilt Cottage

3211 S. Texas Ave. 77802
(979) 775-1681 Fax: (520) 822-0769 Owner: Polly, Millie & Bunny

Largest in the Brazos Valley.
Only Texas Aggie Quilt Dealer.
Top Quality fabrics & notions.
Hand-made gifts.

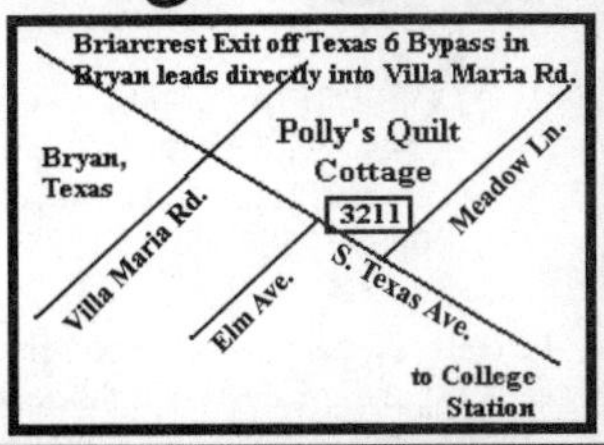

Fairfield, TX #54

Tues - Fri 10 - 5:30
Sat 10 - 3

Cotton Cottage

221 E. Commerce 75840
(903) 389-6528
E-Mail: cottoncottage@hotmail.com
Owner: Pam Beene Est: 1996

100% Cotton fabric, notions, books, patterns. Catering to Quilters & Creative Clothing. Classes and Friendly Service. Husqvarna Viking Dealer.

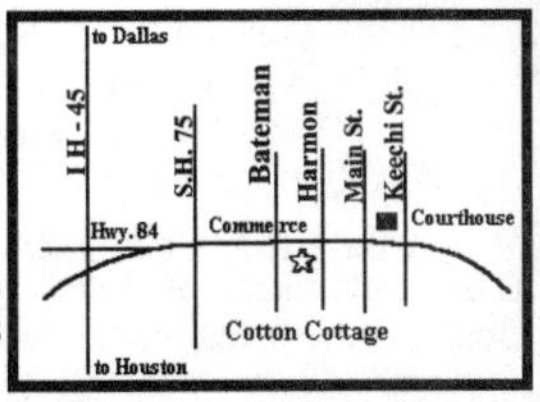

Spring, TX #55

Tues - Sat 10 - 5
Sun 12 - 5

Juliene's Quilt Shop

26303 Preston - B 77373
(281) 355-9820 (800) 976-0633
E-Mail: julienes@pdq,net
Est: 1993 2500 sq. ft. 3000 Bolts.

Full Service Quilt Shop. Fabrics, Patterns, Notions, Classes, Sewing Cabinets, Husqvarna Viking Sewing Machines, Sergers, Machine Embroidery Supplies, Software Sales & Service.

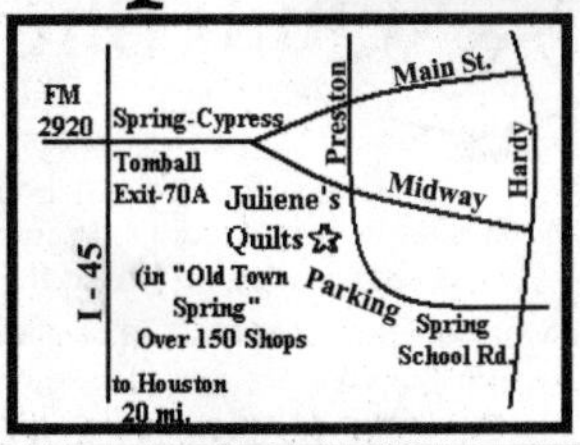

Beaumont, TX #56

The Piecemaker

Mon - Fri 10 - 5
Tues til 6 Sat 10 - 3

3865 Calder Ave. 77706
(409) 835-4736
Owner: Noel Ann McCord

Fabrics — 100% Cottons
Patterns, Books, Notions.
Silk Ribbon,
Cross-Stitch and
Needlepoint Supplies.

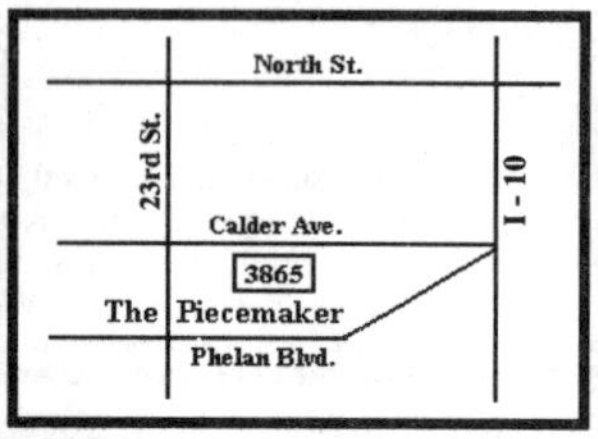

Now Offering:
M & M Quilting Service
Custom Quilting
Gammill Machine
Brochure Available

Located Inside the **Piecemaker**
(409) 833-9256

Humble, TX #57

It's A Stitch

(281) 446-4999
9574 FM 1960 Bypass
77338
Owners: Judy
& John Curtis
Est: 1992 3000 sq.ft.

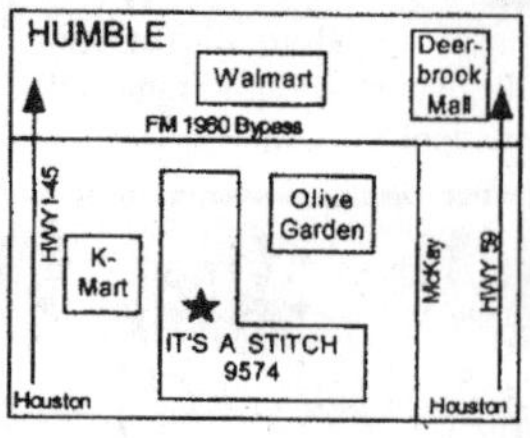

Mon - Fri
10 - 5:30
Sat 10 - 5
Sun 12 - 5

- Large selection of quilting fabrics
- Patterns, books, notions
- Classes
- Bernina and Bernette sewing machines & sergers

Stafford, TX #58

Mon - Fri
10 - 5:30
Sat 10 - 4

Quilt Impressions

12810 Fountain Lake Cir. 77477
(281) 240-4992
Owner: Susan Neal

Located in Fountain Lakes Shopping Center across from the bank and behind Borders Books. Take Corporate Exit off Southwest Freeway.

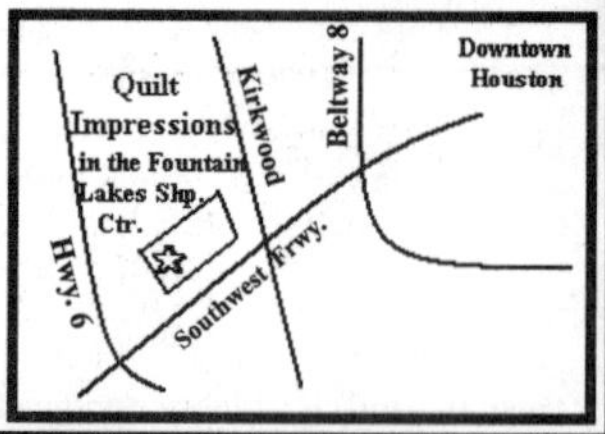

Friendswood, TX #59

Mon - Fri
10 - 5:30
Sat 10 - 4

Quakertown Quilts

180 S. Friendswood Dr. 77546
(888) 464-7845
Web Site: www.QuakertownOnline.com
(281) 996-1756 Fax: (281) 648-9090
Owner: Pat Forke Est: 1988 3500 sq.ft.
Complete Quilt Shop. 3000+ bolts of cotton fabric. Books, Patterns, Notions & Gift Items Blocks of the Month. Wholesale inquiries welcome.

Lake Jackson, TX #60

Mon - Sat
10 - 5
Thurs til 8

Scissortail Quilts

217A Parking Way 77566
(979) 297-8595
Owner: Betty V. G. Meyer
Est: 2000 2500 sq.ft. 1500+ Bolts.

Friendly clerks will help you select from the latest and greatest quilt fabric, notions, books and classes. Fun atmosphere.

Bay City, TX #61

Mon - Sat
9 - 4
Thurs til 7

Sue's Quilt Shop

1840 7th St. 77414
(888) 417-3585 or
(979) 244-8420

Fax: (979) 244-8479
E-Mail: sue@suesquiltshop.com
Web Site: www.suesquiltshop.com Est: 1996
Owner: Sue Bailey 3000 sq.ft. 2000 Bolts
Great selection of 100% cotton fabrics, quilting supplies, books, notions, classes. New Home Machines. Call for current newsletter.

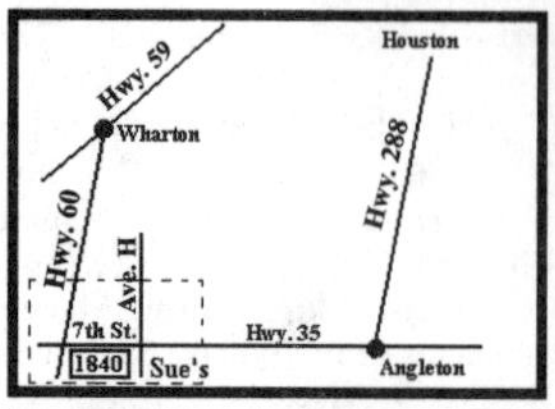

Bay City, TX #62

Mon - Sat
9:30 - 7:30

Threads, Quilts, & Creations

1728 6th St. 77414
(979) 245-5347 or (877) 885-4606
Owner: Beverly Runyan
Est: 1995 3200 sq.ft. 2500 Bolts

Wonderful gifts. Dolls, bears, candles, etc. Over 2500 bolts of 100% Cotton Fabric. Books, patterns, notions, classes. Christmas Room. Antiques.

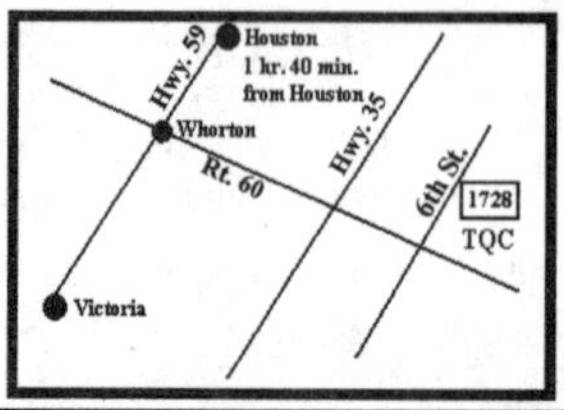

Largest Selection of Fabric in Houston

The Woodlands, TX #63

Plain & Fancy

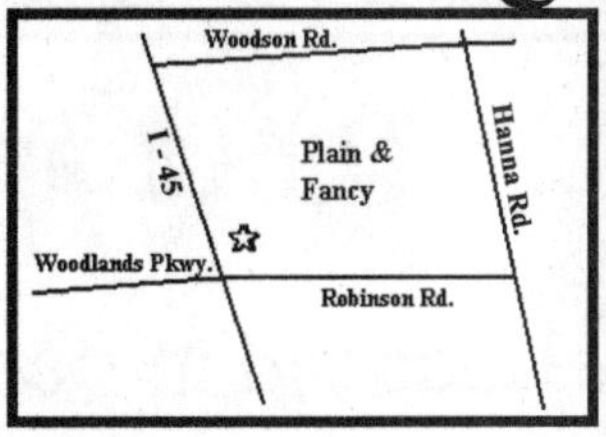

27118 I-45 N
Oak Ridge North, TX
77385
"The Woodlands"
(281) 367-1021
Fax: (281) 367-1172

Mon - Sat 9 - 5

From Houston:
Exit Woodlands Parkway. Stay on the feeder for approx. 2 miles. We are in Woodridge Plaza just past the bowling alley

From Conroe:
Exit Woodlands Parkway. Take the Oak Ridge / Robinson Road exit off the feeder. This will take you up over the freeway. Immediately loop back down on the feeder going north. We are in Woodridge Plaza just past the bowling alley.

Galveston, TX #64

Quilts by the Bay

5923 Stewart Rd. 77551
(409) 740-9296 Est: 1991
Email: qbtb@comwerx.net
Owner: Patricia Stephenson
3500 sq.ft. 4000 Bolts

Mon - Sat 10 - 5:30 Sun 12:30 - 5

Charming shop by Galveston Bay with top quality fabrics, classes, notions, & unique gifts for every occasion.

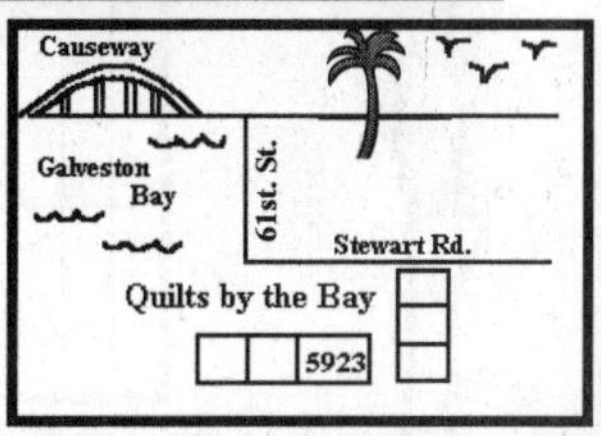

THE FABRIC STORE

and sew much more

We offer a wide selection of quality quilting, fashion and name decorator fabrics, along with patterns, notions & classes. Come see us--We love to sew and quilt as much as you do!

1605 South Hwy. 69,
Nederland, TX 77627
(409) 729-5288 Fax: Same
E-mail: thefabricstore@exp.net
Web Site: www.thefabricstoreonline.com
Over 5,000 bolts of fabric
3500 sq.ft.

Mon - Fri
10 - 5:30
Sat 9:30 - 4

Nederland, TX #65

Front Porch Quilts

5050 FM 1960 W, #127 77069
(281) 444-2882
Fax: (281) 880-6906
E-mail: fpquilts@wt.net
Web Site: www.frontporchquilts.com
Owner: Misty Odenweller
Est: 1996 3250 sq.ft. 2500+ Bolts

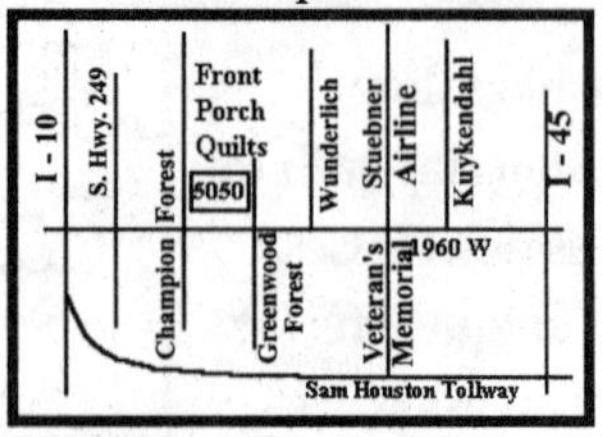

We are a full service quilt store with classes, fabric, notions, patterns, books, commercial quilting machine, living room & children's corner. Newsletter with Mail Order Available.

**Mon - Fri 9:30 - 5
Sat 10 - 5**

Houston, TX #66

Katy, TX #67

**Mon - Sat 10 - 4:30
Thur til 7**

Quilt 'n Sew Studio

1841 N. Mason Rd. 77449
(281) 347-0470 Fax: (281) 347-0474
Owner: Terri Burton
Est: 1993 3000 sq.ft. 4000 bolts

100% cotton Fabrics, Quilting supplies, books, patterns, kits, classes (kids too!). We Quilt - Quilt Tops in the Shop! Custom Quilting

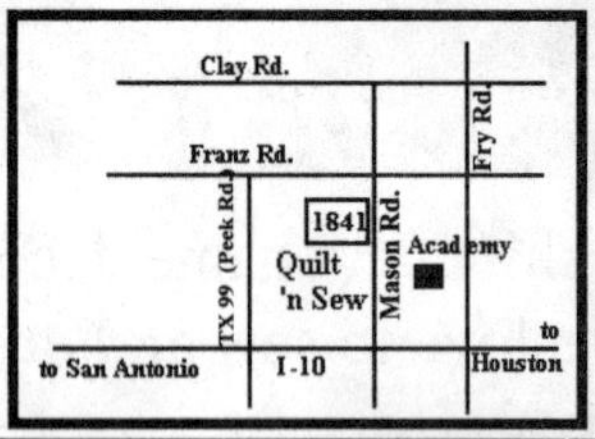

La Porte, TX #68

**Mon - Sat 10 - 5
Thurs til 7**

Painted Pony 'n Quilts

1015 S. Broadway 77571
(281) 471-5735 Fax: (281) 471-1713
E-Mail: ppnqstaff@ppnq.com
Web Site: www.ppnq.com
Owner: Sherrie S. Thomas Est: 1986
8000+ top name quilting fabrics in contemporary, country, plaid and reproduction styles. Notions, Gifts, Janome/New Home Dealer. Friendly, knowledgeable staff to assist in all areas. Samples on display.

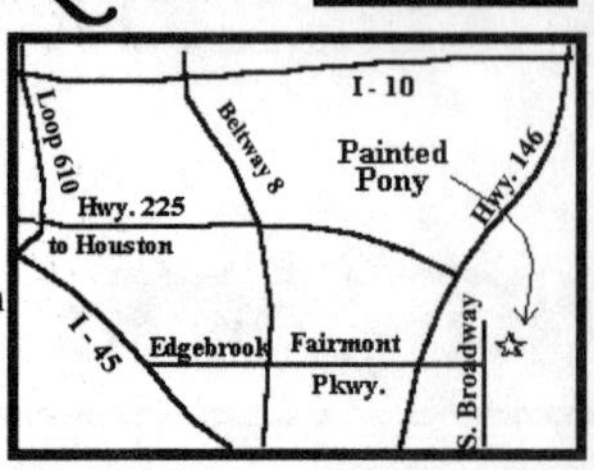

Stitchin Heaven

Quitman, TX #69

Located in Beautiful East Texas!

Featured shop in Quilt Sampler 2000

Over 3000 bolts of quality cotton fabrics in this 4200 square foot "Quilter's Paradise"
The very latest in quilting tools and supplies
A complete library of books & patterns
Machine Quilting Service Available
Free Full-Color Newsletter

Home of "Camp Quilt S'more"

A sewing retreat held once each quarter.
Two nights of uninterrupted sewing and fun!

"The Bunkhouse"

Rent our 2200 square foot log cabin built especially for quilters for your next small group retreat!

Visit our website www.stitchinheaven.com
For a complete listing of happenings in the shop and an incredible on-line shopping experience!
Be sure and register for our "Hot Flashes" - our on-line newsletter!

Owner: Debby Luttrell
502 E. Goode PO Box 1914
Quitman, Texas 75783
Email: info@stitchinheaven.com
Toll free: 800 841-3901
Fax: 903 763-3117

100% Satisfaction Guaranteed!
Be sure and plan to visit when you are in the area!
It's worth the drive!

Jean's Corner
of Feeder's Supply

712 N. Jackson 77351
(409) 327-8817
Fax: (409) 327-6411
E-Mail: sew712@livingston.net
Owner: Jean Yarbrough

Mon - Fri
9 - 5
Sat 9 - 1

Brand name 100% cotton Fabrics
Books - Notions
Janome Sewing Machines
Brother Embroidery Machines

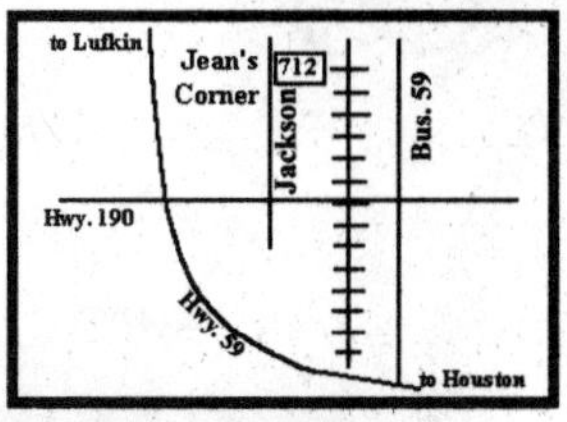

Livingston, TX #70

Palestine, TX #71

Mon - Fri
9 - 5
Sat 9 - 1

Grimes Sewing Center

619 W. Oak St. 75801
(903) 729-2889
Fax: (903) 729-5408
Est: 1991 2600 sq.ft. 2000+ Bolts

Fabrics, Quilting Supplies, Patterns, Books, Notions, Classes

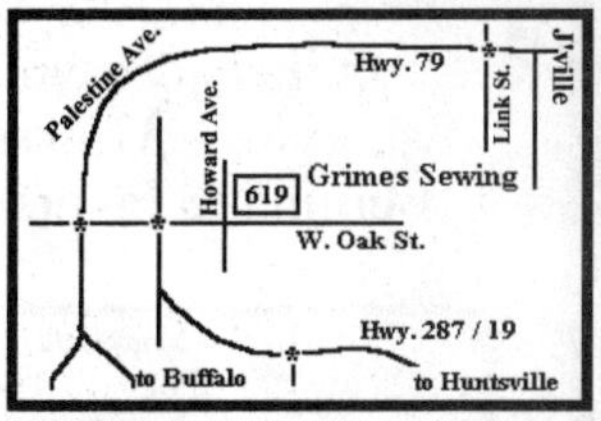

Jefferson, TX #72

Mon - Fri
10 - 5

Quilters Corner

1102 FM 2208 75657
(903) 665-3385
Owners: Gail Thomas, Janis Mayfield, & Dorothy Thompson
Est: 1990 2000 sq.ft.

No quilter's travel through charming Historic Jefferson is complete without stopping here. Browse among fabrics, books and notions. Machine Quilting also available.

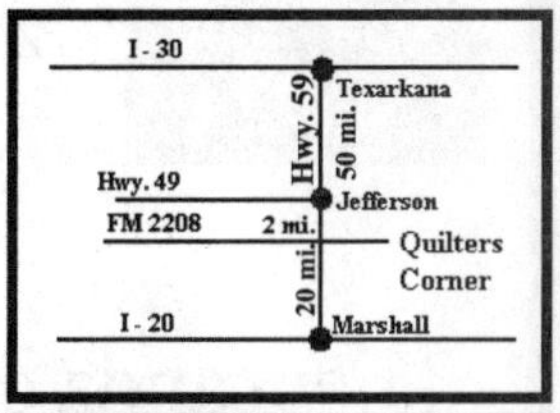

Calico Junction

Mon - Sat
9:30 - 5

(903) 342-3399

107 E. Elm St. 75494

5000 sq.ft. of fabrics, quilts & antiques
Fax: (903) 342-3399 Web Site: www.calico-junction.com

Winnsboro, TX #73

Sewing Notions * Patterns * Classes * Gifts * Antiques * Cappucino * Quilts * Antique Sewing Machines * Custom Machine Quilting

"The friendliest and most helpful shop around"

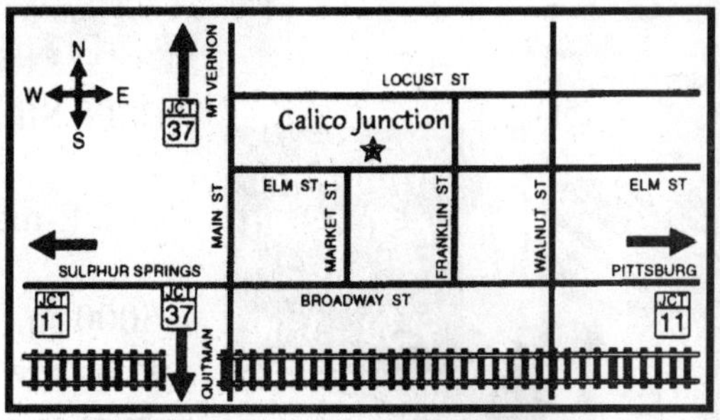

When you're planning a trip to pass thru East Texas, call and we'll send you our newsletter...

Sulphur Springs, TX #74

Sew Many Quilts®
101 Radio Rd. #3
Sulphur Springs, TX 75482
(903) 885-8916 or (888) 855-8916
Fax: (903) 885-9712
quilters@sewmanyquilts.com
Est: 1982 3750 sq.ft. 4000 Bolts
Bernina & Janome Sewing Center

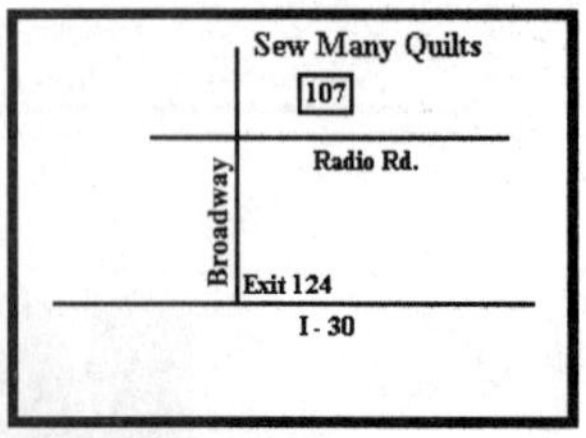

Mon - Fri
9:30 - 5:30
Sat 9 - 4

Owner:
Zella White

Two Great Locations

Texarkana, TX #75

Sew Many Quilts®, Too
4053 Summerhill Square, Texarkana, TX
(903) 792-4630 or (888) 992-4739
texarkana@sewmanyquilts.com
Est: 2002 1500 sq.ft.
1200 Bolts and growing
Janome Sewing Center

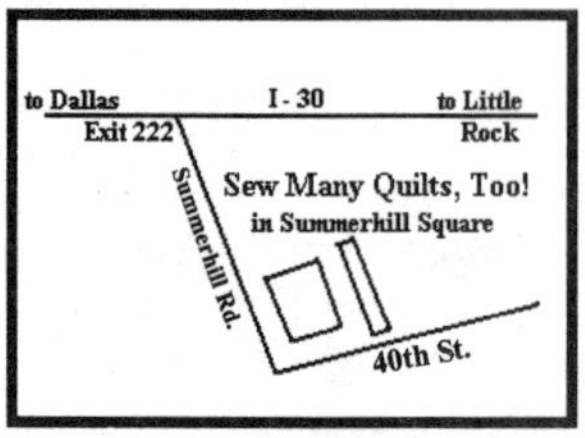

Celebrating Our 20th Anniversary

Mon - Fri
10 - 5:30
Sat 10 - 4

www.sewmanyquilts.com

Thousands of bolts of 100% cotton fabric. 300+ book & pattern titles.

Bernina & Sew Much More

This is a bright, inviting atmosphere to enjoy a huge selection of beautiful cotton fabrics, notions, books, patterns, kits and all the wonderful items that quilters love. We specialize in flannels, orientals and 30's reproduction prints while still offering a full compliment of current quilting fabrics.

Paris, TX #76

Mon - Fri
9:30 - 5:00
Sat
9:30 - 3:00

2400 Stillhouse Rd., Paris, TX 75462
(903) 784-6342
E-mail: dbandel@1starnet.com
Fax: (903) 784-0694
5000 sq.ft. Authorized Bernina Dealer
www.sewmuchmorequilts@1starnet.com

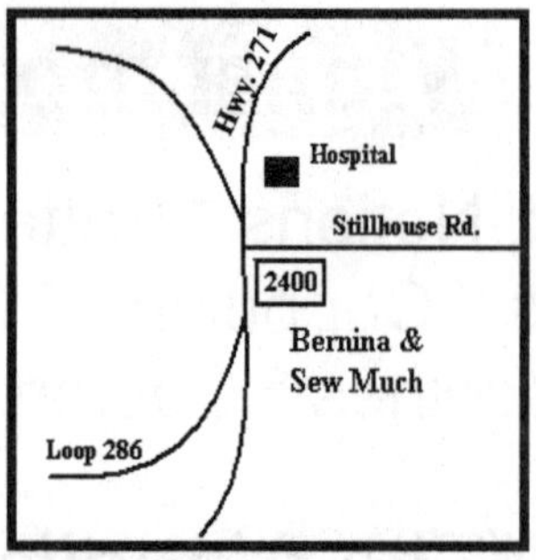

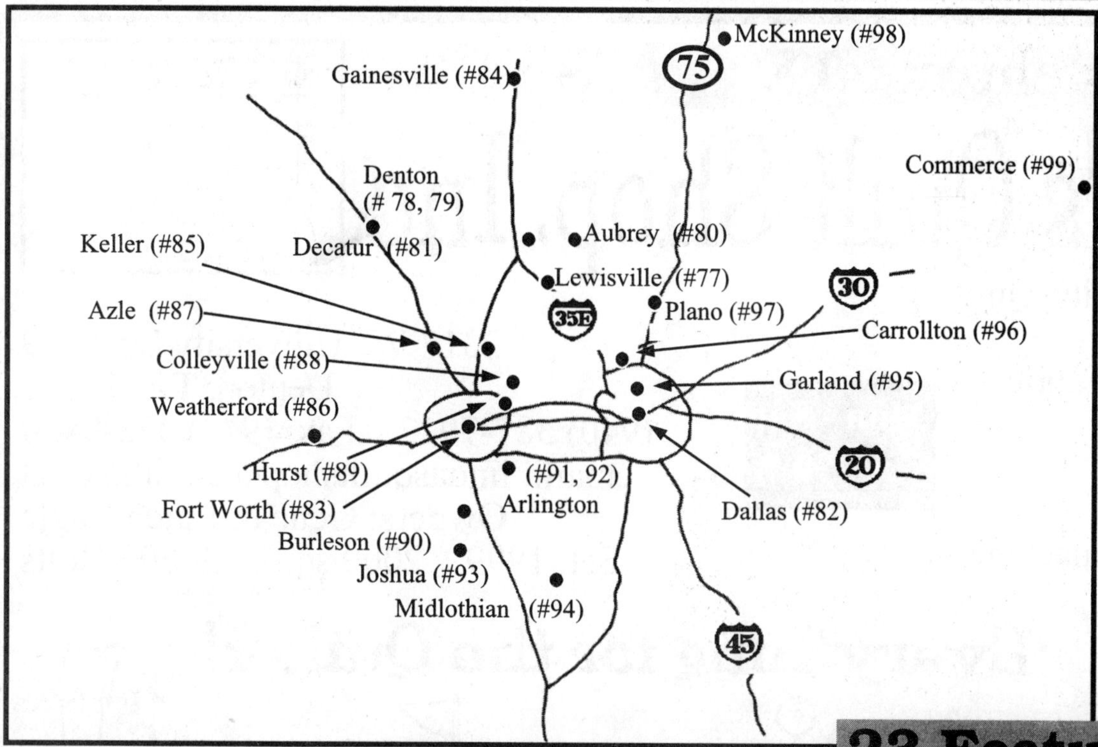

23 Featured Shops

Dallas / Fort Worth Area

Quilt Country

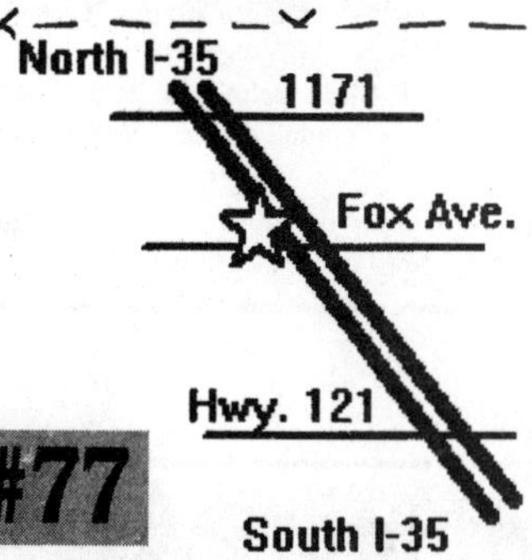

701 South Stemmons #260

Open 7 days a week!

Lewisville, TX #77

Quilt Country is conveniently located right on I-35 E, exit 451. We have a wide variety of fabrics including batiks, plaids, traditional, 30's, novelty prints, bright fun fabrics, and flannels year 'round. We also have many original patterns, and kitted projects. Our tall ceilings provide space to hang lots of models to inspire you!

Monday - Saturday 10:00AM - 5:00PM ~ Sunday 1:00PM - 5:00PM

Owner: Sandy Brawner ~ 5000+ bolts ~ 5000 sq. ft. ~ established 1995

972-436-7022 ~ fax-972-436-6065 www.quiltcountry.com

Denton, TX #78

Linda's Quilt Shop, Inc.

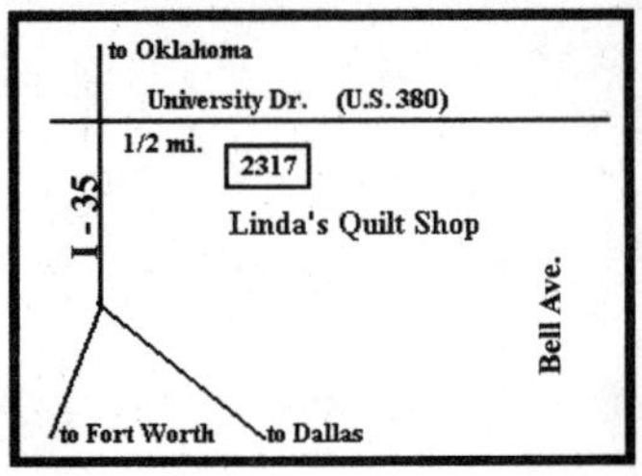

- Custom Machine Quilting
- Quilt Classes
- 100% Cotton Fabric
- Notions
- Patterns
- Books
- A-1 long arm machine sales & service.

Mon - Sat 10 - 6

2317 W. University Dr. #C-9
Denton, TX 76201
(940) 387-7912 Fax: (940) 323-0450
email: lindasquiltshop@earthlink.net
Owners: Gene & Linda Cagle
Est: 1999 2000 sq.ft. 3000+ Bolts

Everything for the Quilter!

Denton, TX #79

Mon - Sat 10 - 5

Stitching Post

2318 San Jacinto Blvd. 76205
(940) 483-9077
E-Mail: stchpost@gte.net
Owner: Donna Graves 5000+ Bolts

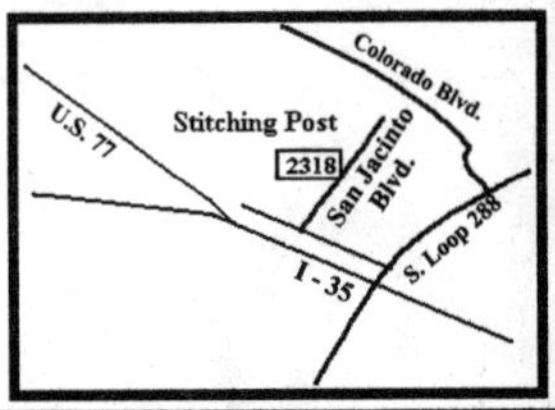

Large selection of fabric, books and quilting supplies. Mail order available.

Aubrey, TX #80

Mon - Sat 9 - 5

The Rail Fence Quilt Shop

4816 Hwy. 377 76227
(940) 440-2243
E-Mail: quilthat@aol.com
Owners: Andrea Meegan & Linda Scott
Est: 2000

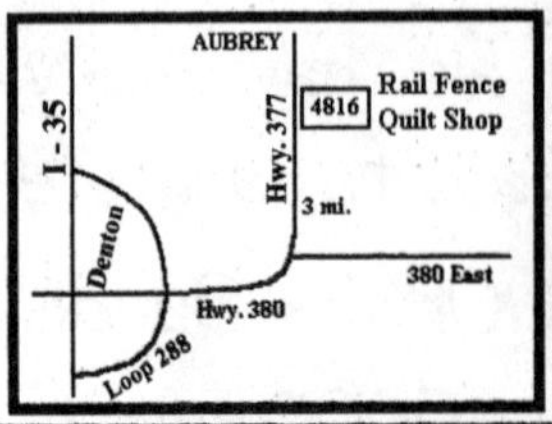

Rustic log interior with 4800 sq.ft. of fabric, notions, books & patterns.

Decatur, TX #81

The Nine Patch

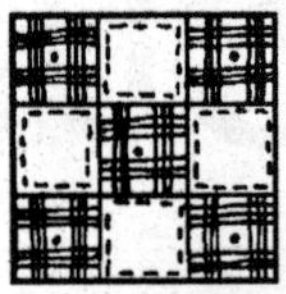

307 W. Main 76234
(940) 627-4422 or (888) 736-5765
Fax: Same Est: 1997
E-Mail: ninepatch@wf.net
Owner: Sandy Smith 4000 sq.ft. 3000 Bolts

Mon - Sat 10 - 5
Sat 10 - 4

Full Service Quilt Shop
Long Arm Quilting Machine

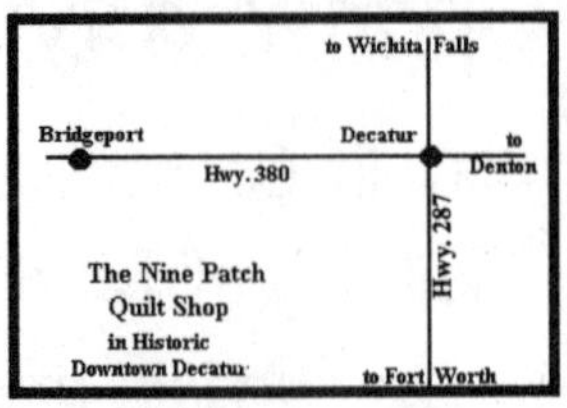

Website: ninepatchquiltshop.com

Quiltmakers inc

social club & supply house

Mon - Sat 10a - 5p
Tue til 8p Sun 1p - 5p

Your source in Dallas for bright, fun & unusual fabrics

◇*Over 4000 bolts of fabric from top manufacturers*
◇*Hundreds of batiks & balis, novelties, and orientals*
◇*Lots of books, patterns and notions*
◇*In-store photo transfer service, using our own* **Creative Copy**™ *Photo Transfer Paper (paper available by mail order)*

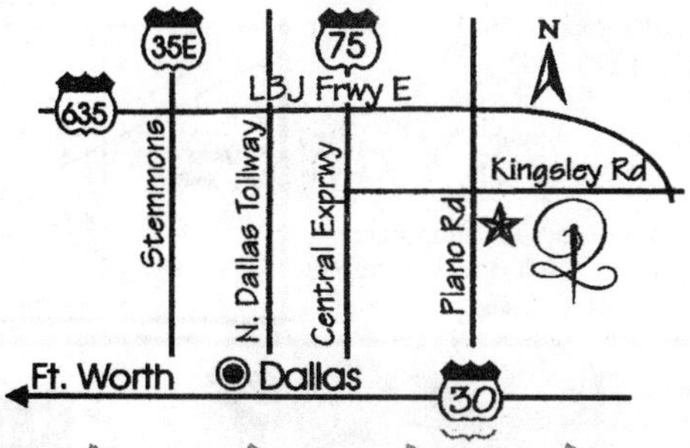

9658 Plano Rd. Dallas, TX 75238 214•343•1440
toll-free 888•494•0291 fax 214•343•2223
www.quiltmakersofdallas.com
e-mail Qltmakers@aol.com
Owner: Kelly J. Baird
Est. 1994 3000 sq. ft. 4200 bolts

#82

Cabbage Rose
Quilts and Gifts

Store Hours
Mon - Sat
10:00 - 5:00
Thurs
10:00 - 7:00

Over 4,000 fabrics in stock, 5,000 sq. ft. of quilting paradise. A complete line of quilting supplies including books, notions, patterns, gifts and classes. Fabrics range from batiks to the largest selection of flannels in North Texas. Located near Fort Worth's Cultural District. Come spend the day with us.

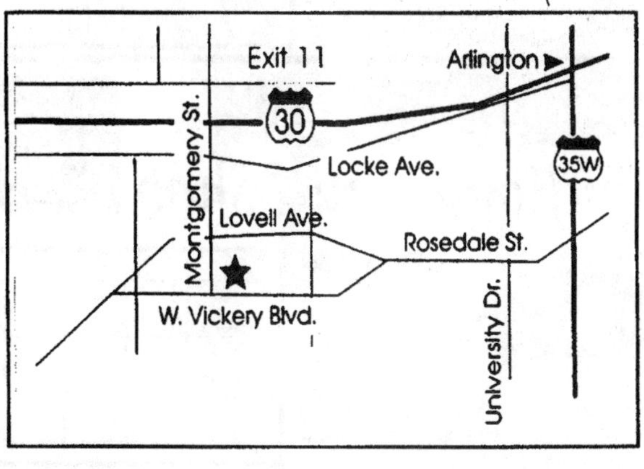

3526 W. Vickery Blvd.
Fort Worth, TX 76107
(817) 377-3993
Est: 1998
e-mail: crquilts@flash.net

Web site: CabbageRoseQuilting.Com

Fort Worth, TX #83

Gainesville, TX #84

Tues - Sat 10 - 5

Pass Time Fabrics

1218 East California 76240
(940) 668-1747
Owner: Fran Scott
Est: 1986

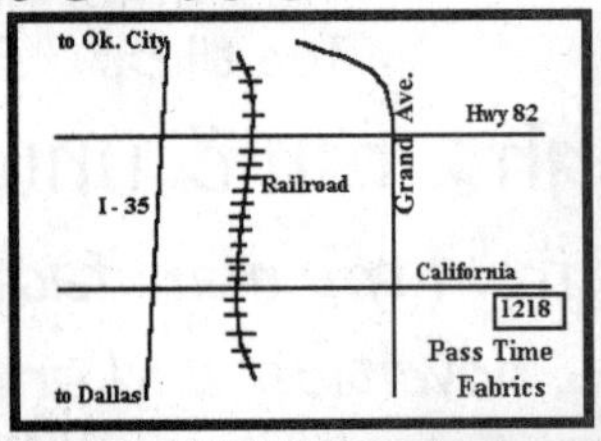

Full line of 100% cotton calicos and solids. Books, notions, patterns, classes - everything for quilters!

Keller, TX #85

Tues - Sat 10 - 3

Grandma's Quilts

111 W. Vine St 76248
(817) 431-1348
E-Mail: qmahln@aol.com
Owner: Helen L. Madden
Est: 1991

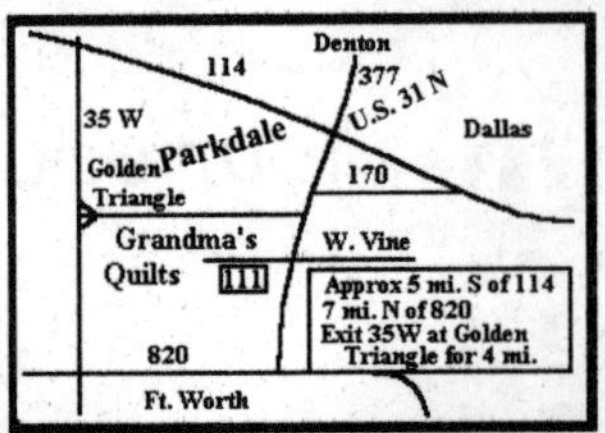

Machine Quilting ◆ Restoration & Repairs
Fabrics ◆ Books ◆ Supplies

Weatherford, TX #86

Mon, Wed, Fri 10 - 5:30 Sat 10 - 5

Grandma Lynn's Quilts

133 N. Waco St. 76086
(817) 599-4114
E-Mail: Lynn@grandmalynnsquilts.com
www.grandmalynnsquilts.com or
www.makeaquilt.com
Est: 1994 1800+ Bolts

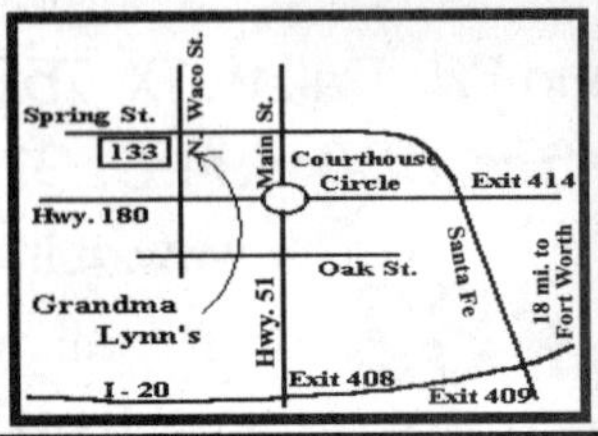

Specializing in Batiks and Designer fabrics
Quilt Kits for all skill levels
Precut Kits for beginners & busy people

Azle, TX #87

Tues - Fri 10 - 6 Sat 10 - 3

Quilts & Stuff

900 NW Parkway 76020
(817) 270-0452
E-Mail: Q-S.inc@juno.com
Owner: Anna Waghalter
Est: 1996 1300 sq.ft.

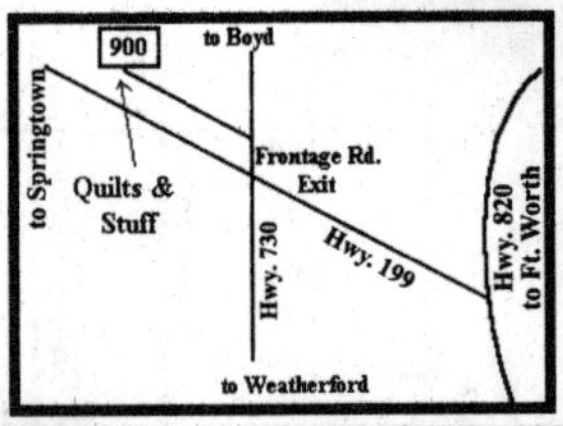

"At Home" take your shoes off atmosphere.
Cotton Fabrics, Notions, Quilt Books, Patterns, Fabric Kits, Classes.

Colleyville, TX #88

Mon & Thur 9 - 6 Tues, Wed, & Fri 9 - 5 Sat 10 - 4

Quilter's Dream

6409 Colleyville Blvd. 76034
(817) 481-7105
Owner: Beverly Ingram

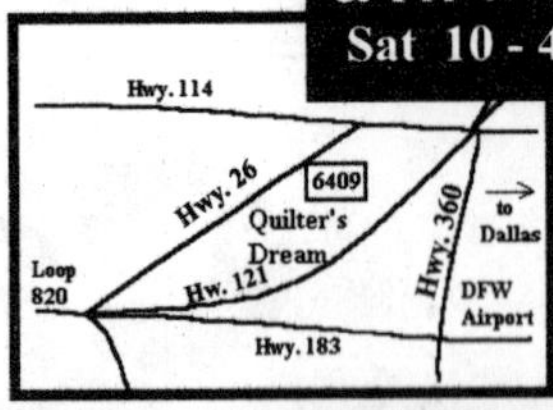

We are known for our knowledgeable, friendly staff and large selection of beautiful 100% cotton fabrics, books & notions.

Hurst, TX #89

Mon - Fri 10 - 6:30 Sat 10 - 5

Quilter's Stash

848 W. Pipeline Rd. 76053
(817) 595-1778
E-Mail: bill@quiltersstash.com
Web Site: www.quiltersstash.com
Owner: Bill Moore
Est: 1999 6000+ Bolts

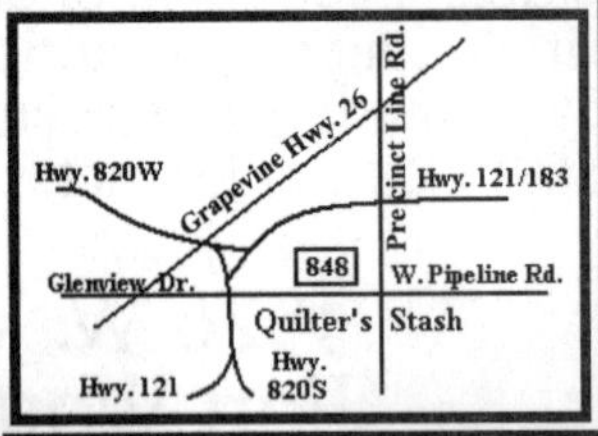

Best Quality 100% Cotton Fabrics, Books, Notions, Patterns and Classes.
Gift Certificates Available.

Burleson, TX #90

Mon - Sat 10 - 6 Sun 12 - 5

Little By Little

109 W Ellison Street, Booth #W31 76097
Nashville Mall # (817) 447-9809
E-Mail: littlebylittle13@aol.com
Web Site: www.littlebylittleonline.com
Owners: Barbara & Joe Loe

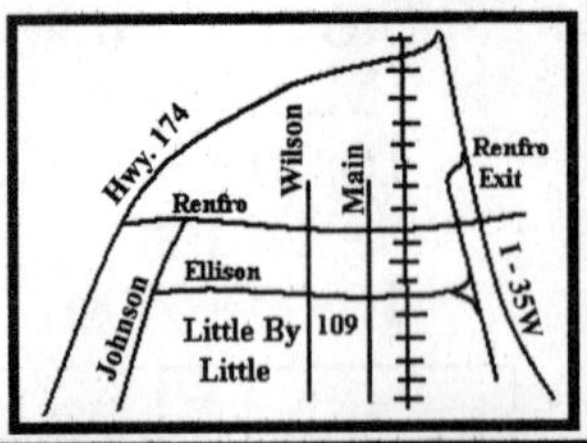

Large selection of quilting books. Quilters gifts/notecards. Boyds Bears! Distributor Farmer Steve's Organic Fat Free Popcorn. Antiques!
(No Fabrics) In a mall of 70 dealers.
Also sell online Hm# (817) 295-4416

Arlington, TX #91

Tues - Fri 10 - 6 Sat 10 - 4

Embroidery & Sewing Place

740 SW Green Oaks Blvd. #204
(817) 467-8585 76017
Fax: (817) 466-3276
Owner: Brenda Griffin
Est: 1999
1800 Bolts

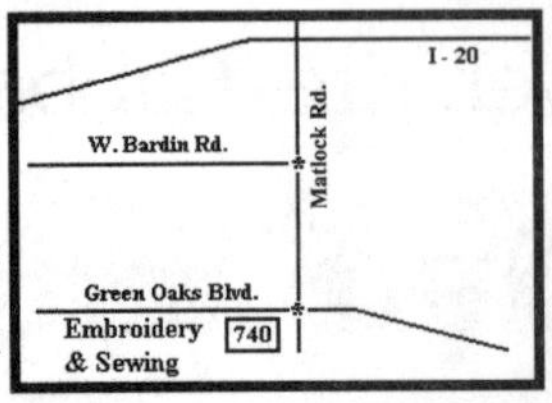

E-Mail: WLGriffin@worldnet.att.net
ESP is 3100 sq.ft. of quilting & heirloom supplies and fabric as well as the full line of Babylock sewing machines and sergers.

Arlington, TX #92

Mon - Fri 10 - 6 Sat 10 - 4

Abram House Quilt Shop

1210 W. Abram
76013
(817) 277-4749
2100+ sq.ft.

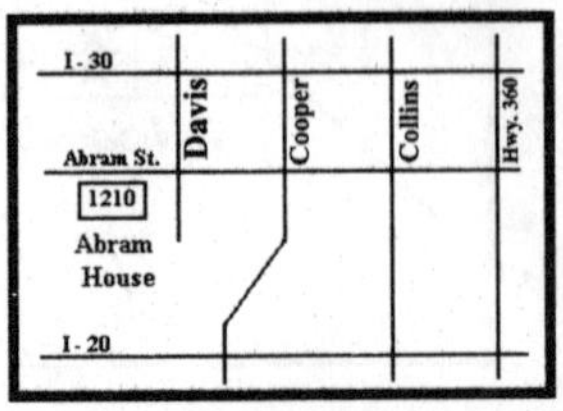

Charming 1903 house filled with large selection of quality 100% cotton fabrics. Books and notions. Antiques and gifts.

Sandy's Quilt Shop

Pfaff Sewing Machine Sales and Service

Over 3000 Bolts of 100% Cotton Fabrics
Notions, Patterns & Books

Sandy's Quilt Shop
301 B 12th St.,
Corner of
Hwys. 174 & 917
P.O. Box 350
76058
(817) 558-2882

Mon - Fri 10 - 5:30
Thur til 9 Sat 9 - 5

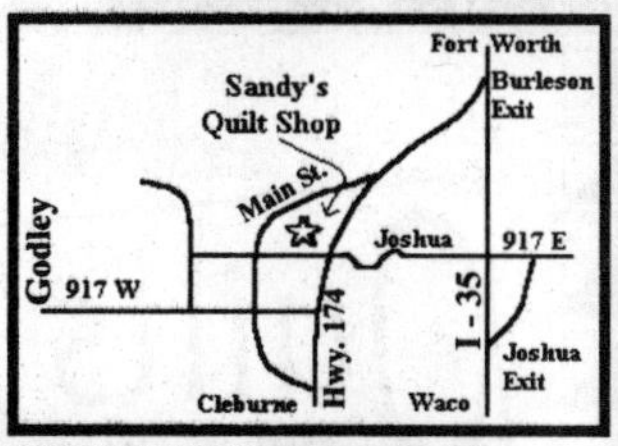

Joshua, TX #93

Quilts 'n More

Est: 2000

Midlothian, TX #94

1200+ bolts of 100% cotton fabrics, notions, books, patterns, classes and longarm quilting. Building space is shared with The Craft Depot, making us the only "mall" in town.

Mon - Fri
10 - 6
Sat 10 - 4

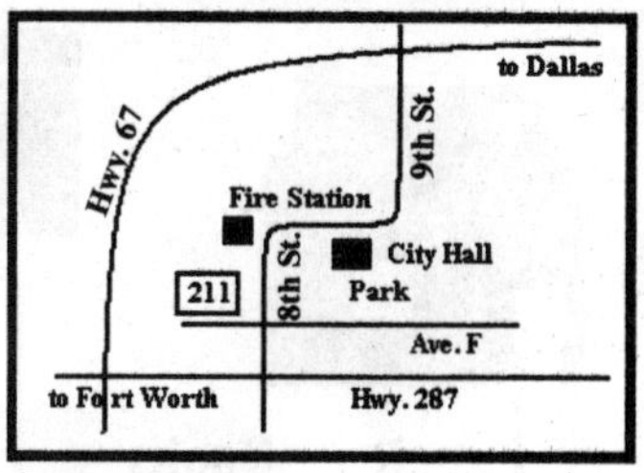

211 W. Ave. "F", Midlothian, TX 76065
(972) 723-8669
E-Mail: quiltsnmore2000@yahoo.com
Owners: Kathleen Allen & Jean McKinney

Garland, TX #95

Suzy's

111 North 6th 75040 972-272-8180

Your Complete Quilt Shop
Owner: Suzanne Cook
Est: 1989 4200 sq.ft.

Mon - Fri 9:30 - 5:00 Sat 9:30 - 4:30

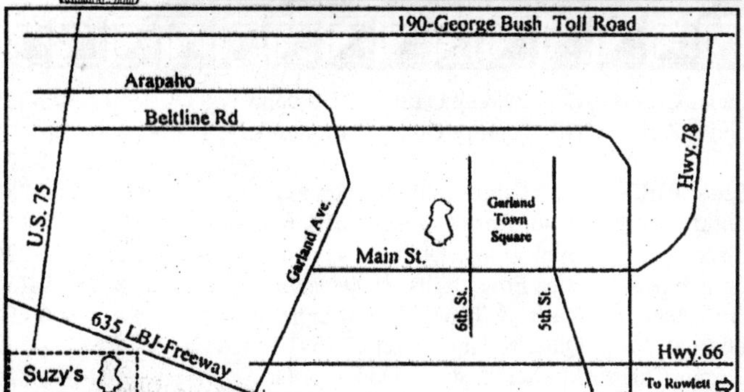

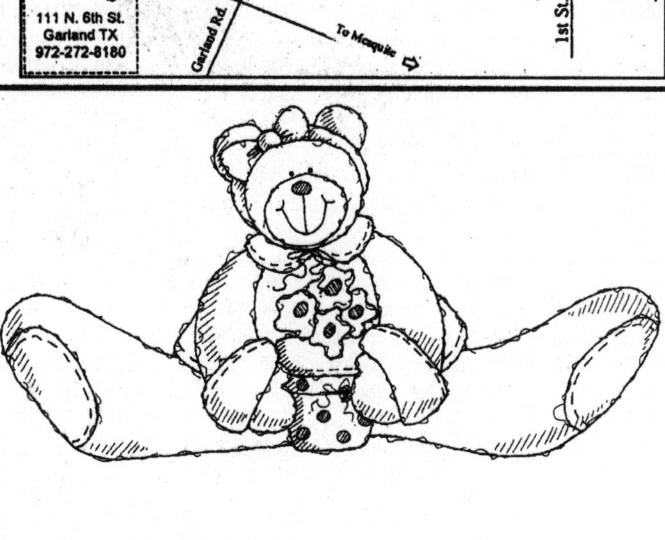

fabrics books patterns notions

Carrollton, TX #96

The Old Craft Store

1110 W. Main Street 75006
(972) 242-9111 Fax: (972) 245-0407
www.theoldcraftstorequilting.com
Owner: Melba Hamrick
Est: 1971 3000 sq.ft.
2500 Bolts

Mon - Sat 10 - 5
Thurs til 7

classes for all Levels us post office

rug hooking redwork embroidery

buyer's club thimbleberries club

Plano, TX #97

Carriage House Quilt Shoppe

3000 Custer, Suite 170
Plano, TX 75075
972-758-9916
E-Mail: chqshoppe@aol.com
Web Site: www.carriagehousequilts.com
Owner: Roxanne Rentzel

Mon - Fri 10 -6
Sat 10 - 5

Fabric — Books
Classes — Notions
We are a full service quilt shop that can help you with all your quilting needs.

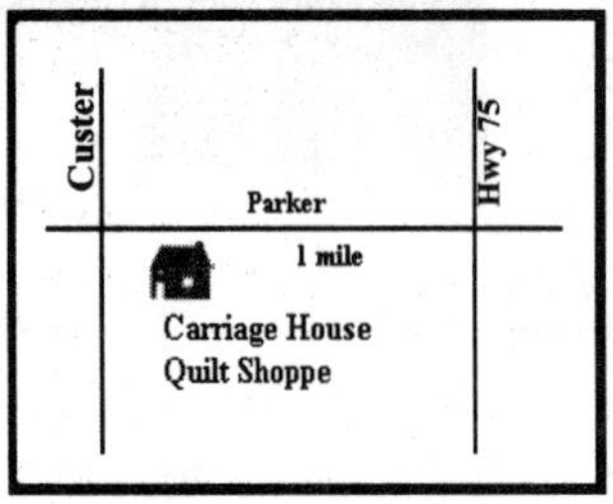

Southeast Corner of Custer and Parker

McKinney, TX #98

Mon - Sat 10 - 5

The Quilt Asylum

405 A N. McDonald St. 75069
(972) 562-2686 Fax: (972) 562-6431
E-Mail: thequiltasylum@aol.com
Owners: Susan and Russell Allen
Est: 2000 2300 sq. ft. 2000 Bolts

McKinney's newest quilt shop featuring batiks, brights, novelties plus books, patterns, notions, and kits.

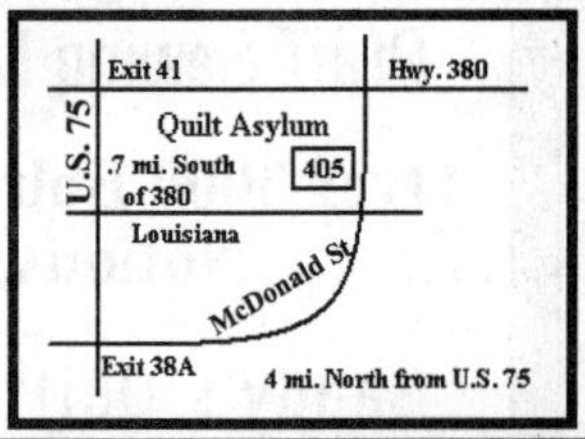

Commerce, TX #99

Quilts on the Square

Mon - Sat 9:30 - 5:30
Tues til 8

100% Cotton Fabric
Books, Patterns
Lots of Notions
Third Saturday Sampler
Great Classes - all levels

Owner: Anne Swartz
Est: 2000
1223 Washington St.
Commerce, TX 75428
(903) 886-2299
quilts@neto.com
www.quiltsonthesquare.com

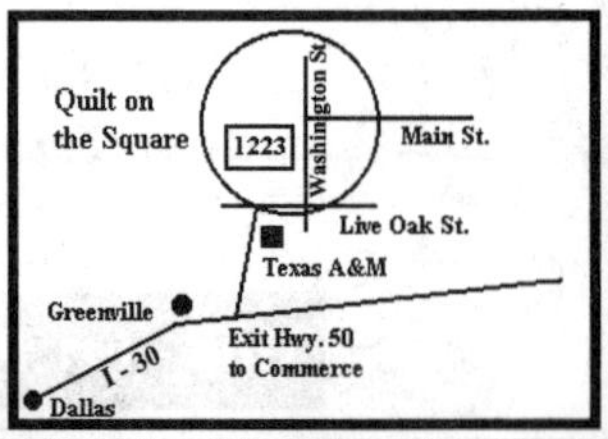

City	Store Name Store Address	Phone
Abilene	Linda's Treasury, 7500 Cty. Rd. 203	915-529-3328
Abilene	Cornerstone Quilting, 1902 Elmwood	915-793-9075
Abilene	Country Pleasures, 2508 S. 7th St.	915-676-8691
Alice	Teresa's Quilts, 1303 W. 2nd St.	361-668-1213
Allen	Quilted for You, 805 New England Ct.	972-727-4347
Allen	Rock Pile Quilters, 701 Victorian Dr.	972-396-8160
Amarillo	Fabric Fotos, 3701 Plains Blvd.	806-359-8241
Amarillo	Quilting Friends, 91 N. Fairmont St.	806-373-8379
Amarillo	Quilting Bee, 8742 River Rd.	806-383-2114
Arlington	Quilted Hearts & Co., 1205 S. Bowen	817-860-1295
Arlington	Antique Sewing Machine Museum, 703 Lombardy Ln	817-275-0971
Arlington	Dee's Quilts Supplies, 2720 Trail Oak	817-496-4854
Athens	Time 2 Quilt, 604 E. Tyler	903-677-3028
Aubrey	Fruit Jar Junction, 5848 Harmony Ranch	940-365-3158
Austin	The Quilting Loft, 301 Hurst Creek	512-261-3389
Austin	Quilts & Patchwork, 4024 Travis Country Cir.	512-892-4101
Austin	Quilts 'N Things, 8210 Briarwood Ln.	512-451-7073
Beeville	Sisters, 1806 N. Washington St.	361-358-6573
Belton	Kay's Quilts, 1668 Jamie	254-933-7140
Boerne	Tea Rose Quilts, 101 S. Main St. #A	830-249-0639
Bowie	Bowie Sewing Center, 217 N. Smythe	940-872-6220
Brownwood	Quilted Heart, 503 E. Anderson St.	915-646-2331
Caldwell	My Spare Time, Rt. 3 Box 264	
Canton	Holdcraft Cottage, 150 E. Terrell St.	903-567-6687
Cedar Creek	Cedar Creek Quilts, 203 Greenway	512-303-7353
Cedar Park	Hill Country Quilts & Embroidery, 117 N. Winecup	512-331-1241
Cedar Park	B J's Quilts, 3404 Shenondoah Dr.	512-258-2852
Childress	Arbor Rose Quilts & Gifts, 611 Ave. F NW	940-937-2797
Cisco	Bunk House Quilting, 418 Cty. Rd. #119	254-442-2205
Colleyville	Blue Frog Quilts, 3809 Oakbrier Ln.	817-514-1515
Comanche	Quilts & Tops, 605 E. Central Ave.	915-356-2047
Conroe	Quilt 'N Time Sisters, 17641 Linda Ln.	409-231-3322
Corpus Christi	My Scraps, 6618 Opengate Dr.	361-993-8552
Dallas	The Copper Lamp, 5500 Greenville Ave.	214-521-3711
Dallas	Carl's Sew Creative, 6465 E Mocking Bird	214-370-4232
Devine	Quiltin Acres, 2702 FM 2200 W	830-663-5088
Edgewood	Bobo's Cupboard, 507 Laura Dr.	903-896-1600
El Paso	El Paso Sewing Center, 1809 Trawood	915-593-0485
El Paso	Bernina of El Paso, 1809 Trawood Dr.	915-599-1909
Elkhart	M & M Shop, 315 S. Hwy. 287	903-764-1160
Fair Oaks Ranch	Sew Special Quilts, 28255 Steeplechase Ln.	210-698-0458
Fairfield	Kathy's Kuilts, 500 Cty. Rd. 228	903-389-4786
Floresville	Center Point Sensations, 680 Cty. Rd. 312	830-393-6978
Fort Stockton	Sue's Quilt Shop, 121 N. Main St.	915-336-8664
Fort Stockton	Sue's Quilt Studios, 1800 W. 7th St.	915-336-8432
Fort Worth	Edwyna's Needleworks, 1705 Fairmount	817-922-9289
Fort Worth	Cherrie's Quilt Shop, 4320 Wichita St.	817-531-0074
Fort Worth	Cotton Works, 8507 Hwy. 377 S.	817-249-0424
Fort Worth	Busy Bee Quilting, 14 Legend Rd.	817-763-8777

Other shops in Texas Cont.

Fredericksburg	Hill Country Collectibles, 249 E. Main St.	830-990-9289
Fredericksburg	Tea Rose Quilts & Gifts, 809 W. Main St.	830-997-9948
Freeport	Broad Street Market, 120 West Broad Street	979-233-6900
Freeport	Pat's Quilts & Crafts, 1822 N. Avenue I	409-233-8900
Friendswood	Cabin Fever Designs, 5010 Centennial Ln.	281-992-8118
Fritch	Kwiltwerks, 505 W. Broadway	806-857-8572
Fulton	Quilt Shoppe, P.O. Box 202	361-727-1075
Garland	Quilting Friends, 318 Saddlebrook Dr.	972-496-3753
Georgetown	Handcrafts Unlimited, 104 W. 8th St.	512-869-1812
Georgetown	Sewing Studio, 3010 Williams Dr. #20	512-863-9201
Granbury	In Stitches, 4909 Fall Creek Hwy. #6	817-326-6444
Grand Prairie	Quilting House, 1009 SE 4th St.	972-264-8380
Grandview	Quilt Lady's Daughter, 8901 Hwy. 171 S	254-854-3028
Hewitt	Wrapped in Quilts, 935 Vail Highlands	254-666-5226
Houston	Quilts Inc., 7660 Woodway #550	713-781-6882
Houston	Granny's Quilting Shack, 11902 Douglas Fir St.	281-583-0344
Houston	Quilts to Treasure, 15219 Stuebner Airline Rd.	713-416-9684
Houston	Cottontail Quilts, 14745 Memorial Dr. #107	713-899-3884
Houston	Great Expectations, 14090 Memorial Dr.	281-496-1366
Houston	Betsy's American Country, 1627-A Blalock Dr.	713-463-7222
Houston Galleria	'N Calicos Too, 10115 Hammerly	713-464-8358
Huntington	Mrs. B Quilt Patch Pond, 110 N. Hwy. 69	409-876-3234
Huntsville	Fabric Carousel, 1101 12th St.	409-295-8322
Iowa Park	Treasured Possessions Quilt, 909 E. Texas Ave.	940-592-4324
Irving	Hobbit's Hollow Quilts, 4021 W. Northgate Dr.	972-259-1415
Jefferson	Victoriana Quilts & Gifts, 211 N. Polk St.	903-665-6144
Jewett	Kountry Klutter, 322 N. Main St.	903-626-6562
Karnes City	Betty's Sewing Room, 713 E. Calvert Ave.	830-780-4044
Keene	Quilt N Stitches, 615 Lawis Ln.	817-645-9860
Keller	Sew Creative, 945 Tealwood Dr.	817-788-2407
Kerrville	Jasmine Heirlooms, 1308 Water St.	830-257-5440
Kountze	Jae's of the Big Thicket, 7616 Old Honey Island Rd.	409-246-4462
League City	The Fabric Hut, 2214 Fair Pointe Dr.	713-477-7531
Livingston	Sew Fancy, 4049 Hwy. 190 W	409-967-3950
Lockney	The Old Blue Quilt Box, 200 S. Main St.	806-652-2183
Longview	Sharman's Sewing Center, 1017 McCann Rd.	903-753-8014
Longview	Peaceful Things, 116 W. Tyler St.	903-984-1720
Lubbock	Kathryn's Quilts, 9707 Nashville Ave.	806-794-1671
Lubbock	Quilt Emporium & Mercantile, 9208 Wayne	806-798-7648
Lufkin	Country Quilting & More, 1200 S. 1st. St.	409-639-1503
Marble Falls	Blue Bonnet Designs, 1011 Ave. G	830-693-2523
McKinney	Quilting Room, 2418 Sherbrooke Ln.	972-569-3936
Memphis	Greene Dry Goods Company, 109 S. Sixth St.	806-259-2912
Midland	Remember When, 2406 Gulf Ave.	915-683-4533
Mineral Wells	Anita's Antiques, 307 N. Oak Ave.	940-325-1455
Monahans	Ye Olde Quilt Shoppe, P.O. Box 1183	915-943-5855
Munday	Prairie Stitches, 111 N. Munday Ave.	940-422-5444
Nacogdoches	The Quilt Cottage, 409 E. Hospital St.	409-559-7000
Natalia	Rose Cottage Quilting, 260 Cty. Rd. 6715	830-665-5053
New Braunfels	The Quilt Barn, 186 E. Garden St.	830-620-5810
Normangee	Esther's Quilts & Things, 13201 FM 3 S	936-855-2088
North Richland Hills	Sue's Creations, 6900 Glenwood Dr.	817-577-1042
Odessa	Heavens Quilting, 1301 McKinney Ave.	915-580-8919
Olney	Grannie's Quilt Box, 811 N Ave. E	940-564-2846
Pampa	Kriss Kross Quilting, 119 Western St.	806-665-8410
Pampa	Sands Fabrics & Quilt Corner, 225 N. Cuyler	806-669-7909
Pilot Point	Quilts in the Attic, 169 Foutch Rd.	940-686-2474
Plano	Plano Singer & New Home Sewing Center 2129 B W. Parker Rd.	972-596-0660
Plano	Carl's Sew Creative, 3237 Independence Pkwy.	972-596-5628
Plano	Heritage Farmstead, 1900 W. 15th St.	972-881-0140
Plano	Pieceful Patchwork, 3417 Parkhaven Dr.	972-964-9678
Plano	Pickin Cotton Quilts, 3117 Pinehurst Dr.	972-867-3607
Portland	Stitches Sewing Center, 801 Houston St.	361-643-1739
Post	Tea Rose Quilts, 209 S. Broadway St.	806-495-3272
Princeton	Seams to Me, 1914 Cty. Rd. 900	972-734-0323
Randolph	The Quilt Cottage, P.O. Box 58	
Richardson	Canyon Creek Quilting, 310 Arborcrest Dr.	972-699-8750
Richardson	Kay Fabrics, 518 W. Arapaho Rd.	972-234-5111
Richardson	The Fabric Affair, 339 Dal-Rich Village	972-234-1937
Roanoke	Seams Like Yesterday, 14 Colonial Ct.	817-430-0004
Round Rock	Color With Quilts, 1003 Parkside Cir.	512-244-3883
San Angelo	Expressions of Joy, 715 W. Ave. H	915-658-3867
San Angelo	Angelo Sewing Center, 5030 Knickerbocker	915-942-9780
San Antonio	Grandby's Quilts, 2519 E. Bitters Rd.	210-490-7813
San Antonio	Amish Quilt Connection, 2219 Fawn Mist	210-492-3882
San Antonio	All To Pieces, 18911 Surreywood	210-479-8969
San Antonio	Herman's Heirlooms, 7731 Apple Grn.	210-509-4578
Santa Anna	Quilters Patch, 705 Wallis Ave.	915-348-3771
Sealy	Country Antiques, 121 Meyer St.	409-885-7976
Sequim	Betsy Rose Quilt Shop Etc., 114 N. River St.	830-372-0965
Smithville	The Pine Cone, 206 Main St.	512-237-4261
Spearman	Country Stitches, 512 S. Townsend St.	806-659-2080
Splendora	Quilts N Gifts, 7979 N. Eldridge Pkwy.	281-469-0502
Spring	The Needle Nest, 2219 Sawdust Rd.	281-292-3153
Sugar Land	Astrid's Creations, 1823 Cheyenne River Cir.	281-265-6429
Sunrise Beach	Patches, 103 Sunrise Dr.	
Temple	Quilting Corner, 1401 S 31st	254-773-8331
The Woodlands	Rosalee's Quilts, P.O. Box 9431	281-364-7579
Troup	QuiltN Bee, 504 E. Duval St.	903-842-4669
Tyler	Ann's Sewing Center, 322 E. Southeast Loop 323 #150	903-581-4926
Tyler	John R. Sauls' Antiques, 310 W. Rusk St.	903-593-4668
Tyler	Granny's Needle Haus, 6004 S. Broadway Ave.	903-561-4637
Victoria	Dunlap's, 2804 N. Laurent St.	361-573-3289
Victoria	Quilt Cupboard, 2805 E. Loma Vista Ave.	361-578-6270
Weatherford	Quilts & More, 1206 N. Main St.	817-599-3552
Webster	Fabrics Etcetera, 571 W. Bay Area Blvd.	281-338-1904
Whitney	Francie's Personally Yours, 5120 FM 933 N	254-694-4950
Whitney	Savior Quilts, R.R. 5, Box 1008	254-694-2720

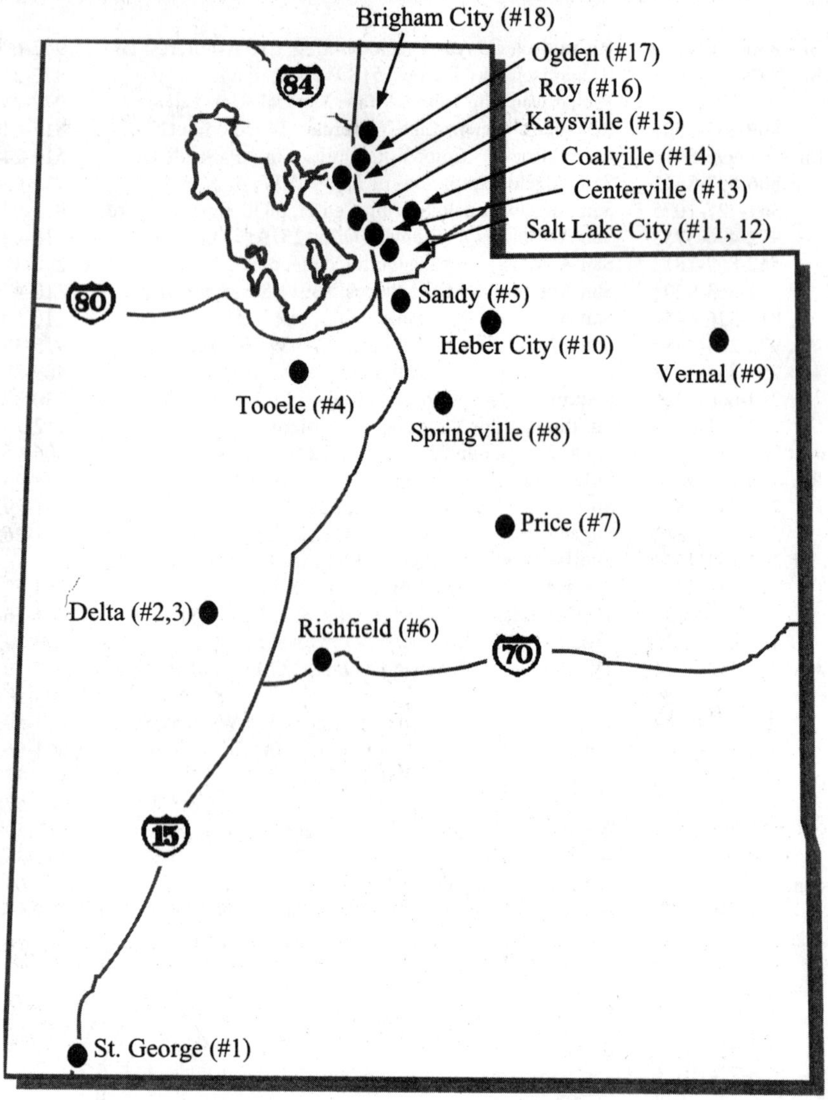

UTAH

18 Featured Shops

St. George, UT #1

Mon - Fri 10 - 5:30
Sat 10 - 4

Sew Suite, Inc.

43 N 700 E 84770
(435) 673-9117 Fax: (435) 673-5931
Est: 1996 3000 sq.ft. 3500 Bolts

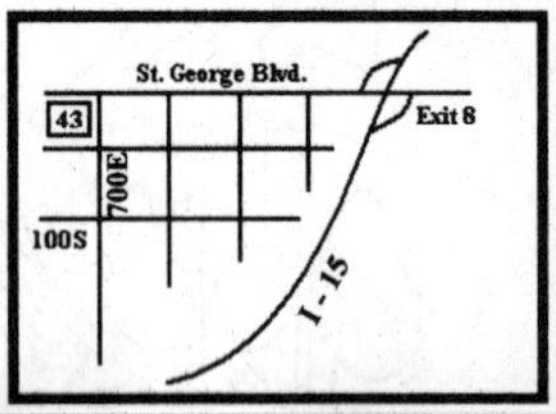

Come and visit the "sweetest" quilt shop in color country. We are a complete quilting resource shop. (There's plenty of great golfing as well.)

Delta, UT #3

Mon - Fri 10 - 5:30
Sat 12 - 5

Heartspun Treasures Quilt Shop

291 E. Main St. 84624
(435) 864-4204
Owners: Ann & Danielle Morgan

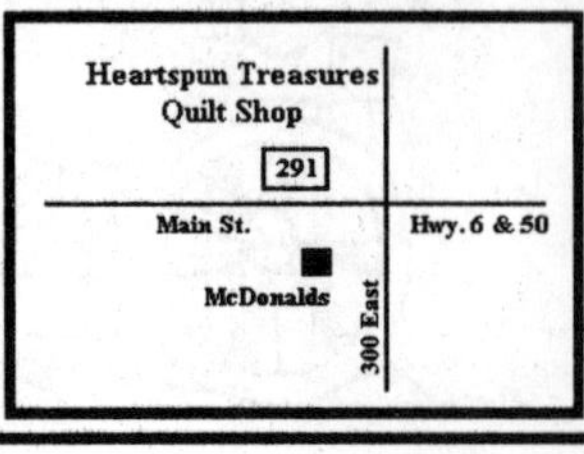

A specialty quilt shop w/ quality 100% cotton fabrics, large selection of homespun plaids! Also, Quilting Supplies, Books, Patterns and Custom Machine Quilting! A vintage display of antique sewing & quilting memorabilia.

"A Quilt Store with a Unique Décor"

Mom's Crafts and Fabrics

Mon - Sat 10 - 6

313 South 100 West 84624

Biggest and Best Selection of Quilting Fabrics South of Provo, Utah. 100 Antique Sewing Machines on Display.
Est: 1973
4800 sq.ft.

(435) 864-3325
Owner: Peggy Overson
E-Mail:
poverson@xmission.com

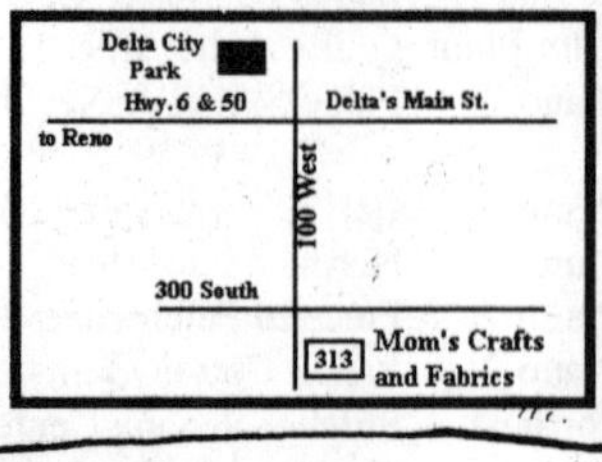

Delta, UT #2

Sew Sweet

986 N Main - Tooele, UT 84074 (435) 833-0370

Tooele, UT #4

2,800 Bolts of high quality quilting fabric
Large selection of Books & Patterns, Notions and Batting

We have over fifteen flavors of our special recipe Gourmet Fudge. You're sure to find one or two flavors you can't live with out! Come in for a FREE sample!

We are proud to announce our own line of patterns; Kitchen Table Quilts. Take a look at our Sweet Weave Quilt on the net!

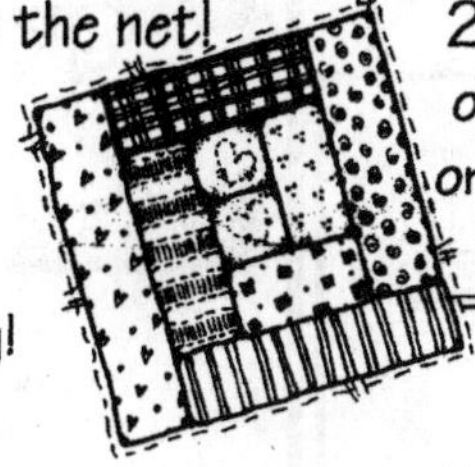

Show us this add to save 20% off one item or 1 cut of fabric

Monday - Friday 10am - 7pm
Saturday 10am - 5pm
Closed Sundays - We're home quilting!

Just 35 miles west of Salt Lake City

From the Salt Lake area, take I-80 west and take exit 99. This is SR 36 and will become Tooele's Main Street in about 12 miles. We are located in the Macey's shopping center on the east side of Main.

Our Internet Shop is Always Open

www.sewsweet.net

Fabric Clubs
Easy Fabric Finder
Large Selections of Notions
Internet Specials
Quilting Tips & Advice
Secure Shopping
FREE Patterns
Quilters@sewsweet.net

Quilt, Quilt, Quilt Etc.

Sandy, UT #5

Weekdays 10 - 9
Saturdays 10 - 5

11 East Main 84070 (8720 South at State)
(877) 422-6765 — (801) 255-2666
Owner: Dorthey Chase Est: 1988 3000 sq.ft.

Notions—all the latest ⌘ Books—all the newest
Patterns—one of the best selections you've seen
Frames ⌘ Classes

15 Minutes South of Salt Lake City

Over 14,000 Bolts of Fabric

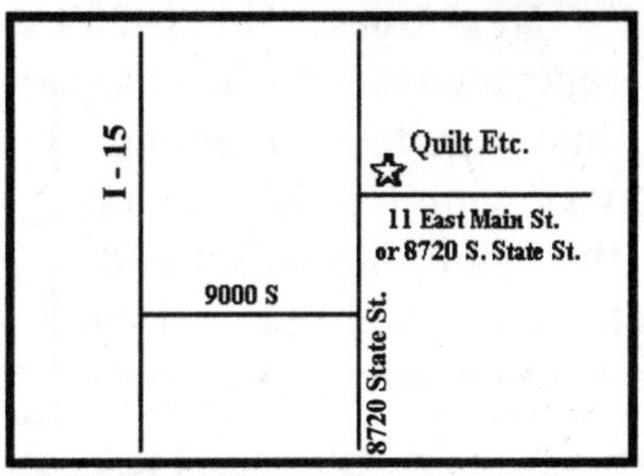

Richfield, UT #6

Mon - Sat 9 - 6

MARCIA'S

25 N. Main St. 84701
(435) 896-8354
Est: 1989

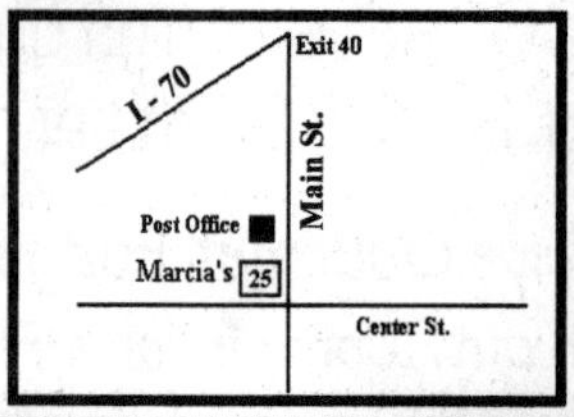

Central Utah's largest fabric shop. We cater to quilters. Custom hand quilting and edging.
Gifts - Fabric - Quilting - Classes

Price, UT #7

Summer Mon - Fri 9 - 6 Sat 10 - 5 Winter Mon - Sat 10 - 5

Fabric Frenzy, Inc.

545 E 100 N 84501
(435) 637-3348

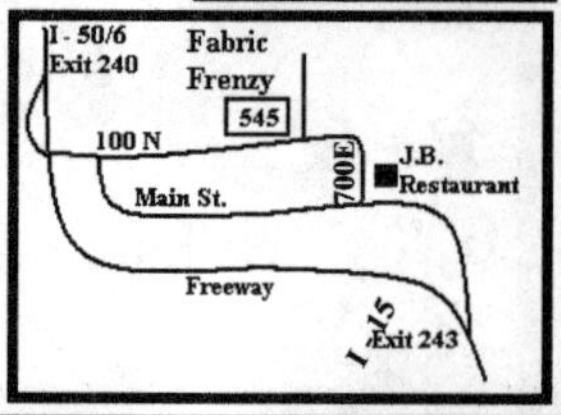

Small quilting shop - Discount to Guild Members. In store discount card - Quilt classes. 1 1/2 miles east from Exit 240. 1 mile northeast to 7th east - Right turn, 1 block - Left 1 1/4 blocks.

Springville, UT #8

Mon - Sat 10 - 6

Corn Wagon Quilt Co.

303 E 400 S 84663
(801) 491-3551 Fax: (801) 491-7256
E-Mail: cornwquilts@aol.com
Owner: Marsha Harward
Est: 1999

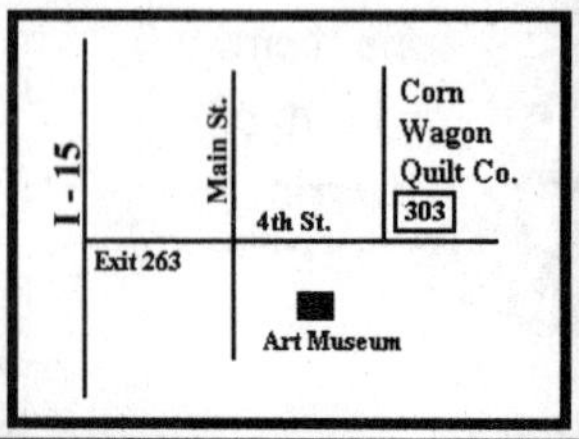

3000+ bolts of 100% cotton fabric & flannels, books, patterns, notions, cross-stitch & stitchery supplies. Beautiful displays of our shop's custom machine quilting.

Vernal, UT #9

Mon - Fri 10 - 6 Sat 11 - 4:30

Quilted Hens

38 South 600 West
84078
(435) 789-2411

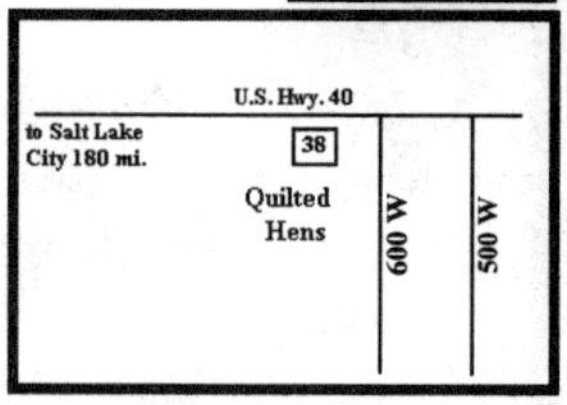

We have a simple abundance of Flannels and Quilting Cottons.

Heber City, UT #10

Whimsy Cottage

350 S. Main St. 84032
(435) 654-7137 Fax: (435) 654-7095
E-Mail: whimsyq@xmission.com
Web Site: whimsycottage.com
Est: 1999 1600 sq.ft.

Mon - Thur 10 - 6 Fri & Sat 10 - 5

Fresh, vibrant fabrics, a creative atmosphere plus friendly, helpful service define our shop. And, across our shared driveway is **The House Next Door.** This 1920's cottage has been renovated just for quilters and is perfect for getting away with friends to do just that...quilt. Details, rates, etc. on our website. Ask for a tour when you stop by!

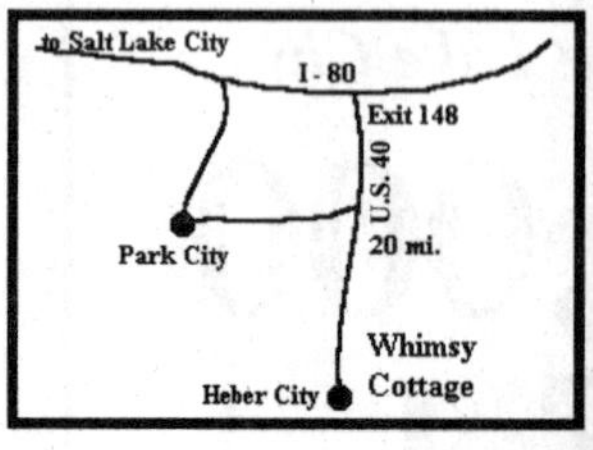

Featured shop in Quilt Sampler 2002

DURABLE GOODS SINCE 1937

MORMON HANDICRAFT

15 WEST SOUTH TEMPLE STREET
SALT LAKE CITY, UTAH 84101
1-801-355-2141 • 1-800-843-1480

The largest inventory of quilting fabrics, supplies, and handmade arts in the Salt Lake area

DISCOVER WHY THOUSANDS VISIT OUR STORES EACH YEAR!

Located directly across the street from historic Temple Square.
ALSO VISIT
OUR ST.GEORGE STORE
735 S. Bluff St. George, Utah
1-435-628-4495 • 1-800-300-0242

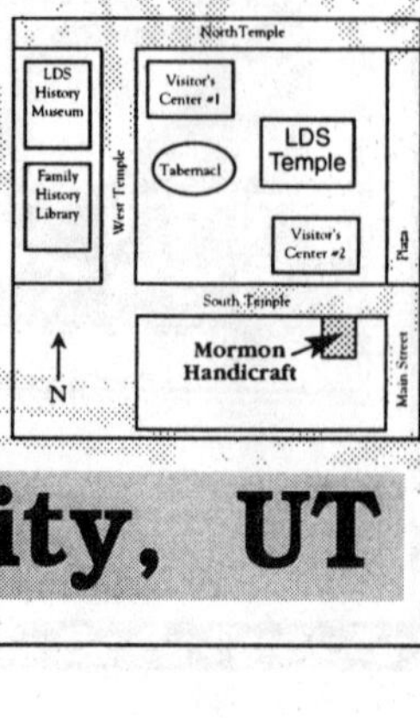

shop 24 hours
mormonhandicraft.com

Salt Lake City, UT

Salt Lake City, UT #12

Mon - Fri 10 - 9
Sat 10 - 6
Sun 12 - 4

Pipers Quilts & Comforts

1944 South 11th East 84106
(801) 484-5890 Fax: (801) 484-5890
E-Mail: info@pipersquilts.com
Web Site: www.pipersquilts.com
Est: 1998 3500 sq. ft. 1500 Bolts.

Located in Historic Sugarhouse's oldest home. An amazing array of fabrics, featuring Moda & Alexander Henry. We specialize in kits!!! Complimentary classes!

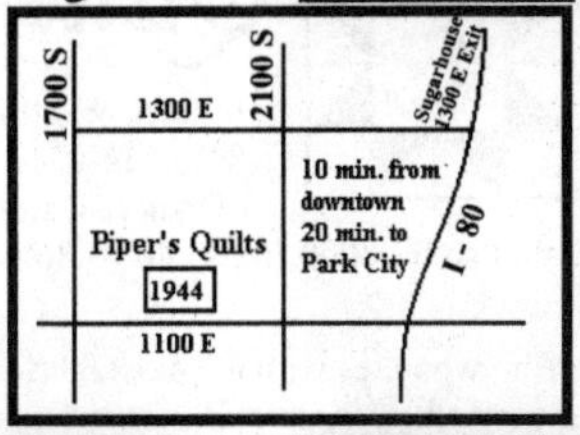

Centerville, UT #13

Mon - Fri 10 - 6
Sat 10 - 5

Threads of Time: Fabric for Quilts

158 W. Parrish Lane 84014
(801) 298-5077 Fax: (801) 298-8780
E-Mail: CherylS@quiltedweb.com
Web Site: www.quiltedweb.com
Owner: Cheryl Styler Est: 1999 4000 sq. ft.

More bolts of fabric than we care to count! Everything that a Quilter could dream of! Books, Patterns, Notions & a huge selection of quality cotton Fabrics. Fun, knowledgeable Staff!

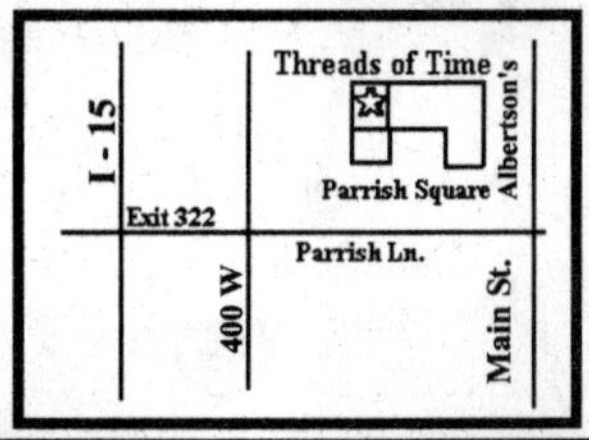

Coalville, UT #14

Tues - Thur 10 - 5:30
Fri & Sat 10 - 5

Gwendolyn's Fabrics

19 S. Main, P.O. Box 38 84017
(435) 336-8770 Fax: (435) 336-8771
E-Mail: gwen@gquilts.com
Web Site: www.gquilts.com
Owner: Gwen Henley
Est: 1997 5300 sq.ft.

Fabrics, Crafts, Machine Quilting, Hemstitching, Lots of flannels, notions, Sewing station rental with all the tools you need for any project! Viking sewing machines.

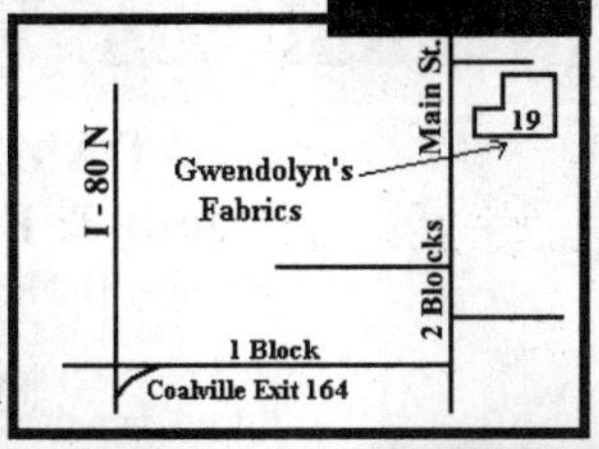

Kaysville, UT #15

Mon - Fri 9 - 9
Sat 9 - 7

Ben Franklin Crafts®

354 N. Main (801) 444-1177
Fax: (801) 444-0429
E-Mail: sbennion@ix.netcom.com
Owners: Steven & Scott Bennion
Est: 1997 20,000 sq.ft. 1500+ Bolts

Over 1500 Bolts of hand picked fabric. Great selection of sewing & quilt items. We also have floral & frame supplies.

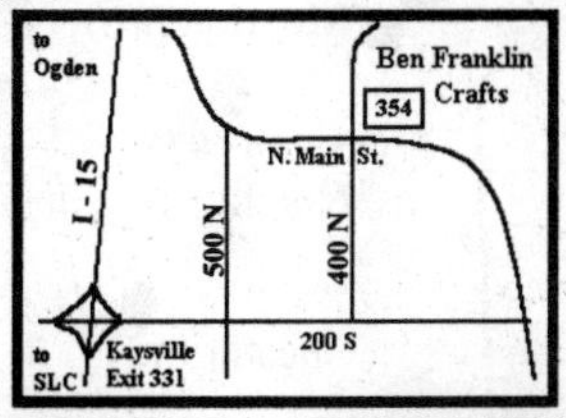

Roy, UT #16

Mon - Fri 9 - 9
Sat 9 - 7

Ben Franklin Crafts®

1946 W 5600 S 84067
(801) 825-7037 Fax: (801) 773-1666
E-Mail: mbennion@ix.netcom.com
Owners: David, Sharon, & Michael Bennion
Est: 1957 21,000 sq.ft. 2000+ Bolts

Over 2000 bolts of hand picked fabric. Great selection of sewing & quilt supplies. Quilt books and patterns, yarn. Plus much more!

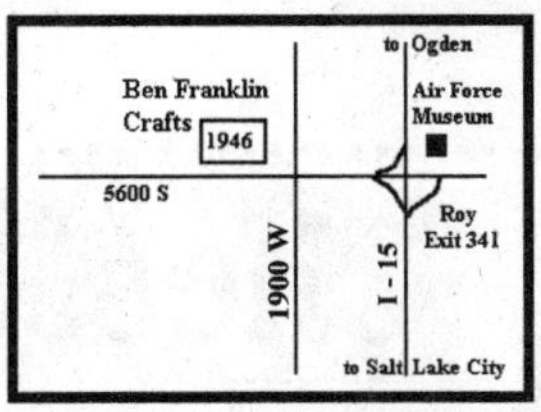

Ogden, UT #17

Mon - Sat 10 - 6

Gardiners Sew & Quilt

2233 Grant Ave. 84401
(801) 394-4466
Owners: Curt & Irene Gardiner
Est: 1975 3000 sq.ft.

Northern Utah's Premier Quilt Shop - 5000+ bolts of 100% cotton, Largest selection of Flannels, Notions, Books, Patterns, Hemstitching, expert machine quilting and classes.

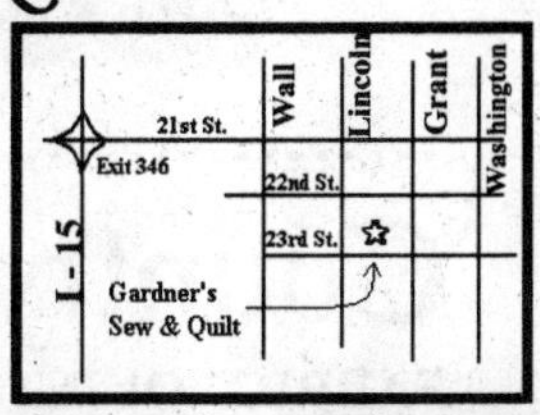

Brigham City, UT #18

Mon - Sat 10 - 6

Village Dry Goods

33 S. Main 84302
(435) 723-1315
Web Site:
www.villagedrygoods.com
(home of Monday's Mail)
Owners: RoLayne & Rosa

A quaint shop in an historic Hotel. Specializing in quality fabric, tons of kits, stitchery, and Block of the Months.

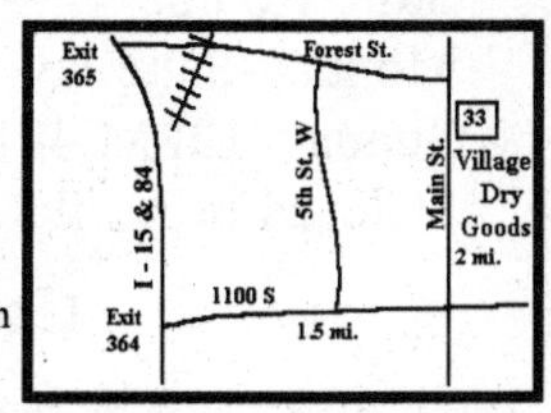

City	Store Name Store Address	Phone
Blanding	Parley Redd Mercantile, 82 S. Main	801-678-2228
Bountiful	Quilter's Haven, 846 S. Main St.	801-292-1846
Cedar City	Color Country Crafts, 622 S. Main St.	801-865-7060
Centerville	Centerville Quilt Works, 322 E 500 N	801-292-7988
Draper	Thimbles & Threads, 12215 S. 900 E.	801-576-0390
Joseph	Friendship Quilts, 95 N. State St.	435-527-3789
Kaysville	Vonda's Quilt Farms, 99 N. Angel St.	801-543-1876
Layton	Nuttalls' Crazy Quilt Shop, 21 E. Gentile St.	801-544-5911
Lehi	Creations by Tish, 127 E. State St.	801-768-8086
Logan	Bernina Fabric Center, 138 N. Main St.	435-752-4186
Logan	Grandma's Quilts, 93 E. 100 S.	435-753-5670
Logan	Needles N Neighbors, 128 S. 1170 E	801-753-6589
Mendon	Quilters' Courtyard, 87 W 300 N	435-755-7065
Midvale	Connie's Quilts & Crafts, 569 Carmel Dr.	801-568-0435
Moab	A Material World, 702 S. Main	435-259-6672
Odgen	Kinsella's Quilts, 1545 24th St.	801-399-2576
Odgen	Envirocraft Posies & Quilts, 990 E 1050 N	801-782-3076
Odgen	Sweet Lavender, 4555 S 700 W	801-627-5005
Ogden	Nuttall Bernina, 3080 Washington Blvd.	801-392-5081
Ogden	Cozy Quilts, 2081 N 4500 W	801-732-1992
Orem	Fabric Mill, 414 E 1400 S	801-225-3123
Orem	The Stitching Corner, 631 E 1700 S	801-426-6900
Panguitch	Snowed in Quilt Shop, 190 N. Main	435-676-8666
Park City	Scrapbaggers, P.O. Box 982124	435-532-3297
Pleasant Grove	Piece Goods Craft & Fabric, 460 W. State	801-785-0437
Providence	The Quilt House, 135 S. 100 E	801-752-5429
Provo	Fabric Mill, 90 W. Center St.	801-375-4818
Riverdale	Fibers & Twigs, 4555 S 700 W	801-627-6475
Riverton	J J Quilts, 2075 W 12130 S	801-253-9747
Roy	Marlene's Quiltsm 3118 W 5200 S	801-825-0547
Roy	The Quilter's Basketm 4684 S 3600 W	888-703-7031
Roy	Utah Quilt Shoppe, 5513 S 2950 W	801-773-3197
Saint George	Quilts Etc., 250 Red Cliffs Dr. #35	
Salt Lake City	Lily Rogers Heirloom Quilts, 602 E 500 S	801-575-6446
Salt Lake City	The Grace Co.-Quilting Frames, 801 W 1850	801-972-5801
Salt Lake City	Gentler Times Quilt Shop, 4880 S. Highland	801-277-9233
Salt Lake City	Quilter's Patch, 2370 S. 3600 W.	801-973-6117
Sandy	The Cotton Shop, 9441 S 700 E	801-572-1412
Sandy	Fabric Warehouse, 9251 S 700 E	801-565-8465
Sandy	Quilts of Utah, 8504 Treasure Mountain Rd.	801-943-7551
Sandy	Quilted Keepsakes, 1897 Falcon Way	801-571-9671
South Jordan	Cottage Comforts & Quilts, 9462 S 3770 W	801-280-9117
St. George	Quilts Etc, 250 Red cliffs Dr. #35	435-674-4911
Tremonton	La Rue's Country Quilts, 145 W. Main	435-257-0801
Tremonton	Miller's Buttons & Bolts, 25 W. Main St.	435-257-5604
Vernal	Dinaland Quiltworks, 2280 S 2000 E	435-789-6426
West Jordan	Fabric Center, 1633 W. 9000 S	801-561-8726
West Jordan	Village Quilt Shop, 1095 W 7800 S	801-566-1846
West Jordan	Cathianne's Quilting Keepsakes, 9231 Tanya Ave.	801-562-1699
West Jordan	The Stitching Corner, 1550 W. 7800 S.	801-566-1400
West Valley	City Quilt Shop, 3601 S 2700 W	801-966-7915

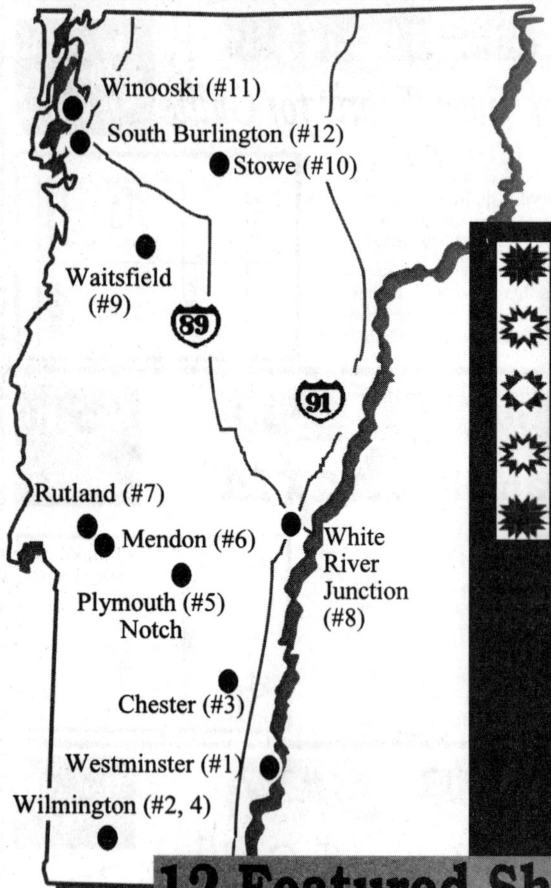

VERMONT

12 Featured Shops

Westminster, VT #1

M, T, Th, F 12 - 4
Sat 10 - 4
or by Appt.

Quilt-a-way

540 Back Westminster Rd.
(802) 722-4743 05159
Owner: Carol Coski
600 sq.ft. 8000 Bolts. 400+ Bolts of Batiks.

"She who dies with the most fabric wins!" Every day is a sale day & we discount everything we sell.

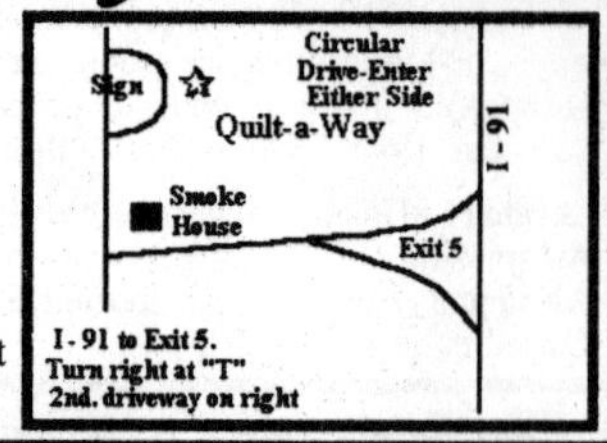

Wilmington, VT #2

Open 10 - 5
Dec - June
Closed Mon
July - Nov
Closed Tues

ADAMS FARM'S
Quilt & Fiber Arts Loft

15 Higley Hill Rd. 05363
(802) 464-3762
Fax: (802) 464-6547
E-mail: farmfun@sover.net
Web : www.adamsfamilyfarm.com
Est: 1998 1500 sq.ft.

Over 150 Family & locally made Quilts & Wallhangings. Handmade Sweaters & Shawls. Join us for "Afternoon Tea" on Wed, Fri or Sat @ 3 p.m.

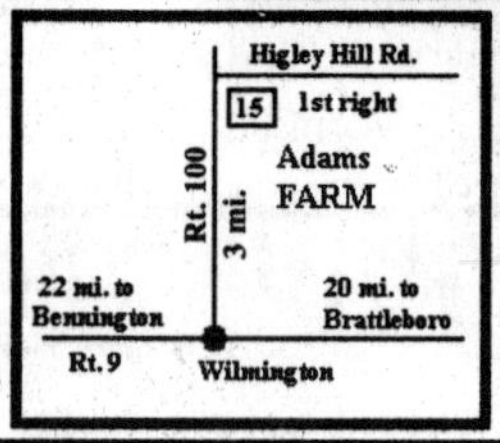

Country Treasures

Chester, VT #3

FABRIC - QUILTS - GIFTS – FOLK ART & BOOKS

P.O. Box 994
12 Common St.
Chester, VT 05143

Phone: (802)875-4377
ww.vermontquilting.com
Email: sue@vermontquilting.com

Store Hours:
Monday-Saturday 10AM-5PM
Sunday, 12PM-4PM
*Closed in April

Country Treasures is one of the premier quilt shops in New England

Over 5,000 bolts of fabric including an entire room of flannels and brushed homespuns.

Established in 1990, Country Treasures is 3000 sq. ft. and has 6,000 bolts of fabric.

Fat quarter bundles done in complete lines or color coordinated are favorites with our customers.

– Large selection of books and patterns – Quilt classes to fit every skill level –
– Gift Department – Will ship anywhere –

Annual Fabric Sale:
Anniversary Sale– Starting the last week of June through July

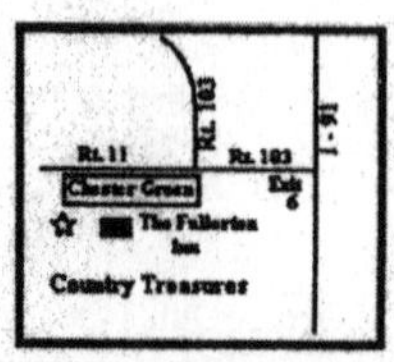

Wilmington, VT #4

Norton House

A Quilter's Paradise !

Over 3000 100% Cotton Fabrics.
The most beautiful fabric at the best prices!

Our friendly competent staff can offer you expert help in quilt planning and fabric coordination.
Books - Notions - Patterns - Quilting Classes
Vermont Made Quilts - Needlework Kits - Candles - Gifts

Our Fabric Sale Attic is stuffed with 100% top quality cottons specially priced at 20 to 50% off.

Open 7 Days a Week, 9 - 5, all year

30 W. Main St., P.O. Box 579 05363
(802) 464-7213
E-Mail: norquilt@sover.net
Owner: Suzanne Wells Wurzberger
Est: 1967 2000 sq.ft.
www.norquilt.com

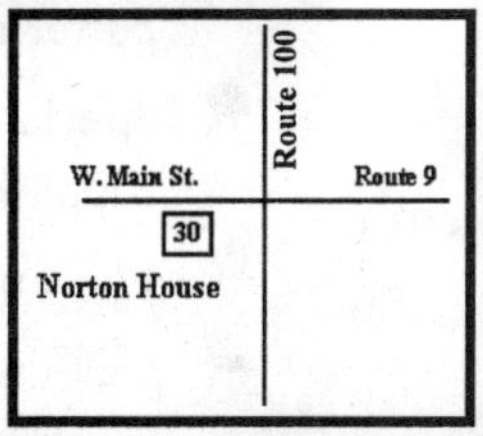

Plymouth Notch, VT #5

Daily Late May - mid Oct 9:30 - 5

President Calvin Coolidge State Historic Site

Plymouth Notch Historic District
(802) 672-3773 Est: 1956
P.O. Box 247 05056
11 Museum Buildings

Several late 19th Century Quilts on Permanent exhibition. Including one pieced by Calvin Coolidge when he was 10 years old. (Tumbling Blocks)

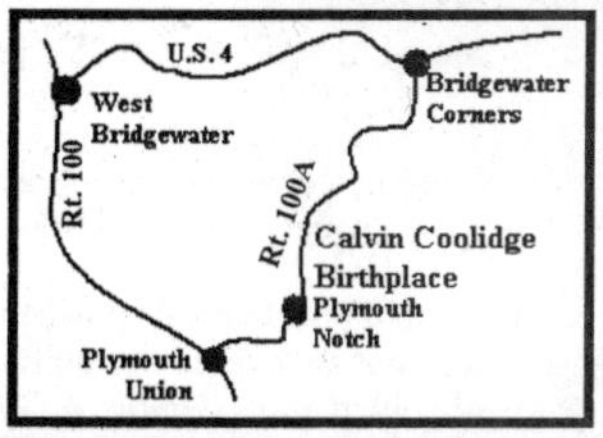

Mendon, VT #6

1 Route 4 East, Mendon, VT 05701
(802) 773-5628

Fax: (802) 773-5641
pbahnson@yahoo.com
Est: 2000 2500 sq.ft. 1500 Bolts

Peggy's Patchwork QUILT SHOP

Quilt Fabric, Patterns, Notions, Books & Quilt Classes

"It is my pleasure to provide you with the best of customer service in an environment which delights your senses."
Peggy Bahnson - Owner

Tues - Sat
9:30 - 6
Sun 12 - 5

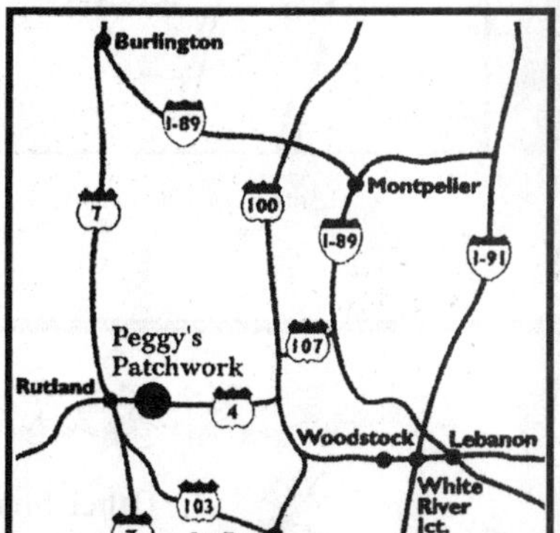

Rutland, VT #7

Mon - Sat 9:30 - 5 Sun 12 - 5

Country Quilt & Fabric

4 U.S. Rt. 4 (Rt. 4E) Mendon, VT 05701
(802) 773-3470
E-Mail: Quilters12@aol.com
Owners: Pat & Lynne Benard
Est: 1982 1400 sq.ft.

3000+ bolts of 100% cotton fabrics -- Hoffman, South Seas, P&B, RJR, plus Notions, Books & Patterns
Custom Orders too.

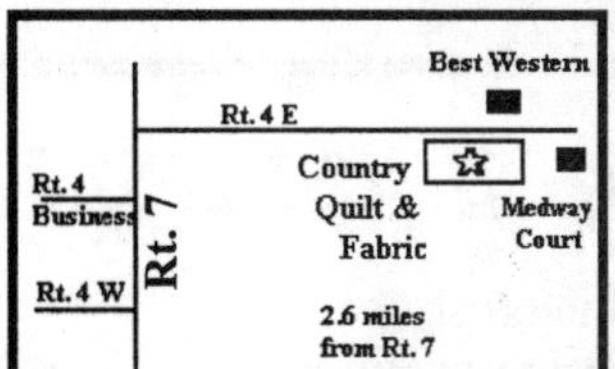

White River Junction, VT #8

Mon - Fri 9:30 - 6 Sat 9 - 4

Country Quilters Emporium

223 Maple St. 05001
(802) 295-1375 Fax: (802) 295-1398
E-Mail: cqemporium@aol.com
Owners: Buzz & Nancy Barr
Est: 2000 1300 sq.ft. 1300 Bolts

Friendly store with quality 100% cotton fabrics, books, patterns, classes and quilting tools. Bernina Dealer, machines serviced, scissors sharpened.

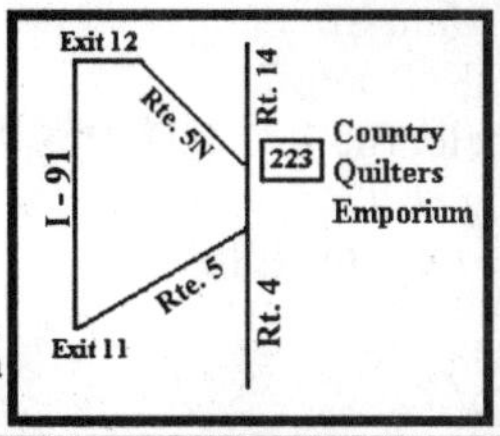

Waitsfield, VT #9

Mon & Wed - Sat 10 - 5

Cabin Fever Quilts

The Old Church Route 100
P.O. Box 443 05673
(802) 496-2287 Owner: Vee Lowell
Est: 1976 1200 Sq.ft.

Cabin Fever Quilts offers Amish/ Mennonite hand quilted quilts plus custom made tied comforters. Fabric, Quilting Supplies, Quilt Kits & much more!

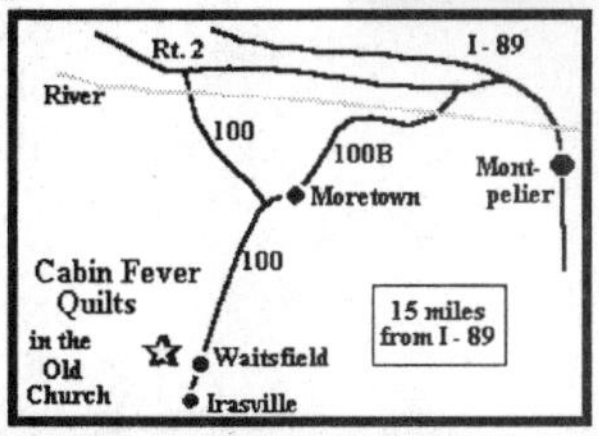

Stowe, VT #10

Mon - Sat 10 - 5

Prints & Patches

Main St., P.O. Box 1205 05672
(802) 253-8643
E-Mail: quilts@stowe.nu
Web Site: www.quiltsvermont.com
Owner: Mary Johnson

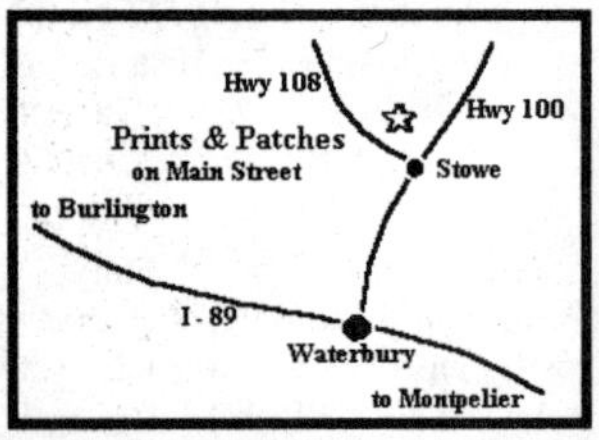

Come on into our Retail shop in Stowe, where we create our own Vermont quilts. Antique & Hand quilted quilts, Fabric, & Gifts.

Winooski, VT #11

**Mon - Sat 10 - 9
Sun 12 - 5**

Yankee Pride

Champlain Mill 05404
(802) 655-0500
Est: 1981 2500 Bolts

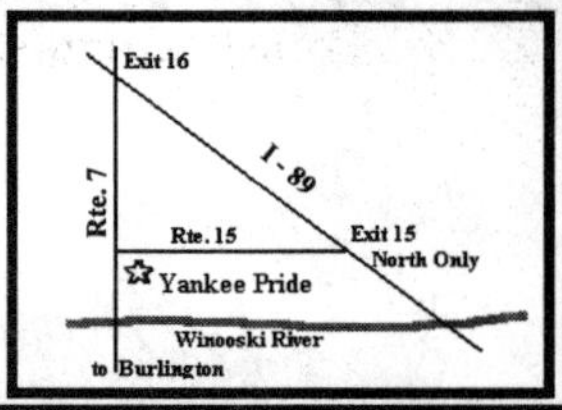

All the top brands of fabrics, the newest books and notions, classes. Friendly, knowledgeable service.

Quilter's Courtyard

A haven for quilters, quilt lovers, and friends.

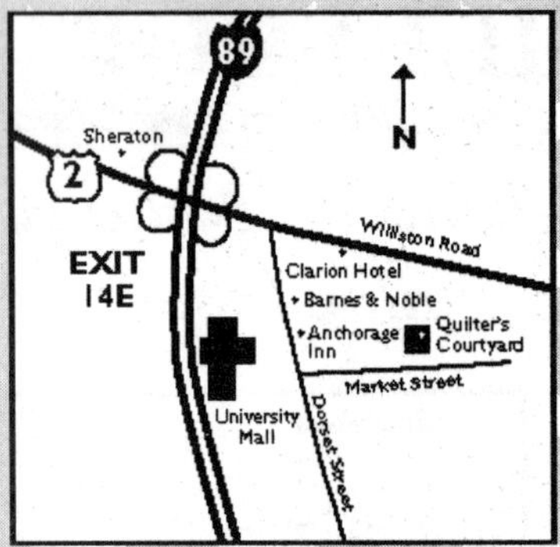

Beth Cousins
Owner

4 Market Street
South Burlington, VT 05403

802.863.4656

www.quilterscourtyard.com

Monday – Friday 10am–9pm
Saturday 9am–9pm
Sunday noon–5pm

Nothing Sews Like A Bernina. Nothing.
BERNINA
Authorized Bernina dealer
for sales and service

Stroll in our beautiful courtyard, just brimming with delightful treasures!

- A spectacular selection of contemporary and traditional fabrics.
- Many unique Blocks-of-the-month.
- A machine quilting studio to finish your quilt tops. We gladly accept quilt tops via mail.
- Personalized weekend getaways for your group or guild.
- Extensive book, notions, thread and pattern collections.
- Special orders for fabrics and quilting supplies.
- Many uniquely wonderful gifts.
- Call us for more details or to place an order.

South Burlington, VT #12

Other Shops in Vermont: We suggest calling first

Essex Junction	Backcountry Threads, 169 Brigham Hill Rd.	802-872-7855
Johnson	Broadwoven Fabric Mill, R.R. # 2	802-635-7880
Ludlow	Clover Knoll Crafter, 140 Main St.	802-228-4830
Lyndonville	Fabrictown, 45 Depot St.	802-626-9367
Newfane	The Log Cabin Quilting Shop, R.R. #1, Box 925	802-365-7974
Newfane	Newfane Country Store, P.O. Box 56 Route 30	802-365-7916
North Clarendon	Quilt Barn of Vermont, 1943 East St.	802-775-0988
Richmond	A Village Quilter, 117 W. Main St.	802-434-4272
Shelburne	The Shelburne Museum, U.S. Route 7	802-985-3346
Shelburne	Hearthside Quilts, 2048 Shelburne Rd., P.O. Box 429	802-985-8077
Vergennes	Lady of the Cloth, 141 King Hill Rd.	802-759-2042
Wills River	Catamount Quilt Studio, 251 Leete Hill Rd.	802-429-2911

VIRGINIA

31 Featured Shops

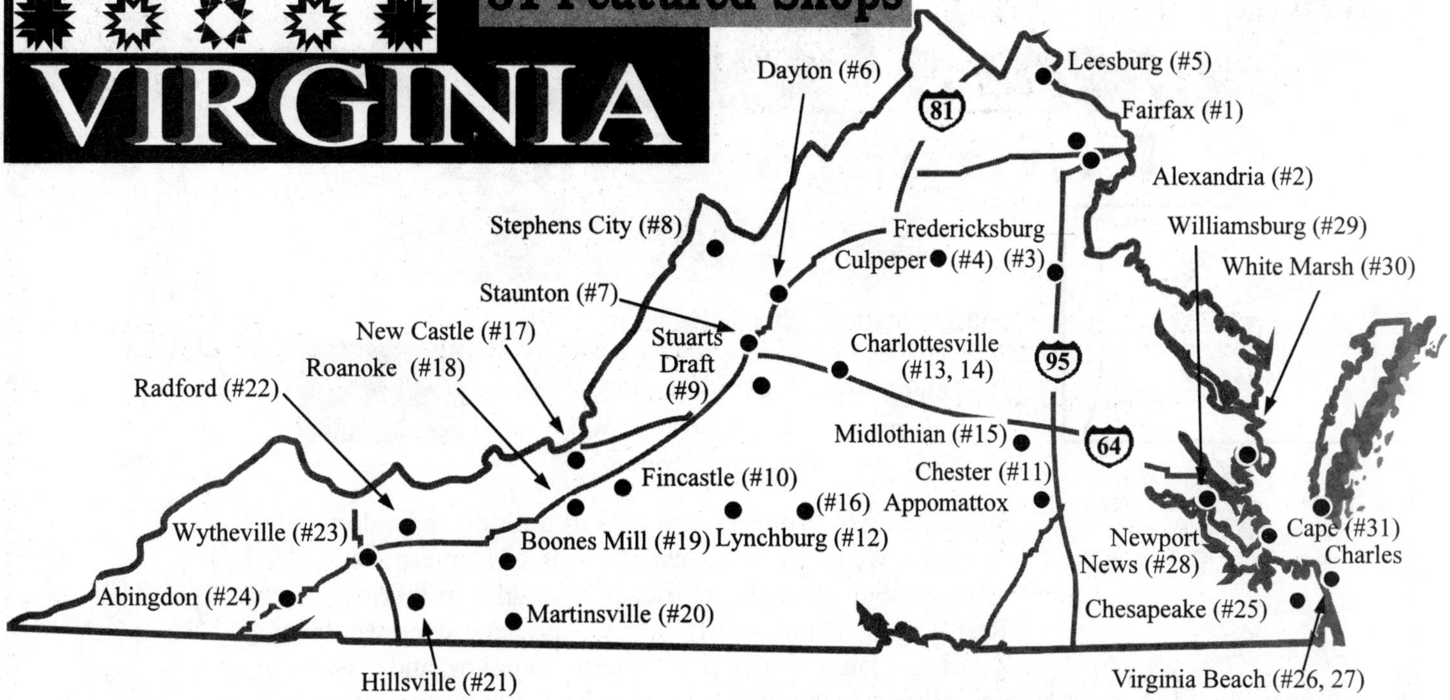

2,500 bolts of 100% Cotton Quilting Fabrics, Quilting Supplies, Notions, Patterns and Books. Classes

The Quilt Patch

Bernina of Northern Virginia

(703) 273-6937
10381 Main St.
Fairfax VA
22030

www.quiltpatchva.com

Monday - Saturday 10 am - 5pm
Thursday 10 am - 8 pm

Fairfax, VA #1

Alexandria, VA #2

Tues - Sat 11 - 5 Sun 1 - 5

Rocky Road to Kansas

215 South Union Street 22314
(703) 683-0116 Est: 1980
Owner: Dixie Kaufman

Large selection antique/vintage Quilts. Tops, Patches, Feedsacks. Quilt Related Items. Gifts and accessories. Vera Bradley Bags.

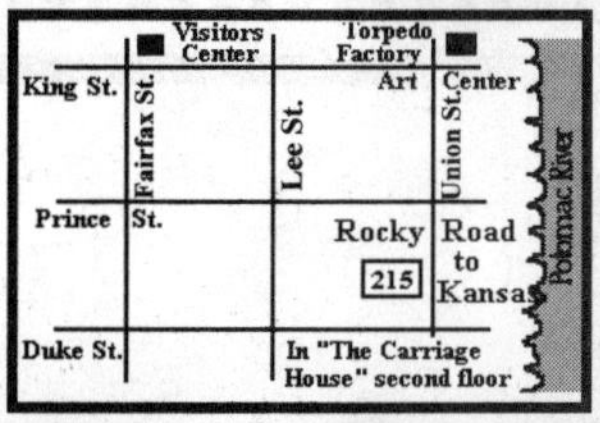

Fredericksburg, VA #3

Tues - Sat 10 - 5 or by Appt.

Quilter's Heaven

1000 Charles St. 22401
(540) 371-9011
Owners: Janice Fletcher & Susan Fulton
Est: 1998 1200 Bolts

Located in Historic Downtown Fredericksburg. 1200 Bolts, Books, Patterns & Notions. Friendly Southern Hospitality.

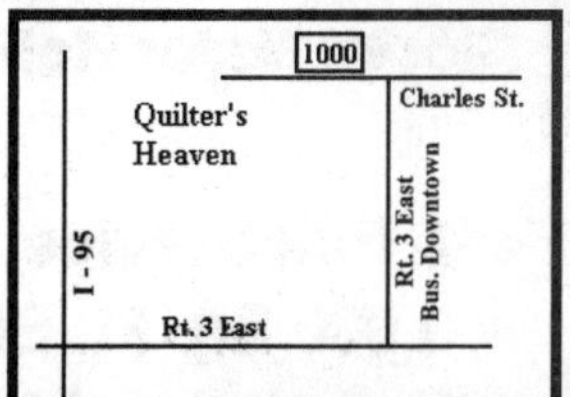

Culpeper, VA #4

Tues & Thurs 7 - 9 Wed & Fri 10 - 2 Sat 9 - 4

Early Times Workshop

129-133 E. Davis St., P.O. Box 748 22701
(540) 829-7200
E-Mail: etwmwm@aol.com
Owner: Marty Moon Est: 1983

Specialty items for Special Needleworkers -- Quilting, Cross Stitch, Canvas work -- Books -- Classes
Hard-to-find notions and fibers -- Fabric
Personal Attention

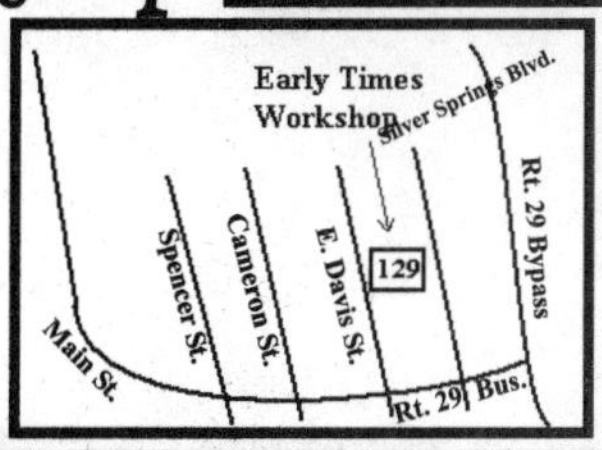

Memere's Garden, Inc.

Fantastic Shop

Historic Leesburg, VA #8

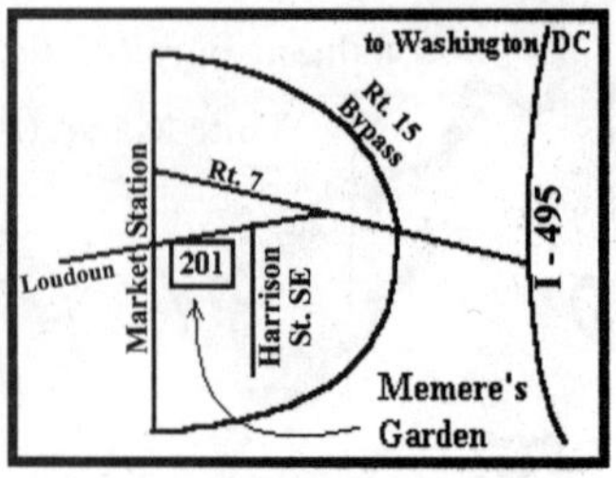

Memere's Garden, Market Station, is located in the Historic Train Depot in Leesburg, VA, Just 20 miles west of Washington DC.

Market Station 201-B Harrison St. SE
Historic Leesburg, VA 20175
(703) 669-0807 Est: 2000 4000+ bolts
E-mail: madym@erols.com
Owner: Dana Sonnenberg

Mon - Sat 10 - 5

Specializing in Primitive and Folkart quilting and colonial crafts, we have the largest selection of Homespuns, Homespun-flannels, reproduction Civil War fabrics, Red Wagon, Thimbleberry fabrics, and hand-dyed wools. We offer a large selection of patterns, supplies, and classes for quilting, rughooking, stenciling, samplers, cross-stitch, primitive stitcheries, and needlepunch. You can also shop in your jammies in our full service webshoppe.

www.memeresgarden.com

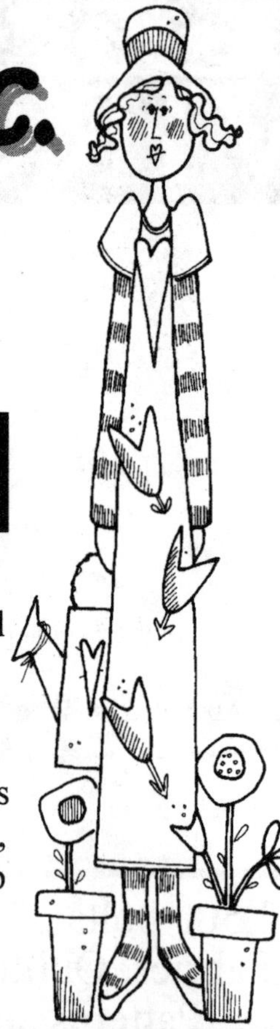

Dayton, VA #6

Patchwork Plus Inc.

HOURS: Mon–Wed 9–5
Thur–Sat 9–6
Closed Major Holidays

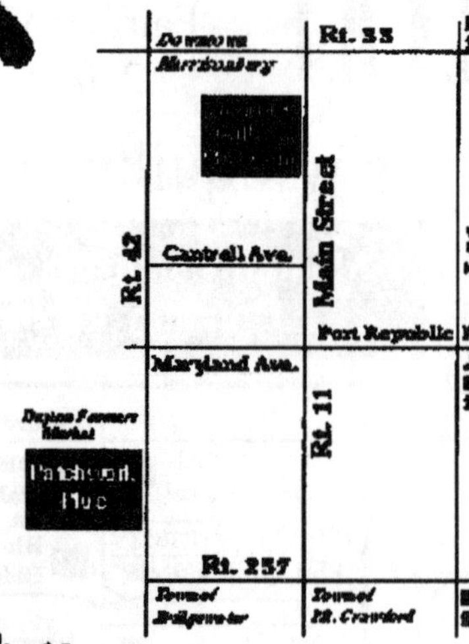

- **A Full Service Shop** offering the best of what quilters need
- **9,000 Sq. Ft.** Showroom, Classroom, Office & Service Area
- **Knowledgeable Staff** with over 600 years combined experience
- **Major Brands** of quality fabrics, notions, books, & patterns
- **A Full Line** of Bernina® sewing machines, sergers, embroidery machines, software and accessories

17 Killdeer Lane (off Rt. 42.), Dayton, VA
(on the hill above Dayton Farmers Market)
Phone 540-879-2505
Toll Free 1-877-674-4821
E-mail: patchwrk@shentel.net

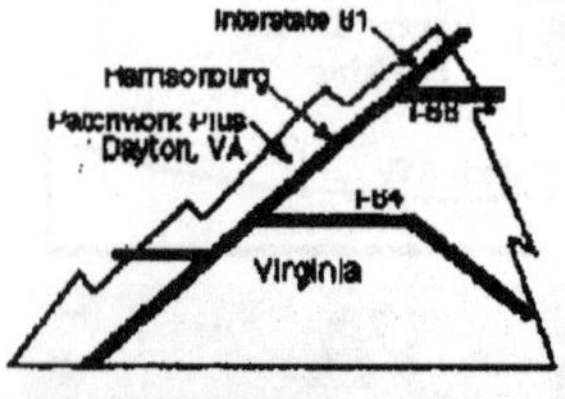

Rachel's QUILT PATCH

Enjoy a unique shop
in Historic Downtown Staunton
at the Train Station

Our shop features
100% cotton fabric collections
from top of the line
designers and manufacturers,
as well as
Patterns, Books, & Notions
selected for today's
Quilter and Fabric Crafter.

*Ask us about
ongoing classes for
quilters and crafters.
Custom made dinner napkins
and ties are available.*

40 Middlebrook Ave. 24401
(540) 886-7728
Owner: Rachel W. N. Brown
www.rachelsquiltpatch.com

Hours
Mon. Wed. Fri. & Sat.
10:00 a.m.- 5:00 p.m.
Tues. & Thurs.
10:00 a.m.- 8:00 p.m.

**We are experienced
quilters dedicated to offering
personal service.**

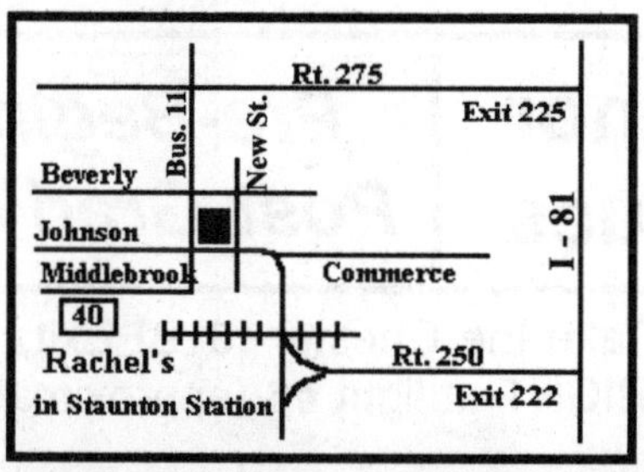

Staunton, VA #7

*Learn the soothing therapy of creating a work of art.
By hand or machine, a quilt is a future heirloom.*

Stephen's City, VA #8

Shenandoah Quilt Patch

1000+ BOLTS OF FABRIC
Hoffman, Moda, Kona Bay, Maywood, Timeless Treasures, Batiks, South Sea Imports, RJR, Thimbleberries, Jinny Beyer, Alexander Henry and many more.

NOTIONS, BOOKS, PATTERNS
Large selection of quilting stencils

!!CLASSES AVAILABLE!!
Call or come in for details and times. Beginner classes available for hand or machine piecing and quilting.

10% discount to all current guild members.

Long Arm Quilting Available

Tues - Fri 10 - 4 Thurs til 6 Sat 10 - 2

5279 Main St. (Rt. 11)
P.O. Box 1284 22655
(540) 868-2150
Fax: (540) 868-2151
Owner: Yvonne E. Orndorff
Est: 2000 1400 sq.ft.
GOD BLESS AMERICA!

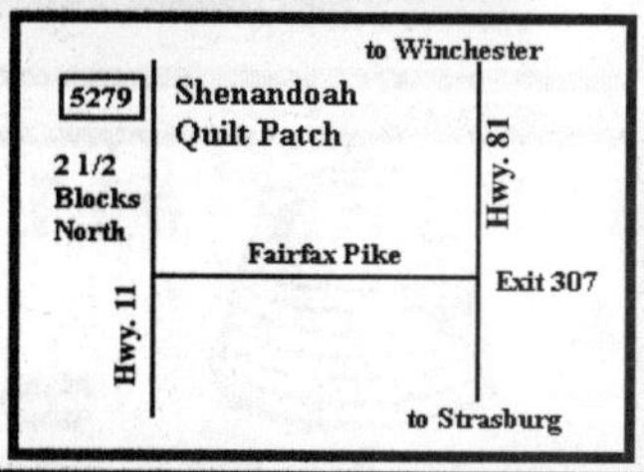

"A Community Sewing Together"

Valley Fabrics

2890 Stuarts Draft Hwy. 24477
540-324-0548 Fax: 540-324-0549
E-Mail: valleyfabrics@rica.net
Est: 2001 1900 sq.ft.

**Mon - Sat
9:30 - 5**

Stuarts Draft, VA #9

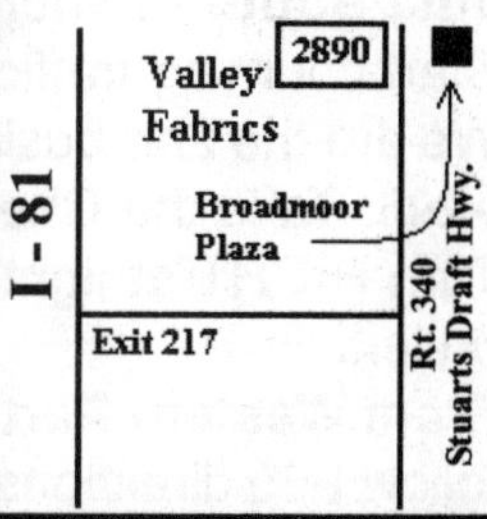

We carry a full line of quilting and apparel fabrics, notions and yarn. We also carry consignment items made by local crafts persons. Quilts, quilt racks, afghans, sweaters, rugs, potholders, dish cloths, aprons, shopping bags, handbags.

Old Trinity Schoolhouse Quilt Shop

Broad Selection of Quilt Fabrics (3000+ Bolts)
Including: Orientals, Hoffman Balis, Jinny Beyer, Thimbleberries, Moda
Specialty: Reproduction Fabrics (1780-1930)
Books: Many with Historical Focus

Notions, Block of the Months, Kits, and Classes

Antique and New Quilts and Quilt Tops

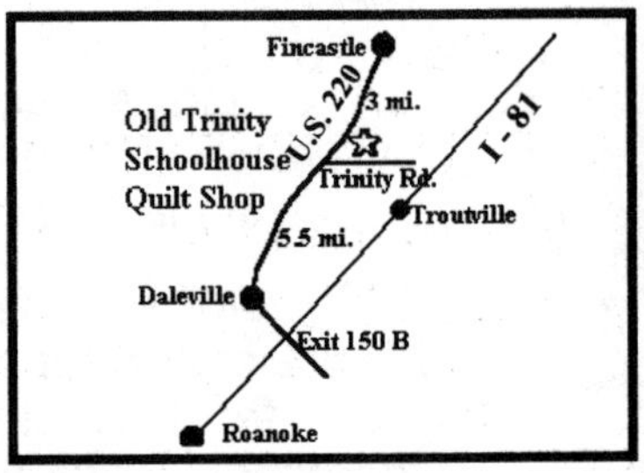

3200 Trinity Road, P.O. Box 189, Fincastle, VA 24090
Corner U.S. 220 and Trinity Rd. (540) 992-1233

Fincastle, VA #10

Mon - Sat 9 - 6

E-Mail: TrinityQuilts@aol.com
Owners: Carolyn and Stan Nelson

#11 The Busy Bea

Est: 1976

Bea & Cathy Chase

11934 Centre St., Chester, Va.

(804) 748-4951

Mon.-Fri., 8:30-6:00
Sat., 8:30-4:00
Closed Sun.

Fax: **(804) 748-2126**
Email: **cathy.bea.chase@worldnet.att.net**

sulky OF AMERICA — **Sulky Threads**

3000 bolts of 100% cotton fabric, notions, books & assorted supplies

elna — **Elna Sewing Machines**

Horn Collection — **Horn Sewing Cabinets**

Cathy is a certified teacher in Eleanor Burns..."QUILT IN A DAY" Techniques

Pre-Beginner to Post-Grad Classes

Just South of Richmond I-95: Take the Chester (61B) Exit, Rt. 10 West. Start counting traffic lights. Turn RIGHT at light #6 (approximately 2 miles). We are the 2nd business on left.

I-295: Take the Chester (15B) exit. Rt. 10 West. Start counting traffic lights. Turn RIGHT at light #10 (approximately 6 miles). We are the 2nd business on left.

From Western Part of State: Follow I-64 East to I-95 South to Chester, then follow I-95 directions.

Quilted Expressions Quilted Expressions

Lynchburg, VA #12

QUILTED EXPRESSIONS
& Sewing Possessions

3622 Old Forest Rd. 24501
(434) 385-6765 or (866) QUILTED
Mon.-Sat.: 10am - 5pm, **Thurs:** 10am - 8pm

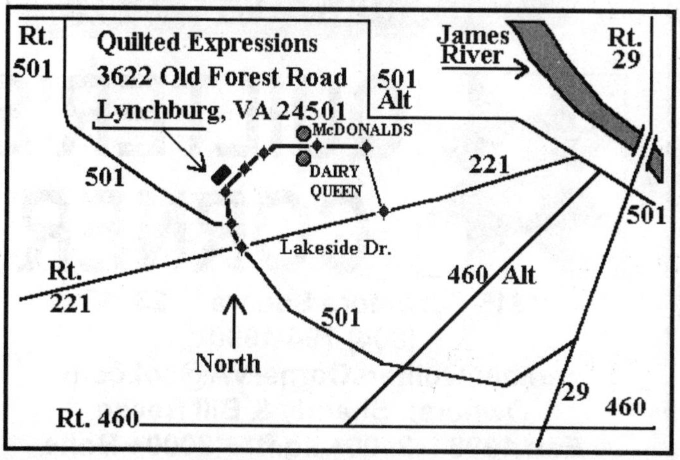

Internet: **www.quiltedexpressions.com**
Email: **info@quiltedexpressions.com**
Owner: **Roberta Whitt**, Opened: 1992

More than **4000 bolts** of Top Quality 100% Cotton Fabrics, such as batiks, Moda, Benartex, 30"s prints, and Thimbleberries. Over a hundred bolts of flannel. We also carry all the popular notions, patterns and books. We offer a variety of classes for quilting, sewing, heirloom sewing and machine embroidery. We have an active **Sewing Club** and handle all **Pfaff & Bernina** Sergers & Sewing Machines offering guide classes for both. **Mail Order** inquiries invited . We offer several kits with patterns and fabric included. Call for more information. **Quilt Guilds/Clubs welcome** - Please call ahead for us to prepare a special event for you.

Authorized Pfaff & Bernina Dealer
** Sales and Service **

Quilted Expressions Quilted Expressions

Sewing Nook

Charlottesville, VA #13

Hours: Winter -- Mon - Fri 10 - 5
Summer -- Mon - Fri 10 - 6
Saturday 10 - 5 (Year Around)

"Where Quilters Gather"

182 Zan Road Charlottesville, VA 22901
(804) 975-1059 sewingnook@aol.com
Visit us online at: www.sewingnook.com
Owner: Amber Goin

- Authorized Husqvarna Viking Dealer
- Horn Cabinet Dealer
- A Great Wall of Fabric
- A Treasure Trove of Fabulous Threads
- Cactus Punch & Amazing Designs for Embroidery
- Notions, 100's of Books and Patterns
- Classes for children through all adult levels
- On-site service for Viking

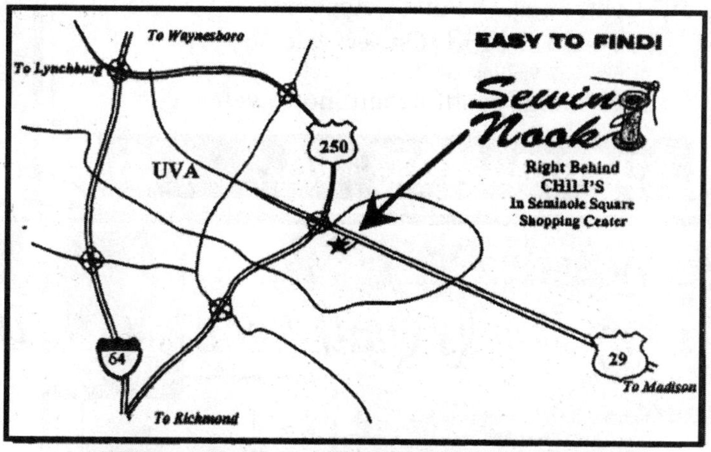

CHARLOTTESVILLE'S PREMIERE QUILT STORE

Charlottesville, VA #14

COTTONWOOD

2039 Barracks Rd. 22903
Meadowbrook Shopping Centre
(434) 244-9975 fax: (434) 244-5072
E-Mail: mary@cottonwoodquiltsshop.com
Web Site: www.cottonwoodquiltshop.com
Est: 1995 1500 sq.ft.

Mon - Sat 10 - 6
Wed til 8

Authorized Bernina Dealer. Over 1000 Bolts of Quilting Cottons, Homespun Plaids, Flannels and Wools, Books, Patterns, Supplies. Gail Wilson Dolls.

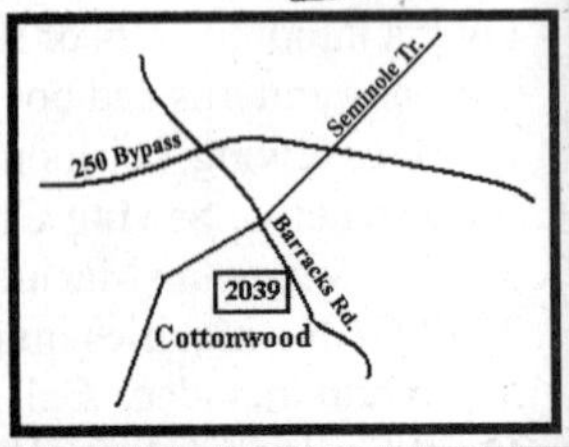

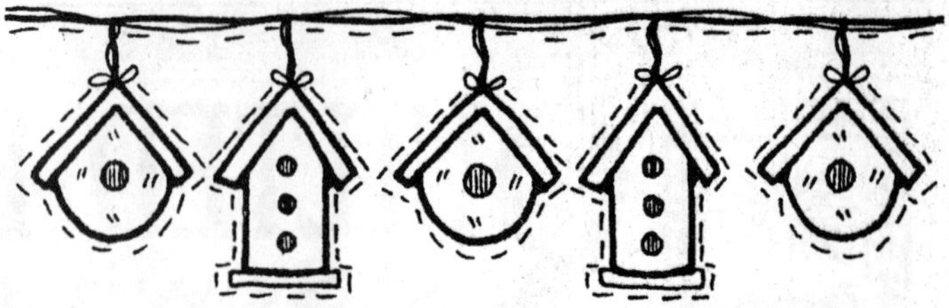

Quilt Shop Everything Beautiful

Quality Fabrics & Gifts

Mon - Fri 10 - 6
Thurs til 8

Large variety of 100% cottons, quilting, supplies, classes and GIFTS! Friendly and helpful staff. Visit Historical Appomattox! It's beautiful!

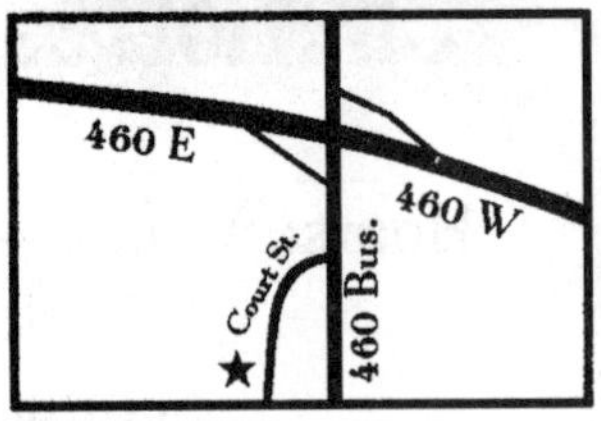

507 Court St., P. O. Box 11, Appomattox, VA 24522
434-352-4432 Owner: Melody Dyson
434-352-9329 facsimile Est. 2001 2,500 sq. ft.
EverythingBeautifulQuiltShop@yahoo.com

Appomattox, VA #16

Midlothian, VA #15

QUILTER'S CORNER

1318 Sycamore Square 23113
(804) 794-1990
email: QuiltersCornerVA@aol.com
Owners: Sheddy & Bill Reese
Est: 1998 2400+ sq.ft. 3000+ Bolts

Mon - Sat 10 - 5
Tues & Thur til 7
Sun 1 - 4

Richmond's premiere quilt Shop. We carry a wide selection of 100% cotton fabrics plus everything from all your quilting needs.

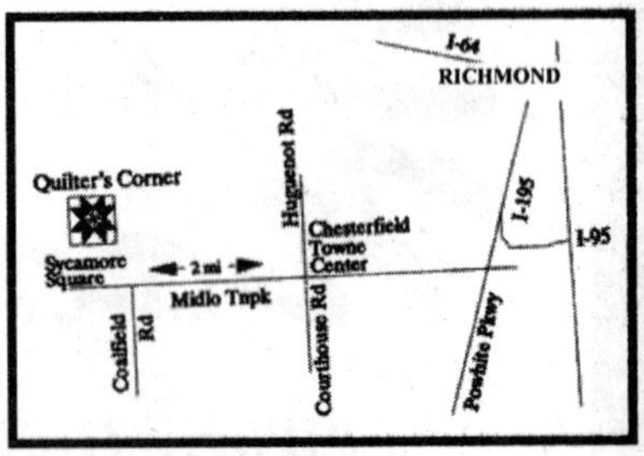

Sycamore Square is a delightful shopping village with many unique shops and restaurants.

New Castle, VA #17

Turkey Tracks Quilt Shop

Thurs - Sat 10 - 5
Sun 1 - 5
Most Wed 10 - 3

326 Main St., P.O. Box 346 24127
(877) 599-0808
Web Site: www.turkeytracksquilts.com

Primitive/folk art quilting, cross stitch & rug hooking supplies. I-81 exits 140 or 141, then north on Rt. 311 approx. 20 miles.

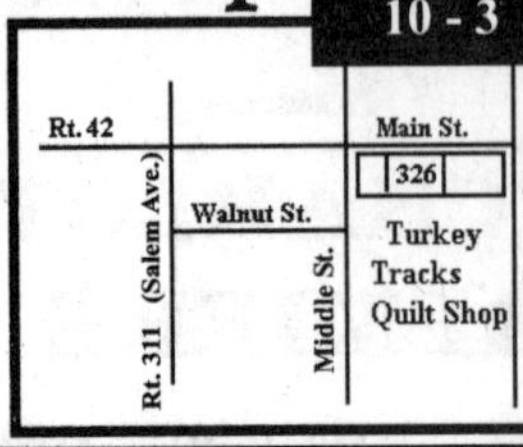

Roanoke, VA #18

The Quilting Connection

Mon - Fri 9:30 - 4
Tues til 6
Sat 10 - 2

2825 Brambleton Ave. 24015
(540) 776-0794
Web Site: www.quiltingconnect.com
Owner: Jill Setchel
Est: 1994 2000 sq.ft.

Large selection of 100% Designer Cottons, Quilting Supplies, Wearable Art, patterns, books, notions and gifts. Personal Service. Classes Available.

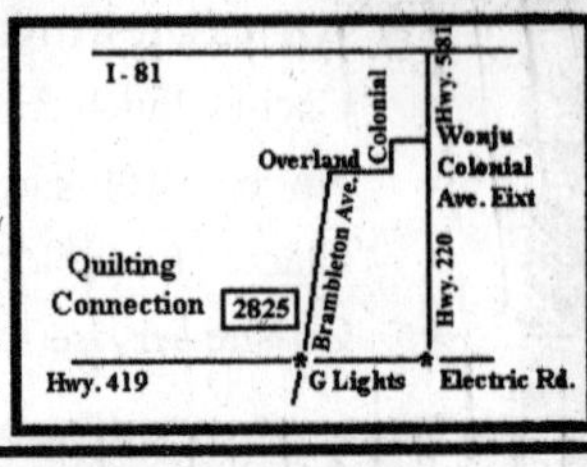

Boones Mill, VA #19

Tues - Sat 9:30 - 5:30

Boone's Country Store

2699 Jubal Early Hwy. 24065
(540) 721-2478
Owners: Randy & Elva Boone
Est: 1975 3588 sq.ft

Old Fashioned Quality -- Up to date Values. Calicoes, broad cloth, sheetings, quilting supplies, books, gifts. Homemade breads, pies, cakes & sweet rolls. 9 miles from Boones Mill.

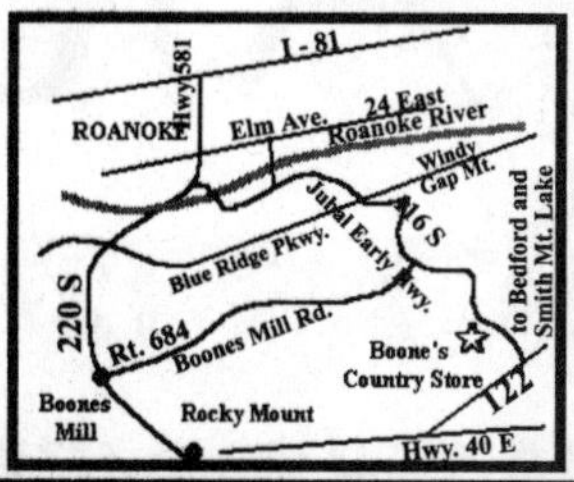

Martinsville, VA #20

Mon - Fri 8:30 - 5
Sat 10 - 2

The Sewing Studio, Inc.

1310 S. Memorial Blvd. 24112
(276) 632-5700 Fax: Same
E-Mail: jfeeny@sitestar.net
Owner: Brenda S. Feeny
Est: 1992 5000 sq.ft. 1500+ Bolts

Large selection of fabric, books & notions. BabyLock dealer. Sales - Service. Classes.

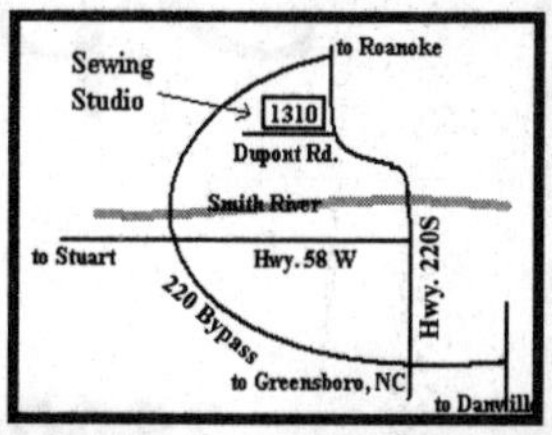

Hillsville, VA #21

Mountain Plains Fabrics

4505 Fancy Gap Hwy.
Hillsville, VA 24343
(276) 728-7517
Owners: Freddie & Hallie Currin

Quilting Fabric & Supplies * Quilt Frames
Buttons * Polyfoam * Lace * Drapery
Upholstery Material * Vinyl * Pillow Tops

Mon - Sat 9 - 5

Est: 1960
8000 sq.ft. 2500 Bolts

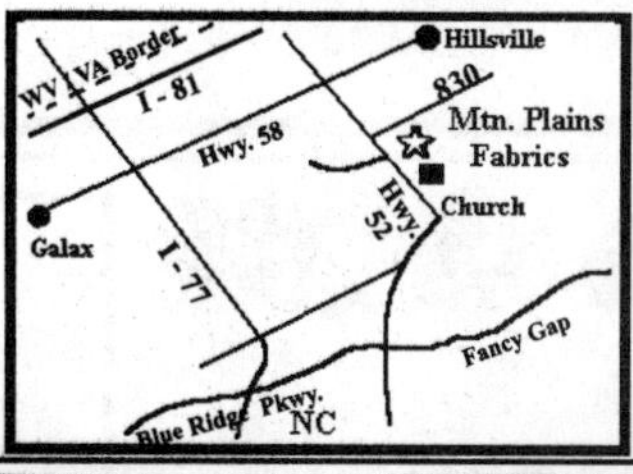

Radford, VA #22

Mon - Sat 9 - 5:30
Thur til 8

Sew Biz inc.

92 & 94 Harvey St. 24141
(540) 639-1138
E-Mail: sewoften@aol.com
Est: 1981
3600 sq.ft.
2000+ Bolts
Web Site: www.sewbiz.com

Two floors of beautiful fabrics for quilting and apparel. Historic building (1889). Extensive selection books, patterns, tools, accessories for Bernina & Elna.

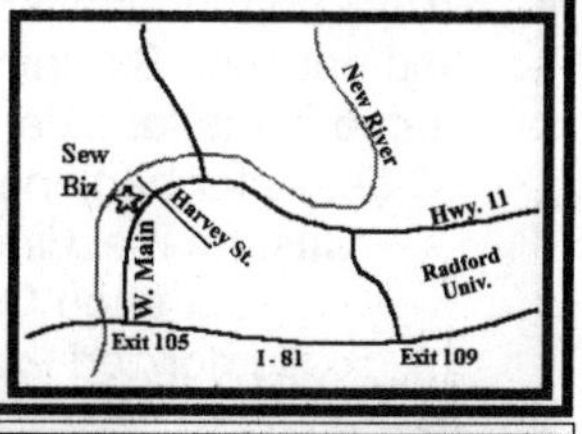

Wytheville, VA #23

Mon - Sat 10 - 5:30

Batiks Etcetera & Sew What Fabrics

460 East Main Street, Wytheville, VA 24382
276-228-6400 or 800-228-4573 Fax: 276-228-9597
Owner: Carol C. Britt www.batiks.com info@batiks.com
Est: 1982 4200 sq.ft. 5250 bolts

The most complete retail source for batik fabrics! Batiks Etcetera & Sew What Fabrics is located in an 1840's home in old town Wytheville, VA Gourmet cottons, Indonesian, Malaysian & Indian batiks, flannel, specialty threads, notions, books and lively classes are available with expert, friendly assistance. Automatic shipment and swatch services are available. Check out our secure web site. Come have a ball!

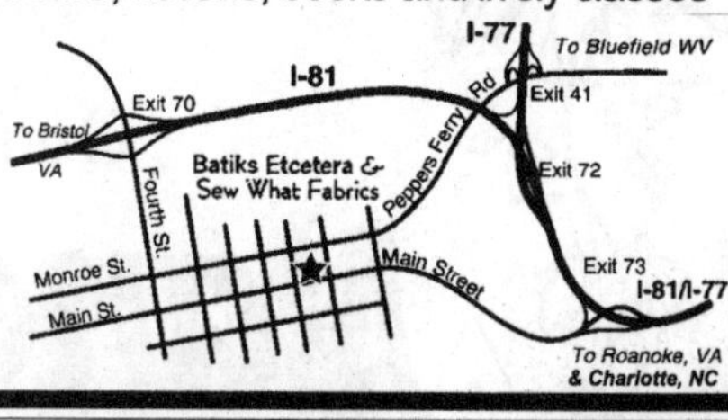

Abingdon, VA #24

Mon - Fri 9:30 - 5:30
Sat 9:30 - 5

Jeannine's Fabrics & Quilt Shop

414 W. Main St. 24210
(276) 628-9586
Owners: Jeannine & Gene Widener
Est: 1968 3000 sq.ft. 1000+ Bolts

Full Line Quilting Supplies including 100% cotton from RJR, P&B, Hoffman, Springs, VIP, Concord, Fabri-Quilt. Books, Patterns, Rulers, Stencils.

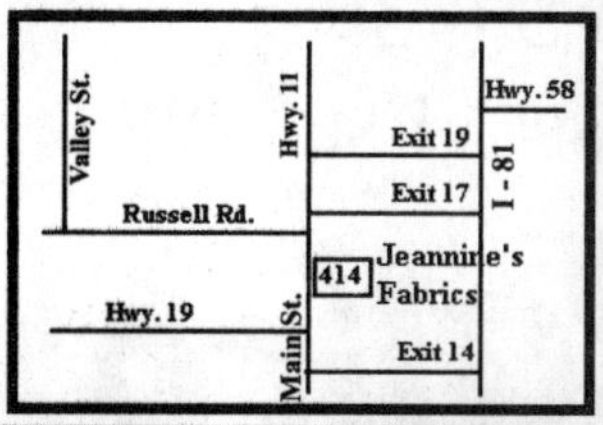

Chesapeake, VA #25

Mon - Fri 10 - 6
Thur til 8
Sat 10 - 5
Sun 12 - 4

Sis 'N Me Quilt Shoppe

3361 Western Branch Blvd. (Hwy 17)
(757) 686-2050 23321
www.sis-n-me.com
Owner: Carole King
Est: 1987 2000 sq.ft. 1500 Bolts

Large selection of 100% cotton Fabrics, Books, Notions, Patterns, Stencils, "Quilter's Cotton" Batting, Prismatic Foil (Glitz Magic) Classes. Mail Order. "Block-a-Month"

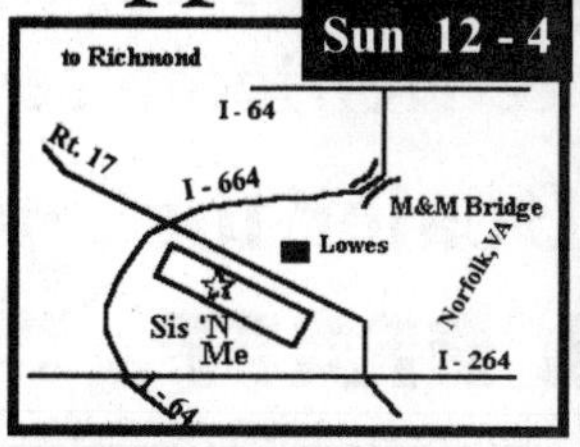

Virginia Beach, VA #26

Mon - Sat 10 - 5:30
Thur til 8
Sun 12 - 4

What's Your Stitch 'N Stuff, Inc.

5350 Kempsriver Dr. #104 23464
(757) 523-2711
Owners: Holly Erdei-Zuber & Irene Erdei
Over 1500 bolts!

100% Cotton Fabrics and Thread, Books, Patterns, Notions, Dolls, Primitive Rug Hooking. PLUS ALWAYS FRIENDLY SERVICE!

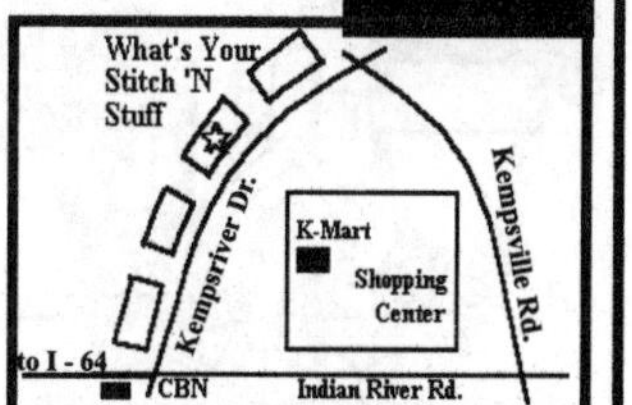

Spooling Around

Virginia Beach, VA #27

3600 Dam Neck Rd. 23456 (757) 368-8962

"No such thing as a stranger, just Friends we haven't met yet." That's how we look at things here.
Come in for a fine selection of 100% cotton fabrics, books, patterns, and notions. Stunning quilts and quilt related items for sale and made locally. Classes for beginners to advanced. Custom machine quilting on our shop Gammill. Authorized Pfaff dealer.

This is your "Full-Service" Quilt Shop

Mon - Sat 10 -6 Sun 12 - 5

Fax: (757) 368-2966
E-Mail: Susan@SpoolingAround.com
Web Site: www.SpoolingAround.com
Owners: Susan Crowder Cyr
Est: 1999 3200 sq.ft.

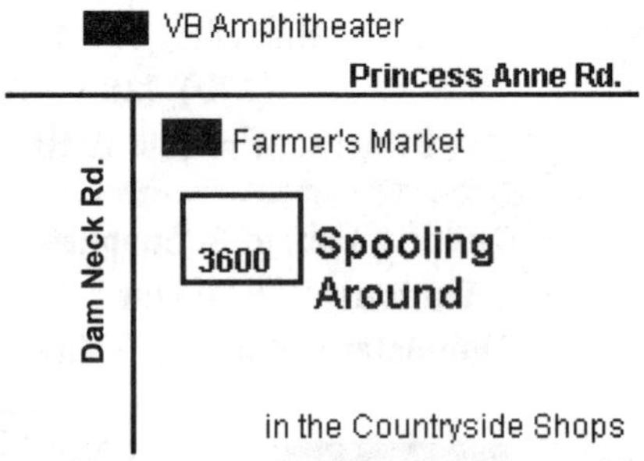

Newport News, VA #28

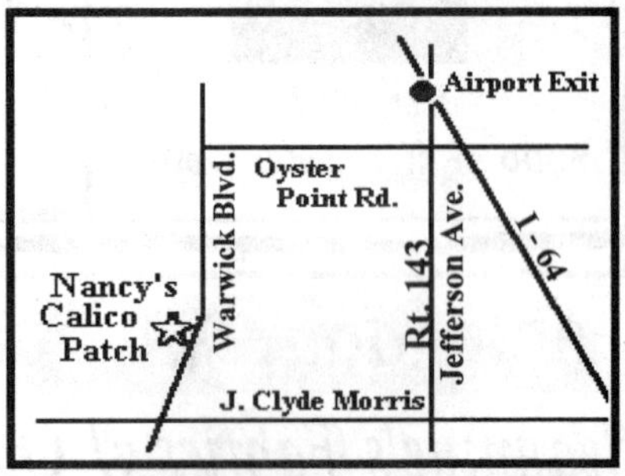

21 Hidenwood Shopping Center
Newport News, VA 23606
(757) 596-SEWS (7397)
Owner: Nancy Gloss Est: 1987

**Mon - Sat 10 - 5
Sun 1- 4**

Nancy's Calico Patch

We have fabrics, books, patterns, supplies, & classes for Quilting, Smocking, & Heirloom sewing.

**Authorized Dealer for
Bernina & PFAFF**

Needlecraft Corner

aka "Sherry's Shop"

Over 2,000 bolts of 100% Cotton Fabrics.

Home of "Granny Nanny's Quilting Gadgets" foundation piecing patterns, needlework kits, fibers, books and accessories.

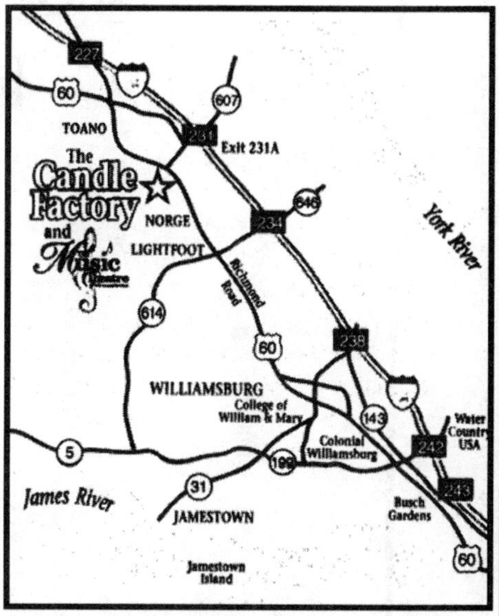

One mile from I - 64 at exit 231A

Williamsburg, VA #29

Everyday
9:30 - 5

7521 Richmond Rd. 23188
(757) 564-3354 Fax: (757) 564-8453
E-Mail: needlecraft@wsac.com
Est: 1977
Owner: Jack Barnett

White Marsh, VA #30

Tues - Sat 10 - 6
Sun 12 - 5

Love2Quilt

4904 George Washington Mem. Hwy. 23183
(804) 695-2700 Fax: (804) 695-2616
E-Mail: love2quilt10@yahoo.com
Web Site: www.love2quilt.net
Owners: Regina, Douglas & Thomas
Est: 2001 1500 sq.ft. 1200+ Bolts

Stop in to see Thomas (the cat), he "Loves" company. He caters to all Quilters, with lovely Quilt Fabrics, Books, Notions and Doo-Dads. He loves kids.

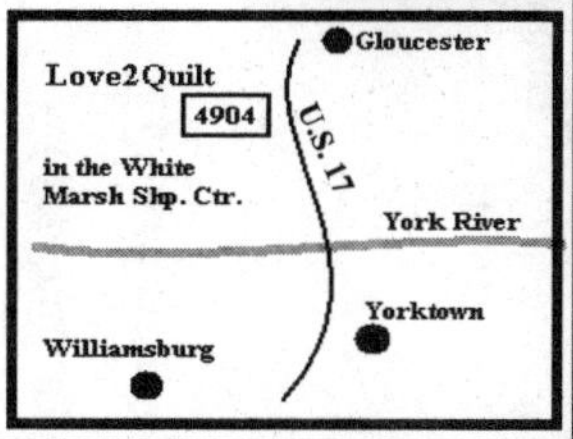

Cape Charles, VA #31

Mon - Sat
10 - 5

Quilts & More Fabric Outlet

27376 Lankford Hwy 23310
(757) 331-3642
Owner: Henrietta Morris
Est: 1990 3900 sq. ft.

Quilting, curtain, upholstery and clothing fabrics, also leather. Sewing supplies & notions. Much more at reasonable prices.

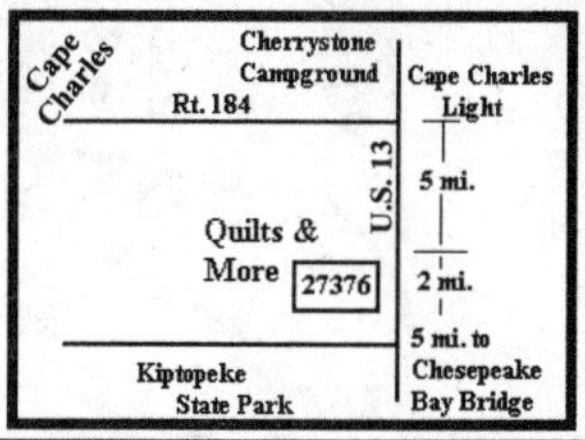

Other Shops in Virginia: We suggest calling first

Abingdon	The Cave House Craft Shop, 279 E. Main St.	540-628-7721
Annandale	Total Crafts, 6910 Bradlick Shopping Ctr., #C	703-256-7110
Arrington	Harmony Hill, 929 Wilson Hill Rd.	804-263-7750
Bristol	The Quilt Shop, 2000 Euclid Ave.	540-466-8552
Cana	Pioneer Village Shop, R.R. #1, Hwy. 52	540-755-3114
Centreville	G Street Fabrics, 5077 Westfields Blvd.	703-818-8090
Charlottesville	Quilts Unlimited, 118 W. Main St.	434-979-0025
Charlottesville	Quilts Unlimited, 1051 Millmont St.	434-979-8110
Chesapeake	A Different Touch, 1107 S Military Hwy	757-366-8830
Clarksville	Patchwork House, 315 Virginia Ave. P.O. Box 1477	804-374-5942
Council	Betty's Fabric & Crafts, HC4, Box 57	
Falls Church	G Street Fabrics, 6250 Arlington Blvd.	703-241-1700
Falls Church	Appalachian Spring, 102 W. Jefferson St.	703-533-0930
Fancy Gap	Pines 'N' Needles, R.R. #1	540-728-9818
Floyd	Schoolhouse, Rte. 8, P.O. Box 9	540-745-4561
Fredericksburg	Quilts 'N' Treasures, 721 Caroline St.	540-371-8166
Gainesville	Quilting Cellar, 4198 Stepney Dr.	703-354-2061
Harrisonburg	Virginia Quilt Museum, 301 S. Main St.	540-433-3818
Hot Springs	Quilts Unlimited, Cottage Row	540-839-5955
Huddleston	Rose Marie's Quilting Cottage, 202 Springs Dr	540-297-1328
Kilmarnock	The Briar Patch, 81 N. Main St., P.O. Box 2040	804-435-9065
Madison	The Little Shop of Madison, 320 S. Main St.	540-948-4147
Manassas	Old Town Needlecrafts, 9774 Center St.	703-330-1846
Manassas	Paint & Threads Designs, 9019 Center St.	703-257-3586
Mechanicsville	Quilt Shack 8107 Mechanicsville Tpke.	804-559-1992
Middletown	The Quilt Shop at Belle Grove Plantation, Belle Grove Plantation Rte. 11 P.O. Box 137	540-869-2028
Midlothian	Sew Special, Inc., 1134 Alverser Dr.	804-379-7727
Newport News	Colonial Quilt Works, 171 Little John Pl.	757-872-0538
Roanoke	Touch of Country, 611 Greenwich Dr.	540-563-4755
Rocky Mount	Fabric Mill Outlet, 453 S. Main St.	540-483-2822
Salem	Quilt Sand Crafts, 1306 Roanoke Blvd.	540-387-0339
Vienna	Vienna Quilt Shop, 109 Park St. NE	703-281-4091
Virginia Beach	Quilters Cotton, 2700 Avenger Dr. #109	757-463-3264
Virginia Beach	Quilt Works, 332 N. Great Neck Rd. #101	757-463-4843
Williamsburg	Quilts Unlimited, 440A W. Duke of Gloucester St.	757-253-8700
Williamsburg	Colonial Williamsburg Foundation, Department of Collections	757-229-1000
Williamsburg	Fabrics Unique, 6510 Richmond Rd.	757-565-0155
Winchester	Quilt Shop at Millwood Crossing, 381 Millwood Ave.	540-662-5157
Wise	Sister Stitches, 7563 Duncan Gap Rd.	540-328-3788
Woodbridge	Ginny Dunning, 4203 Evergreen Dr.	703-670-5733

WASHINGTON
61 Featured Shops
Colville (#6)
Spokane (#1, 2, 3, 4)
Reardan (#5)
Almira (#8)
Clarkston (#15)
Ritzville (#17)
90
Omak (#7)
Chelan (#9)
Odessa (#11)
Moses Lake (#10)
Richland (#18, 19)
Kennewick (#16)
Leavenworth (#13)
Wenatchee (#)
Ephrata (#12)
82
Yakima (#14)
Lynden (#20)
Anacortes (#25)
Sedro Woolley (#23)
LaConner (#24)
Stanwood (#26)
Langley (#22)
Everett (#30)
Bothell (#31)
Seattle (#28, 29)
Bellevue (#27)
Issaquah (#38)
Renton (#36)
Auburn (#37)
University Place (#34)
Puyallup (#46)
Bonney Lake (#39)
Yelm (#40, 41)
Eastsound (#21)
Port Townsend (#52, 53)
Port Angeles (#50)
Sequim (#51)
Gig Harbor (#49)
Port Orchard (#48)
Des Moines (#32)
Federal Way (#33)
Tacoma (#45)
Olympia (#44)
Tumwater (#47)
Centralia (#42, 43)
5
Longview (#56, 57)
Kalama (#58)
Vancouver (#60, 61)
North Bonneville (#59)
Shelton (#35)
Grayland (#54)
Long Beach (#55)

Pacific Crescent Quilting

Spokane's
QUALITY SHOP FOR QUILTERS

Mon - Fri 10 - 8
Sat 10 - 6
Sun 11 - 5

Great fabric, Books, patterns and notions.
We provide mail order service anywhere.
Warm, friendly service in a bright & sunny shop.

(509) 484-4808

AUTHORIZED DEALER FOR NEW HOME / JANOME SEWING MACHINES & SERGERS

7454 N. Division 99208
Fax #: (509) 484-4918
E-Mail: pcq@pcqspokane.com
Web Site: www.pcqspokane.com

Spokane, WA #1

Owners: Sandy & Larry McCauley
Est: 1995 4000 sq.ft.
5000 Bolts

Quality Fabric & Notions for Quilting & Fabric Crafts

BERNINA BERNINA BERNINA BERNINA

The Quilting Bee Inc. BERNINA

Spokane, WA #2

Selected by American Patchwork & Quilting magazine readers as one of the Top 10 quilt shops in the nation for 1998.

12117 E. Mission 99206
(509) 928-6037 (888) 928-6037
Owner: Jackie Wolff Est: 1984 5000 sq.ft.

Spokane's finest Quilting Store!

Filled with quilting books, notions, tools, & 3000 bolts of fabric. Friendly staff and Spokane's only Bernina Dealer.

Mon - Fri 9:30 - 8
Sat 9:30 - 5:30
Sun 12 - 5

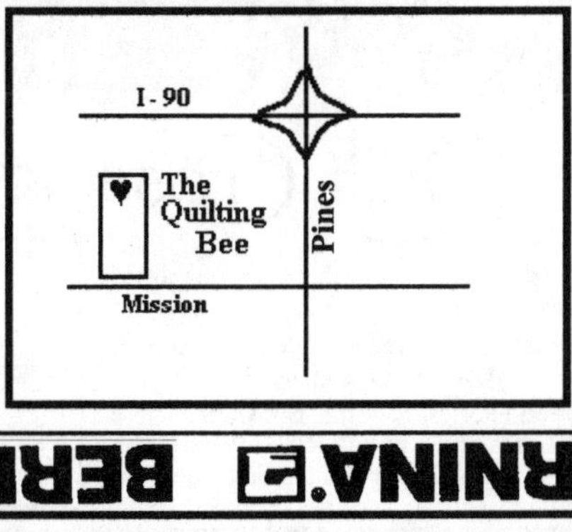

Visit Us At: www.quiltingbeespokane.com

Spokane, WA #3

Mon - Thur 9 - 7
Fri & Sat 9 - 6

Sew E-Z, Too

620 W. Garland 99205
(509) 325-6644
Web Site: www.ezknit.com
Owner: Vickie Black
Est: 1997

Designer Fabrics and More.
Large selection quality cottons, books, patterns.

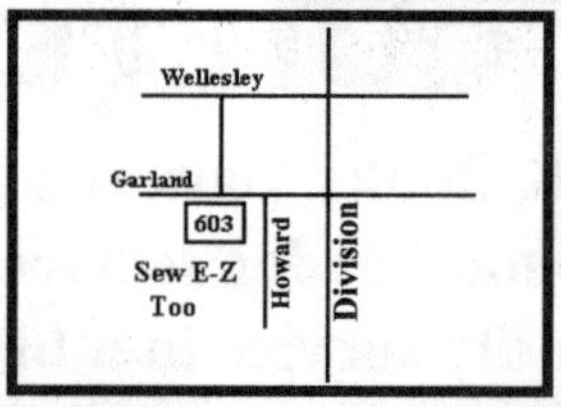

Spokane, WA #4

Mon - Sat 9:30 - 5:30

Kaleidoscope Quilting & Home Decor

1011 E. 2nd Ave. #3 99202
(509) 456-7375 Fax: (509) 444-7333
E-Mail: quilting@kquilting.com
Web Site: www.kquilting.com
Est: 2000 3500 sq.ft. 2000 Bolts

Just off I - 90, near downtown Spokane. Fabric, Notions, Patterns, Books, Classes, Completed Quilts, Wall Hangings, Kits, Racks, Gifts, Home Décor.

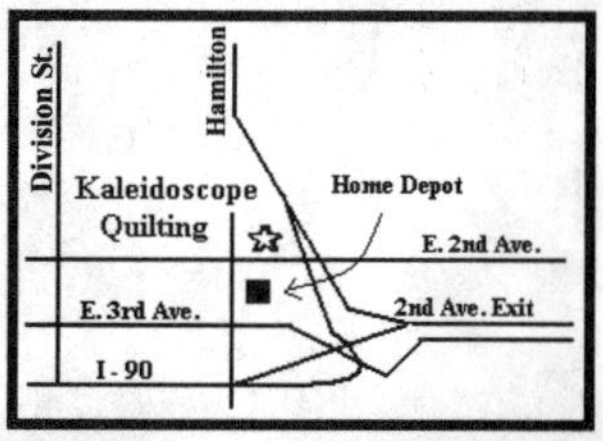

Reardan, WA #5

Tues - Sat 10 - 5

The Buggy Barn

Unique quilt shop in the country!

28848 Tramm Rd. N
99029
(509) 796-2188

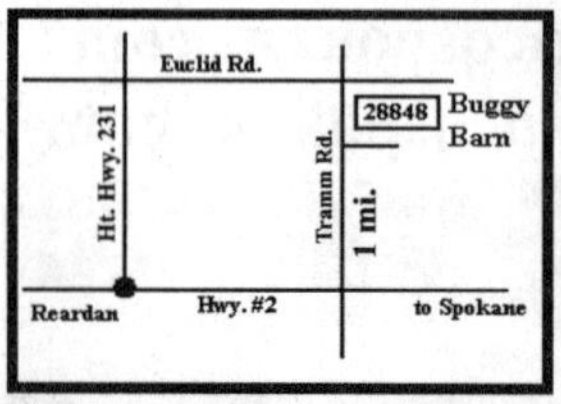

Web Site: www.buggybarnquilts.com
Owners: Pam Soliday & Janet Nesbitt

Unique Quilt Shop in the Country. Featured Shop in *Patchwork & Quilting* May 2002

Colville, WA #6

Mon - Sat 9 - 5:30

E - Z Knit Fabrics

165 N. Main 99114
(509) 684-2644 Fax: (509) 684-6659
E-Mail: ezknit.com
Web Site: www.ezknit.com
Owners: Vickie Black & Helen West
Est: 1969 3000 sq.ft.

3 stores in one — Beads — Fabrics — Yarn
One of the largest selections of fabric in Washington.

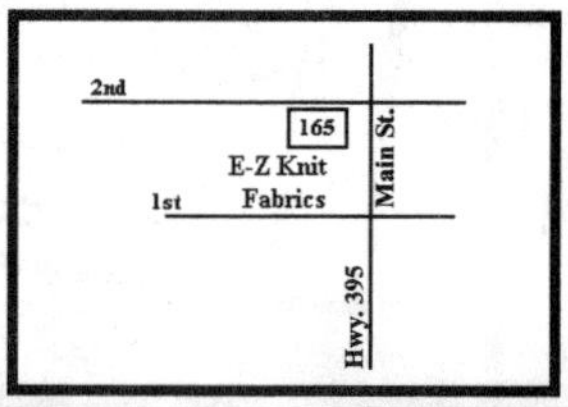

Omak, WA #7

Mon - Fri 9:30 - 6
Sat 9:30 - 5:30

Needlelyn Time

9 North Main 98841
(509) 826-1198
E-Mail: needlyn@televar.com
Web Site: www.needlelyntime.com
Owner: Lyn Hruska
Est: 1986 3000 sq.ft. 1900 Bolts

Quilter's Fabrics, Notions, Quilting Supplies. Pfaff Sewing Machines and Cross-Stitch Supplies. Also Classes.

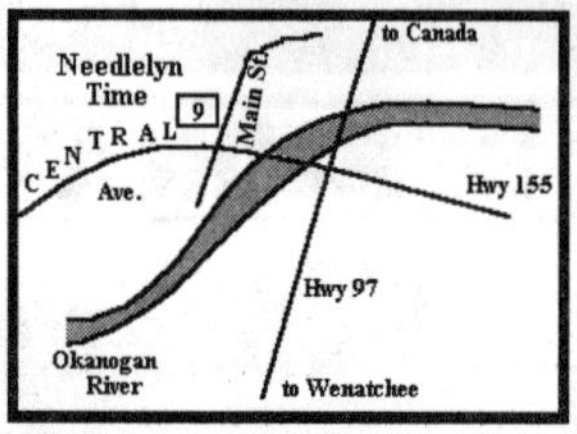

Almira, WA #8

Wed - Thur 11 - 5
Sat 9 - 3

Wheat Country Quilts

403 W. Elm 99103
(509) 639-2552
E-Mail: lmpeha@bossig.com
Owner: Marjorie Peha
Est: 2001

Located in a church in the center of a small town in the middle of wheat country. Fabrics, Books, Patterns & Notions.

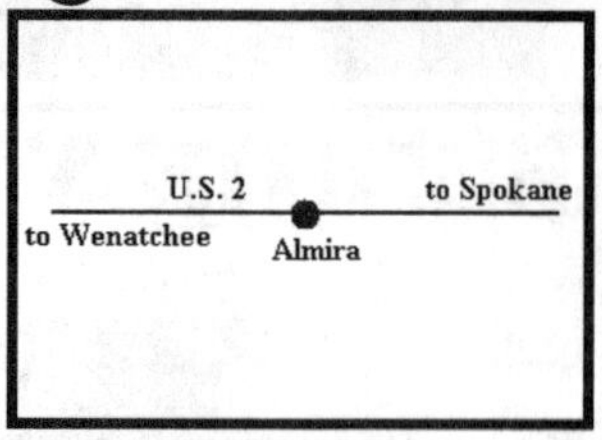

Chelan, WA #9

Mon - Sat 9:30 - 5:30

Woven Threads

"Top Shop 2002"
131 E. Woodin Ave. #B 98816
(509) 682-7714
E-Mail: info@woventhreads.com
Owner: Rose Buhl Est: 1995

We carry a complete line of Books, Patterns & Notions. 100% cotton fabrics. Gifts. Classes. Free Newsletter

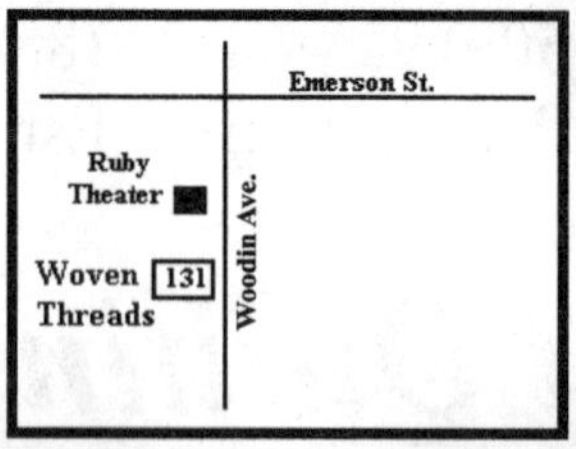

Odessa, WA #11

Mon - Fri 10 - 5
Sat 10 - 4

the Quilt Crossing

4 W. First Ave., P.O. Box 206 99159
(509) 982-2194 Fax: (509) 982-2623
E-Mail: schmidtinsurance@odessaoffice.com
Owner: Lois Fisher

100% Cotton Fabrics, Patterns, Books, Stencils & Notions. Cross stitch & silk Ribbon embroidery supplies. Classes, "Sew Much Fun" quilt-ins. Free Newsletter.

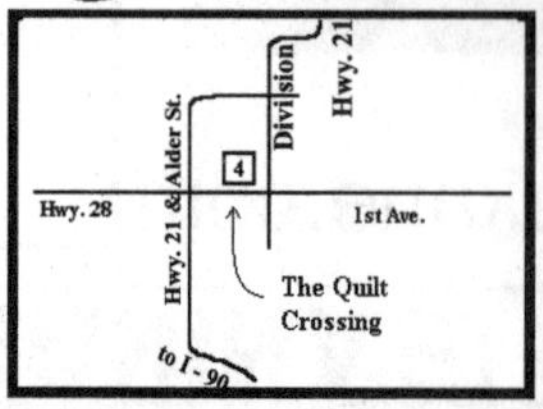

Columbia Basin Quiltworks

AUTHORIZED BERNINA SALES & SERVICE.
A FRIENDLY QUILT STORE WITH 100'S OF BOOKS & PATTERNS PLUS UNFINISHED FURNITURE. LOCATED IN DOWNTOWN MOSES LAKE.

Mon - Fri 10 - 5:30
Sat 10 - 5

122 W. 3rd Ave. 98837
(509) 764-2238
Web: sew2000.com/cbquiltworks
Email: cbquilt@moseslake-wa.com
Owner: Connie Lindell
Est: 1998
4500 sq.ft. 2500+ Bolts

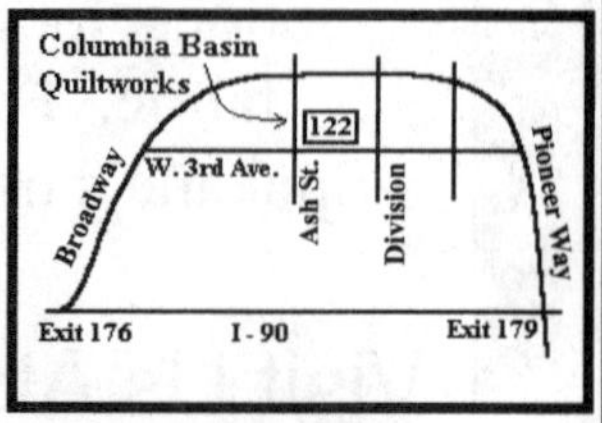

Moses Lake, WA #10

The Fabric Patch

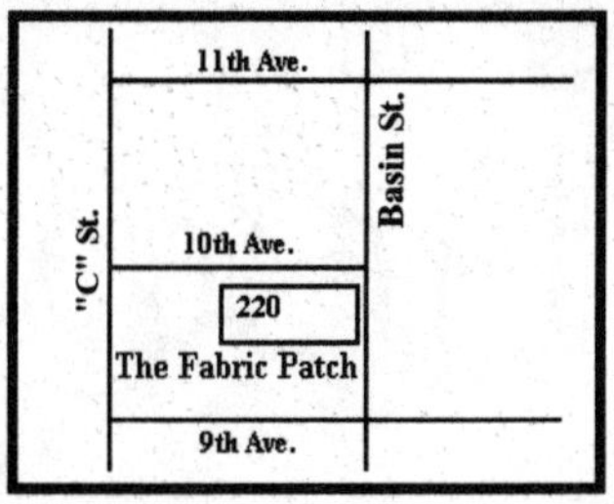

Ephrata, WA #12

220 Tenth Ave. SW, Ephrata, WA 98823
509-754-8280
www.fabricpatch.net
rang@crcwnet.com Est: 1999 2500 sq.ft.
Owners: Cindi & Brianna Rang

2500+ bolts of 100% cotton in Batiks, flannels, novelties and more. 700+ book titles. Complete line of notions and hundreds of patterns. Extensive classroom schedule. Finished samples for sale.

We own two 14 foot Gammill long arm machines that are available for customer use. (Reservations are required) Machine quilt your quilt top in a few hours, or send it in for us to complete.

Mon - Sat 9:00 - 5:30

Leavenworth, WA #13

All Year 9 a.m. to 6 p.m.

Dee's Country Accents

917 Commercial St. 98826
(800) 253-8990
E-Mail: info@quiltersheaven.com
Web Site: www.quiltersheaven.com
Owners: Dee & Al Howie
Est: 1987 1500 Bolts

Incredible Fabrics, Largest selection in the Pacific Northwest of Quilt Books and Patterns. PLUS a Bed & Breakfast decorated with quilts and antiques.

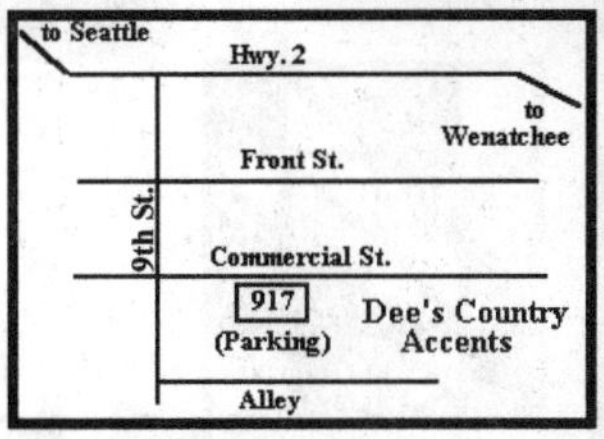

Yakima, WA #14

BERNINA® Sewing Center & Firehouse Fabrics

103 S. 7th Ave. 98902
(509) 248-0078 Fax: (509) 248-0348
E-Mail: bernina@wolfenet.com
Owners: Brad & Sue McMillan
Est: 1968 3500 sq.ft.

Mon - Fri 9 - 5:30 Sat 9 - 5

Over 2500 Bolts of Quilt Fabric. Large Selection of Books, Patterns, Notions, Classes. Bernina Sales & Service.

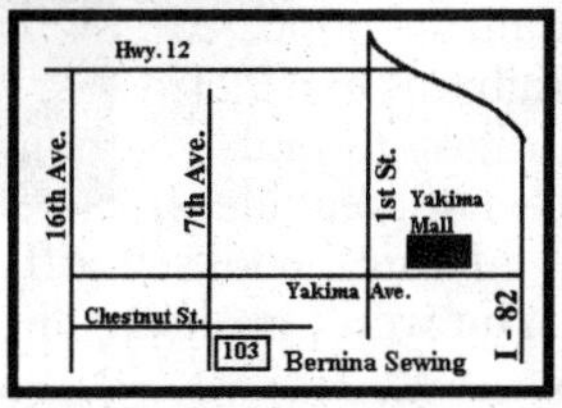

Clarkston, WA #15

Mon - Fri 9:30 - 5 Sat 10 - 5

The Quilt Shoppe

838 6th St. 99403
(509) 751-0618
E-Mail: quiltshoppe@aol.com
Owner: Debby Hupp Est: 1998
3000 sq.ft. 1000 Bolts

Complete Quilt Shop - Friendly Staff - Notions Patterns - Books - Classes - Machine Quilting
We serve SE Washington, NE Oregon and NW Idaho.

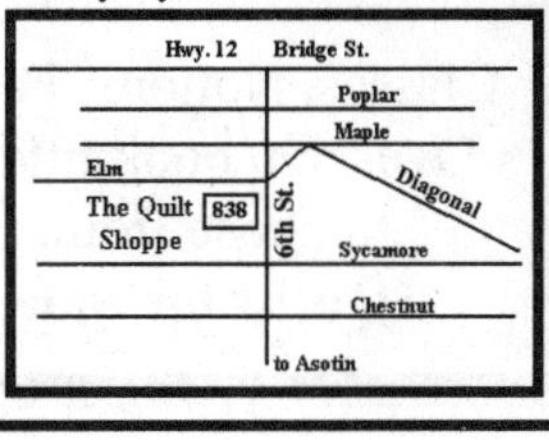

Est: 1991

Kennewick, WA #16

Pieceable Dry Goods

5215 W. Clearwater #106
Marineland Village 99336
(509) 735-6080
Owners: Terry Burkhart
& Barbara Ward
Mon - Fri 10 - 5:30
Sat 10 - 5

"A Country Quilt Store"
Selected by American Patchwork & Quilting magazine as one of the Top 10 Quilt Shops for 1998.

As you step into our cozy country quilt store you'll be inspired by numerous samples and country displays. The courteous and professional staff will help you create your quilt from our large selection of over 2000 bolts of fabric. Specializing in the "Country" look, from Romantic florals to primitive folk art. You'll love our great homespun plaids and extensive selection of primitive stitchery, quit patterns, historical books, wool felt and wool rug hooking.

Professional quilting machine service offered to help you get those projects done.

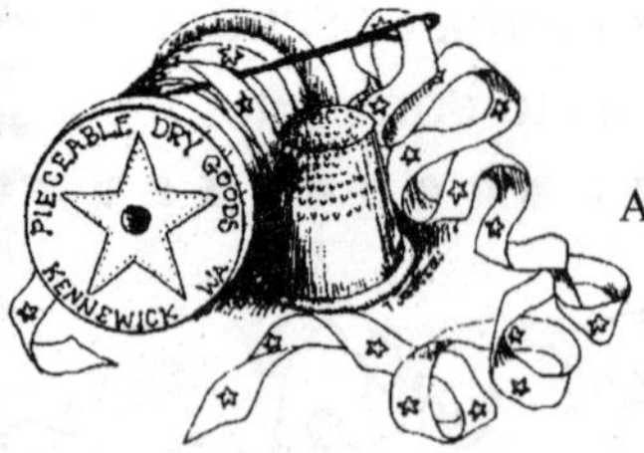

Country Living Quilts
A series of nap-size quilt kits designed by the staff of Pieceable Dry Goods. These quilts capture that primitive antique scrap look we love. Each quilt reminds you of a treasure found in a family trunk or in an antique shop. Each kit is $47.99 and includes fabric and pattern. We add a few new ones each year.

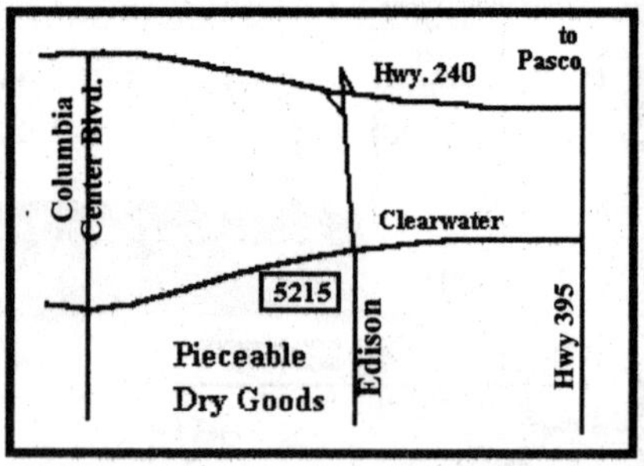

No matter what your age...It's time to start quilting!

Ritzville, WA #17

Garden Gate Quilt Shop

1611 S. Smitty's Blvd. #B 99169
(509) 659-1370
Owner: Celia Benzel 2500 Bolts
Web Site: gardengatequiltshop.com

A fun and friendly quilt shop located right off exit 221. Easy to find. Lots of great ideas, fabrics, books & gifts. You won't be disappointed.

Mon - Sat 10 - 5
Sun 11 - 4

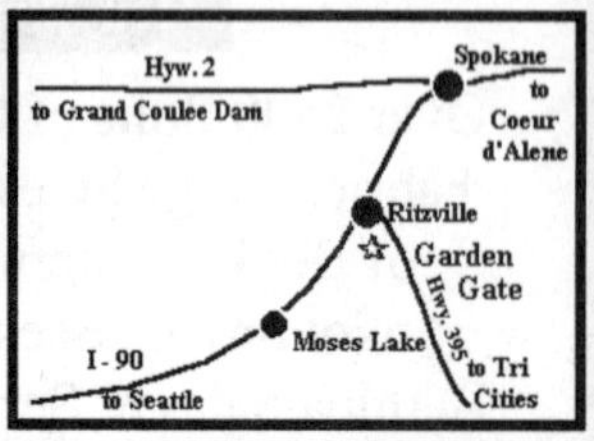

Richland, WA #18

Quiltmania!!

248 Williams 99352
(509) 946-PINS (7467)
Owner: Debi Merhar
Est: 1991 2000 Bolts

Mon - Thur 10 - 9
Fri & Sat 10 - 5

Classes, Notions, Fabric.
Over 600 book titles to choose from.
Quilts for Sale.

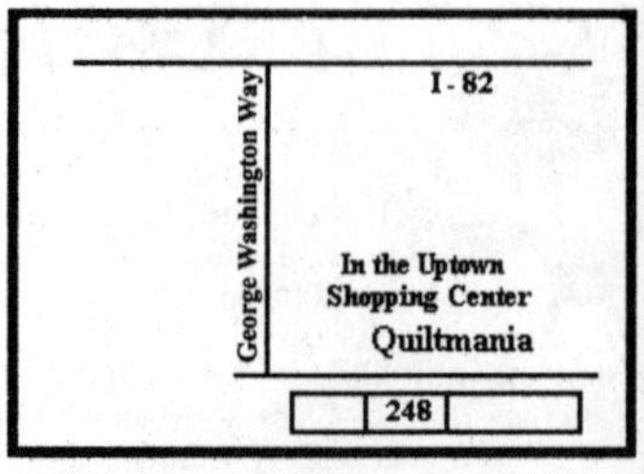

Village Quiltworks

Richland, WA #19

QUEENSGATE VILLAGE
1950 Kenne Road, Suite B, Richland, WA 99352
(509) 628-0652
Est: 2001 3000 sq.ft. Over 2000 bolts

Web Site:
www.villagequiltworks.com

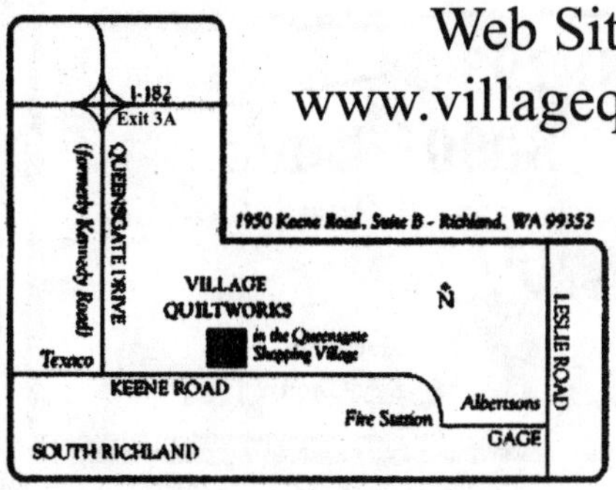

Mon -Fri 10-6
Sat 10-5

PROMOTING the ART of QUILTING

Village quiltworks is a full service quilt shop located in a charming walk-through shopping village.

OFFERING
Unique fabrics Large selection of batting Classes
Machine quilting service Friendly & helpful staff

Lynden, WA #20

CALICO COUNTRY™

1722 Front St.
(Fairway Center) 98264
(360) 354-4832 2500+ Bolts
E-Mail: calico_country@msn.com
Owner: Mary J. Elenbaas

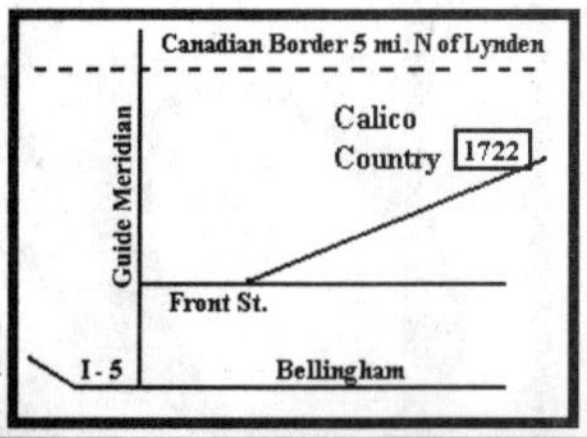

Quilting Supplies, Custom Lampshades, Fabrics, Notions, Crafts, Classes, Alterations & Custom Sewing. 18" Doll Clothes & Accessories.

Eastsound, WA #21

Mon - Sat 10 - 5
Winter Sat 11 - 4

Poppies

294 "A" St., P.O. Box 1075
(360) 376-2686 98245
Owner: Ruth Vandestraat
E-Mail: poppiesfabric.com
Web Site: www.poppiesfabric.com
Est: 1993 1000 sq.ft. 3000 Bolts

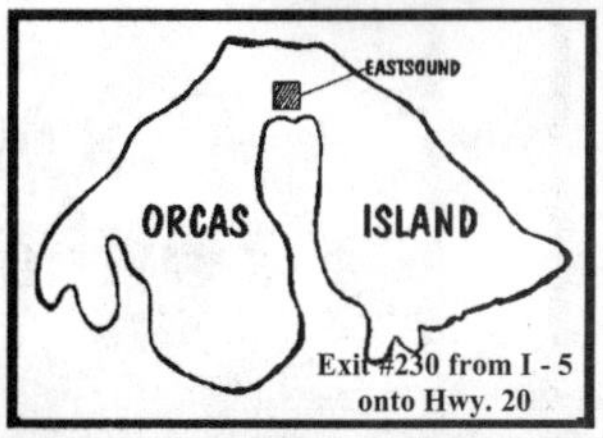

On Lovely Orcas Island — A Complete Quilting Shop plus Yarn, Stitchery, Kits, Notions. Across from the Post Office.

Quilting by the Sea

Langley, WA #22

Voted TOP TEN by American Patchwork & Quilting Magazine

221 Second St. #6, (Langley Village)
P.O. Box 844 98260 (360) 221-8171
E-Mail: marydarby@quiltingbythesea.com
Owner: Mary Darby Est: 1995
2500 sq.ft. 1600+ Bolts 950+ Quilt Titles

Mon - Sat 10 - 5
Sun 12 - 5

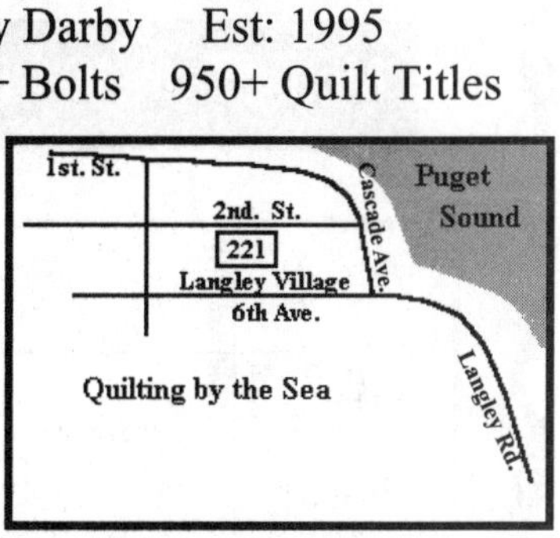

Fabrics, books, patterns, supplies, gifts, & quilts. The friendliest quilt shop for service, inspiration & sharing of ideas. Classroom & Retreat Space with a view of Puget Sound.

www.quiltingbythesea.com

Sedro Woolley, WA #23

Mon - Fri 9:30 - 5:30
Sat 9:30 - 5

Cascade Fabrics

824 Metcalf 98284
(360) 855-0323
Owner: Paul Kelley
Est: 1978 3000 sq.ft.

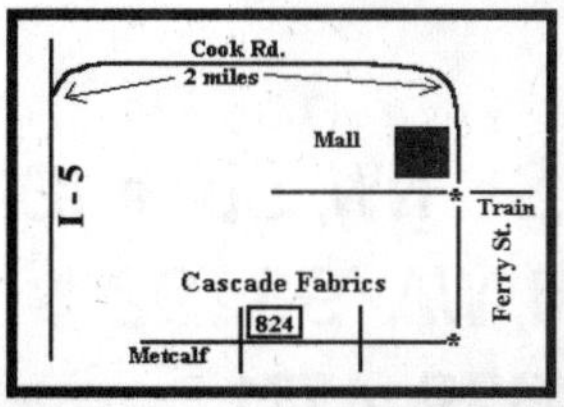

Quilting Supplies and Books, Classes. Experienced Staff. 20% off all quilting cotton always. Additional non-quilting fabrics also.

LaConner, WA #24

Wed - Sat 11 - 4
Sun 12 - 4

La Conner Quilt Museum

703 S. 2nd St.,
P.O. Box 1270 98257
(360) 466-4288 Fax: Same
Director: Rita Hupy
E-mail: lacquiltm@aol.com
www.laconnerquilts.com

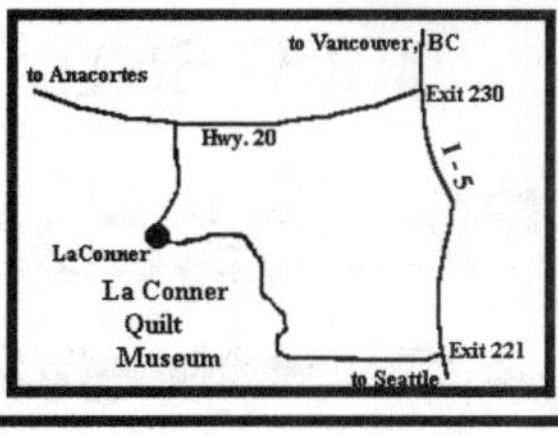

One of only 10 Quilt Museums in the U.S.A. Five shows a year from around the country and the world. Memberships Available.

"Your next quilt starts here"

the Quilt Shop

Anacortes, WA #25

Mon - Sat
9:30 - 5:30
Sun 11 - 4

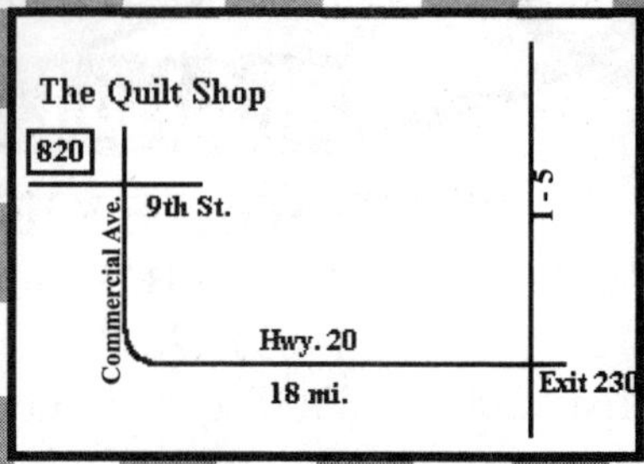

820 Commercial Ave. 98221 (360) 293-2146

Owners: Cathy Berk & Mary Gillman 3000+ Bolts

Everything for the Quilter!

Fabrics, patterns, books, notions & classes.

Stanwood, WA #26

Cotton Pickins'

Choose from a wonderful selection of notions, books, patterns, kits and special gifts. Featuring quality 100% cotton quilting fabrics, homespuns and flannels from Hoffman, Moda, South Seas, Bali, RJR, Thimbleberries, Benartex and More!

Mon - Sat 10 - 5:30

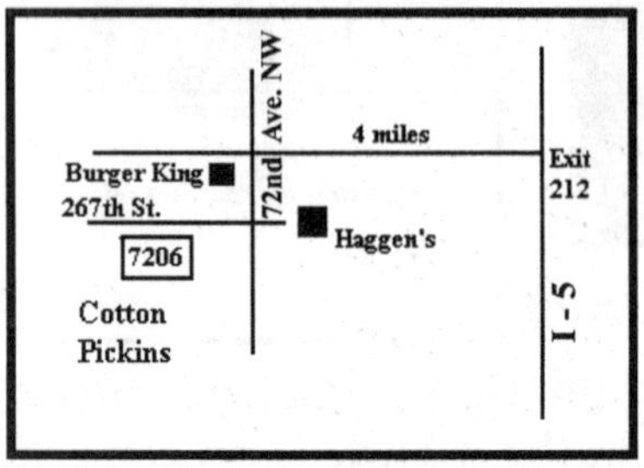

7206 267th St. NW, Suite 102
Stanwood, WA 98292
360-629-4771
email: CottonPickins@aol.com
Owner: Kathy Blank
Fax: 360-629-7530
Est: 2000 3000 Bolts

www.QuiltingwithCottonPickins.com

Bellevue, WA #27

Conveniently located east of Seattle just off I-405 in downtown Bellevue.

QUILTWORKS NORTHWEST

Fabrics Notions Patterns Books

– *The complete line of Electric Quilt products*

Lots of Classes:

- *Traditional and Contemporary Quilting*
- *Photo transfer, Thermafax silk screening*
- *Hands-on computer quilt design*
- *Dyeing and fabric painting*

Hours
M, W, F & Sat: 10 -6
T & Th: 10 - 9
Sun: 12 - 5

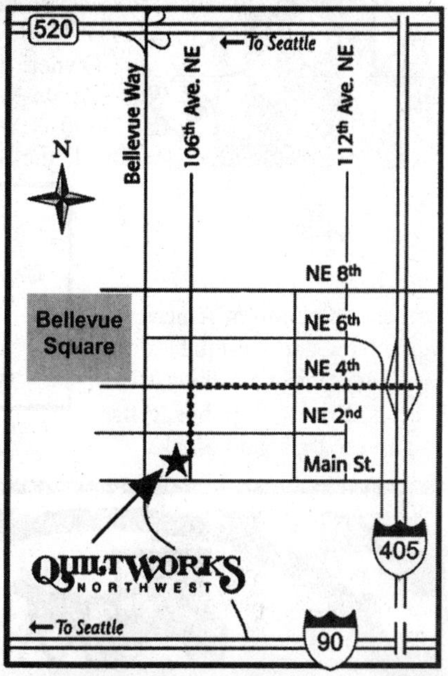

425-453-6005
Toll free 1-877-295-7222
www.quiltworksnw.com • E-mail: info@quiltworksnw.com

145 106th Ave. NE, Bellevue
Located in Bellevue Plaza, 1 block east & 1-1/2 blocks south of Bellevue Square.

In The Beginning *fabrics*

Celebrating 25 years!

One of the Northwest's oldest quilt-fabric shops and its largest. Featuring 1000's of fabrics and books, a huge selection of notions, and classes for all skill levels. The store also showcases many of the fabrics from its wholesale division - which can also be found at quality quilt and fabric shops around the world.
We look forward to your visit.

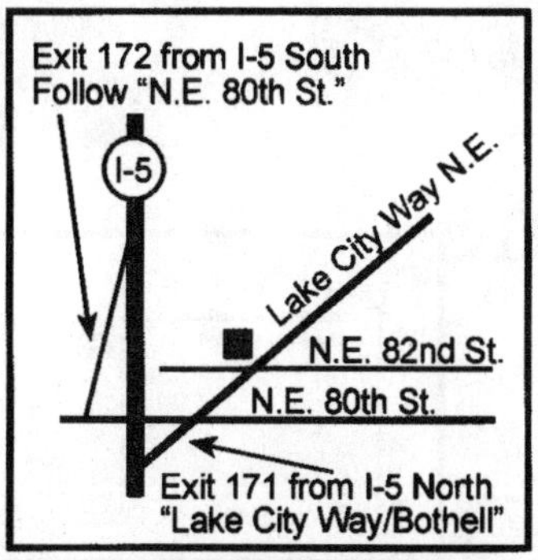

8201 Lake City Way N.E.
Seattle, WA 98115
206-523-8862

Store Hours
Mon., Tues., Fri. & Sat.: 10:00 - 5:30, Wed. & Thurs.: 10:00 - 9:00, Sun.: 12:00- 5:00

www.inthebeginningfabrics.com

Seattle, WA #28

Seattle, WA #29

Mon - Sat 10 - 6
Sun 11 - 5

Undercover Quilts from the U.S.A.

1411 1st Ave. #106 98101
(800) 469-6511 or (206) 622-6382
Fax: (206) 622-6382
E-Mail: quilts@serv.net
Owner: Linda Hitchcock
Web Site: www.undercoverquilts.com
Est: 1990 1000 sq.ft. 1500 Bolts
Inside the South Arcade Bldg.

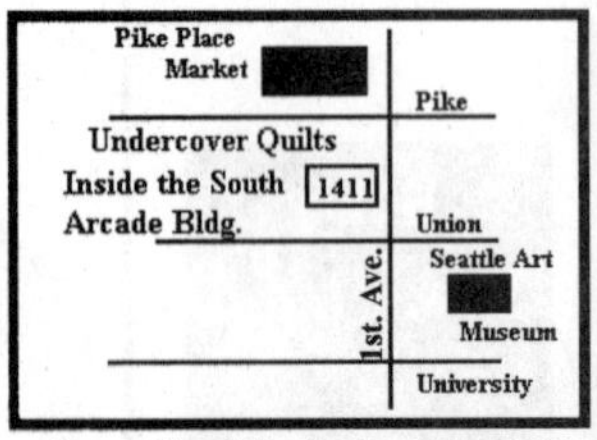

Largest Selection of American Made New and Antique Quilts in the Pacific Northwest! Fabrics, Books, Supplies, gifts, antique tops, and blocks.

From North I - 5 take Exit 165B
From South I - 5 take Exit 165

Everett, WA #30

Mon 12 - 5
Tues - Fri 9 - 7
Sat 9 - 5

Quilt with ease

3122 Broadway
98201
(425) 259-6579

E-Mail: quilt@premier1.net
Owner: Diane Coombs Est: 1982
Over 2500 Bolts of 100% Cotton, Books, Notions, Classes & Quilts!
Plus Quilt Related Tours to National Shows

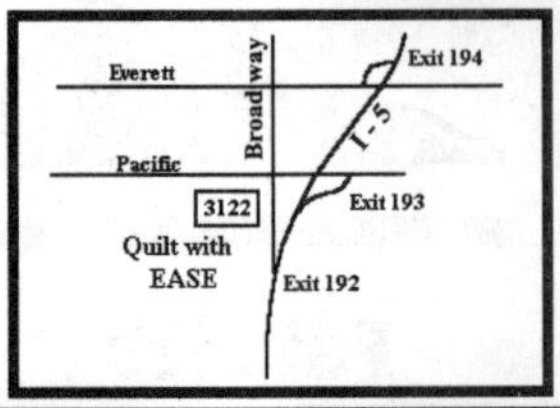

Bothell, WA #31

Mon - Sat 10 - 6
Sun 11 - 5

Keepsake Cottage Fabrics

23732 Bothell-Everett Hwy. 98021
(425) 486-3483
Owners: Delberta Murray & Julie Stewart
Est: 1985 1000 sq.ft.

Quilting Fabrics, patterns and notions. In the heart of Bothell's Country Village.

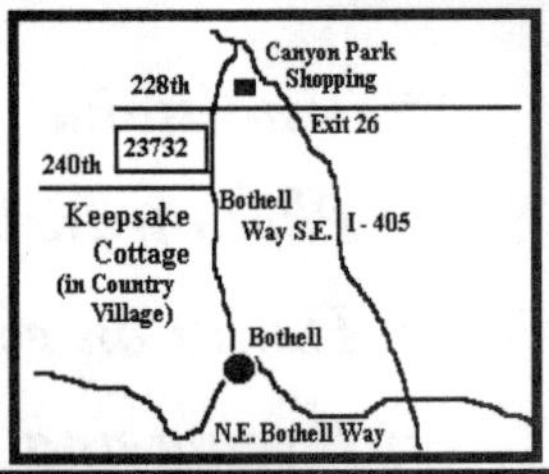

Carriage Country Quilts

Fine Fabrics / Classes
Gifts / Notions
Patterns / Books

Driving Directions: Exit I-5 at exit #149. Head west on the Kent-Des Moines Road. Continue as the road curves and eventually becomes Marine View Dr S as you enter downtown Des Moines. We are in a gray house, between Texaco and Washington Mutual.

#32

22214 Marine View Drive South
Des Moines, Washington 98198
(206) 878-9414

Regular Hours: Mon-Fri 10-7 ♥ Sat 10-5 ♥ Sun 12-4

Federal Way, WA #33

Sues Rags Quilt Shop

1520 S. Dash Point Rd. 98003
(253) 941-5076 or (888) 844-RAGS
Fax: (253) 924-0456 Est: 1994
E-Mail: suesrags@aol.com
Web Site: www.suesrags.com

Mon - Fri 10 - 6
Sat 10 - 5

Announcing: Our New Book: Clever Quilts: Making The Most of Panels, Borders & Theme Prints

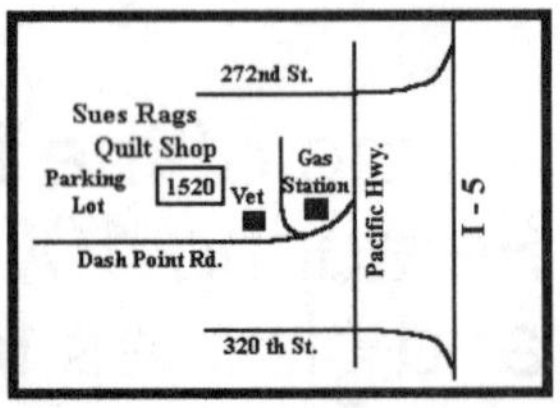

Quilting Fabrics, Books, Notions, Smocking and Heirloom Sewing Supplies, Patterns. Classes and Friendly Staff.

University Place, WA #34

Mon - Fri 10 - 6
Sat 10 - 5

Comfy Quilt Shop

3617 Bridgeport Way W 98466
(253) 565-5745 or (800) 889-0371
Owner: JoAnn Wick
Est: 1995

Large selection of fabric. Hawaiian, Oriental, etc. Custom Machine Quilting. Classes Year Around.

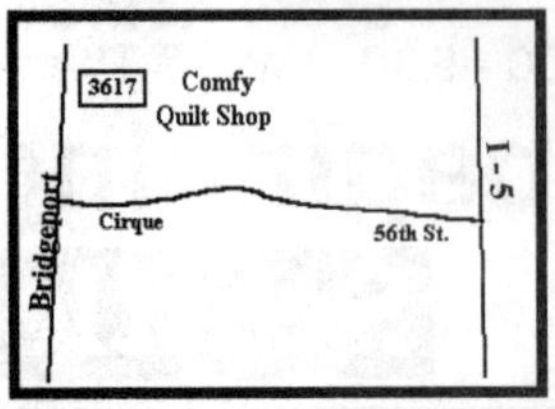

Shelton, WA #35

Mon - Sat 10 - 5:30

Sue's Stitch in Time

927 W. Railroad Ave. 98584
(360) 427-6164
E-Mail: suesstitch@netzero.net
Owner: Sue Bennett
Est: 2000 3400 sq.ft. 2500 Bolts

Beautiful, new, well-lit store offering thousands of bolts of fabrics with professional & enthusiastic customer service

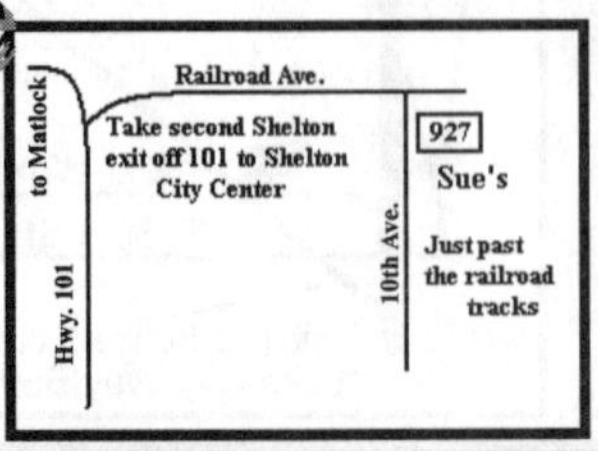

PIECES

Mon - Sat 10 - 7
Sun 12 - 5

364 Renton Center Way SW #59
Renton, WA 98055
(425) 271-7160
Toll Free: (888) 271-7160
E-Mail: mail@piecesquiltshop.com
Web Site: piecesquiltshop.com
Est: 1996
1900 sq.ft. 3600 Bolts

Quality Fabrics & Quilting

Mail Orders.

Quarterly Newsletter.

Specializing in a wide array of color!
Batiks, Collections & Unique Prints !
Classes & Kits year round !

Renton, WA #36

Auburn, WA #37

CALICO CAT
and Bernina Too

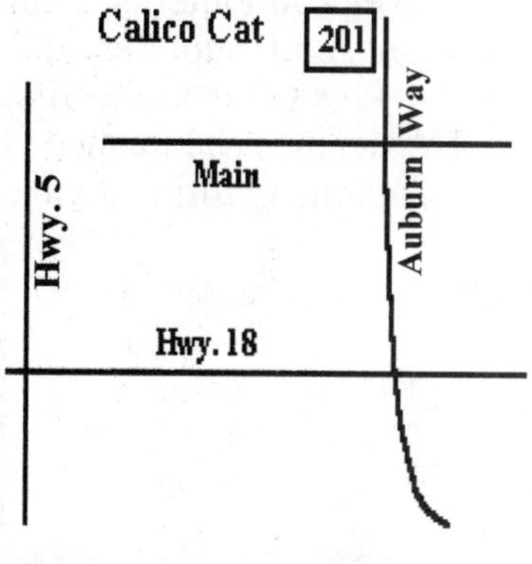

201 N. Auburn Way 98002
Auburn, WA 98002
(800) 908-0885 or (253) 939-0885

Mon - Fri: 10 - 8
Sat: 10 - 5
Sun: 12- 5

Wheel-Chair Accessible

Nothing Sews Like A Bernina. Nothing.
BERNINA®

over 2800 fine cotton fabrics
extensive book collection
notions, patterns, classes
free newsletter
block of the month kits and patterns

Bernina Sewing machines and sergers
accessories and classes
technician on site for service and repair

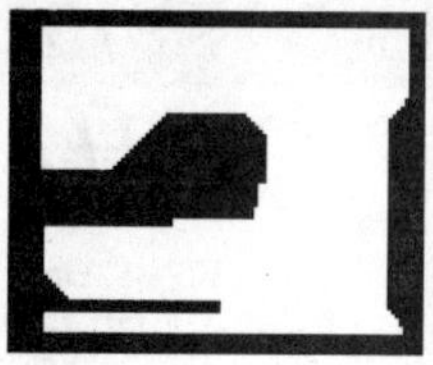

Owner: Mary Stanton Est:1992 5000 sq.ft. Fabric@Thecalicocat.com www.thecalicocat.com

Issaquah, WA #38

The Loft

1480 N.W. Gilman
Blvd. #2
98027
(425) 392-5877
Est: 1972

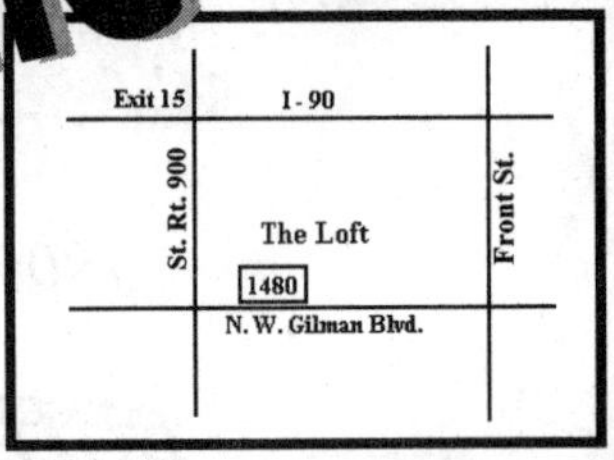

Mon - Fri 10 - 6
Wed til 7
Sat 10 - 5 Sun 12 - 5

Lose yourself for a few minutes or a few hours browsing in our inspiration filled shop. The walls are hung with quilts galore. Our shelves are filled with the latest in fabrics. Bundles and kits abound. Our book collection is huge and we are proud to feature pattern by northwest artists! Located just off the freeway for easy access, parking for large vehicles is available! We look forward to meeting you!

Bonney Lake, WA #39

Quilters Cottage

inside Ben Franklin Crafts

21121 Hwy. 410 98390
(253) 862-6822 2500+ Bolts

Mon - Fri 9 - 8 Sat 9 - 6 Sun 10 - 6

Fine 100% Cotton Quilting Fabrics. Great Selection - Notions, Books, Patterns, Craft Supplies & Classes. Expert Service by our Friendly Knowledgeable Staff

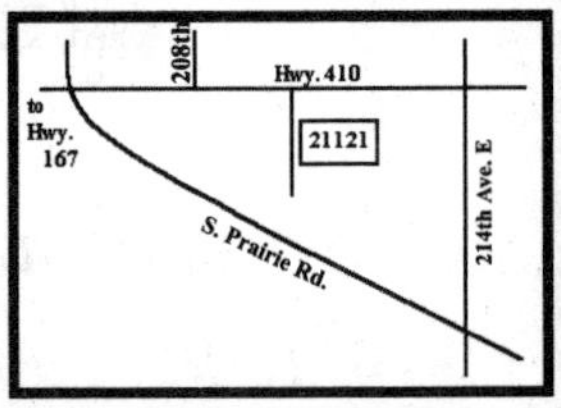

GEE-GEE'S Quilts
Crafts & Gifts

100% Cotton Fabrics, 6000+ bolts,
over 600 Quilting Books,
Over 200 Patterns, stencils,
notions, craft supplies, and yarns.
Plus Collectible Gifts,
TY Beanies & Finished Quilts.
Machine Quilting Available.

Mon - Fri 9 - 6
Sat 9 - 5
Sun 11 - 4

601 Yelm Ave. W 98597
(360) 458-5616
E-Mail: gee-gees
@worldnet.att.net
Est: 1978 6000 sq.ft.

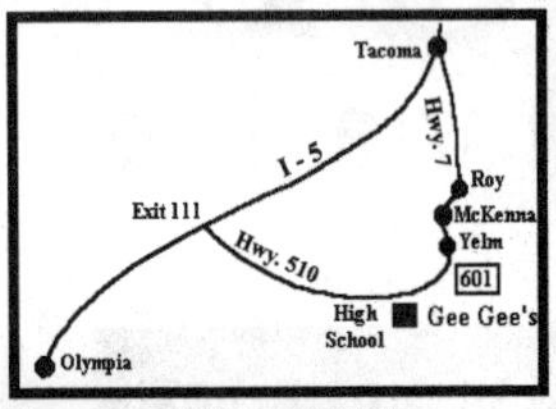

Yelm, WA #40

Yelm, WA #41

By Appt. Only

Quilts by Flo

13242 Rocking "S" Lane SE 98597
(360) 458-6667
Owner: Florence M. Schirman
Est: 1979 784 sq.ft. 380 Bolts
RV Turnaround

Classes, Notions, Fabric, Supplies, Quilts, Quilted Gifts. Relaxed Atmosphere in the Country.

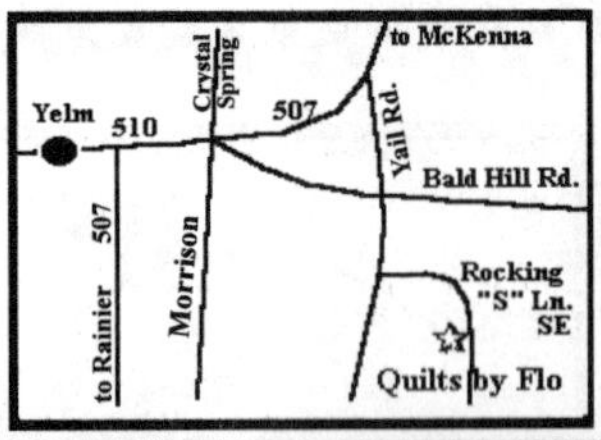

Centralia, WA #42

Mon - Fri 10 - 5
Sat 10 - 4

Quilters Junction

1131 Mellen St. 98531
(888) 553-7865 or
(360) 807-1255
E-Mail: quilters@quik.com
Owner: Evelyna Manier Est: 1997

Located in a large house built in 1916. Take Exit 81 (Mellen St. Exit) off I - 5, and go one block east. Only house with quilts hanging on the porch. Fabrics, Patterns, Books & Notions.

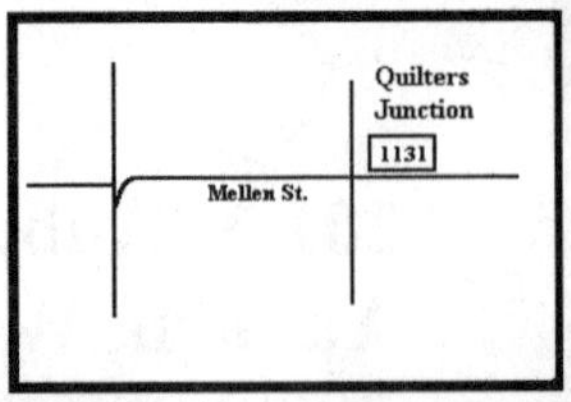

Centralia, WA #43

Mon - Fri 9 - 9
Sat 9 - 6
Sun 11 - 6

Crafts Galore

1724 S. Gold 98531
(360) 330-0200
E-Mail: Craftsgalore@craftsgalore.com
Web Site: www.craftsgalore.com
Est: 1994 17,000 sq.ft. 1200+ Bolts

We cater to Quilters! High Quality Fabrics from top Companies! Rughooking and Supplies. Hundreds of Notions and Buttons. Friendly, helpful Customer Service.

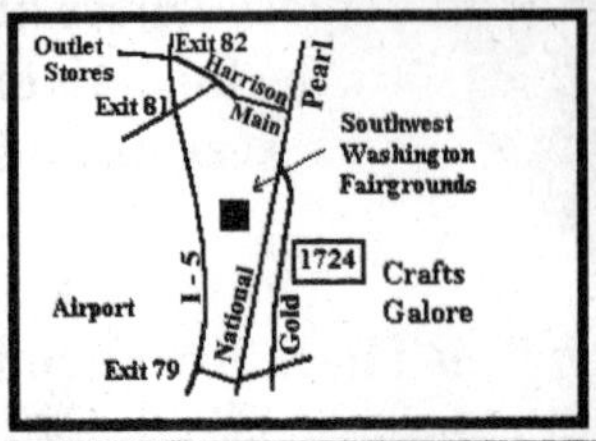

Olympia, WA #44

Mon - Fri 10 - 6
Sat 9 - 5

The Quilt Patch

2747 Pacific Ave. SE, Suite C-1 98506
(360) 754-6732 or (888) 737-2724
Fax: (360) 754-8182
Owner: Pat Seely Est: 1995
1600 sq.ft. 2500+ Bolts Newsletter

100% Cotton Fabric, Quilting & Sewing Supplies, Books, Patterns, Classes. Industrial Quilting Machine.

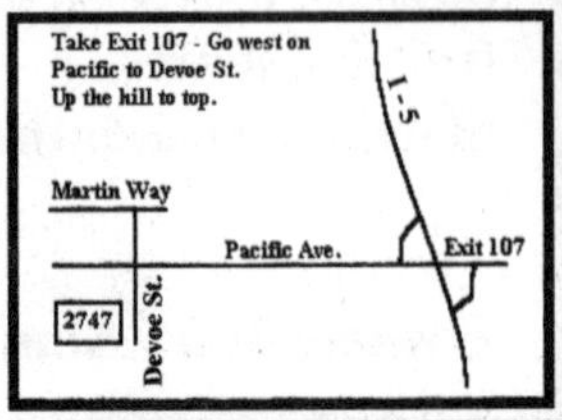

Byrd's Nest Quilting

1613 E. 31st. St. 98404
(253) 274-0336 Fax: 274-0343
E-Mail: byrdsnestquilting@msn.com
Web Site: www.byrdsnestquilting.com

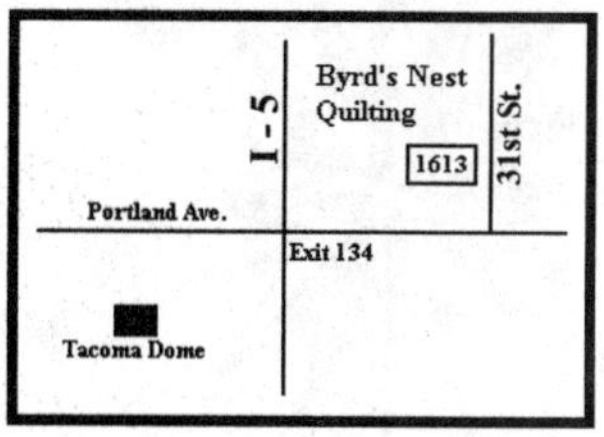

Located 3 Blocks off of I - 5 Exit 134 North Exit 135 South Bound

Over 4000 Bolts of Fabric

Mon - Sat 10 - 6
Sun 12 - 5

Est: 1998
2400 sq.ft.

Owner: Kathy Byrd

Tacoma, WA #45

The Quilt Barn

THE QUILT BARN

Serving Quilters for over 20 years!

1206 E. Main Puyallup, WA 98372
(253) 845-1532 or 1-800-988-BARN
www.quiltbarn.com or e-mail QuiltBarn@aol.com
Regular Business Hours:
Tues., Wed., Fri. 10-7 p.m. Thurs. 10-9 p.m.
Sat. 10-6 p.m. Sun. 12-5 p.m. Closed Mon.
NEW OWNER: Pamela Hewitt 2500 sq. ft.

Puyallup, WA #46

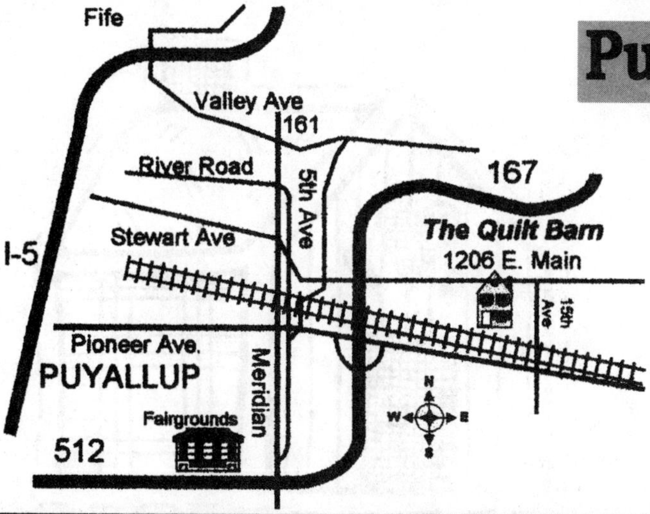

- Fine 100% Cotton Quilting Fabrics
- 3,000 bolt selection
- Complete Quilting supplies and notions
- Large selection of Books and Patterns
- Friendly and knowledgeable staff
- Day and Evening Classes
- Open 6 days a week
- Thimbleberries Quilt Club 2002 in session
- Block-of-the-Month and kits available
- Web Site and Mail Order services

Call for our catalog or details about Classes.

QUILTER'S QUARTERS
BEST SEWING CENTER

100 Ruby Street S.E Tumwater, WA 98501-4546 360-236-0596
Owners: Julie and Joan Bonin Established: 1998 2700 Square Feet

"Your Full Service Quilting Headquarters"

Offering the finest and latest in quality

- 100% Cotton Fabric
- Books and Patterns
- Quilting Supplies and Notions
- Classes at all levels
- Authorized Bernina, Elna, and Babylock Dealership

Store Hours: Monday - Saturday 10-6
Tuesday 10-8 Sunday 12-4

Traveling Northbound I-5: Take exit 102 Trosper Road. Turn right onto Trosper, right on Capital Blvd, and then left on Ruby. We are located behind Pizza Hut.

Traveling Southbound I-5: Take exit 102 Trosper Road. Turn left onto Trosper, right on Capital Blvd, and then left on Ruby.

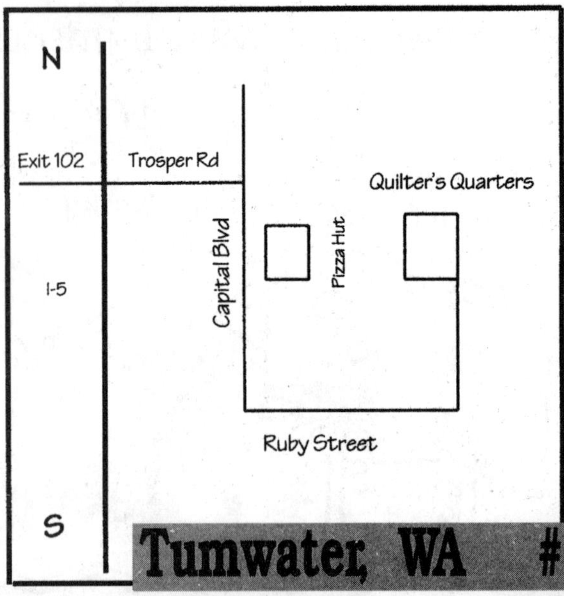

Tumwater, WA #47

Port Orchard, WA #48

Mon - Fri 10 - 8
Sat 10 - 6
Sun 12 - 5

Rochelle's Fine Fabric & Quilting

1700 Mile Hill Drive #200C
South Kitsap Mall: Upper Level
(360) 895-1515 98366
E-Mail: rochelle@oz.net
Owner: Rochelle Savage
Est: 1981 5500 sq.ft.

A complete collection of cotton solids & prints from all the best manufacturers. A large selection of books & notions. Classes too!

Rochelle's is located between Gig Harbor and Bremerton. From Tacoma on Hwy. 16 pass the Gig Harbor exits, 20 minutes, take Fremont St./Port Orchard Exit. Go Rt (east) toward Pt. Orchard. Travel 1.4 miles (4 stoplts) then go left on Bethel. Travel 1 mile and go right on Mile Hill Rd. 1 Block on your right is the So. Kitsap Mall. We are on the Upper level!!

Gig Harbor, WA #49

Mon - Sat 10 - 5
Sun 12 - 5

HARBOR QUILT

3607 Hunt St. NW 98335
(253) 858-5414 or (800) 743-9995
Fax: (253) 858-5416
E-Mail: pgvin@harbornet.com
Web Site: www.harborquilt.com
Owner: Patti Vincent Est: 1999

2000+ bolts of 100% cotton, books, notions, everything for quilting. Batiks, flannels, plaids, 30's reproductions and novelties. Enlarging soon to sell finished quilts.

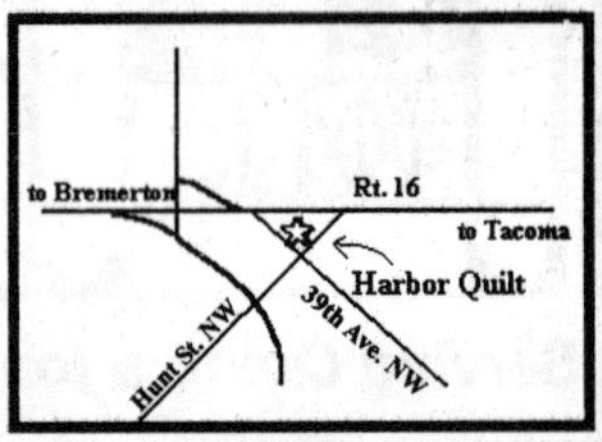

Port Angeles, WA #50

Mon - Sat 10 - 5

QUILTED STRAIT

111 N. Oak St. 98362
Phone / Fax: (360) 457-4733
E-Mail: tomcal@olypen.com
Owners: Calli & Tom Baker
Est: 2001 1500 sq.ft.

Come see our new shop and our extensive collection of flannels, hand dyed wools, fabric, notions, books and patterns.

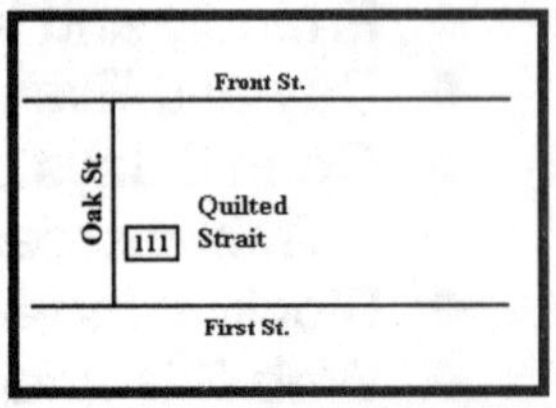

The Stitching Heron

Located on the North Olympic Peninsula in SEQUIM, Washington!

- 2500 square feet and 1500 bolts of cottons, batiks and silks
- Hoffman, Timeless Treasures, Michael Miller, Moda, Robert Kaufman, P&B Textiles, Benartex, Kona Bay, Indo U.S., to name a few!
- An exclusive line of African batiks, a great selection of quality notions and books, and unique quilting frames and hangers
- Come to Sequim, visit us, and take in the Lavender Farms. The Lavender Festival is held annually in July. Call us for motel and restaurant information.
- Family owned and operated! You won't find better service!
- Look for us on the internet in late 2002!

The Stitching Heron
a division of Hatchiko, Inc.

Fabrics, Notions and Books
for Quilting and Fabric Crafts

126 E. Washington Street
Sequim, WA 98382
(360) 582-1230 Phone
(360) 582-1838 Fax

(One Block East of Sequim Ave.)

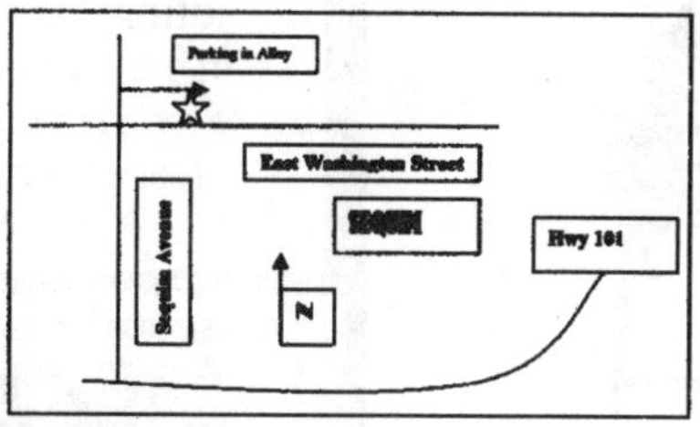

HOURS
10-6 M-F
10-5 Sat.

"A great new quilt shop"

See you in SEQUIM.

Sequim, WA #51

Port Townsend, WA #52

Seaport Fabrics

aka: The Dancing Needle

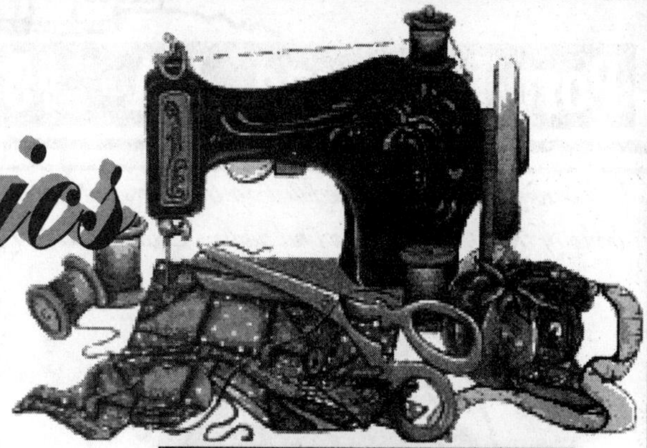

2427 Sims Way 98368
(360) 385-3992 Fax: (360) 379-3961
Owners: Karen Sievert 3800 sq.ft.

Mon - Sat 9:30 - 5:30
Sun 1 - 5

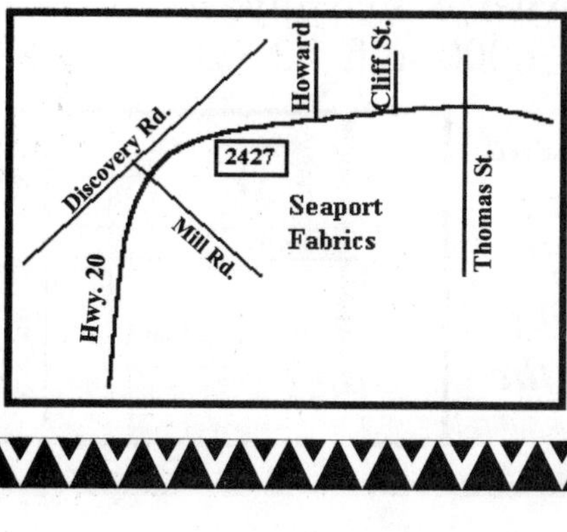

"A Friend is a Present You Give Yourself"

And we so enjoy the friendships we've developed with our customers. Come in for a fine selection of 100% cotton fabrics, books, patterns, notions, kits and gifts. Stunning quilts and quilt related items for sale and made locally. Classes from beginners to advanced. Custom machine quilting on our shop Gammill.

This is your "Full Service" shop.

Quilter's Cove

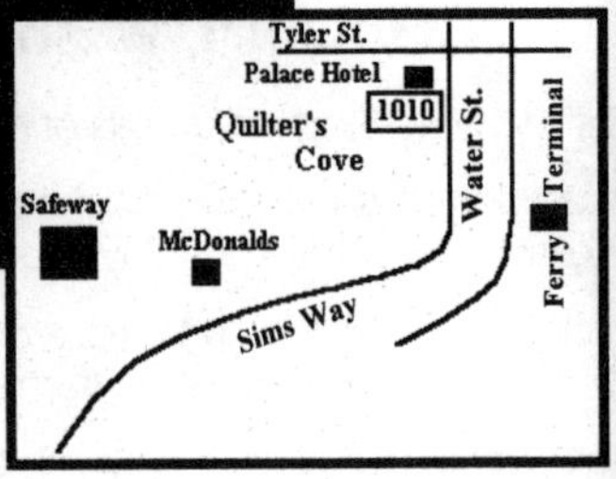

1010 Water St.
98368
(360) 385-4254
E-Mail: Quilterscove@aol.com
Est: 1993 2700 sq.ft.

Mon - Sat 10 - 5:30
Sun 11 - 5

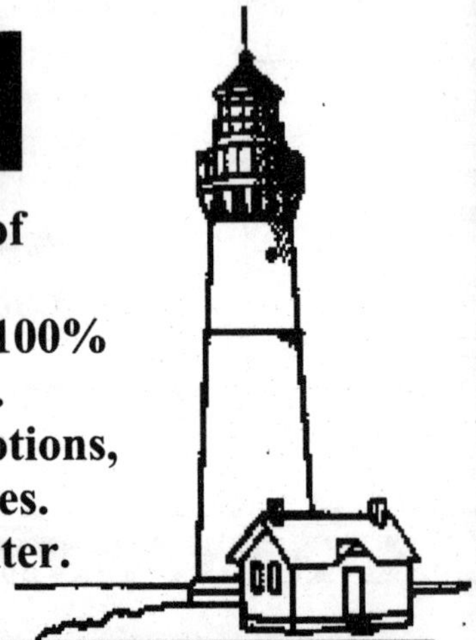

Best Selection of Books.
Large Selection of 100% cotton fabrics.
Complete line of notions, patterns & classes.
Gifts for the Quilter.

Port Townsend, WA #53

Grayland, WA #54

Est: 1999

Quilt Harbor

2172 St. Rt. 105, P.O. Box 771 98547
Toll Free (877) 676-3300
(360) 267-3300 Fax: (360) 267-0129
E-Mail: quiltharbor@olynet.com
Web Site: www.quilt-harbor.com
Owners: Gretchen & George Waham

Mon - Sat
10 - 5
Closed Wed.
Sun 12 - 4

1200 sq.ft. of over 2000 bolts of 100% cotton Fabrics, Notions, Books & Patterns. Coffee's always on. Copy & Fax Service. Authorized Bernina & Elna Dealer Sales & Service.

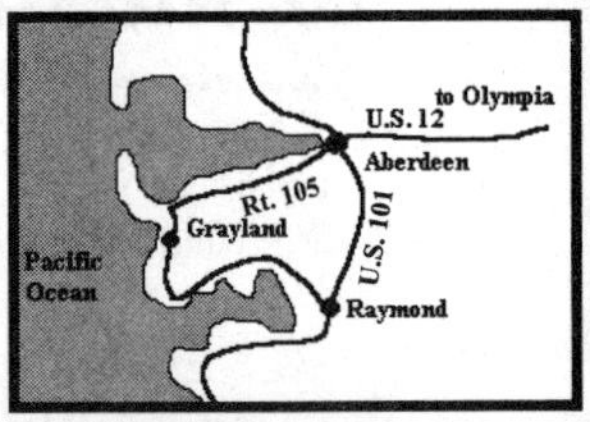

A charming 1930's cottage filled to the brim with over 1,500 bolts of traditional fabrics and quilts. Established in 1996.

MOMMA MADE IT

◆ Fabric & Supplies for Quilters ◆

2035 9th Ave. Longview, WA 98632
360-636-5631 quiltk@solidnet.com

Directions: From I-5 take Exit #39.
Follow the signs to Hwy 4 West (Ocean Beaches)
At Taco Time turn left on 9th Ave.
2nd little house on the right.

Hours:
Mon. – Wed. 10 – 6
Thurs. 10 – 8
Fri. 10 – 5 Sat. 10 – 4

Longview, WA #56

Long Beach, WA #55

7 Days a Week
10 - 5:30

A full line of quilting fabrics & notions including over 3000 bolts of 1930's reproductions & our own line of 30's patterns.

QUILT FABRIC · GIFTS & FUDGE · LONG BEACH · WASHINGTON

Anna Lena's

www.annalena.com

We make our own fudge & espresso. Tables for the family to sit while you shop.

111 Bolstad Ave. 98631
(360) 642-8585 Fax: (360) 642-8948
E-Mail: annalena@willapabay.org
Web Site: www.annalena.com
Owner: Karen Snyder
Est: 1998 6000 sq.ft. 3000 Bolts

We're at the end of the Lewis & Clark Trail! Come see why we're worth the trip!

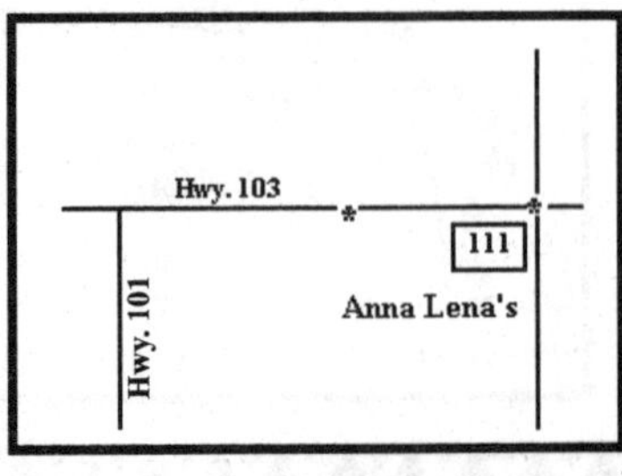

Longview, WA #57

Mon - Fri 9 - 9
Sat 9 - 6
Sun 11 - 6

Crafts Galore

780 Ocean Beach Hwy. 98632
(360) 578-2733 Fax: (360) 578-2734
E-Mail: craftsgalore@tdn.com
Web Site: www.craftsgalore.com
Est: 1991 20,000 sq.ft. 1200+ Bolts

We cater to Quilters! High Quality Fabrics from top Companies! Rughooking and Supplies. Hundreds of Notions and Buttons. Friendly, helpful Customer Service.

Kalama, WA #58

Mon - Sat 10 - 5

THE NINE PATCH

384 N. 1st St. 98625
(360) 673-1725 Fax: (360) 673-1739
E-Mail: theninepatch@kalama.com
Web Site: www.TheNinePatch.net
Owners: Jackie Jamison & LeeAnn Hadaller
Est: 2001 1600 sq.ft.

Our shop has successfully joined the established 'Antique District' and we carry all the fabrics and notions needed to get you started quilting.

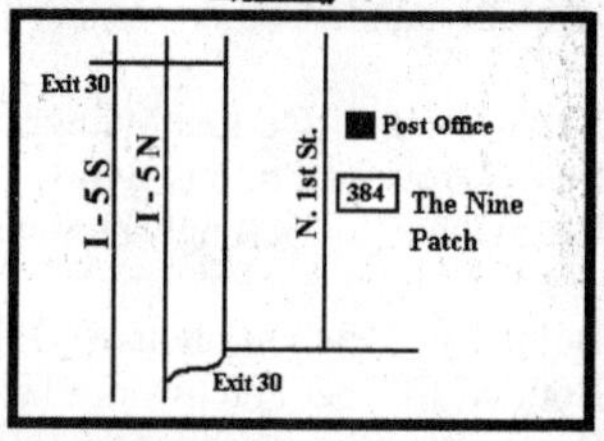

North Bonneville, WA #59

Tues - Sat 10 - 6

Quilters Landing

72 Cascade Mall Dr. 98639
(509) 427-7581 Fax: (509) 427-7641
E-Mail: ottoslanding@yahoo.com
Web Site: www.quilters-landing.com
Owner: Linda Otto Est: 2001

Fabrics, Notions, Books, Patterns, Gifts
All in a park like setting in the Columbia River Gorge--Classes, Friendly Service.

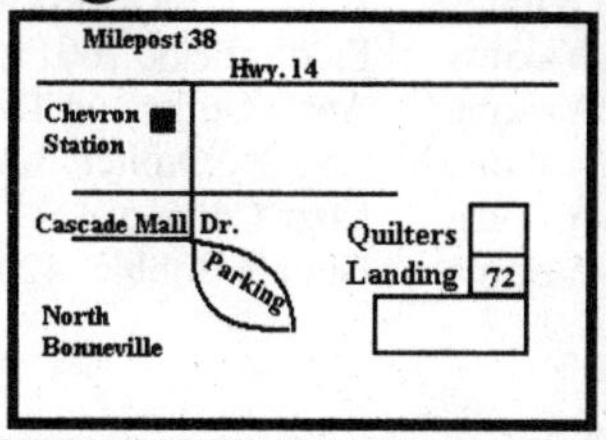

Vancouver, WA #60

Mon - Fri 9 - 5:30
Sat 9 - 5

Quilt-n-Stitch

808 SE Chkalov Dr. #3 98683
(360) 882-9101 fax: (360) 896-4722
Web Site: www.quilt-n-stitch.com
Owner: Betty Markee Est: 2000

A full line of quilting fabric and supplies. Unique kits and patterns designed by our staff. Fun and friendly group.

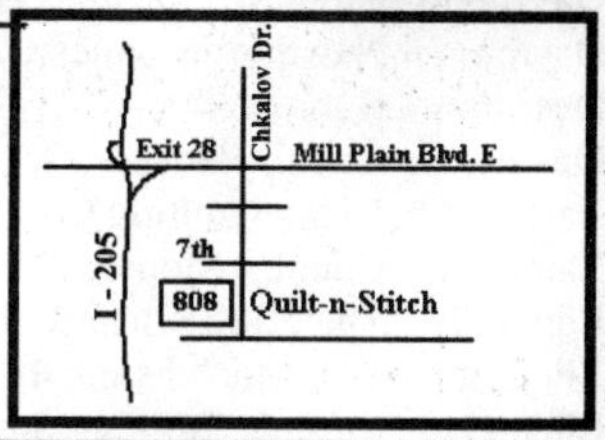

Connecting Threads

You've enjoyed our catalog, now see our store!

- Hundreds of books! Most discounted 20%!
- Hundreds of Tools!
- Latest fabric collections all 100% cotton!
- Exclusive Quilt Kits with Free Patterns included!
- Great Bargains! Catalog fabric overstocks arrive daily! Hundreds of bolts at unbelievable prices everyday!

Open 9 am - 6 pm Monday thru Saturday

Or visit us on the web at

www.ConnectingThreads.com

View the inside pages of hundreds of books and patterns before you buy. Check out every fabric in stock and compare colors and values with 4 different views on our design table. Choose from thousands of tools, notions and supplies. Free pattern downloads!

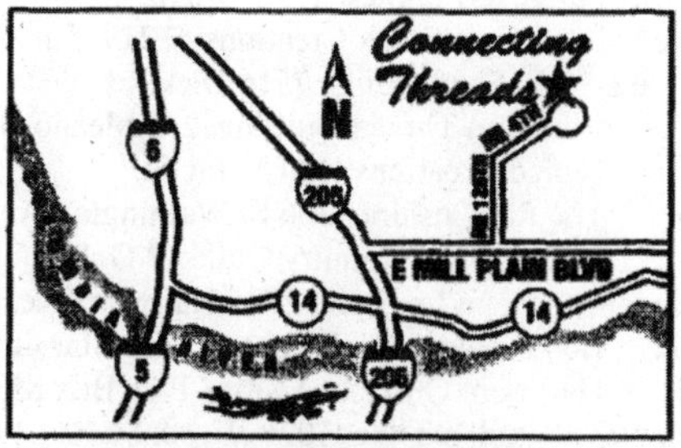

Conveniently located just 10 minutes from the Portland Airport, 20 minutes from downtown Portland.

13118 NE 4th Street
Vancouver, WA 98684
360-260-8900 • 800-574-6454
Call for a free catalog!

Vancouver, WA #61

Other Shops in Washington: We suggest calling first

Aberdeen	Alpha & Omega Quilts, 15 Ocosta 6th St.	360-648-0950
Anacortes	Fabrics Plus, 608 Commercial Ave	360-293-7641
Arlington	Bunny Patch, 24613 27th Ave. NE	360-435-8414
Bainbridge Isle	Rainy Day Quilts, 6516 NE Baker Hill Rd.	206-842-6221
Bainbridge Isle	Esther's Inc., 285 Winslow Way E	206-842-2261
Battle Ground	Country Manor Fabric & Crafts, 7702 NE 179th St.	360-573-6084
Battle Ground	Quilted Memories, 23513 NE 229th St	360-687-9393
Battle Ground	Cottons, 316 E. Main St.	360-666-0366
Bellingham	Bellingham Sewing Center, 3600 Meridian St. #B	360-733-7836
Bothell	The Farmhouse, 23710 Bothell Hwy. SE	425-483-3354
Bothell	That Patchwork Place, P.O. Box 118	425-483-3313
Bremerton	Stormy Stitches, 3602 Madrona St.	360-377-5146
Bremerton	Thread Connection, 1710 15th St.	360-479-2651
Camas	Seed Lady Quilts, 4824 NW 38th Ave.	360-833-9604
Chehalis	Sisters, 476 N. Market Blvd.	360-748-9747
Chehalis	Quilts Sew Easy, 1286 NW Maryland Ave.	360-740-1769
Chehalis	Moir Country Sewing Co., 215 Macomber Rd.	360-748-4517
Chelan	Needle Nook, P.O. Box 1529	509-682-5513
Clinton	Gentle Threads, 2768 Eveing Glory Ct.	360-321-0447
Davenport	Cottonwood Quilts & Collectibles, 537 Morgan	509-725-0700
Dayton	Hawthorne Gallery, 245 E. Main	509-382-3137
Deer Park	Bobbin Along, 831 S. Main, P.O. Box 1128	509-276-1914
Duvall	Duvall Hand Crafters, 15315 1st Ave. NE	425-788-6497
Eastsound	Island Quilting Co., 11 A St.	360-376-6802
Eatonville	Country Mouse, 755 Eatonville Hwy. E	360-832-8065
Edmonds	The Calico Basket, 550 A Main St.	425-774-6446
Ellensburg	Sew Much More, 411 N. Pine St.	509-933-3030
Ellensburg	Moser's Clothing Store, 118 E. 4th Ave.	509-925-1272
Ellensburg	Mom's Fabrics & Crafts, 405 N. Main St.	509-933-1520
Elmer City	Promised Land Quilts, Box 239	509-633-3318
Everett	Quality Sewing & Vacuum, 10121 Evergreen Way Space 14	425-290-8000
Everett	Pacific Fabric, 10203 Evergreen Way	425-353-8866
Everson	The Quiet Garden, 8310 Gillies Rd.	360-966-5238
Federal Way	Federal Way Sewing & Vacuum, 27045 Pacific Hwy S	253-946-5865
Grandview	Georgette's, 1550 Alexander Ext.	509-882-1757
Indianola	Bizarre Bazaar, P.O. Box 356	360-297-4541
Issaquah	Tilton's Treasures, 4611 NE 243red Ct.	425-961-0015
Kelso	Ad's Fabrics, 300 S. 10th Ave.	360-636-1060
Kettle Falls	Red Rooster, 475 S. Meyers St.	509-738-4418
Lopez	Enchanted Needle, P.O. Box 178	360-468-2777
Lyle	Quilter's Market, 452 Hwy 142	
Lynden	Boomers, 1722 Front St.	360-354-1533
Marysville	Fudge & Funnies, 1515 3rd St.	360-659-8455
Metaline Falls	Sweet Creek Creations, E 219 5th Ave.	509-446-2429
Moses Lake	LaFaun Quilts, 7516 Dick Rd. NE	509-762-5614
Moxee	Common Thread Quilting, 240 Meadowlark	509-248-3878
Mt. Vernon	Calico Creations, 400 S. 1st. St.	360-336-3241
Newport	The Pin Cushion, 306 S. Washington Ave.	509-447-5913
Odessa	Laura's Sage Country Quilts, P.O. Box 151	509-982-2908
Olympia	Ben Franklin Store, 2725 Harrison Ave. NW	360-352-0959
Olympia	Ben Franklin Craft Center, 1243 Marvin NE	360-456-3504
Oroville	Heirloom Quilts and More, P.O. Box 853	509-476-2194
Port Angeles	Quilt'n Time, 1026 W. 6th St.	360-457-6125
Port Orchard	Christina's Heritage, 2516 SE Bethel Rd.	360-895-1034
Poulsbo	Heirloom Quilts, 18833-B Front St.	360-697-2222
Poulsbo	Bird House Quilts, 91 NW Beaver Rdg.	360-779-4618
Prosser	The Sewing Basket, 1108 Wine Country Rd.	509-786-7367
Pullman	Artistic Threads Etc., 210 E. Main St.	509-334-2459
Pullman	Quilted Heart, 1709 NW Lamont St.	509-332-1905
Puyallup	Puyallup Sewing & Vacuum, 111 N. Meridian	253-841-4288
Puyallup	Pacific Fabric & Crafts, 3715 S. Meridian St.	253-770-1095
Richland	Perks Sewing, 621 The Parkway	509-943-1149
Seattle	Nancy's Sewing Basket, 2221 Queen Anne N.	206-282-9112
Seattle	Creative Quilting, 900 NW 80th St.	206-297-8270
Seattle	Pacific Fabrics & Crafts, P.O. Box 3637	206-628-6250
Seattle	Pacific Fabrics & Crafts, 838 NE Northgate Way	206-362-0111
Seattle	Glant Pacific Co., 2230 4th Ave S	206-628-6222
Seattle	Quilt Haus, 3511 NE 196th St.	206-362-0719
Seattle	AAA Sewing & Vacuum, 10859 1st Ave S	206-244-5555
Snohomish	Clearview Triangle, 8311 180th St. SE	360-668-4151
Spokane	This N' That, 9826 N. Andrew St.	509-467-9496
Stanwood	Flair Fabric Design, 550 N. Hawk Ridge Pl.	360-387-4034
Stevenson	Rock Creek Fabrics, 390 SW 2nd St.	509-427-8662
Sumner	Mark's Pharmacy, 1119 Main St.	253-863-6223
Tacoma	Gutcheon Patchworks, 917 Pacific Ave. #305	253-383-3047
Toledo	The Bear's Paw, 197 Middlecrest Dr.	360-864-6723
Union Gap	The Threaded Needle, 2640 Main St.	509-469-3838
University Place	Bernina Stitch, 3617 Bridgeport Way W #H	253-473-7420
Valleyford	Dana's Country Quilting, 11017 E. Connor Rd.	509-891-9234
Vancouver	Quilting Etc., 13202 NE 3rd Ave.	360-573-6758
Walla Walla	Suzy's Crafts, 1145 School Ave.	509-525-2388
Walla Walla	Suzanne's Quilt Shop, 425 B St.	509-526-9398
Washougal	Pendleton Woolen Mills, 2 17th St.	360-835-2131
Washtucna	Patchwork Enterprises, 225 E. St.	509-646-3277
Wilbur	Adelia's, P.O. Box 269	509-647-2676
Yakima	Fiddlesticks, 1601 Summitview	509-452-7718
Yakima	Ann's Quilts and Things, 3504 Ahtanum Rd.	509-965-2313
Yakima	Country Quilter, 3280 Marks Rd.	509-966-9130
Yakima	Cozy Cottage, 4111 Englewood Ave.	509-972-8558
Yakima	Double Bobbin, 4202 Garden Park Way	509-966-5327

WEST VIRGINIA

8 Featured Shops

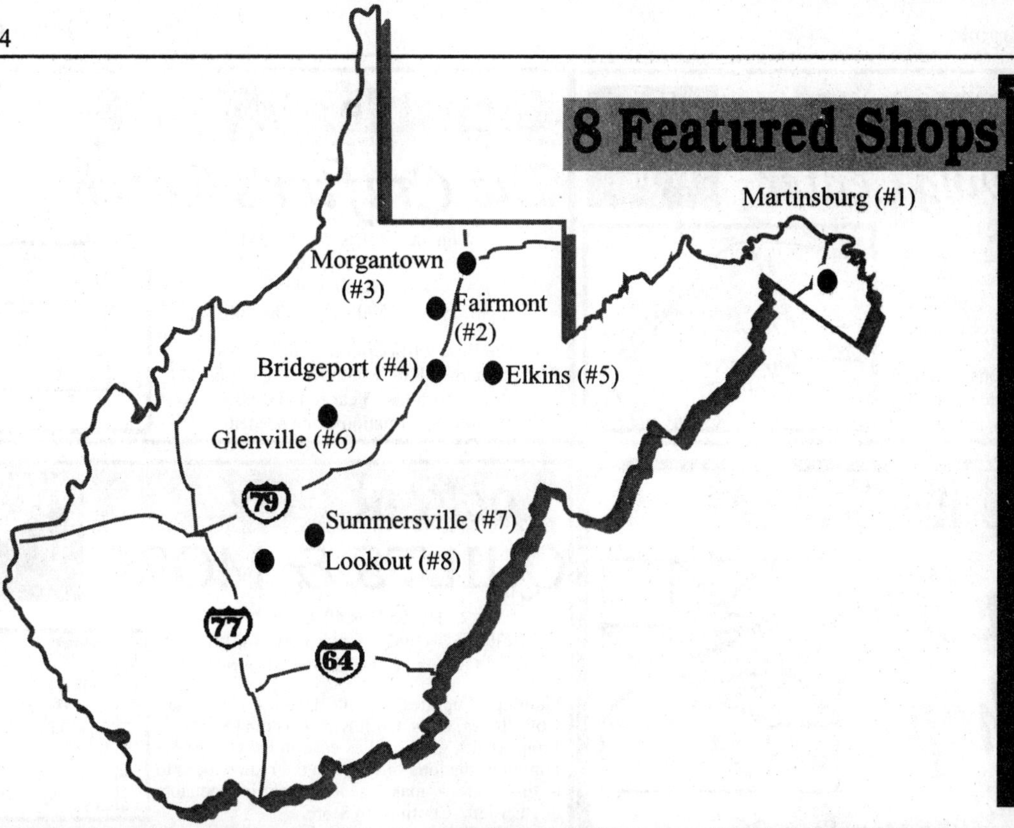

Martinsburg, WV #1

Tues - Fri 10 - 5
Sat 10 - 3

NUTMEG LODGE
318 Wilson St. 25401
(304) 262-6633
E-Mail: nbradley67@msn.com
Owner: Barbara Bradley

A complete Quilt Shop featuring 1500+ bolts of 100% cotton fabric, books, patterns, notions galore. Warm, cozy atmosphere. Pleasant, Friendly Staff!

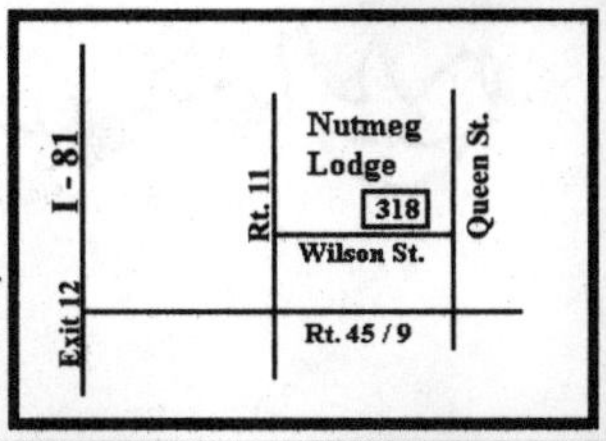

Morgantown, WV #3

Mon - Fri 10 - 6
Sat 10 - 5

The Sew Inn, Ltd.

120 High St. 26505
(304) 296-6802
Owner: Virginia Showers
Est: 1973 1500 sq.ft.

Wonderful collection of quilting cottons, books, notions & classes. Bridal & Special occasion fabrics. Knowledgeable & Friendly service. Authorized Viking Dealer.

Easy Access from I - 79 or I - 68. Located downtown across from The Hotel Morgan.

Bridgeport, WV #4

Mon - Fri 9:30 - 5
Sat 9:30 - 4

The Pine Tree Quilt Shop

132 Thompson Dr. 26330
(304) 842-3200
E-Mail: pinetree@citynet.net
Owner: Kerri E. Smith
Est: 1987 1200 sq.ft.

A quilt shop to satisfy the desires of any quilter. Fabrics include Thimbleberries, MODA, P&B, and many more.

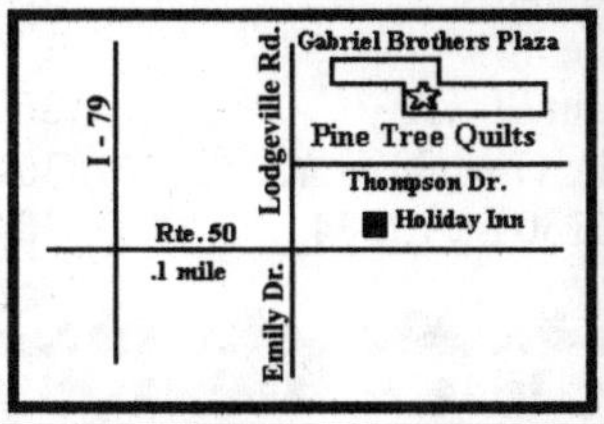

Fairmont, WV #2

Sew Chic

- Over 1500 bolts of designer cottons
- Complete line of quilting supplies, books, patterns, and notions
- Huge thread assortment
- Free newsletter on-line or by request
- Year round classes
- Mail orders welcome

Authorized dealer of Pfaff Sewing Machines, Sergers and Embroidery software

Pfaff creative® 2140

Mon, Tues, Thurs, Fri 10 - 6
Sat 10 - 2
Closed Wednesdays & Sundays

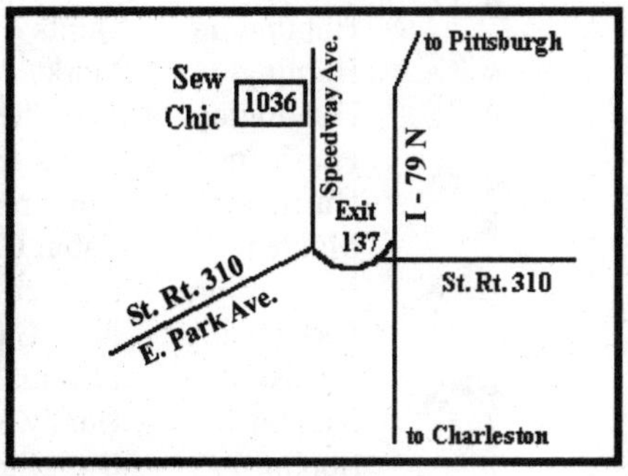

1036 Speedway Ave. 26554
(877) 366-4135 or (304) 366-4135
Fax: (304) 366-6367
E-Mail: sewchic@iolinc.net
Web Site: www.sewchic.com
Owner: Sue Henderson Est: 1996

Elkins, WV #5

Mon - Sat 9 - 5 Fri til 7

Elkins Sewing Center

300 Davis Ave. 26241
(304) 636-9480 or (800) 229-9480
Fax: (304) 636-9486 Est: 1982
E-Mail: SueESC@aol.com 4000 sq.ft.
Owners: Sue & Jim Pifer Free Catalog

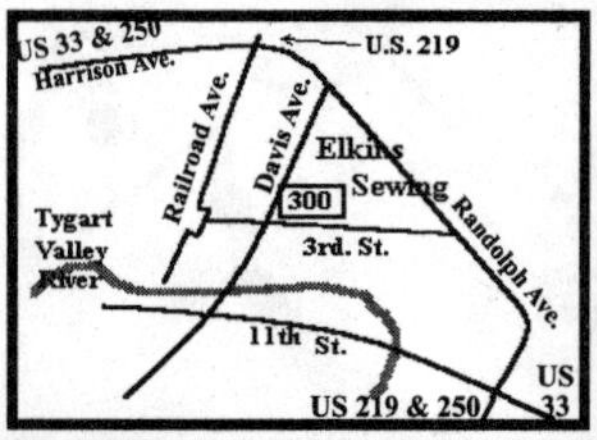

Quilting fabrics, books & notions Specialty threads and trims. Cross stitch supplies. Classes. Viking sewing machines and sergers.

Glenville, WV #6

Tues - Sat 9 - 5

The Crafter's Patch

Main and Morris Sts. 26351
(304) 462-4010
Owner: Sadie Kelble
Est: 1994 1500 sq.ft. 500 Bolts

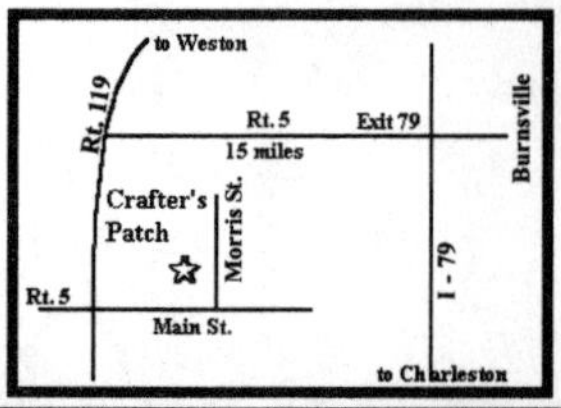

The Best 100% Cotton Quilt Fabrics. P&B, Benartex, RJR, South Seas. Quilting and Sewing Notions. Year round classes. Helpful information when needed.

Summersville, WV #7

Mountain Star Quilt Shop

Mon - Fri 10 - 5 Sat 10 - 1

508A Main St. 26651
(304) 872-0959
E-Mail: mtnstarquilt@hawksnet.net
Owner: Dorleen J. McDowell

Located in historic Summersville, Mountain Star Quilt Shop is a Janome Dealer. We carry quality fabrics, notions, classes and books.
Come Join Us!

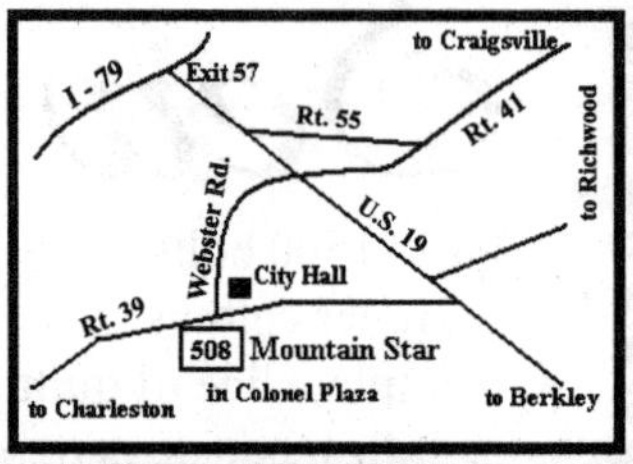

Lookout, WV #8

Tues - Sat 10 - 5 Sun - Mon By Chance Jan 1st - March 31st By Appt.

QUILTS & MORE

HC.65 Box 49 25868
(304) 574-3062 Fax: (304) 574-3910
Owners: Debra & Steve Davis

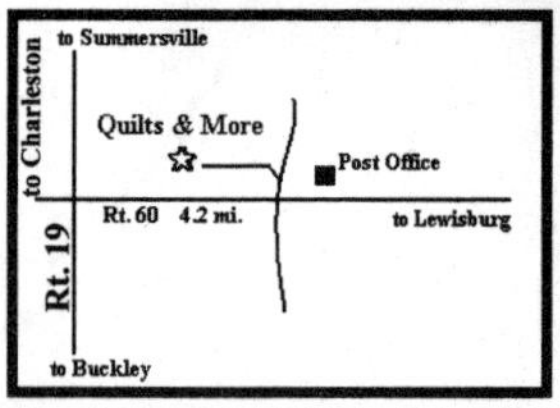

Quilting Supplies, Quilt Classes, Antiques, Collectibles, Gifts, Quilt Kits, Custom Orders. From Rt. 19, go 4.2 miles east on Rt. 60. At the bottom of the long hill - when the road widens to a turn lane - make a left then immediately another left. Continue to Store.

Other Shops in West Virginia: We suggest calling first

Clarksburg	Clarksburg Sewing Center, P.O. Box 353A Route 2	304-622-8112
Dunbar	Mr. Sewing Machine & Vac, 509 Dunbar Ave.	304-768-3939
Farmington	Cotton Patch,. Route 250 N.	304-825-6225
Huntington	Quilts & Crafts, 2887 5th Ave.	304-736-2778
Huntington	Marks Antiques, 617 Fourteenth St. W.	304-525-3275
Huntington	The Cherry Tree Quilt Shop, 6306 E. Pea Ridge	304-736-8086
Hurricane	Quilts & More, 2943 Putnam Ave.	
Hurricane	Quilters Garden, 2730 2nd St.	304-562-7199
Malden	Cabin Creek Quilts, 4208 Malden Dr.	304-925-9499
Martinsburg	Nutmeg Lodge, 318 Wilson St.	304-262-6633
Parkersburg	Rose Garden Quilts, 727 29th St.	304-485-2141
Reedsville	Eleanor's Quilts & Fabric Shop, Rt. 7 E.	304-864-5762
Rippon	Gunny Sack, Rt. 340 S	304-725-3080
Sophia	Quilt Fabrics and Craft Corner, Main St.	304-683-9429
St. Marys	Zepora's Quilt Shop, 116 Lafayette St.	304-684-7113
Summersville	Morning Star Quilt Shop, 508 Main St. #A	304-872-0959
White Sulphur Springs	Morningstar Quilts, The Greenbriar #A	304-536-4003
Winfield	Fern's Fabric and Quilt Shoppe, 6130 St. Rt. 34	304-757-3047

WISCONSIN

80 Featured Shops

Elm Grove, WI #1

Patched Works, Inc.

Owned by a Master Fabricaholic

In a Western Suburb of Milwaukee
13330 Watertown Plank Rd. 53122
(262) 786-1523
Owner: Trudie Hughes
Est: 1978 6000 sq.ft.

Books Patterns Notions

Mon - Fri 9 - 5 Wed til 8
Sat 9 - 4 Sun 12 - 4

8000 bolts of Cotton Fabric
Hundreds of Books &
Patterns for the Quiltmaker

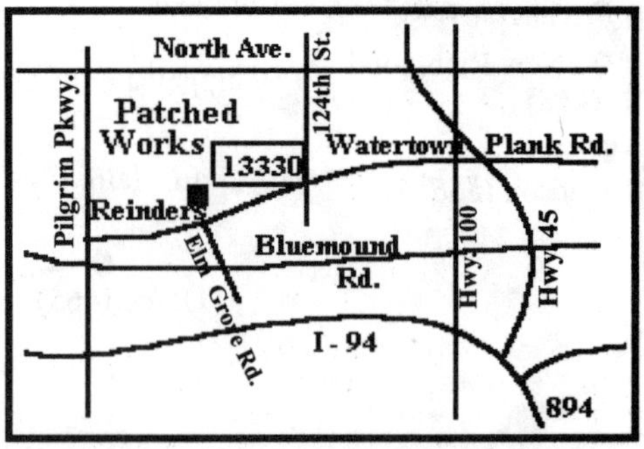

"If it doesn't feel this good, do you really want to use it?"

"If it doesn't feel this good, do you really want to use it?"

2499 S. DELAWARE AVE.
MILWAUKEE, WI 53207
414-744-3747 FAX 414-744-3550
WWW.CUTTINGTABLE.COM

AUTHORIZED ELNA DEALER

elna usa.com

THE CUTTING TABLE®

QUILT AND FASHION FABRIC
SEWING SCHOOL
MACHINE QUILTING SERVICE
BOOKS • PATTERNS • BUTTONS
TRIM • BRIDAL • NOTIONS

HOURS
M-W 9:30am-8pm T-Th-F 9:30-6pm Sat 9:30-4pm Sun 12-4pm
(Closed sundays during summer)

Growing to 6000 sq ft--July 2002

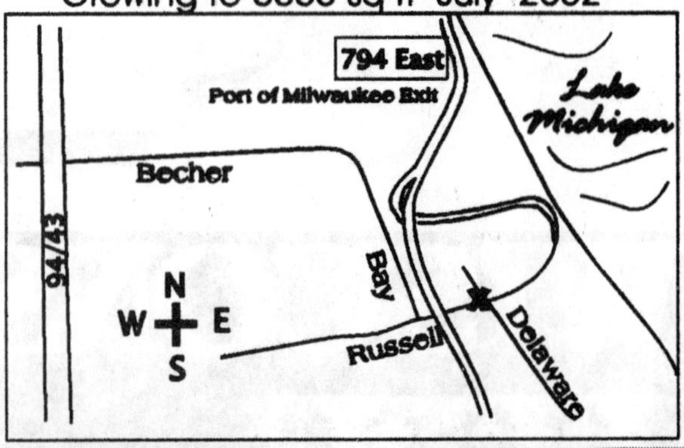

Milwaukee, WI #2

North Prairie, WI #3

Mon - Fri 9:30 - 6
Tues til 8
Sat 9:30 - 4

Pamella's Place

31996 Hwy. 59 53153
(262) 392-3855 Fax: (262) 392-3579
E-Mail: sewing@centurytel.net
Web Site: www.pamellasplace.com
Owner: Pamella Gray
Est: 1987 3200 sq.ft. 2500 Bolts

Bernina and Elna machines.
Inspiring Quilting & Fashion fabrics.
Creating Sewing Excitement!

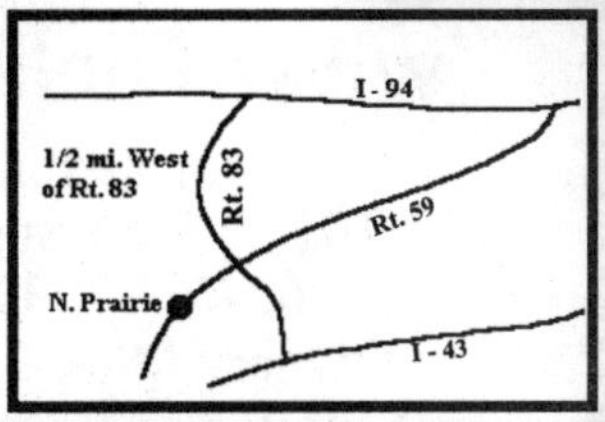

Greenfield, WI #4

QUILTERS HEAVEN

6633 W. Forest Home Ave. 53220
(414) 604-9193 Fax: (414) 327-0496
Owner: Dorothy Dorger

Mon, Wed & Fri 9 - 6
Tues & Thur 9 - 8
Sat 9 - 4

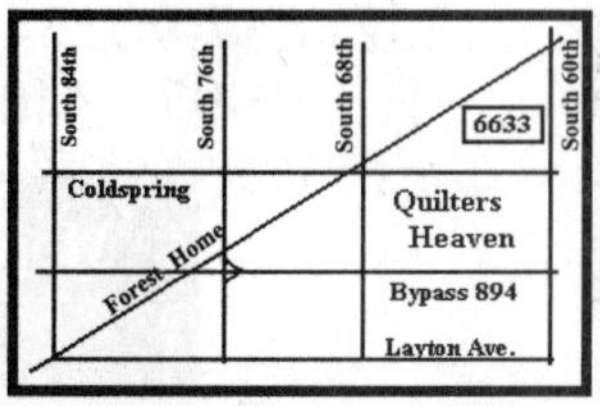

Established in 1999 with Moda, Benartex, RJR, Maywood, South Seas & more. We have grown to 4000 bolts of yummy fabric. We also have a great flannel room and have a second beautiful classroom addition. We have a large selection of books, patterns and samples to inspire you. (We are just north of the 894 bypass using the 60th or 76th exit) We're a fun place to shop, so step in, we'll have the coffee on and you can tell your friends you've been to "Heaven" (Quilter's Heaven)

Rochester, WI #5

Tues - Fri 10 - 5
Thur til 7
Sat 10 - 4

Pieceful Inspirations

200 W. Main St. 53167
(262) 534-5334
E-Mail: pieceful@tds.net
Owner: Dawn Schumacher
Est: 1998 1200 sq.ft. 900 Bolts

High Quality 100% Cotton Fabrics, Notions, Patterns and Classes for Quilters. Gifts and Antiques. Old-Fashioned Friendly Service.

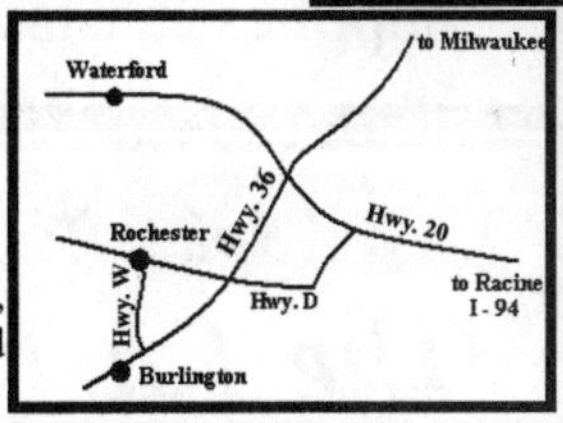

Complete Quilt & Cross-Stitch Shop

Two stories of Wonderful Fabrics, Graphs, Patterns and Gifts with a friendly, knowledgeable staff to help.

Mon, Wed, Fri	**10:00 a.m. - 5:00 p.m.**
Tues, Thurs	**10:00 a.m. - 8:00 p.m.**
Saturday	**10:00 a.m. - 4:00 p.m.**
Sunday	**11:00 a.m. - 4:00 p.m.**

Calico, Canvas & Colors

Racine, WI #6

3305 Washington Ave. 53405
(262) 632-4224

Look for our newly published books and patterns by ***Calico Printworks*** (that's us!)

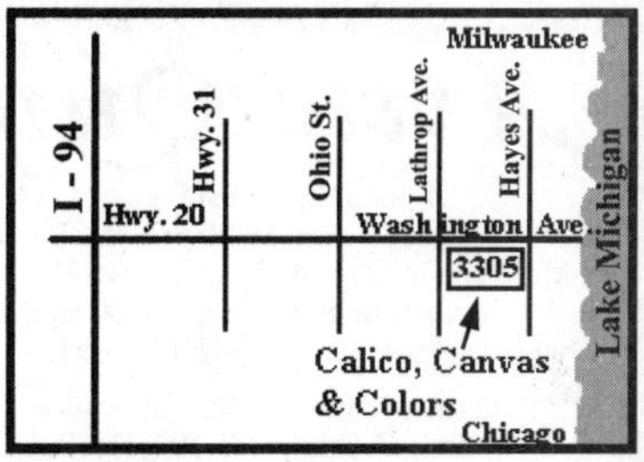

We'd love to have you visit us - in person or on our new web site!
We also have a new toll-free telephone number to make ordering easier.
(888) 3CALICO — (888) 322-5426
Fax: (262) 632-2457 E-Mail: calicocc@execpc.com
Est: 1979 3000 sq.ft
Web Site: www.calicocanvasandcolors.com.

Racine, WI #7

FABRICS FROM THE HEART

2045 Lathrop Ave. 53405
(262) 637-9037 Fax: (262) 637-9038
Est: 1997 3400 sq.ft. 4000 Bolts

Mon - Fri 10 - 5
Sat 10 - 3

WE ARE A FULL SERVICE QUILT SHOP!

We have a large selection of books, patterns, and notions with the largest selection of reproduction fabrics in the area, also an extremely friendly and helpful staff.

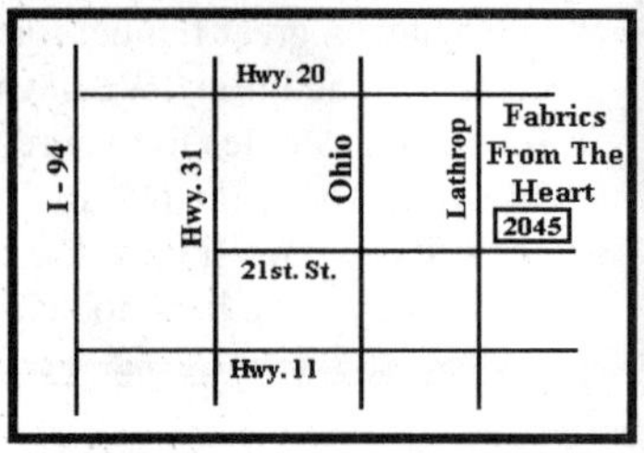

We also do CUSTOM MACHINE QUILTING, with a huge selection of patterns to choose from. Custom one-of-a-kind designs also. Quality Stitching.

Burlington, WI #8

MJ Quilt Works

www.Thelibertyhouse.com

Located in the Liberty House
101 E. State St., Burlington, WI 53105
262-763-7393 Fax: 262-763-8090
Owner: Mary J Shinabarger Est: 2001
E-Mail: alpha@speeddial.net 1200+ bolts

Monday - Friday 10 - 5 Sat 10 - 4

We carry RJR, Moda, Thimbleberries, Benartex. Patterns, Books, Supplies & Classes.

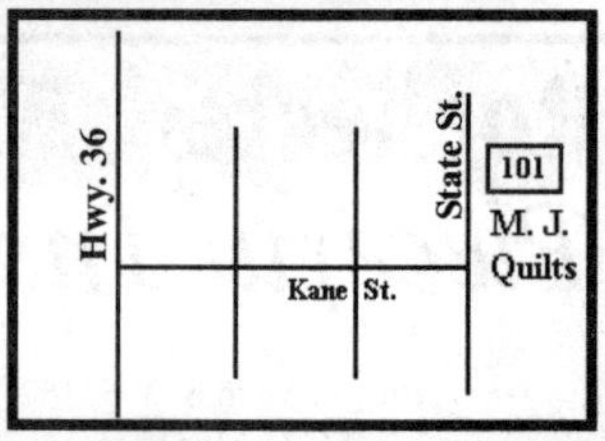

Lake Geneva, WI #9

Tues - Fri 10 - 5
Sat 10 - 3

The Last Stitch

1350 Hwy. H North 53147
(262) 249-1919

Let us custom finish a unique design for you on our long arm machines while you start your next top!

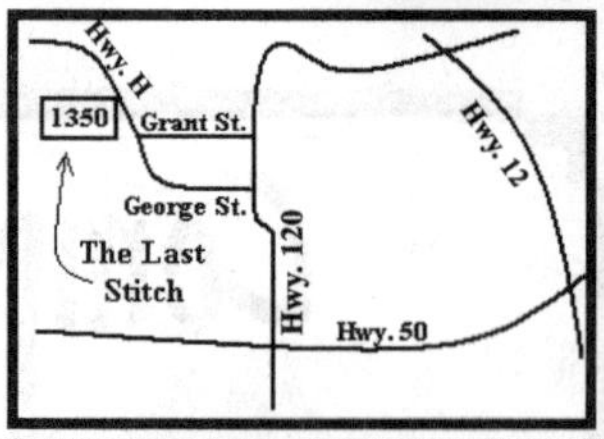

Delavan, WI #10

Tues - Sun 9 - 4
Jan / Feb Weekends

The Stitchery

N 2482 County Road "O" 53115
(262) 728-6318
Owners: Nancy Snyder & Carrie Dodge
Est: 1965 2000 sq.ft. 1800 Bolts

Located in a quaint Pennsylvania Dutch shopping village and restaurant. We carry all your notions and supplies for quilting and needlework.

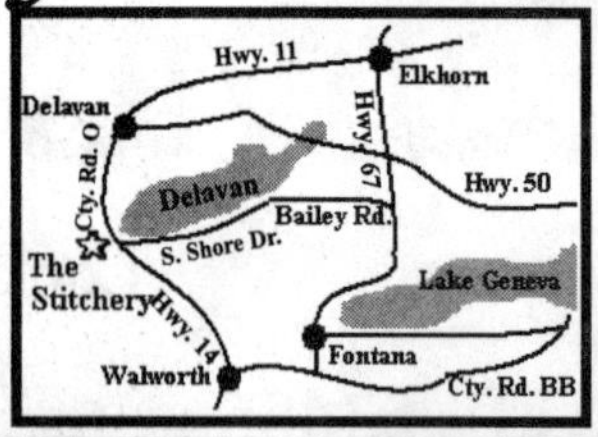

East Troy, WI #11

Tues & Thur 10 - 8
Wed, Fri & Sat 10 - 5
Sun 12 - 4

Quilt Emporium

PIETERS SISTERS DRY GOODS

3290 W. Main St. 53120
(262) 642-4777
Owners: Liz Lois & Sue Weeden

Quilt Emporium offers friendly, personalized service in your search for wonderful fabrics, great ideas, notions, books and classes.

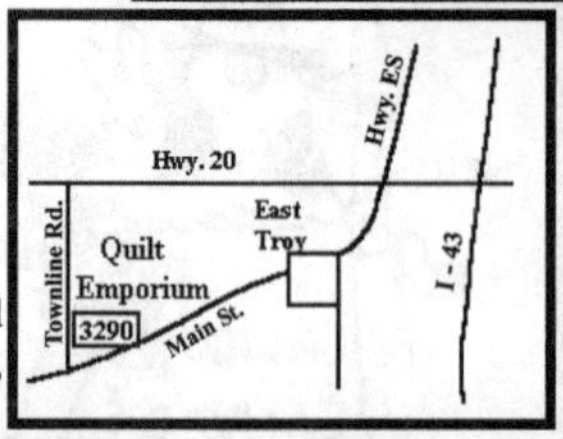

Beloit, WI #12

Mon - Fri 10 - 5:30
Sat 10 - 4

Attic Quilts

314 State St. 53511
(608) 364-4037 Fax: (608) 368-2913
E-Mail: smquilts@aol.com Est: 1997
Web Site: www.atticquilts.com 3000 sq.ft.
Owner: Sally McFerren 2700 Bolts

Books, Patterns, Notions, lots of gadgets. 100% Cotton Fabrics: RJR Hoffman, Benartex, Moda, South Seas, Kona Bay, Clothworks, Thimbleberries, Plaids, Flannels.

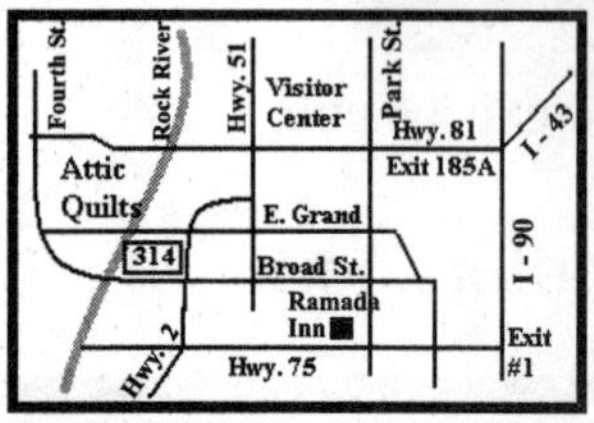

Elkhorn, WI #13

Mon - Fri 10 - 5
Sat 9 - 4

Sawdust & Stitches

13 S. Wisconsin St. 53121
(262) 723-1213 Fax: Same
E-Mail: saw_stitch@hotmail.com
www.elknet.net/Lauds/sawdust&stitches.htm
Owner: Sharon Lauderdale Est: 1996

100% cotton prints & solids for Quilting needs. Patterns, Books, Stitchery & Painting Books. Quilting Classes & Painting classes offered.

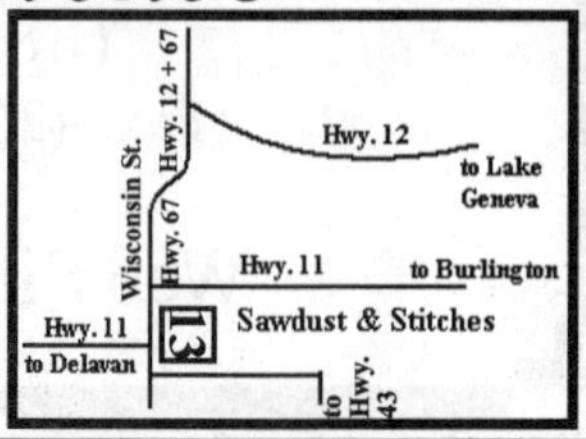

The Quilting Connection

Training and Maintenance
1,2 & 3 Day Class Options
We offer small training classes with only 1 machine head per table. Train on the machine head that you purchase and let us help you with the adjustments!

Authorized APQS
Representative & Trainer
Millennium, Ultimate I, Ultimate II, Ultimate XX & EZ-Q Quilting Machines
Call for a demo appointment or sign up for our "try before you buy" class which includes a coupon toward purchase.

Quilting Supplies
108"-110" wide fabrics, long arm patterns, thread, batting, and the *Quick Zip System* for accurate quilt loading and advance pinning. Pin ahead and load in minutes, or unzip and finish later. Great time-saver!

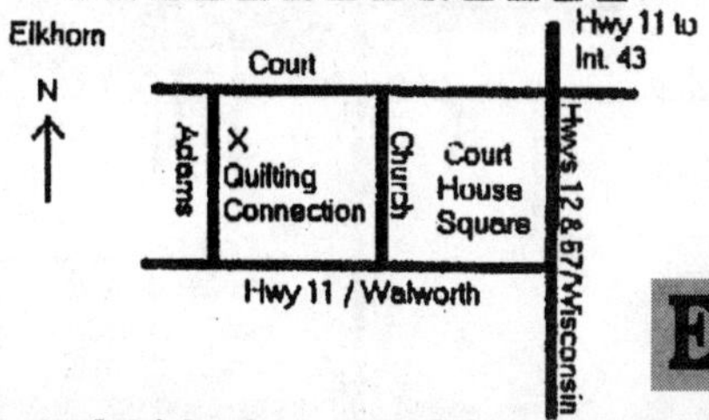

Elkhorn, WI #14

We are located 1 block west of the courthouse square
21 Adams Street, Elkhorn • 262-723-6775
Hours: Tues. - Fri. 10 - 5; Sat. 10 - 3. *Gift Certificates Available*

Belleville, WI #15

13 W. Main St. 53508
(608) 424-1516 Fax: (608) 424-1730
E-Mail: patches1@chorus.net
Est: 1999 3000 sq.ft. 3000 bolts

Tues, Wed
Fri 10 - 6
Thurs 10 - 8
Sat 9 - 4
Sun 12 - 4

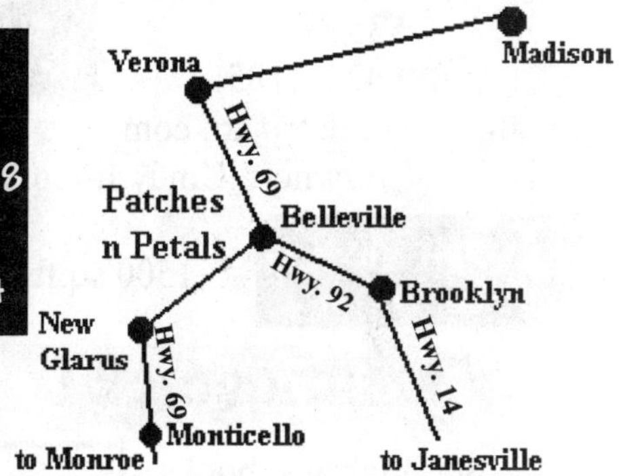

Visit us at: www.patchesandpetals.com
Unique shop featuring fine quilting fabric, books, patterns, quilting supplies, handcrafted gifts, collectibles and antiques. Great Classes.

Patches & Petals

Janesville, WI #16

Fri Only 10 - 4 or By Appt.

Sew Bee Quilting

343 S. Lexington Dr.
53545
(608) 754-2488
Owner: Lynda Short
E-Mail: sewbeequilt@aol.com
Est: 1990 500 sq.ft. Catalog LSASE

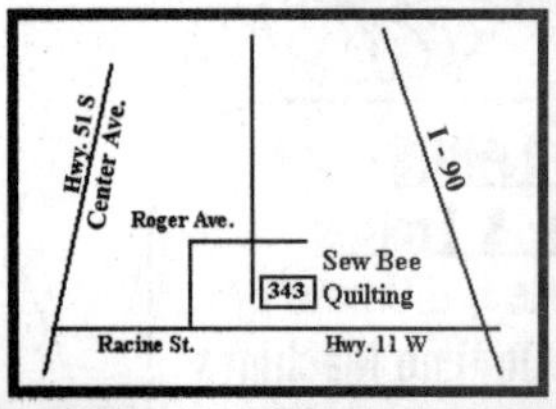

Sew Bee Quilting specializes in custom machine quilting as well as hand-dyed fabrics and features quilts made in Wisconsin.

New Glarus, WI #17

Tues - Sat 10 - 5

Backtown Quilt Shoppe

307 Second St., P.O. Box 854 53574
(608)5276416
E-Mail: backtownquilt@yahoo.com
Owners: Sharon Schlimgen & Teresa Steele
Est: 2000 2000 sq.ft.

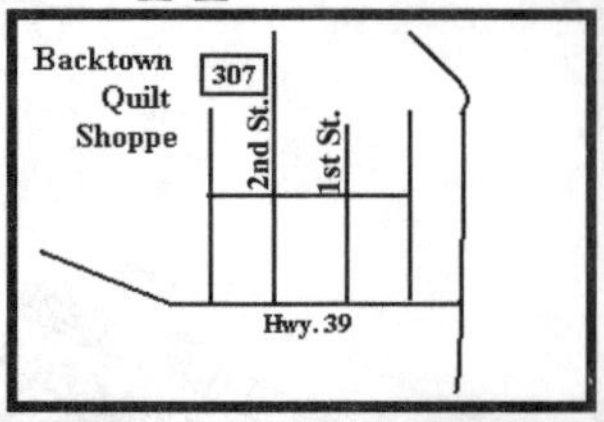

Enjoy our fine fabrics, notions, patterns, books and classes in a warm home-like atmosphere. Machine quilting service too!

Stoughton, WI #18

Mon - Sat 10 - 5 Thur til 7

Saving Thyme

233 W. Main St. 53589
(608) 877-0075 Fax: (608) 877-0076
E-Mail: gstehley@inxpress.net
Owner: Gloria Stehley
Est: 2000 1700 sq.ft.

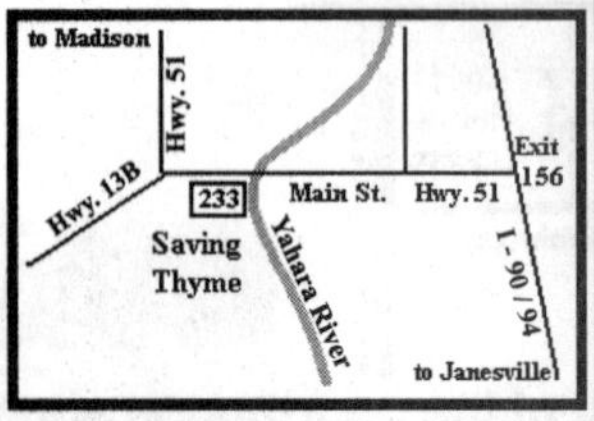

Houses a unique blend of quilting fabric, notions and arts in a Victorian Shop along the Yahara River in Stoughton.

Whitewater, WI #19

Mon - Fri 10 - 5 Sat 10 - 4

Woodland Quilts, LLC

"Over the River & Through the Woods to Woodland Quilts."

135 W. Main St. 53190
(262) 473-2978
E-Mail: woodland@cni-usa.com
Web Site: www.woodlandquilts.com
Owner: Terri Borchardt & Cheryl Kehm

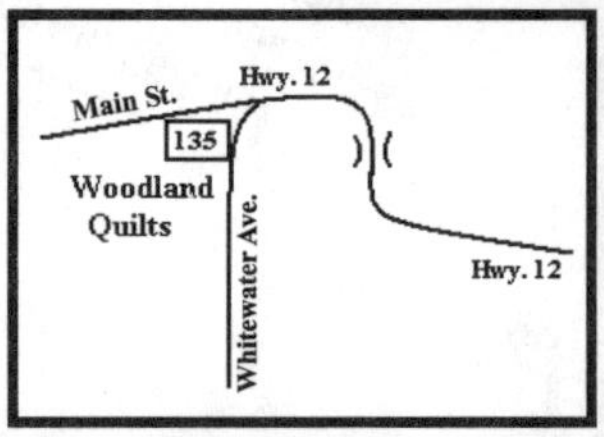

A friendly Quilt Shop offering fabrics, kits, patterns, books and classes for all ages, beginner to advanced. Kids' classes too!

The Quilt Shop

111 Hwy. 18, P.O. Box 280
53523
(608) 423-3185
e-mail: thequiltsh@aol.com
Owner: Cindy Imhoff
Est: 1996
1500 sq.ft. 1000 Bolts

Annual Quilt Show "Quilts On Ice" 1st Weekend in Feb.

Mon - Fri 10 - 5:30 Sat 9:30 - 4

Cambridge, WI #20

100% cotton fabrics, books, patterns, notions & kits. Classes available. Monthly Thimbleberries Club meeting. Visit us on the web!

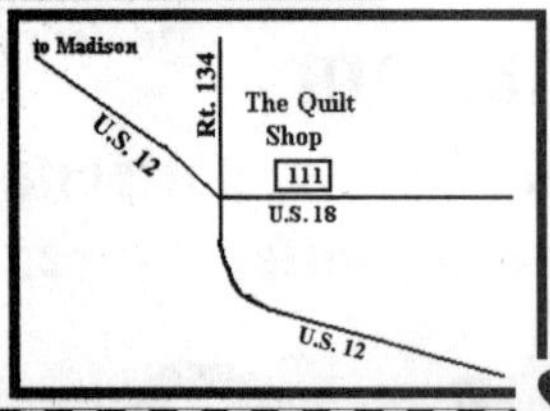

Middleton, WI #22

Mon - Fri 9:30 - 5 Thur til 7 Sat 9 - 3

Quilted Creations

6771 University Ave. 53562
(608) 831-5072 Fax: (608) 831-8347
E-Mail: quilted@execpc.com
Web Site: www.quiltedcreations.com
Owners: Becky Tessmer, Lisa Ruge, & Cheri Conner
Est: 1998 1370 sq.ft. 1300 Bolts

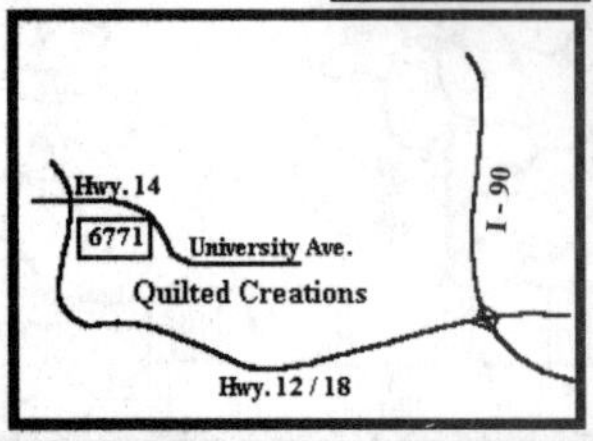

Easy access from both the Beltline and downtown Madison. We carry 100% cotton fabrics, books, patterns and notions. Classes.

The Stitcher's Crossing

Mon - Fri 9:30 - 6 Thur til 8:30 Sat 9:30 -5

6108 Mineral Point Rd. 53705
Tel 608·232·1500 Fax: 608·232·1750
email: info@stitcherscrossing.com
Web: www.stitcherscrossing.com
Owner: Sharon Luehring
Est: 1980 2400 sq.ft.

Great selection of fabrics, books, and patterns for counted cross stitch, quilting, primitive stitching, and soft sculptures. Our wonderful displays will inspire you.

"Where Country Meets Contemporary"

Madison, WI #21

Spring Green, WI #23

Country Sampler

A TOP 10
QUILT SHOP IN 2000

133 E. Jefferson • 53588
608 • 588 • 2510
Fax: 588 • 3528
Email: stchgirl@yahoo.com
Owner: Jeanne Horton
Est: 1983
1800 sq. ft.
2000+ Bolts
Newsletter/Catalog $6.00

You'll find our specialty shop full of Moda designer homespuns and prints, wools, unique kits and patterns. We are also known for our counted cross-stitch samplers and hand-dyed linens. It's all about inspiration and our finishing ideas do just that. You'll be further inspired by our reproduction furniture and Americana CollectibleFolkart showcased in and around our antique decor.

Open Daily
Mon.-Thurs. 10-5
Sat. 10-4:30 • Sun. 12-4

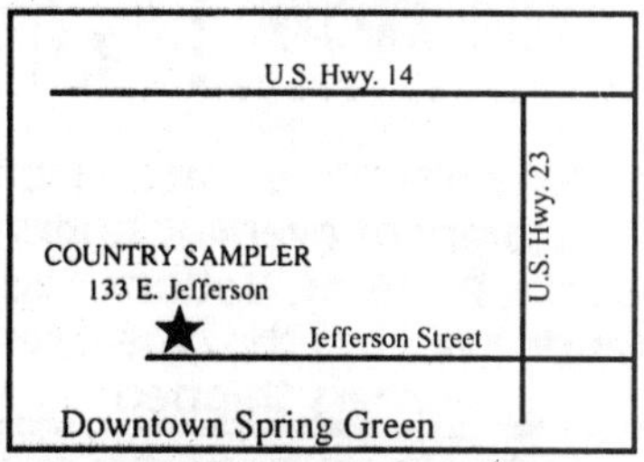

Friendly, knowledgeable Staff and Classical Music all add up to a very enjoyable shopping experience. *VISIT SOON!*

Waunakee, WI #24

100 Baker St. 53597 (608) 849-6473
Owners: Mike & Debbie Kuehn
Website: www.millhousequilts.com
E-mail: quilts@chorus.net
Est: 1995 8000 sq.ft. 4800 Bolts

Mill House Quilts

A Top 10 Shop in 2000!

A Refurbished 1875 Feed Mill featuring over 6000 bolts of fine quilting fabrics, quilting supplies, books, patterns & classes.
Newsletter and mail orders available upon Request.

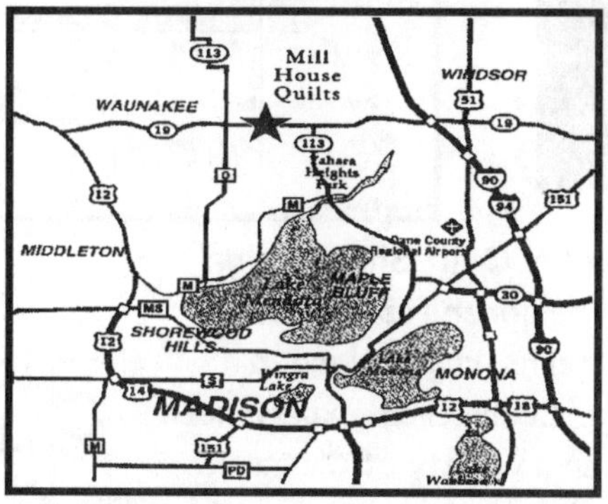

Mon - Sat 9 - 5
Thurs til 8

Off 90 - 94 exit Hwy. 19 West to Waunakee
Located just off Main St. in the "Heart of Waunakee"
7 miles from Madison

Jefferson, WI #25

Tea and Textiles

107 S Main Street
Jefferson, WI 53549
at the corner of Hwy 26 & Hwy 18
(920) 674-9010
email: teaandtextiles@yahoo.com

Mon-Fri 8 AM-9 PM
Sat 8 AM-5 PM
Sun 10 AM-5 PM

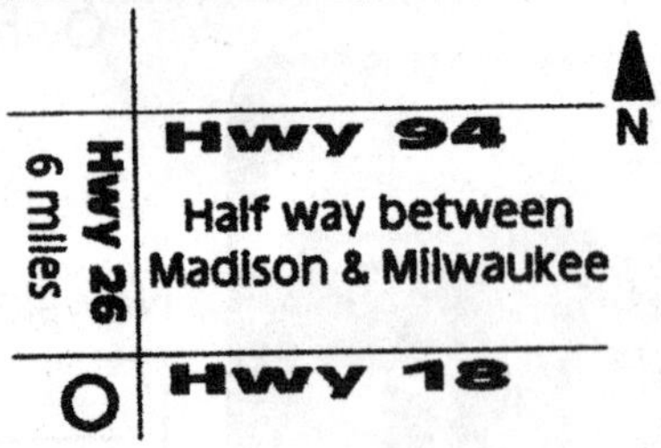

2000 bolts 100% cotton fabric
Library of over 400 books
Books, Patterns, Notions, Classes
Fabric Searches thru the Internet
Orders Shipped

Join us for a Complimentary Cup of Tea

Sun Prairie, WI #26

Mon - Fri 10 - 5
Sat 10 - 4

Prairie Quiltworks, LLC

229 E. Main St. 53590
(608) 837-9201
Owner: Sue Alstad

Quilting fabrics and supplies. Classes.
Hand guided machine quilting.
Warm and friendly atmosphere.

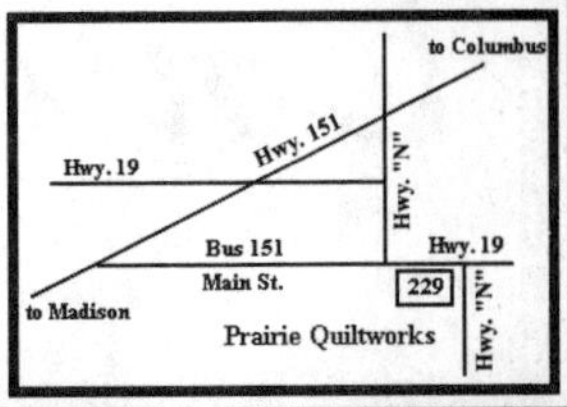

Sun Prairie, WI #27

Mon - Fri 9:30 - 5:30
Sat 10 - 5

J.J. STITCHES

221 E. Main St. 53590
(608) 837-2266
www.jjstitches.com
Est: 1975 5000 Bolts

Featured shop in Quilt Sampler 2002.
Store features homespuns, tickings, and vintage replica fabrics.

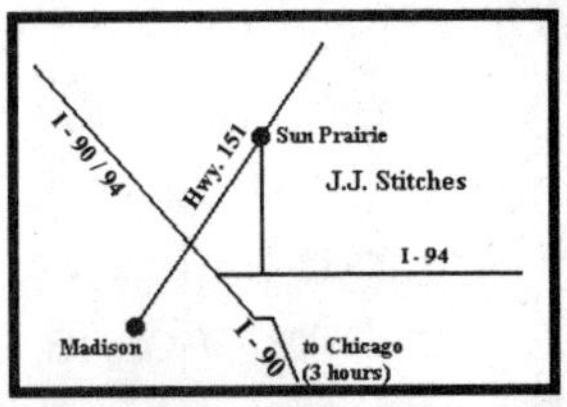

Sun Prairie, WI #28

Mon - Fri 9:30 - 5
Sat 9 - 4

Itchin' To Stitch

509 W. Main St. 53590
(608) 837-4419
Fax: Same
Est: 1983 3500 sq.ft.
7000 Bolts

7000 Bolts of the finest cottons from all major suppliers, notions, books & gifts. Flannels & Homespuns.

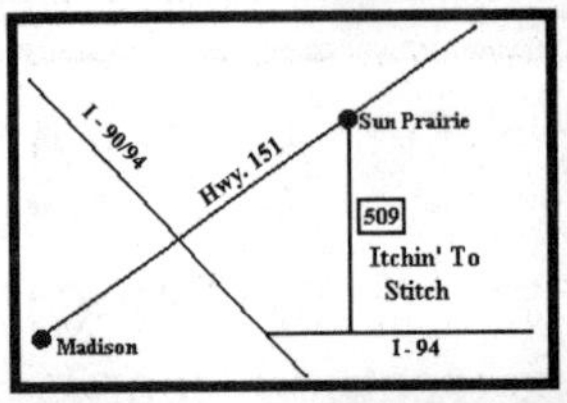

Portage, WI #30

Mon - Fri 9 - 5
Sat 9 - 2

The Gingham Goose

313 DeWitt St 53901
(608) 742-0420 Fax: (608) 742-4068
E-Mail: mgee@jvlnet.com
Owner: Mae Gee
Est: 1989 3000 sq. ft.

Large assortment of 100% cotton fabrics, books, patterns, tools & finished products. Longarm quilting services available. Friendly, helpful employees.

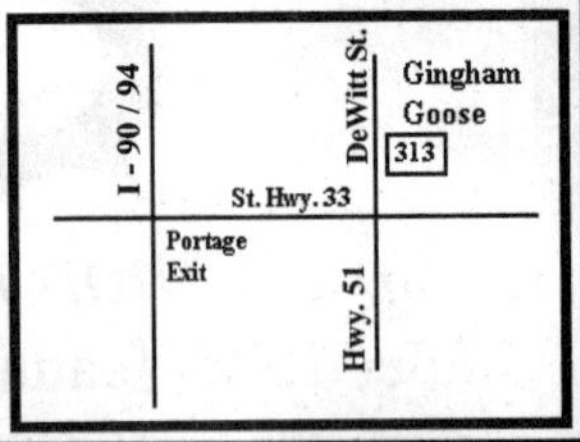

Princeton, WI #31

Mon -Fri 8:30 - 5
Sat 9 - 3

Quilts & Quilting

607 W. Main St. (920) 295-6506
P.O. Box 362 54968 Est: 1971
E-Mail: ronm@vbe.com
Owners: Sandy & Ron Mason
Machine Quilting & Kit Brochure SASE

Custom Machine Quilting Since 1971. Fabric, Notions, Books, Classes. Photos printed on Fabric. Die-Cut Quilt Top Kits—pillows to king size.

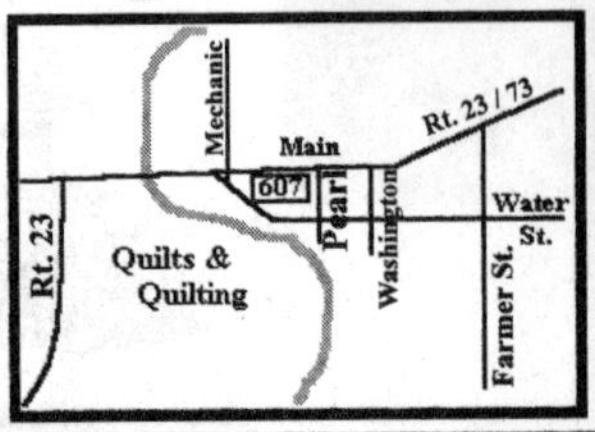

Beaver Dam, WI #29

HOMESPUN PRIMITIVES

Country Quilt Shop

112 S. Spring St., Beaver Dam, WI 53916
(920) 887-3060 Fax: (920) 887-3190
E-Mail: homespun@powercom.net
Owner: John & Peggy Bemis
Est: 2001 4800 sq.ft. 2000+ Bolts

Mon - Fri 9 - 5
Sat 10 - 4

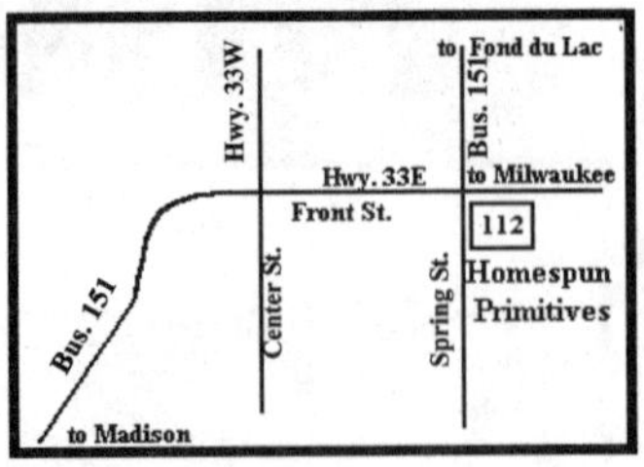

Area's newest Country Quilt Shop. Large selection of Moda designer fabrics, wools, quilting books, patterns, rug hooking, & primitive stitching. Learn from experienced Quilters. We offer a variety of Classes & Workshops, featuring all the latest and traditional quilting techniques. Something for everyone!

Reedsburg, WI #32

Quintessential Quilts

940 East Main 53959 (608) 524-8435
Owner: Terry Antholz Est: 1989 email: qquilts@jvlnet.com
Web Site: www.qquilts.com

WISCONSIN'S BEST KEPT QUILTING SECRET!

Mon - Sat 9 - 5
Sun 12 - 4

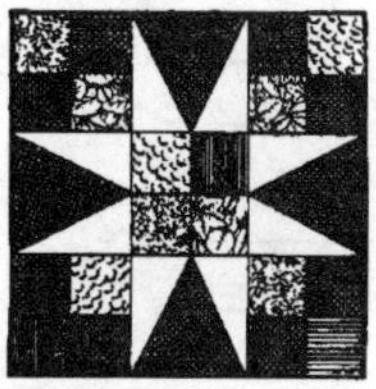

Over 12,000 bolts of fabric.
Large selection of books, patterns & notions. All your quilting needs located under one roof!
Continuous schedule of classes.
Spring & fall weekend seminars.
Mail orders and newsletter available upon request.

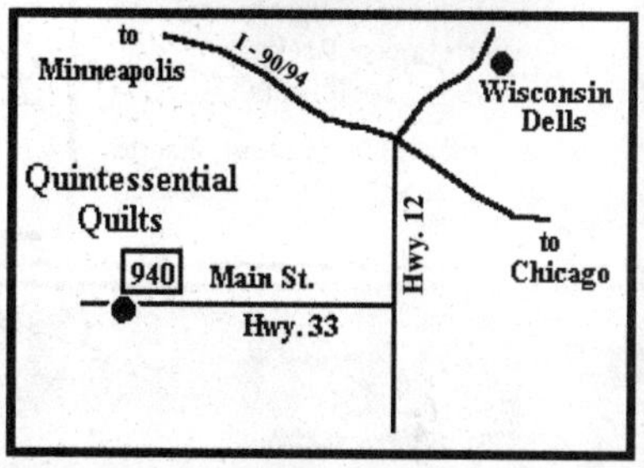

Fond du Lac Quilting & Sewing Center

Fond du Lac, WI #33

Mon - Fri 9:30 - 5
Sat 9:30 - 4

15 North Main Street 54935
(920) 921-3816 or (800) 594-9064
E-Mail: queenbee@fdlquilt.com
Owner: Cathleen Christensen

We are a full service quilting & sewing store featuring thousands of bolts of 100% cotton fabric, patterns & notions.
We carry a full line of Bernina machines and products.
Stop in to browse or take a class

Enjoy!

Nothing Sews Like A Bernina. Nothing.
BERNINA

We are the Host of two of the largest quilting events in the mid-west:
Quilter's Escape & Summer School for Quilters
Please Visit our Website at www.fdlquilt.com

Fond du Lac, WI #34

Mon - Fri 10 - 5
Sat 10 - 2

Wool & Needle

46 N. Main St. 54935
(920) 907-1331 Fax: (920) 907-2974
Web Site: www.woolandneedle.com
Owner: Kathy Geis
Est: 2000 1700 sq.ft. 1200 Bolts.
Unique "country" atmosphere. Hand dyed wool is our specialty. Moda fabrics -- kits -- BOM clubs -- silk ribbon embroidery supplies -- unique yarns & supplies.

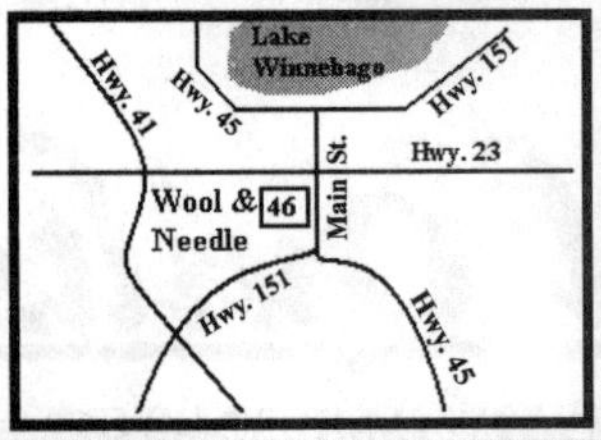

Oakfield, WI #35

Mon - Fri 10 - 5
Sat 10 - 3

Stitches 'N Tyme, LLC

203 S. Main St. 53065
(920) 583-2625
E-Mail: stitchesntyme@hotmail.com
Owners: Jeff & Donna Redman
Est: 2000 1500 sq.ft. 2000+ Bolts
A full service quilt shop; specializing in individualized customer service, long arm machine quilting, and antiques including sewing cabinets and quilting related items.

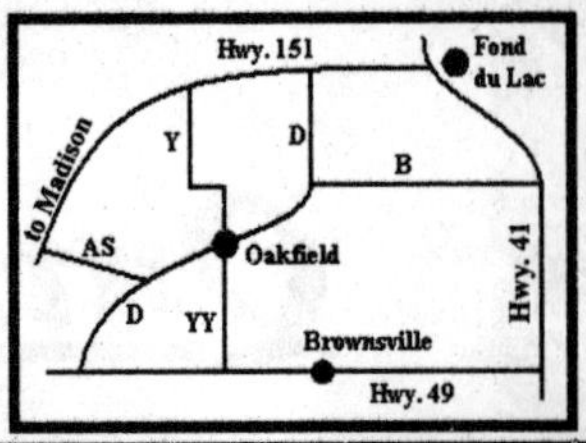

Prairie du Sac, WI #36

Mon - Fri 9 - 6
Sat 9 - 4

Homespun Fabrics

585 Water St. 53578
(608) 643-5083
E-Mail: homespun@shopstop.net
Owner: Louise Back
Est: 1995 1000 Bolts

Great Selection of 100% Cotton Fabrics, Books, Notions & Patterns. Quarterly Newsletter.

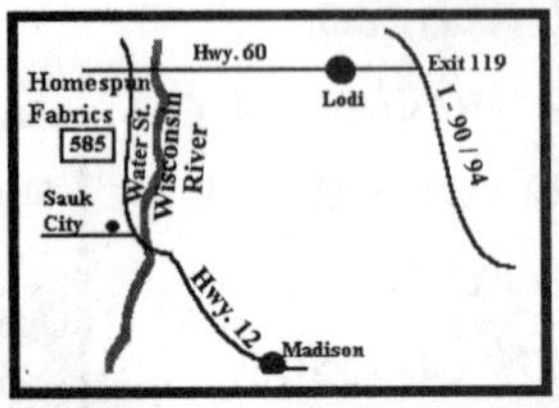

Ferryville, WI #37

Mon - Sat 10 - 5

Olde Tyme Quilt Shoppe

62682 Rush Creek Rd. 54628
(608) 648-2081
Owner: Virginia Johnson
Est: 1986 900 sq.ft.

Virginia's original custom made Quilts--Hand dyed fabric, notions. Hand or machine quilting, outline quilting. Classes

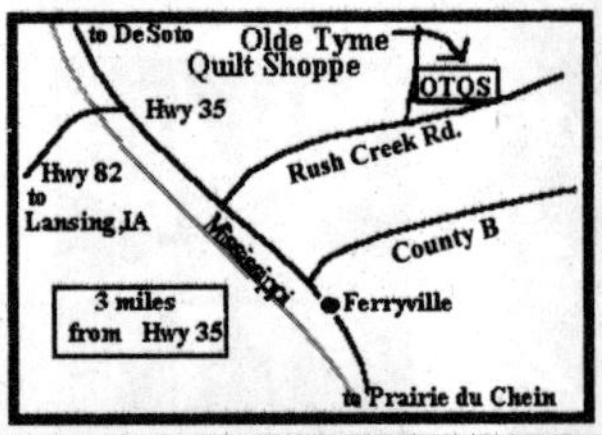

Viroqua, WI #38

Mon - Sat 9:30 - 5
Thur til 7

Quilt Basket 'n' Creations

115 S. Main 54665
(608) 637-7002
Fax: (608) 637-8049
E-Mail: klswens@yahoo.com
Owner: Karen L. Swenson Est: 1999
Great selection of 100% cotton fabrics, books, patterns and notions. We also offer a large selection of gifts.

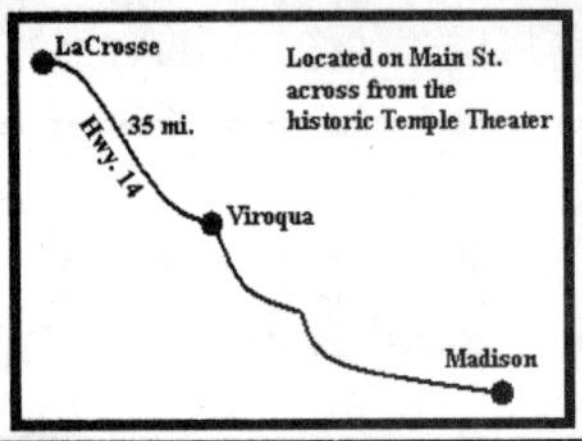

LaCrosse, WI #39

A Stitch In Time

BERNINA

223 N. 3rd St. 54601
(608) 782-3257 Fax: (608) 782-0154
E-Mail: quiltmac@aol.com
Owner: Monica Campbell
Est: 1992 2400 sq.ft. 2000 Bolts

Mon - Sat 10 - 5
Thur til 8

Large selection of fabric, books, patterns, & quilting supplies. The friendliest quilt shop for service, inspiration and sharing of ideas.

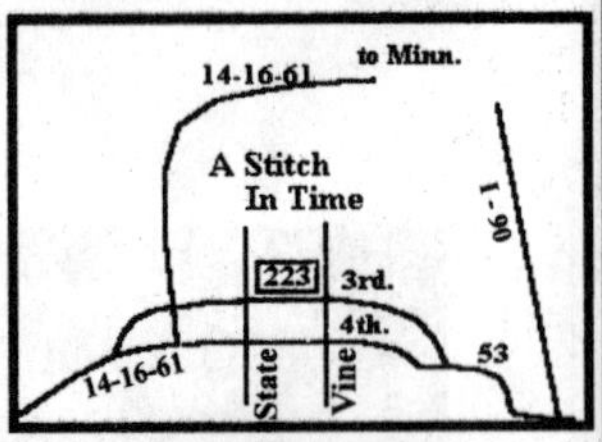

Voted one of America's top 10 Quilt Shops in 1998 Better Homes & Garden Quilt Sampler Magazine!

The Cotton Thimble

FOR YOUR QUILTING NEEDS

Wisconsin Rapids, WI #41

540 Daly Ave. 54494
(715) 424-1122
E-mail: cthimble@wctc.net
Owner: Carol Prahl
Est: 1993

Mon - Fri 10 - 5
Sat 10 - 4

Over 5200 Bolts of 100% Cottons Books, Patterns, Stencils, & Quilting Notions.

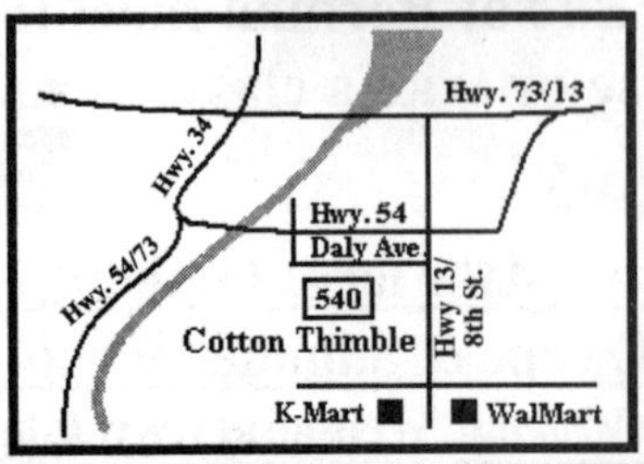

Holmen, WI #40

Tues - Sat 10 - 5
Sun 12 - 5

Wooden Shoe Quilts

W8154 Holland Dr. 54636
(608) 526-3135
Owner: Sharon Slimmen

Classes in and supplies for quilt making. Outlet for quilted items done by customers. Prize winning quilters to teach classes.

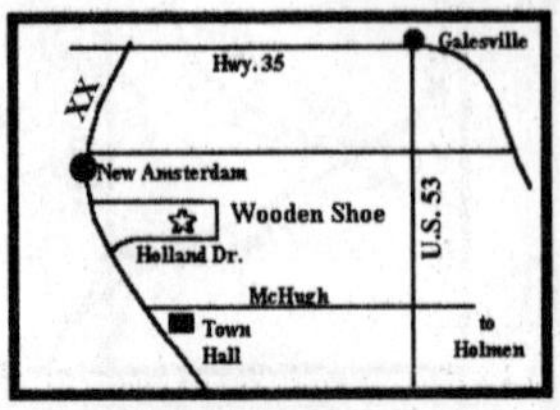

Quilts n' Silks

Fabrics and Supplies

Mon - Fri 9 - 6
Sat 9 - 3

Authorized PFAFF Dealer

Manitowoc, WI #42

711 York St. 54221-2232
(800) 933-1161
(920) 686-0839 Fax: (920) 686-0876
Owner: Elaine A. Springer
Est: 1995 2400 sq.ft. 3000 Bolts
E-Mail: quiltsnsilks@lakefield.net

For all of your quilting fabrics, books, patterns, notions & quilting classes visit Quilts n' Silks!

Spiegel ¤ Kona ¤ South Seas ¤ Bali
Debbie Mumm ¤ Thimbleberries ¤ RJR
Benartex ¤ P&B ¤ Hoffman ¤ Moda
Jinny Beyer ¤ Robert Kaufman

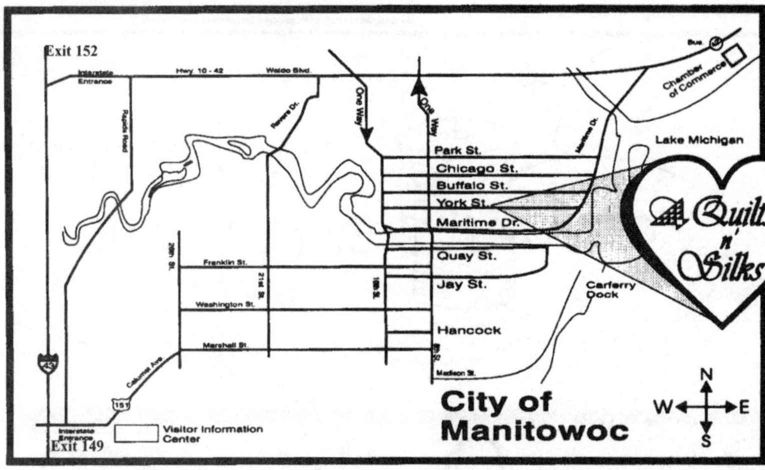

Overlooking the Wisconsin Maritime Museum in historic downtown Manitowoc. Near the Car Ferry dock.

GRAND CREATIONS

QUILTING
Supplies & Classes

THE QUILT SHOP"
IN HISTORIC
DOWNTOWN CEDARBURG

- 4000 BOLTS (TOP DESIGNERS
- 100'S OF SAMPLES
- SPECIALIZING IN KITS
- PATTERNS, BOOKS & NOTIONS

W64 N717 Washington Ave. 53012
(262 377-8400
Virtual tour: www.grandcreations.com

Cedarburg, WI #43

OPEN 7 DAYS A WEEK
Mon - Fri 10AM-6PM
Sat & Sun 11AM - 3PM

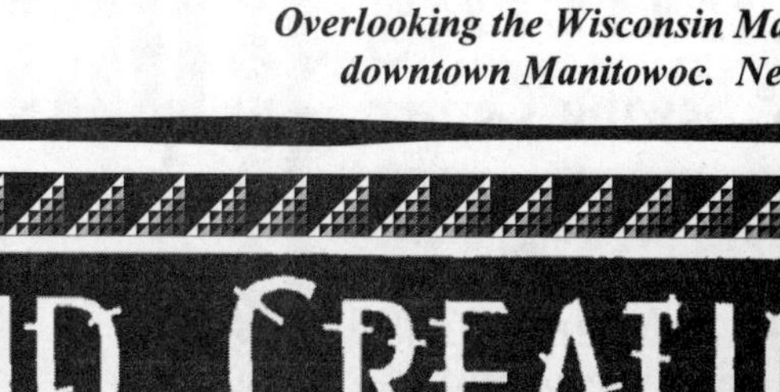

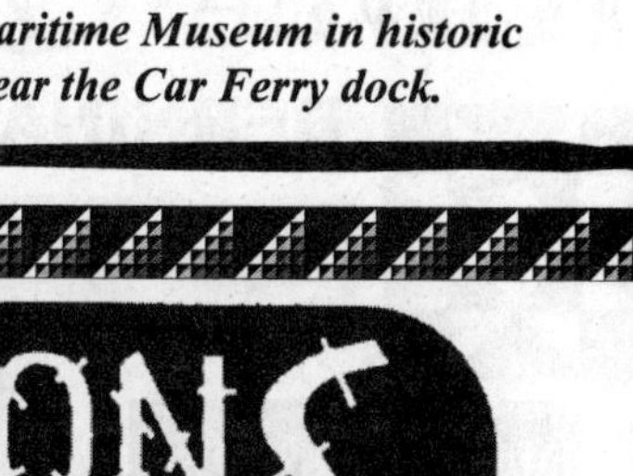

Celebrate the art of Quilting in a charming 1860's historical landmark home, truly a place of inspiration. Bus tours and groups welcome. Special programs available pending notification.

Slinger, WI #44

Mon, Wed, Fri 9 - 5
Tues & Thur 9 - 7
Sat 10 - 4

Common Threads Quilt Shop, LLC.

425 C East Washington St. 53086
(262) 644-0613
E-Mail: commonthread@nconnect.net
Owner: Jenifer Moegenburg
Est: 1995 2300 sq.ft. 2000 Bolts
For women who take pride in their quilting & sewing. Friendly, Expert Service by Knowledgeable Staff.
Husqvarna Viking Authorized Dealer.
Professional Quilting Service Available.

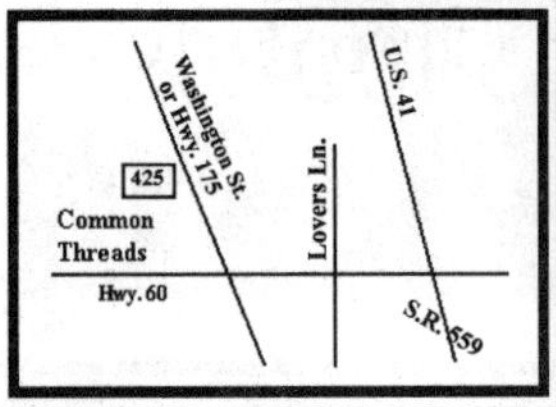

West Bend, WI #45

Mon - Fri 9:30 - 5
Sat 10 - 4

Gingerbread Junction

310 N. Main 53095
(262) 335-3935
E-Mail: qltdonna@netwurx.net
Owner: Donna Domres Est: 1995

Large selection of quilting supplies, kits, cottons, homespuns, flannels, and wool. Friendly, helpful service in a cozy, nostalgic atmosphere.

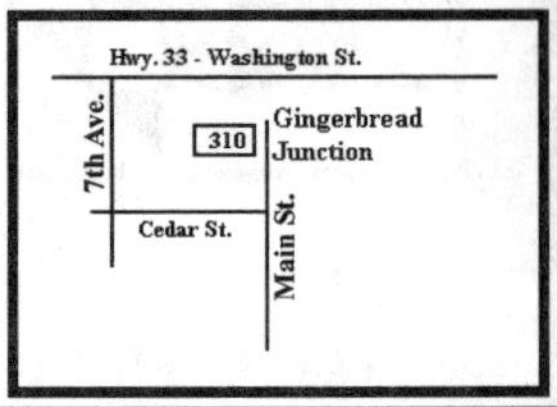

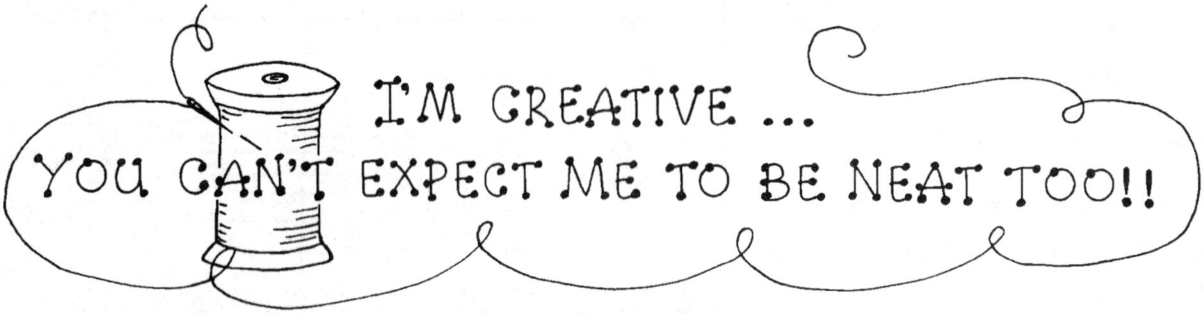

Royce Quilting

BERNINA® Sewing Center

West Bend, WI #46

Mon - Thur 9:30 - 8
Fri & Sat 9:30 - 5
Sun 11 - 4

840 S. Main 53095
(262) 338-0597
E-Mail:
roycequilting@hnet.net
Owner: Jerry Quasius
Est: 1971 3000 sq.ft.

Warm, Friendly and Filled with all the Things Quilters Love.
3000 Quilting Fabrics.
Books, Soft Patterns,
Quilting Classes.

Authorized Sales & Service
Bernina Dealer for 25 Years.

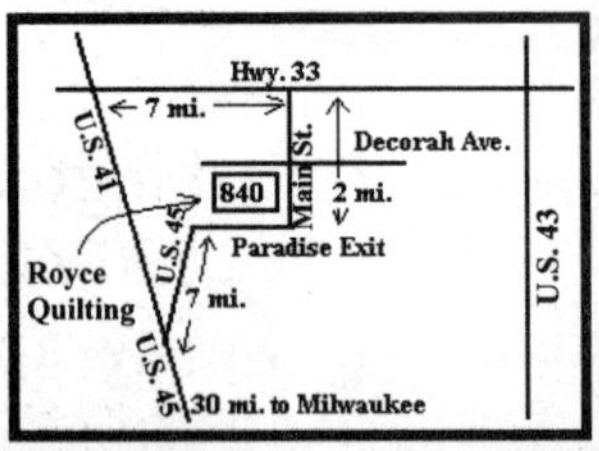

Quilter's Quest

11996 Hwy. 42 Ellison Bay, WI
IN BEAUTIFUL NORTHERN DOOR COUNTY
(Next to the Silly Goose Store)
P.O. Box 346 54210
(920) 854-1824
E-mail quiltersquest@dcwis.com
Linda Batley, Owner

Mon, Tues, Wed, Sat 10 - 5
Thurs & Fri 12 - 7

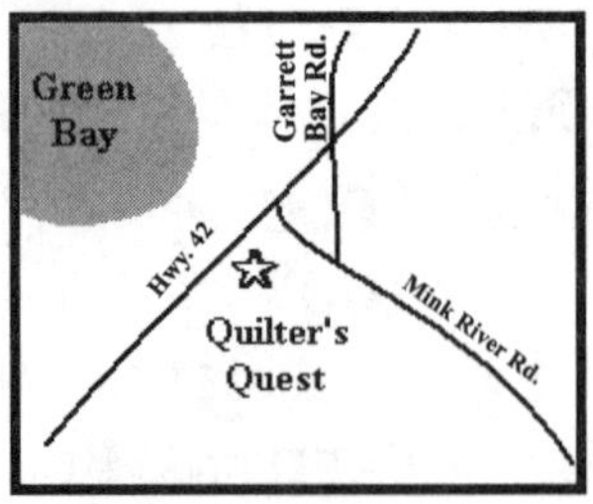

Specialty Notions, Books, Patterns
Over 1500 bolts
Classes, Warm Friendly Service
Access to a Quilting Machine
Contests & Monthly Drawings
Gifts for Quilters & Non-Quilters

Ellison Bay, WI #47

A Truly Unique Shopping Experience!

Plymouth, WI #48

Mon - Sat 9 - 5
Wed til 8
Sun 12 - 4

The Sewing Basket

426 E. Mill St. 53073
(920) 892-4751

We cater to your creative side. Beautiful quality quilting fabrics; quilting books, patterns and notions with a wide variety of cross-stitch fabric, fibers and charts.

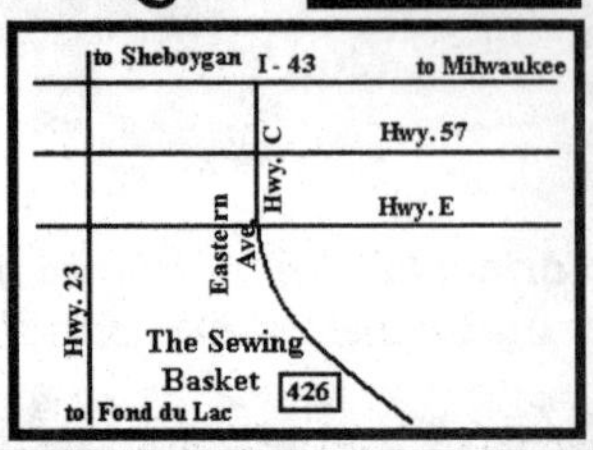

Life's a Stitch

- Learn, Create, Have Fun !
- Over 2500 Bolts of Current 100% Cotton Fabrics
- All your Quilting & Sewing Needs
- Repair all Brands of Sewing Machines
- Quilting Classes for all Levels
- Authorized Bernina Dealer

Located in the Lee Building
On the second floor
124 North Broadway
East De Pere WI 54115
920-338-1381

Owners:
Susan & Mike Carmichael

Hours
10:00 am - 5:00 pm
Monday - Friday
10:00 am - 3:00 pm
Saturday
Or by Appointment

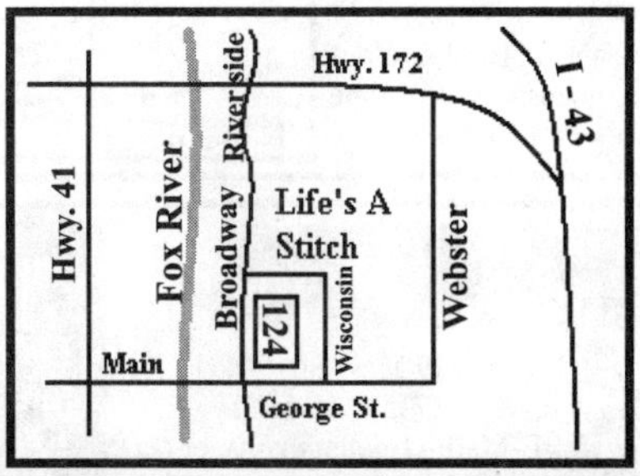

Located Just South of Green Bay

Nothing Sews Like A Bernina. Nothing.
BERNINA

DePere, WI #49

Silver Thimble

Quilt & Gift Shoppe

2475 University Ave.
University Courtyard
54302
(800) 469-1495
(920) 468-1495
Owners: Nanette Guzzonato & Elaine Corson
Est: 1990
Wheelchair Accessible

Mon & Thur 9:30 - 8
Tues & Wed 9:30 - 5
Fri 9:30 - 4 Sun 11 - 4

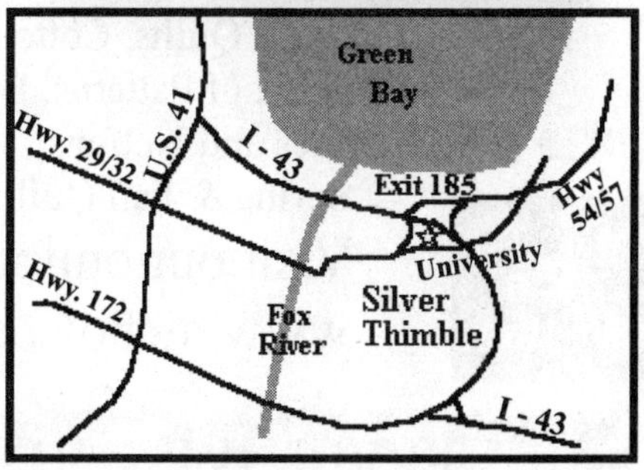

Take I - 43, exit 185, to Green Bay
Turn left at first stoplight.
Go one block & left into parking lot

Green Bay, WI #50

- Over 2000 bolts 100% cotton fabric
- Large Selection Solids
- Books & Patterns
- Notions
- Help selecting colors/fabrics
- Pfaff Sewing Machine Sales
- Complete line Thimbleberries fabric, books & patterns at reduced prices
- Classes
- Gifts
- Hand-dyed Wool
- Custom Sewing
- Hand-dyed Silk Ribbon
- Large Selection of Hoffman Batiks

Green Bay, WI #51

Mon - Fri 10 - 5:30
Sat 10 - 4

Friendship Quilts, Framing & Floral

1235 S. Military Ave. 54303
(920) 490-7877 or (866) 214-6721
Est: 1998

* Over 2000 Bolts of Quality Cotton Fabrics
* Classes, Books, Patterns & Notions
* Custom Machine Quilting
* Custom Framing & Framed Art
* Custom 'Silk' Wedding Floral Designs

Helpful and Always Friendly Staff!

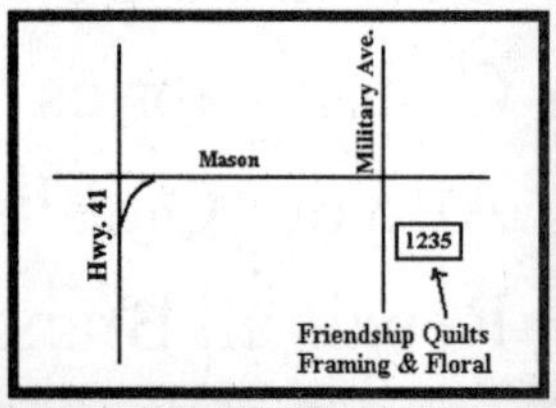

Green Bay, WI #52

Mon & Fri 10 - 6
T, W, Th & Sat 10 - 5

Country Hutch

2158 S. Ridge Rd. 54304
(920) 497-8787
E-Mail: mahrens997@aol.com
Owners: Jan & Mark Ahrens
1500 sq.ft. 1500+ Bolts

A quilter's dream selection of 100% cotton fabric. Experienced and friendly staff waiting to help you.

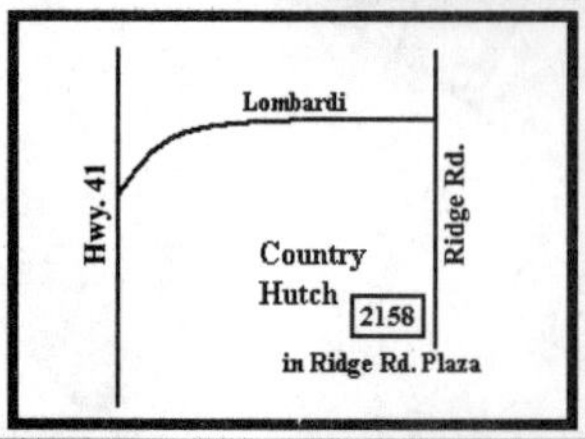

Green Bay, WI #53

Mon - Fri 10 - 6
Tues & Thur til 8
Sat 10 - 4
Sun 12 - 4

Main Street Cotton Works

1812 Main St. 54302
(920) 469-5694
Owners: Patt and Gil Nowak
Est: 1995 1000 Bolts

Located in a 50 yr. old home featuring 100% cotton fabrics, books, patterns & quilting supplies, classes and Friendly, Knowledgeable Staff

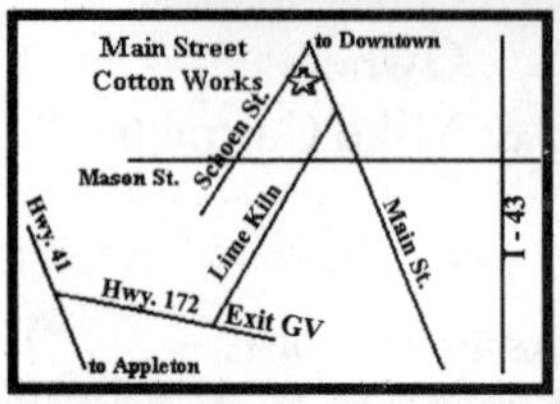

Oshkosh, WI #54

Mon - Fri 10 - 6
Sat 10 - 4:30

JUST SEW SEW &

440 N. Main St. 54901
(920) 303-1166
E-Mail: phs@execpc.com
Owner: Pat Schneider
Custom Machine Quilting

Large selection of cotton Fabric, Books, Craft Patterns, Quilting & Sewing needs. A Welcome for everyone coming in. I enjoy meeting all.

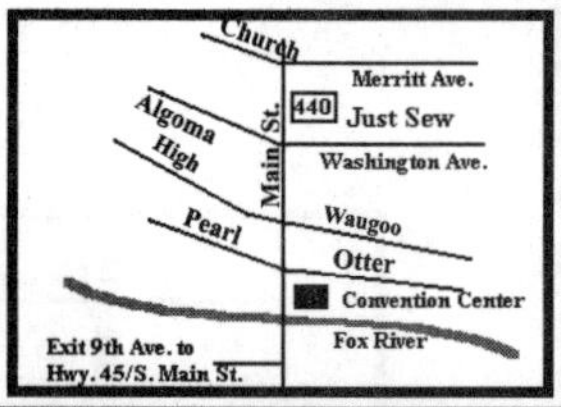

Nichols Creek Quilt Studio

Est: 1994

201 N. Main 54981
(715) 256-1024
E-Mail: ncreek@charter.net
Owner: Nancy M. Oftedahl

Finished Quilts, Cotton Fabric, Large selection of Patterns, Books. Quilting Supplies and Notions. Classes Offered. Spring & Fall Quilting Retreats

Visit our online shop @ www.nicholscreek.com

Mon - Fri 10 - 5
Sat 10 - 4

Waupaca, WI #55

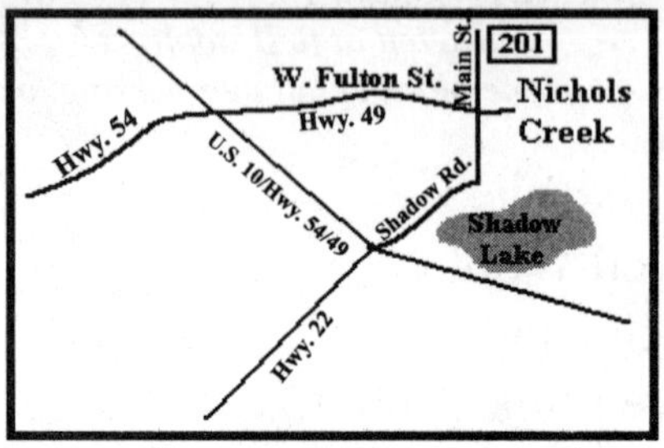

Take the 2nd Waupaca Exit. (Hwy. 22 exit) Turn North at the bottom of the ramp, to S. Main St. Turn left onto S. Main to N. Main.

Stevens Point, WI #56

Mon - Thur 10 - 5
Fri 10 - 6
Sat 10 - 4
Changes in Summer

The Sampler House

BERNINA

1129 Main St. 54481
(715) 341-5540
E-Mail: sampler@voyager.net
Web Site: www.sew2000.com/samplerhouse
Owner: Nina McVeigh

Quaint Shop with quilting, silk ribbon, & Heirloom Sewing. Dealer of Bernina Sewing Machines. Classes & Workshops

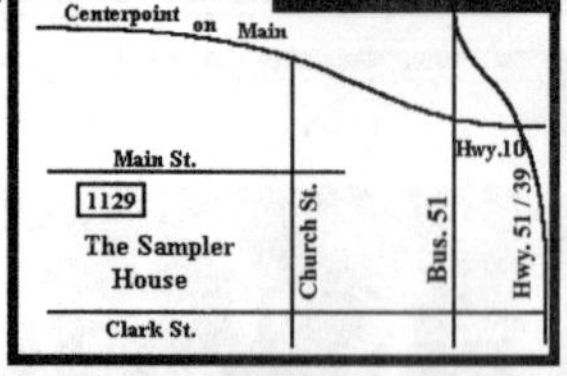

Appleton, WI #57

Mon 12 - 8
Tues, Wed Fri 10 - 5
Thur 10 - 8
Sat 10 - 4

Piece by Piece

formerly Quilters' Corner

1350 W. College Ave. 54914
(920) 749-1957

An inviting unique shop located in an historic Appleton building.

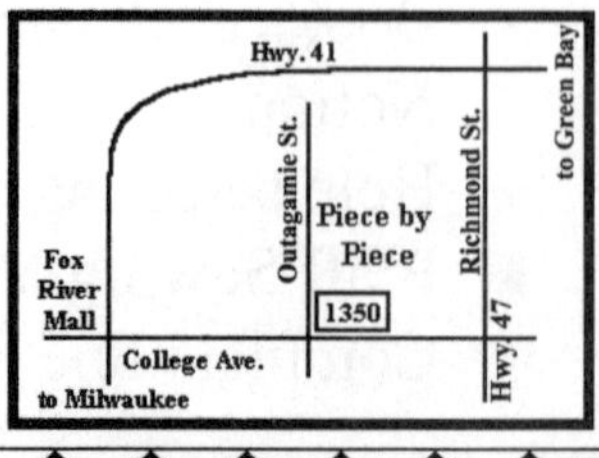

Appleton, WI #58

2306 S. Oneida St. 54915
(920) 991-9021
e-mail PatchworkSampler@aol.com
Owners: Rhonda Roberts & Kim Teigen
Est: 1997 3500 sq. ft. 3500+ bolts

Patchwork Sampler, LLC

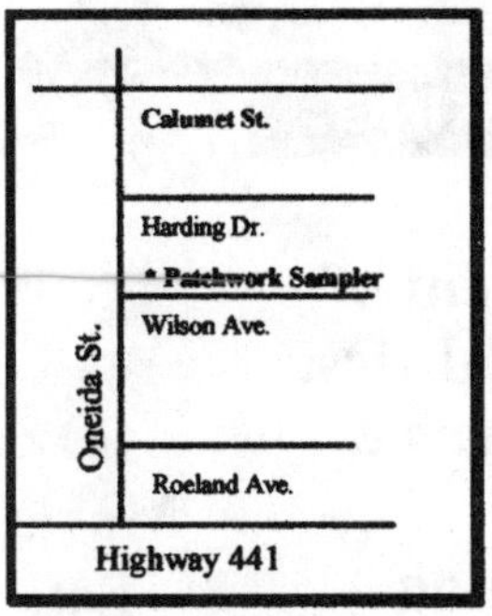

Located just 1/2 mile north of Highway 441 on Oneida Street

Mon & Fri 9:30 - 5:00
Tues - Thurs 9:30 - 8:00
Sat 9:30 - 4:00

We welcome you to visit our charming shop. Come and browse the area's largest selection of quality fabrics for quilters, as well as the latest books and patterns. We feature dozens of classes and events throughout the year. The many samples and displays are sure to inspire and delight you. Our friendly, knowledgeable staff offers personal service to meet all your quilting needs.

Menomonee Falls, WI #59

The Quilted Basket, Inc.

N88 W16599 Main St. 53051
(262) 251-8791
Email: tawanke@execpc.com
Web Site: www.thequiltedbasket.com
Owner: Ann Wanke

M, T, Th, F 9 - 5
Wed 9 - 8
Sat 9 - 4
Sun 11 - 4

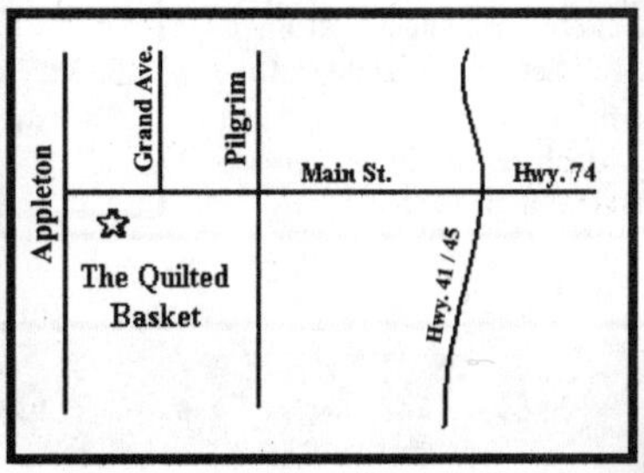

A full service quilt shop featuring over 2000 bolts of fabric, books, patterns, notions and hand dyed wool. Fabrics featured include reproductions, thirties, Moda, Jinny Beyer and more.

Antigo, WI #60

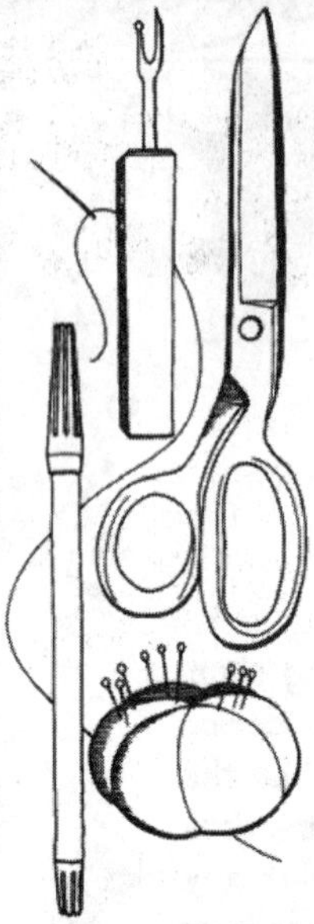

The Cutting Edge

816 5th Ave. 54409
(715) 623-3590

Husqvarna VIKING

Mon - Thur 10 - 6
Fri 10 - 5
Sat 9 - 4

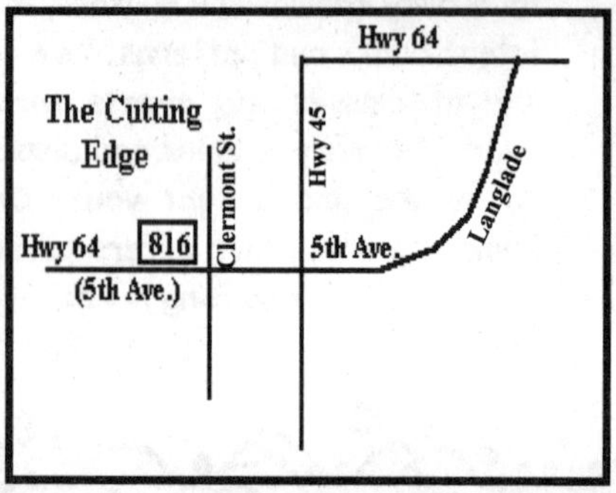

Wide Assortment of 100% Cotton Fabrics, Notions, Patterns & Books
Day & Evening Classes.

Owner: Marla Arndt
Est: 1990
10,000 sq.ft.

Dorchester, WI #61

Mon - Fri 9:30 - 5:30
Sat 9:30 - 4

Cow Country Fabrics & Quilts

800 E. Center Ave. 54425
(715) 654-5250
E-Mail: cowcountry@tds.net
Web Site: cowcountryfabrics.com
Owner: Donna J. Reamer
Est: 1997 2600 sq.ft.

2000 bolts quality Fabrics — Books, Patterns, Notions — Machine quilting services— Classes — Kits — Quilts for Sale.

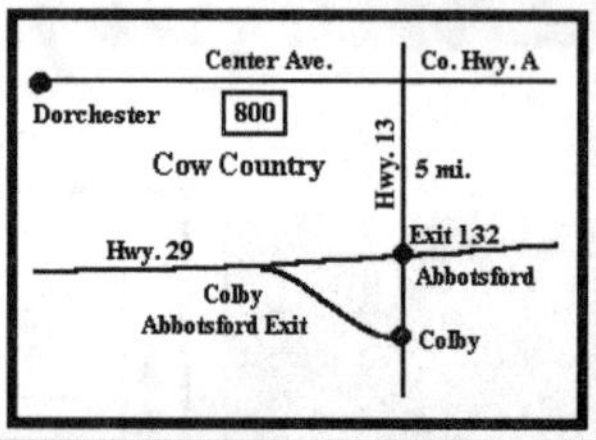

Withee, WI #62

Mon - Fri 8 - 8
Sat 8 - 4

Brubaker Sewing Center

W 7634 Oak Rd. 54498
(715) 669-3224 Fax: (715) 229-4394

Bernina Sewing Machine Sales & Service. Over 2500 Bolts of fabric. Fabric, Quilts & Batting, Baby Supplies, Hosiery, Underwear, Childrens Shoes, Boxed Greeting Cards, Sweaters, Sewing Notions, Disposable Diapers, Stationery & Hair Accessories.

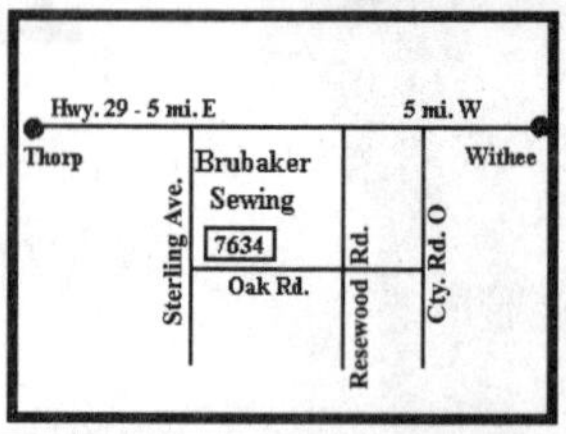

Chippewa Falls, WI #63

Mon - Fri 9:30 - 5
Sat 10 - 3

Hay's Nine Patch

17 W. Central Street 54729
(715) 723-5931
Owner: Kay Hanson
Est: 1993 1500 sq.ft. 750 Bolts

Pieced Quilts & Comforters, Fine Quality Yarns, Quilting & Knitting Supplies, & Gifts. Wool & Poly Batts. Washing & Recarding Service.

Eau Claire, WI #64

Mon - Fri 10 - 5
Sat 10 - 4

The Calico Shoppe

214 S. Barstow St. 54701
(715) 834-9990
Web Site: www.calicoshoppe.com
Owner: Lynn Goelzer
Est: 1993 1600+ Bolts

Great selection of fabrics, patterns, books & quilting supplies. A charming shop specializing in friendly service and abundant ideas!

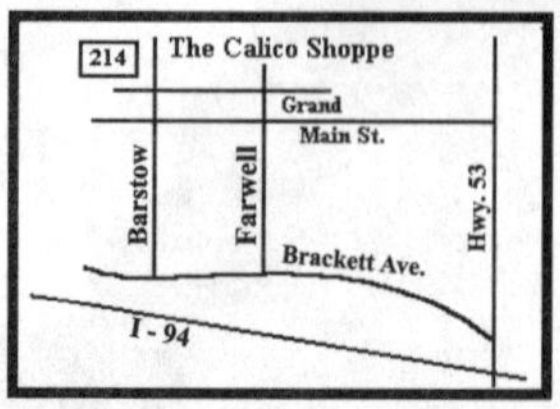

Osseo, WI #65

Corner of 7th and Hwy. 53 54758
(715) 597-2452
E-Mail: quiltyd@triwest.net
Owner: Betty Cotton
Est: 1996 8000 sq.ft. 4000 bolts

The Quilt Yard

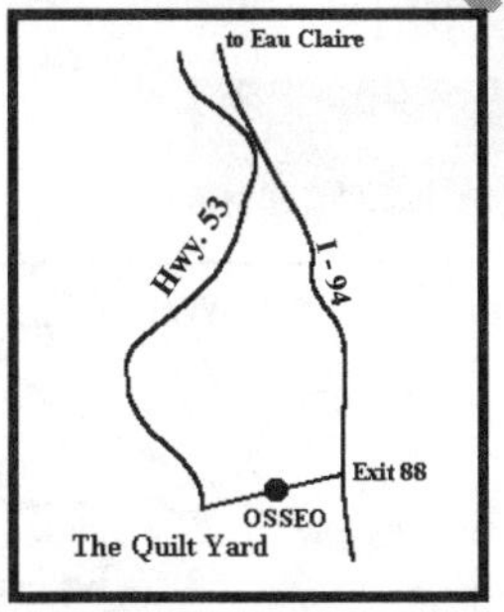

Mon - Sat
9:30 - 5

Located just off I - 94, Exit 88 — at the corner of 7th Street and Hwy. 53

Books, Patterns, Notions and 100% cotton designer fabrics.
Featuring Vintage dry goods and giftware.
Exclusive 'Quilt Yard' patterns and designs.
Handmade Quilts for Sale.
Heirloom Quilting Services.

A large selection of bright contemporary fabrics; specializing in the largest selection of batiks in the Twin Cities area.
Pfaff Sewing Machines and Sergers. **PFAFF®**

A Time To Sew

596 Outpost Circle 54016
(715) 377-0098 Fax: (715) 377-0104
E-Mail: atmtosew@pressenter.com
Web Site: www.atimetosew.com
Est: 2001 1974 sq.ft. 1600 bolts

Hudson, WI #66

Mon - Wed 9 - 6
Thur 9 - 8
Fri - Sat 9 - 5
Sun 12 - 5

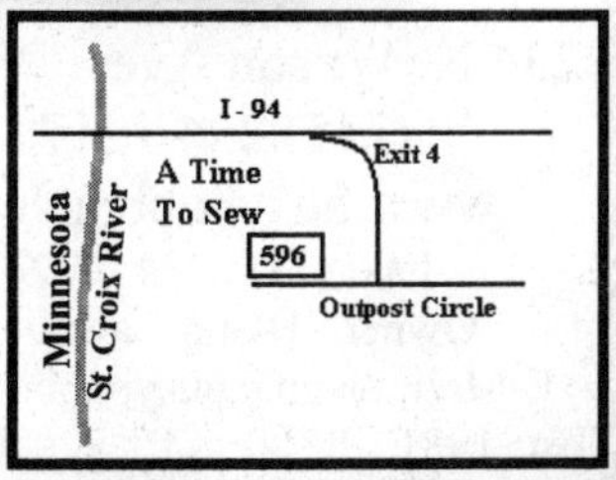

Hudson, WI #67

Mon - Sat
10 - 5
Thur til 8

St. Croix County Dry Goods

220 Locust St.
(715) 386-7405

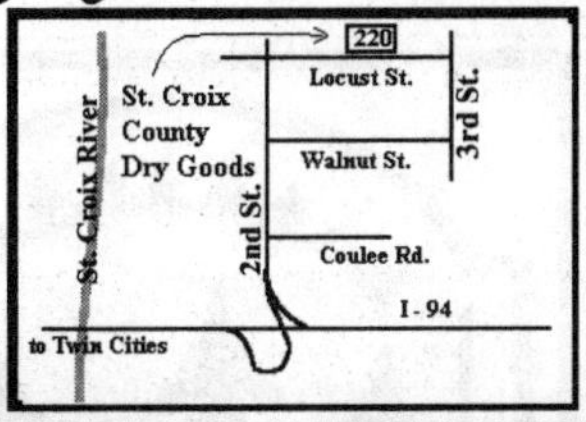

Thousands of bolts of 100% cotton fabric: specializing in reproductions. Books, patterns & supplies. Antiques, accessories and gifts too!

New Richmond, WI #68

Mon - Fri
10 - 6
Sat 10 - 3

Traditions

122 S. Knowles
P.O. Box 26 54017
(715) 246-9910
Fax: (715) 246-9912
E-Mail: traditio@frontiernet.net
Owners: Anna Dzik & Mary Jensen

600+ Bolts fabric, patterns, books, notions, stencils, cross stitch, classes, newsletter.

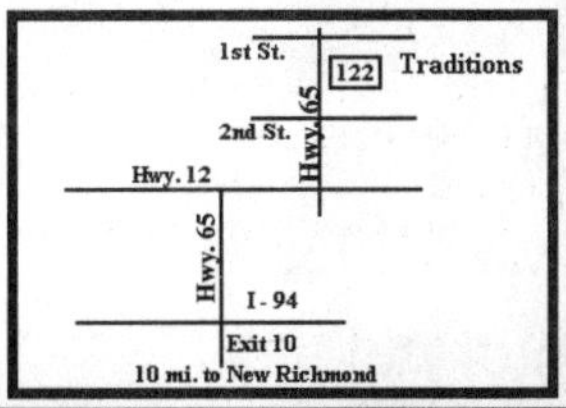

St. Croix Falls, WI #69

Mon - Sat
9:30 - 5:30

Pins 'N' Needles

126 N. Washington 54024
(715) 483-5728
Owner: Mary E. Anderson
Est: 2000 2800 sq.ft.

Over 1500 bolts of fabric along with books, patterns, and notions. Friendly people waiting to help you. Come see us!

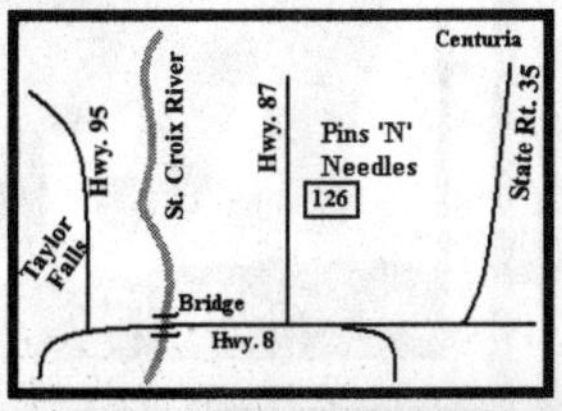

Luck, WI #70

Tues - Fri
9 - 5
Sat 9 - 3

Quilt Country

129 S. Main St. 54853
(715) 472-8088
Owner: Joann Emerson
Est: 1991 3500 sq.ft.
1000+ Bolts

Everything for the Quilter at Reduced Prices.

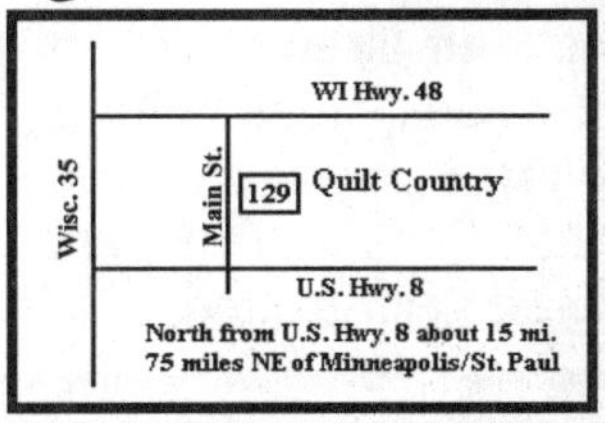

Turtle Lake, WI #71

Mon - Sat
9:30 - 5
Jan 1 - May 1
Closed Mon

Wind in the Willows

P.O. Box 200 54889
612 U.S. Hwy. 8 & 63 W
(715) 986-2983

Quilting, Cross Stitch & Yarn. Books, patterns, buttons & notions. Fabrics include: cottons, flannels, polar fleece and hand-dyed wool. **Also Visit The Gallery Barn.** We carry gifts & collectables. Christian Books & Bibles.

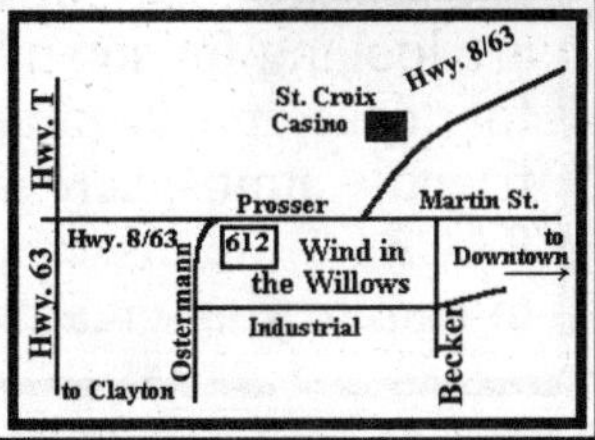

Rice Lake, WI #72

Busy Bobbin

Large selection 100% Cotton fabrics, patterns, books, and quilting notions. Classes offered.

Mon - Fri 9:30 - 5 Sat 9:30 - 3

234 N. Wilson Ave. 54868
(715) 234-1217
www.busybobbin.com
Fax: (715) 234-6326
Owner: Diann Raymond
E-Mail: diann@busybobbin.com
Est: 1981 1300 sq.ft. 2000 Bolts

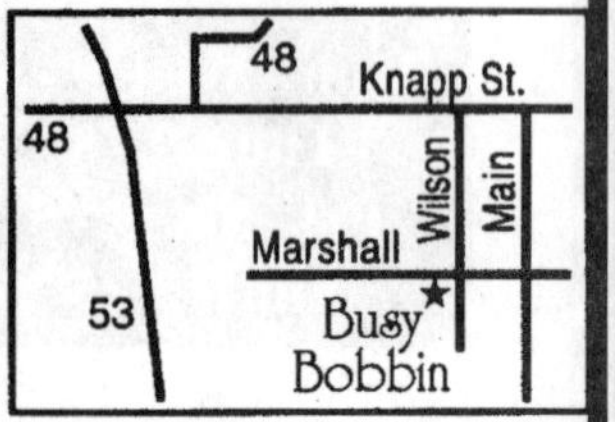

Hayward, WI #73

Hayward Quilters Quarters

Large selection 100% Cotton fabrics, patterns, books, and quilting notions. Classes offered.

Mon - Fri 10 - 5 Sat 10 - 3

10632 Hayward Ct. 54843
(715) 634-3260
www.busybobbin.com
Fax: (715) 234-6326
Owner: Diann Raymond
E-Mail: diann@busybobbin.com
Est: 1995 1800 sq.ft. 1800 Bolts

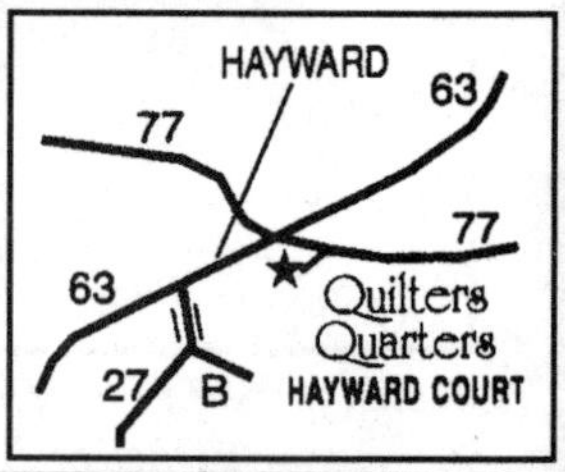

Bear Den Quilt Co.

Siren, WI #74

24665 State Road 35-70, Suite C
Siren, WI 54872
715-349-2250
Fax: 715-349-8939
Owner: Karen Miller
kdmiller@centurytel.net

Hours :

Summer (May 1 - Oct 31)
Mon - Thur 9:30 - 5 PM
Fridays 9:30 - 7 PM
Saturday 9:30 - 4 PM
Sunday Noon - 4 PM
Winter (Nov 1 - April 30)
Tues - Fri 10 - 5 PM
Saturday 10 - 4 PM
Open Evenings during classes

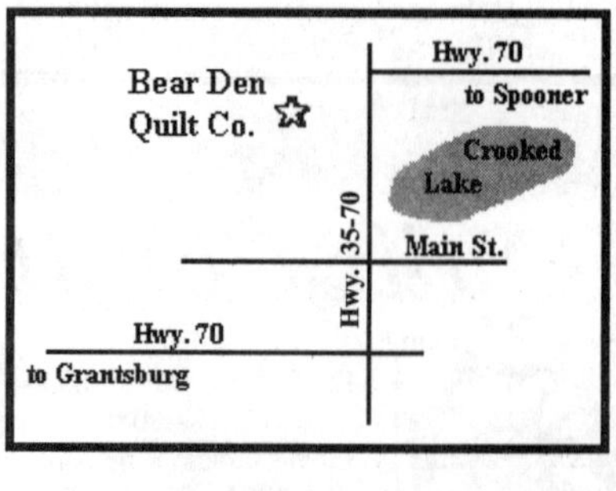

From Main Street in Siren go north 1.5 miles on Hwy. 35-70. Look for us on the west side of the highway.

While visiting beautiful Northwestern Wisconsin don't miss a stop at the area's newest Quilt Shop. Featuring a growing selection of the newest top quality 100% cotton fabrics including Hoffman, Moda, Benartex and more. We feature many of the latest patterns, books, notions and supplies. If you are looking for something unique in "Wearable Art" check our large selection for ideas and inspiration. We specialize in the "Northwoods" look with a friendly atmosphere and personal service. Many unique gift items and Fabric PACs for the discerning quilter. Beautiful quilts, wall hangings and runners to inspire your creativity, many for sale. Classes are offered year around.

Tomahawk, WI #75

Between Friends Quilting & Supplies, LLC

14 W. Wisconsin Ave. 54487
(715) 453-8884 Fax: (715) 453-9026
Est: 1997

Quilting Books, Fabrics, Quilting Supplies, Thread, Floss, Ribbon Embroidery, Classes. Free Newsletter, friendly Service, Inspiration & sharing of ideas.

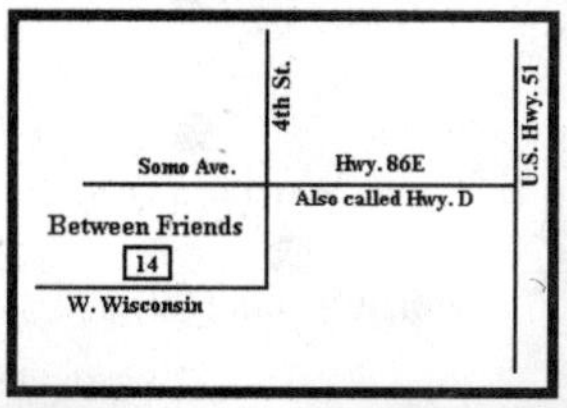

Minocqua, WI #76

Labor Day - Mem.
Mon - Fri 10 - 4
Sat 10 - 3
Memorial - Labor
Mon - Fri 10 - 5
Sat 10 - 3

The Quilt Cottage

510 Chicago Ave.
P.O. Box 910 54548
(715) 358-7074
Fax: (715) 479-3849
Est: 1995 2000+ Bolts
Owners: Barb Zawistowski &

Friendly cottage on the lake carrying cotton fabrics, Hand-dyed wools, Rughooking supplies.

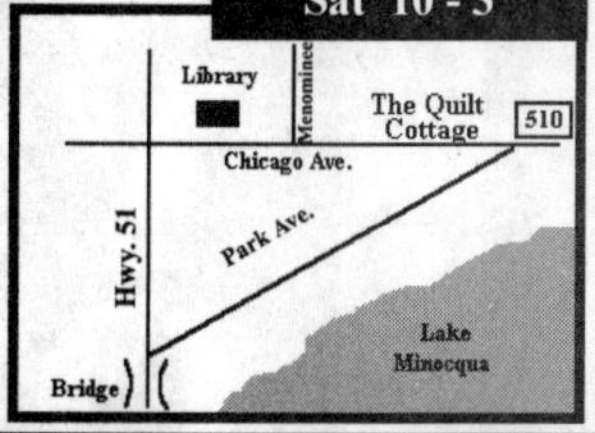

Eagle River, WI #77

Mon - Sat
10 - 5

Heartstrings Quilts & Fabrics

220 S. Main St.,
P.O. Box 194 54521
(715) 479-2313
Owner: Lisa Wood

Est: 1995 1000 sq.ft. 1500+ Bolts
E-Mail: heartstr@newnorth.net

North Woods Quilting at its Best! Fabrics, Patterns, Books, Wool Rug Hooking Supplies, Viking Sewing Machines and Classes.

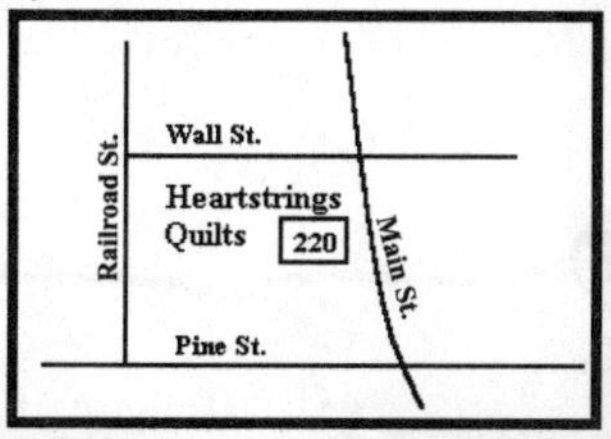

Park Falls, WI #78

Mon - Fri
9 - 5
Sat 10 - 3

Quilters Country Store

409 Division Street 54552
(715) 762-8109
E-Mail: quiltcountrystore@centurytel.net
Owner: Pat Radlinger
Est: 1993 1300 sq. ft.

New store, new location, across from our newly remodeled library. Only quality fabrics & notions, books & patterns. Friendly & helpful customer service.

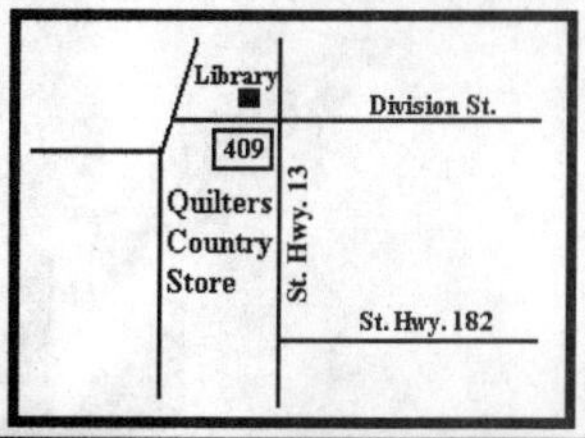

Superior, WI #79

Mon - Fri
9:30 - 5
Thur til 8
Sat 10 - 4

Fabric Works

1320 Tower Ave. 54880
(715) 392-7060
Owner: Barb Engelking
Est: 1991

Over 2000 Bolts of 100% Cotton Fabric. Quilting Books, Patterns and Supplies.

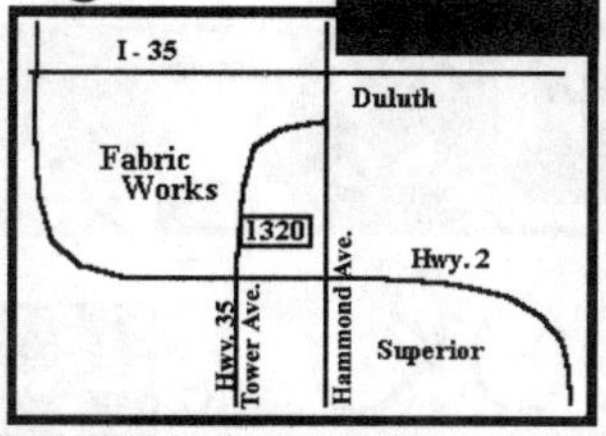

Superior, WI #80

24 Hour Answering Machine

The Country Schoolhouse

5818 Scharte Dr. 54880
(715) 394-9782
E-Mail: CtrySchlhs@aol.com
Owner: Marsha Bergren
Est: 2001 Free Catalog

New mail order business, specializing in "Up North" and Country 100% cotton fabrics. Flannels galore! E-mail or call for catalog.

Local pickup available. Call or write and directions will be provided.

Other Shops in Wisconsin: We suggest calling first

Amery	Rita's Needles, 906 Wisconsin Ln.	715-268-9524
Amherst	Wood Shed Gifts, 291 Packer Ave.	715-824-3848
Beaver Dam	Nancy's Notions, 333 Beichl Ave., P.O. Box 683	920-887-7321
Berlin	West Side Sewing, Highway F, Route 3	414-361-1789
Bloomer	Golden Thimble, P.O. Box 84	715-568-5960
Butternut	Pioneer Quilt Shop, 126 E. Main St.	715-769-3284
Cable	My Favorite Things, Hwy. 63 & Cty. Rd. M	715-798-3665
Cashton	Borntreger Furniture, Box 1978	
Cedarburg	Cedarburg Woolen Mill, W. 62 N. 580 Washington	414-377-0345
Clayton	Pine Cone Quilting, 318 7th Ave.	715-948-2111
Coon Valley	Quilt Basket & Creations, 1155 Main, P.O. Box 234	608-637-7002
Curtiss	LaVerna's Machine Quilting Studio, Route 2	715-223-2133
Darlington	Opera House Shop, 242 Main St.	608-779-2116
Deer Park	What's Sewin', 194 135th St.	715-269-5684
Delafield	Red River Furniture & Gifts, 608 Milwaukee	414-646-8010
Elmwood	Simple Pleasures, 125 E. Race Ave.	715-639-6201
Fond du Lac	Gingerbread Junction, 965 Danbury Ave.	920-924-6050
Green Bay	Door County Quiltworks, 1043 S. Quincy St.	
Green Bay	Koss Quilts & Accents, 2207 Velp Ave.	920-434-1969
Herbster	Cabin Fever Quilt Co., P.O. Box 6	715-774-3309
Janesville	Quilt Center, 1905 Center Ave. #3	608-756-2869
LaCrosse	Carol's Corner, 731 10th St. N	608-784-7860
Madison	Quilting Memories, 4638 Tonyawatha Trl.	608-221-0246
Medford	Treasure Chest Gifts, 345 N. 8th St.	715-748-6860
Menomonee Falls	Fall's Sewing Center, N 81 W 14978 Appleton	414-253-3600
Milwaukee	Diann's Essentials Quilt Shop, 2612 N. Richards St.	414-263-7938
Mineral Point	Old Town Hall, 220 Commerce St.	608-987-2835
Montfort	Moments in Time200 E. Hwy. 18	608-943-6632
New Richmond	Bear Paw Quilting Studio 2325 Arch Ave.	715-246-5854
Omro	Wool & Needle, 5530 St. Hwy. 116	920-582-7196
Osceolo	Quilting Bee, 215 1/2 N. Cascade	715-294-2722
Oshkosh	Patchwork Farm, 438 N. Main St.	920-582-0387
Oshkosh	Country Quilting, 3351 W 20th Ave.	920-233-2916
Platteville	Creative Stitches, 10 E. Main St.	608-348-9276
Sister Bay	Easy Stitchin' Needle Art, 326 Country Walk Ln.	920-854-2840
Spencer	After Hours Creations, 212 S. Pacific, P.O. Box 113	
Spring Green	Sew 'N Sew, 122 N. Lexington	608-588-2273
St. Germain	Hidden Cabin Crafts, 7990 St. Hwy. 70 E	715-542-3731
Stetsonville	Betty White's Fabrics, 109 Mink Ave., P.O. Box 21	715-678-2294
Stockholm	Amish Country, 119 Spring St.	715-442-2015
Superior	Best Friends, 6006 Tower Ave.	715-392-1991
Tomahawk	Tomahawk Quilt Co., W 5158 Piehl Rd.	715-453-1346
Verona	Maple Springs Farm, 1828 Highway PB	608-845-9482
Verona	She Seams Together Quilting, 307 Edward St.	608-848-4119
Viroqua	Bear Paw, 201 N. Main St.	608-637-8007
Waukesha	Just A Little Bit Country, N 4 W 22496 Blue Mound	262-542-8050
Waukesha	Genesee Woolen Mill s, 40 W 28178 Hwy. 59	414-521-2121
Wausau	Wausau Woolen Company, 408 South 4th	715-848-9293
West Bend	Hinterberg Designs, 2805 E. Progress Dr.	800-443-5800
Whitewater	Woodland Quilts, 135 W. Main St.	262-473-2978

WYOMING

16 Featured Shops

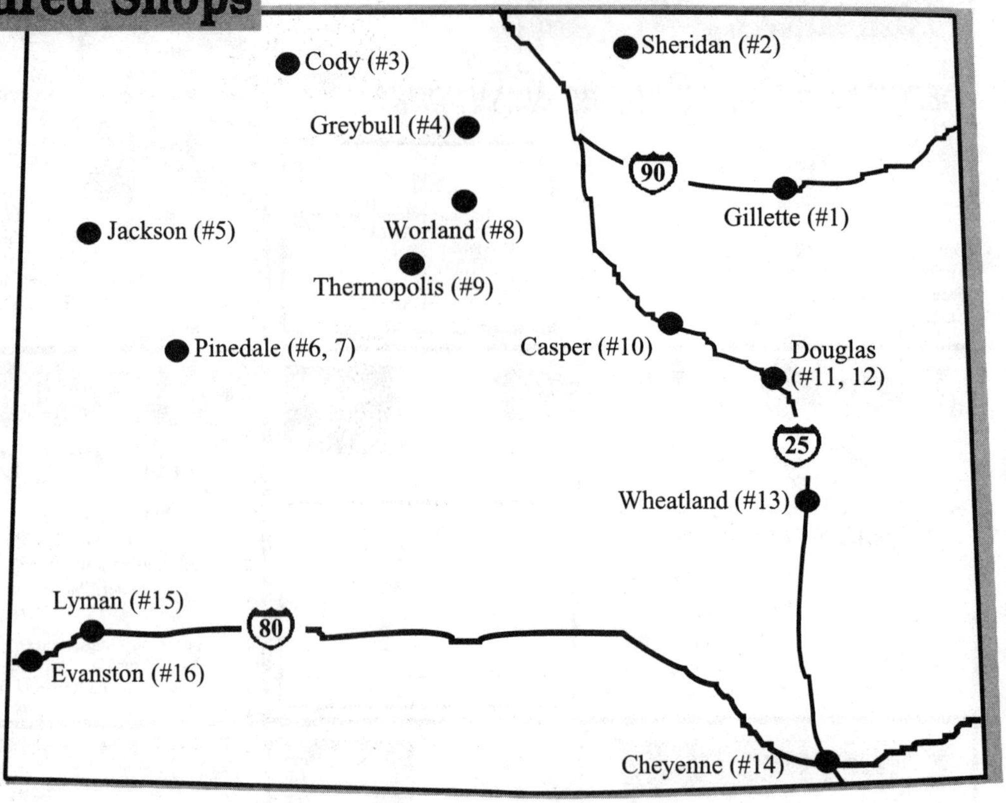

Gillette, WY #1

Quilt Nook, INC.

Northeastern Wyoming's
Quilt Shop!

NEW Location!

101 S. Douglas HWY. STE 120
GILLETTE, WY 82716

(307) 682-9196 (888) 268-3381

* Koala Cabinets
* Kits, Books, Patterns
* Janome Sewing Machines
* Finishing Touch Embroidery Thread
* Quilting Notions, Stabilizers, Needles
* Guterman, YLI, Star Mercerized Thread
* Over 4000 bolts of 100% Cotton Fabrics

HOURS:
MON- FRI 10:00A.M. TO 5:30P.M.
SAT 9:00A.M TO 4:00P.M
CLOSED SUNDAY

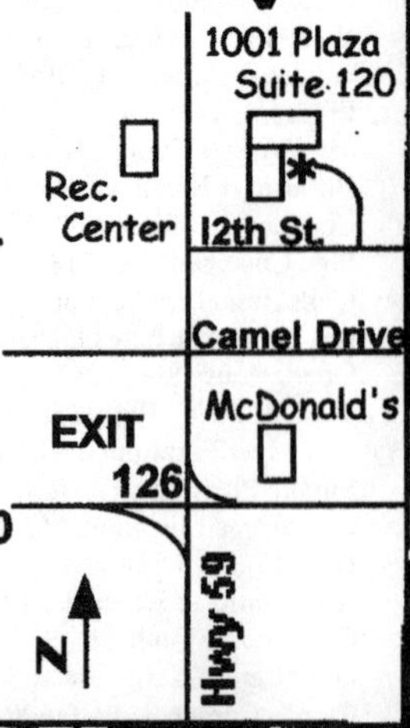

JANOME

Authorized Dealer, Repair and Service Center!

E-mail: quiltnook@vcn.com http://www.quiltnook.com

Sheridan, WY #2

Mon - Fri 10 - 5
Sat 10 - 4

Treasured Stitches

28 N. Main 82801
(307) 674-0558
Owners: Josephine Schreibeis & Rita Baker
Est: 1996

Top quality Fabrics, Patterns, Books, Quilter's Notions, and Supplies. Classes. Silk Flowers and some finished crafts.

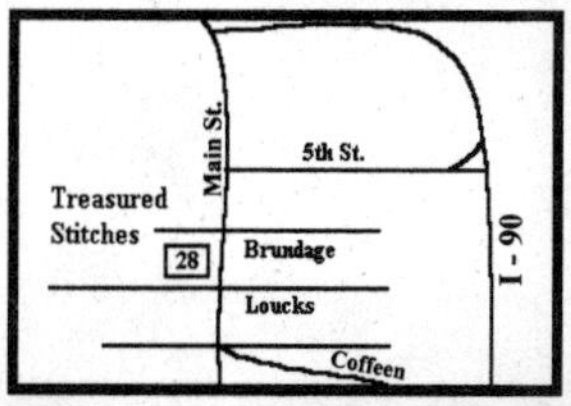

Cody, WY #3

Mon - Fri 9 - 5:30
Sat 9-5

Bobbin & Thimble Quilting Co.

513 16th St. 82414 Est: 1998
(307) 527-9044 or (866) 3-FABRIC
Owners: Marcia Stevens & Jeanie Kieft
mstevens@wtp.net Fax: (307) 587-6298
www.bobbinandthimblequilting.com

Highest quality fabrics at reasonable prices. We are located just 50 miles east of Yellowstone National Park. Warm, friendly service.

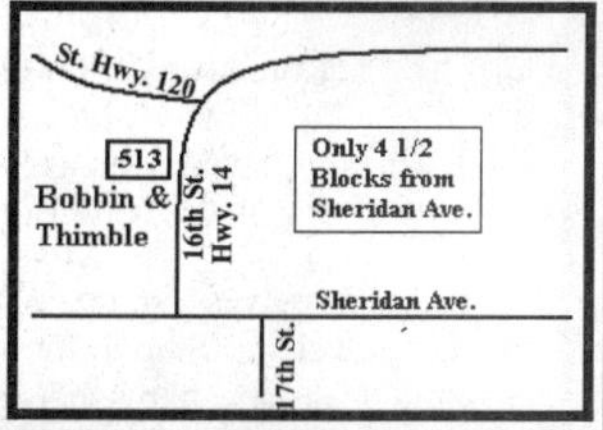

Greybull, WY #4

Mon - Sat 9 - 5

Big Horn Quilts

529 Greybull Ave. 82426
(877) 586-9150
or (307) 765-2604

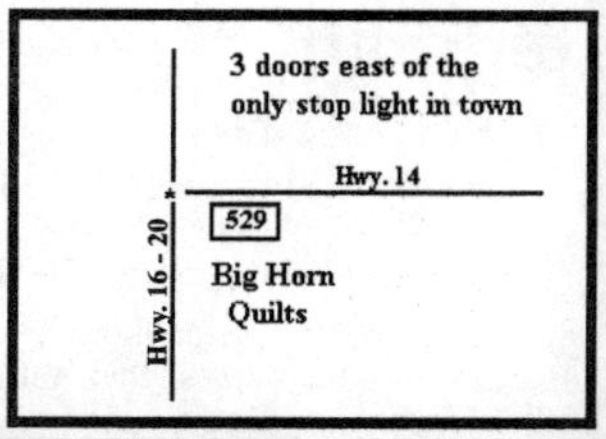

E-Mail: julie@bighornquilts.com
Web Site: www.bighornquilts.com
Owners: David & Julie Owens
Est: 1998 6000 Bolts Full Online Catalog

Jackson, WY #5

Stitch 'n Time

Jaskson Hole's Largest Fabric, Quilting and Sewing Center

Mon - Fri 9 - 6
Sat 9 - 5

185 S. Scott Ln. P.O. Box 13070 83002
(888) 565-5634 or (307) 733-6800
E-Mail: info@stitchntimeinc.com
Web Site: www.stitchntimeinc.com
Owner: Kim Kerr
Est: 1971
4500 sq.ft. 4000 Bolts

A unique array of fabrics and notions that expand the imagination to creative expression

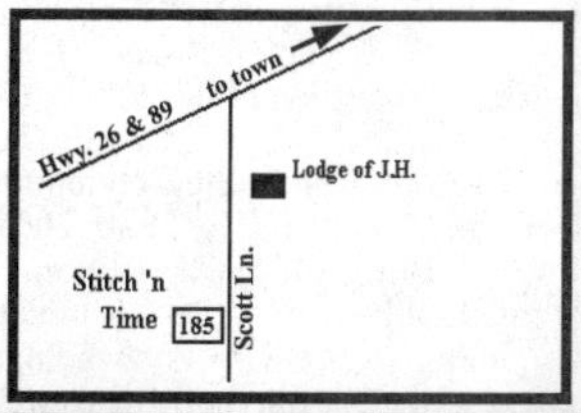

the huckleberry patch

Pinedale, WY #6

Over 2000 Bolts of quality Fabric waiting for you! We specialize in quilt fabrics -- with a special emphasis on western & wildlife prints.

Mon - Sat 9:00 - 5:30

219 E. Pine
Summit Mall #116
(307) 367-6727
P.O. Box 1733,
Pinedale, WY 82941
Fax: (307) 367-2864
Owner: Shirley Roberts
Est: 1994 1500 sq.ft.
2500 Bolts

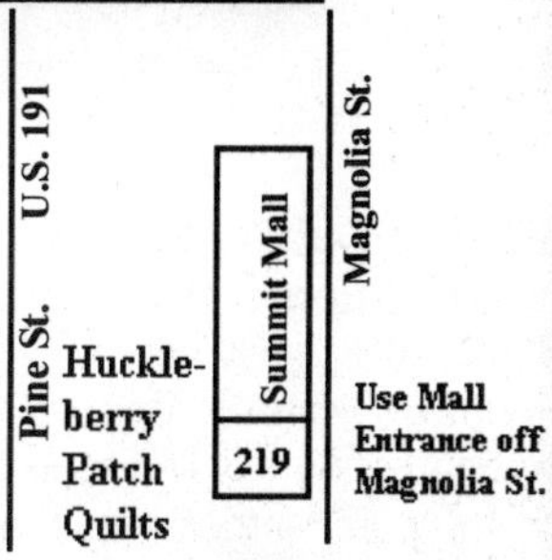

Website: www.huckleberryfabrics.com

Pinedale, WY #7

Mon - Sat 9 - 5:30
Summer Sun 12 - 5

Heritage Quilts & Fabric Shoppe

21 East Pine St., P.O. Box 1517 82941
(307) 367-7397
E-Mail: swells@coffey.com
Owner: Sue & John Wells
Est: 2000 1400 sq. ft. 1500+ Bolts.

Husqvarna Viking Authorized Sales & Service. The ultimate quilt shop - - a fantastic selection of all quilter's fabrics, notions, books and patterns.

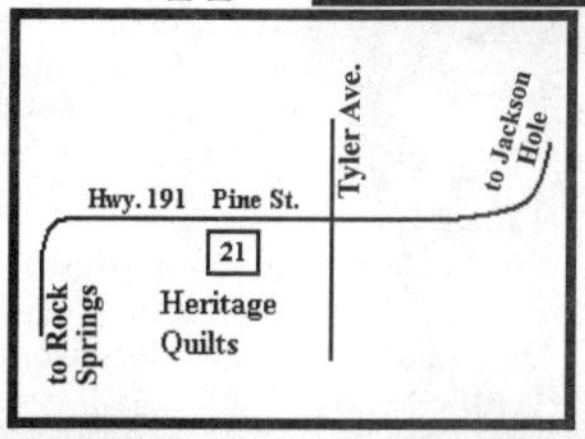

Worland, WY #8

Mon - Sat 9 - 5:30

Hansen's Fabric

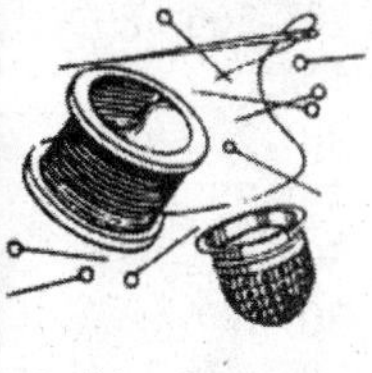

734 Big Horn Ave.
82401
(307) 347-4895

Quilting Cottons & much, much more! Quilt books, notions, patterns etc. PLUS—guaranteed, experienced sewing machine service.

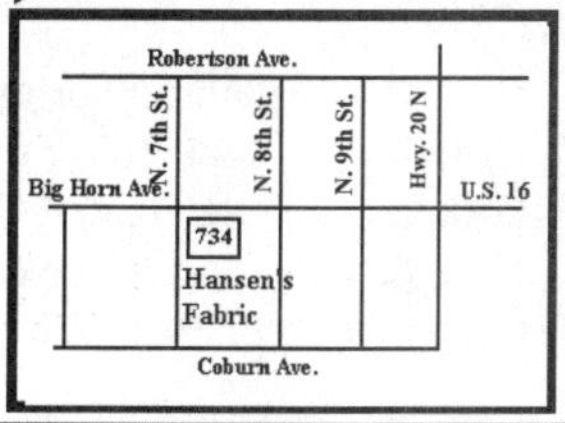

Thermopolis, WY #9

Mon - Sat 9:30 - 5:30
Sun 12 - 4

Keeping You In Stitches

524 Broadway 82443
(307) 864-9490
Owners: Karen & Dennis Sinclair
3000 sq.ft. 3000+ Bolts

We pride ourselves on being the region's favorite quilt shop! Stop in for some quilting inspiration, fabric, patterns, books & more.

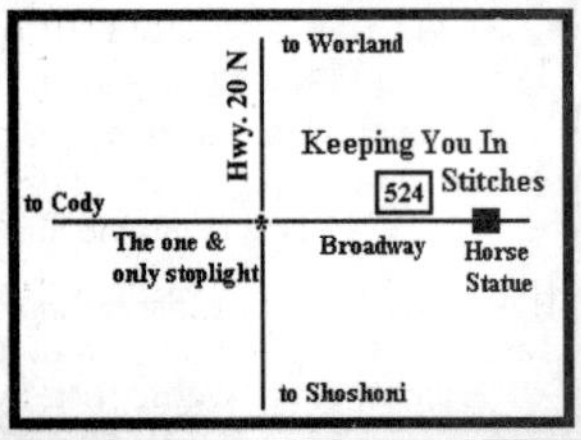

Casper, WY #10

Mon - Sat 10 - 5

Prism Quilt

114 E. 2nd St. 82601
(307) 234-4841
Owners: Becki & Bill Marsh
Est: 1987 4800 sq.ft. 4000+ Bolts

4000+ cotton fabrics, 5000 fat quarters, Pfaff Sewing Machines, Quilts, Books, Patterns, Notions, Quilting Supplies and Service.

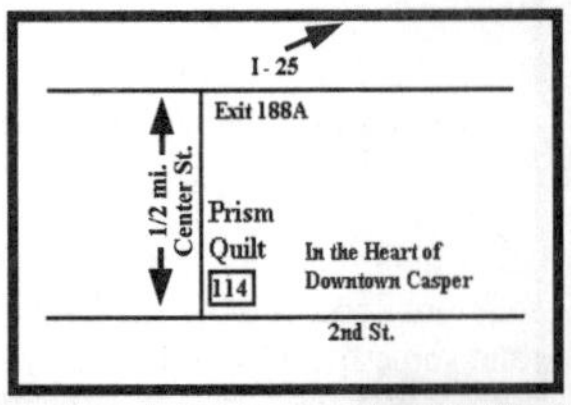

Douglas, WY #11

Mon - Fri 9 - 5:30
Sat 9 - 4

The Prairie Stitcher

120 N. 3rd St. 82633
(307) 358-5571

Complete line of quilting / wearable fabric; books, patterns, notions and stitcheries too. Kits, Thimbleberry, and Kids Clubs. Samples & classes to inspire.

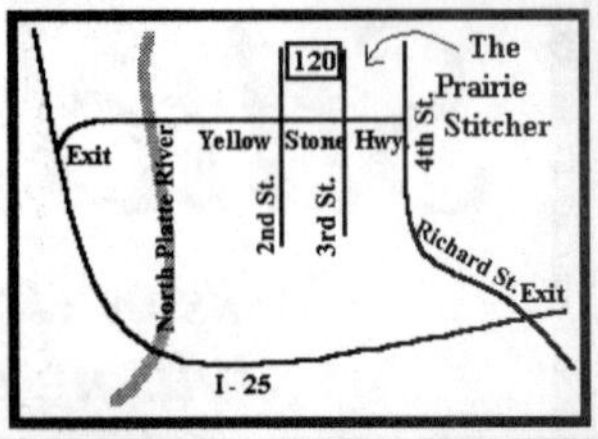

Douglas, WY #12

Tues - Fri 10 - 5:30
Sat 9 - 5

Picket Fence Quilting Co., Inc.

1954 E. Richards #6
82633
Est: 1999
(307) 358-5534 Fax: (307) 358-5534
E-Mail: pktfence@coffey.com
Owner: Pat Linaman 1000 Bolts

Specialize in fabrics for those who use bright and jewel-tone colors in their quilts. Carry a full line of books, patterns and notions.

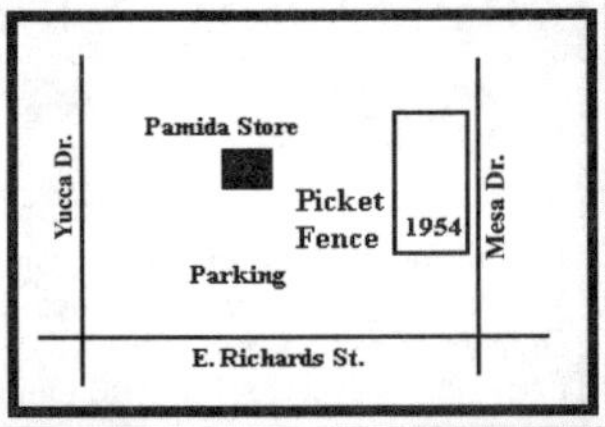

Wheatland, WY #13

Mon - Sat 10 - 6
Sun 1-6
Oct-April Closed Tues

The Quilt Rustler

875 Gilchrist Ave. 82201
(in the Wheatland Mercantile) (307) 322-1725
(800) 620-7897 Fax: (307) 322-1727
E-Mail: wheatmere@communicomm.com
Owner: Joanne Rice Est: 2001 2500 sq.ft.
1000 Bolts of 100% Cotton. Friendly, old fashioned mercantile -- everything from quilting to needlework, beading, gunsmithing and more. "A fiberholic heaven."

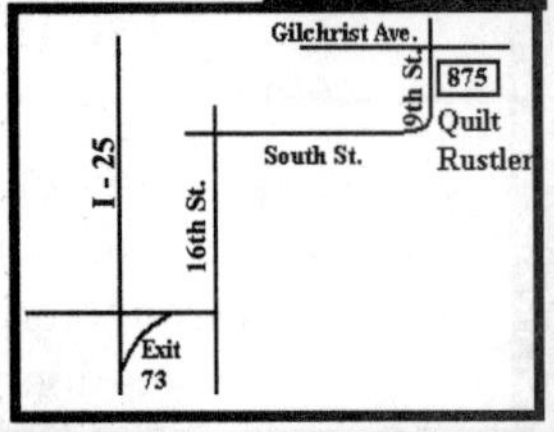

Cheyenne, WY #14

Mon - Sat 10 - 5:30

The Quilted Corner

2015 Warren Ave. 82001
(307) 638-2002 or (877) 282-2002
Web Site: www.WyomingQuilting.com

Cheyenne's only shop devoted to Quilters. Located in historic Home. Large selection - we have 2500 bolts of 100% Cotton Fabric, Books, Notions & Patterns.

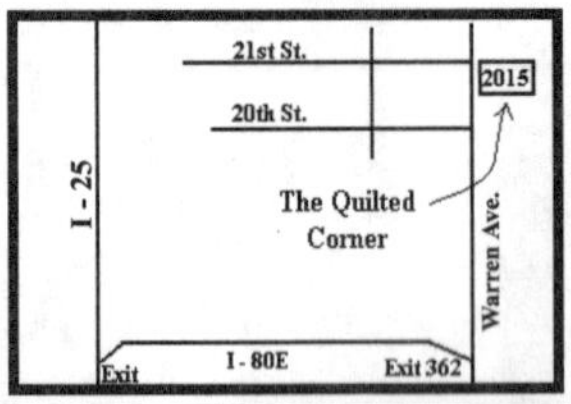

Lyman, WY #15

Mon - Fri 10 - 6
Sat 10 - 5

Valley Fabric Shop

102 Mountain Meadow St.
(Urie) 82937
(307) 786-2653
Fax: (307) 786-2655
Est: 1979 2,000+ Bolts

Wyoming's best kept secret. Quilting Fabrics, flannels, books, notions & patterns. Our sample displays are worth the visit. Terrific Service.

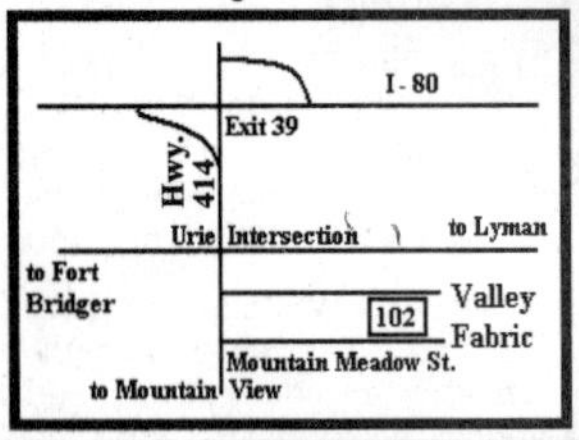

Evanston, WY #16

Mon - Fri 10 - 6
Sat 10 - 5

Quilt Trappings

1029 Main St. 82930
(307) 444-1675
E-Mail: sallyq@attbi.com
Web Site: www.quilttrappings.com
Cyndi Holloman & Sally LeRoy
Est: 1996 2500 sq.ft.

Located in historic downtown Evanston. We specialize in offering personalized, friendly service for your quilting needs.

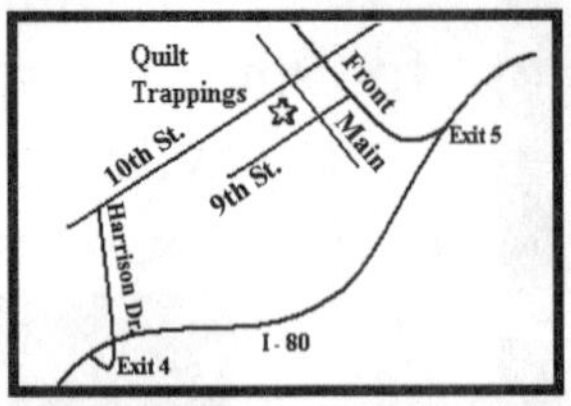

Other Shops in Wyoming: We suggest calling first

Casper	Quilts & Things, 2113 E. 12th St.	307-266-5894
Casper	Wyoming Sewing Center, 2635 E. 2nd St.	307-234-4581
Douglas	Sheila's Fabrics, 515 S. 4th St.	307-358-5333
Gillette	Angel House Quilts, 701 Carey Ave.	307-686-0777
Gillette	Quilt Trail, P.O. Box 4175	307-686-0676
Green River	A Little Character, 1740 Uinta	307-875-7172
Green River	Sew What Sewing, 2020 Colorado Dr.	307-875-7437
Lander	Quilting Bee, 637 W. Main St.	307-332-4123
Laramie	Spencer Fabric & Quilt Shop, 314 S. 2nd	307-742-6156
Marbleton	Fantasy Fabrics, 112 Maxwell Ave.	307-276-3610
Rawlins	Seams to Be, 405 W. Buffalo	307-328-4000
Riverton	Quilted Treasures Studio, 1006 E. Jackson	307-856-9727
Riverton	Country Rose Quilt Shop, 406 E. Main	307-856-4021
Rock Springs	Country Fabrics, 426 S. Main St	307-382-2897
Saratoga	Buggie Bear Station, 106 E. Bridge St.	307-326-9663

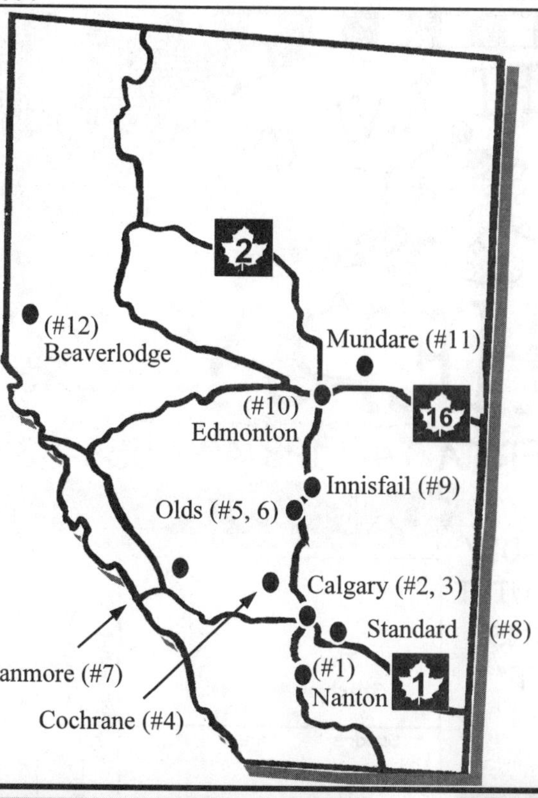

12 Featured Shops

ALBERTA CANADA

Nanton, AB #1

Mon - Fri 9:30 - 5:30
Sat 9:30 - 5

Cottonwoods

2109 - 20 St., P.O. Box 1021 T0L 1R0
(403) 646-2086 Fax: (403) 646-2398
E-Mail: cotwoods@telusplanet.net
Web Site: www.antiquewalk.com
Est: 1998 5000 sq.ft. 1200 Bolts

Quilting fabrics, classes, books, notions & patterns. Quilts for Sale. Authorized Pfaff Dealer.

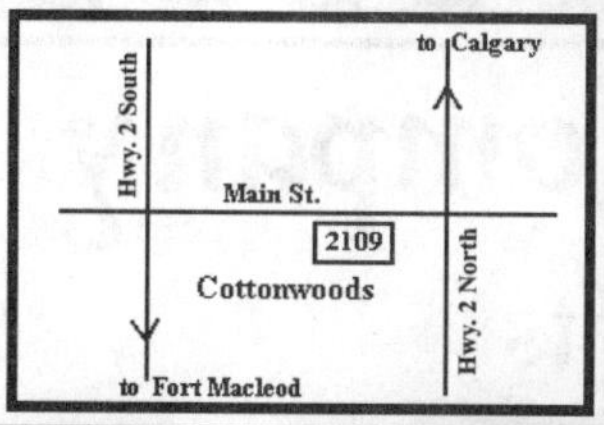

Calgary, AB #2

the Fabric cottage

16 Crowfoot Terrace NW, Calgary, AB T3G 4J8
www.thefabriccottage.com
Info@thefabriccottage.com
(403) 241-3070
Owners: Doreen Folk & Joan Vogel

Mon - Sat 10 - 5:30
Thur til 8:30

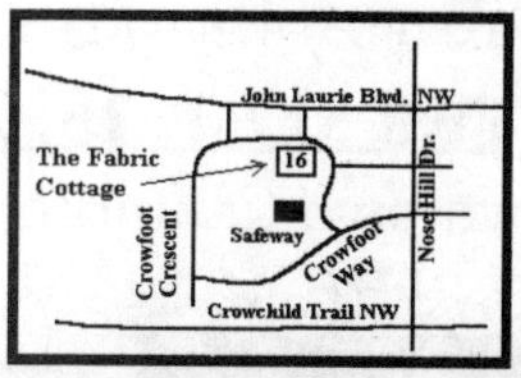

100% quilting cottons, books, patterns, notions & classes. Fully authorized Bernina dealership in sales & service.

"From traditional to contemporary"

Calgary, AB #3

Mon - Fri 10 - 5:30
Thur til 8
Sat 10 - 5

13A-728 Northmount Dr. NW T2K 3K2
(403) 270-2104 or (888) 644-6699
Fax: (403) 283-3709

Est: 1981
3100 sq.ft.
3000+ Bolts

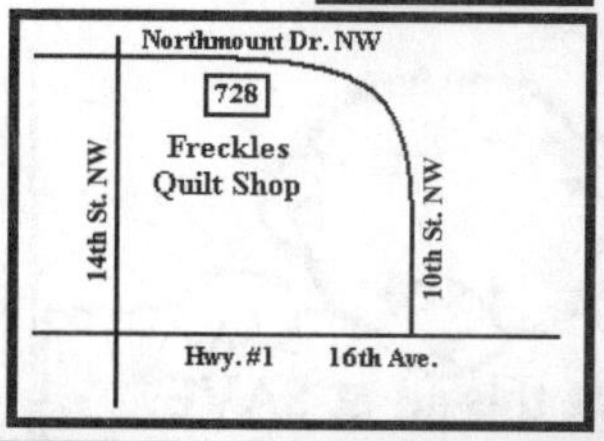

E-Mail: frcklqlt@telusplanet.net
Web Site: www.frecklesquiltshop.com
Owner: Janet E. Samuels

Cochrane, AB #4

Mon - Sat 9:30 - 5:30

Addie's material goods ltd.

420 First St. W, Box 1047 T4C 1B1
(403) 932-1500 Owner: Corlienne Pennell
E-Mail: addies@telusplanet.net
Web Site: www.addiesmaterialgoods.com

A unique turn of the century style Quilt Shop. 100% cotton fabrics, books, patterns & workshops.

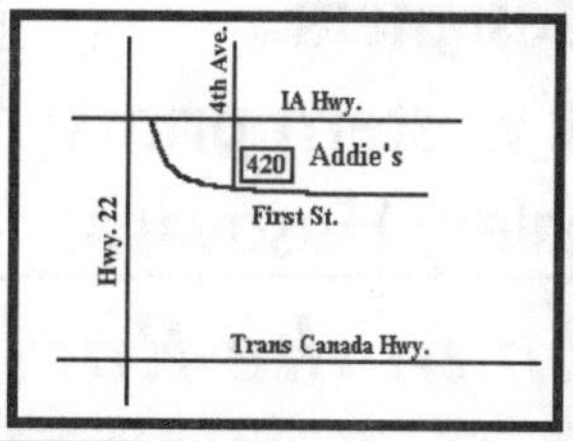

Olds, AB #5

Tues - Sat 10 - 5

The Quilting Bee

5026 51 Street T4H 1P7
(403) 507-8825 Fax: (403) 507-8826
E-Mail: quiltbee@telusplanet.net
Owner: Cheryl Naglis
Est: 2000 2500 sq. ft.

Located in downtown Olds. Large selection of 100% cottons, notions, books and stitchery. Old fashioned prices and hospitality!

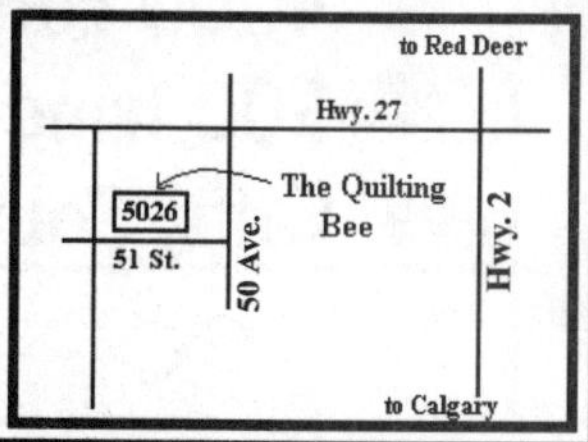

A UNIQUE COUNTRY GIFT AND QUILT SHOP

THE STITCHERY

BOX 6 SITE 1 R.R. #2 OLDS, ALBERTA T4H 1P3 (403)-556-6221

Olds, AB #6

TREAT YOURSELF TO THE RELAXING, FRIENDLY ATMOSPHERE OF OUR UNIQUE COUNTRY QUILT SHOP. ENJOY THE LATEST IN 100% COTTONS, BOOKS, NOTIONS AND OTHER "GOOD STUFF" FOR QUILTERS.

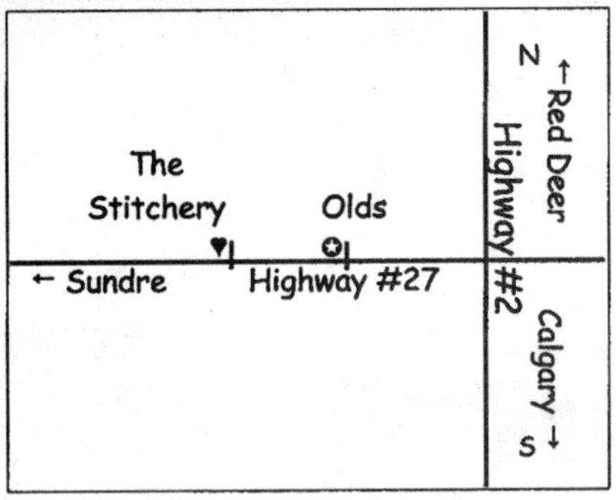

TUE - SAT 10-5
THURSDAY 10-8

Located 2 miles west of Olds on Hwy #27

The Sugar Pine Company

Quilt Shop & Gifts

Canmore, AB #7

Visit us in the beautiful Canadian Rockies, just 20 minutes from Banff!

UNTIL SEPT. 15, 2002: #1-1302 Bow Valley Trail (1A Hwy), Canmore, Alberta T1W 1N6

Phone: (403) 678-9603 / Fax: (403) 678-4703 / www.thesugarpine.com / quilting@thesugarpine.com

NEW ADDRESS **AFTER SEPT. 15, 2002:**

737 Tenth Street, Downtown Canmore, Alberta T1W 2A3 - *SEE MAP*

MON-SAT 9-9
SUN 11-8

Check out QUILT ART ROCKIES at www.quiltartrockies.com

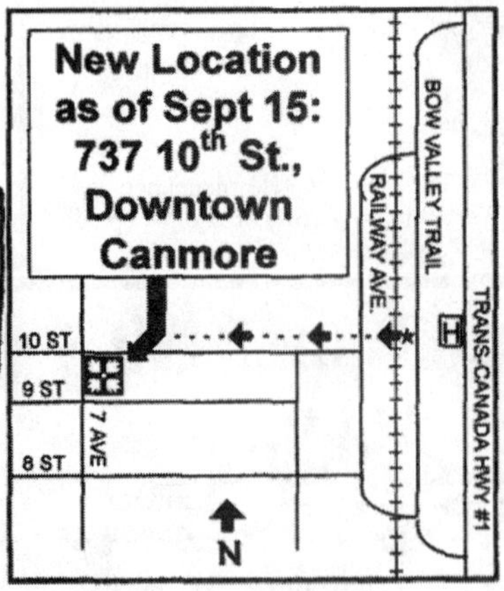

- 4000 cotton fabrics from leading designers
- 500 hand-dyes & batiks, wildlife & western prints
- Gifts, Souvenirs, Ty Authorized Dealer, Husqvarna Viking Machines

Greatest Quilt Shop in the Rockies

Standard, AB #8

Everyday Til 9 pm

Cotton & Candy Country Store

818 The Broadway T0J 3G0
(403) 644-3895 Fax: (403) 644-3820
Owner: Sue Nielsen
Est: 2001 3000 s.q.ft.

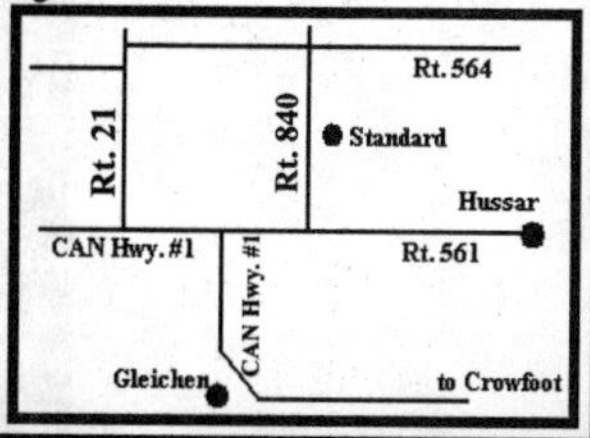

Kaufmann - complete set of quilters spectrum Hoffman - Maywoods - Jenny Beyer - Debbie Mumm, etc. We have it all and we're open til 9 every day with long arm quilting.

Innisfail, AB #9

Mon - Fri 9:30 - 5:30 Sat 10 - 5

Fabric Fantasy

5018 - 50th St.
Box 1645, T4G 1S8
Web Site: www.fabricfantasy.com
(403) 227-4618

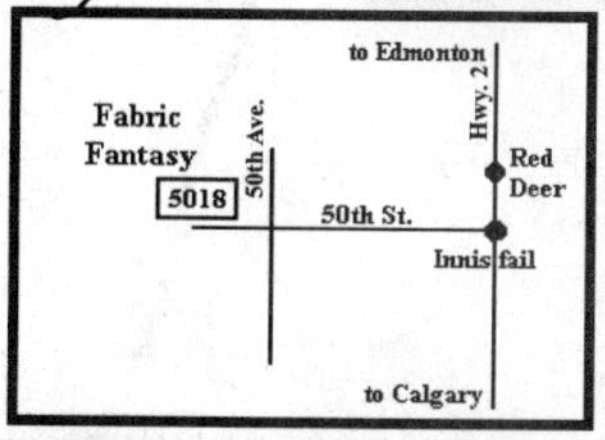

Large selection of quilting supplies, including top quality 100% cotton, notions, patterns and books. We also carry cross stitch supplies.

Edmonton, AB #10

Mon - Fri 9 - 8 Sat 9 - 5 Sun 12 - 5

Earthly Goods

5848 111th St. T6H 3G1
Lendrum Shopping Center
(780) 433-7179 Fax: (780) 430-0817
Est: 1985
Owner:
Sandy Bowhay
4000 sq.ft.
2000 Bolts

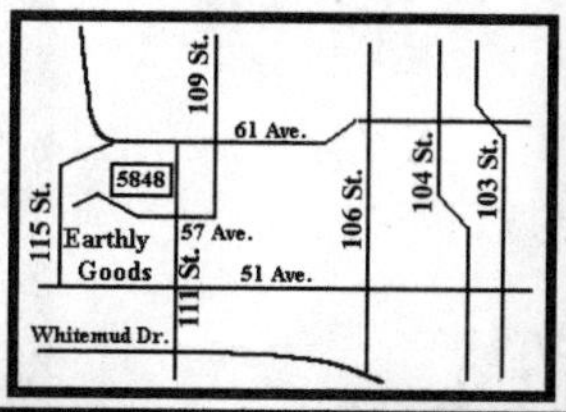

E-Mail: info@earthlygoodsquilting.com
Web Site: www.earthlygoodsquilting.com
Featured in Quilt Sampler Magazine.
Everything you need for quilting including Cottons, Notions & Books. Great Classes.

Beaverlodge, AB #12

Mon - Sat 9 - 6

Around the Block

1040 - 1st Ave. (Box 1078) T0H 0C0
(780) 354-3423 Fax: (780) 354-3430
E-Mail: atblock@telusplanet.net
Owners: Fay & Lyle Sipe Est: 1999

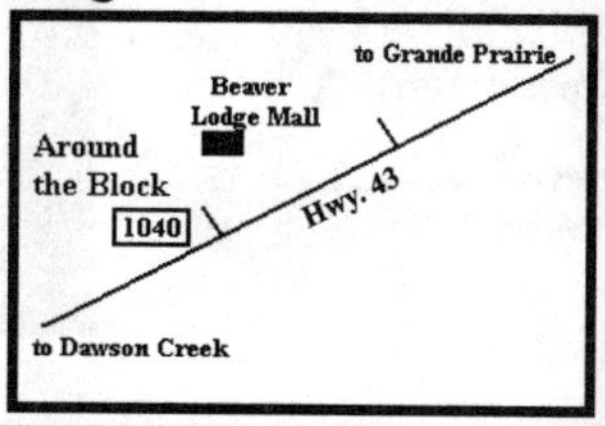

We carry the complete Jinny Beyer Palette, a full line of quilting cottons, kits, books, notions and Block of the Months.

Mundare, AB #11

Tues - Sat 10 - 5

The Chicken Coop

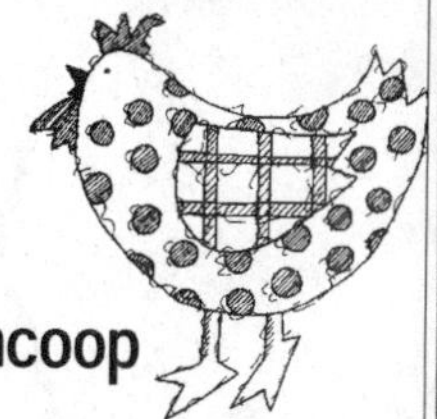

Web Site: redrival.com/chickencoop

Unique gift shop & quilting store.
Fabrics - Notions - Books -
Classes. Large classroom.
Chicken collectibles.
Tole
Painting
Florals

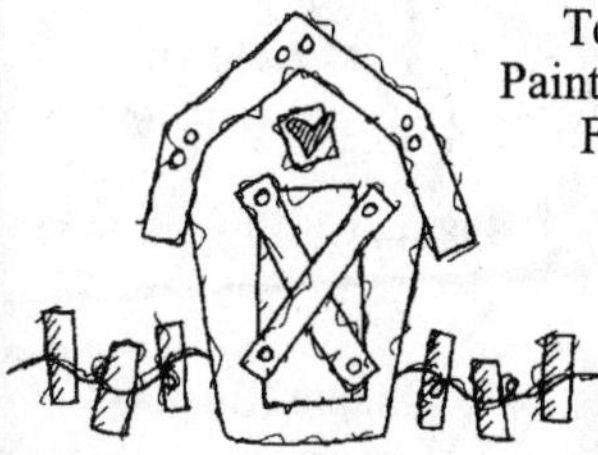

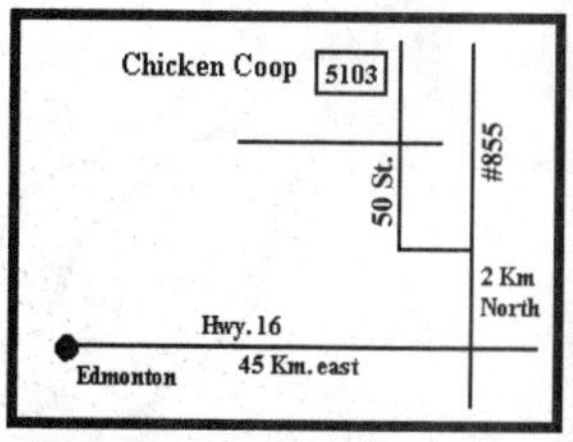

5103 - 50 St. TOB 3HO
(780) 764-3727
Fax: Same

Best smelling Chicken Coop around.

Other Shops in Alberta: We suggest calling first

Boyle	Crystal's Crafts, 5021 - 3rd St.	
Brooks	Family Fabrics, 106 - 2nd St. W, Box 862	403-362-2948
Calgary	The Quilter's Cabin, 118 - 10816 Macleod Tr. S	403-278-4433
Calgary	Ant Hill, 148 10th St. NW	403-283-8989
Calgary	Traditional Pastimes, 7 Parkdale Cres. NW	403-286-9421
Cardston	Imagination Unlimited, 257 Main St.	403-653-2633
Carstairs	Custom Woollen Mill, R.R. # 1	403-337-2221
Claresholm	Wood Lily Florals & Quilting, 4721 1st St. W	403-625-3349
Claresholm	Fabric Boutique, Box 1418	
Cochrane	Fab-Bric House, 2056 3 Ave	403-932-3944
Cold Lake	Quilted Gems, 5214 50 Ave.	780-594-5200
Crooked Creek	Country Stitches Quilts & Fabrics, R.R. #1	780-957-2446
Drayton Valley	Material Matters, 5119 51st St.	403-542-3233
Edmonton	Quilter's Dreamm 10732 - 124 St.	403-452-1133
Edmonton	The Notion Place, 4748 - 99th St.	
Edmonton	Crafts Canada, 4904 - 97th St.	
Edmonton	C & M Cottons & More, 5640 104 St.	780-431-9816
Edmonton	The Quilter's Palette, 522 Carse Ln.	
Fort Kent	Donna's Quilting, Box 26	
Grand Centre	Material World, 5408 - 55A St.	
Grande Prairie	Cotton Candy Crafts & Quilts, #7 11500 100 Street	708-532-2202
Grande Prairie	Patchwork Cottage, 10209 - 102nd St.	708-539-1245
Grimshaw	Cabin Crafts, Main St.	780-332-1160
Hanna	Yesterday's Dreams, Box 34	403-854-2622
High Prairie	Sharon's Quilt Haven, Box 867	
High River	Chinook Fabrics, Box 5482	
Hinton	Dreaming in Colour, 378 Collinge Rd.	403-865-1742
Killam	Tatters, 5007 - 50th St.	
Lac La Biche	Cottage Crafts & Creations, Box 1888	780-623-9477
Lacombe	Wildflower Creations, 5025 50 Ave	403-782-4141
Lamont	L.A. Sewing Centre, 5028 50 Ave.	780-895-2599
Lethbridge	Thistle Down Quilts, 200 4 Ave. S	403-329-1551
Lethbridge	Village Crafts, 227 - 2nd Ave. N	403-320-1817
Lethbridge	Fanny's Fabrics, 1245 2nd Ave. S	403-329-3355
Linden	Jo-Al Styles & Fabrics, 113 Central Ave.	403-546-3882
Lloydminster	Patchwork Junction, 5732 44th St.	403-875-5935
Mayerthorpe	Behind the Seams, P.O. Box 843	403-786-2660
Mayerthorpe	Kountry Krafts, 5015 50 Street, Box 1109	780-786-2821
Mayerthrope	Katherin Kountry Krafts, PO Box 1109	403-786-2821
Medicine Hat	Quilt Art, 520A 4th Ave. SE	403-528-4515
Milk River	Stitch in Time, 207 Main St. NW	
Nanton	Fabrique Boutique, 2119 20 St	403-646-2106
Okotoks	Rainbow End, 2 Elma St. W	
Okotoks	Old Country Store, 64 N. Railway St.	
Okotoks	Patchwork Plus, 1100 Village Ln. Bay 6	403-938-6107
Oyen	The Country Fabric Shop, 513 - 2 St. E, Box 442	403-664-2220
Red Deer	Cotton Threads Quilt Co., 5020 Gaetz Ave.	403-346-4005
Rocky Mountain House	The Fabric Centre, 5116 50 St.	403-845-3740
Sherwood Park	Lori's Fabric Cottage, 20-975 Broadmoor	403-464-9697
Spruce Grove	Continental Quilts & Linens, #2 26510 Township Rd.	403-987-9127
St. Albert	Sherry's Calico Cupboard, #8 Mission Ave.	780-459-5371
Stettler	Stettler Fabric Place, 4909 B 50 St., Box 783	403-742-6145
Stony Plain	Patt's Niche, 5109 - 50th St.	
Strathmore	Darlene's Fabrics, Box 10, Site 3, R.R. #1	403-934-5370
Strathmore	Country Creations, P.O. Box 2142	403-934-4054
Three Hills	Three Hills Sewing Center, 411 Main St.	
Vegreville	McFabrics & More, Box 668	
Viking	Viking Fabric & Gifts, 5116 - 50 St., P.O. Box 218	780-336-3000
Wainwright	Sewing Basket, 213 - 10th St.	
White Court	Sew Right, 5106 50th St., Box 1627	403-778-5717

14 Featured Shops

BRITISH COLUMBIA

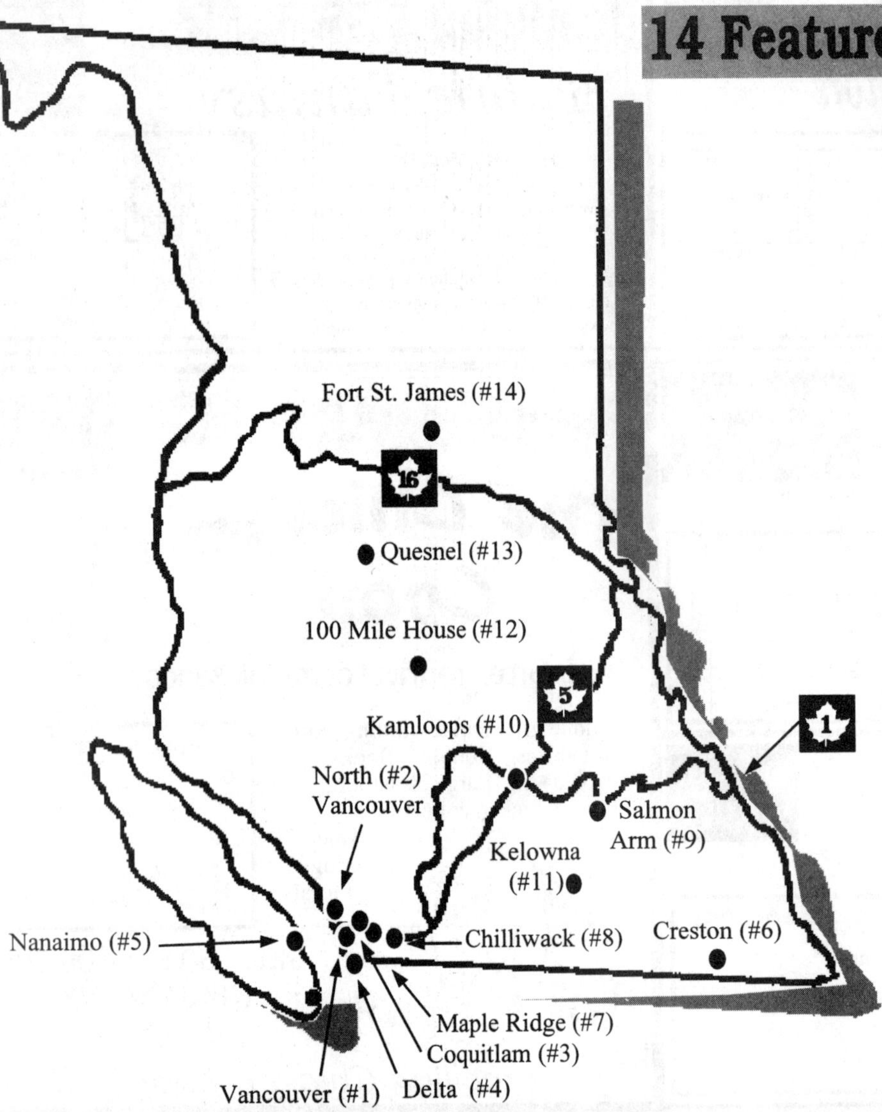

Snip & Stitch
SEWING CENTRE
N A N A I M O

Wander through our store for a refreshing experience. You will find a relaxing atmosphere, warm and friendly staff, and that "something special" you've been looking for!

Conveniently situated, one block off the Island Highway in North Nanaimo, Snip & Stitch offers a wide selection of classes, books and notions as well as the "BEST" selection of quilting cottons on Vancouver Island.

We look forward to meeting you.

Betty MacLean & Staff

Your "One-Stop Quilting & Sewing Machine Store" on Vancouver Island!

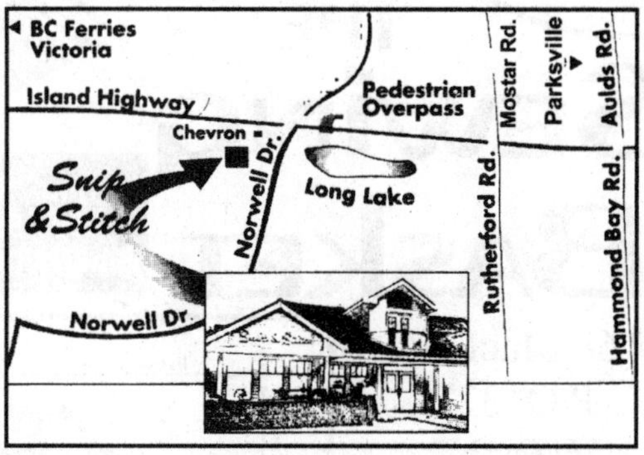

I - 4047 Norwell Dr. V9T 1Y6
(800) 789-1730 or (250) 756-2176

Nanaimo, BC #5

Fax: (250) 756-2178
E-Mail: info@snipandstitch.com
Web-Site: www.snipandstitch.com

9:30 - 5:30 Six days a week
12:00 - 4:00 Sundays

#6

Quiltview CORNER
1-877-PATCH-99

Join us for the
Creston Valley Quilt Festival
September 16 - 21, 2002 & September 2003

• Quilt Show • Classes • Concert • Shop Hop • Vendor & Artisan Market
• Columbia Brewery Tour • Golf Tournament

- 3,000 square ft.
- 1600 bolts of the "BEST" selection of cottons
- Newest notions & gadgets
- Wholecloth Quilts
- Over 250 books

Ph/Fax (250) 428-4891
Toll Free 1-877-PATCH-99

115 - 20 Avenue South
Creston, BC Canada V0B 1G5

Hours Mon - Fri 9:00 - 5:30
Sat 10:00 - 4:00

Owners Jean/Beth Swalwell
quilt@quiltview.com

CALL 1-877-PATCH-99 FOR A BROCHURE OR LOG ON TO WWW.QUILTVIEW.COM/FESTIVAL

Maple Ridge, BC #7

Mon - Sat 9:30 - 5:30

Elizabeth's QUILTER'S QUARTERS

#1 - 22621 Lougheed Hwy. V2X 2V4
(604) 467-8722 Fax: (604) 467-2490
Est: 1990
2600 sq.ft.

E-Mail: Elizabeth_Day@telus.net
Owners: Elizabeth Day, Allison Landerkin

We have a fantastic Quilt Shop. We carry Debbie Mumm, Jinny Beyer, Thimbleberries and more. Books, patterns, notions with knowledgeable, friendly staff.

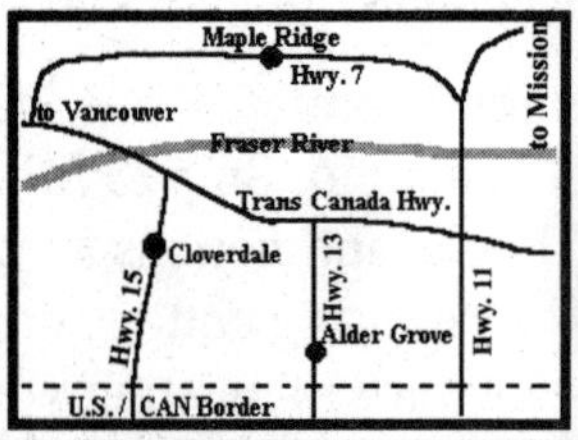

Chilliwack, BC #8

Mon - Sat 9 - 5:30

Hamels Fabrics

#5 - 45802 Luckakuck Way V2R 4E8

Quality Cotton Fabrics.
Books and Quilting Notions.
Mohair for Bears.
Jinny Beyer Kit Member.
Thimbleberries B.O.M.
Brother Sewing Machine Dealer.
Many Quilts on Display.
Mail Order through our Web Site: www.hamelsfabrics.com
Email: hamelsfabrics@shawcable.com
toll free: 1-877-774-2635
Owner: Pauline Southgate

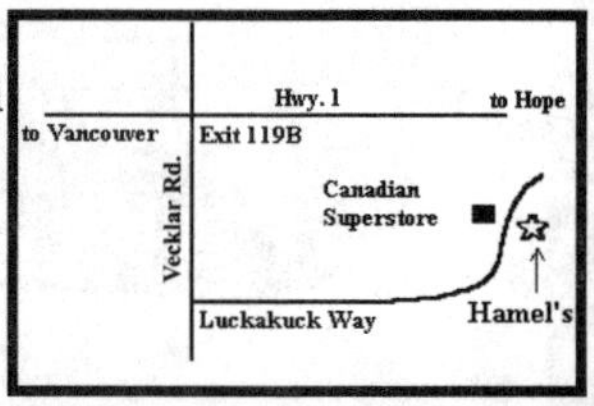

The Sewing Basket

Mon - Sat 9:00 - 5:30 Sun Call First

168 MacLeod
P.O. 327
V1E 4N2
(250) 832-3937
Fax: Same
Est: 1983
2500 sq.ft.

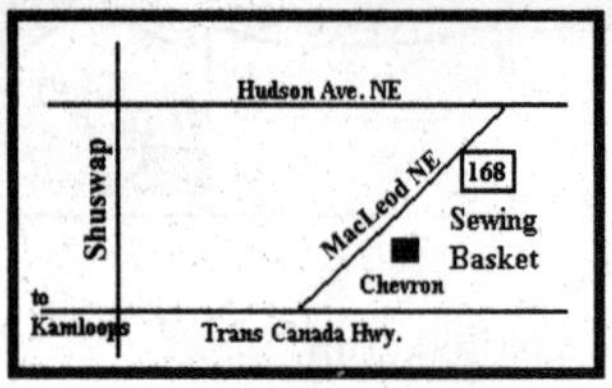

Salmon Arm, BC #9

We carry thousands of bolts of unique fabrics... all for the seamstress at home, or the most selective quilter! We're also a "MacPhee Workshop Dealer" with a great selection of MacPhee Fabrics and Patterns.

~ Craft Supplies ~ Craft Kits ~
~ Needlework ~ Quilting Supplies ~
Plus Many Hard to Find Notions and Accessories...

We offer over 50 'Year Round' Classes
Keeping you Up-to-Date with the latest Techniques.

Katja's Katja's Katja's

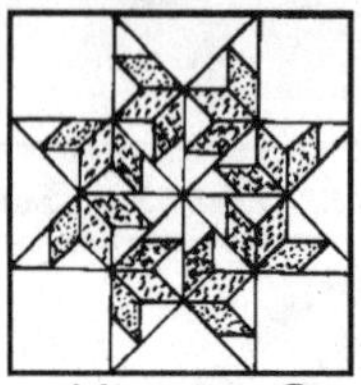

Katja's QUILT SHOPPE

Katja Sayewich – Proprietor
CLASSES / QUILTING SUPPLIES
100% Cotton Fabrics Patterns
Notions Books

"Your source for quilting, with a touch of Country and Christmas"

Kamloops, BC #10

Unit # 101 - 102 1150 Hillside Dr. V2E 2N1
Ph: (250) 851-0324
Fax: (250) 851-0624
E-Mail: katjasquiltshoppe@telus.net

Mon - Sat 9 - 5:30 Fri til 8

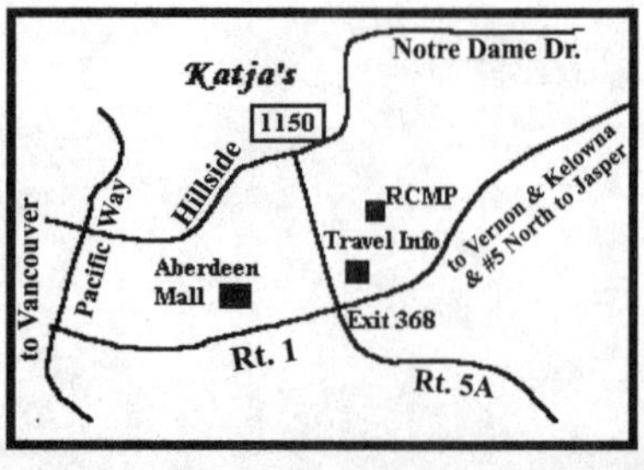

Katja's Katja's Katja's

Kelowna, BC #11

Mon - Sat 9:30 - 5

The Country Schoolhouse

3070 Benvoulin Rd.
V1W 2E3
(250) 861-5487
Fax: (250) 861-5479
E-Mail:
countryschoolhouse@shaw.ca
Owner: Arlene Leystra Est: 1990 2000 sq.ft.

Fabrics • Quilting Supplies
Patterns & Notions • Teddy Bear Supplies

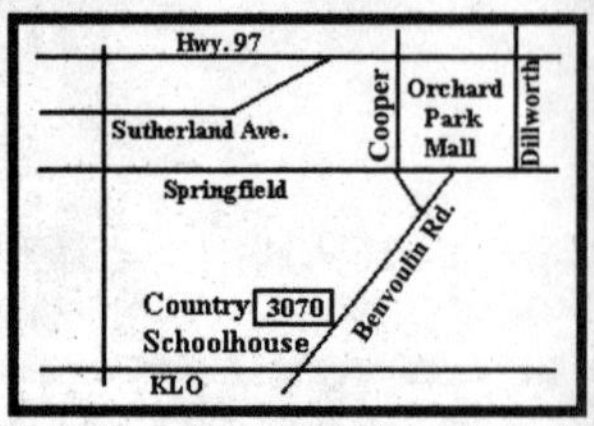

100 Mile House, BC #12

Mon - Sat 9:30 - 5:30

Country Fabrics & Things

257 Hwy. 97 S, P.O. Box 13 V0K 2E0
(250) 395-3377 Fax: Same
Est: 1986 1200 sq.ft.

Very large selection of pillow and crib panels, Quilting fabrics & supplies, lace & trims, denims & southwestern fabrics.

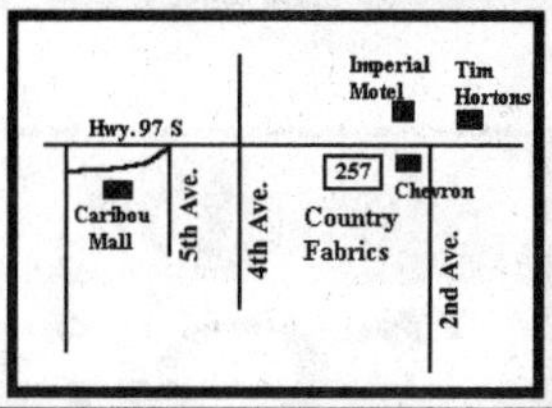

Quesnel, BC #13

Mon - Sat 10 - 5

Expressions By Ewe

222 McNaughton Ave. V2J 2G6
(250) 992-8896
Owner: Marjorie Sales
Est: 1987

More than 1000 bolts of great fabrics. Large selection of books & supplies for quilting & cross-stitch. Authorized Pfaff dealer.

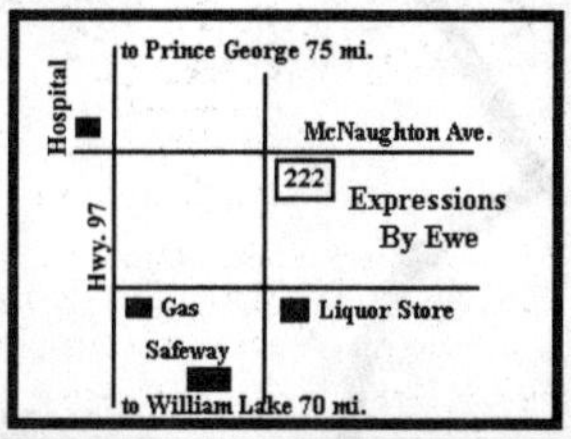

Fort St. James, BC #14

Mon - Sat 10 - 5

Heart n' Sole Quilts

241 2nd Ave. West V0J 1P0
(250) 996-8395 Fax: Same
E-Mail: ckorolek@fsjames.com
Owners: Cathy Korolek & Ginny MacPherson
Est: 2000 500 sq.ft.

Unique little shop situated near beautiful Stuart Lake. Specialities: top quality quilting fabrics, friendly advice & warm smiles.

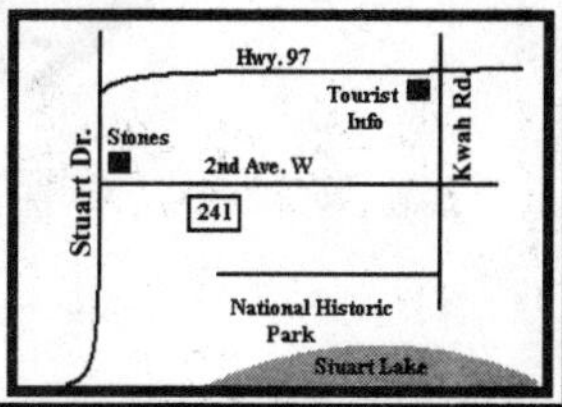

Other Shops in British Columbia: We suggest calling first

100 Mile House	Lillian's Fabric & Quilting 172 S. Birch Ave.	250-395-2625
Ashcroft	Alice's Sewing Shop, 417 Railway, P.O. Box 1090	250-453-2356
Belowna	The Country School House, 3070 Benvoulin	250-861-5487
Burnaby	Quilter's Haven, #9 - 5901 E. Broadway	604-320-0333
Burns Lake	Anna's Fabrics & Craft, 312 Hwy. 16	250-692-7890
Campbell River	Sew 'N' Sew Fabrics, 58 C Adams Rd.	250-923-6065
Campbell River	Calico & Cross Stitch, 910 Island Hwy.	250-287-8898
Campbell River	The Fabric Studio, 908 Island Hwy.	250-286-6451
Comox	Huckleberry's Fabrics, Inc.site 510, C67, RR 5, 1930 Ryan Rd.	250-339-4059
Cranbrook	Shannon's Fabrics Ltd., 16 12th Ave. N	250-426-7877
Dawson Creek	Fabric Place, 10211 13th Ave.	250-782-8388
Delta	Aspidistra, Ste. 493, 7231-120 St.	604-591-7049
Fort Langley	Pat's Quilting & Designs 9217 Glover Rd.	604-882-9411
Fort Nelson	Fabric Fun, 4903 51 Ave W, Box 857	250-774-6468
Hagensbourg	Crafty Lady Gifts & Hobbies, PO Box 114	250-982-2358
Invermere	Stober's, 729 12th St., Box 2259	250-342-9313
Langford	Cloth Castle, 786 Goldstream Ave Hwy 1A	250-478-2112
Madeira Park	The Quilted Path & Country Pleasures, 4982 Gonzales Rd	604-883-2274
Nakusp	The Secret Workshop, 208 Broadway St.	250-265-9966
Nelson	Shannon's Fabrics Ltd., 560 Baker St.	250-352-6104
Penticton	Poppin's Parlour, 425 Main St.	493-1815
Richmond	Fabricana Imports, 4811 Hazelbridge Way	604-273-5316
Sechelt	Sew Easy, Trail Bay Centre	604-885-2725
Smithers	Fabrications, Queen St.	250-847-3250
South Surrey	Creations III Fabrics, 13979 16th Ave	604-531-9311
Squamish	Nothing Finer, 38036 Cleveland Ave.	604-892-6366
Summerland	Art Seen Studio & Boutique, 13216 Henry Ave.	250-494-1677
Surrey	Wineberry Fabrics, 105, 6351 - 152nd St	604-597-1388
Taylor	Windy Willow Fabrics, Collins Rd. Mile 30	250-789-9248
Trail	Allan's Sewing Center, 1268 Pine Ave.	250-368-8485
Vanderhoof	The Stitchery, 173 W. Stewart, PO Box 1655	250-567-4260
Vernon	Definitely Country Treasures, 2801-28th St.	545-9327
Vernon	Mary's Brazilian Embroidery , 1803 36th St.	250-545-3939
Victoria	Capitol Iron, 1900 Store St	250-385-9703
Victoria	Fancyworks, 104 - 3960 Quadra St	250-727-2765
Williams Lake	E & E Sewing Centre, 65 S 1st Ave.	250-392-4055

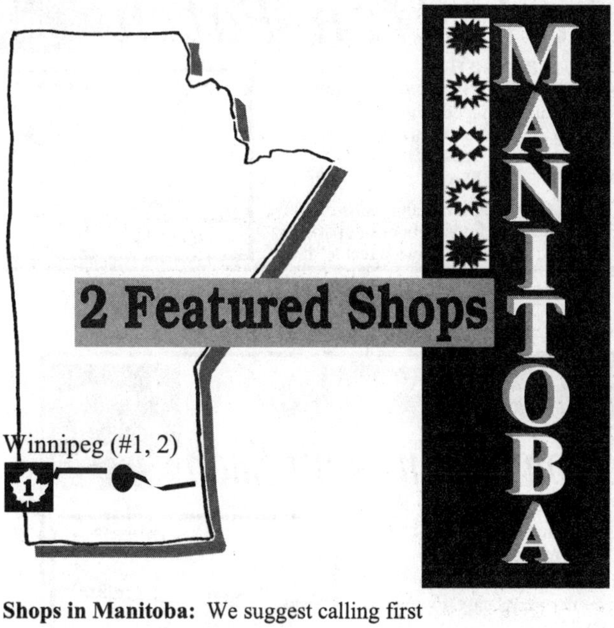

Winnipeg, MB #1

Mon - Sat 10 - 5 Thur til 7

The Quilting Bee

1014 St. Mary's Rd. R2M 3S6
(204) 254-7870 or (888) 518-3300
Fax: (204) 254-7895
Owners: Maria & Gwyneth Ball
2500 Bolts Free Newsletter

Biggest and friendliest shop in Manitoba. Wonderful selection of fabrics, notions, books, patterns and classes. Blocks-of-the-Month Avail

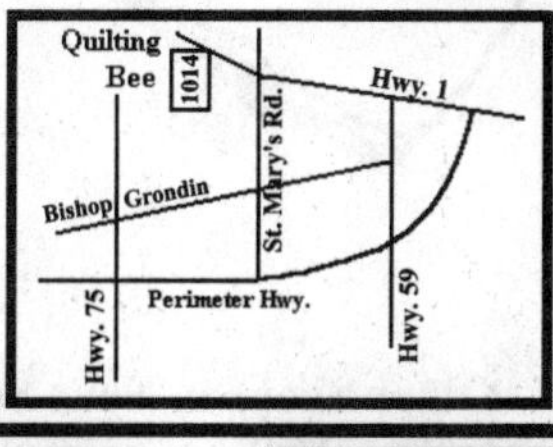

Winnipeg, MB #2

Mon - Fri 9:30 - 5:30 Sat 10 - 4

Croft House Quilt Shoppe

1846 Portage Ave R3J 0G6
(204) 888-3370 or (877) 527-0506
Fax: (204) 889-4774 Est: 1995 1500 sq. ft.
E-Mail: thecroft@escape.ca
Web Site: www.thecroftonline.com
Owners: Aileen & Doug Clarke

The little shoppe in the city with a warm country welcome featuring quilting fabrics, notions, Elna & Husquarna sales & service.

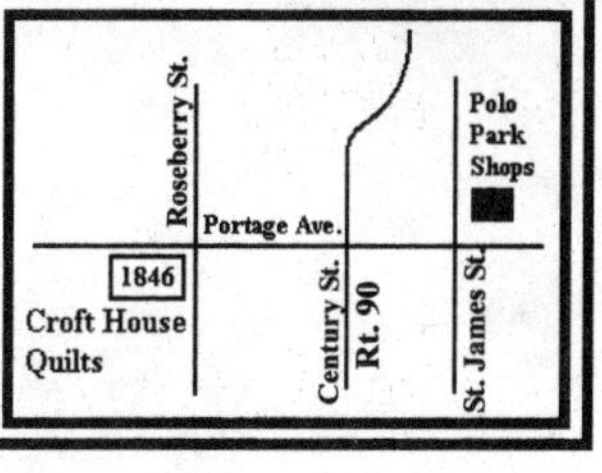

Other Shops in Manitoba: We suggest calling first

Melita	Prairie Patchwork, 53 Front St.	204-522-3540
Plumas	Kick Ass Country Store, Box 178	204-386-2193
Winnipeg	The Old Cotton Shop, 6-935 McLeod	204-663-8774

1 Featured Shop NEW BRUNSWICK

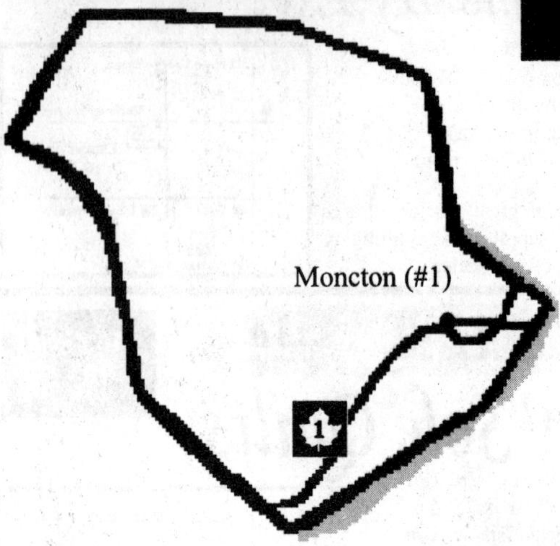

Moncton, NB #1

Mon - Thur 10 - 5
Fri 10 - 8
Sat 10 - 4

The Covered Bridge Quiltery Ltd.

"In Riverview"
630 Pinewood Rd. E1B 4M7
(506) 386-2888 Fax: (506) 386-2800
E-Mail: alj@nbnet.nb.ca
Web Site: www.thequiltery.com
Owner: Martha Davidson

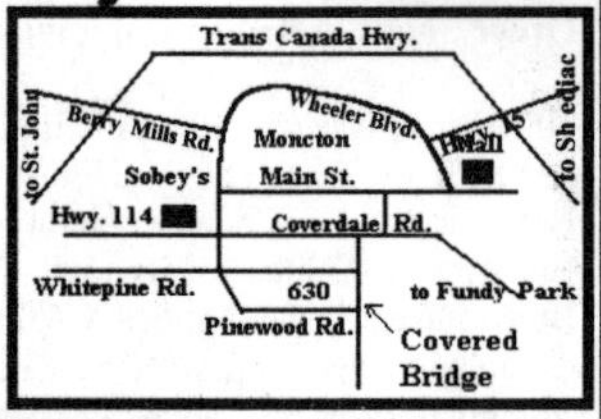

Large Selection of Cottons, Books, Patterns & Notions; Classes; Blocks-of-the-Month Kits.

Another Shop in New Brunswick: We suggest calling first

Fredericton Country Crafts and Curtains, 334 York St. 506-454-2572

2 Featured Shops NOVA SCOTIA

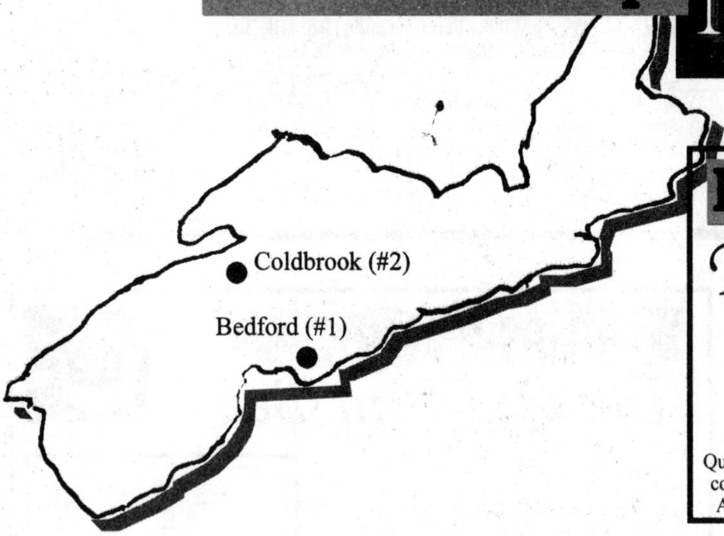

Bedford, NS #1

Mon - Sat 10 - 5
Thurs & Fri til 9

The Cotton Patch

1717 Bedford Hwy. B4A 3X1
(902) 832-0155 Fax: (902) 832-0066
E-Mail: staff@cottonpatch.org
Web Site: www.cottonpatch.org
Owner: Jackie Harris
Est: 1981 1600 sq.ft. 2000 Bolts

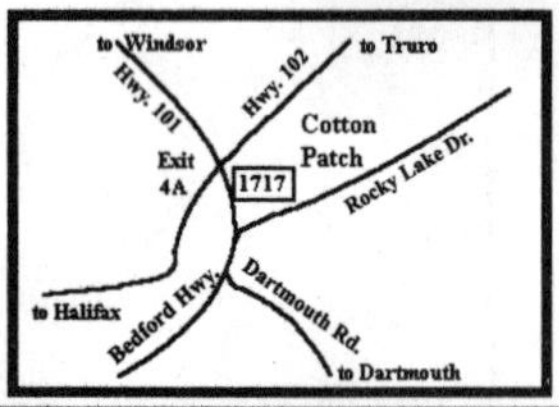

Quilting supplies including 2000 bolts of 100% cotton fabrics. Hundreds of books & patterns. A full line of notions. Knowledgeable staff.

Other Shops in Nova Scotia:
We suggest calling first

Halifax Quilter's Hope Chest
2483 Agricola St. 902-425-5002
Victoria CountyLorraines Yarns & Crafts
P.O. Box 49 902-336-2605

Coldbrook, NS #2

Tues - Fri 9:30 - 5
Sat 9:30 - 4

That Cotton Pickin' Quilt Shop

7130 Hwy. #1, Suite 240 B4R 1C1
(902) 678-0338
E-mail: cpquilter@yahoo.com
Web Site: cpquilter.tripod.ca (No www)

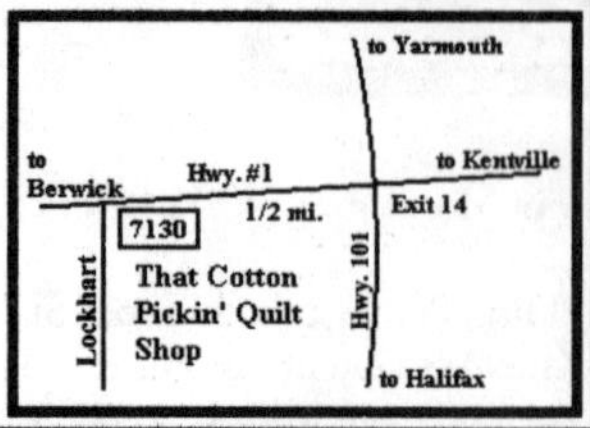

Homespun Pleasures! Flannels, Plaids, Homespun. All the latest Fabrics by your Favourite Designers! Local Handmade Gifts.

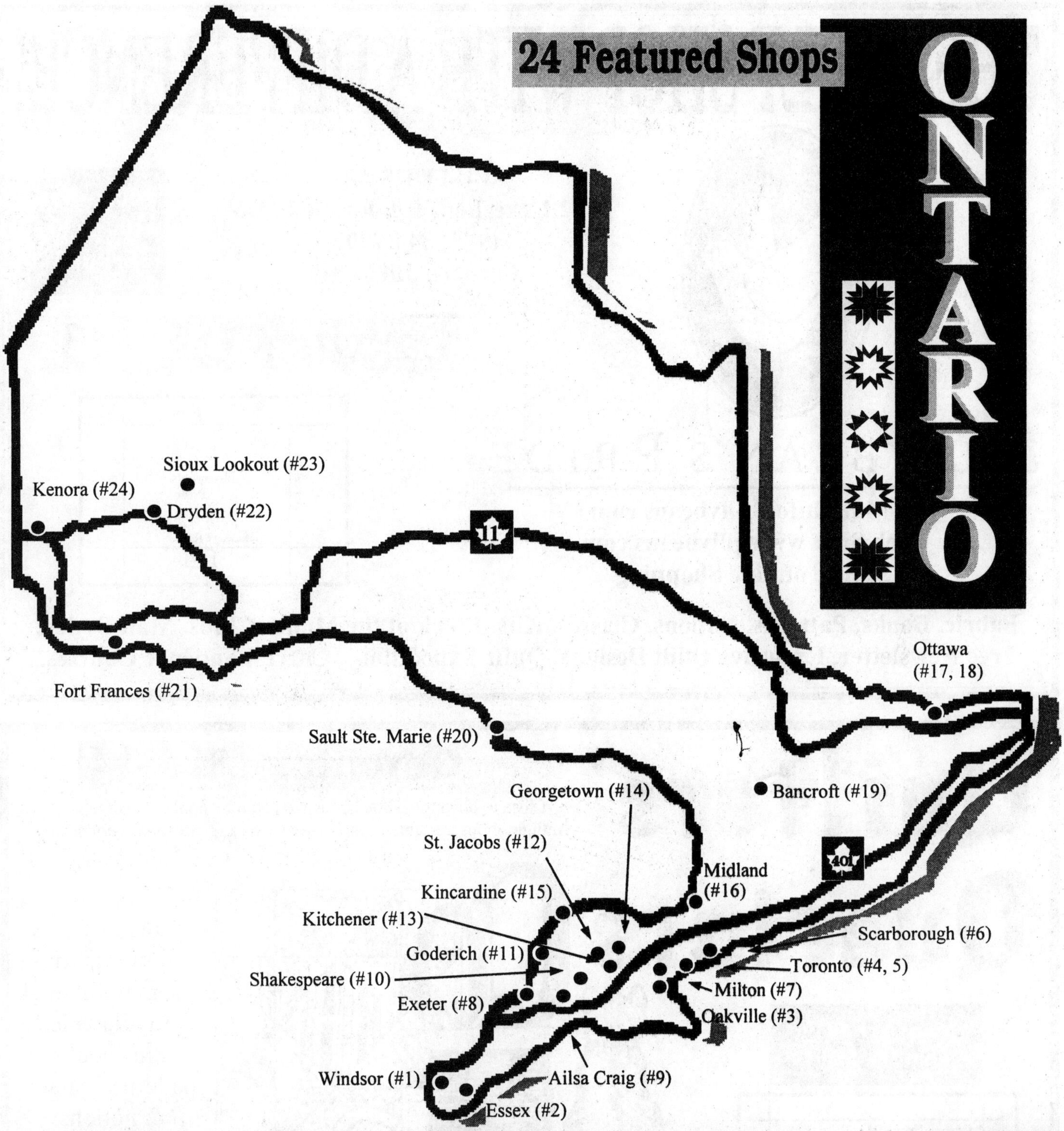

Windsor, ON #1

Mon - Sat 10 - 5:30

The Dresden Rose Sewing Centre

3850 Dougall (at Cabana) N9G 1X2
(519) 966-3355 Fax: (519) 966-9066
E-Mail: gail@dresdenrose.com
Web Site: dresdenrose.com
Owner: Gail Millson Est: 1988 2000 sq.ft.

Husqvarna Viking dealer of distinction; classes, 100% cotton fabrics. Free Lessons w/ machine purchase. Service to all brand machines.

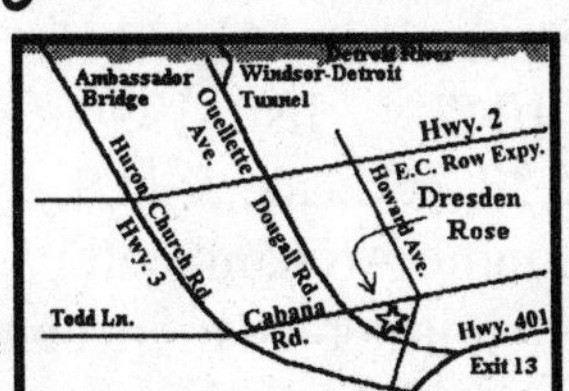

Essex, ON #2

Mon - Fri 9 - 5 Sat 9 - 4

Sew & Sew "The Quilting Store"

183 Talbot St South N8M 1B7
(519) 776-5363 Fax: (519) 776-6805
E-Mail: gwelsh@govital.net
Web Site: www.sewandsew.ca
Owner: Georgeann Welsh

Located in the Hub of Essex County 20 mins. South/East Of Windsor, Ont.

Over 1000 bolts of 100% quality cottons. Sewing & quilting notions, books & patterns. Workshops

THE QUILT SHOP WITH A DIFFERENCE!

VISIT US AT
222 Lakeshore Rd. E L6J 1H6
(905) 844-1793
Owner: Jill Pettit

Mon - Sat
10 - 5:30
Fri til 9

Oakville, ON #3

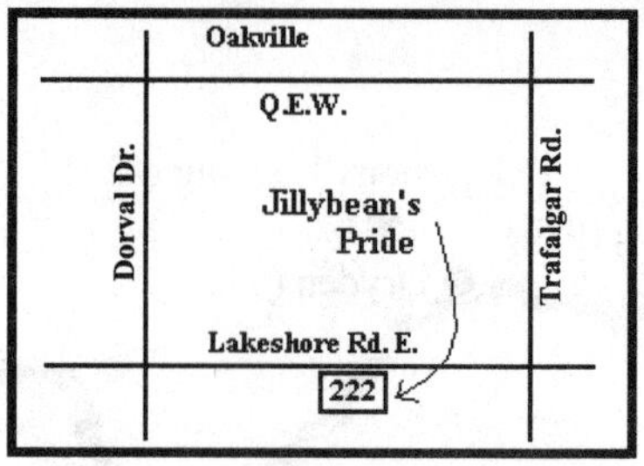

JILLYBEAN'S PRIDE

E-Mail: info@jillybeans.com
Web Site: www.jillybeans.com
Secure on-line Shopping

Fabric, Books, Patterns, Notions, Classes, Kits, Block of the Month Clubs, Mail Order, Free Newsletter, Exclusive Quilt Designs. Quilt Expeditions, Correspondence Courses.

Quilters' Quarters

Toronto, ON #4

Close to downtown hotels, easy to get to by public transit or car.
Antique shops, restaurants, specialty shops and gift shops very nearby.

Lots of 100% cotton fabrics from traditional to dramatic. Plus books, patterns, classes, & notions. Teddybear making supplies, mohair, glass eyes, joints and patterns.

Free Smiles !

Mon - Fri 10 - 6
Sat 10 - 5:30

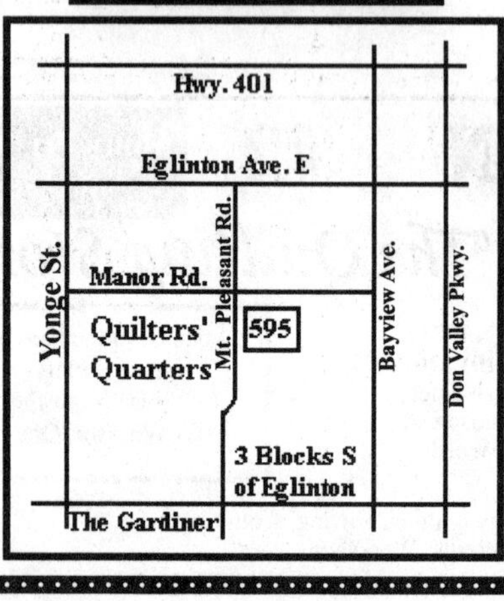

595 Mt. Pleasant Rd. M4S 2M5
(416) 487-1047 Est: 1990
(800) 561-5132 (Canada & U.S.)
Owner: Connie Archambault
E-Mail: connie@quiltersquarters.com

Toronto, ON #5

Quiltmakers

1720 Avenue Road M5M 3Y6
(416) 784-5953

- Wonderful fabrics
- Supplies, books, notions
- Quilting software
- Knowledgeable Staff
- Wheelchair accessible
- Classes at all Levels

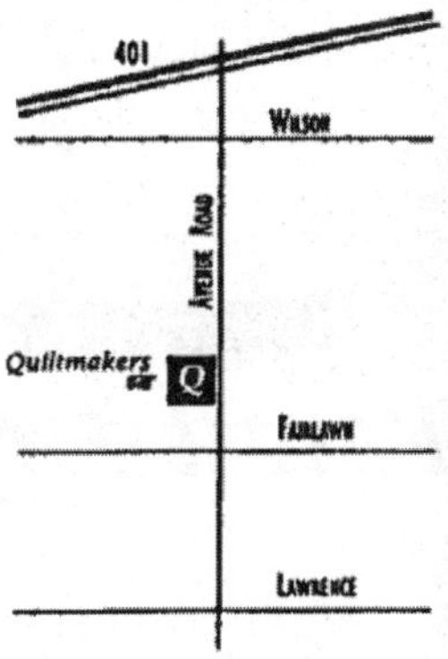

Mon - Sat 10 - 5:30
Thurs til 8

South of Hwy. 401
North of Lawrence Ave.
Plenty of convenient parking

Scarborough, ON #6

Mon - Sat 10 - 5
Thur til 9
Sun 10 - 4

The Quilting Patch, Inc.

86 Dearham Wood M1E 1S4
(416) 281-5561 Fax: (416) 281-3517
E-Mail: qpatch@interlog.com
Web Site: www.interlog.com/~qpatch/start.html
Owner: Donna Edwards
Est: 1977 2000 sq.ft. 2500+ Bolts

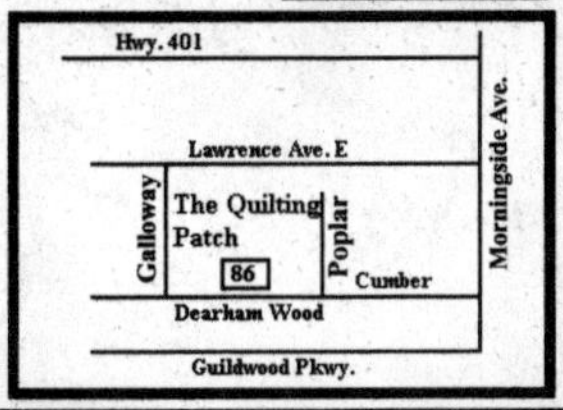

Serving all your Quilting needs with Friendly Service and exceptional Selection for over 25 years. Authorized Bernina Dealer.

Milton, ON #7

Mon - Fri 10 - 6
Sat 10 - 4

The Quilter's Basket, Inc.

264 Bronte St. S, Unit #1 L9T 5A3
(905) 878-7333 Fax: (905) 878-5090
E-Mail: info@quilters-basket.com
Web Site: www.quilters-basket.com
Owner: Dagmar Scherer
Est: 2000 2300 sq.ft. 2500+ Bolts

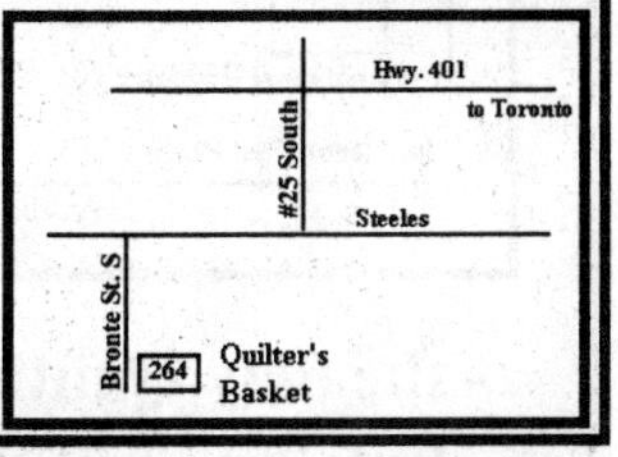

Bright, Beautiful Store. Over 2500 Bolts from Top Supplies. We custom quilt on our Gammill. Year Round classes for all Ages.

QUILTS and CALICOS

Unique quilt shop located in a restored century old building featuring a wide array of 100% cotton fabrics, the latest quilting notions, books, patterns and batting. In short, your one stop quilt shop. We ship anywhere. Bear making supplies available.
10% off for all Guild Members at all times
(with proof of membership) or with this ad.

Exeter, ON #8

392 Main St., P.O. Box 42
Exeter, Ontario N0M 1S6
(888) 305-0949
(519) 235-4084
Fax: (519) 235-4967
E-Mail: quiltscalicos@on.aibn.com
Owner: Linda Bartlett
Est: 1993 2000 Bolts

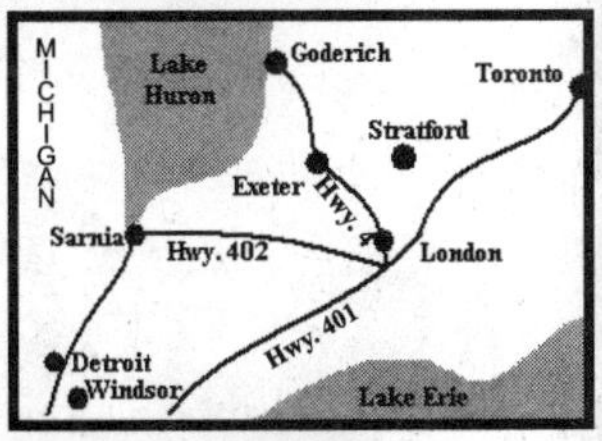

Mon - Fri 9 - 5:30 Sat 9 - 5

www.quilts-calicos.on.ca

Ailsa Craig, ON #9

Mon - Sat 9 - 5

Cotton-By-Post Quilt Shoppe

153 Main St. N0M 1A0
Toll Free: (888) 884-4496
(519) 293-3499 Fax: (519) 232-9199
E-Mail: suzanne@cotton-by-post.com
Web Site: www.cotton-by-post.com
Owners: Suzanne Agnew
Est: 1995 On-line Catalogue

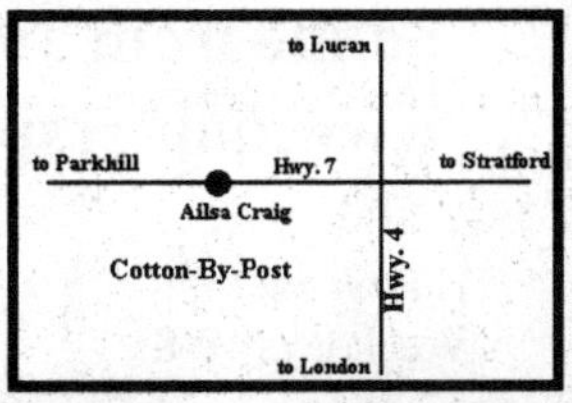

Quality cotton fabrics, cotton batting, books, patterns and all the latest quilting notions. Classes available for all skill levels.

Shakespeare, ON #10

Mon - Sat 10 - 5:30
Sun 12 - 5

THE QUILT PLACE

27 Shakespeare St. N0B 2P0
(519) 625-8435 (888) 457-7077
Owner: Heather Stock
1200 sq.ft.
1500 Bolts
Est: 1986

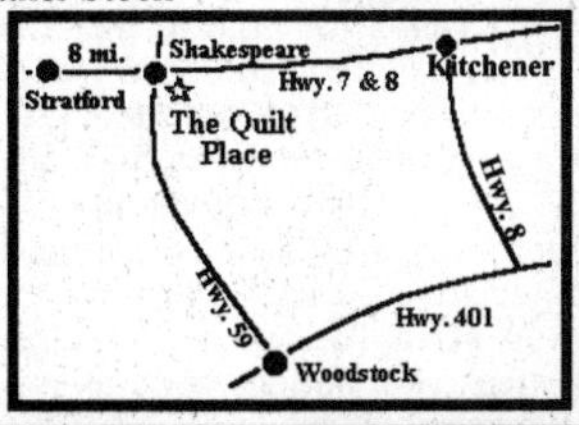

Your place to find a timeless and elegant quilt for your home or choose the supplies to make a family heirloom. Lots of Shops for Everyone To Enjoy in Canada's Antique Capital
Waterloo County Quilt Festival Participant

Goderich, ON #11

Mon - Sat 10 - 5:30

Quilters by the Square

32 West St. N7A 2K3
(519) 524-4333

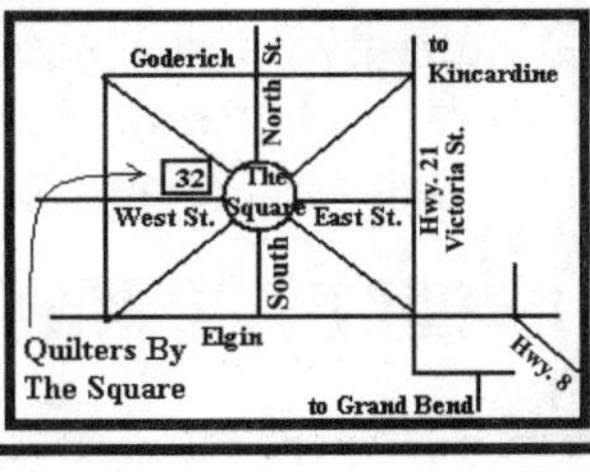

A wide variety of 100% Cotton Fabrics, Quilting Books, Patterns, Notions, DMC floss, Bear Supplies & Classes available. Visit our friendly knowledgeable staff.

St. Jacobs, ON #12

Mon - Sat 9:30 - 8:00
Sun 1 - 5

Ruffled Elegance & Calico

1401 King St. N N0B 2N0
(519) 664-2665 Est: 1984
E-Mail: quilts@ruffledelegance.com
Web Site: www.ruffledelegance.com
Owner: Caroline Verleyen 3000 sq.ft.

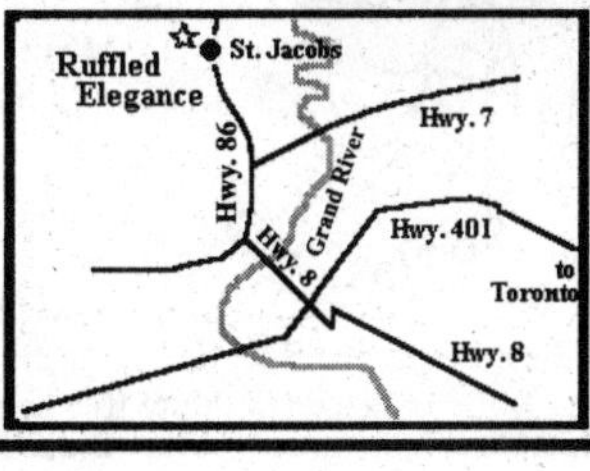

"A Quilter's Delight — A Decorator's Dream"
Name brand fabrics, patterns, notions. Classes. Curtains & Pillows. Handmade quilts by local Mennonite quiltmakers.

Quilter's Paradise

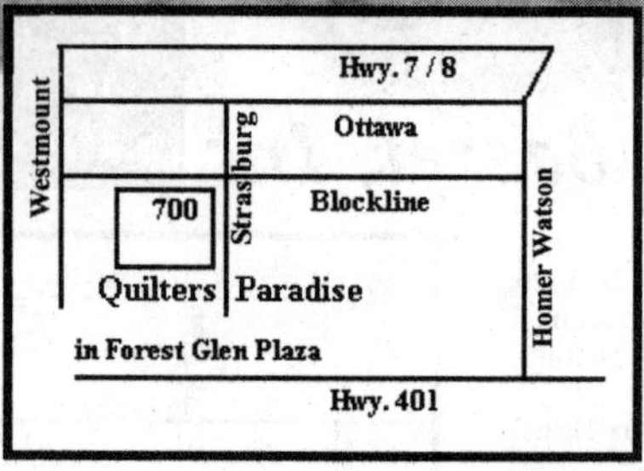

Forest Glen Plaza
700 Strasburg Rd.
Kitchener, Ontario
N2E 2M2

#13

- the only Quilting specialty store In Kitchener-Waterloo!
- 100% cotton fabrics and flannels, Patterns, notions, tools, and more!
- you can also visit us and shop online from anywhere!
www.quiltersparadise.com

Hours: Sat 9-5
Weekdays 10-8

Phone: (519) 579-5618
Toll Free: 1-888-687-0450

Georgetown, ON #14

The Hobby Horse

Mon - Sat 9:30 - 5:30
Sundays & Holiday Mon 12 - 5

12707 9th Line L7G 4S8
(905) 877-9292 or (800) 565-5366
E-Mail: orders@thehobbyhorse.on.ca
Web Site: www.thehobbyhorse.on.ca
Owner: Gail Spence
Est: 1982 Block of the Month Programs

We're filled to the brim with bolts of cotton fabrics, quilting supplies, patterns, books, kits and much more. Come Visit Our Store.

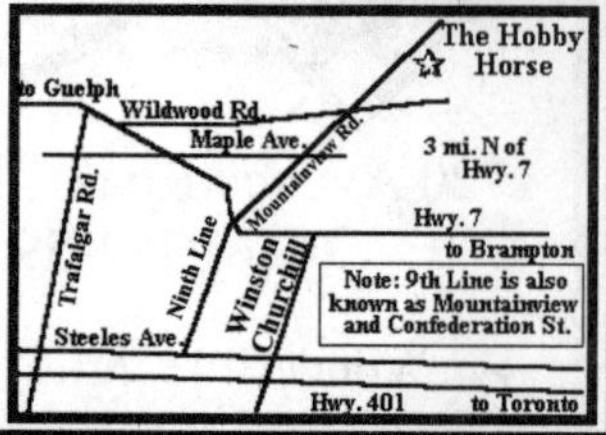

Kincardine, ON #15

Retail Dry Goods

Open Mon, Wed, Fri & Sat All Day Long

R.R. #5, #396 - SDRD 30 Greenock
No Phone N2Z 2X6
Owners: Lloyd & Laura Kuepfer

Large selection of Fabric "over 2500 bolts." Books, Stencils, Threads, Notions, Cross stitch & Floss. Finished Quilts and Quilt Tops. Also visit our second location 3½ mi. west of Linwood.

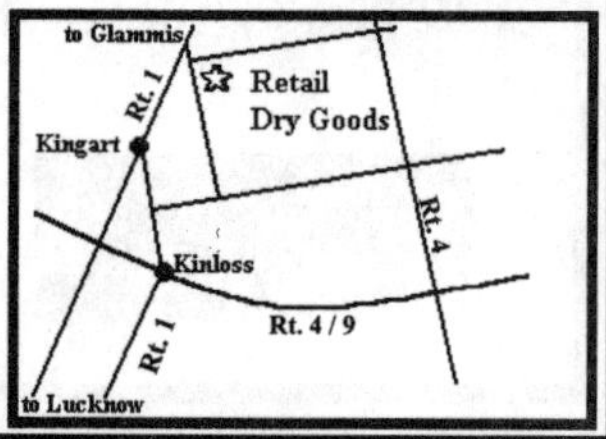

Midland, ON #16

Notions & Sew-Lutions

Tues - Sat 9:30 - 5
Open 7 days July & Aug.

Unit 2 - 559 Bay St. W L4R 1L4
(705) 526-USEW (8739)
Fax: (705) 526-8799 Est: 2000
E-Mail: sewlutions@on-aibn.com
Owner: Betty-Lou Adam 3000 Bolts

Quilt shop overlooking beautiful Georgian Bay. Specializing in 100% cotton fabrics. Authorized dealer for Brother Machines. Extensive notions, patterns & books. Workshops & mail order.

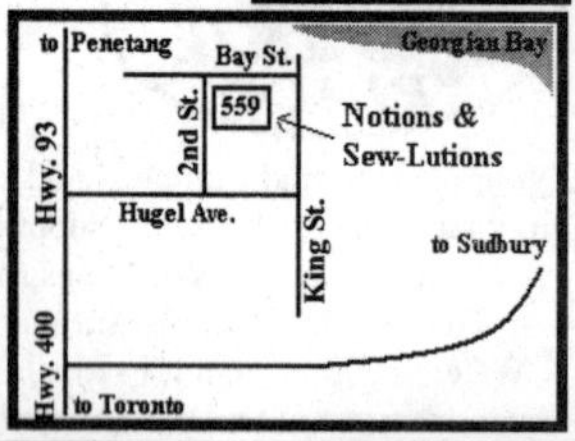

Ottawa, ON #18

Mon - Sat 10 - 5

The Nesting Hen

1797 Kilborn Ave. at Virginia Dr.
K1H 6N1
Owner: Sandra Evans
(613) 521-9839
Est: 1987

All inclusive Quilt Shop. Ottawa's loveliest Fabrics.

Best Books and Supplies. Fine Needlearts and Gifts. Located in Pretty Residential Area.

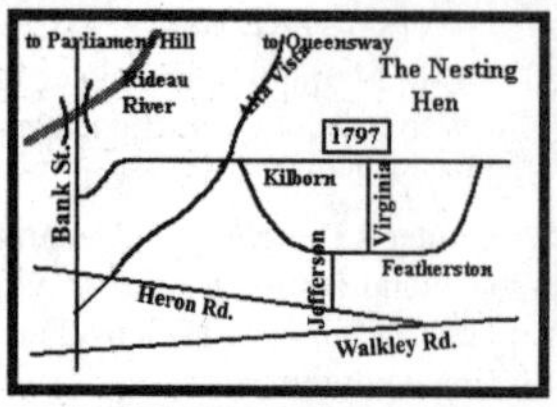

Ottawa, ON #17

Quilts & Seams

175 Richmond Rd. K1Z 6W3
(613) 725-5113 Fax: (613) 798-1952
E-Mail: info@quiltsandseams.com
Owner: Bob & Katuma McLaughlin
Est: 1982 2000 sq.ft.

Mon - Sat 10 - 5
Sun Noon - 4 Seasonal

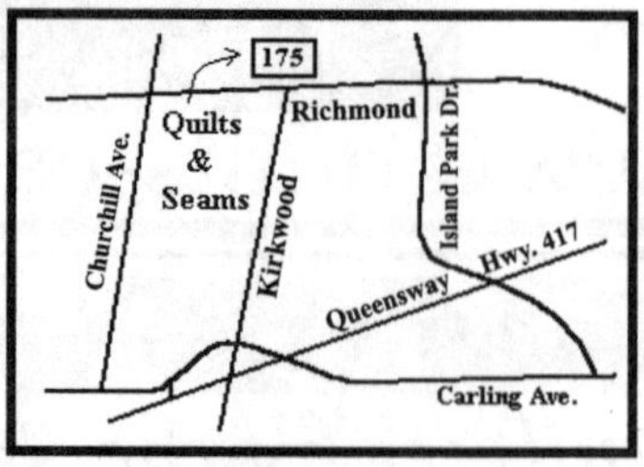

A shop for the discerning quiltmaker featuring quality fabrics, notions, books, patterns, classes & mail order. Machine Service / Repairs—all makes. Authorized Dealer: Bernina, Janome.

Visit us at: www.quiltsandseams.com

Bancroft, ON #19

Mon - Sat 9 - 5:30

Country Quilts & Fabrics

227 Hastings St. N, Box 398
K0L 1C0
(613) 332-2540
Owner: Gwen Schock
Est: 1991 900 sq.ft. 3000+ Bolts

Quilts, Fabrics, Quilting Supplies, Books, Laces, Ribbons, DMC Floss, Stencils, Beads, Patterns, Trims.

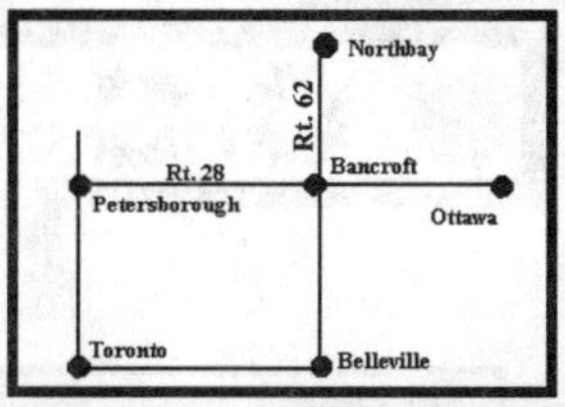

Sault Ste. Marie, ON #20

Mon - Fri 9 - 5 Sat 10 - 4

Cotton Colours

138 Gore St. P6A 1M1
(705) 942-3570 or (866) 447-4404
E-Mail: cottoncolours@on.aibn.com
Web Site: www.cottoncolours.com
Owners: Deone & Kim Avery

"Your one stop quilt shop." Located close to the International Bridge. We also sell corduroy, denim and faux suede.

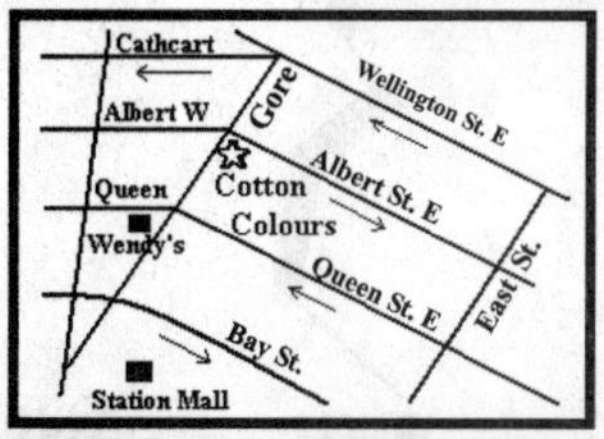

Fort Frances, ON #21

Mon - Fri 10 - 5 Sat 10 - 3

330 Scott Street P9A 1G9
(807) 274-6665
Fax: (807) 274-3168
Web Site: www.crazyladiesfabrics.com
Owner: Phyllis Johnson
Est: 1998 1400 sq. ft. 1000 Bolts.

Located on the U.S.-Canada border in NW Ontario. Carrying the most popular cottons and cotton flannels from top companies.

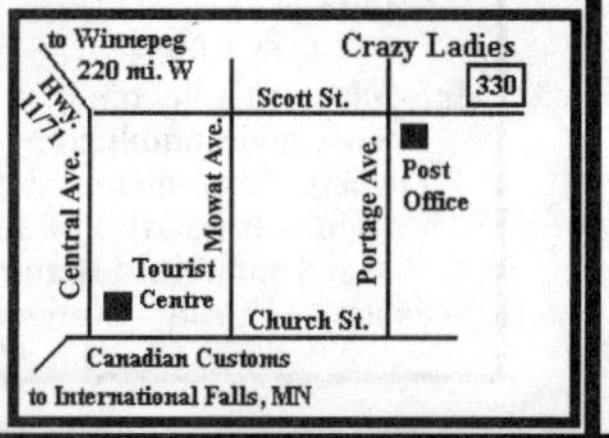

Dryden, ON #22

Mon - Thur 9:30 - 5:30 Fri 9:30 - 6:30 Sat 9:30 - 5

Salavich's Serge 'n Sew

3 - 439 Government St
(807) 223-4362 Fax: (807) 223-2793
E-Mail: esalavich@dryden.ni
Owners: Marj & Ed Salavich
Est: 1995 1200 sq.ft.

Husqvarna Viking Sewing Machines Sales & Service. Large supply of Notions, 100% Cotton Fabric. "Quilters dream come true."

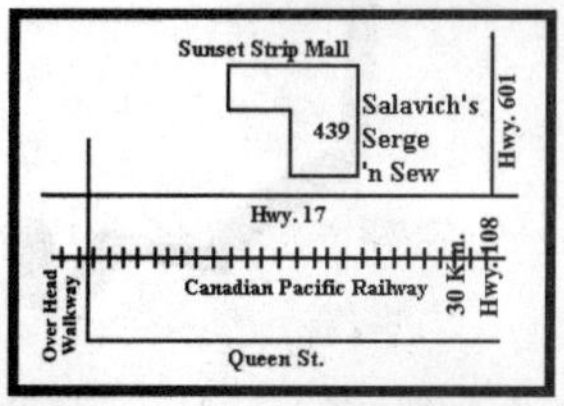

Sioux Lookout, ON #23

Mon - Fri 9 - 5 Sat 10 - 12 Closed Sat May - Sept.

Dori's Sewing Studio

40 Curtis St. P8T 1G8
(807) 737-3674 Fax: (807) 737-3674
E-Mail: dori_sewing@excite.ca
Est: 1998

A full line of quilting cottons & notions. Over 150 different quilting books and patterns to choose from. We carry Elna and Janome Sewing Machines.

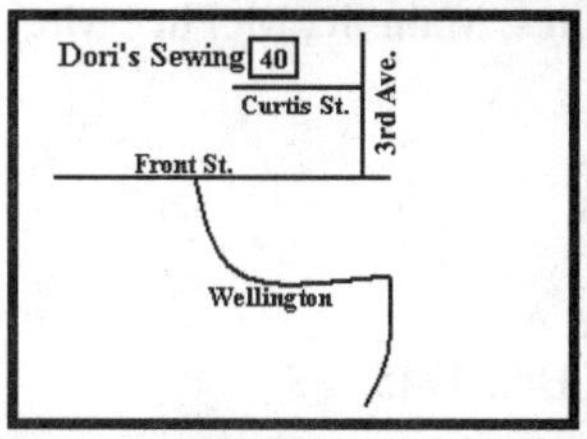

Kenora, ON #24

Mon - Sat 9:30 - 5

Expressions

331 Second St. South P9N 1G3
(807) 468-4452
E-Mail: kenquilt@voyageur.ca
Web Site: Coming Soon
Owner: Audrey Watterson 1000+ Bolts

See beautiful "Lake of the Woods". 1000+ bolts of 100% cotton, books, patterns, notions and classes. Service with a smile!

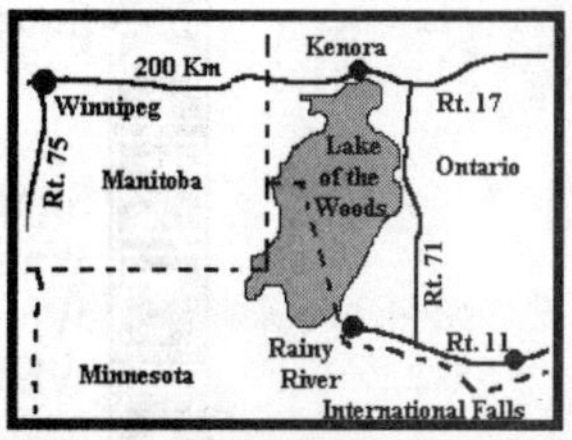

Other Shops in Ontario: We suggest calling first

Aylmer Handmade Quilts, R.R. #1
Barrie The Quilters Shop, Horseshoe Valley 705-739-6875
Burlington The Quilter's Cupboard, 2501 Guelph Line #11 905-332-6640
Cookstown Quilt & Wool Shoppe, 25 Queen St. 705-458-9233
Elmira Reichard's Dry Goods, 3 Arthur St. S 519-669-3307
Elmira Busy Bee Quilts, 48 Arthur St. S 519-669-3441
Floradale Quilts & Crafts, 3 First St. 519-669-5872
Huntsville Pastimes Hobby Centre, 3 Main St. 705-789-3343
Kenora Subtle Creations, 26 Peter St. W 807-468-6650
Kingston Abbey Dawn Quilts & Antiques, 1619 Abbey Dawn Rd. 613-542-6247
Kingston The Quilter's Choice, 650 Progress 613-384-8932
Leamington A Stitch in Time, 275 Talbot St. 519-322-4690
Linwood Retail Dry Goods, R.R. #1 no phone
London Quilters' Supply, 1634 Hyde Park 519-472-3907
Minesing Quilters Shop, R.R. #1, Box 77 705-739-6875
Navuan Aunt Beth's Quilt World, 3217 Navan Rd., R.R. #2 613-837-6222
Nepean Sew for It!, 418 Moodie Dr. 613-820-2201
North Bay Quilts & Other Comforts, 151 Main St. W 705-476-7811
Oakville Quilt Patch, 101A Bronte Rd. 905-847-5105
Red Lake The Yarn Shop, 150 Harvey St. 807-727-2564
Richmond Country Quilter, 3444 McBean 613-838-5541
St. George Lyn Bell's Designs, 14 Main St. 519-448-3739
St. Jacobs Grey Fort Quilts, 14 King 519-664-2130
Sudbury Country Quilter, 463 Falconbridge 705-524-6235
Sudbury It's So Easy, 1313 Lorne St. #4 705-675-1788
Thunder Bay Patchworks, 574 Memorial Ave 807-345-6111
Toronto Quilter's Garden, 931 Kingston Rd. 416-693-1616
Toronto Sawtooth Borders Quilt Gallery, 110 Park Rd. 416-961-8187
Toronto Quilters Fancy, 4 Norbert Crescent 416-232-1199
Uxbridge Quilter's Cupboard, 4 Sandy Hook 905-852-3617
Whitby Olde Silver Thimble Quilt Shoppe, 1380 Hopkins St. 905-430-0297

QUEBEC CANADA

1 Featured Shop

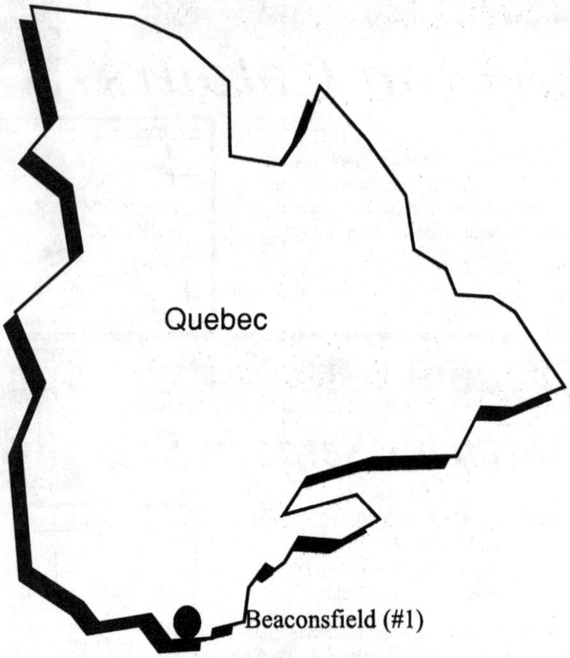

Beaconsfield, QC #1

Tues - Fri 10 - 5
Sat 9 - 6
Sun 12 - 5

La Vie en Quilt

449 Beaconsfield Blvd. H9W 4C2
(514) 693-8934 (866) 693-8934
Info@lavieenquilt.com Fax: (514) 693-8935
www.lavieenquilt.com 2400 sq. ft.
Owners: Sharon Hops & Carol McColl
The shop with heart! Full service quilt shop and authorized Bernina dealer.
Fabric -- Thread -- Notions -- Machines.
We have it all!

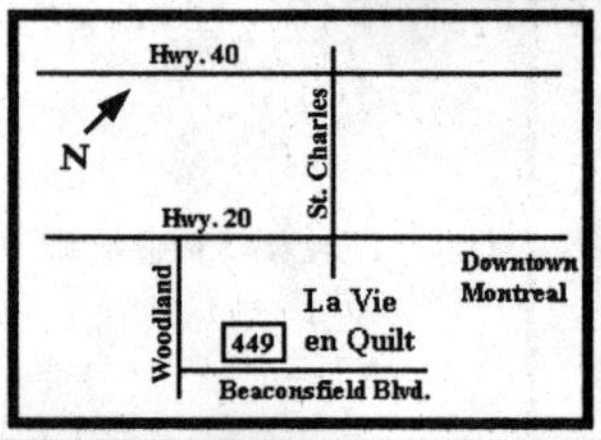

Shops on Prince Edward Island: We suggest calling first

Charlottetown	Quilting B and More, 155 Queen St.	902-628-1998
Souris	Jean's Quilting Crafts & Things, Main St., McPhee Mall	902-687-1367

Shops in the Yukon: We suggest calling first

Watson Lake	The Quilt Cabin, 229 Tamarac, Box 41	867-536-2031
White Horse	A Stitch in Time, 3121 Third Ave.	403-667-6133
Whitehorse	Crocus Creek Quilting, P.O. Box 4745	867-668-7699

Notes

SASKATCHEWAN CANADA

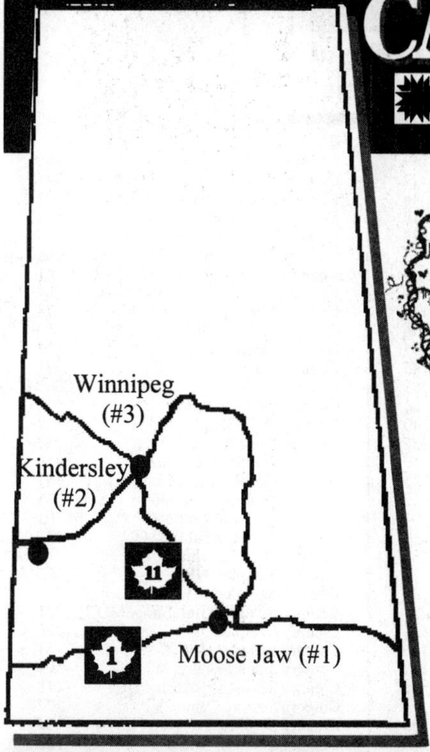

Moose Jaw, SK #1

Mon - Sat
9:30 - 5:30

Prairie Quilters Loft

116 Main St. N - 2nd Level S6H 3J7
(306) 693-7140
Fax: (306) 691-5770

Visit our quilt loft within the Lasting Impressions Craft Mall in historic downtown Moose Jaw. We have quilting fabrics, notions, books & quilting patterns by Canadian designers.

Kindersley, SK #2

Mon - Sat
9 - 5:30
Thur til 9

Veronica's Sewing Supplies

100 Main St., Box 1524 S0L 1S0
(306) 463-4505 Fax: (306) 463-4435
E-Mail: take.care@sasktel.net
owner: Veronica Longmuir BSH. Ec. Est: 1979

6,000 sq. ft. of beautiful fabrics & displays
A Quilter's Gallery. Over 1600 bolts of cottons, pls 60 baby panels, fashion fabrics & More. Janome & Babylock machines & sergers. Welcome.

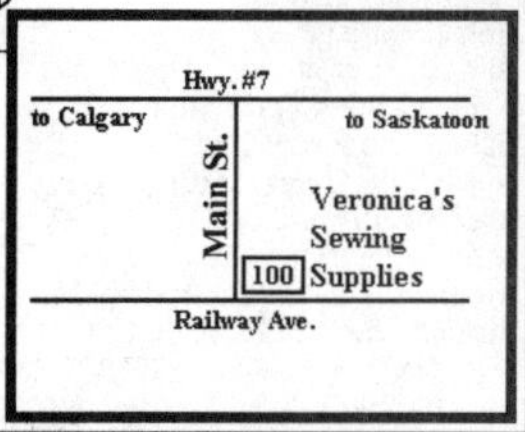

Saskatoon, SK #3

Mon - Sat
9 - 5
Thur til 8

Homespun Craft Emporium, Inc.

16 - 1724 Quebec Ave. S7K 1V9
(306) 652-3585 Fax: (306) 384-9191
E-Mail: homespun86@hotmail.com
Owners: Peggy Grandberg & Sarah Sanduliak
Est: 1986

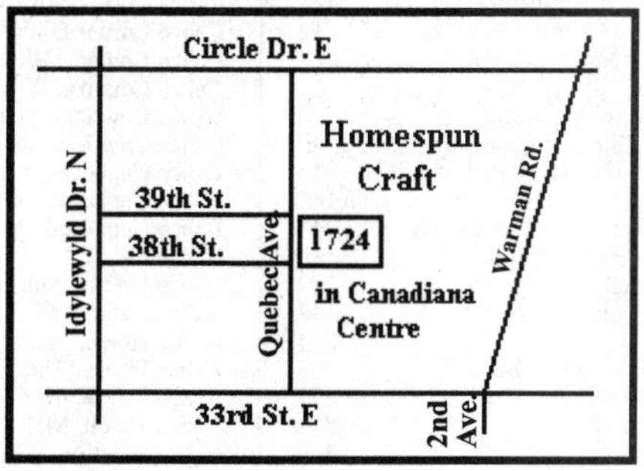

The one stop shop for all your Quilting Supplies.
2500 Bolts of 100% Cotton Fabric, Books, Notions, & Tools.
Authorized Bernina Sewing Machine Dealer, Sales & Service.

Another Shop in Saskatchewan: We suggest calling first

Spirit Wood — Thoughts & Things, 332 First St. E. Box 97
306-883-3800

INDEX

An Alphabetical listing of featured shops by name

We will continue to update our guide on a regular basis. If you own a shop or know of one we should be sure to include in future editions of this guide, please drop us a note, call (719) 685-5041, or visit our website at www.chalet-publishing.com. Also if you have any suggestions for other information we could include that would be helpful when you're traveling, we'd appreciate hearing them.

We welcome wholesale inquiries.

Chalet PUBLISHING
32 Grand Avenue
Manitou Springs, CO 80829